T0137006

Lecture Notes in Computer Science 12631

More information about this subseries at http://www.springer.com/series/7409

Richard Kronland-Martinet ·
Sølvi Ystad · Mitsuko Aramaki (Eds.)

Perception, Representations, Image, Sound, Music

14th International Symposium, CMMR 2019
Marseille, France, October 14–18, 2019
Revised Selected Papers

Editors
Richard Kronland-Martinet
Laboratoire PRISM, CNRS-AMU
Marseilles, France

Sølvi Ystad
Laboratoire PRISM, CNRS-AMU
Marseilles, France

Mitsuko Aramaki
Laboratoire PRISM, CNRS-AMU
Marseilles, France

ISSN 0302-9743 ISSN 1611-3349 (electronic)
Lecture Notes in Computer Science
ISBN 978-3-030-70209-0 ISBN 978-3-030-70210-6 (eBook)
https://doi.org/10.1007/978-3-030-70210-6

LNCS Sublibrary: SL3 – Information Systems and Applications, incl. Internet/Web, and HCI

This Springer imprint is published by the registered company Springer Nature Switzerland AG The registered company address is: Gewerbestrasse 11, 6330 Cham, Switzerland

Preface

The 14th edition of the International Symposium on Computer Music Multidisciplinary Research CMMR2019 "Perception, Representations, Image, Sound, Music" (https://cmmr2019.prism.cnrs.fr/) took place in Marseilles on 14th-18th October 2019. This was the second CMMR event to be organized in Marseilles, but in a slightly different context than in 2013, since the present edition marked the creation of the new interdisciplinary art-science laboratory, PRISM (Perception, Representations, Image, Sound, Music), which we co-founded in 2017 and which very much reflects the spirit of the CMMR conference cycle. PRISM hosts researchers within a large variety of fields, spanning from physics and signal processing, arts and aesthetic sciences to medicine and neuroscience, that all have a common interest in the perception and representation of image, sound and music. The scientific challenge of PRISM is to reveal how the audible, the visible and their interactions generate new forms of sensitive and/or formal representations of the contemporary world.

CMMR2019 was the occasion to inaugurate the PRISM laboratory in the light of the theme of the conference and at the same time honor one of its co-founders, researcher, composer and computer music pioneer Jean-Claude Risset who sadly passed away in November 2016, only two months before the laboratory was officially inaugurated. A scientific session followed by an evening concert was dedicated to him on the first day of the conference. Jean-Claude Risset was also one of the keynote speakers during CMMR2013 in Marseilles and a video of his presentation is available here: https://cmmr2013.prism.cnrs.fr/K1.html

From the first announcement of CMMR2019 we received a large response from both scientists and artists who wanted to participate in the conference, either by organizing special sessions, presenting demos or installations or proposing workshops and concerts. Among the 15 scientific sessions that took place during the conference, eight special sessions that dealt with various subjects from sound design, immersive media and mobile devices, to music and deafness, embodying musical interaction and phenomenology of the conscious experience were scheduled. We were also lucky to have three internationally renowned keynote speakers with us during this edition: John Chowning, Professor Emeritus at Stanford University, Geoffroy Peeters, Professor at Télécom Paris and Josh McDermott, Associate Professor in the Department of Brain and Cognitive Sciences at MIT. Professor John Chowning, who also wrote a foreword that preceded this preface, and strongly encouraged the creation of multidisciplinary laboratories such as PRISM. His piece Turenas was played at the end of his keynote, followed by the concert in tribute to Jean-Claude Risset. Professor Geoffroy Peeters gave a talk on the evolution of Music Information Retrieval, and in particular the deep learning revolution in MIR, while Dr. Josh McDermott presented classic and recent approaches to auditory scene analysis. The videos of the 3 keynotes are available here: https://cmmr2019.prism.cnrs.fr/keynotes.html

As in previous CMMR editions, an artistic program accompanied the scientific sessions. The program was elaborated with "n+n corsino" and "Groupe de Musique Expérimentale de Marseille" (GMEM). The concerts took place at "La Friche la Belle de Mai" (https://www.lafriche.org/) and consisted of a virtual/augmented concert, a contemporary music concert and an interactive music image concert. Sound installations and videomusic were also presented to the participants.

In addition to the oral paper sessions, poster and demo sessions were organized, as well as five "satellite" workshops on Ubiquitous Music, Musicntwrk, Sound Morphing and the Sonic Continuum, and Introduction and Advanced Programming with the bach Library (for more details see https://cmmr2019.prism.cnrs.fr/workshops.html).

The post-proceedings edition of CMMR2019 is the 14th CMMR publication by Springer Verlag in the Lecture Notes in Computer Science Series (LNCS 2771, LNCS 3310, LNCS 3902, LNCS 4969, LNCS 5493, LNCS 5954, LNCS 6684, LNCS 7172, LNCS 7900, LNCS 8905, LNCS 9617, LNCS 10525, LNCS 11265). This year's edition contains 46 peer-reviewed chapters. It is divided into 9 sections. The first three sections are related to music information retrieval, computational musicology and composition tools, followed by a section on notations and instruments distributed on mobile devices. The fifth section concerns auditory perception and cognition, while the three following sections are related to sound design and sonic and musical interactions. The last section contains contributions that relate to Jean-Claude Risset's research.

We would like to thank all the participants of CMMR2019 who made this event possible. A special thanks to our colleagues and students at the PRISM lab as well as n+n corsino and GMEM who took care of the practical organization and insured a smooth and efficient coordination between attendees, speakers, audiences and musicians in both the scientific and artistic programs. We would also like to thank the Program and Music Committee members for their indispensable selection tasks.

Finally, we would like to thank Springer for agreeing to publish the CMMR 2019 post-proceedings edition in their LNCS series.

December 2020

Richard Kronland-Martinet
Mitsuko Aramaki
Sølvi Ystad

Foreword

"Jean-Claude Risset: Humanist, Composer, Musician, and Scientist"

"The impact of Jean-Claude Risset's death in 2016 was immediate and stunning - the news traveled fast in the worlds of music and science that had been so enriched by his life's work. But it was not always so. The path that Jean-Claude had chosen in his first years at Bell Labs, research in acoustics and psychoacoustics, was not guaranteed to be productive in music composition. However, his remarkable ability to hear inside sound pushed him toward discoveries that still resonate these many years later.

I will recount my understanding of his gradual acceptance by the colleagues he cared about, whom he admired, as they learned that there was genius behind his modest presence."

When I wrote these words of introduction to my Keynote address for the International Symposium on Computer Music Multidisciplinary Research (CMMR) on October 14, 2019, I believed that these five days would be a tribute to Jean-Claude's musical and scientific contributions and his person. It was, indeed, with excellent papers exposing the most recent research ranging from computational musicology, tools for music composition, to music and the brain.

At the outset of the symposium, there was another event that was especially important to those of us who know the history of musical and scientific research in France and Marseille in particular - the presentation of the PRISM laboratory as a permanent, formal, funded part of the Aix-Marseille University under the leadership of Richard Kronland-Martinet and Sølvi Ystad. Until then, its future was unsure. Jean-Claude's own research and teaching career was disrupted several times since his first position at Luminy in 1972, because of changes in administrative views regarding computer music. Finally, in his last years, he found a home with PRISM.

Also related to this symposium was another issue, concern for the archiving of Jean-Claude's extensive scientific writings, musical works and scores, and personal notes that he carefully kept of every presentation at every conference that he attended through his career. There seemed to be little interest in France or digital archiving technology, except at Ina-GRM and Daniel Teruggi and Yann Geslin. Beginning in 2010, Jean-Claude, Max Mathews, and I discussed where these materials should go. Finally, following his death, his family decided that the archive should remain in France, and everyone involved agreed that it should remain intact in its entirety.

Those of us involved also agreed that Stanford University Libraries, one of the most advanced digital archiving facilities globally, would be a mirror archive for Jean-Claude's work with on-demand access to his works as they become available from PRISM. But the question remained, could it be done, where are the resources, where should the archived original documents be housed?

Among the papers given at the symposium, there was *"Jean-Claude Risset and his Interdisciplinary Practice: What do the Archives Tell Us?"* Now, as I write these words (27-08-20), I have received an email from Vincent Tiffon, author of the above paper, that he and colleagues are well on their way in the beginning stages of digital documentation.

So, I conclude with the comforting knowledge that the right team is responsible for the ongoing project to digitize and archive Jean-Claude's work; his chronicle of, and contributions to, the beginning of the digital age of music will be available to all.

Link to the keynote video:
https://cmmr2019.prism.cnrs.fr/keynoteChowning.html

John M. Chowning

Organization

The 14th International Symposium on Computer Music Multidisciplinary Research CMMR2019 "Perception, Representations, Image, Sound, Music" was organized by the interdisciplinary art-science laboratory PRISM (Marseilles, France) in collaboration with QMUL (London, UK), and INESC TEC (Porto, Portugal).

Symposium Chairs

Richard Kronland-Martinet	PRISM, CNRS-AMU, Marseilles, France
Mitsuko Aramaki	PRISM, CNRS-AMU, Marseilles, France
Sølvi Ystad	PRISM, CNRS-AMU, Marseilles, France

Paper, Program, and Proceedings Chairs

Mitsuko Aramaki	PRISM, CNRS-AMU, Marseilles, France
Richard Kronland-Martinet	PRISM, CNRS-AMU, Marseilles, France
Sølvi Ystad	PRISM, CNRS-AMU, Marseilles, France
Ivan Magrin-Chagnolleau	PRISM, CNRS-AMU, Marseilles, France
Olivier Derrien	PRISM, CNRS-AMU, Marseilles, France

Committees

Local Organizing Committee

Maurane Andrianaivo	AMU, Marseilles, France
Mitsuko Aramaki	PRISM, CNRS-AMU, Marseilles, France
Corentin Bernard	PRISM, CNRS-AMU, Marseilles, France
Thomas Bordonné	PRISM, CNRS-AMU, Marseilles, France
Antoine Bourachot	PRISM, CNRS-AMU, Marseilles, France
Pascal Cesaro	PRISM, CNRS-AMU, Marseilles, France
Jacques Chatron	LMA, CNRS-AMU, Marseilles, France
Olivier Derrien	PRISM, CNRS-AMU, Marseilles, France
Simon Fargeot	PRISM, CNRS-AMU, Marseilles, France
Antoine Gonot	PRISM, CNRS-AMU, Marseilles, France
Richard Kronland-Martinet	PRISM, CNRS-AMU, Marseilles, France
Claudine Le Van Phu	PRISM, CNRS-AMU, Marseilles, France
Samuel Poirot	PRISM, CNRS-AMU, Marseilles, France
Jocelyn Rozé	PRISM, CNRS-AMU, Marseilles, France
Agnès Saez	PRISM, CNRS-AMU, Marseilles, France
Etienne Thoret	PRISM, CNRS-AMU, Marseilles, France
Adrien Vidal	PRISM, CNRS-AMU, Marseilles, France
Sølvi Ystad	PRISM, CNRS-AMU, Marseilles, France

Paper Committee

Mitsuko Aramaki	PRISM, CNRS-AMU, France
Mathieu Barthet	Queen Mary University of London, UK
Jonathan Bell	PRISM, CNRS-AMU, France
Jonathan Berger	Stanford University, USA
Gilberto Bernardes	University of Porto, Portugal
Tifanie Bouchara	CNAM, France
Sylvain Brétéché	PRISM, CNRS-AMU, France
Lionel Bringoux	ISM AMU-CNRS, France
Marco Buongiorno Nardelli	University of North Texas, USA
Amílcar Cardoso	University of Coimbra, Portugal
Chris Chafe	Stanford University, USA
Roger Dannenberg	Carnegie Mellon University, USA
Matthew Davies	INESC TEC, Portugal
Philippe Depalle	McGill University, Canada
Olivier Derrien	PRISM, CNRS-AMU, France
Christine Esclapez	PRISM, CNRS-AMU, France
Georg Essl	University of Wisconsin-Milwaukee, USA
Clément François	LPL, CNRS-AMU, France
Rolf Inge Gødoy	University of Oslo, Norway
Antoine Gonot	PRISM, CNRS-AMU, France
Keiji Hirata	Future University Hakodate, Japan
Kristoffer Jensen	re-new - Forum for Digital Art, Denmark
Richard Kronland-Martinet	PRISM CNRS-AMU, France
Marc Leman	Ghent University, Belgium
James Leonard	Grenoble Alpes University, France
Luca Ludovico	University of Milan, Italy
Olivier Macherey	LMA, CNRS-AMU, France
Ivan Magrin-Chagnolleau	PRISM, CNRS-AMU, France
Sylvain Marchand	University of La Rochelle, France
David Moffat	Queen Mary University of London, UK
Johan Pauwels	Queen Mary University of London, UK
Samuel Poirot	PRISM, CNRS-AMU, France
Matthew Rodger	Queen's University Belfast, UK
Charalampos Saitis	Queen Mary University of London, UK
Emery Schubert	University of New South Wales, Australia
Diemo Schwarz	IRCAM, France
Rod Selfridge	Queen Mary University of London, UK
Stefania Serafin	Aalborg University Copenhagen, Danmark
Peter Sinclair	PRISM, CNRS-AMU, France
Julius Smith	Stanford University, USA
Bob L. Sturm	KTH Royal Institute of Technology, Sweden
Patrick Susini	IRCAM, France
Atau Tanaka	Goldsmiths, University of London, UK
Etienne Thoret	PRISM, CNRS-AMU, Marseilles, France

Vincent Tiffon	PRISM, CNRS-AMU, France
Bruno Torrésani	I2M, CNRS-AMU, France
Jérôme Villeneuve	Université Grenoble Alpes, France
Jean Vion-Dury	PRISM, CNRS-AMU, France
Grégory Wallet	Université de Rennes 2, France
Marcelo Wanderley	McGill University, Canada
Duncan Williams	University of York, UK
Sølvi Ystad	PRISM, CNRS-AMU, France

Steering Committee

Mitsuko Aramaki	PRISM, CNRS-AMU, France
Mathieu Barthet	Queen Mary University of London, UK
Matthew Davies	INESC TEC, Portugal
Richard Kronland-Martinet	PRISM, CNRS-AMU, France
Sølvi Ystad	PRISM, CNRS-AMU, France

Contents

Auditory Perception and Cognition - From the Ear to the Body

The Process of Sound Design

Sonic Interaction for Immersive Media - Virtual and Augmented Reality

Musical Interaction: Embodiment, Improvisation, Collaboration

Jean-Claude Risset and Beyond

Music Information Retrieval - Music, Emotion and Representation

The Deep Learning Revolution in MIR: The Pros and Cons, the Needs and the Challenges

Geoffroy Peeters(✉)

LTCI, Télécom Paris, Institut Polytechnique of Paris, Paris, France
geoffroy.peeters@telecom-paris.fr
https://www.telecom-paris.fr/geoffroy.peeters

Abstract. This paper deals with the deep learning revolution in Music Information Research (MIR), i.e. the switch from knowledge-driven hand-crafted systems to data-driven deep-learning systems. To discuss the pro and cons of this revolution, we first review the basic elements of deep learning and explain how those can be used for audio feature learning or for solving difficult MIR tasks. We then discuss the case of hand-crafted features and demonstrate that, while those where indeed shallow and explainable at the start, they tended to be deep, data-driven and unexplainable over time, already before the reign of deep-learning. The development of these data-driven approaches was allowed by the increasing access to large annotated datasets. We therefore argue that these annotated datasets are today the central and most sustainable element of any MIR research. We propose new ways to obtain those at scale. Finally we highlight a set of challenges to be faced by the deep learning revolution in MIR, especially concerning the consideration of music specificities, the explainability of the models (X-AI) and their environmental cost (Green-AI).

Keywords: Music information retrieval · Audio feature · Machine-learning · Deep-learning

1 Introduction

Using Deep Neural Network (DNN) algorithms to represent the audio signal has been proposed as early as 1990 when Waibel et al. [121] proposed to use Time Delay Neural Network (TDNN) to allow the representation of the time-varying natures of phonemes in speech. Later, Bourlard et al. [14] convincingly demonstrated in their "connectionist speech recognition" the use of the discriminative projection capabilities of DNN to extract audio features. This has led, among others, to the development of the "tandem features" [48] which uses the posterior probabilities of a trained Multi-Layer-Perceptron (MLP) as audio features or the "bottleneck features" [45] extracted from the bottleneck part of a MLP. This has led today to the end-to-end speech recognition systems which inputs are directly

R. Kronland-Martinet et al. (Eds.): CMMR 2019, LNCS 12631, pp. 3–30, 2021.
https://doi.org/10.1007/978-3-030-70210-6_1

the raw audio waveforms and the output the transcribed text [101,102]. As 2012 is considered a landmark year for Computer Vision (with the AlexNet [66] network wining the ImageNet Large Scale Visual Recognition Challenge), it is also one for speech recognition with the publication of the seminal paper [52], jointly written by the research groups of the University of Toronto, Microsoft-Research, Google, and IBM-Research demonstrating the benefits of DNN architectures for speech processing.

1.1 The Deep Learning Revolution in MIR

The same year, 2012, Humphrey et al. [57] published a manifesto promoting the use of DNN for music audio processing. In this manifesto, the authors demonstrated that any hand-crafted feature (such as Mel-Frequency-Cepstral- Coefficients (MFCC) or Chroma) or algorithms (such as pitch, chord or tempo estimation) used so far are just layers of non-linear projections and pooling operations and can therefore be profitably replaced by the trainable non-linear projections of DNN.

With regard to this "deep learning revolution" announced in 2012, it is striking that the "Roadmap for Music Information Research" [108][1] published in 2013, which was supposed to guide the MIR research for the next decade, has largely missed the warning signs. In this, only one sentence refers to deep learning and in an almost negative way[2].

Since 2012, Deep Learning has progressively become the dominant paradigm in MIR. The large majority of MIR works, whether related to recognition or generation tasks, and whether based on audio, symbolic or optical-score data, rely on deep learning architectures.

1.2 What Is This Paper About?

Deep Learning (DL) is not (only) about a new Machine Learning (ML) algorithm to perform better classification or regression. It is mainly about finding homeomorphisms (performed by a cascade of non-linear projections) which allows representing the data in the manifold in which they live. This *manifold hypothesis* states that real-world high-dimensional data lie on low-dimensional manifolds embedded within this high-dimensional space (such as we perceive the earth as flat while it is a sphere; it is a 2D manifold embedded in a 3D space). Finding this manifold produces a space that makes classification and regression problems easier. It also allows new processes such as interpolation in it or generation from it. In this sense, deep learning does not only provide better representation of the

[1] http://mires.cc/files/MIRES_Roadmap_ver_1.0.0.pdf.

[2] *"More recently, deep learning techniques have been used for automatic feature learning in MIR tasks, where they have been reported to be superior to the use of hand-crafted feature sets for classification tasks, although these results have not yet been replicated in MIREX evaluations. It should be noted however that automatically generated features might not be musically meaningful, which limits their usefulness."*.

data, better solutions to existing problem but also provides new paradigms for data processing. In part Sect. 2, we first review what deep learning is and how it can be used for audio feature learning and for solving difficult MIR tasks.

While Deep Neural Network (DNN) systems are indeed often "deep" learning systems, the authors of those often refer to the non-DNN systems (those based on handcrafted audio features) as "shallow" systems. They admit however that those are more easily explainable. We would like to show here that, while hand-crafted systems were indeed shallow and explainable at the start of MIR, they tended to be deep, data-driven and unexplainable over time. We discuss this in part Sect. 3.

One assumption made by one of the god-father of MIR [50] is that MIR had 4 successive ages: - the age of audio features, - the age of semantic descriptors, - the age of context-awareness systems and - the age of creative systems. It is somehow supposed that *technology developments are driven by the desired applications.* We argue here that most of these applications (semantic, creative) already existed from a long time. However, they were hardly achievable due to the limitation of the technology at that time. It is therefore rather the opposite: *the (possible) applications are driven by the technology developments.* While the idea of "music composition by a computer" dates back to half a century [51], making this a reality, as with the OpenAI "Jukebox generative model for music" [24], was only possible thanks to the latest advances in DL (VQ-VAE and Transformer). We also argue - that the technology developments were mainly possible in MIR thanks to the accessibility of large annotated datasets, - that hand-crafted audio features were "hand-crafted" because of the lack of annotated datasets that prevented using feature learning. When those became available in the 2000s, the first feature-learning systems were proposed (such as the EDS system [88]). Today, thanks to the large accessibility of those, DNN approaches are possible. We therefore support the idea that *dataset accessibility defines the possible technology developments which define the (possible) applications.* In part Sect. 4, we argue that annotated datasets have then become the essential elements in data-driven approaches such as deep learning and we propose new way to obtain those at scale.

Application of DL methods for the processing of audio and music signals, such as done in MIR, has for long ignored the specificities of this audio and music signal and at best adapted Computer Vision networks to time and frequency audio representations. Recently, a couple of DL methods started including such specificities, such as the harmonic structure of audio signals or their sound-production model. Those pave the way to the development of audio-specific DL methods. We discuss this challenge in part Sect. 5 as well as challenges related to the explainability of the DL models (X-AI) and to the development of models with low computational costs (Green-AI).

2 Deep Learning: What Is It?

We define Deep Learning here as a deep stack of non-linear projections, obtained by non-linearly connecting layers of neurons. This process, vaguely inspired by biological neural networks, was denoted by Artificial Neural Network (ANN) in the past and by Deep Neural Network (DNN) since [53]. Deep Learning encompasses a large set of possible algorithms (often considered as a "zoo") which can be roughly organized according to - their **architecture**, i.e. the way neurons are connected to each other, - the way these architectures are combined into **meta-architectures** (defined by the task at hand) - the **training paradigm** which defines the criteria to be optimized.

2.1 DNN Architectures

A DNN architecture defines a function f with parameters θ applied to an input x. Its output $\hat{y} = f_\theta(x)$ approximates a ground-truth value y according to some measurements (a "Loss"). The parameters θ are (usually) trained in a supervised way using a set of input/output pairs $(x^{(i)}, y^{(i)})$. The parameters θ are (usually) estimated using one variant of the Steepest Gradient Descent: moving θ in the opposite direction of the gradients of the Loss function w.r.t. to the θ. These gradients are obtained using the back-propagation algorithm [99]. The function f is defined by the architecture of the network. The three main architectures are:

Multi-Layer-Perceptron (MLP). In this, neurons of adjacent layers are organized in a Fully-Connected (FC) way, i.e. each neuron $a_j^{[l]}$ of a layer $[l]$ is connected to all neurons $a_i^{[l-1]}$ of the previous layer $[l-1]$. The connections are done through multiplication by weights $w_{ij}^{[l]}$, addition of a bias $b_j^{[l]}$ and passing through a non-linear function (activation function) g (the common sigmoid, tanh or ReLu functions). Each $w_{:j}^{[l]}$ therefore defines a specific projection j of the neurons i of the previous layer (as seen in Fig. 1).

Convolutional Neural Network (CNN). While the FC architecture does not assume any specific organization between the neurons of a given layer, in the CNN architecture we assume a *local connectivity* of those. This is done to allow representing the specificities of vision were nearby pixels are usually more correlated[3] than far-away ones. To do so, each "spatial region" (x, y) of $\vec{A}_i^{[l-1]}$ (which is now an image) is projected individually. The resulting projections of the (x, y) are also considered as an image, and is denoted by feature-map and noted $\vec{A}_{i \rightarrow j}^{[l]}$ for the jth projection. CNN also add a *parameter sharing* property: for a given j, the same projection $\vec{W}_{ij}^{[l]}$ (which is now a matrix) is used to project the different regions (x, y), i.e. the weights are shared. Doing so allows to apply the same projection[4] to the various regions (x, y) of $\vec{A}_i^{[l-1]}$. Combining these two properties lead to the convolutional operator [39,68], i.e. the projections are expressed as convolutions. In practice there are several input feature-maps $\vec{A}_{1 \dots i \dots I}^{[l-1]}$, the convolution is performed over x and y with a tensor $\vec{W}_{:j}^{[l]}$ that

[3] such as the adjacent pixels that form a "cat's ear".

[4] such as $\vec{W}_{ij}^{[l]}$ represeting a "cat's ears" detectors.

extends over I (as seen in Fig. 1). The result of this convolution is an output feature-map $\vec{A}_j^{[l]}$. As MLP can have J different projections $w_{:j}^{[l]}$, CNN can have J different convolutions $\vec{W}_{:j}^{[l]}$; resulting in J output feature maps. As in MLP the output feature maps are the inputs of the next layer. CNN is the most popular architecture in Computer Vision.

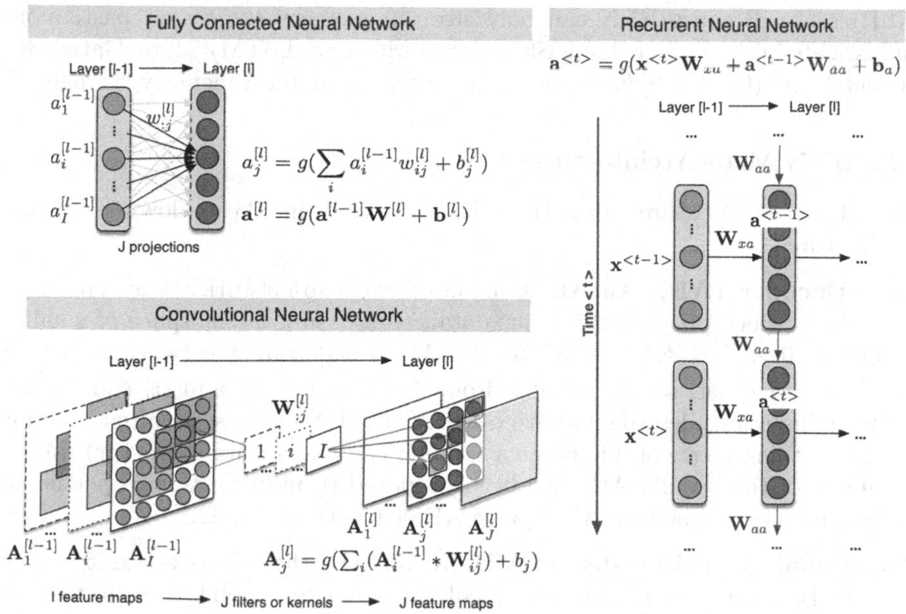

Fig. 1. Fully-Connected (as used in MLP), Convolutional (as used in CNN) and Recurrent (as used in RNN) architectures.

Temporal Convolutional Network (TCN). While attempts have been made to apply CNN to a 2D representation of the audio signal (such as its spectrogram), recent approaches [26] use **1D-Convolution** directly applied on the raw audio waveform. The motivation of using such convolution is to learn better filters than the ones of usual spectral transforms (for example the sines and cosines of the Fourier transform). However, compared to images, audio waveforms are of much higher dimensions[5]. To solve this issue, [86] have proposed in their WaveNet model the use of **1D-Dilated-Convolutions** (also named convolution-with-holes or atrous-convolution). The 1D-Dilated-Convolutions is at the heart of the **Temporal Convolutional Network (TCN)** [7] which is very popular in audio today.

Recurrent Neural Network (RNN). While CNN allows representing the spatial correlations of the data, they do not allow to represent the sequential

[5] 1 s of an audio signal with a sampling rate of 100 Hz is a vector of dimension 44 100.

aspect of the data (such as the succession of words in a text, or of images in a video). RNN [99] is a type of architecture with a memory that keeps track of the previously processed events of the sequence. For this, the internal/hidden representation of the data at time t, $\vec{a}^{<t>}$, does not only depend on the input data $\vec{x}^{<t>}$ but also on the internal/hidden representation at the previous time $\vec{a}^{<t-1>}$ (as seen in Fig. 1). Because of this, RNN architectures have become the standard for processing sequences of words in Natural Language Processing (NLP) tasks. Because RNN can only store in memory the recent past, more sophisticated cells such as Long Short Term Memory (LSTM)[54] or Gated Recurrent Units (GRU)[19] have been proposed for long-term memory storage.

2.2 DNN Meta-Architectures

The above architectures can then be combined in the following "meta-architectures".

Auto-Encoder (AE). An AE is made of two sub-networks: - an encoding network ϕ_e which projects the input data $\vec{x} \in \mathbb{R}^M$ in a latent space of smaller dimensionality: $\vec{z} = \phi_e(\vec{x}) \in \mathbb{R}^d$ $(d << M)$; - a decoding network ϕ_d which attempts to reconstruct the input $\vec{x}$ from $\vec{z}$: $\hat{\vec{y}} = \phi_d(\vec{z})$. ϕ_e and ϕ_d can be any of the architectures described above (MLP, CNN, RNN). AEs are often used for feature learning ($\vec{z}$ is considered as a feature; ϕ_e as a feature extractor). Many variations of this vanilla AE have been proposed to improve the properties of the latent space (Denoising AE, Sparse AE or Contractive AE).

Variational Auto-Encoder (VAE). In an AE, the latent space $\vec{z}$ is not smooth. Because of this, it is not possible to sample a point from it to generate new data $\hat{y}$. To allow this generation, VAEs [64] have been proposed. In a VAE, the encoder and decoder are considered as posterior probability $p_\theta(\vec{z}|\vec{x})$ and likelihood $p_\theta(\vec{x}|\vec{z})$. The encoder actually estimates the parameters of a distribution (here Gaussian for convenience); $\vec{z}$ is then sampled from this estimated distribution and given to the decoder for maximizing the likelihood of $\vec{x}$. Given the smoothness of the latent space $\vec{z}$, it is possible to sample a point from it to generate new data $\hat{y}$.

Generative Adversarial Network (GAN). Another popular type of network for generation is the GAN [41]. GAN only contains the decoder part of an AE here named "Generator" G. Contrary to the VAE, $\vec{z}$ is here explicitly sampled from a chosen distribution $p(\vec{z})$. Since $\vec{z}$ does not arise from any existing real data, the Generator $G(\vec{z})$ must learn to generate data that look real. This is achieved by defining a second network, the "Discriminator" D, which goal is to discriminate between real and fake (the generated ones) data. D and G are trained in turn using a minmax optimization.

Encoder/Decoder (ED). ED [19] or Sequence-to-Sequence [115] architectures can be considered as an extension of the AE for sequences: an input sequence $\{\vec{x}^{<1>} \dots \vec{x}^{<t>} \dots \vec{x}^{<T_x>}\}$ of length T_x is encoded into $\vec{z}$ which then serves as initialization for decoding a sequence $\{\vec{y}^{<1>} \dots \vec{y}^{<\tau>} \dots \vec{y}^{<T_y>}\}$ of length T_y in another domain. Both sequences can have different lengths. This architecture is very popular in machine translation where an input English sentence is translated into an output French sentence (encoder and decoder are then RNNs). It is also used for generating text caption from input images [120] (the encoder is then a deep CNN and the decoder a RNN). Extensions of the ED or Sequence-to-Sequence architecture have been proposed to allows a better encoding of the input sequences information, as in the Attention Mechanism [6] or in the Transformer [119].

Neural Autoregressive Models. Autoregressive model aims at predicting a value x_n as a linear combination of its P preceding values: $x_n = \sum_{p=1}^{P} a_p x_{n-p}$. In Neural Auto-regressive models, this linear combination is replaced by a DNN. For audio, the most popular model is probably **Wavenet** [86]. In this, the conditional probability distribution $p(x_n|x_1, \ldots, x_{n-1})$ is modeled by a stack of TCNs. The model is trained to predict x_n which is here discretized into classes.

2.3 DNN Training Paradigms and Losses

Once the architecture and meta-architecture are defined, one still has to define the criterion to be optimized during the training. This criterion corresponds to the task to be solved and is defined by a "loss" to be minimized by optimizing the parameters θ. Deep learning actually provides a large set of possible training paradigms. The most popular are the following.

Classification. In the simplest case of *binary classification*, the network has a single output neuron (with sigmoid activation) and is trained to estimate the probability of the positive class: $\hat{y} = p(y = 1|x)$. This is done by minimizing a Binary-Cross-Entropy (BCE) loss between y and $\hat{y}$. In the most common case of *multi-class classification* (predicting a given class c among C mutually exclusive classes), the network has C output neurons (with softmax activations) which are trained to estimate the probability $\hat{y_c} = p(y = c|x)$. This is done by minimizing a cross-entropy loss between the y_c and the $\hat{y}_c$. The case of *multi-label classification* (C non-mutually exclusive classes) is processes as a set of C parallel binary classifications.

Reconstruction. When the goal of the network is to reconstruct the input data (such as with AE), the simple Mean Square Error (MSE) between the output and input data is used: $MSE = \sum_{i=1}^{N} ||\vec{x}^{(i)} - \hat{\vec{y}}^{(i)}||^2$.

Metric Learning. Metric learning aims at automatically constructing (using ML) distance metrics from data. DNN provides a nice framework for this. In this, the parameters θ of a network are learnt such that a distance function $g(f_\theta(x), f_\theta(y))$ is minimized for similar training samples x and y and maximized for dissimilar samples. A common choice for g is the Euclidean distance. A popular method for this is the minimization of a "triplet loss" [105]). In this, three data samples are simultaneously considered: an anchor a, a positive p (similar to a) and a negative n (dissimilar to a). The goal is to iteratively train the network on such triplets to ensure that the distance between $f_\theta(p)$ and $f_\theta(a)$ is smaller than between $f_\theta(n)$ and $f_\theta(a)$.

2.4 Deep Learning for Audio Feature Learning

We first highlight here why it make sense to use deep learning for learning audio and music representations. To phrase Humphrey et al. [57] in their manifesto, a DNN is *"a cascade of multiple layers, composed of a few simple operations: affine transforms, point-wise non-linearities and pooling operators. Cascaded non-linearities allow for complex systems composed of simple, linear parts. Music is composed by hierarchies of pitch and loudness forming chords and melodies, phrases and sections, eventually building entirely pieces. Deep structures are well suited to encode these relationships."* At the lowest level, a large part of the most-commonly used audio signal processing algorithms can be formulated as a cascade of affine transformations, non-linear transforms and pooling operations. This is for example the case of the Discrete-Fourier-Transform (DFT). In this the signal is projected on a set of basis (affine transform) from which the absolute value can be taken (point-wise non-linearity). This is also the case of the MFCC or of the Chroma as illustrated in Fig. 2. Principal Component Analysis (PCA) or Non Negative Matrix Factorization (NMF) are also linear affine transformations but are learnt. The only difference between these transformations lies in their parameterization. DL hence provides a convenient framework to learn such parametrization from the data.

Following this idea, the training of "deep-chroma" (a "chroma" representation obtained as the output of a trained DNN) have for example been proposed in [65] (using chord recognition as a pretext task) or [125] (using weakly aligned score-audio pairs as pretext task). In both of these, DL is not used to achieve the final task (chord or alignment) but only to get a better chroma representations.

NMF can also be reformulated using DL as proposed in Smaragdis et al. [113] using a deep AE. In NMF, an observed matrix $X \in \mathbb{R}^+$ is reconstructed as the product of a basis-matrix $W \in \mathbb{R}^+$ with an activation-matrix $H \in \mathbb{R}^+$: $\hat{X} = W \cdot H$. By comparison, in an AE, X is reconstructed by passing z (which plays the same role as H) in the decoder ϕ_d (which plays the same role as W): $\hat{X} = \phi_d(z)$. A positivity can be imposed by using ReLu activations. NMF can then be considered a linear version of the more expressive AE.

2.5 Deep Learning for Solving Difficult MIR Tasks

Apart from audio feature learning, DL can be used to solve difficult MIR tasks. We consider here three of those.

Blind Audio Source Separation (BASS) deals with the development of algorithms to recover one or several source signals $s_j(t)$ from a given mixture signal $x(t) = \sum_j s_j(t)$ without any additional information. For a long time, BASS algorithms relied on the application of Computational Auditory Scene Analysis (CASA) principles [16] or matrix decomposition methods (mostly ICA or NMF).

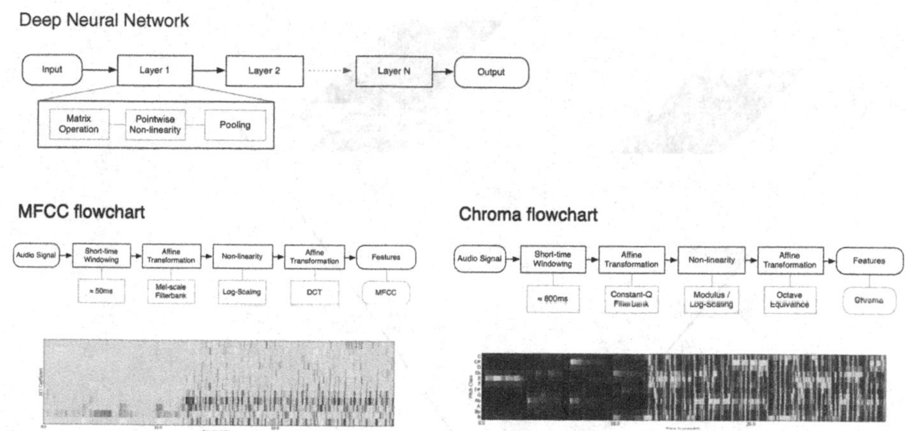

Fig. 2. Deep Neural Network for feature learning. [Top] A neural network as a cascade of matrix multiplication, non-linearity and pooling operations. [Bottom left] MFCC computation flowchart as cascade of affine transforms and non-linearities, [Bottom right] same from Chroma computation. Figure adapted from [56].

In recent years DNN methods have allowed to largely improve the separation quality by formulating it as a supervised task: a model is trained to transform an input mixed signal $x(t)$ to an output separated source $s_j(t)$ or to an output separation mask $m_j(t)$ to be applied to the input $s_j(t) = x(t) \odot m_j(t)$. Such a DNN model often takes the form of a Convolutional Denoising Auto- Encoder (CDAE) (as in Computer Vision) where CNN encoder and decoder are trained to reconstruct the clean signal from its noisy version. However, such a CDAE tends to blur the fine details of the spectrogram. In Jansson et al. [59], a U-Net architecture [98] is then proposed: it is an AE with skip-connections between the encoder and the decoder (see Fig. 3). It has been applied to a spectrogram representation to isolate the singing voice from real[6] polyphonic music. The network is trained to output a Time/Frequency mask $M_j(t, f)$ which is applied to the amplitude Short-Time Fourier Transform (STFT) of the mixture $|X(t, f)|$ to separate the amplitude STFT of the isolated source $|S_j(t, f)| = |X(t, f)| \odot M_j(t, f)$. This simple network has provided a large increase in source separation performances.

Cover Detection. "Covers" denote the various recorded interpretations of a same musical composition (for example "Let It Be" performed by The Beatles or performed by Aretha Franklin). For a long time, two tracks were considered covers of each other if they shared similar harmonic content over time. This content was represented by the sequence of Chroma vectors[7] of the track. Tracks were then compared pair-by-pair by computing the cost necessary to align their respective sequences. This cost was generally obtained using Dynamic Time

[6] non-synthetic.

[7] or more elaborated versions of it.

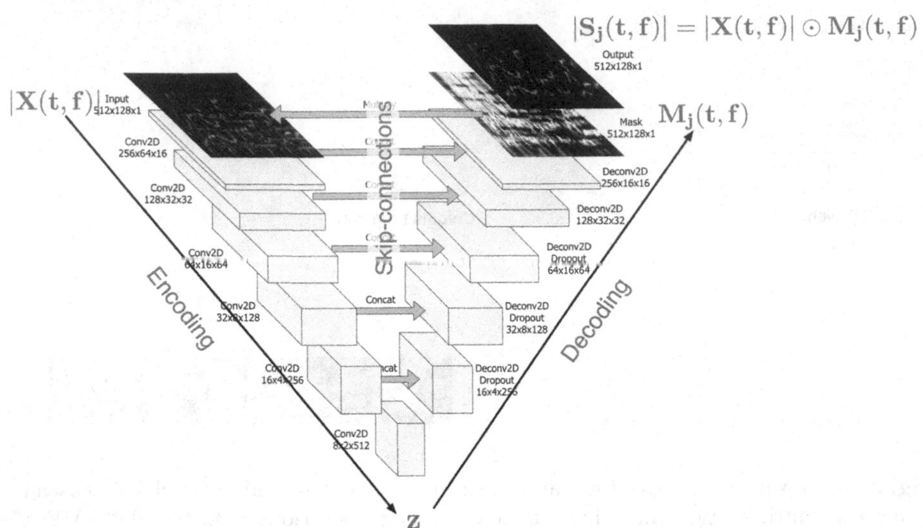

Fig. 3. Source separation using a U-Net architecture. Figure adapted from [58].

Warping[8] as in [107]. This led to a computationally expensive algorithm. Also only one facet of the problem was considered: the harmonic content. While it is hard to define exactly why two tracks are "covers" of each other[9], it is easy to provide examples and counter-examples of those. This is the approach proposed by Doras et al. in [27–29]. In this, the content of a track is represented using jointly a Constant-Q-Transform (CQT), the sequence of its estimated dominant melody and multi-pitches. Those are fed to deep CNN networks which architecture projects them to a time-less vector. The weights of the deep CNN are then trained using a triplet loss paradigm [105], i.e. given simultaneously an anchor track, a positive example (a cover of the anchor) and a negative example (a non-cover of the anchor) a triplet loss is minimized. This simple formulation has provided a large increase in cover-detection performances.

Music Translation aims at translating an input music track $\vec{x}$ with {musical instruments, genres, and style} i to an output y with {musical instruments, genres, and style} j while preserving the musical score. In Mor et al. [83], this ambitious goal is achieved without explicitly extracting the musical score and with a single but smart network illustrated in Fig. 4. We detail this system here since it is quite representative of current audio DL systems. The network has the form of an AE. An encoder E (a single WaveNet [86] for all i) is used to project $\vec{x}$ in the latent space $\vec{z}$. $\vec{z}$ is then used to reconstruct an output music track with {musical instruments, genres, and style} j. This is achieved by specific decoders D^j for each j (which are all WaveNet decoders). The encoder and decoder are

[8] or more elaborated algorithms.

[9] Consider the case of "Blurred Lines" by Pharrell Williams and Robin Thicke and "Got to Give It Up" by Marvin Gaye.

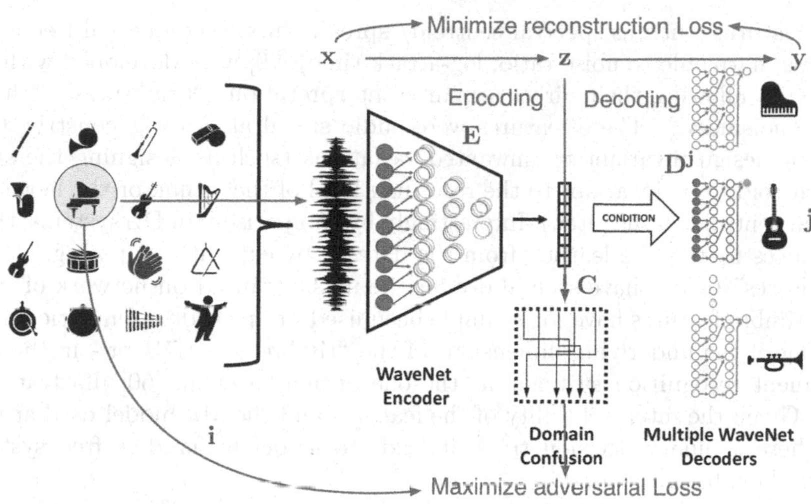

Fig. 4. Music translation using Auto-Encoder with reconstruction and adversarial losses. Figure adapted from [83].

trained to minimize a *reconstruction loss* between $\vec{x}$ and $\vec{y}$. However, for the translation to work, it is important that $\vec{z}$ does not contain information related to the {musical instruments, genres, and style} i, and only contains information related to the musical score. To achieve the *disentanglement* of $\vec{z}$, a classifier C is first trained to recognize i from $\vec{z}$. With C fixed (the parameters are not changed anymore), we then add an *adversarial loss*, i.e. we train the encoder E to maximize a classification loss (to guarantee that it is not possible to recognize i from $\vec{z}$). The final system is then trained to minimize the *reconstruction loss* and maximize the *adversarial loss.* While difficult to quantity, convincing music translation results are obtained with this system[10].

3 Deep Learning: Was the Learning so Shallow and Explainable Before?

Deep learning systems are often denoted as "deep" in comparison to the hand-crafted systems previously used in MIR which are considered "shallow". **We argue here that while hand-crafted systems were indeed shallow and explainable at the start of ISMIR, they tended to be deep, data-driven and unexplainable over time.** To demonstrate this, we consider four main trends (almost chronological) in audio feature design.

3.1 Audio Feature Design: The Timbre Period

Around 2004, the design of audio features was mostly driven by the description of the timbre aspect of the sound or its acoustic characteristics. On one side, timbre

[10] https://research.fb.com/publications/a-universal-music-translation-network/.

scalar features (such as spectral centroid/ spread/ flux, fundamental frequency, loudness, harmonic to noise ratio, log-attack time) [90] were developed with the purpose of allowing their direct semantic interpretation ("brightness", "sharpness", "noisiness"). These features were audio signal algorithms constructured to be by-design invariant to unwanted variations (such as designing the spectral centroid to be invariant to the recording level of the signal, or the harmonic spectral centroid to the pitch). Interestingly by comparison, in DL systems, these invariances need to be learned from the data or by explicitly imposing "adversarial losses" (as we have seen above for the music translation network of [83]). These timbre features have for example been used - to provide a semantic understanding of the underlying dimensions of the "timbre spaces"[11] or - in the first instrument recognition systems, as the one of Jensen et al. [60] illustrated in Fig. 5. Given the interpretability of the features and the ML model used at that time (here a binary decision tree), it leads to associate hand-crafted systems with explainable systems.

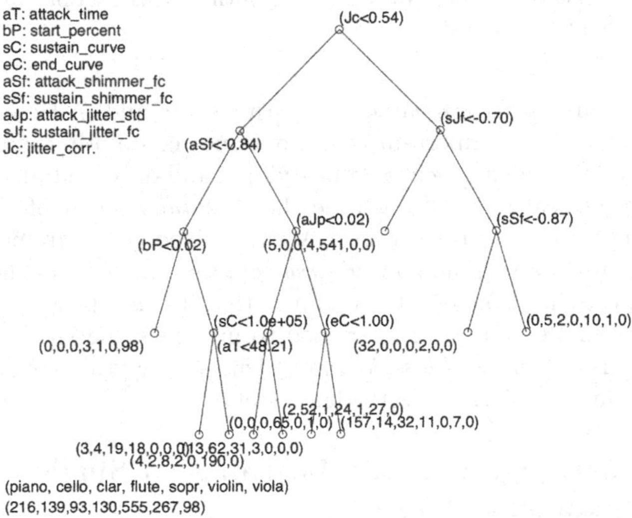

Fig. 5. Instrument classification using timbre features and binary decision tree. Figure from [60].

On the other side, features were developped to provide a representation of the whole timbre characteristics as a single vector. In speech processing, the well-known MFCC [15] were proposed. Those use the underlying model of speech production (the source/filter model) combined with a simplified model of perception (critical bands are modeled by a Mel scale). Without much justification,

[11] The "timbre spaces" are the results of a Multi-Dimensional-Scaling (MDS) analysis of similarity/dissimilarity user ratings between pairs of sounds as obtained through perceptual experiments [78].

those were then considered also as the timbre representation of polyphonic multi-source music [72]. To describe the harmonic content of a signal, a Chroma (also named Pitch-Class-Profile) [38,122] vector representation was proposed.

For complex recognition task (such as drum recognition [49] or large-scale instrument recognition [91]), Automatic Feature Selection algorithms were then developped to allow automatically selecting, from the pool of hand-crafted features, the most relevant for a task at hand. It is interesting to consider that, already at that time, a debate existed related to whether it was better to automatically select the most relevant hand-crafted features or to automatically generate those (using genetic algorithms in [88]).

3.2 Audio Feature Design: The Dynamic Features

All the above representations allowed the description of the sound content around a given time without much consideration of the temporal aspects of the sound (with the exception of the log-attack-time or spectral flux). The temporal evolution of the sound properties was usually simply represented using delta, delta-delta or the first two statistical moments of the features (mean and standard deviation). While this simplification may hold for a stationary process, it surely does not for non-stationary signals as music. Because of this, more sophisticated temporal models were developed around 2010 as the "block-level" features [110]. In those, elaborated summary of the temporal behavior of the audio features are proposed based on the computation of specific percentiles of histogram of the features, temporal correlation pattern or fluctuation pattern (amplitude modulation coefficients weighted by psychoacoustic models).

3.3 Audio Feature Design: Taking Inspiration from Auditory Physiology and Neuro-Science

A completely different path on feature design arose from auditory physiology and neuro-science. As demonstrated in the work of [104] "the mammalian auditory system has a specialized sensitivity to amplitude modulation of narrow-band acoustic signals". This has opened the path to the development of audio features specialized in representing these modulations, such as the modulation spectrogram [4,44] the first and second order modulation spectrogram with inter-band correlation [33,79], the Spectro Temporal Receptive Fields [18] or the well-mathematically-formulated Joint Time/Frequency scattering transform based on a cascade of wavelet transforms [1]. As demonstrated by Mallat [74] this scattering representation actually shares many of the properties of the Deep Learning CNN architecture while providing an explanation to its success.

3.4 Audio Feature Design in Speech: Toward Deep Trained Models

Audio feature design owes speech processing a lot. Between the MFCCs and the Deep Learning era[12], a large set of deep features have been proposed for speech

[12] The idea of using DL for representation learning in audio was initially proposed in the case of speech as described in [52].

processing. For example, the so-called *supervector* features [96] were proposed for speaker identification. Those represent the necessary adaptation[13] of a Universal Background Model (UBM) to represent a target speaker. This UBM is a Gaussian Mixture Model used to pave the space of possible MFCCs values for speech. Joint Factor Analysis [61] or i-Vector [23] further extended this idea by decomposing the *supervector* into speaker independent, speaker dependent, transmission-channel and residual components. Those deep features have been used very successfully to describe non-speech sounds (audio scene classification [32] or music [17], [31]). In these representations, ML is used as a way to find the projection space. Matching pursuit (decomposition of a sound as a set of atoms or molecules), Non Negative Matrix Factorization or Probabilistic Latent Component Analysis have also been used to train projections of the data which facilitate recognition task (for example pitch and instrument in Leveau et al. [70], pitch only in Smaragdis et al. [112] or vocal-imitations in Marchetto et al. [75]).

With the above in mind, we can say that considering hand-crafted systems as shallow and explainable is an over-simplification of the reality. While this was true at the beginning, the last hand-crafted systems (such as the one based on i-Vectors illustrated in Fig. 6) were for sure deep and hardly explainable.

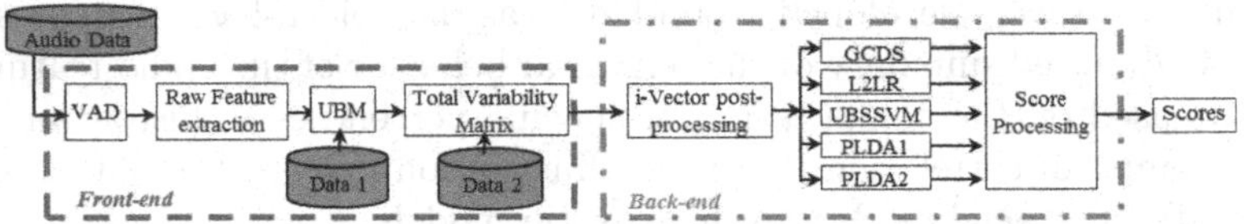

Fig. 6. Advanced system for speaker recognition based on i-Vector representation, Gaussianized Cosine Distance Scoring (GCDS), Regularized Logistic Regression (L2LR), Universal Background Support SVM (UBSSVM) and Probabilistic Linear Discriminant Analysis (PLDA). Figure from [71].

However, a major difference between hand-crafted systems and deep learning system lies in their construction. Hand-crafted systems are designed by optimizing separately the successive stages of the system (such as improving the audio features, their automatic selection/ transformation, the classification algorithm). In the opposite, in deep learning those are just parts of a single DNN which parameters are all jointly optimized (as we have seen above for the music translation network of [83]).

4 Deep Learning: Datasets

We Argue Here that Annotated Datasets are Probably the Most Sustainable Part of Any MIR Research Today. This statement seems obvious if we consider that DL approaches are data-driven approaches and that therefore

[13] using an Expectation-Maximization algorithm.

the knowledge is in the annotated data. Another way to demonstrate this is to consider that the outputs of a research program are: (1) scientific reasoning or experimental results (as published in scientific papers), (2) program code (as published on github.com), (3) annotated dataset (as published on zenodo.org). In audio-content-analysis, (1) is usually achieved by applying the most recent ML algorithms (Gaussian Mixture Model, Hidden Markov Model, Support Vector Machine in the past, DL today). (1) is therefore likely to change as quickly as the advances of ML. (2) is associated to programming environment. While Matlab has been the leading environment for numerical computing for long (hence the development of the Timbre toolbox [90] or the MIR toolbox [67] in Matlab), it has been replaced by the fastest C/C++ (hence the development Marsyas [117], Yaafe [76] or Essentia [13] library in C++); which has been replaced by the much-more-easy-to-use data-science programming language python (hence the development of the librosa [80] package). Only (3) seems sustainable.

However, for long, annotated datasets have only been considered as side tools necessary to validate the scientific reasoning. Regarding this, it is interesting to consider that the GTZAN dataset (one of the most used dataset) was actually not published but only used internally by the authors to validate their experiment in [118]. The first published datasets, AIST-RWC [42,43] and QMUL-Isophonic [77], were only presented as posters or "late-breaking-news/demo" during conferences. Despite that, they all had an enormous influence on MIR research. Today, in the new data-driven area (where knowledge arise directly from the data), things have however changed: a significant part of the papers presented at the ISMIR conference concern such datasets, and the TISMIR journal has a dedicated track for those.

As a proof of the importance and sustainability of this datasets, it is interesting to consider the most cited works of well-known researchers: - Georges Tzanetakis most cited contribution relates to the GTZAN dataset [118]: 3446 citations[14], - Thierry Bertin-Mahieux to Million-Song-Dataset [10]: 1161 citations, - Masataka Goto second and third most cited contributions to AIST-RWC [42,43]: 744 and 586 citations, - Rachel Bittner to Medley-DB [12]: 264 citations.

4.1 New Practices for the Development of MIR Annotated Datasets

The development of such MIR annotated datasets follows several paths: - the recording of new audio material (McGill Sound Library [87], Ircam Studio-On-Line [8], AIST-RWC [42], ENST MAPS [34], Medley-DB [12]), - the use of copyright-free material (Jamendo [94], FMA [22]), - the use of copyrighted material (GTZAN [118], Harmonix [84]). The annotation process also follows different paths: - careful-manual-annotations (AIST-RWC [42]), - crowd-sourced annotations (Million-Song-Dataset [10]), - web-grabbed annotations (Ircam DALI [82]). The size of those also seems to increase over time; according to [58]: from one hour of audio in 2000 to one year of audio in 2020.

[14] The citation figures are derived from Google Scholar as of December 15th, 2020.

It is interesting to consider how trends in DL as used in multimedia, Computer Vision or Natural Language Processing also progressively influence MIR practices for the development of MIR annotated datasets.

Data-Augmentation. Among those, data-augmentation aims at extending the set of training data in order to better cover the distribution $p(x, y)$. Indeed, training a ML system is equivalent to try to approximate the unknown distribution $p(x, y)$ between its inputs x and outputs y. While unknown, the distribution $p(x, y)$ is observed through a set of pairs $(x^{(i)}, y^{(i)})$ (the training data) sampled from this distribution. The goal of training is to minimize a risk on these data (Empirical Risk Minimization). Data augmentation aims at increasing the coverage performed by these samples. This is done by extending the set of $x^{(i)}$ (using processing) while preserving $y^{(i)}$. In audio, such processing are - the addition of noise, - equalization, - distortion, - quantification, - time-stretc.hing, - pitch-shifting. While the data can be augmented automatically, the set of possible augmentations should be decided manually based on a *prior knowledge of the relationship between x and y*. For example, pitch-shifting (time-stretching) cannot be applied blindly to $x^{(i)}$ if the labels $y^{(i)}$ depend on pitch information (on tempo information). This may seem counter-intuitive since the goal of ML is precisely to acquire the knowledge of the relationship between x and y. Data-augmentation has for example been used in Cohen-Hadria et al. [21] to increase the training data for a singing-voice separation task.

Semi-Supervised Learning. Semi-Supervised Learning (Semi-SL) combines training with a small amount of labeled data and training with a large amount of unlabeled data. One popular form of Semi-SL used the so-called *teacher-student paradigm.* It is a supervised learning technique in which the knowledge of a teacher (a model trained on clean labeled data) is used to label a large set of unlabeled data which is used in turn to train student models. It has for example been used in audio - by Aytar et al. [5] in SoundNet to transfer knowledge from Computer Vision models to audio models (using the synchronization of images and audio channels in Audio-Video clips), - by Wu et al. [124] to train deep learning models for drum transcription (using the output of Partially-Fixed-NMF model for the same task), or - by Meseguer-Brocal et al. [81] to train deep learning models for singing-voice detection (by iterating the training using the output of a deep CNN initialized with clean data).

Self-Supervised Learning. Self-Supervised Learning (Self-SL) is a supervised learning technique in which the training data are automatically labeled. To automatically create labels, one can use the natural temporal synchronization between the various modalities of multi-media data as used in the "Look, Listen and Learn" [2], "Object that Sounds" [3] or "Sound of the Pixels" [126] networks. It is also possible to train the network to predict a modification of the input: such as cropping, distorting or rotating an image, or shuffling a video sequence. In audio, such an approach has been proposed by Gfeller et al. [40] in SPICE (Self-supervised Pitch Estimation) to predict the pitch transposition factor applied to the input. As for data augmentation, the set of processes applied to the input is directly governed by the nature of the data to be described by the network. Therefore, as for data augmentation, one should have a prior knowledge of the relationship between x and y to decide on the set of processes to be applied.

The aim of these three approaches is to allow the automatic annotation of audio data and hence to allow the development of very large annotated datasets.

5 Deep Learning: What Are the Challenges for Deep MIR?

We highlight here a set of challenges for deep-MIR.

5.1 Toward Taking into Account Audio and Music Specificities in Models

The first challenge relates to the necessity to develop Deep Learning models that take into account the specificities of audio and music. While it seems obvious to do so, it has not been the case at the start. To understand this, we need to sum up the short history of DNN for audio. We do so by distinguishing four successive periods. Those correspond to increasing consideration/integration of audio/music specificities/knowledge in the models.

First Period: Time-Frequency Representation. The first attempts to use DNN for audio signals date back to 1990 where Waibel et al. [121] proposed a so-called Time-Delay Neural Network (TDNN), an architecture similar to a 1-D convolution over time. As most models proposed in the first period[15], the audio is represented by a time-frequency representation: a Mel-spectrogram in [121]. In MIR, time-frequency representation inputs have also been used at the start of DL. For example, Dieleman [25] used this representation as input to a CNN but only performed convolution over time. In the opposite, Choi et al. [20] considered time/frequency representations as natural images and applied a Computer Vision CNN to it, hence performing convolution both over time and frequency.

However, time/frequency representations cannot be considered as natural images. In *natural images* - the two axis x and y represent the same concept (spatial position), - the elements of an image have the same meaning independently of their positions over x and y, - the neighboring pixels are usually highly correlated (they often belong to the same object). In *time-frequency representations* - the two axis x and y represent profoundly different concepts (time and frequency), - the elements of a spectrogram have the same meaning independently of their positions over time but not over frequency, - the neighboring pixels of a spectrogram are not necessarily correlated (the harmonics of a given sound source can be distributed over the whole frequency in a sparse way

[15] The first period encloses all the models from the "connectionist speech recognition" approaches [14], "tandem features" [48] "bottleneck features" [45] until the seminal paper of [52] (which defines the new baseline for speech recognition system as the DNN-HMM model).

and interleaved with the ones of another source). Because of this, when using CNN architectures, one should carefully choose the shape of the filters and the axis along which the convolution is performed. Therefore, as opposed to Choi et al. [20], Pons et al. [92] specifically addresses these differences by designing musically-motivated filters. The shapes of the CNN filters are carefully chosen to allow representing the timbre (vertical filters extending over the frequency axis) or the rhythm (horizontal filters extending over the time axis) content of a music track.

Second Period: End-To-End Systems. While musically-motivated CNN filter shape is a promising path, one still has to manually design this shape for a given application. Also, one has to decide what is the most appropriate 2D representation (STFT, Log-Mel-Spectrogram (LMS), CQT) and its parameters (window size, hop size, number of bands) for a given application. For these reasons, the so-called "end-to-end" approaches, which consider directly the raw audio waveform as input, have been developed. In those, a 1D-convolution (a convolution over time with 1D-filters) on the waveform is used for the first layer of the network. This is the case of [26] with large temporal filters or of [63,69] in Sample-CNN with a cascade of small temporal filters. While these filters can theoretically re-learn the sines and cosines basis of the Fourier transform (or Gamma-tone filters in [100]), in practice their training often lead to noisy and hardly interpretable temporal basis. One reason for this is the lack of Time Translation Invariance (TTI). TTI is a property of a transform that makes it insensitive to the time translation (or phase shift) of the input. The modulus/amplitude of the DFT (as used in the spectrogram) is TTI.

Third Period: Introducing Audio Signal Knowledge. With this in mind, Ravanelli et al. [95] proposed SincNet, a deep learning model which defines the 1D-filters as a parametric function g (the difference between two sinc functions) which theoretical frequency responses are parameterizable band pass filters. The training therefore consists in estimating the parameters of g. To deal with the TTI property, Noe et al. [85] extended SincNet to the complex domain in the Complex Gabor CNN. It is also possible to use knowledge of the underlying sound-production-model to construct DNN models. Such models can be the source/filter model[16] or the harmonic model[17]. For example, in Basaran et al. [9] the source/filter model is assumed. A NMF source/filter model [30] is first used. A DNN is then fed with the source activation matrix to predict the dominant melody. The Deep Salience network of Bittner et al. [11] assumes an harmonic model. This model leads to the development of an Harmonic CQT which is fed to a DNN to predict the dominant melody. The aims of the Harmonic CQT is to bring back the vicinity of the harmonics of a sound (spread over the whole spectrum) by projecting each frequency f into a third dimension (the depth of

[16] where a sound $x(t)$ is considered as the results of the convolution of a periodic source signal $s(t)$ with a filter $h(t)$: $x(t) = (s * e)(t)$.

[17] where a sound with a pitch f_0 is represented in the spectral domain as a set of harmonically related components at frequencies $hf_0, h \in \mathbb{N}^+$ with amplitudes a_h.

the input) which represents the values of the spectrum at the harmonics hf. Combining the idea of SincNet with the Harmonic CQT leads to the Harmonic-CNN of Won et al. [123]. In this the 1D-convolution is performed with filters constrained as for SincNet but extended to the harmonic dimensions (stacking band-pass filters at harmonic frequencies hf_c).

Fourth Period: Implementing a Sound-Production-Model as a Network. Just as SincNet defines the 1D-filters as parametric functions g and trains the parameters of g, Engel et al. propose in their Differentiable Digital Signal Processing (DDSP) [35] to represent a sound-production-model (here the Spectral Modeling Synthesis (SMS) model [109]) as a network. The network combines harmonic additive synthesis (adding together many harmonic sinusoidal components) with subtractive synthesis (filtering white noise) and extra room acoustics (another convolution by room impulse response). Since the network is differentiable, it can be trained to estimate the SMS parameters and the room impulse response to reproduce a given sound.

It is striking that the most recent fourth period actually brings back the old signal-based SMS model [109] in a deep learning version: the network is trained to predict the parameters of the harmonic-plus-noise model (as were the peak-picking and partial-tracking algorithms in the 90s).

Pursuing this integration of the audio and music specificities in DNN is a challenge. This will allow to prevent audio network simply being Computer Vision networks applied to audio and would facilitate their understanding (X-AI) and reducing their cost (Green-AI) as we see now.

5.2 Explainable AI (X-AI)

Despite their impressive performances, deep neural networks remains largely intriguing. According to Szegedy et al. [116] *"Deep neural networks are highly expressive models that have recently achieved state of the art performance on speech and visual recognition tasks. While their expressiveness is the reason they succeed, it also causes them to learn uninterpretable solutions that could have counter-intuitive properties."*

(a) One such intriguing property is the case of *adversarial examples* as discussed in Szegedy et al. [116]. Those are small, hardly perceptible, perturbations of the input data that lead the network to drastically change its output decision (such as adding a small perturbation to an input image of a "panda" that makes it recognized as a "gibbon"). Kereliuk et al. [62] demonstrated that deep learning systems for music content analysis are also sensitive to these adversarial attacks.

(b) Another intriguing property is the case of *non-trained deep neural networks* (a neural network with random weights) which can achieve significant performances. Saxe et al. [103] show that the classification performance of Support Vector Machines (SVMs) fed with features extracted from a non-trained CNN show significant performances for image classification. This seems to demonstrate that the performances can be attributed to the architecture of the network itself, not to its weights (which are randomly chosen here). As proposed by Pons et al. [93], a possible explanation is the similarity between [103] experiment (which somehow uses CNN as a tool to perform a random projection) and Extreme Machine Learning [55] (which uses a single-layer MLP with random weights to feed a trainable layer). Pons et al. [93] demonstrate the same effect for MIR applications: genre, rhythm class or acoustic event recognition with random projections.

(c) Lastly, the *"lottery ticket hypothesis"* [37] argue that "a large neural network contains a smaller subnetwork that, if trained from the start, will achieve a similar accuracy than the larger structure"; or in another word, that the architecture can be changed but the initialization of the weights for training the amputed-network should be the same. (b) and (c) therefore seems in contradiction: while (b) says that only the architecture matter and not the weight, (c) says that the architecture can be amputed but the initialization weights should be the same. In MIR, Esling et al. [36] demonstrated that this lottery ticket hypothesis can also be used in typical networks performing instrument, pitch, chord or drum recognition with only 10% of the initial network.

Because of these intriguing properties, Explainable AI (X-AI) has been a growing field over the past years. *"X-AI refers to methods and techniques in the application of artificial intelligence technology (AI) such that the results of the solution can be understood by humans. It contrasts with the concept of the "black box" in machine learning where even their designers cannot explain why the AI arrived at a specific decision."* In X-AI, two main approaches have been developed so far. In the *post-hoc approaches*, the network is interpreted afterward. Example of this are the local linear proxy of LIME [97], saliency maps of [111], or the tree explainer of [73]. In the *explainability by design approach*, the architecture of a network is modified to make it interpretable. Example of this are the generation of visual explanations in [47] or the FLINT framework of [89].

In MIR, XAI still need to be developed.

5.3 Green-AI

As stated in the position paper of Schwarz et al. [106], *"The computations required for deep learning research have been doubling every few months, resulting in an estimated 300,000x increase from 2012 to 2018. These computations have a surprisingly large carbon footprint. Ironically, deep learning was inspired by the human brain, which is remarkably energy efficient."* As examples of this carbon footprint, Strubell et al. [114] compare the estimated CO2 emissions of - a round-trip flight (1 passenger, NY $\leftrightarrow$ SF): 1984 lbs, - Human life (avg, 1 year): 11 023 lbs, - a US car including fluel (avg 1 lifetime): 126 000 lbs and - the training of a recent Natural Language Processing DNN (Transformer): 626 155 lbs.

This observation led [106] to promote a "Green-AI", an AI research that yields novel results without increasing computational cost, and ideally reducing it. This "Green-AI" is opposed to the traditional AI, here renamed "Red AI", which is an AI research that seeks to obtain state-of-the-art results in accuracy (or related measures) through the use of massive computational power—essentially, "buying" stronger results. To move toward Green-AI, Henderson et al. [46] propose to report in research papers, along the accuracy results obtained with a given system, the energy and carbon footprints implied in the research of this system (training and hyper-parameters optimization).

While it does not seem at first that MIR is so much concerned by "Green-AI", the recent Jukebox' model for music generation published by OpenAI [24]—which opens a new era of large-size MIR models—surely is. According to the authors of [24]: *"The upsamplers have one billion parameters and are trained on 128 V100s for 2 weeks, and the top-level prior has 5 billion parameters and is trained on 512 V100s for 4 weeks"*.

Acknowledgments. The content of this paper is partly based on a set of keynotes given at the "Berlin Interdisciplinary Workshop on Timbre" (2017/01), at the "Digital Music Research Network Workshop" in London (2018/12), at the "International Symposium on Computer Music Multidisciplinary Research" in Marseille (2019/10) and at the "Collège de France" in Paris (2020/02). The author is grateful to the respective organizers for their invitations. The author is also grateful to Giorgia Cantisani and Florence d'Alché-Buc for sharing materials and Laure Pretet for proof-reading.

References

1. Andén, J., Lostanlen, V., Mallat, S.: Joint time-frequency scattering for audio classification. In: Proceedings of IEEE MLSP (International Workshop on Machine Learning for Signal Processing) (2015)
2. Arandjelovic, R., Zisserman, A.: Look, listen and learn. In: Proceedings of IEEE ICCV (International Conference on Computer Vision) (2017)
3. Arandjelović, R., Zisserman, A.: Objects that sound. In: Ferrari, V., Hebert, M., Sminchisescu, C., Weiss, Y. (eds.) ECCV 2018. LNCS, vol. 11205, pp. 451–466. Springer, Cham (2018). https://doi.org/10.1007/978-3-030-01246-5_27
4. Atlas, L., Shamma, S.A.: Joint acoustic and modulation frequency. EURASIP J. Adv. Signal Process. **2003**(7), 1–8 (2003)
5. Aytar, Y., Vondrick, C., Torralba, A.: Soundnet: learning sound representations from unlabeled video. In: Proceedings of NIPS (Conference on Neural Information Processing Systems) (2016)
6. Bahdanau, D., Cho, K., Bengio, Y.: Neural machine translation by jointly learning to align and translate. In: Proceedings of ICLR (International Conference on Learning Representations) (2015)
7. Bai, S., Kolter, J.Z., Koltun, V.: An empirical evaluation of generic convolutional and recurrent networks for sequence modeling. arXiv preprint arXiv:1803.01271 (2018)
8. Ballet, G., Borghesi, R., Hoffman, P., Lévy, F.: Studio online 3.0: an internet 'killer application' for remote access to ircam sounds and processing tools. In: Proceeding of JIM (Journées d'Informatique Musicale). Issy-Les-Moulineaux, France (1999)
9. Basaran, D., Essid, S., Peeters, G.: Main melody extraction with source-filter NMF and C-RNN. In: Proceedings of ISMIR (International Society for Music Information Retrieval), Paris, France, 23–27 September 2018
10. Bertin-Mahieux, T., Ellis, D.P., Whitman, B., Lamere, P.: The million song dataset. In: Proceedings of ISMIR (International Society for Music Information Retrieval), Miami, Florida, USA (2011)

11. Bittner, R., McFee, B., Salamon, J., Li, P., Bello, J.P.: Deep salience representations for f0 estimation in polyphonic music. In: Proceedings of ISMIR (International Society for Music Information Retrieval), Suzhou, China, 23–27 October 2017
12. Bittner, R.M., Salamon, J., Tierney, M., Mauch, M., Cannam, C., Bello, J.P.: Medleydb: a multitrack dataset for annotation-intensive MIR research. ISMIR **14**, 155–160 (2014)
13. Bogdanov, D., et al.: Essentia: an audio analysis library for music information retrieval. In: Proceedings of ISMIR (International Society for Music Information Retrieval), Curitiba, PR, Brazil (2013)
14. Bourlard, H.A., Morgan, N.: Connectionist Speech Recognition A Hybrid Approach, vol. 247. Springer, US (1994)
15. Bridle, J.S., Brown, M.D.: An experimental automatic word recognition system. JSRU report **1003**(5), 33 (1974)
16. Brown, G.J., Cooke, M.: Computational auditory scene analysis. Comput. Speech Lang. **8**(4), 297–336 (1994)
17. Charbuillet, C., Tardieu, D., Peeters, G.: GMM supervector for content based music similarity. In: Proceeding of DAFx (International Conference on Digital Audio Effects), Paris, France, pp. 425–428, September 2011
18. Chi, T., Ru, P., Shamma, S.A.: Multiresolution spectrotemporal analysis of complex sounds. J. Acoust. Soc. Am. **118**(2), 887–906 (2005)
19. Cho, K., et al.: Learning phrase representations using RNN encoder-decoder for statistical machine translation. In: Proceedings of EMNLP (Conference on Empirical Methods in Natural Language Processing) (2014)
20. Choi, K., Fazekas, G., Sandler, M.: Automatic tagging using deep convolutional neural networks. In: Proceedings of ISMIR (International Society for Music Information Retrieval), New York, USA (2016)
21. Cohen-Hadria, A., Roebel, A., Peeters, G.: Improving singing voice separation using deep u-net and wave-u-net with data augmentation. In: Proceeding of EUSIPCO (European Signal Processing Conference), Coruña, Spain, 2–6 September 2019
22. Defferrard, M., Benzi, K., Vandergheynst, P., Bresson, X.: FMA: a dataset for music analysis. In: Proceeding of ISMIR (International Society for Music Information Retrieval), Suzhou, China, 23–27 October
23. Dehak, N., Kenny, P., Dehak, R., Dumouchel, P., Ouellet, P.: Front-end factor analysis for speaker verification. IEEE Trans. Audio Speech Lang. Process. **19**(4), 788–798 (2011)
24. Dhariwal, P., Jun, H., Payne, C., Kim, J.W., Radford, A., Sutskever, I.: Jukebox: a generative model for music. arXiv preprint arXiv:2005.00341 (2020)
25. Dieleman, S.: Recommending music on spotify with deep learning. Technical report (2014). http://benanne.github.io/2014/08/05/spotify-cnns.html
26. Dieleman, S., Schrauwen, B.: End-to-end learning for music audio. In: 2014 IEEE International Conference on Acoustics, Speech and Signal Processing (ICASSP), pp. 6964–6968. IEEE (2014)
27. Doras, G., Peeters, G.: Cover detection using dominant melody embeddings. In: Proceeding of ISMIR (International Society for Music Information Retrieval), Delft, The Netherlands, 4–8 November 2019
28. Doras, G., Peeters, G.: A prototypical triplet loss for cover detection. In: Proceedings of IEEE ICASSP (International Conference on Acoustics, Speech, and Signal Processing), Barcelona, Spain, 4–8 May 2020

29. Doras, G., Yesiler, F., Serra, J., Gomez, E., Peeters, G.: Combining musical features for cover detection. In: Proceeding of ISMIR (International Society for Music Information Retrieval), Montreal, Canada, 11–15 October 2020
30. Durrieu, J.L., Richard, G., David, B., Févotte, C.: Source/filter model for unsupervised main melody extraction from polyphonic audio signals. IEEE Trans. Audio Speech Lang. Process. **18**(3), 564–575 (2010)
31. Eghbal-zadeh, H., Lehner, B., Schedl, M., Gerhard, W.: I-vectors for timbre-based music similarity and music artist classification. In: Proceeding of ISMIR (International Society for Music Information Retrieval), Malaga, Spain (2015)
32. Elizalde, B., Lei, H., Friedland, G.: An i-vector representation of acoustic environments for audio-based video event detection on user generated content. In: 2013 IEEE International Symposium on Multimedia, pp. 114–117. IEEE (2013)
33. Ellis, D.P.W., Zeng, X., McDermott, J.: Classifying soundtracks with audio texture features. In: Proceedings of IEEE ICASSP (International Conference on Acoustics, Speech, and Signal Processing), pp. 5880–5883. IEEE (2011)
34. Emiya, V., Badeau, R., David, B.: Multipitch estimation of piano sounds using a new probabilistic spectral smoothness principle. IEEE Trans. Audio Speech Lang. Process. **18**(6), 1643–1654 (2010)
35. Engel, J., Hantrakul, L., Gu, C., Roberts, A.: DDSP: differentiable digital signal processing. In: Proceeding of ICLR (International Conference on Learning Representations) (2020)
36. Esling, P., Bazin, T., Bitton, A., Carsault, T., Devis, N.: Ultra-light deep LIR by trimming lottery tickets. In: Proceeding of ISMIR (International Society for Music Information Retrieval), Montreal, Canada, 11–15 October 2020
37. Frankle, J., Carbin, M.: The lottery ticket hypothesis: finding sparse, trainable neural networks. In: Proceeding of ICLR (International Conference on Learning Representations) (2019)
38. Fujishima, T.: Realtime chord recognition of musical sound: a system using common lisp music. In: Proceedings of ICMC (International Computer Music Conference), pp. 464–467. Beijing, China (1999)
39. Fukushima, K., Miyake, S.: Neocognitron: a self-organizing neural network model for a mechanism of visual pattern recognition. In: Amari, S., Arbib, M.A. (eds.) Competition and Cooperation in Neural Nets, pp. 267–285. Springer, Heidelberg (1982)
40. Gfeller, B., Frank, C., Roblek, D., Sharifi, M., Tagliasacchi, M., Velimirović, M.: Spice: self-supervised pitch estimation. IEEE/ACM Trans. Audio Speech Lang. Process. **28**, 1118–1128 (2020)
41. Goodfellow, I., et al.: Generative adversarial nets. In: Advances in Neural Information Processing Systems, pp. 2672–2680 (2014)
42. Goto, M.: Aist annotation for the RWC music database. In: Proceedings of ISMIR (International Society for Music Information Retrieval), Victoria, BC, Canada, pp. 359–360 (2006)
43. Goto, M., Hashiguchi, H., Nishimura, T., Oka, R.: RWC music database: popular, classical, and jazz music databases. In: Proceeding of ISMIR (International Society for Music Information Retrieval), Paris, France, pp. 287–288 (2002)
44. Greenberg, S., Kingsbury, B.E.: The modulation spectrogram: In pursuit of an invariant representation of speech. In: Proceedings of IEEE ICASSP (International Conference on Acoustics, Speech, and Signal Processing), vol. 3, pp. 1647–1650. IEEE (1997)

45. Grézl, F., Karafiát, M., Kontár, S., Cernocky, J.: Probabilistic and bottle-neck features for lvcsr of meetings. In: Proceedings of IEEE ICASSP (International Conference on Acoustics, Speech, and Signal Processing), vol. 4, pp. IV-757. IEEE (2007)
46. Henderson, P., Hu, J., Romoff, J., Brunskill, E., Jurafsky, D., Pineau, J.: Towards the systematic reporting of the energy and carbon footprints of machine learning. arXiv preprint arXiv:2002.05651 (2020)
47. Hendricks, L.A., Akata, Z., Rohrbach, M., Donahue, J., Schiele, B., Darrell, T.: Generating visual explanations. In: Leibe, B., Matas, J., Sebe, N., Welling, M. (eds.) ECCV 2016. LNCS, vol. 9908, pp. 3–19. Springer, Cham (2016). https://doi.org/10.1007/978-3-319-46493-0_1
48. Hermansky, H., Ellis, D.P., Sharma, S.: Tandem connectionist feature extraction for conventional hmm systems. In: Proceedings of IEEE ICASSP (International Conference on Acoustics, Speech, and Signal Processing), vol. 3, pp. 1635–1638. IEEE (2000)
49. Herrera, P., Yeterian, A., Gouyon, F.: Automatic classification of drum sounds: a comparison of feature selection methods and classification techniques. In: Proceedings of ICMAI (International Conference on Music and Artificial Intelligence), Edinburgh, Scotland (2002)
50. Herrera, P.: MIRages: an account of music audio extractors, semantic description and context-awareness, in the three ages of MIR. Ph.D. thesis, Music Technology Group (MTG), Universitat Pompeu Fabra, Barcelona (2018)
51. Hiller Jr, L.A., Isaacson, L.M.: Musical composition with a high speed digital computer. In: Audio Engineering Society Convention 9. Audio Engineering Society (1957)
52. Hinton, G., et al.: Deep neural networks for acoustic modeling in speech recognition: the shared views of four research groups. IEEE Signal Process. Mag. **29**(6), 82–97 (2012)
53. Hinton, G.E., Osindero, S., Teh, Y.W.: A fast learning algorithm for deep belief nets. Neural Comput. **18**(7), 1527–1554 (2006)
54. Hochreiter, S., Schmidhuber, J.: Long short-term memory. Neural Comput. **9**(8), 1735–1780 (1997)
55. Huang, G.B., Zhu, Q.Y., Siew, C.K.: Extreme learning machine: theory and applications. Neurocomputing **70**(1–3), 489–501 (2006)
56. Humphrey, E.J.: Tutorial: Deep learning in music informatics, demystifying the dark art, Part III - practicum. In: Proceeding of ISMIR (International Society for Music Information Retrieval), Curitiba, PR, Brazil (2013)
57. Humphrey, E.J., Bello, J.P., LeCun, Y.: Moving beyond feature design: deep architectures and automatic feature learning in music informatics. In: Proceedings of ISMIR (International Society for Music Information Retrieval), Porto, Portugal (2012)
58. Jansson, A.: Musical Source Separation with Deep Learning and Large-Scale Datasets. Ph.D. thesis, City University of Mondon (2020)
59. Jansson, A., Humphrey, E.J., Montecchio, N., Bittner, R., Kumar, A., Weyde, T.: Singing voice separation with deep u-net convolutional networks. In: Proceedings of ISMIR (International Society for Music Information Retrieval), Suzhou, China, 23–27 October 2017
60. Jensen, K., Arnspang, K.: Binary decision tree classification of musical sounds. In: Proceedings of ICMC (International Computer Music Conference), Bejing, China (1999)

61. Kenny, P., Boulianne, G., Ouellet, P., Dumouchel, P.: Speaker and session variability in GMM-based speaker verification. IEEE Trans. Audio Speech Lang. Process. **15**(4), 1448–1460 (2007)
62. Kereliuk, C., Sturm, B.L., Larsen, J.: Deep learning and music adversaries. IEEE Trans. Multimedia **17**(11), 2059–2071 (2015)
63. Kim, T., Lee, J., Nam, J.: Sample-level CNN architectures for music auto-tagging using raw waveforms. In: Proceedings of IEEE ICASSP (International Conference on Acoustics, Speech, and Signal Processing) (2018)
64. Kingma, D.P., Welling, M.: Auto-encoding variational Bayes. In: Proceedings of ICLR (International Conference on Learning Representations) (2013)
65. Korzeniowski, F., Widmer, G.: Feature learning for chord recognition: The deep chroma extractor. In: Proceedings of ISMIR (International Society for Music Information Retrieval), New York, USA, 7–11 August 2016
66. Krizhevsky, A., Sutskever, I., Hinton, G.E.: ImageNet classification with deep convolutional neural networks. In: Proceedings of NIPS (Conference on Neural Information Processing Systems), pp. 1097–1105 (2012)
67. Lartillot, O., Toiviainen, P.: A matlab toolbox for musical feature extraction from audio. In: Proceeding of DAFx (International Conference on Digital Audio Effects), pp. 237–244. Bordeaux (2007)
68. LeCun, Y., Bottou, L., Bengio, Y., Haffner, P.: Gradient-based learning applied to document recognition. Proc. IEEE **86**(11), 2278–2324 (1998)
69. Lee, J., Park, J., Kim, K.L., Nam, J.: Sample-level deep convolutional neural networks for music auto-tagging using raw waveforms. arXiv preprint arXiv:1703.01789 (2017)
70. Leveau, P., Vincent, E., Richard, G., Daudet, L.: Instrument-specific harmonic atoms for mid-level music representation. IEEE Trans. Audio Speech Lang. Process. **16**(1), 116–128 (2007)
71. Liu, G., Hansen, J.H.: An investigation into back-end advancements for speaker recognition in multi-session and noisy enrollment scenarios. IEEE Trans. Audio Speech Lang. Process. **22**(12), 1978–1992 (2014)
72. Logan, B.: Mel frequency cepstral coefficients for music modeling. In: Proceedings of ISMIR (International Society for Music Information Retrieval), Plymouth, Massachusetts, USA (2000)
73. Lundberg, S.M., et al.: Explainable AI for trees: from local explanations to global understanding. arXiv preprint arXiv:1905.04610 (2019)
74. Mallat, S.: Understanding deep convolutional networks. PhilosophicalTransactions (2016)
75. Marchetto, E., Peeters, G.: Automatic recognition of sound categories from their vocal imitation using audio primitives automatically found by SI-PLCA and HMM. In: Aramaki, M., Davies, M.E.P., Kronland-Martinet, R., Ystad, S. (eds.) CMMR 2017. LNCS, vol. 11265, pp. 3–22. Springer, Cham (2018). https://doi.org/10.1007/978-3-030-01692-0_1
76. Mathieu, B., Essid, S., Fillon, T., Prado, J., Richard, G.: Yaafe, an easy to use and efficient audio feature extraction software. In: Proceedings of ISMIR (International Society for Music Information Retrieval), pp. 441–446. Utrecht, The Netherlands (2010)
77. Mauch, M., et al.: Omras2 metadata project 2009. In: Late-Breaking/Demo Session of ISMIR (International Society for Music Information Retrieval), Kobe, Japan (2009)

78. McAdams, S., Windsberg, S., Donnadieu, S., DeSoete, G., Krimphoff, J.: Perceptual scaling of synthesized musical timbres: common dimensions specificities and latent subject classes. Psychol. Res. **58**, 177–192 (1995)
79. McDermott, J., Simoncelli, E.: Sound texture perception via statistics of the auditory periphery: evidence from sound synthesis. Neuron **71**(5), 926–940 (2011)
80. McFee, B., et al.: librosa: audio and music signal analysis in python. In: Proceedings of the 14th Python in Science Conference, vol. 8, pp. 18–25 (2015)
81. Meseguer Brocal, G., Cohen-Hadria, A., Peeters, G.: Dali: a large dataset of synchronized audio, lyrics and pitch, automatically created using teacher-student. In: Proceedings of ISMIR (International Society for Music Information Retrieval), Paris, France, 23–27 September 2018
82. Meseguer Brocal, G., Peeters, G.: Creation of a large dataset of synchronised audio, lyrics and notes, automatically created using a teacher-student paradigm. Trans. Int. Soc. Music Inf. Retrieval 3(1), 55–67. https://doiorg/105334/tismir30 2020
83. Mor, N., Wolf, L., Polyak, A., Taigman, Y.: A universal music translation network. In: Proceedings of ICLR (International Conference on Learning Representations) (2019)
84. Nieto, O., McCallum, M., Davies, M., Robertson, A., Stark, A., Egozy, E.: The harmonix set: Beats, downbeats, and functional segment annotations of western popular music. In: Proceedings of ISMIR (International Society for Music Information Retrieval), Delft, The Netherlands, 4–8 November
85. Noé, P.G., Parcollet, T., Morchid, M.: Cgcnn: Complex gabor convolutional neural network on raw speech. In: Proceedings of IEEE ICASSP (International Conference on Acoustics, Speech, and Signal Processing), Barcelona, Spain, 4–8 May 2020
86. van den Oord, A., et al.: WaveNet: a generative model for raw audio. arXiv preprint arXiv:1609.03499 (2016)
87. Opolko, F., Wapnick, J.: Mcgill university master samples cd-rom for samplecellvolume 1 (1991)
88. Pachet, F., Zils, A.: Automatic extraction of music descriptors from acoustic signals. In: Proceedings of ISMIR (International Society for Music Information Retrieval), Barcelona (Spain) (2004)
89. Parekh, J., Mozharovskyi, P., d'Alche Buc, F.: A framework to learn with interpretation. arXiv preprint arXiv:2010.09345 (2020)
90. Peeters, G.: A large set of audio features for sound description (similarity and classification) in the cuidado project. Cuidado project report, Ircam (2004)
91. Peeters, G., Rodet, X.: Hierachical gaussian tree with inertia ratio maximization for the classification of large musical instrument database. In: Proceedingg of DAFx (International Conference on Digital Audio Effects), pp. 318–323. London, UK (2003). peeters03c
92. Pons, J., Lidy, T., Serra, X.: Experimenting with musically motivated convolutional neural networks. In: Proceedings of IEEE CBMI (International Workshop on Content-Based Multimedia Indexing) (2016)
93. Pons, J., Serra, X.: Randomly weighted cnns for (music) audio classification. In: Proceedings of IEEE ICASSP (International Conference on Acoustics, Speech, and Signal Processing) (2019)
94. Ramona, M., Richard, G., David, B.: Vocal detection in music with support vector machines. In: Proceedings of IEEE ICASSP (International Conference on Acoustics, Speech, and Signal Processing), Las Vegas, Nevada, USA, pp. 1885–1888 (2008)

95. Ravanelli, M., Bengio, Y.: Speaker recognition from raw waveform with sincnet. In: 2018 IEEE Spoken Language Technology Workshop (SLT). pp. 1021–1028. IEEE (2018)
96. Reynolds, D., Quatieri, T., Dunn, R.: Speaker verification using adapted gaussian mixture models. Digit. Signal Proc. **10**(1–3), 19–41 (2000)
97. Ribeiro, M.T., Singh, S., Guestrin, C.: "why should i trust you?" explaining the predictions of any classifier. In: Proceedings of the 22nd ACM SIGKDD International Conference on Knowledge Discovery and Data Mining, pp. 1135–1144 (2016)
98. Ronneberger, O., Fischer, P., Brox, T.: U-Net: convolutional networks for biomedical image segmentation. In: Navab, N., Hornegger, J., Wells, W.M., Frangi, A.F. (eds.) MICCAI 2015. LNCS, vol. 9351, pp. 234–241. Springer, Cham (2015). https://doi.org/10.1007/978-3-319-24574-4_28
99. Rumelhart, D.E., Hinton, G.E., Williams, R.J.: Learning representations by back-propagating errors. Nature **323**(6088), 533–536 (1986)
100. Sainath, T.N.: Towards end-to-end speech recognition using deep neural networks. In: Proceedings of ICML (International Conference on Machine Learning) (2015)
101. Sainath, T.N., Vinyals, O., Senior, A., Sak, H.: Convolutional, long short-term memory, fully connected deep neural networks. In: Proceedings of IEEE ICASSP (International Conference on Acoustics, Speech, and Signal Processing), pp. 4580–4584. IEEE (2015)
102. Sainath, T.N., Weiss, R.J., Senior, A., Wilson, K.W., Vinyals, O.: Learning the speech front-end with raw waveform CLDNNS. In: Sixteenth Annual Conference of the International Speech Communication Association (2015)
103. Saxe, A.M., Koh, P.W., Chen, Z., Bhand, M., Suresh, B., Ng, A.Y.: On random weights and unsupervised feature learning. In: Proceeding of ICML (International Conference on Machine Learning), vol. 2, p. 6 (2011)
104. Schreiner, C.E., Urbas, J.V.: Representation of amplitude modulation in the auditory cortex of the cat. i. the anterior auditory field (aaf). Hearing Res. 21(3), 227–241 (1986)
105. Schroff, F., Kalenichenko, D., Philbin, J.: Facenet: A unified embedding for face recognition and clustering. In: Proceedings of IEEE CVPR (Conference on Computer Vision and Pattern Recognition), pp. 815–823 (2015)
106. Schwartz, R., Dodge, J., Smith, N.A., Etzioni, O.: Green AI. CACM, Assoc. Comput. Mach. **63**, 54–63 (2020)
107. Serrà, J., Gomez, E., Herrera, P., Serra, X.: Chroma binary similarity and local alignment applied to cover song identification. IEEE Trans. Audio Speech Lang. Process. (2008)
108. Serra, X., et al.: Roadmap for Music Information Research. Creative Commons BY-NC-ND 3.0 license (2013). ISBN: 978-2-9540351-1-6
109. Serra, X., Smith, J.: Spectral modeling synthesis: a sound analysis/synthesis system based on a deterministic plus stochastic decomposition. Comput. Music J. **14**(4), 12–24 (1990)
110. Seyerlehner, K.: Content-based music recommender systems: beyond simple frame-level audio similarity. Ph.D. thesis, Johannes Kepler Universität, Linz, Austria, December 2010
111. Simonyan, K., Vedaldi, A., Zisserman, A.: Deep inside convolutional networks: Visualising image classification models and saliency maps. In: Proceedings of ICLR (International Conference on Learning Representations) (2014)

112. Smaragdis, P., Brown, J.C.: Non-negative matrix factorization for polyphonic music transcription. In: Proceedings of IEEE WASPAA (Workshop on Applications of Signal Processing to Audio and Acoustics), New Paltz, NY, USA, pp. 177–180. IEEE (2003)
113. Smaragdis, P., Venkataramani, S.: A neural network alternative to non-negative audio models. In: Proceedings of IEEE ICASSP (International Conference on Acoustics, Speech, and Signal Processing). pp. 86–90. IEEE (2017)
114. Strubell, E., Ganesh, A., McCallum, A.: Energy and policy considerations for deep learning in NLP. Proceedings of ACL (Conference of the Association for Computational Linguistics) (2019)
115. Sutskever, I., Vinyals, O., Le, Q.V.: Sequence to sequence learning with neural networks. In: Proceedings of NIPS (Conference on Neural Information Processing Systems), pp. 3104–3112 (2014)
116. Szegedy, C., et al.: Intriguing properties of neural networks. In: Proceedings of ICLR (International Conference on Learning Representations) (2013)
117. Tzanetakis, G., Cook, P.: Marsyas: a framework for audio analysis. Organised-Sound **4**(3) (1999)
118. Tzanetakis, G., Cook, P.: Musical genre classification of audio signals. IEEE Trans. Speech Audio Process. **10**(5), 293–302 (2002)
119. Vaswani, A., et al.: Attention is all you need. In: Proceedings of NIPS (Conference on Neural Information Processing Systems), pp. 5998–6008 (2017)
120. Vinyals, O., Toshev, A., Bengio, S., Erhan, D.: Show and tell: a neural image caption generator. In: Proceedings of IEEE CVPR (Conference on Computer Vision and Pattern Recognition), pp. 3156–3164 (2015)
121. Waibel, A., Hanazawa, T., Hinton, G., Shikano, K., Lang, K.J.: Phoneme recognition using time-delay neural networks. In: Readings in Speech Recognition, pp. 393–404. Elsevier (1990)
122. Wakefield, G.H.: Mathematical representation of joint time-chroma distributions. In: Proceedings of SPIE conference on Advanced Signal Processing Algorithms, Architecture and Implementations, Denver, Colorado, USA, pp. 637–645 (1999)
123. Won, M., Chun, S., Nieto, O., Serra, X.: Data-driven harmonic filters for audio representation learning. In: Proceedings of IEEE ICASSP (International Conference on Acoustics, Speech, and Signal Processing), Barcelona, Spain, 4–8 May 2020
124. Wu, C.W., Lerch, A.: Automatic drum transcription using the student-teacher learning paradigm with unlabeled music data. In: Proceedings of ISMIR (International Society for Music Information Retrieval), Suzhou, China, 23–27 October 2017
125. Zalkow, F., Müller, M.: Using weakly aligned score-audio pairs to train deep chroma models for cross-modal music retrieval. In: Proceedings of ISMIR (International Society for Music Information Retrieval), Montreal, Canada, 11–15 October 2020, pp. 184–191
126. Zhao, H., Gan, C., Rouditchenko, A., Vondrick, C., McDermott, J., Torralba, A.: The Sound of Pixels. In: Ferrari, V., Hebert, M., Sminchisescu, C., Weiss, Y. (eds.) ECCV 2018. LNCS, vol. 11205, pp. 587–604. Springer, Cham (2018). https://doi.org/10.1007/978-3-030-01246-5_35

Methods and Datasets for DJ-Mix Reverse Engineering

Diemo Schwarz[1(✉)] and Dominique Fourer[2]

[1] Ircam Lab, CNRS, Sorbonne Université, Ministère de la Culture, Paris, France
schwarz@ircam.fr
[2] IBISC, Université d'Évry-Val-d'Essonne/Paris-Saclay, Evry, France

Abstract. DJ techniques are an important part of popular music culture. However, they are also not sufficiently investigated by researchers due to the lack of annotated datasets of DJ mixes. Thus, this paper aims at filling this gap by introducing novel methods to automatically deconstruct and annotate recorded mixes for which the constituent tracks are known. A rough alignment first estimates where in the mix each track starts, and which time-stretching factor was applied. Second, a sample-precise alignment is applied to determine the exact offset of each track in the mix. Third, we propose a new method to estimate the cue points and the fade curves which operates in the time-frequency domain to increase its robustness to interference with other tracks. The proposed methods are finally evaluated on our new publicly available DJ-mix dataset *UnmixDB*. This dataset contains automatically generated beat-synchronous mixes based on freely available music tracks, and the ground truth about the placement, transformations and effects of tracks in a mix.

1 Introduction

Understanding disc jockey (DJ) practices remains a challenging important part of popular music culture [2,4]. The outcomes from such an understanding are numerous for musicological research in popular music, cultural studies on DJ practices and critical reception, music technology for computer support of DJing, automation of DJ mixing for entertainment or commercial purposes, and others. In order to automatically annotate recorded mixes, the following components are required, put into the larger context of DJ-related music information retrieval in Fig. 1:

Identification of the contained tracks (e.g. fingerprinting) to obtain the playlist,
Alignment to determine where in the mix each track starts and stops,
Time-scaling to determine what speed changes were applied by the DJ to achieve beat-synchronicity,
Unmixing to estimate the cue regions where the cross-fades between tracks happen, the curves for volume, bass and treble, and the parameters of other effects (dynamic range compression, echo, etc.),

R. Kronland-Martinet et al. (Eds.): CMMR 2019, LNCS 12631, pp. 31–47, 2021.
https://doi.org/10.1007/978-3-030-70210-6_2

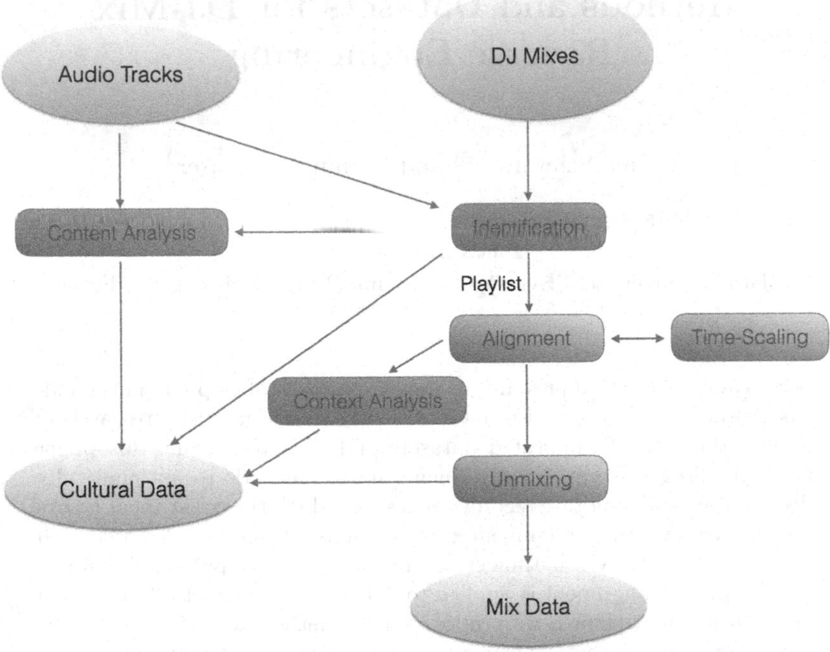

Fig. 1. Overview of the larger context of information retrieval from DJ practices. In red the components for which new contributions are proposed in this work.

Content and context analysis to derive the genre, social tags and other metadata of the music that can inform us about the choices a DJ makes when creating a mix.

The first and last of these components, music identification and content and context analysis, are intensively studied problems by music information retrieval (MIR) research [5,16]. For alignment, time-scaling, and unmixing we propose a method based on multi-scale correlation, dynamic time warping, and time-frequency gain curve estimation to increase its robustness to interferences with other tracks. To come closer to actual DJ practices, we can retrieve the alignment and volume curves from example DJ mixes, and then combine them with content and genre information to investigate the content-dependent aspects of DJ mix methods.

As a working definition, we can roughly distinguish three levels of mixing:

Level 1, *broadcast mixing*, is a simple volume cross fade without paying attention to changing content (as performed by consumer audio players such as iTunes, or in a broadcast context).

Level 2, *lounge mixing*, is beat-synchronous mixing with adaptation of the speed of the tracks and possibly additional EQ fades, while playing the tracks mostly unchanged.

Level 3, *performative mixing*, is using the DJ deck as a performance instrument by creative use of effects, loops, and mashups with other tracks.

This paper addresses the level 1 and 2 cases, while level 3 can blur the identifiability of the source tracks.

2 Related Work

In the audio engineering and signal processing community, rather than on DJ-mixing, existing work has focused on the field of *studio mixing*, where a stereo track is produced from multi-track recordings and software instruments by means of a mixing desk or DAW [4,18,19,22]. It has produced ground truth databases [7] and crowd-sourced knowledge generation [8] with some overlap with DJ mixing. However, when seeing the latter as the mixing of only two source tracks, the studied parameters and influencing factors differ too much from what is needed for DJ mixing.

MIR research has increasingly opened up to the genre family of electronic dance music (EDM) [17], producing research on segmentation and similarity [21,24], event detection [33], and decomposition [17] focused on individual songs, but not on several songs combined in a mix.

There is quite some existing work on methods to help DJs to produce mixes [1,3,6,10,13,15,20], but much less regarding information retrieval from recorded mixes, with the exception of content-based analysis of playlist choices [14], track boundaries estimation in mixes [11,25], and the identification of the tracks within the mix by fingerprinting [30]. To this end, Sonnleitner et al. provide an open dataset[1] of 10 dance music mixes with a total duration of 11 h and 23 min made of 118 source tracks. The included playlists contain hand-annotated time points with relevant information for fingerprinting, namely the approximate instant when the next track is present in the mix. Unfortunately, this information is not accurate enough for estimating the start point of the track in the mix. As a result, it is of limited usefulness as ground truth for our aims of DJ mix analysis, let alone reverse engineering.

Barchiesi and Reiss [2] first used the term *mix reverse engineering* (in the context of multi-track studio mixing) for their method to invert linear processing (gains and delays, including short FIR filters typical for EQ) and some dynamic processing parameters (compression), of interest for our aim of DJ unmixing. Ramona and Richard [23] tackle the unmixing problem for radio broadcast mixes, i.e. retrieving the fader positions of the mixing desk for several known input signals (music tracks, jingles, reports), and one unknown source (the host and guests' microphones in the broadcast studio). They model the fader curves as a sigmoid function and assume no time-varying filters, and no speed change of the sources, which is only correct in the context of radio broadcast. These two latter references both assume having sample-aligned source signals at their disposal, with no time-scaling applied, unlike our use-case where each source

[1] http://www.cp.jku.at/datasets/fingerprinting.

track only covers part of the mix, can appear only partially, and can be time-scaled for beat-matched mixing. There is rare work related to analysis [9] and inversion of non-linear processing applied to the signal such as dynamic-range compression [12] which remains challenging and full of interest for unmixing and source separation.

Hence, this work realizes our idea first presented in [26], by applying it to a large dataset of generated DJ mixes [27]. It extends our preceding CMMR conference article [28], giving more detailed results on the whole dataset, and a simpler measure of the error of the cue region estimation (Sect. 5). This research has already inspired work on a variant of our unmixing method based on convex optimization, and a hand-crafted ground truth DJ mix database [32].

3 DJ Mix Reverse Engineering

The input of our method is the result of the previous stages of identification and retrieval (see Fig. 1) on existing DJ mixes or specially contrived databases for the study of DJ practices. We assume a recorded DJ mix, a playlist (the list of tracks played in the correct order), and the audio files of the original tracks in the playlist. Our method proceeds in five steps, from a rough alignment of the concatenated tracks with the mix by DTW (Sect. 3.1), that is refined to close in to sample precision (Sect. 3.2), then verified by subtracting the track out of the mix (Sect. 3.3), to the estimation of gain curves (Sect. 3.4) and cue regions (Sect. 3.5).

3.1 Step 1: Rough Alignment

Rough alignment uses the Mel Frequency Cepstral Coefficients (MFCC) of the mix $X(k, c)$ (k being the mix frame index and $c \in \{1, 2, ..., 13\}$ the Mel frequency index) and the concatenated MFCCs of the I tracks $S(l, c) = (S_1 \dots S_I)$ as input, l being the frame index of the concatenated matrix S. We use a window size of 0.05 s, and a hop size of 0.0125 s. The motivation for MFCC is that the representation should be compact, capture perceptually important attributes of the signals, and be robust against possible pitch changes from time-scaling of the source tracks in the DJ mix. MFCCs achieve this with only 13 coefficients which model the spectral envelope and capture rhythm and timbre, but not the pitch. This is not the case for a discrete Fourier- or wavelet-based time-frequency representation with at least 10 to 100 times more coefficients, where the matching of spectral peaks of the tonal components would be degraded by the possible pitch changes. Since the tracks' continuity is mostly preserved in level 2 mixes, Dynamic Time Warping (DTW) [31] can latch on to large valleys of low distance, although the fade regions in the mix are dissimilar to either track, and occur separately in the concatenated track MFCC stream $S(l, c)$ (see Fig. 3). To ease catching up with the shorter time of the mix, we provide the extended neighborhood function in Eq. (1), allowing the estimated alignment path to perform larger vertical and horizontal jumps, shown in Fig. 2.

$$p(m,n) = d(m,n) + \min \begin{Bmatrix} p(m-1,n-1) \\ p(m-1,n) \\ p(m-2,n) \\ p(m,n-1) \\ p(m,n-2) \end{Bmatrix} \tag{1}$$

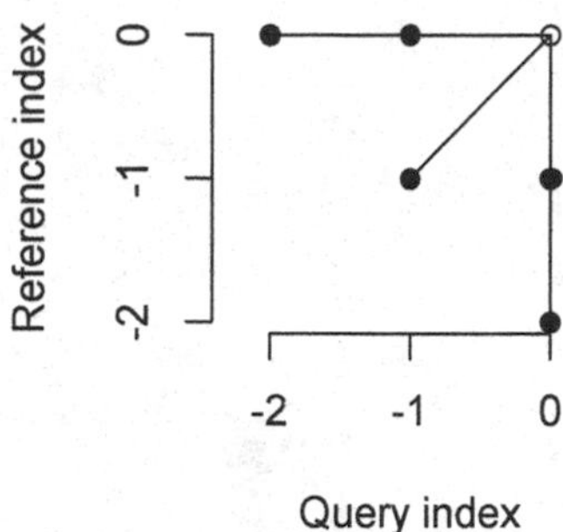

Fig. 2. Extended DTW neighborhood.

The DTW alignment path not only gives us the relative positioning of the tracks in the mix, but also their possible speed change, applied by the DJ to achieve beat-synchronous mixing, see Fig. 3: First, we estimate the speed factor, assumed to be constant for each track, by calculating the mean slope of the alignment path in a window of half the track length, centered around the middle of the track. Then, the intersections of the slope lines with the track boundaries in $S(l,c)$ provide an estimate of the frame start of the tracks in the mix. The start position expresses the offset of the start of the full source track with respect to the mix, not the position from where the track is present in the mix. Since the source tracks are mixed with non-zero volume only between the cue-in and cue-out regions, the value of the track start position can be negative.

3.2 Step 2: Sample Alignment

Given the rough alignment and the speed estimation provided by DTW, we then search for the best sample alignment of the source tracks. To this end, we first time-scale the source track's signal according to the estimated speed factor using resampling. We then shift a window of the size of an MFCC frame, taken from the middle of the time-scaled track, around its predicted rough frame position in the mix, trying displacements up to 2 hop sizes in either direction. The best time shift is simply provided by the maximum of the cross-correlation computed between the mix and the track. Please note that this process is not directly applied during the step 1 due to the high computational cost. The sample

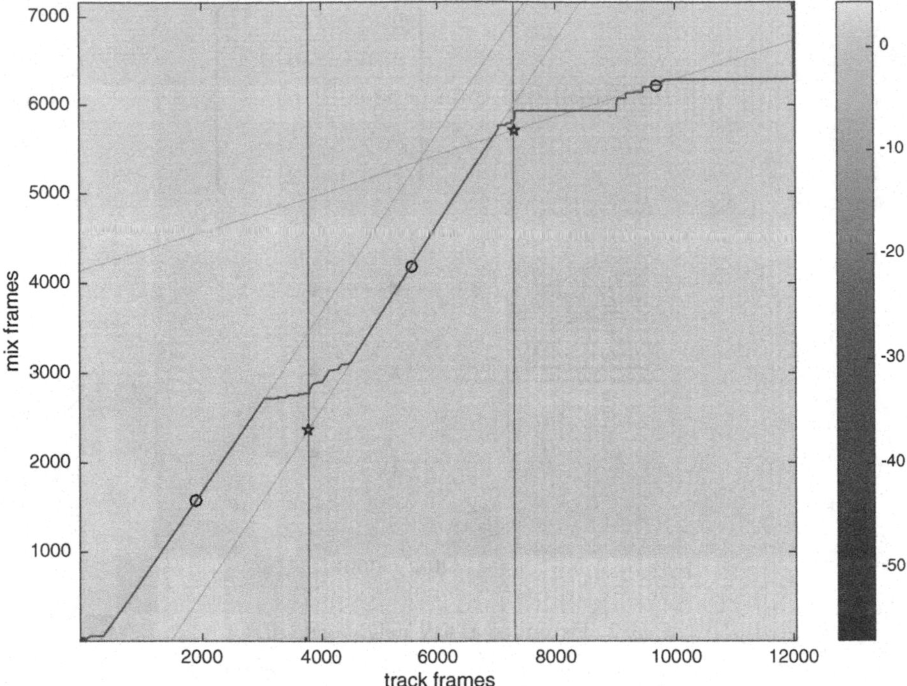

Fig. 3. DTW distance matrix, alignment path (red), track boundaries (vertical lines), found slope lines anchored on track mid-point (circles), and estimated track start (blue marks) on an artificial DJ mix made of 3 tracks from our dataset. (Colour figure online)

alignment considers a maximal delay equal to the size of a window and can be computed in a reasonable time.

3.3 Step 3: Track Removal

The success of the sample alignment can be verified by subtracting the aligned and time-scaled track signal from the mix for which a resulting drop in the root-mean-square (RMS) energy is expected. This method remains valid when the ground truth is unknown or inexact. Figure 4 illustrates the result of track removal applied on a mix in our dataset. We can observe that the resulting instantaneous RMS energy of the mix (computed on the size of a sliding window) shows a drop of about 10 dB. A short increase is also observed during the fades where the suppression gradually takes effect.

3.4 Step 4: Volume Curve Estimation

We introduce a novel method based on the time-frequency representation of the signal to estimate the volume curve applied to each track to obtain the mix.

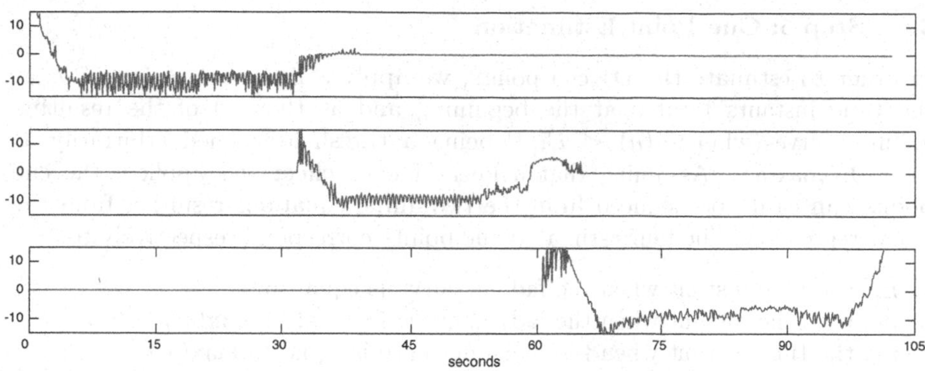

Fig. 4. Resulting RMS energy (in dB) after the subtraction of each track from a mix including fades. Each source track signal is padded with zeros to obtain the same duration than the mix.

Given the discrete-time mix signal denoted $x(n)$ and the constituent sample-aligned and time-scaled tracks $s_i(n)$, we aim at estimating the mixing function $a_i(n)$ as:

$$x(n) = \sum_{i=1}^{I} a_i(n)s_i(n) + b(n), \quad \forall n \in \mathbb{Z} \tag{2}$$

where $b(n)$ corresponds to an additive noise signal.

From a "correctly" aligned track s_i, its corresponding volume curve $\hat{a}_i$ is estimated using the following steps:

1. we compute the short-time Fourier transforms (STFT) of x and s_i denoted $S_i(n, m)$ and $X(n, m)$ (n and m being respectively the time and frequency indices)
2. we estimate the volume curve at each instant n by computing the median of the mix/track ratio computed along the frequencies $m' \in \mathbb{M}$, where $\mathbb{M}$ is the set of frequency indices where $|S_i(n, m')|^2 > 0$, such as:

$$\hat{a}_i(n) = \begin{cases} \text{median}\left(\frac{|X(n,m')|}{|S_i(n,m')|}\right)_{\forall m' \in \mathbb{M}} & \text{if } \exists m' \text{ s. t. } |S_i(n, m')|^2 > 0 \\ 0 & \text{otherwise} \end{cases} \tag{3}$$

3. we optionally post-process $\hat{a}_i(n)$ to obtain a smooth curve by removing outliers using a second median filter for which a kernel size equal to 20 provides good results in practice.

The resulting volume curve can then be used to estimate the cue points (the time instants when a fading effect begins or stops) at the next step. An illustration of the resulting process is presented in Fig. 5.

3.5 Step 5: Cue Point Estimation

In order to estimate the DJ cue points, we apply a linear regression of $\hat{a}_i$ at the time instants located at the beginning and at the end of the resulting volume curve (when $\hat{a}_i(n) < \Gamma$, Γ being a threshold defined arbitrarily as $\Gamma = 0.7 \max(\hat{a})$). Assuming that a linear fading effect was applied, the cue points can easily be deduced from the two affine equations resulting from the linear regression. The four estimated cue points correspond respectively to:

1. n_1, the time instant when the fade-in curve is equal to 0
2. n_2, the time instant when the fade-in curve is equal to $\max(\hat{a}_i)$
3. n_3, the time instant when the fade-out curve is equal to $\max(\hat{a}_i)$
4. n_4, the time instant when the fade-out curve is equal to 0.

In order to illustrate the efficiency of the entire method (steps 4 and 5), we present in Fig. 5 the results obtained on a real-world DJ-mix extracted from our dataset.

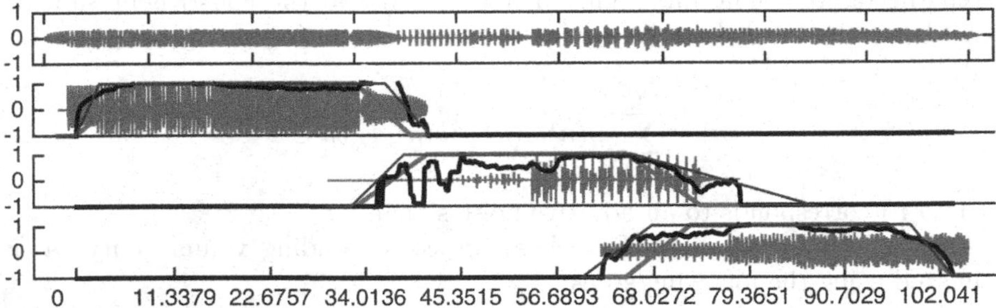

Fig. 5. Estimated volume curve (black), linear fades (blue), ground truth fades (red) (Colour figure online)

4 The *UnmixDB* Dataset

In order to evaluate the DJ mix analysis and reverse engineering methods described above, we created a dataset containing excerpts of open licensed dance tracks and their corresponding automatically generated mixes [27], available via the open data repository *Zenodo*.[2] We use track excerpts of c.a. 40 s due to the high runtime and memory requirements, especially for the DTW that is of quadratic memory complexity.

Each mix is based on a playlist made of 3 track excerpts such that the middle track is embedded in a realistic context of beat-aligned linear cross fading to the other tracks. The first track's BPM is used as the seed tempo onto which the other tracks are adapted.

[2] https://zenodo.org/record/1422385.

Each playlist of 3 tracks is mixed 12 times with combinations of 4 variants of effects and 3 variants of time scaling using the treatments of the *sox* open source command-line program.[3] The 4 effects are:

none
no effect
bass
+6 dB bass boost using a low-shelving biquad filter 100 Hz
compressor
heavy dynamics compression (ratio of 3:1 above −60 dB, −5 dB makeup gain)
distortion
heavy saturation with +20 dB gain

These effects were chosen to cover treatments likely to be applied to a DJ set (EQ, compression), and also to introduce non-linear treatments (distortion) to test the limits of re-engineering and unmixing methods.

The 3 timescale methods are:

none
no time scaling, i.e. the tracks are only aligned on the first beat in the cue region and then drift apart
resample
linked time and pitch scaling by resampling (sox *speed* effect)
stretch
time stretching while keeping the pitch (sox *tempo* effect using WSOLA)

These 3 variants allow to test simple alignment methods not taking into account time scaling, and allow to evaluate the influence of different algorithms and implementations of time scaling.

The *UnmixDB* dataset contains the complete ground truth for the source tracks and mixes. For each mix, the start, end, and cue points of the constituent tracks are given with their BPM and speed factors. Additionally, the song excerpts are accompanied by their cue region and tempo information.

Table 1 shows the size and basic statistics of the six parts (sets) of the dataset. We also publish the Python source code to generate the mixes[4], such that other researchers can create test data from other track collections or other variants.

Our DJ mix dataset is based on the curatorial work of Sonnleitner et al. [30], who collected Creative-Commons licensed source tracks of 10 free dance music mixes from the *Mixotic* net label. We used their collected tracks to produce our track excerpts, but regenerated artificial mixes with perfectly accurate ground truth.

[3] http://sox.sourceforge.net.
[4] https://github.com/Ircam-RnD/unmixdb-creation.

Table 1. Basic statistics of the *UnmixDB* dataset, version 1. Each playlist (Pl.) combines 3 tracks (Tr.) which are mixed in 12 variants.

Set	Number of			Tr. Length		Mix Length		Tr. bpm		Tr. Speed	
	Tr.	Pl.	Mixes	avg	sum	avg	sum	avg	std	avg	std
044	44	44	528	0:46	33:26	1:43	1:15:47	126.4	2.9	1.001	0.043
123	37	37	444	0:46	28:13	1:44	1:04:03	125.8	8.5	1.012	0.175
222	6	4	48	0:49	4:56	1:39	9:54	125.0	2.3	1.114	0.315
230	43	41	492	0:46	32:57	1:42	1:13:21	123.2	5	1.003	0.082
275	32	26	312	0:46	24:26	1:43	55:06	126.5	4.8	1.004	0.088
281	67	53	636	0:46	51:43	1:45	1:57:02	122.9	9	1.007	0.153
All	229	205	2460	0:46	2:55:41	1:44	6:35:12	124.6	6.8	1.007	0.128

5 Evaluation

We applied the DJ mix reverse engineering method on the collection of mixes in our dataset *UnmixDB*, (See footnote 2) version 1, and compared the results to the ground truth annotations. To evaluate the success of our method we defined the following error metrics:

frame error
absolute error in seconds between the frame start time found by the DTW rough alignment (step 1, Sect. 3.1) and the ground truth (virtual) track start time relative to the mix

sample error
absolute error in seconds between the track start time found by the sample alignment (step 2, Sect. 3.2) and the ground truth track start time relative to the mix

speed ratio
ratio between the speed estimated by DTW alignment (step 1, Sect. 3.1) and the ground truth speed factor (ideal value is 1)

suppression ratio
ratio of time where more than 15 dB of signal energy could be removed by subtracting the aligned track from the mix, relative to the time where the track is fully present in the mix, i.e. between fade-in end and fade-out start (step 3, Sect. 3.3, bigger is better)

cue point error
the mean absolute time difference between the four estimated cue points n_i (step 5, Sect. 3.5) and the ground truth cue points in seconds.

Figures 6, 7, 8 and 9 show the quartile statistics of these metrics, broken down by the 12 mix variants (all combinations of the 3 time-scaling methods and 4 mix effects). The sample alignment results given in Fig. 6 (orange) and Table 2 show that the ground truth labels can be retrieved with high accuracy: the median error is in the range of 20–30 ms, except for the mixes with distortion applied, where it is around 190–280 ms. These errors can already be traced back to the rough alignment (Sect. 3.1): Fig. 6 (yellow) shows that it is not robust to heavy non-linear distortion, presumably because the spectral shape changes too much to be matchable via MFCC distances. This error percolates to the speed estimation (Fig. 7), and sample alignment.

The track removal time results in Fig. 8 show sensitivity to the bass and distortion effect (because both of these introduce a strong additional signal component in the mix that is left as a residual when subtracting a track), and also perform less well for time-scaled mixes.

The cue point error in Fig. 9 shows a median between 3 and 4 s, except for the distortion effect and resampling with compression. These results are acceptable, considering that the ground truth fades typically last for 16 s.

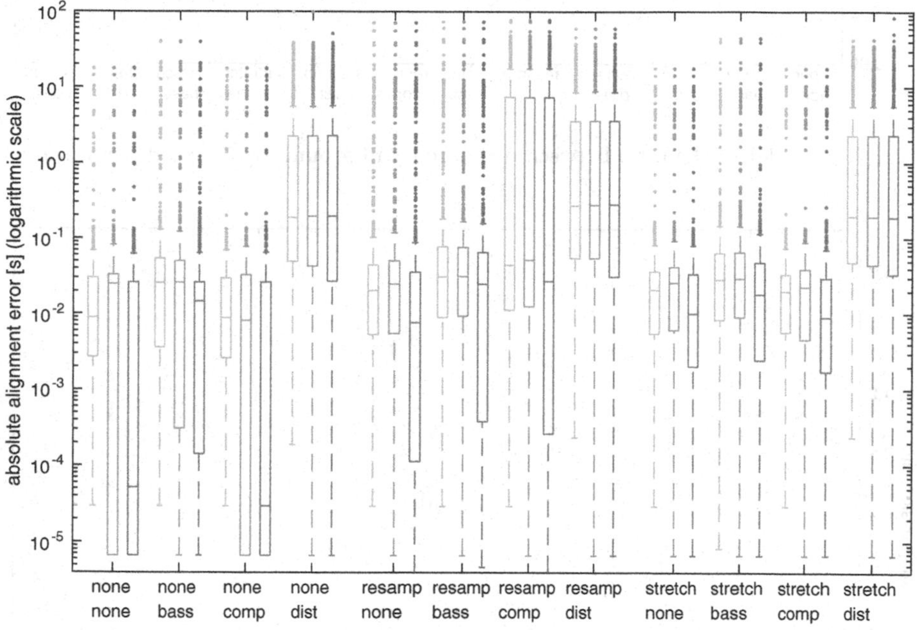

Fig. 6. Box plot of the absolute frame error in seconds in track start time found by DTW (yellow), compared to sample alignment error (orange), and sample alignment error when reinjecting ground truth speed (red, see Sect. 5.1) per variant. (Colour figure online)

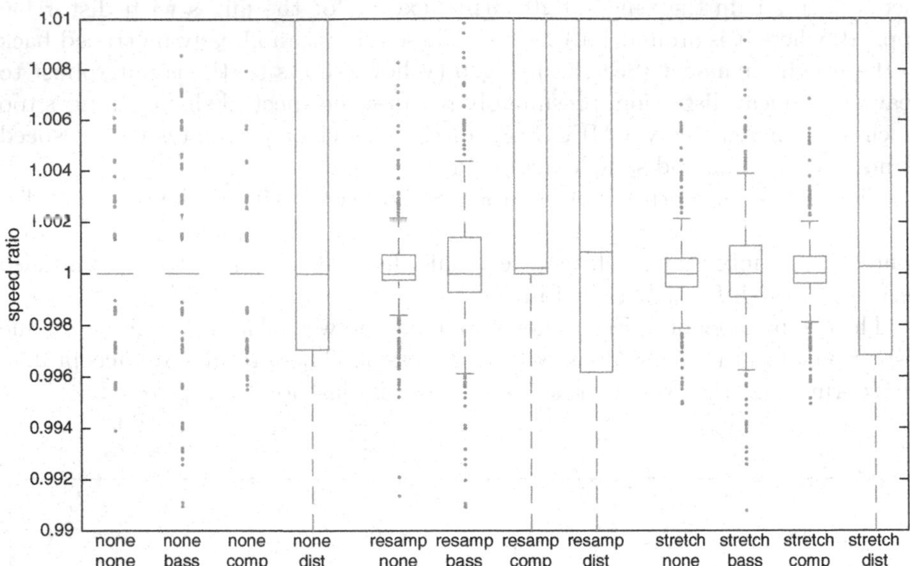

Fig. 7. Box plot of the ratio between estimated and ground truth speed per variant.

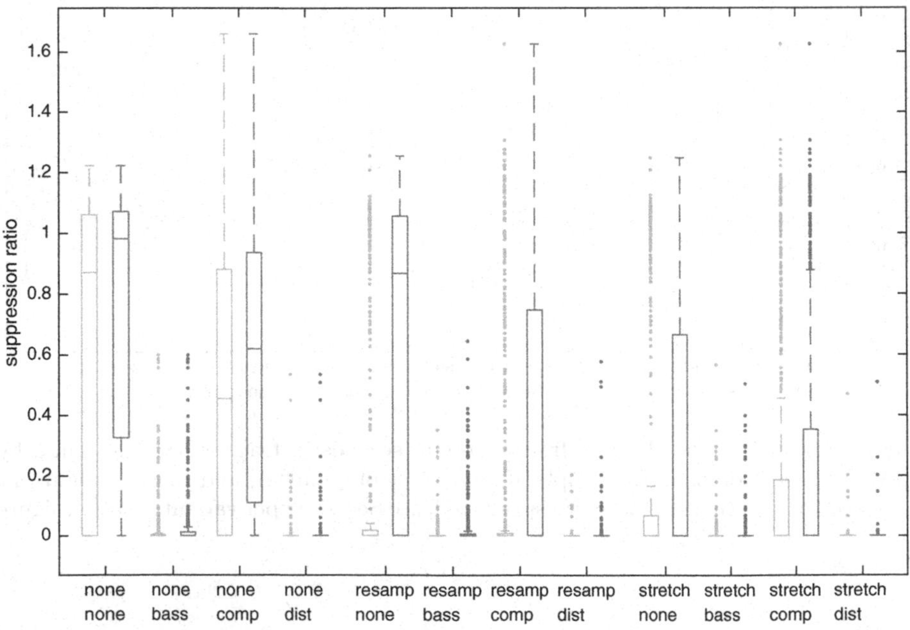

Fig. 8. Box plot of the ratio of removal time (yellow), compared to the ratio when reinjecting ground truth speed (red, see Sect. 5.1) per variant (higher is better). (Colour figure online)

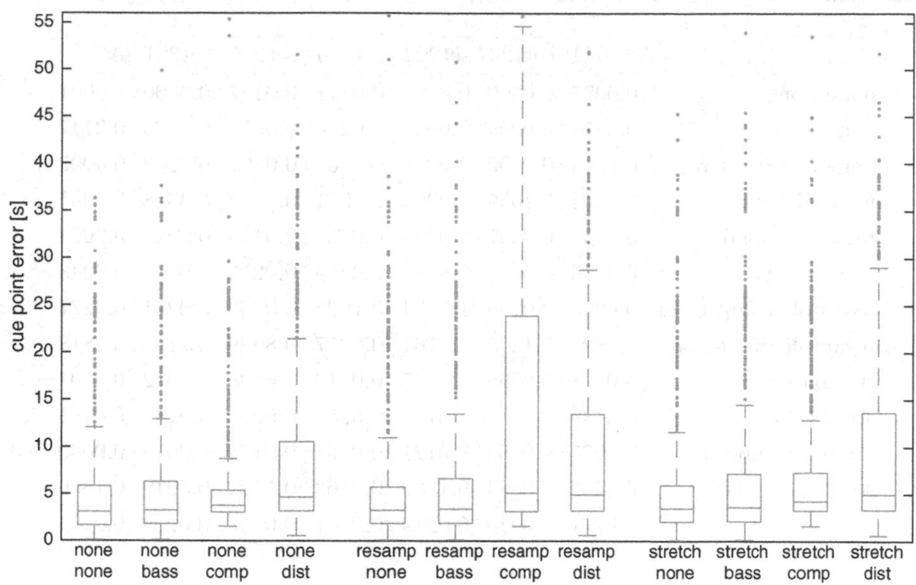

Fig. 9. Box plot of the cue point error in seconds per variant.

Table 2. Median of the absolute error in seconds in track start time found by sample alignment per variant and per set.

	set044	set123	set222	set230	set275	set281	All
none none	0.0261	0.0000	0.0269	0.0261	0.0069	0.0206	0.0247
none bass	0.0261	0.0256	0.0114	0.0261	0.0257	0.0261	0.0260
none compressor	0.0073	0.0000	0.0093	0.0261	0.0261	0.0096	0.0082
none distortion	0.1331	0.1207	2.3638	0.1955	0.3975	0.3364	0.1946
resample none	0.0224	0.0237	0.0373	0.0261	0.0214	0.0261	0.0248
resample bass	0.0269	0.0256	0.0270	0.0318	0.0272	0.0341	0.0313
resample compressor	0.0339	0.0501	1.5816	0.1239	0.0557	0.0471	0.0517
resample distortion	0.1978	0.1271	6.1392	0.2469	0.9214	0.7261	0.2791
stretch none	0.0282	0.0193	0.0216	0.0261	0.0225	0.0261	0.0259
stretch bass	0.0318	0.0269	0.0224	0.0317	0.0256	0.0325	0.0294
stretch compressor	0.0261	0.0174	0.0177	0.0261	0.0216	0.0232	0.0228
stretch distortion	0.1657	0.0895	6.1937	0.2197	0.5349	0.3027	0.1931
All	0.0328	0.0261	0.0352	0.0337	0.0261	0.0327	0.0319

Table 3. Median of the absolute error in seconds in track start time found by sample alignment when reinjecting ground truth speed (see Sect. 5.1) per variant and per set.

	set044	set123	set222	set230	set275	set281	All
none none	0.0077	0.0000	0.0093	0.0261	0.0167	0.0000	0.0001
none bass	0.0076	0.0006	0.0001	0.0256	0.0254	0.0125	0.0147
none compressor	0.0004	0.0000	0.0000	0.0261	0.0197	0.0000	0.0000
none distortion	0.1209	0.1059	2.2966	0.1951	0.4084	0.3388	0.1951
resample none	0.0061	0.0007	0.0209	0.0260	0.0198	0.0006	0.0077
resample bass	0.0215	0.0014	0.0114	0.0255	0.0256	0.0205	0.0248
resample compressor	0.0263	0.0266	1.5424	0.1623	0.0265	0.0261	0.0271
resample distortion	0.1829	0.1249	6.1161	0.2257	0.8969	0.7184	0.2818
stretch none	0.0198	0.0060	0.0137	0.0213	0.0108	0.0072	0.0101
stretch bass	0.0189	0.0080	0.0116	0.0252	0.0224	0.0142	0.0181
stretch compressor	0.0075	0.0055	0.0121	0.0191	0.0171	0.0072	0.0090
stretch distortion	0.1482	0.0884	6.1380	0.2163	0.5422	0.3019	0.1890
All	0.0261	0.0080	0.0219	0.0261	0.0261	0.0259	0.0261

5.1 Reinjecting Ground Truth Speed

While developing our method, we noticed the high sensitivity of the sample alignment and subsequent track removal (steps 2 and 3, Sects. 3.2 and 3.3) on the accuracy of the speed estimation. This is due to the resampling of the source track to match the track in the mix prior to track removal. Even an estimation error of a tenth of a percent results in desynchronisation after some time.

To judge the influence of this accuracy, we produced a second set of the *sample error* and *suppression ratio* metrics based on a run of steps 2 and 3 with the ground truth speed reinjected into the processing. The rationale is that the speed estimation method could be improved in future work, if the resulting reductions of error metrics are worthwhile. Also note that the tempo estimation is inherently inaccurate due to it being based on DTW's discretisation into MFCC frames. In mixes with full tracks, the slope can be estimated more accurately than with our track excerpts simply because more frames are available.

Figures 6 and 8 (red) show the quartile statistics of the sample error (also given in Table 3) and suppression ratio with reinjected ground truth speed. We can see how most variants are improved in error spread for the former, and 4 variants are greatly improved for the latter, confirming the sensitivity of the track removal step 3 on the speed estimation.

6 Conclusions and Future Work

The presented work is a first step towards providing the missing link in a chain of methods that allow the retrieval of rich data from existing DJ mixes and their source tracks. An important result is the validation using track removal in Sect. 3.3 to compute a new metric for the accuracy of sample alignment. This metric can be computed even without ground truth. A massive amount of training data extracted from the vast number of collections of existing mixes could thus be made amenable to research in DJ practices, cultural studies, and automatic mixing methods. With some refinements, our method could become robust and precise enough to allow the inversion of fading, EQ and other processing [2,23]. First, the obtained tempo slope could be refined by searching for sample alignment at several points in one source track. This would also extend the applicability of our method to mixes with non-constant tempo curves. Second, a sub-sample search for the best alignment should achieve the neutralisation of phase shifts incurred in the mix production chain. Various improvements of DTW alignment are possible: relaxed endpoint conditions [29] could allow prealignment per track and thus reduce the memory requirements, and better handle the partial presence of tracks in the mix. Furthermore, the close link between alignment, time-scaling, and unmixing hints at the possibility of a joint and possibly iterative estimation algorithm, maximising the match in the three search spaces simultaneously. In further experiments, we will test the influence of other signal representations (MFCC, spectrum, chroma, scattering transform) on the results, and could extend the *UnmixDB* dataset by other effects commonly used in DJing (cuts and boost on bass, mid and high EQ).

Acknowledgments. This work was carried out within the ABC_DJ project (http://abcdj.eu), which has received funding from the European Union's Horizon 2020 research and innovation programme under grant agreement No 688122.

References

1. Aspillaga, F., Cobb, J., Chuan, C.H.: Mixme: a recommendation system for DJs. In: International Symposium on Music Information Retrieval (ISMIR), October 2011
2. Barchiesi, D., Reiss, J.: Reverse engineering of a mix. J. Audio Eng. Soc. **58**(7/8), 563–576 (2010)
3. Bittner, R.M., et al.: Automatic playlist sequencing and transitions. In: International Symposium on Music Information Retrieval (ISMIR), Suzhou, China, October 2017
4. Brecht De Man, B., King, R., Reiss, J.D.: An analysis and evaluation of audio features for multitrack music mixtures. In: International Symposium on Music Information Retrieval (ISMIR) (2014)
5. Cano, P., Batlle, E., Kalker, T., Haitsma, J.: A review of audio fingerprinting. J. VLSI Signal Process. Syst. Signal Image Video Technol. **41**(3), 271–284 (2005)
6. Cliff, D.: Hang the DJ: Automatic sequencing and seamless mixing of dance-music tracks. Technical report, Hewlett-Packard Laboratories (2000). hPL 104
7. De Man, B., Mora-Mcginity, M., Fazekas, G., Reiss, J.D.: The open multitrack testbed. In: Audio Engineering Society Convention 137 (2014)
8. De Man, B., Reiss, J.D.: Crowd-sourced learning of music production practices through large-scale perceptual evaluation of mixes. Innovation in Music II, p. 144 (2016)

9. Fourer, D., Peeters, G.: Objective characterization of audio signal quality: application to music collection description. In: Proceedings of the IEEE ICASSP, pp. 711–715, March 2017
10. Fujio, T., Shiizuka, H.: A system of mixing songs for automatic DJ performance using genetic programming. In: 6th Asian Design International Conference, October 2003
11. Glazyrin, N.: Towards automatic content-based separation of DJ mixes into single tracks. In: International Symposium on Music Information Retrieval (ISMIR), pp. 149–154, October 2014
12. Gorlow, S., Reiss, J.D.: Model-based inversion of dynamic range compression. IEEE Trans. Audio Speech Lang. Process. **21**(7), 1434–1444 (2013)
13. Ishizaki, H., Hoashi, K., Takishima, Y.: Full-automatic DJ mixing system with optimal tempo adjustment based on measurement function of user discomfort. In: International Symposium on Music Information Retrieval (ISMIR), pp. 135–140 (2009)
14. Kell, T., Tzanetakis, G.: Empirical analysis of track selection and ordering in electronic dance music using audio feature extraction. In: International Symposium on Music Information Retrieval (ISMIR), pp. 505–510 (2013)
15. Kim, A., Park, S., Park, J., Ha, J.W., Kwon, T., Nam, J.: Automatic DJ mix generation using highlight detection. In: Late-breaking Session of the International Symposium on Music Information Retrieval (ISMIR), Suzhou, China, October 2017
16. Lerch, A.: An Introduction to Audio Content Analysis: Applications in Signal Processing and Music Informatics. Wiley-IEEE Press (2012)
17. López-Serrano, P., Dittmar, C., Driedger, J., Müller, M.: Towards modeling and decomposing loop-based electronic music. In: International Symposium on Music Information Retrieval (ISMIR), pp. 502–508 (2016)
18. Maddams, J.A., Finn, S., Reiss, J.D.: An autonomous method for multi-track dynamic range compression. In: Proceedings of the Digital Audio Effects (DAFx) (2012)
19. Mansbridge, S., Finn, S., Reiss, J.D.: An autonomous system for multitrack stereo pan positioning. In: Audio Engineering Society Convention (2012)
20. Molina, P., Haro, M., Jordá, S.: Beatjockey: a new tool for enhancing DJ skills. In: New Interfaces for Musical Expression (NIME), pp. 288–291. Citeseer (2011)
21. Panteli, M., Rocha, B., Bogaards, N., Honingh, A.: A model for rhythm and timbre similarity in electronic dance music. Musicae Scientiae 21 (2016). https://doi.org/10.1177/1029864916655596
22. Perez-Gonzalez, E., Reiss, J.: Automatic gain and fader control for live mixing. In: Proceedings of the IEEE WASPAA, pp. 1–4, October 2009
23. Ramona, M., Richard, G.: A simple and efficient fader estimator for broadcast radio unmixing. In: Proceedings of the Digital Audio Effects (DAFx), pp. 265–268, September 2011
24. Rocha, B., Bogaards, N., Honingh, A.: Segmentation and timbre similarity in electronic dance music. In: Sound and Music Computing (SMC), pp. 754–761 (2013)
25. Scarfe, T., Koolen, W., Kalnishkan, Y.: Segmentation of electronic dance music. Int. J. Eng. Intell. Syst. Electr. Eng. Commun. **22**(3), 4 (2014)
26. Schwarz, D., Fourer, D.: Towards extraction of ground truth data from DJ mixes. In: Late-breaking Session of the International Symposium on Music Information Retrieval (ISMIR), Suzhou, China, October 2017. https://hal.archives-ouvertes.fr/hal-01671768

27. Schwarz, D., Fourer, D.: UnmixDB: a dataset for DJ-mix information retrieval. In: Late-breaking Session of the International Symposium on Music Information Retrieval (ISMIR), Paris, France, September 2018. https://doi.org/10.5281/zenodo.1422385. https://hal.archives-ouvertes.fr/hal-02010431
28. Schwarz, D., Fourer, D.: Methods and Datasets for DJ-Mix reverse engineering. In: Computer Music Multidisciplinary Research (CMMR), Marseille, France, October 2019. https://hal.archives-ouvertes.fr/hal-02172427
29. Silva, D.F., Batista, G.E.D.A.P.A., Keogh, E., et al.: On the effect of endpoints on dynamic time warping. In: SIGKDD Workshop on Mining and Learning from Time Series, II. Association for Computing Machinery-ACM (2016)
30. Sonnleitner, R., Arzt, A., Widmer, G.: Landmark-based audio fingerprinting for DJ mix monitoring. In: International Symposium on Music Information Retrieval (ISMIR), New York, NY (2016)
31. Turetsky, R.J., Ellis, D.P.: Ground-truth transcriptions of real music from force-aligned midi syntheses. In: International Symposium on Music Information Retrieval (ISMIR), October 2003
32. Werthen-Brabants, L.: Ground Truth Extraction & Transition Analysis of DJ Mixes. Master's thesis, Ghent University, Belgium (2018)
33. Yadati, K., Larson, M., Liem, C.C.S., Hanjalic, A.: Detecting drops in electronic dance music: content-based approaches to a socially significant music event. In: International Symposium on Music Information Retrieval (ISMIR) (2014)

Towards Deep Learning Strategies for Transcribing Electroacoustic Music

Matthias Nowakowski[1(✉)], Christof Weiß[2], and Jakob Abeßer[3]

[1] Media Informatics, University of Applied Sciences, Düsseldorf, Germany
matthias.nowakowski@gmail.com

[2] International Audio Laboratories Erlangen, Erlangen, Germany

[3] Semantic Music Technologies Group, Fraunhofer IDMT, Ilmenau, Germany

Abstract. Electroacoustic music is experienced primarily through auditory perception, as it is not usually based on a prescriptive score. For the analysis of such pieces, transcriptions are sometimes created to illustrate events and processes graphically in a readily comprehensible way. These are usually based on the spectrogram of the recording. Although the manual generation of transcriptions is often time-consuming, they provide a useful starting point for any person who has interest in a work. Deep-learning algorithms that learn to recognize characteristic spectral patterns using supervised learning represent a promising technology to automatize this task. This paper investigates and explores the labeling of sound objects in electroacoustic music recordings. We test several neural-network architectures that enable classification of sound objects using musicological and signal-processing methods. We also show future perspectives how our results can be improved and applied to a new gradient-based visualization approach.

Keywords: Electroacoustic music · Acousmatic music · Transcription · Deep learning

1 Introduction

Scientific discourse is based on an intersubjectively accessible object and its representations. Musicology usually treats music as sound or score. Especially when studying electroacoustic art music, the approach must always be an auditive one since the peculiarity of this type of music is to fix the sound and not its prescriptions. Sound material is either synthetically produced or consists of electronically processed recordings [3,25]. Thereby, timbre and its temporal progression become important structural elements, in contrast to harmony [30] or metre. In order to make this music comparable, researchers often create transcriptions, which are mostly colorations or linguistic annotations of spectrograms [10].

There are few attempts to automate this process for electroacoustic music. In particular, the lack of a uniform nomenclature to describe sound objects

R. Kronland-Martinet et al. (Eds.): CMMR 2019, LNCS 12631, pp. 48–59, 2021.
https://doi.org/10.1007/978-3-030-70210-6_3

is an issue to be discussed. Analyzing such properties with signal-processing algorithms has been addressed sparsely [16].

In recent years neural networks have shown promising results for tasks such as genre classification or chord recognition, etc., within the analysis of tonal music [22]. In particular, end-to-end visualization techniques, as well as better scalability on dataset size make this state-of-the-art technology interesting for exploring this task. The few papers dealing with machine learning applied to electroacoustic music either treat this subject superficially, or some advantages where not yet widely accessible at the time of publication, like widely accessible programming libraries or computing infrastructure [21].

Such an endeavor can not only be fruitful for the musicological discourse. Transcriptions are also an communicative device that can be used in an explorative way (find morphologies which were not heard before, reveal macro-forms) or explanatively (backing up individual transcriptions by technical means) and can thus enhance accessibility.

2 Previous Work

In the past, common Music Information Retrieval (MIR) techniques were used to analyze and visualize certain characteristics of elecotracoustic pieces and are also implemented in software [8,19]. Also, further features that capture style-relevant properties could be used for electroacoustic music as well [16,30]. But the interest in using expensive machine- learning algorithms has been rather low so far, although deep learning approaches provide state-of-the-art results in different music related tasks [22].

In a recent study, Collins [6] made thorough analyses of electroacoustic pieces after the release of a large corpus, which is available online.[1] He used fully-connected networks on previously extracted features to estimate publication years, but was not pursuing this approach in subsequent publications [7] since a k-Nearest-Neighbor algorithm outperformed the neural networks in accuracy.

Klien et al. critically discuss the use of machine learning from an aesthetic standpoint [15]. In their view, fully automated annotations are not able to overcome the semantic gap between the "signal" and the "meaning," since electroacoustic (or acousmatic) music tries do defy the definition of music itself. Any algorithm used for analysis therefore should not attempt to "understand" music. Despite their position, we agree that a human annotator is needed to make reasonable assertions about musical structure. In contrast, one could consider the complexity of the task to be particularly suitable for a deep-learning approach.

Using interactive hierarchical clustering, Guluni et al. [13,14] let experts categorize sound events of different timbres of a synthetic data set by putting its results into a feedback loop. The authors use a Support Vector Machine (SVM) classifier, which is fed with the feature coefficients. Both monophonic and polyphonic compositions had results with F-measures ≥ 0.85.

[1] http://www.ubu.com/sound/electronic.html.

Given a sound scene (being musical or not) in which sounds change characteristics according to auditory distance or distortion, form coherent textures with other sounds, or split from them gradually, it might be helpful to view this task as one lying close to the tasks of sound event detection and sound scene analysis. One of the main challenges is high intra-class variance due to the quality of sounds, which may not be clearly separable from each other and appear in multi-source environments [29]. As shown in the regularly held "Detection and Classification of Acoustic Scenes and Events" (DCASE) challenges, best results are produced by neural networks which are trained on some type of a spectrogram representation [1,17]. From this point of view, deep learning seems like a viable approach for elecotracoustic music. The main problem is to develop a suitable set of labels, which show satisfactory results in classification tasks before temporal sound event detection can even take place. Using deep learning also gives the possibility to employ methods for interpreting deep neural networks to generate visualizations [2]. This might show what portions of a spectrogram were actually important while training on sound event classification and so gives visual cues to examine the dataset.

3 Data and Annotation

In this section, we describe the creation and annotation of a dataset of electroacoustic music excerpts. Since there is no consistent or commonly used nomenclature for categorizing sound objects, analysis frameworks can help to develop labels that can be used and understood by musicological experts. For better comparison with previous approaches, we use label names in accordance with commonly used features, which are used in other classification algorithms. Although there are some historically relevant frameworks like Pierre Schaeffer's *Typomorphology* [26], we draw our inspiration for the labels used here from Denis Smalley's *Spectromorphology* [24]. He developed this framework as a tool for describing sound shapes, i. e. the unit of spectral content and their development in time, based on aural perception. Adopting this viewpoint can be helpful to identify such sound-shapes in a spectrogram which is our base baseline feature.

We chose the five descriptors *flux*, *spread*, *noise*, *density*, and *realness* as attributes to describe both the static and dynamic aspects of spectromorphological expectation. For each attribute, the extreme values (0/1) represent poles within a description space.

Flux 0: Stationary; 1: Fluctuating
Spread 0: Narrow spectral range; 1: Wide spectral range
Noise 0: Harmonic; 1: White Noise
Density 0: Single event; 1: Multiple events (uncountable)
Realness 0: Synthetic; 1: Real world sound source

Flux and *density* were selected to reflect the development of a sound event over time. In contrast, *spread* and *noise* describe static sound characteristics. All attributes can be combined to form a label set to provide more complex descriptions of sound events. Each attribute in a label is represented by its initial letter. We obtain 32 possible classes from all combinations of the five attributes. For instance, *f0s0n1d1r0* represents a stationary and narrow sound, which is very noisy, has a high density and a synthetic sound characteristic. As an analogy, one could think of a pass-filtered noise band. Similarly, we can define four separate classes by combining only two attributes. An example of such an annotation w.r.t. *spread* and *noise* could be *s0n1*, which defines a filtered noise-like sound without specifying its temporal characteristics. On the one hand, this way of choosing attributes to form new label sets allows to refine classes during the annotation process. On the other hand, a binary attribution can lead to fuzzy class boundaries, so that event labeling becomes imprecise. For instance, labeling *density* of a drum roll may diverge into labeling each event itself or the whole texture depending on the event frequency. While each event is probably static, the texture could gain fluctuating characteristics due to playing style or instrument manipulation, like a timpani glissando. Therefore, during the annotation process, we focused on sound objects that can be clearly defined by the selected attributes. Note that silence can not be reflected.

The compiled dataset consists of excerpts of 29 electroacoustic pieces from the 1960s to the early 2000s. Longer pieces were cut off at the 5 min mark, while whole pieces were taken if they were shorter or slightly longer than 5 min. This adds up to a total duration of 2.5 h.

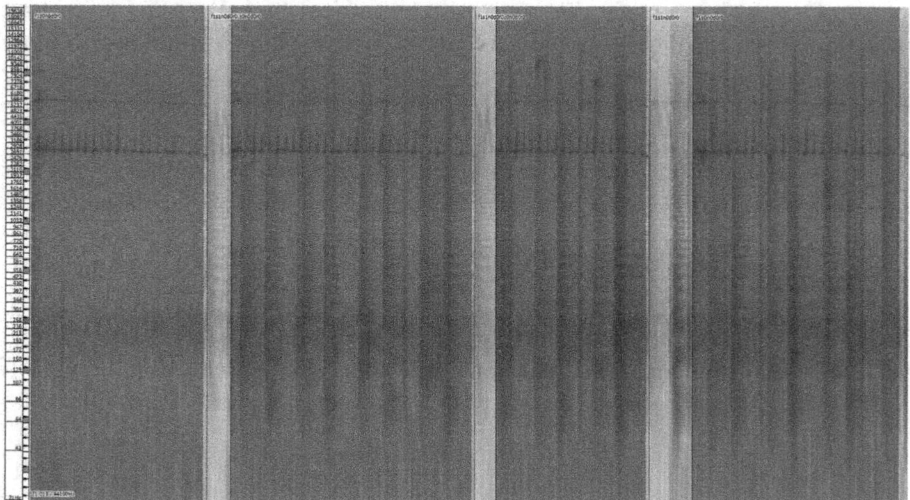

Fig. 1. Example annotation in the log-spectrogram of the first 12 s of the movement *Polyrythmie* in *Vibrations Composés* by François Bayle. Red boxes represent recurring/similar events annotated as *f1s0n0d0r0*, while yellow boxes represent recurring/similar events annotated as *f1s1n0d0r0*. Although more events can be seen (e.g. the dark colored band in the lower half of the spectrogram), all frequencies are used as an input feature for each annotated event as indicated by the boxes. (Color figure online)

Each relevant sound event was then annotated manually including the attack and end of release (Fig. 1). Since almost all recordings are polyphonic, some sound events may appear in multiple longer events. This leads to a total of 3.7 h of extracted material. 3016 separate events were annotated ranging from 0.05 s to 4.5 min. We enlarged the dataset using data augmentation techniques. To this end, we applied mild pitch shifting using step sizes between minus and plus 2 semitones in order to not distort the spectral characteristics. In total, the dataset contains 18.5 h of segmented and augmented material.

Since some classes are stronger represented than others, all the extracted events were resampled to the mean duration of all 32 classes. Resampling on these classes also scales to all other possible label sets. Longer classes were shortened by randomly deleting events. For shorter classes, events were duplicated in turn with slight random modifications to the signal.

In our experiment, we repeat a random dataset split into training, validation, and test set three times using a split ratio of 60%/20%/20% (by number of events). We ensure that the events in the three evaluation sets come from different recordings to reduce overfitting.

4 Experiments

In this paper we focus on reporting results from configurations made with a 4-class label set consisting of the attributes *spread* and *noise* to investigate the impact of a combination of static spectral attributes at first. By using a label set consisting of two attributes, we reduce chances of wrong labeling and have a more manageable number of attributes to compare. For all experiments, the following labels were used: *s0n0*, *s0n1*, *s1n0*, *s1n1*. The deep-learning architectures were implemented using the Keras framework[2], wheras feature extraction algorithms were implemented after [20] or used directly through the librosa library.[3] For our experiments we have focused primarily on the performance of the classification.

4.1 Metrics

Test F1-Score. This measure is used to score the overall classification of a sound event. The F1-score equals the harmonic mean between precision and recall. If classification is done on multiple patches of an event, the mean is computed.

$$F1 = 2 * \frac{Precision * Recall}{Precision + Recall} \tag{1}$$

Training Validation Accuracy Difference (ΔAcc). The accuracy for both training and validation set is computed during the training itself. The goal is

[2] https://keras.io/.

[3] https://librosa.github.io/librosa/.

to have training and validation accuracy as close as possible. A lower value for ΔAcc means less overfitting.

$$Acc = \frac{TP + TN}{TP + TN + FP + FN} \tag{2}$$

$$\Delta Acc = |Acc_{train} - Acc_{val}| \tag{3}$$

All metrics are averaged over the number of folds in the respective configuration. Early stopping on validation accuracy was employed for all the deep-learning experiments after 20 epochs due to usually very short training (one digit numbers of epochs) when using early stopping on the validation loss.

4.2 Baseline

Because we use a self-developed annotation scheme and dataset for this paper, the definition of a baseline performance is challenging. For four classes, we expect the random baseline to be $P(4) = 0.25$. To compare our results to classical approaches, we used a Random Forest (RF) classifier with 100 estimators. For this we used "spectral variation" (also called "spectral flux") for *flux* and "spectral spread" for *spread* as described in [20]. *Noise* is described by the absence of the estimated harmonicity according to a detected fundamental frequency. As a feature for *density* we used the residual part of Harmonic–Percussive–Residual Separation [9]. In lack of a descriptor for *realness* we just used the mean of the mel-spectrogram. All coefficients were computed on the complete event by averaging over time.

Using this classifier also gives the possibility to determine importances of all feature coefficients. Although using five features we expect higher importances for the ones corresponding to our attributes.

4.3 Convolutional Neural Network (CNN)

We now want discuss the CNN architectures used for our experiments. As input representation, we chose mel-spectrograms to keep the aspect ratio of sound shapes independent of vertical position. Time–frequency transformations were made from wavefiles with a sample rate 22050 Hz using a window size of 1024 frames, a hop length of 512 frames and a vertical resolution of 96 bins. Each spectrogram was then cut into patches of 100 frames (around 2 s) with 50% overlap of each subsequent patch. Shorter events were padded by adding low positive noise (up to 10^{-4}) on the spectrogram to reach the desired minimum patch length. Values where scaled by appling zero-mean unit-variance normalization.

For the CNN configurations we chose to use a shallow version of the VGG-Network with 7 Layers [23]. Here, we compare architectures using 2D and 1D convolutional layers. Each architecture consists of two convolutional layers with 32 kernels, followed by two layers with 64 kernels. After each convolution, we applied batch normalization and max pooling. Classification was done with subsequent fully connected layers using one dense layer with 512 nodes as well as a

Table 1. Results of the 4-class classification experiments

	Architecture	F1	Δ Acc
Random baseline	–	0.25	–
Shallow classifier	Random Forest, 100 Estimators	0.27	–
CNN 2D	2 × Conv 2D 32, 2 × Conv 2D 64, 512 FCN	0.335	0.152
CNN 1D	2 × Conv 1D 32, 2 × Conv 1D 64, 512 FCN	0.315	0.207
CRNN 2D	2 × Conv 2D 32, 2 × Conv 2D 64, Bidirectional GRU 32, 512 FCN	0.362	0.112
CRNN 1D	2 × Conv 1D 32, 2 × Conv 1D 64, Bidirectional GRU 32, 512 FCN	0.385	0.022

final dense layer with four output nodes and softmax activation functions. We used dropout (0.25), ℓ_2 kernel regularization (0.01) after the first dense layer, as well as adding Gaussian noise (0.1) on the input in order to regularize the model and reduce overfitting. For the 2D convolutional architecture, we use 3×3 kernels and apply global average pooling before the Fully connected Layer (FCN). Accordingly, we use convolution kernels of size 3 for the 1D architectures before the CNN output is flattened and forwarded to the fully connected layers. Both architectures were chosen due to their different approach on computing features of the given input. While the 2D convolution is able to detect position invariant patterns, 1D convolution focuses on local patterns in a sequence.

4.4 Convolutional-Recurrent Neural Network (CRNN)

For the CRNN, a bi-directional Gated Recurrent Unit (GRU) layer with 32 units was added after the CNN processing for temporal modeling. We chose GRU over Long Short-Term Memory (LSTM) units, because of faster model convergence while showing similar performance to LSTM [4]. The first advantage of using CRNN over CNN alone is that this architecture can better model long-term dependencies. Secondly, such a network architecture can be trained with variable-length input data, while CNNs require fixed-size input. However, we observed a strong model overfitting when training CRNNs on full spectrograms of a piece. Therefore, we will focus on reporting results from the CNN model trained with a fixed input tensor size first. Then, we evaluate, whether the classification results improve if the CRNN is instead initialized with the trained parameters from a CNN model.

5 Results

The feature importance values for the baseline experiment in Table 2 show slight tendency towards the mel spectrogram with 0.22, while the noise feature had the least impact on the classification with 0.16. Importances of the remaining features are balanced.

Table 2. Feature importance values for the baseline experiment (Random Forest classifier)

Flux	Spread	Noise	Density	Mel
0.21	0.21	0.16	0.21	0.22

Comparing our approach (Table 1) with the baseline performance, deep learning improves classification results to some extent. Only using CNN layers for computation, 2D convolution gave best results with an F1-value of 0.335 over 1D convolution with 0.315. Accuracy differences are still relatively high so that we can observe some amount of overfitting. Taking all folds into account, the standard deviation over all accuracy differences in CNN 2D with 0.14 is relatively high as compared to CNN 1D with 0.089. For each fold, a higher ΔAcc usually correlates with higher numbers of training epochs, being a maximum of 98 epochs for CNN 2D and 38 for CNN 1D (Table 3).

Table 3. ΔAcc for each fold in CNN 2D and CNN 1D

CNN 2D Epochs		ΔAcc	CNN 1D Epochs	ΔAcc
Fold 1	3	0.123	16	0.265
Fold 2	98	0.361	38	0.275
Fold 3	1	0.028	3	0.081
Standard Dev	–	0.14	–	0.089

Adding the GRUs to the architectures and initializing weights with the aforementioned models results in improved classification results. Especially, CRNN 1D outperforms all experiments with a F1-value of 0.385, increasing by 0.07, whereas the F1-value for the CRNN 2D increases just by 0.027 to 0.362. ΔAcc decreases for both experiments. For CRNN 1D by 0.185 and 0.04 for CRNN 2D. Also the maximum training time decreased for both experiments being it 12 epochs for CRNN 2D and 14 epochs for CRNN 1D. Overall, a high F1-value correlates with a lower ΔAcc pointing to less overfitting.

6 Discussion

In this paper, we presented a musicologically informed approach for sound object classification of electroacoustic music. Using deep learning, we could show that some improvement could be achieved by architectures more sensitive to sequential data, which can facilitate classifying data as described by our morphological labels. Despite reducing the label space, feature importance values for the selected attributes *spread* and *noise* do not have any significant impact on the classification in the baseline experiment. *Noise* even had the lowest importance. This shows that the semantic implications of the chosen attributes are not transferable to common descriptors easily, so that more complex feature sets might be required.

Although we can see that CNN 2D achieved better classification results, using CNN 1D resulted in constant generalization throughout the folds (Table 3). This indicates that feature generalization depend less on position-invariant sound shapes than on the vertical integrity of the spectrum. Or at least more spectral context is needed than previously expected. One approach to validate this in future experiments is to apply horizontally-shaped CNN filters instead of symmetrical ones to incorporate a larger spectro-temporal context. The importance of temporal succession over the isolated position in the spectrum is then pronounced by the improved scores using CRNN.

Since there are still many questions and many configurations to be tested, this paper is merely a suggestion and baseline on further investigation into this field and even this approach can be still evaluated on more or different attributes, features and architectures. In general, results lagged far behind our initial hopes, which can be attributed to our more explorative approach of this problem.

With regard to the transcription of sound objects, the outcome of such experiments can be used for visualization, using e.g. gradient-based network analysis algorithms. These show portions of the spectrogram, which were relevant for the classification. We suspect these means to be helpful for detecting and displaying sound objects in the spectrogram. For our purposes, we tried layer-wise relevance propagation (LRP) [2] which resulted in relevancy maps which are merely hints to what the network actually learns. But the classification scores are quite low so that mappings at this point are mostly inconclusive and still have to be evaluated.

While developing and evaluating the experiments we noticed some issues that we want to address and propose some future solutions.

Labeling Approach. During the annotation procedure, only one person familiar with electroacoustic music worked on the labels. Thus, no validation could be made. To reduce the bias of the annotator, a group of people could cross-check their annotations. In different classification tasks, as e.g. discriminating cats and dogs, we can expect human experts to classify all samples right. Such bias values for a complex task like the one presented here do not exist so that cross-checking labels could also be a basis for more research. In addition, one could think about continuous values for annotating attributes. This could lead to embeddings of such sound objects which might help constructing new labels or label families.

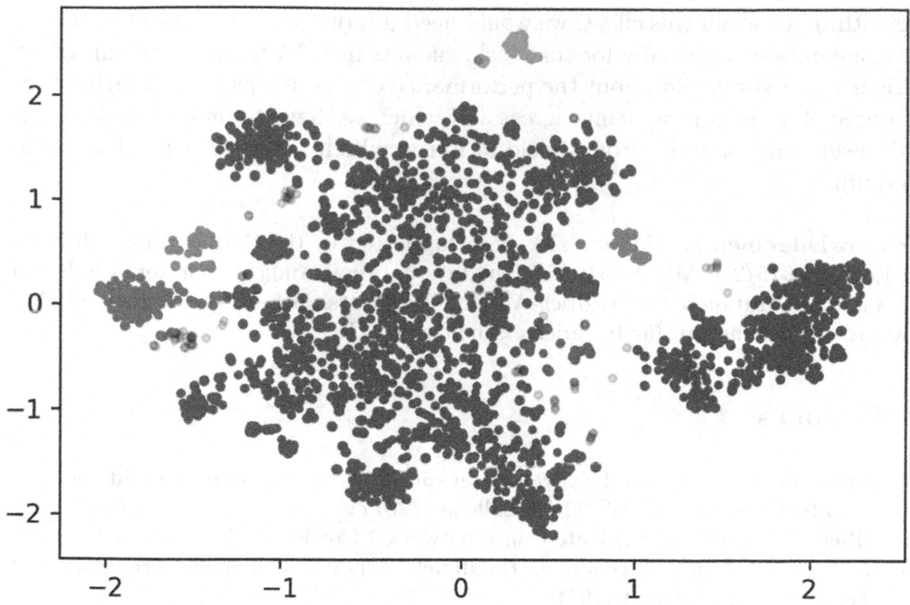

Fig. 2. Visualization using t-SNE for dimensionality reduction and DBSCAN for clustering. Each colored cluster consists of most segments of one piece used in the dataset. The blue cluster consists of segments of all other pieces. (Color figure online)

Dataset Size. The dataset used in this paper is relatively small. Therefore, more elaborate transfer-learning techniques [18,27] could be employed following the assumption that suitable low-level features can be extracted from different music related tasks [5] or even different domains such as images [12]. Beside feature transfer, one could also apply multitask-learning if labels for both source and target task are available [18]. The main idea is to train source and target task simultaneously, provided that both tasks are similar, to extract shared features. Even in the case of negative transfer, analyzing predicted targets could help in investigating the most helpful features. For a source task e.g. electroacoustic sound sources can be used such as *electronic*, *environment*, *instrument*, or *singing* while the target task labels remain morphological attributes.

Studio Effect. To validate the chosen labels, we wanted to see if unsupervised machine-learning techniques could help to figure out if some consistency in the data points can be found beyond our chosen descriptors. To this end, over 160 features were extracted for all segments according to [11] which where used in electroacoustic music related tasks in [13,14]. Using t-SNE [28] for dimensionality reduction and DBSCAN for clustering, we found that the studio effect (the effect of the production conditions for the feature extraction) had large impact on the clustering. In Fig. 2, each colored cluster consists of most segments of one piece used in the dataset, except blue which consists of segments of all other pieces. Grey transparent points are considered to be noisy data points by the clustering algorithm. To avoid this effect, we would need a more uniform dataset composed by some experts especially for that task, such as in [13,14][4], to avoid this effect. This is not a statement about the performance of our descriptors. It rather is an example of a problem we came across and which we have to face when designing a dataset using samples from a field of music which is highly dependent on its medium.

Acknowledgements. This work has been supported by the German Research Foundation (AB 675/2-1, MU 2686/11-1). The International Audio Laboratories Erlangen are a joint institution of the Friedrich-Alexander-Universität Erlangen-Nürnberg (FAU) and Fraunhofer Institut für Integrierte Schaltungen IIS.

References

1. Adavanne, S., Virtanen, T.: A report on sound event detection with different binaural features. In: DCASE 2017 Challenge (2017)
2. Alber, M., et al.: iNNvestigate neural networks! CoRR (2018)
3. Beiche, M.: Musique concrète. Handbuch der musikalischen Terminologie 4, Steiner-Verlag Stuttgart (1994)
4. Chung, J., Gülçehre, C., Cho, K., Bengio, Y.: Empirical evaluation of gated recurrent neural networks on sequence modeling. In: NIPS 2014 Deep Learning and Representation Learning Workshop (2014)
5. Choi, K., Fazekas, G., Sandler, M.B., Cho, K.: Transfer learning for music classification and regression tasks. In: Proceedings of the 18th ISMIR Conference, Suzhou, pp. 141–149 (2017)
6. Collins, N.: The UbuWeb Electronic Music Corpus: An MIR investigation of a historical database. Organised Sound **20**(1), 122–134 (2015)
7. Collins, N., Manning, P., Tarsitani, S.: A new curated corpus of historical electronic music: collation, data and research findings. Trans. Int. Soc. Music Inf. Retr. **1**(1), 34–55 (2018)
8. Couprie, P.: Methods and tools for transcribing electroacoustic music. In: International Conference on Technologies for Music Notation and Representation - TENOR 2018, Montréal, pp. 7–16 (2018)
9. Drieger, J., Müller M., Disch S.: Extending harmonic-percussive separation of audio signals. In: Retrieval Conference (ISMIR 2014), Taipei, pp. 611–616 (2014)
10. Erbe, M.: Klänge schreiben: die Transkriptionsproblematik elektroakustischer Musik. Apfel, Vienna (2009)
11. Essid, S., Richard, G., David, B.: Musical instrument recognition by pairwise classification strategies. IEEE Trans. Audio Speech Lang. Process. **14**(4), 1401–1412 (2006)
12. Grzywczak, D., Gwardys, G.: Deep image features in music information retrieval. Int. J. Electron. Telecommun. **60**(4), 321–326 (2014)
13. Gulluni, S., Essid, S., Buisson, O., Richard, G.: An interactive system for electroacoustic music analysis. In: 12th International Society for Music Information Retrieval Conference (ISMIR 2011), Miami, pp. 145–150 (2011)

[4] We have requested this dataset, but unfortunately it was no longer provided by the creators.

14. Gulluni, S., Essid, S., Buisson, O., Richard, G.: Interactive classification of sound objects for polyphonic electro-acoustic music annotation. In: AES 42nd International Conference, Ilmenau (2011)
15. Klien, V., Grill, T., Flexer, A.: On automated annotation of acousmatic music. J. New Music Res. **41**(2), 153–173 (2012)
16. López-Serrano, P., Dittmar, C., Müller M.: Mid-level audio features based on cascaded harmonic-residual-percussive separation. In: Proceedings of the Audio Engineering Society AES Conference on Semantic Audio, Erlangen (2017)
17. Mesaros, A., et al.: DCASE 2017 challenge setup: tasks, datasets and baseline system. In: DCASE 2017 - Workshop on Detection and Classification of Acoustic Scenes and Events (2017)
18. Pan, S.J., Yang, Q.: A survey on transfer learning. IEEE Trans. Knowl. Data Eng. **22**(10), 1345–1359 (2010)
19. Park, T.H., Li, Z., Wu, W.: Easy does it: the electro-acoustic music analysis toolbox. In: Proceedings of the 10th International Society for Music Information Retrieval Conference (ISMIR 2009), Kobe, pp. 693–698 (2009)
20. Peeters, G.: A large set of audio features for sound description (similarity and classification) in the CUIDADO project (2004). http://recherche.ircam.fr/anasyn/peeters/ARTICLES/Peeters_2003_cuidadoaudiofeatures.pdf
21. Pons, J.: Neural networks for music: a journey through its history (2018). https://towardsdatascience.com/neural-networks-for-music-a-journey-through-its-history-91f93c3459fb (2018)
22. Purwins, H., Li, B., Virtanen, T., Schlüter, J., Chang, S.-Y., Sainath, T.: Deep Learning for Audio Signal Processing. IEEE J. Sel. Top. Signal Process. **14**(8), 1–14 (2019)
23. Simonyan, K., Zisserman, A.: Very deep convolutional networks for large-scale image recognition. In: ILCR (2015)
24. Smalley, D.: Spectromorphology: Explaining Sound-shapes. Organised Sound 2/2, Cambridge, pp. 107–126 (1997)
25. Stroh, W.M.: Elektronische Musik. Handbuch der musikalischen Terminologie 2, Steiner-Verlag, Stuttgart (1972)
26. Thoresen, L., Hedman, A.: Spectromorphological Analysis of Sound Objects: An Adaptation of Pierre Schaeffer's Typomorphology. Organised Sound 12/2, Cambridge, pp. 129–141 (2007)
27. Torrey, L., Shavlik, J.: Transfer learning. In: Handbook of Research on Machine Learning, Algorithms, Methods, and Techniques, pp. 242–264. IGI-Global (2009)
28. van der Maaten, L., Hinton, G.: Visualizing data using t-SNE. J. Mach. Learn. Res. **9**, 2579–2605 (2008)
29. Virtanen, T., Plumbley, M.D., Ellis, D.P.W.: Computational Analysis of Sound Scenes and Events. Springer, Cham (2018). https://doi.org/10.1007/978-3-319-63450-0
30. Weiß, C., Müller M.: Quantifying and visualizing tonal complexity. In: Proceedings of the 9th Conference on Interdisciplinary Musicology (CIM), Berlin, pp. 184–187 (2014)

Ensemble Size Classification in Colombian Andean String Music Recordings

Sascha Grollmisch[1,2(✉)], Estefanía Cano[2], Fernando Mora Ángel[3], and Gustavo López Gil[3]

[1] Institute of Media Technology, TU Ilmenau, Ilmenau, Germany
sascha.grollmisch@tu-ilmenau.de
[2] Semantic Music Technologies, Fraunhofer IDMT, Ilmenau, Germany
[3] Músicas Regionales, Universidad de Antioquia, Medellín, Colombia

Abstract. Reliable methods for automatic retrieval of semantic information from large digital music archives can play a critical role in musicological research and musical heritage preservation. With the advancement of machine learning techniques, new possibilities for information retrieval in scenarios where ground-truth data is scarce are now available. This work investigates the problem of ensemble size classification in music recordings. For this purpose, a new dataset of Colombian Andean string music was compiled and annotated by musicological experts. Different neural network architectures, as well as pre-processing steps and data augmentation techniques were systematically evaluated and optimized. The best deep neural network architecture achieved 81.5% file-wise mean class accuracy using only feed forward layers with linear magnitude spectrograms as input representation. This model will serve as a baseline for future research on ensemble size classification.

Keywords: Ensemble size classification · Music archives · Music ensembles · Andean string music · Deep neural networks

1 Introduction

This work is motivated by the need of robust information retrieval techniques capable of efficiently extracting semantic information from large digital musical archives. With the advancements of deep learning techniques, numerous music information retrieval (MIR) methods have been proposed to address different information retrieval tasks, predominantly from a supervised machine learning perspective. In this work, we focus on the task of ensemble size classification, and aim to automatically classify music recordings according to the number of instruments playing in the track: solo, duet, trio, quartet, etc. Our long-term goal is to develop methods that minimally rely on manually annotated data, and that can exploit commonalities between unlabeled data and the few annotations available (semi-supervised and few-shot learning). This will enable the usage of MIR techniques not only with archives of mainstream music, but also with non-western,

R. Kronland-Martinet et al. (Eds.): CMMR 2019, LNCS 12631, pp. 60–74, 2021.
https://doi.org/10.1007/978-3-030-70210-6_4

under-represented, folk and traditional music archives. As described in Sect. 2, not much work has been conducted on the topic of ensemble size classification in music. Consequently, this work focuses on systematically optimizing a baseline classification model in a fully supervised manner (see Sect. 3) that can serve as a building block for future research on this topic. Detailed descriptions of the dataset used and of the optimization steps taken are presented in Sects. 3.1 and 3.2, respectively. Conclusions are presented in Sect. 4, outlining possibilities to extend this work to semi-supervised and few-shot learning paradigms.

1.1 The ACMus Project

This research work was conducted in the context of the ACMus research project: *Advancing Computational Musicology - Semi-supervised and unsupervised segmentation and annotation of musical collections* [6].[1] The main goal of the project is to improve upon the limits of state-of-the-art machine learning techniques for semantic retrieval of musical metadata. In particular, ACMus focuses on leveraging semi-supervised and unsupervised techniques for segmentation and annotation of musical collections. The music collection in the *Músicas Regionales* archive at the Universidad de Antioquia in Medellín-Colombia is the focus of this research. The archive contains one of the most important collections of traditional and popular Colombian music, including music from the Colombian Andes, indigenous traditions, Afro-Colombian music, among others. The great diversity of the archive in terms of musical traditions, audio quality and formats (analogue, digital, field recordings), and musical sources (instrumental, vocal, speech, mixed), makes it a particularly challenging collection to work with. Besides developing methods for ensemble size classification, the ACMus project will also focus on developing methods for speech/music discrimination, meter recognition, and musical scale detection. The ACMus Project is a collaboration between Fraunhofer IDMT and Ilmenau University of Technology in Germany, and Universidad de Antioquia and Universidad Pontificia Bolivariana in Colombia.

2 Related Work

To the best of the authors' knowledge, automatic ensemble size classification is a vastly unexplored topic in MIR research. Therefore, this section highlights classification methods proposed in related fields such as polyphony estimation, musical instrument classification, and speaker counting. Additionally, a brief description of common data augmentation techniques used to artificially increase datasets is provided.

[1] https://acmus-mir.github.io/.

2.1 Instrument Classification

Several systems have been proposed in the literature that either classify a single instruments in monophonic recordings [8,11], or detect a particular musical instrument in a polyphonic context [4,12]. Machine learning techniques such as Support Vector Machine (SVM) classifiers and Gaussian Mixture Models (GMM) have been frequently applied for the task of instrument classification. In [4] for example, instrument recognition in a polyphonic context is addressed by first applying sound source separation techniques to extract the predominant instrument in the mixture, and then by training a SVM classifier. More recently, convolutional neural networks (CNNs) trained on mel-scaled spectrograms of the audio signal have also been applied to predominant instrument classification in polyphonic music [12]. In an attempt to overcome limitations imposed by the scarce availability of annotated data for instrument recognition, some systems have proposed the use of unlabeled data through semi-supervised machine learning approaches. In [7], a GMM system is proposed where the model parameters are first estimated with labeled data, and then used to estimate the labels for the unlabeled set which is then used for an iterative refinement of the model. Other methods have addressed data limitations by introducing transfer learning techniques into their training procedures in deep learning contexts. In [10] for example, transfer learning is applied in conjunction with a CNN model based on the system proposed in [12], to build a instrument classification model for solo instruments in Jazz music.

2.2 Speaker Counting

While a considerable amount of work on the topic of speaker counting for single channel recordings has been conducted, the problem has often been approached from a feature design perspective, where features are specifically engineered for speech signals [18]. Works using more generic features such as [2,22] often assume that for the most part, only one speaker is active in the recording at a given time instant. In the case of music signals, this would be a strong assumption since musical instruments are expected to play simultaneously.

The task of audio source counting can be seen either as a regression or a classification problem when the number of maximum sources to be expected is known. Stöter et al. [20] investigate the performance of both approaches for speaker counting using bi-directional long-short term memory neural networks (BLSTMs) with different input representations such as the linear magnitude spectrogram, the mel-scaled spectrorgram, and the Mel Frequency Cepstral Coefficients (MFCCs). The dataset comprised 55 h of synthetically generated training material including signals with up to ten speakers. The system was tested on 5720 unique and unseen speaker mixtures. Even though regression could appear to be a good choice since the direct relationship of neighbouring classes is learned as well (a signal with 2 sources is closer to a signal with 3 sources than to a signal with 5), classification performed better for this task using linear magnitude spectrograms as input representation. Following these results, a classification approach was used in this work.

2.3 Polyphony Estimation

Polyphony estimation refers to the task of counting the number of simultaneous notes played by one or several instruments. This can be used as an intermediate step for multi-pitch estimation. It is important to note that polyphony estimation does not directly translate into ensemble size estimation, as several notes can be simultaneously played by a single instrument such as the guitar. Nevertheless, some relevant work on this topic is described here. Using a CNN with constant-Q transform of the audio data, Bittner et al. [3] achieved state-of-the-art performance for multi-pitch estimation. Large losses in accuracy were caused in particular by instruments playing closely harmonically related content. Kareer et al. [13] examine this task separately with different classical instruments playing up to four simultaneous notes. Using training data of 22 min the proposed CNN architecture with mel-scaled spectrogram achieved a file-wise mean class accuracy of 72.7% for three songs.

2.4 Data Augmentation

Classification tasks such as ensemble size classification are often challenging due to the lack of large annotated datasets for training. In general, comprehensive datasets are required to build robust supervised classification models. In this particular case, this would imply a dataset that covers a wide variety of instrument formats and recording conditions. A common method to artificially increase dataset size is data augmentation (DA). The idea behind DA is to apply different transformations to the original training data in order to artificially increase the number of training items. This can potentially make the model more robust to unseen signal characteristics. For audio classification tasks, these methods can be applied directly to the raw audio samples, for example by pitch shifting or time stretching the signal, and have been used in tasks such as chord detection [15] and singing voice separation [17]. Other augmentation methods, developed predominantly for image processing applications, modify a 2D representation of the audio signal such as the magnitude spectrogram. The winning submission of the Urban Sound Tagging task in the Detection and Classification of Acoustic Scenes and Events (DCASE) 2019 challenge[2] combined pitch shifting and time stretching with several image augmentation methods (namely, random erase, random rotate, grid distortion, and mixup) [1]. While random rotate simply rotates the input image by a random angle [5], random erase replaces rectangle regions with random values [24]. Grid distortion deforms the equidistant grid points and interpolates the values in between [5]. Mixup creates new examples by linearly combining pairs of examples and their corresponding labels [23]. A promising augmentation technique in the field of Automatic Speech Recognition is SpecAugment [16]. The technique applies time warping to the spectrogram as well as frequency and time masking. The masking operations replace neighboring time frames or frequency bins over the whole spectral input image with a

[2] Detailed results: http://dcase.community/challenge2019/task-urban-sound-tagging-results.

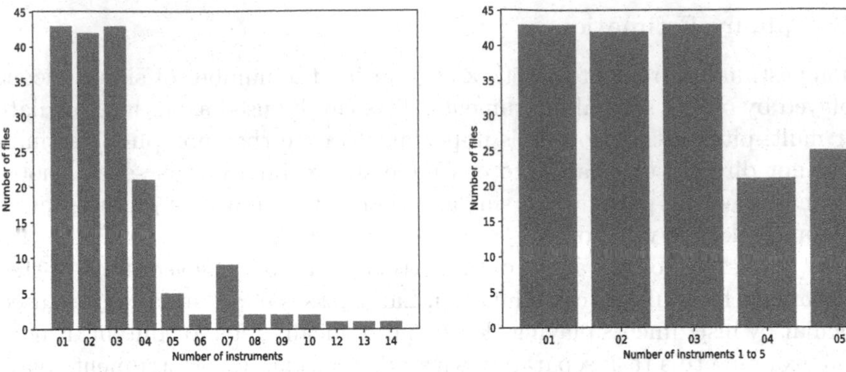

(a) Class distribution in dataset (b) Large ensembles mapped to class *5*

Fig. 1. Distribution of the annotated classes in the dataset. (a) Number of files per ensemble size. (b) Final class distribution with all large ensembles mapped to class 5.

constant value. The authors suggest that time warping can be omitted since it resulted in only minimal performance gains.

3 Proposed Method for Ensemble Size Classification

Since no method had been proposed in the literature that could directly be applied to identify the number of instruments in Andean string music recordings, we focused on developing a baseline model which was systematically evaluated and optimized using different neural network architectures and augmentation methods. In this study, no pre-trained models were used as we wish to build a baseline that shows the potential of different neural networks for unseen tasks, avoiding possible biases from other datasets previously used for training.

3.1 Dataset

For this study, 174 representative song fragments from the *Músicas Regionales* archive were selected and annotated by musicological experts in Universidad de Antioquia.[3] All songs are instrumental pieces performed by ensembles of plucked string instruments from the Andes region in Colombia. The instruments in the dataset include different kinds of acoustic guitars, bandolas, tiples, electric bass guitars, and occasionally percussion instruments such as the maracas. The ensembles sizes considered are soloist, duet, trio, quartet, and large ensembles (five or more instruments). The annotations include the ensemble size, as well as the list of all the instruments in the ensemble.

[3] Dataset published at: https://zenodo.org/record/3268961.

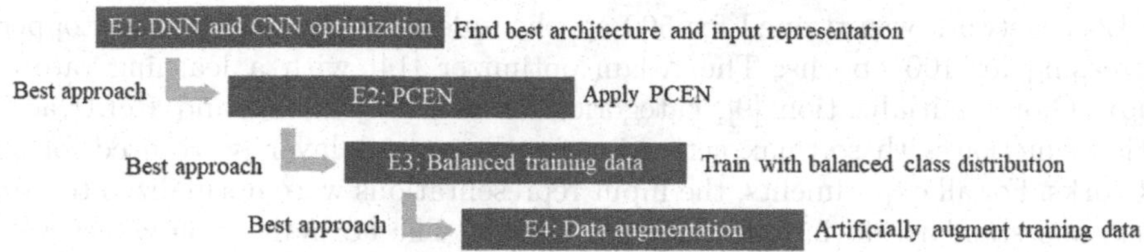

Fig. 2. Four consecutive experiments (E1–E4) were performed to find the optimal network configuration for our task.

In most songs, all annotated instruments are active during the entire file; however, short sections where one instrument is temporarily inactive also occur, leading to some instances of weak labels. The dataset comprises 64 min of audio, with song fragment duration ranging from 7 to 62 s. The distribution of the classes is shown in Fig. 1. Songs containing five or more instruments were mapped to the class 5. No genre or composer bias was found in the class distribution. Given that the original source of the recordings include digitized versions of tape recording as well as more recent digital recordings, these files have been saved with a 96 kHz sampling rate, 24 bit-depth, and in stereo format. However, for monophonic analogue recordings, the stereo was obtained by duplicating the monophonic recording in both channels. Additionally, some of the older recordings only contain information below 8 kHz. To avoid biases during training, all files were downsampled to 12 kHz, mixed to mono, and normalized to a maximum absolute amplitude of 1 for all the experiments.

3.2 Experimental Setup

Four experiments were conducted in order to build a reliable baseline system, showing the upper boundaries for a fully supervised classification system with a neural network trained from scratch. As shown in Fig. 2, our workflow starts with Experiment 1 (E1), where different architectures and input representations are evaluated. The approach that shows best performance in E1 is then used in Experiment 2 (E2) to test the effects of Per-Channel Energy Normalization (PCEN) on the system. Similarly, E3 and E4 evaluate the effects of balancing the training data, and data augmentation, respectively, on the best model from the previous experiment.

In all our experiments, we performed 10-fold cross-validation of random dataset splits for testing all files, and repeated each experiment twice to account the randomness during training. In each step, 80% of the files were randomly picked for training, 10% for early stopping during training, and 10% for the performance evaluation on unseen data. The test set was not balanced. As evaluation measure, we use the file-wise mean class accuracy over all repetition steps plus the standard deviation. To calculate the file-wise accuracy, the class confidences were summed up over all times frames and the class with the highest confidence was chosen.

Each network was trained for 500 epochs unless the validation loss stopped decreasing for 100 epochs. The Adam optimizer [14] with a learning rate of 0.001, Glorot initialization [9], categorical cross-entropy loss, and ReLU activation function with softmax activation for the output layer, were used for all networks. For all experiments, the input representations were normalized to zero mean and standard deviation of one per feature. The normalization values were calculated on the training set and applied to the validation and test sets. All experiments were conducted using Tensorflow[4].

Experiment 1 (E1) - DNN and CNN Models: E1 aimed at finding the best model architecture for a feed-forward neural network (DNN) and a convolutional neural network (CNN) as well as the most fitting input representation. The training data was not balanced in this experiment. Bayesian Optimization [19] was used to obtain an optimal combination of hyper-parameters in a reasonable amount of time, and comparable results for all network architectures.[5] Both the input feature dimensionality and the network architectures were optimized. As input features, a linear magnitude spectrogram obtained from the short-time Fourier transform (STFT) was compared to the mel-scaled spectrogram with a logarithmic frequency axis (Mel) using 128 mel bands.[6] For the DNN model, the spectral frames were smoothed using a moving average filter over time for each frequency bin. The length of the filter, number of layers, number of units per layer, and dropout percentage between the layers were also subject to the Bayesian optimization. For the CNN model, several time frames were combined into patches, where the patch length was also optimized. The maximum patch duration was set to 3 s. The basic CNN architecture was inspired by the model proposed in [12] and the number of layers and filters, amount of Gaussian noise added to the input, and dropout percentage between the layers were included in the optimization. Additionally, a system using MFCCs and their first and second order derivatives as input features with a linear SVM[7] as classifier are also reported for comparison. The number of MFCC coefficients (between 10 and 40) as well as the regularization parameter C (between 0 and 1) were optimized in the same way as the neural networks. The Bayesian optimization process was performed with 30 iterations and was only feasible because of the relatively small dataset (see Sect. 3.1).

Experiment 2 (E2) - Per-Channel Energy Normalization (PCEN): In E2, the best architectures from E1 were taken, and Per-Channel Energy Normalization (PCEN) (see footnote 6) was applied to each audio file. PCEN was evaluated with the default settings S1 ($power = 0.5, time\_constant = 0.4, max\_size = 1$), and with a second parameter setting S2 ($power = 0.25, time\_constant =$

[4] Tensorflow (1.12): www.tensorflow.org.
[5] Implementation from https://github.com/fmfn/BayesianOptimization.
[6] Implementation from librosa (0.7.2): https://librosa.github.io/.
[7] Implementation from scikit-learn (0.22.2): https://scikit-learn.org/.

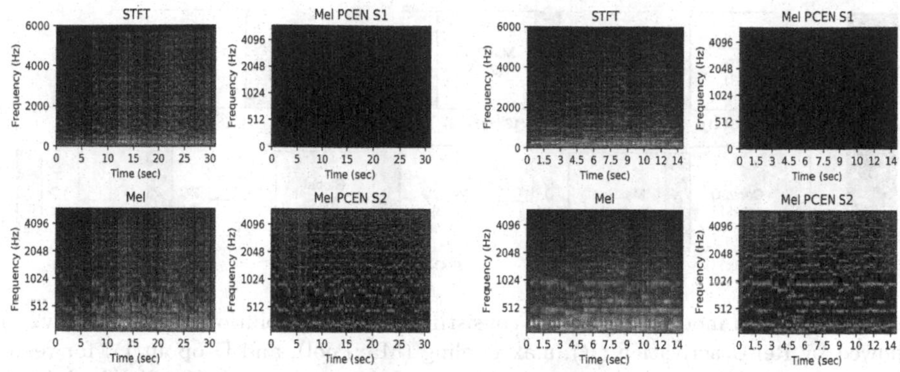

(a) Example with three instruments **(b)** Example with four instruments

Fig. 3. Input representations for two example recordings. (a) Input representations of an example of a trio. (b) Input representations of an example of a quartet.

$0.01, max\_size = 20$) experimentally chosen for highlighting harmonic structures. Figure 3a and 3b show the different input representations and PCEN settings for two audio files, one with three instruments and one with four. While S1 highlights temporal changes, S2 emphasizes harmonic structures. Both versions suppress stable background noise using adaptive gain control and dynamic range compression. This has proved to be beneficial for tasks with high loudness variations such as key word spotting [21]. In this study, PCEN was applied to test its potential to account for the great variability in audio quality in our dataset.

Experiment 3 (E3) - Balanced Training Data: E1 and E2 were conducted using training data with unbalanced classes. In our dataset, the class with the fewest examples (four instruments) has 21 items, while 42 files are available for training the solo and the trio classes. In E3, several methods to deal with unbalanced training data were evaluated. First, the data was randomly downsampled by using the class with the smallest number of examples and randomly subsampling the other classes. Second, the class with the fewest examples was upsampled by randomly repeating examples. Since the balancing was performed on a file level, class weights (see footnote 7) were additionally tested for each balancing method to deal with slightly imbalanced features due to the differences in file duration.

Experiment 4 (E4) - Data Augmentation (DA): The best performing DNNs and CNNs were used to evaluate the performance of DA techniques. On the raw audio, pitch shifting (± 2 semitones) and time stretching (between 90% and 110%) were applied. For the 2D input representation of the CNN, random brightness (default parameters), random erasing (default parameters), random rotate (limited to a max of $5°$ in either direction), grid distortion (default param-

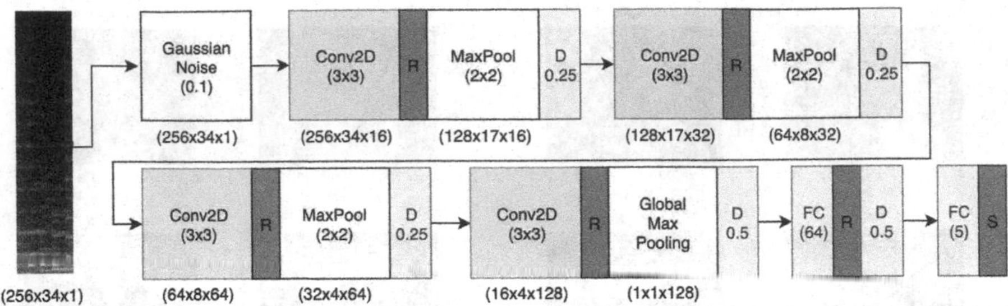

Fig. 4. Best CNN model architecture consisting of four convolutional layers (Conv2D) followed by ReLU activation (R), max pooling (MaxPool), and Dropout(D) for regularization. Global max pooling is applied before the dense layers (FC). The final dense layer uses softmax activation (S) for the classification. The corresponding output shapes are specified for each layer.

eters), mixup (alpha of 0.4), and SpecAugment (without time warping, masking up to 27 spectral bins and 11 time frames) were used.[8] Furthermore, a combination of all of these methods was performed by picking each method randomly with 50% chance. Since the DNN only has one time frame as input, no image augmentation methods were applied. Each augmentation was performed three times with randomized parameters for each batch. This procedure increases the training set size by a factor of three.

3.3 Results

Experiment 1 (E1) - DNN and CNN Models: Table 1 shows the results for E1. To give the reader an idea of the importance of parameter optimization, we present results for the best performing network, as well as for the worst performing one (above chance level 20%). With unbalanced training data and no data augmentation (E1), the highest classification accuracy (81.5%) was obtained by the DNN model with linear magnitude spectrogram (STFT) while the CNN achieved 74.8%. Mel-spectrogram as input representation performed generally worse than linear magnitude spectrograms. This suggests that with small audio training datasets, CNNs do not necessarily lead to the best performance, and that simpler and faster feed forward networks can lead to better results. The SVM classifier with MFCC input features showed inferior performance to all neural network approaches and was therefore not included in the following experiments. Furthermore, linear magnitude spectrograms resulted in higher performance for both DNNs and CNNs. These results go in line with those reported in [20], where linear magnitude spectrogram resulted in better performance than the mel-spectrogram for speaker counting. Table 1 also shows how critical the choice

[8] For random brightness, random rotate and grid distortion implementations were taken from [5]. For random erase, mixup and SpecAugment, we used the implementation provided in the corresponding publications: [23,24], and [16].

of hyper-parameters is. Especially CNNs suffer when parameters are poorly chosen, leading to an accuracy of 20.5% for the worst model above chance level. Since there is so much variability in the CNNs' performance, it is possible that further optimization iterations may lead to better results and architectures than the ones found here.

The final DNN model used a 2048 STFT window size with logarithmic compression of the magnitudes and a moving average filter 10 time frames long, covering 1.7 s. The 1024 unique values in the STFT were passed through a 0.1 dropout layer to one hidden layer with 512 units. The output was passed through a dropout of 0.5 to a final softmax layer with 5 units, one for each class. The best CNN model is shown in detail in Fig. 4. The input representation used was the STFT with a window size of 512 samples and logarithmic compression of the magnitudes. Each patch consisted of 34 STFT frames covering 1.45 s. For the optimized SVM, the regularization parameter C was set to 0.1 with 34 MFCCs.

Table 1. File-wise mean class accuracy and standard deviation for E1.

Optimization	DNN STFT	DNN Mel	CNN STFT	CNN Mel	SVM MFCC
Best	**81.5%, 11.1%**	72.8%, 14.7%	74.8%, 14.2%	73.3%, 17.0%	65.0%, 18.0%
Worst	57.0%, 14.8%	65.5%, 12.1%	20.5%, 1.6%	20.5%, 1.6%	50.5%, 17.5%

Experiment 2 (E2) - PCEN: Table 2 shows the results of applying PCEN-S1 and PCEN-S2 to the input representations, as well as the best performing model from E1 for comparison. As seen in the table, applying PCEN led to worse results with respect to E1 especially for the DNN. The CNN was less affected by PCEN in general. Between the two parameter settings of PCEN, the best results were achieved for S2 which highlights harmonic structures rather than temporal changes. In general, it appears that the suppression of possible background noise in our data when using PCEN results in the loss of discriminative information for ensemble size classification. Therefore, PCEN was discarded as a processing step for the following experiments.

Table 2. File-wise mean class accuracy and standard deviation for E2.

PCEN	DNN STFT	CNN STFT
with PCEN-S1	45.8%, 12.5%	71.0%, 14.6%
with PCEN-S2	72.8%, 9.6%	73.0%, 11.7%
without PCEN (E1)	**81.5%, 11.1%**	74.8%, 14.2%

Experiment 3 (E3) - Balancing Training Data: Table 3 shows the results obtained when the training data was balanced using up- and downsampling, both with and without class weights. Additionally, the results from E1 with unbalanced classes are included for comparison. It can be seen that balancing the training data using downsampling decreases the performance of both neural networks. The possible reason may be the lowered variability of the training data when less data is used. While upsampling lowered the accuracy of the DNN from 81.5% to 79.5% it increased for the CNN from 74.8% to 77.3%. In general, the high standard deviation of more than 10% shows that the performance still depends on which data is used for training. This may be caused by the relatively small size of our dataset. Therefore, no general conclusion that applies to all models could be drawn from these results. Applying class weights led in general to slightly worse performance, and was therefore discarded for the following experiment.

Table 3. File-wise mean class accuracy and standard deviation for E3 with or without (wo) class weights (cw).

Balancing method	DNN STFT	CNN STFT
downsampled with cw	72.5%, 12.3%	63.5%, 15.9%
downsampled wo cw	73.5%, 14.8%	70.0%, 14.8%
upsampled with cw	79.0%, 10.6%	77.3%, 11.5%
upsampled wo cw	79.5%, 10.4%	77.5%, 11.3%
unbalanced with cw	78.8%, 10.5%	71.3%, 12.6%
unbalanced wo cw (E1)	**81.5%, 11.3%**	74.8%, 14.2%

Experiment 4 (E4) - Data Augmentation: Table 4 shows the results obtained with data augmentation, as well as the best performing architectures from E1 and E3 for comparison. For the CNN, DA was applied using upsampling of the training data as it performed best in E3. These results show that artificially increasing the dataset via data augmentation does not necessarily improve classification performance. Augmentation via pitch shift and time stretching did not improve the performance of the DNN; however, accuracy for the CNN increased up to 4.0% in this case. Augmentation methods for 2D data such as random brightness, mixup and random rotate slightly enhanced the performance of the CNN model. Combining all augmentation methods improved the performance of the CNN by 3.3% reaching comparable results to those obtained when using time stretching only. However, it must be noted that this improvement comes at the cost of a training time seven times longer than the one required when no DA is used. None of the CNN models with DA performed better than the best DNN without DA. Possible explanations might be the artifacts produced by the augmentation process which are not present in the original test data and the missing

variability in the training data which cannot be artificially created. Furthermore, most of the augmentation methods were developed for images and only partially capture real-world audio modifications. In general, these results show that the evaluated DA methods do not consistently improve the classification results for our task.

Table 4. File-wise mean class accuracy and standard deviation for E4.

Augmentation (DA)	DNN STFT	CNN STFT
Pitch shift	77.3%, 11.7%	80.0%, 10.3%
Time stretch	79.8%, 9.8%	**81.5%, 11.4%**
Random brightness	-	78.0%, 11.7%
Random erase	-	76.8%, 13.8%
Grid distortion	-	78.8%, 11.7%
mixup	-	79.0%, 12.7%
Random rotate	-	79.8%, 16.3%
SpecAug	-	77.0%, 13.5%
All	-	80.8%, 12.0%
unbalanced wo cw (E1)	**81.5%, 11.3%**	74.8%, 14.2%
upsampled wo cw (E3)	79.5%, 10.4%	77.5%, 11.3%

3.4 Error Analysis

To get a deeper understanding of the classification errors in our models, the mean confusion matrices for the best DNN model (from E1) and the best CNN model (from E4) are shown in Fig. 5. The file-wise mean class accuracy is similar for the DNN and the CNN with 81.5% and most classification errors occurred between neighboring classes. This shows that the network is implicitly capable of learning the relationships between classes (e.g., a duo is closer to a trio than to a quartet), and consequently, of learning useful classification features. This is in line with the findings in [13] and also [20], where better performance was achieved for speaker counting with classification than with regression.

Files containing three instruments were misclassified the most which goes in line with the main challenge of our dataset: Polyphonic melodies can be played by one or several instruments. This blurs the boundaries between the different classes, with trios easily mistaken as duos or quartets due to the high similarity between the neighboring classes. Class 5 (large ensembles) on the other hand, achieved the highest classification accuracy. Since files in this class can contain up to 14 instruments, the difference between these recordings and the other classes is probably much larger in terms of spectral content. This supports the assumption that meaningful features have been learned during training.

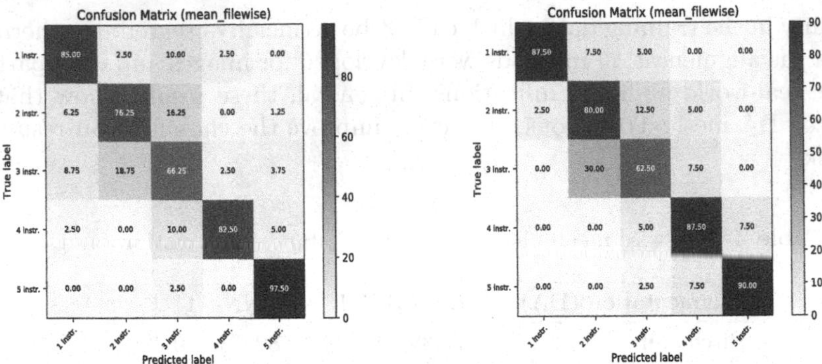

(a) Confusion matrix for best DNN model **(b)** Confusion matrix for best CNN model

Fig. 5. Mean confusion matrices for best models from E3.

4 Conclusions

In this work, the task of classifying the number of instruments in music recordings was addressed using a newly gathered dataset of Colombian Andean string music. Apart from the challenges of the task itself, working with Andean string music comes with its own difficulties: different recording conditions, scarce and expensive annotated data, and high similarity between the different instruments.

To build our baseline system, 174 tracks were annotated by musicological experts in Colombia. Using this relatively small dataset, several neural networks architectures were trained and optimized. The highest file-wise mean class accuracy of 81.5% was achieved for both best CNN and DNN models. Using linear magnitude spectrograms as input representation instead of its mel-scaled version, resulted in better performance in all experiments. All neural network based approaches clearly outperform the 20% chance level baseline and a SVM classifier using MFCCs. In general, all networks had a minimum standard deviation of 10% between repetitions suggesting that the training set does not cover the full variance of recording conditions and instrument combinations. Neither data augmentation nor PCEN increased the robustness against these problems. The optimization procedure showed that hyper-parameter optimization is critical when working with such a small dataset. This system will serve as a baseline for future research on this topic where semi-supervised and unsupervised training techniques will be explored.

Acknowledgments. This work has been partially supported by the German Research Foundation (BR 1333/20-1, CA 2096/1-1).

References

1. Adapa, S.: Urban sound tagging using convolutional neural networks. Technical report, DCASE2019 Challenge (2019)

2. Andrei, V., Cucu, H., Buzo, A., Burileanu, C.: Counting competing speakers in a timeframe - human versus computer. In: Interspeech Conference. ISCA, Dresden, Germany (2015)
3. Bittner, R.M., Mcfee, B., Salamon, J., Li, P., Bello, J.P.: Deep salience representations for F0 estimation in polyphonic music. In: 18th International Society for Music Information Retrieval Conference. Suzhou, China (2017)
4. Bosch, J.J., Janer, J., Fuhrmann, F., Herrera, P.: A comparison of sound segregation techniques for predominant instrument recognition in musical audio signals. In: 13th International Society for Music Information Retrieval Conference, Porto, Portugal, pp. 559–564 (2012)
5. Buslaev, A., Iglovikov, V.I., Khvedchenya, E., Parinov, A., Druzhinin, M., Kalinin, A.A.: Albumentations: fast and flexible image augmentations. Information **11**(2), 125 (2020)
6. Cano, E., et al.: ACMUS - advancing computational musicology: semi-supervised and unsupervised segmentation and annotation of musical collections. In: Late-breaking-demo of the 20th International Society for Music Information Retrieval Conference, Delft, The Netherlands (2019)
7. Diment, A., Heittola, T., Virtanen, T.: Semi-supervised learning for musical instrument recognition. In: 21st European Signal Processing Conference (EUSIPCO). IEEE, Marrakech, Morocco (2013)
8. Essid, S., Richard, G., David, B.: Efficient musical instrument recognition on solo performance music using basic features. In: 25th International AES Conference, London, UK (2004)
9. Glorot, X., Bengio, Y.: Understanding the difficulty of training deep feedforward neural networks. In: International Conference on Artificial Intelligence and Statistics (AISTATS). Society for Artificial Intelligence and Statistics, Sardinia, Italy (2010)
10. Gómez, J.S., Abeßer, J., Cano, E.: Jazz solo instrument classification with convolutional neural networks, source separation, and transfer learning. In: 19th International Society for Music Information Retrieval Conference, Paris, France (2018)
11. Grasis, M., Abeßer, J., Dittmar, C., Lukashevich, H.: A multiple-expert framework for instrument recognition. In: International Symposium on Computer Music Multidisciplinary Research (CMMR), Marseille, France, pp. 619–634 (2013)
12. Han, Y., Kim, J., Lee, K.: Deep convolutional neural networks for predominant instrument recognition in polyphonic music. IEEE/ACM Trans. Audio Speech Lang. Process. **25**, 208–221 (2017)
13. Kareer, S., Basu, S.: Musical polyphony estimation. In: Audio Engineering Society Convention 144, Milan, Italy (2018)
14. Kingma, D.P., Ba, J.: Adam: a method for stochastic optimization. In: International Conference on Learning Representations (ICLR), San Diego, USA (2015)
15. Nadar, C.R., Abeßer, J., Grollmisch, S.: Towards CNN-based acoustic modeling of seventh chords for automatic chord recognition. In: International Conference on Sound and Music Computing, Málaga, Spain (2019)
16. Park, D.S., et al.: SpecAugment: a simple augmentation method for automatic speech recognition. In: INTERSPEECH, Graz, Austria (2019)
17. Prétet, L., Hennequin, R., Royo-Letelier, J., Vaglio, A.: Singing voice separation: a study on training data. IEEE International Conference on Acoustics. Speech and Signal Processing (ICASSP), Brighton, UK, pp. 506–510 (2019)
18. Sayoud, H., Boumediene, T.H., Ouamour, S., Boumediene, T.H.: Proposal of a new confidence parameter estimating the number of speakers - an experimental investigation. J. Inf. Hiding Multimedia Signal Process. **1**(2), 101–109 (2010)

19. Snoek, J., Larochelle, H., Adams, R.P.: Practical Bayesian Optimization of Machine Learning Algorithms. In: 25th International Conference on Neural Information Processing Systems, Lake Tahoe, Nevada, USA, pp. 2951–2959 (2012)
20. Stöter, F.R., Chakrabarty, S., Edler, B., Habets, E.A.P.: Classification vs. regression in supervised learning for single channel speaker count estimation. In: IEEE International Conference on Acoustics. Speech and Signal Processing (ICASSP), Calgary, Alberta, Canada , pp. 436–440. IEEE(2018)
21. Wang, Y., Getreuer, P., Hughes, T., Lyon, R.F., Saurous, R.A.: Trainable frontend for robust and far-field keyword spotting. In: IEEE International Conference on Acoustics. Speech and Signal Processing (ICASSP), New Orleans, LA, USA, pp. 5670–5674. IEEE (2017)
22. Xu, C., Li, S., Liu, G., Zhang, Y.: Crowd ++ : Unsupervised speaker count with smartphones. In: ACM International Joint Conference on Pervasive and Ubiquitous Computing, Zurich, Switzerland, pp. 43–52. ACM (2013)
23. Zhang, H., Cisse, M., Dauphin, Y.N., Lopez-Paz, D.: mixup: beyond empirical risk minimization. In: International Conference on Learning Representations (ICLR), Vancouver, BC, Canada (2018)
24. Zhong, Z., Zheng, L., Kang, G., Li, S., Yang, Y.: Random erasing data augmentation. In: Proceedings of the AAAI Conference on Artificial Intelligence (AAAI), New York, NY, USA (2020)

Tapping Along to the Difficult Ones: Leveraging User-Input for Beat Tracking in Highly Expressive Musical Content

António Sá Pinto[1,2](✉) and Matthew E. P. Davies[1]

[1] INESC TEC, Sound and Music Computing Group, Porto, Portugal
{antonio.s.pinto,matthew.davies}@inesctec.pt
[2] Faculdade de Engenharia da Universidade do Porto, Porto, Portugal

Abstract. We explore the task of computational beat tracking for musical audio signals from the perspective of putting an end-user directly in the processing loop. Unlike existing "semi-automatic" approaches for beat tracking, where users may select from among several possible outputs to determine the one that best suits their aims, in our approach we examine how high-level user input could guide the manner in which the analysis is performed. More specifically, we focus on the perceptual difficulty of tapping the beat, which has previously been associated with the musical properties of expressive timing and slow tempo. Since musical examples with these properties have been shown to be poorly addressed even by state of the art approaches to beat tracking, we re-parameterise an existing deep learning based approach to enable it to more reliably track highly expressive music. In a small-scale listening experiment we highlight two principal trends: i) that users are able to consistently disambiguate musical examples which are easy to tap to and those which are not; and in turn ii) that users preferred the beat tracking output of an expressive-parameterised system to the default parameterisation for highly expressive musical excerpts.

Keywords: Beat tracking · Expressive timing · User input

1 Introduction and Motivation

While the task of computational beat tracking is relatively straightforward to define – its aim being to replicate the innate human ability to synchronise with a musical stimulus by tapping a foot along with the beat – it remains a complex and unsolved task within the music information retrieval (MIR) community. Scientific progress in MIR tasks is most often demonstrated through improved accuracy scores when compared with existing state of the art methods [25]. At the core of this comparison rest two fundamental tenets: the (annotated) data upon which the algorithms are evaluated, and the evaluation method(s) used to measure performance. In the case of beat tracking, both the tasks of annotating datasets of musical material and measuring performance are non-trivial [10]. By

R. Kronland-Martinet et al. (Eds.): CMMR 2019, LNCS 12631, pp. 75–90, 2021.
https://doi.org/10.1007/978-3-030-70210-6_5

its very nature, the concept of beat perception – how an individual perceives the beat in a piece of music – is highly subjective [21]. When tapping the beat, listeners may agree over the phase, but disagree over the tempo or preferred metrical level – with one tapping, *e.g.*, twice as fast as another, or alternatively, they may agree over the tempo, but tap in anti-phase. This inherent ambiguity led to the prevalence of multiple hypotheses of the beat, which can arise at the point of annotation, but more commonly appear during evaluation where different interpretations of ground truth annotations are obtained via interpolation or sub-sampling. In this way, a wide net can be cast in order not to punish beat tracking algorithms which fail to precisely match the annotated metrical level or phase of the beats; with this coming at the expense that some unlikely beat outputs may inadvertently be deemed accurate. Following this evaluation strategy, the performance of the state of the art is now in the order of 90% on existing datasets [4,5] comprised primarily of pop, rock and electronic dance music. However, performance on more challenging material [15] is considerably lower, with factors such as expressive timing (*i.e.*, the timing variability that characterises a human performance, in opposition to a metronomic or "perfectly" timed rendition [11]), recording quality, slow tempo and metre changes among several identified challenging properties.

Although beat tracking has garnered much attention in the MIR community, it is often treated as an element in a more complex processing pipeline which provides access to "musical time", or simply evaluated based on how well it can predict ground truth annotations. Yet, within the emerging domain of creative-MIR [16,22] the extraction of the beat can play a critical role in musically-responsive and interactive systems [18]. A fundamental difference of applying beat tracking in a creative application scenario is that there is a specific end-user who wishes to directly employ the music analysis and thus has very high expectations in terms of its performance [1]. To this end, obtaining high mean accuracy scores across some existing databases is of lower value than knowing "*Can the beats be accurately extracted (as I want them) for this specific piece of music?*". Furthermore, we must also be aware that accuracy scores themselves may not be informative about "true" underlying performance [10,24]. Indeed, within the related field of recommender systems (which has some clear overlap with MIR), it has been observed that incrementing accuracy scores does not, in itself, lead to improvements in user experience [19].

Of course, a user-specific beat annotation can be obtained without any beat tracking algorithm, by manually annotating the desired beat locations, e.g. using software such as Sonic Visualiser [8]. However, manually annotating beat locations is a laborious procedure even for skilled annotators [15]. An alternative is to leverage multiple beat interpretations from a beat tracking algorithm, and then provide users with a range of solutions to choose from [12]. However, even with a large number of interpretations (which may be non-trivial and time-consuming to rank) there is no guarantee that the end-user's desired result will be among them, especially if the alternative interpretations are generated in a

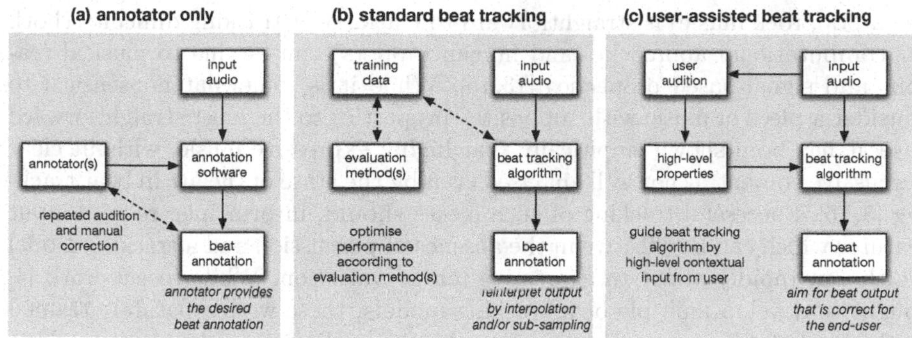

Fig. 1. Overview of different approaches to obtaining a desired beat annotation. (a) The user annotates the beat positions. (b) A beat tracking algorithm is used – whose performance has been optimised on annotated datasets. (c) Our proposed approach, where user input guides the beat tracking.

deterministic manner from a single beat tracking output, *e.g.*, by interpolation or sub-sampling.

In this paper, we propose an alternative formulation which could allow an end-user to drive how the beat tracking is undertaken. Our goal is to enable the user to rapidly arrive at the beat annotation suitable for their purposes with a minimal amount of interaction. Put another way, we envisage an approach to beat tracking where high-level contextual knowledge about a specific musical signal can be given by the user and reliably interpreted by the algorithm, without the need for extensive model training on annotated datasets, as shown in Fig. 1. In this sense, we put aside the concept of "universal" beat tracking models which target equal performance irrespective of the musical input signal, in favour of the more realistic goal of identifying different classes of the beat tracking problem, which require different beat tracking strategies. While the end goal of retrieving beat locations may be the same for fast-paced techno music and highly expressive classical guitar recordings, the assumptions about what constitutes the beat and how this can be extracted from audio signals are not. Conversely, constraints should not be placed on what musical content can be creatively re-purposed based on the limitations of MIR algorithms.

The long-term challenges of our approach are as follows: i) determining a low-dimensional parameterisation of the beat tracking space within which diverse, accurate solutions can be found in order to match different beat tracking conditions; ii) exposing these dimensions to end-users in a way that they can be easily understood; iii) providing an interpretable and understandable mapping between the user-input and the resulting beat annotation via the beat tracking algorithm; and finally iv) measuring the level of engagement among end-users who actively participate in the analysis of music signals.

Concerning the dimensions of beat tracking, it is well-understood that music of approximately constant (medium) tempo, with strong percussive content (*e.g.*, pop, rock music) is straightforward to track. Beat tracking difficulty (both for computational approaches and human tappers) can be due to musical reasons and signal-based properties [13,15]. While it is somewhat nonsensical to consider a piece of music with "opposite" properties to the most straightforward case, it has been shown empirically that highly expressive music, without clear percussive content, is not well analysed even by the state of the art in beat tracking [5,15]. Successful tracking of such pieces should, in principle, require input features which can be effective in the absence of percussion and a tracking model which can rapidly adapt to expressive tempo variation. While recent work [4] sought to develop multiple beat tracking models, these were separately trained at the level of different databases rather than according to musical beat tracking conditions.

In our approach, we reexamine the functionality of the current state of the art in beat tracking, *i.e.*, the recurrent neural network approach of Böck et al. [5]. In particular, we devise a means to re-parameterise it so that it is adapted for highly expressive music. Based on an analysis of existing annotated datasets, we identify a set of musical stimuli we consider typical of highly challenging conditions, together with a parallel set of "easier" examples. We then conduct a small-scale listening experiment where participants are first asked to rate the perceptual difficulty of tapping the beat, and subsequently to rate the subjective quality of beat annotations given by the expressive parameterisation vs the default version. Our results indicate that listeners are able to distinguish easier from more challenging cases, and furthermore that they preferred the beat tracking output of the expressive-parameterised system to the default parameterisation for the highly expressive musical excerpts. In this sense, we seek to use the assessment of perceptual difficulty of tapping as a means to drive the manner in which the beats can be extracted from audio signals towards the concept of user-informed beat tracking. To complement our analysis, we explore the objective evaluation of the beat tracking model with both parameterisations.

The remainder of this paper is structured as follows. In Sect. 2 we detail the adaption of the beat tracking followed by the design of a small-scale listening experiment in Sect. 3. This is followed by results and discussion in Sect. 4, and conclusions in Sect. 5.

2 Beat Tracking System Adaptation

Within this work our goal is to include user input to drive how music signal analysis is conducted. We hypothesise that high-level contextual information which may be straightforward for human listeners to determine can provide a means to guide how the music signal analysis is conducted. For beat tracking, we established in Sect. 1 that for straightforward musical cases, the current state of the art [5] is highly effective. Therefore, in order to provide an improvement over the state of the art, we must consider the conditions in which it is less effective, in particular those displaying expressive timing. To this end, we first summarise the main functionality of the beat tracking approach of Böck et al., after which we detail how we adapt it.

The approach of Böck et al. [5] (originally presented in [6]) uses deep learning and is freely available within the madmom library [3]. The core of the beat tracking model is a recurrent neural network (RNN) which has been trained on a wide range of annotated beat tracking datasets to predict a beat activation function which exhibits peaks at likely beat locations. To obtain an output beat sequence, the beat activation function given by the RNN is post-processed by a dynamic Bayesian network (DBN) which is approximated by a hidden Markov model [20].

While it would be possible to retrain this model from scratch on challenging data, this has been partially addressed in the earlier multi-model approach of Böck et al. [4]. Instead, we reflect on the latter part of the beat tracking pipeline, namely how to obtain the beat annotation from the beat activation function. To this end, we address three DBN parameters: i) the minimum tempo in beats per minute (BPM); ii) the maximum tempo; and iii) the so-called "transition-λ" parameter which controls the flexibility of the DBN to deviate from a constant tempo[1]. Through iterative experimentation, including both objective evaluation on existing datasets and subjective assessment of the quality of the beat tracking output, we devised a new set of expressiveness-oriented parameters, which are shown, along with the default values in Table 1. More specifically, we first undertake a grid search across these three parameters on a subset of musical examples from existing annotated datasets for which the state of the art RNN is deemed to perform poorly, *i.e.*, by having an information gain lower than 1.5 bits [26]. An informal subjective assessment was then used to confirm that reliable beat annotations could be obtained from the expressive parameterisation.

Table 1. Overview of default and expressive-adapted parameters.

Parameter	Default	Expressive
Minimum Tempo (BPM)	55	35
Maximum Tempo (BPM)	215	135
Transition-λ (unitless)	100	10

As shown in Table 1, the main changes for the expressive model are a shift towards a slower range of allowed tempi (following evidence about the greater difficulty of tapping to slower pieces of music [7]), together with a lower value for the transition-λ. While the global effect of the transition-λ was studied by Krebs et al. [20], their goal was to find an optimal value across a wide range of musical examples. Here, our focus is on highly expressive music and therefore we do not need to pursue a more general solution. Indeed, the role of the expressive model is to function in precisely the cases where the default approach cannot.

[1] The probability of tempo changes varies exponentially with the negative of the "transition-λ", thus higher values of this parameter favour constant tempo from one beat to the next one [20].

3 Experimental Design

Within this paper, we posit that high-level user-input can lead to improved beat annotation over using existing state of the art beat tracking algorithms in a "blind" manner. In order to test this in a rigorous way, we would need to build an interactive beat tracking system including a user interface, and conduct a user study in which users could select their own input material for evaluation. However, doing so would require understanding which high-level properties to expose and how to meaningfully interpret them within the beat tracking system. To the best of our knowledge, no such experiment has yet been conducted, thus in order to gain some initial insight into this problem, we conducted a small-scale online listening experiment, which is split into two parts: **Part A** to assess the perceptual difficulty of tapping the beat, and **Part B** to assess the subjective quality of beat annotations made using the default parameterisation of the state of the art beat tracking system versus our proposed expressive parameterisation.

We use **Part A** as a means to simulate one potential aspect of high-level context which an end-user could provide: in this case, a choice over whether the piece of music is easy or difficult to tap along to (where difficulty is largely driven by the presence of expressive timing). Given this choice, **Part B** is used as the means for the end-user to rate the quality of the beat annotation when the beat tracking system has been parameterised according to their choice. In this sense, if a user rates the piece as "easy", we would provide the default output of the system, and if they rate it as "hard" we provide the annotation from the expressive parameterisation. However, for the purposes of our listening experiment, all experimental conditions are rated by all participants, thus the link between **Part A** and **Part B** is not explicit.

3.1 Part A

In the first part of our experiment, we used a set of 8 short music excerpts (each 15 s in duration) which were split equally among two categories: i) "easy" cases with near constant tempo in 4/4 time, with percussive content, and without highly syncopated rhythmic patterns; and ii) "hard" cases typified by the presence of high tempo variation and minimal use of percussion. The musical excerpts were drawn from existing public and private beat tracking datasets, and all were normalised to −3 dB.

We asked the participants to listen to the musical excerpts and to spontaneously tap along using the computer keyboard at what they considered the most salient beat. Due to the challenges of recording precise time stamps without dedicated signal acquisition hardware (*e.g.*, at the very least, a MIDI input device) the tap times of the participants were not recorded, however this was not disclosed. We then asked the participants to rate the difficulty they felt when trying to tap the beat, according to the following four options (Fig. 2):

- Low - *I could easily tap the beat, almost without concentrating*
- Medium - *It wasn't easy, but with some concentration, I could adequately tap the beat*

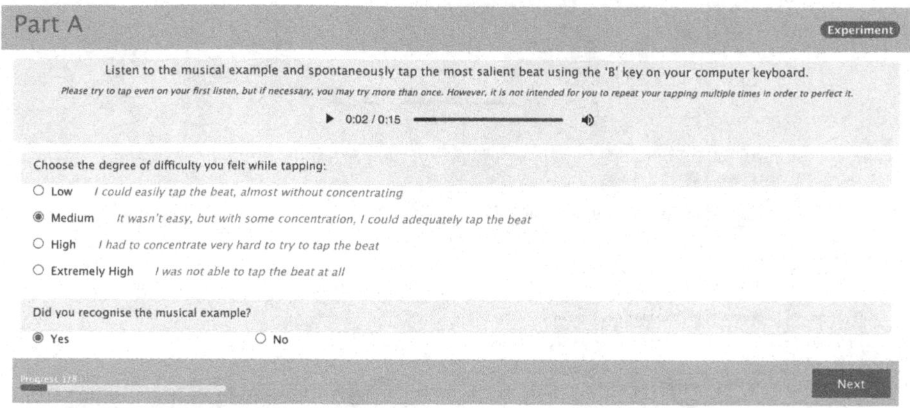

Fig. 2. Listening experiment - graphical interface of Part A.

- High - *I had to concentrate very hard to try to tap the beat*
- Extremely high - *I was not able to tap the beat at all.*

Our hypothesis for **Part A** is that participants would consistently rate those drawn from the "easy" set as having Low or Medium difficulty, whereas those from the "hard" should be rated with High or Extremely High difficulty.

3.2 Part B

Having completed **Part A**, participants then proceeded to **Part B** in which they were asked to judge the subjective quality of beat annotations (rendered as short 1 kHz pulses) mixed with the musical excerpts. The same set of musical excerpts from **Part A** were used, but they were annotated in three different ways: i) using the *default* parameterisation of the Böck et al. RNN approach from the madmom library [3]; ii) using our proposed *expressive* parameterisation (as in Table 1); and iii) a control condition using a completely *deterministic* beat annotation, *i.e.*, beat times at precise 500 ms intervals without any attempt to track the beat of the music. In total, this created a set of $8 \times 3 = 24$ musical excerpts to be rated, for which participants were asked to: *Rate the overall quality of how well the beat sequence corresponds to the beat of the music* (Fig. 3).

For this question, a 5-point Likert-type item was used with (1) on the left hand side corresponding to "Not at all" and (5) corresponding to "Entirely" on the right hand side. Our hypothesis for **Part B** was that for the "hard" excerpts, the annotations of the expressively-parameterised beat tracker would be preferred to those of the default approach, and for all musical excerpts that the deterministic condition would be rated the lowest in terms of subjective quality. In this part of the experiment we draw inspiration from evaluation of automatic musical accompaniment driven by real-time beat tracking where our three conditions of: default, expressive, and deterministic can be deemed similar

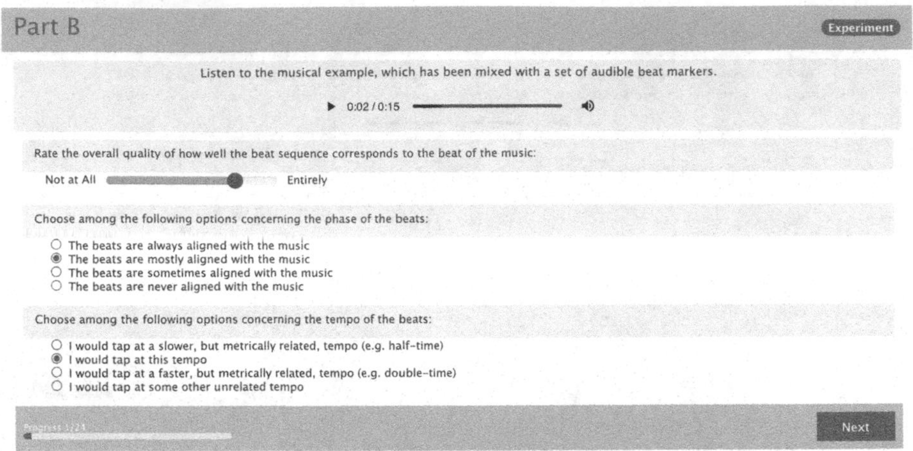

Fig. 3. Listening experiment - graphical interface of Part B.

to the use of a beat tracking system, a human tapper, and a quantised beat sequence, by Stowell et al. [23].

3.3 Implementation

The experiment was built using HTML5 and Node.js and run online within a web browser, where participants were recruited from the student body of the University of Porto and the wider research network of the Sound and Music Computing Group at INESC TEC. Within the experimental instructions, all participants were required to give their informed consent to participate, with the understanding that any data collected would be handled in an anonymous fashion and that they were free to withdraw at any time without penalty (and without their partial responses being recorded). Participants were asked to provide basic information for statistical purposes: sex, age, their level of expertise as a musician, and experience in music production.

All participants were encouraged to take the experiment in a quiet environment using high quality headphones or loudspeakers, and before starting, they were given the opportunity to set the playback volume to a comfortable level. Prior to the start of each main part of the experiment, the participants undertook a compulsory training phase in order to familiarise themselves with the questions. To prevent order effects, each participant was presented with the musical excerpts in a different random order. In total, the test took around 30 min to complete.

4 Results and Discussion

4.1 Listening Experiment

A total of 10 listeners (mean age: 31, age range: 23–43) participated in the listening test, 9 of whom self-reported amateur or professional musical proficiency.

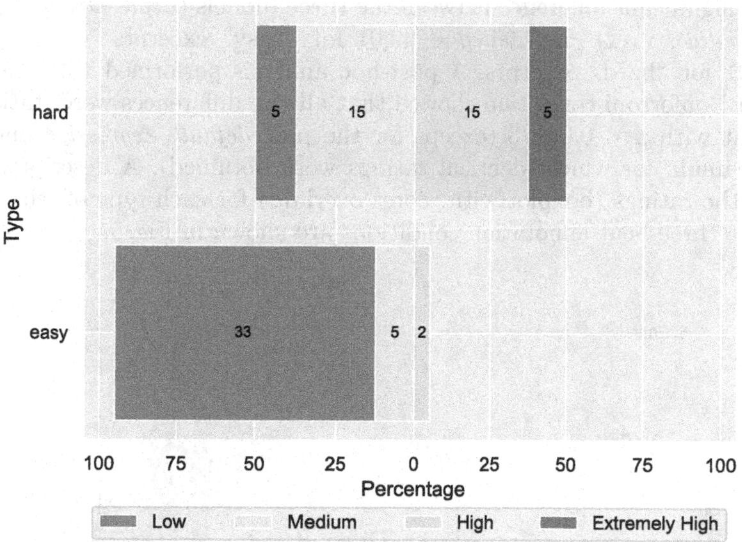

Fig. 4. Subjective ratings of the difficulty of beat tapping.

For **Part A**, we obtained 40 ratings for each stimuli group "easy" and "hard", according to the frequency distribution shown in Fig. 4. The most frequent rating for the first group was "low" (82.5%), followed by the "medium" rating (12.5%). For the "hard" group, a symmetrical rating was obtained: the adjacent ratings "medium" and "high" (37.5% each), complemented by the more extreme ratings "low" and "extremely high" (12.5% each). A Mann-Whitney test showed that there was a statistically significant difference between the ratings for both groups, with $p < 0.001$.

From these results we interpret that there was greater consistency in classifying the "easy" excerpts as having low difficulty, with only two excerpts rated above "medium", than for the "hard" excerpts which covered the entire rating scale from low to extremely difficult, albeit with the majority of ratings being for medium or high difficulty. We interpret this greater variability in the rating of difficulty of tapping to be the product of two properties of the participants: their expertise in musical performance and/or their familiarity with specific pieces. Moreover, we can observe a distinction between the understanding of the perceptual difficulty in tapping on the part of the participant and the presence of expressive timing in the musical excerpts; that experienced listeners may not have difficulty in tapping along with a piece of expressive music for which they knew well. Thus, for expert listeners it may be more reasonable to ask a direct question related to the presence of expressive timing, while the question of difficulty may be more appropriate for non-expert listeners who might lack familiarity with the necessary musical terminology.

For **Part B**, we again make the distinction between the ratings of the "easy" and the "hard" excerpts. A Kruskal-Wallis H test showed that there was a statistically significant difference between the three models (*expressive*, *default* and *deterministic*): $\chi^2(2) = 87.96$, $p < 0.001$ for "easy" excerpts, $\chi^2(2) = 70.71$, $p < 0.001$ for "hard" excerpts. A post-hoc analysis performed with the Dunn test with Bonferroni correction showed that all the differences were statistically significant with $p < 0.001/3$ (except for the pair *default–expressive* under the "easy" stimuli, for which identical ratings were obtained). A descriptive summary of the ratings (boxplot with scores overlaid) for each type of stimuli, and under the three beat annotation conditions are shown in Fig. 5.

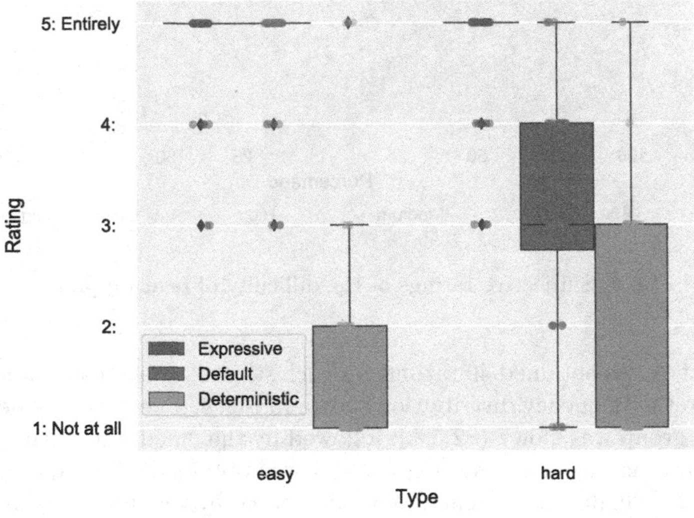

Fig. 5. Subjective ratings of the quality of the beat annotations.

The main results from Part B are as follows. For the "easy" excerpts there is no difference in performance for the *default* and *expressive* parameterisations of the beat tracking model, both of which are rated with high scores indicating high quality beat annotations from both systems. We contrast this with the ratings of the *deterministic* output (which should bear no meaningful relationship to the music) and which are rated toward the lower end of the scale. From these results we can infer that the participants were easily able to distinguish accurate beat annotations and deliberately inaccurate annotations, a result which is consistent with the well-known Beat Alignment Test [17]. Concerning the ability of the expressively parameterised model to achieve such high ratings, we believe that this was due to very clear information concerning the beat in the beat activation functions from the RNN, and thus there was no alternative "expressive" path for this model to follow.

Conversely, the ratings of the "hard" excerpts show a different picture. Here, the ratings of the expressively-parameterised model are similar to the "easy" excerpts, but the ratings of the *default* model [3] are noticeably lower. This suggests that the participants, in spite of their reported higher perceptual difficulty in tapping the beat, were able to reliably identify the accurate beat predictions of the *expressive* model over those of the *default* model. It is noteworthy that the ratings of the *deterministic* approach are moderately higher for the "hard" excerpts compared to the "easy" excerpts. Given the small number of samples and participants for this experiment, we should not draw strong conclusions about this difference, but for highly expressive pieces, the *deterministic* beats may have inadvertently aligned with the music in brief periods compared to the "easy" excerpts, which may have been unrelated in a more obvious way to listeners.

4.2 Beat Tracking Accuracy

In addition to reporting on the listening experiment whose focus is on subjective ratings of beat tracking, we also examine the difference in objective performance of using the *default* and *expressive* parameterisations of the beat tracking model. Given the focus on challenging excerpts for beat tracking, we initially focus on the SMC dataset [15]. It contains 217 excerpts, each of 40 s in duration. Following the evaluation methods described in [10] we select the following subset: F-measure, CMLc, CMLt, AMLc, AMLt, and the Information Gain (D) to assess performance. In Tables 2, we show the recorded accuracy on the SMC for both the default and expressive parameterisations. Note, for the default model we use the version in the madmom library [3] which has been exposed to this material during training (via cross-validation), hence the accuracy scores are slightly higher than those in [5] where 8-fold cross validation was used. In addition to showing the performance of each parameterisation we also show the theoretical upper limit achievable by making a perfect choice (by a hypothetical end-user) among the two parameterisations. Since multiple evaluation scores are reported, and there is no accepted single metric to use within the beat tracking community, we make the optimal choice per excerpt according to each individual evaluation metric.

From Table 2, we see that for all the evaluation methods, with the exception of the Information Gain (D), the default parameterisation outperforms the expressive one. This result is not unexpected result as the SMC dataset is not entirely comprised of highly expressive musical material. We consider the more important result to be the potential for our *expressive* parameterisation to track those excerpts for which the *default* approach fails. To this end, the increase of approximately 10% points across each of the evaluation methods demonstrates how these two different parameterisations can provide greater coverage of the dataset.

Table 2. Overview of beat tracking performance on the SMC dataset [15] comparing the default and expressive parameters together with upper limit on performance.

	F-measure	CMLc	CMLt	AMLc	AMLt	D
Default [3]	0.563	0.350	0.472	0.459	0.629	1.586
Expressive	0.540	0.306	0.410	0.427	0.565	1.653
Optimal Choice	0.624	0.456	0.611	0.545	0.703	1.830

While the SMC dataset is well-known for containing a high proportion of challenging material, we also believe that it is worthwhile to explore the effectiveness of our method on other musical material. Since the expressive parameterisation should only be effective when applied to music with a slow average tempo and high expression, the gains on datasets comprised primarily of pop or rock music will be much lower. In addition, many of the existing beat tracking datasets have been used to train the approach of Böck et al. [5] and thus cannot provide insight into the effectiveness of our approach on truly unseen data. To this end, we make use of a more recently annotated dataset which was used in the 2017 IEEE Signal Processing Cup (SP Cup) [18]. While the dataset is quite small, containing 98 excerpts of 30 s it was compiled in a community-driven fashion where teams participating in the competition selected the audio material and annotated it themselves. In line with the competitive element of the SP Cup many teams chose to submit challenging musical excerpts. On this basis, we believe it represents a highly appropriate choice for additional validation of our approach. A summary of the results containing the same three conditions: default, expressive, and the optimal choice between the two, is shown in Table 3.

Table 3. Overview of beat tracking performance SP Cup dataset [18] comparing the default and expressive parameters together with upper limit on performance.

	F-measure	CMLc	CMLt	AMLc	AMLt	D
Default [3]	0.833	0.660	0.687	0.846	0.877	2.968
Expressive	0.783	0.564	0.581	0.805	0.826	2.955
Optimal Choice	0.860	0.733	0.762	0.873	0.897	3.062

Contrasting the results in Tables 2 and 3 we can observe a similar pattern of lower overall performance for the expressive approach compared the default parameterisation. However, once again, the optimal choice between the two provides a notable improvement (of up to 7% points) depending on the evaluation method. Given the improvement under both presented datasets we believe this supports the need for different parameterisations to tackle different types of musical content, a concept related to Collins' discussion of "style-specific" beat tracking [9]. In addition, it suggests that training a classifier to choose between expressive and non-expressive pieces would be a promising area for future work.

4.3 Individual Example

While results shown in Tables 2 and 3 focus more on the global effect of these different paramaterisations across entire datasets, it is important to consider the practical impact at the level of individual musical excerpts. In this section we consider an annotation workflow perspective, which might rely on the correction of an automatic annotation of the beat of a piece of music, as opposed to completely annotating a piece by hand. In this context, we contend that an informed choice of how to first estimate the beat automatically may have a significant impact in terms of the subsequent work required to obtain an output which is acceptable for the end-user, i.e. by inserting, deleting, and shifting the automatically estimated beats.

To this end, we focus on one specific example within the Hainsworth dataset [14]; an excerpt from the composition "Evocaciòn" by Jose Luis Merlin. It is a solo piece for classical guitar which features extensive *rubato* and as such can be considered one of the more challenging pieces within the dataset. In the absence of any other musical instruments, together with the clear guitar plucking technique, this piece is rather a paradox since it is quite straightforward for onset detection, but notoriously difficult for beat tracking. The challenge lies not in the ability to precisely identify where in time the notes are played, but to decode which of these onsets correspond to the beat over a highly variable underlying tempo. To explore this specific musical excerpt in greater detail, we contrast the outputs of the default and expressive parameterisations together with the ground truth annotation (taken from the supplementary material from [2]) in Fig. 6.

As can be seen from the figure, the output of the expressive parameterisation (in the bottom plot) is much closer to the ground truth annotations than the default (in the top plot). Across this 30 s section there are just 6 beats in need of correction for the expressive output, with no fewer than 18 for the default output. The number of atomic operations to correct each annotation can be broken down as follows: 13 shifts and 6 deletions for the default output vs. 3 shifts and 3 deletions for the expressive output. Taking into account the number of annotations in this excerpt, the amount of editing effort required to converge on the ground-truth annotation is even more illustrative: 21% of the expressive beats output vs 61% of the default beat outputs. Thus, from the user (annotator) perspective, it is clearly more efficient to correct the expressive output.

In this example, we have explicitly used the ground truth as a means to illustrate the fewer number of errors made by the expressive parameterisation. However, when such ground truth annotations exist, the need for automatic analysis is negated. Yet, in real-world uses, where there is no ground truth, we would replace this visual comparison with an interactive process whereby the user verifies the output of the algorithm by listening and iterative adjustment. The number of edit operations to achieve the desired output indicates the amount of interactions between the user and the beat-tracking system, and can thus provide a direct indicator of the impact of user-informed beat tracking in the annotation workflow.

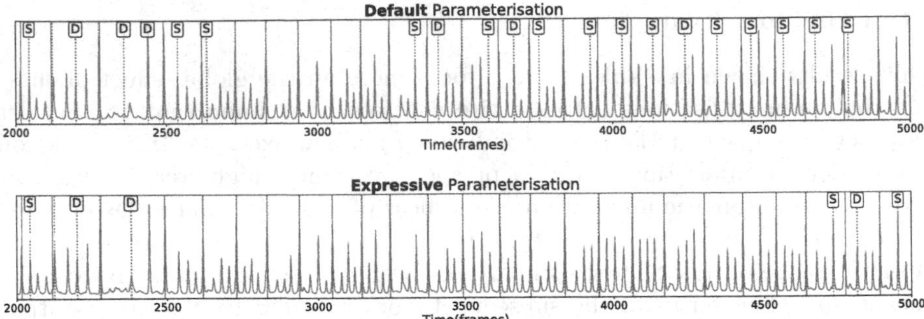

Fig. 6. Comparison of different beat tracking outputs. The blue solid line indicates the beat activation function given by the Böck et al. approach [5]. The vertical red solid lines show the ground truth annotations. The vertical green dashed lines show: the default output (top) and the expressive output (bottom). The incorrect beat outputs are labelled with the required operations (**D**elete, **S**hift, **I**nsert) to correct the annotation. The temporal axis represents frames at a rate of 100 frames per second. (Color figure online)

5 Conclusions

In this paper we have sought to open the discussion about the potential for user-input to drive how MIR analysis is performed. Within the context of beat tracking, we have demonstrated that it is possible to reparameterise an existing state-of-the-art approach to provide better beat annotations for highly expressive music, and furthermore, that the ability to choose between the default and expressive parameterisation can provide significant improvements on very challenging beat tracking material. We emphasise that the benefit of the expressive model was achieved without the need for any retraining of the RNN architecture, but that the improvement was obtained by reparameterisation of the DBN tracking model which performs inference on the prediction of the RNN.

To obtain some insight into how user input could be used for beat tracking, we simulated a scenario where user decisions about perceptual difficulty of tapping could be translated into the use of a parameterisation for expressive musical excerpts. We speculate that listener expertise as well as familiarity may play a role in lowering the perceived difficulty of otherwise challenging expressive pieces. Our intention is to further investigate the parameters which can be exposed to end-users, and whether different properties may exist for expert compared to non-expert users. Despite the statistical significance of our results, we acknowledge the small-scale nature of the listening experiment, and we intend to expand both the number of musical excerpts uses as well as targeting a larger group of participants to gain deeper insight into the types of user groups which may emerge. Towards our long-term goal, we will undertake an user study not only to understand the role of beat tracking for creative MIR, but also to assess the level of engagement when end-users are active participants who guide the analysis.

Acknowledgments. This work is supported by Portuguese National Funds through the FCT-Foundation for Science and Technology, I.P., under the grant SFRH/BD/120383/2016 and the project IF/01566/2015.

References

1. Andersen, K., Knees, P.: Conversations with expert users in music retrieval and research challenges for creative MIR. In: Proceedings of the 17th International Society for Music Information Retrieval Conference, pp. 122–128 (2016)
2. Böck, S., Davies, M.E.P., Knees, P.: Multi-task learning of tempo and beat: learning one to improve the other. In: Proceedings of the 20th International Society for Music Information Retrieval Conference, pp. 486–493 (2019)
3. Böck, S., Korzeniowski, F., Schlüter, J., Krebs, F., Widmer, G.: Madmom: a new python audio and music signal processing library. In: Proceedings of the 2016 ACM Multimedia Conference, pp. 1174–1178 (2016). https://doi.org/10.1145/2964284.2973795
4. Böck, S., Krebs, F., Widmer, G.: A multi-model approach to beat tracking considering heterogeneous music styles. In: Proceedings of the 15th International Society for Music Information Retrieval Conference, pp. 603–608 (2014)
5. Böck, S., Krebs, F., Widmer, G.: Joint beat and downbeat tracking with recurrent neural networks. In: Proceedings of the 17th International Society for Music Information Retrieval Conference, pp. 255–261 (2016)
6. Böck, S., Schedl, M.: Enhanced beat tracking with context-aware neural networks. In: Proceedings of the 14th International Conference on Digital Audio Effects, pp. 135–139 (2011)
7. Bååth, R., Madison, G.: The subjective difficulty of tapping to a slow beat. In: Proceedings of the 12th International Conference on Music Perception and Cognition, pp. 82–55 (2012)
8. Cannam, C., Landone, C., Sandler, M.: Sonic visualiser: an open source application for viewing, analysing, and annotating music audio files. In: Proceedings of the 18th ACM International Conference on Multimedia, pp. 1467–1468 (2010). https://doi.org/10.1145/1873951.1874248
9. Collins, N.: Towards a style-specific basis for computational beat tracking. In: Proceedings of the 9th International Conference on Music Perception and Cognition (ICMPC), pp. 461–467 (2006)
10. Davies, M.E.P., Böck, S.: Evaluating the evaluation measures for beat tracking. In: Proceedings of the 15th International Society for Music Information Retrieval Conference, pp. 637–642 (2014)
11. Desain, P., Honing, H.: Does expressive timing in music performance scale proportionally with tempo? Psychol. Res. **56**(4), 285–292 (1994). https://doi.org/10.1007/BF00419658
12. Goto, M., Yoshii, K., Fujihara, H., Mauch, M., Nakano, T.: Songle: a web service for active music listening improved by user contributions. In: Proceedings of the 12th International Society for Music Information Retrieval Conference, pp. 311–316 (2011)
13. Grosche, P., Müller, M., Sapp, C.: What makes beat tracking difficult? A case study on chopin mazurkas. In: Proceedings of the 11th International Society for Music Information Retrieval Conference, pp. 649–654 (2010)
14. Hainsworth, S.: Techniques for the Automated Analysis of Musical Audio. Ph.D. thesis, University of Cambridge (2004)

15. Holzapfel, A., Davies, M.E.P., Zapata, J.R., Oliveira, J., Gouyon, F.: Selective sampling for beat tracking evaluation. IEEE Trans. Audio Speech Lang. Process. **20**(9), 2539–2548 (2012). https://doi.org/10.1109/TASL.2012.2205244
16. Humphrey, E.J., Turnbull, D., Collins, T.: A brief review of creative MIR. In: Late-breaking Demo Session of the 14th International Society for Music Information Retrieval Conference (2013)
17. Iversen, J.R., Patel, A.D.: The Beat Alignment Test (BAT): surveying beat processing abilities in the general population. In: Proceedings of the 10th International Conference on Music Perception and Cognition, pp. 465–468 (2010)
18. Jin, C.T., Davies, M.E.P., Campisi, P.: Embedded systems feel the beat in new orleans: highlights from the IEEE signal processing cup 2017 student competition [SP Competitions]. IEEE Signal Process. Mag. **34**(4), 143–170 (2017). https://doi.org/10.1109/MSP.2017.2698075
19. Konstan, J.A., Riedl, J.: Recommender systems: from algorithms to user experience. User Model. User-Adap. Inter. **22**(1), 101–123 (2012). https://doi.org/10.1007/s11257-011-9112-x
20. Krebs, F., Böck, S., Widmer, G.: An efficient state space model for joint tempo and meter tracking. In: Proceedings of the 16th International Society for Music Information Retrieval Conference, pp. 72–78 (2015)
21. Moelants, D., McKinney, M.: Tempo perception and musical content: what makes a piece fast, slow or temporally ambiguous? In: Proceedings of the 8th International Conference on Music Perception and Cognition, pp. 558–562 (2004)
22. Serra, X., et al.: Roadmap for music information research (2013), Creative Commons BY-NC-ND 3.0 license, ISBN: 978-2-9540351-1-6
23. Stowell, D., Robertson, A., Bryan-Kinns, N., Plumbley, M.D.: Evaluation of live human-computer music-making: quantitative and qualitative approaches. Int. J. Hum. Comput. Stud. **67**(11), 960–975 (2009). https://doi.org/10.1016/j.ijhcs.2009.05.007
24. Sturm, B.L.: Classification accuracy is not enough. J. Intell. Inf. Syst. **41**(3), 371–406 (2013). https://doi.org/10.1007/s10844-013-0250-y
25. Urbano, J., Schedl, M., Serra, X.: Evaluation in music information retrieval. J. Intell. Inf. Syst. **41**(3), 345–369 (2013). https://doi.org/10.1007/s10844-013-0249-4
26. Zapata, J.R., Holzapfel, A., Davies, M.E.P., Oliveira, J.L., Gouyon, F.: Assigning a confidence threshold on automatic beat annotation in large datasets. In: Proceedings of the 13th International Society for Music Information Retrieval Conference, pp. 157–162 (2012)

Drum Fills Detection and Generation

Frederic Tamagnan(✉) and Yi-Hsuan Yang

Academia Sinica, Taipei, Taiwan
frederic.tamagnan@gmail.com, yang@citi.sinica.edu.tw

Abstract. Drum fills are essential in the drummer's playing. They regularly restore energy and announce the transition to a new part of the song. This aspect of the drums has not been explored much in the field of MIR because of the lack of datasets with drum fills labels. In this paper, we propose two methods to detect drum fills along a song, to obtain drum fills context information. The first method is a logistic regression which uses velocity-related handcrafted data and features from the latent space of a variational autoencoder. We give an analysis of the classifier performance regarding each features group. The second method, rule-based, considers a bar as a fill when a sufficient difference of notes is detected with respect to the adjacent bars. We use these two methods to extract regular pattern/ drum fill couples in a big dataset and examine the extraction result with plots and statistical test. In a second part, we propose a RNN model for generating drum fills, conditioned by the previous bar. Then, we propose objective metrics to evaluate the quality of our generated drum fills, and the results of a user study we conducted. Please go to https://frederictamagnan.github.io/drumfills/ for details and audio examples.

Keywords: Drum fills detection · Drum fills generation

1 Introduction

Percussions and drums are a fundamental core aspect of music. One important part of long-term drums generation is the drum fills issue. In recent works on music generation using generative deep learning models, drum fills have often been treated implicitly. The main challenge of drum fills generation comes from the lack of labelled data. So that, drum fills detection is an important preliminary task. The second tricky issue that comes in mind when dealing with drum fills is the lack of rules that defined them. Nevertheless, our empirical observations can lead to these properties: 1) a greater use of toms, snares or cymbals, than in the regular drum pattern; 2) a difference of played notes between the regular pattern and the drum fill; 3) an appearance in general at the end of a cycle of 4 or 8 bars. The task of detecting and generating drum fills explicitly has at least the following two use cases: first, segmenting the parts of a music piece, as important drum fills are often located as a transition between two parts of a song, from the verse to the chorus for example; second, allowing the generation

R. Kronland-Martinet et al. (Eds.): CMMR 2019, LNCS 12631, pp. 91–99, 2021.
https://doi.org/10.1007/978-3-030-70210-6_6

of long music sequences, in order to be able to create drum patterns with real evolution and ruptures.

In this paper, we present an initial attempt towards generating drum fills. Our goal is first to address drum fills detection and to build-up a dataset of regular pattern/drum fills couples (Fig. 1). Secondly, we use this dataset to train a model able to generate a drum fill based on a regular pattern. In particular, this work allows us to answer three research questions: (1) Can we train a fill detector from isolated fills? or Is it mandatory to take into account the context? (2) Is a rule-based method effective enough to detect fills? (3) How objectively a human can rate a drum fill? In Sects. 4–5, we develop two methods to detect and classify drum fills. The first is a logistic regression based on two different groups of features: velocity-related handcrafted features and variables from a variational auto-encoder latent space. The classifier has been trained on drums kits from Native Instruments and OddGrooves.com with regular pattern and drum fills labels. The second method is a rule-based method that reflects the interpretation of a drum fill as a variation. Then, in Sect. 6 using these two classifiers, we extract regular pattern/drum fills couples in the Lakh pianoroll dataset to build-up two generation datasets. After cleaning these extracted datasets to provide clean and balanced enough datasets to our further generation model, we evaluate the extraction. Our generation model, whose architecture is precisely described in Sect. 7, is able to generate a drum fill based on the regular pattern given as a input. We use a many-to-many RNN with 2 layers of GRU units, followed by fully-connected and batch-normalization layers. Section 8 shows the results of the user-study we have conducted with musicians and non musicians where our model trained on our two different datasets is confronted with a rule-based method to generate drum fills.

2 Related Works

Lopez-Serrano *et al.* [7] have proposed a method to detect drum breaks in the audio domain. In this paper it is not a question of detecting short drum fills but rather percussion-only passages. The authors address this problem inspired by a baseline method initially designed for singing voice detection. In order to detect frames that contain percussion-only passages, they use features in the audio domain as included in [6], and a random forest model to define a median filtered decision function over the frames, and then apply a decision threshold. Roberts *et al.* [9], wrote a paper about learning and generating long term structure music. Recurrent Variationnal Auto-Encoder (VAE) having difficulties to model a piece of music made up of several bars, they use a VAE including a hierarchical decoder. The VAE encoder produces a latent vector from n bars using a bi-directional recurrent layer. The first level of the decoder, the conductor, generates a series of embedding vectors from the latent vector, each corresponding to a bar. A second level of recurrent decoder decodes these embeddings into notes sequences. The most interesting thing in this paper related to our topic, is that their model is able to produce drum fills implicitly as we can hear in their demo files.

3 Preliminaries

In this paper, we do not care about the precise boundaries of a drum fills. To simplify the problem, we decide to detect and generate bars containing drum fills. We also reduce the problem by working with only 9 different drums instruments as [9]: kick (abbreviated BD for bass drum), snare (SD), low, mid and high tom (LT, MT and HT), closed and open hi-hat (CHH and OHH), crash and ride cymbals (CC and RC). We work only with bars having a 4/4 time signature. We decide to work with a precision of 4 time steps for each beat. This gives us a tensor with a 9×16 dimensions filled with the velocity of each note. In the next sections, we use the term "reduced pianoroll" to call a pianoroll transformed to a 9×16 tensor and "binarized pianoroll" to call a pianoroll filled with 0 and 1 instead of velocity.

3.1 Datasets

Labelled Datasets. The Native Instruments' Battery Kits and the oddgrooves website's fill pack are composed by loops with different time signatures and length. We decided to crop and add paddings to these loops to form bars with a 4/4 signature. The concatenation of these bars from the two datasets gives us a dataset composed of 5,317 regular patterns and 1,412 drum fills.

Unlabelled Dataset. The dataset we would like to label is the Lakh Pianoroll Dataset [2], a derivative of Lakh Midi Dataset [8], which contains 21,425 songs with their related drums pianorolls.

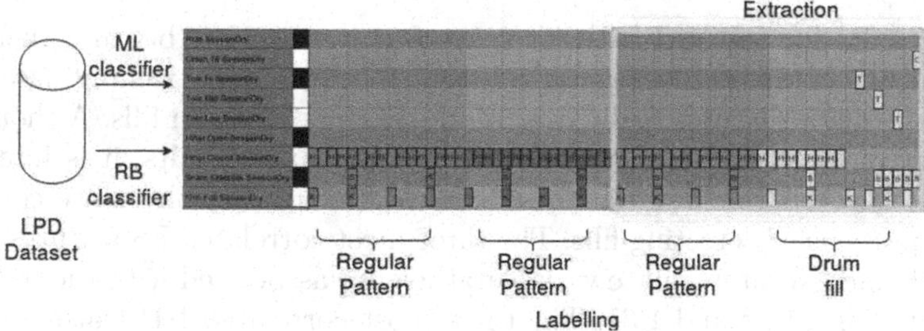

Fig. 1. Flowchart of the labelling/extraction: we use two different classifiers to label the LPD dataset. Then, we extract regular pattern/drum fill couples to constitute a drum fills dataset for generation

4 Machine Learning Classifier

4.1 Features Used and Model

We use two groups of features to train our model. For each bar of our labelled dataset, we decide to compute the maximum, the standard deviation and the mean of the velocity for each instrument of the reduced drums classes along the time axis. It give us a 27 dimensions-vector. This vector represents the use, the amount of notes and the dynamics of playing of each drum class for each bar. We trained a VAE over thousands of bars of the Lakh pianoroll dataset [2], to obtain features that capture a good compressed representation of the drums patterns. Then, we use the encoder of this VAE to encode the data of our labelled dataset and to obtain the latent space features. It gives us a 32-dimensions vector.

We train a logistic classifier with regularization on our whole labelled dataset using *LogisticRegressionCV* from the Sklearn API [1]. We use standardization as pre-processing of our data and automatic-cross validation to tune the regularization hyperparameter.

4.2 Validation

Using the $L2$ regularization that performs better in our case, we obtain the result shown in Table 1.

Table 1. Validation metrics of our classifier. HD: Handcrafted features, LS: VAE's latent space features

Feature set	Precision	Recall	F1 Score
HD	0.80	0.79	0.79
LS	0.58	0.06	0.10
HD+LS	0.89	0.81	0.85

The results for the VAE's latent space features are low because there were few drum fills compared to regular patterns in the VAE's training dataset. So that, latent space features badly capture the essence of drum fills. Although the training with $L1$ regularization has worse performance results, it is interesting to have a look on the weights, to see which features are the most correlated with the purpose of detecting fills. The three most correlated LS features are the 18th, 20th and 1st latent space variables; they are associated with the regression coefficients 2.06, 1.92 and 1.61. The three most correlated HD features are the max velocity of high tom, the standard deviation of mid tom and the max velocity of low tom; they are associated with the regression coefficients 1.26, 1.26 and 1.26. That confirms our intuition that fills are related with toms and cymbals and that gives us a better comprehension of our VAE. The drawback of this approach is that we characterize a drum fill with absolute rules, and not with the relative difference between bars.

5 Rule-Based Classifier

Fills can be seen as a variation regarding the regular pattern of the song they belong to. In order to answer to research question 2, we build another approach, rule-based. Let A, B be two binarized pianorolls (tensors) of dimension $t \times n$ (time steps $\times$ number of instruments), we define the difference of notes DN between A and B as:

$$DN(A, B) = \sum_{\substack{0 \leq i < t \\ 0 \leq j < n}} max(0, A_{i,j} - B_{i,j}) \tag{1}$$

Iterating over the binarized and reduced bars of our unlabelled dataset, we decide to consider the current bar as a drum fill if the difference of notes between the current bar and the two adjacents bars respectively is above a threshold. We use a threshold of 7 notes for the extraction part.

6 Extraction of Fills

We apply our machine learning classifier and our rule-based classifier to our unlabelled dataset. Then, we extract 2-bars sequences composed by a drum fill following a regular pattern. So, we obtain two datasets from our two labelling methods that we will call ML dataset (extracted with the machine learning classifier) and RB dataset (extracted with the Rule-based classifier).

6.1 Data Cleaning

In order to have a good enough datasets for the generation we apply the three following rules (Table 2) to clean our datasets: removing duplicated rows (Rule 1), removing all the couples where the regular pattern or the drum fill have fewer than 7 notes (Rule 2), removing all the couple where the drum fill has a too high density of snare notes, above 8 (Rule 3).

Table 2. Influence of the cleaning process on our datasets size. The RB dataset is less sensitive to our filtering rules.

	#ML dataset	#RB dataset
Raw	13,476	97,023
After rule 1	6,324	45,723
After rule 2	5,271	39,108
After rule 3	3,283	32,130

6.2 Analysis of the Extracted Datasets

Total of Notes by Instrument. A Pearson's chi-squared test between the total of notes by instrument of the regular patterns and the drum fills certifies us that the distributions are significantly different for the two extracted datasets. The drum fills of the two datasets contains more toms and cymbals notes than the regular patterns, as we can see for example in the Fig. 2.

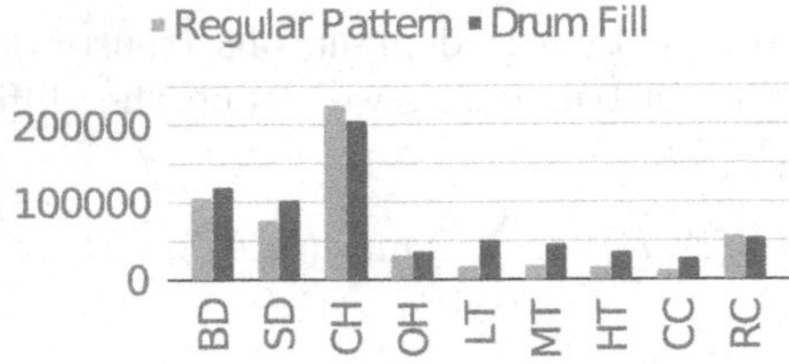

Fig. 2. Amount of notes by instrument for the ML dataset

Proximity of Drum Fills. We want our extracted drum fills not too close to each other, as we consider that fills only appear every 4, 8, or 16 bars. Thus, we compute the length of the longest serie of adjacent fills in every song of our dataset. The average lenght is 0.68 and 1.90 for the ML dataset and the RB dataset respectively. The perfect result would be 1, so it is close to what we expect.

Distribution of Genres. We compute the average amount of fills extracted over genres. We expect to find more fills in the following genres: Metal and Jazz. Our RB dataset follows well this intuition but this is not the case for our ML dataset.

7 Generation of Drum Fills

Our main goal is to generate a bar containing a drum fill, conditioned by a previous bar containing a regular pattern. We decide to use an architecture often found in the Natural Language Processing state-of-the-art, many-to-many Recurrent Neural Networks (RNN), whose architecture is described in Fig. 3.

7.1 Training

We train our model over 300 epochs with a batch size of 4096 for the RB dataset and 256 for the ML dataset. We use Adam [4] as optimization algorithm with a learning rate of 0.001 and binary cross-entropy as loss function. We remove from each dataset the intersection of the two datasets which we use later as a test dataset, in order to evaluate the model trained on different datasets. We use a split of 80/20 for the training/validation datasets.

7.2 Evaluation

We use the test dataset to generate two set of fills with our model trained on the ML dataset and the RB dataset. Then, we compare the original fills (ground truth fills) from our test dataset with the two other sets of generated fills (ML fills and RB fills).

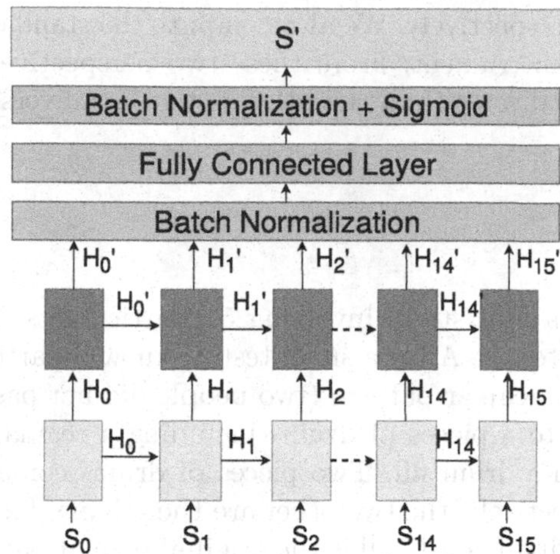

Fig. 3. Our model architecture is composed by two stacked GRU layers followed by batch norm and fully connected layers

Total of Notes by Instrument. Applying the Pearson's chi-squared test between the total of notes by instrument of the three datasets (pair-wise), the p-value is less than 0.01, that shows that the fills are different in the three sets.

As main differences, we can see that the RB fills includes more bass drum and closed hit-hat than the other sets of fills. The ML fills include more low tom notes than the other set of fills as well. Unfortunately, our datasets, substracted from their high-density snares fills, do not allow us to create drum fills with snare rolls (Fig. 4).

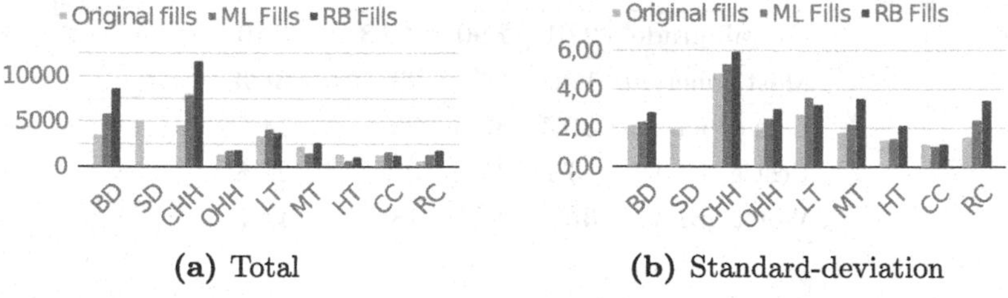

(a) Total **(b)** Standard-deviation

Fig. 4. Total and standard-deviation of the amount of notes in the generated/original fills by instrument

Diversity of Fills. We take each set of fills, and we encoded them in the VAE's latent space of the Sect. 4.1. So, for each set of fills, we compute the sum of the Euclidean distance between fills (pair-wise) as a measure of diversity for each set of fills. And give us 93012, 93844 and 102135 for the ML fills, the RB fills and the original fills respectively. We also compute the standard deviation of the amount of notes by instrument. From these two perspectives, we can see that the RB fills are more diverse than the ML fills but less diverse than the original fills.

8 User Study

Finally, we conduct a user study involving 51 participants (66% of musicians) recruited from the Internet. After a small test to know if participants are able to recognize a fill from a regular pattern (two people did not pass the test), people were asked to listen to 4 pieces of drums including a regular pattern repeated three times and then a drum fill. Two pieces of drums come from the ML fills and the RB fills respectively, the two other are the original fill and a "Rule based composed fill" (RC fill). The RC fill is the original regular pattern with the same toms/crash pattern added each time. We report in Table 3 the results. We can see that our methods do not beat a human for the task of composing a drum fill, even when the fill is composed with the same rule. Nevertheless, the RB fills are getting closer from the original fills. The original fill is not rated with a good grade in our experiment. In other words, human listeners do not think the human composed fills are good enough. Additionally, the RC fill has almost the same grade as the original fill. This indicates the subjective nature of the task and answers to the research question 3.

Table 3. Results of the user study, averaged over 49 subjects. The mean of the five-point scale grade is given in the first line. For the rest of the lines, the ratio of vote is given.

	ML	RB	Original	RC
Overall grade	2.61	2.90	**3.13**	3.10
Most coherent	17%	18%	29%	**36%**
Less coherent	**30%**	**30%**	23%	18%
Best groove	13%	25%	**34%**	28%
Worst groove	**35%**	30%	18%	17%

9 Conclusion

We have presented several axes to research in the field of drum fills detection and generation. We have shown the importance of considering a fill as a variation rather than through an absolute view. The results of our generation pipeline (detect drum fills with a rule-based method and then generate them with an RNN) are getting closer from the human-composed fills. In future work, we will explore fusion-method that combines machine-learning and rule-based method to improve the results of the drum fills detection with the help of more hand labelled data.

Acknowledgments. This work was done when FT was a visiting student at Academia Sinica.

References

1. Buitinck, L., et al.: API design for machine learning software: experiences from the scikit-learn project. In: ECML PKDD Workshop: Languages for Data Mining and Machine Learning, pp 108–122 (2013)
2. Dong, H.W., Hsiao, W.Y., Yang, L.C., Yang, Y.H.: MuseGAN: multi-track sequential generative adversarial networks for symbolic music generation and accompaniment. In: Thirty-Second AAAI Conference on Artificial Intelligence (2018)
3. Dong, H. W., Yang, Y. H.: Convolutional generative adversarial networks with binary neurons for polyphonic music generation. In: ISMIR (2018)
4. Kingma, P., Ba, D., Adam, J.: A method for stochastic optimization. In: ICLR 2015 (2015)
5. Kingma, D.P., Welling, M.: Auto-encoding variational bayes. In: The International Conference on Learning Representations (2014)
6. Lehner, B., Widmer, G., Sonnleitner, R.: On the reduction of false positives in singing voice detection. In: ICASSP, pp. 7480–7484. IEEE (2014)
7. López-Serrano, P., Dittmar, C., Müller, M.: Finding drum breaks in digital music recordings. In: Aramaki, M., Davies, M.E.P., Kronland-Martinet, R., Ystad, S. (eds.) CMMR 2017. LNCS, vol. 11265, pp. 111–122. Springer, Cham (2018). https://doi.org/10.1007/978-3-030-01692-0_8
8. Raffel, C.: Learning-based methods for comparing sequences, with applications to audio-to-midi alignment and matching. PhD Thesis (2016)
9. Roberts, A., Raffel, C., Engel, J., Hawthorne, C., Eck, D.: A hierarchical latent vector model for learning long-term structure in music. In: ICML 2018 (2018)
10. Play Drums Today. Hal Leonard, Milwaukee (2001). ISBN 0-634-02185-0

End-to-End Classification of Ballroom Dancing Music Using Machine Learning

Noémie Voss[1(✉)] and Phong Nguyen[2]

[1] Sevenoaks School, Sevenoaks, UK
noemievoss@gmail.com
[2] Tokyo Techies, Tokyo, Japan
phong.nguyen@tokyotechies.com

Abstract. The term 'ballroom dancing' refers to a social and competitive type of partnered dance. Competitive ballroom dancing consists of 10 different types of dances performed to specific styles of music unique to each type of dance. There are few algorithms attempting to differentiate between pieces of music and classify them into the categories, making it hard for beginners to identify which dance corresponds to a certain piece of music they may be listening to. In our research, we attempted to use an end-to-end machine learning approach to easily and accurately classify music into the 10 different types of dance. We experimented with four types of machine learning models and received the highest accuracy of 83% using a Deep Neural Network with three hidden layers. With this algorithm, we can facilitate the learning experience of beginner ballroom dancers by aiding them to distinguish between different types of ballroom dancing music.

Keywords: Ballroom dancing · Classification · Deep neural network · Machine learning

1 Introduction

The term 'ballroom dancing' refers to a social and competitive type of partnered dance, famously performed at the Blackpool Dance Festival [3]. Competitive ballroom dancing is split into 10 distinct types of dance: Chacha, Foxtrot, Jive, Paso Doble, Quickstep, Rumba, Samba, Tango, Viennese Waltz and Waltz.

Each type of competitive ballroom dance is danced to a different type of music specific to the dance type. Though some of the differences are obvious, many are subtle, and it can therefore be difficult for a beginner dancer's ear to distinguish the musical features and classify music.

Machine learning can facilitate this process of music classification. Professional and amateur ballroom dancers can use models to categorise a piece of music based on the unique characteristics of each dance type. Anyone interested in the field of ballroom dancing can make use of this kind of model when curious about a specific song, or when learning how to ballroom dance.

The two authors contributed equally to this work

R. Kronland-Martinet et al. (Eds.): CMMR 2019, LNCS 12631, pp. 100–109, 2021.
https://doi.org/10.1007/978-3-030-70210-6_7

In recent times, machine learning has become a frequently used form of technology, used to create applications and models to solve a variety of issues. Using data, machines can be trained to recognise patterns between characteristics which can be applied to new data. In the field of ballroom dancing, machines can be trained to identify the musical features of each type of dance and apply the patterns to classify new pieces of music. This can help avoid the need for manual rule-based classification of each piece of data, which is less accurate and less efficient.

In our research, we evaluated four different types of machine learning models to classify ballroom dancing music: Support Vector Machine (SVM), k-Nearest Neighbours (k-NN), Random Forest, and Deep Neural Network (DNN). In the future, we would like to create a mobile application for beginner dancers which incorporates our classification model, in order to facilitate their learning experience. Using a public dataset with approximately 4000 tracks of audio data, our models achieved a classification accuracy of 60%, 50%, 76% and 83% respectively.

2 Related Work

This section contains references and descriptions of previously existing research using machine learning for music classification.

Recently, machine learning has been vastly applied to classification tasks, including in the signal processing field. Classifying music into different categories has been a frequently studied process for many years. Tzanetakis and Cook [4] addressed this problem with supervised machine learning approaches including a Gaussian Mixture model and k-Nearest-Neighbour classifiers [4]. The three sets of features utilised in this task were timbral structure, rhythmic content and pitch content. Support Vector Machines (SVM) were introduced later by Scaringella and Zoia [10, 14]. With the new development of Deep Neural Networks, many studies have attempted to apply such techniques to speech and audio data, such as by Gemmeke et al. [6, 8]. Representing audio in the time domain as an input into neural networks is challenging due to the high sampling rate of audio signals. Therefore, feature engineering for audio data is still the more popular technique when working with audio signals. H. Bahuleyan [1] extracted frequency features and time-domain features from audio data, and used these features to accurately classify music genres using a Deep Neural Network (DNN) [1].

U. Marchand, G. Peeters (2016) [11] proposed a method to classify music into different ballroom dance types. This was done by representing audio data along the two dimensions of time and frequency based on the application of Scale Transform. However, this technique does not use machine learning, but rather rule-based classification.

3 Music and Sound Data

Audio data consist of waves transformed into electrical signals. Initially, sound waves are converted into analog signals, which are continuous digital representations of sound waves. These analog signals are then converted into digital signals through an analog-digital converter (ADC). Digital signals can be stored digitally and consist of a continuous sequence of numerical samples. These signals are formed from the original analog signal, from which the digital values of the amplitude of the signal are extracted.

The frequency of a sound wave is representative of the pitch of the sound. Hence, the higher the frequency of a sound wave (measured in Hz, hertz), the higher the pitch of the sound. The human ear can hear between a range of frequencies: from 20-20 kHz. To ensure that all frequencies are captured in an audio signal, ADCs sample audio signals at a frequency of 44,100 Hz (roughly double the human hearing range) [7].

4 Features Engineering for Sound Data

4.1 Data Collection and Preprocessing

The first step in creating a machine learning music classification model is the collection of data, consisting of pieces of music corresponding to a known type of ballroom dance.

Our model was trained with a public dataset, the Extended Ballroom dataset [12], containing ballroom dancing tracks collected from the website www.ballroomdancers.com. The Extended Ballroom dataset includes 4180 tracks, corresponding to a total of 13 dance types as shown in the table (Table 1) below.

Table 1. Number of tracks in Extended Ballroom dataset

Ballroom dance category	Number of audio tracks
Chacha	455
Jive	350
Samba	468
Viennese Waltz	252
Waltz	529
Tango	464
Rumba	470
Quickstep	497
Foxtrot	507
Paso Doble	53
Salsa	47
Slow Waltz	65
West Coast Swing	23
Total	**4180**

Our model was focused only on the competitive types of ballroom dance, and hence we decided to omit Salsa, Slow Waltz and West Coast Swing. After some consideration, we decided to also omit Paso Doble as the dataset only included 53 Paso Doble tracks which would have imbalanced the model and not been sufficient to train it. The final dataset consisted of 3992 tracks.

The audio data was cut into smaller 10 s segments called ‘windows’, each with a 5 s overlap. This was done to standardise the length of each piece of data and increase the number of samples for the model to learn from. This process facilitated the extraction of statistical features from the pieces of data.

4.2 Feature Extraction

37 features were extracted from each track. The first extracted feature was the tempo (BPM, beats per minute), representing the speed of the music. Each type of ballroom dance is danced to music within a specific BPM range, as shown in Table 2 below.

Table 2. BPM of different categories of ballroom dancing [2]

Ballroom dance category	BPM
Chacha	120–128
Jive	168–184
Samba	96–104
Viennese Waltz	174–180
Waltz	84–90
Tango	120–140
Quickstep	200–208
Rumba	100–108
Foxtrot	112–120

The next feature extracted from the tracks was the time signature (beats per measure) which represents the rhythm of the music. This feature was of significant use in distinguishing between the Waltzs and the other types of dance; Waltz and Viennese Waltz both have a time signature of 3/4, whereas the other dance categories all have time signatures of either 2/4 or 4/4.

A third feature extracted was the ‘fingerprint’ of each piece of music. A fingerprint consists of a list of five values combined to form one hashtag. Each value represents a certain pitch present in the piece of music; they represent the *most common frequencies* (most common pitches) of the piece of music from within five specific frequency ranges. The five ranges were: 30–40 Hz, 41–80 Hz, 81–120 Hz, 121–180 Hz, and 181–300 Hz [8].

The next 34 features extracted from the data consisted of both short-term and mid-term features. Short-term features are features extracted from the data after having split each original piece of music into several short-term windows. Statistics were then extracted from these short-term features (eg. Mean, standard deviation), making up the mid-term features (Table 3).

Table 3. Features of the PyAudioAnalysis program [5]

Feature ID	Feature name	Feature description
1	Zero crossing rate	The rate of sign-changes of the signal during the duration of a particular frame
2	Energy	The sum of squares of the signal values, normalized by the respective frame length
3	Entropy of energy	The entropy of sub-frames' normalized energies. It can be interpreted as a measure of abrupt changes
4	Spectral centroid	The center of gravity of the spectrum
5	Spectral spread	The second central moment of the spectrum
6	Spectral entropy	Entropy of the normalized spectral energies for a set of sub-frames
7	Spectral flux	The squared difference between the normalized magnitudes of the spectra of the two successive frames
8	Spectral rolloff	The frequency below which 90% of the magnitude distribution of the spectrum is concentrated
9–21	MFCCs	Mel Frequency Cepstral Coefficients form a cepstral representation where the frequency bands are not linear but distributed according to the mel-scale
22–33	Chroma vector	A 12-element representation of the spectral energy where the bins represent the 12 equal-tempered pitch classes of western-type music (semitone spacing)

4.3 Classification Models

Our classification process consists of three separate models. The first model uses the distinguishing time signature of Waltz and Viennese Waltz as the main criteria to classify between these and the other 7 types of dance. A second model is then used to distinguish Waltz and Viennese Waltz from each other. The third model classifies between the other seven types of dance: Tango, Samba, Chacha, Rumba, Quickstep, Foxtrot Blues, and Jive.

The overall process (illustrated in Fig. 1 below) results in a program able to classify music into the nine categories of ballroom dancing music.

When designing models to classify the music, we compared four types of classification models: Support Vector Machines (SVM), k-Nearest Neighbors, Random Forest and Deep Neural Network (DNN).

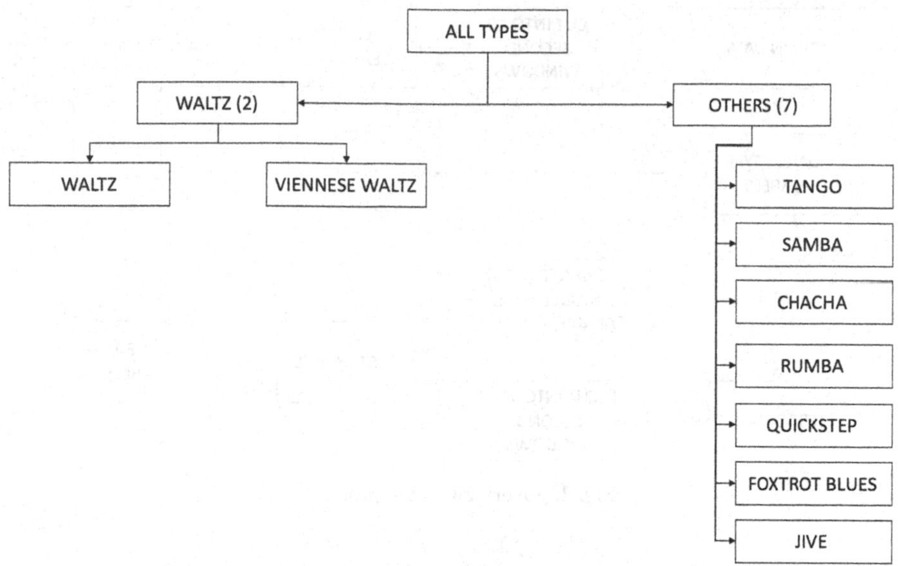

Fig. 1. Overview of the classification method.

Support Vector Machines (SVM) is a machine learning algorithm used for classification. Training data is inputted into the SVM model to create an optimal decision boundary called a 'hyperplane'. This boundary marks the extremes of the different classes of data, and hence separated it into different categories [13].

K-Nearest Neighbours uses a certain number (k) of a data point's 'nearest neighbours' (nearest data points), regardless of their label, to classify the data. The data point is assigned a label based on the modal label of its neighbours, meaning it takes the same label as the one which appears most frequently [15].

A Random Forest Model uses a multitude of decision trees to classify data into categories. Each individual tree in the model generates a predicted label for the data. The data is then given the label which was predicted by the most individual trees [9].

A Deep Neural Network attempts to mimic the process of the human brain using machine learning algorithms to recognise patterns in features of data. These models contain hidden layers to analyse and apply patterns to classify data points [14].

Figure 2 below is a visual description of the data processing involved in training our machine learning model to classify music and be evaluated for accuracy.

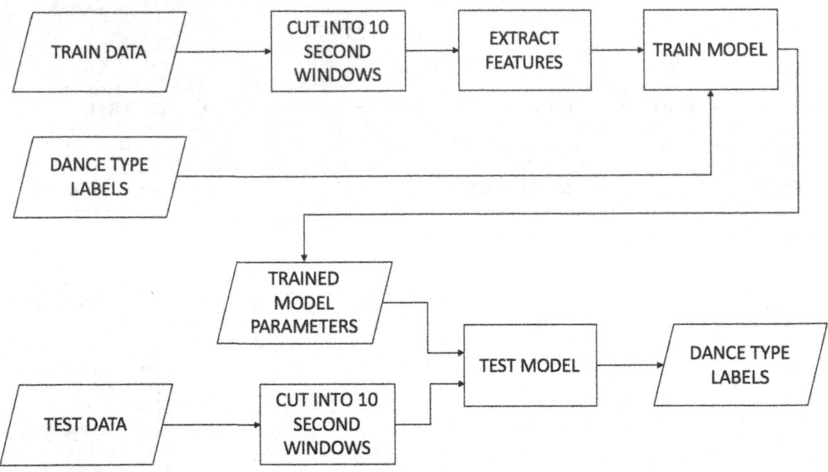

Fig. 2. Overview of the process.

4.4 Classification of a New Song

To classify a new song, we began by preprocessing the audio track. It was split into 10-s windows with a 5 s overlap like the train data. We extracted all the features from these windows and ran them through our algorithm to group each window into a specific dance category.

This outputted a classification label for each of the windows. We were able to determine the label of the original song based on which dance category the algorithm predicted the majority of the windows belonged to.

5 Experimental Settings

To create our model, we began by collecting data from the public Extended Ballroom dataset previously mentioned above. We removed the audio data for four types of dances: Paso Doble, Slow Waltz, Salsa and West Coast Swing, which left us with a total of 3992 tracks.

We split our data randomly, splitting the dataset into 90% train data and 10% test data. We evaluated our model with the 10% of test data as well as our own self-collected dataset including songs chosen by professional ballroom dancers (10 per dance type).

After splitting the audio data into the 10 s windows, we were left with a total of 45000 pieces of data as the train data, and 4100 pieces as the test data. The 37 features were then extracted for each individual window and used to train the four types of classification models we were testing: SVM, k-NN, Random Forest, and DNN. We obtained an accuracy and weighted F1-score for each model to evaluate which model was best suited for our project. The hyperparameters of each model were tuned to their highest accuracy by trial and error.

6 Results

The four classification models we trained and tested were: 'Support Vector Machine', 'K-Nearest-Neighbours' with neighbours = 101, 'Random Forest' with 100 trees, and a 'Deep Neural Network' with three hidden layers (Fig. 3).

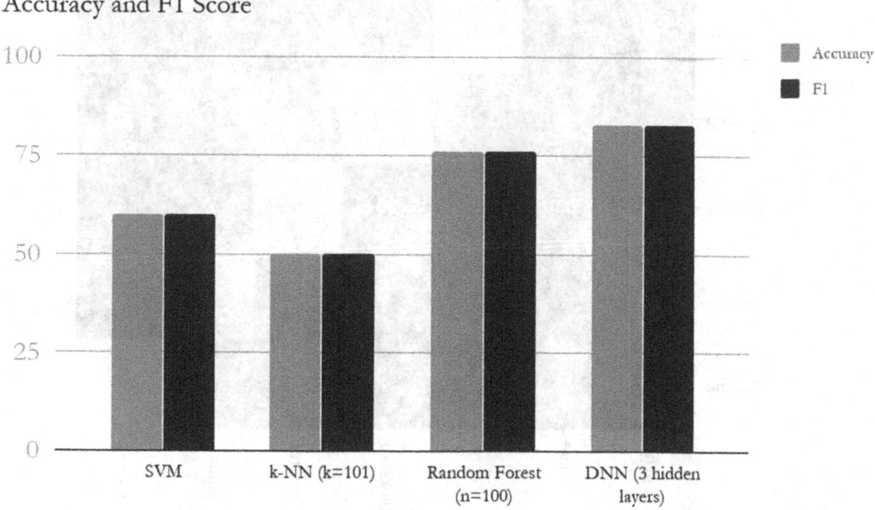

Fig. 3. A graph comparing the F1 scores and accuracies of each type of classification model.

The accuracy and F1 scores of the models are specified in Table 4.

Table 4. Accuracy and F1 scores of different classification models

Model	Accuracy	F1 score
SVM	60%	60%
k-NN (n = 101)	50%	50%
Random Forest (n = 100)	76%	76%
DNN (3 hidden layers)	83%	83%

Our results found that the model which achieved the highest accuracy was the Deep Neural Network with 3 hidden layers. The model achieved 90% accuracy when tested on our self-collected data set of 30 professional ballroom dancing songs, correctly assigning 27 labels out of 30 (Fig. 4).

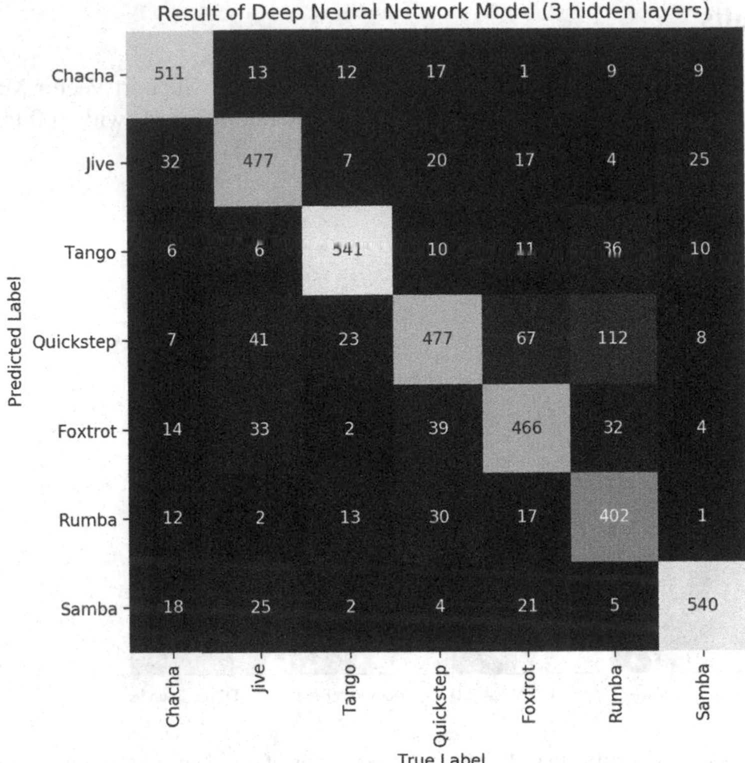

Fig. 4. Confusion matrix of Deep Neural Network model with three hidden layers for the 'Extended Ballroom' dataset, excluding Waltz and Viennese Waltz.

Above is a confusion matrix showing the results of the classification model responsible for classifying the dance types excluding Waltz and Viennese Waltz (which were classified separately, as explained earlier). We found that although the model was able to accurately classify most dance types, it was less accurate when classifying Rumba and Quickstep, often confusing the two: 112 Rumba tracks were given an incorrect label of Quickstep. The model also had difficulty distinguishing between Quickstep and Foxtrot, mislabelling 67 Foxtrot tracks as Quickstep.

The overall accuracy of the model is 83%.

Our aim is to incorporate our algorithm into a mobile application. Beginner and amateur ballroom dancers would be able to use this application to help them learn how to ballroom dance and to ameliorate their experience with ballroom dancing. This application could also be gamified to encourage learners to guess a song's dance type before using the app to reveal what the correct answer would be. This would not only provide an entertaining way for dancers to familiarise themselves with the different types of music, but would also help improve beginners' confidence in ballroom dancing. This mobile application has not yet been implemented, but could be feasible in the future.

7 Conclusion

We have evaluated an end-to-end method using machine learning which is able to classify pieces of music into categories of ballroom dancing. The Deep Neural Network with three hidden layers achieved an accuracy of 83%. We have opened our source-code of the processing to train the model at: https://bitbucket.org/xphongvn/ballroom_music_classification.

This method could be improved in the future by finding more musical features which could be extracted from the audio data and lead to a higher accuracy of classification. Alternatively, a larger training dataset could be used to train the model.

References

1. Bahuleyan, H.: Music genre classification using machine learning techniques. arXiv preprint arXiv:1804.01149 (2018)
2. Beats Per Minute Online: Tempo Indications and Beats Per Minute (BPM) Reference for Social Dance Genres. https://www.beatsperminuteonline.com/en/home/bpm-beats-per-minute-reference-for-dance-genres. Accessed June 2018
3. Blackpool Dance Festival. https://www.blackpooldancefestival.com/. Accessed Aug 2018
4. Tzanetakis, G., Cook, P.: Musical genre classification of audio signals. IEEE Trans. Speech Audio Process. **10**(5), 293– 302 (2002)
5. Giannakopoulos, T.: 3. Feature Extraction. https://github.com/tyiannak/pyAudioAnalysis/wiki/3.-Feature-Extraction. Accessed Aug 2018
6. Gemmeke, J.F., et al.: Audio set: an ontology and human-labeled dataset for audio events. In: 2017 IEEE International Conference on Acoustics, Speech and Signal Processing (ICASSP), pp. 776–780. IEEE (2017)
7. Jovanovic, J.: How does Shazam work? Music Recognition Algorithms, Fingerprinting, and Processing. https://www.toptal.com/algorithms/shazam-it-music-processing-fingerprinting-and-recognition. Accessed Sept 2018
8. Jovanovic, J.: Music Recognition: Fingerprinting a Song. https://www.toptal.com/algorithms/shazam-it-music-processing-fingerprinting-and-recognition. Accessed Sept 2018
9. Koehrsen, W.: Random Forest Simple Explanation. Medium, Medium (2017). medium.com/@williamkoehrsen/random-forest-simple-explanation-377895a60d2d. Accessed Sept 2018
10. Scaringella, N., Zoia, G.: On the modeling of time information for automatic genre recognition systems in audio signals. In: ISMIR, pp. 666–671 (2005)
11. Marchand, U., Peeters, G.: Scale and shift invariant time/frequency representation using auditory statistics: application to rhythm description. In: 2016 IEEE 26th International Workshop on Machine Learning for Signal Processing (MLSP), pp. 1–6. IEEE, September 2016
12. Marchand, U., Peeters, G.: The extended ballroom dataset (2016)
13. Ray, S., Business Analytics: Understanding Support Vector Machine Algorithm from Examples (along with Code). Analytics Vidhya, 11 March 2019. analyticsvidhya.com/blog/2017/09/understaing-support-vector-machine-example-code
14. Skymind: A Beginner's Guide to Neural Networks and Deep Learning. skymind.ai/wiki/neural-network. Accessed Sept 2018
15. Srivastava, T.: Introduction to KNN, K-nearest neighbors: simplified. Analytics Vidhya (2018). www.analyticsvidhya.com/blog/2018/03/introduction-k-neighbours-algorithm-clustering/. Accessed Mar 2019

Computational Musicology

Modal Logic for Tonal Music

Satoshi Tojo(✉)

Japan Advanced Institute of Science and Technology, Nomi, Japan
tojo@jaist.ac.jp

Abstract. It is generally accepted that the origin of music and language is one and the same. Thus far, many syntactic theories of music have been proposed, however, all these efforts seem mainly to concern the generative syntax. Although such syntax enables us to construct hierarchical tree, the mere tree representation is not sufficient in representing mutual references in music. In this research, we propose the annotation of tree with modal logic, by which the reference from each pitch event to harmonic regions are clarified. In addition, while the conventional generative syntax constructs the tree in the top-down way, the modal interpretation gives the incremental construction according to the progression of music. Therefore, we can naturally interpret our theory as the expectation–realization model that is more familiar to our human recognition of music.

Keywords: Generative syntax · Modal logic · Kripke semantics

1 Introduction

What is the semantics of music? In general, the semantics is understood as the link between symbols and their targets to which the symbols refer. A written music score consists of a sequence of musical notes, and on the whole, it is linked to an actual music, being rendered to physical sounds. In this, the semantics of written score could be music as sequences of sounds, however, these sounds still possess further external references.[1]

On the contrary, both written scores and sequences of sounds can refer to their internal structures. Meyer [17] argued that we could define an innate meaning of music, independent of the external references. Although there should be a big discussion more for this, we contend that we could devise a formal method to clarify the internal references.

Assuming that the origin of music and language is one and the same [24], we consider incorporating Montagovian semantics [8], as a parallelism between

[1] Koelsch [15] distinguished the three levels of the reference to the outer worlds; (i) the simple imitation of sounds by instruments, (ii) the implication of human emotions, and (iii) the artificial connection to our social behavior.

R. Kronland-Martinet et al. (Eds.): CMMR 2019, LNCS 12631, pp. 113–128, 2021.
https://doi.org/10.1007/978-3-030-70210-6_8

syntactic structure and logical forms, into music.[2] In this work, we propose to employ modal logic to represent internal references in music, where a certain note or a chord can refer others if they are *accessible* in them. However, music symbols in the score are aligned on a time axis, and thus, we should include the notion of proximity in each other. Therefore, we adopt here an extended modal logic to represent *neighborhood*, to clarify the inter-region relationship in a piece.

Thus far, many linguistic approaches have been made to analyze the music structure, however, almost all these efforts concern the generative syntax, based on Context-free Grammar (CFG) by Chomsky [3,4]. However, the non-terminal symbols in the production rules, which appear as nodes in the tree, are often ambiguous or meaningless in music; in some cases they may represent the salience among pitch events and in other cases overlaying relations of functional regions. Also, the hierarchical construction of tree is weak in representing mutual relationship in regions.

In this work, we reinterpret those generative grammar rules in the X-bar theory [5], and show their *heads* explicitly. Then, we translate them into logical formulae, and show a deduction system to attach these formulae to the tree structure. This reinterpretation accompanies one more significant aspect. The tree structure is constructed by production rules, in general in the top-down way. However, when we listen to or compose music, we recognize it in the chronological order according to the progression of time. With our method, those rules would be transformed to construct a tree in the incremental way.

This paper is organized as follows. In Sect. 2, we survey the syntactic studies in music. Next in Sect. 3, we introduce the modal logic as formal language to represent semantics. regarding the neighborhood semantics. Thereafter in Sect. 4, we translate the syntactic rules to logical formulae, as semantics to be attached in each node in a tree. Then in Sect. 5, we apply our methodology of translation to grammar rules of music. We give a concrete example of analysis by modal logic. In the final Sect. 6, we summarize our contribution and discuss our future tasks.

2 Syntactic Theory of Music

Thus far, many linguists and musicologists have achieved to implement the music parser, beginning from Winograd [25]. Some works were based on specific grammar theories, such as Head-driven Phrase Structure Grammar (HPSG) [23] or Combinatory Categorial Grammar (CCG) [10] though their theoretical generative power is almost the same as the context-free grammar. In recent years, furthermore, two distinguished works are shown; one is exGTTM by Hamanaka et al. [12] based on Generative Theory of Tonal Music (GTTM) [16] and the other is Generative Syntax Model (GSM) by Rohmeier [22].

[2] We need to take care of the ambiguity of what *semantics* means. In Montagovian theory, the syntax of natural language is those written by categorial grammar and the semantics is written by logical formuale, while in mathematical logic the formal language (logic) has its own syntax and its semantics is given by set theory or by algebra.

2.1 Brief Introduction of GSM

We briefly introduce GSM with its abridged grammar for convenience. First we introduce the basic sets

$$\mathbb{R} = \{TR, SR, DR\} \quad \text{(region)}$$
$$\mathbb{F} = \{t, s, d, tp, sp, dp, tcp\} \quad \text{(function)}$$

as well as $\mathbb{K}$: a set of key names and $\mathbb{O}$: a set of chord names.

The P (piece) is the start symbol of production rules. It introduces TR (tonic region)

$$P \rightarrow TR,$$

In the next level, TR generates DR (dominant region) and SR (subdominant region), and in the further downward level they result in t (tonic), d (dominant), s (subdominant).

$$\begin{array}{ll} TR \rightarrow DR\ t & TR \rightarrow t \\ DR \rightarrow SR\ d & DR \rightarrow d \\ TR \rightarrow TR\ DR & SR \rightarrow s \end{array}$$

Also, each of t, d, s may result in tp (tonic parallel), tcp (tonic counter-parallel), dp (dominant parallel), sp (subdominant parallel) of Hugo Riemann [11].

$$t \rightarrow tp \mid tcp, \ \ s \rightarrow sp, \ \ d \rightarrow dp$$

where the vertical bar ('|') shows the 'or' alternatives. In addition, there are scale-dgree rules, which maps function names to degrees, *e.g.*,

$$t \rightarrow \mathrm{I}, \ tp \rightarrow \mathrm{VI} \mid \mathrm{III}, \ s \rightarrow \mathrm{IV}, \ d \rightarrow \mathrm{V} \mid \mathrm{VII}, \ \text{and so on.}$$

Furthermore, [22] employed the rules of secondary dominant, and that of modulation.

However, the formalism of GSM is partially inconvenient since the interpretation of

$$XR \rightarrow XR\ XR\ (XR \in \mathbb{R})$$

is ambiguous as to which is the head. Rather, we prefer to rigorously define heads, distinguishing region rules from harmonic function rules.

2.2 X-barred GSM

Here, we introduce the notion of *head*, employing the X-bar theory [5].[3] A binary production in Chomsky Normal Form (CNF) should be rewritten with the parent category X' and the head daughter category X, as follows.

$$X' \rightarrow Spec\ X \tag{1}$$
$$X' \rightarrow X\ Comp \tag{2}$$

[3] The latest Chomskian school has abandoned X-bar theory, and instead they explain every syntactic phenomena only by *merge* and *recursion* [6].

where *Spec* stands for specifier and *Comp* for complement.[4] When X in the right-hand side already includes a prime ($'$), X' in the left-hand side becomes doubly primed ($''$) recursively.

Since we do not use those degree rules, our simplified GSM rules becomes as follows, where $\mathbb{F} = \{tonic, dom, sdom\}$.

$$\begin{array}{ll} TR' \rightarrow DR\ TR & TR \rightarrow tonic \\ DR' \rightarrow SR\ DR & DR \rightarrow dom \\ TR'' \rightarrow TR'\ TR & SR \rightarrow sdom \\ TR'' \rightarrow TR\ TR' & \end{array}$$

We show an example of syntactic tree by our rules in Fig. 1.

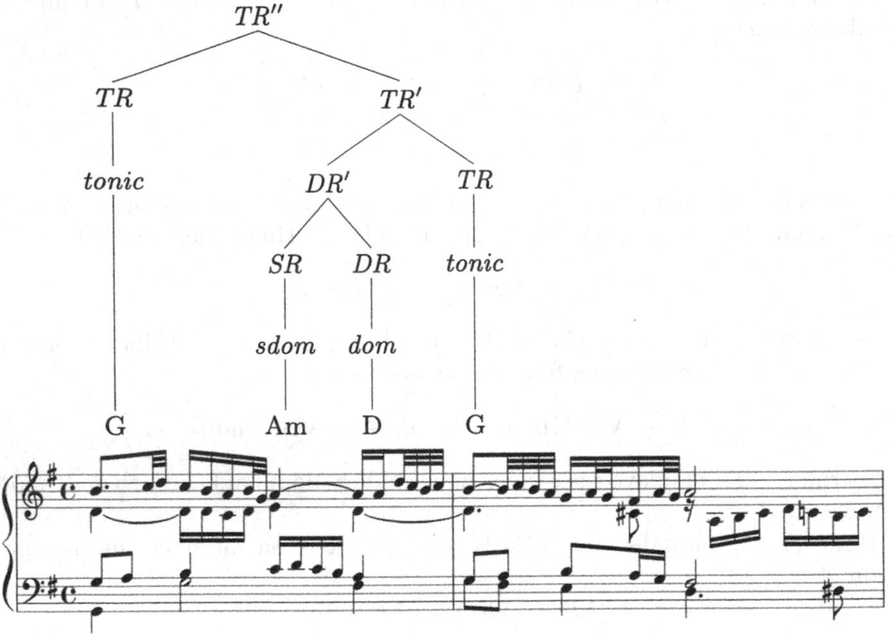

Fig. 1. J. S. Bach: "*Liebster Jesu, Wir Sind Hier*", BWV731

3 Semantics in Logic

3.1 Kripke Semantics

A modal logic [1,2,14] consists of such syntax as follows.

$$\phi := p \mid \neg\phi \mid \phi \vee \phi \mid \Box\phi$$

[4] Note that notion of head resides also in Combinatory Categorial Grammar (CCG), as $X \rightarrow X/Z\ Z$ implies that X/Z is the principle constituent of X.

where $\Box\phi$ represents, intuitively, 'necessarily ϕ.' In order to give a formal semantics to modal logic, we provide a *Kripke* frame which is a triplet $\mathcal{M} = \langle W, R, V \rangle$. W is a set of possible worlds and R is an accessibility relation among worlds, and when w' is accessible from w we write wRw'. V is a valuation for each atomic proposition. Employing the negation connective, we also introduce[5]

$$\phi \wedge \phi \equiv \neg(\neg\phi \vee \neg\phi),\ \ \phi \supset \psi \equiv \neg\phi \vee \psi,\ \text{and}\ \Diamond\phi \equiv \neg\Box\neg\phi.$$

Now, we give the semantics of '$\Box$' operator, and its *dual* operator '$\Diamond$', as follows.

$$\begin{array}{lll} \mathcal{M}, w & \models \Box\phi \textit{ iff} & \text{for all } w'(wRw') \in W,\ \mathcal{M}, w' \models \phi \\ \mathcal{M}, w & \models \Diamond\phi \textit{ iff} & \text{there exists } w'(wRw') \in W \text{ and } \mathcal{M}, w' \models \phi \end{array}$$

that is, $\Box\phi$ holds in w if and only if ϕ holds in all the accessible worlds w' from w, and $\Diamond\phi$ holds in w if and only if there exists an accessible world w' where ϕ holds.

We also read '$\Box\phi$' as '(a certain agent) knows ϕ' in epistemic logic since the knowledge of agent is a part of propositions which are true to her after considering (accessing) every possibility. In deontic logic '$\Box\phi$' means 'ϕ is obligatory.' In our study, this formula means ϕ persists for a certain extent of time.

In conventional Kripke semantics, we have not considered the distance in accessibility. However, we can naturally introduce the notion of distance and restrict the accessibility only to those stay near the current world. Here, the distance is the very strong notion in mathematics, so that we call *topology* as its generalized sense.

3.2 Topology and Neighborhood

Given a mother set X, let $\mathcal{P}(X)$ be the powerset of X and let $\mathcal{T} \subset \mathcal{P}(X)$. We call $\mathcal{T}$ is a topology if it satisfies

1. $X, \emptyset \in \mathcal{T}$.
2. for $\mathcal{O}_1, \mathcal{O}_2 \in \mathcal{T}$, $\mathcal{O}_1 \cap \mathcal{O}_2 \in \mathcal{T}$.
3. for any (possibly infinite[6]) index set Λ, if each $\mathcal{O}_i (i \in \Lambda) \in \mathcal{T}$, $\cup_{i \in \Lambda} \mathcal{O}_i \in \mathcal{T}$.

Each member of $\mathcal{T}$ is called an *open set* that, intuitively, does not have hard boundary. Among various topologies, the *discrete topology* consists of all the subset of mother set X, that is, $\mathcal{T} = \mathcal{P}(X)$. Then, every point is distinguished from each other. In contrast, $\mathcal{T} = \{\emptyset, X\}$ is called *indiscrete topology.*

A set of open sets induces the notion of *neighborhood*; set $V \subset X$ is a neighborhood of point $w \in X$ if $w \in V^\circ$, where V° is the maximum open set in V. Given neighborhoods $\mathcal{N}(w)$ for each w, that is $w \in V^\circ \subset V \in \mathcal{N}(w)$, we can show

[5] Note that '$\supset$' is not a set inclusion but a logical implication.

[6] As for '$\cap$' sets are finite; if we admit infinite sets, *e.g.*. in Euclidean space, $\cap_{n \in \mathbb{N}, \geq 1} [0, 1/n) = [0]$ is not an open set.

1. $V \in \mathcal{N}(w)$ and $V \subset V'$ implies $V' \in \mathcal{N}(w)$.
2. $V_1, V_2 \in \mathcal{N}(w)$ implies $V_1 \cap V_2 \in \mathcal{N}(w)$.
3. For any $V \in \mathcal{N}(w)$ there exists $V'' \in \mathcal{N}(w)$ such that for any $y \in V''$ $V \in \mathcal{N}(y)$.

On the contrary, if we give $\mathcal{N}(w)$ for each $w \in X$ the neighborhoods induces a topology in X by *filtration*.[7]

3.3 Topological Semantics

The topological semantics of modal logic adopts a topology $\mathcal{T}$ instead of accessibility relation R, rereading possible worlds as geometric *points* in a more general way. Let $\mathcal{M} = \langle X, \mathcal{T}, \mathcal{V} \rangle$ where $\mathcal{V}$ is the valuation for atomic propositions.

The syntax is changed as

$$\phi := p \mid \neg\phi \mid \phi \vee \phi \mid \langle\rangle\phi \mid \langle]\phi$$

with $[\rangle\phi \equiv \neg\langle]\neg\phi$ and $[]\phi \equiv \neg\langle\rangle\neg\phi$, as well as $\phi \wedge \phi \equiv \neg(\neg\phi \vee \neg\phi)$ and $\phi \supset \psi \equiv \neg\phi \vee \psi)$.

The semantics of modal operators is given as follows.

$$\mathcal{M}, w \models \langle]\phi \textit{ iff } \text{there exists } \mathcal{O} \in \mathcal{N}(w), \text{ and for all } w' \in \mathcal{O}, \mathcal{M}, w' \models \phi$$
$$\mathcal{M}, w \models \langle\rangle\phi \textit{ iff } \text{there exists } \mathcal{O} \in \mathcal{N}(w), \text{ and for some } w' \in \mathcal{O}, \mathcal{M}, w' \models \phi$$

that is, $\langle]\phi$ holds if and only if there is such a neighborhood in $\mathcal{N}(w)$ that at all the points in which ϕ holds, while $\langle\rangle\phi$ holds if and only if there is such a neighborhood in $\mathcal{N}(w)$ that at some point in which ϕ holds.

When we call *neighborhood semantics* in general, each w may not necessarily belong to every $\mathcal{O} \in \mathcal{N}(w)$ [21]. However, in this research we observe the original notion of neighborhood in topology, that is, $w \in \mathcal{O}$ for any $\mathcal{O} \in \mathcal{N}(w)$. When $w \models \phi$ and $\mathcal{N}(w)$ is not empty, there exists a neighborhood $\mathcal{O}$ in which there is such a point w that $\mathcal{M}, w \models \phi$. Therefore, $\mathcal{M}, w \models \langle\rangle\phi$. Thus,

$$\phi \supset \langle\rangle\phi \tag{3}$$

inevitably holds and the frame becomes **S4**.[8]

3.4 Application to Temporal Structure

Now, we apply the notion of neighborhood to temporal structure, since we assume music is a sequence of pitch events that resides on the time axis. We may conceive that the time is one continuous line, however in this paper, we simply assume that the time is a set of discrete points, corresponding to beats

[7] $\mathcal{N}(w)$ is a *filter* when for any $U \in \mathcal{N}(w)$ there exists $V(\subset U) \in \mathcal{N}(w)$ and for all $w' \in V, U \in \mathcal{N}(w')$.

[8] This is based on Axiom **T**: $\Box\phi \supset \phi$ and its dual form **T***: $\phi \supset \Diamond\phi$ [1,2,14].

or occurrences of pitch events, though they are totally-ordered. From now on, we write point as τ, mnemonic to time, instead of w. The total order (*aka* the linear order) is connected,[9] anti-symmetric,[10] and transitive;[11] for any τ_1 and τ_2, either $\tau_1 \geq \tau_2$ or $\tau_1 \leq \tau_2$, and $\tau_1 \leq \tau_2$ and $\tau_2 \leq \tau_3$ implies $\tau_1 \leq \tau_3$.

In this study, we simply define a set of neighborhoods at τ as those of closed intervals that include τ, as

$$\mathcal{N}(\tau) \ni \mathcal{O} = \{[\tau', \tau''] \mid \tau' \leq \tau'' \ \& \ \tau \in [\tau', \tau'']\}.$$

4 From Syntactic Rules to Logical Formulae

In this section, we translate the syntactic rules in Sect. 2 to logical formulae in Sect. 3. Hereafter, we often write $\tau \models \phi$ when ϕ holds at time τ omitting the frame $\mathcal{M}$ for simplicity. Also, we employ a set notation on the left-hand side of '$\models$' if the same formula ϕ is valid in multiple time points, as $\{\tau_1, \tau_2, \cdots\} \models \phi$.

4.1 Modality for *Head*

Syntactically, the *head* is the most salient lexical item in a given phrase, clause, or sentence. We call such local contexts *regions* as well. Then, for any lexical item,

- Its head is found in its neighborhood ($\langle\rangle$).
- Its head can be accessed from anywhere in the neighborhood ($\langle]$).

And thus, the head is represented by '$\langle]\langle\rangle$'. For visibility, we rename it as **H** hereafter. In addition, we also restrict a neighborhood by '$\langle\rangle$' to the future including now, naming **N**.

$\mathbf{N}\phi \cdots \phi$ appears either <u>n</u>ow or in a <u>n</u>ear future.

$\mathbf{H}\phi \cdots \phi$ is the <u>h</u>ead in a neighborhood.

Therefore, the definitions of **N** and **H** operator are stated as follows.

$$\tau \models \mathbf{N}\phi \iff \exists \mathcal{O} \in \mathcal{N}(\tau) \text{ such that } \forall \tau' (\in \mathcal{O}) \geq \tau,\ \exists \tau'' \in \mathcal{O}\ \tau'' \models \phi. \quad (4)$$

$$\tau \models \mathbf{H}\phi \iff \exists \mathcal{O} \in \mathcal{N}(\tau)\ \forall \tau' \in \mathcal{O},\ \tau' \models \mathbf{N}\phi. \quad (5)$$

---

[9] For any x, y, either $x < y$, $x > y$, or $x = y$.

[10] $x \geq y$ and $x \neq y$ then $x \not\leq y$.

[11] $x \leq y$ and $y \leq z$ implies $x \leq z$.

4.2 Translation

We provide the first-order formulae of predicate-argument structure, corresponding to each syntactic rule. Let predicate $f \in \{head, spec, comp\}$, standing for X, *Spec*, and *Comp* in X-bar rules (1) and (2), respectively.

In order to implement a progression model instead of a generation model, we employ the top-down chart parser (*aka* Earley's algorithm) [9]. Let us consider a generative (production) rule '$A \rightarrow B\ C$' where the right-hand side consists of either two non-terminal symbols or a terminal symbol.[12] Then the rule is evoked and executed in the following process.

1. Observe a pitch event with a harmonic function.
2. Find such generative rule(s) whose first item of the right-hand side (B) matches the observation.
3. To complete the upper category (A) residing at the left-hand side, predict the second item in the right-hand side (C) of the rule.

Here, we translate X-bar rules (1) and (2) to logical formulae in a stepwise manner.

(Step 1) According to the above progression model, we write the first item of the left-hand side first.

- For (1), observe *Spec*, then predict X and X' holds.
- For (2), observe X, and if *Comp* is accompanied then X' holds.

(Step 2) Translate them with logical connectives.

- For (1), $Spec \supset [X \wedge X']$.
- For (2), $X \wedge [Comp \supset X']$.

The adequacy of ($\supset$) and ($\wedge$) is explained in (Step 4).

(Step 3) Replace them for formuale with predicates and chord variables.

- For (1), $spec(x) \supset [head(y) \wedge head'(y)]$.
- For (2), $head(x) \wedge [comp(y) \supset head'(x)]$.

Note that the variable in $head'$ is common with that in $head$.

(Step 4) Now, we need to quantify variables. Since the syntactic head must exist, we quantify *head* by the existential quantifier ($\exists$) while *spec* and *comp* may appear arbitrarily so that these two should be quantified with the universal quantifier ($\forall$). Namely, $\exists x[head(x)]$, $\forall x[spec(x)]$, and $\forall x[comp(x)]$.

[12] It is shown that every context-free rule is transformed into this binary branching, known as Chomsky Normal Form (CNF).

Employ the usual *dual* relation[13] of ($\forall$) and ($\exists$), so as to be consistent with the logical connectives in (Step 2), and thus,

- For (1), $\forall x[spec(x) \supset \exists y[head(y) \wedge head'(y)]]$.
- For (2), $\exists x[head(x) \wedge \forall y[comp(y) \supset head'(x)]]$.

(Step 5) Finally, we enrich the formulae with modal operators, to externalize the future expectation. To denote a time point, either now or in future, in the neighborhood, we employ (**N**). Also, to denote the neighborhood region covered by the head (′) pitch event, we apply (**H**).

- For (1),
$$\forall x[spec(x) \supset \exists y[\mathbf{N}head(y) \wedge \mathbf{H}head(y)]]. \tag{6}$$
The intuitive reading is that if we observe $spec(x)$ there exists a head event $head(y)$ in its neighborhood $\mathcal{O}$ and in any point in $\mathcal{O}$ it becomes the head.
- For (2),
$$\exists x[head(x) \wedge \forall y[\mathbf{N}comp(y) \supset \mathbf{H}head(x)]]. \tag{7}$$
This means that if we first observe $head(x)$ it is possibly accompanied by $comp(y)$ in the neighborhood. Then, there might be a wider region $\mathcal{O}$, anywhere in which $head(x)$ holds.

4.3 Deduction System

To deduce valid formulae, we employ a labeled deduction system.[14] Again, let $f \in \{head, spec, comp\}$. In the deduction schemata, $\tau_i \models \phi$ is abbreviated to $i\colon \phi$. Also, $\exists \mathcal{O} \in \mathcal{N}(\tau_i)$ & $\tau_j \in \mathcal{O}$ is abbreviated to $j\colon \mathcal{O}(i)$. $\phi[c/x]$ represents that each occurrence of x in ϕ is substituted for c.

First, $\forall$-elimination is the easiest as *Modus Ponens* (MP).

$$\frac{i\colon f(c) \quad i\colon \forall x[f(x) \supset \phi]}{i\colon \phi} \tag{8}$$

We need to be careful of $\exists$-elimination, in general, as the existing variable may be different from a found constant. However in our case, since one event occurs at a time, we invoke the formula and simply replace the existing variable with a found variable.

$$\frac{i\colon f(c) \quad i\colon \exists x[f(x) \wedge \phi]}{i\colon \phi[c/x]} \tag{9}$$

Next, we formalize the meaning of (**N**), as follows.

$$\frac{i\colon \exists x \mathbf{N} f(x) \quad j\colon f(c) \quad j\colon \mathcal{O}(i)}{i\colon f(c)}$$

[13] $\forall x[\phi \supset \psi]$ versus $\exists x[\phi \wedge \psi]$. We obtain one from the other by negating the whole formula.

[14] Formulae are labeled by indices of temporal points [13].

Namely, when we expect $f(x)$ at τ_i ($i\colon \mathbf{N}f(x)$), if we can find $f(c)$ at τ_j in the neighborhood of τ_i ($\leq \tau_j$) by (4) as $j\colon \mathcal{O}(i)$, $i\colon f(c)$ holds.

In accordance with (5), (**H**) disseminates **N** in a neighborhood.

$$\frac{i\colon \mathbf{H}f(c) \quad j\colon \mathcal{O}(i)}{j\colon \mathbf{N}f(c)}$$

where there is a neighborhood $\mathcal{O} \in \mathcal{N}(\tau_i)$ and at every point in $\mathcal{O}$ $\mathbf{N}f(c)$ holds.

5 Logical Annotation in Tree of Music

Our task in this paper is to annotate the syntactic tree by logical formulae and to identify the harmonic regions on the time structure. To be precise, according to a pitch event found at each time point τ, we aim at fixing the neighborhood $\mathcal{N}(\tau)$ to validate the formula at τ, and name those neighborhoods as regions.

5.1 Formulae for Chord Progression

According to (6) and (7), we translate syntactic rules X-barred GSM where we employ $f \in \mathbb{F} = \{tonic, dom, sub\}$, instead of $\{head, spec, comp\}$.

For example, for $DR' \rightarrow SR\ DR$, since *dom* is the head, we translate it for the following formula.

$$\forall x[sdom(x) \supset \exists y[\mathbf{N}dom(y) \wedge \mathbf{H}dom(y)]].$$

For $TR'' \rightarrow TR'\ TR$, we write

$$\exists x[tonic(x) \wedge \forall y[\mathbf{N}tonic(y) \supset \mathbf{H}tonic(x)]].$$

The translations for intrinsic rules are shown in Table 1.

Table 1. Logical formulae for X-barred GSM

$TR' \rightarrow DR\ TR$	$\forall x[dom(x) \supset \exists y[\mathbf{N}tonic(y) \wedge \mathbf{H}tonic(y)]]$	(10)
$DR' \rightarrow SR\ DR$	$\forall x[sdom(x) \supset \exists y[\mathbf{N}dom(y) \wedge \mathbf{H}dom(y)]]$	(11)
$TR'' \rightarrow TR'\ TR$	$\exists x[tonic(x) \wedge \forall y[\mathbf{N}tonic(y) \supset \mathbf{H}tonic(x)]]$	(12)
$TR'' \rightarrow TR\ TR'$	$\forall x[tonic(x) \supset \exists y[\mathbf{N}tonic(y) \wedge \mathbf{H}tonic(y)]]$	(13)
$TR \rightarrow tonic$	$\forall x[tonic(x) \supset \mathbf{H}tonic(x)]$	(14)
$DR \rightarrow dom$	$\forall x[dom(x) \supset \mathbf{H}dom(x)]$	(15)
$SR \rightarrow sdom$	$\forall x[sdom(x) \supset \mathbf{H}sdom(x)]$	(16)

5.2 Valuation with Key

In general, a logical formula ϕ in modal logic is evaluated, or decided true or false, given a Kripke frame or simply *model* $\mathcal{M}$ with possible world w as follows.

$$\mathcal{M}, w \models \phi.$$

In our case, a possible world is a time point τ and the frame $\mathcal{M}$ is either topology $\mathcal{T}$ or the neighborhoods, thus

$$\mathcal{M}, \tau \models \phi.$$

Especially, when ϕ includes modal operators, our task has been to fix a member of $N(\tau)$ so as to validate ϕ.

If we consider music, we need key information in our context of music on the left-hand side of '$\models$'. When we observe a set of notes {D, E♯, A} at a certain time point in a music piece, we recognize the pitch event as chord D, though we may not yet be aware of the scale degree and its key. Whether a chord in $\mathbb{O}$ possesses a function in $\mathbb{F}$ depends on the key. If the context is G major, we can assign the *dominant* function to this *D*. That is, *tonic*(G), *dom*(D), *sdom*(C) all hold in G major while not in C major.

Since we have provided a topology or a neighborhood, we need to detail the left-hand side of '$\models$', as

$$\text{Gmaj}, \mathcal{M}, \tau \models \mathit{dom}(\text{D}).$$

Or, in general, $K.\mathcal{M}, \tau \models \phi$ where $K \in \mathbb{K}$. For simplicity, in the remaining discussion we omit such key information as long as there is no confusion.

5.3 Analysis

First, we show how the deduction system works.

Example 1. Let $\tau_1 \models \mathit{tonic}(\text{G})$. Consulting Table 1, we can find three applicable rules. First by (14),

$$\frac{1\colon \mathit{tonic}(\text{G}) \quad 1\colon \forall x[\mathit{tonic}(\text{x}) \supset \mathbf{H}\mathit{tonic}(\text{x})]}{1\colon \mathbf{H}\mathit{tonic}(\text{G})}$$

that is, G forms a region of tonic on its own. Second by deduction (9) and rule (12),

$$\frac{1\colon \mathit{tonic}(\text{G}) \quad 1\colon \exists x[\mathit{tonic}(x) \land \forall y[\mathbf{N}\mathit{tonic}(y) \supset \mathbf{H}\mathit{tonic}(x)]]}{1\colon \forall y[\mathbf{N}\mathit{tonic}(y) \supset \mathbf{H}\mathit{tonic}(G)]}$$

suggests a possibility that the tonic prolongs in the neighborhood. Third by deduction (8) and rule (13),

$$\frac{1\colon \mathit{tonic}(\text{G}) \quad 1\colon \forall x[\mathit{tonic}(x) \supset \exists y[\mathbf{N}\mathit{tonic}(y) \land \mathbf{H}\mathit{tonic}(y)]]}{1\colon \exists y[\mathbf{N}\mathit{tonic}(y) \land \mathbf{H}\mathit{tonic}(y)]}$$

that is, G is overcome by another later tonic. □

Table 2. Chronological recognition of pitch events; two G's at the beginning and at the end are distinguished by indices. (i)–(v) correspond to the subtrees in Fig. 2.

$\tau_1 \models$	$tonic(\mathrm{G}_1)$	We observe chord G_1 at τ_1 as tonic.
	$\mathbf{N}tonic(\mathrm{G}_1)$	By (3).
	$\mathbf{N}tonic(x)$	By (12), still another tonic may follow for tonic prolongation,
		that is, $\forall u[\mathbf{N}tonic(u) \supset \mathbf{H}tonic(u)]$. $(\star)$
	$\mathbf{H}tonic(\mathrm{G}_1)$	$\{\tau_1\} \in \mathcal{N}(\tau_1)$, and $\{\tau_1\} \models tonic(\mathrm{G}_1)$.
		By (13), $\tau_1 \models \exists w[\mathbf{N}tonic(w) \wedge \mathbf{H}tonic(w)]$ (†)
$\tau_2 \models$	$sdom(\mathrm{C})$	We observe C at τ_2 as subdominant. (i)
		as a result, $(\star)$ $\tau_1 \not\models \mathbf{N}tonic(x)$ and $\{\tau_1\}$ is *TR* on its own.
	$\mathbf{N}sdom(\mathrm{C})$	By (3).
	$\mathbf{H}sdom(\mathrm{C})$	$\{\tau_2\} \in \mathcal{N}(\tau_2)$ and $\{\tau_2\} \models sdom(\mathrm{C})$, that is *SR*.
	$\mathbf{N}dom(y)$	We expect a dominant coming in a neighborhood. (ii)
		Applying (8), we obtain $\tau_2 \models \exists y[\mathbf{N}dom(y) \wedge \mathbf{H}dom(y)]$
$\tau_3 \models$	$dom(\mathrm{D})$	We observe D as dominant at τ_3. (iii)
	$\mathbf{N}dom(\mathrm{D})$	By (3).
		$\tau_2 \models \mathbf{N}dom(\mathrm{D}) \wedge \mathbf{H}dom(D)$ by $y = \mathrm{D}$.
		Then recursively $\tau_2 \models \exists z[\mathbf{N}tonic(z) \wedge \mathbf{H}tonic(z)]$. (‡)
	$\mathbf{N}tonic(z)$	Also, we expect a tonic follows. (iv)
		Applying (8), we obtain $\tau_3 \models \exists y[\mathbf{N}tonic(y) \wedge \mathbf{H}tonic(y)]$
	$\mathbf{H}dom(\mathrm{D})$	$\{\tau_2, \tau_3\} \in \mathcal{N}(\tau_2)$ and for $\{\tau_2, \tau_3\} \models dom(D)$, that is *DR*.
$\tau_4 \models$	$tonic(\mathrm{G}_2)$	We observe G_2 as tonic. (v)
	$\mathbf{N}tonic(\mathrm{G}_2)$	By (3).
		$\tau_3 \models \mathbf{N}tonic(\mathrm{G}_2) \wedge \mathbf{H}tonic(\mathrm{G}_2)$ by $y = \mathrm{G}_2$.
		$\tau_2 \models \mathbf{N}tonic(\mathrm{G}_2) \wedge \mathbf{H}tonic(\mathrm{G}_2)$ by $z = \mathrm{G}_2$. (‡)
		$\tau_1 \models \mathbf{N}tonic(\mathrm{G}_2) \wedge \mathbf{H}tonic(\mathrm{G}_2)$ by $w = \mathrm{G}_2$. (†)
	$\mathbf{H}tonic(\mathrm{G}_2)$	$\{\tau_3, \tau_4\} \in \mathcal{N}(\tau_3)$ and $\{\tau_3, \tau_4\} \models tonic(\mathrm{G}_2)$, that is *TR*.
		From (‡), $\{\tau_2, \tau_3, \tau_4\} \in \mathcal{N}(\tau_2)$ and $\{\tau_2, \tau_3, \tau_4\} \models tonic(\mathrm{G}_2)$, that is *TR*.
		From (†), $\{\tau_1, \tau_2, \tau_3, \tau_4\} \in \mathcal{N}(\tau_1)$ and $\{\tau_1, \tau_2, \tau_3, \tau_4\} \models tonic(\mathrm{G}_2)$, that is *TR*.

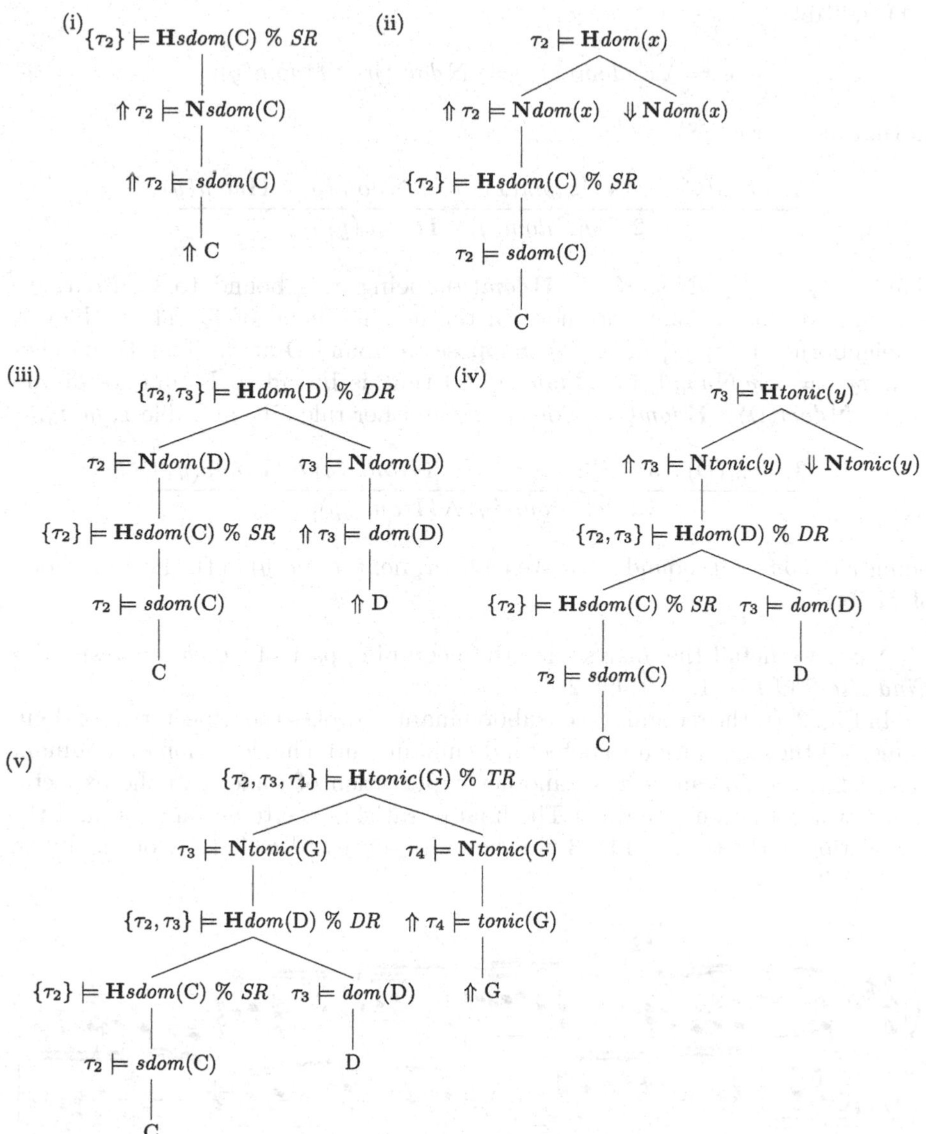

Fig. 2. Expectation-based Tree Construction of the bottom half of Table 2. The upward arrows mean the observation of pitch events in the bottom-up process and the downward arrows show the expectation.

Example 2. Let C be a subdominant in G major found at τ_2 as $\tau_2 \models sdom(\mathrm{C})$. Since $\{\tau_2\} \in \mathcal{N}(\tau_2)$, by (4) $\tau_2 \models \mathbf{N}sdom(\mathrm{C})$ as well as $\tau_2 \models \mathbf{H}sdom(\mathrm{C})$. The latter implies that this region of $\{\tau_2\}$ becomes *SR*. According to translated rule (11) in Table 1,

$$\tau_2 \models \forall x[sdom(x) \supset \exists y[\mathbf{N}dom(y) \wedge \mathbf{H}dom(y)]],$$

so that at τ_2, from (8)

$$\frac{2\colon sdom(\mathrm{C}) \quad 2\colon \forall x[sdom(x) \supset \exists y[\mathbf{N}dom(y) \wedge \mathbf{H}dom(y)]}{2\colon \exists y[\mathbf{N}dom(y) \wedge \mathbf{H}dom(y)]}$$

that is, $\tau_2 \models \exists y \mathbf{N}dom(y) \wedge \mathbf{H}dom(y)$, being x is bound to C. Next, we envisage we find a dominant chord in the neighborhood of τ_2. Then, there is a neighborhood $\{\tau_2, \tau_3\}$ of $\mathcal{N}(\tau_2)$. Suppose we found D at τ_3. This D matches y in $\tau_2 \models \exists y[\mathbf{N}dom(y) \wedge \mathbf{H}dom(y)]$ so that is bound to D and we obtain $\tau_2 \models \mathbf{N}dom(\mathrm{D}) \wedge \mathbf{H}dom(\mathrm{D})$. Consulting another rule (10) in Table 1, at τ_3,

$$\frac{3\colon dom(\mathrm{D}) \quad 3\colon \forall x[dom(x) \supset \exists y[\mathbf{N}tonic(y) \wedge \mathbf{H}tonic(y)]]}{3\colon \exists y[\mathbf{N}tonic(y) \wedge \mathbf{H}tonic(y)]}$$

being x in $dom(x)$ is bound to D. We look for, next, $tonic(y)$ in the neighborhood of τ_3. □

Next, we detail the analysis for the beginning part of "*Liebster Jesu, Wir Sind Hier*" of Fig. 1, in Table 2.

In Fig. 2, (i) the recognition of subdominant C evokes the expectation of dominant, (ii) the expectation to detect a dominant, (iii) The detection of dominant D satisfies the *DR* and evokes another expectation of tonic, (iv) the expectation towards the tonic, and (v) The final G satisfies the tonic function and the completion of the tree. In Fig. 3, we show the suggested regions by our analysis.

Fig. 3. Time points and regions in the beginning of BWV731

6 Conclusion

In this paper, we have proposed the logical semantics of music. We employed the X-bar theory and reinterpreted the existing GSM rules according to the X-bar notation. Thereafter, we have shown the translation of these rules to logical formulae, together with its deduction system. Then, we applied the translated formulae to music, and illustrated the incremental process of tree construction.

Our contributions are two-fold. First, we have assigned logical formulae in parallel to the syntactic rules. These formulae represent references as to what pitch events are expected in each time step. Also this logical formalism could identify tonal regions, that are the temporal extents each of which is represented by a head pitch event. As a result, we have rigorously annotated the meaning of nodes in the tree.

Second, the top-down procedure of generation, consisting of a chaining of multiple generative rules can be reinterpreted to the progressive model. When we listen to music, or compose a music, we construct the music in our mind in accordance with the time progression. By our reinterpretation, now each rule works as our cognitive model. We have implemented such an incremental parser and have shown its efficacy by jazz standards [20].

Finally, we discuss various future tasks. (a) We have divided a music piece in a disjoint, hierarchical regions in accordance with GTTM's grouping analysis [16], however, a short passage, including pivot chords, may be interpreted in multiple ways. Thus, we need to consider flexible overlapping regions. (b) Though we have introduced the semantics by topology, this formalism occasionally seem to be unnecessarily complicated. We may be able to simplify the model only with the necessary operations by, for example, Computational Tree Logic (CTL) [7]. (c) We need also to consider how such expectation corresponds to the existing implication–realization model (I-R model) [19], or to tension–relaxation structure in GTTM [16] in general. (d) In the progressive process, the chart parser produces so many futile subtrees though we only have shown meaningful ones in Table 2 and in Fig. 2. How we can reduce such useless production is another computational interest. (e) Finally, we have treated only intrinsic chord progression rules. If we were to apply our formalism to practical music processing, we need to acquire a non-trivial set of rules, consulting a large music corpus. Considering (d) and (e) together, the study on probabilistic grammar rules would be the most important future target.

Acknowledgments. This work is supported by JSPS kaken 16H01744.

References

1. Blackburn, P., de Rijke, M., Venema, Y.: Modal Logic, Cambridge Tracts in Theoretical Computer Science. Cambridge University Press, Cambridge (2002)
2. Chellas, B.: Modal Logic: An Introduction. Cambridge University Press, Cambridge (1980)
3. Chomsky, N.: Sytactic structures, mouton & Co (1957)

4. Chomsky, N.: Aspects of the Theory of Syntax. The MIT Press, Cambridge (1965)
5. Chomsky, N., Jacobs, R., Rosenbaum, P.: Remarks on nominalization. Read. English Transformational Grammar **184**, 221 (1970)
6. Chomsky, N.: The Minimalist Program. The MIT Press, Cambridge (1995)
7. Clarke, E.M., Emerson, E.A.: Design and synthesis of synchronization skeletons using branching time temporal logic. In: Kozen, D. (ed.) Logic of Programs 1981. LNCS, vol. 131, pp. 52–71. Springer, Heidelberg (1982). https://doi.org/10.1007/BFb0025774
8. Dowty, D.R., Wall, R.E., Peters, S.: Introduction to Montague Semantics. D. Reidel Publishing Company **17**, 3300 (1981)
9. Earley, J.: An efficient context-free parsing algorithm, communications of the association for computing. Machinery **13**(2), 94–102 (1970)
10. Granroth-Wilding, M., Steedman, M.: A robust parser-interpreter for jazz chord sequences. J. New Music Res. **43**, 354–374 (2014)
11. Gollin, E., Rehding, A.: The Oxford Handbook of Neo-Riemannian Music Theories, oxford, USA (2011)
12. Hamanaka, M., Tojo, S., Hirata, K.: Implementing a general theory of tonal music. J. New Music Res. **35**(4), 249–277 (2007)
13. Hatano, R., Sano, K., Tojo, S.: Cut free labelled sequent calculus for dynamic logic of relation changers. In: Yang, S.C.-M., Lee, K.Y., Ono, H. (eds.) Philos. Logic: Curr. Trends Asia, pp. 153–180. Springer, Singapore (2017)
14. Hughes, G.E.: A New Introduction to Modal Logicand Cresswell. Routledge, M. J., London (1996)
15. Koelsch, S.: Brain and Music. John Wiley & Sons Ltd., Hoboken (2015)
16. Lehrdahl, F., Jackendoff, R.: A Generative Theory of Tonal Music. The MIT Press, Cambridge (1983)
17. Meyer, L.E.: Meaning in music and information theory. J. Aestheticsex Art Criticism **15**(4), 412–424 (1957)
18. Narmour, E.: The Analysis and Cognition of Basic Melodic Structures: The Implication-Realization Model. The University of Chicago Press, Chicago (1990)
19. Narmour, E.: The Analysis and Cognition of Melodic Complexity: The Implication-Realization Model. The University of Chicago Press, Chicago (1992)
20. Ogura, Y., Ohmura, H., Uehara, Y., Tojo, S., Katsurada, K.: Expectation-based parsing for Jazz chord sequences. In: The Proceedings of 17th SMC Sound and Music Computing Conference (2020)
21. Pacuit, E.: Neighborhood Semantics for Modal Logic. Springer, Berlin (2017)
22. Rohmeier, M.: Towards a generative syntax of tonal harmony. J. Math. Music **5**(1), 35–53 (2011)
23. Tojo, S., Oka, Y., Nishida, M.: Analysis of chord progression by HPSG. In: Proceedings of 24th IASTED International Conference on Artificial Intelligence and its Applications (2006)
24. Wallin, N.L., Merker, L., Brown, S.: The Origins of Music. The MIT Press, Cambridge (2000)
25. Winograd, T.: Linguistics and the computer analysis of tonal harmony. J. Music Theory **12**(1), 2–49 (1968)

John Cage's Number Pieces, a Geometric Interpretation of "Time Brackets" Notation

Benny Sluchin[1(✉)] and Mikhail Malt[2]

[1] IRCAM/EIC, Paris, France
sluchin@ircam.fr
[2] IRCAM/IReMus, Paris, France
mikhail.malt@ircam.fr

Abstract. Conceptual musical works that lead to a multitude of realizations are of special interest. One can't talk about a performance without considering the rules that lead to the existence of that version. After dealing with similar works of open form by Iannis Xenakis, Pierre Boulez and Karlheinz Stockhausen, the interest in John Cage's music is evident. His works are "so free" that one can play any part of the material; even a void set is welcomed. The freedom is maximal and still there are decisions to consider in order to make the piece playable. Our research was initially intended to develop a set of conceptual and software tools that generates a representation of the work as an assistance to performance. We deal here with the *Number Pieces* Cage composed in the last years of his life. Over time, we realized that the shape used to represent time brackets, brought important information for the interpretation and musical analysis. In the present text, we propose a general geometric study of these time brackets representations, while trying to make the link with their musical properties to improve the performance.

Keywords: Computer aided performance · Notation · Musical graphic representation

1 Introduction

The interpreter who approaches the music of John Cage composed after the middle of the 20th century is often disconcerted by a great freedom of execution, associated with a set of precise instructions. The result is that, each time, the musician is led to determine "a version," and to decide on a choice among the free elements proposed by the piece. A fixed score is thus created, which can be used several times. The musician interprets "his version" while thinking that it conforms to the composer's intentions. But in fact, most works of Cage composed after the 1950s should not be preconceived, prepared, "pre-generated" for several executions. Each interpretation should be unique and "undetermined." It is in this sense that the use of the computer can help the performer: a program will allow the latter to discover without being able to anticipate what and when he plays. The performance of the work thus escapes the intention of the musician to organize the musical text.

R. Kronland-Martinet et al. (Eds.): CMMR 2019, LNCS 12631, pp. 129–141, 2021.
https://doi.org/10.1007/978-3-030-70210-6_9

2 John Cage's Number Pieces

The corpus of John Cage's late compositions (composed between 1987 and 1992) is known today as *Number Pieces*. Each work is named after the number of musicians involved; and the exponent indicates the order of the piece among the other compositions containing the same number of musicians [5].

2.1 Silence and Indeterminacy

In the course of his creative research as a composer, Cage has laid down essential structural elements. Thus, silence has been posited as an element of structure to be thought of in a new and positive way; not as an absence of sound, but as a diachronic element, a presence, an acoustic space. This innovative work concerning silence has itself evolved: at first it was conceived as giving the work its cohesion by alternating with sound, then Cage extended the reflection to a spatial conception: the silence is composed of all the ambient sounds which, together, form a musical structure. Finally, silence was understood as "unintentional," sound and silence being two modes of nature's being unintentional [4].

Moreover, in this desire to give existence to music by itself, Cage has resorted to various techniques of chance in the act of composition and principles of performance.

The principles of indetermination and unintentionality go in that direction. The principle of indetermination leads the musician to work independently from the others, thus introducing something unexpected in what the musical ensemble achieves. The performer, unaware of the production of his fellow musicians, concentrates on his own part and on the set of instructions. This requires great attention, even if the degree of freedom of the playing is high [8].

2.2 Time Brackets

In Cage's Number Pieces each individual part contains musical events with *time brackets*. Generally, an event consists of a score endowed with two pairs of numbers: time brackets (Fig. 1).

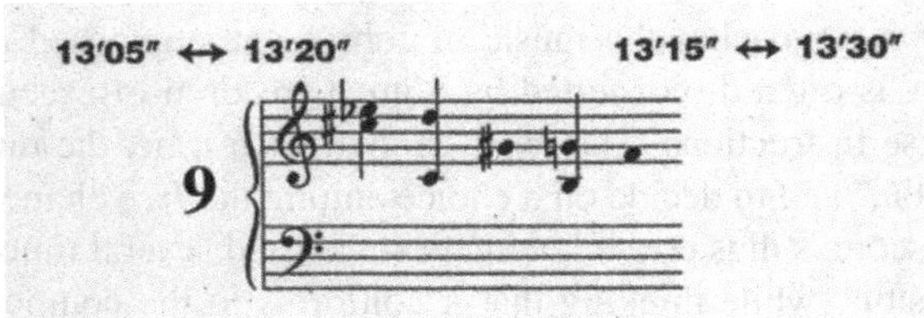

Fig. 1. John Cage's *Two*^{5}, piano, 9th event

This gives the interpreter lower and upper-time bounds to begin and end each event. The composition has a defined total duration and the events are placed inside a pair of the *time brackets*. Although there are only individual parts, a score for the group is implicitly present and leads to a form.

2.3 Earlier Research

In previous work [12] we modeled these time brackets by parallelograms (see Figs. 2 and 3) to build computer interfaces for interpretation assistance in the context of Cage's *Two*^{5} (Fig. 2).

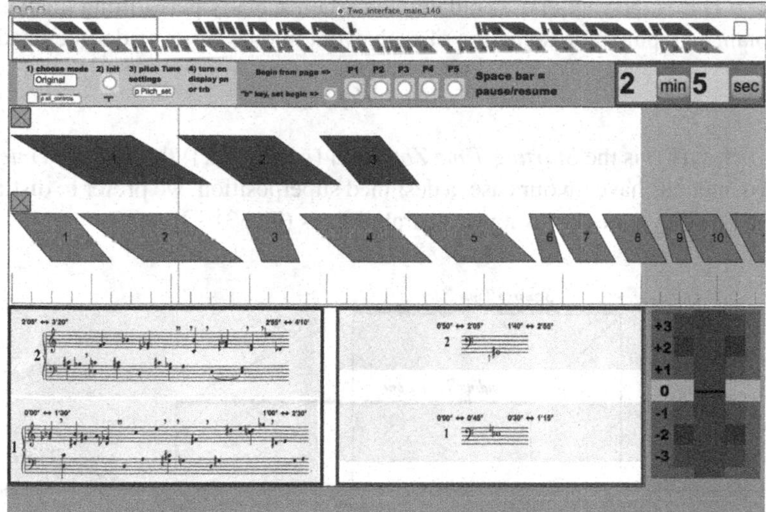

Fig. 2. Cage's *Two*^{5} main computer interface

Over time [1–3], we realized that the shape used to represent time brackets, brought important information for the interpretation and musical analysis. The unusually long duration of this piece, 40 min, and the use of time brackets show that the temporal question, and its representation, is essential in the Number Pieces, in general, and in *Two*^{5} in particular.

> *The computer interface whose use has become obvious, has created for us a climate of confidence in our relationship to the piece. Random encounters of synchronicity as well as intervals bring unexpected situations...* [9].

In the present text, we propose a general geometric study of these time brackets representations, while trying to make the link with their musical properties to improve the performance.

3 The Geometry of Time Bracket

The first step in the process was to model a graphic representation of each part as a succession of musical events in time. For this purpose, the temporal structure of the piece has been represented as quadruples on a timeline $(s_l(k), s_u(k), e_l(k), e_u(k))$.

In order to place an event k on the timeline, time brackets are defined as quadruples to indicate the time span allocated to it. Each quadruple consists of two pairs. More precisely, each pair gives the interpreter lower and upper time bounds to start $(s_l(k), s_u(k))$ and to end $(e_l(k), e_u(k))$. Theses closed time intervals give to the performer, a choice of the pair$(s(k), e(k))$, where $(s_l(k) \leq s(k) \leq s_u(k))$ and $(e_l(k) \leq e(k) \leq e_u(k))$. One could choose the starting time $(s(k))$, while performing and, then accordingly, the end time $(e(k))$. This is the way one would employ when actually performing the work.

To obtain a graphic representation of each event in time we consider the quadruple:

$$(s_l(k), s_u(k), e_l(k), e_u(k))$$

where $(s_l(k), s_u(k))$ is the *Starting Time Zone* and $(e_l(k), e_u(k))$ the *Ending Time Zone*. As the two intervals have, in our case, a designed superposition, we prefer to distinguish starting and ending zones by using two parallel lines (Fig. 3).

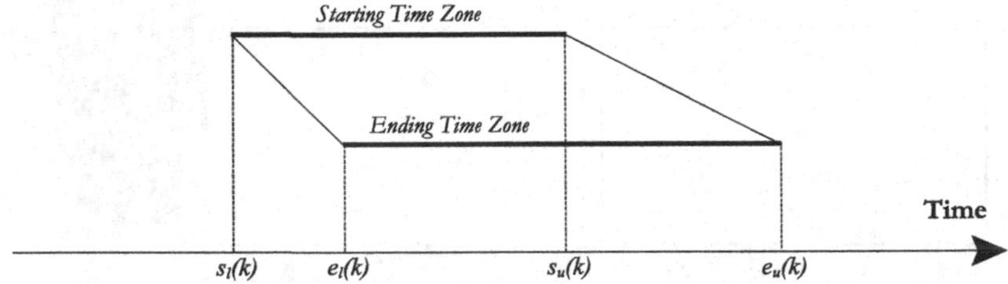

Fig. 3. Graphic representation for a generic time event

The graphic event obtained by connecting the four points has a quadrilateral shape. The height has no particular meaning. The *starting duration* $\delta_s(k)$ is defined as the difference: $(s_u(k) - s_l(k))$, which is the time span the performer has to start the event. In the same way the *ending duration* $\delta_e(k)$ will be the time span given to end the event $(e_u(k) - e_l(k))$. In the general case, these values are not the same, and the form we get is asymmetrical. When dealing with Cage's *Number Pieces*, one generally has: $\delta_s(k) = \delta_e(k)$, both durations are the same, and the figure to represent an event is a trapezoid (Fig. 4). This is the case in the majority of the corpus we are treating. Special cases will be mentioned later on.

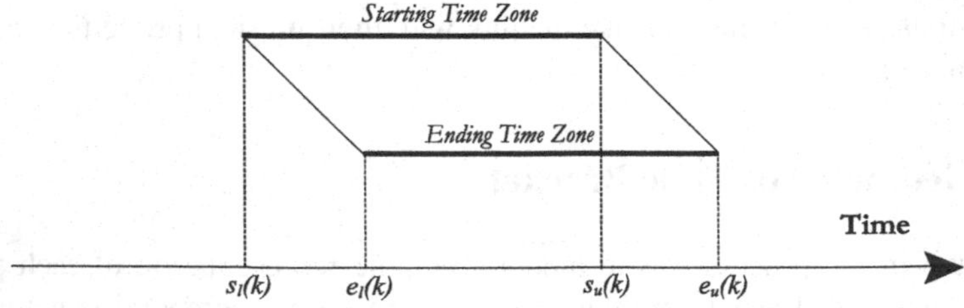

Fig. 4. Graphic representation for a time event in Cage's *Number Pieces*

There is mostly an overlapping of the two time zones, $(s_l(k), s_u(k))$ and $(e_l(k), e_u(k))$ but it can happen that those are disjoined. We can define a variable $\gamma(k)$ where: $s_l(k) + \gamma(k) = e_l(k)$. In Cage's *Number Pieces,* $\gamma(k)$ depends generally on the event duration. Thus, we don't have a big variety of forms. For example, in *Five*[3], we have only 4 different time brackets sorts, for a total number of 131 events for the five instruments and $\gamma(k) = \frac{2}{3}\delta(k)$ for all quadruples.

We make a distinction between a *generic musical event* and a *real* (or determined) *musical event.* A real musical event is the one whose starting point (s) and end point (e) are defined, that is, where there is a concretization of choice. One could represent this by a straight line from $s(k)$ to $e(k)$ (Fig. 5).

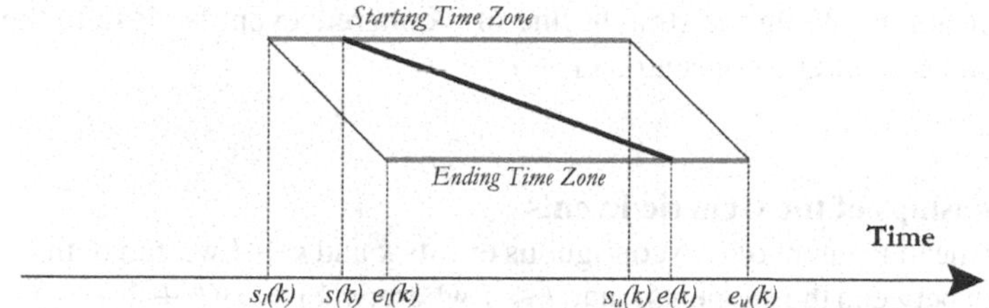

Fig. 5. A real music event represented by a straight line, joining the starting to ending time zones

There are certain properties of a generic event that can easily be deduced from the trapezoidal graphic representation:

1. The *starting* or *ending durations*: $\delta_s(k)$ or $\delta_e(k)$ are a kind of a nominal duration that Cage gives to an event.
2. The maximum duration, $e_u(k) - s_l(k) = \delta_{max}(k)$, is the maximum length (duration) an event can have.
3. The fact that, $s_u(k) > e_l(k)$ means that we can choose a starting point $s(k)$ placed after the end, which leads to an empty musical event ∅ (an important idea of Cage: he often indicates that the artist can choose, all of, a part of, or nothing of the material placed at its disposal). In this case, $s(k) > e(k)$.
4. An alternative way to present a quadruple will be: $(s_l(k), \delta_s(k), \delta_e(k), \gamma(k))$ where $\gamma(k)$ is the value previously discussed. This representation can easily display the regularity in the time brackets construction (Fig. 6). It is easy to see that

$$\delta_{max}(k) = \frac{(\delta_s(k) + \delta_e(k))}{2} + \gamma(k).$$

5. An implicit parameter that is important is the straight line's slope of the concrete event (Fig. 5). This value is inversely proportional to the concrete event duration. The slope is strongly related to performance: it shows how much time the performer has for a particular event k. In regard to a wind instrument part, often only composed by held notes, knowledge of this parameter allows the artist to better manage his air capacity, in order to respect the composer's indications. As far as the pianist is concerned, the slope

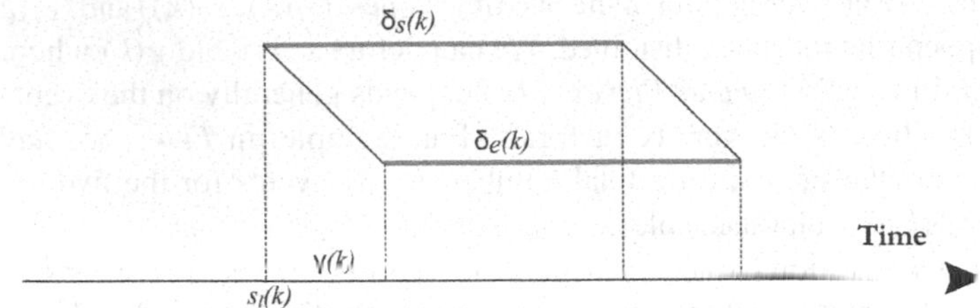

Fig. 6. An event represented as $(s_l(k), \delta_s(k), \delta_e(k), \gamma(k))$

gives some information that allows him to manage his interpretation with reference to the time indications. When the straight line of a concrete event is close to the vertical, the event will be short and concentrated.

The Relationships of the Generic Events

Concerning the placement of two contiguous events k and $k+1$ we can define a variable $\varepsilon(k)$, the gap between the elements k and $k+1$ where: $\varepsilon(k) = s_l(k+1) - e_u(k)$ (Fig. 7).

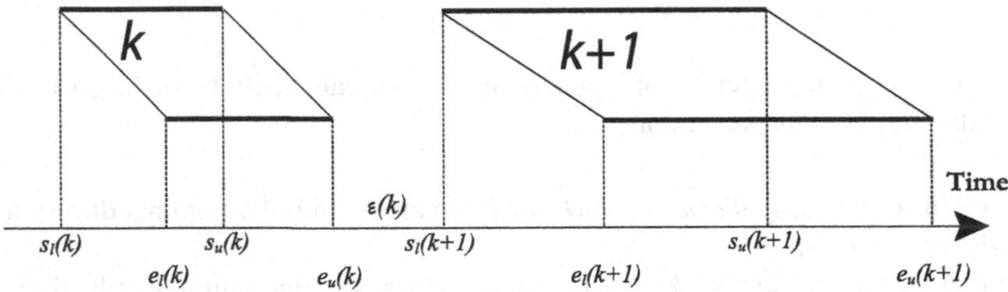

Fig. 7. $\varepsilon(k)$, The gap between the elements k *and* $k+1$

We will observe five typical placements of two contiguous events.

1. $\varepsilon > 0$.
The two events are separated on the timeline. There is a minimum length of silence between the two events, which will probably be longer according to the choice of $e(k)$ and $s(k+1)$. In *Five*[3] for example, we have events 1 and 2 of violin 2 separated by more than 8 min, or 3 min between events 6 and 7 of violin 1. Here the piece could also be considered from the point of view of the relative density of the musical elements. One should mention the global statistical approach done elsewhere [6, 7].

2. $\varepsilon = 0$.
The two events are adjacent (Fig. 8).

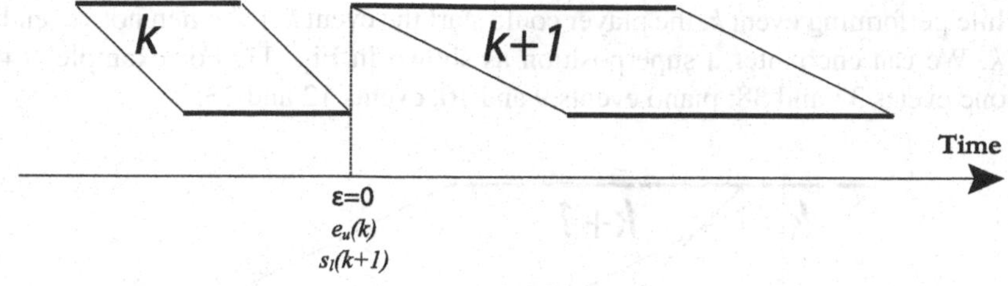

Fig. 8. $\varepsilon = 0$

Again, a gap may occur between the two events as the actual ending of event k: $e(k)$, and/or the actual starting of event $k + 1$, $s(k + 1)$ will differ from $e_u(k)$, and $s_l(k + 1)$ correspondingly. For example, *Two*[5], trombone, events 21 and 22 (Fig. 9), events 27 and 28.

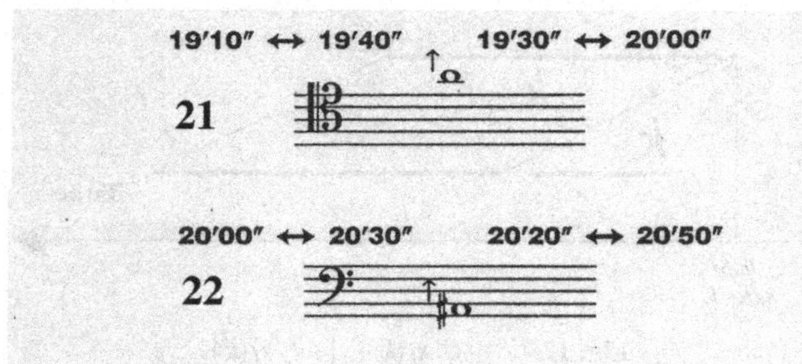

Fig. 9. *Two*[5], trombone, events 21 and 22

3. $\varepsilon < 0$.

In this case, the performer's opinion and attitude can determine the performance. There are many remarkable cases of interest in this situation; we could mention some cases that presently occur in Cage's *Number Pieces*. For example (Fig. 10), *Two*[5], trombone events 28 and 29, and piano events 6 and 7.

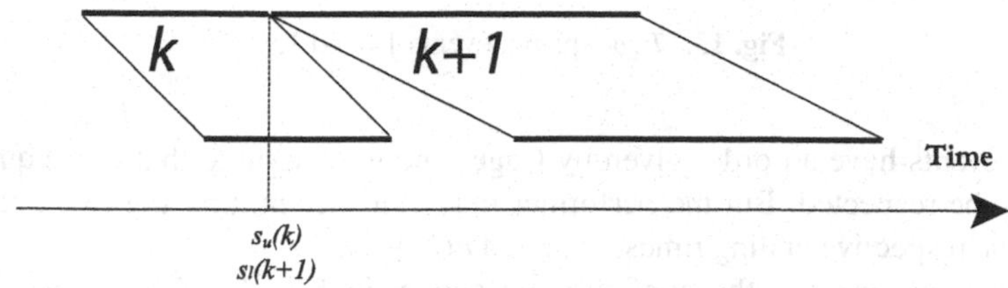

Fig. 10. $\varepsilon < 0$, $s_l(k + 1) = s_u(k)$

While performing event *k*, the player could start the event *k* + *1* when not yet ending event *k*. We can encounter a superposition as shown in Fig. 11. For example, *Two*[5], trombone events 37 and 38; piano events 9 and 10, events 12 and 13.

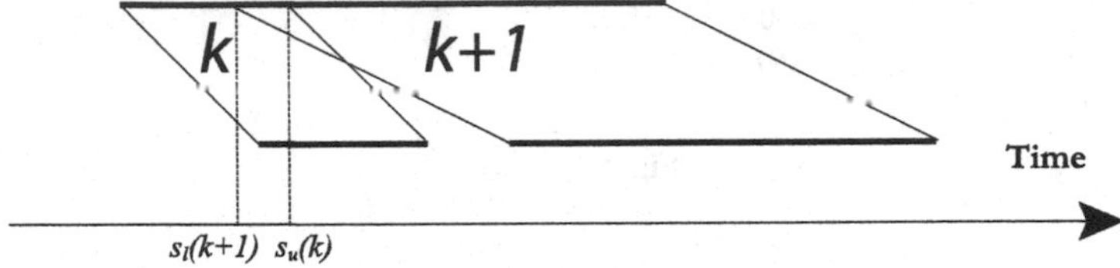

Fig. 11. $\varepsilon < 0, s_l(k+1) < s_u(k)$

And even the same starting time for the two events: $s_l(k+1) = s_l(k)$ (Fig. 12). For example, *Two*[5], piano, events 14 and 15 (Fig. 13).

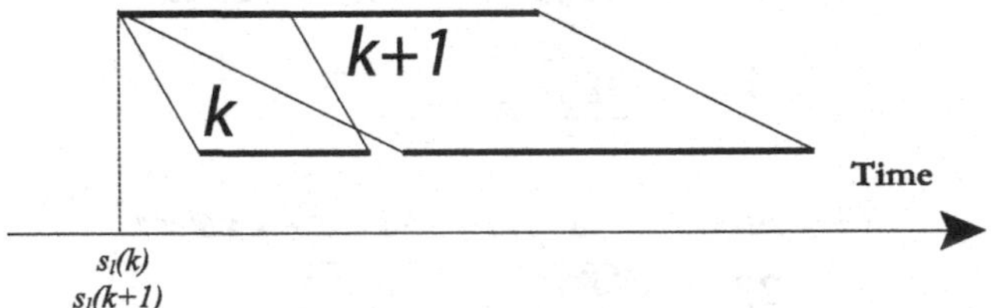

Fig. 12. $\varepsilon < 0, s_l(k+1) = s_l(k)$

Fig. 13. *Two*[5], piano, events 14 and 15

As the events have an order given by Cage, one may assume that the sequence of events is to be respected. But the performer may consider mixing the two events and choosing the respective ending times, $e(k)$ and $e(k+1)$.

In some case one has the configuration shown in Fig. 14. For example, *Two*[5], trombone events 31 and 32, events 39 and 40.

This may be a mistake, in calculation or in printing. Again, without change the order of events, one could start with the event *k*, and continue with the event *k* + *1*, mixing or

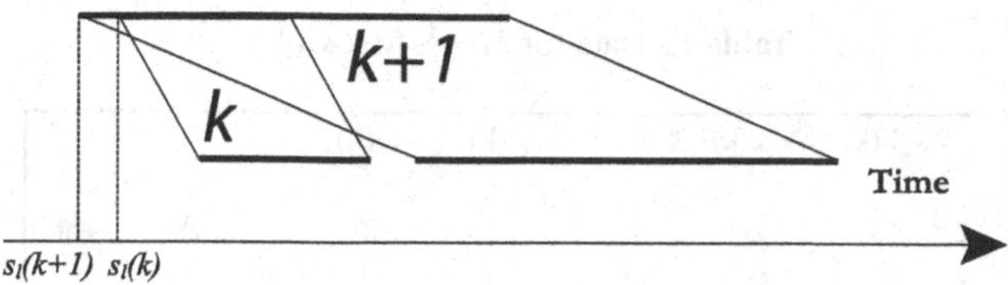

Fig. 14. $\varepsilon < 0$, $s_l(k+1) < s_l(k)$

separating. Starting with the event $k + 1$ would mean that mixing has to happen, or the event k, should be skipped, that an idea dear to Cage: the event k wouldn't be performed.

The presentation of the time brackets as geometric figures and the variables we have defined lead to calculate some constants related to each of the instruments involved. The *average filling rate* ($\overline{Fr}$) gives an indication of how much a particular instrument is present during the piece. This value will be the ratio of the sum of all the events' duration by the overall length of the work (Δ), where the event duration, $\delta(k)$, is the arithmetic mean between $\delta_s(k)$ and $\delta_e(k)$ (1).

$$\overline{Fr} = \frac{\sum_1^n \delta(k)}{\Delta} \tag{1}$$

In the analog way, if we set: $\varepsilon(0)$ be the gap before the first event, and $\varepsilon(n)$ the gap after the last event n, the *average silence rate* ($\overline{Sr}$) will be the ratio of the sum of all the gaps between the events by the overall length of the work (2).

$$\overline{Sr} = \frac{\sum_0^n \varepsilon(k)}{\Delta} \tag{2}$$

These interesting values are based on the lengths of events, the gaps between them and their number, independent of the contents of the events.

If instead of using $\delta(k)$, the event duration, we consider $\delta_{max}(k)$, then:

$$\sum_{k=1}^{n} \delta_{max}(k) + \sum_{0}^{n} \varepsilon(k) = \Delta \tag{3}$$

4 Musical Analysis Application

Table 1 shows the values for the 21 events of violin 1 in *Five*[3], and the constants we just defined. The time values, onsets and durations, are defined in seconds.

The following Table 2, compares these constants for the five instruments. We can observe how these two constants ($\overline{Fr}$ and $\overline{Sr}$) are strongly related to the presence of the instruments. For example, trombone will be more present, more active than the string instruments. One can see that $\overline{Sr}$ may be negative. This occurs when many of the events are superposed (All cases with $\varepsilon < 0$).

These values are clearly reflected in the form of the piece seen in the upper part of Fig. 15. We had implemented several models, some offline in "OpenMusic"[1] computer

[1] "OpenMusic" is a software developed by Ircam by Gerard Assayag, Carlos Augusto Agon and Jean Bresson. See: https://recherche.ircam.fr/equipes/repmus/OpenMusic/.

Table 1. Data for *Five*^{3}, first violin

	s_1 (k)	δ_s (k)	δ_e (k)	γ (k)	ε (k)		
1	10	45	45	30	10	Δ=	2400
2	150	45	45	30	65		
3	215	30	30	20	-10		
4	290	45	45	30	25	$\sum_{k=1}^{n} \delta(k) =$	810
5	405	45	45	30	40		
6	465	45	45	30	-15		
7	740	45	45	30	200	$\sum_{k=0}^{n} \varepsilon(k) =$	1030
8	1225	45	45	30	410		
9	1315	15	15	10	15		
10	1325	45	45	30	-15	$\overline{Fr} =$	0,3375
11	1475	15	15	10	75		
12	1570	30	30	20	70	$\overline{Sr} =$	0,4292
13	1625	45	45	30	5		
14	1685	45	45	30	-15		
15	1865	30	30	20	105		
16	1900	45	45	30	-15		
17	2060	45	45	30	85		
18	2165	45	45	30	30		
19	2235	15	15	10	-5		
20	2245	45	45	30	-15		
21	2305	45	45	30	-15		

Table 2. Comparison values in *Five*^{3}

	#Events	$\overline{Fr}$	$\overline{Sr}$
Violin 1	21	0.34	0.43
Violin 2	12	0.16	0.74
Viola	26	0.34	0.44
Violoncello	25	0.23	0.5
Trombone	47	0.74	−0.24

aided composition software, and in a real-time "Max" software [12]. Figure 15 presents a generic computer interface we are exploring, to perform most part of Cage's *Number Pieces*.

The medium part of this figure, displays one of the instruments chosen (here violin 1) and bottom part displays the musical score corresponding to the time (here 30 s after beginning). The global view displays a presentation of the entire duration of *Five*^{3}, using the trapezoidal event representation. It allows the performer to have a global view of the piece at a glance. As Cage mention about the context-specific character of his time-bracket notation:

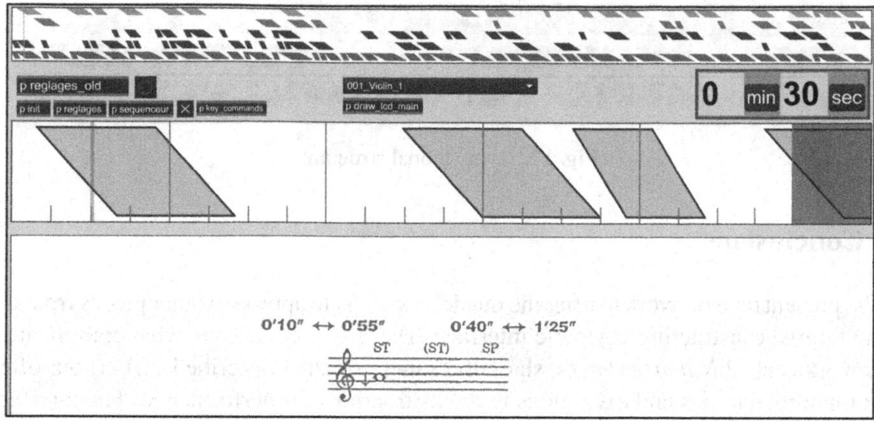

Fig. 15. Computer interface used for performing *Five*^{3}

Then, we can foresee the nature of what will happen in the performance, but we can't have the details of the experience until we do have it. [10].

This global representation enables another perspective of the piece. The printed score orients a natural local view. More than being a graphic representation for each time bracket, it allows us to identify similarities between generic musical events. Figure 16, a detail from Fig. 15, presents the first ten minutes of the global representation of *Five*^{3}.

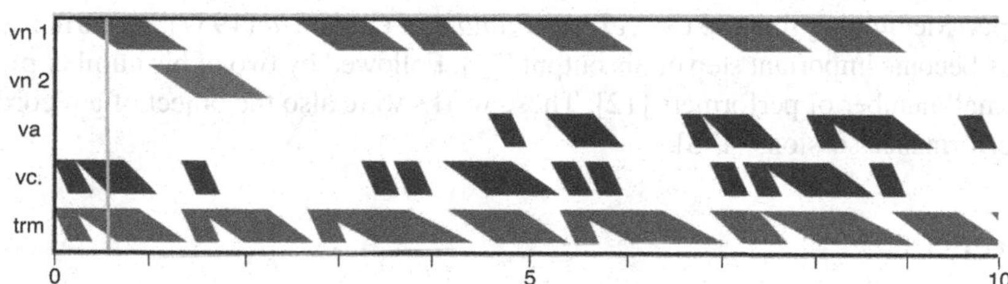

Fig. 16. The first ten minutes of the global representation in Cage's *Five3*

In an analog way Table 3 presents $\overline{Fr}$ and $\overline{Sr}$ constants for *Two*^{5}, and Fig. 17 shows the global structure of the piece. One can clearly distinguish the difference in the presence of the two instruments.

Table 3. Comparison values in *Two*^{5}

	#Events	$\overline{Fr}$	$\overline{Sr}$
Piano	29	0.33	0.15
Trombone	40	0.46	−0.14

Fig. 17. Two^5 global structure

5 Conclusions

At the present time we work to offer the musicians a way to approach other pieces from the same family, constructing a generic interface. The task may be somewhat complicated. The works called *Number Pieces*, share the same principal described earlier, but often contain particularities and exceptions in the instructions for performance. The interface then has to be adapted to cover these.

The interface is a substitute to the printed score. It reveals the structure of the work and provides the performer with the tool to achieve the "meditative concentration" needed. The few instructions given by Cage are integrated in the interface.

Considering the graphic representation, we presented above, our main goal was to find geometric properties and strategies to enhance the performance of these pieces through computer interfaces. John Cage's works have been the target of our work for several years now. We have developed computer tools for the interface, and used it in practice. Both concerts and recordings have been the tests for the usefulness of the approach towards performance. The modeling process is transformed in a pragmatic analysis of the musical phenomena that leads us, step by step, to model some of Cage's concepts. Mentioning first the *Concert for Piano and Orchestra* (1957), an earlier work that has become important step of his output [11]. Followed by two of his number pieces for a small number of performers [12]. These works were also the object of a recording and performance sessions [1–3].

References

1. Cage, J.: *Two*^{5}. On John Cage Two^5 [CD]. Ut Performance (2013)
2. Cage, J.: *Music for Two.* On John Cage, Music for Two [CD]. Ut Performance (2014)
3. Cage, J.: *Ryoanji.* On John Cage, Ryoanji [CD]. Ut Performance (2017)
4. Chilton, J.G.: Non-intentional performance practice in John Cage's solo for sliding trombone. DMA dissertation, University of British Columbia (2007)
5. Haskins, R.: The Number Pieces of John Cage. DMA dissertation, University of Rochester (2004). Published as Anarchic Societies of Sounds, VDM Verlag (2009)
6. Popoff, A.: Indeterminate music and probability spaces: the case of John Cage's number pieces. In: Agon, C., Andreatta, M., Assayag, G., Amiot, E., Bresson, J., Mandereau, J. (eds.) Mathematics and Computation in Music. MCM 2011. Lecture Notes in Computer Science, vol. 6726, pp. 220–229. Springer, Heidelberg (2011). https://doi.org/10.1007/978-3-642-21590-2_17
7. Popoff, A.: John Cage's number pieces: the meta-structure of time-brackets and the notion of time. Perspect. New Music **48**(1), 65–83 (2010)
8. Pritchett, J.: The Music of John Cage. Cambridge University Press, Cambridge (1993)
9. Rappaport, S., Sluchin, B.: On Panorama [CD]. Liner notes. Ut Performance (2019)

10. Retallack, J.: Musicage: Cage Muses on Words, Art, Music, p. 182. Wesleyan university Press, Middletown (1996)
11. Sluchin, B., Malt, M.: Interpretation and computer assistance in John Cage's Concert for piano and Orchestra (1957–58). In: 7th Sound and Music Conference (SMC 2010), Barcelona, 21–24 July 2010 (2010)
12. Sluchin, B., Malt, M.: A computer aided interpretation interface for John Cage's number piece Two5. In: Actes des Journées d'Informatique Musicale (JIM 2012), Namur, Belgique, 9–11 mai 2012), pp. 211–218 (201)

Modelling 4-Dimensional Tonal Pitch Spaces with Hopf Fibration

Hanlin Hu(✉) and David Gerhard

Department of Computer Science, University of Regina, Regina S4S 0A2, Canada
{hu263,gerhard}@cs.uregina.ca

Abstract. The question of how to arrange harmonically related pitches in space is a historical research topic of computational musicology. The primitive of note arrangement is linear in 1-D, in which ordered ascending pitches in one direction correspond to increasing frequencies. Euler represented harmonic relationships between notes with a mathematical lattice named Tonnetz, which extends the 1-D arrangement into 2-D space by reflecting consonances. Since then, mathematicians, musicians, and psychologists have studied this topic for hundreds of years. Recently, pitch-space modelling has expanded to mapping musical notes into higher-dimensional spaces. This paper aims to investigate existing tonal pitch space models, and to explore a new approach of building a pitch hyperspace by using the Hopf fibration.

Keywords: Tonal pitch space · Hopf fibration · Human pitch perception

1 Introduction

Pitch represents the logarithmic value of the fundamental frequency, which is used by humans to distinguish different sounds [10]. The distance between pitches p and q, which has a measurement with the usual metric on $\mathbb{R}$ with an absolute value of the difference, $\mid q - p \mid$, shows the degree of relatedness, with closely related pitches near to each other, and less closely ones far apart. A collection of distances between pitches is denoted as a *scale*, which consists of a number of pitches and their order of the organization [24]. For example, the western 12-tone equal tempered (12-TET) scale, also called the chromatic scale, has twelve pitches. Each pitch has a semitone distance higher or lower than its adjacent one. In the $\mathbb{R}$ Euclidean space, a musical scale could be visualized with a line segment connecting all 12 pitches, since a line segment indicates the range of the collection as well as the increment of all values upon it.

In addition to being logarithmic, human pitch perception is also *periodic* [11]. The distance between one pitch and its double-frequency pitch is called an octave or perfect octave, and this distance can be considered a unit distance in a periodic scale. In different octaves, the denotation of a pitch class – a set of all pitches with a whole number of octaves apart (in 12-TET, a pitch class is presented

R. Kronland-Martinet et al. (Eds.): CMMR 2019, LNCS 12631, pp. 142–156, 2021.
https://doi.org/10.1007/978-3-030-70210-6_10

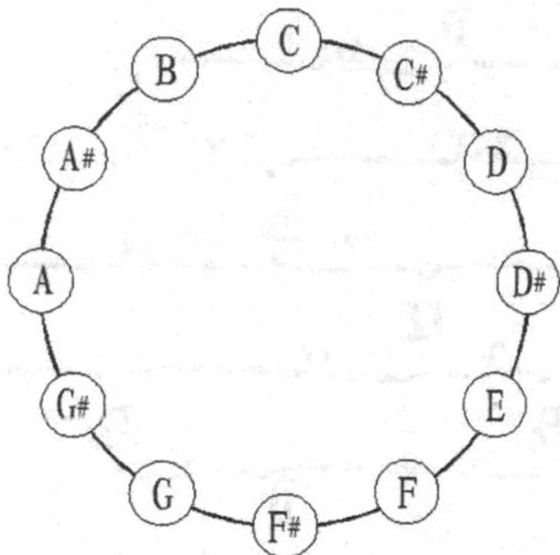

Fig. 1. Circular chroma of a western 12-tone equal tempered scale [13]

by a set of points in the quotient space $\mathbb{R}/12\mathbb{Z}$) – is repeatable with the same symbols or characters but different subscripts, which allows visualization in the $\mathbb{R}^n$ space to show a periodic relationship regardless the hierarchy of tone heights. For example, Fig. 1 shows a *chroma*, an attribute of pitch referring its quality in human pitch-perception, just like hue is an attribute of color, in 1-sphere ($\mathbb{S}^1$ that can be embedded in $\mathbb{R}^2$ Euclidean space) that is the inherent circularity of the chromatic scale in an arbitrary octave. A 12-TET chromatic scale can begin on any note, and proceed through all others before returning to the same note, one octave further in tone height.

In spite of the fact that variations of frequencies describe the interval – a physical distance between pitches – some special collections of pitches or pitch-class sets show "closer" distance (pitches sound more consonant) in perception [9]. For instance, a pair of pitches that have the Perfect fifth relationship sounds more harmonious than a pair of two adjacent pitches in chromatic scales, even though the frequency distance between the notes of a Perfect fifth is much larger than the frequency distance between two adjacent pitches [20]. The physical cause of this perception of consonance relates to the alignment of harmonics in the harmonic series. In a Perfect fifth, every second harmonic of the higher note aligns closely with every third harmonic of the lower note, since the frequency ratio of the two notes is close to 3:2. Dissonant intervals have larger denominator ratios (e.g. 16:15 for a just-tuned semitone, $1 : 2^{12}$ for an equal tempered semitone), with fewer aligned harmonics and more harmonics interfering with each other. Thus, intervals with frequencies close to a small whole-number ratio contain pairs of notes that are somehow "closer together" in terms of perceptual harmonic relationships. In this way, we can imagine a collection of "distance" metrics besides linear frequency distance, in an attempt to indicate the harmonic or musical "closeness" of a pair of notes, relating to the interval between them rather than the distance between them.

Since any two non-identical intervals are independent to each other, the perceptual distance of harmonic closeness can be represented by orthogonal vectors

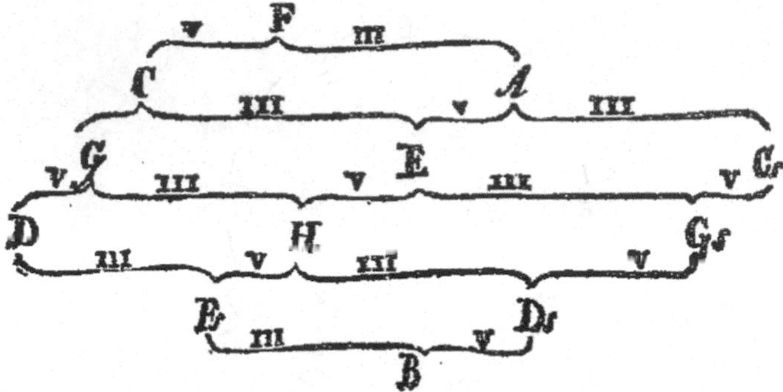

Fig. 2. Euler's Tonnetz (1737) [5]

representing the intervals between them. Mathematically, the selective combination of these vectors can be bundled into groups. To visualize these groups, researchers have modeled the relationships between notes using graphs, tilings, lattices and geometrical figures such as helices. All models like these, which may be multidimensional, are named *pitch spaces* or *tonal pitch spaces* [13]. To model an n-dimensional pitch space, an $\mathbb{R}^n$ pitch space is needed due to the orthogonality of the groups whose order (the number of elements in its set) is n. Each relationship between a set of pitches is represented as a vector in $\mathbb{R}^n$ pitch space, and the distance along that vector corresponds to an accumulated number of the indicated interval (a distance of 3 Minor thirds, for example).

Tonal pitch space research relating to groups in $\mathbb{R}^n$ lies at the intersection of two seemingly independent disciplines: human pitch perception and algebra topology. Human pitch perception is a part of psychoacoustics that studies the psychological and physiological responses associated with sound. Algebra topology leverages tools of abstract algebra to study topological spaces. In this paper, existing tonal pitch space lattices and human pitch perception models will be reviewed in Sect. 2 to Sect. 4. An exploration of modelling tonal pitch spaces in $\mathbb{R}^4$ space with Hopf fibration, which associates with all the lattices and models mentioned in previous sections, will be described in Sect. 5, before the conclusion in Sect. 7.

2 Tonnetz in $\mathbb{R}^2$ Space and Its Isomorphism

A Swiss mathematician, Leonhard Euler, introduced a conceptual $\mathbb{R}^2$ lattice diagram named *Tonnetz* (Tone-network in German) representing 2-dimensional tonal pitch spaces in 1737 [5]. Euler's Tonnetz (Fig. 2) shows the triadic relationships of the Perfect fifth and the Major third. Proceeding from the top of the figure, between note F and note C, there is a Perfect fifth (marked as Roman numeral "V"), while from F to A there is a Major third (marked as "III").

In 1858, the $\mathbb{R}^2$ pitch space was rediscovered by Ernst Naumann. Later in 1866, it was disseminated in Arthur von Oettingen and Hugo Riemann's publication of exploration to chart harmonic motion between chords [4]. Oettingen and Riemann show that the relationships in the chart can be extended through *Just intonation* (requiring strict whole number frequency ratios between notes) to form a never-ending sequence in every direction without repeating any pitches [21]. Modern music theorists generally construct the Tonnetz with an equilateral triangular lattice based on Neo–Riemannian theory. As shown in Fig. 3, the equilateral triangular lattice demonstrates the equal temperament of triads since a minor third (C–$E\flat$) followed by a major third ($E\flat$–G) is equivalent to a Perfect fifth (C–G).

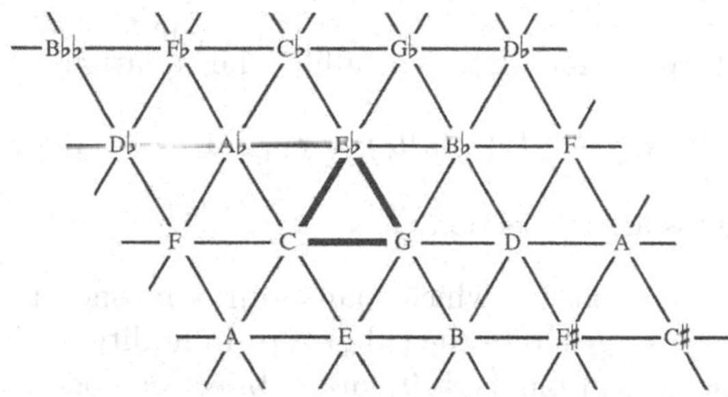

Fig. 3. Modern rendering of the Tonnetz with equilateral triangular lattice [21]

The musical relationships in the lattice can be explained by using group and set theory. The collection of notes along each direction can be considered as a *subgroup* (a subset of a group which is also a group) of a chromatic scale denoted as $\mathbb{R}/12\mathbb{Z}$ under the operation of addition denoted as $+$. For example, the Major third relationship exists as four subsets of the complete chromatic scale: $\{0, 4, 8\}$, $\{1, 5, 9\}$, $\{2, 6, 10\}$ and $\{3, 7, 11\}$. In each of these instances, a collection of notes selected from a chromatic scale are all related as Major thirds. For example, for the chromatic scale starting at C, the subset $\{0, 4, 8\}$ corresponds to the notes C, E, $A\flat$, which appear aligned in Fig. 3 (note that in 12-TET, $F\flat$ is an enharmonic spelling of the note E and thus equivalent in pitch).

Similarly, the Minor third relationship exists as three subsets of the chromatic scale, as $\{0, 3, 6, 9\}$, $\{1, 4, 7, 10\}$ and $\{2, 5, 8, 11\}$. The Perfect fifth has the same collection of notes with chromatic scale but in different order of arrangement, which is $\{0, 7, 2, 9, 4, 11, 6, 1, 8, 3, 10, 5\}$, and this is also considered as a subgroup [6,17]. In this way, although only some notes can be reached by any combination of jumps of Major thirds, all notes can be reached by some number of jumps of Perfect fifths.

In abstract algebra, a group isomorphism presents a one-to-one correspondence between two groups when a group operation is given. The general definition of group isomorphism is:

Considering two groups G and H, where G is under the operation of $\odot$ and H is under the operation of $\Diamond$, where $\odot$ and $\Diamond$ can only be the operations of addition *(denoted as +) or multiplication (denoted as* $*$*). G and H are isomorphic when there exists a function* $f : G \longmapsto H$ *that fulfills the equation* $f(x) \Diamond f(y) = f(x \odot y)$ *where* $x, y \in G$*, and also they are bijection* [1].

where bijection corresponds to a one-to-one mapping from one group to the other. Applied to tonal pitch spaces, the additive group is sufficient for the consideration of isomorphism. It is easy to show that two subgroups of $\mathbb{R}/12\mathbb{Z}$ are isomorphic under the operation of + in a certain collection of relationships such as Major third, Minor third and Perfect fifth. For example, there are two subgroups under the operation of + from Major third: the subgroup A:$\{0, 4, 8\}$ and the subgroup B:$\{1, 5, 9\}$. A and B are isomorphic if two requirements are fulfilled:

1. A function $f(x)$ can be found, which fulfills the equation

$$f(\{0,4,8\}) + f(\{1,5,9\}) = f(\{0,4,8\} + \{1,5,9\})$$

2. The two subgroups are a bijection.

The Major third relationship, which spans four semitones, requires the target function $f(x) = x \pm 4$ to generate the subgroup. In addition, the elements from $\{0, 4, 8\}$ and the elements from $\{1, 5, 9\}$ are a bijection (one-on-one correspondence) as $0 \mapsto 1$, $4 \mapsto 5$, and $8 \mapsto 9$ respectively. Therefore, these two subgroups are isomorphic.

This group isomorphism is directly manifest in music theory as *transposition invariance* (where changing the degree of the starting note of a musical construct does not change the perception of the musical construct, notwithstanding perfect pitch perception) and *tuning invariance* (where changing the frequency of the starting note of a musical construct does not change the perception of the musical construct, notwithstanding perfect pitch perception) [15]. Moreover, the isomorphism of the equilateral triangular lattice in Fig. 3 is useful of building musical keyboards since the dual of equilateral triangle is the hexagon which is a regular polygon of the dihedral group that is a unified tile capable of implementing transpositional invariance [8].

3 Shepard's Double Helix Model in $\mathbb{R}^3$ and Its Winding Torus in $\mathbb{R}^4$

In addition to mathematicians and musicians trying to chart the relationships of pitches, psychologists also explore ways to depict the psychological responses of musical sounds. In human pitch perception, Roger Shepard introduced a double helix model of visualizing ascending chroma and Perfect fifth relationship simultaneously [22].

Figure 4(a) shows an equilateral triangular lattice in $\mathbb{R}^2$ space. The arrangement in vertical direction represents the whole-tone relationship such as C to D, and the zigzag between the two vertical edges depicts the semi-tone relationship such as C to $C\sharp$. As shown in Fig. 4(b), when twisting the lattice along the

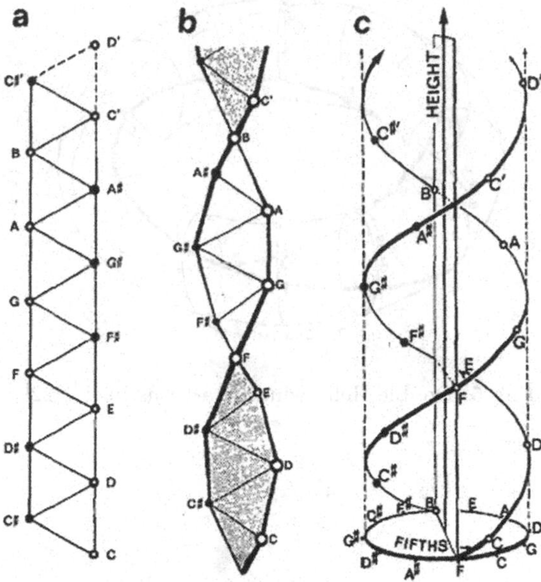

Fig. 4. Shepard's Double Helix model of human pitch perception. [22] (a) the flat strip of equilateral triangles in $\mathbb{R}^2$; (b) the strip of triangles given one complete twist per octave; (c) the resulting double helix shown as a winding around a cylinder in $\mathbb{R}^3$.

vertical direction which indicates the ascending (or descending) of octave, the lattice of equilateral triangles form a double helix structure. If this double helix structure is mapped onto a cylinder in $\mathbb{R}^3$ space, the resulting cylindrical lattice is as shown in Fig. 4(c).

The cylindrical double helix structure can collapse vertically so as to continuously vary the structure that representing the pitches between the double helix with the rectilinear axis in Fig. 4(c), and eventually becomes the variant with a completely circular axis in Fig. 5. This new structure is a torus in $\mathbb{R}^4$ space, and it embeds the cylindrical lattice. In addition, the pair of edges in Fig. 4(a) becomes two circles linked together in the torus, which actually is a "Hopf link" [12]. In Fig. 5, one circle consists of notes *C, D, E, F♯, G♯* and *A♯*, and the other circle includes notes *C♯, D♯, F, G, A* and *B* respectively.

4 Multidimensional Pitch Space Torus and Phases of Pitch-Class Sets

In the last two decades, the exploration of modelling higher dimensional tonal pitch space shown solid results, such as Dmitri Tymoczko in 2006 exploited non-Euclidean geometry space to represent a musical chord, and pointed out that the structure is an n-orbifold [23]. In 2013, Gilles Baroin introduced a model in $\mathbb{R}^4$ space which derived from two planar graphs: Triangle (C3) and Square (C4).

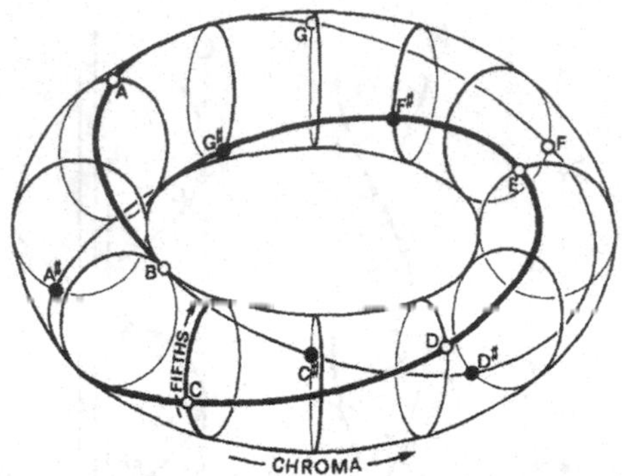

Fig. 5. Double Helix winding a torus in $\mathbb{R}^4$ [22]

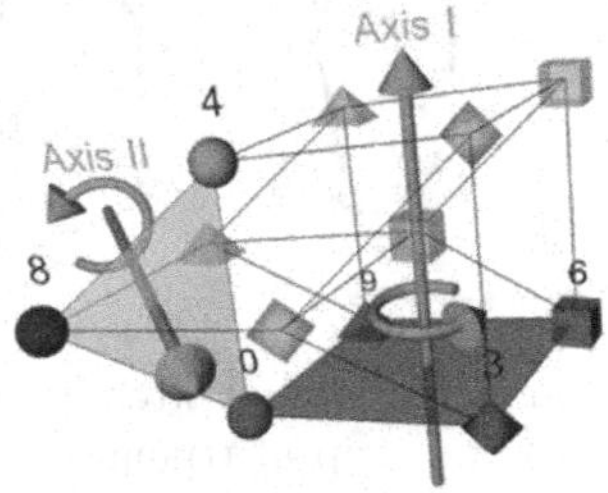

Fig. 6. Major Axes of the 4D model [3]

There are two axes in the model which indicate the rotation directions. The two axes in Fig. 6 are represented by straight lines. However, if a straight line was considered as the special case of an infinite circle $\mathbb{S}^1$ mapped into a $\mathbb{R}$ space, the Cartesian product of these two perpendicular circles is represented by a torus ($\mathbb{T}^2 = \mathbb{S}^1 \times \mathbb{S}^1$) in $\mathbb{R}^4$ space. Conclusively, it turns out the traditional Tonnetz can be embedded into a 4-dimensional hypersphere [3].

Besides leveraging algebraic topological structures to extend dimensions, another approach is mapping pitches from real space into complex space. In 2012 Emmanuel Amiot decomposed the phases of the pitch-class sets with Fourier coefficients, which delivered an even finer result on mapping chromatic scale notes onto a 4-dimensional torus surface [2].

5 Villarceau Circles and Hopf Fibration

Before introducing Villarceau circles and Hopf fibration, it is necessary to have a review of the 4-dimensional torus $\mathbb{T}^2$ as used in human pitch perception models.

Since a pitch class from the 12-tone equal tempered scale is presented by a set of points in the quotient space $\mathbb{R}/12\mathbb{Z}$, n pitch classes can be denoted as $\mathbb{R}^n/12\mathbb{Z}^n$. Hence, an n-torus can be represented by the equation $\mathbb{T}^n = \mathbb{R}^n/12\mathbb{Z}^n$. Whereas a chromatic scale is represented by a circle which is denoted as $\mathbb{S}^1$

in algebraic topology, there is the other equation $\mathbb{S}^1 = \mathbb{R}/12\mathbb{Z}$. Combining two equations together, it is easy to have $\mathbb{T}^n = (\mathbb{R}/12\mathbb{Z})^n = (\mathbb{S}^1)^n$. When n equals 2, the equation becomes $\mathbb{T}^2 = (\mathbb{S}^1)^2 = \mathbb{S}^1 \times \mathbb{S}^1$. This indicates a torus in $\mathbb{R}^4$ space could be represented by the Cartesian product of two circles $\mathbb{S}^1$ in $\mathbb{R}^2$ space. One of the circles is around its axis of rotational symmetry and the other one is around a circle in the interior of the torus.

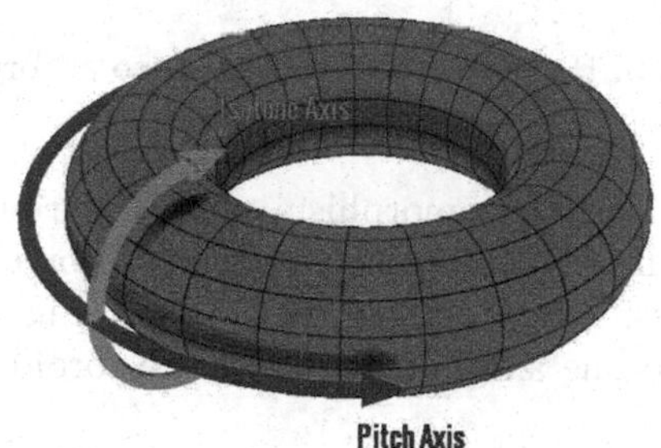

Fig. 7. Two axes for mapping Neo-Riemannian Tonnetz

Comparing to the torus in Fig. 5, the toroidal model makes sense in human pitch perception when the circle around its axis of rotational symmetry (or a.k.a. along "Toroidal" direction) represents chroma, and the circle around a circle in the interior of the torus (along the "Poloidal" direction) represent the repetition of pitches. According to [19], the repetition of the pitch direction is named "Isotone Axis", and the ascending chroma direction is named "Pitch axis" respectively. The torus in Fig. 7 can be used to map the Neo-Riemannian Tonnetz onto the surface. It should be noted that this arrangement (chroma/pitch in the torodial direction, isotone in the polodial direction) may be reversed without losing generality of the model, but most researchers have used this first arrangement and we maintain that approach.

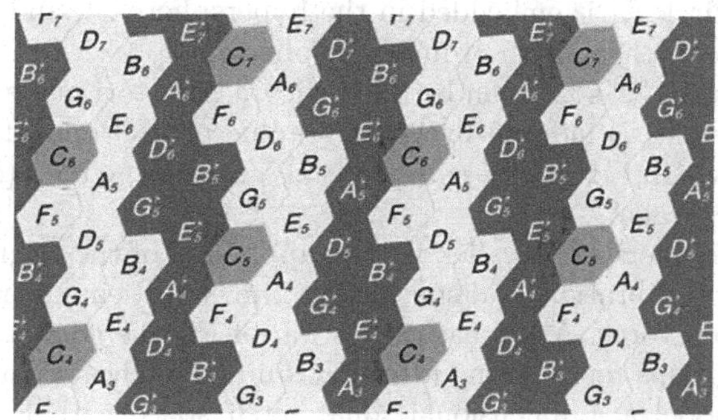

Fig. 8. Isomorphic Tessellation: Harmonic Table

Fig. 9. Harmonic Table mapping to a Torus

As an example consider the isomorphism called "Harmonic Table" presented in Fig. 8. This isomorphism uses the intervals of Major third and Minor third along the heagonal axes. When mapped to a torus (Fig. 9), this isomorphism shows the pitch and isotone axes aligned with the toroidal and poloidal directions, as discussed.

In geometry, cutting a torus with a plane bitangent to two symmetrical poloidal circles results in a pair of *Villarceau circles.* This can be seen in Fig. 10 where the bitangent plane ε is shown in pink and the coplanar pair of Villarceau circles ($M1$ and $M2$, marked in red and blue) are produced by this cutting. These two Villarceau circles are linked to each other [16]. Since the torus has symmetry of its centre, a pair of mirrored Villarceau circles can easily be generated by rotating the torus along toroidal direction with 180°. Each Villarceau circle and its 180-degree mirrored circle are also linked together. This link is a Hopf link, and the circle of a Hopf link is a Hopf fiber [14].

The *Hopf fibration* (also known as the Hopf bundle or Hopf map), named after German geometer and topologist Heinz Hopf [7] is a foundation stone in the theory of Lie Groups. The Hopf fibration describes a hypersphere (called a 3-sphere in $\mathbb{R}^4$ space) in terms of circles (the "fiber") and an ordinary sphere [14].

The denotation of fiber bundle (bundle of linked circles) is:

$$\mathbb{S}^1 \hookrightarrow \mathbb{S}^3 \overset{p}{\mapsto} \mathbb{S}^2$$

which means a circle $\mathbb{S}^1$ is embedded in the hypersphere $\mathbb{S}^3$, and the Hopf map $p : \mathbb{S}^3 \mapsto \mathbb{S}^2$ projects $\mathbb{S}^3$ onto an ordinary 2-sphere $\mathbb{S}^2$.

Theoretically, an $\mathbb{R}^3$ space can be filled with nested tori made of linking Villarceau circles, which is induced by Stereographic projection of the Hopf fibration [14]. As shown in Fig. 11, the same type of Villarceau circles (or Hopf fibers) are considered "parallel".

Because these fibers are parallel, we can apply any of the original pitch-class mappings onto this fibration, and specifically, the Neo-Riemannian Tonnetz can be mapped onto a torus. Along each direction of Fig. 3's equilateral triangular lattice, the subgroups representing a relationship of pitches are always parallel. Therefore, to model a 4-dimensional tonal pitch space with Hopf fibers, two subgroups of the pitches (in $\mathbb{R}/12\mathbb{Z}$ space) need to be selected to map onto the a Hopf link (including two types of Hopf fibers). For example, the Perfect fifth

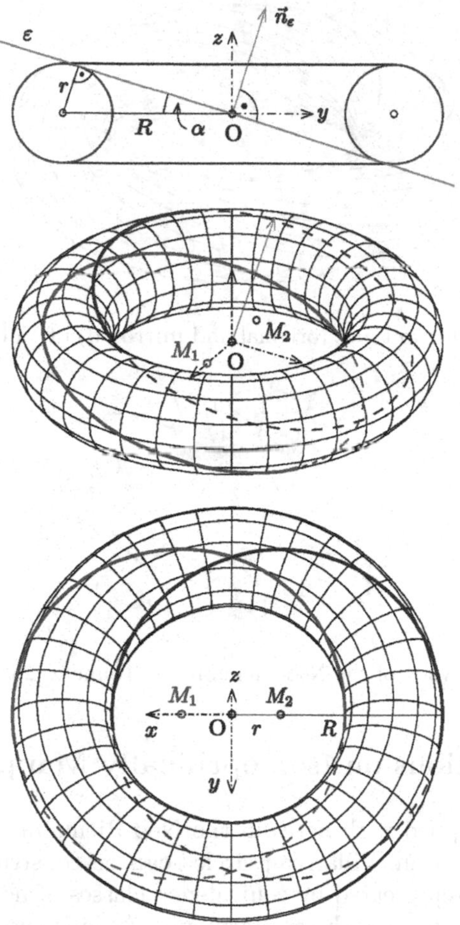

Fig. 10. Villarceau circles on a Torus [25] (Color figure online)

is mapped onto one type of Hopf fiber, and the Major third is mapped onto the other type of Hopf fiber, where two Hopf fibers combine to make a Hopf link.

However, the poloidal direction of the torus may not always show the partition of same pitch in a single octave. Instead, it could show the partition of the pitch that is several octaves when the poloidal circle of the torus gets larger. To force the poloidal circle to show a relationship of pitches in a single octave, the paralleled Villarceau circles have to vary to non-round closed curves but still keep parallel structure. For example, in Fig. 12, the Perfect fifth (in blue) and the Major third (in red) represent two relationship of pitches individually, the Minor third (in green) has been laid along the poloidal direction. Because the Minor third poloidal circle represents a subgroup of pitches in $\mathbb{R}/12\mathbb{Z}$ space rather than Minor third pitches with partition in $\mathbb{R}$ space, it is obvious that the paralleled red curves and blue curves are not, in fact, circles anymore.

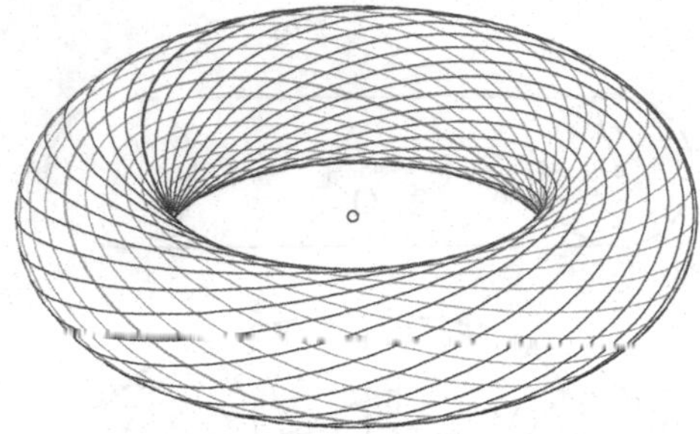

Fig. 11. Torus with two types (original and mirrored) of Villarceau circles [25]

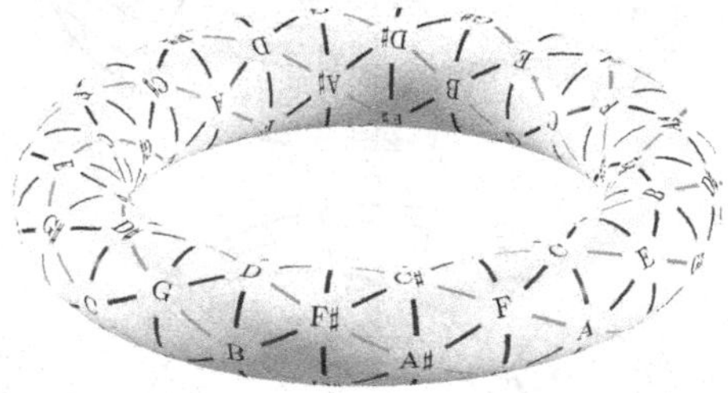

Fig. 12. One toroidal view of the Neo-Riemannian Tonnetz [26] (Color figure online)

6 Hopf Fibrations on Isomoprhically Mapped Torus

When a torus is mapped with notes in the Neo-Riemannian sense, or with an isomorphic representation, Villarceau circles can be constructed by linking the points on the torus represented by equivalence classes of notes. As an example, consider the torus mapped with the Harmonic Table isomorphism as it Fig. 13. We can connect the Major third equivalence classes on one axis, consisting of the following sets of notes C-E-A♭-C; D♭-F-A-D♭; D-G♭-B♭-D; E♭-G-B-E♭. Similarly, we can connect the Minor third equivalences classes on the other axis, using these sets of notes C-E♭-G♭-A-C; D♭-E-G-B♭-D♭; D-F-A♭-B-D

Fig. 13. Hopf link (consisting of two Villarceau circles) on Harmonic Table Torus

Fig. 14. Hopf bundle on Harmonic Table Torus (Color figure online)

In Fig. 14, we can see the Major third equivalence classes in red, and the Minor third equivalence classes in blue. Each set forms one Villarceau circle, and the collection of these orthogonal sets creates a complete Hopf fibration.

7 Conclusion and Future Work

In this paper, the existing human pitch perception models and tonal pitch spaces lattices are well studied. Through the line segments in $\mathbb{R}$ space, the circular chromatic scale in $\mathbb{R}^2$ space, the double helix model in $\mathbb{R}^3$ space, and the torus in $\mathbb{R}^4$ space, we attempted to find a generic way of modelling the tonal pitch space onto manifolds. After exploring the approaches in the interaction of two seemingly independent disciplines human pitch perception and algebra topology, a new method of modelling 4-dimensional tonal pitch spaces is presented, which leverages the knowledge of Hopf fibration.

In the future, one possible research could be the torus knots which presenting the sinusoidal phases of the musical notes on a Hopf fibers bundled torus. Topologically, a knot is a continuous looped path that may be intertwined with itself in one or more ways. When a knot lies on the surface of a torus in $\mathbb{R}^3$ space,

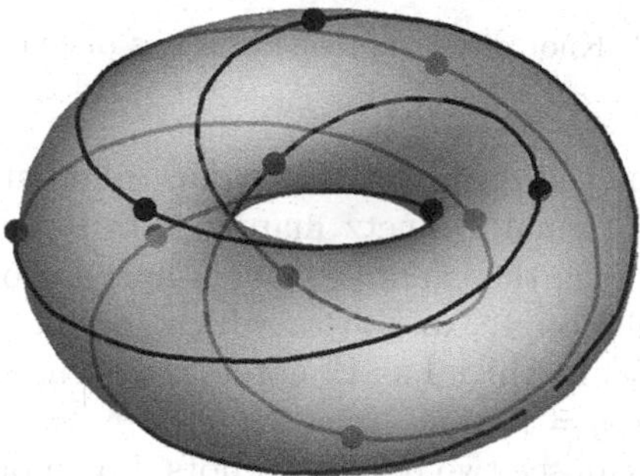

Fig. 15. Torus knot (3,4) shows the continuous orbits of all pitches of the chromatic scale in a $\mathbb{T}^2$ Torus [3]

it is called torus knot. This torus knot is denoted with two numbers: (p, q), where p indicates the number of times the knot's path goes around its axis of rotational symmetry, and q indicates the number of times the knot's path goes around a circle in the interior of the torus [18]. For example, Fig. 15 shows a torus knot that could be applied to a Neo-Riemannian Tonnetz mapping torus. The 12 black dots indicate the 12 notes within a chromatic scale with different phases in complex space [2]. It is easy to count the number of rounding the rotational symmetrical axis and the number of rounding circle of interior of the torus. Apparently, in this example, this torus knot is a (3, 4) knot.

Fig. 16. Knot of the equivalence class of Major thirds (C-E-A♭-C)

Fig. 17. Knot of the equivalence class of semitones

Knots can represent the path of a subgroup different from the subgroups used to construct the original Tonnetz mapping. In other words, the different combinations of p and q, in the example, reflect how a group of chromatic scale can be divided into subgroups. No matter which combination is used, in order to map the chromatic scale which has 12 notes, the torus knot (p, q) would need to fulfil the equation $p \cdot q = 12$.

As an example, we can see two different knots drawn on the Harmonic Table isomorphic torus example from before. In Fig. 16, the equivalence class of Major thirds (C-E-A♭-C) is shown, and in Fig. 17, the equivalence class of semitones is shown. In both cases, a Hopf fibration is not created, but instead, a knot.

Though the mathematical model for the torus knots can easily be created, more exploration and research are needed to study the position of musical notes on the surface of the knot, which potentially presents the sinusoidal phases of the musical notes. In addition, the torus knots can be further utilized in the research of human pitch perception.

References

1. Allenby, R., Rings, Fields and Groups: An Introduction to Abstract Algebra. Butterworth-Heinemann, Oxford (1991)
2. Amiot, E.: The Torii of phases. In: Yust, J., Wild, J., Burgoyne, J.A. (eds.) MCM 2013. LNCS (LNAI), vol. 7937, pp. 1–18. Springer, Heidelberg (2013). https://doi.org/10.1007/978-3-642-39357-0_1
3. Baroin, G.: The planet-4D model: an original hypersymmetric music space based on graph theory. In: Agon, C., Andreatta, M., Assayag, G., Amiot, E., Bresson, J., Mandereau, J. (eds.) MCM 2011. LNCS (LNAI), vol. 6726, pp. 326–329. Springer, Heidelberg (2011). https://doi.org/10.1007/978-3-642-21590-2_25
4. Cohn, R.: Introduction to Neo-Riemannian theory: a survey and a historical perspective. J. Music Theory **42**(2), 167–180 (1998)
5. Euler, L.: De Harmoniae Veris Principiis per Speculum Musicum Repraesentatis. In: Novi commentarii academiae scientiarum Petropolitanae, St. Petersburg, pp. 330–353 (1774)
6. Fiore, T.M., Noll, T.: Commuting groups and the topos of triads. In: Proceedings of Mathematics and Computation in Music - Third International Conference, MCM 2011, Paris, France, pp. 69–83 (2011). https://doi.org/10.1007/978-3-642-21590-2_6
7. Hopf, H.: Über die Abbildungen der dreidimensionalen Sphäre auf die Kugelfläche. Mathematische Annalen **104**(1), 637–665 (1931). https://doi.org/10.1007/BF01457962
8. Hu, H., Gerhard, D.: WebHexIso: a customizable web-based hexagonal isomorphic musical keyboard interface. In: Proceedings of the 42th International Computer Music Conference, Utrecht, Netherlands, pp. 294–297 (2016)
9. Hu, H., Park, B., Gerhard, D.: Mapping tone helixes to cylindrical lattices using Chiral Angles. In: Proceedings of the 12th International Sound and Music Computing Conference, Maynooth, Ireland, pp. 447–454 (2015)
10. Klapuri, A., Davy, M.: Signal Processing Methods for Music Transcription. Springer, Heidelberg (2006). https://doi.org/10.1007/0-387-32845-9
11. Krumhansl, C.L.: Perceptual structures for tonal music. Music Percept. **1**, 28–62 (1983)
12. Kusner, R.B., Sullivan, J.M.: On distortion and thickness of knots. In: Whittington, S.G., De Sumners, W., Lodge, T. (eds.) Topology and Geometry in Polymer Science (IMA), vol. 103, pp. 67–78. Springer, New York (1998). https://doi.org/10.1007/978-1-4612-1712-1_7
13. Lerdahl, F.: Tonal Pitch Space. Oxford University Press, Oxford (2001)
14. Lyons, D.W.: An elementary introduction to the Hopf fibration. Math. Mag. **76**(2), 87–98 (2003). http://www.jstor.org/stable/3219300
15. Milne, A., Sethares, W., Plamondon, J.: Tuning continua and keyboard layouts. J. Math. Music **2**, 1–19 (2008)
16. Monera, M.G., Monterde, J.: Building a Torus with Villarceau sections. J. Geom. Graph. **15**(1), 93–99 (2011)

17. Morris, R.D., Rahn, J.: Basic Atonal Theory. Longman, New York (1980). Music Theory Spectrum 4(1), 138–154 (1982). https://doi.org/10.2307/746016
18. Murasugi, K.: Knot Theory and Its Applications. Birkhäuser, Boston (2008). https://doi.org/10.1007/978-0-8176-4719-3
19. Park, B., Gerhard, D.: Discrete isomorphic completeness and a unified isomorphic layout format. In: Proceedings of the Sound and Music Computing Conference. Stockholm, Sweden (2013)
20. Piston, W., DeVoto, M.: Harmony. W. W. Norton & Company, New York (1987)
21. Riemann, H.: Ideen zu einer â Lehre von den Tonvorstellungen, â Jahrbuch der Bibliothek. Peters, pp. 21–22 (1914–1915)
22. Shepard, R.N.: Geometrical approximations to the structure of musical pitch. Psychol. Rev. **89**(4), 3005 (1982)
23. Tymoczko, D.: The geometry of musical chords. Science **313**(5783), 72–74 (2006). https://doi.org/10.1126/science.1126287. https://science.sciencemag.org/content/313/5783/72
24. Tymoczko, D.: Three conceptions of musical distance. In: Chew, E., Childs, A., Chuan, C.-H. (eds.) MCM 2009. CCIS, vol. 38, pp. 258–272. Springer, Heidelberg (2009). https://doi.org/10.1007/978-3-642-02394-1_24
25. Wikipedia contributors: Villarceau circles – Wikipedia, The Free Encyclopedia. https://en.wikipedia.org/w/index.php?title=Villarceau_circles&oldid=875134100 (2018). Accessed 10 July 2019
26. Wikipedia contributors: Neo-Riemannian theory – Wikipedia, The Free Encyclopedia (2019). https://en.wikipedia.org/w/index.php?title=Neo-Riemannian_theory&oldid=893433197. Accessed 10 July 2019

Automatic Dastgah Recognition Using Markov Models

Luciano Ciamarone(✉), Baris Bozkurt(✉), and Xavier Serra(✉)

Universitat Pompeu Fabra, Barcelona, Spain
luciano.ciamarone@libero.it, {baris.bozkurt,xavier.serra}@upf.edu

Abstract. This work focuses on automatic Dastgah recognition of monophonic audio recordings of Iranian music using Markov Models. We present an automatic recognition system that models the sequence of intervals computed from quantized pitch data (estimated from audio) with Markov processes. Classification of an audio file is performed by finding the closest match between the Markov matrix of the file and the (template) matrices computed from the database for each Dastgah. Applying a leave-one-out evaluation strategy on a dataset comprised of 73 files, an accuracy of 0.986 has been observed for one of the four tested distance calculation methods.

Keywords: Mode recognition · Dastgah recognition · Iranian music

1 Introduction

The presented study represents the first attempt in applying Markov Models to a non-western musical mode recognition task. The proposed approach focuses on Persian musical modes which are called *Dastgah*. Several different approaches to the same task have already been documented. In 2011 Abdoli [1] achieved an overall accuracy of 0.85 on a 5 Dastgahs classification task by computing similarity measures between Interval Type 2 Fuzzy Sets. In 2016 Heydarian [9] compared the performances of different methods including chroma features, spectral average, pitch histograms and the use of symbolic data. He reported an accuracy of 0.86 using Manhattan metric as a distance calculation method between a signal and a set of templates that are constructed in a former training stage. Another contribution to the field comes from research works in Turkish music [13] and [3] from which this work inherit some analysis techniques [8]. None of these previous works uses Markov models for their classification purposes while for western music several applications has been explored [10,11] although only for chord progression thus under the point of view of music harmony. The presented work, instead, investigates the music melodic aspect[1] developing a mathematical model able to

[1] Markov Models have been extensively used in the past for composition purposes as melodic progressions generators, see for example some Xenakis's works like *Analogique B* [4].

L. Ciamarone—Independent researcher.

R. Kronland-Martinet et al. (Eds.): CMMR 2019, LNCS 12631, pp. 157–165, 2021.
https://doi.org/10.1007/978-3-030-70210-6_11

encode the typical melodic interval progression of Persian Dastgahs in the form of Markov Transition Probabilities Matrices (Sect. 3.2). A subsequent distance evaluation method between matrices has been applied in order to carry out the classification task (Sect. 3.3). Finally, standard machine learning evaluation has been carried to measure system performances. An accuracy of 0.98 has been reached on a database of 73 audio files belonging to the seven main Persian Dastgahs. The complete algorithm has been publicly shared on a github repository [6] for the sake of reproducibility. In the final part of the presented paper future developments of this research have been identified.

2 Persian Traditional Music

Persian music is based on a set of seven principal Dastgahs: *shur*, *homayun*, *segah*, *chahargah*, *mahour*, *rast-panjgah* and *nava*. The seven main modes and their five derivatives (*abu ata*, *bayat-e tork*, *afshari*, *dashti* and *bayat-e esfehan*) are collectively called the twelve dastgahs, they cover most of the structures in Persian music [1,9].

Traditional Persian music has the octave concept and one octave always contains seven principal notes. The tuning system of Persian music applies 24 quarter tones per octave [14] and does not rely on equal temperament. The most authentic definition has been given by Farhat [7] who teaches that Persian music has very characteristic intervals, one of them is the neutral second. This is a flexible interval but in all its variations it is noticeably larger then the minor second (western semitone) and smaller then the major second (western whole tone). Another typical interval [7] is an interval which is larger then the major second (western whole tone) but smaller then the western minor third. Rhythmic structure of Persian music is generally strictly connected to voice and speech, often music is conceived as accompaniment for singers. Each *Dastgah* consists of some partial melodies called *Gushe*, the arrangement of *Gushe*s during the performance is called *Radif*. Conceptually Persian music is conceived like melodic motives around a central tone and modulation is conceived as changing the central tone.

3 Methodology

The presented Dastgah recognition system applies a sequence of three processes: pitch estimation and quantization, Markov Modeling, and classification. Markov chains have been used for modeling the sequence of musical intervals. The concept behind Persian musical intervals is the same as in western music, which is a frequency ratio between two notes. For example the western musical fifth is defined as $\sqrt[12]{2^7} \cong 3/2$[2]. The presented Markov algorithm models in the form of

[2] An example of western fifth is the interval between A4 = 440 Hz and E5 = 659.25 Hz (659.25/440 = 1.498 $\cong \sqrt[12]{2^7}$.

Transition Probability Matrix, the sequence (in time) of musical intervals contained in each audio file. The synthetic example in Fig. 1 can help understanding the Markov Matrix building strategy. Frequency values in time like in Fig. 2 are converted in a vector of consecutive musical intervals; in this example [*3/2, 3/2, 2, 2, 2, 3, 3, 2*]. Thus we have three Markov states: $A = 3/2$, $B = 2$ and $C = 3$. Finally, transitions between consecutive states are counted and cumulated to build up the Markov matrix. As we can see transitions from B to A never occurs (neither C to A and A to C), furthermore if we had a state $D = 5/2$ it would have occurrence count equal to *0* in this example.

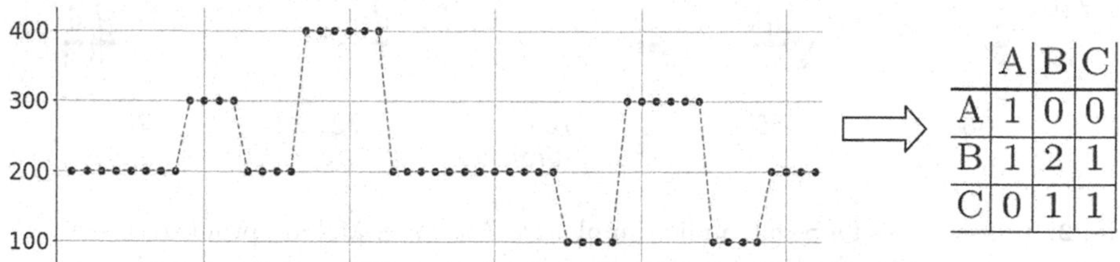

	A	B	C
A	1	0	0
B	1	2	1
C	0	1	1

Fig. 1. Example of Markov Matrix building strategy starting from quantized pitch data (this is not real data).

3.1 Pitch Detection and Quantization

For pitch detection, we have used the algorithm explained in [2] (more specifically the implementation by its authors[3]) which mainly applies post-filters to the output of the Melodia algorithm [12]. According to the implementation[3] of [2], pitch quantization is achieved by mapping each pitch value to the closest pitch histogram peak where pitch histograms are computed as in [8]. Frequency quantization has the effect of stabilizing the values given by the pith detection algorithm forcing them to be equal to the closest pitch histogram peak [8] (for example the sequence of pitches: [200.1, 200.2, 199.85] is forced to be [200, 200, 200] 200 Hz is the closest pitch histogram peak).

Secondly, spurious and very short duration notes has been removed because they are assumed to be detection errors. When a quantized note is removed (because of too short in duration) it is replaced (and merged) with the following stable note (a stable note is assumed to be at least 15 ms long). The quantized pitch data obtained as a result of these two post processing steps are exemplified in Fig. 2.

3.2 Markov Model

The Markov Model builder block uses the data generated by the pitch detection and quantization algorithm in order to create a vector of musical intervals

[3] https://github.com/MTG/predominantmelodymakam.

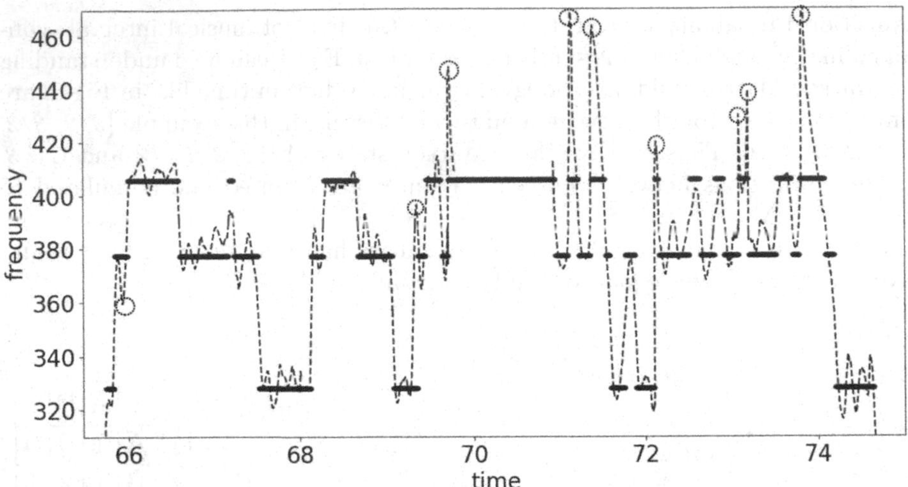

Fig. 2. Ten seconds of a Segah audio sample. *Dashed Line:* Melody profile of the audio input as analyzed by the Essentia monophonic pitch detection algorithm. *Continuous Line:* Same melody profile after post processing for stabilizing the frequency values. *Dotted Circles:* Peaks that generated too short duration quantized notes which have been replaced and merged with the following stable note.

which are calculated from the ratio between two consecutive frequency values (as explained at the beginning of this Sect. 3 and in Fig. 1). The resulting sequence of musical intervals (from one audio file) can be concatenated (using several audio files) in case one wants to build up the database matrix associated with one of the seven possible Dastgah considered in the present work.
Building the Transition Probability Matrix associated with the sequence of musical intervals consists in counting the number of transition occurrences between consecutive intervals (as exemplified in Fig. 1). All probability values have been normalized to one in the end. After that a vector containing the count of the occurrences of each Markov Model state has been created, the Fig. 3 shows this vector calculated for a small audio chunk belonging to Dastgah-e Segah.

The vector plotted in Fig. 3 is a sort of one-dimensional view of a Markov Matrix, on the x axis there are the Markov Matrix indexes from one to ns (where ns is the total number of Markov States); on y axis there is the normalized frequency of occurrence of each state. The presented Dastgah Recognition system does not use a previously defined TET musical system, furthermore there are no octave folding operations and the dimension of the Markov Matrix does not need to be predefined; it just needs to be greater then the maximum number of playable musical intervals and sufficiently small not to overload the computational cost of the whole algorithm. Results presented in this paper have been obtained using 98 Markov States (ns = 98). Each Markov State represents a bin

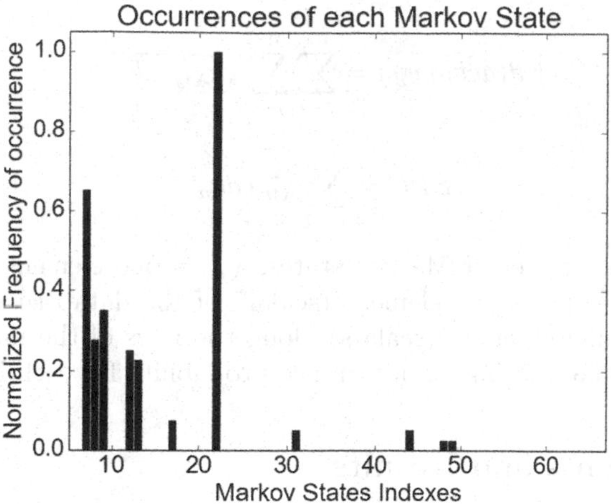

Fig. 3. Markov states frequency of occurrence for a small chunk of Dastgah-e Segah.

whose width is equal to $(\frac{1}{ns}+1)^4$, the computed musical intervals are mapped into these bins (this means that small fluctuations of frequency ratios are mapped into the same bin if those fluctuations are contained in the bin width) [6]. In Fig. 3 there are lots of Markov states with number of occurrences equal to zero, this means that for that audio sample, no musical intervals have been mapped into those bins, this is why this vector can be considered as a first raw fingerprint of the Dastgah to which the audio file belongs to.

3.3 Classification

In order to classify one unknown audio file as belonging to one of the seven considered families of Dastgah it is necessary to implement a metric able to measure the distance between the matrix associated to the unknown audio file and the seven database matrices associated to the seven Dastgah. In this work four distance candidates have been tested: Euclidean distance (Eq. 1), Kullback-Leibler distance (Eq. 2), Bhattacharyya likelihood (Eq. 3) and the last metric (which is also in the form of a likelihood) State Probability Correlation (Eq. 4). This last metric basically performs the dot product between *Frequency of Occurrence* vectors like the one showed in Fig. 3.

$$euclidean = \sqrt{\sum_{i=1}^{ns}\sum_{j=1}^{ns}(\chi_{ij} - db_{ij})^2}\ . \tag{1}$$

$$kullback = \sum_{i=1}^{ns}\sum_{j=1}^{ns}\chi_{ij}\cdot log\left(\frac{\chi_{ij}}{db_{ij}}\right)\ . \tag{2}$$

[4] Using 98 Markov States each bin width is equal to $\frac{1}{98}+1 = 1.0102$ which is smaller then the western music semitone $\sqrt[12]{2} = 1.0595$.

$$battacharyya = \sum_{i=1}^{ns}\sum_{j=1}^{ns} \sqrt{\chi_{ij} \cdot db_{ij}} \,. \tag{3}$$

$$SPC = \sum_{n=1}^{ns} \bar{\chi_n} \cdot \bar{db_n} \,. \tag{4}$$

Where ns is the number of Markov states, χ_{ij} is one element (scalar) of the unknown matrix, db_{ij} is one element (scalar) of the database matrix; $\bar{\chi_n}$ and $\bar{db_n}$ are the cumulated values (scalars) along the rows of the matrices in order to obtain a cumulative value of occurrence probability for each Markov state.

4 Experiments and Results

The experiments carried out had the goal of testing and validating the classification algorithm, a standard machine learning evaluation procedure has been applied. A *Leave One Out* testing strategy has been implemented and in the end, standard machine learning evaluation parameters have been calculated. A github repository [6] has been created where the testing package can be downloaded and executed again for obtaining the same results presented in this paper.

4.1 Dataset

In the aforementioned github repository an *annotation.json* file can be found. In this file is contained the formal description of the used database of audio files. A total amount of 73 audio files has been collected with average duration of about two minutes each (maximum 4:50, minimum 1:10), they belongs to the seven Dastgah category considered in this work: Segah (16 files), RastPanjgah (5 files), Nava (7 files), Mahour (15 files), Homayun (10 files), Chahargah (8 files) and Shur (12 files). The recordings are monophonic (recording of a single instrument) and does not include mode transitions/modulations. There are no constraints concerning the instruments, there are file audio containing voice samples, tar, se-tar, santur among the others.

4.2 Testing Strategy and Results

A *Leave One Out* validation procedure has been considered for the presented work. The procedure uses one sample for testing and all the rest for modeling. This is repeated for each sample and the results are averaged. At the end of validation process the following standard machine learning evaluation measures has been calculated: Recall, Specificity, Precision, False Positive Rate, False Negative Rate, F1 and Accuracy. The four different distance calculation methods are explicated in Eqs. 1, 2, 3 and 4. Table 1 shows the evaluation measures obtained for each distance metric.

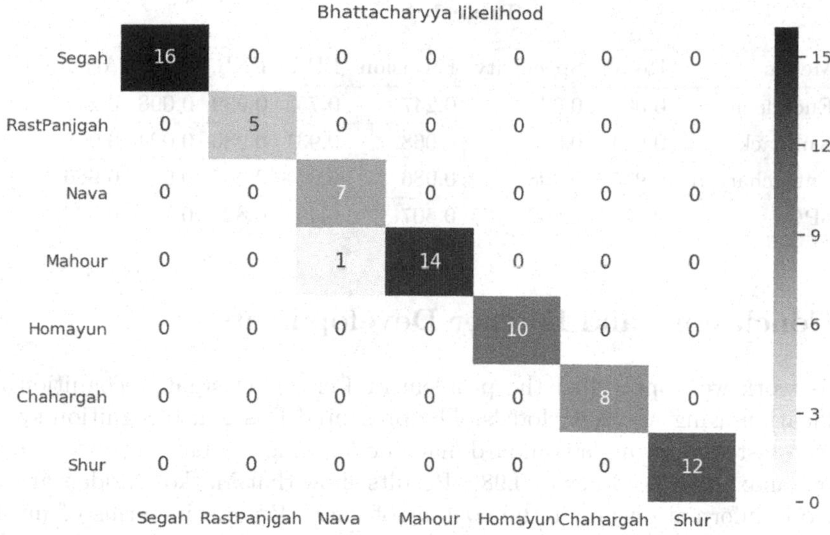

Fig. 4. Confusion matrix for the Bhattacharyya likelihood calculation method

The first two methods gave very poor results below the 50% of correct answers. The logarithmic terms in Eq. 2 makes this metric particularly suitable for very smooth distributions like Gaussian ones; in our case this metric suffers the big entropy (from a statistical point of view) of the data it is applied to. The last method (SPC) gave an *Accuracy* of 0.507 and a *FPR* (*False Positive Rate*) of 0.493. The third distance calculation method (*Bhattacharyya likelihood*) gave instead an *Accuracy* of 0.986 and a *FPR* of 0.014. Figure 4 shows the confusion matrix for the Bhattacharyya likelihood.

Results clearly state that Eq. 3 is the best way of calculating similarities between Markov Transition Probability Matrices; in fact this method resulted in only one error on 73 audio file which means a percentage of correct answers equal to 98.6%. The only error of the *Bhattacharyya* classification method is an audio file belonging to the *Mahour* family which has been classified as *Nava*. The reason why all the other metrics are so far from the Battacharyya metric in terms of results, is that Eq. 3 is the only one which uses an *element by element* product between Markov Matrices, this produces the effect that only values different from zero contribute to the total sum; non-zero values represent specific transitions between consecutive musical intervals and these transitions are the musical core of *Dastgahs*.

Table 1. Scores.

Metric	Recall	Specificity	Precision	FPR	FNR	F1	Accuracy
Euclidean	0.061	0.663	0.247	0.753	0.939	0.098	0.247
Kullback	0.014	0.306	0.068	0.931	0.986	0.024	0.068
Battacharyya	0.935	0.998	0.986	0.014	0.065	0.960	0.986
[illegible]	0.170	0.860	0.507	0.493	0.829	0.255	0.507

5 Conclusions and Further Developments

In this work we approached the problem of Persian Dastgah recognition and classification using Markov Models. The presented Dastgah recognition system has been tested following a standard machine learning evaluation procedure and it gave a maximum accuracy of 0.986. Results show that Markov Models are able to encode information about the content of each Dastgah in terms of musical intervals and their temporal sequence. The presented system has been tested on monophonic recordings of short duration. Our further efforts will be dedicated to building a larger dataset including longer recordings and improvisations as well as multi instrumental recordings.

References

1. Abdoli, S.: Iranian traditional music dastgah classification. In: Proceedings of the 12th International Conference on Music Information Retrieval, ISMIR, Miami (2011)
2. Atli, H. S., Uyar, B., Senturk, S., Bozkurt, B., Serra, X.: Audio feature extraction for exploring Turkish makam music. In: Proceedings of 3rd International Conference on Audio Technologies for Music and Media, Ankara, pp. 142–153 (2014)
3. Bozkurt, B., Ayangil, R., Holzapfel, A.: Computational analysis of Turkish makam music: review of state-of-the-art and challenges. J. New Music Res. **43**(1), 3–23 (2014)
4. Ciamarone, L.: Towards a real time implementation of Analogique B. In: Proceedings of the international Symposium Xenakis. Xenakis, The electroacoustic music, université Paris 8 (2012)
5. C++ library for audio and music analysis, description and synthesis, including Python bindings. https://github.com/MTG/essentia
6. Dastgah-Recognition-System Github repository. https://github.com/luciamarock/Dastgah-Recognition-System
7. Farhat, H.: The dastgah concept in Persian music. Cambridge University Press, Cambridge (1990)
8. Gedik, A.C., Bozkurt, B.: Pitch-frequency histogram-based music information retrieval for Turkish music. Sig. Process. **90**(4), 1049–1063 (2010)
9. Heydarian, P.: Automatic recognition of Persian musical modes in audio musical signals. Ph.D. thesis, London Metropolitan University (2016)
10. Noland, K.: Computational tonality estimation: signal processing and Hidden Markov models. Ph.D. thesis, Queen Mary, University of London (2009)

11. Noland, K., Sandler, M.: Key estimation using a Hidden Markov Model. In: Proceedings of the 7th International Conference on Music Information Retrieval (ISMIR), Victoria, Canada (2006)
12. Salamon, J., Gomez, E.: Melody extraction from polyphonic music signals using pitch contour characteristics. IEEE Trans. Audio Speech Lang. Process. **20**(6), 1759–1770 (2012)
13. Senturk, S.: Computational analysis of audio recordings and music scores for the description and discovery of Ottoman-Turkish makam music, Ph.D. dissertation, Universitat Pompeu Fabra, (2016)
14. Vaziri, A.N.: Dastur-e Tar, Tehran (1913)

Chord Function Identification with Modulation Detection Based on HMM

Yui Uehara[1(✉)], Eita Nakamura[2(✉)], and Satoshi Tojo[1(✉)]

[1] Japan Advanced Institute of Science and Technology, 1-1 Asahidai, Nomi, Ishikawa 923-1292, Japan
{yuehara,tojo}@jaist.ac.jp

[2] Kyoto University, Yoshida-honmachi, Sakyo-ku, Kyoto 606-8501, Japan
enakamura@sap.ist.i.kyoto-u.ac.jp

Abstract. This study aims at identifying the chord functions by statistical machine learning. Those functions found in the traditional harmony theory are not versatile for the various music styles, and we envisage that the statistical method would more faithfully reflect the music style we have targeted. In machine learning, we adopt hidden Markov models (HMMs); we evaluate the performance by perplexity and optimize the parameterization of HMM for each given number of hidden states. Thereafter, we apply the acquired parameters to the detection of modulation. We evaluate the plausibility of the partitioning by modulation by the likelihood value. As a result, the six-state model achieved the highest likelihood value both for the major keys and for the minor keys. We could observe finer-grained chord functions in the six-state models, and also found that they assigned different functional roles to the two tonalities.

Keywords: Chord function · Hidden Markov model · Modulation detection

1 Introduction

The chord functions are one of the most fundamental bases of tonal music to identify the key. Although the traditional functional harmony theory well describes the general roles of chords, the functions should have been diversified in accordance with the target music.

Previously chord function identification has been carried out mainly by statistical clustering algorithms [4,8]. Since these statistical methods learn from raw data instead of the textbook theory, they have the potential to reflect the difference of music styles. A recent study proposed a generative model [12], which is advantageous in its predictive power and in its applicability to practical problems such as melody harmonization [11]. However, this study focused on popular music and the key was assumed to be invariant within each piece. In our research, we consult J. S. Bach's music, thus the modulation detection

R. Kronland-Martinet et al. (Eds.): CMMR 2019, LNCS 12631, pp. 166–178, 2021.
https://doi.org/10.1007/978-3-030-70210-6_12

would be inevitable. Thus far, modulation detection has been carried out either by heuristics [8] or by a key-finding algorithm [4] though there have been still several difficult cases to determine the key [10].

We conceive that the local keys could be also determined by the functional progression of chords. Therefore, we propose a new dynamic modulation detection method, applying the statistically found chord functions. Here, the optimal number of functions would be also determined computationally so that it maximizes the likelihood of chord progressions in the entire corpus. In this research, we achieve the detection of the data-oriented chord functions, together with the detection of modulation. We envisage that we would obtain finer-grained chord functions which faithfully reflect the targeted music style. Our method is new in that we do not need to prefix the scope of modulation as opposed to the algorithm using the histogram of pitch classes [3,5,10,13].

We begin this paper by reviewing related works, especially the key detection algorithms and the statistical learning methods of the chord functions in Sect. 2. Then, we propose our method in Sect. 3, and thereafter show the experimental results in Sect. 4. We conclude in Sect. 5.

2 Related Work

2.1 Key Detection Algorithms

Among the key detection algorithms based on the histogram of the pitch classes [3,5,10,13], the most well-known one is the Krumhansl-Schmuckler algorithm that adopts the key-profile obtained by a psychological experiment [5]. More recently, the key-profile was obtained from music data by using a simple Bayesian probabilistic method [10] and the Latent Dirichlet Allocation (LDA) [3]. Although histogram-based key detection algorithms are widely used, they impose us a restriction to fix a scope beforehand.

Sakamoto et al. [9] employed the distance between chords by using Tonal Pitch Space (TPS) [6] rather than the pitch classes. Given a sequence of Berklee chord names, the key is detected by the Viterbi algorithm, not requiring a fixed scope. A Berklee chord can be interpreted in multiple keys; for example, the chord **C** is **I** of C major key as well as **IV** of G major key. Therefore, the network of candidate nodes consists of keys with degree names. Since TPS does not have adjustable parameters, it cannot reflect the difference in music styles.

2.2 Statistical Learning of the Chord Functions

Statistical learning of the chord functions has been studied by classifying the chords using clustering algorithms. Rohrmeier and Cross [8] adopted the hierarchical cluster analysis to find the statistical properties of the chords, where the most distinctive cluster of the pitch class sets reflected the dominant motion in both major and minor keys. They also found that the result for the minor key was significantly different from that for the major key. The clusters that represent the Tonic and Dominant of the relative major key were obtained.

Jacoby et al. [4] also carried out the clustering of the chords in J. S. Bach's chorales and some other datasets. They proposed the evaluation method using two criteria, accuracy and complexity, inspired by the information theory. They introduced the optimal complexity-accuracy curve, which is formed by the maximal accuracy for each complexity. When using diatonic scale degrees as the surface tokens, the functional harmony theory that uses Tonic, Dominant, Sub-dominant clustering was plotted on the optimal curve, while the Major, Minor, Diminished clustering was far less accurate. This means that the functional harmony theory is more favorable than Major, Minor, Diminished clustering when using the diatonic scale degrees as the surface tokens. In addition, they employed the analysis with automatically labelled data. They adopted the key-detection algorithm of White and Quinn [13] that employed the Krumhansl-Shmuckler algorithm [5] on windows of eight slices, and picked up the most common 22 pitch classes (with the bass notes) as the surface tokens. They reported that the obtained clusters were quite close to the Tonic, Dominant, Sub-dominant classification when the number of the categories was 3.

On the other hand, Tsushima et al. [12] found the chord functions in datasets of popular music pieces, using generative models rather than clustering: HMM and Probabilistic Context Free Grammar (PCFG). They reported that when the number of states was 4, the output probability of HMM trained with a popular music dataset could be interpreted as the chord functions: Tonic, Dominant, Sub-dominant, and Others [12], though the model achieved less perplexity with more states. Although PCFG is more advantageous since it can represent more external structures such as long-range dependency of cadence, the reported performance did not exceed that of the HMM. Using a trained HMM as the initial value of PCFG was also found to be clearly effective. However, for the melody harmonization task, PCFG was reported more effective than HMM [11]. For training the HMM, they tested the expectation-maximization (EM) algorithm and Gibbs Sampling (GS) since GS showed significantly higher accuracy than the EM algorithm in the part-of-speech tagging task [2]. They reported that the GS algorithm may perform better especially for a large number of hidden states since it can avoid being trapped in bad local optima.

3 Chord Function Identification with HMM

Following the previous works, we employed a statistical approach to identify chord functions. We chose the HMM for our model because its structure agrees well with that of the functional harmony theory. We expect that the states of the HMM represent chord functions, instead of another possible approach that assumes chord symbols as the hidden states and surface notes as the output tokens.

We obtained the chord functions with the plausible number of states that was fed back by the modulation detection in the following steps.

1. Train the HMM in the range of 2–12 states and choose the best parameterization for each number of states in terms of perplexity.

2. Calculate the likelihood of the chord progression of every candidate partition of key blocks by using the obtained HMM, and determine the intervals of modulation that maximize the sum of the likelihoods of key blocks with the set partitioning model.[1]
3. Obtain the best number of states that scores the highest sum of likelihoods on an entire corpus.

3.1 Dataset

We used J. S. Bach's four-part choral pieces BWV253-438 from the Music21 Corpus [1] as our dataset. Several pieces in the chorales have complicated modulations which are not compatible with the modern tonalities. We should also consider that the key signatures of several pieces are different from the modern tonal system. We excluded 24 pieces which obviously differed from the major and the minor key: 22 dorian, 1 mixolydian, and 1 phrygian, and targeted the remaining 94 major pieces and 68 minor pieces. However, there were still pieces that retained the feature of the church modes, especially in minor mode pieces.

To train the HMMs, we used only the first and the last phrases[2] that were identified by the fermata[3] notation in each piece because we supposed to be able to identify the key of these phrases from the key signature. Those pieces whose first and last chords were different from the tonic of the key signature were excluded. Thereafter, when we calculated the sum of likelihoods of chord progressions, we used the entire phrases and all the pieces.

3.2 Functional Chord Progression Model Based on HMM

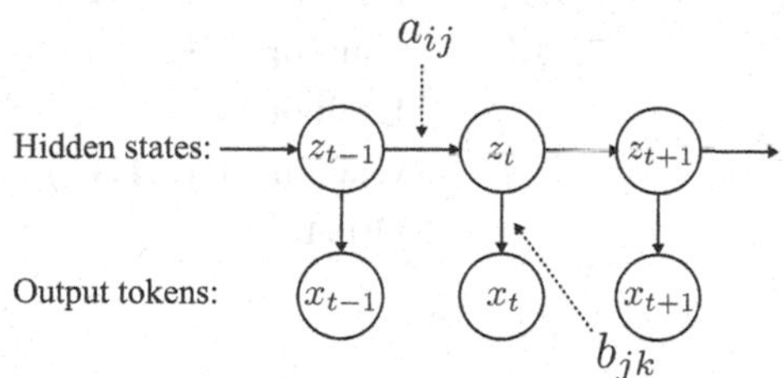

Fig. 1. Graphical representation of the hidden Markov model (HMM).

Model. We regarded chord degrees as output tokens for the HMM in Fig. 1, and states as chord functions. Here, z_t denotes the hidden state and x_t the output token at each time step. The state-transition probability is denoted by

[1] The set partitioning model is a sort of the linear programming.

[2] In this paper, a phrase means a section divided by fermatas.

[3] Fermata is a notation which usually represents a grand pause. However, in the chorale pieces, it represents the end of a lyric paragraph.

a_{ij} and the output probability b_{jk}. The number of distinct states is denoted by N_s, and that of output tokens N_v. When we need to specify a state, we use $(z_t =)s_i, i \in \{1, \ldots, N_s\}$, and for output tokens we use $(x_t =)v_k, k \in \{1, \ldots, N_v\}$.

Surface Tokens. We modelled the chord functions of the major key and the minor key by the HMM, and investigated the number of states in the range from 2 to 12. To train the models, we transposed all the major keys to C major and all the minor keys to A minor.

Basically, we used chord degrees on the diatonic-scale as the surface tokens because we trained the models only for C major and A minor, and used them for other keys by transposing the surface tokens. We needed to use more tokens for the minor key considering the all possible chords that were created by introducing the leading-tone in addition to the natural **VII**. The surface tokens of the major and minor keys are listed in Table 1.

Table 1. Surface tokens.

Major		Minor	
Chord name	Proportion	Chord name	Proportion
C major (**I**)	30.50%	A minor (**i**)	28.59%
G major (**V**)	19.56%	E major (**V**)	14.94%
D minor (**ii**)	12.35%	C major (**III**)	7.91%
A minor (**vi**)	10.76%	B diminished (**ii**°)	7.22%
F major (**IV**)	9.57%	D minor (**IV**)	6.23%
B diminished (**vii**°)	5.44%	G major (**VII**)	6.13%
E minor (**iii**)	4.37%	G♯ diminished (**vii**°)	5.24%
Others	7.45%	F major (**VI**)	5.14%
		E minor (**v**)	3.46%
		C augmented (**III**$^+$)	2.08%
		Others	13.06%

Here, we simply removed chords that were not classified to major, minor, diminished, and augmented by using a function to classify the qualities of chords in the Music21 library [1]. We treated the remaining chords that were not in the diatonic scale as 'Others'. In addition, we treated a succession of the same chord as a single surface token since we do not expect any change of chord functions in it.

Optimization Method. We adopted the simple EM-based approach known as the Baum-Welch algorithm for learning the HMM parameters from data. While the GS would be effective to avoid bad local optima [2,12], we rather employed the optimization from a large number of initial values to study the variance of locally optimal parameterizations. For each number of states, we used 1000 different initial values to learn the parameters. We randomly initialized the state-transition probability matrix, while the output probability matrix was initialized uniformly. For each initial value setup, the training data consisting of randomly connected pieces, where we shuffled the opus numbers of the pieces and put them into one sequence.

Evaluation Measures. We evaluated the parameterizations of the HMM obtained from 1000 different initial values on each number of states (among 2–12) to find the optimal one. For each number of states, we selected the optimal parameterization which scored the lowest perplexity defined by following equation:

$$\mathcal{P} = \exp\left(-\frac{1}{|\boldsymbol{x}|}\ln P(\boldsymbol{x}|\boldsymbol{\theta})\right). \tag{1}$$

Here, the θ denotes the set of model parameters. Although we trained the HMMs on randomly connected pieces as mentioned before, we calculated the perplexity by each piece and summed up the results.

We also calculated the variance of the 1000 optimal parameterizations for each number of states by employing the k-means clustering around the best optimal parameterization. A large variance indicates larger difficulty to consistently obtain the optimal parameterization.

3.3 Modulation Detection as the Set Partitioning Problem

The remaining problem is to select the best number of hidden states. We obtain it by feeding back the score of the modulation detection described below. We select a key that maximizes the likelihood, calculated by the obtained HMM. If we simply apply the HMM, we can only obtain one optimal key for a target piece. By the set partitioning algorithm to detect modulations, we can assign the optimal key blocks to the target piece. The chord functions are expected to work well for detecting a key, especially when there are modulations in the target pieces.

This idea can be formulated as a special case of the set partitioning model, regarding that a music piece is composed of locally optimal key blocks. Here, we use the following notation (Table 2).

Table 2. Notation in the set partitioning model.

$T = \{1, \cdots, N_t\}$	Serial number of chords in a target sequence
$C = \{1, \cdots, N_c\}$	Set of indices of candidate blocks
$j \in C$	Index of blocks
C_j	Set of chords in candidate block j
e_{ij}	$e_{ij} = 1$ if chord $i \in C_j$ and otherwise $e_{ij} = 0$
d_j $(j \in C)$	$d_j = 1$ if C_j is chosen in the partition and otherwise $d_j = 0$
r_j	Score (the likelihood and penalty) of candidate block C_j

The objective of this set partitioning model is to maximize $\sum_{j=1}^{N_c} r_j d_j$, which means that we select the set of blocks that gives the highest score. The imposed constraints are $\sum_{j=1}^{N_c} e_{ij} x_j = 1, i \in T, d_j \in \{0,1\}, j \in C$, which means that a surface token must be included in one and only one block.

Since we used only the chords on the diatonic scales for each key, there were many tokens that were classified as 'Others' described in Table 1 when considering all the candidate keys. We imposed penalty on 'Others' tokens. The penalty value was empirically set to log(0.01).

4 Experimental Results

Here we present the experimental results. First, we show the evaluation measures of the obtained parameterizations in Sect. 4.1 and Sect. 4.2. Thereafter, we discuss the fine-grained chord functions that could be seen in the best parameterization in Sect. 4.3. Finally, we show an example of the modulation detection in Sect. 4.4.

4.1 Evaluation for Each Number of Hidden States

Perplexity. For each number of states, we assumed that a parameterization with a lower perplexity is better. With this criteria, we sorted the results by the perplexity and selected the best one in all the results from 1000 initial values. The best perplexity decreased as the number of states increased (Fig. 2). This result is consistent with the previous work that used a popular music dataset [12].

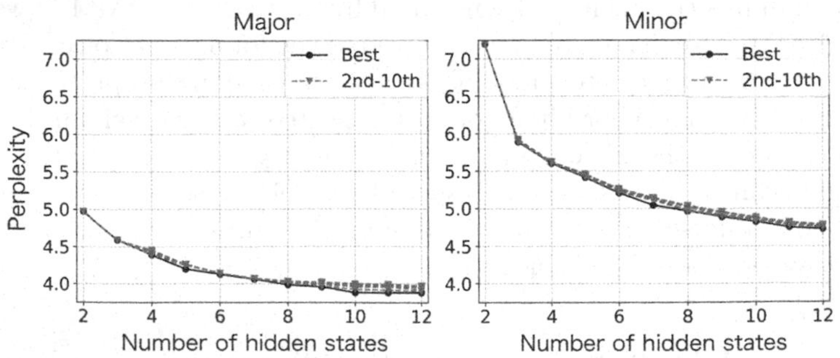

Fig. 2. Perplexities of 10-top parameterizations for each number of states.

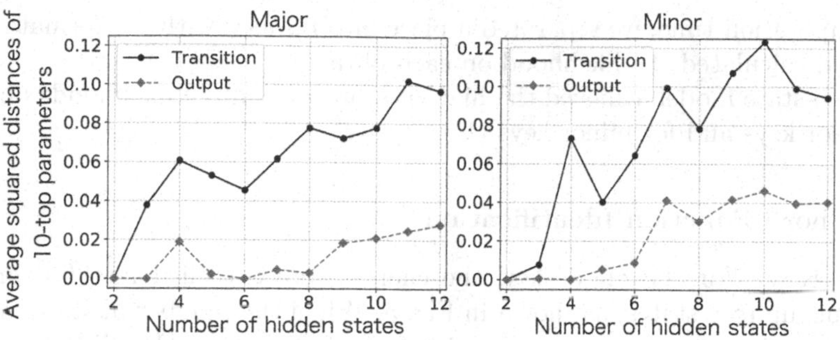

Fig. 3. Average squared distances of 10-top parameters with k-means clustering.

Variance. Next, we studied the variance of the optimal parameterizations. For each number of states, we calculated the average squared distances of each of the output and transition probabilities among the top 10 optimal parameterizations. To eliminate the influence of the permutation ambiguity of the state labels, we adopted the k-means clustering method for calculating the squared distance between two parameterizations of output/transition probabilities. More specifically, we used the Scikit-learn library [7] and fixed the centroids of the clusters as the best optimal parameter values.

As shown in Fig. 3, the distances of the optimal parameterizations increase along with the number of hidden states. This suggests that when the number of hidden states is large there are many different optimal parameterizations and it is difficult to uniquely find the best parameterization solely based on the perplexity.

4.2 Selecting the Number of Hidden States

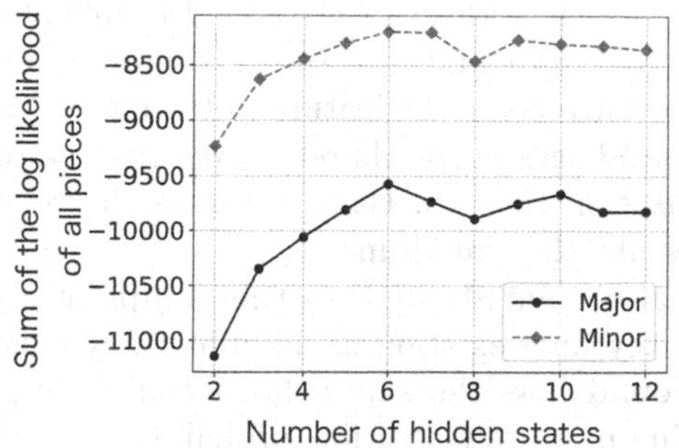

Fig. 4. Sum of the log likelihood of all pieces.

As explained in Sect. 3.3, we obtained the appropriate number of states by calculating the score of the modulation detection with the learned HMMs. To reduce the computation time, we separated a piece into phrases with the fermata notation, and calculated the likelihood on each phrase.

The 6-state model achieved the highest score *i.e.* sum of likelihoods both for the major keys and for minor keys (Fig. 4).

4.3 Chord Function Identification

Major Key. For the major key, the chords were classified into fine-grained functions, up to 6 states, as shown in Fig. 5. When the number of states is 3, in addition to the clear functions of Tonic $\{\mathbf{I}\}$ and Dominant $\{\mathbf{V}, \mathbf{vii}^\circ\}$, there is a mixed function of Tonic and Sub-dominant to which $\{\mathbf{ii}, \mathbf{iii}, \mathbf{IV}, \mathbf{vi}\}$ are assigned. This mixed function is separated into Tonic $\{\mathbf{iii}, \mathbf{vi}\}$ and Sub-dominant $\{\mathbf{ii}, \mathbf{IV}\}$ when the number of states is 4. And then, the state of Dominant is separated into $\{\mathbf{V}\}$ and $\{\mathbf{vii}^\circ\}$ with 5 states. Finally, when the number of states is 6, most chords are assigned to an almost unique state, except that $\{\mathbf{iii}, \mathbf{vi}\}$ form one state. Here, we see that $\{\mathbf{iii}\}$ is mainly assigned to Tonic, which recovers the result of Tsushima et al. for popular music datasets [12].

The fine-grained state-transition probability is also meaningful. As shown in Fig. 6, we can find detailed functions. For example,

1. The state s_2 for **V** and state s_6 for **vii°** both tend to proceed to state s_4 for **I**, while state s_6 less often proceeds to s_3 for $\{\mathbf{iii}, \mathbf{vi}\}$.
2. Although both states s_1 and s_5 have the function Sub-dominant, s_1 for **ii** more often proceeds to Dominant chords (state s_2 and state s_6) than state s_5 for **IV**.

Minor Key. The results for the minor key were significantly different from those for the major key, where states corresponding to Tonic and Dominant of the relative major key were obtained when the number of states was larger than 4. With 6 hidden states, in addition to Tonic, Dominant and Sub-dominant, the Tonic of the relative major and that of the Dominant of the relative major were obtained. This result reflects the feature of the choral, whose melodies were composed in the medieval ages in the church modes instead of modern tonalities, prior to the harmonization by J. S. Bach, because the relative keys share the common pitch classes like the church modes.

Rohrmeier et al. also pointed out that the groups of chords corresponding to the relative major key were existing in the minor key clusters [8]. In addition to this finding, we found how the same chord could have different functions by observing the value of state-transition probability. As shown in Fig. 6, **ii°** appears in both hidden states s_3 and s_5. Here, state s_5 is Sub-dominant since it tends to proceed to state s_2 which is clearly Dominant. On the other hand, **ii°** in state s_3 can be interpreted as the Dominant of the relative major key since it mainly proceeds to state s_6, which represents **III** corresponding to **I** of relative major key.

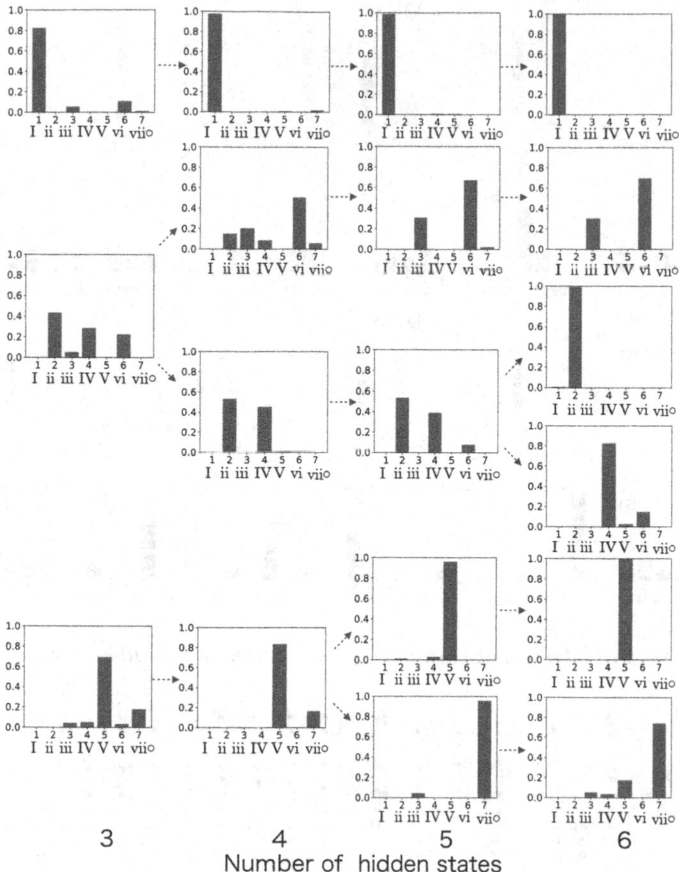

Fig. 5. Output probabilities of the best HMMs for the major key.

4.4 Example of the Modulation Detection

Although we calculated the sum of the likelihood on separated phrases to reduce the computation time as mentioned in Sect. 4.2, we could detect the modulation on the entire piece. Since pieces of classical music often have a number of modulations and their phrase boundaries are usually not explicitly indicated, this fully dynamic modulation detection is practically useful.

For example, Fig. 7 shows the modulation detection for the piece BWV271. The initial key of this piece is D major, while the key at the end is B minor with a half cadence. This piece has key blocks in D major, B minor, E minor, and A major. The proposed method captured the modulations for the most part.

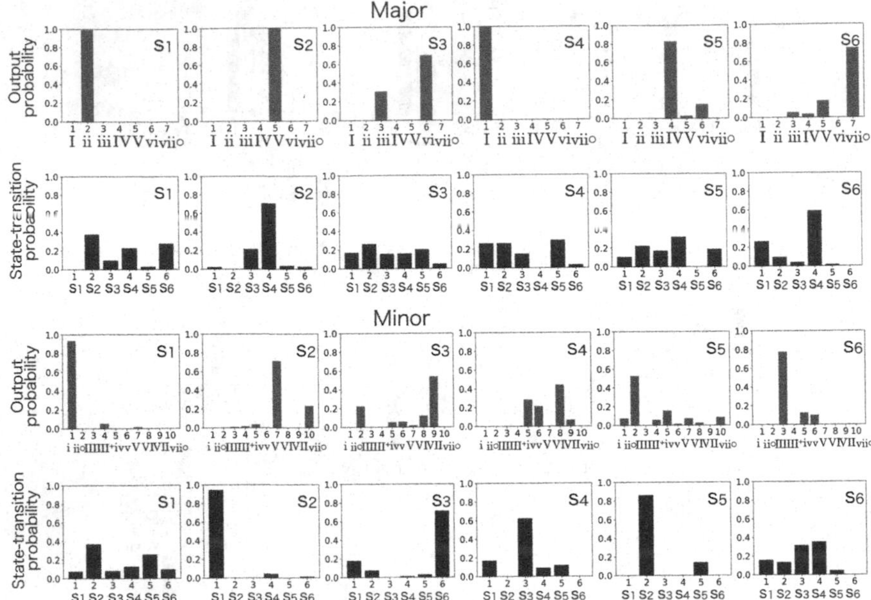

Fig. 6. Output and transition probabilities of 6 hidden states.

Fig. 7. Modulation detection for the piece BWV271. The 'No.' denotes serial numbers, 'Chord' denotes chord names, 'Key' denotes keys and block numbers obtained by the proposed method, and 'State' denotes HMM state labels.

5 Conclusion

We have employed the Hidden Markov Model (HMM) to identify the chord functions, regarding the surface chord degrees as observed outputs. First, we have looked for the best parameterization for each number of hidden states by perplexity, and then, we evaluated the best likelihood of partitioning by modulation. We found that the most adequate number of hidden states was six, which is not large, and thus we could give the finer-grained interpretations for chord functions; *e.g.*, the Dominant **V** and **vii**$^{\circ}$ had different tendency towards $\{\mathbf{iii}, \mathbf{vi}\}$, or the Sub-dominant **IV** and **ii** behaved differently toward the Dominant.

We have applied those chord functions to the partitioning by modulation. The interval of modulation was determined dynamically without fixing the scope beforehand, however, the resultant score of partitioning was also fed back to the number of hidden states. Thus, this process is a tandem model, which is one of the most important features of our work.

Another important feature is the characterization of music styles by parameters. In our example, the set of parameters reflects the specific feature of Bach's chorales, where the basic melodies are of church modes while the harmonization is in the Baroque style. In general, other sets of parameters may have a potential to characterize different music styles such as post-romanticism.

Since our main objective was to investigate the functional progression of chords that determine keys, we excluded those borrowed chords and assigned an artificial penalty value to them. However, we found the minor key model could properly distinguish the functions of the relative major key. This result suggests that we would not need to exclude borrowed chords beforehand. Thus, to investigate the key recognition with extraneous chords is our immediate future work. And also, the evaluation with human annotations is also our important future work, even though the human recognition of modulations could admit multiple interpretations. In addition, we admit our model intrinsically cannot distinguish locally optimal keys from globally optimal ones. To solve this issue, we plan to consider prolongation of the influence of preceding chords.

Acknowledgments. This research has been supported by JSPS KAHENHI Nos. 16H01744 and 19K20340.

References

1. Cuthbert, M.S., Ariza, C.: music21: a toolkit for computer-aided musicology and symbolic music data. In: 11th International Society for Music Information Retrieval Conference, pp. 637–642 (2010)
2. Goldwater, S., Griffiths, T.L.: A fully Bayesian approach to unsupervised part-of-speech tagging. In: 45th Annual Meeting of the Association of Computational Linguistics, pp. 744–751 (2007)
3. Hu, D.J., Saul, L.K.: A probabilistic topic model for unsupervised learning of musical key-profiles. In: 10th International Society for Music Information Retrieval Conference, pp. 441–446 (2009)

4. Jacoby, N., Tishby, N., Tymoczko, D.: An information theoretic approach to chord categorization and functional harmony. J. New Music Res. **44**(3), 219–244 (2015)
5. Krumhansl, C.L., Kessler, E.J.: Tracing the dynamic changes in perceived tonal organisation in a spatial representation of musical keys Key-Finding with Interval Profiles. Psychol. Rev. **89**(2), 334–368 (1982)
6. Lerdahl, F.: Tonal Pitch Space. Oxford University Press, Oxford (2004)
7. Pedregosa, F., et al.: Scikit-learn: machine learning in Python. J. Mach. Learn. Res. **12**, 2825–2830 (2011)
8. Rohrmeier, M., Cross, I.: Statistical properties of tonal harmony in Bach's chorales. In: 10th International Conference on Music Perception and Cognition, pp. 619–627 (2008)
9. Sakamoto, S., Arn, S., Matsubara, M., Tojo, S.: Harmonic analysis based on Tonal Pitch Space. In: 8th International Conference on Knowledge and Systems Engineering, pp. 230–233 (2016)
10. Temperley, D.: The tonal properties of pitch-class sets: tonal implication, tonal ambiguity, and tonalness. Comput. Musicol. **15**, 24–38 (2007). Center for Computer Assisted Research in the Humanities at Stanford University
11. Tsushima, H., Nakamura, E., Itoyama, K., Yoshii, K.: Function-and rhythm-aware melody harmonization based on tree-structured parsing and split-merge sampling of chord sequences. In: 18th International Society for Music Information Retrieval Conference, pp. 502–508 (2017)
12. Tsushima, H., Nakamura, E., Itoyama, K., Yoshii, K.: Generative statistical models with self-emergent grammar of chord sequences. J. New Music Res. **47**(3), 226–248 (2018)
13. White, C.W., Quinn, I.: The Yale-classical archives corpus. Empir. Musicol. Rev. **11**(1), 50–58 (2016)

Audio Signal Processing - Music Structure, Analysis, Synthesis and Composition Tools

Deploying Prerecorded Audio Description for Musical Theater Using Live Performance Tracking

Dirk Vander Wilt(✉) and Morwaread Mary Farbood

New York University, New York, NY, USA
{dirk.vanderwilt,mfarbood}@nyu.edu

Abstract. Audio description, an accessibility service used by blind or visually impaired individuals, provides spoken descriptions of visual content. This alternative format allows those with low or no vision the ability to access information that sighted people obtain visually. In this paper a method for deploying prerecorded audio description in a live musical theater environment is presented. This method uses a reference audio recording and an online time warping algorithm to align tracks of audio description with live performances. A software implementation that is integrated into an existing theatrical workflow is also described. This system is used in two evaluation experiments that show the method successfully aligns multiple recordings of works of musical theater in order to automatically trigger prerecorded, descriptive audio in real time.

Keywords: Audio description · Blind · Visually impaired · Accessibility · Disability · Musical theater · Time warping

1 Introduction

Audio description (AD) is an accommodation used by people who are visually impaired or blind. It is a spoken description of the visual elements of an accompanying work, providing an accessible alternative to obtaining information that sighted individuals may obtain visually. Users of AD should be able to ascertain with audio what a sighted person at the same time and place may ascertain with vision. At live theatrical events that provide AD, such as some Broadway musicals, patrons are either provided with a wireless audio receiving device or are asked to download a software application onto their smartphone, so the transmission of the AD will not disrupt other theatergoers. For an overview on the art and practice of AD, see Fryer [7] and Snyder [14].

Live theatrical events pose an interesting problem for AD services. Like fixed media, the descriptions must be timed appropriately so as not to disrupt other aural aspects of the show (musical numbers, dialogue, etc.) [7,14]. However, since repeated live performances are by design never identical, a fixed AD track cannot be aligned in advance. In live situations, either a professional audio describer

R. Kronland-Martinet et al. (Eds.): CMMR 2019, LNCS 12631, pp. 181–189, 2021.
https://doi.org/10.1007/978-3-030-70210-6_13

describes the visual elements in real time, or a system is created to allow pre-recorded AD to be triggered [9]. Developing and deploying this type of service is expensive and time-consuming. A recent study showed that media producers view AD as "a costly service with no revenue potential." Creating audio description for a 30-min television show with 24 cues may cost between $698 and $1,462, depending on how the description is produced [12]. According to Szarkowska [15], "A lengthy preparation process and high production costs are among the greatest obstacles to the wider availability of audio description."

This paper proposes an inexpensive and novel method to trigger AD for a live theatrical performance by only using audio obtained from a show's previous performance. The process described in this paper warps the audio from the live show in real time to a reference recording using an established online time warping algorithm [5]. This method is a step towards being able to reduce the cost of deploying live theatrical audio description, thus making it more available to visually impaired people.

2 Method

Live audio-to-audio alignment has been used successfully in music score following [1,2] and audio-transcription alignment [8] tasks. In this implementation, a reference recording is aligned to live input using an online time warping algorithm [5]. During the live alignment, descriptive audio tracks are also aligned, based on their pre-aligned position in the reference recording, and played back in real time to theatergoers using the service.

First, a performance of the entire production is recorded in advance. Relevant features from that audio are then extracted and stored in frames of vectors. A second audio track is also created, containing only the AD which aligns to that recorded performance. The descriptive track is broken up into multiple smaller tracks such that one sub-track contains the audio for a single described event within the recorded performance, and the points where each sub-track should be triggered are marked. Once the marks, descriptive track, and extracted features of the reference recording are obtained, the live alignment may begin.

2.1 Audio Features

In the system described here, Mel-frequency cepstrum coefficients (MFCCs) are extracted from both the live input and reference recording. MFCCs are a well-established set of features used when analyzing audio signals for human speech recognition and music information retrieval applications. Both uses are applicable here since theatrical productions often contain both speech (dialogue) and music (showtunes). The coefficients are derived from the Mel scale, which captures patterns audible to the human ear. Although the system does not recognize speech explicitly, it uses MFCCs to compare different (but similar) samples of speech and music patterns. The code implemented to extract MFCCs here was based on [6].

Starting with audio at a sampling of 8 kHz, the MFCC extraction process begins with the application of a pre-emphasis filter so that the higher frequencies of the signal have greater energy. The signal is then segmented into frames, and a Hamming window and FFT are applied to each frame. The results are filtered through a Mel filterbank with 40 filters, which is where the raw frequency data gets "refined" to frequencies based on the Mel scale. A discrete cosine transform is performed on the log-amplitudes of the filter output, resulting in 13 coefficients which are the MFCCs for that frame. To account for change over time, a first-order difference of each coefficient from the previous frame is appended to the 13 current coefficients, making the total number of coefficients used for analysis 26 per frame. Given the real-time nature of this system, the features must be extractable in less time than it takes the corresponding audio to play out in real time. In this case, the system extracts one MFCC feature vector at a frame length of 100 ms and a hop size of 40 ms. For a description of MFCC feature extraction, see [8,10,11].

2.2 Online Time Warping

Dynamic Time Warping (DTW) uses dynamic programming to recursively compare two time series U and V of lengths m and n. The output is an m- by- n matrix D where each element $D(x, y)$ is a cumulative (in this case Euclidean) distance between $U(x)$ and $V(y)$. The value of each cell is the cumulative "path cost" from $D(1,1)$ up to that point [13]:

$$D(i,j) = d(i,j) + min \begin{Bmatrix} D(i-1,j) \\ D(i-1,j-1) \\ D(i,j-1) \end{Bmatrix} \tag{1}$$

Every cell in the matrix is calculated by obtaining the distance between $U(i)$ and $V(j)$, and adding it to the least of one of three adjacent (previous) cells. In this way, the cumulative path cost between $D(1,1)$ and the current cell is determined. The smaller the cumulative cost, the better the match up to that point. When the whole matrix is calculated through $D(m,n)$, backtracking the smallest distance back to $D(1,1)$ will be the warp path which relates the closest points of U to V. Unfortunately, this algorithm requires both series to be fully available in advance and has a running time of $O(N^2)$, making it unsuitable for live performance tracking.

This online time warping algorithm, developed by Dixon [5], requires only one of the series to be available in advance, while the other series may be obtained in real time (V is known fully in advance, and U is only partially known, but increases as new live input is received). The algorithm outputs a similar matrix D, but it builds as the input is received, one row and/or column at a time, and only in the forward direction. Plus, it is only able to estimate the total size of the resulting matrix, so it is instead bounded by a constant, which is determined in advance. Thus, it does not have the advantage of being able to backtrack from future input.

In online time warping, whenever a new frame of input is received in real time as $U(t)$, where t is the current live input frame, the system must determine whether to add another row, or column, or both, to matrix D. It does this by checking all the path cost's previous c elements of the current row t and column j of the matrix. If the lowest cost is in a row, it increments the row. If the lowest path is in the column, it increments the column. If the lowest cost is $D(t, j)$, the current cell, it increments both. Also, if a row or column has been incremented $MaxRunCount$ times, it then increments the other, thus preventing the system from running away in one direction. This implementation sets $c = 500$ and $MaxRunCount = 3$ as described in [5].

Indices t and j are pointers to the current real-time position in U and V. At any point $U(t)$ (the current frame in the real-time input), the value of j is the current estimated location in V. Since index t is the current live input frame, it will always increment steadily. Index j, however, will increment based on where the online time warping algorithm estimates the current temporal location to be in the reference recording. AD is inserted based on the real-time current value of j.

3 The Alignment Process

Three inputs are needed to trigger AD: the reference recording V, one or more frames of ongoing live input U, and an array of frame numbers F, where $F(1...x)$ represents the frame at which AD number x should be triggered. U and V are arrays of feature vectors. Both $U(n)$ and $V(n)$ are a single feature vector at frame n. Prior to the live performance commencing, all features of the reference recording are extracted and placed in V. U is extracted in real time during the live performance.

When the show begins, $t = 1$ and $j = 1$, which are references to the indices of the first frames of U and V, respectively. Each time t increases (meaning the live recording has progressed by one frame), the new value of j is determined, based on the online time warping algorithm. If the algorithm determines that U is progressing faster than V at that moment, then $t+ = 1$. If U is slower than V, then $j+ = 1$. If they are both moving at the same speed at that moment, then both t and j are incremented. Index j will keep increasing until it matches t's estimated location, and a new t (live input frame) is obtained (or, alternately, j will not increase while t catches up). The AD number x is triggered when $j = F(x)$. In this way, the descriptive tracks are able to align with the live performance based on the online time warping's estimation of the current index j of the reference.

Since the actual size of the matrix is unknown, an empty square matrix of 40,000-by-40,000 was created in the current implementation, which holds approximately 25 min of data on either t or j given the feature extraction parameters presented earlier. During the alignment, when one index is incremented up to the size of the matrix, the matrix is reset and the path cost returns to 0. In this manner, the alignment can run indefinitely, and the calculated path cost does not increase indefinitely. During the feature extraction phase, the MFCCs for each minute of audio was calculated and extracted in less than 2 s while running on a 2.7 GHz MacBook Pro using a C/C++ implementation. Offline tests of the online algorithm were able to process one hour of alignment (including extraction and matrix calculation) in about 4 min. This process therefore runs comfortably in a real-time scenario.

4 Evaluation

To evaluate this method, two different audio recordings of the same theatrical productions were used, with one recording as a reference and the other as live input. Markers were placed manually in both recordings to represent specific moments in the production (such as lines of spoken words or musical cues). The algorithm was then run in real time and the mark locations found during the alignment were compared to the actual mark locations in the live input.

In the first evaluation experiment, two recordings of Gilbert and Sullivan's *H.M.S. Pinafore* were used: a D'Oyly Carte recording from 1949 and a Malcolm Sargent recording from 1957. In both recordings 213 specific points were marked; these points were meant to simulate where AD may be triggered. This experiment used the D'Oyly Carte version as the reference and the Malcolm Sargent version as the live input.

After completing the alignment, the ground truth was compared with the marks automatically located by the algorithm. A total of 161 marks (76%) were found less than 1 s from the mark's actual location in the reference; 183 marks (86%) were found less than 2 s from the actual location; and 200 marks (94%) were less than 5 s. The mean difference between the marks indicated by the algorithm and the ground truth was 1.2 s (SD = 2.68 s).

To test the algorithm in a more realistic situation, a second experiment using two recordings with notable, audible differences were obtained: the Broadway (2007) and London (2010) cast recordings of *Legally Blonde, The Musical.* The London version was recorded in front of a live audience and contains audience noise, laughter, ambience, etc. that is not present in the Broadway recording. The only alteration made to the recordings was the removal of one track from the London version because it was out of order in the Broadway recording.

In both versions of *Legally Blonde*, 169 locations were manually marked, and the alignment was run in real time using the London recording as the reference, and the Broadway recording as the live input. The results showed that 117 marks (69%) were found within 1 s of the reference, 133 (79%) were within 2 s, and 147 (87%) were within 5 s. The mean difference between the generated marks and ground truth was 1.79 s (SD = 3.32 s).

In both experiments, the total duration of each recording was over an hour, and the algorithm was able to keep up with the long live input, and automatically correct itself after moments of difference between the reference and the live input. If there is a "mistake" between productions and the AD becomes misaligned, the algorithm may correct itself as the production progresses. For

Table 1. Results of the two evaluation experiments. Marks refers to the total number of annotated marks for each show; values in the < 1, 2, 5 s columns indicate the percentage of marks found within 1, 2, and 5 s of the ground truth; St. dev refers to standard deviation of the differences between the found marks and the ground truth.

	Marks	<1 s	<2 s	<5 s	St. dev.
Pinafore	213	75.57%	85.92%	93.92%	2.68 s
Blonde	169	69.23%	78.70%	86.98%	3.32 s

example, the longest difference between reference and live for all experiments was about 21 s, which occurred during a significant period of divergence between the two recordings of *Legally Blonde*. However, the algorithm was back to correctly aligning once again less than 2 min later, with the next marks falling 120 ms from the reference (Fig. 1).

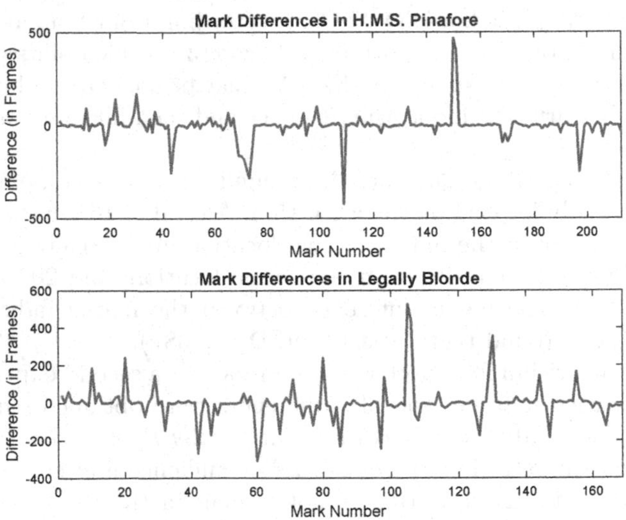

Fig. 1. Accuracy of all marks shown for *H.M.S. Pinafore* and *Legally Blonde*, shown as deviations from ground truth in frames. X axis indicates mark number; Y axis indicates difference in number of frames (25 frames = 1 s).

Within the context of a live theatrical environment, these results show that most (79–86%) AD will be triggered within two seconds of the actual event occurring. These metrics indicate that theatergoers would be able to follow the visual elements of the production in a timely way.

5 Implementation

Software implementations to increase the availability of audio description generally take the form of automating some task of AD creation or deployment, thus decreasing cost and complexity, and ultimately increasing availability. For example, the *CineAD* system [4] uses information from existing closed captions and a teleplay or screenplay of a fixed film or television program to generate a descriptive script automatically, which may then be read by a synthetic voice or by a human. Alternately, *LiveDescribe* [3] seeks to recruit amateur describers to describe videos; it does this in part by analyzing a video and allowing describers to record descriptive audio only during breaks in dialogue.

In a live setting, and in particular when a live performance is imperfectly repeated, automated AD must accommodate for variations, but must still be able to follow some static representation of the performance in order to correctly align the description. Thus, we propose both a software implementation and workflow that takes into account existing theatrical technology (audio recording) as well as established music information retrieval techniques (feature extraction and online time warping) to align AD in real time. The previous sections of this paper have discussed the algorithm and parameters of the software; this section describes how the software may be ideally used in a live setting.

Computer and Theatrical Requirements. The software in this implementation runs comfortably on a 2012-era MacBook Pro with a solid-state hard drive and 16 gigabytes of memory. The computer must be able to obtain two channels of mono input simultaneously—one input to capture the reference recording and (later) the live input, and the other to capture the live audio describer. Importantly, both channels must be isolated from each other such that they do not capture audio from each other, meaning the describer must be listening with headphones so that the reference recording is not captured on the descriptive audio track. The computer must also have a single mono audio output channel, though this will not run simultaneously with the input. This output is transmitted (by either wireless or some other mechanism) to audience members using the descriptive service.

Software Interface. The software's core functions are *Record* and *Begin Show* buttons. The *Record* button activates the two mono inputs simultaneously to capture both the reference recording and the descriptive audio. The software records the reference's alignment to the AD by detecting when the speaker begins to talk, and the corresponding frame number is retained for the particular mark. Alternately, a third function, *Add Mark*, can be manually activated each time the describer wishes to add a new mark.

The software may have supplemental editing features. The ability to replace portions of the reference recording may be helpful if a long-running show has scene changes. Additionally, the ability to minutely correct the trigger timing of specific descriptive audio may help with fine tuning the AD between performances.

Capturing the Reference and Audio Description. With the software running, the setup configured as above, and the show commencing, the live describer presses *Record* on the computer and the system begins to capture both the performance and describer's voice. The system records the entirety of both mono inputs, capturing the sample numbers for each audio described event. By the end, the system will have captured all relevant data needed to play back the description to future audiences. After this point, the human describer is no longer needed, and the system may be automated.

Providing Audio Description to Audiences. A theatrical technician activates the *Begin Show* button as the production commences. At this point, the mono output (to the wireless receivers of audience members) and the mono input for the live recording (which is the same input as for the reference) is activated. The online time warping process is activated, and the AD is triggered at the correct moment.

6 Conclusion and Future Work

In this paper we presented an automated approach to triggering audio description for a live musical theater performance using audio from a previous performance and an online time warping algorithm. The method is able to correct itself and adapt to variations between the reference and live performance, which is necessary for an effective real-time method. Although the method could be further refined in the future by taking into account very large variations due to intermissions and audience applause that are typical in live performances, the evaluation experiments showed that significant differences such as changes in casting, script, and instrumentation, are already handled robustly.

The software implementation of the system described here can be integrated into a theater's existing setup with minimal interference. For example, the system is able to capture, process, and deploy AD independent from the existing software or hardware controls, since it only uses an audio signal which is readily available in the performance space. Other than an initial reference recording and the descriptive tracks themselves, no other setup or configurations were required. The simplicity of the method's technical setup and its overall flexibility provide a new way to make theater experiences for visually impaired audience members more inclusive and accessible.

Given the proliferation of accessibility on personal computing devices, using a smartphone to align and deliver the description would improve the overall success of the system. Being able to track a live performance from a mobile device without having to be connected to a wireless transmission mechanism would allow AD to be completely in control of the user, not reliant on the setup of the theater.

Audio description is a quickly expanding service for those with visual impairments. While it is becoming more common in film and television, AD for live theatrical performances remains rare. Decreasing the cost and complexity of creating and deploying AD would increase its availability, thus making the enjoyment of live theater more accessible to blind and visually impaired individuals.

References

1. Arzt, A.: Flexible and robust music tracking. Ph.D. dissertation, Johannes Kepler University, Linz (2016)
2. Arzt, A., Widmer, G., Dixon, S.: Automatic page turning for musicians via real-time machine listening. In: Proceedings of the European Conference on Artificial Intelligence, pp. 241–245 (2008)
3. Branje, C.J., Fels, D.I.: LiveDescribe: can amateur describers create high-quality audio description? J. Vis. Impair. Blind. **106**(3), 154–165 (2012)
4. Campos, V.P., de Araujo, T.M.U., de Souza Filho, G.L., Goncalves, L.M.G.: CineAD: a system for automated audio description script generation for the visually impaired. Universal Access in the Information Society, pp. 1–13 (2018)
5. Dixon, S.: Live tracking of musical performances using on-line time warping. In: Proceedings of the 8th International Conference on Digital Audio Effects, pp. 92–97 (2005)
6. Dubagunta, S.P.: A simple MFCC extractor using C++ STL and C++11. Source code at (2016). http://www.github.com/dspavankumar/compute-mfcc
7. Fryer, L.: An Introduction to Audio Description: A Practical Guide. Routledge, London (2016)
8. Lertwongkhanakool, N., Kertkeidkachorn, N., Punyabukkana, P., Suchato, A.: An automatic real-time synchronization of live speech with its transcription approach. Eng. J. **19**(5), 81–99 (2015)
9. Litsyn, E., Pipko, H.: System and method for distribution and synchronized presentation of content. U.S. Patent Application 16/092,775, 2 May 2019
10. Logan, B.: Mel frequency cepstral coefficients for music modeling. ISMIR. **270**, 1–11 (2000)
11. Muda, L., Begam, M., Elamvazuthi, I.: Voice recognition algorithms using mel frequency cepstral coefficient (MFCC) and dynamic time warping (DTW) techniques. J. Comput. **2**(3) (2010)
12. Plaza, M.: Cost-effectiveness of audio description process: a comparative analysis of outsourcing and "in-house" methods. Int. J. Prod. Res. **55**, 3480–3496 (2017)
13. Sakoe, H., Chiba, S.: Dynamic programming algorithm optimisation for spoken word recognition. IEEE Trans. Acoust. Speech Signal Process. **26**, 43–49 (1978)
14. Snyder, J.: The visual made verbal: A comprehensive training manual and guide to the history and applications of audio description. American Council of the Blind (2014)
15. Szarkowska, A.: Text-to-speech audio description: towards a wider availability of AD. J. Spec. Transl. **15**, 142–162 (2011)

MUSICNTWRK: Data Tools for Music Theory, Analysis and Composition

Marco Buongiorno Nardelli[1,2,3,4,5,6](✉)

[1] CEMI, Center for Experimental Music and Intermedia, University of North Texas, Denton, TX 76203, USA
mbn@unt.edu
[2] iARTA, Initiative for Advanced Research in Technology and the Arts, University of North Texas, Denton, TX 76203, USA
[3] Department of Physics, College of Science, University of North Texas, Denton, TX 76203, USA
[4] Division of Composition Studies, College of Music, University of North Texas, Denton, TX 76203, USA
[5] IMéRA - Institut d'Études Avancées of Aix-Marseille Université, Marseille 13004, France
[6] Aix Marseille Univ, CNRS, PRISM, 31 Chemin Joseph Aiguier, CS 70071, Cedex 09, 13402 Marseille, France
http://www.musicntwrk.com,
http://www.materialssoundmusic.com

Abstract. We present the API for MUSICNTWRK, a python library for pitch class set and rhythmic sequences classification and manipulation, the generation of networks in generalized music and sound spaces, deep learning algorithms for timbre recognition, and the sonification of arbitrary data. The software is freely available under GPL 3.0 and can be downloaded at www.musicntwrk.com or installed as a PyPi project (pip install musicntwrk).

Keywords: Computational music theory · Computer aided composition · Data tools · Machine learning

1 Introduction

Big data tools have become pervasive in virtually every aspects of culture and society. In music, application of such techniques in Music Information Retrieval applications are common and well documented. However, a full approach to musical analysis and composition is not yet available for the music community and there is a need for providing a more general education on the potential, and the limitations, of such approaches. From a more fundamental point of view, the abstraction of musical structures (notes, melodies, chords, harmonic or rhythmic progressions, timbre, etc.) as mathematical objects in a geometrical space is one of the great accomplishments of contemporary music theory. Building on this

R. Kronland-Martinet et al. (Eds.): CMMR 2019, LNCS 12631, pp. 190–215, 2021.
https://doi.org/10.1007/978-3-030-70210-6_14

foundation, we have generalized the concept of musical spaces as networks and derive functional principles of compositional design by the direct analysis of the network topology. This approach provides a novel framework for the analysis and quantification of similarity of musical objects and structures, and suggests a way to relate such measures to the human perception of different musical entities. The original contribution of this work is in the introduction of the representation of musical spaces as large-scale statistical mechanics networks: uncovering their topological structure is a fundamental step to understand their underlying organizing principles, and to unveil how classifications or rule-based frameworks (such as common-practice harmony, for instance) can be interpreted as emerging phenomena in a complex network system. Results from this research, the theoretical and technical foundation for this paper and some application of this techniques in composition and analysis can be found in Ref. [3,6,7]. In the following we give the full API of the software library after summarizing some important definitions.

2 Background

Network analysis methods exploit the use of graphs or networks as convenient tools for modeling relations in large data sets. If the elements of a data set are thought of as nodes, then the emergence of pairwise relations between them, edges, yields a network representation of the underlying set. Similarly to social networks, biological networks and other well-known real-world complex networks, entire data-set of sound structures can be treated as a network, where each individual descriptor is represented by a node, and a pair of nodes is connected by a link if the respective two objects exhibit a certain level of similarity according to a specified quantitative metric. Pairwise similarity relations between nodes are thus defined through the introduction of a measure of distance in the network: a metric. In MUSICNTWRK we use the Euclidean norm (generalized Pythagoras theorem in N-dimensions) to quantify similarity between descriptors:

$$\text{distance}(I, J) = \sqrt{\sum_i \left(x_i^I - x_i^J\right)^2}, \tag{1}$$

where $\mathbf{x}$ is the chosen sound descriptor for sound I and J. We specialize in the following the metric for the two major musical spaces in MUSICNTWRK and define two of the operators that are central to many of the algorithms in the MUSICNTWRK package:

1. Metric in the interval vectors space: the distance operator for interval vectors can be written as:

$$d(\mathbf{x}, \mathbf{y}) = \sqrt{\sum_i (\mathbf{x}_i - \mathbf{y}_i)^2} \tag{2}$$

   where $\mathbf{x}$ and $\mathbf{y}$ are interval vectors of dimension INT($\mathrm{N}_C/2$), where N_C is the cardinality of the pcs (number of total pitches). This is a quantity that measures the change in the harmonic content of two pcs, and thus contains a quantification of the rules of harmony in arbitrary musical spaces.

2. Metric in the ordered pcs space (voice leading): the distance operator for pcs provides instead a quantification of voice leading, the study of the linear progression of individual melodic lines at the foundation of counterpoint. For this we use minimal Euclidean voice leading distance [1] for arbitrary TET-notes temperaments (12, 24, etc.):

$$d_{\min}(\mathbf{x}, \mathbf{y}) = \min_{\mathbf{TET}_j} \sqrt{\sum_i (\mathbf{x}_i - (\mathbf{y}_j \pm \mathbf{TET}_j))^2} \tag{3}$$

Here $\mathbf{x}$ and $\mathbf{y}$ are the pcs in normal order and TET = (0, 0, ..., 0, ±TET, 0, ...), a vector of dimension N_C that raises or lowers the jth pitch of the ordered pcs by TET. It is easy to verify that this definition of distance operator is equivalent to finding the minimal distance between all possible cyclic permutations of the pcs. Such definition is easily extended to non-bijective voice-leadings, by an iterative duplication of pitches in the smaller cardinality pcs, and then looking for the multiset that produces the minimal distance. Note that, although we use eucledean distance throughout this discussion, the metric can be chosen by the user from the full palette of metrics available in `sklearn` through the `distance` variable.

From the definition of metrics above we can introduce two essential operators in the vector spaces of interval vectors or ordered pcs:

1. The distance operators: $O(\{n_i\})$ as defined in MUSICNTWRK is an operator that raises or lowers by an integer n the ith component of a vector. In the interval vector space, these are vector operators of dimension INT($N_C/2$); in the voice-leading space, they have dimension N_C. With this definition, if $\mathbf{x}$ is transformed into $\mathbf{y}$ by $O(\{n_i\})$, then:

$$d(\mathbf{x}, \mathbf{y}) = \sqrt{\sum_i n_i^2} \tag{4}$$

The distance operator defined above is assumed to be raising or lowering by the specified amount one of the pitches of the pcs (or components of interval vector (IV)) with no information on the positional ordering (i is left unspecified). As such it is a function that acts upon the vector of all the permutations of the input pcs. For instance, the voice leading operator, O(1) applied to the [0, 4, 7] pcs (C Maj chord) generates the following chords: [0, 3, 7] (C min), [0, 4, 6] (C incomplete half-diminished seventh), [0, 4, 8] (C augmented), [5, 7, 0] (F quartal trichord), [1, 4, 7] (C# diminished), [4, 7, 11] (E min). If the number of specified components is smaller than the cardinality of the pcs or the dimension of the IV, all unspecified components are assumed to be 0.

2. Based on the metric in voice leading space, we can introduce the normal-ordered voice leading operator VL(**n**), that given a normal-ordered pcs, transform it into the successive normal-ordered pcs in the chord progression. Here **n** is an ordered vector of positive or negative integers where each component represents the minimal number of steps that need to be applied to the corresponding pitches of the ordered pcs. So, for instance, VL $(-1, -2, 0)$ applied to [0, 4, 7] produces [7, 11, 2] (the I-V progression from the C major triad to its dominant in the key of C).[1]

3 MUSICNTWRK

The MUSICNTWRK package (www.musicntwrk.com), is a python library written by the author and available as a PyPi project at www.pypi.org/project/music-ntwrk/ or on GitHub: https://github.com/marcobn/musicntwrk. `musicntwrk` is the main module of the project and contains helper classes for pitch class set classification and manipulation in any arbitrary temperament (`PCSet`, `PCSetR` and `PCSrow`), `RHYTHMSeq` for the manipulation of rhythmic sequences, and the main class `musicntwrk` that allows the construction of generalized musical space networks using distances between common descriptors (interval vectors, voice leadings, rhythm distance, etc.); the analysis of scores, the sonification of data and the generation of compositional frameworks. `musicntwrk` acts as a wrapper for the various functions organized in the following sub-projects:

1. `networks` - contains all the modules to construct dictionaries and networks of pitch class set spaces including voice leading, rhythmic spaces, timbral spaces and score network and orchestarion analysis
2. `data` - sonification of arbitrary data structures, including automatic score (musicxml) and MIDI generation
3. `timbre` - analysis and characterization of timbre from a (psycho-)acoustical point of view. In particular, it provides: the characterization of sound using, among others, Mel Frequency or Power Spectrum Cepstrum Coefficients (MFCC or PSCC); the construction of timbral networks using descriptors based on MF- or PS-CCs
4. `harmony` - helper functions for harmonic analysis, design and autonomous scoring
5. `ml_utils` - machine learning models for timbre recognition through the TensorFlow Keras framework
6. `plotting` - plotting function including a module for automated network drawing
7. `utils` - utility functions used by other modules

[1] A full treatment of the mathematical properties of VL operators will be the subject of a forthcoming publication.

MUSICNTWRK is written in python 3 and requires installation of the following dependencies (done automatically when pip install musicntwrk):[2]

1. System modules: sys, re, time, os
2. Math modules: numpy, scipy
3. Data modules: pandas, sklearn, networkx, python-louvain, tensorflow, powerlaw, ruptures, numba
4. Music and audio modules: music21, librosa, pyo, pydub
5. Visualization modules: matplotlib, vpython, PySimpleGUI
6. Parallelization modules: mpi4py (optional)

The reader is encouraged to consult the documentation of each package to get acquainted with its purposes and use. In particular, MUSICNTWRK relies heavily on the music21 package for all the music theoretical and musicological functions. [8] In what follows we provide the full API of MUSICNTWRK only. The display of musical examples in musicxml format requires the installation of a score app like MuseScore (https://musescore.org/). See Section 08 of the music21 documentation for a step by step guide of installing a musicxml reader.

Finally a full set of examples and application of the library for a variety of tasks can be downloaded from the MUSICNTWRK repository on GitHub.[3]

3.1 musicntwrk

The PCSet *Class.* The PCSet class deals with the classification and manipulation of pitch set classes generalized to arbitrary temperament systems (arbitrary number of pitches). The following methods are available:

def class PCSet

- def __init__(self,pcs,TET=12,UNI=True,ORD=True)
  - pcs (int) pitch class set as list or numpy array
  - TET (int) number of allowed pitches in the totality of the musical space (temperament). Default = 12 tones equal temperament
  - UNI (logical) if True, eliminate duplicate pitches (default)
  - ORD (logical) if True, sorts the pcs in ascending order (default)
- def normalOrder(self)
  Order the pcs according to the most compact ascending scale in pitch-class space that spans less than an octave by cycling permutations.
- def normal0Order(self)
  As normal order, transposed so that the first pitch is 0
- def T(self,t=0)
  Transposition by t (int) units (modulo TET)

[2] This step might be unnecessary if running on a cloud service like Google Colaboratory.

[3] https://github.com/marcobn/musicntwrk/tree/master/musicntwrk-2.0/examples.

- def zeroOrder(self)
  transposed so that the first pitch is 0
- def M(self,t=1)
  multiply pcs by an arbitrary scalar mod. 12
- def multiplyBoulez(self,b)
  pitch class multiplication of self * b according to P. Boulez
- def I(self)
  inverse operation: (-pcs modulo TET)
- def primeForm(self)
  most compact normal 0 order between pcs and its inverse
- def intervalVector(self)
  total interval content of the pcs
- def LISVector(self)
  Linear Interval Sequence Vector: sequence of intervals in an ordered pcs
- def Op(self,name)
  operate on the pcs with a distance operator
  - name (str) name of the operator O(ni)
- def VLOp(self,name)
  operate on the pcs with a normal-ordered voice-leading operator
  - name (str) name of the operator $R(n_0, n_1, ..., n_{N_c})$
- def forteClass(self)
  Name of pcs according to the Forte classification scheme (only for TET = 12)
- def commonName(self)
  Display common name of pcs (music21 function - only for TET = 12)
- def commonNamePrime(self)
  As above, for prime forms
- def commonNamePitched(self)
  Name of chord with first pitch of pcs in normal order
- def displayNotes(self,xml=False,prime=False)
  Display pcs in score in musicxml format. If prime is True, display the prime form.
  - xml (logical) write notes on file in musicxml format
  - prime (logical) write pcs in prime form

The PCSetR *Class.* The PCSetR class and its methods (listed below) parallels the PCSet class by adding recursive capabilities to it: in practice any method returns an instance of the class itself. This facilitates the construction of method chains for compositional or analytical tasks. The following methods are available:

def class PCSetR

- def __init__(self,pcs,TET=12,UNI=True,ORD=True)
  - pcs (int) pitch class set as list or numpy array
  - TET (int) number of allowed pitches in the totality of the musical space (temperament). Default = 12 tones equal temperament

- UNI (logical) if True, eliminate duplicate pitches (default)
- ORD (logical) if True, sorts the pcs in ascending order (default)

– def normalOrder(self)
Order the pcs according to the most compact ascending scale in pitch-class space that spans less than an octave by cycling permutations.
– def normal0Order(self)
As normal order, transposed so that the first pitch is 0
– def T(self,t=0)
Transposition by t (int) units (modulo TET)
– def M(self,t=1)
multiply pcs by an arbitrary scalar mod. 12
– def I(self)
inverse operation: (-pcs modulo TET)
– def multiplyBoulez(self,b)
pitch class multiplication of self * b according to P. Boulez
– def zeroOrder(self)
transposed so that the first pitch is 0
– def inverse(self,pivot=0) invert pcs around a pivot pitch
– def primeForm(self)
most compact normal 0 order between pcs and its inverse
– def intervalVector(self)
total interval content of the pcs
– def LISVector(self)
Linear Interval Sequence Vector: sequence of intervals in an ordered pcs
– def Op(self,name)
operate on the pcs with a distance operator

- name (str) name of the operator $O(n_i)$

– def VLOp(self,name)
operate on the pcs with a normal-ordered voice-leading operator

- name (str) name of the operator $R(n_0,n_1,...,n_{N_c})$

– def NROp(self,ops=None)
operate on the pcs with a Neo-Rienmanian operator

- ops (str) name of the operator, P, L or R

– def opsNameVL(self,b,TET=12)
given a pcs returns the name of the normal-ordered voice-leading operator R that connects self to it
– def opsNameO(self,b,TET=12)
given a pcs returns the name of the distance operator O that connects self to it

The PCSrow *Class.* PCSrow is a helper class for 12-tone rows operations (T, I, R, M, Q)

```
def class PCSrow
```

– def __init__(self,pcs,TET=12)

- pcs (int) 12 tone row as list or numpy array

- def normalOrder(self)
  Transpose the row so that first pitch class is 0
- def intervals(self)
  vector of intervals of the row
- def T(self,t=0)
  Transposition by t (int) units (modulo TET)
- def I(self)
  inverse operation: (-pcs modulo TET)
- def R(self,t=1)
  Retrograde plus transposition by t (int) units (modulo TET)
- def M(self,t=1)
  Multiplication by t (int) units (modulo TET)
- def Q(self,t=1)
  cyclic permutation of stride 6 so that the result is an All Interval Series in normal form
- star(self)
  star of the row in prime form
- def constellation(self)
  constellation of the row

The RHYTHMSeq *Class.* The RHYTHMSeq class and its methods (listed below) encode various functions for rhythmic network manipulations. The RHYTHMSeq class deals with the classification and manipulation of rhythmic sequences. The following methods are available:

def class RHYTHMSeq

- __init__(self,rseq,REF='e',ORD=False)
  - rseq (str/fractions/floats) rhythm sequence as list of strings or fractions or floats
  - REF (str) reference duration for prime form âĂŞ the RHYTHMSeq class contains a dictionary of common duration notes that uses the fraction module for the definitions (implies import fraction as fr):

    {'w': fr.Fraction(1,1), 'h': fr.Fraction(1,2),'q': fr.Fraction(1,4), 'e': fr.Fraction(1,8), 's': fr.Fraction(1/16),'t': fr.Fraction(1,32), 'wd': fr.Fraction(3,2), 'hd': fr.Fraction(3,4),'qd': fr.Fraction(3,8), 'ed': fr.Fraction(3,16), 'sd': fr.Fraction(3,32),'qt': fr.Fraction(1,6), 'et': fr.Fraction(1,12), 'st': fr.Fraction(1,24), 'qq': fr.Fraction(1,5), 'eq': fr.Fraction(1,10), 'sq': fr.Fraction(1,20)}.

    This dictionary can be extended by the user on a case by case need.
  - ORD (logical) if True sort durations in ascending order
- def normalOrder(self)
  Order the rhythmic sequence according to the most compact ascending form.
- def augment(self,t='e')
  Augmentation by t units
  - t (str) duration of augmentation

- **def diminish(self,t='e')**
  Diminution by t units
  - t (str) duration of diminution
- **def retrograde(self)**
  Retrograde operation
- **def isNonRetro(self)**
  Check if the sequence is not retrogradable
- **def primeForm(self)**
  reduce the series of fractions to prime form
- **def durationVector(self,lseq=None)**
  total relative duration ratios content of the sequence
  - **lseq (list of fractions)** reference list of duration for evaluating interval content; the default list is:

    fr.Fraction(1/8), fr.Fraction(2/8), fr.Fraction(3/8), fr.Fraction(4/8), fr.Fraction(5/8), fr.Fraction(6/8), fr.Fraction(7/8), fr.Fraction(8/8), fr.Fraction(9/8)
- **def durationVector(self,lseq=None)**
  inter-onset duration interval content of the sequence
  - **lseq (list of fractions)** reference list of duration for evaluating interval content; the default list is the same as above.

The **musicntwrk** *class* Defines wrappers around calls to the main functions of the different packages. The variables passed in the **defs** are used to call the specific function requested. See documentation of the functions in the separate sections.

- **def dictionary(self, space=None, N=None, Nc=None, order=None, row=None, a=None, prob=None, REF=None, scorefil=None, music21=None, show=None)**
  define dictionary in the musical space specified in 'space'. All other variables are as defined in **pcsDictionary**, **rhythmDictionary**, **orchestralVector**, and **scoreDictionary**, in Sect. 3.2 depending on the choice of 'space'
  - **space (string)** = 'pcs', pitch class sets dictionary; 'rhythm' or 'rhythmP', rhythm dictionaries; 'score', score dictionary; and 'orch' orchestral vector.

    Returns

    See description in Sect. 3.2 for individual functions.
  - **def network(self, space=None, label=None, dictionary=None, thup=None, thdw=None, thup_e=None, thdw_e=None, distance=None, prob=None, write=None, pcslabel=None, vector=None, ops=None, name=None, ntx=None, general=None, seq=None, sub=None, start=None, end=None, grphtype=None, wavefil=None, cepstrum=None, color=None)**

  define networks in the musical space specified in 'space':

- **space (string)** = 'pcs', pitch class sets network, both full and ego network from a given pcs; 'rhythm' or 'rhythmP', rhythm dictionaries (see below for details); 'score', score dictionary; and 'orch' orchestral vector. See description in Sect. 3.2.
  Returns
  See description in Sect. 3.2 for individual functions.

– **def timbre(self, descriptor=None, path=None, wavefil=None, standard=None, nmel=None, ncc=None, zero=None, lmax=None, maxi= None, nbins = None, method=None, scnd=None, nstep=None)**
Define sound descriptors for timbral analysis: MFCC, PSCC ASCBW in regular or standardized form. See description of variables in Sect. 3.3.

– **def harmony(self,descriptor=None,mode=None,x=None,y=None)**
handler for calculating tonal harmony models, tonnentz and to launch the tonal harmony calculator. See description of variables in Sect. 3.6.

– **def sonify(self, descriptor=None, data=None, length=None, midi=None, scalemap=None, ini=None, fin=None, fac=None, dur=None, transp=None, col=None, write=None, vnorm=None, plot=None, crm=None, tms=None, xml=None)**
sonification strategies - simple sound (spectral) or score (melodic progression). See description of variables in Sect. 3.5.

3.2 networks

networks contains specific functions for network generation and analysis in different musical spaces.

Networks of pitch class sets

– **def pcsDictionary(Nc,order=0,TET=12,row=False,a=None)**
Generate the dictionary of all possible pcs of a given cardinality in a generalized musical space of TET pitches. Returns the dictionary as pandas DataFrame and the list of all Z-related pcs
  - **Nc (int)** cardinality
  - **order (logical)** if 0 returns pcs in prime form, if 1 retrns pcs in normal order, if 2, returns pcs in normal 0 order
  - **row (logical)** if True build dictionary from tone row, if False, build dictionary from all combinatorial pcs of Nc cardinality given the totality of TET.
  - **a (int)** if row = True, a is the list of pitches in the tone row
    Returns
  - **dictionary (pandas dataframe object)** dictionary as dataframe (name, pitch class set, interval vector)
  - **ZrelT (list of strings)** pitch class sets that have a Z-relation

- def pcsNetwork(input_csv, thup= 1.5, thdw=0.0,TET=12, distance= 'euclidean', col=2,prob=1)
  generate the network of pcs based on distances between interval vectors
  In output it writes the nodes.csv and edges.csv as separate files in csv format
  - input_csv (str) file containing the dictionary generated by pcsNetwork
  - thup, thdw (float) upper and lower thresholds for edge creation
  - distance (str) choice of norm in the musical space, default is 'euclidean'
  - col (int) metric based on interval vector, col = 1 can be used for voice leading networks in spaces of fixed cardinality (OBSOLETE)
  - prob (float) if not 1, defines the probability of acceptance of any given edge
    Returns
  - nodes, edges (pandas dataframe objects) dataframe of nodes and edges of the network
- def pcsEgoNetwork(label, input_csv, thup_e=5.0, thdw_e=0.1, thup= 1.5, thdw=0.1, TET=12, distance='euclidean')
  Generates the network for a focal node (ego) and the nodes to whom ego is directly connected to (alters). In output it writes the nodes_ego.csv, edges_ego.csv and edges_alters.csv as separate files in csv format
  - label (str) label of the ego node
  - thup_e, thdw_e (float) upper and lower thresholds for edge creation from ego node
  - thup, thdw (float) upper and lower thresholds for edge creation among alters
  - distance (str) choice of norm in the musical space, default is 'euclidean'
    Returns
  - nodes(ego), edges(ego), edges(alters) (pandas dataframe objects) dataframes of nodes and edges of the ego network
- def vLeadNetwork(input_csv,thup=1.5,thdw=0.1,TET=12,w=True, distance='euclidean',prob=1)
  Generation of the network of all minimal voice leadings in a generalized musical space of TET pitches - based on the minimal distance operators - select by distance. In output returns nodes and edges tables as pandas DataFrames.
  - input_csv (str) file containing the dictionary generated by pcsNetwork
  - thup, thdw (float) upper and lower thresholds for edge creation
  - distance (str) choice of norm in the musical space, default is 'euclidean'
  - w (logical) if True it writes the nodes.csv and edges.csv files in csv format
    Returns
  - nodes, edges (pandas dataframe objects) dataframe of nodes and edges of the network
- def vLeadNetworkByName(input_csv, thup=1.5, thdw=0.1, TET=12, w=True, distance= 'euclidean', prob=1)
  Generation of the network of all minimal voice leadings in a generalized musical space of TET pitches - based on the minimal distance operators - select by name. In output returns nodes and edges tables as pandas DataFrames. Available also in vector form for computational efficiency as vLeadNetworkByNameVec

- `input_csv (str)` file containing the dictionary generated by pcsNetwork
- `name (str)` name of operator for edge creation
- `distance (str)` choice of norm in the musical space, default is 'euclidean'
- `w (logical)` if True it writes the nodes.csv and edges.csv files in csv format

  Returns
- `nodes, edges (pandas dataframe objects)` dataframe of nodes and edges of the network

Score networks

– def scoreNetwork(seq, ntx, general, distance, TET)
Generates the directional network of chord progressions from any score in musicxml format, See Fig. 1 for an illustration.
- `seq (int)` list of pcs for each chords extracted from the score
- `ntx (logical)` if True produces the network (directed and undirected) as a `networkx` graph object
- `general (logical)` if True classifies the chord progressions with the voice-leading operators, else with the distance operators
- `distance (string)` defines the metric using the definitions in sklearn.

  Returns
- `nodes, edges (pandas dataframe objects)` dataframe of nodes and edges of the network
- `counts (list of integers)` number of occurrences for each chord (histogram)
- `avgdeg, modul (floats)` if ntx = True: average degree and modularity
- `Gx, Gxu (networkx graph objects)` if ntx = True: directed and undirected graph as `networkx` objects

– def scoreSubNetwork(seq, start, end, ntx, general, distance, TET)
Generates the directional sub- network of chord progressions from a range of pcs in the sequence defined by start and stop (int). All other variables as above. It returns the sub-network in the same format as above.

– def scoreDictionary(seq, TET=12)
Builds the dictionary of pcs in any score in musicxml format

- `seq (list of lists)` list of the pitch class set sequence (from readScore)

  Returns
- `dictionary (pandas dataframe object)` dictionary as dataframe (name, pitch class set, interval vector)

– def readScore(inputxml,TET=12,music21=False)
Reads musicxml score and returns chord sequence
- `inputxml (str)` score file
- `music21 (logical)` if True search the music21 corpus

  Returns
- `seq (list of lists)` list of the pitch class set sequence

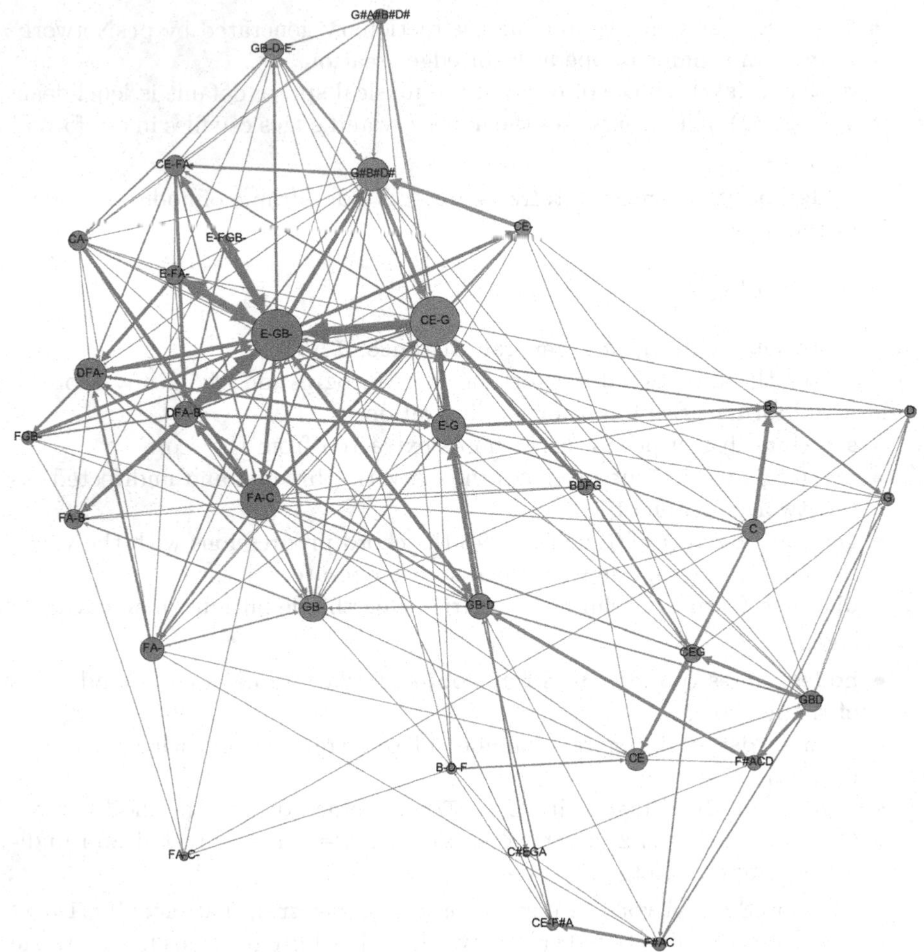

Fig. 1. Score network of the first movement of L. van Beethoven string quartet Op. 127 n. 12 in E♭ Major. Different coloring of the nodes displays their modularity class and reflects the tonal regions used by Beethoven in this piece. (Color figure online)

  - `chords (music21 chord object)` list of the chord sequence as extracted by `music21`

Rhythm networks

- `def rhythmDictionary(Nc,a=None,REF='e')`
  Generates the dictionary of all possible rhythmic sequences of Nc length in a generalized meter space of N durations. Returns the dictionary as pandas DataFrame and indicates all non retrogradable and Z-related cells
  - `Nc (int)` cell length
  - `a (str)` list of durations in the rhythm sequence

Returns

- `dictionary (pandas dataframe object)` dictionary as dataframe (name, rhythm sequence, duration vector)
- `ZrelT (list of strings)` rhythm sequences that have a Z-relation

– def rhythmPDictionary(N,Nc,REF='e')

Generate the dictionary of all possible rhythmic sequences from all possible groupings of N REF durations. Returns the dictionary as pandas DataFrame and indicates all non retrogradable and Z-related cells

- `Nc (int)` cell length
- `N (int)` number of REF units

Returns

As above.

– def rhythmNetwork(input_csv, thup=1.5, thdw=0.0, distance= 'euclidean', prob=1, w=False)

Generates the network of rhythmic cells based on distances between duration vectors. In output it writes the nodes.csv and edges.csv as separate files in csv format

- `input_csv (str)` file containing the dictionary generated by rhythmNetwork
- `thup, thdw (float)` upper and lower thresholds for edge creation
- `distance (str)` choice of norm in the musical space, default is 'euclidean'
- `prob (float)` if not 1, defines the probability of acceptance of any given edge
- `w (logical)` if True it writes the nodes.csv and edges.csv files in csv format

Returns

- `nodes, edges (pandas dataframe objects)` dataframe of nodes and edges of the network

– def rLeadNetwork(input_csv, thup=1.5, thdw=0.1, w=True, distance= 'euclidean', prob=1)

Generation of the network of all minimal rhythm leadings in a generalized musical space of N_C-dim rhythmic cells based on the rhythm distance operator. Returns nodes and edges tables as pandas DataFrames

- `input_csv (str)` file containing the dictionary generated by rhythmNetwork
- `thup, thdw (float)` upper and lower thresholds for edge creation
- `distance (str)` choice of norm in the musical space, default is 'euclidean'
- `prob (float)` if not 1, defines the probability of acceptance of any given edge
- `w (logical)` if True it writes the nodes.csv and edges.csv files in csv format

Returns

As above.

Orchestration networks

- def orchestralVector(inputfile,barplot=True)
  Builds the orchestral vector sequence from score in musicxml format. Returns the score sliced by beat; orchestration vector.
  - barplot=True plot the orchestral vector sequence as a matrix
    Returns
  - score (music21 object) score sliced by beat
  - orch (list of lists) orchestral vectors for every beat (in binary format: 1 if instrument is playin, 0 if not)
  - num (list) beat vector identifier (integer corresponding to the binary number encoded in the orchestral vector)
  - def orchestralNetwork(seq)

  Generates the directional network of orchestration vectors from any score in musicxml format. Use orchestralVector to import the score data as sequence. Returns nodes and edges as Pandas DataFrames; average degree, modularity and partitioning of the network.
  - seq (int) list of orchestration vectors extracted from the score
    Returns
    As scoreNetwork.
- def orchestralVectorColor(orch, dnodes, part, color=plt.cm.binary)
  Plots the sequence of the orchestration vectors color-coded according to the modularity class they belong. Requires the output of orchestralNetwork(). See Fig. 2
  - orch (int) list of orchestration vectors extracted from the score
  - dnodes (pandas dataframe object) dataframe of nodes of the network (for labelling)
  - part (list of int) list of partitions for orchestration vectors

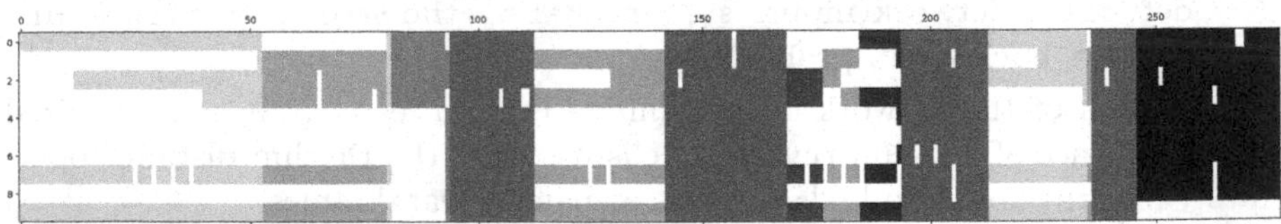

Fig. 2. Orchestration map of the first movement (Allegro) of J.S. Bach's Brandenburg Concerto n. 2, BWV 1047, as produced by the orchestralVectorColor function. Different shades of gray represent the sections of similar orchestral color as measured by their modularity class in the network.

Timbral networks

- def timbralNetwork(waves,vector,thup=10,thdw=0.1)
  generates the network of MFCC vectors from sound recordings. Returns the nodes and edges tables as pandas DataFrames

- **seq (float)** list of MFCC vectors
- **waves (str)** names of sound files

  Returns
- **nodes, edges (pandas dataframe objects)** dataframe of nodes and edges of the network

See Sec. 3.3 for a full discussion on the **timbre** modules.

3.3 timbre

timbre contains all the modules that deal with analysis and characterization of timbre from a (psycho-)acoustical point of view and provides the characterization of sound using, among others, Mel Frequency or Power Spectrum Cepstrum Coefficients (MFCC or PSCC) that can be used in the construction of timbral networks using these descriptors

Sound Classification. The sound classification section, **timbre**, comprises of modules for specific sound analysis that are based on the **librosa** python library for audio signal processing. We refer the interested reader to the **librosa** documentation at https://librosa.github.io/librosa/index.html. For a more complete discussion on the descriptors defined in MUSICNTWRK please refer to the work in Ref. [5].

Audio Descriptors and Metrics in the Generalized Timbre Space. The Power Cepstrum of a signal gives the rate of change of the envelope of different spectrum bands and is defined as the squared magnitude of the inverse Fourier transform of the logarithm of the squared magnitude of the Fourier transform of a signal:

$$\text{PSCC} = \left|FT^{-1}\left\{\log(|FT\{f(t)\}|^2)\right|^2$$

MUSICNTWRK defaults to the first 13 cepstrum coefficients (PSCC), where the 0th coefficient corresponds to the power distribution of the sound over time. The number of coefficient can be controlled by the user.

The Mel Frequency Cepstrum of a signal is obtained as in the equation for the PSCC and differ from the power cepstrum by the choice of the spectrum bands that are mapped over the Mel scale using triangular overlapping windows. The mapping of the frequency bands on the Mel scale better approximates the human auditory system's response than the linearly-spaced frequency bands used in the normal cepstrum. MUSICNTWRK defaults to 16 bands Mel filter. As for the PSCC, the 0-th coefficient corresponds to the power distribution of the sound over time. Both PSCC and MFCC are obtained using 64 bins in the short time Fourier transform (default).

As an illustration, in Fig. 3 we show the network of the MFCC built from 1620 sounds produced by either wooden or metallic objects that were analyzed by a deep learning model trained on a perceptually salient acoustic descriptor or on a signal descriptor based on the energy contents of the signal for a study on automatic timbre characterization. [5] In the figure we display the principal component of the timbral network for which less than 2% of all possible edges are built, that is, we allow an edge only if two MFCCs are at a distance that is less than 3% of the maximum diameter of the network. This representation reveals that the classification is coherent with material categories, as it can be observed from the emergence of clusters of sounds belonging to the same material (see for instance the green cluster of wood sounds on the lower left part of the network and the cyan, pink and orange clusters of metallic sounds in the upper part). This result validates the corpus with respect to the sound quality.

Fig. 3. Section of the network of the MFCCs built from the 1620 sounds that have been used to train the machine learning models. Colors indicate the classification based on their modularity class: Green, mostly high frequency tones from wood; Gray, mostly high to mid-frequency tones of wood; Purple, mostly deep frequency tones of wood; Cyan, mostly dry metal tones; Pink, mostly metal; and Orange, mostly "choked" metal sounds. (Color figure online)

- **def computeMFCC(input_path,input_file,barplot=True,zero=True)**
read audio files in repository and compute a normalized MEL Frequency Cepstrum Coefficients and single vector map of the full temporal evolution of the sound as the convolution of the time-resolved MFCCs convoluted with the normalized first MFCC component (power distribution). Returns the list of files in repository, MFCC0, MFCC coefficients.
  - `input_path (str)` path to repository
  - `input_file (str)` filenames (accepts "*")
  - `barplot (logical)` plot the MFCC0 vectors for every sound in the repository
  - `zero (logical)` If False, disregard the power distribution component.

  Returns
  - `waves (list of strings)` filenames of the .wav files in the repository
  - `mfcc0 (list)` vector of MFCC0 (MFCC with DC component taken out)
  - `mfcc (list)` vector of MFCC (full MFCC)
  - **def computeStandardizedMFCC(input_path,input_file,nmel=16, nmfcc=13,lmax=None,nbins=None)**

Reads audio files in repository and compute a normalized Power Spectrum Frequency Cepstrum Coefficients and single vector map of the full temporal evolution of the sound as the convolution of the time-resolved PSCCs convoluted with the normalized first PSCC component (power distribution). Returns the list of files in repository, PSCC0, PSCC coefficients. Other variables and output as above.

- **def computeStandardizedMFCC(input_path,input_file,nmel=16, nmfcc=13,lmax=None,nbins=None)**

read audio files in repository and compute the standardized (equal number of samples per file) and normalized MEL Frequency Cepstrum Coefficient. Returns the list of files in repository, MFCC coefficients, standardized sample length.
  - `nmel (int)` number of Mel bands to use in filtering
  - `nmfcc (int)` number of MFCCs to return
  - `lmax (int)` max number of samples per file
  - `nbins (int)` number of FFT bins

  Returns

  As above.

- **def computeStandardizedMFCC(input_path,input_file,nmel=16, nmfcc=13,lmax=None,nbins=None)**

read audio files in repository and compute the standardized (equal number of samples per file) and normalized Power Spectrum Frequency Cepstrum Coefficients. Returns the list of files in repository, PSCC coefficients, standardized sample length.
Variables defined as for MFCCs.

  Returns

  As above.

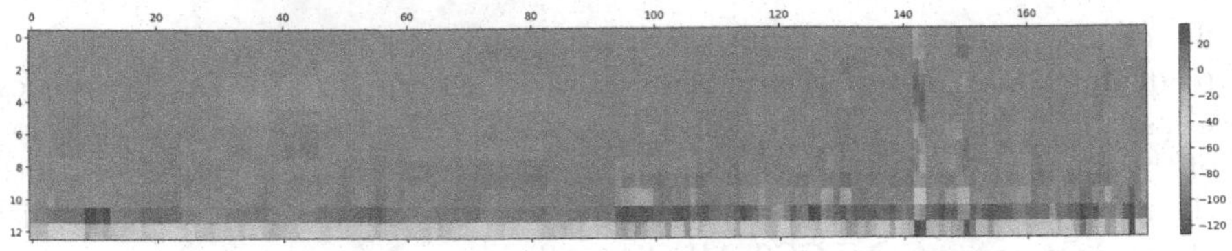

Fig. 4. Map of the MFCC for a repository of 180 impact sounds.

3.4 Machine Learning Models (Ml_utils)

The definition of machine learning models for sound recognition requires standard techniques of data science (like the separation of data entries in training and testing sets, definition of neural network architectures, etc.) that will not be discussed here. Basic knowledge of Keras is also assumed. **ml_utils** contains many auxiliary functions to deal with such tasks. We implemented a deep learning model based on convolutional neural network (CNN) architecture inspired by similar approaches used in image and sound recognition [9]. The CNN is built using the Keras kernel of Tensorflow [1] and it is trained on the full PSCC or MFCC data, after proper scaling and normalization. We retained only models with validation accuracy higher than 90%. After an appropriate model is chosen, it is tested on the set initially chosen for the human perception experiment. Each model chosen retains a similar accuracy on this set. A typical result of a training session on 30 epochs is shown in Fig. 5. Here we limit to report the API for the main machine learning functions and refer the user to the full example available of GitHub:

- **def trainNNmodel(mfcc, label, gpu=0, cpu=4, niter=100, nstep = 10, neur = 16, test=0.08, num_classes=2, epoch=30, verb=0, thr=0.85, w=False)** train a 2 layer neural network model on the ful MFCC spectrum of sounds. Returns: model, training and testing sets, data for re-scaling and normalization, data to asses the accuracy of the training session.
  - **mfcc (float)** list of all the MFCCs (or PSCCs) in the repository
  - **gpu, cpu (int)** number of GPUs or CPUs used for the run
  - **niter (int)** max number of model fit sessions
  - **nstep (int)** how often the training and testing sets are redefined
  - **neur (int)** number of neurons in first layer (it is doubled on the second layer
  - **test (float)** defines the relative size of training and testing sets
  - **num_classes=2 (int)** dimension of the last layer
  - **epoch (int)** number of epochs in the training of the neural network
  - **verb (int)** verbose - print information during the training run
  - **thr (float)** keep the model if accuracy is > test
  - **w (logical)** write model on file if accuracy is above **thr**
- **def trainCNNmodel(mfcc, label, gpu=0, cpu=4, niter=100, nstep=10, neur=16, test=0.08, num_classes=2, epoch=30, verb=0, thr=0.85, w =**

False)
train a convolutional neural network (CNN) model on the full MFCC/PSCC spectrum of sounds. Returns: model,training and testing sets,data for re-scaling and normalization,data to asses the accuracy of the training session. Parameters are defined as above.

For a complete description and example see the notebook on GitHub.

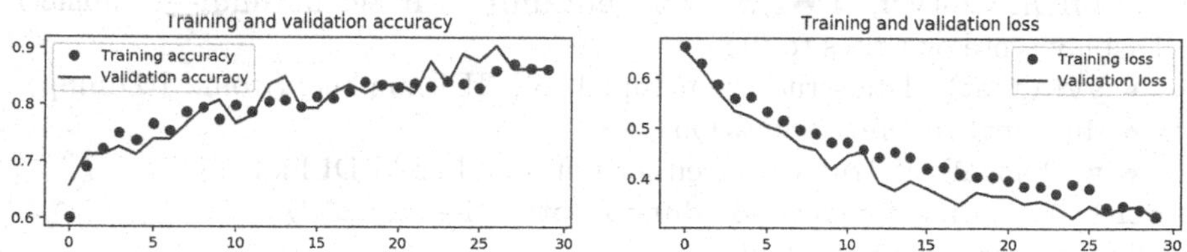

Fig. 5. Training and validation accuracy and loss in a typical Neural Network model learning run

3.5 data

data contains functions for the sonification of data in multi-column or csv format and produces output as WAV either via csound (it requires an installation of csound and direct reference to the **ctcsound** module), **pyo** or pure python, and **musicxml** or MIDI. Two sonification protocols are available: spectral - data are mapped to a single sound using subtractive synthesis (FIR filter); and linear - individual data points are mapped to pitches in a time-series structure. See Ref. [2,4] for a complete description of this protocol. **data** contains:

- **def r_1Ddata(path,fileread)**
  Read data file in a multicolumn format (csv files can be easily put in this format using Pandas). Returns the data values as (x, y).
  - **path (str)** path to data file
  - **fileread (str)** data file
- **def i_spectral2(xv,yv,itime,path='./',instr='noise')**
  Use subtractive synthesis to sonify data structure. Returns the sound file.
  - **xv,yv (float)** data structure to sonify
  - **path (str)** path to data file
  - **fileread (str)** data file
- **def i_time_series(xv,yv,path='./',instr='csb701')**
  Use csound instruments to sonify data structures as time-series. Returns the sound file.
  - **xv,yv (float)** data structure to sonify
  - **path (str)** path to data file
  - **fileread (str)** data file
  - **instr (str)** csound instrument (it can be modified by user)

- def MIDImap(pdt,scale,nnote)
  Data to MIDI conversion on a given scale defined in scaleMapping (see below). Returns the MIDI data structure.
  - pdt (float) data structure mapped to MIDI numbers
  - scale (float) scale mapping (from scaleMapping)
  - nnote (int) number of notes in the scale (from scaleMapping)
- def scaleMapping(scale)
  Scale definitions for MIDI mapping. Returns: scale, nnote (see above).
- def MIDIscore(yvf,dur=2,w=None,outxml='./music',outmidi='./music')
  Display score or writes to file
  - yvf (float) data structure mapped to MIDI numbers (from MIDImap)
  - dur (int) reference duration
  - w (logical) if True writes either musicxml or MIDI file)
- def MIDImidi(yvf,vnorm=80,dur=4,outmidi='./music')
  Display score or writes to file
  - yvf (float) data structure mapped to MIDI numbers (from MIDImap)
  - vnorm (int) reference velocity
  - outmidi (str) MIDI file

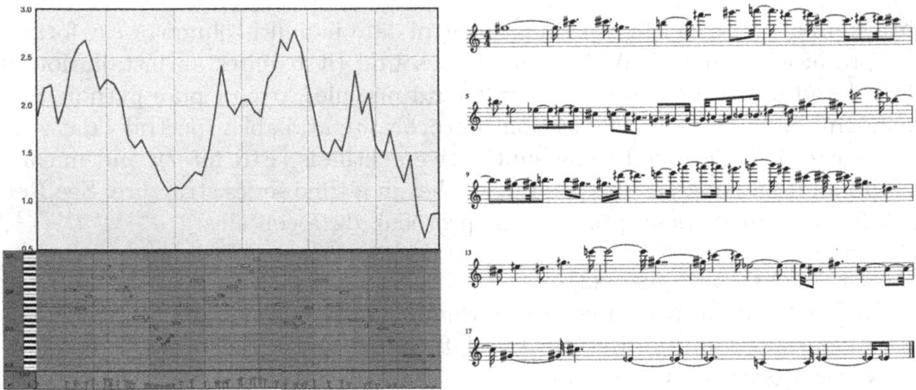

Fig. 6. Data, MIDI map and score from the sonification protocol in MIDIscore

3.6 harmony

Utilities for harmonic analysis, design and autonomous scoring

See example in the notebooks on GitHub and Ref. [7] for possible uses of the modules contained here.

Harmonic analysis functions:

- def scoreFilter(seq,chords,thr=0,plot=False)
  filter out low recurring chords to facilitate change point detection and score partitioning in regions. Needs the output of readScore

- seq (int) list of pcs for each chords extracted from the score
- chords (music21 object) chords as extracted by music21

  Returns
- value, valuef (int) integer identifier for the full and filtered chord sequence
- filtered (int) sequence of filtered chords (by identifier as defined above)
- fmeasure (int) measure number to which the filtered chord belongs

– def changePoint(value, vmodel='rbf', penalty=1.0, vbrakepts=None, plot = False)
run a change point detection algorithm to isolate sections on the filtered score. Uses the implementation in ruptures.

- value (int) list of pcs for each chords as extracted from scoreFilter
- other variables documentation for the other variables at https://pypi.org/project/ruptures/

  Returns
- sections (list of int) list of breakpoints in the score sectioning (by position in the filtered chord sequence)

– def keySections(sections, GxsecDi, dnodes)
region key identification

- sections (int) list of region identified by the changePoint algorithm
- GxsecDi (networkx graph object) score sub-network as computed by scoreSubNetwork
- dnodes (pandas dataframe) dataframe of node label of the full score network

  Returns
- key (string) key associated with given chord in the sequence as identified by a "prevalent chord" algorithm
- keySections (pandas dataframe) dataframe that summarizes the key analysis results by 'section', 'chord range', 'prevalent_chord' ,'region'

– def tonalAnalysis(chords, sections, key, enharm=[['C','C']], write=None)
roman numeral analysis of regions in the full score

- sections (int) see above
- chords (music21 object) see above
- key (string) see above
- enharm (list of strings) optional enharmonic table for pitch respelling

  Returns
- analysis (pandas dataframe) dataframe that summarizes the full analysis of the score, including roman numerals - the results can be visualized in musicxml format if write = True.

Harmonic design functions and autonomous scoring

– def chinese_postman(graph, starting_node)
solve the optimal routing problem of the Chinese postman on an assigned network

- graph (networkx graph object) graph on which to find the optimal path
- starting_node (int) node from where to start the path

Returns

- graph (networkx graph object) directed graph with optimal path (used in harmonicDesign

– def networkHarmonyGen(mk, descriptor=None, dictionary=None, thup=None, thdw=None, names=None, distance=None, probs=None, write=None, pcslabel=None)
probabilistic chord distribution based on geometric distances. It is a wrapper around the modules in networks. See the discussion in Sect. 3.2 for the description of the variables. Only additions are:
  - names (list of strings) list of operators to slice the network of pitches using vLeadNetworkByName
  - probs (list of floats) list of probabilities to slice the network of pitches using vLeadNetwork by distance

  Returns

  - nodes, edges (pandas dataframe) nodes and edges of the generated network

– def harmonicDesign(mk, nnodes, nedges, refnodes, refedges, nstart = None, seed=None, reverse=None, display=None, write= None)
generate a scale-free network according to the Barabasi-Albert model of preferential attachment and assign chords to nodes using the output of networkHarmonyGen
  - mk (musicntwrk class)
  - nnodes, nedges (int) number of nodes and edges per node used to generate the scale free network using networkx.barabasi_albert_graph. See documentation on networkx for details.
  - nodes, edges (pandas dataframe) nodes and edges of the network generated by networkHarmonyGen

  Returns

  - pitches (list of lists of int) chord sequence of the generated network. If display = True it draws the graph, if write = True it writes the sequence as musicxml.

– def rhythmicDesign(dictionary, nnodes, nedges, refnodes, refedges, nstart = None, seed=None, reverse=None, random=None)
builds a scale-free network according to the Barabasi-Albert model of preferential attachment and assign rhythmic figures to nodes. Details as above using the result of any of the rhythm network generation function of Sect. 3.2.
  - durations (list of lists of int) duration sequence of the generated network.

– def scoreDesign(pitches, durations, fac=1, TET=12, write=False)
using the sequences of pitches and rhythms from the above, generate a score in musicxml

Helper functions

- def tonalHarmonyCalculator()
  multi-function harmony calculator: pitches, roman numerals, voice leading operations and more. See the in app HELP for a description of usage.
- def tonalHarmonyModel(mode='minimal')
  build a minimal *harmony model* based on voice leading operators (to be used in the calculator)
- def tonnentz(x,y)
  build the *tonnentz* for the specified x, y relation

3.7 Plotting and General Utility Functions

There are many utility functions (in utils) that are used by other modules and that should be transparent to the average user. We recall here only the ones that are used for computing distances in pitch space, since they relate directly to the discussion of Sect. 2:

- def minimalNoBijDistance(a, b, TET, distance)
  calculates the minimal distance between two pcs of different cardinality (non bijective)
  - a,b (int) pcs as lists or numpy arrays
  - distance (str) choice of norm in the musical space

  Returns
  - dist (float) minimal distance
  - r (array of int) multiset corresponding to minimal distance
- generalizedOpsName(a,b,TET,distance)
  finds the voice leading operator that connects two pcs (also for non bijective transformations)
  - a,b (int) pcs as lists or numpy arrays
  - distance (str) choice of norm in the musical space

  Returns
  - r (array of int) multiset corresponding to minimal distance
  - Op (string) VL operator that connects the two pcs

Finally, it is worth mentioning the network plotting utility drawNetwork in plotting:

- drawNetwork(nodes, edges, forceiter=100, grphtype='undirected', dx = 10, dy=10, colormap='jet', scale=1.0, drawlabels=True, giant=False)
  draws the network using networkx and matplotlib
  - nodes, edges (pandas dataframe) nodes and edges of the network
  - forceiter (floats) iterations in the networks force layout
  - grphtype (string) 'directed' or 'undirected'
  - dx, dy (floats) dimensions of the canvas
  - colormap (string) colormap for plt.get_cmap(colormap)

- **scale (float)** scale factor for node radius
- **drawlabels (logical)** draw labels on nodes
- **giant (logical)** if True draws only the giant component of the network

The most computationally intensive parts of the modules can be run (optionally) on parallel processors using the MPI (Message Passing Interface) protocol. Communications are handled by two additional modules: communications and load_balancing. Since the user will never have to interact with these modules, we omit here a detailed description of their functions.

4 Conclusions

We have presented the API for the MUSICNTWRK software package. The software is freely available under GPL 3.0 and can be downloaded from GitHub and at www.musicntwrk.com, or installed directly via pip install musicntwrk.

Acknowledgments. We acknowledge the support of Aix-Marseille University, IMéRA, and of Labex RFIEA+. It must be understood that MUSICNTWRK is a continuously evolving library, so it is likely that at the time of publication of this paper more functionalities will be available. We invite the reader to explore the GitHub distribution that will always provide the most recent version of the software. Finally, we thank Richard Kronland-Martinet, Sølvi Ystad, Mitsuko Aramaki, Jon Nelson, Joseph Klein, Scot Gresham-Lancaster, David Bard-Schwarz, Roger Malina and Alexander Veremyer for useful discussions.

References

1. Abadi, M., et al.: TensorFlow: large-scale machine learning on heterogeneous systems (2015). https://www.tensorflow.org/. Software available from tensorflow.org
2. Buongiorno Nardelli, M.: materialssoundmusic: a computer-aided data-driven composition environment for the sonification and dramatization of scientific data streams. In: International Computer Music Conference Proceedings, vol. 356 (2015)
3. Buongiorno Nardelli, M.: Topology of networks in generalized musical spaces. Leonardo Music J. (2020). https://doi.org/10.1162/lmj_a_01079, arXiv:1905.01842
4. Buongiorno Nardelli, M.: Beautiful data: reflections for a sonification and post-sonification aesthetics, in leonardo gallery: scientific delirium madness 4.0. Leonardo **51**(3), 227–238 (2018)
5. Buongiorno Nardelli, M., Aramaki, M., Ystad, S., Kronland-Martinet, R.: 14th International Symposium on Computer Music Multidisciplinary Research CNMR: Oct 2019, Marseille, France (2019)
6. Buongiorno Nardelli, M.: The hitchhiker's guide to the all-interval 12-tone rows (2020). https://arxiv.org/abs/2006.05007
7. Buongiorno Nardelli, M.: Tonal harmony, the topology of dynamical score networks and the Chinese postman problem, submitted (2020). https://arxiv.org/abs/2006.01033

8. Cuthbert, M., Ariza, C., Hogue, B., Oberholtzer, J.: music21: a toolkit for computer-aided musicology, Massachussetts Institute of Technology. http://web.mit.edu/music21/
9. Piczak, K.J.: Environmental sound classification with convolutional neural networks. In: 2015 IEEE 25th International Workshop on Machine Learning for Signal Processing (MLSP), pp. 1–6 (2015)

Feasibility Study of Deep Frequency Modulation Synthesis

Keiji Hirata[1(✉)], Masatoshi Hamanaka[2], and Satoshi Tojo[3]

[1] Future University Hakodate, Hokkaido, Japan
hirata@fun.ac.jp
[2] Riken AIP, Tokyo, Japan
masatoshi.hamanaka@riken.jp
[3] JAIST, Ishikawa, Japan
tojo@jaist.ac.jp

Abstract. Deep Frequency Modulation (FM) synthesis is the method of generating approximate or new waveforms by the network inspired by the conventional FM synthesis. The features of the method include that the activation functions of the network are all vibrating ones with distinct parameters and every activation function (oscillator unit) shares an identical time t. The network learns a training waveform given in the temporal interval designated by time t and generates an approximating waveform in the interval. As the first step of the feasibility study, we examine the basic performances and potential of the deep FM synthesis in small-sized experiments. We have confirmed that the optimization techniques developed for the conventional neural networks is applicable to the deep FM synthesis in small-sized experiments.

Keywords: Frequency Modulation synthesis · Neural networks · Activation function · Backpropagation

1 Introduction

Frequency Modulation (FM) synthesis is a well-known technique for generating musical sound [1] and has been employed for many commercial products of digital synthesizers such as DX7 of Yamaha, which is one of the bestselling synthesizers [7]. Also many variations of the FM synthesis have been developed [6, pp. 224–250]). FM synthesis can generate rich sounds despite a simple configuration, i.e., the small number of parameters; on the other hand, it is known that FM synthesis requires some skills for manipulating parameters when generating new desired sounds. It is mainly because the relationships among output sounds, parameter values, and configurations of connecting oscillators are not sufficiently intuitive. Hence, to create new sounds easily, many of digital synthesizers employing the FM synthesis provides the presets which are built-in connection patterns of oscillators with predefined parameters of amplitudes and carrier and modulating frequencies.

R. Kronland-Martinet et al. (Eds.): CMMR 2019, LNCS 12631, pp. 216–224, 2021.
https://doi.org/10.1007/978-3-030-70210-6_15

After considering these presets provided, we would come up with an idea of a general form of the FM synthesis which looks like a neural network, the activation functions of which are oscillators. Suppose, in the network, an oscillator X at a layer can receive modulating waveforms from the ones at one-level lower layer $Y_1, Y_2, \cdots$. The weight of the connection between X with Y_k corresponds to amplitude parameters. The carrier and modulating frequencies are defined as parameters within each oscillator. Then, all the oscillators should refer to an identical current time and simultaneously generate waveforms along with the time as in the conventional FM synthesis. If we would apply the learning techniques developed for conventional neural networks to the network inspired by the conventional FM synthesis, we might generate target sounds without taking care of the relationships among output sounds, parameter values, and configurations of connecting oscillators.

Gashler and Ashmore [2] have surveyed various networks to model and predict time-series data and offered a useful idea for categorization of approaches. Gashler and Ashmore claim that at a high level, the neural networks to predict time-series data are broadly categorized into three major approaches: here we refer to them as WaveNet approach, RNN approach, and extrapolation approach. Among them, there have been proposed several neural networks that belong to the extrapolation approach and employ vibrating activation functions such as a sinusoidal function and wavelet [2,3,5]. In these architectures, the current time for generating a waveform is treated as the explicit input given at an input layer. That is, neither all the activation functions (i.e., oscillators) share the current time, nor the activation functions at the hidden layers refer to it.

In the paper, we propose deep Frequency Modulation (FM) synthesis, which is the method of generating an approximating waveform based on the network inspired by the conventional FM synthesis. According to the Gashler and Ashmore's categorization, the deep FM synthesis basically belongs to the extrapolation approach. Thus, we hope the deep FM sysntesis could generate unknown yet good sounds by extrapolating already existing sounds in a different way from prevalent sound generation methods such as sampling and WaveNet. To study the feasibility and utility of the deep FM synthesis, we investigate the basic characteristics and performances of it; for instance, how accurate the deep FM synthesis can approximate a target waveform, what size of the network we need for reconstructing a target waveform, how and what conventional techniques for optimizing networks can be applied to the deep FM synthesis, and so on.

2 Deep Frequency Modulation Synthesis

2.1 Architecture

For theoretical consideration, we think of a simple, typical architecture shown in Fig. 1, which presents how oscillator units are interconnected with weights w; the depth is $M+1$, the width is $N+1$, and Σ^w stands for weighted sum. The input to the network is vector $\{A_0, A_1, \cdots A_N\}$, and the output is waveform S. For an oscillator unit by a typical vibrating function, we here adopt a sinusoidal function

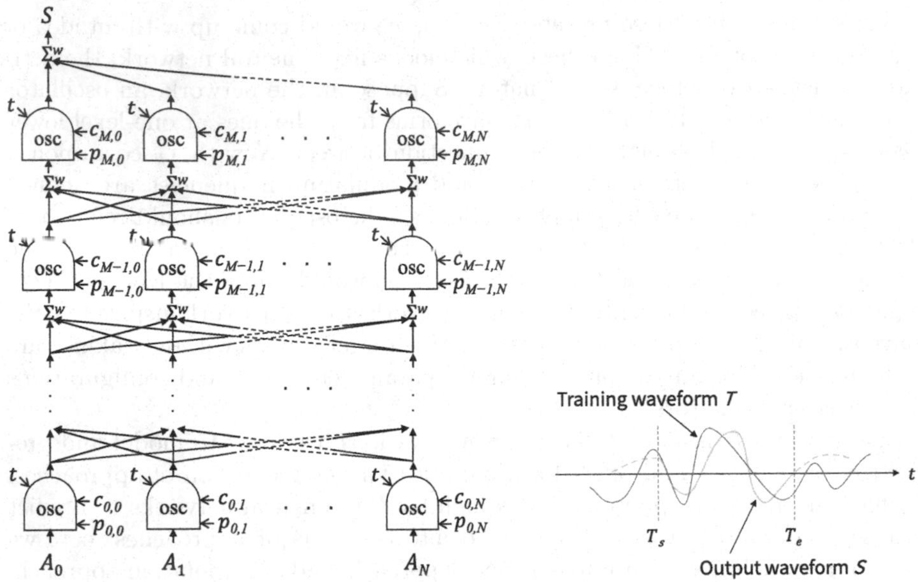

Fig. 1. Network configuration of deep FM synthesis (Color figure online)

$y = \sin\ 2\pi((x + c)\ t + p)$ with input x (the bottom of the oscillator unit in the figure) and output y (the top). Each oscillator unit has two parameters c and p to be tuned corresponding to frequency and phase, respectively. All oscillator units share the identical timing signal t, which moves between starting time T_s and ending time T_e, to compute the output waveform (the red solid curve in Fig. 1). The network attempts to fit the output waveform to the training waveform only between T_s and T_e (dark blue). Thus, in the ranges out of the interval between T_s and T_e, the network does not take care of the output waveform (red dashed curves).

The forward propagation in the deep FM synthesis works as conventional neural networks; at layer n, input waveform x is given to each oscillator unit to compute output y with parameters $c_{m,n}$ and $p_{m,n}$ at time t. Then, the output waveforms calculated at layer n, that is y, are summed up with weights, and the sum is provided to the input waveform at layer $n+1$ as x. An output waveform is made of the series of values S_t, which represent the samples at time instant t between T_s and T_e. In other words, given time t at which we want to obtain value S_t, the network calculates S_t in a bottom-up manner.

We may assume that all the elements of the input vector $\{A_0, A_1, \cdots A_N\}$ are constant values. The assumption is justified by the design decision we made that the deep FM synthesis works as a multiple-wave generator depending on the input vector. In reality, the input vector can be made of either constant values or any waveforms synchronized by the timing signal t. Theoretically, the input vector can be either constants or any waveforms synchronized by the timing signal t, since giving waveforms to the input is equivalent to the extension of the network in the direction of depth with constants given to the input. Therefore, the multi-layered architecture absorbed such subtle differences, and we can put the assumption without loss of generality.

2.2 Backpropagation

We would apply the standard backpropagation technique to optimize the deep FM synthesis as follows [4]. For notational simplification, we assume the network size is depth $M+1$ by width $N+1$, and the width is unchanged from the top layer to the bottom. The final output of the deep FM synthesis at time t is denoted as S_t. The input and output of the n-th oscillator unit at layer m are denoted as $x_{m,n}$ and $y_{m,n}$, respectively. The weight between adjacent layers is denoted as $w_{m,n',n}$, which stands for the weight from n'-th unit at layer m to n-th unit at layer $m+1$. Only at the topmost layer, we write $w_{M,n}$, omitting the second n. Then, the final output is straightforwardly defined in a topdown manner:

$$S_t = \sum_{n=0}^{N} w_{M,n} \cdot y_{M,n} \tag{1}$$

For m = M .. 1 and n = 0 .. N, we define $y_{m,n} = \sin 2\pi((x_{m,n} + c_{m,n})t + p_{m,n})$ and $x_{m,n} = \sum_{n'=0}^{N} w_{m-1,n',n} \cdot y_{m-1,n'}$. For m = 0 and n = 0 .. N (the bottom layer), we define $y_{0,n} = \sin(x_{0,n}t + p_{0,n})$, and $x_{0,n} = A_n$. We always put $c_{0,n} = 0$ because the elements of the input $\{A_0, A_1, \cdots A_N\}$ are all assigned to constant values.

A single network of deep FM synthesis is trained, considering the set of time instants within the designated period between T_s and T_e. Let us denote the training waveform (target waveform) at time t as T_t. Then, the loss function is defined as follows:

$$E = \sum_t E_t = \sum_t \frac{1}{2}(S_t - T_t)^2 \, , \tag{2}$$

where $\sum_t$ means the summation over the set of the time instants ($T_s \leq t \leq T_e$).

We present the gradient descent method for optimizing the network [4]; let us compute the partial differential of the loss in Eq. (2) with respect to each parameter contained in the network in the standard manner. First of all, for the topmost weights $w_{M,n}$, from Eq. (1) we have

$$\frac{\partial E_t}{\partial w_{M,n}} = \frac{\partial E_t}{\partial S_t} \cdot \frac{\partial S_t}{\partial w_{M,n}} = (S_t - T_t) \cdot y_{M,n}$$

Note that although the same timing signal t is provided to all oscillator units, the gradient of the loss can be derived as in conventional neural networks. Also for the parameters within each oscillator, $\frac{\partial E_t}{\partial c_{M,n}}$ and $\frac{\partial E_t}{\partial p_{M,n}}$ can be derived similarly. Then, to simply express the derivatives of $y_{m,n}$, we introduce term $\cos 2\pi((x_{m,n} + c_{m,n})t + p_{m,n})$ and denote it as $z_{m,n}$. Due to space limitation, we omit the technical details and show only the result of parameter optimization. We derive the following entire inductive definition of the gradient chain Γ and the feedback values for gradient descent:

Base step: $\Gamma^A_{M,n} = (S_t - T_t) \cdot w_{M,n}$
Induction step:

$$\Gamma^A_{m,n} = \sum_{i=0}^{N} \Gamma^B_{m+1,i} \cdot w_{m,n,i} \quad (m = 0 \mathrel{..} M-1)$$
$$\Gamma^B_{m,n} = \Gamma^A_{m,n} \cdot 2\pi t \; z_{m,n} \quad (m = 0 \mathrel{..} M) \tag{3}$$

Using the series of the gradient chain above, we obtain the partial differentials of the parameters as follows:

$$\frac{\partial E_t}{\partial w_{M,n}} = (S_t - T_t) \cdot y_{M,n}$$
$$\frac{\partial E_t}{\partial w_{m,n',n}} = \Gamma^B_{m+1,n} \cdot y_{m,n'} \quad (m = 0 \mathrel{..} M-1)$$
$$\frac{\partial E_t}{\partial c_{m,n}} = \Gamma^A_{m,n} \cdot 2\pi t \; z_{m,n} \quad (m = 0 \mathrel{..} M)$$
$$\frac{\partial E_t}{\partial p_{m,n}} = \Gamma^A_{m,n} \cdot 2\pi \; z_{m,n} \quad (m = 0 \mathrel{..} M)$$

3 Experiments and Results

3.1 Implementation

Following the standard backpropagation techniques [4], for optimization, we employ stochastic gradient descent, Adam, and L^2 regularization with soft threshold. Within an epoch, as many time instants at which the loss is calculated as the size of the mini-batch are generated by the uniform random number generator over the designated temporal interval. In the following experiments, the mini-batch size is always set to 5. For simplicity, all parameters c's, p's, and w's are initialized by the normal distribution with the average being 0.0 and the variance being 0.1. Each layer, consisting of the oscillator units, is fully-connected to adjacent layers.

Here, we give a notice in setting the period of time t to preserve stability for the deep FM synthesis. As some may already noticed in Eq. (3), the gradient chain inevitably includes term t^n, where n is the depth from the top layer. It follows that the amount of the loss feedback is proportional to t^n. Thus, if $0.0 < t < 1.0$, t^n may always become almost 0.0; on the other hand, if $t > 1.0$, t^n may become a larger value. Therefore, in the following experiments, the period of time t is put from 1.0 to 2.0. These values have been determined through several trials we made.

3.2 Loss Convergence

At the very first step, we would check if the backpropagation technique introduced in the previous section can work for the deep FM synthesis. Figure 2 shows the loss convergences calculated by mean squared error as the epoch increases (Eq. (2)), when the network size is depth 5 by width 5 and the training waveforms are rectangle and sawtooth with two cycles in the period of 1.0 to 2.0.

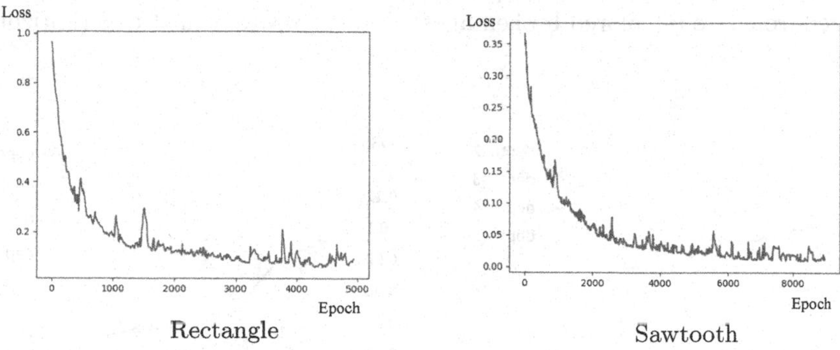

Fig. 2. Loss convergences along with Epoch

Figure 3 shows the intermediate waveforms generated by the network at epochs 0, 500, and 4400 for rectangle and at epochs 0, 1000, and 8400 for sawtooth, respectively. Note that the training and output waveforms are shown only between T_s and T_e (i.e., 1.0 and 2.0). To obtain the above results, it took several minutes or less for each training phase, using Surface Pro 3 featuring Intel Core i7 CPU @ 1.70 GHz.

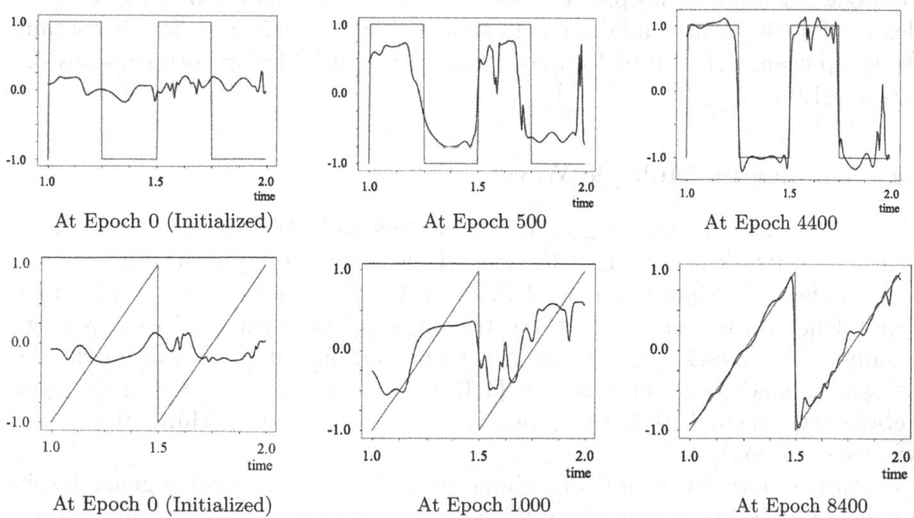

Fig. 3. Waveforms generated during training for rectangle and sawtooth

3.3 Network Size

We examine the relationship between the network size (depth × width) and the loss. The left-hand graph in Fig. 4 shows the results for rectangle as the training waveform, and the right-hand graph sawtooth. In the both graphs, the depth is changed from 2 to 5 (colored broken lines), and the width from 1 to 8 (horizontal axes).

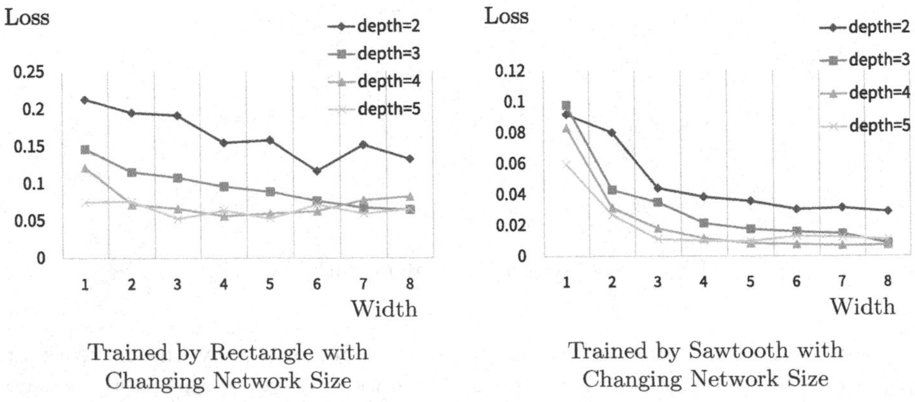

Fig. 4. Network size and loss

The loss in sawtooth converges faster along with the width increased than rectangle. At present, we presume the result could be understood by the complexity of a waveform as a figure. For example, while a cycle of rectangle contains two steep changes (−1.0 to 1.0 and 1.0 to −1.0), that of sawtooth contains one (1.0 to −1.0).

3.4 Training by Multiple Waves

We are interested in the learnability of the network, that is, how many wave forms the network can learn at the same time. Then, for training, the network is given the more than one pair of input vector and output wave form. In the experiment, during an epoch, three trainings are performed. During a single training, the network is given a pair of input and output by a mini-batch. The first pair is made of input vector of $\{1, 0, 0, \cdots\}$ and output signal of two-cycle rectangle; the second $\{0, 1, 0, \cdots\}$ two-cycle sawtooth, and the third $\{0, 0, 1, \cdots\}$ two-cycle sinusoid.

Figure 5 shows the results of training the three pairs; the waves generated by the deep FM synthesis are drawn in the colored curves, and the training waves in black. We use the network of depth 5 by width 5.

The leftmost graph in the figure is obtained at epoch 23000 with loss of 6.57 $\times 10^{-2}$ (near the optimal point for the rectangle), when given input $\{1, 0, 0, \cdots\}$.

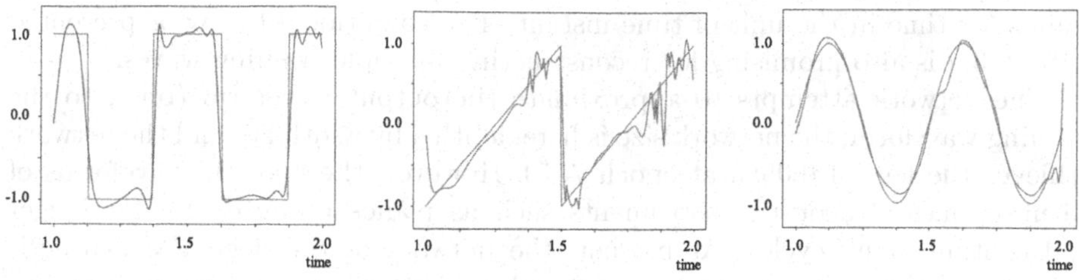

Fig. 5. Three waves generated by network when given three distinct input vectors (Color figure online)

Similarly in the middle for sawtooth, the graph is obtained at epoch 21370 with loss of 2.12 $\times 10^{-2}$, and for sinusoid, at epoch 11680 with loss of 6.62 $\times 10^{-3}$.

For instance, let us compare the leftmost colored graph in Fig. 5 with the upper rightmost in Fig. 3 ("At Epoch 4400"). It seems that the generated wave form in the former is hardly deteriorated, even if that network learns three different wave forms at the same time, however, the epochs required for training is about 5 times larger.

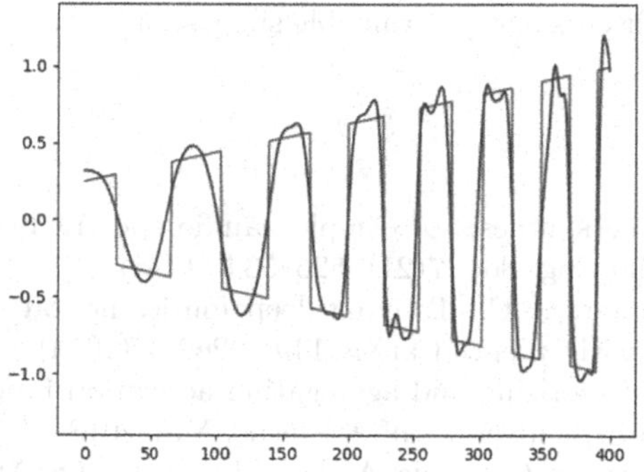

Fig. 6. Approximating unsteady waveform

4 Concluding Remarks

We propose the deep FM synthesis which is inspired by the conventional FM synthesis; it has the network architecture like neural networks and can be optimized by the backpropagation technique as neural networks. We have demonstrated that the deep FM synthesis works well to some extent for small-sized artificial training waveforms. Figure 6 shows an example when an unsteady, a little complicated training waveform (black curve in the figure) is given; the wave length and amplitude of it is varied along time. The horizontal axis in the figure stands for time in the unit of time instant. The conditional behavior presented in Sect. 3.4 is also promising for reconstructing multiple training waves.

The network attempts to approximate the output waveform (blue) to the training waveform; the network size is here depth 4 by width 20, and the network achieves the loss of 0.0583 at epoch 7570. However, the realistic waveforms of natural tones of acoustic instruments such as pianos or flutes are far longer and contain many cycles. At present, the network of the deep FM synthesis cannot properly learn and reconstruct such real waveforms, unfortunately. The output waveform of the network does not sufficiently converge on a given training waveform under the current optimization method.

Future work will include improving the approximation to the simple waveforms as given in Sects. 3.2 and 3.3, and developing a tractable optimization method that can work effectively when learning realistic, long, complicated waveforms such as natural tones of acoustic instruments and voices. For the purpose, we would investigate other vibrating functions to be used for an activation function which must be differentiable and not necessarily periodic such as wavelet and phase modulator.

Acknowledgments. This work has been supported by JSPS Kakenhi 16H01744. The authors would like to thank to Prof. Ichiro Fujinaga of McGill University, Mr. Adrien Ycart of Queen Mary University, and Mr. Masafuji Takahashi of Future University Hakodate for fruitful discussions and valuable suggestions.

References

1. Chowning, J.M.: The synthesis of complex audio spectra by means of frequency modulation. J. Audio Eng. Soc. **7**(21), 526–534 (1973)
2. Gashler, M.S., Ashmore, S.C.: Training deep fourier neural networks to fit timeseries data (2014). arXiv preprint arXiv:1405.2262v1 (2014)
3. Godfrey, L.B.: Parameterizing and aggregating activation functions in deep neural networks. Ph.D. thesis, University of Arkansas, May 2018
4. Goodfellow, I., Bengio, Y., Courville, A.: Deep Learning. The MIT Press, Cambridge (2016)
5. Mingo, L., Aslanyan, L., Castellanos, J., Daz, M., Riazanov, V.: Fourier neural networks: an approach with sinusoidal activation functions. Int. J. Inf. Theories Appl. **11**, 52–55 (2004)
6. Roads, C.: The Computer Music Tutorial. The MIT Press, Cambridge (1996)
7. Wikipedia: Yamaha DX7. https://en.wikipedia.org/wiki/Yamaha_DX7. Accessed 24 Jan 2019

Musical Note Attacks Description in Reverberant Environments

Thiago de Almeida Magalhães Campolina(✉)
and Mauricio Alves Loureiro(✉)

Center for Studies on Musical Gesture and Expression (CEGeME), School of Music, Federal University of Minas Gerais (UFMG), Belo Horizonte, Brazil
thicampolina@gmail.com, mauricio.alves.loureiro@gmail.com
http://www.musica.ufmg.br/cegeme/

Abstract. This paper addresses the description of musical note attacks considering the influence of the reverberation. It is well known that attacks have an essential role in music performance. By manipulating note attack quality, musicians are able to control timbre, articulation, and rhythm, which are essential parameters for conveying their expressive intentions. Including information about the interaction with room acoustics enriches the study of musical performances in everyday practice conditions where reverberant environments are always present. Spectral Modeling decomposition was applied to evaluate independently, three components along the attack: (i) the harmonics of the note being played, (ii) the harmonics of the reverberation, (iii) the residue energy. The description proposal covers two stages: A 2D confrontation of the energy from the extracted components, and a profile representing the first nine harmonics' structure. We tested the approach in a case study using recordings of an excerpt from a clarinet piece from the traditional classical repertoire, played by six professional musicians. MANOVA tests indicated significant differences ($p < 0.05$) when considering the musician as a factor for the 2D confrontation. Linear Discriminant Analysis applied for supervised dimensionality reduction of the harmonic profile data also indicated group separation to the same factor. We examined different *legato*, as well as articulated note transition presenting different performance technique demands.

Keywords: Note attacks description · Empirical performance analysis · Music information retrieval

1 Introduction

Research related to the note attack region in musical signals has been conducted since the 1960s. Several studies demonstrated the importance of the attack on the perception of a musical note [7,10,12]. In [10], for example, it was shown that the musical instrument identification was possible with only 60 ms of the attack, whereas more than twice as long (150 ms) was necessary using only the note sustain.

R. Kronland-Martinet et al. (Eds.): CMMR 2019, LNCS 12631, pp. 225–247, 2021.
https://doi.org/10.1007/978-3-030-70210-6_16

Experimental studies on spectral content analysis of musical note attacks have been usually conducted in low reverberant environments, in order to better isolate parameters variations, disregarding the interaction between musician and performance environment. However, adapting the performance to a specific room or concert hall acoustics is part of musicians' routine. In [9], an experiment with professional musicians revealed that they consciously adjust their performing style under different room acoustic conditions. An interview with the performers indicated that each participant consciously adjusted the performing style according to some of the following attributes: tempo, vibrato, harmonics, sound quality, articulation, agogics, and dynamics. Also, studies have focused on the objective investigation of adjustments of performances made by professional musicians under different room acoustic conditions [1,6,9,14]. In [14] for example, computer models of 14 rooms were tested by dynamic binaural synthesis with performers playing physically in an anechoic chamber, while wearing aural headphones simulating corresponding virtual acoustic environments. This experiment revealed distinct concepts of adjustment to room acoustical conditions as well as significant individuality concerning musicians' interaction with room acoustics.

Inspired by these studies, we explored in [2] the audio content of monophonic musical note attacks, considering the reverberated harmonics of the previous note as relevant information. Spectral Modeling Synthesis (**SMS**) decomposition [15] was applied for estimating the energy of the harmonic and residual components, using this information for audio description as proposed by [8]. In [2], however, an additional step was included in the description considering the harmonic content of reverberation independently from the harmonic content of the note being attacked. We proposed a 2D representation aiming at comparing three components for characterizing note attacks: the harmonic energy of the attacked note, the harmonic energy of the previous note reverberation, and the residual component. This approach enabled inferences about the interaction with room acoustics, enriching the study of musical performances in everyday practice conditions where reverberant environments are always present. The results here shown extends [2] to further approaches, by providing an additional description tool, the Harmonic Profile of the Attack (**HPA**), aimed at representing the starting harmonic structure of the attacked note. As in the previous study, a comparison of the efficiency of different spectral modeling techniques is beyond the scope of this paper. For the present analysis, we used the same experimental data from [2]: two different performance situations of note articulation (*legato* and *staccato*), as well as note transitions demanding different performance techniques.

Figure 1 illustrates the primary motivation of this study. The spectrogram of a fragment extracted from a recording used in this study, delimited by the rectangle on the score of the fragment, summarizes the three acoustic elements we observed on the attack region: (1) the harmonic content of the previous note reverberation (highlighted by the circle); (2) the specific behavior of harmonics magnitude increase and onset lags in individual attacked notes (highlighted by the ellipse); (3) an element that is neither a part of the note's harmonic structure, nor from the reverberation, usually treated as noise, that could originate from instrument keys, air blowing, or any turbulence (highlighted by square).

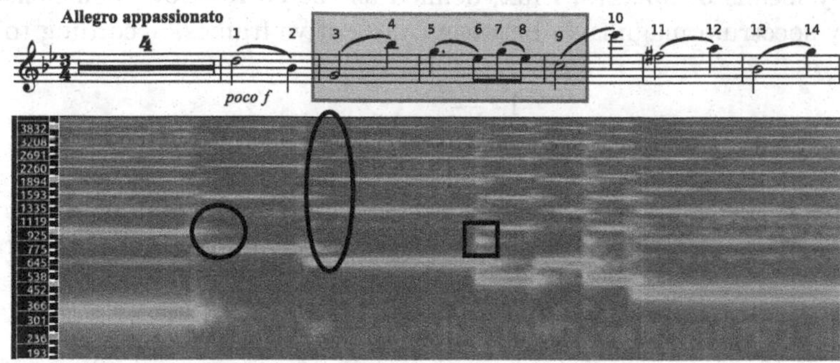

Fig. 1. A Spectrogram of a fragment extracted from a recording used in the analysis. Three elements found in the note attacks are highlighted.

2 Methods

We divided the proposed methodology into three stages: (1) Audio segmentation (pre-processing); (2) Spectral modeling and decomposition; (3) Characterization of attacks using the extracted components. Stage (2) decomposes the signal by modeling three components from the attack spectrum: harmonic content of the attacked note ($H1$), the harmonic content of reverberation ($H2$) and the residues ($R2$). Stage (3) is divided into two parts: the first describes the Plane **H2R2**, a 2D representation of the three components we proposed in [2]; the second, named Harmonic Profile of the Attacks (**HPA**), introduces an additional tool, proposed in this paper.

2.1 Segmentation

We used MATLAB from MathWorks for audio processing. Figure 2 shows a diagram of the audio segmentation processing. First, note onsets were detected by energy and pitch criteria combined. Root Mean Square (**RMS**) and Fast Fourier Transform (**FFT**) were used to represent the energy envelop and the frequency spectrum of the signal. For all windowing calculations, we used a Hamming window with size of 1024 samples (23.2 ms) and hop size of 256 samples (5.8 ms) at the sample rate of 44.1 kHz. The pitch was estimated by choosing the local maximum of the spectrum that presents the highest harmonic series energy sum. Onsets of consecutive notes with equal pitch were detected by crossing the **RMS** curve by an auxiliary **RMS** with a window size of 1 s [5]. In transitions involving notes with different pitches, onsets were detected by variations in the pitch curve above 6%. Techniques for transients detection in musical signals are based on four principles: variations in signal energy, variations in frequency spectrum magnitude, variations in phase spectrum and detection by modeling [4]. Here, variations in frequency spectrum magnitude was chosen to detect the attacks by means of Spectral Flux, defined as the correlation coefficient of the frequency spectrum magnitude between consecutive frames, according to Eq. 1.

$$F(q) = 1 - \frac{1}{M}\sum_{p=1}^{M}|r(X(p)_q, X(p)_{q-1})| \quad (1)$$

where $F(q)$ is the Spectral Flux value in frame q, M is the window size, r is the correlation coefficient, and X is the frequency spectrum of the current frame.

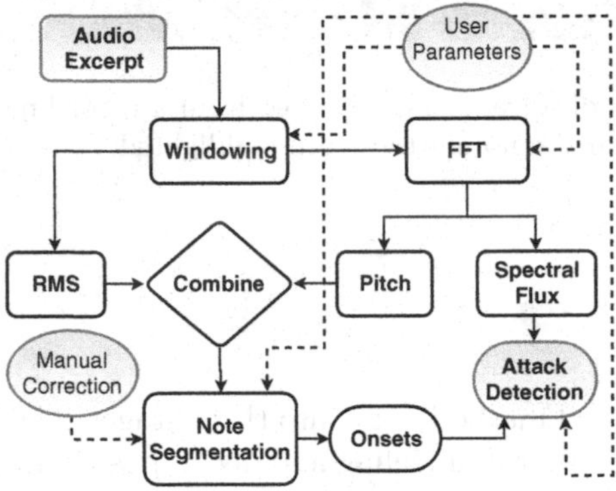

Fig. 2. Diagram of pre-processing.

Spectral Flux value decreases in regions with small variation in the temporal evolution of the frequency spectrum, tending to stabilization in the region of note sustain. The end of the attack was estimated as the first instant of Spectral Flux stabilization below a threshold defined as 10% of the average Spectral Flux of the entire note. Attack region was assumed as the region delimited by the note onset and the end of the attack.

2.2 Spectral Modeling and Decomposition

Initially we used the **SMS** implementation published in [16] to decompose the frequency spectrum of the attack region (Fig. 3) into components $H1$, $R1$, $H2$ and $R2$, corresponding to the harmonic and the residual content of the note being played and of the previous note. First, spectral modeling synthesis **SMS(1)** returns $H1$ by modeling the harmonics with frequency restriction around the pitch of the attacked note (*Pitch Restriction 1*). Spectral Subtraction returns the first residue $R1$. Then, we applied spectral modeling **SMS(2)** in $R1$ with frequency restriction around the pitch of the previous note (*Pitch Restriction 2*), resulting in a second pair of components: $H2$, the energy of the modeled harmonics from the reverberation of the previous note and $R2$, the energy of the second residue. Frequency restriction of five percent was adopted. The components $H1$, $R1$, $H2$, and $R2$ will be latter expressed in terms of their proportions to the original energy.

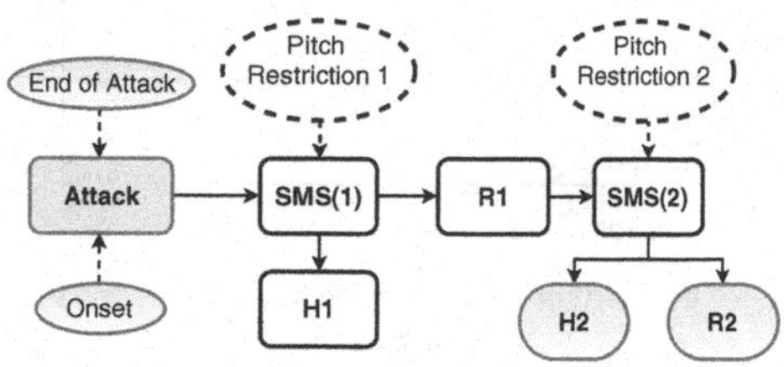

Fig. 3. Diagram of the spectral modeling and decomposition process.

2.3 Characterization of Attacks

Plane H2R2. The first tool for characterizing note attacks is the 2D confrontation of components $H2$ and $R2$, as described in [2]. Considering the total energy (root mean square) of the signal during the attack as S_E, we can write Eq. 2:

$$S_E = H1 + H2 + R2. \tag{2}$$

where $H1$, $H2$ e $R1$ e $R2$ are the energy (root mean square) of the components defined in Subsect. 2.2. Then we want to confront $H2$ x $R2$ (Eqs. 3 and 4) normalized by the total energy S_E in decibels:

$$\mathbf{H2} = 10 \log_{10}(\frac{H2}{S_E}), \tag{3}$$

$$\mathbf{R2} = 10 \log_{10}(\frac{R2}{S_E}). \tag{4}$$

With this representation we have negative values for **R2** and **H2** limited to 0 dB (zero decibels). Hence, higher values of any of these two variables correspond to lower harmonic energy from the current note ($H1$), since the sum of $H2$ and $R2$ equals to $R1$. Figure 4 shows the superior limit for the values of **R2** and **H2** alternating with each other, when $H1$ has no energy.

Harmonic Profile of the Attack (HPA). The second tool for characterizing note attacks aims at representing the structure of the first nine harmonics of the component **H1**, considering the influence of the reverberation.

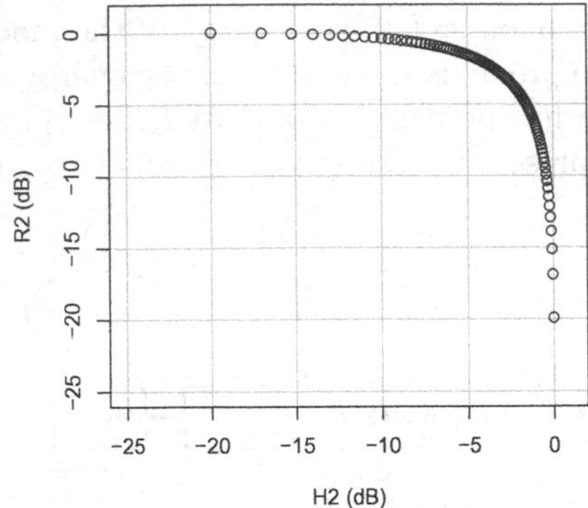

Fig. 4. Plane **H2R2:** 100 points simulating the superior limit for **R2** and **H2**, when **H1** remains without energy.

The profile starts in the fundamental frequency and goes through the first nine harmonics crossing each one at the frame immediately before reaching a threshold (Thr) defined as stated in Eq. 5:

$$Thr(i) = 10\log\left(E_f(i)\right) + 0.5\left[\,\left|10\log\left(E_f(i)\right)\right| - \left|10\log\left(E_{min}(i)\right)\right|\,\right], \qquad (5)$$

where $Thr(i)$ is the energy limit to define the crossing point for the ith harmonic with i varying from 1 (the fundamental frequency) to 9, $E_f(i)$ is the energy of the final frame of the ith harmonic inside the attack, and $E_{min}(i)$ is the minimum energy of the ith harmonic. As can be noted in Eq. 5, if the minimum energy of the ith harmonic coincides with the energy of the final frame, the term inside the brackets become zero, leading the crossing point of the **HPA** to the last frame, the end of the attack.

The **HPA** carries time and energy information from each of the nine harmonics, resulting in an 18-dimensional representation of the attack. These values are then normalized by the note duration and note maximum energy in decibels. Figure 5 panel (a) shows the **HPA** in dashed line over the harmonics (continuous lines) of the attack of note 4, at take **T1**, by clarinetist **C2**, and panel (b) shows the **HPA** in dashed line and its projections (dot-dashed lines) in planes Harmonics x Magnitude (**HxM**) and Harmonics x Time (**HxT**). Section 3 presents a detailed description of the data used in the analysis.

2.4 Statistical Methods

In order to verify whether the proposed tools are capable of describing musicians' individuality in reverberant environments, as observed by [14], we carried out statistical tests to verify significant difference among the musician's group means. All the statistical analysis was conducted using the programming environment R [11].

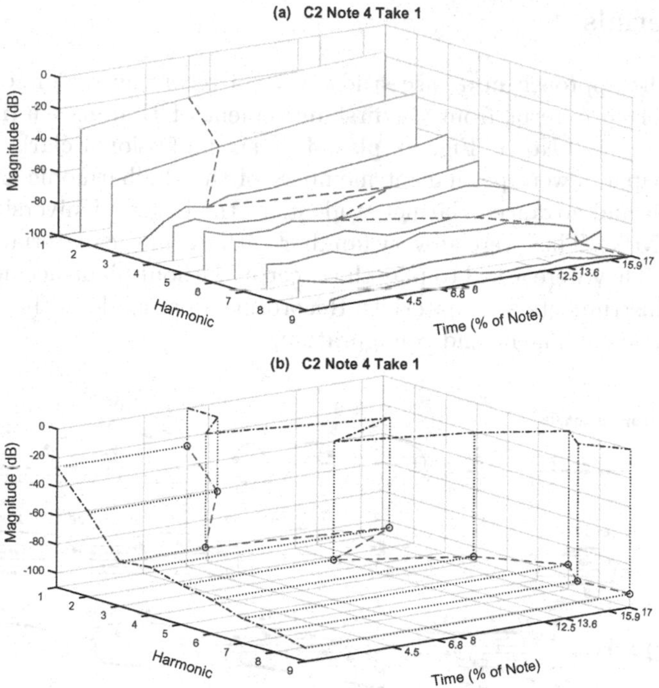

Fig. 5. Panel (a): **HPA** in dashed line over the harmonics (continuous lines) from the attack of the note 4 take 1 clarinetist **C2**. Panel (b): Projections in planes Harmonics x Magnitude (**HxM**) and Harmonics x Time (**HxT**).

First, we applied MANOVA (with Pillai's trace[1]) to test the effect of musician as a factor on Plane **H2R2** dimensions. Variances of the covariance matrix were also used to infer about musicians' consistency.

The Plane **H2R2** was also useful in the analysis of the Harmonic Profiles of the Attack. We used a threshold of −3 dB in both dimensions for identifying note attacks considered as unsuccessfully executed categorized by too low energy of harmonic content of the note being attacked. We excluded from the tests participants with three or more unsuccessful executions for that note in order to avoid bias in the statistical analysis.

We applied Linear Discriminant Analysis associated with the MANOVA to reduce the 18-dimensional representation of **HPA** and to verify grouping separation considering musician as a factor. Besides, ANOVA was also applied to test grouping separation to each Linear Discriminant separately.

[1] The Pillai's trace is the default test option used in R function MANOVA and considered the most robust statistic for general use, here chosen due to the exploratory characteristics of the research.

3 Materials

We tested the approach in a case study using a recording set of selected note transitions of an excerpt from the first movement of Brahms Clarinet Sonata in F minor, op. 120 No. 1 (Fig. 6), played by six professional clarinetists in six takes. Participants were permanent members of the Philharmonic Orchestra of Minas Gerais and advanced clarinet students of the Federal University of Minas Gerais (**UFMG**). They were all very familiar with the music material used in the experiment. They were asked to play the excerpt, without piano accompaniment, using their instruments and materials. Recordings were made in the same room, using the same equipment and configuration.

Fig. 6. Excerpt from the first movement of Brahms Clarinet Sonata in F minor, op. 120 No. 1, used in the analysis (written pitch for B flat clarinet).

4 Results

We selected seven cases of consecutive note transition to examine our representation for characterizing note attacks, considering different levels of performance technique demands, due to note articulation type and note interval leap. Five of them are *legato* transitions (connected by a slur on the score): notes 3 to 4, 9 to 10, 11 to 12, 13 to 14 and 21 to 22 (Fig. 6). Two are articulated (detached) transitions (indicated by a slur break): notes 8 to 9 and 12 to 13.

4.1 Plane H2R2

Figure 7(a) shows the Plane **H2R2** for the attacks from all observations of note 4, composed by six takes played by six clarinetists (**C1** to **C6**). **T1** and **T2** represent two takes executed by the same clarinetist **C2**. Figure 7(b) and (c) show **T2** and **T1** waveforms, spectrograms and Spectral Flux confirming the distance between both executions observed on the Plane **H2R2**, where execution **T2** exhibits much lower harmonic content ($H1$) then execution **T1**. In this figure, waveforms and spectrograms were extracted with the software Sonic Visualizer [3] and Spectral Flux (continuous white line) using the plugin MIR.EDU [13]. The elliptical shapes are data-concentration delimiters. These shapes were estimated as bivariate-normal probability-contour at confidence level 80 %. Associated solid points in these figures represent the center of the ellipses.

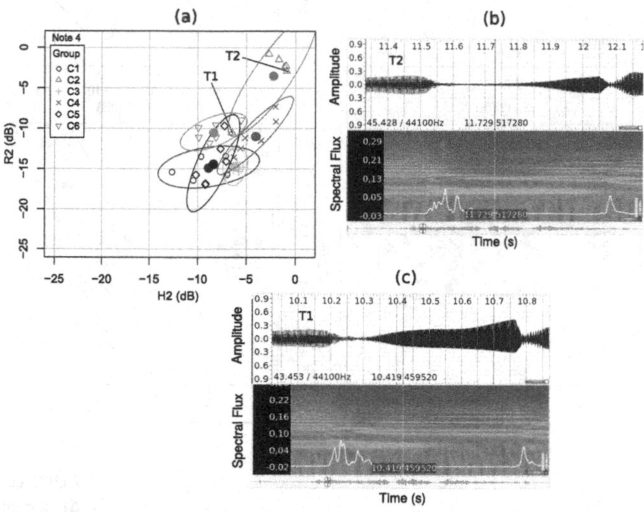

Fig. 7. Panel (a): Plane **H2R2** for all executions by the six clarinetists (**C1** to **C6**) of attacks of note 4. **T1** and **T2** indicate two takes executed by clarinetist **C2**. The other panels shows the waveform and spectral flux (spectrogram in background) of **T2** (panel b) and **T1** (panel c).

Panels (a) to (e) of Fig. 8 show the Planes **H2R2** for the attacks of the notes 22, 12, 14, 10 and 4, within *legato* note transitions, where blowing pressure is maintained across the transition to minimize vibration interruption. Panels (f) and (g), show attacks of notes 9 and 13 after detached articulation, where blowing pressure is interrupted by touching the reed with the tongue.

Table 1 shows the results of MANOVA (p-values) considering the clarinetists (**C1** to **C6**) as a factor for each of the selected notes, the variances of **R2** and **H2** for each clarinetist by note and, finally, the group pairs with Maximum Contrast.

4.2 Harmonic Profile of the Attack (HPA)

As mentioned before, we did not include note attacks considered as unsuccessfully executed in the Harmonic Profile analysis, as revealed by a threshold on the Plane **H2R2** representation. Figure 9 shows the Plane **H2R2** with the established threshold of -3 dB in dashed line. Clarinetists that failed three times or more to execute a note, were discarded from the analysis of that note.

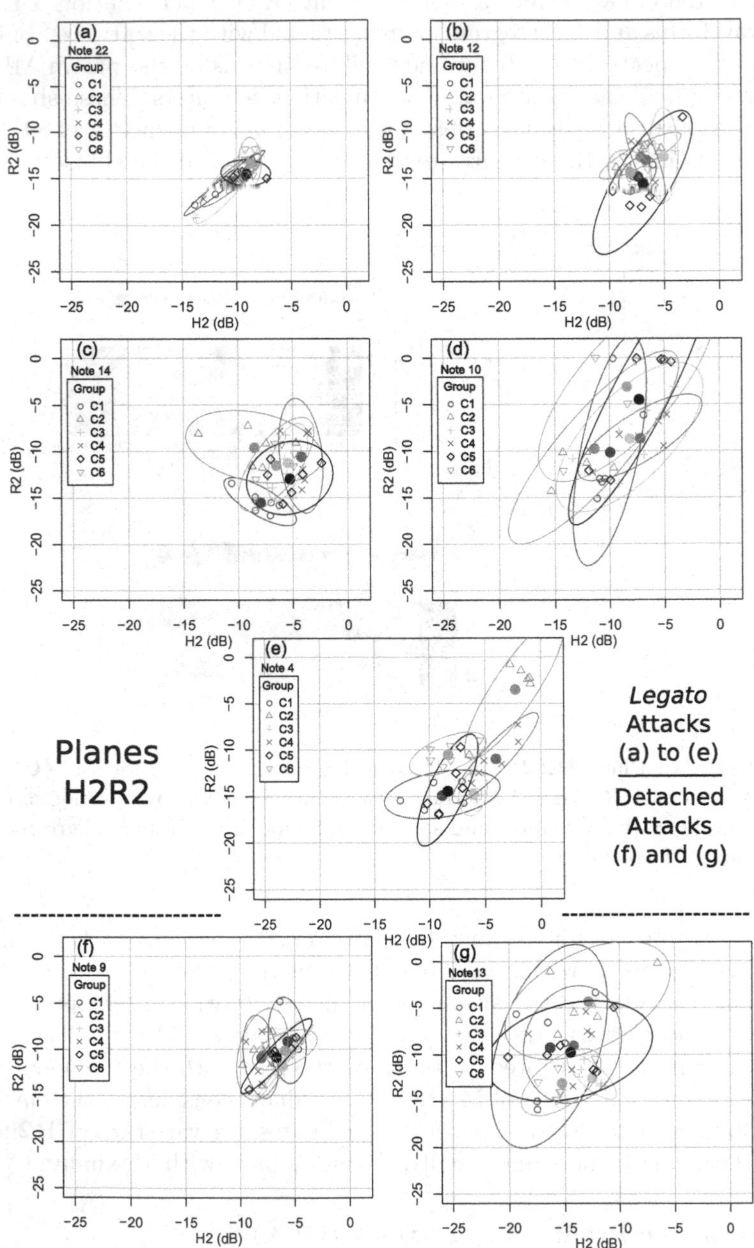

Fig. 8. Planes **H2R2** for the attacks from the *legato* transitions to notes 22, 12, 14, 10 and 4 in panels (a) to (e) and from the detached transitions to notes 9 (f) and 13 (g).

Table 1. Results of MANOVA testing clarinetists as a factor in Plane **H2R2** data. Variances of **R2** and **H2** for each clarinetists (**C1** to **C6**), Maximum Contrast pairs, and p-values.

	Variance						Max. contrast	MANOVA
	C1	C2	C3	C4	C5	C6	in dB (pair)	P-value
Note 4							4.4 (C1–C4)	<0.001*
R2	1.5	12.9	1.3	5.2	8.0	1.2	–	–
H2	6.0	4.5	0.4	3.3	1.7	2.6	–	–
Note 9							2.1 (C1–C4)	0.007
R2	4.8	5.3	4.3	4.4	3.6	1.0	–	–
H2	0.7	1.3	1.8	0.6	2.4	1.9	–	–
Note 10							4.8 (C2–C6)	0.015
R2	33.6	23.7	14.2	4.7	40.9	23.6	–	–
H2	2.5	13.3	10.0	7.1	9.2	14.3	–	–
Note 12							2.4 (C3–C5)	0.013
R2	0.9	1.4	5.8	5.3	13.1	1.2	–	–
H2	0.7	3.1	0.4	0.7	4.6	0.9	–	–
Note 13							5.6 (C2–C6)	<0.001
R2	26.5	8.8	1.3	8.8	6.4	2.8	–	–
H2	6.2	12.5	1.12	4.4	12.6	2.9	–	–
Note 14							4.3 (C1–C4)	<0.001
R2	1.5	3.4	3.8	8.4	3.5	5.6	–	–
H2	2.4	8.6	0.8	0.9	3.4	2.7	–	–
Note 22							2.3 (C1–C6)	0.027
R2	2.7	0.7	3.8	1.8	0.4	1.6	–	–
H2	3.1	0.5	2.1	1.7	1.2	0.2	–	–

*Group **C2** of note 4 was discarded from MANOVA due to strong rejection in normality test.

Figures 10, 11, 12, 13 show two-dimensional projections of **HPA** for all executions (takes) by each clarinetist of four selected notes, two attacked in *legato* transition, notes 4 and 14, and two attacked after detached articulation, notes 9 and 13. Panels (1a) to (1f) show the **HPA** projections on the Harmonic x Time (**HxT**) plane and panels (2a) to (2f) show the projections on the Harmonic x Magnitude (**HxM**) plane. The time dimension is expressed by percentage of note duration and the magnitude in dB normalized by the maximum energy of the note.

The results of the Linear Discriminant Analysis applied to the Harmonic Profile of the Attack are shown in Figs. 14 and 15. Figure 14 shows all Linear Discriminants (**LD**) data projections by note and clarinetists groups in columns. Under each **LD** label in this figure, three values are displayed: **TP**, the cumulative percentage of true positive from the discriminant functions classification; the

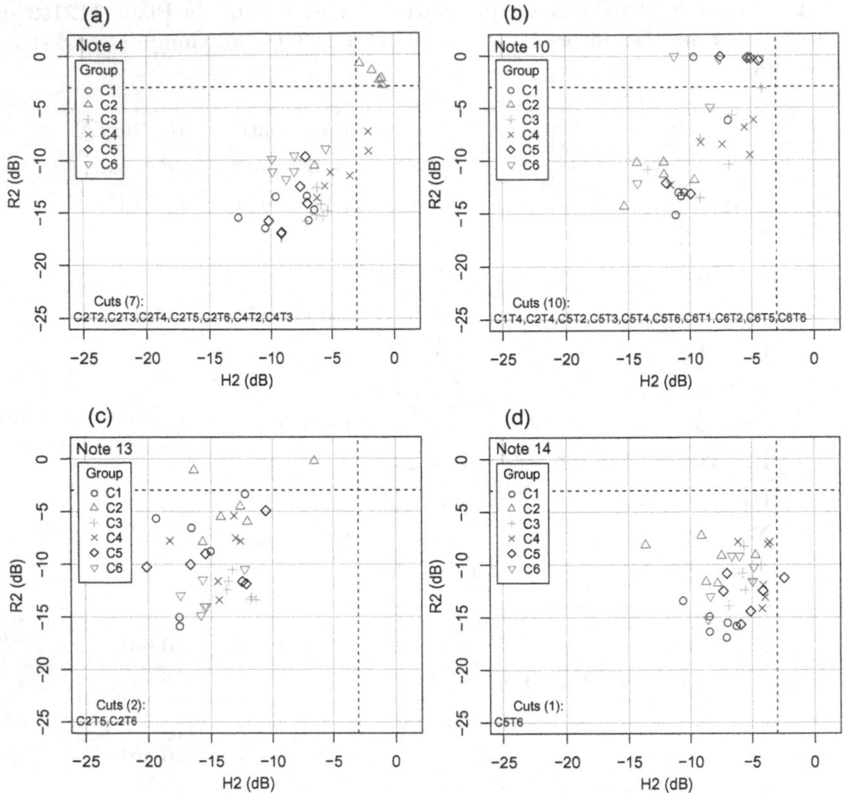

Fig. 9. Plane **H2R2** for notes that have at least one of the takes above the threshold of −3 dB.

ANOVA p-value for each **LD** (in parenthesis); and **E**, the cumulative percentage of explanation after the inclusion of each **LD**. We used all data to generate the linear discriminant functions and then applied the classification to the same data. We intended to verify clarinetists groups separability and coherence but not to evaluate a classifier.

Table 2 shows the percentages of true positives in the classification accomplished by the firsts and also by all Linear Discriminants, for notes and clarinetist groups (**C1** to **C6**).

Figure 15 shows for all notes the maximum correlations between the dimensions of the Harmonic Profile of the Attack (**HPA**) and the Linear Discriminants (**LDs**). The corresponding **LD** with the maximum correlation is indicated bellow the values for each dimension.

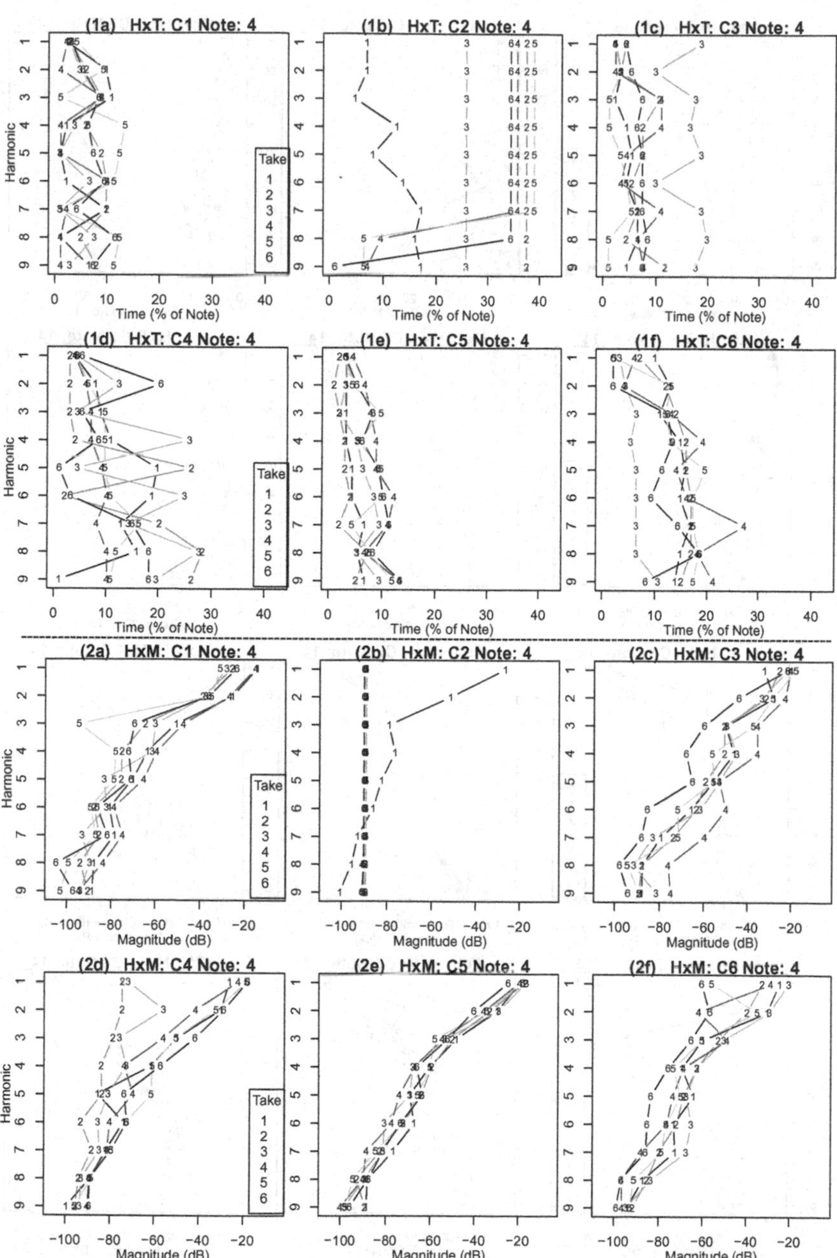

Fig. 10. HPA Projections for note 4 played by each clarinetist (**C1** to **C6**). Harmonic x Time (**HxT**) plane in panels (1a) to (1f) and Harmonic x Magnitude (**HxM**) plane in panels (2a) to (2f). Time axis in percentage of the note duration and Magnitude in dB, normalized by the maximum energy of the note.

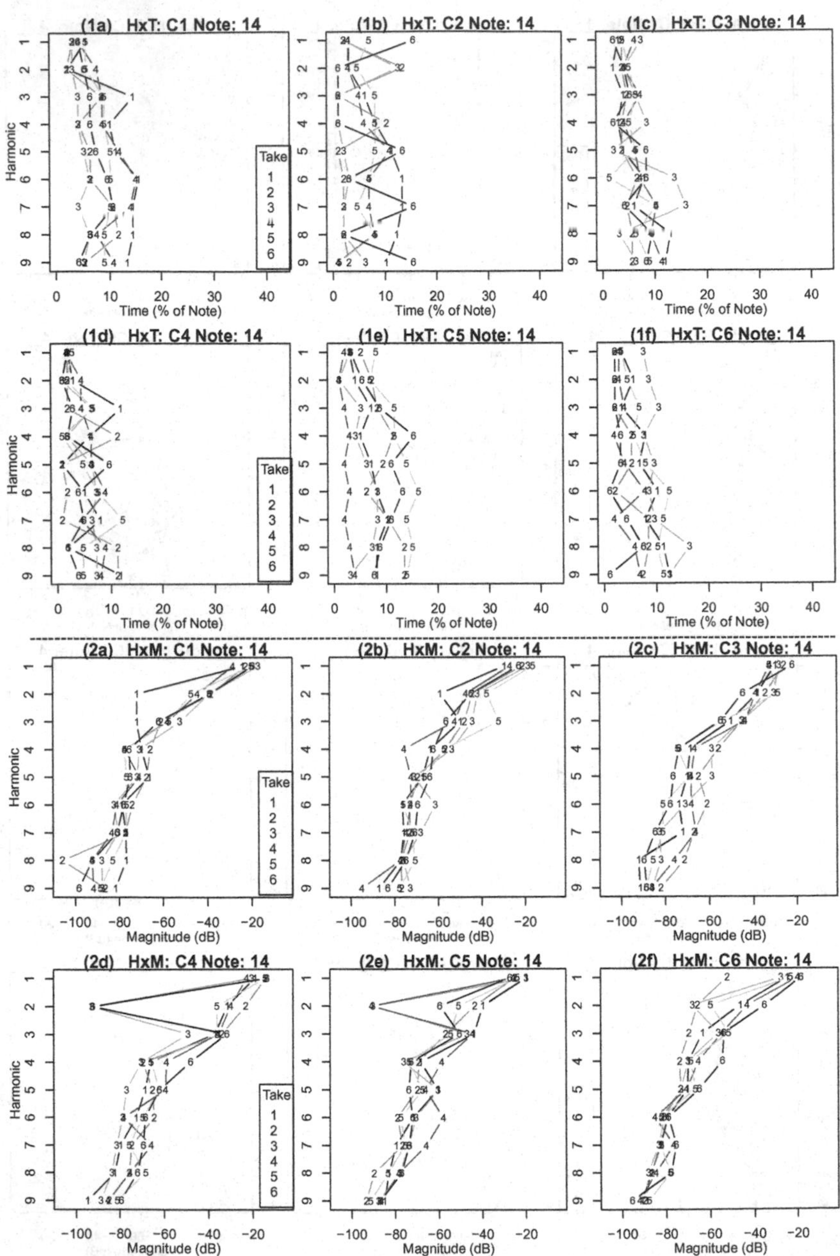

Fig. 11. HPA Projections for note 14 played by each clarinetist (**C1** to **C6**). Harmonic x Time (**HxT**) plane in panels (1a) to (1f) and Harmonic x Magnitude (**HxM**) plane in panels (2a) to (2f). Time axis in percentage of the note duration and Magnitude in dB, normalized by the maximum energy of the note.

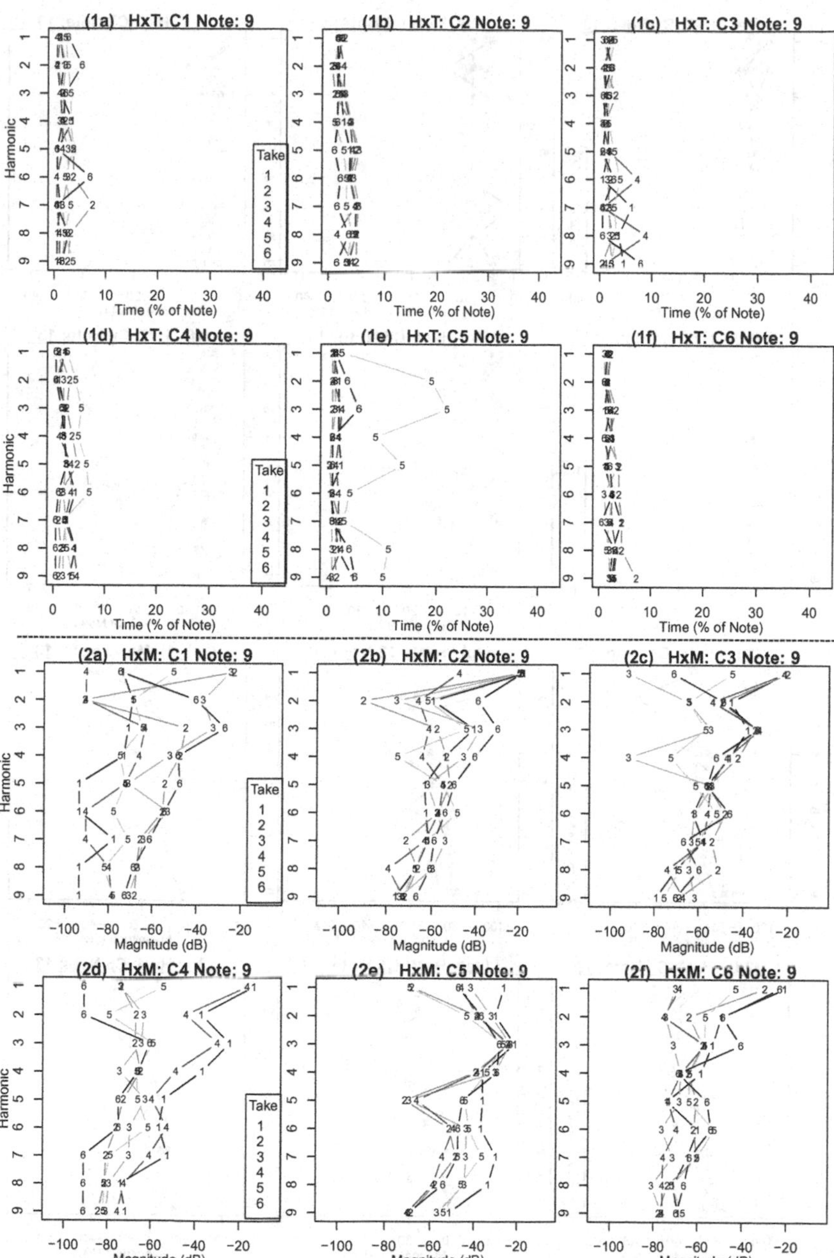

Fig. 12. HPA Projections for note 9 played by each clarinetist (**C1** to **C6**). Harmonic x Time (**HxT**) plane in panels (1a) to (1f) and Harmonic x Magnitude (**HxM**) plane in panels (2a) to (2f). Time axis in percentage of the note duration and Magnitude in dB, normalized by the maximum energy of the note.

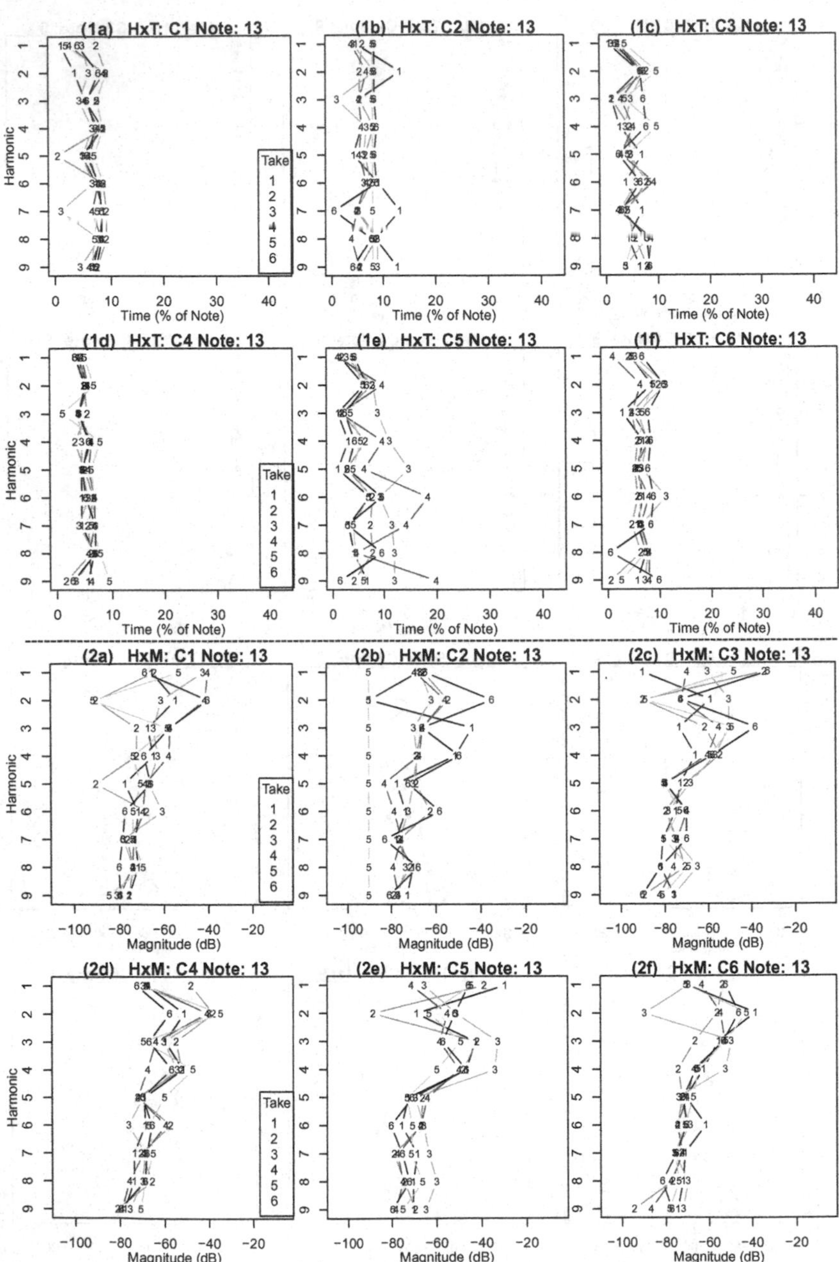

Fig. 13. HPA Projections for note 13 played by each clarinetist (**C1** to **C6**). Harmonic x Time (**HxT**) plane in panels (1a) to (1f) and Harmonic x Magnitude (**HxM**) plane in panels (2a) to (2f). Time axis in percentage of the note duration and Magnitude in dB, normalized by the maximum energy of the note.

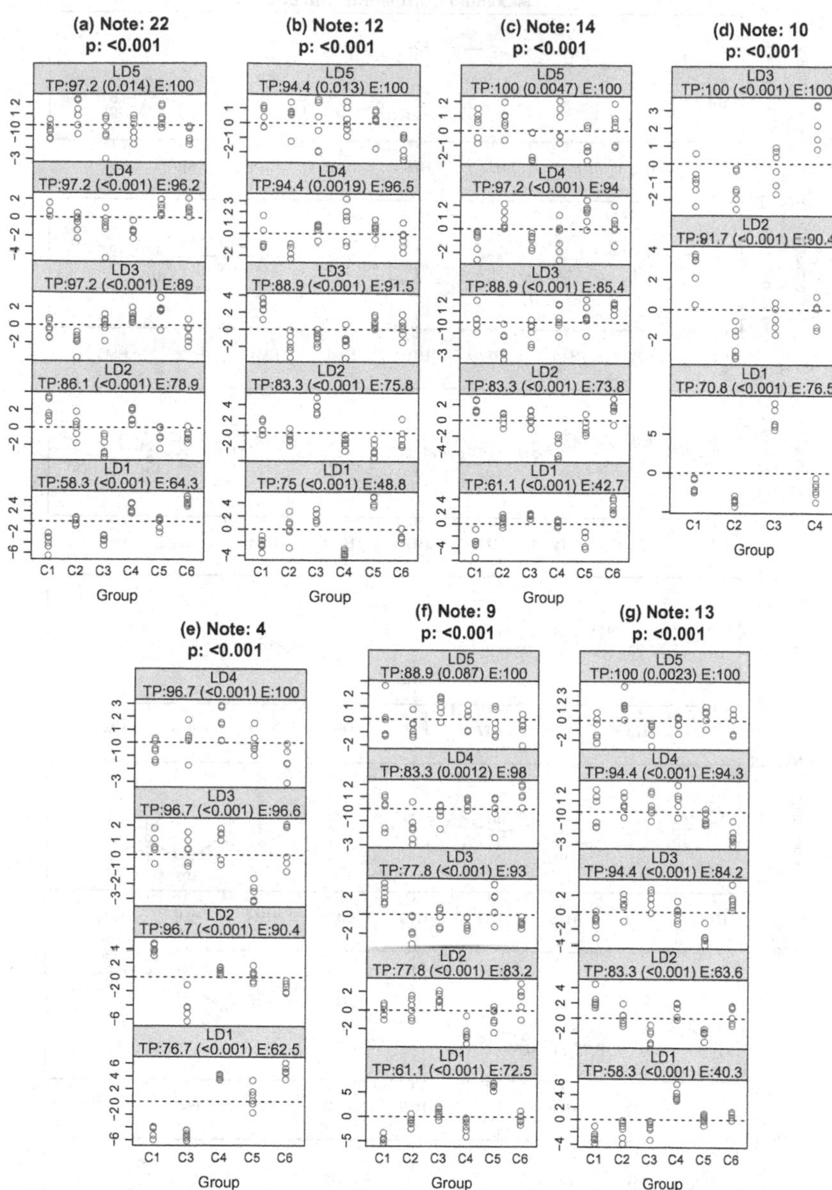

Fig. 14. Linear Discriminants (**LDs**) data projections by note and clarinetists groups in columns. Under each **LD** label: **TP**, the cumulative percentage of true positive from the discriminant functions classification; the ANOVA p-value for each **LD** (in parenthesis); and **E**, the cumulative percentage of explanation after the inclusion of each **LD**.

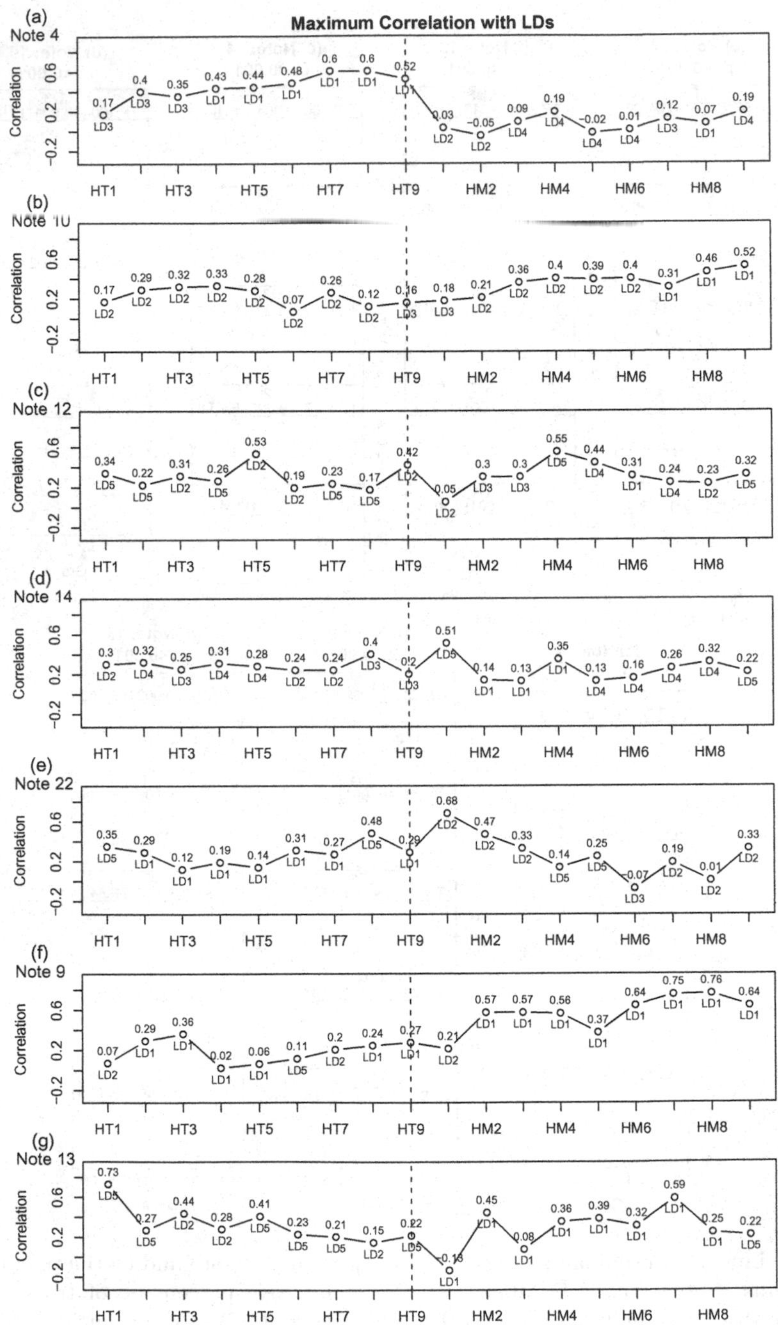

Fig. 15. Maximum correlations between **HPA** dimensions and **LDs**. The corresponding **LD** with the maximum correlation is indicated bellow the values for each dimension.

Table 2. Percentages of true positives in the Linear Discriminant (**LD**) classification by the firsts and also by all **LDs**, for clarinetist groups (**C1** to **C6**) and each note.

				True	Positive	(%)	Note (firsts LDs)	Note (all LDs)
	C1	C2	C3	C4	C5	C6		
Note 4							96.7 (2)	96.7 (4)
2 LDs	100	*	100	100	83.3	100	–	–
4 LDs	100	*	100	100	83.3	100	–	–
Note 9							77.8 (3)	88.9 (5)
3 LDs	100	83.3	66.7	83.3	100	33.3	–	–
5 LDs	100	83.3	83.3	83.3	100	83.3	–	–
Note 10							91.7 (2)	100 (3)
2 LDs	83.3	100	100	83.3	*	*	–	–
3 LDs	100	100	100	100	*	*	–	–
Note 12							88.9 (3)	94.4 (5)
3 LDs	83.3	83.3	100	83.3	100	83.3	–	–
5 LDs	83.3	83.3	100	100	100	100	–	–
Note 13							94.4 (3)	100 (5)
3 LDs	100	83.3	83.3	100	100	100	–	–
5 LDs	100	100	100	100	100	100	–	–
Note 14							88.9 (3)	100 (5)
3 LDs	100	83.3	66.7	100	83.3	100	–	–
5 LDs	100	100	100	100	100	100	–	–
Note 22							97.2 (3)	97.2 (5)
3 LDs	100	100	100	100	83.3	100	–	–
5 LDs	100	100	100	100	83.3	100	–	–

*Discarded groups.

5 Discussion

The results of the MANOVA testing the two dimensions (**R2** and **H2**) of the Plane **H2R2** indicated differences between the means ($p < 0.05$) when considering musician as a factor for all evaluated note transitions. The results of the Linear Discriminant Analysis applied to the Harmonic Profile of the Attack (**HPA**) data showed the same separability. Only the Linear Discriminant **LD5** of note 9 (Fig. 14f) did not separate the clarinetists with 95% of confidence level. All others **LDs** tested alone with ANOVA and together with MANOVA indicated separation ($p < 0,05$).

Note transitions in *Legato* condition, as to notes 4, 10, 12, 14, and 22, are achieved by maintaining blowing pressure across the transition, i.e., the reed vibration should be interrupted neither by any decrease of the blowing pressure nor by touching the reed with the tongue. The quality of *legato* transitions between consecutive notes is almost entirely dependent on the musician's ability to keep the blowing pressure stability. Moreover, as the width of the interval-leap between the notes increases, the execution of such transitions may impose additional technical demands that can vary according to the leap width. It may demand precision on synchronizing movements that involve more fingers, sometimes of different hands.

Additionally, some leaps may also demand additional skills for synchronizing the required finger movement with the mouth pressure adaptation to the vibration mode on the instrument tube changing to the next note, especially when the transition involves register change.

The transition to note 22 involves a downward semitone that requires merely the release of a key to close a hole, driven by a steel spring, while the transition to note 12 requires lifting one left-hand finger simultaneously with one right-hand finger, demanding precision of synchronization of the movement of both fingers. The Plane **H2R2** shows higher harmonic content **H1** in the attack of note 22 (Fig. 8a) than of note 12 (Fig. 8b), hence less reverberation (**H2**) and less noise (**R2**), which may indicate a higher *legato* quality on this transition. We also observe lower variance of both dimensions for note 22, either considering all executions, or executions within participants. Linear Discriminant Analysis of the Harmonic Profile of the Attack (**HPA**) reveled yet higher percentage (97.2 %) of true positive in the classification for note 22 (Fig. 14a), when compared to 94.4 % for note 12 (Fig. 14b), which may indicate more coherence of the harmonic structures during the attacks of note 22. It might suggest that players can achieve more success in executing the transition to note 22.

The *legato* to note 14 and to note 4 involve an upward major sixth and a minor tenth leap, respectively, crossing from the low to the high register of the instrument. The difficulty in these transitions lies not only in the multiple simultaneous finger action, but also in maintaining the blowing pressure stable and coupling the mouth pressure with the finger movement. Comparing the executions of both transitions we can observe in the Planes **H2R2** a higher variance of both dimensions for note 4 (Fig. 8e) than for note 14 Fig. 8c), which might suggest that players have more difficulty to achieve better *legato* quality for that transition. Linear Discriminant Analysis of the Harmonic Profile of the Attack (**HPA**) also revealed higher percentage of true positive in the classification for note 14 (100%), when compared to note 4 (96.7%), as shown in panels c) and e) of Fig. 14, respectively. It may indicate more coherence of the harmonic structures during the attacks of note 14 compared to note 4. In fact, other than involving a wider interval leap, the transition from **G4** to **B** flat 5 (note 4) requires complex actions of simultaneous hole covering and key pressing with fingers of both hands. This might also explain the higher importance of almost all **HPA** time dimensions (**HT**s), for the LDA separation, for note 4, as revealed by higher correlation values for these dimensions, when compared to note 14, as shown in panels a) and d) of Fig. 15, respectively. The correlation of **HT**s dimensions of **HPA** observed for note 4 might also explain the lower percentage of true positive in note 4.

The most demanding of these passages is the transition to note 10. Like for note 4, note 10 is also reached by an upward minor tenth leap in *legato*, but involving a more demanding register change, from a low note of the high register to the *altissimo* register. This passage imposes additional technical difficulty due to the acoustic instability of the instrument in the *altissimo* register, where players always have to make use of various alternative fingerings in order to correct the intonation, which imposes additional demand for coupling the mouth pressure with finger movement. It is common for players to fail to execute this passage correctly, regardless of their degree of expertise, as observed in some executions. The particular complexity of this passage shall explain the 10 unsuccessfully executions of this note that were excluded by the established threshold of −3 dB, the highest number of exclusions of all analyzed notes. Moreover, the Plane **H2R2** for note 10 (Fig. 8d), shows also the highest variance of both dimensions of all notes.

Comparing the Planes **H2R2** for both articulated transitions (notes 9 and 13) shown in Fig. 8(f) and (g) respectively, we can observe that note 9 exhibits higher overall harmonic content of the target note, except for one outlier execution, if compared to note 13. It might be explained by the longer articulation length imposed by the register change (high to low register) involved in the transition to note 13. As stated before, register changes demand more finger actions synchronization and mouth pressure adaptation, which might require longer articulation time between notes. It might also explain the higher variance of executions of note 13, probably reflecting the player's attempts to perform the articulation with less sound interruption ("hole") between the notes. The **LDA** revealed higher percentage (100%) of true positive in the classification for note 13 (Fig. 14g), when compared to 88.9% for note 9 (Fig. 14f), which may indicate more coherence of the harmonic structures during the attacks of note 13. Another possible consequence of this longer articulation to note 13 might be associated with the greater balance between the correlation values observed in both dimension, **HT**s an **HM**s for that note (Fig. 15g), while to the note 9 (Fig. 15f), the correlation of **HT**s dimensions are lower than the **HM**s dimensions.

6 Conclusion

In this paper, we proposed two description tools for characterizing the content of musical note attacks in reverberant environments. The first tool (presented in previous work) is a confrontation between the energy of two components estimated by Spectral Modeling Synthesis decomposition: (1) **H2**, the harmonic component due to the previous note reverberation; and (2) **R2**, the residual component obtained by subtracting the harmonic components (**H1** and **H2**) from the original signal. The **H1** is the harmonic component of the note being attacked. The confrontation of both components, **H2** and **R2**, in terms of their energy proportions to the original signal, allowed us to infer about them, together with **H1**, in a single 2D visualization, the Plane **H2R2**. In this paper, we proposed an additional description tool for characterizing note attack, also aimed at examining the influence of the reverberation, the Harmonic Profile of the Attacks (**HPA**). The **HPA** is a representation of the first nine harmonics' structure of component **H1** between the note onset and the end of the attack. The profile starts in the fundamental frequency and goes through the first nine harmonic components, crossing each at the frame immediately before reaching the half of the energy (in dB) of the end of the attack. Hence, **HPA** carries time and energy magnitude information about the behavior of the nine harmonic components within the attack region, which results in an 18-dimensional representation of the attack. Both approaches were able to provide a detailed description of the spectral content of the attack region, which allowed inferences about the interaction with room acoustics, enriching the study of musical performances in everyday practice conditions where reverberant environments are always present. We tested the approach using a recording set of an excerpt from a clarinet piece of the traditional classical repertoire, the first movement of Brahms Clarinet Sonata in F minor, op. 120 No. 1, played by six professional clarinetists. We examined different *legato*, as well as articulated note transition presenting different performance technique demands. MANOVA testing of dimensions (**R2** and **H2**) indicated differences ($p < 0.05$) when considering musician as a factor for all evaluated note transitions. A higher variance of both dimensions was observed for notes with higher performance technique demands. This analysis approach was also able to reveal note attacks not successfully executed, as observed for the executions of note 4 by clarinetist **C2**. Linear Discriminant Analysis applied for supervised dimensionality reduction of the **HPA** indicated group separation to the same factor in MANOVA testing ($p < 0.05$).

Future investigations with the description tools here presented may be unfolded to unravel how musicians adapt their execution of note attacks to different room acoustics, by attempting to find other factor's effects, such as estimates of acoustic impedance of individual note or variations in the room acoustic. This study, restricted to note attacks on only one monophonic instrument (the clarinet) shall also be extended to different wind instruments. The approach also shows potentials for analysing chord onsets of polyphonic instruments (or ensembles) by informing the pitch of each chord note to the **SMS** signal decomposition into the correspondent **H1**. Moreover, the synchronization of polyphonic chord attacks may be evaluated with the **HPA** adapted for crossing only the fundamental frequencies of each note of the chord.

Acknowledgments. This work was supported by CNPq (Brazilian National Council for Scientific and Technological Development).

References

1. Bolzinger, S., Warusfel, O., Kahle, E.: A study of the influence of room acoustics on piano performance. Le J. Phys. IV **4**(C5), C5–617 (1994)
2. Campolina, T.A., Loureiro, M.A.: Description of monophonic attacks in reverberant environments via spectral modeling. In: 14th International Symposium on Computer Music Multidisciplinary Research, p. 534 (2019)
3. Cannam, C., Landone, C., Sandler, M.: Sonic visualiser: an open source application for viewing, analysing, and annotating music audio files. In: Proceedings of the ACM Multimedia 2010 International Conference, Firenze, Italy, pp. 1467–1468, October 2010

4. Daudet, L.: A review on techniques for the extraction of transients in musical signals. In: Kronland-Martinet, R., Voinier, T., Ystad, S. (eds.) CMMR 2005. LNCS, vol. 3902, pp. 219–232. Springer, Heidelberg (2006). https://doi.org/10.1007/11751069_20
5. De Poli, G., Mion, L.: From audio to content. In: Algorithms for Sound and Music Computing, chap. 5. Unpublished book. Dipartimento di Ingegneria Dell'Informazione-Università degli Studi di Padova, Padova (2006)
6. Fischinger, T., Frieler, K., Louhivuori, J.: Influence of virtual room acoustics on choir singing. Psychomusicol.: Music Mind Brain **25**(3), 208 (2015)
7. Grey, J.: Multidimensional perceptual scaling of musical timbres. J. Acoust. Soc. Am. **61**(5), 1270–1277 (1977)
8. Herrera, P., Serra, X., Peeters, G.: A proposal for the description of audio in the context of MPEG-7. In: Proceedings of European Workshop on Content-based Multimedia Indexing. Citeseer (1999)
9. Kato, K., Ueno, K., Kawai, K.: Musicians' adjustment of performance to room acoustics, part III: understanding the variations in musical expressions. J. Acoust. Soc. Am. **123**(5), 3610 (2008)
10. Luce, D.: Physical correlates of nonpercussive musical instrument tones. Ph.D. thesis, MIT (1963)
11. R Core Team: R: A Language and Environment for Statistical Computing. R Foundation for Statistical Computing, Vienna, Austria (2018). https://www.R-project.org/
12. Risset, J.: Computer study of trumpet tones. J. Acoust. Soc. Am. **38**, 912 (1965)
13. Salamon, J., Gómez, E.: MIR. EDU: an open-source library for teaching sound and music description. In: Proceedings of the 15th International Society for Music Information Retrieval (ISMIR), Tapei, Taiwan (2014)
14. Schärer Kalkandjiev, Z., Weinzierl, S.: The influence of room acoustics on solo music performance: an experimental study. Psychomusicol.: Music Mind Brain **25**(3), 195 (2015)
15. Serra, X., Smith, J.: Spectral modeling synthesis: a sound analysis/synthesis system based on a deterministic plus stochastic decomposition. Comput. Music J. **14**(4), 12–24 (1990)
16. Zölzer, U.: DAFX: Digital Audio Effects. Wiley, Hoboken (2011)

Generating Walking Bass Lines with HMM

Ayumi Shiga and Tetsuro Kitahara(✉)

College of Humanities and Sciences, Nihon University, Chiyoda City, Japan
{shiga,kitahara}@kthrlab.jp

Abstract. In this paper, we propose a method of generating walking bass lines for jazz with a hidden Markov model (HMM). Although automatic harmonization has been widely and actively studied, automatic generation of walking bass lines has not. With our model, which includes hidden states that represent combinations of pitch classes and metric positions, different distributions of bass notes selected at different metric positions can be learned. The results of objective and subjective evaluations suggest that the model can learn such different tendencies of bass notes at different metric positions and generates musically flowing bass lines that contain passing notes.

Keywords: Jazz bass · Automatic generation · Hidden Markov model

1 Introduction

Creating walking bass lines is a fundamental skill required for jazz bassists, because bass lines in general are not explicitly described in musical scores that jazz musicians use. Since each score that they use, called a *lead sheet*, includes only a dominant melody and chord progression, they have to create a musically appropriate bass line from that melody as well as the chord progression to play jazz bass. However, that process is challenging for novice bassists, because it requires constructing bass lines that satisfy both simultaneity (i.e., harmonic congruency between the bass line and chord backing) and sequentiality (i.e., smooth succession of notes within the bass line).

Although many systems for harmonization—that is, for outputting chord progressions or four-part harmonies—have been developed [2,5–7,12,14], few have attempted to generate walking bass lines. Dias et al. [4] developed a walking bass line generator following the contour-based approach, in which the user can specify whether the pitch of the bass line ascends or descends according to two parameters: direction and openness. Whereas *direction* specifies whether the first bass note in the next chord is higher or lower than that in the current chord, *openness* specifies how directly the bass line progresses from the first bass note in the current chord to that in the next chord. In particular, *low openness* indicates a direct path—for example, C–D–E–E–F—whereas *high openness* indicates an indirect path—for example, C–E–G–G$^{\flat}$–F. When choosing passing notes, the

R. Kronland-Martinet et al. (Eds.): CMMR 2019, LNCS 12631, pp. 248–256, 2021.
https://doi.org/10.1007/978-3-030-70210-6_17

system applies the idea that stronger beats tend to have chord tones and that the last beat of each bar can have a chromatic approximation to the first note in the next bar.

In other studies, Kunimatsu et al. [8] developed a system that automatically composes pieces of blues music consisting of a melody, a chord progression, and a bass line using genetic programming. To generate a bass line, bass line candidates are evaluated in a fitness function based on integrity with the chord progression and music entropy. Ramalho et al. [13] developed a jazz bass player agent that memorizes existing bass-line fragments and reuses them by means of case-based reasoning to generate bass lines. Meanwhile, Piedra [3] developed a bass line generating agent by using a probabilistic model to extract musical knowledge from a collection of MIDI-based bass line loops, although he focused on electronic dance music, and thus did not consider walking bass lines for jazz. Indeed, no researchers have previously attempted to generate walking bass lines for jazz from a data-driven probabilistic model.

In this paper, we propose a method of generating walking bass lines using a hidden Markov model (HMM). HMMs allow estimating the most likely sequence of hidden states from a sequence of observed symbols and are commonly used in *harmonization*—that is, creating a chord progression for a given melody—in which a *chord progression* is a sequence of hidden states, whereas a *melody* is a sequence of observed symbols (e.g., [7]). HMMs are widely considered to be good models for learning relations between a chord progressions and a melody to be performed under the chord progression. Therefore, despite the lack of previous attempts to do so, we expected our HMM to be effective in generating a walking bass line for a given chord progression.

2 Method

2.1 Problem Statement

Our aim was to generate a bass line for a given chord progression. Ideally, a melody should also be considered, because the most musically appropriate bass line depends on the melody even if the chord progression is the same. However, we did not consider melodies in our work given the lack of any database of walking bass lines involving dominant melodies. For simplicity's sake, we assumed chord progressions to have only one chord for each bar, and bass lines are assumed to have quarter notes only. The chord candidates were 12 major and 12 minor chords—that is, the elements in the set $\mathcal{C} = \{\mathrm{C}, \mathrm{C}^\sharp, \cdots, \mathrm{B}\} \times \{\mathrm{maj}, \mathrm{min}\}$. We also assumed the measure and key to be 4/4 and C major, respectively. In sum, the input was an m-bar chord progression $C = (c_0, \cdots, c_{m-1})$ $(c_i \in \mathcal{C})$, while the output was a bass line consisting of four quarter notes for each of m bars, for a total of $4m$ quarter notes, denoted by $B = (b_0, \cdots, b_{4m-1})$, in which each b_i is a MIDI note number.

2.2 Formulation with HMM

An HMM is a model in which an observed symbol is probabilistically emitted from a hidden state. In our case, we regarded given chords to be observed symbols and bass notes to be hidden states. Given a chord progression $C = (c_0, \cdots, c_{m-1})$, the observation $X = (x_0, \cdots, x_{4m-1})$ is defined so that $x_i = c_{[i/4]}$, in which [ ] is the floor function. Given $C = (\mathrm{C}, \mathrm{Am}, \mathrm{Dm}, \mathrm{G})$, for example, $X = (\mathrm{C}, \mathrm{C}, \mathrm{C}, \mathrm{C}, \mathrm{Am}, \mathrm{Am}, \mathrm{Am}, \mathrm{Am}, \mathrm{Dm}, \mathrm{Dm}, \mathrm{Dm}, \mathrm{Dm}, \mathrm{G}, \mathrm{G}, \mathrm{G}, \mathrm{G})$.

We designed a set of hidden states $\mathcal{S}$ in three ways:

Method 1 The simplest, octave-ignored method
$\mathcal{S}$ was a set of pitch classes such that $\mathcal{S} = (0, 1, 2, \cdots, 11)$, where $0, 1, 2, \cdots, 11$ correspond to C, C$^\sharp$, D, $\cdots$, B, respectively.

Method 2 The simple, but non-octave-ignored method
In Method 2, $\mathcal{S}$ was a set of pitches in a specific pitch range such that $\mathcal{S} = (28, 29, 30, \cdots, 60)$, in which each integer represents a MIDI note number. This pitch range was determined so that it covered the pitches used in typical bass lines.

Method 3 The octave-ignored but metrical-position-considered method
$\mathcal{S} = (0, 1, 2, \cdots, 47)$ was a combination of pitch classes and metric positions. Specifically, each element s in $\mathcal{S}$ was calculated by $s = n + 12q$ where $n \in \{0, 1, 2, \cdots, 11\}$ is a pitch class and $q \in \{0, 1, 2, 3\}$ is a metric position. With that model, distribution of emission probability can be learned separately for each metric position. Because bass note selection obviously depends on its metric position—for example, the root note frequently occurs at the first beat in a bar but seldom at the last beat—we expected Method 3 to be superior to the others.

We did not consider the fourth possiblity, i.e., the non-octave-ignored metrical-position-considered method, because our dataset was too limited to learn such a large model.

Let $H = (h_0, \cdots, h_{4m-1})$ be a sequence of hidden states for a given observation $X = (x_0, \cdots, x_{4m-1})$. The following probabilities were learned from the dataset:

- the initial probabilities $\{P(h_0 = s) \mid s \in \mathcal{S}\}$,
- the emission probabilities $\{P(x_i = c | h_i = s) \mid c \in \mathcal{C}, s \in \mathcal{S}\}$, and
- the transition probabilities $\{P(h_{i+1} = s' | h_i = s) \mid s, s' \in \mathcal{S}\}$.

2.3 Algorithm for Determining Pitches

Given the chord progression $C = (c_0, \cdots, c_{m-1})$, we estimated the most likely sequence of hidden states $H = (h_0, \cdots, h_{4m-1})$ based on the HMM.

Because Methods 1 and 3 determined not pitches but pitch classes, we had to determine the octave for each bass note in order to determine the pitch. Let o_i be the octave—specifically, the MIDI note number of the octave's C—for the bass note b_i. For Method 1, $b_i = o_i + h_i$, whereas for Method 3, $b_i = o_i + \mathrm{mod}(h_i, 12)$, in which mod is the modulo operation.

For the initial note, the lowest pitch within the specified pitch range (28 to 60) is selected, that is,

$$o_1 = \begin{cases} 24 \ (\mathrm{mod}(h_1, 12) \geq 4) \\ 36 \ (\mathrm{mod}(h_1, 12) \leq 3) \end{cases}$$

The octave of each other notes is determined so that the note is smoothly connected from the previous note, that is,

$$o_i = \begin{cases} \max(o_{i-1} + 12, 24) & (\mathrm{mod}(h_i, 12) - \mathrm{mod}(h_{i-1}, 12) < -5) \\ \min(o_{i-1} - 12, 48) & (\mathrm{mod}(h_i, 12) - \mathrm{mod}(h_{i-1}, 12) > 5) \\ o_{i-1} & (\text{otherwise}) \end{cases}$$

For Method 2, $b_i = h_i$ for every i.

3 Experiments

3.1 Dataset

We used data collected from "Jazz Bass Running 104: Examples Collections 1–3" [9–11] and the website Projazz Lab [1]. Of the bass lines collected and the transcriptions of chord progressions, ones with multiple chords in any bar were excluded as well as ones with bass notes beyond the specified bass pitch range (i.e., 28 to 60). We transposed all remaining bass lines to C major and divided them into four bars each. If a bass line contained non-quarter notes (e.g., a dotted quarter note plus an eighth note), we manually simplified it to a sequence of quarter notes. The total number of the four-bar bass lines collected was 206, 103 of which we used as training data, whereas we used the other 103 as test data.

3.2 Examples

The bass lines generated by Methods 1–3 for three chord progressions appear in Figs. 1, 2 and 3, which show the following:

Figure 1 In the bass lines generated with Methods 1 and 2, repetitions of the same notes appear in the second half. By contrast, the bass line generated by Method 3 is smooth overall, although a non-chord note appears in the first bar.

Figure 2 The bass lines generated by Methods 1 and 2 are highly monotonous because the same notes appear repeatedly, whereas the one generated by Method 3 has many passing notes, which makes it smooth and melodious.

Figure 3 Similarly to the other two examples, the bass lines generated by Methods 1 and 2 repeat the same notes, whereas the one generated by Method 3 has many passing notes that make it smoother.

Fig. 1. Bass lines generated for D–B$^\flat$–F$^\sharp$–D

Fig. 2. Bass lines generated for Em–Em–A–Dm

Fig. 3. Bass lines generated for Dm–F–C–A

3.3 Objective Evaluation

We evaluated the bass lines generated with the 103 test data from two points of view. One evaluation involved note-wise comparison, in which we computed the rate of concordance with the ground truth (**C1**). If this rate is higher, the result can be considered better. The other evaluation is a statistics-based comparison, in which statistics such as **C2**–**C9** were computed from the bass lines generated and the ground truth. If those statistics are closer to the ones computed from the ground truth, the result can be considered better.

C1 Rate of concordance with the ground truth
C2 Rate of the root note of the chord at each bar
C3 Rate of the root note of the chord at the first beat of each bar

C4 Rate of the chord note at the first beat of each bar
C5 Rate of dissonant notes (notes with intervals of the minor 2nd from any chord notes)
C6 Rate of flat motions (here meaning a motion from a pitch to the same pitch)
C7 Rate of conjunct motions (motions with intervals of minor or major 2nd)
C8 Rate of distinct motions (motions with intervals of more than major 2nd)
C9 Number of pitch classes appearing in the bass line

The results listed in Table 1 can be summarized as follows:

Table 1. Results of the objective evaluation. (The bolded values are the best results, that is, the highest for **C1** and the closest to the ground truth for **C2** to **C9**).

	Method 1	Method 2	Method 3	Ground truth
C1	38.47%	35.32%	**41.75%**	–
C2	**54.79%**	56.55%	32.89%	51.33%
C3	53.88%	52.91%	**76.46%**	90.29%
C4	85.68%	81.07%	**96.36%**	98.05%
C5	11.10%	17.05%	**24.33%**	25.36%
C6	51.13%	**49.19%**	17.67%	41.88%
C7	31.59%	28.67%	**53.07%**	66.21%
C8	17.28%	22.14%	**29.26%**	43.04%
C9	4.20	5.40	**7.78**	8.68

C1 Method 3 showed the highest rates of concordance with the ground truth.
C2, C9 Method 3 generated bass lines containing various pitch classes (7.78) whereas Methods 1 and 2 generated bass lines in which the numbers of pitch classes were 4.2 and 5.4 on average, respectively. In addition, bass lines generated by Methods 1 and 2 contained many root notes (54.79% and 56.55%, respectively), as shown from **C2**. Of those results, bass lines generated by Methods 1 and 2 were more monotonous than those generated by Method 3.
C2, C3 Method 3 generated bass lines in which the first note at each bar was mostly the root note. In Methods 1 and 2, **C3**'s values were exceptionally close to **C2**'s values, because the distribution of the emission probabilities was common among all metric positions. By contrast, in Method 3, **C3**'s value was high (76.46%) even though **C2**'s value was low (32.89%), because that method prescribed separate distributions of emitted bass notes for each metric position.
C5 Method 3 generated bass lines with the highest rate of dissonant notes; however, that outcome was not problematic because the ground truth also had a similar rate of dissonant notes.

C6, C7, C8 Methods 1 and 2 generated bass lines with high rates of flat motions. By contrast, Method 3 generated bass lines with 53.07% of conjunct motions. This is a successful result since the high rate of distinct motions is a characteristic feature of walking basslines.

To summarize, Method 3 generated the most melodious bass lines, with a tradeoff of melodiousness and low dissonance. Method 1 mostly generated consonant bass lines, but half notes in the generated bass lines were root notes and had many flat motions. In contrast, the basslines generated by Method 3 included many non-root notes and moderate conjunct motions.

3.4 Subjective Evaluation

We asked an expert bassist with 25 years of experience in playing jazz bass to evaluate the bass lines generated by the three methods. We selected 50 chord progressions at random from the ones used in the objective evaluation and prepared four bass lines (i.e., Methods 1–3 and the ground truth) for each chord progression. We gave the bassist the scores and MP3 data of the prepared bass lines and asked him to evaluate them in the following ways:

S1 Marking musically inapporopriate notes in the scores—the fewer, the better.
S2 Rating the bass lines from the following criteria on a scale of 1 to 5, in which higher ratings indicated better bass lines:
  (a) Overall quality
  (b) Overall smoothness
  (c) Congruency with the chord progression

Table 2. Subjective evaluation results

	Method 1	Method 2	Method 3	Ground truth
S1	1.40	1.88	0.60	0.98
S2 (a)	3.52	3.00	3.70	3.96
S2 (b)	3.40	2.96	3.80	3.96
S2 (c)	3.54	3.16	3.82	4.10

The results of the expert's evaluation appear in Table 2 and can be summarized as follows:

S1 The number of musically inappropriate notes was minimal for Method 3 among the three methods and ground truth, for two possible reasons. One is that some bass lines of the ground truth consisted primarily of root notes to allow novice players to play. The other is that some bass lines may have been made too simple by the simplification mentioned in Sect. 3.1.
S2 For all of (a) to (c), Method 3 obtained scores between 3.7 and 3.9 and was superior to the other methods, even though it was slightly worse than the ground truth.

4 Conclusion

In this paper, we have proposed a method of generating walking bass lines for jazz using an HMM. By designing hidden states consisting of combinations of pitch classes and metric positions, the model successfully learned different tendencies of bass notes at different metric positions. As a result, the bass lines generated contained passing notes and were thus musically flowing.

Our study involved several limitations. For one, we considered four-bar bass lines only. For longer musical pieces, a bass line should vary along the progress of the music. In the first verse and another verse later, for example, the bassist may play different bass lines even if the melody and chord progression remains the same. In response, we need to consider the relationship of bass lines and musical context in order to generate appropriate bass lines for long pieces. Moreover, advanced bassists often add ornamentation to bass lines, which we also did not consider in our study. Also, it could be more useful to adapt generated bass lines to the user's performing skill.

Acknowledgments. This project was supported by JSPS Kakenhi (JP16K16180, JP16H01744, JP17H00749, and JP19K12288) and the Kawai Foundation for Sound Technology and Music.

References

1. http://www.projazzlab.com/study-tools
2. Buys, J., van der Merwe, B.: Chorale harmonization with weighted finite-state transducers. In: Twenty-Third Annual Symposium of the Pattern Recognition Association of South Africa, pp. 95–101. PRASA South Africa (2012)
3. Calopa Piedra, P.: Bassline generation agent based on knowledge and context. B.Sc. thesis, Universitat Pompeu Fabra (2015)
4. Dias, R., Guedes, C.: A contour-based jazz walking bass generator. In: Sound and Music Computing Conference (SMC 2013), pp. 305–308 (2013)
5. Ebcioglu, K.: An expert system for harmonizing four-part chorales. Comput. Music J. **12**(3), 43–51 (1988)
6. Hild, H., Feulner, J., Menzel, W.: HarmoNet: a neural net for harmonizing chorales in the style of J.S. Bach. In: Advances in Neural Information Processing Systems, pp. 267–274 (1992)
7. Kawakami, T., Nakai, M., Shimodaira, H., Sagayama, S.: Hidden Markov model applied to automatic harmonization of given melodies. In: IPSJ SIG Notes, pp. 59–66. 99-MUS-34 (2000, in Japanese)
8. Kunimatsu, K., Ishikawa, Y., Takata, M., Joe, K.: A music composition model with genetic programming –a case study of chord progression and bassline. In: Proceedings of Internatinal Conference on Parallel and Distributed Processing Techniques and Applications (PDPTA 2015), pp. 256–262 (2015)
9. Nakamura, S.: Jazz bass running 104: examples collection 1. Saber Incorporated (2017, in Japanese)
10. Nakamura, S.: Jazz bass running 104: examples collection 2. Saber Incorporated (2017, in Japanese)

11. Nakamura, S.: Jazz bass running 104: examples collection 3. Saber Incorporated (2017, in Japanese)
12. Phon-Amnuaisuk, S., Smaill, A., Wiggins, G.: Chorale harmonization: a view from a search control perspective. J. New Music Res. **35**(4), 279–305 (2006)
13. Ramalho, G.L., Rolland, P.Y., Ganascia, J.G.: An artificially intelligent jazz performer. J. New Music Res. **28**(2), 105–129 (1999)
14. Suzuki, S., Kitahara, T.: Four-part harmonization using Bayesian networks: pros and cons of introducing chord nodes. J. New Music Res. **43**(3), 331–353 (2014)

Programming in Style with *bach*

Andrea Agostini[1(✉)], Daniele Ghisi[2], and Jean-Louis Giavitto[3]

[1] Conservatory of Turin, Turin, Italy
andreaagostini@conservatoriotorino.eu
[2] University of California, CNMAT, Berkeley, USA
danieleghisi@berkeley.edu
[3] Sciences et Technologies de la Musique et du Son (STMS) CNRS, IRCAM, Sorbonne Université, Paris, France
jean-louis.giavitto@ircam.fr

Abstract. Several programming systems for computer music are based upon the data-flow family of programming paradigms. In the first part of this article, we shall introduce the general features and lexicon of data-flow programming, and review some specific instances of it with reference to computer music applications. We shall then move the discussion to Max's very peculiar take on data-flow, and evaluate its motivation and shortcomings. Subsequently, we shall show how the *bach* library can support different programming styles within Max, improving the expression, the readability and the maintenance of complex algorithms. In particular, the latest version of *bach* has introduced *bell*, a small textual programming language embedded in Max and specifically designed to facilitate programming tasks related to manipulation of symbolic musical material.

Keywords: Programming paradigms · Computer-aided composition · Max · *bach* · *bell*

1 Introduction

In spite of the way it is advertised, its own Turing-completeness and the sheer amount and complexity of things that have been done with it, programming in Max is difficult. Whereas setting up simple interactive processes with rich graphical interfaces may be immediate, it has long been observed that implementing nontrivial algorithms is far from being straightforward, and the resulting programs are often very difficult to analyse, maintain and debug.

Several other popular programming languages and environments for computer music, such as OpenMusic [1], PWGL [15] and Faust [19], share with Max a superficially similar, but profoundly different, *dataflow* programming paradigm, which makes them better suited for 'real' programming and less for setting up highly interactive and responsive systems. This is reflected in the types of artistic practices these systems are typically used for, and mirrors the oft-discussed rift between composition- and performance-oriented tools in computer music [22].

R. Kronland-Martinet et al. (Eds.): CMMR 2019, LNCS 12631, pp. 257–278, 2021.
https://doi.org/10.1007/978-3-030-70210-6_18

We are convinced that this rift is by no means necessary or natural and that, on the contrary, it has proven problematic with respect to a wide array of practices lying somehow between the two categories, such as extemporaneous, 'intuitionistic' approaches to composition (including, but not limited to, improvisation), sound-based and multimedia installations, live coding and more.

In this paper, we shall investigate this divide and its reasons from the point of view of computational models, and consider how it can be bridged, or at least narrowed, through the use of the *bach* package for Max [1].

2 Dataflow Computational Models

The concept of dataflow is an old one, dating back at least to [8], where the idea of independent computational modules communicating by sending data (discrete items) among directed links was first introduced. Over the years, many kinds of dataflow computation models have been developed. In this section, we shall review some of them and how they apply to different languages and software systems for computer music.

2.1 The Dataflow Model

The term *dataflow* refers to a whole family of execution models that can be described by autonomous entities called *actors* or *processes* and interacting only through links connecting their *input* and *output ports*[1]. An actor triggers a computation according to the availability of data on its input ports and delivers its results on its output ports. The sequence of data passing through a link constitutes a *stream* and each value in the sequence is called a *token*. A token is sent through an output port and received by one or more destination actors, each of which retrieves the token through an input port. Often a dataflow graph (DFG) defines a whole computation that must be iterated periodically on a sequence of data (periodic dataflow). This graph can be simply modelled by considering the stream of inputs.

The different dataflow execution models differ in the static or dynamic nature of the connection graph, the activation strategy of the actors, the ability of the links to temporarily store the data produced (often through a FIFO buffer), and the type of computation performed by each actor. By varying these parameters, the dataflow model is able to describe, in a unified manner, execution models as diverse as electronic circuits, computer programs in functional style and signal processing graphs.

2.2 Homogeneous Synchronous Dataflow

One specific dataflow model is particularly useful, since it corresponds to the kind of computations done in real-time signal processing: the *synchronous dataflow*

[1] In the usual Max terminology, actors correspond to boxes (object or message) and input and output ports correspond respectively to inlets and outlets.

(SDF), also called the *static dataflow*. In this specific model, the graph is fixed and the order in which actors trigger their computations does not depend on the data that is processed (i.e. the value of the token).

In an *homogeneous SDF*, an actor fires its computation when there is a token on each of its input ports, and it produces a token on each output port. In other words, the connections are FIFO queues of size one and the activation of actors never leads to a buffer overflow. The homogeneous SDF model can represent conveniently audio graphs where tokens correspond to audio buffers and actors to unit generators, delays, filters and other effects. This model also matches well the behavior of synchronous (clocked) electronic digital circuit: an actor is an electronic gate and a token is the value of the voltage on a pin. A clock is used to acquire and deliver the tokens simultaneously for all the gates.

2.3 Dynamic Dataflow

The SDF model is not particularly expressive. A number of dataflow variants have been developed that relax the constraints of SDF. We loosely refer to their general computational model as *dynamic* dataflow (DDF). In the DDF model, the activation of an actor can be more complicated and the firing strategy may change in time, for instance according to some internal state of the actor. The number of tokens produced can also vary on each output ports. This makes possible to express conditional firing, a situation in which an actor triggers its computation only if the input token has a particular value.

For instance, the audio graph in Max[2] matches the SDF model, whereas the control graph is of the DDF kind: the firing of an actor is driven by the so-called 'hot' inlets, and not by the availability of the incoming messages on all inlets. Which inlet is 'hot' may also depend on the specific data arriving in non-'hot' (or 'cold') inlets (as for example in the `switch` box). Moreover, the activation of a box does not necessarily cause necessarily all its outlets to fire (this happens, for example, in the `gate` box). As for patchcords, the ones connecting an outlet to a cold inlet do not store the whole sequence of messages in transit before being consumed by the target, as only the last one (*i.e.*, the most recent) is kept until its consumption.

DDF is also needed to handle several rates in an audio graph, for instance for handling multimedia streams (audio and video).

2.4 Data-Driven and Demand-Driven Implementation Strategies

Historically, there have been two main approaches for the software implementation of dataflow: the *data-driven* approach and the *demand-driven* one.

The Data-Driven Approach. In the data-driven implementation, tokens travel in the interconnection graph and fire according to the actors. The activation of the actors propagates in the graph like a wave starting at the inputs and

[2] We shall talk diffusely about Max in the later chapters, and only introduce it as an example here for readers already familiar with it.

ending at the outputs, that is, actors that have no output ports and that are used to 'deliver' the result of the calculation (be it in the form of text, audio, MIDI data, image display, etc.).

In SDF, tokens can be presented asynchronously to the input ports but the actors only fire when all their inputs bear a token. If the graph is homogeneous, then a token is produced on each of the output ports and, subsequently, actors located at distance 1 from the inputs are activated, and so on. Therefore, the functioning of the dataflow graph in time can be seen as a sequence of 'rounds', that is, transactions in which the first token of each input streams is consumed and a token is produced for each output streams (hence the term "synchronous"). In this context, the order of activation of the actors can be fixed *a priori*, through a static analysis of the graph itself, and can be computed by a simple topological sort of the graph, as long as it is acyclical (also see below).

Both Max's and Pure Data's audio and control graphs are implemented using a data-driven approach. Once the user has laid out graphically the audio graph, the program analyses it statically and, if there are no errors (typically resulting from a feedback connection) an internal representation of it is generated, also establishing a fixed sequence of activations. Things are different for the control graphs: since their behavior depend on the data they receive, their scheduling cannot be fixed statically.

The Demand-Driven Approach. The demand-driven approach is more convenient to handle DDF. In this approach, the outputs of the graph require a token from their connected actors, which in turn transmit the request to their inputs, so that a wave of requests propagates through the graph, from its outputs to its inputs. Each input of the graph answers the request by sending the requested token, which is then processed, thus creating a second wave of computations from the inputs to the outputs.

The demand-driven approach is interesting because it may handle easily non-homogeneous dataflow graphs. It is not by chance that it was chosen as a model for the Patchwork family of tools, OpenMusic and PWGL. For instance, in OpenMusic's dataflow graphs, each node implements a function. Functions can be non-strict, that is, they may use only part of the inputs to produce the output. An example is the conditional operator `if`, which returns the value of either of its two inlets according to the boolean value present on a third inlet. Handling correctly non-strict functions is necessary for defining recursive functions: if the conditional operator were strict, the retrieval of both inputs would be required and the computation of recursive functions would loop forever, since even in the terminal case all branches would be computed.

In demand-driven models, the firing of an actor may consume an arbitrary number of tokens on each input, and may produce an arbitrary number of tokens on each output. In this case, an actor would request to its inputs the number of tokens it needs. This can be used to simplify the handling of multirate audio graphs.

Assessment of Demand-Driven and Data-Driven Approaches. Demand-driven and data-driven approaches have both their pros and cons. Generally speaking, we might say that the demand-driven approach is more suitable for highly dynamic computations in which the focus is placed on the result to be obtained, whereas the data-driven approach is more suitable for static calculations.

An advantage of demand-driven models is that they greatly reduce the need for initialisation: all the parameters needed for performing the computation are retrieved automatically as a direct or indirect consequence of the evaluation request, whereas in data-driven models an explicit mechanism for entering the initialisation data in the graph must be specified.

On the other hand, data-driven models can model in a more straightforward way reactive systems, which can be simply activated by the arrival of new data at one of the sources of the graph, whereas demand-driven models need both the data to be made available at the source and a request to be submitted at the sink, causing the 'upward' request wave to be propagated for the 'downward' wave to happen.

2.5 The Kahn Principle: Reconciling the Operational and the Algebraic View

The previous considerations sketch an *operational* view of the functioning of a dataflow graph: the graph is a machine similar to an electrical circuit and the functioning of the graph amounts to moving tokens along the links and to transforming the values of the tokens when passing through an actor.

Another, more abstract, view of the graph has an algebraic flavour. The idea is to assign a variable to each connection from an output port to an input port and to describe the interaction graph through a set of equations linking such variables—one equation for each output port. We can assume that there is only one output port labeled with variable y for an actor **a**.[3] Then, the equation $y = a(x_1, x_2, \dots)$ represents the relationships between the inputs $x_1, x_2, \dots$ and the output y (cf. the diagram below, at left). The symbol a refers to the behavior of actor **a** and there are several mathematical ways to model this behavior. For instance, a can be a function of the tokens. In this case, the variable denotes the "current token value" instead of the entire stream.

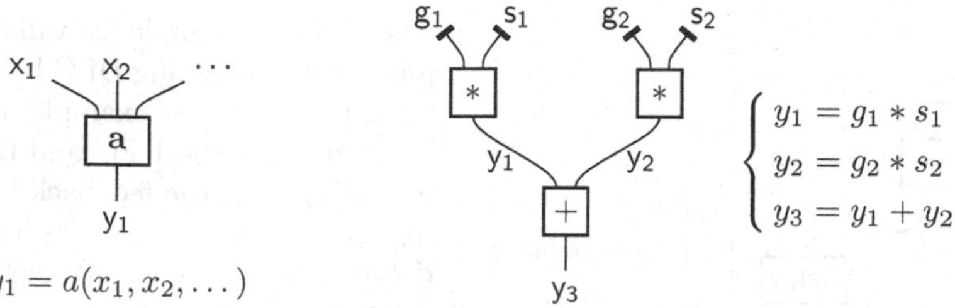

[3] If an actor has multiple output ports, it can be divided into as many actors as outputs, each taking the same inputs and having only one output.

With this interpretation, the set of equations associated to a DFG can be interpreted as an ordinary set of equations between real values. The right side of the diagram above models a simple two-input mixer, with gain g_1 and g_2. Notice that the set of equations is a set of *fixed point equations*, that is, each equation takes the form

$$\textit{variable} = \text{expression-involving-variables}\,.$$

The interesting point is that, in this example, solving the algebraic equations associated with the DFG gives the same result as the operation of the DFG in terms of movement and transformation of the tokens (the operational view).

However, restricting the behavior of a node to a function of the current input tokens is too restrictive: for instance, this mathematical model cannot represent a node whose behavior depends of an internal memory, like a delay (see next section). But the actor operation in the example above can be interpreted as function acting on entire streams, the operators $*$ and $+$ being the point-wise multiplication and the point-wise addition of the stream's elements.

A DFG where the behavior of each actor can be modeled as a continuous function of the entire input streams to the output streams is said to be *pure*. It has been postulated by Kahn [14], and proven only ten years later by Faustini in [11], that the operational behavior of a pure DFG computes *the least fixed point solution of its associated set of equations.* The understanding of this result requires to define precisely what is meant by *continuous* and *least.* Intuitively, we can say that a set of equations may have zero or more solutions. This result states that there is at least one solution, and that the graph computes the stream solution that is minimal according to a carefully chosen stream comparison order [16].

2.6 Feedback Loops

The previous example of fixed point equations is not very interesting: these equations remain simple because there is no circular dependencies between variables. Fixed point equations of this kind are easily solved by substituting known variables (here g_1, s_1, g_2 and s_2) in the expressions at the right hand side of the equations and repeating this process until there is no further unknown variable. In the example, the first iteration defines variables y_1 and y_2 and the second iteration defines y_3.

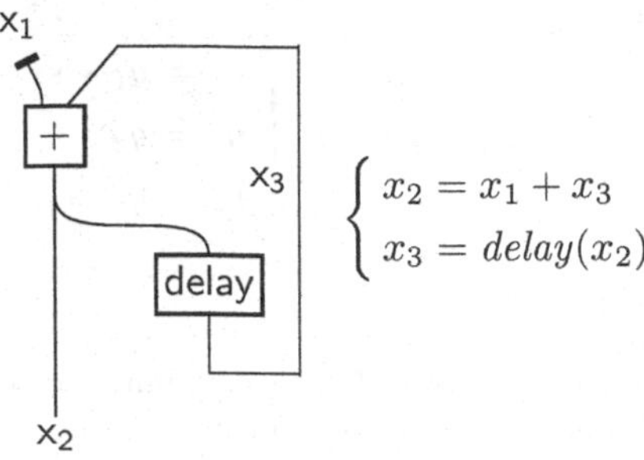

The Kahn principle is valid for any pure DFG, including DFG having feedback loops. In the example at left, x_1 is an input of the DFG and the operator *delay* is on the feedback loop going from the output of + to its input. Here *delay* is a function shifting the entire stream $s = v_0 \cdot v_1 \cdot v_2 \cdot \ldots$ in time: $delay(s) = 0 \cdot v_0 \cdot v_1 \cdot v_2 \cdot \ldots$. Operationally, the delay is a memory initially filled with 0.

When a token is present at the input, the *delay* outputs the value in the memory and then updates the memory with the input value. Thus, this DFG computes the sum of its successive inputs.

The corresponding equations exhibit a self-dependency: if we substitute the definition of x_2 into the right hand side of x_3, we get $x_3 = delay(x_1 + x_3)$ which cannot be solved by substituting the variables. But we can look at what happens at the level of the stream's elements instead: let the stream x_i be $x_i^0 \cdot \ldots \cdot x_i^j \cdot \ldots$

$$x_3^0 \cdot \ldots \cdot x_3^j \cdot \cdots = 0 \cdot (x_1^0 + x_3^0) \cdot \ldots \cdot (x_1^j + x_3^j) \cdot \ldots$$

that is,

$$x_3^0 = 0, \qquad x_3^{j+1} = x_1^j + x_3^j$$

or, in other words, x_3 is the running sum of the successive values of x_1.

2.7 Time in Dataflow: Synchronous Languages

In the previous example, one may notice that *delay* is a function acting on streams, not a function acting on tokens. This allows the specification of behaviors implying a transfer of information from one token to the next one. However, this is not enough to model the behavior of a node acting to merge two streams.

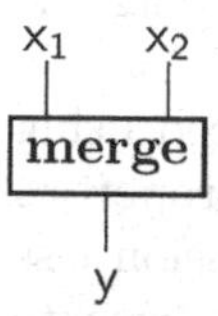

The merge actor simply transmits the tokens that present themselves at its inputs towards its outputs, in their arrival order. The first problem is to decide what happens when tokens are simultaneously available on the two inputs. One may chose to transmit the token on the first input and to drop the second token. This way, the merge operator has a deterministic behavior. But even so, it cannot be modeled as a stream function.

The reason is that SDF does not provide enough information on the passing of time. For instance, suppose that stream s represents the value 0 produced every two seconds starting from date 0, while s' represents the value 1 produced every two seconds, starting from date 1. Then merge(s, s') has for result the stream $0 \cdot 1 \cdot 0 \cdot 1 \cdot \ldots$ Let s'' be the stream representing the value 1 produced every four seconds, starting from date 1, then we have merge$(s, s'') = 0{\cdot}1{\cdot}0{\cdot}0{\cdot}0{\cdot}1{\cdot}0{\cdot}0{\cdot}0{\cdot}1{\cdot}\ldots$ even if $s' = s''$. The lack of temporal information in the stream makes the streams s' and s'' indistinguishable, even if they model two different processes and so there is no function *merge* on streams.

The problem was recognized in the real-time programming community and lead to the development of synchronous languages like LUSTRE [13]. In this dataflow programming language, the idea is to "align" each stream so the production of the ith value of any stream takes place on the same date. This is achieved by introducing a special token value $\perp$ meaning "an actual value is not available". With this token, the *synchronized streams* s' and s'' are presented by:

$$s' = \perp \cdot 1 \cdot \perp \cdot 1 \cdot \perp \cdot 1 \cdot \perp \cdot \ldots$$
$$s'' = \perp \cdot 1 \cdot \perp \cdot \perp \cdot \perp \cdot 1 \cdot \perp \cdot \ldots$$

The Kahn principle holds for fixed point equations on these synchronized streams and more actors can be specified as stream functions.

2.8 Declarative Programming

If we insist on Kahn's principle, it is because it leads to a *declarative programming language*. It is commonly said that that declarative programming focuses on what the program should accomplish (whereas imperative or procedural programming focuses on how the program should achieve the result). This description is rather vague, and a more effective way to look at it is to characterize declarative programming languages as programming languages making possible equational reasoning, where an entity may always be substituted by its definition. In other words, each statement of the language can be seen as a set of mathematical definitions, that is, a set of fixed point equations, and program execution amounts to finding a solution to these equations.

In this context, a variable in a program is handled exactly as a mathematical variable: a reference to a well-defined although possibly unknown value. This departs considerably from the notion of variable in an imperative program, where a variable refers to a memory location that can hold various values during the program execution.

By definition, declarative programming enjoys *transparential referency*: any expression can be replaced with its corresponding value without changing the program behavior [24].

A program becomes a mathematical object that can be manipulated using classical mathematical methods, so as to, for instance, prove program properties for efficient compilation, replace an expression by an equivalent expression less costly to compute, rearrange the order of the computation, possibly execute some tasks in parallel.

The Kahn principle gives us a tool to solve some equations on streams. It also allows us to reason algebraically on the operational properties of a dataflow program.

3 Dataflow and Computer Music Programming Languages

The previous section may seem very technical, but it has far-reaching consequences in the realm of computer music programming languages. Several languages and systems, such as OpenMusic, PWGL and Faust, are based upon more or less pure SDF:

- The core of OpenMusic and PWGL is a demand-driven implementation of a pure dataflow. However, the language embeds some imperative features that are useful for interacting with users (e.g.. fixing some computed value to be reused in later evaluation). Interestingly, a specific version of OpenMusic, OM#, extends the demand-driven execution model towards an hybrid

data- and demand-driven execution model which simplifies considerably the programming of reactive system [5].
- Faust [18] is a perfect example of data-driven, pure synchronous dataflow. Equational reasoning is heavily used in the Faust compiler, for code generation (by program transformation) but also for the automatic parallelisation [20].
- Synchronous programming—which involves synchronous streams, either in the context of dataflow or in the context of imperative languages—is the model embraced by signal processing languages like CHUCK [25] or KRONOS [17].

3.1 Dataflow Programming in Max and Pd

As previously mentioned, Max and PureData implement two different dataflow systems, respectively devoted to control messages and audio signals. The earliest versions of Max only implemented the former system, as Max itself had been originally conceived as a tool for building interfaces controlling external audio hardware. The audio system was only added to Max in the late 1990s, and was so distinctly separated from the 'core' of Max itself that it used to be sold separately under a different name, MSP.

The Max audio graph is a relatively simple case of pure SDF, whose functional nature is somewhat less explicit than that of Faust, but not too different from it. Our discussion will only focus on the control graph, its significantly different paradigm and the consequences this bears with respect to the different applications Max lends itself to, with a specific focus on the implementation of compositional processes.

In what follows, we shall assume in the reader a basic, practical knowledge of Max, and only review some fundamental concepts when needed.

A Max patch can be seen as a set of nodes working asynchronously with respect to each other: if, when and how each module 'fires' depends on the data processed, and, generally speaking, only one message can traverse the patch at any given time. This means that nodes with more than one input link must have mechanisms for storing data for later use. This is accomplished through the so-called 'hot' and 'cold' inlets (that is, input links in the Max jargon): when a hot inlet receives a message, it performs its computation and delivers the result; but when a message is received in a cold one, it gets stored for later use and nothing else happens. Most Max objects have at least one hot inlet, and many have one or more cold inlets.

This structure, which actually involves many other details and is not without exceptions, has profound consequences: there is no transparential referency in the control DFG.

For example, multiple links ('cords' in the Max jargon) can be connected to a single inlet corresponding to an implicit merge. But there is no notion of synchronous stream in Max: there is no notion of timestamp that can be used to "align" the streams values and to recover transparential referency. Another example of non-transparential referency: sending the same message, that is, outputting a token on some link, does not always achieve the same effect if done on the timer thread or on the main thread (because of different message priorities, its subsequent handling may differ).

3.2 Pros and Cons of Different Computational Models

Max's computational model is motivated by the fact that, unlike the other systems described above, it was not conceived as a programming language but, in its own creator's words [21], as a *musical instrument*. With respect to this end, Max has the merit of being extremely economical in terms of its basic principles and quite adaptable to very different use cases.

On the other hand, as hinted at above, representing nontrivial algorithms in Max is often more complicated than with other systems. Two of the authors became painfully aware of this complicatedness while working at the *cage* package [2], which implements a comprehensive set of typical computer-aided composition operations. *cage* is entirely composed of abstractions, and during its development the shortcomings of Max programming became so evident that the seeds for the work presented in this article were planted.

The reasons for this difficulty are multiple, and include the following:

- The greater freedom Max grants in building the program graph easily leads to far more intricate patches than functional dataflow models, with spaghetti connections that can grow very hard to analyse.
- Typical Max patches often have their state distributed through many objects whose main, individual purpose is not data storage.
- Max lacks, or implements in quite idiosyncratic ways, some concepts that are ubiquitous in modern programming languages, such as complex, hierarchical data structures, iteration, data encapsulation, functions and parametrization of a process through other processes.

On the other hand, Max allows to incorporate, on top of its basic paradigm, traits reminiscent of various programming styles, such as imperative, object-oriented and functional. Moreover, it includes various objects enclosing entire language interpreters, thus allowing textual code in various languages to be embedded in a patch.

These features may prove useful when nontrivial processes have to be implemented, as is the case when working in contexts like algorithmic and computer-aided composition. Whereas Max was not conceived with these specific applications in mind, it quickly became clear that it could be a valuable environment for them, and several projects have been developed in this sense [10,23,26]. We shall focus on one of them, the *bach* package, which has been conceived and is maintained by two of the authors.

3.3 The *bach* Package

The *bach* package[4] for Max is an open source library of more than 200 modules aimed at augmenting Max with advanced capabilities of symbolic musical representation. At its forefront are two objects called `bach.roll` and `bach.score`, capable of displaying, editing and playing back musical scores composed of both traditional notation and arbitrary time-based data, such as parameters for sound synthesis and processing, textual or graphical performance instructions, file paths and more.[5]

One of the main focuses of *bach* is algorithmic generation and manipulation of such scores. To this end, *bach* implements in Max a tree data structure called *llll* (an acronym for Lisp-like linked list), meant to represent arbitrary data including whole augmented scores. *bach* objects and abstractions exchange *lllls* with each other, rather than regular Max messages, and their majority is devoted to performing typical list operations such as reversal, rotation, search, transposition, sorting and so on.

Generally speaking, *bach* objects abide by the overall design principles and conventions of Max, but it should be remarked that, whereas standard Max objects can control the flow of *lllls* in a patcher just like they do with regular Max messages, they cannot access their contents unless *lllls* are explicitly converted into a Max-readable format, which on the other hand has other limitations (for a detailed explanation, see [4]). Thus, *bach* contains a large number of objects that somehow extend to *lllls* the functionalities of standard Max objects. For example, whereas the `zl.rev` object reverses a plain Max list, the `bach.rev` object reverses an *llll* by taking into account all the branches of the tree, each of which can be reversed as well or not according to specific settings. While it is possible to convert an *llll* into the Max format and reverse it with `zl.rev`, in general the result will not be semantically and syntactically correct.

Since its beginnings, *bach* has been strongly influenced by and related to a number of other existing projects: for an overview of at least some of them, see [4]. The synthesis of different approaches that lies at the very basis of the conception itself of *bach* has been validated by a large community of users, who have developed many artistic and research projects in several domains[6], and by the fact that it provides the foundation for the *cage* and *dada*[7] libraries [12].

In the following sections, we shall review a few programming styles and approaches and see how *bach* can be helpful with adopting them in Max: namely, we shall show how some fundamentally imperative, functional and objected-

---

4 www.bachproject.net.

5 `bach.roll` and `bach.score` differ in that the former represents time proportionally, whereas the latter implements a traditional representation of time, with tempi, metri, measures and relative temporal units such as quarter notes, tuplets and so on.

6 The website of *bach* showcases some interesting works that have been developed with the library, mostly by people unrelated to its developers.

7 The *dada* library contains interactive two-dimensional interfaces for real-time symbolic generation and dataset exploration, embracing a graphic, ludic, explorative approach to music composition.

oriented traits of Max can be leveraged through the use of specific *bach* objects and design patterns; moreover, we shall discuss a recent addition to *bach*, that is, a multi-paradigm programming language called *bell* and meant to facilitate the expression of complex algorithms for manipulating *lllls*.

4 Different Programming Styles and Approaches in Max

4.1 Imperative Approach

It has been observed that Max is essentially an imperative system in disguise [9]: as stated before, any nontrivial program in Max requires to take care of states and the order of operations, and analysing even a moderately complex patch can only be done by following the flow of data and the evolution of states over time. This is complicated by the fact that many objects whose purpose is carrying out specific operations also maintain a state that can be used to store values for later use. For example, most arithmetic operators have two inlets: the left one, called *hot*, sets the first term of the operation and triggers the calculation; the right one, called *cold*, only sets the second term of the operation. So, the typical way to perform, say, a sum of two numbers is first setting the right term, and then the left term, thus calculating the result. This somewhat idiosyncratic design can be leveraged to perform more complex tasks in quite a synthetic way. For example (see Fig. 1), a typical way to build a running accumulator is to feed each new number to be accumulated in the hot inlet of a `+` operator, and feeding back the result in the right inlet, so as to have it ready to be summed to the next incoming value. Likewise, a differentiator can be built by sending each new value to the hot inlet of a `-` object first and the cold inlet immediately after, so that it is ready to be subtracted from the next incoming value. Whereas this may be convenient for such simple cases, it can become extremely complicated as the complexity of the problem grows.

Fig. 1. The typical design of a simple accumulator in Max: the `int` module stores the current number in a hidden state; when the top button is clicked, the state is output, incremented, and stored in the `int` module anew. Notice that, as a general rule in Max, the internal state is hidden from the user: at the moment in which the screenshot was taken the internal state had been updated to 8 (as the bottom number displays) although the argument of the `int` module still shows '0', which represents the *initial* state. Note also that the functioning here is asynchronous and controlled through hot and cold inlets which differs from the synchronous functioning of the DF accumulator in Sect. 2.6

On the other hand, it is possible to make this imperative style more explicit by adopting some good practices, like widely using specific objects (such as `trigger` and `bangbang`) that can help with keeping the evaluation order under control. Moreover, Max contains two objects whose only purpose is holding data associated with a name: `value` and `pv` (for 'private value'), whose role can be seen as corresponding to that of variables in traditional imperative programming languages. Each instance of those objects has a name, and every time it receives a piece of information it retains and shares it with all the other objects with the same name. It is subsequently possible to retrieve the stored data from any of them. The `value` and `pv` modules differ in their scope: the former's is global, that is, data are shared through all the open patches in the Max session, whereas the latter's is local, in that data are only shared within the same patcher or its

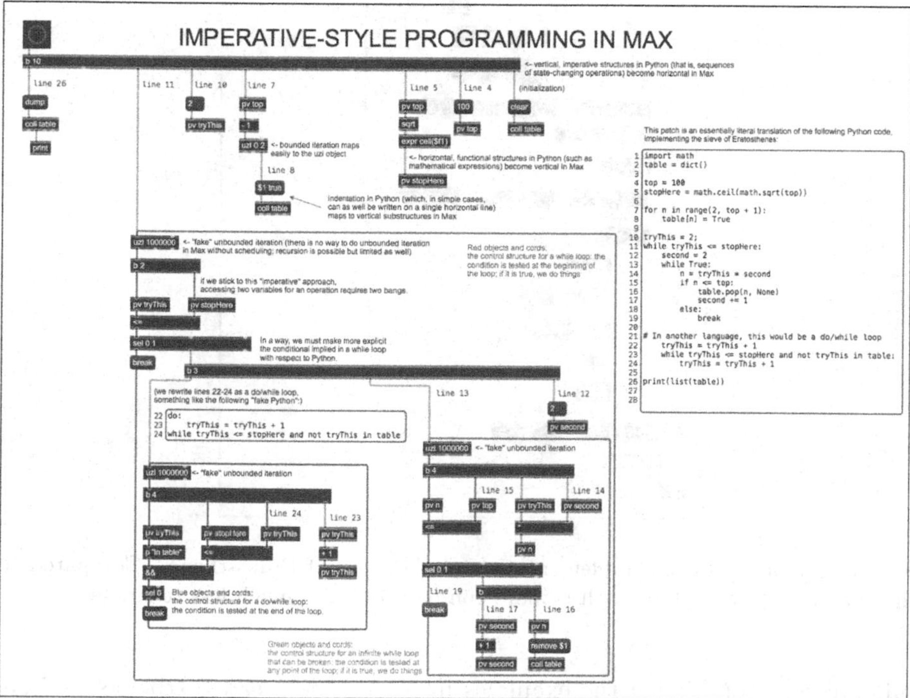

Fig. 2. An implementation in strict imperative style of the sieve of Eratosthenes, an algorithm for finding prime numbers. The patch is a direct translation of the Python code shown in the box. We have chosen not to write very idiomatic Python code to make it closer to pseudocode. In the patch, we have avoided—among the other things—storing data in the cold inlets of objects: every piece of data meant to be reused is stored in `pv` objects, from which they are retrieved at need. The result is quite redundant, but the structure of calculation is clear. Among the other things, it is interesting to notice how the three `while` 'loops' in the Python code correspond to three actual graphical loops in the Max patch.

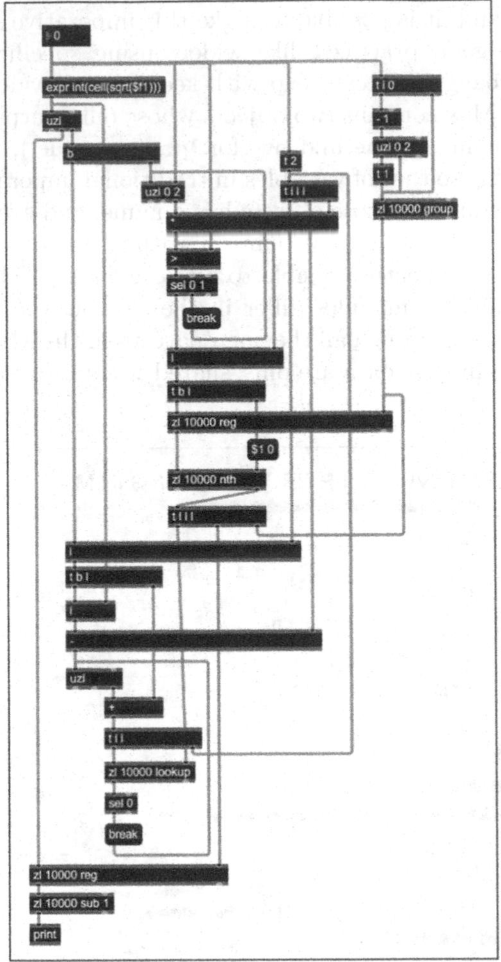

Fig. 3. A more synthetic implementation of the sieve of Eratosthenes. Compared to the example of Fig. 2, the patch is more compact but also much less readable.

subpatchers. Considering the examples in some widespread textbooks [6,7,26] and the Max documentation, as well as some informal reckoning of the patches that users share on the official Max forum, it seems to us that these objects are seldom used. One likely reason is that they are virtually never necessary, and tend to make patches larger and slightly less efficient. On the other hand, by combining `value` and `pv` with the aforementioned sequencing objects, it is possible to use Max in a much more readable, essentially imperative programming style (Fig. 3).

bach implements its own variants of these objects, respectively named `bach.value` and `bach.pv`. Besides dealing correctly with *lllls*, they can open a text editing window if double-clicked, allowing to view and modify the data they hold. Moreover, *bach* contains an object called `bach.shelf`, which acts as a container of an arbitrarily large set of *lllls*, each associated to a unique name. `bach.shelf` objects can be themselves named, thus defining namespaces: this means that *lllls* associated to a name within one named `bach.shelf` object will be shared only with other `bach.shelf` objects with the same name. Although still somewhat crude (it might be interesting, for example, to allow non-global namespaces), this is a way to improve data localization and data encapsulation, and reduce the proliferation of storage objects in complex scenarios.

4.2 Object-Oriented Approach

The fact that a Max program is built of independent blocks responding to messages they send to each other in consequence of callbacks triggered by events gives it a strong object-oriented flavour, and the Smalltalk influence is both apparent and declared. At a lower level, in fact, each Max object in a patch is an instance of a specific class, with member variables containing the object's state and methods roughly corresponding to the messages it accepts for modifying and/or querying the state.

The two main *bach* editors, `bach.roll` and `bach.score`, comply with this object-oriented approach. However, a distinction can be made about the kinds of messages they accepts: some control and query the object's appearance (background color, zoom level, etc.), whereas others are dedicated to the direct management of the editor's content.

In fact, there are several ways to modify a score. One of the simplest involves dumping its parameters from some outlets, modifying them via appropriate Max and *bach* modules, and feeding the result into a different editor object.

In contrast, one can send direct messages to the editor, asking for specific elements of the score to be created or modified through the so-called *bach in-place syntax*, with no output from the object outlets (unless explicitly requested). The operations are immediately performed and the score is updated (see Fig. 4). These messages enable the creation, the edition and the deletion of individual notation items, such as a single measure or a single note, and can actually be seen as methods of the items themselves, arranged according to a precise hierarchy and sharing a certain number of common properties (such as having a symbolic name, being selectable, etc.).

This mechanism is strongly inspired by object-oriented programming: references to the notation items to be modified are acquired via a selection mechanism, and then messages are sent to them. A set of items can be selected graphically, or through a query in the form of a message such as `sel note if voice == 2 and pitch % C1 == F#0`, and then modified by means of messages such as `duration = velocity * 10`. Most musical properties can be modified in this way, and the expressions determining the assignation support a standard set of predefined variables, capturing the current state of the object (`onset`, `cents`, `duration`, `velocity`, `index`, `part`, `grace`, and so on).

In fact, this kind of approach allows much more complex operations than the ones described here, as there are many classes of notation items, each having a large number of properties and related messages. In spite of the richness of the data it can manipulate, though, the in-place syntax is not very flexible, but there are plans to extend it through the *bell* language (see below).

Moreover, there are available methods to perform routine tasks such as copying/pasting score content or slot[8] information, inserting or deleting pitch breakpoints, modifying portions of score, snapping items to a temporal grid, making selection monophonic, adding or modifying slot content, renaming, distributing elements evenly in time, and so on. Notation objects send notifications whenever their state is changed, so that any of the aforementioned methods can be also triggered by user operations on the score, in a reactive way. Some of these messages work in conjunction with the playback system, so that users can, among other things, retrieve properties of the currently played notes or move the playback cursor.

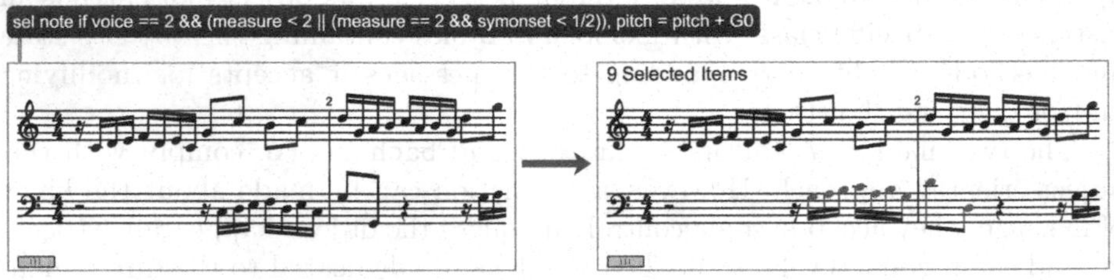

Fig. 4. A very simple example of in-place modification: notes belonging to the second voice and whose onset lies before the middle of the second measure are selected and transposed up a perfect fifth (the image shows the state of the score both before and after the click on the message).

4.3 Functional Approach

Max shares some similarities with functional languages, firstly because it manupulates values through a variety of nodes implementing functions on them. It is then possible to build patches that somehow behave functionally, and whose appearance is extremely similar to that of equivalent ones in a functional graphical system such as PWGL. *bach* extends the functional traits of Max in a few areas.

As hinted at before, it implements the *llll*, a tree data type quite similar to a Lisp list, and provides a large number of modules for dealing with *lllls*. Although, of course, list operators are not inherently functional, they are quite customary in functional languages, and the corresponding *bach* objects can be connected in a way corresponding to the composition of list functions in functional languages such as Lisp or Haskell.

Secondly, generalized versions of functions such as *sort* and *find* require some way to specify, respectively, a custom ordering or an arbitrary search criterion.

[8] Slots are containers of arbitrary data attached to notes and chords.

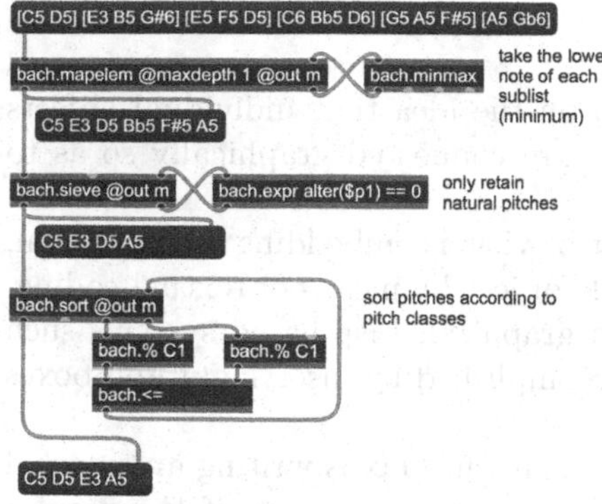

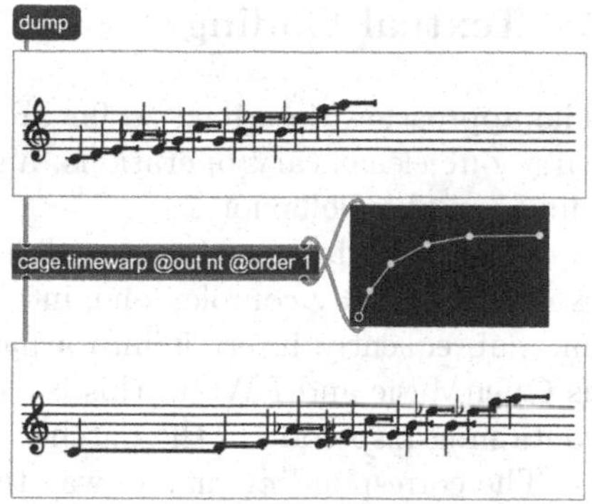

Fig. 5. The cross-connected and loop-connected patch cords attached to `bach.mapelem`, `bach.sieve`, `bach.sort` and `cage.timewarp` modules form several instances of the so-called lambda loop. The left-side example should be straightforward. In the right-side example, the temporal distribution of events in a musical score is altered through the provided transfer function, with time on the X axis and speed on the Y axis. At a superficial level, patches like these appear to be quite similar to how the same processes might be implemented in a functional dataflow system.

In several languages, these generalized functions are conveniently implemented as higher-order functions, i.e. functions taking other functions as arguments. This requires to handle functions like ordinary data. A Max patcher lacks the concept of function, but several *bach* objects implement a design pattern called the *lambda loop* (see Fig. 5), whose role is somehow akin to that of higher-order functions.

A lambda loop is a patching configuration in which one or more dedicated outlets of a module output data iteratively to a patch section, which must calculate a result (either a modification of the original data, or some sort of return value) and return it to a dedicated inlet of the starting object [4].

Lambda loops are used by some *bach* modules directly inspired by functional programming practices, such as `bach.mapelem` (performing a map operation) and `bach.reduce` (recursively applying a binary function on elements); all these modules can be helpful to translate programs conceived functionally into Max patches. The number of modules taking advantage of this design pattern is, however, much larger, and includes basic operators such as `bach.sieve` (only letting some elements through) and `bach.sort` (performing sort operations), but also advanced tools such as `bach.constraints` (solving constraint satisfaction problems) as well as some of the modules in the *cage* package.

It might be interesting to remark that, although the high-level concepts at play are quite different from those required by an actual implementation of lambda functions, the way lambda loops are implemented under the hood is quite similar to the callback-based low-level implementation that is typical of higher-order functions in functional languages.

5 Textual Coding

The approaches described so far are based on the idea that individual objects carry out elementary operations, and they are connected graphically so as to build complex behaviors.

A different, but not incompatible, point of view is embedding an algorithm, even a potentially complex one, into a single object by means of textual coding, and subsequently insert it into a patch. In graphical, Lisp-based systems such as OpenMusic and PWGL, this is easily accomplished by inserting graph boxes containing Lisp code in the patcher.

The corresponding, native way to do the same in Max is writing an external object in C. Whereas this was originally meant to be a part of the regular Max workflow, it is undoubtedly a rather complicated task for today's average Max user, requiring to master the C programming language and the compilation chain. Moreover, the write-test-debug cycle requires to restart the whole Max environment at every modification made to the object, and errors in the code are not unlikely to crash Max. Finally, unlike what happens with Lisp snippets in OM and PWGL, the code for a Max object is required to include a relatively bulky infrastructure taking care of the communication with the Max environment and only remotely related to the actual problem meant to be tackled.

As expressing algorithms through textual coding can be quite convenient but the C API has the aforementioned drawbacks, over the years various other programming languages have been embedded into Max through higher-level APIs, including Java, JavaScript and Lua, all included in the Max distribution. Although very effective for various kinds of operations, these bindings are not optimal for interacting with *bach*, for a number of reasons that are detailed in [3], mostly related to the two following points:

- As mentioned before, the all-encompassing data structure of *bach* is the *llll*, which is not easily expressed in any of the above languages.
- All these bindings require some pieces of quasi-boilerplate infrastructure, such as the explicit management of inlets, outlets and messages sent to the enclosing object, that make the writing of code significantly more complex, compared to the ease and directness of embedding Lisp code in Open Music and PWGL.

On the other hand, Max contains a family of objects, namely `expr`, `vexpr` and `if`, that allow defining textually mathematical expressions and simple conditionals which might otherwise require fairly complicated constellations of objects in a patch. *bach* adds another member to the family, called `bach.expr`, allowing to define mathematical expressions to be performed point-wise on *lllls*.

While the `expr` family syntax is not a full-fledged programming language, it can be seen as the basis for one. We therefore decided to add in the latest release of *bach* a new object to the family, called `bach.eval`, implementing a new, simple programming language conceived with a few, conceptually simple points in mind:

- Turing-complete, functional syntax, in which all the language constructs return values, but also including imperative traits such as sequences, variables and loops.
- Full downward compatibility with the `expr` family.
- Inclusion of list operators on *lllls* respecting, as far as possible, the conventions and naming of the corresponding *bach* objects.
- Implicit concatenation of elements into *lllls*, meaning that by simply juxtaposing values (be they literals, or the result of calculations) they are packed together into an *llll*. In this way, a program can be seen as an *llll* intermingled with calculations, not unlike what happens by combining the `quote` operator and `unquote` macro in Lisp.
- Maximum ease of embedding of the object into a Max patcher, with, among the other things, no need for explicit management of inlets and outlets.

The resulting language is called *bell* (standing for *bach evaluation language for llls*, but also paying homage to the historic Bell Labs). A detailed description of its syntax can be found in [3], whereas, for the scope of this article, a few examples should suffice (see Fig. 6, 7 and 8).

bell code can be typed in the `bach.eval` object box or into a dedicated text editor window, loaded from a text file and even passed dynamically to the host object via Max messages.

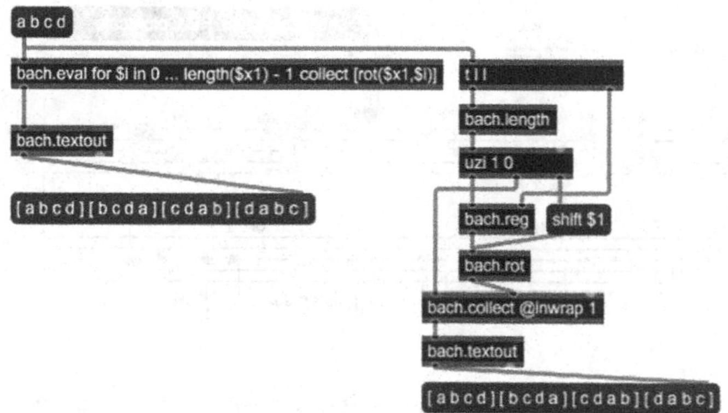

Fig. 6. A comparison between an *llll* manipulation process described through a snippet of *bell* code (in the `bach.eval` object box) and the corresponding implementation within the standard graphical dataflow paradigm of Max. The code should be mostly straightforward for readers familiar with the *bach* library and a textual programming language such as Python, considering that the `[ ... ]` paired operator encloses one or more elements into a sublist, according to the general syntax of *lllls*.

The intended usage paradigm of `bach.eval` is similar to that of the `expr` family: `bach.eval` objects are meant to carry out relatively simple computational tasks, and to be disseminated around the patcher among regular *bach* and Max objects taking care of the UI, MIDI, DSP, event scheduling and so on. Snippets

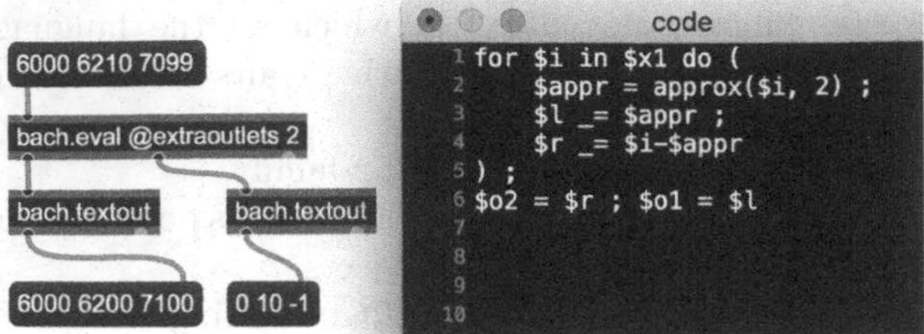

Fig. 7. A snippet of *bell* code approximating a list of cents to the nearest semitone, and returning the distances from the semitone grid from a different outlet. Here, the code has been typed in a separate text editing window (shown on the right). The `$o1` and `$o2` pseudovariables assign results to the extra outlets declared in the `bach.eval` object box. The main, rightmost outlet returning the actual result of the computation (which, in this example, is the last term of the sequence defined by the ; operators, that is, the value of the `$l` variable as passed to the first extra outlet) is left unused here. The language has several other features not shown here, including named and anonymous user-defined functions with a rich calling mechanism.

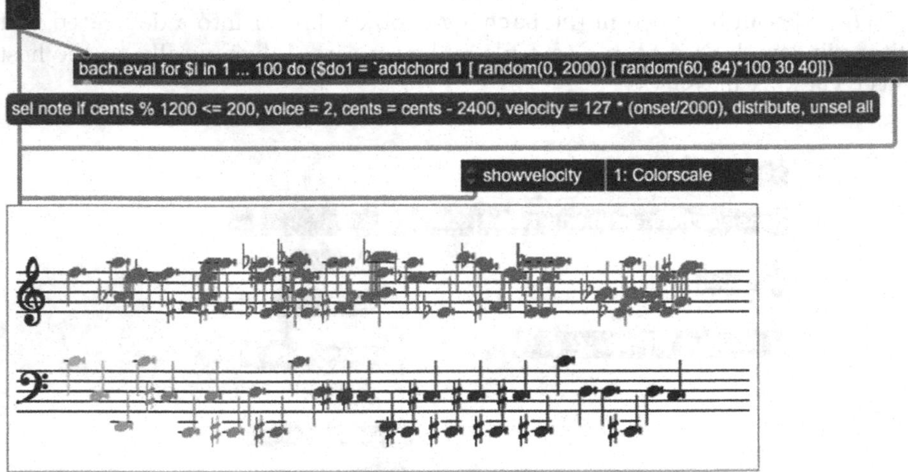

Fig. 8. An example of usage of *bell* in combination with `bach.roll`'s in-place syntax: 100 notes are generated in the first voice with random onsets (between 0 and 2 s) and random pitches (between middle C and the C two octaves above, on a tempered semitonal grid); then all C's, C♯'s and D's are selected (i.e. notes whose remainder modulo 1200 is less than or equal to 200), assigned to the second voice, transposed two octaves below, remodulated with a velocity crescendo and distributed evenly in time.

of *bell* language can also be passed to other objects for the fine-tuning of their behavior as a replacement for lambda loops. Moreover, as hinted at before, an intended (albeit not straightforward) development is to allow `bach.score` and `bach.roll` to be scripted in *bell*, thus allowing far more complex interactions than what is already possible through the syntax described above.

6 Conclusions and Future Work

We have presented some historical and theoretical background about the computational models of Max and other related programming languages and environments, and subsequently described how the *bach* library can be helpful with writing clear and maintainable programs, through some specific features aimed at implementing different programming approaches and styles on top of it. These features are rooted in practical considerations and experience, and allow one to escape the limitations of pure formal models.

More generally, we think that time is ripe for advocating the adoption of more structured and theoretically grounded approaches to working with this successful and widely used tool. We hope that this article may be a step in that direction: further steps should involve, on the one hand, an actual survey of real-life use cases, possibly with the involvement of the community of *bach* users; a more precise and organic formalisation of good and scalable programming practices in Max, which might prove quite different from the ones typical of more traditional programming languages; and, most likely, the conception and development of new tools to encourage them and facilitate their adoption.

References

1. Agon, C.: OpenMusic: un language visuel pour la composition musicale assistée par ordinateur. Ph.D. thesis, University of Paris 6 (1998)
2. Agostini, A., Daubresse, E., Ghisi, D.: Cage: a high-level library for real-time computer-aided composition. In: Proceedings of the International Computer Music Conference, Athens, Greece (2014)
3. Agostini, A., Giavitto, J.: Bell, a textual language for the bach library. In: Proceedings of the International Computer Music Conference (to appear), New York, USA (2019)
4. Agostini, A., Ghisi, D.: A max library for musical notation and computer-aided composition. Comput. Music J. **39**(2), 11–27 (2015). https://doi.org/10.1162/COMJ_a_00296
5. Bresson, J., Giavitto, J.L.: A reactive extension of the openmusic visual programming language. J. Visual Languages Comput. **25**(4), 363–375 (2014)
6. Cipriani, A., Giri, M.: Musica Elettronica e Sound Design. ConTempoNet (2013)
7. Colasanto, F.: Max/MSP: Guía de Programación para Artistas. CMMAS (2010)
8. Conway, M.E.: Design of a separable transition-diagram compiler. Commun. ACM **6**(7), 396–408 (1963)
9. Desain, P., et al.: Putting max in perspective. Comput. Music J. **17**(2), 3–11 (1992)
10. Didkovsky, N., Hajdu, G.: Maxscore: music notation in Max/MSP. In: Proceedings of the International Computer Music Conference (2008)
11. Faustini, A.A.: An operational semantics for pure dataflow. In: Nielsen, M., Schmidt, E.M. (eds.) ICALP 1982. LNCS, vol. 140, pp. 212–224. Springer, Heidelberg (1982). https://doi.org/10.1007/BFb0012771
12. Ghisi, D., Agostini, A.: Extending bach: a family of libraries for real-time computer-assisted composition in max. J. New Music Res. **46**(1), 34–53 (2017)
13. Halbwachs, N., Caspi, P., Raymond, P., Pilaud, D.: The synchronous data flow programming language LUSTRE. Proc. IEEE **79**(9), 1305–1320 (1991)

14. Kahn, G.: The semantics of a simple language for parallel programming. In: proceedings of IFIP Congress 1974, North Holland, pp. 471–475 (1974)
15. Laurson, M., Kuuskankare, M.: PWGL: a novel visual language based on common Lisp, CLOS and OpenGL. In: Proceedings of International Computer Music Conference, Gothenburg, Sweden, pp. 142–145 (2002)
16. Mosses, P.D.: Handbook of theoretical computer science, vol. 2, chap. Denotational Semantics, pp. 575–631. Elsevier Science (1990)
17. Norilo, V., Rautatiekatu, P.: Introducing kronos-a novel approach to signal processing languages. In: Proceedings of the Linux Audio Conference, pp. 9–16. Maynooth: NUIM (2011)
18. Orlarey, Y., Fober, D., Letz, S.: Syntactical and semantical aspects of Faust. Soft. Comput. **8**(9), 623–632 (2004)
19. Orlarey, Y., Fober, D., Letz, S.: Faust: an efficient functional approach to DSP programming. New Comput. Pradigms Comput. Music **290**, 14 (2009)
20. Orlarey, Y., Fober, D., Letz, S.: Parallelization of audio applications with Faust. In: Proceedings of the 6th Sound and Music Computing Conference, Porto, PT, pp. 99–112 (2009)
21. Puckette, M.: Max at seventeen. Comput. Music J. **26**(4), 31–43 (2002)
22. Puckette, M.: A divide between 'compositional' and 'performative' aspects of Pd. In: Proceedings of the First International Pd Convention. Graz, Austria (2004)
23. Scholl, S.: Musik – Raum – Technik. Zur Entwicklung und Anwendung der graphischen Programmierumgebung "Max", chap. Karlheinz Essls RTC-lib, pp. 102–107. Transcript Verlag (2014)
24. Søndergaard, H., Sestoft, P.: Referential transparency, definiteness and unfoldability. Acta Informatica **27**(6), 505–517 (1990). https://doi.org/10.1007/BF00277387
25. Wang, G., Cook, P.R., Salazar, S.: Chuck: a strongly timed computer music language. Comput. Music J. **39**(4), 10–29 (2015)
26. Winkler, T.: Composing Interactive Music. The MIT Press, Cambridge (1998)

Generative Grammar Based on Arithmetic Operations for Realtime Composition

Guido Kramann(✉)

Brandenburg University of Applied Sciences, Brandenburg, Germany
kramann@th-brandenburg.de

Abstract. Mathematical sequences in $\mathbb{N}_0$ are regarded as time series. By repeatedly applying arithmetic operations to each of their elements, the sequences are metamorphised and finally transformed into sounds by an interpretation algorithm. The efficiency of this method as a composition method is demonstrated by explicit examples. In principle, this method also offers laypersons the possibility of composing. In this context it will be discussed how well and under what kind of conditions the compositional results can be predicted and thus can be deliberately planned by the user. On the way to assessing this, Edmund Husserl's concept of "fulfillment chains" provides a good starting point. Finally, the computer-based board game MODULO is presented. Based on the here introduced generative grammar, MODULO converts the respective game situation directly into sound events. In MODULO, the players behave consistent to the gaming-rules and do not care about the evolving musical structure. In this respect, MODULO represents an alternative draft to a reasonable and common use of the symbols of the grammar in which the user anticipates the musical result.

Keywords: Algorithmic composition · Phenomenology · Arithmetic operations · Realtime composition · Live coding · Edmund Husserl · Notation system

1 Introduction

This thesis deals with a generative process in the field of real-time composition, which is essentially based on the fact that different arithmetic operations are repeatedly applied to the elements of a mathematical sequence. In the following, this basic procedure shall be abbreviated as **AOG** (**A**rithmetic-**O**peration-**G**rammar).

"Every human is a composer" – with this casual modification of a saying by Joseph Beuys I would like to express that generative composition processes basically open up the possibility that even people with little knowledge of music theory can compose, since in the sense of Chomsky's division of generative grammars those of level 3 – the one presented here is one of this kind – help to produce exclusively meaningful/wellformed musical structures [2,3].

R. Kronland-Martinet et al. (Eds.): CMMR 2019, LNCS 12631, pp. 279–303, 2021.
https://doi.org/10.1007/978-3-030-70210-6_19

Typically, generative methods of composition are judged from the point of view of what kind of structures they produce and if so what relation they have to music [21].

However, in the second part of this work, the actual process is discussed under another aspect, namely the extent to which the generative process chain can also be mapped in the mind of a person who produces it, especially with regard to its possible use as a composition aid for laypersons. To even consider taking such a direction is motivated by the fact that the overall procedure presented here works in such a way that the process of generating the composition from its symbolic representation is straightforward, without the need for automatic corrections or optimizations of the linear or harmonic structure. At least this ensures a relative transparency of the generating process.

But first the actual procedure is described in detail both theoretically and in examples and its special characteristics are analyzed:

2 A 3rd Order Generative Grammar Based on Arithmetic Operations Applied to Mathematical Sequences

The overall shape of the sequence $a_{i+1} = a_i + 1$ (identity on natural numbers $id(\mathbb{N}_0) = \{0, 1, 2, 3, 4, ...\}$) is to be changed by applying an arithmetic operation to each of its sequence members. This can be repeated on the resulting sequence with another operation, and so on. One gets a metamorphosis of sequences which have a close structural relation to each other.

For musical use, from now on all sequences are to be understood as time sequences which deliver their values in a fixed time interval ΔT within a real-time composition process.

$\mathbb{N}_0$ is also the permitted number range. So that this number range is never left, a filter is set after the execution of any operation, in which the decimal places are truncated and values smaller than zero are set to zero. In Table 1 some operators are suggested to be used for this grammar. There the symbols used for the operations and their meaning are shown together with an example. In addition, it is shown here how the corresponding operator is represented in the game "MODULO" introduced at the end of this presentation.

The operators proposed here go a little beyond of what is common in arithmetic. In order to understand the table, the operators $\neq$, $==$, $\nmid$, $|$ should also be regarded as a type of filter that allows a number to pass when the condition meant is fulfilled.

2.1 Sound Generation on the Basis of a Mathematical Sequence

For sound generation, $id(\mathbb{N}_0)$ is now executed as a counting process with constant speed. The introduced grammar makes it easy to gradually increase the complexity of simple structures by adding an operation. Thus, adding a symbol on the symbol level typically results in an increase of complexity at the score level.

Table 1. Used operators with examples

Symbol	Symbol in MODULO	Meaning	Example
$+$	$+$	Addition	$\{0,1,2,3,4\}+3=\{3,4,5,6,7\}$
$-$	$-$	Subtraction	$\{0,1,2,3,4\}-3=\{0,0,0,0,1\}$
$\cdot$	$\cdot$	Multiplication	$\{0,1,2,3,4\}\cdot 2=\{0,2,4,6,8\}$
$\neq$	++	Not equal	$\{0,1,2,3,4\}\neq 3=\{0,1,2,0,4\}$
$==$	−−	Identity	$\{0,1,2,3,4\}{==}\,3=\{0,0,0,3,0\}$
$\div$	..	Division	$\{0,1,2,3,4\}\div 2=\{0,0,1,1,2\}$
$\nmid$	+++	Does not divide	$\{0,1,2,3,4\}\nmid 2=\{0,1,0,3,0\}$
$\equiv$	−−−	Modulo	$\{0,1,2,3,4\}\equiv 3=\{0,1,2,0,1\}$
$\vert$	...	True divider	$\{0,1,2,3,4\}\vert 2=\{0,0,2,0,4\}$

Each intermediate result of the successive operations is used in parallel for the sound generation. This means that not only the sequence is used for sound generation, which is the final result after all successive operations have been applied, but also each individual sequence, which is the intermediate result after each individual operation. Thus, also the members of each intermediate resulting sequence are regarded as divisors of the base number b, with for example $b = 2520 = 2\cdot 2\cdot 2\cdot 3\cdot 3\cdot 5\cdot 7$.

Whenever the divisibility is actually given and a number between for example 55 and 1760 (A1 and A6) comes out, this is understood as frequency, which is then mapped in the best possible way to the equally tempered scale, so that this tone can then be played in real time e.g. as a piano tone by a sequencer. This mechanism plays the role of a filter that suppresses pitches that have a too large harmonic difference to the overall structure.

2.2 "$\equiv 7\cdot 5\equiv 3\cdot 5$" – a Simple Composition as an Example

"$\equiv 7\cdot 5\equiv 3\cdot 5$" is meant as a symbolic representation of a tiny composition (for sound and complete score see [9]). As it is a convention to apply all operators to $id(\mathbb{N}_0)$ first this information can be neglected in the symbolic representation. As an additional convention one operation is applied after the other with a time delay of twelve times ΔT which can be interpreted as two three-four time bars. Figure 1 shows how the unfolding of this composition could take place starting from the symbolic representation. Obviously, as we go through the successive stages of the unfolding process, there is a steady increase of information and complexity in the resulting structure.

2.3 Analysis of the Musical Structure

At first glance the resulting musical structure seems to be very similar to (repetitive) minimal music. This will be analysed in more detail here.

First of all, the musical structure does not have to be analyzed at the level of the score, but it already becomes apparent after all mathematical operations have

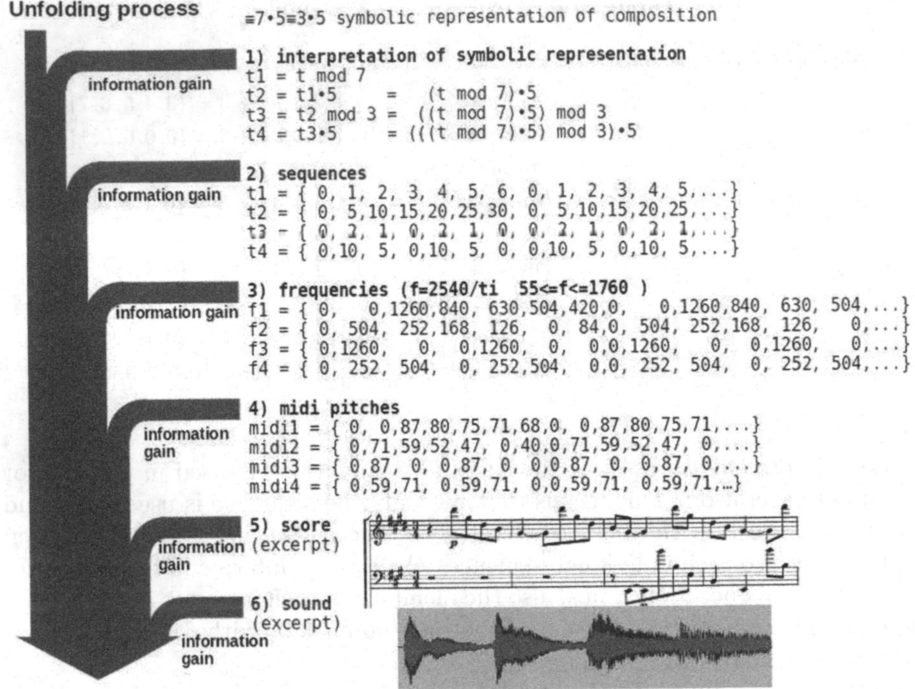

Fig. 1. Unfolding process from symbolic representation to sound.

been applied, but before the resulting sound events are determined. These do not yet represent sound events, but indices of potential sound events (see Fig. 1). As a result of the successively applied operations, generally several superimposed structures appear. By looking at the individual intermediate results, one already obtains an analytical view of the structure without additional effort.

Some operations can easily be related to known musical forms, for example a subtraction applied to $id(\mathbb{N}_0)$ corresponds to the emergence of the same sequence only time-delayed and thus to the structure of an imitation canon, e.g.. $\{0, 1, 2, 3, 4, 5, 6, 7, 8, ...\} - 2$ results in $\{0, 0, 0, 1, 2, 3, 4, 5, 6, ...\}$.

As already mentioned above, values smaller than zero are always set to zero and decimal places are neglected.

The modulo division is mainly responsible for the repetitive structures that frequently occurs here, e.g. $\{0, 1, 2, 3, 4, 5, 6, 7, 8, 9, ...\}$ *modulo* 5 results in $\{0, 1, 2, 3, 4, 0, 1, 2, 3, 4, ...\}$.

The division applied to $id(\mathbb{N}_0)$ results in a slowed down sequence of the same indices when successive identical indices are joined together, e.g. $\{0, 1, 2, 3, 4, 5, 6, 7, 8, 9, ...\}/2$ results in $\{0, 0, 1, 1, 2, 2, 3, 3, 4, 4, ...\}$. Thus, the structures occurring during division show a certain similarity with the musical structure with the musical form of an augmentation canon.

On the whole, the actual minimal music effect results from the fact that the surgery through a newly applied operation always torments the entire picture to a not too extreme extent, instead of changing individual things in isolation.

2.4 Analysis of the Harmonic Structure

The creation of musical structures with **AOG** is constructive. There is no harmonic analysis and no correction of the harmonic interactions performed in this algorithm. This is also not necessary for **two** reasons:

The individual numbers in the sequence obtained from an arithmetic operation are used as divisors of the so-called base number. Thus, these numbers result in a certain picking of prime factors from the base number. The product of the selected prime factors – respectively the result of the division – is then interpreted as the frequency of the tone to be heard. Finally, this frequency is mapped to the tempered tone system.

The frequencies that can be generated in this way have only a limited degree of dissonance to each other. Leonhard Euler has already provided a method to measure this. He called his method "gradus suavitatis" (GS) g. It is very well suited to this task because, like the approach here, it is based on integer frequencies f, which are then broken down into their prime factors p_i.

In order to calculate the degree of dissonance g between two frequencies f_1 and f_2 according to Euler, all prime factors of both values are first searched for in which f_1 and f_2 do not coincide. The product of these prime factors we call z. g is now derived from z in the following way: For $z = \prod_{i=1}^{n} p_i^{k_i}$ the "gradus suavitatis" is $g = 1 + \sum_{i=1}^{n} p_i.k_i - \sum_{i=1}^{n} k_i$ [1]. (The much discussed problems in the direct application of the gradus to classical harmony theory will be ignored in this context but are discussed e.g. here: [11]).

Thus, the degree of dissonance between two frequencies is then the gradus function for the prime factors in which the two compared frequencies differ from each other. Since the prime factors of the base number consist of relatively small prime numbers, it is immediately obvious that when comparing two frequencies that can be generated from, only relatively small degrees of dissonance are produced according to the gradus function.

In addition to this fundamental limitation of the degree of dissonance, a **second factor** that plays a role, that the harmonic event that results in **AOG** generally seems to be reasonable. It can be found in a meaningful organization not only of sound events, but also of their harmonical relationships by the algorithm.

It is anything but trivial to explain here what makes sense and what does not. Since the examples of Bach's monophonic polyphony and at the latest since the tintinabuli harmony of Arvo Pärt, it is clear that even sound events that are far apart can be related melodically or harmonically to each other if they are in the same register in the first case and even not in the second.

Since the sequences of numbers resulting from the arithmetic operations are applied as divisors of the base number used, **AOG** does not only result in a multi-level rhythmic musical structure right from the start, but they also bring the harmonic relationships of the tones into a rhythmic order.

This principle will be illustrated in a small (a bit academic) example: The base number is $b = 2 \cdot 3 \cdot 5 = 30$. For the sequence $\{0, 1, 2, 3, 4, 5, 6, 7, 8, 9, 10, 11, 12\}$ modulo 7 is applied. The result is the sequence $\{0, 1, 2, 3, 4, 5, 6, 0, 1, 2, 3, 4, 5, 6\}$. Each sequence element is used as a divider of b. In those cases where this operation is not possible without a remainder, a zero is set as the result (no sound). This results in the following frequency sequence. $\{0, 2 \cdot 3 \cdot 5, 3 \cdot 5, 2 \cdot 5, 0, 2 \cdot 3, 5, 0, 2 \cdot 3 \cdot 5, 3 \cdot 5, 2 \cdot 5, 0, 2 \cdot 3, 5\}$.

If one looks at the prime factors of the occurring tone frequencies separately, it turns out that not only the frequencies of the sound events themselves occur in rhythmic order, but also the individual prime factors of these frequencies: $\{0, 2, 0, 2, 0, 2, 0, 0, 2, 0, 2, 0, 2, 0\}$, $\{0, 3, 3, 0, 0, 3, 0, 0, 3, 3, 0, 0, 3, 0\}$, $\{0, 5, 5, 5, 0, 0, 5, 0, 5, 5, 5, 0, 0, 5\}$.

Several real-time composition tools that implement **AOG** were done so far. The **CFE** (**C**omposing **F**or **E**veryone) app, for example, allows formulas to be entered according to **AOG** syntax and makes the compositional result immediately audible (see Fig. 2).

3 The Role of Natural Numbers for AOG

In the following we shall try to show that the deeper reason why the structures resulting from the arithmetic operations show the affinity to music shown above is that the natural numbers themselves also show this affinity.

Fig. 2. Android app **CFE** (**C**omposing **F**or **E**veryone) is a direct implementation of **AOG** and can be obtained on google play.

Any arbitrary integer positive divisor d occurs regularly in the sequence of natural numbers at a constant distance, which is also d.

Two arbitrary but different divisors d_1 and d_2 occur simultaneously relative to their size, the less dissimilar they are to each other. Corresponding to the gradus suivitatis (GS) introduced above, the degree of dissimilarity can be taken as the number of prime factors that they do not have in common, or more differentiated, it can also be demanded that the dissimilarity is greater the larger the prime factors in which the numbers do not match.

Now the sequence of numbers, which have a certain divisor d in common, itself forms a progression, thus fulfilling the Peano axioms, see e.g. [19].

All in all, all these progressions are interwoven in such a way that such pairs whose divisors d_1 and d_2 have a high GS, seldom occur simultanously in the identical element of the sequence of natural numbers, whereas those with a low GS occure more often simultanously.

If one understood these dividers directly as frequencies of tones, then such tones appear more often in combination, which harmonize well, and such rarely appear in combination, which harmonize less well, all within the context of the concept introduced here.

It is quite clear that what is said here for the natural numbers is of course not identical with classical harmony or counterpoint, but it shows – and this cannot be denied – amazing similarities with it.

Listing 1.1. Simple sonification of the natural numbers

```
int BASENUMBER = 2*2*2*3*3*5*7; // == 2520
... public void draw() { //  ... loop
  int t = t_N;
  int f = BASENUMBER;
  //Extract primefactors 2,3,5,7 from t
  //and take them away from the BASENUMBER (% is modulo):
  while(t>=2 && t%2==0 && f>=2 && f%2==0) {t/=2;f/=2;}
  while(t>=3 && t%3==0 && f>=3 && f%3==0) {t/=3;f/=3;}
  while(t>=5 && t%5==0 && f>=5 && f%5==0) {t/=5;f/=5;}
  while(t>=7 && t%7==0 && f>=7 && f%7==0) {t/=7;f/=7;}
  //Interpretate the result as a frequency and play it:
  if(f>=55 && f<=1760) play(f);
  t_N++;  // next number from id(N) }
```

In addition, a very short program is presented here (code 1.1), which sonifies the natural numbers in a very simple way. It was implemented in Processing/Java, see example BASIC_Sound_of_N in contributed library "Composing-ForEveryone" at https://www.processing.org. To keep it short, no effort was made to achieve a particularly interesting sound. A more elaborate realization of the same thing can be watched as a youtube video: https://youtu.be/e81wd1b3FEE. According to what has been said so far about **AOG**, not the entire actual natural number is taken, but only its parts of 2s, 3s, 5s and 7s. And also these parts are not used directly, but they are taken as divisors of the base number. Finally, the result of this division is interpreted as frequency and translated musically. Only if this division is possible without remainder and the result lies in the frequency range of the used musical instrument, a tone sounds. The procedure thus filters out those tones that are in simple ratios to each other and are playable. It should be seen as a kind of humanization process that is applied to the original natural numbers. The musical form is essentially created by not playing parts that lie outside this frame.

3.1 Musical Interpretation and Sound Generation

In principle, the fact that the entire intermediate stages of the generative process on the way from the symbolic representation to the representation of the sequence of the sound events are available offers a multitude of starting points for controlling musical parameters in the field of musical interpretation. In particular, it is possible to take into account by which partial sequence of the applied operations a certain tone was produced.

However, in order not to increase the complexity on the currently treated level, methods have already been used for the musical interpretation of the tone frequencies to be played, which simply remember a part of the pitches that have arisen in the past and determine parameters such as dynamics or the choice of playing technique of a new tone based on the context of this new tone to the past ones.

A rather minimalist procedure results quasi automatically with **AOG**: Each note is assigned a sample of a percussive instrument. If it turns out that the same frequency has to be played several times simultaneously at a certain point in time – and this is exactly the case if several currently applied operations result in the same frequency – these events are just played in addition and thus form acoustically one event with a corresponding increase of volume. The whole software was implemented in Java (Processing) and for the actual sound generation a simple sequencer, which is also implemented in Java, is responsible, which allows to stream wav files (also superimposed).

4 The Concept of Transparency Considering Generative Grammars

> *"I am giving a performance in Toronto ... I call it Reunion. It is not a composition of mine, though it will include a new work of mine, 0'00" II, ...* [12]".

John Cage represents to an extreme degree an attitude towards the work in which the maker, the composer, steps back behind the work. This attitude can be read from his late works in that arrangements of things found by chance often form the basis for a musical structure. This basic attitude has strongly influenced the art world both in the visual arts and in music, and the trend is that the composer is no longer the creator of a musical structure, but determines the setting in which the composition then happens [16]. Especially in the field of algorithmic composition there is the widespread basic attitude that the composing subject has no direct imaginative access to what the algorithm itself produces. During the discussion on [22] Sever Tipei notes that music is experimental for him when the result of the generation process is unpredictable. One may or may not follow this paradigm, the fact is that the creation of a setting creates a certain void, which is then often filled by interaction with the (active) recipients. And it is also a fact that these people who are involved in the artistic process bring their own ideas about what music or art is. If one admits this and takes it seriously, and thus gives human interaction a higher meaning than that of a mere random generator, the question immediately arises to what extent the setting provided allows the active recipient to consciously design a (musical) performance according to his or her own ideas.

As mentioned above, in terms of Chomsky's division of generative grammars, **AOG** is one of level 3: Its application ensures that only meaningful/well-formed musical structures arc created ([2,3]) and can thus in principle also enable people with little knowledge of music theory to compose. On the other hand, this advantage is bought at the price of a certain lack of transparency with regard to the relationship between a sequence of symbols and the musical form they represent, and is thus directly opposed to the claim of being able to mentally foresee the resulting musical structures.

Can this shortcoming in **AOG** somehow be compensated by the fact that we are already well versed in dealing with arithmetic operations and infinite sequences, which together form the basis for **AOG**, due to our school education in general? So does this kind of mathematical education in **AOG** allow us to mentally understand the connection between symbolic representation and the musical form it represents?

In order to prepare an answer to this question by first gaining an approximate understanding of how a corresponding mental process can be imagined, a suitable description Husserl's will first be referred to below. It deals with the mental process of how we obtain out of an arithmetic term an idea of the set represented by it.

4.1 Husserl's "Philosophy of Arithmetic"

Husserl's "Philosophy of Arithmetic" comes from a time before he founded his phenomenological method.

The starting point for the development of mathematical concepts in this text is the set as a phenomenon directly accessible to man.

This fact alone should legitimize a deliberately phenomenological reading of this early text, as it is carried out here below. This attitude is also supported by the work of Lohmar [14], and also by the fact that Husserl again, in his later work "logical investigations" ("*Logische Untersuchungen*"), which co-founded the phenomenological method, cites the example of the mental unfolding of mathematical expressions down to the set (see below) to illustrate the difference between the instant imagination of a phenomenon ("*eigentliche*

Vorstellung eines Phänomens") and a symbolically intermediated imagination ("*uneigentliche Vorstellung eines Phänomens*") [8].

4.2 Imaginating Sets

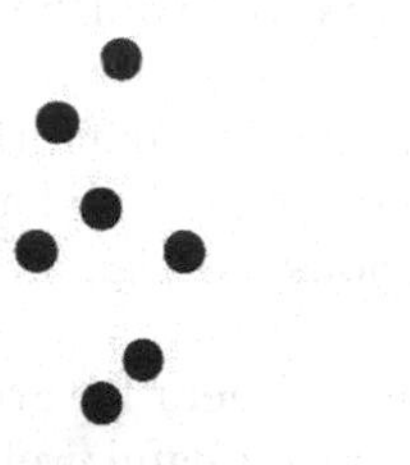

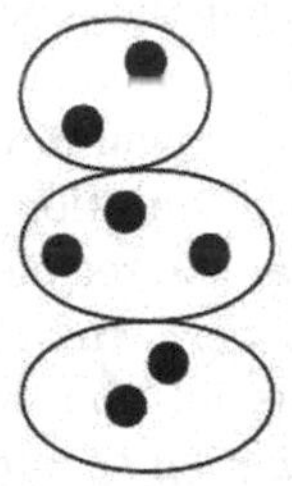

7

intermediated
symbolic
representation
of a set
("*uneigentliche*
Vorstellung")

Fig. 3. How to imagine sets.

Husserl regards sets as an elementary phenomenon. He emphasizes that an instant imagination of sets is possible [7, 201–203], but only for very small sets. And even for very small sets, we still manage by dividing them into subgroups in order to capture their extent ("*figurales Moment*") [7, 203–210] (Fig. 3).

In the course of human history, number systems have become the symbolic representation of sets and also of mechanized procedures which operate on these numbers (arithmetic), in order to merge the different sets behind them (addition), to merge several sets of the same size (multiplication), etc.

According to Husserl, the reason for this is our mental inability to perform these operations directly on the sets [7, 239–240].

4.3 The Stepwise Unfolding of Arithmetic Expressions to the Set Represented by Them

After Husserl the set is the elementary phenomenon and that the representation of numbers in the place-value system is a symbolic representation of this set, from which this set can be recovered at any time. Again, arithmetic expressions are symbolic representations, from which a certain number can be obtained unambiguously. As already mentioned above, Husserl also explains this fact at the end of the second part of his "Logical Investigations" in order to explain the representational meaning of symbols. He explains in an exemplary way (translated from German original):

"*We make the number* $(5^3)^4$ *clear to ourselves by falling back to the definitory idea: 'Number which arises when one forms the product of* $5^3 \cdot 5^3 \cdot 5^3 \cdot 5^3$*'. If we want to make this latter idea clear again, we have to go back to the sense of* 5^3*, i.e. to the formation* $5 \cdot 5 \cdot 5$*. Going even further back, 5 can be explained by the definition chain* $5 = 4 + 1, 4 = 3 + 1, 3 = 2 + 1, 2 = 1 + 1$". [8] (Translation. Original is in German.)

4.4 Fulfillment Chains

In the course of the following explanations in [8], Husserl generalizes the step-by-step process of the unfolding of arithmetic expressions described here and postulates that it typically leads to an increase in the richness of content if one, starting from an imagined idea, arrives at an actual representation of a phenomenon over several unfolding steps.

An example of an imagined idea could be the memory of the name of a particular person and the actual representation of a phenomenon could then be to vividly imagine the person to me.

The area of validity of this description shall not be discussed further at this place, but only its applicability to the area of interest here. For this area it can be said without further ado: The transformation of symbolic expressions into musical structures is clearly a process in which a structure containing relatively little information is transformed into a structure with a larger amount of information (see again Fig. 1). If this process is also mentally reproduced, this basically corresponds to the scheme of gradually increasing abundance described by Husserl and called "fulfillment chains" ("Erfüllungsketten" GE) by him.

The prerequisite for this information enhancement is always the availability of suitable prior knowledge: With generative grammar, I know how the algorithm works. In the example mentioned above, I remember details of the person to whom the name I came across, refers. In the following we discuss to what extent the arithmetic operations of **AOG** can be performed mentally. The necessary prior knowledge consists on the one hand in the awareness of the corresponding algorithm and on the other hand in our knowledge of arithmetic.

4.5 Phenomenological Investigation

Against the background of the eye-catching parallels of the above example to the unfolding processes described by Husserl with arithmetic expressions, the representation quoted above from Husserl's work is used, so to speak, as a blueprint for the following explanations.

In the examination of the development process described in Sect. 2.2, it is noticeable that the generation of the sequence $t \equiv 7$ can still be easily comprehended. But already here it must be said restrictively that this applies only with exclusive consideration of the first sequence members of this potentially infinite sequence. Also the following multiplication of the resulting sequence by

3 can still be imagined well. At the latest, however, when trying to apply $\equiv 5$ to the preceding result, it becomes very difficult not to lose sight of the previously obtained results.

After all: With pen and paper you can create the score from the symbol series without any problems. Only here, as with every written fixation of a score, there is still the discrepancy between writing and musical interpretation.

Even though in the development of this generative grammar great care was taken to use generally familiar structures and even though the steps in the unfolding process are completely transparent in detail, here one is still far from being able to comprehend the unfolding process in its entirety in the mind. The system of symbols on the highest level with the rules belonging to it enables the composer to produce very complex compositions very quickly. However, the price for this is that a very multi-stage unfolding process has to be passed through in order to come down to the sound level.

Basically, all of this was to be expected, too, if one realizes that in Husserl's presentation the unfolding to a single number and finally to a set is not quite easy and that in the generative grammar introduced here we are dealing with mathematical sequences, which are sets of sets. And the latter do not even form the end point of the unfolding process here, but are followed by the transformation into a score and finally into a musical performance.

Now you can ask yourself how it is even possible to generate a relatively complex score from a few symbols. Where does that come from, what is represented in Fig. 1 as information growth? - Obviously this unfolding complexity has been bought with a limitation of the amount of possible compositions. Because the fact that grammars of the third order provide for the rule-compliant generation of scores at the same time states that everything in structures that cannot be obtained by applying these rules cannot be represented with the respective grammar either. And what has been said applies to any generative tool. In the present case, music arises with an affinity to (repetitive) minimal music. The musical event is shaped by the metamorphosing structurally related (tone) sequences.

Overall, the use of familiar structures as the basis of a generative grammar is a qualitative prerequisite of being able to imagine the structures unfolding from the representation of symbols, but the practical implementation fails due to the relative limitations of the human imagination.

Nevertheless, the possibility of presenting compositions as formulas has a great advantage: even if one cannot become aware of the fully developed composition purely by looking at the formula, this concise presentation refers to the composition behind it in a way that is easy to remember. The compactness of the presentation allows us to get an overview of the common features of two compositions and on this basis to build up a pool of individual compositional expressions.

What has been disregarded in the entire consideration so far is the possibility given today of enabling an immediate sonic implementation of symbol writing via a software in which an arbitrary change of the symbol representation instant is expressed in a corresponding sonic one. Through this feedback mechanism between generative tool and composer, an intuitive knowledge of the direct connection between symbol and sound is established over cycles of intensive use. The compactness of the symbol notation introduced plays an important role here: it creates a good overview of the entire musical structure on an abstract level and supports the consciously executed influence on the sound event. Even further thought, over time a synaesthesia between symbolic structure, sound and emotional feeling arises, as expressed literarily in the following description of a chess game in Nabokov's "The Defence":

> "*He saw then neither the Knight's carved mane nor the glossy heads of the Pawns – but he felt quite clearly that this or that imaginary square was occupied by a definite concetrated force, so that he envisioned the movement of a piece as a discharge, a shock, a stroke of lightning – and the whole chess field quivered with tension, and over this tension he was sovereign, here gathering in and there releasing electric power* [17]".

5 MODULO

But there is even another way to learn how to control the power of generative grammar:

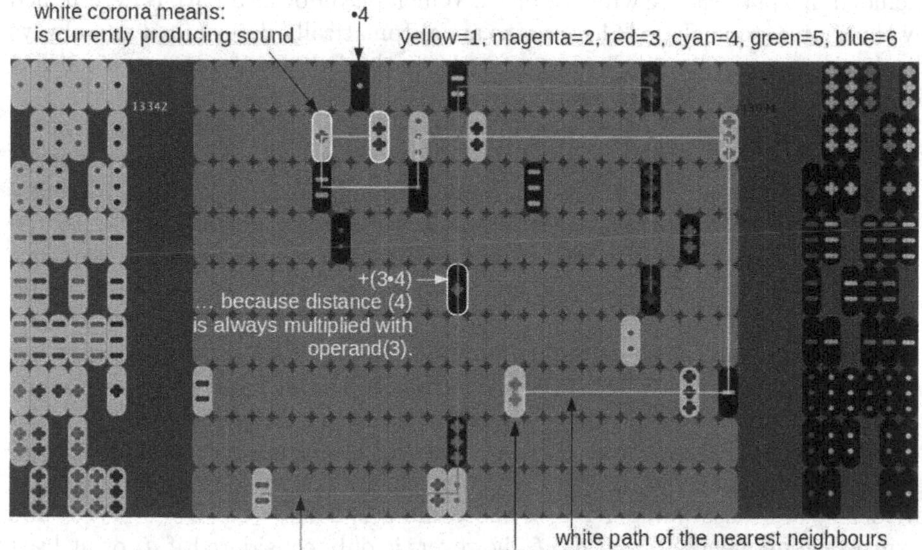

Fig. 4. View of the MODULO playing field. (Color figure online)

In the computer-based board game MODULO (Fig. 4), the players behave consistent to the gaming-rules and do not care about the evolving musical structure. In this respect, MODULO represents an alternative draft to a reasonable and common use of the symbols of the grammar in which the user anticipates the musical result.

In MODULO, the game pieces are arithmetic operations. These are applied along a path of the shortest adjacent distances starting from a source tile representing $id(\mathbb{N}_0)$. Thus, such a path can be understood as a symbolic representation of a piece of music in the sense of the example given in Sect. 2.2.

Above this level is the level of the game rules for the two-person game, who alternately place tiles on the board or move them. The goal of the game is to establish an own path by skilful moves, which consists of operations and operands as mutually different as possible and at the same time to prevent the opponent from doing so. Points are awarded after each move.

Each of the opponents (white/black) in the game has a source tile. The source tile supplies the elements of the mathematical sequence $id(\mathbb{N}_0)$ at fixed time intervals ΔT: $t = 0, 1, 2, 3, 4, 5, 6, ...$ All other tiles represent mathematical operations. Starting from a source tile representing t, the arithmetic operations represented by the other tiles are applied sequentially along the path of the shortest orthogonal distances. This path is continued from tile to tile, beginning with the source tile, until one reaches a point where the condition "shortest orthogonal distance" is no longer unambiguous, or the continuation of the path would include a tile that is already part of the same previous path. The pieces included in a path can be white or black. Which player owns a path is determined by the source stone alone. These paths are automatically determined and always displayed: A green line is displayed for the path of the white player, a red line for the path of the black player.

Each tile that is not a source tile represents an arithmetic operation o_i, represented by the symbols $., .., ..., -, --, ---, +, ++, +++$ and an integer z_i (in the game currently: $1, 2, 3, 4, 5, 6$, represented by the colors yellow, magenta, red, cyan, green, blue). The number z_i multiplied by the distance s_i to the preceding tile in the path gives the operand which is applied to the sequence t_{n-1} produced by the preceding tile, i.e..: $t_n = o_i(t_{n-1}, z_i \cdot s_i)$, see Table 1 and Fig. 4.

If, for example, a piece represents a division by two, the new sequence $t' = t/2$ with $t' = 0, 0, 1, 1, 2, 2, 3, 3, 4, 4...$ results from t. The decimal places are omitted in all operations and values smaller than zero are set to zero. In order to finally obtain sounds from such a sequence, in accordance with the procedure described above for **AOG**, each element of a sequence is interpreted as a divider d_i of a base number b – in the game b is $2520 = 2^3 \cdot 3^2 \cdot 5^1 \cdot 7^1$ – and returns the frequency $f_i = b/d_i$. f_i, however, is only considered if d_i or at least b *modulo* d_i is a true divider of b. What is more, only those frequencies are converted into sounds, which lie within a certain range. In the game it is 55 Hz and 1760 Hz. This corresponds to the tones A1 to A6. The sounds are represented by samples that are played by a sequencer program. If the operation of a piece produces an audible sound, it is played immediately and the piece flashes briefly (white border). The integer frequencies are mapped to the tempered tuning. Within the given limits for the frequencies and the given base number, the following scale (midi) results as a summary of all tones that can be formed: $33, 35, 37, 38, 40, 42, 44, 47, 49, 52, 54, 56, 59, 61, 63, 66, 68, 71, 75, 80, 87$.

5.1 Strategies

You may only move tiles of your own colour, but the paths are formed taking into account all tiles lying on the playing field. This way, enemy structures can be used or disturbed.

Not all actions on the playing field lead to immediate changes in the musical structure, but they prepare it in so far as a later action can result in a path which then includes the previously musically inactive elements.

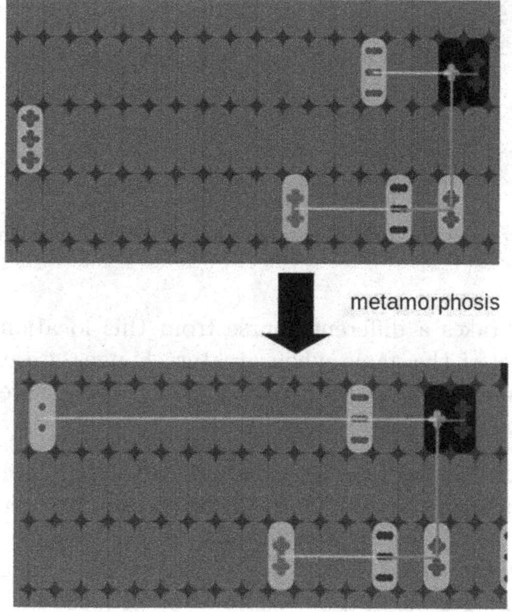

Fig. 5. Addition of an operation towards an existing path (metamorphosis).

Metamorphosis. Typically, an existing path that represents the successive mathematical operations is extended by one element with another move. This causes the existing related mathematical sequences to be extended by another relatively similar one. In terms of sound, this means that another voice appears that varies the existing one (Fig. 5).

Context Switch and/or Hostile Takeover. If, during the course of a path, an element is suddenly moved or added and another neighbor appears as the next

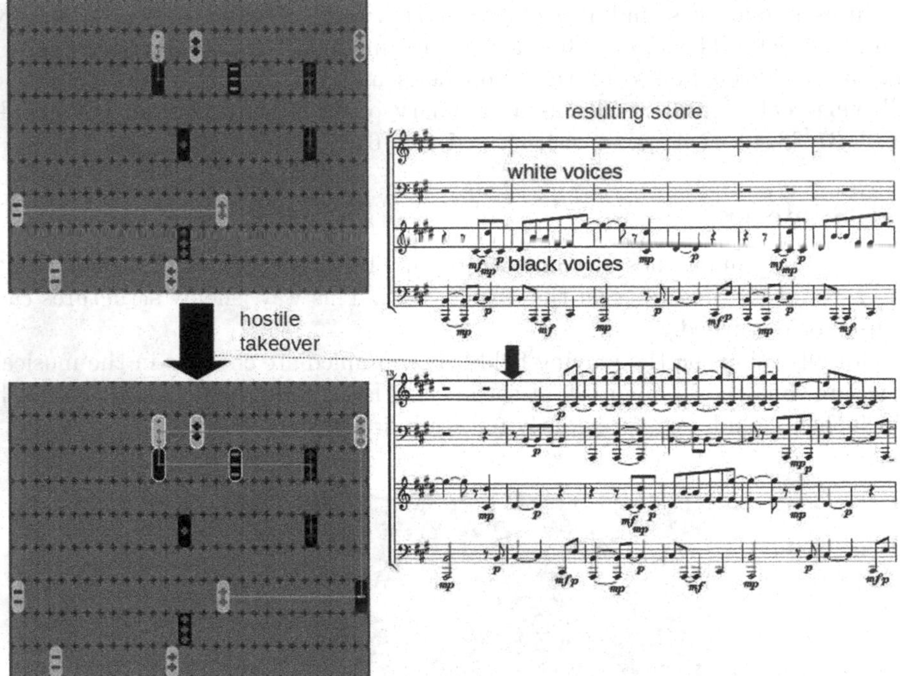

Fig. 6. Switching path by adding element close to source tile (hostile takeover).

element, the path takes a different course from this location after this move. Later in the course of the game when greater changes are expected from the point of view of musical dramaturgy either, in this way, several sequences are typically exchanged at the same time (Fig. 6).

Blockade, Sudden Silence. For both opponents the path is constantly formed, which always leads from the own source piece to the next neighbour, until this rule can no longer be applied unambiguously, or a piece already integrated into the path has to be connected. If a player causes such a ambiguity in the opponent's path by placing a tile in the neighborhood of a tile involved in the opponent's path in such a way that it lies at the same distance as the nearest neighbor there, the complete following path disappears immediately and in extreme cases sudden (partial) silence occurs.

5.2 MODULO Seen as a Composition Tool

One way to prove that the rules of the game have been chosen in a meaningful way, as far as the resulting musical result is concerned, is to prove a positive correlation between the number of points achieved by both opponents in a game and the quality of the resulting music. In order to be able to make at least a preliminary statement about this, the game was extended by a component, in which the moves are carried out automatically, whereby from the multitude of possible moves one is always selected, which results in relatively many points. The quality of the resulting sound result can at least be seen intersubjectively in a video [10].

6 Summary

Theorem 1. *It seems impossible in principle that a powerful generative grammar to be presented in a compact way is at the same time designed in such a way that the structures unfolded from it can also be imagined mentally. Theoretically this is possible, but in practice it fails because of the limitations of human imagination.*

Theorem 2. *Furthermore, an increase in the power of the symbolic language is always linked to a restriction of the overall structures that can be generated.*

One might now conclude that the fact that the symbolic representation does not correspond to the pure phenomenon, but only represents it and thus conceals it, is the reason why generative grammars are powerful tools for the composer, but can in principle not guarantee good control over the sound process, i.e. control based on knowledge.

In doing so, however, one overlooks the decisive advantage that every abstracting representation or model building brings with it, namely the possibility of identifying characteristically similar phenomena on the basis of structural differences in the representation of symbols and, on this symbolic linguistic basis, building up a pool of individual compositional possibilities of expression.

One way of actively establishing the connection between symbolic representation and sound, however, is to present both to the composer coincidentally (real-time composition tool), trusting that the composer can thus learn this connection as intuitive knowledge.

A second way is to make what makes sense measurable and then to give this measure to the composer as feedback and to trust that the composer learns at some point to intuitively maximize this measure through his actions. Such a thing takes place in a sonified, competition-driven performance, if a really meaningful connection between the rules of the game and the sound events has been established. Thus, MODULO is integrated into a series of sonified games in which an attempt is made to establish a clear connection between the course of the game and its musical implementation [5,20]. As a special feature in comparison to the listed examples it has to be emphasized once again that the game structure and the game rules of MODULO were obtained directly from musical considerations. Specifically, sequences of a grammar based on arithmetic operations are generated with the help of the game moves.

6.1 About Virtuososos and Sumo Robots

Unfortunately, it must be said that this work does not end with the solution of a problem, but in the best case with its sharper contouring:

The possibility to execute real-time composition either leads to trivial results if one has complete knowledge about what one is doing, or symbolically complex actions are triggered, whose non-trivial, but in the best case interesting results will never be completely transparent, especially not in real-time. In fact, however, at least the culture of classical music seems to live from the illusion that the virtuoso interpreter would react spontaneously and knowingly, for example, to the orchestra accompanying him: Through constant repetition of the same phrases in a piece, musicians learn to master a piece of music from a meta-level and can put emotional expression into these phrases, while the actual mechanical process of instrumental playing sinks into the subconscious and is thus mastered perfectly. The recipient, on the other hand, lets himself be drawn into the illusion of a spontaneous, fully conscious play in classical concerts: The enjoyment of a musical performance lies above all in experiencing the totality of technically perfect playing and apparently spontaneous emotional expression as a real fact.

While the virtuoso concert creates the illusion that the musical event unfolds directly from the moment, the illusion in automatically created compositions that are realized in real time lies in the fact that no consciously acting individual is the cause of the musical event. We only project consciousness into the machines [13]. And while in the virtuoso concert the task of the classical composer is above all to anchor the illusion of spontaneity in the structural arrangement of the composition, as a consequence of the preceding considerations the task and special challenge of the developer of real-time composition programs can be seen above all in evoking the illusion of consciously made musical decisions in the recipient.

This is where the embodiment comes into play: A box with a loudspeaker is hardly seen by the recipients as a source for conscious decisions, whereas a humanoid robot, which plays a musical instrument much more likely. This statement needs further explanation: Why do people watch competitions between sumo robots [18]? - It is the fascinating speed with which the opponents (robots) try to push each other from the battlefield. The spectators project consciously acting beings into these opponents. Such a substitution and a transcendental aspect seem to be the two basic ones at most, if not all cultural events: A lot of people come together. On a stage, something emerges that the audience would not normally be capable of representing them. The challenge for those acting on stage is to stage this illusion as perfectly as possible.

6.2 What Sense Does it Actually Make to Include Phenomenological Considerations in the Development of New Computer-Aided Compositional Techniques?

First of all, in a context of artistic performance and phenomenology, one will think first of the concept of embodiment coined by Merleau Ponty rather than – as used here – of Husserl's remarks on mathematics. But phenomenology is first and foremost a special way of dealing with something, and there is nothing that is particularly predestined to be considered phenomenologically in comparison to other fields of subject matter. So why is there this special emphasis on embodiment in art and music, like e.g. in [4]? In "The Primacy of Perception" Merleau-Ponty emphasizes:

> "A phenomenology of perception abandons perceptual models that work with the dualistic assumption of sensations on the one hand and unconscious operations on the other, and instead turns to the importance of the body for perception." [15] (Translation. Original is in French.)

In the manifold ways of experiencing our physicality, we find the original expression of our perception. So if we want to deal with perceptions, from a phenomenological point of view, according to Merleau-Ponty, it makes sense to turn our attention towards our physicality. But also in general, phenomenology strives to look at an object in the way it shows itself, or as Martin Heidegger expresses it in "Sein und Zeit" (Being and time):

> "The meaning of the expression 'phenomenon' is therefore: that which shows itself in itself, the obvious." [6] (Translation. Original is in German: Als Bedeutung des Ausdrucks 'Phänomen' ist daher festzuhalten: das Sich-an-ihm-selbst-zeigende, das Offenbare).

Basically, this claim is already the essence of phenomenology. And the phenomenological aspect of the approach in the present work lies essentially in a continuous effort to, on the one hand, repeatedly get a view of the subject areas dealt with as they show themselves from their own point of view and, on the other hand, to proceed in one way or another to justify certain decisions from this point of view.

Looking back on the previous explanations, I would like to illustrate this with a few examples: The use of mathematical operations played a central role in this work and one could have regarded it as a game with symbols. This point of view could have been motivated by an external observation, in which a person is watched as he or she handles mathematical symbols. On the basis of such a perspective, a composition tool could have been developed in which the users playfully handle these symbols and music is generated from them. However, such a perspective would not take into account the fact that the symbols used represent manipulations applied to sets. In this work, extensive use has been made of Husserl's analysis of arithmetic, in which sets are represented as the original "eigentliche" phenomenon, but their symbolic representation by numbers as a non-original "uneigentliches" phenomenon. In the sense described above of looking at an object in the way it shows itself, this is what we have here: "7" not a set, but this: "* * * * * * *". With reference to exactly the same claim, one could now say that symbols can also be viewed phenomenologically and that there is therefore no compelling reason to go from a symbolic representation down to a representation of sets if one decides to choose symbols as the subject area. On the other hand, it can be argued that here, however, sets and thus mathematical notions of multiplying, dividing, increasing and decreasing were chosen as the subject matter and that, against this background, the symbolic representation of mathematical operations is not the type of representation of these notions that takes the original phenomenon into account. If, on the other hand, symbols had been chosen instead as the subject matter, the adequate phenomenological approach would be one in which the symbols were examined as graphic objects.

The effort to abstract an object area in order to be able to handle it better always brings with it the danger of losing the object area in the way it shows itself. What this means for music is also immediately obvious: a score is not music. Treating music phenomenologically can never mean analysing symbols in a score in terms of their occurrence and spatial arrangement. Rather, treating music phenomenologically can only mean describing it in terms of the acoustic experience of time. In the former case, one can at most claim to take a phenomenological view of the score, but not of the music.

On the other hand, however, this work also showed that only abstracting representations (here arithmetic formulas) enable us to deal with an object area (here the resulting composition). One can, I think, even say without restriction that every imagination is abstract.

How Has all This Phenomenological Classification of the Various Subject Areas Dealt with Influenced the Direction Taken in the Development of a Compositional Tool in This Work?
Against the background of the previous remarks, the image of a compass is obvious when describing the benefits of the phenomenological approach for the present work: The design of a compositional tool can be described as successful precisely if the connection with the level of meaning is not cut off or obscured by the level of symbol and the handling of it, but on the contrary, direct references to this level of meaning are preserved/promoted/perceivable/imaginable.

In this specific case, there are at least two levels of semantic meaning: the mathematical level and the musical level resulting from the use of the compositional tool.

From the phenomenological point of view, questions such as the following have arisen:

- Does the mathematical level of semantic meaning conceal the musical one?
- Can the resulting musical form be guessed on the basis of the mathematical symbolic form?
- If we take the natural numbers as a temporal sequence and consider the divider structures underlying the individual numbers, are they then congruent with musical phenomena?

However, these questions have by no means all been answered satisfactorily in the course of the work. In the sense of the above given metaphor of the compass, however, they have only arisen on the basis of the phenomenological approach and have only given something like a basis of assessment for the design of the described composition tools, i.e. specifically for composing directly by entering arithmetic formulas, or by playing a board game (**MODULO**).

6.3 Further Work

To conclude, to show phenomenology in action, so to speak, the question will be raised how **AOG** (**A**rithmetic **O**peration **G**rammar – the central generative method for musical structures based on arithmetic operations presented here) can be made usable for children, say for first graders. One thing is clear: at such an age there is no familiarity with arithmetic and its symbolic language. WITHOUT any reference to phenomenological perspectives, one could simply say that children could just learn to use the formula editor to create real-time compositions. A corresponding context sensitivity of the editor could ensure that nothing "wrong" can ever be entered, for example two operators that follow each other directly without an operand in between. With this implementation, nothing would have been done to create a mentally ascertainable connection between what the children do and what effect it has. They would have been degraded to an underage element of an artistic setting in the sense described here in chapter four. It could be the intention to do something like this. But it would contradict a basic phenomenological approach, which strives for an inner participation for all participants that corresponds to the external phenomena.

Now, however, the outer world with its things, which can be the theme of a picture, and mathematics, in which, among other things, sets are handled, are intimately interwoven: Everything in the world is also set and structure of sets. And extended to music: Everything in the material world can also be viewed in relation to rhythmic and harmonic relationships in space and it is possible to transfer this to the temporal level. This second possibility of establishing a connection between an image and music is naturally obvious and is often implemented. It is also the way in which a (graphic) score works. The first mentioned connection, that is the one between things and sets, will be further elaborated here: We go back to the fact that the symbolic formulas of arithmetic represent manipulations on sets and can be traced back to them at any time via the Husserl chains of fulfilment mentioned above. So instead of "somehow" extracting mathematical symbols from an image, it is much more appropriate to capture quantitative structures in an image.

In order to get from there to the desired arithmetic operations, one can ask oneself how one gets from the one set that can be captured in the picture to the other, for example from a pictorial object of the form "* * *" to one of the form "* * * * *"? – Answer: by doubling, or adding three.

Based on this basic idea, the Android app "ComposingWithCamera" is now an experimental way for children to deal with AOG, without knowledge of arithmetic, but with the certainty that they can get a clear idea that set considerations in the painted picture form the basis for its musical realization:

With "ComposingWithCamera", when the picture is painted or created on a light table using a layering technique, contiguous areas are segmented in the colours red, green, blue and yellow and also displayed on the screen as feedback so that it is clear "what is important in the picture" (Fig. 7). Now it is typical that there are groups in the image analysed in this way, which consist of several of these connected areas of different colours. In order to form numbers out of

Fig. 7. Working with "ComposingWithCamera". The app is available at google play and the source code is available as an example inside the processing library ComposingForEveryone, see processing.org or kramann.info/cfe.

them, which have the advantageous property for music that they consist of small prime factors and at the same time ensure that the set examinations are very little sensitive to image rotations and shifts, these groups are evaluated in the following way: Each red area of such a colourful group is assigned the number three, each green one the number five, each blue one the number two and each yellow one the number seven. The product of all these individual numbers then results in the number assigned to the colored group. For example, if such a colored group consists of two red and one green area, the corresponding number of this colored group is $3 \cdot 3 \cdot 5 = 45$ (Fig. 8).

In the concrete implementation, it is now determined for each colored group how far (center of gravity) each other group is from it and a ranking is derived from this (next neighbor first). The sum of the ranking numbers for a particular colored group, as it appears in all other groups, indicates how central (small sum) this group is, or how peripheral (large sum). The four (if so many are available) most central colorful groups are assigned to one of four voices in the musical performance. By ranking each of these four selected colored groups according to how close each of the other groups is to it, you "naturally" get an order of colored groups. Always from one to the next, the question is asked, in accordance with the considerations mentioned above, which arithmetical operation is best suited to proceed from this number to the next number assigned to it. Addition and subtraction always work, of course, and so the corresponding algorithm first

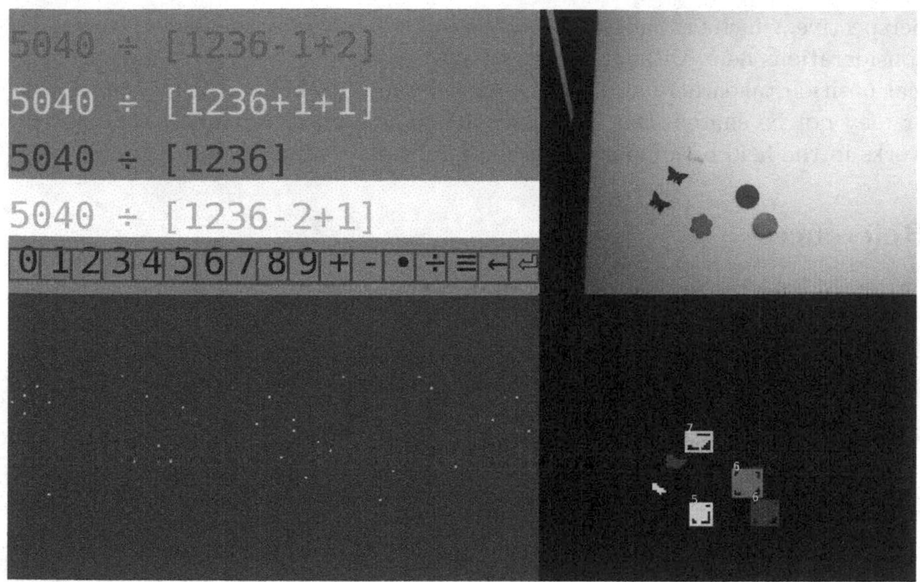

Fig. 8. Screenshot from "ComposingWithCamera". A demo video can be obtained from here: youtu.be/escAY5vmv3Q (Color figure online)

asks whether division or multiplication works, if that doesn't work modulo is tried, and only then addition or subtraction. In this way, an arithmetic formula is obtained from an image for each voice. By means of the special procedure of the ranking and the selection of central colorful groups, relationships arise, as one often finds in modulo, in which over certain distances in two voices partly exactly the same operations appear. This has proven to be musically particularly advantageous.

As with the other composition tools discussed here, ComposingWithCamera cannot be said purely on the basis of the theoretical considerations that led to its design, whether it can ultimately be used to compose comprehensibly. But if this is the case, it is not by chance, but because the prerequisites for this have been created based on the phenomenological approach. If, on the other hand, it turns out that this tool does not work in the desired way, the phenomenological approach provides the necessary tools to investigate why it is not possible for the user to work with the tool in an understandable way. In initial tests, for example, it turned out that children simply do not notice a less intensive or less convincing sound implementation. They then concentrate exclusively on painting pictures and not at all on the resulting sound events.

It was not always easy to find the balance between the sometimes somewhat theoretical phenomenological considerations and the presentation of the pure functionality of the tools for real-time composition. But in the best case, this presentation has shown that the direction that technical developments have taken is also strongly influenced by their assessment from a phenomenological perspective, which of course is a good reason not to ignore the phenomenological considerations here. Ultimately, the scientific or respectively the phenomenological position taken here also represents a certain aesthetic attitude, which may or may not be shared. But of course, this also applies to many other scientific works in the field of computational music, if not to all of them.

References

1. Busch, H.R.: Leonhard Eulers Beitrag zur Musiktheorie, p. 34. Gustav Bosse, RegensburgD (1970)
2. Chomsky, N.: Three models for description of language. IRE Trans. Inf. Theory **2**(3), 113–124 (1956). https://chomsky.info/wp-content/uploads/195609-.pdf. Accessed 4 Apr 2019
3. Chomsky, N.: On certain formal properties of grammars. Inf. Control **2**, 137–167 (1959). http://twiki.di.uniroma1.it/pub/LC/WebHome/chomsky1959.pdf. Accessed 4 Apr 2019
4. Cox, A.: Music and Embodied Cognition: Listening, Moving, Feeling, and Thinking. Indiana University Press, Bloomington (2017)
5. Hamilton, R.: Musical sonification of avatar physiologies, virtual flight and gesture. In: Aramaki, M., Derrien, O., Kronland-Martinet, R., Ystad, S. (eds.) CMMR 2013. LNCS, vol. 8905, pp. 518–532. Springer, Cham (2014). https://doi.org/10.1007/978-3-319-12976-1_31
6. Heidegger, M.: Sein und Zeit, p. 28. Max Niemeyer, Tübingen (2006)
7. Husserl, E.: Philosophie der Arithmetik. Martinus Nijhoff, The Hague (1970)
8. Husserl, E.: Stufenreihen mittelbarer Erfüllungen. Mittelbare Vorstellungen. In: Logische Untersuchungen, second part, pp. 601–602. Felix Meiner, Hamburg (2009)
9. Kramann, G.: "$\equiv 7 \cdot 5 \equiv 3 \cdot 5$" – a simple composition as an example (2019). http://www.kramann.info/cmmr2019a
10. Kramann, G.: M O D U L O (2019). http://www.kramann.info/cmmr2019b
11. Kramann, G.: An overtone based algorithm unifying counterpoint and harmonics. In: Music, Mind and Embodiment (CMMR 2015), Plymouth, pp. 791–805 (2015). https://cmmr2019.prism.cnrs.fr/Docs/proceedingsCMMR2015.pdf. Accessed 17 Feb 2021
12. Kuhn, L.D. (ed.): The Selected Letters of John Cage, p. 382. Wesleyan University Press, Middletown (2016)
13. Leidlmair, K.: Künstliche Intelligenz und Heidegger – Über den Zwiespalt von Natur und Geist. Wilhelm Fink, Paderborn (1999)
14. Husserls Phänomenologie als Philosophie der Mathematik. Doctoral dissertation, Faculty of Philosophy, University of Cologne, Cologne (1987)
15. Merleau-Ponty, M.: Das Primat der Wahrnehmung, p. 86. Trans. Jürgen Schröder. Suhrkamp, Frankfurt am Main (2016). Trans. of: Le primat de la perception et ses consequences philosophiques. Éditions Verdier, Paris (1996)
16. de la Motte-Haber, H.: Selbständigkeit als Prinzip künstlerischer Settings. Neue Zeitschrift für Musik **6**, 52–56 (2018)
17. Nabokov, V.: The Defence, pp. 72–73. Granada Publishing Limited, London (1971)
18. McGregor, R.: Robot Sumo (2017). https://www.youtube.com/watch?v=QCqxOzKNFks. Accessed 4 Apr 2019
19. Russel, B.: Introduction to Mathematical Philosophy, pp. 1–10. Routledge, London (1993)

20. Sinclair, P., Cahen, R., Tanant, J., Gena, P.: New Atlantis: audio experimentation in a shared online world. In: Aramaki, M., Kronland-Martinet, R., Ystad, S. (eds.) CMMR 2016. LNCS, vol. 10525, pp. 229–246. Springer, Cham (2017). https://doi.org/10.1007/978-3-319-67738-5_14
21. Supper, M.: A few remarks on algorithmic compositions. Comput. Music J. **25**(1), 48–53 (2001)
22. Tipei, S.: Emerging composition: being and becoming - an experiment in progress. In: Proceedings of the Sound and Music Computing Conference 2016, Hamburg, pp. 477–482 (2016). https://llaudioll.de/proaudio/pdfs/SMC2016_proceedings.pdf. Accessed 17 Feb 2021

Notation and Instruments Distributed on Mobile Devices

Mobile Music with the Faust Programming Language

Romain Michon[1,2](✉), Yann Orlarey[1], Stéphane Letz[1], Dominique Fober[1], and Catinca Dumitrascu[1]

[1] GRAME-CNCM, Lyon, France
michon@grame.fr
[2] CCRMA, Stanford University, Stanford, USA

Abstract. The FAUST programming language has been playing a role in the mobile music landscape for the past ten years. Multiple tools to facilitate the development of musical smartphone applications for live performance such as `faust2ios`, `faust2android`, `faust2api`, and `faust2smartkeyb` have been implemented and used in the context of a wide range of large scale musical projects. Similarly, various digital musical instruments leveraging these tools and based on the concept of augmenting mobile devices have been created. This paper gives an overview of the work done on these topics and provide directions for future developments.

Keywords: FAUST, Mobile music, Digital Lutherie

1 Introduction

The field of mobile music has been active for the past fifteen years [1]. It started with early experiments on programmable smartphones around 2004 [11,12] but it really took off in 2007 when the iPhone was released and smartphones started to spread out to quickly become a standard [13]. The FAUST[1] project [10] through its core developer team at GRAME-CNCM[2] involved itself in this action in 2010 with initial experiments on running FAUST programs on iOS devices. Since then, a panoply of tools to generate standalone smartphone applications and audio engines for different mobile platforms (i.e., Android and iOS) have been developed and used as part of a wide range of musical and pedagogical projects.

In this paper, we give an overview of the work that has been done around mobile music in the context of the FAUST programming language. We present `faust2ios`, `faust2android`, `faust2api`, and `faust2smartkeyb` which are tools that can be used to create musical mobile apps at a high level using FAUST. Work carried out on the idea of augmenting mobile devices with passive and

[1] https://faust.grame.fr (All URLs presented in this paper were verified on May 6, 2020).
[2] http://www.grame.fr.

R. Kronland-Martinet et al. (Eds.): CMMR 2019, LNCS 12631, pp. 307–318, 2021.
https://doi.org/10.1007/978-3-030-70210-6_20

active elements to turn them into specific musical instruments is described. An overview of various musical projects such as *SmartFaust*, *SmartMômes*, and *Geek-Bagatelles* is presented. Finally, we talk about current developments and future directions for this type of work.

2 faust2ios

Pushed by the interest around mobile music in the early 2010s (see Sect. 7), we worked at GRAME-CNCM on a tool to convert FAUST programs into ready-to-use iOS applications: `faust2ios`. As any other FAUST "architecture",[3] the user interface of such apps is based on the UI description provided in the FAUST code, and is therefore typically made out of sliders, knobs, buttons, groups, etc.

Figure 1 presents a screenshot of sfCapture,[4] an app made with `faust2ios` as part of the *SmartFaust* project (see Sect. 7.1).

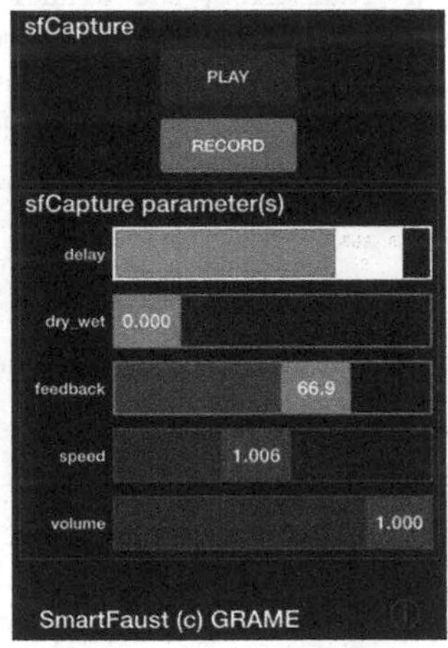

Fig. 1. Screen-shot of sfCapture, an app made with `faust2ios`.

`faust2ios` works as a command line tool taking a FAUST program as its main argument and producing in return either a ready-to-install iOS app or the Xcode project corresponding to this app. For example, running the following command in a terminal:

```
faust2ios myFaustProgram.dsp
```

[3] Architectures in the FAUST vocabulary refer to wrappers allowing to turn a FAUST program into a specific object such as standalone desktop program, an audio plug-in, a smartphone app, an audio engine for a specific platform, etc.

[4] https://itunes.apple.com/us/app/sfcapture/id799532659?mt=8.

will produce an iOS app corresponding to the FAUST program implemented in `myFaustProgram.dsp`.

Various features can be added to the generated app such as MIDI, OSC and polyphony support simply by using specific flags (options) when running `faust2ios`. Regular FAUST options are also available to generate parallelized DSP[5] code, change sample resolution, etc. Any parameter of a FAUST program can be assigned to a specific axis of a built-in motion sensor (i.e., accelerometer, gyroscope, etc.) of the smartphone simply by using metadata. Complex non-linear mappings can be implemented using this mechanism.[6]

Implementing `faust2ios` was relatively straightforward since the FAUST compiler can generate C++ code and that iOS applications can be implemented in Objective-C which allows for the direct use of C++.

3 faust2android

Motivated by the success of `faust2ios` (see Sect. 2) among composers and developers at GRAME-CNCM, we started the development of a similar system for the Android platform in 2013 [2]. This proved to be way more challenging than we anticipated, mostly because Android was never designed with real-time audio applications in mind. First, the fact that JAVA is used as the preferred programming language to develop Android apps was problematic since it doesn't perform well in the context of real-time DSP. Hence, the audio portion of the app must be implemented in C++ and the higher level elements in JAVA. This implies the use of wrappers between these two languages which is not straightforward to implement. Another issue with Android was that despite the use of low-level native code for the DSP portion of the app, audio latency used to be dreadful around 2013 (greater than 200 ms), discarding any potential use in a musical context.

Despite these difficulties, the first version of `faust2android` was released in the first quarter of 2013 [2]. It had similar features than `faust2ios` (see Sect. 2) and worked in a very similar way as a command line tool. Figure 2 presents a screenshot of an app generated with `faust2android`.

As time passed and the market for real-time audio applications on smartphone grew up, Google slowly addressed the audio latency issue of Android and acceptable performances matching that of the iOS platform (less than 20 ms) were achieved by 2016. Additionally, Google released in 2017 a new C++ API named Oboe,[7] for real-time audio on Android which significantly simplified the design of apps involving this kind of element.

On the `faust2android` front, various new features were added to replace the standard FAUST user interface of Android apps by advanced interfaces more usable in a musical context such as piano keyboards, X/Y controllers, etc. [3] These opened the path to `faust2smartkeyb` which is presented in Sect. 5.

[5] *Digital Signal Processing.*
[6] https://faust.grame.fr/doc/manual#sensors-control-metadatas.
[7] https://github.com/google/oboe/.

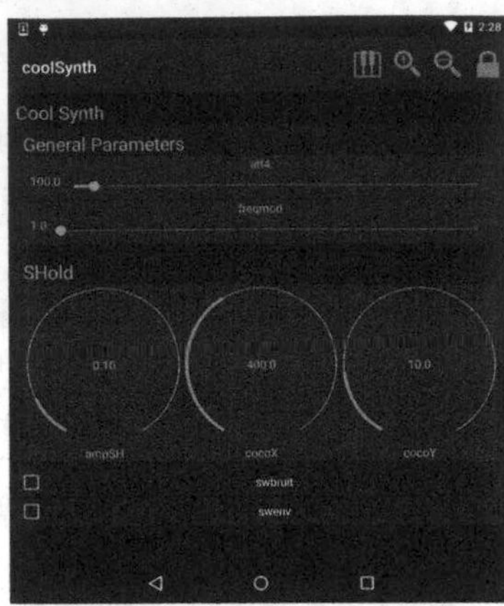

Fig. 2. Example of interface generated by `faust2android` containing groups, sliders, knobs and checkboxes.

4 faust2api

With `faust2ios` (see Sect. 2) and `faust2android` (see Sect. 3) appeared the need for a generic system to generate audio engines with a high-level API similar across languages (i.e., JAVA, C++, etc.) using FAUST: `faust2api` [4]. The main goal of this tool was to offer iOS and Android developers with little background in audio DSP a simple way to generate ready-to-use engines for sound synthesis and processing.

`faust2api` is a command line tool working in a similar way than `faust2ios` and `faust2android`. It takes a FAUST program as its main argument and accept more or less the same options than `faust2ios` and `faust2android`. The format of the generated engines varies between platforms but the same API can be used to configure and control it.

`faust2api` was released in 2017 and was used as the basis for `faust2smartkeyb` (see Sect. 5). `faust2ios` and `faust2android` were simplified by using `faust2api` to carry out real-time audio DSP tasks. Because of its large success among developers, the concept of `faust2api` was spread to most of FAUST's targets and it can now be used to generate audio engines for desktop applications, plug-ins, etc.

5 faust2smartkeyb

With the latest developments of `faust2android` (see Sect. 3), we started exploring the idea of replacing the standard FAUST user interface made out of sliders, buttons, groups, etc. with more advanced interfaces, better adapted to a use in a live music performance context and to touch-screens. We extended this idea with SMARTKEYBOARD which is a highly configurable keyboards matrix where keys can be seen both as discrete buttons and continuous X/Y controllers.

For example, a keyboard matrix of size 1×1 (a single keyboard with a single key) will fill up the screen which can then be used as a multi-touch X/Y controller.

This type of interface is available as part of the `faust2smartkeyb` command line tool [5] which allows us to turn a FAUST program into an iOS or an Android app with a SMARTKEYBOARD interface. The interface can be configured directly from the FAUST code using a metadata. For example, the following program:

```
declare interface "SmartKeyboard{
  'Number of Keyboards':'2'
}";
import("stdfaust.lib");
f = nentry("freq",200,40,2000,0.01);
g = nentry("gain",1,0,1,0.01);
t = button("gate");
envelope = t*g : si.smoo;
process = os.sawtooth(f)*envelope <: _,_;
```

implements a synthesizer based on a sawtooth wave oscillator and a simple exponential envelope controlled by two parallel piano keyboards on the touch-screen (see Fig. 3). Connection between the interface and the DSP part is carried out by the use of standard parameter names. Hence, `freq` is automatically associated to the pitch on the keyboard, `gain` to velocity, and `gate` to note-on/off events.[8]

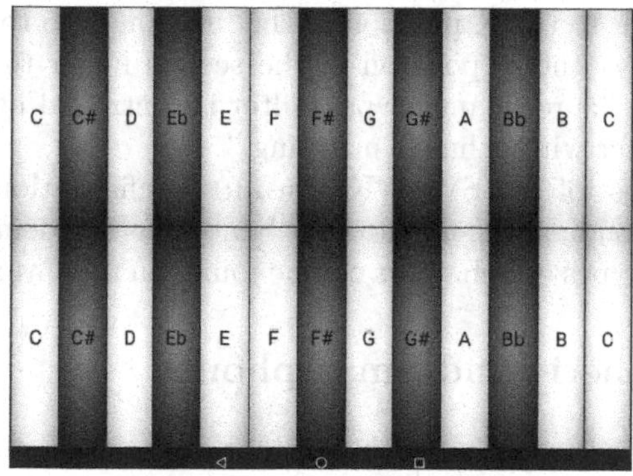

Fig. 3. Simple SMARTKEYBOARD interface.

Complex behaviors can be implemented to handle polyphony, monophony (e.g., voice stealing, priority to upper or lower keys, etc.), and continuous pitch control (e.g., quantization, "pitch rounding" to be in tune and allow for vibrato and glissandi to be performed at the same time, etc.).

In the following example, a completely different app is implemented where a single key on a single keyboard is used to control a simple synthesizer producing a constant sound (no key on/off):

[8] https://faust.grame.fr/doc/manual#standard-polyphony-parameters.

```
declare interface "SmartKeyboard{
  'Number of Keyboards':'1',
  'Max Keyboard Polyphony':'0',
  'Keyboard 0 - Number of Keys':'1',
  'Keyboard 0 - Send Freq':'0',
  'Keyboard 0 - Static Mode':'1',
  'Keyboard 0 - Piano Keyboard':'0',
  'Keyboard 0 - Send Numbered X':'1',
  'Keyboard 0 - Send Numbered Y':'1'
}";
import("stdfaust.lib");
//////// parameters ////////
x0 = hslider("x0",0.5,0,1,0.01) : si.smoo;
y0 = hslider("y0",0.5,0,1,0.01) : si.smoo;
y1 = hslider("y1",0,0,1,0.01) : si.smoo;
q = hslider("q[acc: 0 0 -10 0 10]",30,10,50,0.01) : si.smoo;
//////// mapping ////////
impFreq = 2 + x0*20;
resFreq = y0*3000+300;
//////// putting it together ////////
process = os.lf_imptrain(impFreq) : fi.resonlp(resFreq,q,1) :
ef.cubicnl(y1,0)*0.95 <: _,_;
```

Here, x0 corresponds to the X position of the first finger to touch the screen, y0 its Y position and y1 the Y position of the second finger to touch the screen. The q parameter of the resonant lowpass filter is controlled by the X axis of the built-in accelerometer with a linear mapping.[9]

An exhaustive list of the SmartKeyboard configuration keywords can be found in its corresponding documentation[10] and tutorials demonstrating how to implement various types of behaviors can be found on the Faust tutorial page.[11]

6 Digital Lutherie and Smartphones

In parallel of the development of the various tools presented in the previous sections, an important work has been carried out at GRAME-CNCM and at CCRMA[12] (Stanford University) around the concept of augmenting mobile devices to implement advanced musical instruments. The core idea of this project was to use mobile devices as the platform for computing and sound synthesis/processing of physical Digital Musical Instruments (DMIs) built around this type of device. Two kinds of "smartphone augmentations" were developed in this context:

[9] https://faust.grame.fr/doc/manual#sensors-control-metadatas.

[10] https://ccrma.stanford.edu/~rmichon/smartKeyboard/.

[11] https://ccrma.stanford.edu/~rmichon/faustTutorials/#making-faust-based-smartphone-musical-instruments.

[12] *Center for Computer Research in Music and Acoustics.*

- **passive augmentations** [6] based on digitally fabricated elements leveraging existing sensors on the device, allowing us to hold it in a specific way, or modifying the acoustical properties of its built-in speaker and microphone, etc.,
- **active augmentations** [7] implying the use of additional sensors connected to the mobile device through the use of a microcontroller, etc.

Figure 4 presents an overview of the type of passive augmentations that have been explored as part of this project.

The BladeAxe [8] is a good example of an active mobile device augmentation. It provides a plucking system based on piezo to capture sound excitations created by the performer on plastic tines to drive waveguide physical models running on an iPad in an app implemented with `faust2smartkeyb` (see Sect. 5). This allows for a very natural and intuitive control of the plucking since the sound of each excitation is different.

7 Performances and Pedagogy

7.1 From SmartFaust to Geek-Bagatelles

`faust2ios` and `faust2android` (see Sect. 2, 3) served as the platform for the development by GRAME-CNCM of a series of large scale musical projects involving the use of smartphones as early as 2013. The first of them – *SmartFaust* – was a participatory concert for smartphones which was commissioned to composer Xavier Garcia for the 2014 Biennale Musique en Scène and funded by the INEDIT ANR[13] project.

Garcia worked closely with a developer/computer music assistant (Christophe Lebreton) to the development of a series of iOS and Android applications using `faust2ios` and `faust2android`. The instruments/applications and their corresponding musical pieces were co-written simultaneously. Another remarkable feature of these instruments is the lack of graphical interface: only motion sensors were used. The performer never needs to look at the phone to play it: everything is done between the hand and the ear! (Fig. 5).

The fruit of this work was performed for the first time at the Subsistances in Lyon (France) in March 2014. The concert was organized in two sections: the performance of three pieces for "chorus" of Smartphones and soloists, and then a fourth piece involving the audience.

After this first performance, *SmartFaust* met a large success and started an Asian tour with participatory concerts and workshops that were organized in June 2015 in Wuhan, Hong-Kong and Chengdu. In this context, new pieces for the *SmartFaust* apps corpus were written, in particular by composer Qin Yi in Shanghai.

The original *SmartFaust* project also gave birth to other performances such as:

---

[13] *Agence Nationale de Recherche*: French National Research Agency.

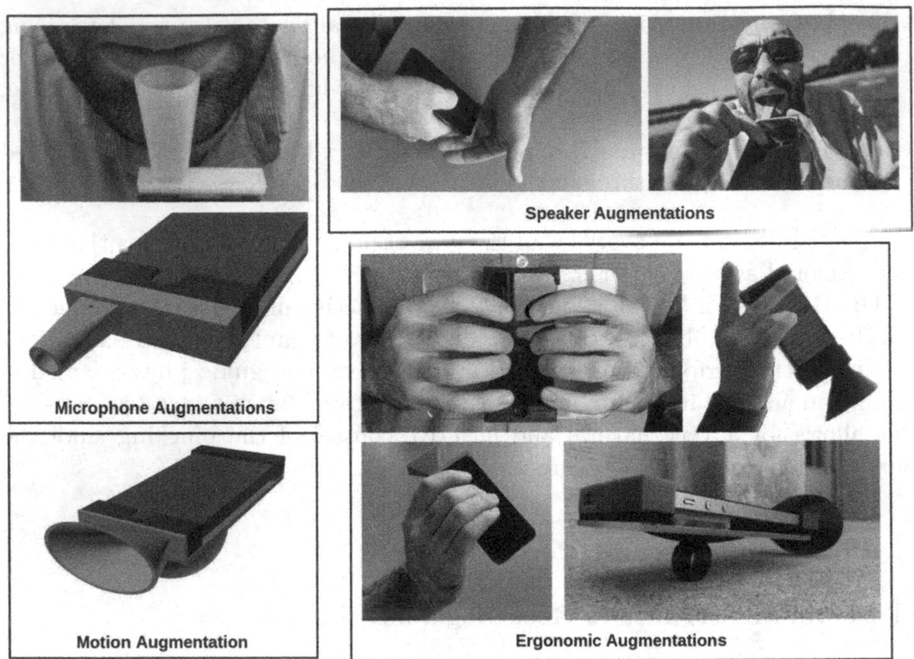

Fig. 4. A few examples of passive smartphone augmentations.

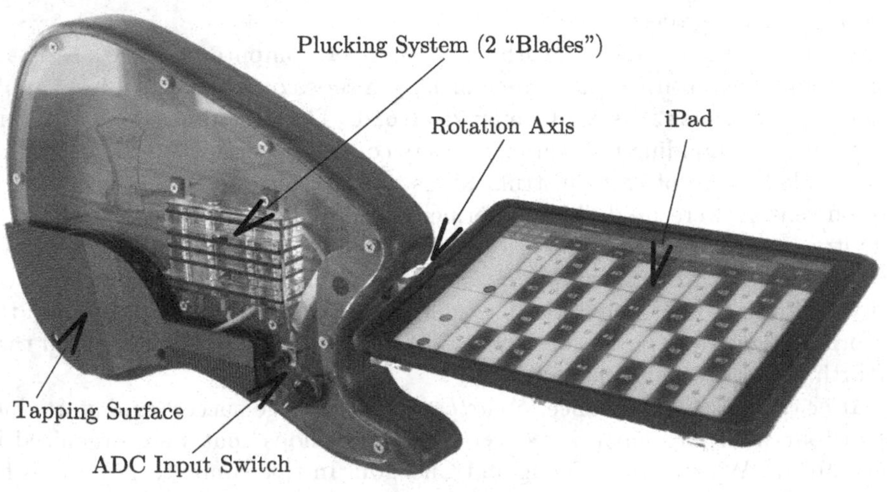

Fig. 5. The BladeAxe.

Fig. 6. Left: *SmartFaust* performance at the subsistances in Lyon (France) on March 16, 2014. Right: *SmartMômes* performance at the Saint-Étienne (France) City Hall in March 2016.

- *SmartFaust on Air* at the 2015 Design Biennale in Saint-Etienne (France),
- participatory concerts in the TGV[14] in partnership with the SNCF,[15]
- sound installations with the *Smartland Divertimento* piece presented at the Museum of the Confluences at the 2016 Biennale Musique en Scène (Lyon, France).

The latter, proposed by Christophe Lebreton and composer Stéphane Borrel, is like a bush of smartphones that communicate with each other and sparkle independently, a bit like fireflies.

The most recent project of this series was created as part of the ONE project (Orchestra Network for Europe) with the Picardy Orchestra (France). It was finalized in September 2014, approved by the European Commission in April 2015, and finally resulted in a commission to composer Bernard Cavanna for a piece for orchestra and smartphones: *Geek-bagatelles, introspections sur quelques fragments de la IXe symphonie de Beethoven.* The performance was premiered on November 20, 2016 by the Picardy Orchestra at the Paris Philharmoni.e. It combined a chorus of 20 smartphones and an orchestra of 38 musicians. The audience participated as well thanks to the *Geek-Bagatelles* app on their smartphone.

The performance was a success and a tour was initiated in the countries part of the ONE network, each time with a new orchestra and a new amateur smartphones chorus formed for the occasion (Fig. 7).

7.2 SmartMômes

After the initial performance of *SmartFaust*, Mômeludies which is a nonprofit promoting the creation and the diffusion of new musics towards kids commissioned composer Xavier Garcia a new piece for smartphones: *SmartMômes* (see Fig. 6). They asked him to teach a series of workshops on this topic in multiple

[14] High speed train system in France.
[15] French National Railway Company.

Fig. 7. *Geek-Bagatelles* performance at the Paris Philharmonie on November 20, 2016.

middle schools as well. As a publisher, Mômeludies also published the score of *SmartMômes*.

Because of the interest around the pedagogical aspect of this approach, GRAME-CNCM organized a series of *SmartFaust* workshops during which the FaustPlayground[16] was used to create musical smartphone apps using Faust at a very high level with a Graphical User Interface.

8 Current and Future Directions

The various tools and technologies presented in the previous sections of this paper reached a certain level of maturity and are now broadly used at GRAME-CNCM and elsewhere. They significantly contributed to the success of most of the recent musical productions of our center thanks to their universal aspect and to their tangibility. Performing with independent standalone and tangible DMIs is quite appealing in a world where everything tends to become completely virtual. Hence, while we keep adding new features to our toolkit for mobile development, we also started exploring new paths to work with embedded systems for low latency/high quality audio. Indeed, microcontrollers are now powerful enough to run complex sound synthesis and processing algorithms in real-time. Similarly, embedded computers such as the Raspberry Pi (RPI) when used without operating system ("bare-metal"), FPGAs[17], GPUs[18] and other low-level DSPs offer new possibilities to create embedded/embodied instruments at a low cost and with un-paralleled performances. While we currently investigate the use of FAUST on FPGAs and bare-metal RPI, FAUST targets have already been implemented for microncontrollers [9] and DSPs such as the SHARC Audio Module.[19]

[16] https://faust.grame.fr/faustplayground.

[17] *Field Programmable Gate Arrays.*

[18] *Graphical Processor Units.*

[19] https://wiki.analog.com/resources/tools-software/sharc-audio-module/faust.

These new developments recently allowed us to create a new programmable musical instruments: the *Gramophone* (see Fig. 8) that we plan to use for pedagogical purpose and for future musical productions at GRAME-CNCM. Based on Teensy 3.6 board[20] for sensor acquisition and sound synthesis, it can be powered by its internal battery for about ten hours, it is equipped with a powerful speaker and amplifier, and it hosts a wide range of sensors (i.e., accelerometer, gyroscope, compas, force sensing resistors, knobs, buttons, photo-resistor, etc.) that can be assigned to FAUST parameters directly from the FAUST code using metadata. It is better than a smartphone in many ways as it offers more affordances and it is more flexible and much louder. We plan to release the first version in Fall 2020.

Fig. 8. The Gramophone.

9 Conclusion

After fifteen years, mobile music has reshaped the computer music landscape partly by reintroducing the concept of standaloneness/independence in DMIs and by making this type of instrument more approachable by the general public. FAUST played a role in this revolution by providing high level tools to develop musical apps for live performance. GRAME-CNCM took advantage of these technologies to place mobile music at the heart of various large scale musical productions/projects. By offering the possibility to easily create orchestras of DMIs, mobile music opened the way to new paths for creation that we intend to keep exploring by developing new programmable instruments taking advantage of recent developments in embedded real-time signal processing such as the Gramophone.

[20] https://www.pjrc.com/store/teensy36.html.

References

1. Gaye, L., Holmquist, L.E., Behrendt, F., Tanaka, A.: Mobile music technology: report on an emerging community. In: Proceedings of the International Conference on New Interfaces for Musical Expression (NIME-06), Paris (2006)
2. Michon, R.: faust2android: a faust architecture for Android. In: Proceedings of the 16th International Conference on Digital Audio Effects (DAFx-13), Maynooth, Ireland (2013)
3. Michon, R., Smith, J.O., Orlarey Y.: MobileFaust: a set of tools to make musical mobile applications with the faust programming language. In: Proceedings of the International Conference on New Interfaces for Musical Expression, Baton Rouge (2015)
4. Michon, R., Smith, J.O., Letz, S., Chafe C., Orlarey, Y.: faust2api: a comprehensive API generator for Android and iOS. In: Proceedings of the Linux Audio Conference (LAC-17), Saint-Étienne, France (2017)
5. Michon, R., Smith, J.O., Chafe, C., Wang, G., Wright, M.: faust2smartkeyb: a tool to make mobile instruments focusing on skills transfer in the faust programming language. In: Proceedings of the International Faust Conference (IFC-18), Mainz, Germany (2018)
6. Michon, R., Smith, J.O., Wright, M., Chafe, C., Granzow, J., Wang, G.: Passively augmenting mobile devices towards hybrid musical instrument design. In: Proceedings of the International Conference on New Interfaces for Musical Expression (NIME-17), Copenhagen (2017)
7. Michon, R., Smith, J.O., Wright, M., Chafe, C., Granzow, J., Wang, G.: Mobile music, sensors, physical modeling, and digital fabrication: articulating the augmented mobile instrument. Appl. Sci. **7**(12), 1311 (2017)
8. Michon, R., Smith, J.O., Wright, M., Chafe, C.: Augmenting the iPad: the BladeAxe. In: Proceedings of the International Conference on New Interfaces for Musical Expression (NIME-16), Brisbane, Australia (2016)
9. Michon, R., Orlarey, Y. Letz, Y., Fober D.: Real time audio digital signal processing with Faust and the Teensy. In: Proceedings of the Sound and Music Computing Conference (SMC-19), Malaga, Spain (2019). Paper not published yet but accepted to the conference
10. Orlarey, Y., Letz, S., Fober, D.: FAUST: an efficient functional approach to DSP programming. In: New Computational Paradigms for Computer Music. Delatour, Paris (2009)
11. Schiemer, G., Havryliv, M.: Pocket Gamelan: tuneable trajectories for flying sources in Mandala 3 and Mandala 4. In: Proceedings of the International Conference on New Interfaces for Musical Expression (NIME06), Paris (2006)
12. Tanaka, A.: Mobile music making. In: Proceedings of the International Conference on New Interfaces for Musical Expression (NIME04), National University of Singapore (2004)
13. Wang, G.: Ocarina: designing the iPhone's magic flute. Comput. Music J. **38**(2), 8–21 (2014)

COMPOSITES 1: An Exploration into Real-Time Animated Notation in the Web Browser

Daniel McKemie(✉)

New York, USA

Abstract. *COMPOSITES 1 for Modular Synthesizer Soloist and Four Accompanists* is a real-time, graphically notated work for modular synthesizer soloist and four accompaniment parts that utilizes the power of Node.js, WebSockets, Web Audio, and CSS to realize an OS-agnostic and web-deliverable electroacoustic composition that can be accessed on any device with a web browser. This paper details the technology stack used to write and perform the work, including examples of how it is used compositionally and in performance. Recent developments in web browser technology, including the Web Audio API and Document Object Model (DOM) manipulation techniques in vanilla JavaScript, have improved the possibilities for the synchronization of audio and visuals using only the browser itself. This paper also seeks to introduce the reader to the aforementioned technologies, and what benefits might exist in the realization of creative works using this stack, specifically regarding the construction of real-time compositions with interactive graphic notations.

Keywords: JavaScript · Node.js · WebSockets · CSS · Animated notation · Web browser · Web audio API · Mobile device music

1 Introduction

During my studies with John Bischoff and Chris Brown [1], I developed my aesthetic of network music that is largely influenced by West Coast Experimentalism. However, it is only recently that have I made serious developments in my own work through the use of web-based technologies, and in particular, the construction and realization of network-based pieces and real-time compositions for live performance. The work of Georg Hajdu, most notably for this context his Quintet.net [2, 3], has served as a great example of contemporary approaches to network music; bringing the traditions of tethered, machine-based network music [1] into the age of mobile devices and wireless capabilities [4, 5].

D. McKemie—Independent Author.

R. Kronland-Martinet et al. (Eds.): CMMR 2019, LNCS 12631, pp. 319–328, 2021.
https://doi.org/10.1007/978-3-030-70210-6_21

2 Full Stack Web Technology

JavaScript is the language of the web, and over the last decade it has expanded greatly into server-side tools and technology. The Document Object Model (DOM) is used to create dynamic changes to, and interactions between, HTML elements on the webpage, and can be linked to a number of processes afforded to work in the browser. For the realization of *COMPSOITES 1*, there is a great degree of nested communication in Node.js using WebSockets, with the Web Audio API treating audio data on the front end, all linked through JavaScript as the primary mode of construction. This architecture is very similar to that implemented in the *Soundworks* framework built by Sébastian Robaszkiewicz and Norbert Schnell at IRCAM [6]. In this section, I will briefly give an overview of these primary components used to write *COMPOSITES 1 for Modular Synthesizer Soloist and Four Accompanists.*

2.1 Web Audio API

The Web Audio API (Application Programming Interface) is a high-level JavaScript API that enables audio synthesis and digital signal processing (DSP) in the browser. The dynamic nature of JavaScript allows the API to be used in conjunction with an array of libraries and tools available in web development, including those on the server side with Node.js. The structure of the API, specifically the modular nature of audio node routing, is similar to other audio software environments in that it provides the user with a large array of options for the synthesis and processing of audio.

2.2 Node.js

Node.js is an open source environment that allows JavaScript to run on the server and return content to the client. This is used to power data flow from back end databases all the way to the browser page using a single language. Global modules, variables, and functionalities can be spread across multiple pages in the server and can be used with a multitude of frameworks to maximize the efficient construction of an API. In this case, the popular framework Express was used as it is lightweight and wide support.

2.3 WebSockets/Socket.IO

WebSocket technology allows for real-time data transfer to and from the server, without the need to refresh the webpage. This enables the manipulation of back end data through client activity, the broadcasting of unique front-end HTML/CSS stylings to multiple devices or individuals, and the projection of real-time manipulations of said stylings to multiple URLs.

Socket.IO is a client and server-side library that uses WebSockets, with some added features that can open thousands of connections vs other methods [7]. Socket.IO is optimized to implement real-time binary streaming, and for this reason was chosen as the best option for the needs of this project.

3 COMPOSITES 1

In the musical work *COMPOSITES 1 for Modular Synthesizer Soloist and Four Accompanists*[1], there is one host point (the soloist) who goes to the homepage/server site, hooks a modular synthesizer in to be the performance instrument, and assists in score generation. Each of the four accompanying parts can be assigned to any pitched instruments and can be augmented with electronics if desired. The soloist is instructed to send out a simple waveform from the synthesizer, with sine, triangle, and sawtooth working best in that order, into the computer (via an audio interface) which will then send the signal to the web browser to be pitch-tracked. The resultant data of the pitch will be used to generate the notational material for the accompanists. While this waveform is uninterrupted in its signal path directly to the server site, the soloist is to construct a performance patch around that patch point before it reaches the server. The performer may modulate that waveform's frequency but is advised not modulate too heavily: a "cleaner" tone, such as a sine wave, will lead to a more legible performance score for the accompanists. The frequency is tracked, and certain frequency thresholds lead to the generation of visuals and/or "decisions" to change the existing visuals. The visuals include color changes, projected pitches on the staff, shapes, shade contours, and so on. These visuals are broadcast to individual URLs, and each of the four accompanists can then access on their own device. For the sake of brevity, I will only discuss examples of one accompanying part, and the technology used to create the server and client pages.

3.1 File Structure

The file directory is set up with client-side scripts in the public folder that are sent to the browser screen which is nested inside the working directory of the Node.js and Socket scripts. Beginning with the client-side calls, there is an HTML and JavaScript file for the host and each accompanist respectively. The host file holds the connections to the server, sockets, and analysis code for the incoming audio stream.

3.2 Client-Side Input and Analysis

An audio input stream is created using the Web Audio DAW (Wad) library [8]. Based on the same concept as a guitar tuner, the signal's frequency is tracked, and because the signal is a simple waveform from an electronic source, the stability of tracking is far better than that of an acoustic instrument (Fig. 1). A major benefit of the Web Audio API is that the hardware synchronization is all done globally. The audio configurations in the computer's system preferences are automatically picked up by the browser, which frees the need for any external drivers or OS dependencies.

The code in Fig. 1 calls for the input and runs the signal through the logPitch() function which is a product of the Wad library. This function calls to analyze the frequency of the incoming signal, and also return its corresponding note name as it coincides on the staff.

[1] Demonstration video: https://www.danielmckemie.com/composites1.

```
// host.js
let input = new Wad({ source: 'mic' });
let tuner = new Wad.Poly();

// Sets the library to begin tracking input signal info
tuner.setVolume(0);
tuner.add(input);
input.play();
tuner.updatePitch();

// Logs the signal to frequency number and note name
let inputFreq = null;
let inputNote = null;
let logPitch = function() {
  requestAnimationFrame(logPitch);
  inputFreq = tuner.pitch;
  inputNote = tuner.noteName; };
```

Fig. 1. Code to declare input and track frequency. The frequency and note name captured by the logPitch() function is assigned to the global inputFreq and inputNote, to allow for transfer and broadcast to the clients.

4 Client to Server Connection

4.1 Client-Side

After the input, analyses, and assignments on the client-side have been rendered, the WebSockets must connect this information to the server in order for it to be broadcast

```
// host.js
// A trigger that automates a button click every 20ms
const buttonBroadcast = docu-
ment.getElementById('broadcaster');
setInterval(function() {
  buttonBroadcast.click()}, 20);

// Clicking the button sends the pitch data to the server
buttonBroadcast.addEventListener('click', function(e) {
  e.preventDefault();
  socket.emit('frequency', {
buttonBroadcast.addEventListener('click', function(e) {
  e.preventDefault();
  socket.emit('frequency', {
    pitch: inputFreq,
    note: inputNote })
});
```

Fig. 2. The frequency assignment sends the pitch and note keys with the values of the global variables, inputFreq and inputNote, which were declared prior. This sends/emits this data to the server environment via Socket.IO

to the client's webpages. The 'broadcast' button calls for the host data to be emitted via the socket, and back to the server, and this occurs automatically every 20 ms in order to simulate the transmission of real-time data flow. A number of sockets can be implemented to send data, and each are identified with unique IDs created by the user. In the following case 'frequency' is the unique ID associated with the analysis of the incoming audio stream (Fig. 2).

4.2 Server Side

The server connection to the localhost and the incoming sockets are all housed within the primary application file in Node.js. Following the thread from the client, the socket connections must be written in such a way that the host data can pass to anywhere on the server via Socket.IO. In this case, the data is broadcast to all clients on the server; and while there are options to broadcast to select clients instead of broadcasting all data in one stream (frequency) while avoiding others, it is beyond the scope of this paper, and not necessary for the success of the piece (Fig. 3).

```
// app.js
io.on('connection', function(socket) {
  socket.on('frequency', function(data) {
    io.sockets.emit('frequency', data) });
```

Fig. 3. This code enables global data sharing and accessibility among all the clients but must be called later by specific clients for their own use.

4.3 Return to Client

The data received from the host and brought to the server, can now be pulled back through to any of the four remaining clients (accompanists) through their respective script.js files. In order to see unique transmissions and treatments of this data, a route must be set up in our app.js file so that a connector can access for their own broadcast (Fig. 4).

The JavaScript calls the data emitted by Socket.IO and can be treated in any number of ways. In this example, the frequency number is run through a switch statement, and as certain conditionals are met, the background color of our <body> is changed accordingly (Fig. 5). This data can be sent to clients in many fashions, from private messages to select clients, and so on, but for the sake of brevity we will emit data to all clients equally.

```
// app.js
// Piping the pitch data back up to the client-side page
app.get('/player1', function(req, res) {
  res.sendFile(__dirname + '/public/player1.html');
});

// script1.js
// As the data is read, a connection is made between the
// background color of the web page and the pitch
// material. A switch statement changes the colors
// according to frequency range

let backColor = null;
socket.on('frequency', function(data) {
  switch (true) {
    case (data.pitch < '200'):
      backColor = 'red';
      break;
    case (data.pitch < '300'):
      backColor = 'orange';
      break;
  };
  document.body.style.backgroundColor = backColor });
```

Fig. 4. The app.js file sends our player1.html file to the browser, which is linked to our script1.js file, which can treat the data sent out to the server through WebSockets.

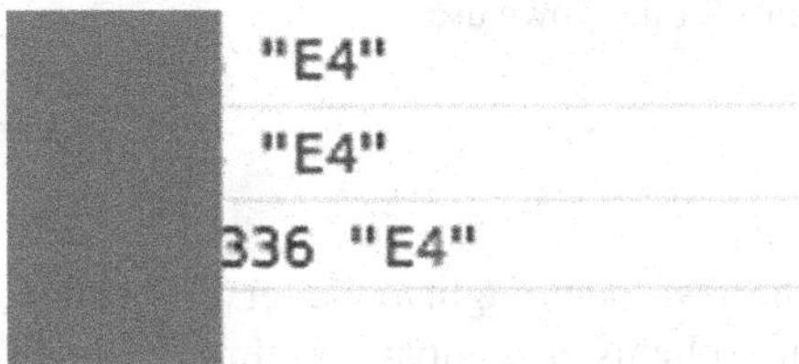

Fig. 5. Example of the frequency to color relationship as seen through the host's console (right) and Player 1's yellow background (left). (Color figure online)

5 Use as a Compositional Tool

The browser houses a healthy number of ways to compose, manipulate, and animate visual elements, and CSS and DOM manipulation techniques alone include a large number of options to create scores that convey musical information to performers. As outlined in previous sections, these elements can be synchronized through the server and delivered to individually unique locations. The following will outline a number of examples as to how *COMPOSITES 1* uses these techniques to create a real-time score for the accompanying parts.

The elements of the score include the background color, shapes, words and staff notation. Changes to these elements are based on the host input's frequency and/or note name values. The goal of the work was to not inundate the performers with instructions and elements, but rather let them choose pathways in which to realize musical material.

This was to lessen the problems that can arise when constructing notation in real-time. [9].

5.1 Colors

The use of color as a notational element has seen more traction in recent years, but no consistent practice has been established. Lindsay Vickery's research into the topic suggests the need for further exploration into the field, especially in regard to multimedia works [10]. As opposed to leaving the interpretation of colors open or to be designated for assignment, the decision was made to give the performer overall qualities to enhance the stylistic qualities of their playing. A classic and notable example of color usage is that of John Cage's Aria (1958), in which he uses color to denote different singing styles for each line [11]. I wanted to take a similar approach in *COMPOSITES 1*, to denote a type of executable action in response to color as opposed to a specific executable action. The colors of the spectrum are at play, and call for the following:

- Red: Poignant
- Orange: Fleeting
- Yellow: Bright
- Green: Stable
- Blue: Metastatic
- Indigo: Dark
- Violet: Razor-like

5.2 Shapes

Shapes have been a centerpiece in the evolution of western music notation and maintain an important role in certain brands of music education and vocal music [12]. While I did not seek to morph and modulate the current staff notation system, I did want to use basic shapes to convey a musical response, but not have any shapes that were simply a one-dimensional linear contour. This decision stems from not wanting to encourage a correlation of pitch with vertical placement [10], though if players wish to interpret the two-dimensional shapes this way, that is quite acceptable. With the circle, triangle, and square, the instruction to the performer is to assign a very focused action that best reflects the given shape and execute it regardless of surrounding context. Simple shapes were chosen as they can be easily recognizable compared to the others, and should result in a more focused performance [13]. This achieves two desired goals, the first being a consistent execution of sonic events that will occur throughout the piece; and the second, to allow the performer to have more unrestricted decision making in the performance process. The shapes are called by a change in the *<img>* tag source path and are set to appear when specific parameters are met (Fig. 6).

Fig. 6. The triangle shape used in COMPOSITES 1 (one of three shapes to appear), with the yellow background. (Color figure online)

5.3 Words

The use of written words to enhance musical expression and performance has been around for centuries. In the case of *COMPOSITES 1*, instead of indicating musical results that could be achieved by using traditional markings (ie. *ff* instead of 'very loud' or a crescendo instead of 'get louder'), I sought to explore the use of words to allow for variations upon the already present situation. To expand, when 'pointed' is displayed, this can result in a number of different outcomes based on both decisions made by the performer, and the context in which it appears (Fig. 7).

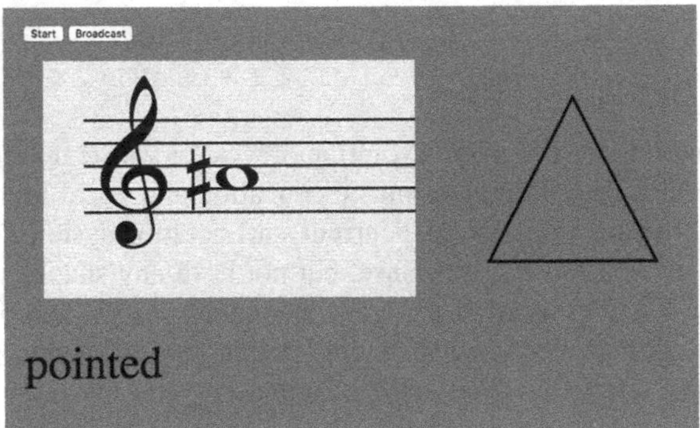

Fig. 7. An example of all elements displayed on one page as seen by an accompanying performer.

The words are generated independently from the host's incoming audio signal by a random number generator and a switch statement assigned to the DOM. Inserting one independently timed element that is separate from the host's actions gives the accompanying part its own pace. This decision grew out of a desire to eliminate any sort of perceptible rigidity in the performing group as a whole, without having completely asynchronous events.

Additionally, the use of simple, non-musical phrases enhances the space that the performer can work in, and at the same time not be overbearing. The words and shapes are the only elements of the score that appear and are then removed as opposed to remaining stationary and changing over time.

5.4 Pitch/staff Notation

The images of the staff are the most straightforward of all the elements in the score. As the note changes, the performer uses it as a pitch reference to construct their material, and they also have the option to ignore any number of other elements and continue holding that pitch. The note indicated on the staff is directly correlated to the note name of the incoming waveform.

5.5 Goals and Challenges

As stated earlier, the resulting notation structures are designed to produce varying interpretations by the accompanying performers. The instructions provided encourage the performer to choose pathways and focus on or ignore elements as they choose. Granting the performers this flexibility helps to relieve any desire, whether purposeful or accidental, to simply follow the soloist. The use of colors, shapes, words, and traditional staff notation provides varying degrees of openness to closedness, and players can find their own level of comfort in the notational structures provided.

The chaotic nature of analyzing audio signals for pitch detection becomes potentially problematic for the stability of the display of accompaniment scores. For example, an input signal that accidentally becomes frequency-modulated would in turn send the accompanists' notation screens into a tail spin, with elements rapidly changing well beyond any realistic readability. Instead of leaving this open to cause an otherwise well executed performance to be ruined, this has been dealt with in two ways: firstly, the soloist is instructed to extensively practice with their synthesizer and this setup and to take note of reactions based on their actions; and second, if the notation system were to fall into chaos, accompanying performers are informed to do the same. Instead of treating this as a hinderance, the inherent fragility in the technology becomes an interesting musical element when executed properly.

6 Future Work

The ever-expanding collection of libraries and development tools can be seamlessly integrated into and inspire works like *COMPOSITES 1*. More involved data visualizations can be built using libraries like D3 [14], and the sharing of data over common networks to control and manipulate individual Web Audio streams could lead to very interesting results, as it did in similar settings that came before it [1].

The back-end server is what supports the delivery of the parts to individual screens for each player and allows for a greater depth of concentration and execution of each player's part for a more effective performance. Taking inspiration from Kelly Michael Fox's *Accretion* [15], which uses individual monitors as opposed to a projected screen in which all players read from, not only maximizes the efficiency of the space in which to render elements, but also injects a sense of mystery for the audience: what are they all looking at?

The fact that the projected parts can be accessed via a multitude of different devices, so long as they support modern web browsers, is key in broadening accessibility and ease of performance of works such as *COMPOSITES 1* and those that choose to employ the same architecture. As stated earlier, the Web Audio API uses the global settings of the computer, which allows for a wider range of device types to be used, and the option to deploy the entire piece as a cloud-based app [16], removes the need to deliver code in any form, requiring nothing more than a simple URL.

References

1. Bischoff, J., Brown C.: Indigenous to the net: early network music bands in the san francisco bay area (2002). https://crossfade.walkerart.org/brownbischoff/IndigenoustotheNetPrint.html
2. Hajdu, G.: Quintet.net: an environment for composing and performing music on the internet. Leonardo **38**(1), 23–30 (2005)
3. Hajdu, G.: Real-time composition and notation in network music environments. In: Proceedings of the International Computer Music Conference. Belfast, N. Ireland (2008)
4. Hajdu, G.: Composing for networks. In: Proceedings of the Symposium for Laptop Ensembles and Orchestras, Baton Rouge, Louisiana, pp. 98–102 (2012)
5. Carey, B.: SpectraScore VR: networkable virtual reality software tools for real- time composition and performance. In: International Conference on New Interfaces for Musical Expression, Brisbane, Australia, pp. 3–4 (2016)
6. Robaszkiewicz, S., Schnell, N.: Soundworks – a playground for artists and developers to create collaborative mobile web performances. In: 1st Web Audio Conference, Paris, France (2015)
7. Carey, B., Hajdu, G.: Netscore: an image server/client package for transmitting notated music to browser and virtual reality interfaces. In: The International Conference on Technologies for Music Notation and Representation, Cambridge, UK, pp. 151–156 (2016)
8. Serota, R.: Web Audio Library. https://github.com/rserota/wad
9. Freeman, J.: Extreme sight-reading, mediated expression, and audience participation: Real-time music notation in live performance. Comput. Music J. **32**(3), 25–41 (2008)
10. Vickery, L.: Some approaches to representing sound with colour and shape. In: The International Conference on Technologies for Music Notation and Representation, Montreal, Canada, pp. 165–173 (2018)
11. Poast, M.: Visual color notation for musical expression. Leonardo **33**(3), 215–221 (2000)
12. Johnson, D.C.: Tradition with Kodály applications. Kodály Envoy **35**(1), 11–15 (2008)
13. Smith, R.R.: An atomic approach to animated music notation. In: The International Conference on Technologies for Music Notation and Representation, Paris, France, pp. 40–48 (2015)
14. Data-Driven Documents. https://d3js.org
15. Fox, M.K.: Flexible, networked animated music notation for orchestra with the Raspberry Pi. In: TENOR: The International Conference on Technologies for Music Notation and Representation, Paris, France, pp. 104–109 (2015)
16. Deploying Node.js Apps on Heroku. https://devcenter.heroku.com/articles/deploying-nodejs

Distributed Scores and Audio on Mobile Devices in the Music for a Multidisciplinary Performance

Pedro Louzeiro(✉)

Universidade de Évora, Évora, Portugal Centro de Estudos de Sociologia e Estética Musical (CESEM), Lisbon, Portugal
pedrolouzeiro@gmail.com

Abstract. In an attempt to uncover the strengths and limitations of web technologies for sound and music notation applications, driven by aesthetic goals and prompted by the lack of logistic means, the author has developed a system for animated scores and sound diffusion using browser-enabled mobile devices, controlled by a host computer running Max and a web server. Ease of deployment was seen as a desirable feature in comparison to native application computer-based systems – such as Comprovisador, a system which has lent many features to the one proposed herein. Weaknesses were identified motivating the design of mitigation and adaptation strategies at the technical and the compositional levels, respectively. The creation of music for a multidisciplinary performance entitled GarB'urlesco has served as a case study to assess the effectiveness of those strategies. The present text is an extended version of a paper presented at CMMR 2019, in Marseille.

Keywords: Animated notation · Electro-acoustic composition · Web applications · Multidisciplinary performance · Networked music performance

1 Introduction

Recently, we were invited to compose music for a multidisciplinary performance entitled GarB'urlesco, which includes elements of theatre, dance, costume design and music (Fig. 1) [22]. In addition to the new music created for this purpose, the performance also includes pieces of baroque music, played on period instruments. The narrative explores the sociocultural contrasts that can be observed in the Algarve. Algarve is a southern Portuguese region marked by densely populated coastal areas and scattered rural communities, and with an economy driven by a very seasonal tourist activity. To enhance the idea of contrast in the composition, it seemed aesthetically relevant to include electro-acoustic elements clashing with the period instruments. However, there were no logistical or financial resources for this, especially regarding sound projection. Not allowing ourselves to give

R. Kronland-Martinet et al. (Eds.): CMMR 2019, LNCS 12631, pp. 329–344, 2021.
https://doi.org/10.1007/978-3-030-70210-6_22

up, we looked for alternatives in recent examples in the field of network musical performance where mobile devices are used as musical instruments, sound projectors, animated scores or as an interface for audience participation.

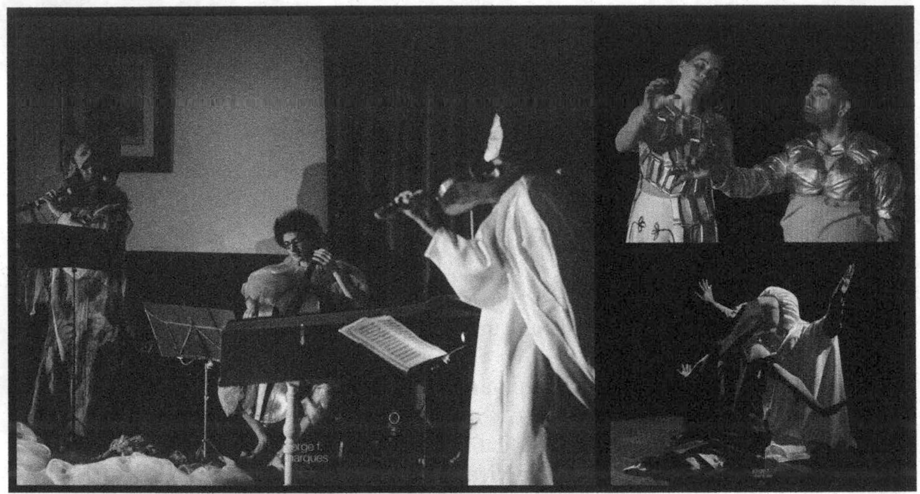

Fig. 1. GarB'urlesco – a multidisciplinary performance combining theatre, dance, costume design and music (early and contemporary), played on period instruments.

Regarding our previous experience, as of 2015 we have been developing Comprovisador, a system designed to enable mediated soloist-ensemble interaction using machine listening, algorithmic compositional procedures and dynamic notation, in a networked environment [18–20]. In real-time, as a soloist improvises, Comprovisador's algorithms produce a score that is immediately sight-read by an ensemble of musicians, creating a coordinated response to the improvisation. To this date, Comprovisador has been used in ten public performances. In each performance, the system is presented with new features. The introduction of composed electro-acoustic tracks in synchronisation with the animated scores is to be expected soon.

Like any other tool, Comprovisador has its strengths and its weaknesses. Weaknesses are often problems for which a solution has not yet been found or represent a trade-off from other aspects considered more important. One such case is the fact that Comprovisador is not compatible with mobile devices (namely, tablets). Not only does it require proper computers but it also requires software installation procedures[1] that are not very complex for someone experienced, but can be so for someone who is not computer oriented. Thus, it can

[1] Both host and client applications of Comprovisador run in the Max environment [25] using the bach library [6,12] and also Java.

be tedious or discouraging for users and it always entails increased preparation time when preparing a concert. These issues would be problematic in the context of GarB'urlesco and would not solve the fundamental issue of sound projection logistics.

For Comprovisador's objectives, processing speed and reliability of laptop computers running native applications outweigh ease of deployment of tablets running web applications. Other applications with different objectives may benefit more from a mobile device-based approach. Apart from musical performance with real-time generated scores, we envisage possibilities in the educational field – Soundslice [15], a web platform where users can learn to play pieces of music through dynamic notation synchronised with Youtube videos is a good example, but there are also possibilities in the fields of ear training and sight reading (see [21]).

In the field of music and multimedia networked performance, there are many examples that use mobile devices with as many different strategies. Following are only a few examples.

"Flock" [10,11], a piece by Jason Freeman for saxophone quartet, video, electronic sound, dancers, and audience participation premiered in 2007, uses PDA's mounted on each player's instrument. Those devices display music notation generated from the locations of musicians, dancers, and audience members as they move and interact with each other.

Decibel ScorePlayer [16] is an iPad application developed by the Decibel New Music Ensemble, a group led by composer Cat Hope. This application enables network-synchronised scrolling of proportional colour music scores and audio playback. It has been used by many composers worldwide.

Cheng Lee proposes an approach for incorporating computer music and virtual reality practices into a multimedia performance installation requiring the audience members to use their own smartphones as 360-degree viewing devices [17]. The author also proposes the use of wireless speakers carried around the venue as a means of achieving immersive sound and music effects in substitution for a multi-channel surround-sound system.

Composer Jonathan Bell, who also has used bluetooth speakers as networked sound projectors, has created a system called SmartVox [7] – a web-based distributed media player as notation tool for choral practices. The audio-visual scores are created with the bach environment for Max. In a choral context, singers hear (using earphones) and see their own part displayed in the browser of their smartphone. The whole is synchronised through the distributed state of the web application.

In May 2019, a networked music performance dubbed Symphony for a Tunnel for 144 musicians and distributed score display system took place in Hamburg's St. Pauli Elbe Tunnel [14]. The performance featured Drawsocket [13], a recently developed system which was able to draw and synchronise scores across the required 144 iPads, connected via Wi-Fi. The system provides control over diverse media features of web browsers, notably SVG[2] which can be used to draw animated graphic notation. Through integration with MaxScore[3] [14], the system also enables common-practice notation. On the server side, Drawsocket uses Max as its primary controller interface and Node.js (Node for Max (N4M)) for server-client communication. Of the examples given here, only SmartVox and Drawsocket use purely web technologies on the client side.

Finally, we should mention a.bel [8] – a system presented in 2015 at Casa da Música, in Porto, Portugal, in a concert where almost 1000 smartphones were used as musical instruments by the members of the audience. The event featured pieces by four composers – Carlos Guedes, José Alberto Gomes, Neil Leonard and Rui Penha – using different approaches to audience participation via their smartphones and the a.bel system.

In this paper, based on a case study – the music composed for GarB'urlesco, we will attempt to demonstrate a possible application for web resources (HTML5, JavaScript (JS) and open-source libraries) which includes animated precomposed scores and distributed sound diffusion on a local network. Since synchronisation is not easily achievable in this context, we will discuss certain mitigation and adaptation strategies that were adopted, regarding the technical and the compositional sides, respectively. The compositional strategies also took into account the sound characteristics of this type of devices.

The motivation for carrying out this practical application is therefore related to research on easily deployable solutions and sharpened by the will to perform electro-acoustic music in a context with scarce logistical resources.

2 HTML5-based Solutions

General advantages of mobile devices for animated score and sound applications include ubiquity (most especially in the case of smartphones), ease of transportation and set-up (from one's pocket directly to the music stand), and a fair processing power despite being small and lightweight. As for the advantages of web-based software we count being completely cross-platform and cross-type (laptops, tablets, smartphones, etc.), having no need for additional software installation (any required libraries are loaded by the browser at runtime), being free of charge, capable of performing animation at an adequate frame rate (HTML5 Canvas element/`window.requestAnimationFrame()` method, which we find to have a superior performance than Max's `jsui` or `lcd` options (cf. [20])), and including access to powerful open-source tools for graphics and sound (p5.js, p5.sound [2], tone.js [3]) and for interfacing with Max (Miraweb and its underlying library – xebra.js [4]).

[2] Scalable Vector Graphics (SVG) is an Extensible Markup Language (XML)-based vector image format for two-dimensional graphics with support for interactivity and animation.

[3] MaxScore is a music notation library for the Max environment [1].

This approach also has disadvantages, specifically the inability to use UDP[4] and the unavailability to the best of our knowledge of an open-source[5] music notation library with suitable quality for generative applications[6]. Furthermore, there are important timing issues with three different origins: 1) network latency, which is aggravated by the use of the Transmission Control Protocol (TCP) (since UDP as an alternative is unavailable); 2) imprecise JavaScript clock (accessing the audio subsystem's hardware clock through the Web Audio API can improve precision although not to our desired levels, as will be discussed in Sect. 3.1); and 3) latency originating in other factors.

Considering the above disadvantages, can we nonetheless accomplish interesting musical results by implementing mitigation and adaptation strategies? This question is what we attempt to answer in the following sections.

3 Case Study

GarB'urlesco is a multidisciplinary performance with elements of theatre, dance, costume design and music (both early music and purposely composed music), using period instruments and a traditional cane flute, composed electronics for networked mobile devices and animated score. The score uses standard notation which is dynamically updated also featuring a bouncing ball cueing system for synchronisation between instrumentalists and electronics.

Regarding space, the devices are arranged according to Fig. 2 (left). Smartphones are hidden under the audience's chairs, which are arranged in double rows on each side of the room. Device number 1 (a tablet) is the only device in charge of displaying the score and it sits on the flautist's music stand.

The intent of hiding the devices in close proximity to the audience is to create immersive sound effects while causing some strangeness (hearing sound but not being able to see its source) and to compensate for the weak sound output of these devices.

In addition, there is a host computer running Max that coordinates sound and score events, being also connected to a small 2.1 sound system, located in the musicians' space, enabling low frequency sound effects.

We have designed a system that uses xebra.js to establish WebSocket[7] communication between Max and the browser of each device. Besides Max, the host

[4] UDP (User Datagram Protocol) is a communications protocol used primarily for establishing low-latency and loss-tolerating connections between network applications.

[5] Paid solutions are not included in the scope of this research.

[6] At the cmmr 2019 conference, we have learnt about the Guido Project [5], an open source project that encompasses a music notation format, a score rendering engine and various music score utilities. The Guido engine is a library that can be embedded on different platforms using different programming languages, among which JavaScript. We find both the music notation format and the score rendering engine to be adequate for the type of generative applications we envisage.

[7] WebSocket is a computer communications protocol, providing full-duplex communication channels over a single TCP connection.

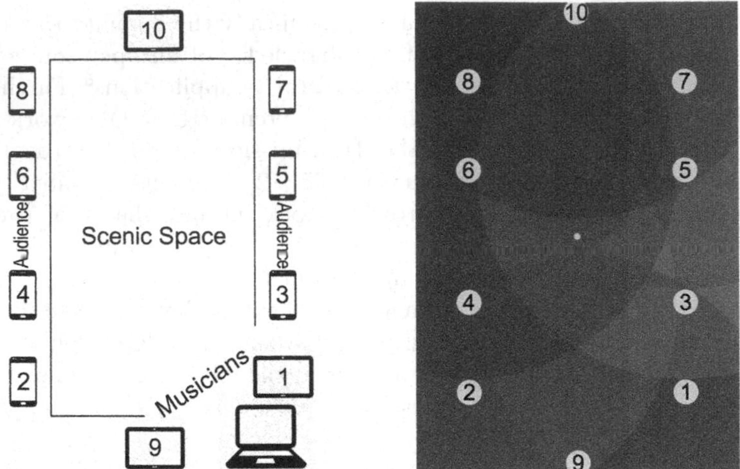

Fig. 2. Left: space arrangement of mobile devices in GarB'urlesco; right: Swarm Spatialiser GUI - `nodes` Max object.

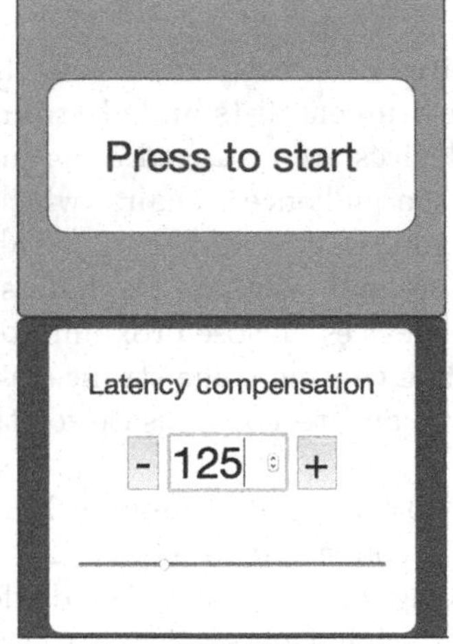

Fig. 3. HTML-based GUI for default devices – audio playback only.

computer runs a server hosting two HTML files, two JavaScript libraries (xebra.js and tone.js), various audio files and the score (comprised of png files, designed in Max using the `bach` library [6] for notation and Computer Assisted Composition (CAC) features – see Sect. 3.1). One of the HTML files is destined for audio playback only (see Fig. 3) and the other for displaying the score as well (device number 1, Fig. 4).

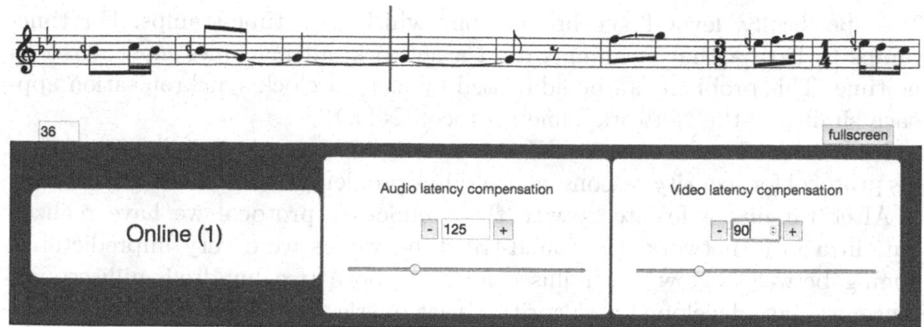

Fig. 4. HTML-based GUI for device 1 – audio playback and score display.

The loading steps occur as follows:

- the browser of each device is pointed to the appropriate HTML file;
- the user is prompted to input a unique label for easy identification by Max;
- the relevant audio files and, if applicable, the score png files are then loaded by the script;
- meanwhile, a WebSocket connection is established with Max;
- by user interaction ('press to start' button), the audio context is started up, Max is notified of the client's status (online) and initial clock synchronisation takes place;
- clock sync continues in background (preventing drift), during performance.

3.1 Technical Problems and Mitigation

Battery operated devices turn off their screens and other resources when left idle with no user interaction. In our case, it makes sense to leave the screen off as it saves up battery power, avoiding the need to plug everything to the mains, also helping conceal the devices. The problem is that other resources such as sound output and Wi-Fi connection also go to sleep or run in low consumption mode, thus hampering performance.

One possible workaround for this issue is to play a dummy sound file every few seconds, triggered from Max over the network. This keeps both resources awake[8]. The dummy sound file must contain some audio data otherwise it is dismissed by the system. On the other hand, we obviously could not do with an audible repeating sound. Hence our sound file contains a very short (100 ms), low amplitude (−21 dB) and low frequency (30 Hz) sine wave which cannot be heard from the devices' speakers though having enough information to trick the system into keeping both resources active.

In Comprovisador, we had implemented a system to attain suitable synchronisation which was based on Dannenberg's concept of "time-flow"

[8] – in devices running older Android versions – see Sect. 4.

[9] – specifically, level 1 synchronisation[9] which uses time-stamps. For time-stamps to have actual meaning within a network, all machines must agree on the time. This problem can be addressed by using a clock synchronisation approach similar to the Network Time Protocol (NTP).

NTP is based on low-latency UDP. However, browsers do not allow the use of this protocol for security reasons, which raises problems for applications like ours.

After running a few tests with the WebSocket protocol we have realized that, in a local network, the round-trip time values were very unpredictable, ranging between below one millisecond and above two hundred milliseconds. Hence, we have developed an algorithm that queries the server time repeatedly, during 2 s. By probability, the fastest round trip within this interval will be under eighty milliseconds – although very often under one millisecond. By selecting this iteration we maximise precision and use the reported server time to make the necessary adjustments to the client's clock. Every few minutes the algorithm runs again to compensate for clock drift. The algorithm is presented below.

```
function queryNow(){     // Called repeatedly during a 2s interval
  if (querying) {
    var wrong_time = now(); // client time is assumed wrong
    var message = ["queryNow",wrong_time];
    sendMax(message);         // query Max to get server time
  }
}
function timedResponse(t){  // Called upon Max response
  var wrong_time = t[0];     // Max echoes the client time
  var reported_time = t[1]; // and reports server time
  var received_time = now(); // Client time-stamps the response
  var round_trip = received_time - wrong_time;
  if (round_trip < best_lap) {
    best_lap = round_trip;  // Store the fastest iteration
                            // calculate our offset
    ntp_off = reported_time - round_trip/2 - wrong_time;
  }                         // after 10ms, recall queryNow
  Tone.context.setTimeout(queryNow, 0.01);
}
function queryEnd() {       // Called when the 2s interval ends
  querying = false;
  Tone.Transport.seconds += ntp_off; // adjust client time
}
```

[9] This concept aims at solving synchronisation problems in real-time music and media systems. The author describes four approaches to synchronisation in increasing levels of sophistication: Synchronisation Levels 0 through 3. Level 1 consists on applying time-stamps to events, computing the events in advance within a "control stage" and delivering the computed events with time-stamps to a "rendering stage". There, events are delayed according to time-stamps in order to produce accurately timed output.

On the server side, time is obtained with the Max `cpuclock` object, which is the most accurate [25]. On the client side, we obtain it with `Tone.Transport` (from the tone.js library) which is based on Web Audio's `audioContext.currentTime` property. It is indeed more accurate than the JS clock. Nevertheless, it is not as accurate as we would like it to be. A simple experiment consisting on scheduling a repeated event every 500 ms with `Tone.Transport.scheduleRepeat` using various latency hint values revealed noticeable jitter in every device we have tested (Android only).

We have encountered additional latency originating in other factors at a later stage than the network and the Web Audio clock. The latency value varies from device to device, being higher on older Android devices (cf. [23]) – sometimes surpassing 400 ms. In iOS devices, values were more consistent – around 100 ms. Within the same device it stays relatively stable (see Sect. 4).

To tackle this problem we have implemented a graphic user interface (GUI) allowing manual adjustment of the latency compensation for audio (see Fig. 3) and also for video (score version) , which in many cases required a different value (see Fig. 4). To perform this adjustment, one needs to be physically placed between the sound output of the server (hard-wired) and the client device; then, we trigger a repeating sharp sound on both devices and adjust the value until the resulting sound is perceptually centered. Since our approach uses time-stamps delaying the sound onset by one second in relation to triggering, it is possible to account for all latency contributions (network transfer, software and hardware processing) within a safe margin. In the future, this procedure can be automated using the server audio input to measure the client output delay and calculate the adjustment.

As for the score, since we were unable to find a suitable JS notation library, we have turned to the idea of using image files. This is possible thanks to an image-export feature included in the recently-released version 0.8.1 of bach[10], on which we were allowed to beta-test a pre-release.

Our approach is well suited for precomposed music and can, in the future, be modified for real-time generative scores. Here are its characteristics (see Fig. 5):

- measures are unitary (1/4, 3/8, 3/16, 5/16, etc.);
- each measure consists of an independent png file of a constant pixel size;
- the number of measures per system depends on screen resolution and is optimized for 8 measures on the more common screens;

[10] The bach library enables music notation and CAC tools inside the Max environment. Its most prominent objects are bach.score (for standard metric notation) and bach.roll (for proportional notation). Both objects are notation editors (meaning a user can interact with them via mouse and keyboard to create/modify the score) and score players (they can read back score data and drive a MIDI synth or similar). Moreover, they feature Max type inputs and outputs in order to be controlled by and/or to control other Max processes in real time [6].

- measures are dynamically updated in cycle in such a way as not to disturb the reading process – replacing the ones that have been read at the distance of half a system (half a cycle)[11].

This approach was adapted from a previous one recently introduced in Comprovisador, the difference being that, in Comprovisador, notation is generated and drawn in real-time using bach objects.

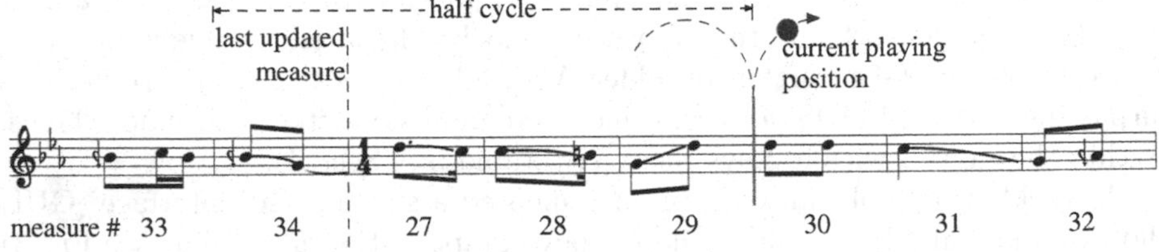

Fig. 5. Score with measures dynamically updated in cycle and bouncing ball.

Another approach inherited from Comprovisador is the bouncing ball as a visual synchronisation and score navigation device. Other authors have used similar approaches (see [26,28]) and consider them preferable when comparing to other types of score navigation strategies [24].

In our web-based application, two overlaid canvas elements are used: one holds the score while the other renders the bouncing ball. The former is redrawn the least number of times possible – once only whenever the measure is updated and only in the corresponding rectangle. The latter is redrawn around 60 times per second (with JS's `requestAnimationFrame()` method). It would be possible to use only one canvas but it seemed unnecessary to redraw all the png images in every frame.

Since rendering of the bouncing ball is done by a different clock[12], a drift may occur. The correction for such drift is obtained as follows:

- Max host sends the message `syncScore(n, t)` every few measures, where `n` is the measure to reach at time `t`;
- if at `t` the bouncing ball is lagging behind, then jump forward to `n`;
- else if ball is early, reduce velocity by a factor in order to reach `n+1` on time `t+period` (skew).

The last step of this algorithm helps avoiding jitter, which would occur if the bouncing ball had to jump backward.

[11] For a standalone interactive example of the score in action, visit https://glitchscore.glitch.me/.

[12] Trying to render graphics with the more precise Web Audio clock would result in a much lower frame rate. Synchronisation is nonetheless controlled by the Web Audio clock using the Tone.Draw.schedule() method of the tone.js library (see [3,27]).

3.2 Compositional Problems and Adaptation

Several problems are faced when composing mixed music with mobile devices as sound projectors:

low power output – a smartphone cannot balance with an acoustic instrument;
poor quality – absence of low frequency spectrum and some degree of distortion; audible dynamic compression in iOS devices;
latency – even with our mitigation strategies, it is not possible to have the required level of timing precision to perform phase-accurate spatialisation.

Regarding the lack of power, we adapt by using number – at least one device for every four people – and textural reduction, using electronics mainly against solo instruments. On the issue of poor quality, we can restrict to using high-pitched sounds. As for latency, "if you can't beat it, join it", which in this case means to embrace non-simultaneity – to use granulation-based effects.

In fact, we have built a granular synthesiser controlled from a bach score. Thanks to bach's slot system, it allows sequencing all the granular synth's temporal parameters, as well as the transposition parameters (the musical notes) in the same notation environment used for the instrumental parts (see Fig. 6).

Fig. 6. A `bach.score` object featuring slots of type *function* (coloured lines) and type *intlist* (coloured numbers). (Color figure online)

Although phase-accurate spatialisation is not feasible, we have conceived a strategy thus allowing to convey spatial sensations encompassing temporal inaccuracies. It uses the characteristics of granulation – namely, the probability of a given grain to be emitted by a particular source.

In Fig. 2 (right), we see a GUI made with the object `nodes`. Here, each ellipse represents the field of influence of each source while the cursor's position in relation to each ellipse represents the probability weight of a grain, at a given moment, to be emitted by the respective source.

To avoid phase problems due to temporal inaccuracies, a grain can never be emitted by more than one source simultaneously. The amplitude is based on the same weight assignment (`nodes` GUI) but with normalised and scaled values.

This system is intended to simulate, to a certain extent, a graphic system of particles where each particle revolves around a point in space, with apparent free will. Although we never see the centre point, we get a sense of where it is by the way particles express their desire towards it. The same happens in our granular spatialiser – which we name Swarm Spatialiser.

However, when we apply an automated trajectory generator to our GUI to get a stream of probability weights, and then apply further calculations of norm and scale to those values before feeding them to the granular synth, our system's CPU utilization becomes dangerously high. We have solved this by recording the stream of weights (post-calculations) to a `bach.roll` object as slot content of type llll[13]. Then, when we read back the values from `bach.roll` as a lookup table, we avoid performing all the calculations within the trajectory generator (Lissajous curves and other functions), the `nodes` GUI (translation of coordinates into probability weights and graphic rendering of the GUI object) and beyond. Furthermore, we can access the recorded information in `bach.roll` and perform simple time stretching and compressing operations in order to obtain slower or faster trajectories.

Another advantage of using bach is its microtonal support which we have taken advantage of (see Fig. 6). In fact, some traditional melodies were used as a basis for the composition and those melodies contain various microtonal inflections. Therefore, it seemed relevant to extrapolate that feature to the remaining musical elements. Bach works in midicents, which our granular synth accepts. Regarding notation, it supports pitch breakpoints in the duration lines (see Figs. 4 and 5), allowing glissandi to be defined and played back.

4 Results

The system was assessed by composer and musicians during rehearsals (April to July 2019) and performance (6 and 7 July 2019).

The animated score was found to perform suitably, with faster performance of the bouncing ball when compared to previous experiments in the Max environment. Also, the appearance of the staff, despite being comprised of individual image files, is seamless.

Synchronisation between flautist and electronics guided by the bouncing ball was considered effective, but it must be taken into account that there were no

[13] llll stands for Lisp Like Linked List.

events requiring very precise synchronisation (as part of our adaptation strategy). Other instruments' lines were subject to that of the flute and were easy to follow along with the paper version of the score.

Manual latency compensation was found relatively easy to adjust sensorially. Once adjusted, there was some probability of a change in the latency value, causing the device to be slightly out of sync. In slower devices running older Android versions, this was more noticeable. However, this probability was not very significant. Moreover, our compositional strategy accounts for these imprecisions.

The dummy sound workaround for keeping resources active was effective with many of the devices available to us. However, it did not work with iOS devices nor with devices running Android version 8 or later. On iOS devices, the solution was to simply set the display to not enter sleep mode. Recent Android devices revealed more disadvantages: developer options had to be enabled and devices had to be connected to a power source in order to stay awake during the show.

At the sequencing level, the probability-based granular spatialiser was considered effective, being analogous to a graphic particles system simulating swarm intelligence. The use of the `bach.roll` for trajectory sequencing has enabled better performance by eliminating the need to perform a substantial number of calculations, replacing it with a lookup table approach.

Furthermore, using bach to sequence our granular synth's pitch and temporal parameters has proved advantageous in regards to the integration with the instrumental melody representation. It is noteworthy that the slot system enables a kind of interaction similar to the one enabled in Digital Audio Workstations (DAW) for automation control, with the advantage of a deeper integration with notation. On top of that, it allows us to sequence data for instruments created in Max which therefore are not available in any DAW software.

Finally, at the composition level, our adaptation strategies have made it possible to circumvent inherent problems in this type of system and achieve results with pleasing aesthetics. Regarding the sound spectrum restriction and the instrumental texture reduction, our choice was to use granulated instrumental sounds taken from the ensemble in order to create a dialogue with the respective acoustic instruments, as a duet. This approach offered timbre cohesion and balance, overcoming the poor quality and sound power of the devices. With regards to sound design, the system adapted well to the effects required by the narrative – namely, 'countryside' (represented by the bells of a flock of sheep), 'sea' (filtered white noise and seagulls), 'frantic tourism and its bipolar seasonality': extreme calmness vs chaos (smartphone ringtones, camera shutters, DTMF tones[14] and glitchy sounds). These sounds were chosen firstly based on their energy in the high spectrum and secondly because they were in some way associated with the concept of flock – sheep, seagulls, tourists with their smartphones and cameras – and therefore appropriate for our Swarm Spatialiser.

[14] Dual-tone multi-frequency (DTMF) signaling is a telecommunication signaling system using the voice-frequency band over telephone lines between telephone equipment and other communications devices and switching centers.

Sensations of sound source displacement were felt clearly around the room as expressed by a few audience members who came to us once the show had ended.

Also appreciated was the satirical use of the ringtones emitted by actual smartphones: it starts with only one phone ringing, thus leading the audience to think someone forgot to turn off their phone (remember: the devices are hidden under the audiences' chairs). After a short while and a blatant ringtone crescendo, the purpose becomes obvious.

In addition to the mobile devices, it was possible to obtain sound effects with stronger dynamics and lower frequencies by using a 2.1 sound system. Effects consisted in certain soundscapes and reinforcement of instrumental passages.

GarB'urlesco was conceived for a particular venue, in Lagos, Portugal. If the possibility ever comes of performing it elsewhere, some adaptation will likely be needed. For example, a larger venue will require a larger number of devices – which could raise problems regarding network capability – or the use of portable speakers, which would change the original sound characteristics.

5 Conclusions

A system of this nature can hardly compete with native application computer-based systems for distributed music in contexts where the music requires great accuracy and reliability. A notation system like Comprovisador takes advantage of the timing accuracy of Max's scheduler and bach's CAC tools enabling distributed computing of real-time generated scores with great flexibility and scalability. An array of speakers will deliver the full range of audible frequencies with the dynamic range of an orchestra and unsurpassable timing precision. But these systems involve significant preparation time and/or logistic resources.

Hence, in situations where it is possible to adapt the music creation to the idiosyncrasies of a web-based system, it is possible to take advantage of its best features (notably, ease of deployment) and achieve aesthetically pleasing results.

The case study presented herein showed the usefulness of some of the features available in the bach library for achieving the desired results. On one hand, the new image-export feature allowed us to create a dynamic, nice-looking score on the browser using png files as discrete measures. On the other hand, the slot system present in the `bach.score` and `bach.roll` objects allowed integrated sequencing of parameter values and microtonal notation for our granular synth and respective Swarm Spatialiser. These latter tools were crucial in the accomplishment of the outlined compositional strategies.

Acknowledgments. I should like to thank my supervisors Christopher Bochmann and António de Sousa Dias for their advice and Sara Ross for proofreading. I would also like to thank Elsa Santos Mathei and all artists who made GarB'urlesco possible.

References

1. MaxScore. http://www.computermusicnotation.com/. hochschule für Musik und Theater Hamburg
2. p5.js. https://p5js.org. Processing Foundation
3. tone.js. https://tonejs.github.io
4. xebra.js (2018). https://cycling74.github.io/xebra.js/index.html. cycling74
5. The Guido project (2020). https://guidodoc.grame.fr/about/. grame-CNCM
6. Agostini, A., Ghisi, D.: A max library for musical notation and computer-aided composition. Comput. Music J. **39**(2), 11–27 (2015). https://doi.org/10.1162/COMJ_a_00296
7. Bell, J.: Audiovisual scores and parts synchronized over the web. In: Bhagwati, S., Bresson, J. (eds.) Proceedings of the International Conference on Technologies for Music Notation and Representation - TENOR 2018. Concordia University, Montreal, Canada, pp. 17–23 (2018). https://www.tenor-conference.org/proceedings.html
8. Clément, A.R., Ribeiro, F., Rodrigues, R., Penha, R.: Bridging the gap between performers and the audience using networked smartphones: the a.bel system. In: Proceedings of the International Conference on Live Interfaces, Brighton (2016). http://users.sussex.ac.uk/~thm21/ICLI_proceedings/2016/Papers/Short_Papers/127_Abel.pdf
9. Dannenberg, R.B.: Time-flow concepts and architectures for music and media synchronization. In: Proceedings of the 43rd International Computer Music Conference, Shanghai, pp. 104–109 (2017). https://www.cs.cmu.edu/~rbd/papers/timeflow2017.pdf
10. Freeman, J.: Flock (2007). http://distributedmusic.gatech.edu/flock/
11. Freeman, J.: Extreme sight-reading, mediated expression, and audience participation: real-time music notation in live performance. Comput. Music J. **32**(3), 25–41 (2008). http://www.jstor.org/stable/40072645
12. Ghisi, D., Agostini, A.: Extending bach: a family of libraries for real-time computer-assisted composition in max. J. New Music Res. **46**(1), 34–53 (2017). https://doi.org/10.1080/09298215.2016.1236823
13. Gottfried, R., Hajdu, G.: Drawsocket: a browser based system for networked score display. In: Hope, C., Vickery, L., Grant, N. (eds.) Proceedings of the International Conference on Technologies for Music Notation and Representation - TENOR 2019. Monash University, Melbourne, Australia, pp. 15–25 (2019). https://www.tenor-conference.org/proceedings.html
14. Hajdu, G., Gottfried, R.: Networked music performance in the old elbe tunnel. In: Hope, C., Vickery, L., Grant, N. (eds.) Proceedings of the International Conference on Technologies for Music Notation and Representation - TENOR 2019, Monash University, Melbourne, Australia, pp. 55–60 (2019). https://www.tenor-conference.org/proceedings.html
15. Holovaty, A., Richardson, C., O'Riordan, E.: Soundslice (2019). https://www.soundslice.com
16. Hope, C., Vickery, L., Wyatt, A., James, S.: The decibel scoreplayer - a digital tool for reading graphic notation. In: Battier, M., et al. (eds.) Proceedings of the First International Conference on Technologies for Music Notation and Representation - TENOR 2015, Paris, France, pp. 58–69 (2015). https://www.tenor-conference.org/proceedings.html

17. Lee, C.: Multimedia performance installation with virtual reality. In: Proceedings of the 43rd International Computer Music Conference, Shanghai, pp. 347–350 (2017). http://www.icmc2017.com/en/download.html
18. Louzeiro, P.: Mediating a comprovisation performance: the comprovisador's control interface. In: Proceedings of the 43rd International Computer Music Conference, Shanghai, pp. 362–367 (2017). http://www.icmc2017.com/en/download.html
19. Louzeiro, P.: Real-time compositional procedures for mediated soloist-ensemble interaction: the comprovisador. In: Agustín-Aquino, O.A., Lluis-Puebla, E., Montiel, M. (eds.) MCM 2017. LNCS (LNAI), vol. 10527, pp. 117–131. Springer, Cham (2017). https://doi.org/10.1007/978-3-319-71827-9_10
20. Louzeiro, P.: The comprovisador's real-time notation interface (extended version). In: Aramaki, M., Davies, M.E.P., Kronland-Martinet, R., Ystad, S. (eds.) CMMR 2017. LNCS, vol. 11265, pp. 489–508. Springer, Cham (2018). https://doi.org/10.1007/978-3-030-01692-0_33
21. Louzeiro, P.: Improving sight-reading skills through dynamic notation - the case of Comprovisador. In: Bhagwati, S., Bresson, J. (eds.) Proceedings of the International Conference on Technologies for Music Notation and Representation - TENOR 2018. Concordia University, Montreal, Canada, pp. 55–61 (2018). https://www.tenor-conference.org/proceedings.html
22. Louzeiro, P.: Distributed scores and audio on mobile devices in the music for a multidisciplinary performance. In: Proceedings of the 14th International Symposium on Computer Music Multidisciplinary Research, Marseille, pp. 401–412 (2019). https://cmmr2019.prism.cnrs.fr/downloads.html
23. Michon, R., Orlarey, Y., Letz, S., Fober, D., Dumitrascu, C.: Mobile music with the faust programming language. In: Proceedings of the 14th International Symposium on Computer Music Multidisciplinary Research, Marseille, pp. 371–382 (2019). https://cmmr2019.prism.cnrs.fr/downloads.html
24. Picking, R.: Reading music from screens vs paper. Behaviour & Information Technology 16(2), 72–78 (1997). https://doi.org/10.1080/014492997119914
25. Puckette, M., et al.: Max 7: documentation. https://docs.cycling74.com/max7/
26. Shafer, S.: VizScore: an on-screen notation delivery system for live performance. In: Proceedings of the International Computer Music Conference, Denton, TX, pp. 142–145 (2015). http://hdl.handle.net/2027/spo.bbp2372.2015.027
27. Wilson, C.: A tale of two clocks - scheduling web audio with precision (2013). https://www.html5rocks.com/en/tutorials/audio/scheduling/
28. Zagorac, S., Alessandrini, P.: ZScore: a distributed system for integrated mixed music composition and performance. In: Bhagwati, S., Bresson, J. (eds.) Proceedings of the International Conference on Technologies for Music Notation and Representation - TENOR 2018, Concordia University, Montreal, Canada, pp. 62–70 (2018). https://www.tenor-conference.org/proceedings.html

The BabelBox: An Embedded System for Score Distribution on Raspberry Pi with INScore, SmartVox and BabelScores

Jonathan Bell[1(✉)], Dominique Fober[2], Daniel Fígols-Cuevas[3], and Pedro Garcia-Velasquez[4]

[1] Aix Marseille Univ, CNRS, PRISM, Marseille, France
belljonathan50@gmail.com
[2] GRAME CNCM, Lyon, France
fober@grame.fr
[3] King's College London, London, England
daniel.figols-cuevas@kcl.ac.uk
[4] BabelScores, Paris, France
pgarcia@babelscores.com

Abstract. The slow but steady shift away from printed text into digital media has not yet modified the working habits of chamber music practitioners. If most instrumentalists still heavily rely on printed scores, audiences increasingly access notated music online, with printed scores synced to an audio recording on youtube for instance. This paper proposes to guide the listener and/or the performer with a cursor scrolling on the page with INScore, in order to examine the consequences of representing time in this way as opposed to traditional bars and beats notation. In addition to its *score following* interest for pedagogy and analysis, the networking possibilities of today's ubiquitous technologies reveal interesting potentials for works in which the presence of a conductor is required for synchronization between performers and/or with fixed media (film or tape). A *Raspberry Pi*-embedded prototype for animated/distributed notation is presented here as a *score player* (such as the *Decibel ScorePlayer*, or *SmartVox*), in order to send and synchronize mp4 scores to any browser capable device connected to the same WIFI network. The corpus will concern pieces edited at BabelScores, an online library for contemporary classical music. The BabelScores pdf works, composed in standard engraving softwares, will be animated using INScore and video editors, in order to find strategies for animation or dynamic display of the unfolding of time, originally represented statically on the page.

Keywords: Distributed scores · Animated notation · Music publishing · Embedded system · Networked music performance

Electronic supplementary material The online version of this chapter (https://doi.org/10.1007/978-3-030-70210-6_23) contains supplementary material, which is available to authorized users.

R. Kronland-Martinet et al. (Eds.): CMMR 2019, LNCS 12631, pp. 345–359, 2021.
https://doi.org/10.1007/978-3-030-70210-6_23

1 From Paper Towards Animated Notation: The Quantum Leap

A great majority of orchestral musicians today would still consider cumbersome the idea of replacing sheet music by screens. And yet, as early as 1999, thorough research had already been undertaken (see J. McPherson [21]) in a realm which is now identified as *animated notation* or *screen-scores*.[1] In his works and its surroundings [3], questions relative to scrolling vs turning pages, resolution and number of systems per pages, were addressed for the first time, and already gave substantial elements of response to issues which now concern most music theory educational games.

1.1 Where Gaming Meet Musical Notation

The representation of time in the age of *screen scores* opens a wide array of questions. Thinking of tablature[2] notation, if we understand scores as a set of prescribed actions to be performed in time, video games such as Guitar Hero or Beatmania will show that such new forms of music-making offer unprecedented control over the sequential realisation of rhythmic patterns. If, on the other hand, notation is defined as something to be interpreted, and performed on an acoustic instrument, perhaps these games will hardly be recognised as "musical" experiences by musicians.

Compared to traditional score written on paper or *Common Music Notation* (hereafter referred to as CMN), graphical notation scrolling on a screen offers a more mimetic (more direct, less codified) approach to music reading, which evokes video games in many ways. With the exception of the Decibel Score Player (see Mezareon for instance) or composers cited in the animatednotation.com website, this rather ludic or *gamified* approach to score reading has only gained visibility in education so far. In the pedagogical context indeed, recent applications such as Simply Piano take great advantage from their ability to validate/invalidate the performer's actions, again as a way to *gamify* apprenticeship of music reading. Unfortunately *Simply Piano* is an exception, and the general tendency in software development (as shown in the case of *Guitar Hero, Synthesia* or *Beatmania* for instance) is simply to bypass CMN altogether (both for in term of pitches and rhythm). Whilst some of this games might help developing music skills among amateur practitioners (such as those youtube videos tagged

[1] The term *screen-scores* is attributed to Lindsey Vickery and Cat Hope [17].

[2] Tablature, as opposed to common music notation, can be conceived as prescriptive notation, in the sense defined by Mieko Kanno: 'Prescriptive notation specifies the means of execution rather than the resultant configurations of pitch and rhythm' (Kanno, 2007, p.1). The distinction between prescriptive and descriptive notation (or common music) was already discussed in the fifties, as can attest the following statement by Charles Seeger: 'Prescriptive and descriptive uses of music writing, which is to say, between a blue-print of how a specific piece of music shall be made to sound and a report of how a specific performance of it actually did sound (...)' (Seeger, 1958, p. 1).

[Piano Tutorial] (Synthesia)), effort remains to be made in order to find bridges between those emerging amateur practices and the art of musical notation as it is used by contemporary classical composers and performers, both still active in concert halls and academia.

1.2 Animation in the Context of Distributed Musical Notation

Ryan Ross Smith's animatednotation.com website features many examples of composers elaborating scores taking advantage of the possibilities of screen scores. Most of these example rely on the projection on one single score projected on a screen visible to the audience and the performers. The networking capacities of today ubiquitous technologies would however easily allow each performer to receive only his own part of the score. Indeed, composers and researchers increasingly acknowledge the strong analogy which can be drawn between the traditional 'score and parts' musical practice led by a conductor, and the modern distributed systems or web applications (Zscore [26] - MASD [22] - SmartVox [5]), in which multiple clients coordinate their actions by passing messages to one another. Several attendees of the Tenor Conference[3] have proposed elements of response in an emerging realm which can be called "distributed musical notation". Some performance-oriented systems (INScore [11], SmartVox [5,6], Zscore [26], Decibel [16,18], MaxScore [15], Comprovisador [20]) endeavour to distribute and synchronise each part of the score on the performer's devices (whether Smartphones, tablets or laptops).

1.3 Animated Notation and the Composers of the New Complexity

Only a few composers of contemporary classical notated music feel the necessity to acknowledge this sudden growth of animated/distributed notation, since the software they use (Finale, Sibelius or pen and paper in great majority) are designed to render still images. Also these scores are dedicated to classically trained performers, all familiar with CMN and in great majority also aware of complex experimental forms of "static" notation. In academia, composers and music analysts are trained to read and follow these complex scores in which the notation is sometimes overloaded and detached from the acoustic result, as can be exemplified with the experimental music of the so called *new complexity*, with extremely complex rhythms (famously led by Brian Ferneyhough), or with some of its more recent (post-Lachenmanian) manifestations with large amounts of extended techniques and graphical notation.

The Score Follower project helps such composers getting their music heard and understood by simply synchronising a recording to each page of the score and share it on social media (youtube). To some unexperienced readers/listeners, the sound to sign relationship may still be difficult to follow which is one of the reasons why the cursor was introduced here. The representation of musical time in the examples below will propose an attempt of *hybridised* situations in which (often complex) contemporary classical scores take advantage of the possibilities

[3] http://www.tenor-conference.org/.

of animated notation (DENM being a major influence [2]). The case of *New Complexity* or post-Lachenman types of aesthetics will be of particular interest here (see Malaussena), as the proposed cursor solution may provide elements of response to composers whose rhythmic complexity seeks *rubato* in the first place. Indeed, beyond the exact realisation of nested tuplets, some of these composers seek in rhythmic complexity the absence of a clear sense of pulse and fluidity.

1.4 Scrolling Versus Beating Time

In the above-mentioned video games and musical examples, whether notation is scrolling from right to left (as in *Simple Piano* or *Decibel ScorePlayer*) or top to bottom (Guitar Hero - [Piano Tutorial] (Synthesia)), the basic principal relies on a continuous or scrolling movement (either of a cursor, or of the score itself) representing the passage of time. Cursors, as will be seen below, present great possibilities of synchronisation, in terms of *duration* rather than *rhythm*: when instruments need to synchronise with electronics or video for instance. In terms of pulse however, cursors remain quite approximate in comparison with the arm movement of a conductor dictating a beat. In none-pulsed music therefore, and in spite of the great conducting tradition in chamber music and orchestral works, such scrolling displays (as in the Decibel ScorePlayer or SmartVox) seem a far more straightforward strategy to obtain synchronisation in comparison to the bars and beats 'encoding' (quantified by the composer's choice of bars and beats) and decoding processes (a compromised interpretation by the instrumentalist, between the rhythmic values written on the page and the gestures of the conductor), inherited from a scoring tradition in which a regular meter was assumed.

We therefore propose here a solution for animation of pre-existing scores, with the help of a cursor scrolling on a static page. INScore [11] is in no small part designed for cursor animation, and will be of particular relevance to extend the practice of animated screen scores to a wider community of composers and performers, through BabelScores[4] in particular.

2 SmartVox, BabelScores, and INScore, An Introduction

BabelBox, the project envisaged here proposes a collaboration between two existing technologies (INScore and SmartVox) and BabelScores, a publishing company specialised in contemporary classical scores, which will now be presented.

2.1 SmartVox

SmartVox [5,6] is a distributed web application that delivers and synchronizes audiovisual scores in the video mp4 format to the performerbile devices,

[4] Babelscores (https://www.babelscores.com/) is an online score database for classical contemporary music, currently actively supporting the SmartVox project: http://1uh2.mj.am/nl2/1uh2/lgi4u.html.

in compositions involving up to 80 simultaneous performers such as in Le temps des Nuages. The ability to synchronise *screen scores* and *audio-scores* [4] through the browser of the performer's phones allows for various kinds of assistance, such as free movement on stage and around the audience, audio guide for singers, simplified synchronisation with tape and/or visuals... Recent developments include the use of head-mounted displays (HMDs) for technology-aided performance, as in the pieces In Memoriam Jean-Claude Risset I and Mit Allen Augen, In Memoriam J.C. Risset II (Fig. 1).[5]

Fig. 1. Singer wearing HMD for technology-aided performance.

SmartVox was developed in the *SoundWorks* framework.[6] *SoundWorks* provides a set of services – such as synchronization, network messages, distributed states, creation of groups of clients – that aims to solve problems common to distributed and synchronized web applications centered on multimedia rendering. The framework is written in Javascript, with a server side based on Node.js.[7] The SmartVox application consists of two web clients, the player and the conductor, that can be executed in any recent web browser on mobile devices (e.g. smartphones, tablets) and laptops. The real-time communication between clients is achieved through the WebSocket protocol[8] The application is typically deployed over a *local area network*, but it may also be used over the internet.[9]

2.2 The 'BabelBox', SmartVox Embedded on a Raspberry Pi

In search of a light plug-and-play dedicated system to be sent over the post, the Raspberry Pi quickly appeared as the best option to host SmartVox on an embedded system. Node.js runs on Raspbian, and SmartVox proved to be very stable on a Raspberry Pi 3, so, once installed, the only two steps for a *0-conf* deliverable hardware were:

[5] Those three pieces are respectively available at: https://youtu.be/SyFdR2HiF00, https://youtu.be/hQtyu1dcCaI, and https://youtu.be/ET_OBgFWx04.
[6] *SoundWorks* was initiated by the CoSiMa research project funded by the French National Research Agency (ANR) and coordinated by Ircam.
[7] https://nodejs.org/en.
[8] https://www.w3.org/TR/WebSockets/.
[9] https://youtu.be/83ub6-Q5oj0.

- Setting up a static address for a dedicated router (e.g. tp-link...).
- Starting SmartVox at boot using linuxstemdrvice.

Starting a script at boot can be done on Raspbian with a file containing the following in the etc./systemd/system:

```
[Unit]
Description=My service
[Service]
ExecStart=/home/pi/Desktop/hello.sh
[Install]
WantedBy=multi-user.target
```

With the hello.sh script containing the following to launch the server:

```
#!/bin/bash
cd /home/pi/Desktop/risset
npm run start
exec bash
```

This low-cost system (less than 65 €, for a Raspberry and a router) now allows the sending of ready-to-use scores. Once the system is power-supplied, all the performers need to do is to join the dedicated Wi-Fi, and type the static IP address of the server on their smartphone/tablet (i.e. for the performers: 192.168.0.100:8000, and for the conductor: 192.168.0.100:8000/conductor). In January 2019, the first system was rented to the Caen French conservatoire via BabelScores,[10]. Later, the system facilitated the performance of *Common*

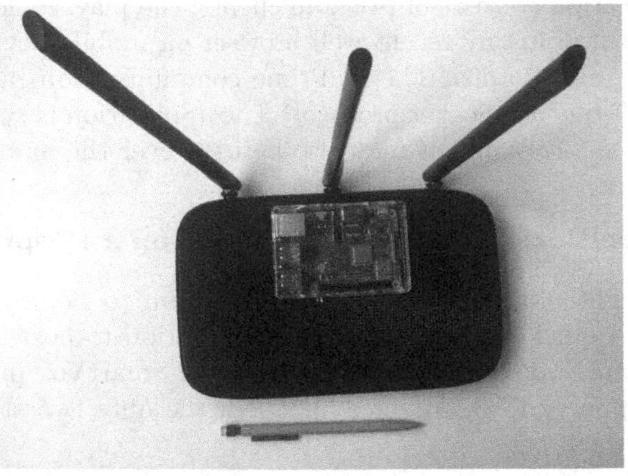

Fig. 2. BabelBox kit.

[10] Babelscores (https://www.babelscores.com/) currently supports actively supporting the SmartVox project: http://1uh2.mj.am/nl2/1uh2/lgi4u.html. The first piece performed in Caen with the Babelbox is available at the following address: https://youtu.be/wUyw0KQa5Wo.

Ground [7][11], a vocal whose performance would have been compromised otherwise: the show took place in Melbourne, without the presence of the composer, who sent the kit from Madrid (Fig. 2).

2.3 BabelScores

BabelScores is a France-based organization arising from the need to circulate and promote contemporary music from the last 50 years, rendering information more easily available to everyone worldwide. Through an international network, BabelScores looks into and selects the works of the most creative, original and innovative composers of the past few decades. BabelScores offers a wide and constantly growing catalogue, setting up a powerful circulation platform especially addressed to instrumentalists, ensembles, orchestras, composers, musicologists, conservatories, universities and festivals throughout the world. BabelScores offers the possibility to consult online all the material in its catalogue. Scores, which are the central element of BabelScores' material, may be consulted bookwise, turning pages, by means of a special reader which allows a comfortable and detailed reading (Fig. 3).

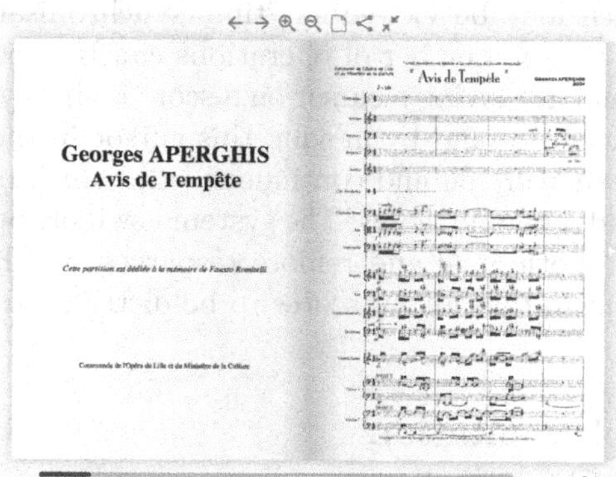

Fig. 3. BabelScore's virtual reader.

In the framework of its purpose to promote, excite, support and diffuse the written music creation in connection with web technologies, BabelScores cooperates with the world's leading universities, conservatoires, as well the Bibliothèque Nationale de France (BNF) in order to find and conjointly develop a robust, relevant and pragmatic way to handle music scores in this web and digital era, particularly their preservation and automatic (server-to-server) deposit to archive centres. BabelScores also works on the topic of native digital sketches, in order to asset which formats to use, how to transfer them and how to expose them in the most meaningful way in the BNF's collections once processed. BabelScores

[11] A recording is available here.

also collaborate with researchers and emerging projects such as SmartVox and INScore in order to support research applied to the domain of notation and web technologies. Based on current research in progress, BabelScores seeks partnerships in order to solve problems through pragmatic and large scale use of these techniques. The main vision BabelScores has is to create an interface between researchers, orchestras, creators, institutions and musicians that will allow these new usages to express their potential at their best.

2.4 INScore

INScore [9] is an environment for the design of augmented interactive music scores, opened to unconventional uses of music notation and representation, including real-time symbolic notation capabilities. It can be controlled in real-time using Open Sound Control [OSC] messages as well as using an OSC based scripting language, that allows designing scores in a modular and incremental way. INScore supports extended music scores, combining symbolic notation with arbitrary graphic objects. All the elements of a score (including purely graphical elements) have a temporal dimension (date, duration and tempo) and can be manipulated both in the graphic and time space. They can be synchronized in a master/slave relationship i.e. any object can be placed in the time space of another object, which may be viewed as "time synchronisation in the graphic space". As a result, a large number of operations can be performed in the time domain and in particular, moving a cursor on a score is simply achieved using the synchronization mechanism and by moving this cursor in the time space. Time in INScore is both event-driven and continuous [12], which makes it possible to design interactive and dynamic scores. The system is widely open to network uses [11]: it allows to use both local and remote resources (via HTTP), it provides a forwarding mechanism that allows scores to be distributed in real time over a local network.

3 Cursor Implementation

A cursor emphasizes the continuous unfolding of time while common practice musical notation implicitly relies on the rhythmic accents defined by bars and beats. The aim here is to find with INScore an efficient solution to incorporate animated cursors to a large number of pieces in the most automated and efficient possible way. Indeed, the *BabelBox* project consists in generalising to use of distributed notation and make it available to composers using those standard engraving softwares. From a given pdf score of the *BabelScores* corpus to its rendering on phone and tablet, one of the main issues will concern cursor implementation. Recent strategies for score distribution (such as pieces realised with the Decibel Score Player[12] or the quintet.net/drawsocket server) tend to let a score scroll over a fixed cursor. Whilst this solution remains envisageable, the BabelBox realisations achieved so far tend to use a moving cursor over fixed images, with page turns.

[12] See for instance The Dying Pillow by Cat Hope.

3.1 Cursors with INScore

Space Time Mapping: INScore has built-in solutions for monitoring the position and the speed of cursors in an efficient way. Since common practice notation is rarely proportional (i.e. a 4/4 is not necessarily twice longer on the page than a 2/4 bar), a cursor moving at constant speed across a whole system will never accurately fall at each bar accurately according to musical time. To tackle this issue, INScore provides a mechanism to describe the relationship between the graphic and the time space in the form of "mappings" which are actually a relation (in the mathematical sense) between a set of graphic segments and a set of temporal segments. A graphic segment is described with two intervals: the first one on the x-axis, and the second one on the y-axis. With images, these intervals are expressed in pixel positions. A time segment is an interval expressed by rationals that represent dates in musical time (where 1 is a whole note). INScore mappings describe arbitrary relationships between time and any graphical resource. It is mainly used to solve the problem of non-proportionality of symbolic musical notation (see for example in Fig. 4 and Fig. 5).

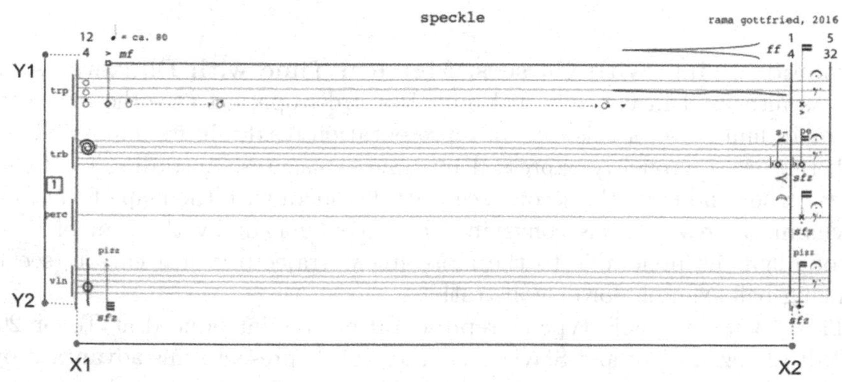

Fig. 4. One bar's coordinates expressed in pixel coordinates

These two segments (X1 – X2 and Y1 – Y2, see Fig. 4) define a rectangle corresponding to one bar in the score. The pixel coordinates of this rectangle are then attached to the duration of the bar, expressed in regular time signatures, with the following syntax: *([one graphical segment on x axis [[one graphical segment on y axis[) ([one temporal segment[).*

```
([144, 623[ [227, 745[) ([0/4, 1/4[)
# x1    x2    y1    y2      t1    t2
([635, 1203[ [705, 744[) ([1/4, 2/4[)
# x2+1  x3    y1    y2      t2    t3
```

The same procedure is then repeated with each bar (see Fig. 5). A specific INScore script allows you to draw mappings directly on the page and to retrieve

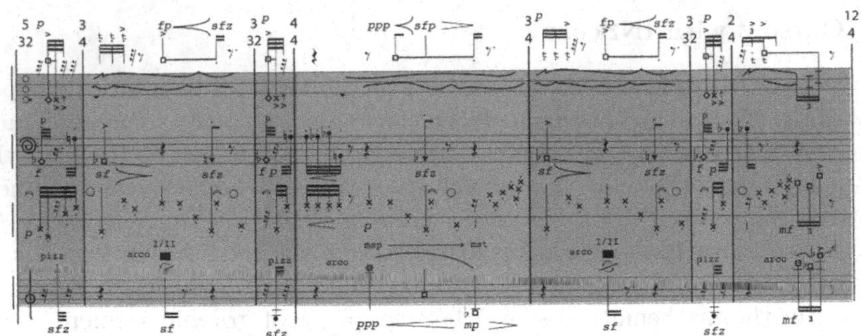

Fig. 5. Rectangles monitoring the position of the cursor: Time and space relationship is linear inside a box.

them in a "nearly ready to use" form, with default time intervals that need to be specified.[13] This type of cursor seems to facilitate video part extraction by simply cropping the section of the screen corresponding to one particular instrument.[14]

Continuous Time with Cursors, Metrical Time with Blinkers: A cursor was also used in extracts of Emily Howard's opera To see the invisible[15]. The main limitation of this type of representation resides in its impossibility to mark the beats implicitly expressed by time signatures. According to Richard Baker - who conducted the second scene of the opera with the help of *SmartVox* -, dynamic representations conveying the accent meant by the arm of a conductor might be preferable to the more linear trajectory of a cursor (see the bouncing ball example for demonstration).

This "Bouncing ball" type of representation was introduced at Tenor 2018 by Pedro Louzeiro [20] and Slavko Zagorac [26]. It presents this advantage over cursors mark upbeats and downbeats, like the arm of a conductor, but one may argue that this form of representation might be disturbing for the eye.

Kocher (see [19] Sect. 2.1: "The Virtual Conductor"), in a similar way, uses two animated bars located on the left and top edges of the screen.

Another strategy for marking the bar's beats more clearly might be to make a static cursor blink on each beat, with different colour for upbeat and downbeat (see examples realised with INScore on compositions by Lemme-Icône-Epigramme/Brian Ferneyhough and Aeon/Daniel Fígols).

---

[13] The corresponding tools are available at the following address: https://github.com/grame-cncm/inscore/tree/dev/scripts/Tools/drawmap.

[14] See Figols - Fullscore for demonstration, together with the corresponding separate part here).

[15] https://snapemaltings.co.uk/concerts-history/aldeburgh-festival-2018/to-see-the-invisible/.

3.2 Cursors Without INScore: Standard Engraving Softwares, *bach*, and *ianalyse*

A great majority of the pieces performed with SmartVox were composed in *bach* [1], a realtime computer-aided composition package for Max/MSP. This environment inherits lots of its functionalities from *Open Music*, and therefore remains grounded in computer-aided composition rather than score engraving. Objects like *bach.roll* or *bach.score* are well-suited to animation and provide built-in cursor support, but they cannot compete (graphically) with the engraving capacities of dedicated softwares like Finale or Sibelius.

Latest versions of Sibelius (7.5 and 8.0) offer the possibility of exporting a video of the score with a cursor following the beats with the metronomic parameters marked in the score. This possibility could facilitate the creation of the video material needed for the *BabelBox*. However, the procedure demands a well configured MIDI encoding of the tempo - including tempo changes - in the original file in order not to miss the synchronisation between the notated score and the sound recording. Finale and Sibelius offer advanced MIDI controls that will have to be taken into account necessarily if this procedure is taken.

Finally, Pierre Couprie's *ianalyse* software[16] also provides a useful set of tools for cursor implementation.

3.3 Page Turn and Animated Notation, An Example with *bach* and *bell*

bach now implements a small domain specific language entitled *bell* (short for bach evaluation language for llll) [13]. It allows to code expressions (in a similar way as the Max"expr" object, inside a *bach.eval* object), which would otherwise be cumbersome to write in Max/MSP boxes. This language was used in our case to built an automatic cueing system for singers (see [7], Chap. 3.4.4), and also proved to be useful to automatise the visual layout and page turns of scores realised in *bach.roll*. In the piece *Deliciae*[17], the singers received audiovisual score (such as, for instance, soprano 1) whose page turns required special attention. since the standard behaviour of *bach.roll* doesn't allow the singer to foresee his/her next phrase, two *bach.roll* objects reading the same score were used here. The first object (called "play bach.roll") is the only one really playing with a scrolling cursor, and the second one (called "preview bach.roll') is only displaying what comes next. In order to avoid page turns in the middle of a phrase, we collected a list of onsets slicing the *bach.roll* at strategic moments (see Fig. 6 at the top, with time expressed in milliseconds, 1st onset = 0, 2nd onset = 29.5 s, 3rd onset = 42.9 s etc.). *bach.eval* is then used to generate 'addmarker' message (see Fig. 6 at the bottom), in order to determine the domain to be displayed during playback: in this example, at 39.5 s, a marker will command the "play bach.roll" to display the score between 39.4 s and 42.9 s. At the same

[16] https://logiciels.pierrecoupri.e.fr/.

[17] A video of the performance is available here.

time, the marker will command the "preview bach.roll" to display what comes next (between 42.9 s and 48.5 s). In the *bach.eval* box (i.e. in *bell*) $x1 and $x2 correspond to the left and right inlets of the object. The message is output when an integer hits the left inlet (here the integer's value is "3"). The object looks up in the list ($x2), and takes the third element ($x2:$x1 = $x2:3 = 39487). Each time the cursor hits a marker, the position of the "play bach.roll" and "preview bach.roll" switch up and down, thus giving the impression of a cursor moving up and down in alternation between the upper and lower system(such as in the soprano 1 part.)

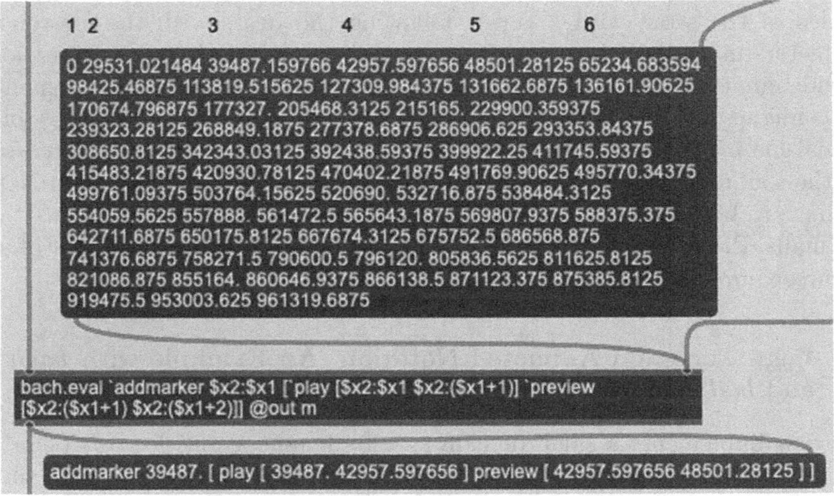

Fig. 6. One bar's coordinates expressed in pixel coordinates

4 Conclusion

This paper presents the early stages of a research project which could help musicians access distributed/animated notation easily[18]. Indeed for pieces for chamber groups with electronics or video for instance, synchronisation through the browser of the performer's phone/tablet/computer seem a costless and promising way of making music. Solutions such as the BabelBox however, - local NPMs - only constitute a temporary solution if we acknowledge the exponential growth of the internet. In a few years' time, simple urls such as www.smartvox.eu should be sufficiently robust to let performers access the same piece via different terminals and through the internet directly, even in concert situations.[19]

[18] BabelScores now has partnerships with the world's most prestigious universities, see: https://www.babelscores.com/partners.

[19] Rather than a static address (such as http://37.59.101.205:8000/), a bootstrap or a web-application may be more appropriate here.

INScore allows for the precise temporal control of animated cursors in the graphical domain. Thanks to its OSC support, it is possible to control the cursor's position via automations in Ableton Live.[20] This setup suits particularly well sound-to-visual synchronisation as in Julien Malaussena's piece, in which the cursor follows the audio recording. This methods however needs to be compared to the different tools and approaches exposed in Sect. 3, which might allow for faster results.

Once these practical problems elucidated, a more definitive solution for score elaboration workflow will be defined. Figure 6 presents its current state (Fig. 7).

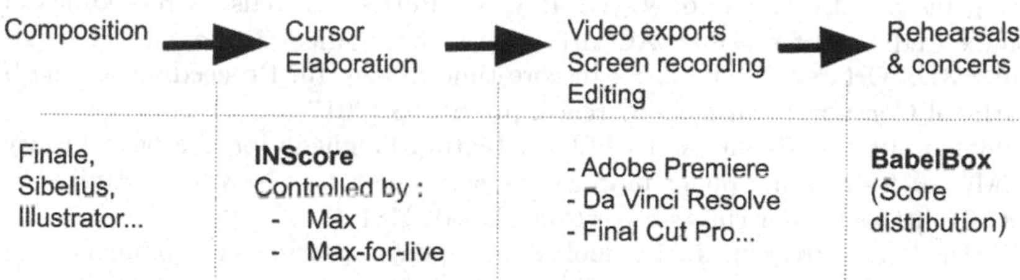

Fig. 7. Score elaboration workflow.

References

1. Agostini, A., Ghisi, D.: BACH: an environment for computer-aided composition in Max. In: Proceedings of the 38th International Computer Music Conference (ICMC), Ljubljana, Slovenia (2012)
2. Bean, J.: DENM (dynamic environmental notation for music): introducing a performance-centric musical interface. In: Proceedings of the First International Conference on Technologies for Music Notation and Representation (TENOR), Ann Paris, France (2015)
3. Bell, T. C., Church, A., McPherson, J., Bainbridge, D.: Page turning and image size in a digital music stand. In: Proceedings of the International Computer Music Conference, Barcelona, Spain (2005)
4. Bell, J. Audio-scores, a resource for composition and computer-aided performance, Ph.D. dissertation, Guildhall School of Music and Drama (2016). http://openaccess.city.ac.uk/17285/
5. Bell, J., Matuszewski, B.: SmartVox. a web-based distributed media player as notation tool for choral practices. In: Proceedings of the 3rd International Conference on Technologies for Music Notation and Representation (TENOR). Universidade da Coruña, Coruña, Spain (2017)
6. Bell, J.: Audiovisual scores and parts synchronized over the web. In: TENOR 2018, Montreal, France (2018). https://hal.archives-ouvertes.fr/hal-01779806
7. Bell, J., Wyatt, A.: Common ground, music and movement directed by a Raspberry PI. In: TENOR 2020, Montreal, France, 2018. Tenor, Hambourg (2020). https://hal.archives-ouvertes.fr/hal-02774082/document

[20] Via Max-for-Live, see https://youtu.be/rLy8DW_p2JE for demonstration.

8. Bresson, J., Agon, C., Assayag, G.: OpenMusic - visual programming environment for music composition, analysis and research. In: ACM MultiMedia (MM 2011), Scottsdale, United States (2011). https://hal.archives-ouvertes.fr/hal-01182394
9. Fober, D., Orlarey, Y., Letz, S.: INScore - an environment for the design of live music scores. In: Proceedings of the Linux Audio Conference - LAC 2012, pp. 47–54 (2012). INScore-ID12-2.pdf
10. Fober, D., Gouilloux, G., Orlarey, Y., Letz, S.: Distributing music scores to mobile platforms and to the internet using INScore. In: Proceedings of the Sound and Music Computing conference – SMC 2015, pp. 229–233 (2015). inscore-web-SMC15.pdf
11. Fober, D., Orlarey, Y., Letz, S.: Towards dynamic and animated music notation using inscore. In: Ciciliato, V., Orlarey, Y., Pottier, L. (eds.) Proceedings of the Linux Audio Conference – LAC 2017, pp. 43–51, Saint-Etienne. CIEREC (2017)
12. Fober, D., Orlarey, Y., Letz, S.: Inscore time model. In: Proceedings of the International Computer Music Conference, pp. 64–68 (2017)
13. Giavitto, J.L., Agostini, A. Bell, J.: A textual language for the bach library. In: ICMC 2019 - International Computer Music Conference, New York, United States (2019). https://hal.archives-ouvertes.fr/hal-02348176
14. Gottfried, R., Bresson, J.: Symbolist: an open authoring environment for user-defined symbolic notation. In: Proceedings of the International Conference on Technologies for Music Notation and Representation - TENOR 2018, Bhagwati, S., Bresson, J. (eds.) Concordia University, Montreal, Canada, pp. 111–118 (2018)
15. Hajdu, G., Didkovsky, N.: MaxScore: recent developments. In: Proceedings of the International Conference on Technologies for Music Notation and Representation - TENOR 2018, Bhagwati, S., Bresson, J. (eds.) Concordia University, Montreal, Canada, pp. 138–146 (2018)
16. Hope, C., Vickery, L., Wyatt, A., James, S.: The DECIBEL Scoreplayer - a digital tool for reading graphic notation. In: Proceedings of the First International Conference on Technologies for Music Notation and Representation - TENOR 2015, Battier, M., Bresson, J., et al. (eds.) Paris, France, pp. 58–69 (2015)
17. Hope, C.: Electronic scores for music: the possibilities of animated notation. Comput. Music J. **41**(3), 21–35 (2017)
18. Hope, C. Wyatt, A., Thorpe, D.: Scoring an animated notation opera - the decibel score player and the role of the digital copyist in 'Speechless'. In: Proceedings of the International Conference on Technologies for Music Notation and Representation - TENOR 2018, Bhagwati, S., Bresson, J. (eds.) Concordia University, Montreal, Canada, pp. 193–200 (2018)
19. Kocher, P.: Polytempo network: a system for technology-assisted conducting. In: Proceedings of the 3rd International Conference on Sound and Music Computing (SMC), Athens, Greece (2014)
20. Louzeiro, P.: Improving sight-reading skills through dynamic notation - the case of comprovisador. In: Proceedings of the International Conference on Technologies for Music Notation and Representation - TENOR 2018, Bhagwati, S., Bresson, J. (eds.) Concordia University, Montreal, Canada, pp. 55–61 (2018)
21. McPherson, J.: Turning-score automation for musicians. Honours report, University of Canterbury, New Zealand (1999)
22. Nathan Magnus, D.G.: Musician assistance and score distribution (MASD). In: Proceedings of The International Conference on New Interfaces for Musical Expression - NIME 2012. University of Michigan, Ann Arbor (2012)
23. Rottondi, C., Chafe, C., Allocchio, C., Sarti, A.: An overview on networked music performance technologies. IEEE Access **4**, 8823–8843 (2016)

24. Schnell, N., Robaszkiewicz, S.: Soundworks - a playground for artists and developers to create collaborative mobile web performances. In: Proceedings of the first Web Audio Conference (WAC), Paris, France (2015)
25. Vickery, L.: Hybrid real/mimetic sound works. In: Proceedings of the International Conference on Technologies for Music Notation and Representation - TENOR 2016, Hoadley, R., Nash, C., Fober, D. (eds.) Anglia Ruskin University, Cambridge, UK, pp. 19–24 (2016)
26. Zagorac, S., Alessandrini, P.: ZScore: a distributed system for integrated mixed music composition and performance. In: Proceedings of the International Conference on Technologies for Music Notation and Representation - TENOR 2018, Bhagwati, S., Bresson, J. (eds.) Concordia University, Montreal, Canada, pp. 62–70 (2018)
27. Vickery, L.: Some approaches to representing sound with colour and shape. In: Proceedings of the International Conference on Technologies for Music Notation and Representation - TENOR 2018, Bhagwati, S., Bresson, J. (eds.) Concordia University, Montreal, Canada, pp. 165–173 (2018)

Auditory Perception and Cognition - From the Ear to the Body

Modeling Human Experts' Identification of Orchestral Blends Using Symbolic Information

Aurélien Antoine(✉), Philippe Depalle, Philippe Macnab-Séguin, and Stephen McAdams

Schulich School of Music, McGill University, Montreal, QC, Canada
{aurelien.antoine,philippe.depalle,stephen.mcadams}@mcgill.ca
philippe.macnab-seguin@mail.mcgill.ca

Abstract. Orchestral blend happens when sounds coming from two or more instruments are perceived as a single sonic stream. Several studies have suggested that different musical properties contribute to create such an effect. We developed models to identify orchestral blend effects from symbolic information taken from scores based on calculations related to three musical parameters, namely onset synchrony, pitch harmonicity, and parallelism in pitch and dynamics. In order to evaluate the performance of the models, we applied them to different orchestral pieces and compared the outputs with human experts' ratings available in the Orchestration Analysis and Research Database (Orchard). Using different thresholds for the three parameters under consideration, the models were able to successfully retrieve 81% of the instruments involved in an orchestral blend on average. These results suggest that symbolic representation of music conveys perceptual information. However, further developments including audio analyses to take into account timbral properties could alleviate some of the current limitations.

Keywords: Orchestral blend · Computer modeling · Perception · Music information retrieval

1 Introduction

Orchestration offers myriad possibilities to combine instruments and create potential sonic effects that could not necessarily be achievable with a smaller ensemble. This musical practice is a challenging subject that is being investigated from a wide range of research perspectives. The aim of our project is to explore perceptual effects of orchestration in order to understand which are the prominent characteristics. It has been suggested that different perceptual effects can emerge from the combinations of instrumental properties, such as the blending or separation of musical instrument sounds to name but two [5]. The fusion of two or more instruments results in a blend effect in which the

R. Kronland-Martinet et al. (Eds.): CMMR 2019, LNCS 12631, pp. 363–378, 2021.
https://doi.org/10.1007/978-3-030-70210-6_24

sounds are perceived as belonging to a single musical event [14,15], whereas segregation happens when there is a clear separation between different concurrent sound events [10,11]. This paper focuses on the factors affecting orchestral blend and introduces our approach for developing computer models capable of identifying groups of instruments involved in blend effects. Previous research has proposed computational models of auditory scene analysis [16] but not specifically for instrument blend effects in a musical context. Our aim is to investigate the extent to which the blend effects could be modeled using only symbolic information in order to formalize the processes involved, which would then be utilized for comparisons between computational outputs and data from perceptual experiments. Such developments could be incorporated into systems designed to perform orchestration analysis from machine-readable musical scores and also in computer-aided orchestration systems.

The remainder of this paper is organized as follows. First, we introduce the different characteristics that contribute to the creation of orchestral blends and define the properties that have been utilized in our models. Section 3 provides technical details of the implementation of the orchestral blend models. Then, we apply the models to a selection of orchestral pieces and compare the outputs with human experts' ratings in order to assess the performance of the models. The results of these analyses are then discussed in Sect. 5. Finally, the last section presents concluding remarks and suggests different ideas to enrich the current models.

2 Orchestral Blend

As mentioned in the previous section, orchestral blend is the perception of different sounds as being grouped into a single event. This perceptual effect is the result of the fusion of instruments properties, an important aspect in orchestration [2]. Several treatises on orchestration have discussed blending techniques and have suggested methods for combining instruments to create this effect [1,12,13], which can be a punctual event or happen over several measures. Such techniques can be utilized for enriching the quality of a dominating instrument by adding other instruments or for completely fusing instrument sounds to create a unique mixture with a new, emerging timbre [12,13,15]. These treatises usually offer guidance for selecting instruments that are most likely to result orchestral blends when combined. For example, Rimsky-Korsakov suggests that woodwind and string instruments tend to blend well [13].

Blend has also been investigated within perception and cognition research. It has been suggested that different acoustical properties play an important role in grouping musical events into a single stream. Following Gestalt principles, sounds evolving similarly are more likely to be grouped together [3]. For instance, onset synchrony, harmonicity, and similar changes in frequency and amplitude across successive sounds might lead the auditory system to group sound components together [6,9]. Moreover, two or more instruments with a low overall spectral centroid and with close centroids tend to blend better. Characteristics related to the musicians' performance nuances, the spatial position of the instruments, and the room acoustics also contribute to blend effects [7,8]. In regards to musical properties linked to studies in auditory perception and cognition, having instruments playing in a harmonic series, in synchrony, and with perfect parallelism in pitch and dynamics often leads to a blend. An example of a blend effect is shown in Fig. 1, in which oboes 1 and 2 in major thirds and clarinets 1 and 2 in major thirds an octave below the oboes play together in harmonic relations (roughly harmonics 4, 5, 8, 10), in synchrony, and with perfect parallelism in pitch and dynamics. Figure 2 shows another blend example, in which two flutes, two clarinets, and two bassoons are playing together, with two oboes coming in and out throughout the phrase.

Given that we are processing only symbolic information, we have disregarded spectral properties and information related to performance, spatial position, and room acoustics for the first phase of this project. Instead, we have decided to process musical properties that can be estimated from a musical score. Therefore, for our models, we have estimated the onset synchrony, pitch harmonicity, and parallelism in pitch and dynamics between instruments, recognizing that timbral aspects derivable from the audio signal often also play a role.

3 Score-Based Modeling of Orchestral Blend

This project aims to model human experts' identification of orchestral blends using symbolic information. Thus, the initial stage is to define methods to retrieve the musical information from computer-readable scores before developing models for estimating orchestral blend.

3.1 Retrieving Symbolic Score Information

For computer-readable scores, we selected MusicXML, a format based on the markup language XML, which is used to represent Western musical notation and provides more comprehensive musical information than other formats, such as MIDI. We used `MusicXML 3.1`[1] to encode the symbolic score information. Several databases offer orchestral pieces encoded in this format. However, in order to minimize missing information or errors and variations in the output of different notation software platforms, we decided to use MusicXML files created by the company OrchPlayMusic (OPM)[2], which are exported with individual staves for each instrument (e.g., first and second flutes). They have also developed a specific mapping for extensive information related to percussive instruments, in particular for pitched percussion in the current research, which is not necessarily present in standard MusicXML files or in other formats. OPM proposes high-quality simulations of orchestral pieces and musical scores exported as MusicXML files, along with a multichannel audio player especially designed

[1] www.w3.org/2017/12/musicxml31/.
[2] www.orchplaymusic.com.

Fig. 1. Example of a blend between two oboes and two clarinets (annotated with a red box) in Mozart, Don Giovanni, mm. 62–66. (Color figure online)

for orchestral music. While this currently limits us to the content available in the OPM library, it allows us to have consistent and validated machine-readable scores along with their audio renderings for immediate listening purposes and for additional developments in audio analysis that are beyond the scope of the present paper.

In order to retrieve the specific musical information required for estimating the characteristics involved in a blend effect, we process MusicXML files within `Python 3.7`, using the `xml.etree.ElementTree`[3] module for parsing and creating XML data. It allows us to retrieve information from the MusicXML files,

[3] https://docs.python.org/3/library/xml.etree.elementtree.html.

Fig. 2. Example of a blend between two flutes, two oboes, two clarinets, and two bassoons (annotated with a red box) in Mozart, Don Giovanni, mm. 223–227. (Color figure online)

which are parsed into three objects, following a macro- to micro-events approach. The first one contains metadata related to the orchestral piece such as the composer's name and the title and movement name of the piece, but also the list of instruments, the total number and list of measures in the excerpt, and information about the tempo. Then, we have an object with information about the instruments. For each instrument, we assign its name, along with its section and instrument family, key, clef, whether it is a transposing instrument, list of notes and dynamics. The last object is related to a note event, which contains its pitch, octave, note (combination of pitch and octave), duration (both as MusicXML duration value and as duration in milliseconds), type of note (as rhythmic symbol such as eighth note), its moment of onset within the measure (both as in MusicXML duration value and converted to milliseconds), the instrument name the event is attached to, whether it is part of a chord, and whether it is tied or not. These objects can then be manipulated and processed by our models to estimate potential orchestral blends, as detailed in the following section.

3.2 Estimating Orchestral Blend

The process for estimating orchestral blend from computer-readable scores is divided into different steps. First, we had to define the segmentation of the musical pieces. We decided to perform the analysis on a measure-by-measure basis, as orchestral effects most often occur over the course of at least a measure. The rationale is that performing the calculations on a shorter frame (i.e., note by note) would result in a significant increase in the amount of information to compute and compare. It would also prevent the temporal properties, such as parallelism, from being observed. A longer analysis frame could overlook effects occurring in a single measure. Thus, a measure worth of information appeared to be an appropriate analysis time frame to start with.

The estimations of orchestral blend are computed in three steps: first the onset synchrony, then the pitch harmonicity, and finally comparing the parallelism in pitch and dynamics. Figure 3 presents a diagram of the different processes for estimating orchestral blend, which are detailed below.

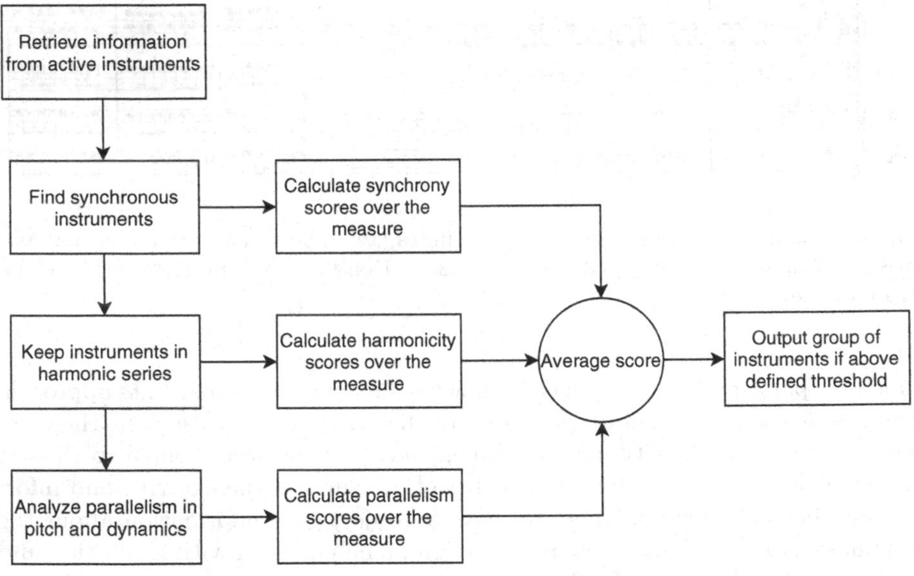

Fig. 3. Synopsis of the orchestral blend estimation algorithm.

Onset Synchrony. The first step is to list all the onset values for each active instrument in the measure. MusicXML's note duration being represented as divisions per quarter note, it is necessary to convert the symbolic duration into time, defined in milliseconds using tempo values and note types (e.g., eighth, quarter, half note). It is then possible to calculate the onset value for each note. Furthermore, using duration in milliseconds allows us to specify a threshold for considering notes being synchronized. We set the default threshold at 30 ms, following suggestions by research on attack time [4]. Thus, notes are considered synchronized if their onset values fall within a 30-ms window. Then, the instruments sharing the most onset values are grouped together. Finally, the synchrony score is calculated with the cardinality of the intersection of the different sets of onset values. The groups of synchronous instruments are then passed to the function for pitch harmonicity calculations. Also, if there is no group of synchronous instruments, the algorithm bypasses the other functions and moves to the next measure.

Pitch Harmonicity. In the second step, this function takes as input the groups of synchronous instruments. For each onset value, the function retrieves the pitch for each active instrument and calculates the interval in semitones between the different pitches. It determines whether they are in a harmonic series, using the lowest pitch as the root. If the instruments are not all in a harmonic series, the function lists all the different instrument pitches and checks if a tonal chord is involved, following a framework of standard Western musical chords. This characteristic is often present in a punctuated blend involving a large number of instruments. If no harmonic chord is found, it keeps the largest list of instrument pitches that are in a harmonic series, similar to applying a harmonic template. This step also removes instruments that share onset values but are not in the harmonic series and potentially not involved in the blend. Once the intervals for all the onset values are analyzed, the function returns a harmonicity score for the instruments that are either playing in a harmonic series or forming a tonal chord.

Parallelism in Pitch and Dynamics. The final step looks at the evolution of the pitches and the dynamics over the course of a measure. The function estimates whether the different instruments are playing in parallel. For each instrument, it lists the note sequence by examining if the next note is higher (+1), lower (−1), or the same (0) in pitch as the initial note of the measure, which is set to 0. Then, it compares each element of the different lists of note sequences and adds 1 if for each note they all have the same value (i.e. +1, −1 or 0) and 0 if at least one is different. The resulting score is then divided by the number of elements in the list, giving us a proportion that is then used for the parallelism score. A similar procedure is applied for the dynamics, where the function examines whether the instrument is playing the notes harder, softer, or at the same dynamic, and then calculates the parallelism.

Output Decision. Once the three properties have been calculated, their corresponding scores are averaged and compared to a defined threshold. If the average score is above the threshold, the group is output as a potential blend. If it is below, the group is ignored and the next group is tested or the program moves to the next measure if there is no other group of instruments to analyze. A threshold defined as 100 would mean that all the instruments in the group would have perfect synchrony, harmonicity, and parallelism in pitch and dynamics. Lowering the output threshold would allow for more flexibility in the calculations of the musical characteristics and would tolerate deviations from the theoretical rules. This would also account for the different strengths of the blend effect. Furthermore, the properties are set as having the same weights in the calculations. For instance, synchrony is as important as parallelism and harmonicity.

For each measure, the algorithm lists the group(s) of blended instruments with their scores, if a blend has been detected. Nevertheless, orchestral effects can happen over several measures. Thus, we also apply a post-blend analysis function in order to find groups of blended instruments that span consecutive measures. It compares the list of instruments in two neighboring measures and groups them if all the instruments are in both measures. The grouping continues until the instruments are not present in the next measure. The blend is then listed as happening from measure a to measure b, with the names of the instruments involved in the effect. Using the example shown in Fig. 1, the blend occurs from measures 62 to 66, with oboes 1 and 2 and clarinets 1 and 2 playing in every measure and returned as blending instruments. Here, the model would return the group of instruments (oboe 1–2 and clarinet 1–2) and specifies that the effect starts at measure 62 and finishes at measure 66.

4 Comparison Between Score-Based Models and Human Experts' Identification

In order to test and evaluate the performance of the score-based modeling of orchestral blend, we decided to apply the models to orchestral excerpts and compare the output with blends that have been previously identified by human experts. This section details the evaluation corpus that has been used along with the results of the evaluations. The list of excerpts processed and the approaches to compare the model's output with labeled examples to provide an accuracy score are described.

4.1 Evaluation Corpus

To evaluate the performances of the models, we used data available in the Orchestration Analysis and Research Database (Orchard)[4], which contains numerous annotations of orchestral effects derived from the analysis of several orchestral pieces, with the majority spanning the period from 1787 to 1943. These pieces have been analyzed and annotated by musical experts who had access to musical scores and professional audio recordings. Our evaluation corpus was limited to excerpts available in both the OPM library and the Orchard database. This resulted in using 32 orchestral excerpts, which represented 229 labeled blends across all pieces, with a total of 1032 measures having a blend effect. A list of orchestral excerpts used in this evaluation corpus can be found in Table 3.

[4] https://orchard.actor-project.org.

Table 1. Blend-detection score using an output decision threshold set at 100 for a blend in Mozart, Don Giovanni, mm. 62–66, shown in Fig. 1.

Measure number	Human experts	Model	Score (ratio)
62	Oboe 1, Oboe 2, Clarinet 1, Clarinet 2	Oboe 1, Oboe 2, Clarinet 1, Clarinet 2	1.0
63	Oboe 1, Oboe 2, Clarinet 1, Clarinet 2	Oboe 1, Oboe 2, Clarinet 1, Clarinet 2	1.0
64	Oboe 1, Oboe 2, Clarinet 1, Clarinet 2	Oboe 1, Oboe 2, Clarinet 1, Clarinet 2	1.0
65	Oboe 1, Oboe 2, Clarinet 1, Clarinet 2	Oboe 1, Oboe 2, Clarinet 1, Clarinet 2	1.0
66	Oboe 1, Oboe 2, Clarinet 1, Clarinet 2	Oboe 1, Oboe 2, Clarinet 1, Clarinet 2	1.0

4.2 Evaluation Metrics

As detailed in Sect. 3.2, the blend estimations are executed on a measure-by-measure basis. Therefore, we performed the comparison between human expert annotations and model outputs similarly. The aim is to determine whether the model can retrieve the same instruments as those identified by experts as creating an orchestral blend. For example, Table 1 details the results of the comparison for a blend identified in the Overture to Mozart's Don Giovanni (shown in Fig. 1). Here, using an output decision threshold set at 100, the model has output the same group of instruments (oboe 1–2 and clarinet 1–2) as the human experts for the five measures, obtaining a score of 1.0 (4/4 instruments) for each measure. Table 2 details the results for the blend shown in Fig. 2, also taken from Don Giovanni. Here, the output decision threshold was set at 80. Note that the model has output the same instruments as the ones labeled by the experts for measure 223 (i.e., flute 1–2, clarinet 1–2, and bassoon 1–2), resulting in a score of 1.0. However, for the measures 224 to 227, the model missed the oboe 1–2, thus, obtaining a proportional score of 0.75 (6/8 instruments). This process was applied to the 229 labeled blends from the 32 orchestral excerpts withing our evaluation corpus.

4.3 Results

We performed the comparison between human expert annotations and model outputs on a measure-by-measure basis in order to evaluate whether the model retrieved the same instruments identified by the experts using the 32 orchestral excerpts for the evaluation corpus. However, we evaluated the model output using two ways to consider the orchestral blend examples. The initial approach considers each blend as one entity, regardless of the number of measures that composes it. Therefore, 229 blends labeled by experts were used to evaluate the model outputs. We evaluated three different output decision threshold values

Table 2. Blend-detection score using an output decision threshold set at 80 for a blend in Mozart, Don Giovanni, mm. 223–227, shown in Fig. 2.

Measure number	Human experts	Model	Score (ratio)
223	Flute 1, Flute 2, Clarinet 1, Clarinet 2, Bassoon 1, Bassoon 2	Flute 1, Flute 2, Clarinet 1, Clarinet 2, Bassoon 1, Bassoon 2	1.0
224	Flute 1, Flute 2, Oboe 1, Oboe 2, Clarinet 1, Clarinet 2, Bassoon 1, Bassoon 2	Flute 1, Flute 2, Clarinet 1, Clarinet 2, Bassoon 1, Bassoon 2	0.75
225	Flute 1, Flute 2, Oboe 1, Oboe 2, Clarinet 1, Clarinet 2, Bassoon 1, Bassoon 2	Flute 1, Flute 2, Clarinet 1, Clarinet 2, Bassoon 1, Bassoon 2	0.75
226	Flute 1, Flute 2, Oboe 1, Oboe 2, Clarinet 1, Clarinet 2, Bassoon 1, Bassoon 2	Flute 1, Flute 2, Clarinet 1, Clarinet 2, Bassoon 1, Bassoon 2	0.75
227	Flute 1, Flute 2, Oboe 1, Oboe 2, Clarinet 1, Clarinet 2, Bassoon 1, Bassoon 2	Flute 1, Flute 2, Clarinet 1, Clarinet 2, Bassoon 1, Bassoon 2	0.75

(i.e, 100, 80, 60) in order to observe the performances with greater flexibility with respect to the theoretical rules. The results for each excerpt and across all of them are presented in Table 3, which shows that the best average ratio score, 0.816, was obtained with the output decision threshold set at 60.

In Sect. 2, it was mentioned that orchestral blend effects can happen over one to several consecutive measures. Therefore, we chose to also evaluate the model outputs by considering each measure of a blend individually. Using the 32 orchestral excerpts previously listed, the 229 blends happened over 1032 measures. Thus, the evaluation was performed using 1032 labeled blends. Here, the denominator is the number of measures per excerpt instead of the number of blends per excerpt. Again, the model was applied with the same three different output decision threshold values as mentioned above. The results for each excerpt and across all of them using the three different thresholds are presented in Table 4. As for the other comparative approach, the best average ratio score, 0.808, was again achieved with the output decision threshold of 60.

5 Discussion

The results of the evaluations performed using 32 orchestral excerpts, presented in the previous section, show that the models have been able to retrieve around 81% of the instruments involved in a blend effect on average. By considering a blend as one global event and using the 229 blends identified by the experts within the 32 orchestral excerpts of our evaluation corpus, the model successfully

Table 3. Summary of the average ratio scores for the evaluations considering a blend as a whole event and number of blends for each orchestral piece and across all of them.

Musical pieces	Average ratio scores			
	Output decision threshold = 100	Output decision threshold = 80	Output decision threshold = 60	Number of blends
Berlioz, Symphonie Fantastique, IV (mm. 1–77)	0.522	0.819	0.778	8
Bizet, Carmen, Overture (mm. 121–147)	0.559	0.606	0.613	7
Borodin, In the Steppes of Central Asia (mm. 40–71)	0.244	0.244	0.244	2
Brahms, Symphony No. 4, I (mm. 1–57)	0.334	0.815	0.821	3
D'Indy, Choral Varié (mm. 70–78)	0.207	0.800	0.864	2
Debussy, La Mer, I (mm. 1–141)	0.292	0.699	0.764	47
Debussy, La Mer, III (mm. 31–52, 171–186)	0.439	0.504	0.584	14
Haydn, Symphony No. 100 (Military), II (mm. 1–70)	0.737	0.889	0.889	8
Haydn, Symphony No. 100 (Military), III (mm. 50–65)	0.643	0.794	0.917	2
Mahler, Symphony No. 1, I (mm. 1–22, 356–363)	0.673	0.897	0.904	8
Mendelssohn, Symphony No. 3 (Scottish), II (mm. 1–40, 242–273)	0.735	0.796	0.818	2
Mendelssohn, Symphony No. 3 (Scottish), IV (mm. 161–182)	1	1	1	1
Mussorgsky, Pictures at an Exhibition, Baba Yaga (mm. 106–124)	0.730	0.730	0.771	3
Mussorgsky, Pictures at an Exhibition, Catacombæ (mm. 1–22)	0.704	0.704	0.704	7
Mussorgsky, Pictures at an Exhibition, Gnomus (mm. 57–109)	0.359	0.776	0.761	18
Mussorgsky, Pictures at an Exhibition, Promenade (1st) (mm. 1–24)	0.130	0.997	0.924	12
Mussorgsky, Pictures at an Exhibition, Promenade (2nd) (mm. 1–12)	0.089	0.889	0.910	3
Mussorgsky, Pictures at an Exhibition, Goldenberg and Schmuÿle (mm. 1–9)	0.444	1	1	1
Mussorgsky, Pictures at an Exhibition, Vecchio Castello (mm. 30–52)	0.166	0.75	0.75	4
Mozart, Don Giovanni, Overture (mm. 1–284)	0.416	0.968	0.971	17
Schubert, Symphony No. 8, I (mm. 1–62)	0.541	0.763	0.796	7
Schubert, Symphony No. 9, II (mm. 300–310)	0	1	1	1
Schubert, Symphony No. 9, III (mm. 187–221, 336–359)	0.807	0.935	0.935	6
Schubert, Symphony No. 9, IV (mm. 543–564)	0.5	0.5	0.5	1
Sibelius, Symphony No. 2, II (mm. 150–203)	0.378	0.812	0.824	11
Smetana, The Bartered Bride, Overture (mm. 9–59)	0.522	0.781	0.781	4
Smetana, Ma vlast, Die Moldau (mm. 185–228)	0.305	0.520	0.551	2
Williams, Symphony No. 8, I (mm. 140–161)	0.409	0.880	0.891	4
Williams, Symphony No. 8, II (mm. 71–107)	0.729	1	1	5
Williams, Symphony No. 8, IV (mm. 12–25, 54–96)	0.450	0.901	0.910	8
Verdi, Aida, Act II, Scene 1 (mm. 41–57)	0.39	0.98	0.98	5
Verdi, La Traviata, Prelude (mm. 17–37)	0.894	0.957	0.957	6
Across all pieces	**0.480**	**0.804**	**0.816**	**229**

Table 4. Summary of the average ratio scores for the evaluations considering each measure of a blend and number of measures for each orchestral piece and across all of them.

Musical pieces	Average ratio scores			
	Output decision threshold = 100	Output decision threshold = 80	Output decision threshold = 60	Number of measures
Berlioz, Symphonie Fantastique, IV (mm. 1–77)	0.558	0.853	0.838	67
Bizet, Carmen, Overture (mm. 121–147)	0.588	0.814	0.847	35
Borodin, In the Steppes of Central Asia (mm. 40–71)	0.114	0.114	0.114	32
Brahms, Symphony No. 4, I (mm. 1–57)	0.433	0.761	0.768	23
D'Indy, Choral Varié (mm. 70–78)	0.206	0.793	0.853	9
Debussy, La Mer, I (mm. 1–141)	0.267	0.619	0.682	123
Debussy, La Mer, III (mm. 31–52, 171–186)	0.411	0.468	0.560	54
Haydn, Symphony No. 100 (Military), II (mm. 1–70)	0.733	0.903	0.903	41
Haydn, Symphony No. 100 (Military), III (mm. 50–65)	0.634	0.843	0.918	13
Mahler, Symphony No. 1, I (mm. 1–22, 356–363)	0.570	0.900	0.907	22
Mendelssohn, Symphony No. 3 (Scottish), II (mm. 1–40, 242–273)	0.677	0.751	0.778	23
Mendelssohn, Symphony No. 3 (Scottish), IV (mm. 161–182)	1	1	1	4
Mussorgsky, Pictures at an Exhibition, Baba Yaga (mm. 106–124)	0.710	0.710	0.742	16
Mussorgsky, Pictures at an Exhibition, Catacombæ (mm. 1–22)	0.461	0.461	0.461	18
Mussorgsky, Pictures at an Exhibition, Gnomus (mm. 57–109)	0.422	0.779	0.773	74
Mussorgsky, Pictures at an Exhibition, Promenade (1st) (mm. 1–24)	0.108	0.991	0.912	20
Mussorgsky, Pictures at an Exhibition, Promenade (2nd) (mm. 1–12)	0.089	0.889	0.910	6
Mussorgsky, Pictures at an Exhibition, Goldenberg and Schmuÿle (mm. 1–9)	0.444	1	1	9
Mussorgsky, Pictures at an Exhibition, Vecchio Castello (mm. 30–52)	0.285	0.857	0.857	14
Mozart, Don Giovanni, Overture (mm. 1–284)	0.442	0.969	0.973	85
Schubert, Symphony No. 8, I (mm. 1–62)	0.684	0.863	0.888	41
Schubert, Symphony No. 9, II (mm. 300–310)	0	1	1	1
Schubert, Symphony No. 9, III (mm. 187–221, 336–359)	0.743	0.839	0.839	32
Schubert, Symphony No. 9, IV (mm. 543–564)	0.5	0.5	0.5	16
Sibelius, Symphony No. 2, II (mm. 150–203)	0.402	0.787	0.794	37
Smetana, The Bartered Bride, Overture (mm. 9–59)	0.636	0.918	0.918	32
Smetana, Ma vlast, Die Moldau (mm. 185–228)	0.042	0.298	0.356	43
Williams, Symphony No. 8, I (mm. 140–161)	0.455	0.889	0.900	22
Williams, Symphony No. 8, II (mm. 71–107)	0.731	0.992	1	23
Williams, Symphony No. 8, IV (mm. 12–25, 54–96)	0.418	0.893	0.902	41
Verdi, Aida, Act II, Scene 1 (mm. 41–57)	0.228	0.980	0.980	21
Verdi, La Traviata, Prelude (mm. 17–37)	0.894	0.980	0.980	35
Across all pieces	**0.466**	**0.795**	**0.808**	**1032**

Table 5. Percentage of extra instruments on average across the 32 excerpts for each decision output threshold value.

	Average extra instruments			
	Threshold = 100	Threshold = 80	Threshold = 60	Number of instruments to retrieve
Across all pieces	4.2%	7.6%	13.8%	7911

retrieved 81.60% of the 7911 instruments involved in the effect, achieved with the output decision threshold set at 60. When considering each measure as one blend, the model successfully retrieved 80.80% of the instruments on average for the 1032 measures analyzed, also achieved with a threshold of 60. These results suggest that models based on ASA principles processing only symbolic information can successfully retrieve on average over 81% of the instruments involved in an orchestral blend.

We observe a significant improvement between the output decision thresholds set at 100 and at 80, while the difference between 80 and 60 is minimal. As mentioned in Sect. 3.2, an output threshold set at 100 means that each estimation has to strictly follow the rules based on ASA principles (i.e., perfect onset synchrony, pitch harmonicity, and parallelism in pitch and dynamics). This suggests that these cues do not need to be perfect to create a blend effect and that flexibility from the theoretical rules in the models is required. Lowering the threshold increases the performance of the model, but it may also result in grouping instruments that share characteristics with others but which were not included by the expert annotators as part of the orchestral effect. Table 5 shows the percentage of extra instruments on average across the 32 excerpts used in the evaluation corpus for each decision output threshold value. The average extra instruments goes from 4.2% with the threshold set at 100 to an extra 13.8% of odd instruments with the output threshold value 60. Furthermore, the small increase in accuracy between the output decision thresholds values 60 and 80 in comparison to the significant increase of false positives suggests that a ceiling has been reached.

Although our model has successfully retrieved over 80% of the instruments involved in an orchestral blend, some limitations have emerged from the evaluations, which could explain the remaining 20% of instruments unsuccessfully retrieved. For instance, in the blend shown in Fig. 2, the model missed oboes 1–2 in measures 224 to 227. This is due to them playing one note in each measure, and thus, having a low score for onset synchrony (1 common onset value out of 4 with all the other instruments) as well as for the parallelism properties. The current implementation is not able to retrieve instruments involved in a blend and playing sporadically compared to the rest of the blended instruments. Another limitation is illustrated with Fig. 4. Here, the four bassoons switch from one group of blend (annotated with a red box) to another (annotated with an orange box) in the middle of the measure 63. The model grouped the bassoons with the flutes, oboes, clarinets, horns, trumpets, and cornets instead of with the tuba and timpani for measures 63 and 64. Due to performing the analysis on

Fig. 4. Example of a blend between a tuba, two timpani, and four bassoons later in the phrase (annotated with an orange box), mm. 60–65, and a blend between two flutes, two oboes, two clarinets, four bassoons, four horns, two trumpets, and two cornets (annotated with a red box), mm. 62–65, in Berlioz, Symphonie fantastique IV. (Color figure online)

a measure-by-measure basis, the model cannot notice a change of blended group if it occurs within a measure. Furthermore, given that the pitch harmonicity function is based either on harmonic series of semitone intervals or on a succession of tonal chords, if instruments play notes that do not follow this framework, they would be discarded. This could be another reason that the model did not retrieve all of the instruments involved in an orchestral blend.

The missing 20% could also be explained by the absence of information related to instrument timbre, musicians' performance, spatial position of the instruments, and room acoustics in the symbolic representation of music. As mentioned in Sect. 2, these characteristics are also important in creating orchestral effects and were part of the human experts' annotations. Thus, incorporating these cues from analyses of the audio files could overcome some of the current limitations.

6 Conclusion and Future Directions

In this paper, we have presented our approach to modeling human experts' identification of orchestral blends using symbolic information from computer-readable scores. Our partnership with OrchPlayMusic has allowed us to get standard, precise, and consistent MusicXML files of orchestral pieces from which to process symbolic score information. We based our model on the evaluation of three musical characteristics suggested by previous research on orchestral blend: onset synchrony, pitch harmonicity, and parallelism in pitch and dynamics, as described in Sect. 3. In order to evaluate the performance of the model, we decided to compare its output with blends that had been labeled by human experts. Here, we used resources available in the Orchestration Analysis and Research Database. The results of the performance evaluations, detailed in Sect. 4, have shown that the model has successfully retrieved over 80% of the instruments involved in a blend effect on average, either by considering a blend as a global event or each measure as a blend. The best average scores were achieved using output decision threshold values set at 80 and 60, providing a significant improvement from estimations strictly limited to the rules. This suggests that some flexibility in the estimations is required for modeling perceptual effects of orchestration. Yet, lower thresholds could result in grouping extra instruments, as shown in Table 5 for our evaluation.

The developments presented in this paper suggest that estimations based on the processing of symbolic information can account for a significant part in modeling orchestral blends. However, further investigations are still necessary to overcome the current limitations discussed in Sect. 5 and to match human auditory perception. For instance, tuning the weights of the different calculations could be an aspect to consider, as perhaps onset synchrony is a more prominent characteristic than pitch harmonicity. Here, the use of supervised machine learning techniques combined with a large set of labeled blend examples could potentially aid in addressing this question and help in refining the calculations of the current models. Another important aspect to incorporate is information related to timbre, which is a central characteristic in perceptual effects of orchestration. Information resulting from audio analyses that take into account timbral characteristics as well as data about musicians' performance nuances, spatial position of the instruments, and room acoustics would help to alleviate the current limitations in developing computational models designed to automatically identify orchestral blend effects.

Acknowledgments. This research is supported by a NSERC SPG-P/507004-17 research grant.

References

1. Berlioz, H.: Grand Traité d'Instrumentation et d'Orchestration Modernes. Henry Lemoine, Paris, France (1844)

2. Blatter, A.: Instrumentation and Orchestration, 2nd edn. Schirmer Books, New York (1997)
3. Bregman, A.S.: Auditory Scene Analysis: The Perceptual Organization of Sound. MIT Press, Cambridge (1990)
4. Bregman, A.S., Pinker, S.: Auditory streaming and the building of timbre. Canadian J. Psychol./Revue Canadienne de Psychologie **32**(1), 19 (1978)
5. Goodchild, M., McAdams, S.: Perceptual processes in orchestration. In: Dolan, E.I., Rehding, A. (eds.) The Oxford Handbook of Timbre. Oxford University Press, New York (2018)
6. Kendall, R.A., Carterette, E.C.: Identification and blend of timbres as a basis for orchestration. Contemp. Music Rev. **9**(1–2), 51–67 (1993). https://doi.org/10.1080/07494469300640341
7. Lembke, S.A.: When timbre blends musically: perception and acoustics underlying orchestration and performance. Ph.D. thesis, McGill University, Montreal, QC, Canada (2014)
8. Lembke, S.A., Parker, K., Narmour, E., McAdams, S.: Acoustical correlates of perceptual blend in timbre dyads and triads. Musicae Scientiae **23**, 1–25 (2017). https://doi.org/10.1177/1029864917731806
9. McAdams, S.: The auditory image: a metaphor for musical and psychological research on auditory organization. In: Crozier, W.R., Chapman, A.J. (eds.) Cognitive Processes in the Perception of the Art, pp. 289–323. Elsevier, North-Holland (1984)
10. McAdams, S.: Musical timbre perception. In: Deutsch, D. (ed.) The Psychology of Music, 3 edn., pp. 35–67. Academic Press, San Diego (2013)
11. McAdams, S., Bregman, A.S.: Hearing musical streams. Comput. Music J. **3**(4), 26–43 (1979)
12. Piston, W.: Orchestration. WW Norton, New York (1955)
13. Rimsky-Korsakov, N.: Principles of Orchestration, 1st edn. Dover Publications, New York (1964)
14. Sandell, G.J.: Concurrent timbres in orchestration: a perceptual study of factors determining "blend". Ph.D. thesis, Northwestern University, Evanston, Illinois, United States of America (1991)
15. Sandell, G.J.: Roles for spectral centroid and other factors in determining "blended" instrument pairings in orchestration. Music Percept. **13**(2), 209–246 (1995). https://doi.org/10.2307/40285694
16. Wang, D., Brown, G.J. (eds.): Computational Auditory Scene Analysis: Principles, Algorithms and Applications. Wiley-IEEE Press, New York (2006)

The Effect of Auditory Pulse Clarity on Sensorimotor Synchronization

Prithvi Kantan[1(✉)], Rares Stefan Alecu[1], and Sofia Dahl[2]

[1] Sound and Music Computing, Aalborg University, Copenhagen, Denmark
{pkanta18,ralecu18}@student.aau.dk

[2] Department of Architecture, Design and Media Technology, Aalborg University, Copenhagen, Denmark
sof@create.aau.dk
https://vbn.aau.dk/da/persons/118552

Abstract. This study investigates the relationship between auditory pulse clarity and sensorimotor synchronization performance, along with the influence of musical training. 29 participants walked in place to looped drum samples with varying degrees of pulse clarity, which were generated by adding artificial reverberation and measured through fluctuation spectrum peakiness. Experimental results showed that reducing auditory pulse clarity affected phase matching through significantly higher means and standard deviations in asynchrony across musical sophistication groups. Referent period matching ability was also degraded, and non-musicians were impacted more than musicians. Subjective ratings of required active concentration also increased with decreasing pulse clarity. These findings point to the importance of clear and distinct pulses to timing performance in synchronization tasks such as music and dance.

Keywords: Pulse clarity · Sensorimotor synchronization · Rhythm · Movement · Perception · Musical training · Timing

1 Introduction

Sensorimotor synchronization (SMS) [25] is a form of referential behavior in which an action is coordinated with a predictable external event, the referent, where both are usually periodic. Examples of SMS are dance (where movements are synchronized with both music and the movements of other dancers), music performance and marching. The vast majority of studies primarily use finger tapping [25,27]. While, for instance, foot tapping, could be assumed to be just as common as tapping in every-day SMS, the prevalence of finger tapping studies most likely has its explanation in the fact that finger tapping is the most practical to measure. There are, however, an increasing number of studies on SMS involving lower-limb activities such as stepping in place [4], locomotion [29], and dance [2,3].

R. Kronland-Martinet et al. (Eds.): CMMR 2019, LNCS 12631, pp. 379–395, 2021.
https://doi.org/10.1007/978-3-030-70210-6_25

Another noteworthy observation concerns the choice of stimuli in SMS studies, where music is comparatively rare [25]. Instead, studies tend to use auditory stimuli consisting of brief tones or clicks. Such stimuli generally have sharp temporal profiles, which along with low noise in testing environments are likely to exhibit prominent and effortlessly perceptible periodicities or *pulses*. Real-life SMS referents, however, such as music performed in a reverberant hall, often have less pulse salience due to time-smearing and masking effects. Dynamics processing and speaker distortions can further undermine the strength of rhythmic pulsations. In extreme situations, the pulse may no longer even be readily perceptible, subject to individual perceptual ability and musical training or experience.

In this study, we used computational methods for *pulse clarity (PC)* estimation [17], to design ecologically valid stimuli for the investigation of systematic relations between pulse clarity and SMS task performance. In-phase walking in place was chosen for greater ecological validity with regard to general bodily movement.

2 Related Work

The extensive study of SMS is comprehensively reviewed in [25] and [27]. With respect to tapping to simple isochronous stimuli, Madison et al. [19] showed that the response mode, feedback received and training have an effect on SMS, with feedback and training resulting in lower local variability. In general, taps tend to precede sequence tones by a few tens of milliseconds, rather than being symmetrically distributed around tone onsets. Possible causes of this *Negative Mean Asynchrony (NMA)* have generated a considerable amount of research (see [27] for a summary). Research has shown that the magnitude of NMA is influenced by a number of factors such as effector used, feedback, event density (subdivision) and expertise. Trained musicians exhibit both smaller NMA [11,15] and a smaller standard deviation in asynchrony than non-musicians [26].

Chen et al. [5] studied the behavioral and neural effect of increased metrical complexity on SMS in musicians and non-musicians. Measuring SMS performance in terms of intertap interval and asynchrony, they found that musicians were significantly more accurate than non-musicians in terms of period and phase synchronization. Although these abilities were degraded in both groups with increasing rhythmic complexity, there was a significant interaction between asynchrony and music training across rhythm types. In other words, the performance of the musician group was not as severely degraded as the nonmusician group due to greater stimulus complexity (c.f. Fig. 3 in [5].) The authors attributed this superior performance to a more efficient recruitment of motor neural regions, as well as superior abilities in timing, error correction and general auditory discriminatory processes.

In another study, Chen et al. [4] investigated lower-limb SMS to a variable metronome for different types of response (uni- or bilateral heel tapping when sitting, bilateral heel tapping when standing, or the toe or heel strike when stepping on the spot). For the steady-state baseline part of the stimuli, they reported more negative asynchronies for stepping on the spot than bilateral heel tapping in standing. The details of the automatic detection of heel and toe strike during stepping were not reported. While the constraints of keeping balance in bilateral stepping and standing did show an effect on error correction, results also showed reduced variability for stepping compared to bilateral heel tapping in standing. The authors suggested that the reduced variability could be an effect of the increased sensory feedback to participants from the load of the body weight, which would explain the difference between stepping compared to heel tapping. Similarly, Palmer et al. [22] reported that tactile feedback appears to be important in reducing timing errors for clarinetists.

Lower-limb SMS such as stepping in place is particularly interesting because it relates to every-day activities such as walking, dancing and also to the use of SMS in rehabilitation [20,28]. While these activities can be synchronized with metronomes it is also common with live or recorded music, often with a clear pulse. With varying stimuli in less controllable surroundings, it seems reasonable to assume that most real-life SMS occurs in situations where the referent characteristics is distinct from the majority of laboratory settings.

Perceptual Centers. Ecological stimuli may exhibit varied temporal envelopes with distinct sub-band spectral evolution. For instance, the sound of a regular snare drum hit has a very well-defined onset with a sharp attack and fast decay, whereas a wind or string instrument can produce onset envelopes of varying length and shape. The *Perceptual Center* (P-center) of a sound is understood as the specific moment of perceived occurrence [7]. Synchronization then involves aligning P-centers, which studies [7,13] have shown to depend upon envelope characteristics. The P-center seems to be located between the perceptual onset and the energy peak of a sound. For impulsive sounds this is close to a single location, while tones with gradual onsets tend to show a range of equally 'correct' sounding locations [13]. Danielson et al. [7] found that in general, sounds with slower attacks and longer durations had later P-centers with greater variability in their exact location. In a synchronization task with musical and quasi-musical stimuli, NMA with respect to the physical onsets was small to non-existent, but significant with respect to the P-center. This aligned with the hypothesis of Vos et al. [32] that participants use P-centers, rather than the physical onset of the tone as the target for SMS tasks.

Pulse Clarity. The ease of perception of the underlying pulsation in temporally organized stimuli such as music may determine the ease with which the body can be synchronized to them. Lartillot et al. [17] define *Pulse Clarity (PC)* as a high-level musical measure conveying how easily listeners can perceive the underlying rhythmic or metric pulsation. There is evidence that pulse clarity affects corporeal movement characteristics during SMS tasks [2,3]. Burger et al. [2] found that music with greater pulse clarity elicited greater temporal and spatial regularity in dance. Van Dyck et al. [30] found that when the bass drum was made louder in the music mix, dancers increased their motor activity and entrained better to the beat. In addition to exploring internal SMS mechanisms [12,16], neuroscience studies show that the extent to which cortical or subcortical motor activations are coupled with the auditory cortex depends on beat salience and music training [6]. As stable pulse perception underlies all SMS tasks, lowering the perceived pulse salience of a referent is likely to have a detrimental impact on SMS performance.

We now examine some ways in which Pulse Clarity has been modelled in the past. Lartillot et al. [17] quantified the temporal evolution of music in terms of its *Onset Detection Curve (ODC)*, where peaks indicate pulses. They then characterized pulse clarity by describing the ODC in terms of local configurations or the presence of periodicities. In the former, PC characterizations do not relate to periodicity, and focus on articulation and attack characterization. Specifically, the attack slope [24] and local maxima of the time derivative of the amplitude envelope [14] can be considered as possible factors for PC prediction. Periodic characterizations are made in terms of the autocorrelation function of the ODC, which can be either full-band or multi-band. The principle is that peaks in the autocorrelation function indicate the most probable periodicities, and resonance functions can be used to model these in terms of perceptual salience [14]. Lartillot et al. [17] described pulse clarity in terms of the global maximum, global minimum, kurtosis and entropy of the ODC autocorrelation curve. In perceptual tests, they found that the best predictor of perceptual pulse salience was the global minimum.

Pampalk et al. [23] extracted a rhythm pattern representation of music pieces based on the *amplitude modulation(AM)* of the loudness sensation per critical band [9], weighting its coefficients based on the psychoacoustic model of fluctuation strength [8]. The effect on hearing depends on the modulation frequency, and is most intense 4 Hz [23]. Within each frequency band, gradient and Gaussian filters were used to emphasize distinctive beats, characterized through high fluctuation strength at these modulation frequencies relative to neighboring frequencies. They found that pieces of music dominated by strong beats had high fluctuation strength values, which were also correlated to bass. PC estimation metrics based on both ODC methods [17] and fluctuation strength [23] can be easily evaluated for audio recordings using the MIRtoolbox [18]. In the stimulus design process of the present study, both types of methods are assessed in terms of their correspondence to subjective beat perception.

3 Stimulus Design

The creation of suitable auditory referents necessitated 1) The design of rhythmic stimuli spanning the entire range of perceptual pulse salience by systematic manipulation of a single base stimulus. 2) The objective assessment of these stimuli by PC measures.

We made drastic changes to perceived pulse salience by simply altering the decay time of a digital reverberation (reverb) effect with a flat frequency decay, applied to a looped snare drum sample (EZDrummer 2 VST instrument). Increasing the decay time reduced perceptual pulse salience, due to the increasing masking effect of previous decay tails on subsequent onsets, along with the reduction in overall dynamic range. The reverb plugin used was the 64 bit version of WAVES TrueVerb, with early reflections and high frequency roll-off disabled. Finally, the audible pulsation of the primary resonance of the drum sample was suppressed using a narrow notch filter.

To determine the range of reverb decay times that fit the required perceptual range, we blindly adjusted decay time to yield pulses that were subjectively *'Very Clear', 'Moderately Clear', 'Moderately Unclear' and 'Very Unclear (but perceptible)'.* We then analyzed these four preliminary sample points of the perceptual range using the MIRToolbox [18] and 1) Entropy of *Onset Detection Function (ODF)* Autocorrelation [17]; 2) Max ODF Autocorrelation; 3) Min ODF Autocorrelation; and 4) Peakiness of Fluctuation Spectrum [3,23]. The fourth approach estimates PC by the relative Shannon entropy of the fluctuation spectrum [23], in terms of peak magnitude, regularity of spacing and noise between peaks. The calculated values can be seen in Table 1.

Table 1. Comparison between different methods for PC computation [17,18]

Sr. No.	Salience	Fluct. spectrum peak	EntropyAutocor	MinAutocor	MaxAutocor
1	Very clear	293961.77	0.5066	0.398	0.9899
2	Moderately clear	146677.66	0.6314	0.335	0.9749
3	Moderately unclear	24224.66	0.721	0.3891	0.7672
4	Very unclear (but perceptible)	17082.21	0.7439	0.3342	0.5134

Similar to what was reported in [3], the fluctuation spectrum of the perceptually clearer stimuli exhibited peaks with markedly higher magnitude at the beat frequency, and less inter-peak noise than the unclear stimuli (see Fig. 1). Perceptually, increasing the reverb decay time was always found to reduce pulse salience, and this behavior was reproduced in preliminary tests with the fluctuation spectrum peakiness but not always with ODF-based measures. Hence, we used the fluctuation spectrum peakiness to model the perceptual range. Note that 4 Hz peaks in the fluctuation spectrum plots are higher than 2 Hz peaks (true frequency), and this could be attributed to the weighting of the AM coefficients in the algorithm [23].

From the total range of reverb times, we empirically found that *nine* total stimuli would sample the perceptual range with enough inter-stimulus difference to minimize redundancy. To determine the necessary fluctuation peak magnitudes, we fitted a 3rd order polynomial curve to the four previously determined values and designed stimuli S1–S9 to match nine equi-spaced curve values in the same range, in decreasing order of PC. Stimulus tempo was centered around 120 BPM, close to the preferred human movement tempo [10], but varied by ±1 BPM between successive stimuli to prevent short-term training effects [19]. The onset peak amplitude was kept constant across stimuli. The loudness of the base

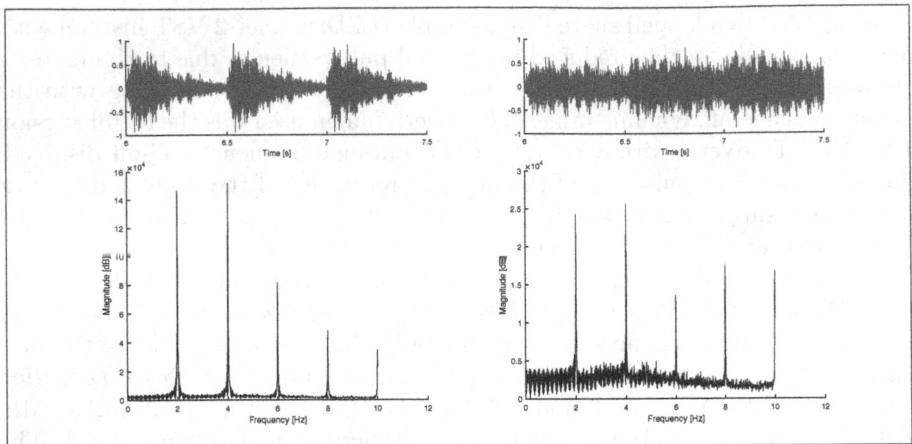

Fig. 1. Pulse clarity measurement using fluctuation spectra. For the signal to the right, the spectrum peaks have lower overall magnitude, and greater noise in between peaks, implying lower pulse clarity. This is also evident from the time domain waveform.

stimulus (dry snare drum sample) was kept constant between stimuli, so the perceived overall loudness increased with reverb decay time. This is an ecologically valid effect, as sounds are generally perceived to be louder in acoustically 'live' environments than in 'dead' (reverberation-free) ones.

4 Experiment

In order to test whether our stimuli with degrading pulse clarity would affect SMS performance we designed a within participant experiment. We hypothesized the following effects of pulse clarity manipulations of the referent stimulus:

- Decreased PC leads to smaller NMA across participants and greater asynchrony variance (greatest for nonmusicians).
- Decreased PC leads to greater tempo deviation from the referent tempo, and greater variance in the reproduced interval duration. Nonmusicians are affected to a greater extent than musicians.
- Decreased PC leads to higher ratings of required concentration across participants, independent of music training.

4.1 Participants

A convenience sample of 29 participants (6 women, 21–35 years, $MeanAge = 26$), mainly students at Aalborg University, volunteered in return for a film voucher. Participants were briefed on the length of the experiment (9 stimuli $\times$ 50 s) and that they could withdraw at any time without losing their remuneration.

4.2 Experimental Setup and Procedure

Participants were tested individually in a quiet, medium-sized room on campus. The stimuli was played via a set of Focusrite Studio Headphones, while recordings of the activity were captured with a Focusrite CM25 large-diaphragm cardioid condenser microphone. The audio was digitized to a 44.1 KHz/24-bit WAV format using a Focusrite Scarlett Solo Studio audio interface.

After obtaining the participants' informed consent, we asked them to complete an online musical background questionnaire to determine their Ollen Musical Sophistication Index (OMSI) [21]. The OMSI reflects the probability that a music expert would categorize a respondent as *"more musically sophisticated"*, with regard to musical knowledge, skill, and composition ability.

Subsequently, participants were instructed to assume a standing position in front of the microphone such that their feed were approximately 30 cm from the diaphragm of the microphone. They were then asked to walk in place, stepping in exact synchronization with each of the stimuli, which were presented in random order with brief pauses in between. After each trial, participants were asked to rate on a scale of 1–10 the amount of active concentration required to maintain synchronization with the stimulus. This procedure was repeated for all 9 stimuli.

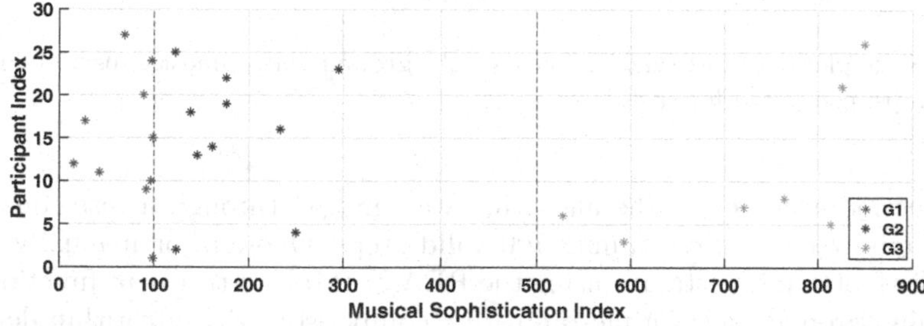

Fig. 2. Distribution of participants based on Musical Sophistication Index and the design of clusters for statistical analysis. The dotted lines indicate the segregation thresholds between groups G1, G2 and G3. Participants with OMSI scores greater than 500 should be classified as "more musically sophisticated" [21].

4.3 Data Analysis

Recordings of two participants were discarded in entirety due to poor signal quality, yielding 27 $\times$ 9 trials = 243 recordings for analysis.

The OMSI scores of the participants covered a considerable range (see Fig. 2). In order to study the effect of musical training on task performance, we therefore further grouped participants on the basis of their OMSIs into 3 *MSoph* groups G1 (OMSI $<$ 100, **10** participants), G2 (OMSI 100–500, **10** participants), and G3 (OMSI 500–1000, **7** participants).

Onset Detection Algorithm. From each recording, the extraction of footstep timestamps was carried out in MATLAB using an onset detection algorithm, based on [1]. The first 10 s of each recording (containing the initial rhythm acquisition phase) were discarded. The remaining audio was processed using a sliding window approach, with a frame size of 512 samples and a hop ratio of 0.5. From the obtained audio frames, the algorithm computes a signal reflecting the temporal evolution of spectral magnitude difference between short-term Fourier spectra of successive frames across bands. This is used as the *onset detection function* [1]. Spectral difference is a useful indicator in this case, since footstep onsets are accompanied by transient increases in spectral magnitude, resulting in detection function peaks. Finally, an adaptive threshold in the form of a moving median filter is used to pick peaks and record their associated timestamps.

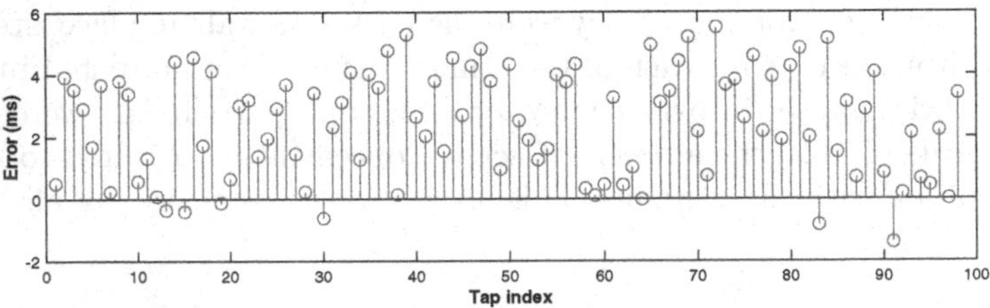

Fig. 3. Stem plot of error deviation between the ground truth timestamps and detected timestamps, computed for each foot.

Detection accuracy of the algorithm was gauged through a test conducted on one trial recording containing 100 valid steps. One author manually annotated the footstep timestamps using the REAPER tab-to-transient functionality to obtain "ground truth" timestamps for comparison with algorithm-detected timestamps. No false positives or false negatives were observed. As shown in Fig. 3 the algorithm detections showed a high degree of agreement with the annotated ground truths over 100 steps, with a mean error of 2.41 ± 1.72 ms. The positive mean error can be attributed to the sliding window (11.6 ms) and hop size (50%) of the spectral energy difference computation. For the purposes of data analysis, we deemed the onset detection error and sound propagation delay low enough to be neglected.

Statistical Analysis. From the timestamps obtained using the onset detection algorithm, SMS performance was analyzed in terms of the participants' ability to match stimulus period and phase. For phase matching, *mean asynchrony (MA)* and *standard deviation - asynchrony (STD-A)* were compared across stimuli (S1–S9) using mixed-design repeated-measures ANOVAs, with 'Stimulus' as the within-subject factor and musical sophistication 'MSoph Group' as the between-subjects factor. For period matching, *inter-tap interval coefficient of variation (ITI-CoV)* and mean tempo deviation (MTD) in *beats per minute* were similarly compared. Additionally, we calculated the groupwise percentages of participants deviating from the correct stimulus tempo by over *0.2 BPM* for all stimuli. The threshold of 0.2 BPM corresponds to a timing mismatch of 100 ms after one minute at 120 BPM assuming the first tap was in phase, and this mismatch exceeds most echo perception thresholds [33]. Finally, A Friedman Test was conducted on the participants' subjective concentration ratings. Pairwise comparisons were performed with a Bonferroni correction for multiple comparisons. All statistical analysis was done in SPSS 25.0 (IBM Corp).

5 Results

5.1 Phase Matching

Figures 4 and 5 show the average MA across participants and STD-A for each of Stimulus 1 to 9 (S1 to S9, decreasing PC) The effects of the independent variables on each dependent variable are considered in turn.

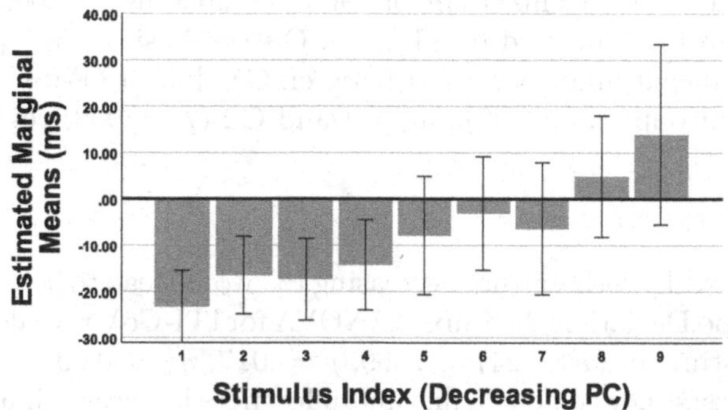

Fig. 4. Average MA across all participants for Stimuli 1 (maximum PC) through 9 (minimum PC). Vertical axis ticks are in ms and 95% confidence intervals are shown in error bars. The negative asynchrony gradually beocomes more positive with decreasing pulse clarity.

We tested the hypothesis that lower PC would lead to smaller NMA in a 9 Stimuli × 3 MSoph Groups mixed-design ANOVA. Results showed a significant main effect of stimulus ($F(2,\ 24)\ =\ 7.351$, $p\ =\ <.0001$, $\eta_p^2\ =\ 0.776$) and no significant interaction between stimulus and MSoph Group ($F(2,\ 24) = 1.379$, n.s., $\eta_p^2\ =\ 0.393$). A Tukey post-hoc test revealed that MA was statistically significantly more negative for stimulus S1(-23.3 ± 19.6 ms) as compared to S7(-6.4 ± 36.13 ms, $p\ =\ 0.028$), S8(4.8 ± 33.1 ms, $p < .0001$), and S9(13.9 ± 49.1 ms, $p < .0001$, see Fig. 4). There were no significant differences in pairwise comparisons between MSoph groups.

Another mixed-design ANOVA tested the hypothesis that STD-A would increase with decreasing PC. We found a main effect of stimulus ($F(2,\ 24) = 5.628$, $p = .001$, $\eta_p^2 = 0.726$) with no significant interaction between stimulus and

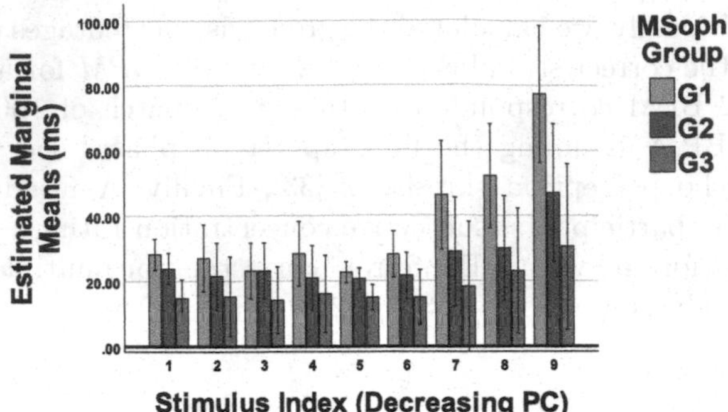

Fig. 5. Group wise *mean* STD-A for Stimuli 1 (maximum PC) through 9 (minimum PC). Vertical axis ticks are in ms and 95% confidence intervals are shown in error bars. Overall standard deviations increase with decreasing pulse clarity.

MSoph group. Post-hoc pairwise comparisons showed that STD-A was significantly less for S1(23.0 ± 8.8 ms) than for S9(53.9 ± 36.8 ms, $p = .002$), with a clear positive trend from S7 onward (see Fig. 5). On the basis of MSoph, significant and nearly-significant differences exist between G1 (lowest OMSI group) and G3 (highest OMSI group) ($p = 0.02$), and G1 and G2 ($p = .069$) respectively.

5.2 Period Matching

We tested the next hypothesis that decreasing PC would lead to increased ITI-CoV and Mean Tempo Deviation. The mixed ANOVA for ITI-CoV revealed a significant main effect of stimulus ($F(2, 24) = 2.399$, $p = .017$, $\eta_p^2 = 0.091$), although pairwise post-hoc tests showed non-significant differences between stimuli and MSoph groups. Despite this, it is noteworthy that S5 had the lowest mean ITI-CoV (3.6%)

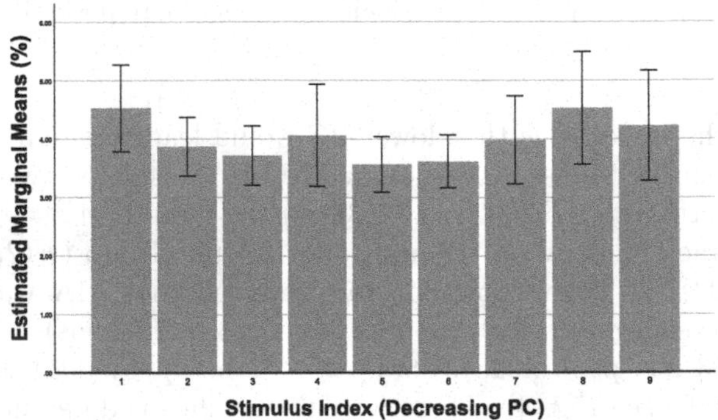

Fig. 6. Average ITI CoV across participants for Stimuli 1 (maximum PC) through 9 (minimum PC). Vertical axis ticks are in percentage and 95% confidence intervals are shown in error bars.

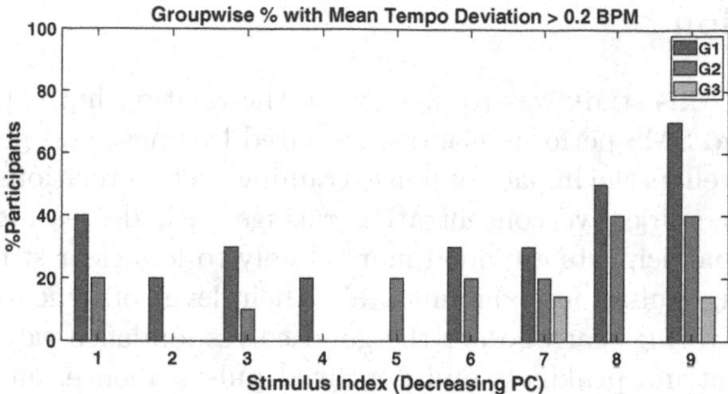

Fig. 7. Group wise % of participants with mean tempo deviation over 0.2 BPM for Stimuli 1 (maximum PC) through 9 (minimum PC). Vertical axis ticks are in percentage.

across participants (see Fig. 6) while S1 (max PC) had a mean value (4.59%) similar to S8 (4.64%) and S9 (4.32%) (min PC). The mixed ANOVA for MTD did not show a significant main effect of stimulus ($F(2, 24) = 1.022$, $p = .421$, $\eta_p^2 = 0.041$). Figure 7 shows the groupwise percentages of participants with MTD > 0.2 BPM. For the majority of stimuli, this percentage appears inversely related to musical sophistication; G1 has the highest incidence and G3 the minimum. Contrary to our hypothesis, however, the percentages were minimum *not* for S1 but for S4 and S5, before increasing as expected towards S9.

5.3 Concentration Ratings

For the stimulus-wise subjective concentration ratings, a Friedman Test found significant differences among stimuli ($\chi^2 = 144.12$, $p < .001$), and Dunn-Bonferroni-based post-hoc comparisons showed significant differences between multiple pairs of stimuli and non-significant differences between MSoph groups, with a general increasing trend from S1 to S9 as shown in Fig. 8.

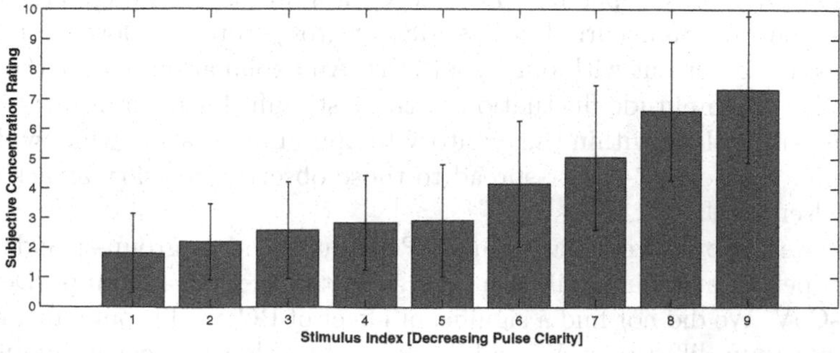

Fig. 8. Subjective concentration ratings for each of the nine stimuli across participants and groups. Vertical axis ticks are in the subjective scale unit, and 95% confidence intervals are shown in error bars.

6 Discussion

The purpose of this study was to investigate the relationship between auditory pulse clarity and SMS performance (as measured by phase and period matching measures), as well as the impact of music training on this relationship. The clear trend of higher subjective concentration ratings with decreasing pulse clarity indicates that participants attended more closely to less clear stimuli to deduce their underlying pulsations, and maintain their level of synchronization performance. The ratings corroborate the good correspondence we found between fluctuation spectrum peakiness and perceived pulse salience, and were aligned with our hypothesis regarding them.

The phase-related results from the mixed ANOVAs showed good agreement with finger-tapping literature [27], firstly in that the mean asynchrony across participants was found to be negative for most high PC stimuli (see Fig. 4). Secondly, the hypothesis of lower PC leading to smaller NMA was supported. Measured MA for all MSoph groups showed an increasing trend, with G2 and G3 having more positive mean values. This could be attributed to the masking of *true* perceptual onsets by previous reverb tails, and increased stimulus duration, ultimately leading to later P-centers and correspondingly later taps [7,32]. However, we did not find significant mean asychrony differences across MSoph groups resembling the findings of Chen et al. [5]. This could be attributed to the use of OMSI as a general measure of musical training as opposed to the more detailed and stringent group segregation done by Chen et al. [5] on the basis of several skill criteria.

G3 uniformly exhibited lower average STD-A than G1 and G2, in line with past literature [26]. We hypothesized that reducing PC would increase STD-A, but the results indicate that this relationship may not be linear, as the STD-A values across groups only begin to increase markedly beyond S6. The result seems reasonable, considering that most people would have experienced synchronizing to stimuli with some degradation in pulse clarity, e.g. due to natural reverberation. This points to there being a tolerated level of pulse degradation before regular phase synchronization begins to break down, which may affect individuals differently depending on their level of musical training. The increase in STD-A beyond S6 occurred across MSoph groups but was lower for trained musicians, in agreement with our hypothesis. An explanation is that the diminished extent of amplitude fluctuation of these stimuli during transients implied a smaller attack slope within the auditory temporal integration window, leading to a similar temporal P-center spread to those observed for slow-attack sounds by Danielsen et al. [7].

Next, we hypothesized that reduced PC would lead to group-specific degradation in period matching ability, measured in terms of Mean Tempo Deviation and ITI-CoV. We did not find a significant effect of PC on this outcome, nor any significant group differences. We did, however, find that was generally only participants from the lower MSoph groups (G1 and G2) who exceeded the 0.2 BPM deviation threshold, while G3 seemed largely unaffected in this regard. However, the percentage of these incidences did not steadily increase from S1–S9 as we had hypothesized. Interestingly, the percentages were lower for S4 and S5 than S1-3 as shown in Fig. 7. A possible explanation could stem from the differences between the stimuli. S1-3 had greater PC with shorter reverb tails, meaning that they were sparser in the time domain. S6-9 had the lowest PC but were also the least sparse signals. We deduce that similar to the subdivision advantage [27], the presence of non-zero auditory information (reverb tails) in between two pulses may have an assistive effect on synchronization ability. S4 and S5 may thus have been 'sweet-spot' referents balancing the tradeoff between providing non-sparse inter-pulse assistive information and compromising the salience of the underlying pulsation itself. A possible support for this would be that listeners have been reported to use different strategies for judging duration of tones with flat or decaying envelope shape [31]. Another possibility is that higher PC gave participants greater awareness of their own synchronization errors, affecting confidence and worsening performance. Simultaneous masking of the higher PC transients due to bone conduction while stepping may also have imparted advantages to synchronizing with stimuli having longer decay times.

The tactile feedback from whole-body weight shifting when stepping is different from that of finger tapping but, as noted by Chen et al. [4], also involves the constraint of maintaining balance. Chen et al. suggested that the lower variability in stepping compared to heel tapping found in their study might be explained by the tactile feedback. Unlike their study, we recorded the sounds of the steps rather than the movement of markers. Comparing their reported mean asynchronies for toe (−61.45 ms) and heel (33.88 ms) [4], our mean values fall in between (see Fig. 4). While we cannot be exactly sure how participants purposefully aligned their steps and the perceived tactile feedback to the stimuli sounds, we would argue that our approach of sound detection makes sense from an ecological perspective.

Our hypothesis that ITI CoV would increase with decreasing PC was not supported by the data. In particular for G1, ITI CoV did not increase proportionally with STD-A as would be expected. This conflict is explained by these participants stepping in a regular fashion but drifting from the stimulus tempo. The lack of significant differences between groups resembling the results of [5] could similarly be attributed to our choice of musical sophistication index. Another measure more sensitive to differences in general rhythmic ability, along with a stringent group segregation based on concrete skill criteria might have given another result. Nevertheless, it is noteworthy that mean ITI-CoV was lowest for S5, which when combined with the superior tempo performance and low STD-A indicates that participants performed best here in terms of both period and phase matching. A more thorough investigation of this performance improvement observed in the intermediate stimuli would make an interesting topic for a follow-up study on a larger population sample.

Overall, these findings indicate that the clarity of the periodic referent has a considerable influence on SMS performance, which would have direct implications for music and dance performance. The type of degradation present in our stimuli bears resemblance to what might appear in real environments where music or dance activities are performed. For lower PC, beat entrainment not only consumes more cognitive resources, but is also less accurate and stable to a perceptible extent (mean STD-A of 54 ms for S9 v/s 23 ms for S1), highlighting the importance of clear pulse audibility for timing during performance. Interestingly, performance appeared to remain fairly consistent until a certain 'threshold' was crossed, around S7 ('Moderately Unclear') (see Fig. 5), implying a certain sensory 'robustness' to referent degradation.

Limitations of the study include the static modality of PC manipulation, short length of the trials and relatively small number of participants, particularly with extensive musical training. Another shortcoming was the lack of detailed background information on the level of training the participants had; the use of OMSI may have blurred inherent inter-group differences. Pulse degradations in real-life situations may be time-varying due to the changing spectral content of referents, and unpredictably varying masking effects. Interpersonal entrainment and visual cues during group performance are also important factors. Future studies can address whether the different types of pulse degradation similarly impact SMS performance, and whether these can be accurately modeled by fluctuation spectrum measurements.

7 Conclusion

The present study concluded that reducing auditory pulse clarity influences sensorimotor synchronization performance in terms of both phase and period matching abilities, in addition to subjective ratings of required concentration. We found evidence that a certain degree of temporal pulse degradation is not only tolerated, but may also lead to performance improvements upto a point, beyond which pulse degradation detrimentally affects the performance of musically untrained participants more than trained ones. These results have direct relevance to timing performance in dance, music and timing practice, although further studies must be conducted on a larger sample, exploring other ecological pulse degradation methods to explore their true implications for real SMS contexts.

Acknowledgments. We thank the participants in our experiment. Authors PK and RSA were mainly responsible for the experiment, data analysis and writing of the manuscript. Author SD supervised the project, and assisted in writing. SD's contribution is partially funded by NordForsk's Nordic University Hub Nordic Sound and Music Computing Network NordicSMC, project number 86892.

References

1. Bello, J.B., Daudet, L., Abdallah, S., Duxbury, C., Davies, M., Sandler, M.B.: A tutorial on onset detection in music signals. IEEE Trans. Speech Audio Process. **13**(5), 1035–1047 (2008). https://doi.org/10.1109/TSA.2005.851998
2. Burger, B., Thompson, M. R., Luck, G., Saarikallio, S., Toiviainen, P.: Music moves us: beat-related musical features influence regularity of music-induced movement. In: Proceedings of the 12th International Conference on Music Perception and Cognition and the 8th Triennial Conference of the European Society for the Cognitive Sciences of Music, pp. 183–187 (2012)
3. Burger, B., Thompson, M.R., Luck, G., Saarikallio, S., Toiviainen, P.: Influences of Rhythm- and Timbre-related musical features on characteristics of music-induced movement. Front. Psychol. **4**, 183 (2013). https://doi.org/10.3389/fpsyg.2013.00183
4. Chen, H.Y., Wing, A.M., Pratt, D.: The synchronisation of lower limb responses with a variable metronome: the effect of biomechanical constraints on timing. Gait Posture **23**(3), 307–314 (2006). https://doi.org/10.1016/j.gaitpost.2005.04.001
5. Chen, J., Penhune, V., Zatorre, R.: Moving on time: brain network for auditory-motor synchronization is modulated by rhythm complexity and musical training. J. Cogn. Neurosci. **20**(2), 226–239 (2008). https://doi.org/10.1162/jocn.2008.20018
6. Chen, J.L., Penhune, V.B., Zatorre, R.J.: The role of auditory and premotor cortex in sensorimotor transformations. Ann. New York Acad. Sci. **1169**(1), 15–34 (2009). https://doi.org/10.1111/j.1749-6632.2009.04556.x
7. Danielsen, A., et al.: Where Is the beat in that note? Effects of attack, duration, and frequency on the perceived timing of musical and quasi-musical sounds. J. Exp. Psychol.: Hum. Percept. Perform. **45**(3), 402 (2019). https://doi.org/10.1037/xhp0000611
8. Fastl, H.: Fluctuation strength and temporal masking patterns of amplitude-modulated broad-band noise. Hear. Res. **8**(1), 59–69 (1982). https://doi.org/10.1016/0378-5955(82)90034-X
9. Feiten, B., Günzel, S.: Automatic indexing of a sound database using self-organizing neural nets. Comput. Music J. **18**(3), 53–65 (1994). https://doi.org/10.2307/3681185
10. Fraisse, P.: Rhythm and Tempo. Psychol. Music **1**, 149–180 (1982)
11. Fujii, S., Hirashima, M., Kudo, K., Ohtsuki, T., Nakamura, Y., Oda, S.: Synchronization error of drum kit playing with a metronome at different tempi by professional drummers. Music Percept.: Interdisc. J. **28**(5), 491–503 (2011). https://doi.org/10.1525/mp.2011.28.5.491
12. Fujioka, T., Trainor, L.J., Large, E.W., Ross, B.: Internalized timing of isochronous sounds is represented in neuromagnetic beta oscillations. J. Neurosci. **32**(5), 1791–1802 (2012). https://doi.org/10.1523/JNEUROSCI.4107-11.2012
13. Gordon, J.W.: The perceptual attack time of musical tones. J. Acoust. Soc. Am. **82**(1), 88–105 (1987). https://doi.org/10.1121/1.395441
14. Klapuri, A., Eronen, A., Astola, J.: Analysis of the meter of acoustic musical signals. IEEE Trans. Audio Speech Lang. Process. **14**(1), 342–355 (2006). https://doi.org/10.1109/TSA.2005.854090

15. Krause, V., Pollok, B., Schnitzler, A.: Perception in action: the impact of sensory information on sensorimotor synchronization in musicians and non-musicians. Acta Psychol. **133**(1), 28–37 (2010). https://doi.org/10.1016/j.actpsy.2009.08.003
16. Large, E.W.: On synchronizing movements to music. Hum. Mov. Sci. **19**(4), 527–566 (2000). https://doi.org/10.1016/S0167-9457(00)00026-9
17. Lartillot, O., Eerola, T., Toiviainen, P., Fornari, J.: Multi-feature modeling of pulse clarity: design, validation and optimization. In: ISMIR, pp. 521–526 (2008)
18. Lartillot, O., Toiviainen, P., Eerola, T.: A Matlab toolbox for music information retrieval. In: Preisach, C., Burkhardt, H., Schmidt-Thieme, L., Decker, R. (eds.) Data Analysis, Machine Learning and Applications, Studies in Classification, Data Analysis, and Knowledge Organization. Springer, Heidelberg (2008). https://doi.org/10.1007/978-3-540-78246-9_31
19. Madison, G., Karampela, O., Ullén, F., Holm, L.: Effects of practice on variability in an isochronous serial interval production task: asymptotical levels of tapping variability after training are similar to those of musicians. Acta Psychol. **143**(1), 119–128 (2013). https://doi.org/10.1016/j.actpsy.2013.02.010
20. Mainka, S., Wissel, J., Völler, H., Evers, S.: The use of rhythmic auditory stimulation to optimize treadmill training for stroke patients: a randomized controlled trial. Front. Neurol. **9**, 755 (2018). https://doi.org/10.3389/fneur.2018.00755
21. Ollen, J.E.: A criterion-related validity test of selected indicators of musical sophistication using expert ratings. Doctoral Dissertation, The Ohio State University (2006)
22. Palmer, C., Koopmans, E., Loehr, J.D., Carter, C.: Movement-related feedback and temporal accuracy in clarinet performance. Music Percept.: Interdisc. J. **26**(5), 439–449 (2009). https://doi.org/10.1525/mp.2009.26.5.439
23. Pampalk, E., Rauber, A., Merkl, D.: Content-based organization and visualization of music archives. In: Proceedings of the 10th ACM International Conference on Multimedia, pp. 570–579 (2002)
24. Peeters, G.: A large set of audio features for sound description (similarity and classification) in the CUIDADO project (version 1.0). In: Report, Ircam (2004)
25. Repp, B.H.: sensorimotor synchronization: a review of the tapping literature. Psychonom. Bull. Rev. **12**(6), 969–992 (2005). https://doi.org/10.3758/BF03206433
26. Repp, B.H.: Sensorimotor synchronization and perception of timing: effects of music training and task experience. Hum. Move. Sci. **29**(2), 200–213 (2010). https://doi.org/10.1016/j.humov.2009.08.002
27. Repp, B.H., Su, Y.-H.: Sensorimotor synchronization: a review of recent research (2006–2012). Psychonom. Bull. Rev. **20**(3), 403–452 (2013). https://doi.org/10.3758/s13423-012-0371-2
28. Schaffert, N., Janzen, T.B., Mattes, K., Thaut, M.H.: A Review on the Relationship Between Sound and Movement in Sports and Rehabilitation. Front. Psychol. **10**, 244 (2019). https://doi.org/10.3389/fpsyg.2019.00244
29. Styns, F., van Noorden, L., Moelants, D., Leman, M.: Walking on music. Hum. Mov. Sci. **26**, 769–785 (2007). https://doi.org/10.1016/j.humov.2007.07.007
30. Van Dyck, E., Moelants, D., Demey, M., Deweppe, A., Coussement, P., Leman, M.: The impact of the bass drum on human dance movement. Music Percept.: Interdisc. J. **30**(4), 349–359 (2012). https://doi.org/10.1525/mp.2013.30.4.349

31. Vallet, G.T., Shore, D.I., Schutz, M.: Exploring the role of the amplitude envelope in duration estimation. Perception **43**(7), 616–630 (2014). https://doi.org/10.1068/p7656
32. Vos, P.G., Mates, J., van Kruysbergen, N.W.: The perceptual centre of a stimulus as the cue for synchronization to a metronome: evidence from asynchronies. Q. J. Exp. Psychol. Sect. A **48**(4), 1024–1040 (1995). https://doi.org/10.1080/14640749508401427
33. Wallach, H., Newman, E.B., Rosenzweig, M.R.: The precedence effect in sound localization. Am. J. Psychol. **62**, 315–336 (1949). https://doi.org/10.2307/1418275

A Proposal of Emotion Evocative Sound Compositions for Therapeutic Purposes

Gabriela Salim Spagnol[1](✉), Li Hui Ling[2], Li Min Li[1], and Jônatas Manzolli[3]

[1] School of Medical Sciences, University of Campinas, Campinas, Brazil
gabrielaspagnol21@hotmail.com
[2] Proactive Cultural Studio, Campinas, Brazil
[3] Interdisciplinary Nucleus of Sound Communication (NICS), São Paulo, Brazil
https://www.nics.unicamp.br

Abstract.. Recognition and understanding of emotions is a path for self healing. We have worked with Mandalas of Emotions, derived from the Traditional Chinese Medicine (TCM), as a complementary therapy. In this paper, we present the conceptual framework related to the creation of sound collages for the five elements of TCM and assessment of these compositions by experienced holistic therapists. Results present quantitative data, according to scales for relaxation, arousal and valence, and qualitative data from transcription and analysis of the recorded responses of volunteers. In our study, the most common perceptions were warmth, irritation, peace and fear. The innovation of this proposal may stimulate further research on emotion-evoking sounds, and in sound composition.

Keywords: Sounds · Music · Emotions · Integrative Therapies

1 Introduction

Music and emotion has been long discussed, but systematic efforts to understand this relation are recent [1]. Its origin in the late 19th century occurs under a perspective of general psychology focused on psychophysics and experimental control. At this time, music psychology favored a more 'basic' perceptual and cognitive process related to music listening [2]. In the 1980s, Sloboda played an important role in developing the field of 'music cognition'. When his book, The Musical Mind [3], received recognition in the field, Sloboda had already started research in another field: music and emotion. Through a revival of Leonard B. Meyer's classic theory about musical expectations [4], Sloboda posed a correlation between 'cognition' and 'emotion'. Sloboda is now considered one of the driving forces in bringing 'music and emotion' to the spotlight, as a primary topic in music psychology [5].

Emotions, according to Koelstra et al. [6], are a psychophysiological process triggered by conscious and/or unconscious perception of an object or situation and are often associated with mood, personality, and motivation. Evoking emotions, including by means of music appreciation, is important to allow the recognition of feeling and to improve coping. In a healthcare service environment, sounds may be used as a masking

R. Kronland-Martinet et al. (Eds.): CMMR 2019, LNCS 12631, pp. 396–408, 2021.
https://doi.org/10.1007/978-3-030-70210-6_26

tool, as a mean to improve patient-healthcare professional relation, and to elucidate the emotional response to the current body and mind condition. This process may also mediate the creation of a therapeutic bound between patient and healthcare professional, the isolation of external sound interferences and improve patient experience and outcomes.

A specific dimensional approach for emotions, called the circumplex model of affection, proposes that all affective states result from two fundamental neurophysiological systems, one related to valence (a continuum of pleasure-dislike) and another to arousal or alertness [7]. According to the circumplex model, each emotion can be understood as a linear combination of two dimensions, or as varying degrees of valence and excitation. Joy, for example, is defined as an emotional state product of strong activation in the neural systems associated with valence or positive pleasure, together with the moderate activation in neural systems associated with excitation [8]. The affective states beyond joy also arise from the same two neurophysiological systems, but differ in the degree or extent of activation.

Specific emotions, therefore, arise from activation patterns within these two neurophysiological systems, along with cognitive interpretations and labeling of these central physiological experiences. Studies have applied the circumplex model to create and use musical parameters. In the study of Wassermann et al. [9], Sonification for Synthetic Emotions was used through the creation of an intelligent space, named as ADA. This artificial organism integrated a great number of sensorial modalities, so as to interact with the visitors through receptor systems. ADA used a language of sound and light to communicate their states of mind, emotions and behaviors.

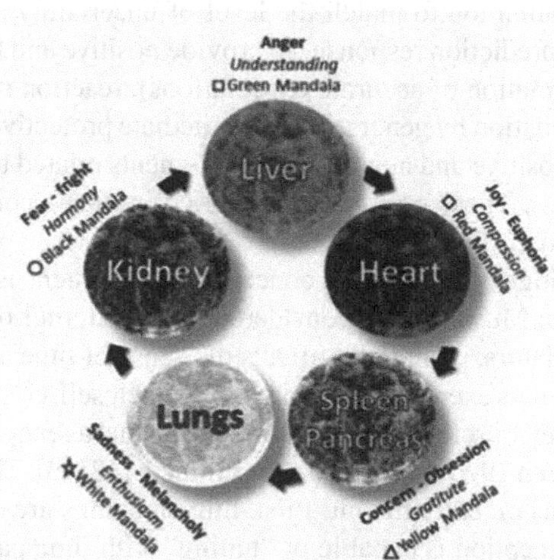

Fig.1. The cycle of mandalas in the sequence: spring/green, summer/red, high summer/yellow, autumn/white, winter/black.

We propose the use of circumplex model in a different context, in which we consider the five emotions based on Traditional Chinese Medicine (TCM), whose aims is to establishment a psychophysical balance. For this reason, the technique called Mandalas of Emotions (ME) applies nine steps to welcome emotions and develop abilities for reflection, as follows: identifying, accepting, accessing, revisiting, understanding, resignifying, reflecting, releasing emotions [10].

For this process, this technique uses five colored, walnut-sized stones that are placed around the patient or on the person's abdomen for periods of 10 to 15 min, creating mandalas that correspond to five colors (green, red, yellow, white, black) and five emotions with its positive and negative correspondents (anger/comprehension, euphoria/ compassion, concern/gratitude, joy/ sadness, fear/courage) (Ling, 2013). These five colors establish a relation to the five seasons (spring, summer, high summer, fall, winter) and to the five functional systems (liver, heart, spleen and pancreas, lungs and kidney) [10], as depicted in Fig.1.

In this paper, we present the conceptual framework related to the creation of sound collages for the five Chinese elements (Wu Xing) and assessment of these compositions by holistic therapists. This relation was established by a strategy of sound collage, composing five pieces, one corresponding to each emotion.

Related Work

Research has shown that sounds may translate emotions, as above mentioned, and also evoke emotions. In this sense, variations in sounds may elucidate what Huron [11] describes as the expectation-related emotion response system, which arouse corresponding limbic activations and contrasts.

Huron [11] defines five expectation-related emotion response systems: imagination (to motivate an organism to behave in ways that increase the likelihood of future beneficial outcomes), tension response (to prepare an organism for an impending event by tailoring arousal and attention to match the level of uncertainty and importance of an impending outcome), prediction response (to provide positive and negative inducements that encourage the formation of accurate expectations), reaction response (to address a possible worst-case situation by generating an immediate protective response), appraisal response (to provide positive and negative reinforcements related to the biological value of different final states). These concepts are applied in music composition in order to create absorbing sounds.

Moreover, psychologists describe the concept of entrainment as essential to perceive, react and enjoy music. Music, when considered as an external oscillator entraining a person's internal oscillators, potentially affects the sense of time and the sense of being in the world. Also, listeners exercise a great amount of their self-control in directing music entrainment, through unconscious processes and individual agency. Jones and colleagues published works between 1976 and 2002 on entrainment [12, 13]. This research considers three main assumptions on entrainment. First, human beings are considered inherently rhythmical, whose perception is capable of "tuning" with time patterns in the physical world. There is a tendency of synchronizing an individual's endogenous rhythms with perceived and expected rhythmic processes. Second, entrainment takes place as both period and phase present synchronization. At last, entrainment may vary in degrees.

In this paper, we illustrate the use of the Affective Slider[1] and other qualitative and quantitative data collection strategies performed to present sound compositions for expert assessment. Therefore, our methods section is intended to support further studies with similar approaches. Results present quantitative data, according to scales for relaxation, arousal and valence, and qualitative data, which derive from transcription and analysis of the recorded responses of volunteers. In our study, the most common perceptions were warmth, irritation, peace and fear; drawing a parallel to its corresponding mandalas.

2 Methods

This section will present the method for creation of sound collages and its assessment by holistic therapists.

2.1 Creation of Sound Collages

We created five compositions, one for each mandala, using Audacity 2 with sound collages. These sound collages were chosen based in the elements of its corresponding mandala, which will be further elucidated in Table 1. We also considered the stages of the relaxation process defined in the method, as three main phases (receive the emotion, reflect, and release the emotion). The duration of each composition was defined as 2.30 min, which creates a cycle that can be repeated for therapeutic purposes. Components followed the rationale described in Table 1.

Table 1. Elements, emotions, concepts and sound elements for each mandala.

Mandala	Elements	Emotions	Concepts	Sound elements
Green	Wood	Peace or Harmony	Beginning, birth of intentions	Shakuhachi and sound landscape of wind through bamboo
Red	Fire	Anxiety and confort	Growth, expansion	Sounds of hang drum, rattle and burning wood
Yellow	Earth	Gratitude and Concern	Harvest results	Sounds of two slowed hang drum rhythms
White	Metal	Joy and sadness	Reflection	Sounds of koshi bells and wind
Black	Water	Fear and courage	Conclusion	Sounds of ocean waves and rain

[1] The Affective Slider, developed by Betella and Verschure [14] represents a model for data collection on reported valence and arousal, as described in the Methods Section. It is an advantage to use this model, since it will reflect a certain approximation to reality for experimental purposes.

Original sounds have been altered from YouTube relaxation pieces to serve as samples and test the composition method. In order to create a database of sounds, we searched for videos on YouTube that presented a reference to the element of each mandala. For instance, wood is the element of the green mandala. The Japanese flute called Shakuhachi was chosen due to its relation to traditional knowledge and the possibility of having a melody with few notes, allowing collage-based techniques. We also used a sound of wind through bamboo to depict a sound landscape that posed a direct reference to wood and green, which the concept of mandalas (Table 1) associates with a calm and comprehensive atmosphere. For the red mandala, whose element is fire, there is a greater activity, with a rhythmic and repetitive melody, presented with a sound landscape of burning wood. This composition was expected to convey a feeling of warmth and a minor level of excitement or anxiety. For the yellow mandala, we searched for sounds of traditional tribal drums as a reference to earth or desert, and we reduced the pace of the rhythm. For the white mandala, we searched for sounds created with metal, such as bells and chimes. At last, the black mandala comprises sounds related to water: sound waves, rain and a rain rattle.

The sound collages were organized to follow the nine stages of emotion recognition, as previously mentioned in the introduction section (identifying, accepting, accepting, accessing, revisiting, understanding, resignifying, reflecting and releasing emotions), which were comprised in three main steps: identify, revisit and release. Translated into sound composition, we created the rationale depicted in Fig. 2 below.

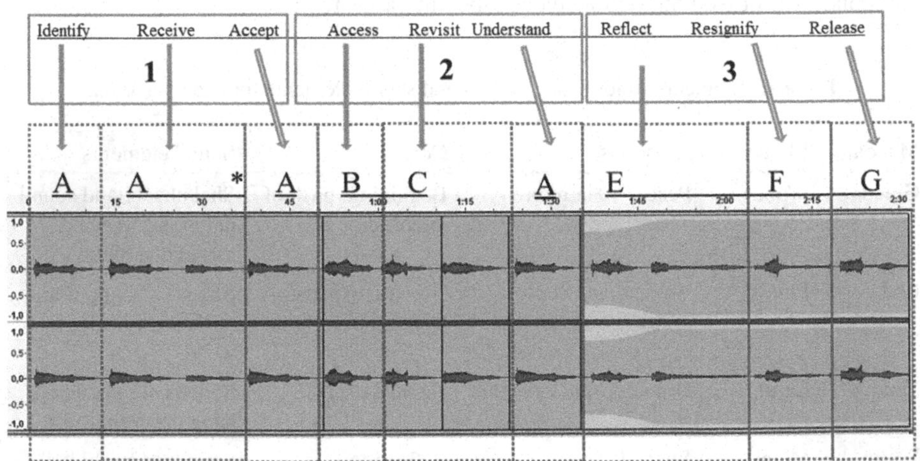

Fig. 2. The figure illustrates a print from the Audacity 2, in which A represents the arrival of the emotion, repeated throughout the composition.

In the next stage of this study, these collages will be reformulated, using original sounds and instruments, in order to be released for therapeutic purposes.

2.2 Assessment by Holistic Therapists

This study was performed with 8 participants on June 2018 from 8 am to 6 pm, with sessions of 30 min with each volunteer. In terms of sample size, we applied the first round of the Delphi method for validation of materials with experts as described by Alexandre and Colucci [15]. Selection process of volunteers included only professionals with more than one year of experience in applying Mandalas of Emotions, after signing an Informed Consent Term under Ethics Committee approval from University of Campinas. We prepared a controlled environment in which the volunteer laid down and listened to the compositions with a Microsoft Headset LX-3000. The volunteer listened to the 2.30 min samples in a randomized order, which was unknown to the researcher who performed the experiment.

Data collection started with questions regarding relaxation (visual Likert-scale, which ranges from 1, not relaxed, to 5, completely relaxed), valence and arousal levels with a validated visual scale called Affective Slider, that we printed in A4 white sheets to be marked with a pencil [14]. According to these authors, the "Affective Slider" (AS) is "a digital self-reporting tool composed of two sliders that measure arousal (top) and pleasure (bottom) on a continuous scale. The AS does not require written instructions and it is intentionally displayed using a neutral chromatic palette to avoid bias in ratings due to the emotional connotation of colors".

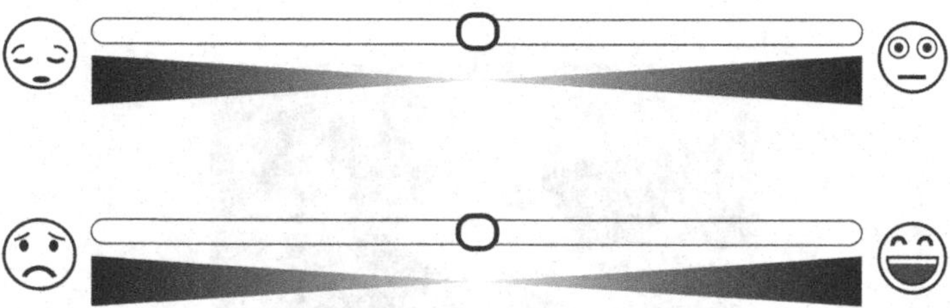

Fig. 3. This original Affective Slider is used in a touch-screen device, that allows to scroll the marker, placed in the center of each scale. We deleted this marker, printed this scale and instructed the participant to mark with a pencil.

Each mark on these scales was converted in centimeters, in order to elaborate graphs for further analysis. See the experiment flow in Fig. 4.

Before listening to any composition, participants fulfilled the scales as mentioned in step A. In B, the researcher asked the volunteer response considering its body and mind perceptions, which include memories and colors. In C, the researcher presents a series of images (Fig. 5) and materials (Fig. 6) that represent each element (wood, fire, earth, metal and water) in forms that correspond to those used in the compositions. Those images and elements are depicted in Figs. 3 and 4. This strategy aimed to recall timbre perceptions, using these materials to enable characterizing the musical perception, once that volunteers did not present a background in musical knowledge.

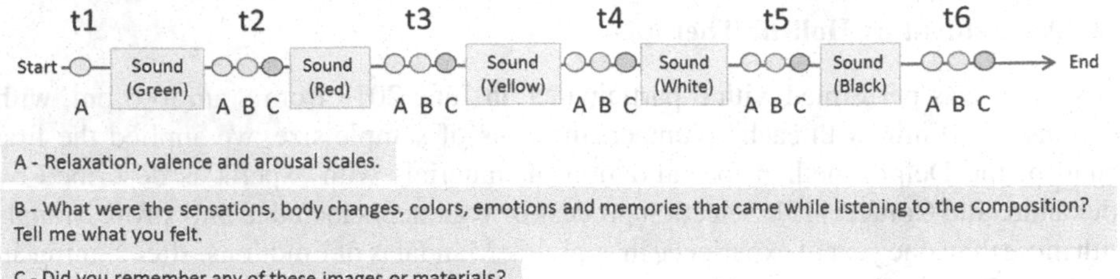

Fig. 4. Illustration of the experiment flow. The first period of data collection (t1) to the last (t6); A, B and C represent the qualitative and quantitative data collection questions and each box shows the presentation of sound. For each volunteer, the order of these compositions was different, in a randomized distribution. The sound was also unknown to the researcher who collected data.

Fig. 5. Pictures presented to volunteers that corresponded to elements of timbre in each composition.

Fig. 6. Materials presented to volunteers corresponded to elements of timbre in each composition.

3 Results

This section will present quantitative results, according to data collected using the scales for relaxation, arousal and valence, and qualitative data, which derives from transcription and analysis of the recorded responses of volunteers.

3.1 Quantitative Results

Volunteers presented the level of relaxation in a continuous scale that ranged from 0 to 100 mm, marked with five possibilities of levels (1 = not at all, 5 = very much). Data in Fig. 7 represents measurement from the first period (t1) to the last (t6). Results show a progressive relaxation effect throughout the experiment, with a plateau between t5 and

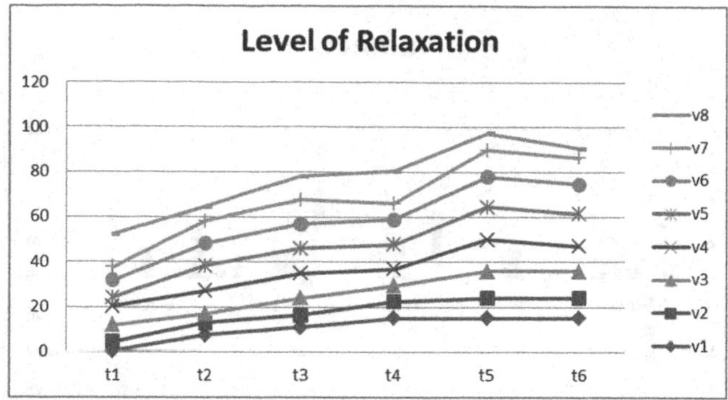

Fig. 7. Level of relaxation for each of the data collection periods, which range from t1 to t6. The initial period (t1) depicts the volunteer's baseline, before any sound intervention.

t6. It is important to mention that the compositions were in a randomized order; therefore, graph 1 depicts the isolated effect of the experiment, showing that any combination of compositions provokes a similar outcome throughout time.

Volunteers were also required to fulfill the Affective Slider scale, which was printed in a paper, indicating with a pencil the current position of their arousal level, as shown in Fig. 8. The same was performed for valence (Fig. 9). In these graphs, we present the isolated results per composition (green, red, yellow, white or black).

Considering media and standard deviation, results indicate a greater effect in terms of arousal variations in the following order: white, 0.7 (1.3); black, 0.3 (1.5); green, 0.4 (2.0); red 0.3 (1.5); yellow, 0.0 (2.0) and in terms of valence variations: green, 2.35 (2.2); white 1.1 (2.0); red, 0.55 (0.75); black, 0.1 (2.1) and yellow, 0.0 (1.5). For therapeutical purposes, arousal levels must present a minor change, since the subject is expected to have a steady state of mind and body but, at the same time, present a variation related to the emotion-evoking process.

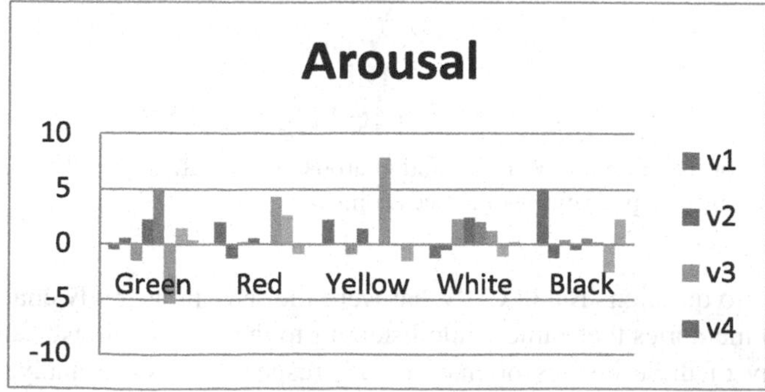

Fig. 8. Level of arousal for each mandala composition (green, red, yellow, white and black) and volunteers (v1 to v8).

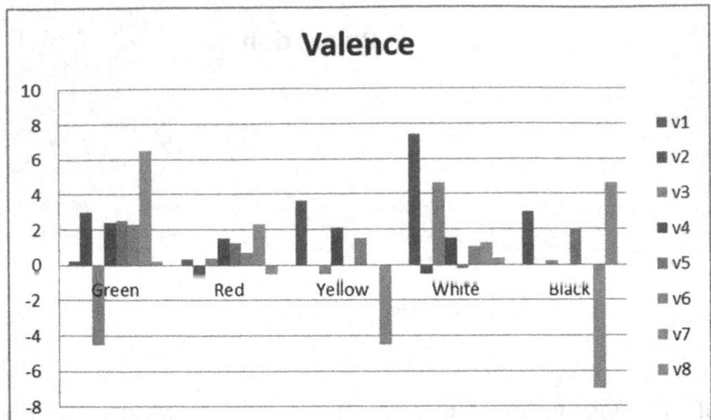

Fig. 9. Level of valence for each mandala composition (green, red, yellow, white and black) and volunteers (v1 to v8).

3.2 Qualitative Results

For each period illustrated in Fig. 4, that depicts the experiment flow, we asked questions that would convey the perceptions of our volunteers. For each composition, volunteers were asked to describe it as an emotion. We present this data in the form of a word cloud in Fig. 10, showing a wide range of outcomes.

Fig. 10. Results of the question "Which emotion arouse when listening to the sound composition?". Created with < https://www.wordclouds.com/ >

Responses to questions B and C: "What were the sensations, body changes, colors, emotions and memories that came while listening to the compositions?" and "Did you remember any of these images or materials?", respectively, were analyzed for each composition in order to convey the main topics of outcomes, as described in the following paragraphs and in Table 2.

In general, the composition of the green mandala brought a feeling of opening, beginning, with light tones. Six of eight volunteers pointed out as very relaxing, and that it should be the first of all compositions. According to volunteers, this sound referred to the green, wood, bamboo, as well as the desert and the vastness. These perceptions confirm that specialists related this composition to the green mandala. The sound of the red mandala was indicated by 7 of the 8 volunteers as related to warmth, comfort. Volunteers attributed this sensation to the cracking of fire sounds, but referred that its intensity could be reduced.

Specialists related the composition of yellow mandala to elements of earth (sand), wind, wood, and feelings of trust and gratitude. The sound of the white mandala brought elements of metal, water, wind, peace, but also irritation and anxiety associated with metallic sounds. Volunteers suggested reducing the information in this mandala. The sound of the black mandala was related to the sounds of waves, sand and also fear. Participants referred that there were several elements in this composition, and that these could be reduced.

Table 2. Responses for emotions, colors, elements and memories indicated by volunteers for each sound composition.

Mandala	Volunteers report
Green	Emotion: hope, peace, calm Colors: light colors, green Elements: bamboo, wood Memories: forest, wind
Red	Emotions: trust, gratitude, good memories Colors: red, dark colors Elements: fire Memories: fire, bonfire
Yellow	Emotions: peace, irritation, anxiety Colors: light and warm colors Elements: sand Memories: wide field, horses
White	Emotions: peace, irritation, anxiety Colors: dark, blue, black Elements: metal, water Memories: wind, desert
Black	Emotions: fear, irritation, affliction, determination Colors: black, yellow, blue, dark Elements: sand, water Memories: storm, beach

4 Discussion

This study presents the application of a method to assess specialists' response to collage-based compositions. These compositions are related to the five emotions derived from the Traditional Chinese Medicine (see Table 1). Quantitative and qualitative data conveyed participants' perceptions and suggestions concerning the sounds, which will be later considered to compose the final version of each mandala.

The composition aesthetics followed characteristics of American Minimal Music and music commonly used for therapeutic purposes. According to a systematic review of randomized controlled trials that applied music interventions in a Neonatal Intensive Care Unit (NICU), music for therapies should be "soothing and not use too many different elements in terms of instruments, rhythms, timbres, melodies and harmonies" [16]. Considering this definition, the review study shows that the preferable choice of music is a lullaby, softly sung or played on an instrument. Also, we understand that familiarity plays an important role in music appreciation, so this strategy aimed at creating some degree of recognition related to a music style. In a study by Pereira et al. [17], brain activation data revealed that broad emotion-related limbic and paralimbic regions as well as the reward circuitry were significantly more active for familiar relative to unfamiliar music.

Instead of presenting a classification of emotions for participants to choose from, we performed open-ended questions, which were recorded and later analyzed. We also used physical elements and images related to elements of the five emotions to question whether participants identified sound landscapes and concepts applied in compositions. When comparing results in Table 2 with emotions in Table 1, we may state that there is a considerable parallel, and adjustments that can be implemented to reduce unwanted reactions, such as irritation.

Considering that these compositions allowed emotion arousal, as described in the Results section, we may compare our findings to those of Sloboda [18]: seventy-six college students were asked to indicate which of 25 emotions they had experienced to music. Sadness and joy were the two emotional states experienced by most listeners (96.2 and 93.4%, respectively). In our study, the most common perceptions were warmth, irritation, peace and fear as shown in Table 2. We understand that the emotion of joy (55%) may be related to feelings of gratitude, welcoming, peace, comfort and calm, whereas sadness (37%) may be associated with fear, affliction, not to mention the report of "sadness" itself.

Limitations of this study are related to the sample size, which could be later expanded, and the application of only one round with experts. Once we apply changes in the compositions, we expect to organize a second round of experts' assessment to validate our compositions. Our results are limited to the self-reported perceptions of volunteers, using visual scales that may not correspond to physiological changes in arousal and valence. Since this research project is under development, at some point, new research could be incorporated in this study. Also, quantitative and qualitative methods of conveying perception may be later complemented by physiological measures, such as heart rate and skin conductance, and, if applicable, brain activation experiments.

5 Conclusion

Mandalas of Emotions derive from a secular culture, Chinese Medicine, and establish a bridge between East and West for a need as ancient and complex as human beings: self-healing. Evoking, communicating and understanding emotions have been widely developed through integrative therapy and music, paths to reestablish a balance in the body and mind. The creation of sound compositions based in an emotion-evoking therapy may enhance its potential and, therefore, the possibility of self-healing.

This study provides a conceptual framework for creation of sound collages and testing of these with experts, based in Mandalas of Emotions. The innovation of this proposal may stimulate further research on emotion-evoking sounds, in sound composition and, possibly, in computational music. We understand that the creation of modulated music and systematization of sounds must be preceded by a process of applying and validating a conceptual framework, which could be pursued as we proposed. In the next stages of this ongoing project, we intend to use a music software tool to transform these compositions based on the listener's response in real time, and improve data collection methods.

Ackowledgements. We thank the support provided by the Interdisciplinary Nucleus for Sound Studies (NICS), UNICAMP, the Brazilian Research Institute of Neuroscience and Neurotechnology (BRAINN) and the Mandalas of Emotions experts. We also thank for the valuable insights from Charles de Paiva, researcher at NICS. This work was developed with the financial support of the Coordination for the Improvement of Higher Education Personnel - Brazil (CAPES), Financing Code 001.

References

1. Juslin, P.N., Sloboda, J.A.: The past, present, and future of music and emotion research. In: Juslin, P.N., Sloboda, J.A. (eds.) Handbook of Music and Emotion: Theory Research, Applications, pp. 933–955. Oxford University Press, New York (2010)
2. Deutsch, D. (ed.): The Psychology of Music, 2nd edn., Academic Press, New York (1999)
3. Sloboda, J.A.: The Musical Mind. Clarendon Press, London (1986)
4. Meyer, L.B.: Emotion and meaning in music. IL, Chicago University Press, Chicago (1956)
5. Thompson, W.F.: Music, Thought, and Feeling Understanding the Psychology of Music. Oxford University Press, Oxford (2009)
6. Koelstra, S., Muhl, C., Soleymani, M., Lee, J.-S., Yazdani, A., Ebrahimi, T., Patras, I.: Deap: a database for emotion analysis; using physiological signals. IEEE Trans. Affect. Comput. **3**(1), 18–31 (2012)
7. Russell, J.A.: A circumplex model of affect. J. Pers. Soc. Psychol. **39**, 1161–1178 (1980)
8. Posner, J., Russell, A., Bradley, J., Bradley, P.: The circumplex model of affect: an integrative approach to affective neuroscience, cognitive development, and psychopathology. Dev. Psychopathol. **17**, 715–734 (2005). https://doi.org/10.1017/S0954579405050340
9. Wassermann, K.C., Eng, K., Paul, F.M.J., Manzolli, J.: Live soundscape composition based on synthetic emotions. IEEE Comput. Soc. **10**, 82–90 (2003). ISSN: 1070–986X/03
10. Ling, L.H. Dialogando com as emoções e promovendo a saúde. Curitiba, Insight (2013)
11. Huron, D.: Sweet Anticipation: Music and the Psychology of Expectation. The MIT Press, New York (2006)
12. Jones, M.R.: Time, our lost dimension: toward a new theory of perception, attention, and memory. Psychol. Rev. **83**(5), 323–355(1976)
13. Jones, M.R., Boltz, M.: Dynamic attending and responses to time. Psychol. Rev. **96**(3), 459–491 (1989). https://doi.org/10.1371/journal.pone.0027241
14. Betella, A., Verschure, P.F.M.J.: The affective slider: a digital self-assessment scale for the measurement of human emotions. PLoS ONE **11**, e0148037 (2016). https://doi.org/10.1371/journal.pone.0148037

15. Alexandre, N.M.C., Coluci, M.Z.O.: Content validity in the development and adaptation processes of measurement instruments. Ciência Saúde Coletiva **16**(7), 3061–3068 (2011)
16. van der Heijden, M.J.E., Oliai Araghi, S., Jeekel, J., Reiss, I.K.M., Hunink, M.G.M., van Dijk, M.: Do hospitalized premature infants benefit from music interventions? A systematic review of randomized controlled trials. PLoS ONE **11**(9), e0161848 (2016). https://doi.org/10.1371/journal.pone.0161848
17. Pereira, C.S., Teixeira, J., Figueiredo, P., Xavier, J., Castro, S.L., et al.: Music and emotions in the brain: familiarity matters. PLoS ONE **6**(11), e27241 (2011). https://doi.org/10.1371/jornal.pone.0027241
18. Sloboda, J.A.: Empirical studies of emotional response to music. In: Riess-Jones, M., Holleran, S. (eds.) Cognitive bases of musical communication, pp. 33–46. American Psychological Association, Washington, DC (1992)

Why People with a Cochlear Implant Listen to Music

Jérémy Marozeau(✉)

Hearing System Group, Department of Health Technology,
Technical University of Denmark, Lyngby, Denmark
jemaroz@dtu.dk
https://www.hea.healthtech.dtu.dk

Abstract. The cochlear implant (CI) is the most successful neural prosthetic device in the market. It allows hundreds of thousands of people around the world to regain a sense of hearing. However, unlike a pair of glasses that can restore vision perfectly, the CI still has some shortcomings for non-speech sounds such as music and environmental sounds. Many studies have shown that most CI users have great difficulties perceiving pitch differences or recognizing simple melodies without words or rhythmical cues. Consequently, CI users report finding music less pleasant compared to their pre-deafness period. Despite this, many of those users do not entirely reject music, and it is not uncommon to see young CI users listening to music all day, or even playing an instrument. Listening to music is an experience that arises from more than the sum of the sensations induced by the basic elements of music: pitch, timbre and rhythm. Listening to music is a pleasant experience because it prompts high-level cognitive aspects such as emotional reactions, needs to dance, or the feeling of musical tension. Therefore, CI users still engaged in musical activities might experience some of these high-level features. In this paper, I will review recent studies on music perception in CI listeners and demonstrate that, although most CI users have difficulties with perceiving pitch, additional music cues such as tempo and dynamic range might contribute positively to their enjoyment of music.

Keywords: Cochlear implant · Music and deafness

1 Introduction

The cochlear implant, CI, is a medical device that allows the direct stimulation of the auditory nerve fibers to restore some sense of hearing in severe to profoundly deaf people. Although it successfully helps many patients to perceive speech, the CI shows some limitations when reproducing musical signals [27]. Because of the inadequate frequency resolution created by the device, many CI users show scanty abilities in perceiving pitch, harmony, and timbre [24,25]. However, despite these limitations, it is not uncommon to see young CI users engaged in musical activities. In this review, I will argue that, although their perception of

R. Kronland-Martinet et al. (Eds.): CMMR 2019, LNCS 12631, pp. 409–421, 2021.
https://doi.org/10.1007/978-3-030-70210-6_27

pitch and harmony is limited, music is such a rich and complex signal that CI users can rely on other high-level features to find some genuine enjoyment in musical activities.

2 The Cochlear Implant

In a healthy human cochlea, the sound is conveyed to the brain by the activation of the auditory nerve fibers connected to about 3.500 sensory receptors, called inner hair cells, located along of the cochlea. Unfortunately, damages to those inner hair cells, for example by exposure to loud music, are irreversible. This injury, commonly known as a sensorineural hearing loss, will prevent the acoustic wave from triggering any action potentials along the auditory nerve fibers. In that case, even the most powerful hearing aid will not be able to provide sufficient amplification to restore sound perception. A person suffering from such loss will be considered as candidate for a CI as this device can directly stimulate the auditory nerve and replace the function of the damaged inner hair cells.

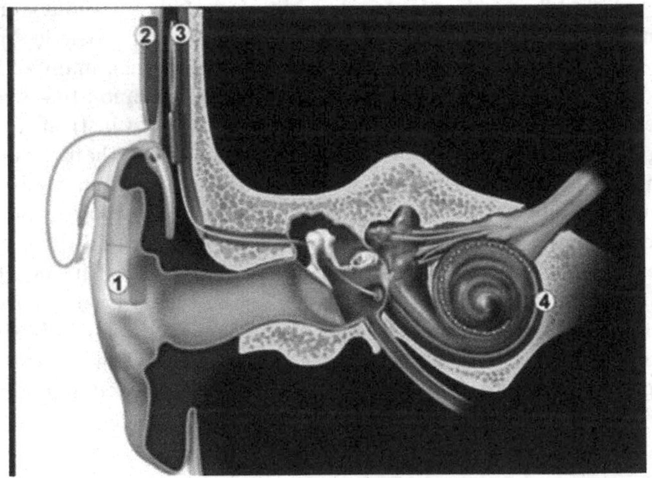

Fig. 1. Schema of a cochlear implant. The sound processor (1) captures a sound via its external microphone and converts it into a corresponding electrical signal. This signal is then transmitted through the skin by a radio-frequency from an external transmission coil (2) to the internal component (3). The electrical signal is then converted into an electric pulse that can generate an action potential in the auditory nerve (4) (Drawing by S. Blatrix for R. Pujol, www.cochlea.eu; used with permission of R. Pujol)

Figure 1 summarises the different parts and function of a cochlear implant. It is composed of an outer and an internal part. The outer part (#1) is a shelf that contains one or more microphones, the batteries, and the DSP chip that converts the acoustic signal into electric pulses based on a predefined sound coding strategy. Those pulses are transmitted as radio-frequency waves via a wireless link antenna (#2) through the skin to the implant's receiver (#3). The antenna and the internal receiver are aligned by a pair of magnets. Finally, the pulses are delivered into the cochlea through a linear array of up to 22 electrodes (#4) and stimulate the auditory nerve directly, thus replacing the function of the hair cells that are lost or damaged in sensorineural deafness. The number of neurons activated will depend on the overall electric charge produced, the distance to the neurons, and the number of functional neurons.

3 The Perception of Music with a Cochlear Implant

Unfortunately, with the current technology, the CI cannot replace perfectly the role of the hair-cells. Therefore, many aspects of sound, important for music perception, will not be restored.

3.1 Pitch

The perception of pitch in normal-hearing listeners relies mainly on two possible coding mechanisms: the place and temporal coding. In the place coding, a pure tone will induce a maximum displacement on the basilar membrane at a specific location. Therefore, the brain will have an indication of the frequency of the sound by analyzing the position of the auditory nerve fibers activated. Given the high number of nerve fibers that homogenously innervate the cochlea, and the active behavior of the basilar membrane, such a cue could provide reliable information to extract a pitch. In the temporal coding, the overall activity of the auditory nerve fibers creates a temporal pattern that is linked to the frequency of the sound (at least up to about 1–4 kHz), giving a possible additional cue to form a pitch percept.

A cochlear implant has a limited number of electrode positions restricting the place coding dramatically. Furthermore, as the electrodes are located at a relatively large distance from the auditory nerve fibers, the current spread inside the cochlea will induce a substantial overlap between the region of neurons activated by each electrode. Additionally, most of the current coding strategies will use a fixed pulse rate that samples the envelope at a low frequency (typically around 500 to 900 Hz). Therefore, both natural pitch coding mechanisms will be only weakly represented in the current CI technology. It is therefore not surprising that studies on CI listeners found very weak abilities to discriminate pitch direction.

In most western music, the smallest pitch difference, the semitone, is about 6% change in fundamental frequency. However, Looi et al. [21] have shown that CI users need an average difference of at least 25% in fundamental frequency between notes, more than a minor third, to start to assess the direction of pitch change accurately. Such a low accuracy creates a clear challenge for CI listeners to follow a melody, in which the most common musical intervals between two notes are below a third [10]. Additionally, many studies using different tasks, such as pitch discrimination, melody recognition, or pitch change detection, have shown that CI users perform, on average, significantly worse than normal-hearing listeners (e.g., [13,18]).

3.2 Harmony

This weak ability to discriminate pitch will also result in an inability to perceive harmony and chord structure. Caldwell et al. [4] have asked ten CI users and 12 normal-hearing (NH) listeners to rate on a Likert scale from −5 (very unpleasant) to +5 (very pleasant) 36 piano pieces especially composed for that study. Those pieces were created based on 12 different melodies played with three possible types accompanying chords: 1) consonant triads, 2) minor seven chords, 3) dissonant minor seven with an augmented fifth. As expected, NH listeners judged consonant triads as the most pleasant, and dissonant chords as the least pleasant. On the other hand, CI users rated all three types of chords as equally pleasant. It is worth noting that despite having a very weak pitch percept, CI users report to enjoy every pieces. Recently, Knobloch et al. [14] showed that CI users rate major chords as more consonant than other types. These results suggest that consonance is somewhat accessible to at least some CI users. However, they are not able to differentiate an authentic cadence from a modified version in which the final tonic was replaced either by a transposed major chord or by a dissonant chord. Similar results were found with young implanted children [35].

3.3 Timbre

Along with the perception of pitch, timbre is also of paramount importance in music appreciation. It is a complex percept that can be divided into three main dimensions influenced by the temporal characteristic (impulsiveness), the spectral envelope (brightness) and spectro-temporal fluctuations [26]. Although the temporal variation of sound can be relatively well conveyed by the CI, it shows some limitations on spectral information [16,17]. This results in a reduced accuracy of CI users to identify musical instruments [7] despite extensive training [6]. However, based purely on the attack time, CI users are still able to differentiate impulsive instruments, like the piano or the guitar, from non-impulsive instruments, like the flute or the violin [11,28]. One might argue that the perception of timbre is not so important to enjoy music. Do we really need to be able to differentiate a trumpet from a saxophone to appreciate a tune from Miles Davis' Quintet? Do we really need to listen to music with a high-fidelity sound system to experience some great joy out of it? While this might be true, it is worth noting that timbre is of paramount importance to segregate different instruments. Without that ability, a beautiful and sophisticated symphony may turn into a giant sonic mess.

3.4 Rhythm

It can be argued that rhythm is at the core of music. Fortunately, studies have shown that CI users can perform at nearly comparable levels as NH listeners on simple rhythmical tasks such as pattern reproduction and discrimination [8], tempo discrimination [15], or dance in rhythm [30]. However, Jiam and Limb [12] argued that many of the studies on rhythm perception in CI users were based on relatively simple perception tasks, that differed from real-world music composed of multiple streams of many different notes. Such a dichotomy might reduce the ecological validity of those studies. In fact, the perception of tempo in music will depend on the ability to detect strong and weak beats. It relies on the ability to segregate different musical streams and on accurately identifying loudness differences. As both of those cues are affected by the CI sound coding scheme, it remains unclear how CI users can detect complex polyphonic rhythms or get an accurate sense of *groove*.

4 Why Do CI Users Listen to Music?

In the previous section, I have discussed many studies that showed that CI users have great difficulties in most of the building blocks of music. It should be natural then to assume that CI users would avoid music at any cost. In fact, Looi and She [22] have found with a survey on musical habits of over a hundred CI listeners that music was overall less enjoyable post-implantation. However, some CI listeners reported to enjoy music and to listen to it very often. Migirov et al. [29] showed that among 53 CI users tested, only 27% reported to never listen to music post-implantation. Interestingly, 30% of them still have a musical activity (playing an instrument or singing). A similar result was shown in a study by Brockmeier et al. [3], who found that 65% of their CI users regularly listen to music and 50% of them rate the quality via their CI as *pleasant.* One might wonder why do CI users still listen to music, given all the difficulties they have to perceive it. I will argue in the rest of the paper, that CI users can understand some higher-level features of music that allow them to find genuine enjoyment in musical activities.

4.1 The Perception of Musical Emotion

Music is often considered as the language of emotion. It is, therefore, essential to understand the emotional content of a piece to enjoy it. Given that emotion is mostly conveyed in Western music by mode (major or minor) and tempo, CI users might have some difficulties to perceive it. Surprisingly different studies have shown that although they are not as precise as NH listeners, CI users are able to classify a piano piece accurately as *Happy* or *Sad* [1,2,33]. Given the lack of frequency resolution in the CI, it is unlikely that they only rely on the mode to perform this task. However, the question remains whether they are able to identify the emotional content based solely on pulsation.

For the sake of clarity, I will make a clear distinction in the rest of the document between the tempo, a musical instruction as noted by the composer on the music score, and the pulsation, a perceptual quality that can be defined as the heartbeat of the music or the pace at which someone will tap along the music.

If tempo is fixed and objective, pulsation can vary dramatically for a listener to another. For example, when a crowd starts clapping during a live performance, some people will tape every beat, some every downbeat, some every upbeat and some all over the place. However, after a few seconds, a consensus will appear, and most of the crowd will be more or less in sync. Therefore, although it can be argued that there is no single objective way to tap one music, one can extract a pulsation pace that will suit most people.

Vannson et al. [33] have asked 19 CI users to rate the intended emotion of 28 piano pieces specially composed to induce a specific feeling on a continuous slider labeled *Happy* and *Sad*. Among those 28 pieces, 14 were written in major mode, with tempi that varied from moderate to fast to convey happiness and 14 in minor, with tempi that ranged from slow to moderate to express sadness [34]. The published data suggest that the judgment of CI users can be modeled based solely on tempo.

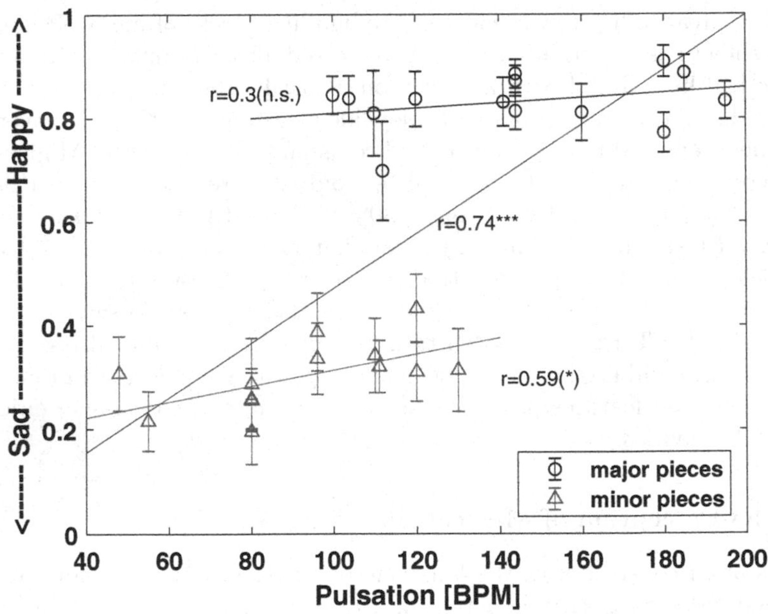

Fig. 2. Replot of the data from Vannson et al. [33]. The average emotional of rating 28 musical pieces is plotted as function of pulsation. The error bars represent the standard errors. Three regression lines and their corresponding correlations scores are shown: in blue for all the stimuli, in black for the subset of minor songs, and in red the major songs. (Color figure online)

A recent re-analysis of this data suggests a slightly different conclusion. Figure 2 replots the data as a function of the pulsation (collected and averaged across eight normal-hearing listeners). All the pieces in major mode (dark circles) are classified as *Happy* and all the pieces composed in minor mode (red triangles) as *sad*. On average, all the major pieces were played with a faster pulsation, ranging from 100 to 200 BPM, than the minor pieces, ranging from 45 to 130 BPM. Because of the collinearity between the two factors (mode and pulsation), it is difficult, in a purely statistical point of view, to disentangle their respective effects on emotional judgments. However, given the difficulties of CI users to perceive the harmony, it can be assumed that the temporal cues alone are driving their emotional judgment. The question remains of which temporal cues are used. Although pulsation is significantly correlated with the judgment of CI users ($r(27) = 0.7390, p < 0.0001$), it cannot explain all the data. First, a large difference can be observed between the minor pieces played at pulsation above 100 BPM, and the major ones played at a pulsation below 140 BPM. If the CI listeners had relied purely on pulsation, then those pieces should have been rated with similar emotion. Furthermore, it can be seen that a major piece with a pulsation of 100 BPM is judged as happier than minor pieces with similar or faster paces. Additionally, when considering the subset of the pieces in one specific mode, the correlation was much weaker for the minor pieces alone ($r(13) = 0.5913, p = 0.0259$) and not significant for the major pieces alone ($r(13) = 0.3013, p = 0.2951$). Different hypotheses can be put forward to explain this result. First, the pulsations were derived from NH listeners tapping along with the piece. These estimations might not be accurate. For example, the major piece at 110 BPM might be perceived as double by CI users. Second, it has been shown that CI users rate major chords as more consonant than minor chords [14]. Therefore, it cannot be excluded that CI users have access to the mode and will use it to form their judgments. Third, happy pieces have not only higher tempi, but they also have usually more syncopated rhythm, faster notes, and overall higher pitch. Therefore, CI users might have learned those subtle additional cues to extract the emotional content of the pieces accurately.

The audio signal was processed through the miningsuite toolbox[1] to extract possible temporal descriptors that could correlate strongly with the emotional judgment. Different temporal cues were tested, such as the nPVI, the duration of the notes, syncopation. The most promising descriptor evaluates the log of the geometric mean of the difference between the onset of two consecutive events. We will call this descriptor: Mean Onset-to Onset Difference, *MOOD*:

$$MOOD = log(\sqrt[n-1]{\prod_{i=1}^{n-1} (t_{i+1} - t_i)}) \tag{1}$$

This descriptor is highly negatively correlated with the pulsation. However, *MOOD* can be considered as a quantity more accessible or more primary than the pulsation. To extract a pulsation, a listener needs to extract a specific time interval from a structure that might be complex. This might be straightforward for some musics with a define beat (like techno music) but can be more challenging for music like free jazz. The MOOD, on the other hand, requires only to estimate the average duration between successive events that can be easily convey

[1] http://olivierlar.github.io/miningsuite/.

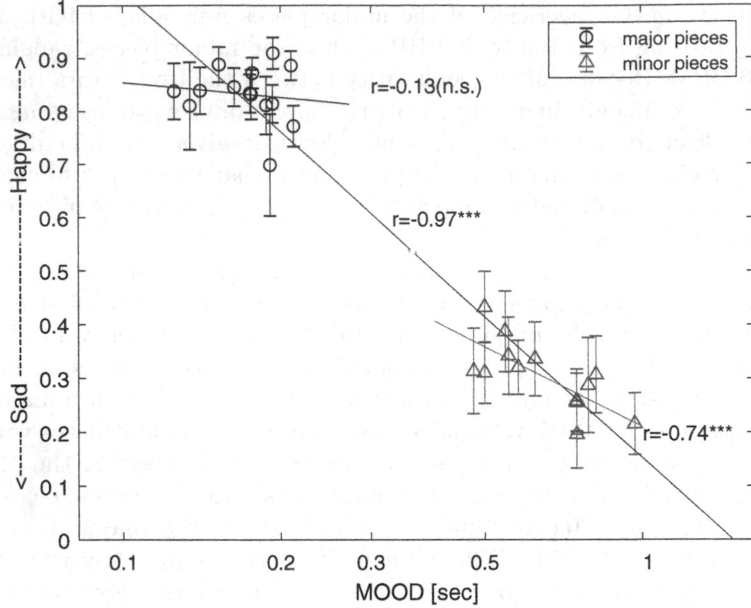

Fig. 3. Replot of the data from Vannson et al. [33]. The average emotional of rating 28 musical pieces is plotted as function of MOOD. See Fig. 2 for more detail. (Color figure online)

by a CI. The log of the geometric mean was implemented to reproduce our logarithm perception of time. Figure 3 plots the emotional judgement as a function of the MOOD. The correlation between all the pieces and the MOOD is much stronger than with the pulsation ($r(27) = 0.9702, p < 0.0001$). Furthermore, the two groups are clearly separated. When considering the subset, the minor pieces were strongly correlated with MOOD ($r(13) = -0.7495, p = 0.0025$). However, no correlation was found for the between the major pieces and the MOOD.

4.2 The Perception of Musical Tension

An intense musical experience can often be linked to changes in musical intensity, or tension, in which the music gets gradually more dissonant and louder to reach a climax and then resolve into a smoothing and consonant moment that brings relief [19,31]. Therefore, it can be hypothesized that to enjoy music, CI users must experience those different stages of musical intensity.

Tension rating can be modeled by a combination of tonal entropy, novelty, spectral centroid, and sound intensity [9]. **Tonal entropy** is related to the harmonic structure of music. In western music, tension is often created by subtle cues such as a dissonant chord, a delayed resolution or the resolution of a dominant chord on the tonic [19,20]. However, as CI users cannot discriminate between a consonant and dissonant chord progression [4] nor identify a cadence [14], it is unlikely that they will be able to use this cue to experience musical tension. **Novelty** relies on the capacity to memorize and identify pitch sequences. Given the weak ability of CI users to recognize well-known melody [5] it is unlikely that they will be able to rely on the novelty cue. **Spectral centroid** is related to the perception of the averaged energy content of the spectrum. Although as discussed Sects. 3.1 and 3.3, CI users cannot perceive fine differences in the spectral shape, they are still able to detect large variations of frequency, as needed to perceive vowels, and could perceive the spectral centroid in a similar way as NH listeners [23]. Finally, although the dynamic range of CI is limited to about 40 dB and often includes some heavy compressions, a monotonic relationship between the **sound intensity** and loudness can be achieved with CI users. Therefore, if CI users experience musical tension, they should rely mainly on loudness cues.

To test that hypothesis, Spangmose-Pedersen, Hjortkjær and Marozeau [32] have asked 9 NH and 9 CI listeners to rate the musical tension on a continuous analog slider of the Mozart's Piano Sonata No. 4 (K282) performed by an experienced pianist. In addition to the original piece, two modified versions were also tested in which 1) all the notes were altered, 2) the intensity of each keystroke was kept constant.

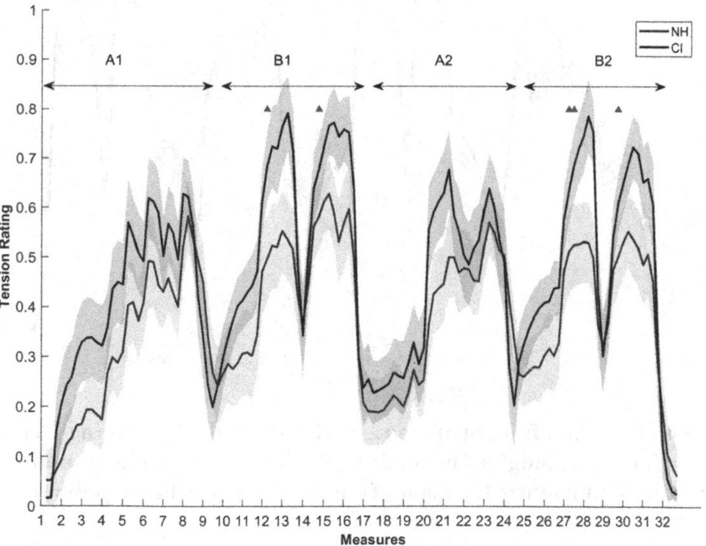

Fig. 4. Replot of the data from Spangmose-Pedersen et al. [32]. Average tension ratings of CI listeners (in black) and NH listeners (in blue) as a function of the musical measures. Horizontal double arrows outline the 4 parts of the piece (A1, B1, A2, B2). Shaded areas represent standard errors. Red triangles indicate the period in which the two ratings differ significantly. (Color figure online)

Figure 3 represents the average rating for both groups as a function of the musical measure. The piece can be divided into two repeating parts (A1, B1, A2,

B2). The first 9 measures include the first part (A1) with a climax of maximal tension between the measures 6 and 7, and a release in 9. Measures 10 to 20 form the second part (B1), with two climaxes (12–13 and 15–16) and a long period of release (17–20). Then the piece is repeated with the same notes in parts A2 and B2 (20 til the end), but with a different interpretation of the musician. Surprisingly, the average rating pattern of CI users is highly correlated with the ratings of the NH users ($r(126) = 0.92385, p < 0.0001$). Additional statistical analysis (for more detail see [32]) outlined only few moments, during the climaxes of the section B1 and B2, in which the ratings of the CI users were significantly larger than those of NH listeners. This result suggests that CI users report a more intense experience of music. However, this interpretation should be taken with a caution, as CI listeners might have interpreted the task differently than the NH listeners.

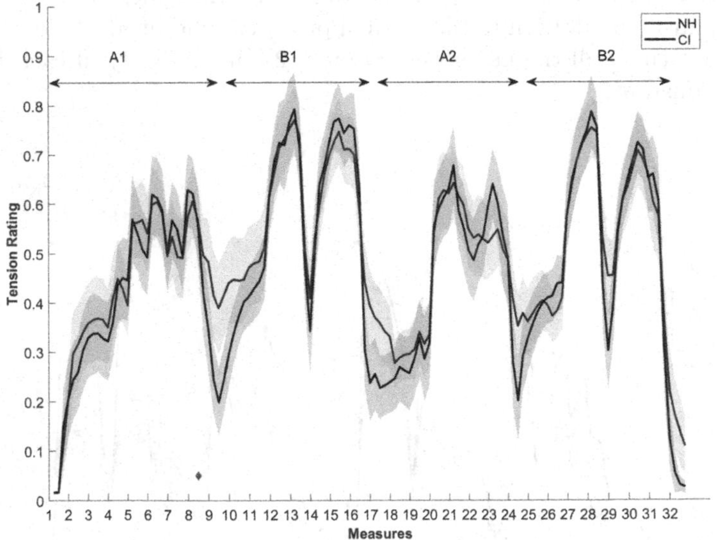

Fig. 5. Replot of the data from Spangmose-Pedersen et al. [32]. Average tension ratings of CI listeners (in black) judging the original piano piece (as in Fig. 4) and NH listeners (in blue) judging a randomized version of the piece. (Color figure online)

In a follow-up condition, the listeners were presented with a modified version of the piece, where the pitch of each note was set to a random value. All other information, such as the timing and the velocity of the keystrokes were kept identical to the original piece. Results showed that removing tonal information had a much larger effect on the ratings of the NH listeners compared to the CI listeners. In fact, the average judgment of NH listeners with this atonal version reproduced astonishingly well the original judgment of the CI listeners (see Fig. 4). A third condition was tested in which the stimulus was a version of the piece where the velocity of the keystrokes was kept constant. This manipulation had a more pronounced effect on the ratings of the CI listeners than for the NH listeners. Overall, this experiment confirms that CI users can rate musical tension in a very similar way as NH listeners, but that they rely mostly on intensity cues while NH listeners integrate many cues along with intensity such as pitch and harmony (Fig. 5).

5 Conclusions

Although the cochlear implant (CI) can be highly successful in restoring speech perception in quiet, it still has some important shortcomings to convey the signals. Many studies have demonstrated that, overall, CI users perform below normal-hearing listeners in tasks relative to pitch, harmony, and timbre. However, they are still able to follow a rhythm change and a variation of intensity accurately. Based on this capacity, they can identify musical emotion, and follow changes in musical intensity. Although their overall percept of music is degraded, they seem to receive enough information to still be engaged in musical activities or simply enjoy listening to music.

Acknowledgments. Data on pulsation with NH listeners presented in Sect. 4.1 was collected by Tanmayee Pathre during her final research project for her master degree. I would like to thank Niclas Janssen for his useful comments on an earlier version of the manuscript.

References

1. Ambert-Dahan, E., Giraud, A.L., Sterkers, O., Samson, S.: Judgment of musical emotions after cochlear implantation in adults with progressive deafness. Front. Psychol. **6**, 181 (2015)
2. Brockmeier, S.: Emotional response to music in combi 40/40+ users. Cochlear Implants International (S1) (2003)
3. Brockmeier, S., et al.: Correlation of speech and music perception in postlingually deafCombi 40/40+ users. In: Kubo, T., Iwaki, T. (eds.) Cochlear Implants - An Update, p. 599. Kugler Publications (2002)
4. Caldwell, M.T., Jiradejvong, P., Limb, C.J.: Impaired perception of sensory consonance and dissonance in cochlear implant users. Otol. Neurotol. **37**(3), 229–234 (2016)
5. Gfeller, K., et al.: Recognition of familiar melodies by adult cochlear implant recipients and normal-hearing adults. Cochlear Implants Int. **3**(1), 29–53 (2002)
6. Gfeller, K., et al.: Effects of training on timbre recognition and appraisal by postlingually deafened cochlear implant recipients. J. Am. Acad. Audiol. **13**(3), 132–145 (2002)
7. Gfeller, K., Witt, S., Mehr, M.A., Woodworth, G., Knutson, J.: Effects of frequency, instrumental family, and cochlear implant type on timbre recognition and appraisal. Ann. Otol. Rhinol. Laryngol. **111**(4), 349–356 (2002)
8. Gfeller, K., Woodworth, G., Robin, D.A., Witt, S., Knutson, J.F.: Perception of rhythmic and sequential pitch patterns by normally hearing adults and adult cochlear implant users. Ear Hear. **18**(3), 252–260 (1997)

9. Hjortkjær, J.: Toward a cognitive theory of musical tension. Ph.D. thesis, Copenhagen University (2011)
10. Huron, D.: Tone and voice: a derivation of the rules of voice-leading from perceptual principles. Music Percept. **19**(1), 1–64 (2001)
11. Innes-Brown, H., Marozeau, J., Storey, C.M., Blamey, P.J.: Tone, rhythm, and timbre perception in school-age children using cochlear implants and hearing Aids. J. Am. Acad. Audiol. **24**(9), 789–806 (2013)
12. Jiam, N.T., Limb, C.J.: Rhythm processing in cochlear implant-mediated music perception. Ann. New York Acad. Sci. **1453**, 22–28 (2019)
13. Kang, R., et al.: Development and validation of the University of Washington clinical assessment of music perception test. Ear Hear. **30**(4), 411–418 (2009). https://doi.org/10.1097/AUD.0b013e3181a61bc0
14. Knobloch, M., Verhey, J.L., Ziese, M., Nitschmann, M., Arens, C., Böckmann-Barthel, M.: Musical harmony in electric hearing. Music Percept.: Interdisc. J. **36**(1), 40–52 (2018)
15. Kong, Y.Y., Cruz, R., Jones, J.A., Zeng, F.G.: Music perception with temporal cues in acoustic and electric hearing. Ear Hear. **25**(2), 173–185 (2004)
16. Kong, Y.Y., Mullangi, A., Marozeau, J.: Timbre and speech perception in bimodal and bilateral cochlear-implant listeners. Ear Hear. **33**(5), 645–659 (2012)
17. Kong, Y.Y., Mullangi, A., Marozeau, J., Epstein, M.: Temporal and spectral cues for musical timbre perception in electric hearing. J. Speech Lang. Hear. Res. **54**, 981–994 (2011)
18. Laneau, J., Moonen, M., Wouters, J.: Factors affecting the use of noise-band vocoders as acoustic models for pitch perception in cochlear implants. J. Acoust. Soc. Am. **119**(1), 491–506 (2006)
19. Lerdahl, F.: Tonal Pitch Space. Oxford University Press, New York (2001)
20. Lerdahl, F., Krumhansl, C.L.: Modeling tonal tension. Music Percep.: Interdisc. J. **24**(4), 329–366 (2007)
21. Looi, V., McDermott, H., McKay, C.M., Hickson, L.: Pitch discrimination and melody recognition by cochlear implant users. Int. Congr. Ser. **1273**, 197–200 (2004)
22. Looi, V., She, J.: Music perception of cochlear implant users: a questionnaire, and its implications for a music training program. Int. J. Audiol. **49**(2), 116–128 (2010)
23. Macherey, O., Delpierre, A.: Perception of musical timbre by cochlear implant listeners: a multidimensional scaling study. Ear Hear. **34**(4), 426–436 (2013)
24. Marozeau, J., Lamping, W.: Timbre perception with cochlear implants. In: Siedenburg, K., Saitis, C., McAdams, S., Popper, A.N., Fay, R.R. (eds.) Timbre: Acoustics, Perception, and Cognition. SHAR, vol. 69, pp. 273–293. Springer, Cham (2019). https://doi.org/10.1007/978-3-030-14832-4_10
25. Marozeau, J., Simon, N., Innes-brown, H.: Cochlear implants can talk but cannot sing in tune. Acoust. Aust. **42**(2), 131–135 (2014)
26. McAdams, S., Winsberg, S., Donnadieu, S., De Soete, G., Krimphoff, J.: Perceptual scaling of synthesized musical timbres: common dimensions, specificities, and latent subject classes. Psychol. Res. **58**(3), 177–192 (1995)
27. McDermott, H.: Music perception with cochlear implants: a review. Trends Amplif. **8**(2), 49–82 (2004)
28. McDermott, H., Looi, V.: Perception of complex signals, including musical sounds, with cochlear implants. Int. Congr. Ser. **1273**, 201–204 (2004)
29. Migirov, L., Kronenberg, J., Henkin, Y.: Self-reported listening habits and enjoyment of music among adult cochlear implant recipients. Ann. Otol. Rhinol. Laryngol. **118**(5), 350–355 (2009). https://doi.org/10.4324/9780429493485

30. Phillips-Silver, J., Toiviainen, P., Gosselin, N., Turgeon, C., Lepore, F., Peretz, I.: Cochlear implant users move in time to the beat of drum music. Hear. Res. **321**, 25–34 (2015)
31. Schoenberg, A.: Style and Idea. St. Martins Press, New York (1975)
32. Spangmose-Pedersen, S., Hjortkjær, J., Marozeau, J.: Perception of musical tension in cochlear implant listeners. Front. Audit. Cogn. Neurosci. **13**, 987 (2019)
33. Vannson, N., Innes-Brown, H., Marozeau, J.: Dichotic listening can improve perceived clarity of music in cochlear implant users. Trends Hear. **19** (2015). https://doi.org/10.1177/2331216515598971
34. Vieillard, S., Peretz, I., Gosselin, N., Khalfa, S., Gagnon, L., Bouchard, B.: Happy, sad, scary and peaceful musical excerpts for research on emotions. Cogn. Emot. **22**(4), 720–752 (2008)
35. Zimmer, V., Verhey, J.L., Ziese, M., Böckmann-Barthel, M.: Harmony perception in prelingually deaf, juvenile cochlear implant users. Front. Neurosci. (2019)

The Deaf Musical Experience

Bodily and Visual Specificities: Corpaurality and Vusicality

Sylvain Brétéché(✉)

Aix Marseille Univ, CNRS, PRISM, Marseille, France
breteche@prism.cnrs.fr

Abstract. This paper focuses on the bodily and visual specificities of the Deaf musical experience, by first focusing on the investigation of a fundamental principle of the human experience, the *corpaurality*, that engages to consider the sono-sensitive bodily qualities and the natural hearing modalities of Deaf; and secondly considering the visual dimensions of music, based on the Deaf practices, that reveal a denormalized musical expression, namely the *vusicality*.

Keywords: Deaf people · Deaf musical experience · Deaf listening · Corpaurality · Somato-sensitivity · Vibratory sensation · Vusicality · Vusic · Sign-singing

1 Introduction

The Deaf[1] relationships to music are often thought to be altered, deteriorated, or reduced because the ordinary consideration of deafness is that of the 'alteration'. Nevertheless, far from presenting only themselves as 'impaired beings' in their capacities of perception and representation of the world, Deaf take on this latter a singular view and, even more singular, give him attentive 'ear' and 'eye', in tune with its sensitive manifestations.

A priori paradoxical, the 'Deaf listening' is yet very real and upset our ordinary conceptions, emphasizing that while deafness is a human condition, it does not reveal

[1] Following the Deaf revendications, I write 'Deaf' with a capital D which, as specified by Charles Gaucher, "announces a quest for identity which falls into very precise historicity and is stated in terms which seek to turn the deaf difference into a cultural particularity detached from the physical incapacity which stigmatizes it" [1, p. 17]. In this way, deafness proposes itself as a social and cultural group, where the constitutive dimensions of the community rely on Deaf specific features. In this article, I use the term Deaf to designate all the individuals who claim the Deaf identity and specificities – cultural, sensorial, social, linguistic,… – but also these specificities, which present themselves like particular qualities: "the attitudinal deafness" [2].

For information, around 466 million people worldwide have disabling hearing loss (over 5% of the world's population – disabling hearing loss refers to hearing loss greater than 40 decibels (World Health Organization estimations). Also, and according to the SIL International census and estimates (2019), there are 144 Sign Languages around the world. However, the number of native speakers of these Sign Languages remains difficult to establish formally but can be estimated at around 10 million (information available via www.ethnologue.com).

R. Kronland-Martinet et al. (Eds.): CMMR 2019, LNCS 12631, pp. 422–448, 2021.
https://doi.org/10.1007/978-3-030-70210-6_28

'alteration' but more especially 'otherness' [3]. Perceptive otherness or representational otherness, in the face of a reality that phenomenologically is not altered. Because the Deaf listening does not concern another sound world, but quite the contrary brings another approach of the common world, of this shared world that we define and fix from a 'normalized' point of view, audio-centered and finally limited to what our ears endeavor to state.

Nevertheless, Deaf people culturally define themselves as 'visual beings' and the specificities of their condition necessarily imply that their capacities for perceiving the reality rest on particularly on its visual and dynamic aspects. But beyond to specify only a characteristically Deaf perceptive feature, the visible presents itself for the 'People of the Eye' - typical Deaf expression – as a founding principle for the development of artistic practices and, in this way, as the primary sense of all aesthetic experiences. Rather than simply content with the visible arts, Deaf also seize on practices that may initially seem inaccessible to them, unreachable or even 'forbidden', such as dance and more specifically music. With their cultural affiliation to a community rich to its specificities, Deaf produce an extra-ordinary music that goes beyond the ordinary conceptions of musical practices, developing what they call the *vusic* – contraction of visual and music. Music of the eye, for the eye, that gives itself to see abandoning the aural dimensions commonly established to define the musical experience. More culturally still, they develop a typically deaf practice of sung in sign language, the sign-singing, where the signifying gesture takes musical values, the words becoming a visual melody, silent and embodied.

In this article[2], I would like to consider the bodily and visual specificities of the Deaf musical experience, by first focusing on the Deaf listening and more specifically on the involvement of the body in the Deaf musical experience [4]; precisely, by the investigation of a fundamental principle of the human experience, the *corpaurality* [5]. It engages to consider the sono-sensitive bodily qualities and the natural hearing modalities of Deaf, modalities which, detached from the ordinary aural perceptions, position the body at the core of the musical experience. In a second part, I will mostly consider the visual dimensions of music, based on the Deaf practices represented by the vusic and the sign-singing, seeking to think how they can bring to a denormalized consideration of music, namely the *vusicality*.

2 Bodily Specificities: The *Corpaurality*

Essential base of sensoriality, the body presents itself as a sense vector and, faced with the sound reality, reveals a dimension inherent in the human condition, what I call the *corpaurality*. Convergence of 'aurality' (what is perceived by the ear) and 'corporeality' (what is experienced by the body), two sensory modalities revealing the perceptible world, corpaurality designated the fundamental connection of the individual

[2] This article is based on 2 papers pre-published in the 14th CMMR-proceeding (ed. by M. Aramaki, O. Derrien, R. Kronland-Martinet & S. Ystad, Marseille 2019): "The 'Deaf listening'. Bodily qualities and modalities of musical perception for the Deaf" (p. 276–285) & "Visual-music? The Deaf experience. 'Vusicality' and Sign-singing" (p. 846–852).

and the sound world: the body is anchored in the sensory world and the audible takes shape through it, form part of corporeality and reveals itself in an embodied way.

The 'hearing norm' that determines the ordinary delineation of the musical experience focuses primarily on the aural aspect of music. Indeed, "we must admit that when we play an instrument or listen to a disc, we use the sense that is socially intended for this purpose - hearing - and we consider most of the time that only the ear has a role to play in the listening function" [6, p. 54].

However, corpaurality as an essential principle of sound perception reveals that the music listening is naturally multi-sensory and confirms what is already known, that it is not only and exclusively located in the aural sphere of the perceptible world. As a sensory reality, the sound phenomenon fundamentally produces a material diffusion of mechanical vibrations, and for that "hearing is only one aspect of vibratory sense. The ear is not the exclusive receptor of sound vibrations, this function involves the whole body" [6, p. 56].

2.1 The Vibratory Sensation

The vibratory sensation informs about the sensory data perceived by the sense organs [7]. The vibratory bodily sensitivity falls within *somesthesia*, that designates specificities of the body to perceive sensorial stimuli [8]. The somatosensory system - or somesthetic system - concerns the sensitivity to stimuli perceived to whole the body, in association or in addition to those directly concerning the sense organs. Somatic sensations can thus give or supplement information on the environment. Unlike the sense organs, which concentrate their receptors in localized parts of the body (ears, eyes,…), the somesthetic system has receptors distributed over the entire body and positioned in the various layers that compose it: skin, bones, and musculotendinous or visceral levels.

The somato-sensitivity is based on specific sensory neurons, the mechanoreceptors, which perceive the stimuli and are attentive to mechanical transformations or deformations of the sensitive environment [8]. Mechanoreceptors concern more specifically – and among others – the vibratory sensations; the human body is, in its entirety, sensitive to vibration frequencies, and this characteristically: "faced with the vibrations transmitted to the whole body, the human body behaves as a complex group […]. At a given frequency, all or some parts of the body will react by amplifying the vibratory" [9, p. 45]. Thus, exposed to mechanical vibrations,

> the human body can be considered like an adaptable mechanical system, consisting of different entities connected to each other by springs and dampers that are the ligaments, muscles, intervertebral discs. When the body is exposed to vibrations, not all organs react in the same way. Each part of the body having its own resonant frequency [10, p. 6].

According to the work of Michael J. Griffin, the whole-body human vibration exploits a frequency field that ranges from about 0.5 to 1,250 Hz [11]. Studies conducted on the resonance frequencies of the human body determine two spaces of vibratory reception and precise notably:

> Human exposure to vibration may be classified due to their peculiarities, in (1) Whole Body Vibrations (WBV): vibrations that, as the name suggests, affect the whole body, particularly in a frequency range 0.5 to 80 Hz […]; (2) Hand-Arm vibration (HAV): vibrations that affect and are transmitted specifically to the hand-arm system, in a frequency range from 6.3 to 1,250 Hz (…) [12, p. 282].

With this specification, it is possible to identify a specific somato-sensitive organization mainly developed – for an overall threshold of perception around 80 dB – at the level of the head, arms, bust, legs, and spinal column, but several studies establish different results for the level distinctions of organ sensitivity. The table below reports 4 of these classifications of the human resonance frequencies (classifications resumed and summarized on Fig. 1):

Table 1. Classifications of the human resonance frequencies (in Hz).

	Rasmussen [13]	Mandal and Srivastava [14]	Duarte et al. [15]	Cardinaels [9]
Skull		50–70		
Head	25	1–2	20–40	25
Shoulders	4–5		4–8	4–5
Maxilla			100–200	
Ocular Globe	20–90	20–25	60–90	30–80
Spinal Column	10–12		8	10–12
Chest Wall	50–100	4–8	60	60
Abdominal	4–8		4–8	4–8
Lungs			4–8	
Hands	150 a 200	30–50	20–70	60
Arms	16–30	15–30		16 à 30
Wrist				50–200
Legs	2 (sit.)–20 (sta.)	2 (sit.)–20 (sta.)		2 (sit.)–20 (sta.)
Knees		1–8		
Feet		16–31		

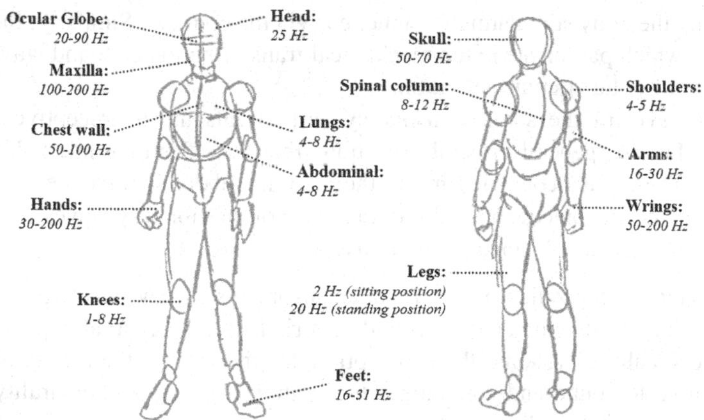

Fig. 1. Presentation of human resonance frequencies

2.2 Modalities of the Sono-Sensitive Body

Indeed, "the human body, despite its higher complexity, can be considered as a biomechanical system for analysis of vibration" [12, p. 282], and the modes of bodily reception of mechanical vibrations are integrated into the somesthetic system, which can be classified in several different ways. Depending on the Sherrington's distinction [16], the sensory system can be categorized according to three distinct levels of sensitivity:

1) first, the exteroceptive sensation, which refers to the external perceptions – cutaneous – of mechanical variations. The body is directly in contact with the sensitive environment through the skin, which contains many sensory receptors – the exteroceptors – that react to air vibrations and oversee the vibrotactile perception. The cutaneous mechanoreceptors reveal the sensitivity of the skin and are associated with three stimuli: pressure, touch, and vibration. Among the exteroceptors, two are more specifically engaged in the perception of mechanical vibrations [8]: the Pacinian corpuscles (which are sensitive to vibrations in the 40 to 1,000 Hz frequency range with an optimal sensitivity around 300 Hz) and Meissner corpuscles (responsible for the 'fine touch' and particularly present in the dermis of hands, feet, lips, and tongue, which are more sensitive to vibrations from 10 to 400 Hz).
2) The second level of somatic receptivity is the proprioceptive sensations, which brings together muscular, bony and tendon perceptions. Considered as the 'in-depth' reception, in opposition to the 'surface' perception represented by the exteroceptive sensation, the proprioceptive sensation allows the reception and transmission of sound vibrations through the musculoskeletal receptors. The bony reception of vibrations also concerns a particular aspect of the transmission of sound to the inner part of the auditory system: the sound is not only transmitted by the sound waves to the middle ear, but also by bone conduction, the vibrations perceived by the body stimulating the inner ear via the cranium. Similarly, the auditory ossicles, which participate in the mechanical transformation of sound waves, can be stimulated by the cranium vibration.
3) The last level of the somatosensory system reveals the interoceptive sensation, which refers to "general visceral sensations that arise from the internal organs"[8, p. 549]. The organs contained in the thoracic and abdominal cavities also contain numerous mechanoreceptors and the transmission of vibratory waves is carried out by the soft tissues contained in the body.

This specific organization of the somatic sensory system reveals the possibilities of the body in the face of sound elements and materializes the corpaurality principle in its physiological reality. The somesthetic reception determines thus the faculty of the body to be sensitive to sound and concretizes the complexity of the corpaurality that formalizes the embodied qualities of listening.

2.3 The 'Deaf Listening'

Corpaurality states this fundamental dimension of music reception and disrupts somehow the ordinary considerations of the musical experience. However, as the Deaf percussionist Evelyn Glennie reminds us, "for some reason we tend to make a distinction between hearing a sound and feeling a vibration, in reality they are the same thing" [17]. Listening to music is feeling the mechanical vibrations of space, which concern the ear, but also and simultaneously the body. Within this context, Evelyn Glennie establishes a relevant connection with the Italian language, to highlight the fundamental link between listening and feeling:

> It is interesting to note that in the Italian language this distinction does not exist. The verb *sentire* means to hear and the same verb in the reflexive form *sentirsi* means to feel. Deafness does not mean that you can't hear, only that there is something wrong with the ears. Even someone who is totally deaf can still hear/feel sounds [17].

Fundamentally, the sound world is felt and the otherness of the Deaf musical experience thus rests on this reality of feeling. Given their specificities, deafness situations reveal a singular apprehension of music that is fundamentally related to ordinary practices, but changes and reconsiders it outside the aural sphere. To be deaf is to feel the music vibrate, and as Danièle Pistone points out, "the hearing-impaired people themselves perceive the sound vibrations" [18, p. 69].

This Deaf musical otherness unveils the peculiarities of deafness as a human condition which, beyond revealing a hearing problem, suggests more precisely another modality of listening, 'denormed' and 'denormative' because fundamentally based on the materiality of sound reality. As Evelyn Glennie once again emphasizes, "to understand the nature of deafness, first one has to understand the nature of hearing" [17], and this can be extended by saying that, in a way, it is through deafness that could be to find out the deep nature of the hearing. Because the corpaurality principle determines the sono-sensitive qualities of the body in its anatomical constitution and its sensory possibilities, even though, in the ordinary musical experience, the listening remains focused on the ear as the privileged sensory organ. The hearing experience cannot escape the aural primacy, essential and natural medium of the musical experience, and it turns out that "only the deaf know what this means not to hear" [6, p. 56]. Therefore, the Deaf musical experience seems capable to restore a hidden but essential facet of hearing, which is in the first instance and in essence "a specialized form of touch" [17]. Basically, the listening aims to be "acoustical prehension" [19, p. 236], namely the grasp of the sound materiality in its vibratory consistency, which touches the ear but also the body in its entirety. The deaf experiences of music appear able to reveal this essential nature of hearing as a grasping medium of audible reality. Listening to music is thus in the Deaf musical experience relocated from the ear to the body, which presents itself as the main base for understanding and expression of musicality.

In the Deaf musical experience, the listening is revealed therefore primarily embodied and the modalities of the Deaf listening refer more specifically to the three levels of somato-sensitivity.

Firstly, we find a cutaneous perception, and indeed "the skin, as a sensory system with all its aptitudes, is therefore an essential organ for the deaf" [6, p. 58], and according to the study conducted by Maïté Le Moël, the most sensitive areas are "the fingers and the palm of the hand, the toes and the soles of the feet" [6, p. 57] – where we find, in particular, Meissner's corpuscles. As outlined the music therapist Alain Carré, "very often, deaf people make music 'bare ears' and often barefoot to have a complete vibratory perception" [20, p. 15]. The sense of vibrations transmitted from the floor passes directly "by the soles of the feet on a massive scale" [6, p. 57], and the air perception of sounds is commonly experienced naturally, without hearing aids ("bare ears") in order to give sustained attention to the vibratory qualities of the music.

Even if elements can be perceived aurally, the Deaf prefer to listen to the music naturally, without artificial deformations. The abandonment of hearing aids during the musical practice is in line with the will of a 'natural practice' (the perceived sounds are not transformed) but also with the desire to avoid the amplification of sounds that are often unpleasant to the ear. Deaf people prefer to live the experience of music in the most natural manner possible, to keep a sound experience not deformed; and as pointed out Alain Carré:

> For the deaf person, the most pleasant perception will often be bare ears, natural since there is no deformation or discomfort of this amplification compared to the wearing of hearing aids, even if they are the best. But in terms of music, deaf musicians often prefer to work with their natural perception, especially since they rely heavily on the processing of vibratory information, even if it does not produce an aural sensation. This vibration becomes relevant for the profoundly deaf person [20, p. 15].

It seems obvious that "the deaf are very sensitive to tactile perception" [6, p. 57] and pay specific attention to structure-born vibrations of the objects and materials that surround them. Claire Paolacci specifies that "the tactile listening is more immediate for the deaf" [21, p. 15] and that the aural perceptions are very often secondary, or less meaningful. The Deaf "know how subtle the answer given by the skin constantly caressed by the sound waves from various origins" [6, p. 57], and they are indeed able to identify a usual or everyday object from the vibrations it produces, without necessarily perceive their aural quality. As the Deaf musician Maati El Hachimi explains: "the Deaf person feels the vibrations in a car, knows if it is going faster or slower, if he/she is in a tractor or in a small car" [21, p. 49]. Hearing people are also endowed with this somato-sensitive capacity of identification of sound elements, but it is primarily their aural perceptions which are significant and meaning; by contrast, "for the people deprived of hearing, the sensory discrimination of the waves by the bodily perception can reach a subtlety that hearing people can hardly suspect" [22, p. 226].

In accordance with this, sono-sensitive experiences are essential in the daily life of Deaf, and as David Le Breton emphasizes,

> vibration sensitivity allows deaf people to gather information about their environment: recognize the voices of relatives, detect footsteps, identify musical moments, the passage of a car, the fall of an object [23, p. 171].

In the instrumental practice, the sonic variations of instruments are also perceived cutaneously, mainly through the hands (directly in contact with the object). This perception of sound vibrations by touch is often sought by the deaf person during the musical experience, and the use of specific objects which materially restore and amplifying the air vibrations (balloon, rigid pipe, wooden crate) is common. Similarly, the Deaf put their hands on the speakers to feel the air vibration produce the sound emission. Cutaneous reception is thus presented as a fundamental sensory modality in the Deaf musical experience,

> the sense of touch can reach, through long learning and multiple experiences, a maximum sensitivity. It can give to hearing-impaired people the pleasure of feeling their skin receive every sound wave [6, p. 58].

This cutaneous perception is associated with a bony reception of sound vibrations, which is based mainly on a structure-borne perception of the acoustic elements: "the bones are actively touched and precisely vibrated by the sound waves which they receive and transmit through the limbs and the whole body" [6, p. 58]. The vibrations of the floor are perceived on the feet and "by the knees where they produce a rotational movement on the kneecaps" [6, p. 57]. Bone perception develops initially by the contact of a body part with a material element, primarily through the legs, which are in contact with the floor; and as a young Deaf reports: "*when I try to listen to music (without hearing aids) I feel by the feet the vibrations. It taps through the body*" [24, p. 44]. The structure-borne reception of the musical vibratory movement seems to begin with the feet and invests in the rest of the body, and according to Maïté Le Moël, "the most sensitive bone areas are the spine, the pelvis (ilium, sacrum, coccyx), the shoulder girdle (clavicles and shoulder blades) and the thoracic cavity (sternum, ribs, vertebrae)" [6, p. 58].

During the instrumental practice, the body is vibrated by the instrument, primarily on the arms, and the bone perception of acoustic variations is also efficient by air conduction because "the head is a bone region frequently vibrating with the acoustic waves and in particular the cranium, the frontal area and the lower jaw" [6, p. 58].

More complex to describe, the internal sensations induce by sound vibrations make it possible "to hypothesize that soft tissues are also good receptors of sound waves" [6, p. 58]. These contain many mechanoreceptors, and the descriptions offered by the deaf [5] of 'resonances' and 'vibrations' on the torso or 'bubbling' in the stomach indicate that the transmission of the vibratory waves is also performed via visceral conduction, which mainly concerns the thoracic and abdominal cavities.

This consideration of the sono-sensitivity of the Deaf musical experience confirms the reality of a specific bodily musical experience. The Deaf perceive and feel the music in and through their body, the latter receiving the sounds according to different perception modalities and develops a truly fine approach to sounds. The music therapist and anthropologist Alain Cabéro specifies that the pitch is felt differently by the body:

> when the sound was low, they located it in the stomach, but also on the face, when the sound was rather high-pitched, they located it along the arms and the head. We also had as answers for the low sounds: knee and hand. The high-pitched is not always very well perceived in its delicacy, it was more by a feeling of pain, in the ears [25, p. 67–68].

These elements show the complexity of the Deaf musical experience which, as the ordinary musical experience, reveals as many facets as it implies of individuals. Each deafness is different, and each experience of the music reports a singular lived experience, deeply embodied, but conveying different meaning values. Evelyn Glennie's testimony shows this complexity of the relation to the sound and the possible diversity of the bodily experiences of the music that it induces:

> I spent a lot of time in my youth (with the help of my school percussion teacher Ron Forbes) refining my ability to detect vibrations. I would stand with my hands against the classroom wall while Ron played notes on the timpani (timpani produce a lot of vibrations). Eventually, I managed to distinguish the rough pitch of notes by associating where on my body I felt the sound with the sense of perfect pitch I had before losing my hearing. The low sounds I feel mainly in my legs and feet and high sounds might be particular places on my face, neck, and chest [17].

To make more concrete this somatic sensitivity of the Deaf, we can see the body areas stimulated during the musical experience (Fig. 2), areas specified by the Deaf in a survey conducted in 2015 [5] and which precisely correspond to the human resonance frequencies (Fig. 1):

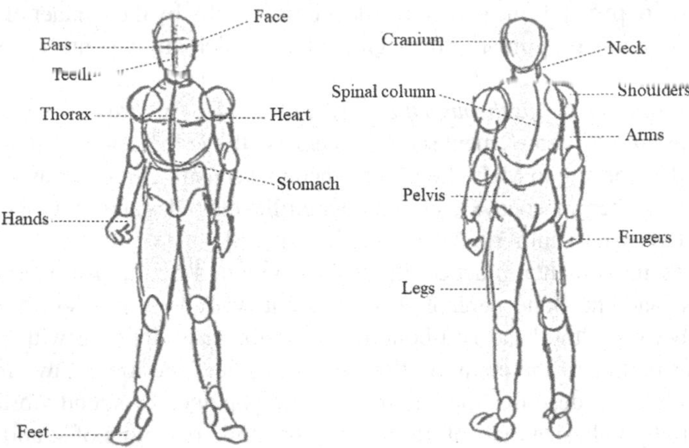

Fig. 2. Body perceptions of Deaf [5, p. 588]

Despite the diversity of their musical experiences, we note that, for the Deaf, the body proposes itself as the privileged place of the musical realization. In this way, "regarding the direct experience of music since it is vibration, deafness, including profound, does not prevent sound contact, but displaces the privileged sense of the ear to the body" [22, p. 221]. The Deaf musical experience is fundamentally anchored in the corpaurality principle and thus affirms, in the words of a young Deaf, that "*[we] can listen to music through the body and not through the ears. This is another way of listening. As if the body is the ear*" [26, p. 247]. Music is, therefore, fundamentally lived by the body and flourishes to become a sensitive reality, revealing specific aesthetic values: "the whole body becomes 'the organ' of hearing […]. By the vibrations that touch it, it replaces the ear" [26, p. 249–250].

Giving itself to feel, music imposes itself on the body; however, if "the link between the body and the music is complex and indissoluble" [27, p. 103], when the aural primacy is overcome, the musical experience finds within the body its space of realization. it seems that once sidelined the aural primacy, the musical experience reveals its natural embodiment. This is how to observe the Deaf musical practices makes it possible to pass beyond the a priori fundamental aurality of music by highlighting the primordial place of the body. In other words, the Deaf otherness restores an extraordinary experience of music, detached from the ordinary conventions dependent to the ear performances, and seems to be able to reveal an unknown aspect of music, the one doing the body the primordial listening support, affirming thus that "hearing is not prerequisite to appreciating music" [28, p. 441]. And as the Deaf percussionist Evelyn Glennie specified: "so far we have the hearing of sounds and the feeling of vibrations. There is one other element to the equation: sight" [17].

3 Visual Specificities: The *Vusicality*

Given the sensory specificities that characterize them, the Deaf develop a singular relationship to the world, putting aside the auditory realities and focusing primarily on visual and bodily qualities; because as Oliver Sacks specified, the Deaf community is "a community adapted to another sensory mode" [29, p. 251]. It is recognized today that the absence or the deterioration of a sensory modality can lead to the development of other sensory modalities, and recent studies emphasize this Deaf visual specificity [30–33].

3.1 "Attitudinal Deafness"[3]: The Deaf Visual Specificity

Therefore, and in the words of Owen Wrigley, "deafness is primarily a visual experience" [34, p. 29], and the Deaf willingly take possession of this 'visible' specificity that represents their singular relationship to the world. As writes Yves Delaporte:

> Deaf culture is a visual culture. Because hearing people also have a sense of sight, it is not sure that there is not much in common in the use that each makes of their eyes. Their eye gaze is invested with language functions [...] [35, p. 36].

The Deaf visual qualities are characteristic of the Deaf identity, because "if for hearing people, being Deaf is defined by not hearing, for the deaf, being deaf is defined by the fact that to be visual" [36, p. 29]. The eyesight is thus essential for the Deaf sensory modality of the world apprehension. In a paper devoted to the issue of the 'Deaf eye gaze' [37], Yves Delaporte is interested in this self-designation of the Deaf as 'being-visual' and states:

> There is a specifically deaf way to permanently immerse yourself in all that the world can bring as visual information. The eye gaze is never passive or at rest, it is constantly attracted by everything in motion [...]. This extreme sensitivity to everything within the visual field reflects recurring behaviors in time sand space that we must consider them for what they are: cultural characteristics [37, p. 50].

For the Deaf, the visual plays a fundamental role in their experiences of the world, exceeding the simple function of sensitive expression becomes the main modality of understanding and realization of the real. In addition, the specificities of gestural languages, fundamentally embedded into a visual expression, emphasize the importance given to the visual field by the Deaf. Thus, in the words of Yves Delaporte, we approach "what it is for the deaf to be deaf: it is to have capacities that hearing people do not have" [35], p. 38]. Indeed, for the Deaf, their condition is not defined primarily from their 'losses' but their abilities. They do not primarily think itself like beings

[3] "The most basic factor determining who is a member of the deaf community seems to be what is called 'attitudinal deafness'. This occurs when a person identifies him/herself as a member of the deaf community, and other members accept that person as part of the community" [2, p. 4].

whose the auditory system is impaired, but rather as individuals whose visual system is particularly operative: "We are visuals: this is the self-definition of the deaf" [35, p. 50]. This first cultural representation leads to consider the 'Deaf world' as a visuo-centered universe opposing the audiocentrism characteristic of the hearing world.

Moreover, the Deaf are fundamentally 'speech beings'. This is the main cultural feature of the Deaf identity, and the Sign Language formalizes the essential criterion of membership of the Deaf community. The latter is defined as a linguistic and cultural minority; Sign Language is the natural language of the Deaf, their language which "reflects the culture, the traditions and how the individuals who use it to communicate see the world" [38, p. 61]. More than a mere means of communication, the Sign Language represents for the Deaf the physical and ideological support of their identity representations. It is from their linguistic specificity that the Deaf have affirmed throughout History their identity and that they have elaborated their community gathering. Thus, the Deaf identity develops around another norm, visuo-centered and deeply embodied, which defines their relationship to the real, but also to music.

3.2 "*Vusicality*": Seeing Music

Indeed, in the Deaf musical experiences, the visual occupies a fundamental place. The Deaf specificities making the sight the dominant reception to perceive the material realities, in the musical experience, the eye complements the impaired ear to give meaning to sound phenomena. As Claire Paolacci points out, the Deaf "have a highly developed visual listening" [21, p. 55]; in this way, the music agrees with another sensitive dimension and takes on a specific value, singularly expressed in the 'musical' paintings by the deaf painter Chuck Baird which illustrate this *music for the eyes*.

However, the sounds are not materially seen and remain elements to hear and to feel; in the Deaf consideration of musical reality, certain elements involved in the creation of sounds become carriers of musical qualities. The deep sensitivity to vibrations that animate the body of the Deaf agrees also with the elements perceived by the eye [7], attentive to visible movements that animate - in music, for music or by music - the visual space. As Emmanuelle Laborit explains:

> The concert show influences me too. The effects of light, the atmosphere, the many people in the concert hall, are also vibrations. I am conscious that we are all together for the same thing. The saxophone shining with golden flashes, it is fantastic. The trumpeters who inflate their cheeks [39, p. 30].

Thus, the music exceeds its only sound dimension, the musician bodies and musical objects are invested with a profound significance for the realization of the musical experience. Separated from its ordinary nature, music is no longer simply an Art that 'is listened' but is primarily an Art that 'is looked'. As an artistic activity, music is a living Art that is performed in live and the concert represents a fundamental dimension of musical reality both to the Deaf and to the hearing people. To attend a concert is to see music being performed and the visual dimension, which also concerns the hearing audience, assumes a deep musical signification for the Deaf audience; in the words of Pierre Schmitt, "When music becomes a show, it is also through an increased focus on the visual aspects of the live performance that the musical experience takes on a particular significance for the deaf" [22, p. 228].

Deaf musical listening is not only perception and feeling of sounds, but it is also and fundamentally visualization of dynamics and movements that participate in the creation of the sensitive environment. Thereby, in the Deaf musical experience "the sight is a sense that draws the sound" [40] and brings to sound reality a more concrete existence revealing another form of materiality. Because the eye is sensitive to movements and visual rhythms, and as the deaf musician Maati Hel Hachimi points out,

> the deaf can understand the rhythm, to feel it without hearing, if only visually. For example, the train that passes with the wheels turning, the subway windows that scroll: we know very well if it goes more or less quickly and we feel the rhythm of what we see [21, p. 49].

Thus, the movement and rhythm of the visual elements contribute to animate the Deaf musical experience. In this way, the movements of the musicians seem essential, both for their participation in the reception of sound (felt and seen) and for their fundamental involvement in the musical practice. The gesture produced by the instrumentalist participates in this way to realize the perception of the sound elements, by bringing them a concrete origin and by giving to the vibratory feeling a visual base. As Maïté Le Moël points out: "every gesture is the cause of a bodily perception of the sound vibrations transmitted by the musical instrument" [6, p. 52]. Thus, the gestuality gives meaning to the Deaf music listening, but also contributes to the understanding of the dimensions and qualities peculiar to the musical practices.

Indeed, like for the hearing people, the musical practice for the Deaf requires a perfect command of specific technical gestures for producing the musical sounds with the instrument; however, in the Deaf practices, the gesture also presents itself as the fundamental understanding support of the musical elements, by participating to determine the sound differences and to define the notions of nuance, intensity or even rhythm. In fact, "it is by the meticulous control of the gesture and by the fine analysis of the bodily perceptions [that the Deaf] can discover the different variations of the sounds […] and apprehend the notions of intensity, duration, and height" [6, p. 53], making musician gesture an essential element for the musical practice. For the perfect command of the gestuality leads in a first instance to a control of the body in the musical activity, but it also leads to an understanding of the bodily perception capacities of sounds. The gesture presents itself as "a preferred means to feeling sensations and integrating certain sensory data transmitted by a sound emission" [21, p. 36]. Therefore, the musical gesture makes it possible to realize the sound event based on visual and corporal elements.

But the gestuality is also for the Deaf the basis of their communication modality, and the Sign Language participates to define a singular facet of the Deaf musical reality revealing a specific practice, the sign-singing.

3.3 The Sign-Singing: The Body Sings Silently

Real musical practice from the Deaf world, the sign-singing proposes a soundless expression of a verbal text in the form of a signed song, where the body carries the melodic and rhythmic values by the exploitation of a "choreographed Sign Language, abstract and poetic" [22, p. 222]. Beyond presenting a simple translation of a vocal song into Sign Language, the sign-singing is deeply invested with musical dimensions that transform the common practice of Sign Language [41, 42]. Here, the musical experience accords with the Deaf specificities: the melodicity takes the body as the production space of the musical expression, whereas the rhythmicity of the gesture exploits the visual space as the realization place of the musical event. The signed song performances synthesize the specificities of the Deaf musical reality: the visual modality and the embodied practice of the musical experience. Affirming part of their musical identity with this singular practice, the Deaf distort the ordinary codes of the singing to produce a visual music that borrows the expressive values of the vocal to develop an exclusively bodily song [43, 44]. The sign-singing is, in a way, a silent musical expression, the silence of the Deaf expressed through the body like musical expressiveness support [45, 46].

Musical Criteria

The musical qualities of sign-singing are close to ordinary musical parameters, although using them in specific ways according to the Sign Language characteristics. In this way, we can identify 6 criteria that allow us to consider the musical dimensions of a signed song performance:

Criterion 1. Rhythmicity

We find in the sign-singing a rhythmic transformation of the signs production; in a musical situation, these are indeed produced with a particular movement, which exploited the discourse energy with a specific dynamic more structured and orderly but less natural than the spoken communication.

The rhythm is also integrated into the whole body, which characterizes the global musical dynamics and animates the gestural production of lyrics. During the gestural communication, the body is not engaged in regular movements and is often adapted to the gestural specificities to the signs produce. In a musical situation, it is more specifically invested with structured movements, rhythmically organized, that bring to the gestural production a specific expressiveness and give it these aesthetic qualities.

Illustration 1.
In his song "October" (2015), Ian Sanborn rhythmically uses the manual alphabet (dactylology) to express the word [OCTOBER] as a chorus. It is possible to note the rhythmic dynamics of gestural expression, rhythmicity replicated identically every time the chorus even occurs. The figure below shows the gestural production (isolation of alphabetical signs) and the corresponding rhythmic formula.

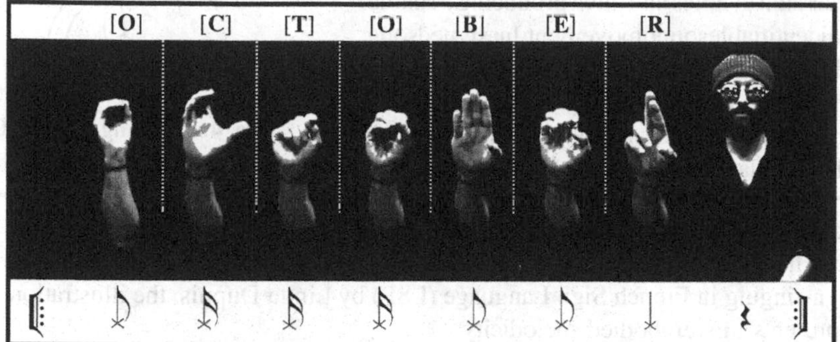

Fig. 3. Rhythmicity: [OCTOBER] [47]

Criterion 2 – Melodicity
The melodicity of a signed song rests on the development of the gestures in the communicational space and on the enlargement of signs production framework. In everyday gestural communication, Sign Language involves mostly the upper body – above the waist – in defined proportions; the 'signing space' designates the signs production sphere in the spoken communication, which defines

> the space surrounding the signer and that is reachable by these two hands. The signing space is used to locate the entities or notions associated with certain signs, possibly to specify their shape and size properties and to establish the spatial relations between the entities [48, p. 220].

The signing space (Fig. 4) thus reports a specific area on the front of the signer's body, mainly between the shoulders and the waist. Forming "roughly a volume with a depth, a width and a height equal to the length of the speaker's arms" [49, p. 9], it defines the communicational framework of signs realization.

The sign-singing, in its musical exploitation of Sign Language parameters, broadens the communicational signspaceproposinganenlargementinheight,width,and depth of signs production. The amplitude of signed song performances thus distinguishes the spoken production from its musical expression, bringing to the discourse its melodicform.Themelodyofsign-singingstandsoutfrom ordinaryconceptionsofthemelodicity,whichassociateit with a succession of notes and pitch producing a characteristicandidentifiablesoundmovement.Inasignedsong, the melody is coming from a movement, not a sounding movement but a visual expression; the dynamics succession of signs produces a silent melody based on a specific usage of the sign place poetically.

Fig. 4. 'Signing space' [50]

Illustration 2.
Extracted from the song "Amoureux d'un ange" (2011) by the slam poet Lhomé [51], sign-singing in French Sign Language (LSF) by Linda Dupuis, the illustration below presents this embodied melodicity.

Here, the exemplary sung phrase – that says: "*Elle, qui m'inspire / She, who inspires me*" (<01:10-01:14>) – can be divided into 2 phases in its signing expression:

- *1*st *phase:* the verbal expression [SHE + WHO + INSPIRES ME]:

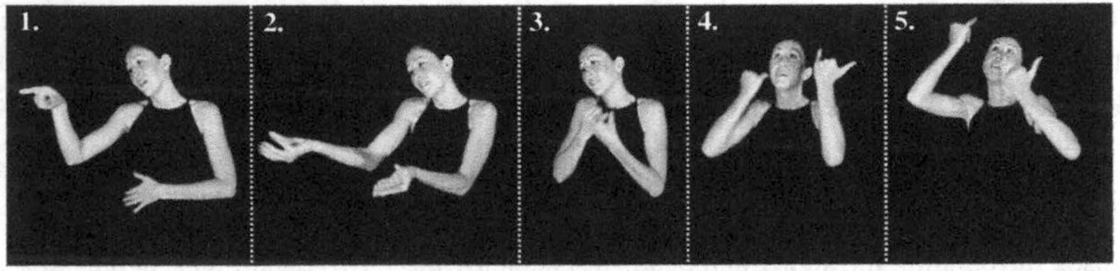

Fig. 5a. Melodicity I. verbal expression: [SHE + WHO + INSPIRES ME] [51]

- *2*nd *phase:* the expansion of the signing space, for aesthetic purposes:

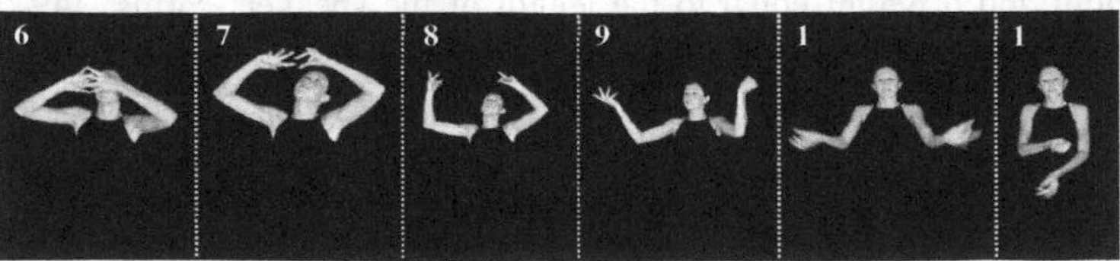

Fig. 5b. Melodicity II. Sign expansion: [INSPIRE ME] [51]

Figure 5a: pictures 4 and 5 show the verb [TO INSPIRE/ TO IMAGINE] in LSF (Fig. 6).

Figure 5b: pictures 6 to 11 show the extra-verbal exploitation that corresponds to an evocation of [INSPIRATION], visually materialized by the hands that extend above the head and then form a sphere coming down to the waist.

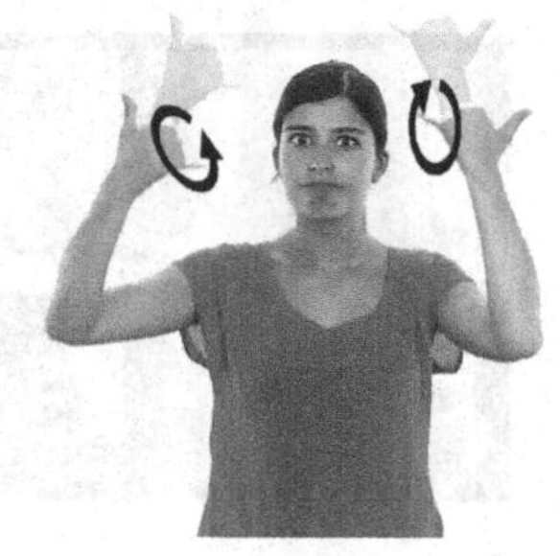

Fig. 6. [TO IMAGINE] in LSF [52]

Criterion 3 – Nuances and Intensities

The sign-singing is based on nuances, which do not appear here as sound qualities but as dynamic intensities. Rhythmicity and melodicity of the gestures are associated with a diminution or an enlargement of the verbal signs, formal transformations that intensify the musicality of the performance defining its aesthetic qualities. In a musical context, the body extends or reduced giving to the sign's significant values, a phenomenon that is also found, to a lesser extent, in current gestural communication. Indeed, the sign-singing intensifies the expressive dimensions inherent in Sign Language, to requalify them into vusical elements.

Illustration 3.

The illustration below is a cover of Serge Gainsbourg's song "Chanson de Prévert", interpreted by the French duo Albaricate (2020) - Samuel Genin (voice) and Clémence Colin (sign) [53]. The extract used here is part of the chorus: *"Jours après jours, les amours mortes / Day after day, dead loves"* (<00:43–00:50>); it shows in different ways the visual nuances and the intensity of the musical expressiveness:

1) the expressiveness of Clémence Colin's face accompanies the musicality of gestures and intensifies the textual content.
2) the first expression *"Day after day"* is divided into 2 parts:
   a. pictures 1 to 4. [DAY], the first expression: the left arm describes a circular arc passing in front of the face, from left to right, from one end to each other of the right arm on a horizontal plane. This relatively rapid movement evokes the sun's path (left arm) on the horizon (right arm). *(cf. Criterion 6 - 'transposition')*.

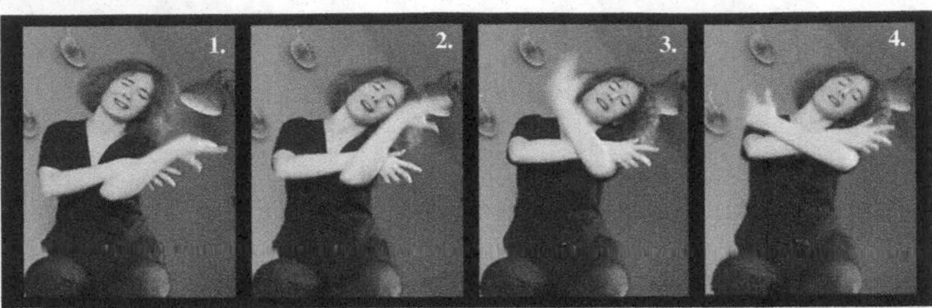

Fig. 6a. Nuances I: [DAY] [53]

b. Pictures 5 to 8. [DAY] is expressed this time with the right arm performing the same movement, left arm horizontally. The movement is slower, to signify the [SUCCESSION] of the days, the word [AFTER] being omitted in the gestural expression because it is not necessary: the successive executions of [DAY] with a different dynamic (slower the second time) expresses the 'succession of days'.

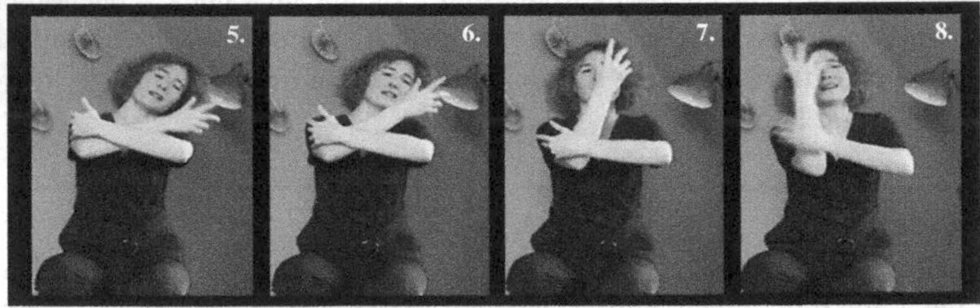

Fig. 6b. Nuances II: [AFTER + DAY] [53]

3) Pictures 9 and 10. The [DAY] turns into [LOVE], the pictures 10 and 11 presenting its gestural expression in LSF (Fig. 7).

Fig. 7. [LOVE] in LSF [54]

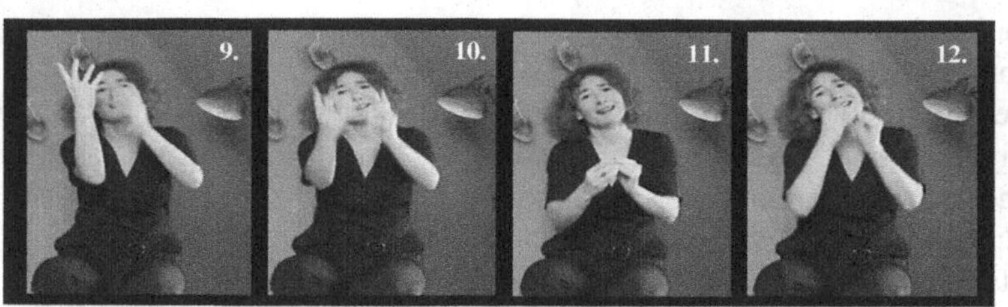

Fig. 6c. Nuances III: [LOVE] [53]

Pictures 13 and 14, [LOVE] is put in the plural, and loves [DIE] (expressed by the sign [DISAPPEAR] (Fig. 8), pictures 15 and 16).

Fig. 8. [TO DISAPPEAR] in LSF [55]

Fig. 6d. Nuances IV: [DEAD LOVES] [53]

Criterion 4 – Repetition

The repetition process is significantly used in the sign-singing, firstly to add an expressive effect, consistent with text content, but also to inject dynamism into the musical performance or accentuate its rhythmicity. It is common to find repeated signs sometimes several times in a row, in a purely visual aesthetic perspective that transforms the gestural expression into a vusical – melo-rhythmic – interpretation.

Illustration 4.

This process of repetition is explicitly exploited in the chorus from the sign-song "Watch these hands" (2012) by Sean Forbes [56], the text itself resting on a repetition: *"Watch, Watch, Watch these hands".*

Fig. 9. [WATCH] in ASL [57]

In its linguistic expression in American Sign Language (ASL), we find the sign [WATCH] (Fig. 9) used 3 times successively in a different way, more or less in accordance with the initial configuration of the verbal sign: 2 fingers (evocation of the gaze) which indicate the direction "where to watch".

1. Firstly, the sign is proposed in a two-hand expression, with all the fingers (except the thumbs) oriented towards the song-signer's face. This first expression is a way to concern the audience members: "Watch!" (Several fingers express several "watchers").

Fig. 10a. Repetition I: [WATCH] 'all'! [56]

2. The repetition of the sign is a one-hand expression; it respects the initial configuration of the verbal sign (2 fingers) and is addressed individually to the audience member: "You, watch!" (2 fingers express one individual).

Fig. 10b. Repetition II: 'you', [WATCH]! [56]

3. The last evocation of the sign is again a one-hand expression, performed with the right hand directed towards the left hand, a gestural expression for: "you, watch this hand!"

Fig. 10c. Repetition III: 'You' [WATCH] 'this hand' [56]

Criterion 5 – Visual Rhyme

The association of the criteria of rhythmicity, melodicity, and repetition reveals a new parameter[4], more singular because distorting a principle usually associated with the language sonority, that of visual rhyme. Indeed, to add a vusical character to a gestural production, the sign-singing relies on elements sharing visual characteristics that produce an effect of recurrence or similarity and participate in the dynamic and aesthetic expressiveness of linguistic performance. These visual rhymes can be in the order of the formal resemblance (the configuration of the verbal sign or the shape of the hand. Cf. Fig. 10a, 10b and 10c), in the range of the sign positions in relation to the song-signer's body, or also in the order of the recurring movements that participate to the discourse structuration.

Illustration 5.

Although revealing a fundamental parameter of the sign-singing's vusicality, the principle of visual rhyme remains complex to identify and isolate in a gestural production. We can nevertheless take as an example an excerpt from "Smells like victory" (2009) by Signmark [58]. In the second part of his chorus, we find vocal rhymes in the text: *"What you're doing over there / There's a party over here / Winners over here / Losers over there"*. In the same way, we can identify visual rhymes:

1. the general rhythmicity used animates the gestural production regularly and synchronously
2. It may be noted several visual or rhythmic symmetry:
   - pictures 1, 4, and 6: repetition of the gesture (2 times) over the same rhythmic duration.
   - pictures 1, 4, 6, and 8: sign positioning on the upper of the body (beginning of verses)
   - pictures 5 and 7: identical gestures.
   - pictures 5, 7, and 9: directional parallelism (unidirectional movement of the 2 hands)
   - pictures 3, 5, and 7: sign positioning on the lower of the body (end of verses)

[4] I develop here this new criterion to the other musical parameters of the sign-singing established since my doctoral research [5].

Fig. 11a. Visual rhyme I: [*"What you're doing over there"*] [58]

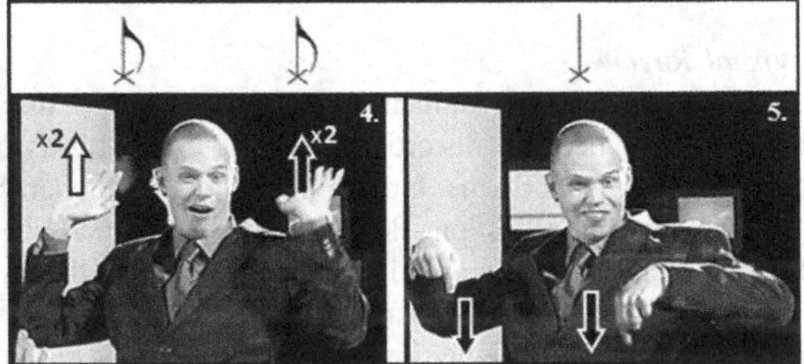

Fig. 11b. Visual rhyme II: [*"There's a party over here"*] [58]

Fig. 11c. Visual rhyme II: [*"There's a party over here"*] [58]

Fig. 11d. Visual rhyme II: [*"There's a party over here"*] [58]

Criterion 6 – Transposition of signs

Finally, we find a transposition of the usual form of the verbal signs, which can sometimes be modified in their production (gestures enlargement or reduction; the speed of execution; production delocalized in the sign space) or totally transformed to perform the lyrics visually or poetically (close to mime).

Illustration 6.

In the sign-song "Against the Wall", performed in ASL by Signmark, we can find a formal transposition of the sign [WALL], whose usual configuration in ASL (Fig. 12) is transformed into a mimetic expression in the sign-singing execution (Fig. 13).

Initial configuration

Final configuration

Fig. 12. [WALL] in ASL [57]

We can see that the musical using of the verbal sign [WALL] (hands side by side on the front of the body, which separate laterally at the shoulder width) transforms its initial disposition (in Signmark's performance, the hands are not side by side on the front of the body in the center of the torso, but at the shoulders close to the body) and its final resolution is extended (the hands do not stop at shoulders; the arms are outstretched). This transposition of the sign agrees with the expressive orientation of the lyrics: "against the wall", words that the sign-singer performs physically.

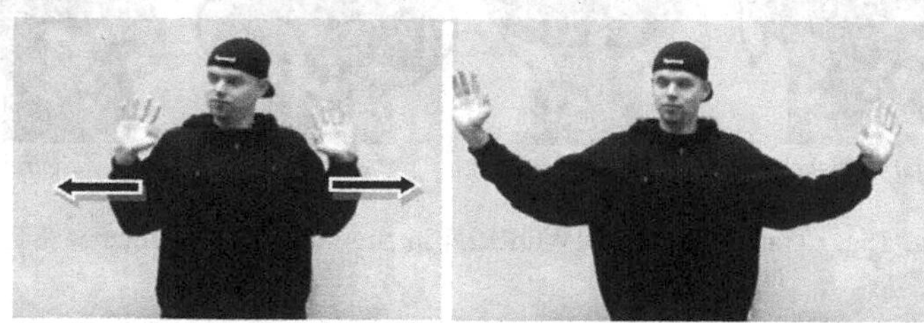

Initial configuration *Final configuration*

Fig. 13. Transposition I. [WALL] in Signmark's performance [58]

We can take another example of musical transposition, more explicit this time. In the same Signmark's song, the production of the verbal sign [WORLD] is totally detached from the usual sign to be closer to a formal expression of the World (Fig. 14), formal expression that the linguistics of Sign Language calls the 'highly iconicity' [60], namely the insertion into the language of "structural indications of an illustrative representation of the sensory experience" [61, p. 23].

ASL configuration [57] *Formal representation*

Fig. 14. [WORLD] [57]

In his signed song, Signmark uses two configurations to perform [WORLD], which stand out from the usual sign. The first (Fig. 15a) is related to the round shape of the World and in no way to the verbal sign [WORLD]. In ASL, the sign [WORLD] is based on a configuration reflecting a low degree of iconicity (few illustrative values) and consists of two 'W' (the form of the hands into the manual alphabet), which rotate around each other to symbolize the Earth's rotation. In this, this sign has little iconic dimensions but refers more specifically to the word itself in its writing.

Initial configuration *1st movement* *2nd movement* *Final configuration*

Fig. 15a. Transposition II. [WORLD] in Signmark's performance 1 [58]

In the second evocation of [WORLD], the round shape evoking the Earth is transformed into a new expression (Fig. 15b), which presents again the shape of the world without referring to the usual verbal sign. This second expression is again part of an expressive process; to musically produce the lyrics "Even if the world comes crashing down", Signmark formalizes and choreographs the Sign Language to make visible his poetic and musical intentions. The WORLD is represented in its round shape (with the clenched fist) and this expression is used to express the lyrics in a mimetic way: the clenched fist 'crashes on' the hand. The expressiveness of the lyrics leads to transform the usual dimensions of Sign Language to bring a concrete and illustrative dimension to the sign-singing performance.

Initial configuration [WORLD] — *1st movement* [COMES] — *Final configuration* [CRASHING DOWN]

Fig. 15b. Transposition III. [WORLD] in Signmark's performance II [58]

The sign-singing thus reveals the silent appropriation of the musical codes of the ordinary song, adapting its expressive modalities to the Sign Language specificities. The music then becomes specifically Deaf and reveals the culture that defines the Deaf community, offering a singular way to claim a 'musical otherness'. The sign-singing involves the Sign Language in a musician practice that, transcending the ordinary norms of the song, revalorizes the notion of silence: *by the hands, for the eyes*, the sign-singing becomes a visual expression of music. So, we can consider with Pierre Schmitt that

> the musical experience claimed by the deaf exceeds the only sound sphere. Its meeting with the Sign Language poses the visual dimension not as a further or an additional dimension, but as a constitutive value of a musical form whose conception is enlarged [22, p. 229].

More than just a communication mode, the Sign Language unveils aesthetic qualities that lead to the realization of original Deaf music, revealing singular creative perspectives and a strong musical identity, embodied and integrating primarily visual dimensions. Thus, the Deaf practices, by revealing the 'corpaural dimensions' and the 'vusical qualities' of the music, make it possible to relocate the currentss conceptions of the music and offer to think the musical in its multimodal dispositions: the ear, but also the eye and more broadly the body proposing to concretize, together and jointly, the musical experience.

References

1. Gaucher, C., Vibert, S. (eds.): Les Sourds : Aux origines d'une identité plurielle. Peter Lang, Bruxelles (2010)
2. Baker, C., Padden, C.: American Sign Language: A look at its history, structure and community. T.J. Publishers, Silver Spring Md (1978)
3. Brétéché, S.: Through the prism of disability. For an experience of alterity: the being-Deaf as figure of world. In: Dario, M. (ed.) The Role of Humanities in Contemporary Society: Semiotics, Culture, Technologies, pp. 25–35. Kaunas Univ. of Tech., Kaunas (2017)

4. Brétéché, S., Esclapez, C.: Music(s), Musicology and Science: Towards an Interscience Network. In: Aramaki, M., Davies, M.E.P., Kronland-Martinet, R., Ystad, S. (eds.) CMMR 2017. LNCS, vol. 11265, pp. 637–657. Springer, Cham (2018). https://doi.org/10.1007/978-3-030-01692-0_42
5. Brétéché, S.: L'incarnation musicale. L'expérience musicale sourde. Thèse de doctorat en musicologie. Esclapez, C., Vion-Dury, J., (dir.). Aix-Mars. Univ. (2015)
6. Le Moël, M.: L'univers musical de l'enfant sourd. Marsyas **39**(40), 51–58 (1996)
7. Brétéché, S.: Body Ways: the extra-ordinary music of the Deaf. In: Hoppe, C., Muller, A. (ed.) Göttingen Studies in Musicology. Olms-Verlag, Hildesheim (to be published)
8. Campbell, W., Barhon, R.J.: Dejong's. The neurologic examination. Wolter Kluwer, Philadelphia (2020)
9. Cardinaels, J.: Vibrations. Wolter Kluwer, Waterloo (2009)
10. CNAC (ed.) Bruit et vibrations. Fascicule n°112. Carl Heyman, Bruxelles (2006)
11. Griffin, M.: Handbook of human vibration. Elsevier, London (1996)
12. Gomes, H.M., Savionek, D.: Measurement and evaluation of human exposure to vibration transmitted to hand-arm system during leisure cyclist activity. Revista Brasileira de Engenharia Biomedica **30**(4), 291–300 (2014)
13. Rasmussen, G.: Human Body vibration exposure and its measure. Technical Rev. Bruel & Kjaer **1**, 3–1 (1982)
14. Mandal, B., Srivastava, A.K.: Risk from vibration in Indian mines. Indian J. Occupational and Environ. Med. **10**(2), 53–57 (2006)
15. Duarte, M.L., De Brito Pereira, M.: Vision influence on whole-body human vibration comfort levels. Shock and Vibration **13**, 367–377 (2006)
16. Sherrington, C.S.: The integrative action on the nervous system. CTYale University Press, New Haven (1906)
17. Glennie, E.: Hearing essay. https://www.evelyn.co.uk/hearingessay/
18. Pistone, D.: Imaginaire et sens musical : des héritages aux réalisations. In : Grabócz, M. (ed.) Sens et signification en musique, pp. 35–49. Hermann éditeurs, Paris (2007)
19. Sayeux, A.S.: Le corps-oreille des musiques électroniques. Une approche anthropologique sensuelle. In: Communications **86**, 229–246 (2010)
20. Cité de la musique (ed.) Rencontre Musique et surdité. Cité de la Musique, Paris (2003) https://drop.philharmoniedeparis.fr/content/GPM/pdf/02Metiers04/Musique-et-surdite-cite-2003-06-24.pdf
21. Cité de la musique (ed.) Journée d'étude professionnelle Musique et surdité. Cité de la Musique, Paris (2005). www.citedelamusique.fr/pdf/handicap/260305_musique-et-surdite.pdf
22. Schmitt, P.: De la musique et des sourds. Approche ethnographique du rapport à la musique de jeunes sourds européens. In: Bachir-Loopuyt, T., Iglesias, S., Langenbruch, A., Zur Nieden, G. (eds.) Musik – Kontext – Wissenschaft. Interdisziplinäre Forschung zu Musik, pp. 221–233. Peter Lang, Frankfurt am Main (2012)
23. Le Breton, D.: La saveur du monde. Anthropologie des sens. Métailié, Paris (2006)
24. Cabéro, A.: La musique du silence. Éd. du Non Verbal/A.M. Bx, Parempuyre (2006)
25. Cabéro, A.: De l'ouïe à l'audition. Éd. du Non Verbal/A.M. Bx, Parempuyre (1998)
26. Cabéro, A.: Différent, différence et différends. Essai anthropologique sur les dissonances de la surdité mal-entendue. Doctoral Thesis, Traimond, B. (dir.), Univ. Bordeaux (2009)
27. Csepregi, G.: La musique et le corps. Vladimir Jankélévitch sur l'art du piano. In: Csepregi, G. (dir.) Sagesse du corps, pp. 103–114. Éd. du Scribe, Bruxelles (2001)
28. Loeffler, S.: Deaf music: embodying language and rhythm. In: Bauman, H-D.L., Murray, J. (ed.) Deaf gain: raising the stakes for human diversity, pp. 436–456. University of Minnesota Press, Minneapolis (2014)

29. Sacks, O.: Des yeux pour entendre. Voyage au pays des sourds. Seuil, Paris (1990)
30. Codina, C., Buckley, D., Port, M., Pascalis, O.: Deaf and hearing children : a comparison of peripheral vision development. Dev. Sci. **14**(4), 725–737 (2011)
31. Stivalet, P., Moreno, Y., Richard, J., Barraud, P.-A., Raphel, C.: Differences in visual search tasks between congenitally deaf and normally hearing adults. Cogn. Brain Res. **6**, 227–232 (1998)
32. Parasnis, I., Samar, V.J.: Parafoveal attention in congenitally deaf and hearing young adults. Brain Cogn. **4**, 313–327 (1985)
33. Proksch, J., Bavelier, D.: Changes in the spatial distribution of visual attention after early deafness. J. Cogn. Neurosci. **14**, 687–701 (2006)
34. Wrigley, O.: The Politics of Deafness. Gallaudet University Press, Washington (1996)
35. Delaporte, Y.: Les sourds, c'est comme ça : Ethnologie de la surdimutité. Éd. de la Maison des sciences de l'homme, Paris (2002)
36. Lachance, N.: Territoire, transmission et culture Sourde. Perspectives historiques et réalités contemporaines. Presses de l'Univ. de Laval, Québec (2007)
37. Delaporte, Y.: Le regard sourd. «Comme un fil tendu entre deux visages…». In: Terrain, **30**, 49–66 (1998)
38. Dubuisson, C.: Signer ou le sort d'une culture. Nouvelles pratiques sociales **6**(1), 57–68 (1993)
39. Laborit, E.: Le cri de la mouette. Robert Laffont, Paris (1994)
40. Boyer, M.: La musique chez les enfants sourds. Mémoire du CAAPSAIS Option A (2001) https://atelieroptiona.free.fr/accat/accate.htm
41. Cripps, J., Rosenblum, E., Small, A.: Signed Music: An Emerging Inter-performative Art. In: Stringham, D., Jarashow, B., Eldredge, B.K (ed.) Deaf Studies Today! **6**, 179–186 (2019)
42. Cripps, J., Rosenblum, E., Small, A., Supalla, S.: A case study on signed music: the emergence of an inter-performance art. In: Liminalities: A Journal of Performance Studies **13** (2) (2017). https://liminalities.net/13-2/signedmusic.pdf
43. Maler, A.: Songs for hands: analyzing interactions of sign language and music. In: Music Theory Online, **13**(1) (2013), https://mtosmt.org/issues/mto.13.19.1/mto.13.19.1.maler.html
44. Maler, A.: Musical expression among deaf and hearing song signers. In: Howe, B., Jensen-Moulton, S., Neil Lerner, N., Straus, J. (eds.) The Oxford Handbook of Music and Disability Studies, pp. 73–91. Oxford Univ. Press, New-York (2015)
45. Holmes, J.A.: Singing beyond hearing. J. Am. Musicol. Soc. **69**(2), 542–548 (2016)
46. Jones, J.: Imagined hearing: music-making in deaf culture. In: Howe, B., Jensen-Moulton, S., Neil Lerner, N., Straus, J. (eds.) The Oxford Handbook of Music and Disability Studies, pp. 54–72. Oxford Univ. Press, New-York (2015)
47. Ian, S.: "October" https://www.youtube.com/watch?v=kF6UKQyrxnA
48. Ben, M.M.: Analyse automatique de discours en langue des signes : Représentation et traitement de l'espace de signation. In: Actes de la conférence conjointe Jep-Taln-Recital, **3**, pp. 219–232. Grenoble (2012)
49. Segouat, J.: Modélisation de la coarticulation en Langue des Signes Française pour la diffusion automatique d'informations en gare ferroviaire à l'aide d'un signeur virtuel. Doctoral Thesis, Braffort, A. (dir.). Univ. Paris XI (2010)
50. Guitteny, P., Legouis, P., Verlaine, L.: La langue des signes. Centre d'Information sur la Surdité d'Aquitaine (2004)
51. Lhomé, "Amoureux d'un ange". https://www.youtube.com/watch?v=y3s39AKsmOE
52. 'Le Dico Elix'. https://dico.elix-lsf.fr/dictionnaire/imaginer/v.-175026
53. Clémence, C., Samuel, G.: "Chanson de Prévert" (cover). https://www.youtube.com/watch?v=KrsmAiW_Cqw
54. 'Le Dico Elix'. https://dico.elix-lsf.fr/dictionnaire/amour/n.m.-129494

55. 'Le Dico Elix'. https://dico.elix-lsf.fr/dictionnaire/dispara%C3%AEtre/v.-155650
56. Sean Forbes, "Watch these hands". https://www.youtube.com/watch?v=7lQx1f5lEFo
57. 'American Sign Language University' (ASLU). https://www.lifeprint.com
58. Signmark, "Smells like victory". https://www.youtube.com/watch?v=oUtM8_DOVUI
59. Signmark, "Against the Wall". https://www.youtube.com/watch?v=JYOYvjhzy84
60. Marie-Anne, S., Cuxac, C.: Iconicity in sign language: a theoretical and methodological point of view. In: Wachsmuth, I., Sowa, T. (eds.) GW 2001. LNCS (LNAI), vol. 2298, pp. 173–180. Springer, Heidelberg (2002). https://doi.org/10.1007/3-540-47873-6_18
61. Sallandre, M-A.: Va et vient de l'iconicité en langue des signes française. In: Acquisition et interaction en langue étrangère no. 15 (2001). https://aile.revues.org/1405

How Would You Reproduce a Synthetic Sound of an Ellipse in Water? A Phenomenological Investigation of Pre-reflexive Contents of Consciousness

Jean Vion-Dury[1,2(✉)], Marie Degrandi[2], Gaëlle Mougin[1], Thomas Bordonné[1], Sølvi Ystad[1], Richard Kronland-Martinet[1], and Mitsuko Aramaki[1]

[1] Aix Marseille Univ, CNRS, PRISM, Marseille, France
jvion-dury@ap-hm.fr
[2] Pôle de Psychiatrie "Solaris", Centre Hospitalier Universitaire de Sainte-Marguerite, 270 Bd de Sainte-Marguerite, 13009 Marseille, France

Abstract. This article describes a listening experiment based on elicitation interviews that aims at describing the conscious experience of a subject submitted to a perceptual stimulation. As opposed to traditional listening experiments in which subjects are generally influenced by closed or suggestive questions and limited to predefined, forced choices, elicitation interviews make it possible to get a deeper insight into the listener's perception, in particular to the pre-reflexive content of the conscious experiences. Inspired by previous elicitation interviews during which subjects passively listened to sounds, this experience is based on an active task during which the subjects were asked to reproduce a sound with a stylus on a graphic tablet that controlled a synthesis model. The reproduction was followed by an elicitation interview. The trace of the graphic gesture as well as the answers recorded during the interview were then analyzed. Results revealed that the subjects varied their focus towards both the evoked sound source, and intrinsic sound properties and also described their sensations induced by the experience.

Keywords: Phenomenology · Elicitation interview · Auditory perception · Sound synthesis · Graphic gestures · Audio-motor loop

1 Introduction

When preforming perceptual evaluations of sounds, it is important to be aware of the fact that listeners may focus on different aspects. Gaver [9] distinguished everyday listening from analytical listening. In the case of everyday listening of a simple source, the listener pays attention to the sound producing object, such as its size [15] and the material of which it is composed [1,12]. In the case of more complex situations reflecting for instance interactions between sound sources, the listener perceives properties related to the event as a whole. Warren and Verbrugge [32] showed that objects that bounce and break can be distinguished by listeners with a high degree of accuracy, while Repp [21] revealed that

R. Kronland-Martinet et al. (Eds.): CMMR 2019, LNCS 12631, pp. 449–461, 2021.
https://doi.org/10.1007/978-3-030-70210-6_29

subjects were able to recognize their own recorded clapping and the hand position from recordings when someone else is clapping. More recently, Thoret et al. [27,28] showed that subjects were able to recognize biological motions and certain shapes from friction sounds produced when a person is drawing on a paper. To favor analytical listening where the listeners focus on intrinsic sound properties linked, for instance, to loudness, pitch, and timbre, other approaches have been used. Merer [18] used acousmatic sounds which source could not be easily recognized to reveal sound structures responsible for the evocation of movement categories. Other approaches such as sensory analysis during which a group of subjects identify sensory descriptors such as onomatopoeias have been used, for instance to characterize the formantic transition from "ON" (pronounced [ɔ̃]) to "AN" (pronounced [ɑ̃]) that characterizes sounds from car engines [22,25]. Other approaches, such as vocal imitations, that do not specifically focus on everyday or analytical listening have been used to extract relevant features of kitchen sounds [16], and more recently to reveal invariant structures responsible for the evocation of movements and materials [4,5]. Psycholinguistic analyses have been used to characterize sounds from musical instruments through spontaneous verbalizations. One such study that investigated violinists' preference judgements during a playing task, led to a model that linked auditory and haptic sensations to timbre, quality, and playability of the instrument [23,24]. Sound perception is a conscious experience that can be described not only in so-called "third person" protocols (from the point of view of the experimenter within a given paradigm, e.g. a psycho-physical paradigm), but also by protocols aiming at describing the experience from the subjects' perspective (subjective methods) mainly based on the Husserlian phenomenology. Most of the time, spontaneous descriptions of experiences and cognitive processes are poor [20] because the experience does not guarantee immediate access to its background contents [29]. Several kinds of information usually remain undisclosed, masked or "pre-reflexive" as they are called in phenomenological language [20]. Various methods allow to accurately describe the conscious experience in its reflexive and mostly pre-reflexive part. Among them, the elicitation interview (EI) [17,30] is a disciplined introspection method conceptually based both on neurolinguistic programming (NLP) and Husserlian phenomenology [14]. EI makes it possible to return to the non-reflexive part of the conscious experience of a subject, hereby limiting influences from closed or suggestive questions. Whereas the qualitative research methods used in sociology, such as Glaser and Strauss' anchored theory (see [23]) or the "repertory grid" method use textual corpora of reflexive descriptions of experiences to extract emerging themes and their variations, EI is essentially interested in the non-reflexive component of the experience. For this reason, whereas in the qualitative methods, the subjects use their autobiographical memory, in the EI, the subjects must relive their experience and activate their "integral memory", in particular corporeal. We previously described pre-reflexive conscious experiences in passive listening of sounds [19]. In the current work we analyze pre-reflexive content of conscious experiences in an active task consisting in reproducing a sound by drawing on a graphic tablet.

2 Materials and Methods

In this section, we describe the interactive device used by the participants, the experimental protocol and the elicitation interview.

2.1 Equipment: The "Tablet-Synthesizer" Device

Sound synthesis is a powerful tool to create any kind of sounds that either imitate real or virtual situations. Current synthesis models enable high quality resynthesis of natural sounds that can be generated in real-time. One challenging aspect linked to sound synthesis is the control of the synthesis parameters that is not always intuitive. To meet this challenging control issue, we have developed a synthesizer based on perceptual features linked to the evocation of actions and objects [1,2]. This device is based on the ecological approach to perception proposed by Gibson [11] which considers that actions and objects are recognized through invariant structures. The sound synthesizer makes it possible to create sounds from verbal labels that describe the action (e.g. hitting, scraping, rolling) and the object (e.g. material, size, shape) associated with the sound. Any combination between actions and objects can hereby be simulated, such as scratching a small metallic bell or hitting a big wooden bar [8]. Unrealistic situations can also be simulated this way, such as rubbing the wind or scratching a wave.

In the present study we decided to use a sound texture that evoked a movement in water, since the timbre of liquid sounds vary strongly with the dynamic action. To create the reference sound that the subjects were asked to reproduce, the synthesized sound was combined with an elliptic movement recorded by the experimenter who drew on a WACOM INTUOS PRO graphic tablet. The experimenter freely chose the eccentricity and the orientation of the ellipse that he/she was asked to draw ten times. To induce a periodic movement, we used a 60 bpm metronome while the experimenter was drawing to help him/her maintain a regular speed. Among the ten repetitions, the three most regular ellipses were selected. The position of the stylus was recorded by a Max/MSP interface at a sampling rate 129 Hz. We then derived the position to get the velocity profile. The scalar product that quantifies the difference between the two profiles (the reference profile and the profile performed by the subject) was calculated. If the two profiles are completely different, the scalar product will have a low value, whereas if they are identical, it will have a maximum value (around 1).

2.2 Experimental Protocol

The subjects were first asked to listen to the reference sound which nature and origin they ignored. They were then asked to reproduce this reference sound on the WACOM INTUOS PRO graphic tablet with the gesture that best imitated the reference sound. The subjects produced the sound in real time while they performed the gesture on the graphic tablet (Fig. 1).

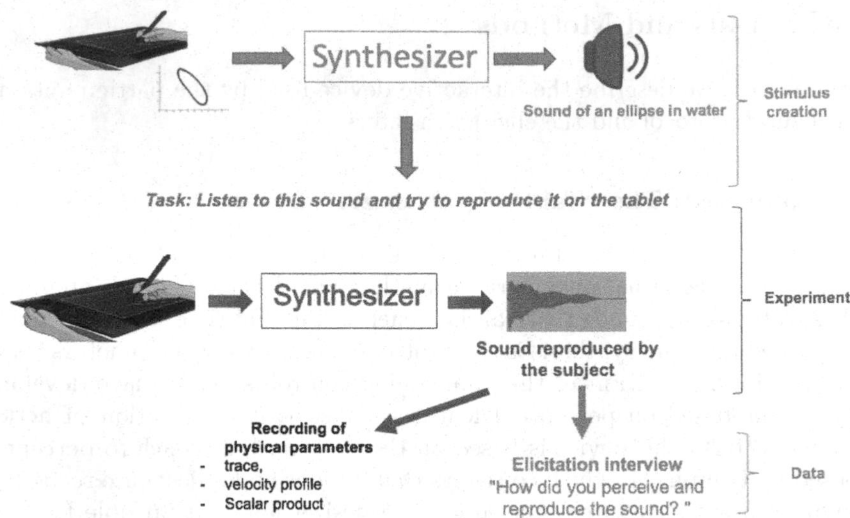

Fig. 1. Experimental protocol

Participants. Ten subjects, 7 women and 3 men (aged from 26 to 70 years) were included in this experiment. Five subjects were experienced musicians practicing an instrument on a regular basis and the remaining 5 participants were not musicians. The ten subjects were right handed. Subjects did not have any hearing or neurological problems, such as memory-related problems or attention difficulties. The interview was conducted by one of the three medical doctors involved in the study: MD, GM, JVD. An audiogram was performed for each subject before the beginning of the experiment to make sure that none of the subjects had hearing impairments.

The Elicitation Interview. In a second step (just after the reproduction of the sound), the subjects were asked to review their experience while listening to and reproducing the sound by means of an elicitation interview, by answering the question "how did you perceive and reproduce the sound?". The EI was conducted by three experienced researchers in phenomenology and EI. The EI is based on a certain number of methodological specificities:

a) The first key of the interview is to lead the subjects to describe their experience, that is to tell what they experienced and not what they thought, believed or imagined their experience had been like [20].
b) The interviewer should lead the subjects to discuss their past experiences by helping them to find the sensory and emotional dimensions.
c) The interview consists in helping the subjects redirect their attention from the content of their experience (the "what"), to its diachronic and synchronic structure oriented towards the experiential (non-causal) "how". The diachronic structure of the experience corresponds to the stages of its

deployment over time. The synchronic structure of the experiment corresponds to the configuration at a given moment of the sensory registers used, the type of mobilized attention... etc. The aim is to make the subjects relive their experience rather than to remember it.

d) To collect such a description, the interviewer's questions should be "empty of content", non-inductive and "point" to the structure of the experiment without providing any content. Questions are, for example: "From what did you start? What did you feel ? How did it appear to you?", etc. This mode of questioning emphasizes the "how" of the conscious experience and excludes the "why".

e) The structure of an interview is iterative while guiding the attention of the subject towards a diachronic or synchronic mesh which progressively becomes more detailed each time. The average duration of an interview is about an hour to describe a few seconds of experience (as Stern puts it, "there is a world in a grain of sand" [26]). The interviewer must remain totally neutral. A good harmonization of affects (motor and prosodic affective tuning [26]) is a critical condition for the quality of the interview.

Data Collection and Analysis. All the EIs were recorded, with the subjects' agreement. The physical data (pen movement, speed, pressure etc. ...) were collected from the computer connected to the graphic tablet. The records of EIs were entirely transcribed. The analysis of verbatim was carried out to extract the descriptive categories (saliencies) from each interview. The choice of descriptive categories for each interview was validated by 7 people in an inter-judge session.

3 Results

The physical data from the tablet were analyzed together with the EIs. Only the data from the EIs, and the drawings recorded on the tablet are presented in Tables 1 and 2.

Types of Sound Listening. The EI enabled to collect the synchronic and diachronic structure from the listening experience of each subject. These data respond to both the "what" of their experience but also to "how", to the proper way of perceiving and reproducing this sound. They give a fine and precise description of an experience that lasted for a few seconds by allowing an awareness of the different processes. Each of the 3 types of listening can be analyzed from a) the main sensory modalities used, b) the attentional disposition of the subject, c) the position of the subject with respect to the sound (sound-auditor position) and d) the moment this type of listening occurs. Each subject has a preferred type of listening (in this experiment), but this does not mean that he or she does not use other types of listening in a less marked way. This part of the analysis is presented in Table 1.

Table 1. Three types of listening experiences

Types of listening experiences						
Listening focus (LF)	Main LF in subjects	Number of subjects presenting this LF	Main sensory modalities involved	Attentional disposition	Sound/ auditor position	Moment of appearance
Origin of sound	2, 4 and 5	8/10	Scenes (sea, beach…) perceived by the auditory and visual modalities	Directed attention towards the source. Active search remembrance, familiar scenes evoking the source.	Location of the subject in relation to the scene.	Appears spontaneously first while listening
Acoustic characteristi cs of sound	1, 7, 8 and 10	8/10	Timbre, intensity, rhythm, height perceived by the auditory modality but may be associated with other modalities (rhythm with kinesthetic sensitivity)	Attention directed towards the different parts of the sound Active position of the subject in relation to the sound.	Accurate location of the sound, external to the subject....	Appears when subjects focus on the task of reproduction
Effect of the sound	3, 6 and 9	8/10	Dynamics of the sound perceived by kinesthetic sensitivity, mainly	Attention less focused, more global Position of the subject rather passive compared to the sound	Blurred boundary between body space and sound Effect of sound throughout the body.	Particular listening modality, generally not described spontaneously rather evoked at the end of EI.

The first type of listening is turned to the source of the sound and involves attention directed to the origin of the sound with an active search for familiar scenes associated with the source. In this type of causal listening the imagination is very active. The subject is thus projected into an imaginary scene evoked by the sound heard which is integrated into the scene, and a given context in the visual modality. This listening structure appears spontaneously and early in the diachronic description of the experience. This type of listening, characterized as everyday listening by Gaver [9], represents the main listening mode for three subjects but is, for 8 out of 10 subjects, used in addition to their main listening mode.

The second type of listening, characterized as analytic listening by Gaver, is directed to the characteristics of the sound. This way of perceiving sounds appears when subjects focus on the reproduction task. This time the sound is brought back to its different components (rhythm, pitch, timbre, intensity), and the subjects focus on the sound itself and not on the causality. This is the main listening type for four subjects, but 8 out of 10 subjects used it in addition to their main listening mode.

The third level of listening is a particular listening modality that is usually not spontaneously described in our daily lives and rather evoked at the end of the diachronic description of the listening experience. It focuses on the effect of the sound, specifically the dynamics, the movement it induces relative to the whole body. It is an "internal" or "embodied" listening modality in which the boundaries between the sound and the corporal space become porous. Subjects adopt a more passive position related to the sound, in a way they are "impregnated" by the sound. This is the main listening modality for three out of ten subjects, but 8 out of 10 subjects used it in addition to their main listening mode.

Finally, concerning the musical expertise of the subjects, we did not observe any difference.

Reproductive Strategies. The drawings made by the subjects can be classified into 5 shapes: ellipses (n = 2), lemniscates (n = 1), sinusoids (n = 2), lines (back and forth) (n = 3), complex shapes (n = 2, Table 2).

Table 2. Recorded traces, velocity profiles and scalar product related to the reproduction task of each subject.

Subject n°	Recorded trace	Velocity profiles	Scalar product
2			0,89
4			0,93
5			0,89
1			0,87
7			0,90
8			0,95
10			0,92
3			0,98
6			0,99
9			0,91

The velocity profiles of the movements used to draw the different shapes are perceived as dynamic variations in the sounds and serve as auditory cues to recognize different shapes [28]. The velocity profiles drawn by the subjects are broadly similar to the reference profiles, regardless of the drawn shapes that vary across subjects. These velocity profiles, like the drawings on the tablet, show that the subjects actually try to reproduce an alternate motion. The scalar products comparing the subjects' velocity profiles with the reference velocity profile are rather high (>0.87) reflecting a correct reproduction of the reference velocity profile.

Several unexpected results are observed in the reproduction task which can be analyzed according to three criteria: a) how the subject conceptually represents the sound, i.e. what the sound "looks like" (Table 3, column 3), b) the imaginary visual content (an imaginary scene) associated with the sound (Table 3, column 4), and c) how the subject actually drew the sound on the tablet (Table 3, column 6).

Table 3. Results of the elicitation interviews related to type of sound listening and reproduction task. The coherency between the representation of the sound and the imaginary content or the reproduction gesture is given by following symbols: (+) = good coherence, (+/-) = medium coherence, (-) = poor coherence.

1	2	3	4	5	6	7	8
Subject n°	Listening focus	The sound is like a... (= representation) (Sound listening)	Associated imaginary visual content (Sound reproduction)	3 vs 4	Recorded trace (movement)	6 vs 4	6 vs 3
2	Origin of sound	Wave	Scene of waves. I'm riding the waves.	+		+	+
4		Waves and bubbles	Scene of close waves with bubbles bursting, like scum.	+		-	-
5		Waves and bubbles	Scene of wave with splashing droplets. Slow "glou glou"	+		-	-
1	Acoustic parameters of sound	Something perfectly rounded with rythm	Ellipse on a table, or a cardiac motion, "wroum wroum"	+		+	+
7		Dynamics, a sinusoid, a wave	I wanted to make sinusoid shapes	+		-	-
8		A growing flow	It is like a refrain.	-		-	-
10		Waves	Scene of waves, with"vrrr" and "boum"	+		+	+
3	Effect of the sound	Oscillation, oval shape (hourglass)	I am washing a sweater by hand. I sing the rhythm, I dance	+/-		+	+
6		Dynamics. A zigzag shape, an ellipse	I danse on the sound. I'm rowing on the water.	+/-		-	+
9		Pulsation, a spindle	I wanted to do a spindle, or a wave, with internal movements	+		+	+

The representation of the sound contents to reproduce the sound heard depends on each subject's main listening mode (Table 3, comparison of columns 2 and 3). For all the subjects with predominant listening based on the origin of the sound (i.e. everyday listening), the sound heard resembles more or less typical waves. For subjects presenting predominant listening based on the acoustic characteristics of the sound (i.e. analytical listening) the reproduction strategy (4 subjects out of 4) is based on the physical dynamics of the sound (rhythm, oscillations, intensity). For subjects whose predominant listening is based on the sound effect, the reproduction strategy is based more on the feeling of oscillations and pulsations (2 subjects out of 3).

The visual scenes associated with the task consisting of reproducing movements in a liquid are summarized in column 4, Table 3. These visual scenes are consistent with the subjects' representation of sounds (column 5) in 7 subjects. The coherence between the produced shape and the imaginary scene is good for half of the subjects (column 7). The coherence between the produced shape and the sound representation is good for 6 subjects (column 8), who are mainly the same as those with a good coherency in the other representation.

4 Discussion and Conclusion

The phenomenological analysis of the pre-reflexive contents of the consciousness in a reproduction task of a sound using a sound-based graphic tablet makes it possible to confirm the main types of listening previously described by Gaver [9] or Petitmengin et al. [19]. The fact of having a reproduction task to be accomplished modifies, with respect to an isolated passive listening, the diachronic and synchronic content of this experience (the moment of appearance of the experiential content, in particular). In this preliminary work involving a small population of subjects, we did not find differences in listening and sound reproduction based on age, gender, or musical experience. It would be interesting to increase the number of subjects to assess whether differences appear according to these factors. However, we can not perform EIs on large populations because of the considerable time required for data processing. We (GM, JVD) are currently testing faster and more efficient data processing methods to increase the number of subjects involved in this type of study.

When comparing our current and previous studies [19], several differences must be reported. The initial study focused on describing the listening modalities of the sound, as such, and without any task required at the end of the listening. The study aimed to highlight the descriptive categories of the non-reflexive part of the sound listening experiences and to define the general structure of such an experience. For this reason, various sounds were used (sounds from nature, sounds from everyday life, abstract sounds). Some individual differences linked to the way subjects listened to sounds were observed, but the constitution of subgroups of subjects did not appear. In our current study, only one sound is proposed with an associated reproduction task. If the same types of non-reflexive experiences can be observed, the task to be done changes the type of intentionality [11] and attentional focus.

Perceptual modalities also change between listening and reproducing tasks. During a listening task, it is the auditory system that is mainly solicited, whereas in a reproduction task, perception is multimodal with a solicitation of auditory, visual and proprioceptive activities in addition to motor skills. Note that in this study we did not focus on the way in which the heard sound is transformed (or not) in the consciousness at the moment of initiating the drawing on the tablet, just after hearing the sound. This probably depends on the type of listening that the subject adopts and probably on the time it takes before he/she starts moving the pen on the tablet. In phenomenological terms, this amounts to asking the question of how retention and protention [13] are respectively organized in this pivotal moment (this thick present) between listening and reproduction. This study also made it possible to highlight the fact that even if each subject possesses a preferential type (focus) of listening, other types of listening are also mobilized to find the resources for carrying out the reproduction task. In reality, perceptual processes are rarely unimodal. The so-called primary receptor areas of the cerebral cortex that were thought to be specific to a sensory modality are in fact multimodal [10]. Multimodality in perception seems to be the rule and the degree of synaesthesia varies from one individual to another [6]. This, for example, could explain why we find an entanglement of different types of listening in all the subject responses, along with the presence of a preferential type. This entanglement of available perceptual dispositions reveals the complexity of the processes involved in the reproduction task and opens a new field of research on the co-presence of pre-reflexive perceptual processes.

Taking into account only the traces obtained, transcribed by the velocity profiles and the scalar products (Table 2), we can conclude from this study that the subjects reproduce the dynamic structure of an alternating motion correctly, i.e. they make a sketch or a summary of the transformational invariant underlying the evoked action. However, the two parameters (velocity profile, and scalar product) do not enable to deduce the specific shape drawn during the reproduction and from the drawings it is clear that the sounds do not contain the spatial cues that would lead all the subjects to draw the same figure.

When the subjects are asked how they represent the sound, i.e. what it looks like (Table 3, column 3), they call upon characteristics which are also related to the dynamics of a movement, according to three categories: a) oscillation: waves, oscillations, pulsations in 6 subjects, b) rhythm in 2 subjects and c) dynamics (without precision of nature) in 2 subjects. Probably this "representation" of sound participates in sound semiosis, that is to say in the sense that the subject gives to the sound. However, the variety of semiotic processes involved should be noted.

The way in which the subjects represent the sound is globally in agreement with their predominant type of listening (column 2). Subjects with a preferred listening type related to the origin of the sound (alternating movement in a liquid) hear waves and therefore focus on the structural and/or transformational invariant. Subjects who present a preferential listening oriented towards acoustic characteristics propose representations more related to signal structures and focus on the intrinsic sound properties. Subjects whose preferential listening mode is the effect of sound do not represent the sound but describe what they feel more than what they represent themselves: in this sense they have a more phenomenological approach than the other two types of subjects.

When the subjects are asked about the imaginary content (visual scenes) associated with sound reproduction (column 4), we observe a good correlation (in 7 subjects) between the representation of sound and this imaginary content (column 5). However, the imaginary content adds additional information about how the subjects were involved in the task. For example, subject 3 saw himself washing a sweater by hand. Of the 7 subjects for whom a good coherence between the sound representation and the imaginary visual scene was observed, only 5 of them generated a shape that was coherent with the representation and the imagination (comparison of columns 5 and 6).

All these results can be summarized in a simplified and hypothetic model of the processes involved (Fig. 2). It turns out that the audio-motor loop leads to the reproduction of sound dynamics, i.e. the reproduction of alternating movement, while the associated shape, which cannot be predicted from the sound itself, depends on the subjects and their representation of the sound. This shape is modulated by the subject's preferred type of listening. The associated visual imaginary content, which is richer than the representation, might modulate the generation of the shape, giving it a kind of imaginary context. The type of preferential listening is also likely to modulate the imaginary content.

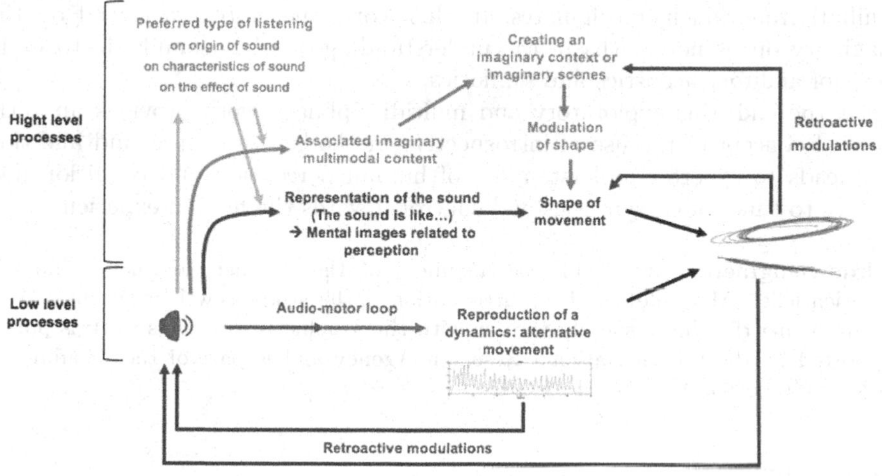

Fig. 2. Hypothetic model of the reproduction task.

One of the most important results of this study is the ability of EIs to highlight the role of imagination in the reproductive process. However, it is important to differentiate between mental imagery associated with perception and imagination. This mental imagery is either unimodal or multimodal. Imagination is that mental activity associated or not with a perception or an action. It is the imagination (fantasia) that we find liberated in dreams or hypnosis. Thus, at the level of the representation of the sound, the subjects, describe for example sinusoids for which they might either have an image in the visual modality, or an amodal thought in the form of a concept. Recent studies show that this type of multimodal mental imagery is very often associated with perception and is either conscious or unconscious (pre-reflective in phenomenology) [3]. It seems that this mental imagery is correlated to the activation of numerous cerebral areas, especially visual areas [7]. On the other hand, when subjects imagine how they are going to reproduce the sound, they often insert the shapes to be reproduced in a rich and systematically multimodal context. Imagination creates scenes (with motor, kinesthetic, and sometimes olfactory components) in which the subject does an action more or less related to the task, but which is not the task. This imagination creates a context, a scene or a story (washing a sweater, playing on the string of a harpsichord) related to the subject's habits. It is very difficult, if not impossible, to study such rich and evanescent imaginary processes with current means of neuroscience.

Imagination is undoubtedly the blind spot of cognitive and neurophysiological approaches. Its richness and complexity defy any reduction to simple activations or to logico-semantic or computational processes. Only introspective approaches that leave room for the subject's mental landscape, such as the Experiential Phenomenological Interview [31] (or microphenomenology) can account for the richness of this imagination and the multiple backgrounds (historical, cultural, familial) from which it originates. In this work, the emphasis placed on the imaginary opens new paths in the understanding of what sounds do to us in terms of auditory acoustics and semiotics.

At the end, this exploratory and multidisciplinary work provides an early proof of concept of the use of introspective methods in acoustics and audition that leads to a better understanding of human perception and cognition and enables to tune sound synthesis and control towards the human experience.

Acknowledgments. We thank the members of the "Atelier de Phénoménologie Expérientielle" (Marseille) for their participation to this study as well as Dr Dias-Alvez for producing the ellipse sound in water with the graphic tablet. This work is partly supported by the French National Research Agency and is part of the "Sonimove" project (Grant No. ANR-14-CE24-0018).

References

1. Aramaki, M., Besson, M., Kronland-Martinet, R., Ystad, S.: Controlling the perceived material in an impact sound synthesizer. IEEE Trans. Audio Speech Lang. Process. **19**(2), 301–314 (2011)
2. Aramaki, M., Gondre, C., Kronland-Martinet, R., Voinier, T., Ystad, S.: Imagine the sounds: an intuitive control of an impact sound synthesizer. In: Ystad, S., Aramaki, M., Kronland-Martinet, R., Jensen, K. (eds.) CMMR/ICAD -2009. LNCS, vol. 5954, pp. 408–421. Springer, Heidelberg (2010). https://doi.org/10.1007/978-3-642-12439-6_21
3. Nanay, B.: Multimodal mental imagery. Cortex 105, 125134 (2018)
4. Bordonné, T., Dias-Alves, M., Aramaki, M., Ystad, S., Kronland-Martinet, R.: Assessing sound perception through vocal imitations of sounds that evoke movements and materials. In: Aramaki, M., Davies, M.E.P., Kronland-Martinet, R., Ystad, S. (eds.) CMMR 2017. LNCS, vol. 11265, pp. 402–412. Springer, Cham (2018). https://doi.org/10.1007/978-3-030-01692-0_26
5. Bordonné, T., Kronland-Martinet, R., Ystad, S., Derrien, O., Aramaki, M.: Exploring sound perception through vocal imitations. J. Acoust. Soc. Am. **147**(5), 3306–3321 (2020)
6. Spence, C.: Crossmodal correspondences: a tutorial review. Attent. Percept. Psychophys. **73**, 971995 (2011)
7. Winlove, C.I.P., et al.: The neural correlates of visual imagery: a co-ordinate-based meta-analysis. Cortex **105**, 425 (2018)
8. Conan, S., et al.: An intuitive synthesizer of continuous-interaction sounds: rubbing, scratching, and rolling. Comput. Music J. **38**(4), 24–37 (2014)
9. Gaver, W.W.: What in the world do we hear? An ecological approach to auditory event perception. Ecol. Psychol. **5**(1), 1–29 (1993)
10. Ghazanfar, A., Schroeder, C.E.: Is the cortex essentially multisensory? Trends Cogn. Sci. **10**(6), 278285 (2006)
11. Gibson, J.J.: The Ecological Approach to Visual Perception: Classic Edition. Psychology Press (2014)
12. Giordano, B.L., McAdams, S.: Material identification of real impact sounds: effects of size variation in steel, wood, and plexiglass plates. J. Acoust. Soc. Am. **119**(2), 1171–1181 (2006)

13. Husserl, E.: Leçons pour une phénoménologie de la conscience intime du temps. Presses Universitaires de France (19051964)
14. Husserl, E.: Idées directrices pour une phénoménologie. Gallimard (1985)
15. Lakatos, S., McAdams, S., Chaigne, A.: The representation of auditory source characteristics: simple geometric form. Percept. Psychophys. **59**, 1180–1190 (1997)
16. Lemaitre, G., Dessein, A., Susini, P., Aura, K.: Vocal imitations and the identification of sound events. Ecol. Psychol. **4**(23), 267–307 (2011)
17. Maurel, M.: The explicitation interview: example and applications. J. Conscious. Stud. **16**, 20–57 (2009)
18. Merer, A., Aramaki, M., Ystad, S., Kronland-Martinet, R.: Perceptual characterization of motion evoked by sounds for synthesis control purposes. ACM Trans. Appl. Percept. **10**(1), 1–24 (2013)
19. Petitmengin, C., et al.: Listening from within. J. Conscious. Stud. **16**, 252–284 (2009)
20. Petitmengin, C., Bitbol, M., Ollagnier-Beldame, M.: Vers une science de l? Expérience vécue. Intellectica - Rev. Assoc. Pour. Rech. Sur. Sci. Cogn. ARCo **64**, 53–76 (2015)
21. Repp, B.H.: The sound of two hands clapping: an exploratory study. J. Acoust. Soc. Am. **81**(4), 1100–1109 (1987)
22. Roussarie, V., Richard, F., Bezat, M.C.: Validation of auditory attributes using analysis synthesis method. In: Congrés Francais d'Acoustique/DAGA, Strasbourg (2004)
23. Saitis, C., Fritz, C., Scavone, G., Guastavino, C., Dubois, D.: A psycholinguistic analysis of preference verbal descriptors by experienced musicians. J. Acoust. Soc. Am. **141**(4), 2746–2757 (2017)
24. Saitis, C., Giordano, B., Fritz, C., Scavone, G.: Perceptual evaluation of violins. A quantitative analysis of preference judgments by experienced players. J. Acoust. Soc. Am. **132**(6), 4002–4012 (2012)
25. Sciabica, J., Olivero, A., Roussarie, V., Ystad, S., Kronland-Martinet, R.: Dissimilarity test modelling by time-frequency representation applied to engine sound. In: Audio Engineering Society Conference: 45th International Conference: Applications of Time-Frequency Processing in Audio (2012)
26. Stern, D.: The Present Moment in Psychotherapy and Everyday Life. W. W. Norton & Company (2010)
27. Thoret, E., Aramaki, M., Bringoux, L., Ystad, S., Kronland-Martinet, R.: Seeing circles and drawing ellipses: when sound biases reproduction of visual motion. PLoS One **11**(4), e0154475 (2016)
28. Thoret, E., Aramaki, M., Kronland-Martinet, R., Velay, J.L., Ystad, S.: From sound to shape: auditory perception of drawing movements. J. Exp. Psychol. Hum. Percept. Perform. **40**(3), 983 (2014)
29. Vermersch, P.: Conscience directe et conscience réfléchie. Intellectica **31**, 269–311 (2000)
30. Vermersch, P.: Describing the practice of introsopection. J. Conscious. Stud. **16**, 20–57 (2009)
31. Vion-Dury, J., Mougin, G.: L'exploration de l'expérience consciente: archéologie d'une démarche de recherche. vers l'entretien phénoménologique expérientiel (epe). Chron. Phénoménol. **11**, 4357 (2018)
32. Warren, W.H., Verbrugge, R.R.: Auditory perception of breaking and bouncing events: a case study in ecological acoustics. J. Exp. Psychol. Hum. Percept. Perform. **10**(5), 704–712 (1984)

The Process of Sound Design

Exploring Design Cognition in Voice-Driven Sound Sketching and Synthesis

Stefano Delle Monache[1(✉)] and Davide Rocchesso[2]

[1] Faculty of Industrial Design Engineering, Delft University of Technology, Delft, The Netherlands
s.dellemonache@tudelft.nl

[2] Department of Mathematics and Computer Science, University of Palermo, Palermo, Italy
davide.rocchesso@unipa.it

Abstract. Conceptual design and communication of sonic ideas are critical, and still unresolved aspects of current sound design practices, especially when teamwork is involved. Design cognition studies in the visual domain represent a valuable resource to look at, to better comprehend the reasoning of designers when they approach a sound-based project. A design exercise involving a team of professional sound designers is analyzed, and discussed in the framework of the Function-Behavior-Structure ontology of design. The use of embodied sound representations of concepts fosters team-building and a more effective communication, in terms of shared mental models.

Keywords: Sound design · Collaboration · Design cognition

1 Introduction

We witness an essential process of convergence of inquiries in sound design towards the broader field of design research. From different angles, sound studies, sonic interaction design (SID), computer science, auditory cognition studies, and sonification research are challenging the inherent cooperative and collaborative, yet ambiguous nature of listening and hearing, as method and means to contribute to better everyday environments for the living [2,43]. More recently, sound design research has been unfolding its interest in the interaction- and information-centered use of sound in computational artefacts, towards the study of the process of designing sound. There are a variety of reasons to study sound designing. Researchers may want to have an understanding of the actual activities carried out by practitioners and their status [52]. Others may investigate the design process with the goal of improving the practice [12,16]. Other loci of interest may inquiry designing sound with the aim of developing appropriate design tools and supporting technologies throughout the various stages of

R. Kronland-Martinet et al. (Eds.): CMMR 2019, LNCS 12631, pp. 465–480, 2021.
https://doi.org/10.1007/978-3-030-70210-6_30

the process [7,14]. Finally, other research approaches, whether bottom-up (e.g., case studies and design explorations [32,44]) or top-down (e.g., reference frameworks and systems [4,50]), may wish to achieve and provide a more general and abstracted explanation of thinking patterns in sound design tasks, the design process and methods that practitioners may look at.

Indeed, one main problem that sound practitioners strive to deal with is the communication and evaluation of a design, that is sound, in which the distance between the intermediary representations and the final product is perceived as very short. The intrinsic ambiguity of sound and listening do affect both the collaboration between peers and the contact points with stakeholder in general [10, p. 35]: Communicating and elaborating concepts through sound can be hazardous, especially in the early interactions with clients; design solutions on sound are difficult to argue, especially when designers overindulge in the description of the sound-producing mechanisms rather than accounting for the global sensory experience; as a consequence, the evaluation of sound design proposals often takes the prosaic form of the individual preference of the client, whenever it is not based on psychoacoustic metrics for sound quality assessment [36,40].

In the practice, sound creation and production rather unfold, within the overall design process, as an individual activity kept separate and asynchronous from the global product development, the effect of which undermines the participation and communication with stakeholders, both horizontally and vertically, and brings about a tendency to anticipate, early in the process, the creation of assortments of selected variations of highly refined sounds [46,47].

Since the 2nd International Symposium "Les Journées du Design Sonore"[1] in 2004, a growing corpus of additive knowledge on sound design has been produced (see [3,17,18,24,37,39,43,49], for a comprehensive overview). Such body of knowledge outlines a landscape of descriptive models of designing sound, whose central proposal is a closed loop of sound evaluation and design that advances through rapid prototyping and iterative improvement: Research through design workshops, design critique and explorations, and controlled experiments with sonic interactive artifacts and tools are primarily focused on the design activity in the conceptual and embodiment stages of the design process.

It turns out, however, that little is known about how sound designers think, generate and develop ideas. Given their multidisciplinary background [38], how do sound designers approach projects? For example, do they favor a search process in the problem space, like industrial designers do, or in the solution space, like engineers apparently prefer [28]?

Designing (sound) takes place in people's minds. Despite the market availability of countless types of computational tools for sound analysis and production, the very first creative act happens in the designer's mind. Understanding sound design thinking becomes crucial to create the next generation of design tools,

[1] The symposium, organized by Frédérique Guyot (LAPS-design) and Patrick Susini (Ircam) in collaboration with the French Acoustical Society, took place at Centre Pompidou, Paris, France, in 2004 (https://www.centrepompidou.fr/cpv/resource/cazjxnn/rLLRyR).

computational or not, to aid the generation and communication of auditory concepts. In this respect, sound design research may look at design cognition studies in the visual domain, as reference framework of relevant topics, and rigorous and formal methods and ontologies to investigate individual and collaborative design dynamics involving sound [11,25].

In this area of study, protocol analysis is the established, empirical method, commonly used to inquiry well-defined design phenomena, such as novice-expert differences in problem structuring and organization of cognitive actions, the effect of the "structeredness" of ideation methods on cognition, the role of design representations and sketching, the conditions for design fixation and its effect on the novelty of ideas, and in general the cognitive processes involved in design moves [15]. Typically, audiovideo documentations of design sessions are transcribed and parsed in segments, that is the smallest units of analysis that can be time-based, reflect turn-taking (e.g., in team dynamics) or other rationale (e.g., decision-making), according the granularity and the objective of the study. Segments are coded according to meaningful schemes that may well-represent the particulars of the case in question. Finally, various kinds of qualitative and quantitative analyses can be carried out in order to derive an understanding of the design phenomena under scrutiny [23,29].

In this work, we analyze the protocol of a design session involving a team of professional sound designers engaged in vocal sketc.hing the sound of two car models (e.g., idle engine, driving, braking), with the aid of a computational tool for voice-driven sound synthesis [14]. We apply the Function-Behavior-Structure (FBS) ontology of design [29, chap. 13] as coding scheme, from which we derive information on the team dynamics and productivity, the role-taking, the designing style and process unfolding. The FBS ontology is a formal coding scheme which takes in account the cognitive processes emerging as transitions in the design space, and precisely in terms of transformations between classes of issues which are intrinsic to any design domain: i) the purpose of the artifact, that is the Function; its imagined performance, that is the Behavior Expected; iii) its form and configuration, that is the Structure; iv) the resulting performance, that is the Behavior derived from the Structure (see further, Sect. 3).

The paper is organized as follows: the next Section provides an overview of topics on cognition in conceptual design activity which can be relevant to investigate in design teamwork involving sound; Sect. 3 introduces the sound design session, and the coding procedure using the FBS ontology of design; we analyze and discuss the session in Sect. 4.

2 Conceptual Design Cognition at a Glance

It has been argued that the next generation of CAD systems will be defined by four main characteristics, and namely cognition, collaboration, concepts, and creativity [20]. The majority of the research in design cognition concerns the disciplines of architectural design, engineering design, and product design. The research revolves around the two main paradigms of design as search in the problem space [21] or design as exploration and co-evolution [22,48], and focuses on the processes of information gathering and structuring, the role of long-term memory, schema activation in working memory, semantic processing, mental synthesis and sketch-based reasoning (see [25,26] for a systematic review of protocol studies on conceptual design cognition). These processes are essentially inspected from a visuo-spatial perspective, if one excludes the role of the phonological loop for verbal design information [8,42].

Such a structured knowledge and methodological approach are still missing in the realm of aural collaborative creativity and design. Certainly, auditory imagery and cognition represent a vast field of research which received an increasing attention in the past several years. The majority of the studies, originating from experimental psychology and neuroscience, are aimed at the understanding of the human abilities to generate and manipulate mental auditory images, where music and language are the preferred foci of interest: For instance, it has been shown that auditory images contain both depictive and descriptive components, that is some relationships of the auditory stimuli are preserved (e.g., pitch and temporal properties), while others rather "sound like" (e.g., loudness), and that the reinterpretation (i.e., figure-ground segregation) of a given stream of sounds is more difficult in auditory imagery than in auditory perception, especially when subvocalization is blocked [27]. Functional MRI studies showed that conceptual acoustic processing, that is thinking about a sound even when implicitly presented through visual words, involves a partial reinstatement of the brain activity during the perceptual experience of the same acoustic features [31].

Empirical frameworks on the role of the active body as inherent mediator between perception and the cognitive processing of music (and sound) have been proposed, wherein the sonic experience emerges in interaction, as complex network of intentional states and internal models of observable patterns, that are acquired through knowledge and skills [35]. Within this framework, recent researches not only showed that vocal imitations of nonverbal sounds encode salient acoustic features into some other vocal features [33], while gestural metaphors are exploited to illustrate auditory sensations and causal representations of sonic concepts [34], but also explored their use as cognitive devices to enable and support sketc.h-based reasoning in conceptual sound design [13].

Embodied cognition, concepts, and creativity are at the center of frameworks for designing the next generation of sonic information and interactions [43,45], where experimental applications of body-centered auditory display and sonification are finding their way in walking interactions in mixed reality, physical rehabilitation and motor learning, sensory alteration and emotional design [51]. On the other side, process-based studies on sound design are still embryonic [11], if one excludes the existing literature on creative thinking in music processes: The ill-defined problem of composing a piece of music is solved through iterative, non-linear stages of insight (i.e., musical inspiration), problem restructuring and proliferation [9]. Cognitive processes in music composition can reflect an analytic, horizontal approach to the sequential writing of the musical parts, or develop vertically, that is implying a strong conceptualization phase of the whole in advance, before the actual production: The "sound designer" style has been characterized by an in-depth, horizontal exploration and original use of tools, where iterations are especially concentrated in the re-execution and revision of sound segments in the recording phases [1].

Horizontal and vertical compositional strategies strongly resonate with the dual mechanism model of design problem-solving: Lateral transformations of an idea are divergent and associative, are facilitated by ill-structured representations (i.e., conceptual sketches), and widen the problem space, while vertical transformations are convergent and inferential, are facilitated by well-structured representations (e.g., prescriptive sketches and blueprints), and deepen the problem space [21]. It has been shown how sketch-based reasoning facilitates the reorganization and creation of new knowledge [5]. It can be argued that the main criticality of sound design is the unbalanced use of well-structured representations [12], due to the lack of proper tools that afford sketching in the established workflow, at least in the acceptation widespread in the visual domain [10, p. 35].

Cooperation and collaboration in conceptual sound design are not common practices, where design in a natural setting, e.g. in a design firm, is typically carried out by teams with multidisciplinary background. The study of design teams may reveal several insights on design thinking. One main advantage of examining design teams is that think-aloud protocols are naturally enforced and concurrent with the execution of the task. It has been shown that early collaborations are the most effective and improve consistency in mental models, and yet that design teamwork do not necessarily brings about a higher productivity, compared to the individual activity: Apparently, the experienced individual designer is equipped with all the necessary expertise to act as a unitary system (i.e., a team, in which the expertise are allocated by role-taking instead), whereby the semantic coherence of the team composition affects positively the quality of the final designs [15].

Design ontologies have been proposed to formalize and analize the design process. The Function-Behavior-Structure (FBS) coding framework was used to observe an industry team (a business consultant, three mechanical engineers, an electronic business consultant, an ergonomicist, and an industrial design student), involved in a brainstorming session: The distribution of word count and turns variation throughout the design episodes provided coarse quantitative observations on the quality of the team interaction, in terms of producing a shared mental model, whereby the analysis of transitions between FBS design issues produced fine-grained representations of the design process at the individual and team level [30].

The same coding scheme was applied to measure the designing styles of teams of industrial design students and mechanical engineering design students, that is observing whether the designers' focus on the problem space or on the solution space may be specific to design disciplines, and how it may affect the team building and composition [28]: The Problem-Solution Index (PSI) was proposed as ratio measurement, computed over the total occurrences of design issues representing problem formulations (i.e., the function and the expected behavior) and design issues representing solutions to the formulated problem (i.e., the structure, and the behavior derived from the structure). The same measurement was applied to investigate how the structuredness of concept generation techniques affects the cognitive focus of teams towards the problem space or the solution space in the early stage of the design process [19].

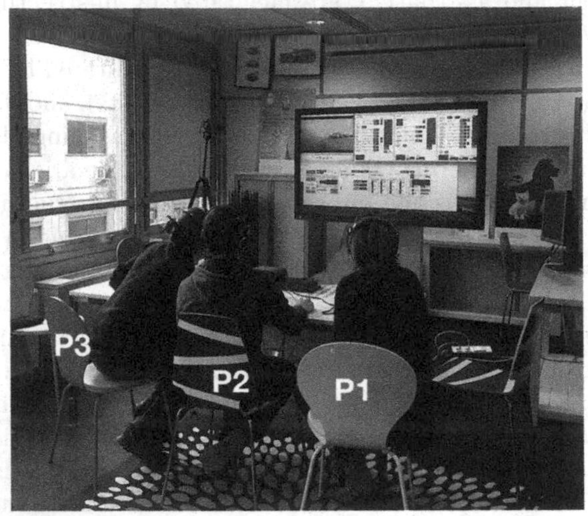

Fig. 1. Team composition: project manager (P1), audio engineer (P2), sound designer (P3).

Taken together, this concise survey of relevant studies on team design cognition prompts a path of open questions in the domain of aural creativity and design. While the discipline of sonic interaction design has been proposing and accumulating a variety of methods, frameworks and techniques [4,6,13,16,18], to our knowledge no formal and structured inquiries have been carried out yet, in terms of their impact on sound design cognition. In the next Section we describe the sound design task, along with a brief, operational discussion of the FBS ontology, the coding procedure and the conventions.

3 Collaborative Sketching with Voice-Driven Sound Synthesis

The vocal sketching exercise took place during a sound design workshop organized in collaboration with the audio research team of a vehicle manufacturing company. The team, including two sound designers, two audio engineers, and one project manager, was split in two groups in order to derive two protocols that could be analyzed and compared. The fictitious task was to re-design the EV (i.e., Electric Vehicle) engine sound version of two combustion engine car models. The assignment was delivered as follows:

Theme - A brand-new voice for an old car: How would the Citröen 21DS Rally and the Peugeot 205 GTI sound today if they were electric?
Objective: Re-think and design their sound according to the current brand values, optimistic, smart, human.
Time constraints: The design task duration is 90 min, split in 2 sessions of 45 min per car model.

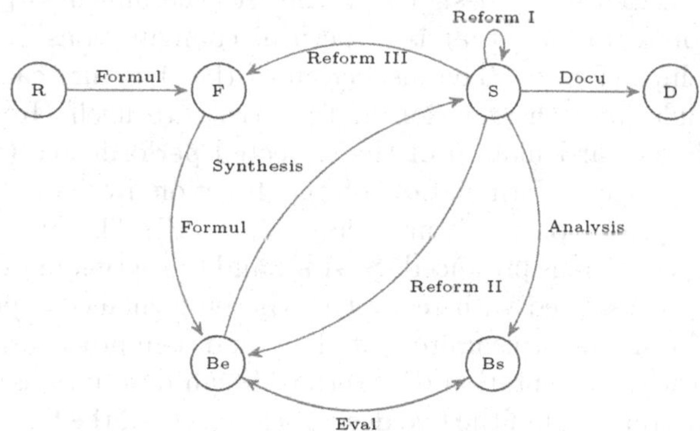

Fig. 2. The FBS framework. The codes represent the issues. Arcs are labeled according to the design processes.

The teams were provided with a computational tool for voice-driven sound synthesis, to support their sketc.hing activity: The tool affords the externalization of synthetic sound impressions by means of mixtures of sound models that can be set, played and shared as instances of vocal utterances. We refer to our previous work for the in-depth description and evaluation of the tool[2] [14]. The groups were also provided with silenced videos of the two car models, in order to vidco-prototype their design. The teams tackled the Citröen sound first, and the Peugeot sound design later. All the design tasks were video-recorded. In this paper, we report the protocol analysis of one team composed by one sound designer, one audio engineer and the project manager, shown in Fig. 1.

3.1 The Function-Behavior-Structure Coding Procedure

According to the FBS framework, any design artifact can be described and modeled as a set of semantic transitions, that is cognitive processes, between three classes of ontological variables, and namely the purpose of the artifact, its imagined and emerging performances, the components of the artifact and their compositional relationships. As shown in Fig. 2, the FBS coding scheme maps these three classes on six design issues, which are represented as codes: The final goal

[2] The tool in action: https://vimeo.com/271826511.

of any designing activity is to transform a set of requirements (R) and functions (F) into a set of design descriptions of the artifact at hand (D).

In the practice, the transcript of the design session is parsed in design moves, that is segments of utterances, gestures, and any other kinds of representation, which are labeled according to the design issues. Design moves-issues are linked according to causal transformations. Typically, the designer formulates the function (F), based on the requirements (R→F), which are usually derived from the brief. The expected behavior (Be) reflects the performance imagined to fulfill the function (F→Be). Hence, the designer synthesizes the imagined performance in externalized representations, that is structural configurations of elements and formal relationships (Be→S). The inspection of the structure can lead to three types of reformulations: the revision of the structure itself (Reformulation I, S→Bs); the different articulation of the expected performance (Reformulation II, S→Be); the proper reformulation of the function by lateral thinking the actual sketch or prototype (Reformulation III, S→F). The analysis transition occurs once the structure is produced (S→Bs), and the actual performance based on the structure is assessed with respect to the performance expected (evaluation, Be↔Bs). Eventually, this finite-state loop of design processes among design issues leads to the documentation of external design descriptions (S→D).

In coding the transcript of the two design sessions (i.e., the Citröen 21DS rally and the Peugeot 205 GTI), we followed a set of conventions, extensively reported in [11], that we introduced to fully capture the sound designers' intentions, as they find themselves involved in discussing by means of verbalizations, vocalizations, iconic gestures accompanying the utterances, and synthesized sounds driven by both the vocal control and the mouse interaction on the graphic user interface of the sketching tool.

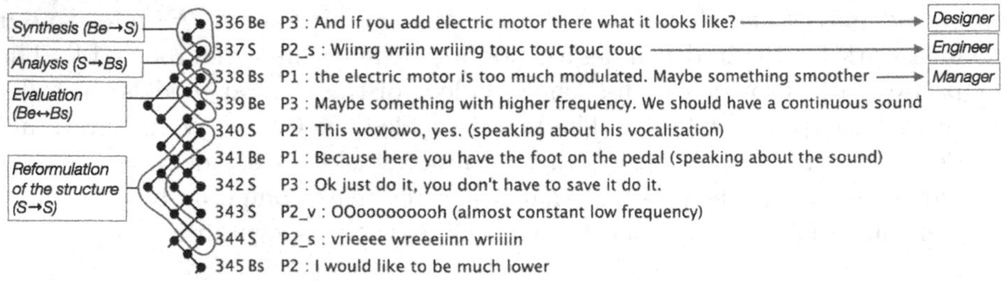

Fig. 3. Linkograph of an excerpt of 12 FBS-coded moves, extracted from the Citröen protocol in Fig. 4a. Links and nodes are visible, and examples of transitions between issues are highlighted: synthesis (e.g., 336→337), reformulation of the structure (e.g., 340→344), analysis (e.g., 337→338) and evaluation (e.g., 338→339).

Once the coding procedure is completed, the emerging network of design moves can be organized and represented as a linkograph, where the relations among nodes, such as the density, the distance between links, the amount of links, their direction, distribution and patterns, are used to inspect the productivity and the behavior of the designer(s) involved in the actual process [23]. Figure 3 shows the linkographic representation of 12 moves extracted from the protocol of the Citröen sound design session. The linkograph is generated by feeding the software LiNKODER[3] with the FBS-coded protocol [41]. In the next Section, we analyze and compare the two episodes, in order to derive a global picture of the team cooperation and dynamics.

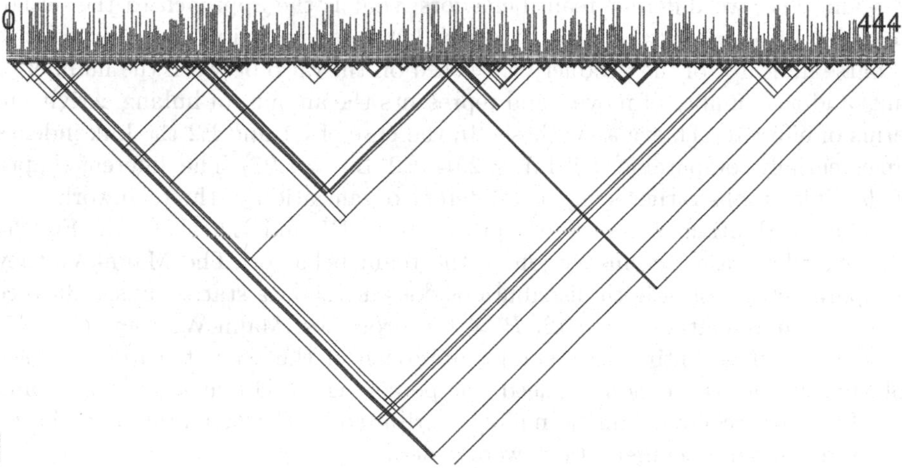

(a) Linkograph of the Citröen sound design session, computed over 444 segments, FBS-coded protocol.

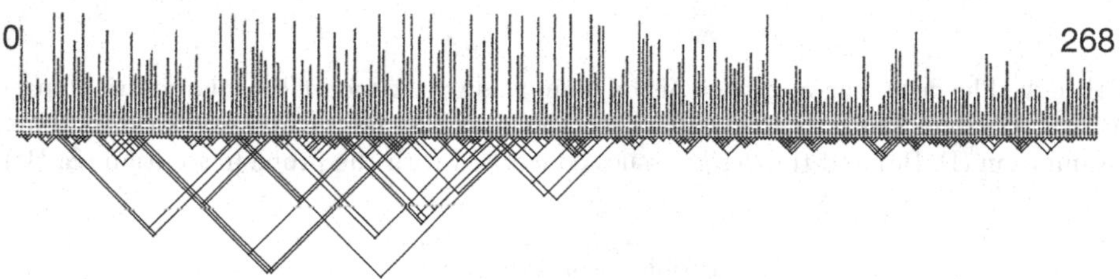

(b) Linkograph of the Peugeot sound design session, computed over 268 segments, FBS-coded protocol.

Fig. 4. Linkographic representations of the two sound design episodes, as generated by the software LiNKODER [41].

4 Analysis and Discussion

The Citröen sound session (E1) resulted in a protocol of 444 moves, whereas 268 segments were retained for coding the Peugeot sound session (E2). From

[3] LiNKODER, a design protocol analysis tool: https://sites.google.com/a/linkoder.com/linkoder/home.

the visual inspection of their linkographic representations, shown respectively in Fig. 4a and 4b, we can notice that E1 is characterized by a longer link span (mean 10.5, STD 45.5), which denotes either a longer incubation of ideas, where sketching serves as external memory function, or a typical team behavior where members may relate to their previous moves, regardless of the other moves intervened in the meanwhile. E2 linkograph is much more cohesive, with a shorter link span (mean = 5.3, STD = 10.3), which suggests a rather unitary behavior of team. The two different team behaviors, that is the approach to the design task, do not necessarily imply a higher or lower productivity. The link index is a coarse indicator of the productivity, based on the ratio between the number of links and the number of moves, and represents the amount of linking activity in terms of effort to achieve a synthesis. In the case of E1 and E2 the link indexes are essentially comparable (E1, L.I. = 2.04; E2, L.I. = 1.97). The different shapes of the linkographs rather suggest a different organization of the teamwork.

The distribution of issues and processes in E1 and E2, shown in Fig. 5a and 5b, allows a closer inspection of the team behavior. The Mann-Whitney non-parametric test of both distributions does not show a statistical significance (issues, Mann-Whitney, $U = 12$, $P > .05$; processes, Mann-Whitney, $U = 17$, $P > .05$), hence hinting at a similar approach of the team towards the task solution, in the two sessions. Indeed, the percentage of D issues is identical and yet the low percentage can be mainly attributed to the fact that only shared and agreed-upon documentations were coded.

Taken together, the two episodes reveal a design activity especially centered on structural issues (S, Bs, >60%), where the cognitive efforts are mainly allocated to the reformulation of the structure and the evaluation of the resulting sound design.

Table 1. The designing approach of the team was rather focused on the solution space (PSI < 1.). The PSI is the ratio between the design issues representing the problem formulation (F, Be) and the design issues concerned with the problem solution (S, Bs).

	Problem-solution index
E1	0.42
E2	0.56

Table 2. Team activity: Occurrence of types of expressions in the two design sessions E1 and E2 (P1 = manager; P2 = engineer; P3 = designer).

	Verbalizations		Vocalizations		Gestures		Synth Snd	
	E1	E2	E1	E2	E1	E2	E1	E2
P1	67	58	0	0	0	0	0	0
P2	77	54	19	1	28	4	32	2
P3	141	87	34	19	18	22	28	21
Tot %	285 (64, 2)	199 (74, 2)	53 (11, 9)	20 (7, 5)	46 (10, 4)	26 (9, 7)	60 (13, 5)	23 (8, 6)

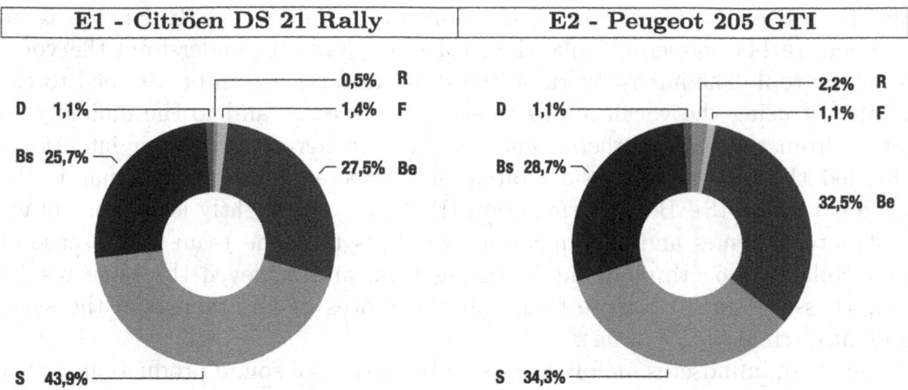

(a) Distribution of issues. The structural issues (S, Bs) represent more than the 60% of all the codes.

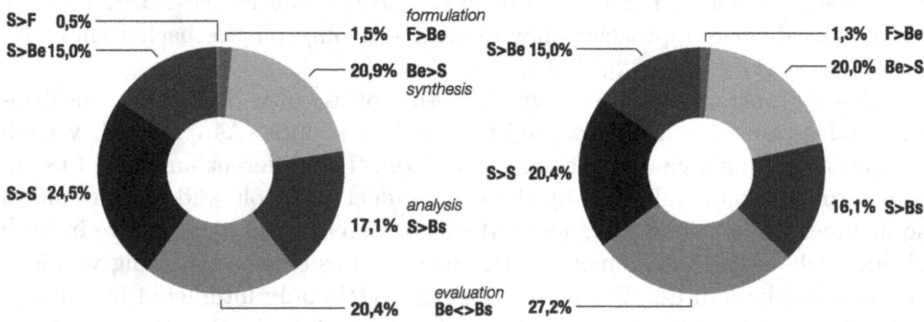

(b) Distribution of the processes. The team efforts are especially focused on producing and evaluating the sound (S→S; Be↔Bs).

Fig. 5. Distribution of issues and processes in the two design sessions (Citröen on the left, Peugeot on the right).

Table 3. Backward, forward and bidirectional critical moves in the two design sessions E1 and E2. The superscript indicates the criticality threshold.

	- P1 - Manager		- P2 - Engineer		- P3 - Designer		Team (Tot)	
	E1	E2	E1	E2	E1	E2	E1	E2
$<CM^4$	1	3	8	7	18	14	27	24
$CM^4>$	3	8	29	8	26	15	58	31
$<CM^4>$	1	1	5	2	3	8	9	11

In the practice, the two linkographic representations depict a shift in the effectiveness of the team's communication and collaboration. In E1, the team members rather cooperate, take their roles, explore and understand the vocal sketching tool. The intense work on the structural issues can be ascribed to the novelty of using the vocalizations as sketching means, and to the difficulty to obtain from the tool synthetic representations coherent with their intentions. This led the team to reconsider often the expected performance, that is the imagined sound (S$\rightarrow$Be, Reformulation II). In E2, the slightly lower percentage of structural issues and reformulations suggests that the team made sense of their collaboration through the sketching tool, and achieved the same results (i.e., D issues) in little more than half the moves of E1, though in the same amount of time (i.e., 45 min).

The team mindset is mainly addressed to the actual sound production, rather than its conceptualization (i.e., F$\rightarrow$Be, Be$\rightarrow$S). More in detail, Table 1 reports the problem-solution index value for E1 and E2, which reflects the attitude of the team towards the design process, whether focused on the conceptualization of the design problem (P-S I. $>$ 1.) or of the design solution (P-S I. $<$ 1.). The shift to the diverse approaches may depend not only on the background, but also on the specific design task [28].

Table 2 reports the group activity in terms of use of verbalization, vocalizations and gestures, and externalized synthesized sounds. As expected, verbal-thinking is the main channel of communication. The different amount of use of other forms of communication by the team reflects the role and background of the members. The sound designer (P3) was apparently the most active in both episodes, where the audio engineer (P2) became less engaged in using vocalizations and gestures in E2. The project manager (P1) only interacted by talking.

However, the quality of the individual contribution in the two episodes is reported in Table 3: The critical moves (CMs) are moves with a high number of links, based on a significant threshold typically set in order to obtain around 10–12% CMs from the total number of moves [23, p. 73]. The links between the critical moves are arranged in nodes of reasoning which may lead forward, thus denoting acts of synthesis (CM>), or backward, thus representing acts of evaluation (<CM). Bidirectional moves (<CM>) are associated to rapid shift of divergent and convergent thinking. Critical moves represent turning points in the unfolding of the design process. Whereas P2 and P3 were the main drivers of the process in E1, the team found a stronger integration and produced a more balanced process in E2.

In this respect, the count of the types of expressions in the two halves of the protocols of the two sessions is shown in Fig. 6: Although the total percentage of verbalizations is even increasing in E2 (see Table 2, last row, second column), the two halves in E2 are very different in nature, whereby the drop of verbalizations and increase of nonverbal representations in the second half stresses the achievement of shared mental models, as a consequence of a better integrated conceptualization phase in the first half of the session (see also the peculiar shape of the corresponding linkograph in Fig. 4b). To conclude, the

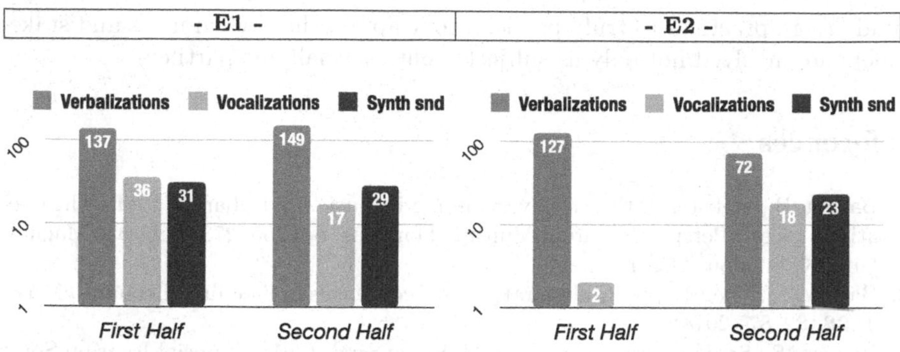

Fig. 6. Verbal and nonverbal expressions in the two design sessions.

design exercise acted throughout the two design sessions as an effective team-building tool, fostering more effective communication and collaboration between members with multidisciplinary background.

5 Conclusions

Designing is a process of construction of representations, from early, unstructured ideas of products, systems, services, etc. held in the mind towards the final artefacts. We showed how a cognition-based inquiry of sound design can reveal several aspects of team dynamics in conceptual design activities, which are considered critical and still unresolved in the current practices.

In the post-workshop comments, the participants reported a major frustration caused by several limitations of the computational sketching tool, that is first and foremost a lack of immediacy of use of the user interface and of technical integration in their established workflow (i.e., DAWs), whereby the voice-driven sound synthesis approach prompted clear expectations on the creation and shaping of the sound sketches. Nonetheless, the participants remarked the high value of collaboration experienced, by sketching through voice-based representations. They reported that for the first time, at least in their everyday workflow, they experienced to work collaboratively around a project. They especially remarked how through collaboration diverse approaches and ideas emerged. They found the overall workshop useful for team-building and reflecting on the role of creativity in their everyday sound design practice.

Protocol studies and ontologies of design, such as the FBS framework, represent valuable resources to investigate the process of sound design. In this respect, the establishment of design cognition studies in the sound design domain provides a novel, yet complementary perspective on the study of embodied sound cognition.

Understanding how representations of sound designs are externalized for communication and collective transformation purposes becomes crucial to open sound design practices to truly participatory approaches, when users and stakeholders are involved not only as subjects, but especially as partners.

References

1. Barbot, B., Webster, P.R.: Creative thinking in music. In: Lubart, T. (ed.) The Creative Process: Perspectives from Multiple Domains, pp. 255–273. Palgrave Macmillan UK, London (2018)
2. Barney, A., Voegelin, S.: Collaboration and consensus in listening. Leonardo Music J. **28**, 82–87 (2018)
3. Barrass, S.: Sonic information design. J. Sonic Stud. (2018). Special Issue on Sonic Information Design. https://www.researchcatalogue.net/view/558606/558686
4. Brazil, E.: A review of methods and frameworks for sonic interaction design: exploring existing approaches. In: Ystad, S., Aramaki, M., Kronland-Martinet, R., Jensen, K. (eds.) CMMR/ICAD - 2009. LNCS, vol. 5954, pp. 41–67. Springer, Heidelberg (2010). https://doi.org/10.1007/978-3-642-12439-6_3
5. Brun, J., Le Masson, P., Weil, B.: Designing with sketches: the generative effects of knowledge preordering. Design Sci. **2**, e13 (2016)
6. Caramiaux, B., Altavilla, A., Pobiner, S.G., Tanaka, A.: Form follows sound: designing interactions from sonic memories. In: Proceedings of the 33rd Annual ACM Conference on Human Factors in Computing Systems, CHI 2015, pp. 3943–3952. ACM, New York (2015)
7. Carron, M., Rotureau, T., Dubois, F., Misdariis, N., Susini, P.: Speaking about sounds: a tool for communication on sound features. J. Design Res. **15**(2), 85–109 (2017)
8. Cash, P., Maier, A.: Prototyping with your hands: the many roles of gesture in the communication of design concepts. J. Eng. Des. **27**(1–3), 118–145 (2016)
9. Collins, D.: A synthesis process model of creative thinking in music composition. Psychol. Music **33**(2), 193–216 (2005)
10. Delle Monache, S., et al.: Interactive prototypes realized with the SkAT-VG tool. Deliverable, SkAT-VG project (2017)
11. Delle Monache, S., Rocchesso, D.: Cooperative sound design: a protocol analysis. In: Proceedings of the Audio Mostly, AM 2016, pp. 154–161. ACM, New York (2016)
12. Delle Monache, S., Rocchesso, D.: To embody or not to embody: a sound design dilemma. In: Fontana, F., Gulli, A. (eds.) Machine Sounds, Sound Machines - Proceedings of the XXII CIM Colloquium on Music Informatics, pp. 93–100, November 2018
13. Delle Monache, S., Rocchesso, D.: Sketching sonic interactions. In: Filimowicz, M. (ed.) Foundations in Sound Design for Embedded Media, A Multidisciplinary Approach, pp. 79–101. Routledge, New York (2019)
14. Delle Monache, S., Rocchesso, D., Bevilacqua, F., Lemaitre, G., Baldan, S., Cera, A.: Embodied sound design. Int. J. Hum. Comput. Stud. **118**, 47–59 (2018)
15. Dinar, M., et al.: Empirical studies of designer thinking: past, present, and future. J. Mech. Des. **137**(2), 021101–0211013 (2015)
16. Erkut, C., Serafin, S., Hoby, M., Sårde, J.: Product sound design: form, function, and experience. In: Proceedings of the Audio Mostly 2015 on Interaction With Sound, AM 2015, pp. 10:1–10:6. ACM, New York (2015)

17. Filimowicz, M.: Foundations in Sound Design for Embedded Media: A Multidisciplinary Approach. Routledge, London (2019)
18. Franinović, K., Serafin, S.: Sonic Interaction Design. MIT Press, Cambridge (2013)
19. Gero, J.S., Jiang, H., Williams, C.B.: Design cognition differences when using unstructured, partially structured, and structured concept generation creativity techniques. Int. J. Design Creat. Innov. **1**(4), 196–214 (2013)
20. Goel, A.K., Vattam, S., Wiltgen, B., Helms, M.: Cognitive, collaborative, conceptual and creative-four characteristics of the next generation of knowledge-based cad systems: a study in biologically inspired design. Comput. Aided Des. **44**(10), 879–900 (2012)
21. Goel, V.: Creative brains: designing in the real world. Front. Hum. Neurosci. **8**, 241 (2014)
22. Goldschmidt, G.: The backtalk of self-generated sketches. Des. Issues **19**(1), 72–88 (2003)
23. Goldschmidt, G.: Linkography: Unfolding The Design Process. MIT Press, Cambridge (2014)
24. Grimshaw, M.: Game Sound Technology and Player Interaction: Concepts and Developments. IGI Global (2010)
25. Hay, L., Duffy, A.H.B., McTeague, C., Pidgeon, L.M., Vuletic, T., Grealy, M.: A systematic review of protocol studies on conceptual design cognition: Design as search andÂ exploration. Design Sci. **3**, e10 (2017)
26. Hay, L., Duffy, A.H.B., McTeague, C., Pidgeon, L.M., Vuletic, T., Grealy, M.: Towards a shared ontology: a generic classification of cognitive processes in conceptual design. Design Sci. **3**, e7 (2017)
27. Hubbard, T.L.: Auditory imagery: empirical findings. Psychol. Bull. **136**(2), 302 (2010)
28. Jiang, H., Gero, J.S., Yen, C.-C.: Exploring designing styles using a problem–solution division. In: Gero, J.S. (ed.) Design Computing and Cognition 2012, pp. 79–94. Springer, Dordrecht (2014). https://doi.org/10.1007/978-94-017-9112-0_5
29. Kan, J.W., Gero, J.S.: Quantitative Methods for Studying Design Protocols. Springer, Heidelberg (2017). https://doi.org/10.1007/978-94-024-0984-0
30. Kan, J.W., Gero, J.S., Tang, H.H.: Measuring cognitive design activity changes during an industry team brainstorming session. In: Gero, J.S. (ed.) Design Computing and Cognition 2010, pp. 621–640. Springer, Dordrecht (2011). https://doi.org/10.1007/978-94-007-0510-4_33
31. Kiefer, M., Sim, E.J., Herrnberger, B., Grothe, J., Hoenig, K.: The sound of concepts: four markers for a link between auditory and conceptual brain systems. J. Neurosci. **28**(47), 12224–12230 (2008)
32. Lemaitre, G., Houix, O., Visell, Y., Franinović, K., Misdariis, N., Susini, P.: Toward the design and evaluation of continuous sound in tangible interfaces: the Spinotron. Int. J. Hum. Comput. Stud. **67**(11), 976–993 (2009)
33. Lemaitre, G., Jabbari, A., Houix, O., Misdariis, N., Susini, P.: Vocal imitations of basic auditory features. J. Acoust. Soc. Am. **139**(1), 290–300 (2016)
34. Lemaitre, G., Scurto, H., Françoise, J., Bevilacqua, F., Houix, O., Susini, P.: Rising tones and rustling noises: metaphors in gestural depictions of sounds. PLoS One **12**(7), e0181786 (2017)
35. Leman, M., Maes, P.J., Nijs, L., Van Dyck, E.: What is embodied music cognition? In: Bader, R. (ed.) Springer Handbook of Systematic Musicology, pp. 747–760. Springer, Heidelberg (2018). https://doi.org/10.1007/978-3-662-55004-5_34
36. Lyon, R.H.: Product sound quality-from perception to design. Sound vibr. **37**(3), 18–23 (2003)

37. Meelberg, V., Özcan, E.: Editorial: Designing our sonic lives. J. Sonic Stud. (6) (2018). Special Issue on Sound Design. https://www.researchcatalogue.net/view/239747/239748/0/0
38. Özcan, E., van Egmond, R.: Product sound design: an inter-disciplinary approach? In: Undisciplined! Design Research Society Conference (2009). http://shura.shu.ac.uk/531/
39. Pauletto, S.: Perspectives on sound design. The New Soundtrack **4**(2), v–vi (2014)
40. Pedersen, T.H., Zacharov, N.: How many psycho-acoustic attributes are needed. J. Acoust. Soc. Am. **123**(5), 3163 (2008)
41. Pourmohamadi, M., Gero, J.S.: LINKOgrapher: an analysis tool to study design protocols based on FBS coding scheme. In: Culley, S., Hicks, B., McAloone, T., Howard, T., Clarkson, J. (eds.) ICED 2011 Proc. of the 18th International Conference on Engineering Design, Impacting Society through Engineering Design. Design Theory and Research Methodology, vol. 2, pp. 294–303 (2011)
42. Purcell, A., Gero, J.S.: Drawings and the design process: a review of protocol studies in design and other disciplines and related research in cognitive psychology. Des. Stud. **19**(4), 389–430 (1998)
43. Rocchesso, D., Delle Monache, S., Barrass, S.: Interaction by ear. Int. J. Hum.-Comput. Stud. (2019). Accepted for publication
44. Rocchesso, D., Polotti, P., Delle Monache, S.: Designing continuous sonic interaction. Int. J. Design **3**(3), 13–25 (2009)
45. Roddy, S., Bridges, B.: Sound, ecological affordances and embodied mappings in auditory display. In: Filimowicz, M., Tzankova, V. (eds.) New Directions in Third Wave Human-Computer Interaction: Volume 2 - Methodologies. HIS, pp. 231–258. Springer, Cham (2018). https://doi.org/10.1007/978-3-319-73374-6_12
46. Sander, H.: Listen! Improving the cooperation between game designers and audio designers. In: DiGRA 2011 - Proceedings of the 2011 DiGRA International Conference: Think Design Play. DiGRA/Utrecht School of the Arts, January 2011
47. Sanz Segura, R., Manchado Pérez, E.: Product sound design as a valuable tool in the product development process. Ergon. Design **26**(4), 20–24 (2018)
48. Schon, D.A.: The Reflective Practitioner: How Professionals Think in Action. Basic Books (1984)
49. Serafin, S., Franinović, K., Hermann, T., Lemaitre, G., Rinott, M., Rocchesso, D.: Sonic interaction design. In: Hermann, T., Hunt, A., Neuhoff, J.G. (eds.) The Sonification Handbook, chap. 5, pp. 87–110. Logos Publishing House, Berlin (2011)
50. Susini, P., Houix, O., Misdariis, N.: Sound design: an applied, experimental framework to study the perception of everyday sounds. New Soundtrack **4**(2), 103–121 (2014)
51. Tajadura-Jiménez, A., Väljamäe, A., Bevilacqua, F., Bianchi-Berthouze, N.: Body-centered auditory feedback. In: Norman, K.L., Kirakowski, J. (eds.) The Wiley Handbook of Human Computer Interaction, pp. 371–403. Wiley, Hoboken (2017)
52. Zattra, L., Misdariis, N., Pecquet, F., Donin, N., Fierro, D.: Analysis of sound design practices [ASDP]. Research methodology. In: Fontana, F., Gulli, A. (eds.) Machine sounds, Sound machines - Proceedings of the XXII CIM Colloquium on Music Informatics, pp. 168–175, November 2018

Morphing Musical Instrument Sounds with the Sinusoidal Model in the Sound Morphing Toolbox

Marcelo Caetano[1,2(✉)]

[1] Aix Marseille Univ, CNRS, PRISM "Perception, Representations, Image, Sound, Music", Marseille, France
marcelo.caetano@prism.cnrs.fr
[2] Schulich School of Music & CIRMMT, McGill University, Montreal, Quebec, Canada
marcelo.caetano@mcgill.ca
https://www.prism.cnrs.fr, https://www.cirmmt.org

Abstract. Sound morphing stands out among the sound transformation techniques in the literature due to its creative and research potential. The aim of sound morphing is to gradually blur the categorical distinction between the source and target sounds by blending sensory attributes. As such, the focus and ultimate challenge of most sound morphing techniques is to interpolate across dimensions of timbre perception to achieve the desired result. There are several sound morphing proposals in the literature with few open-source implementations freely available, making it difficult to reproduce the results, compare models, or simply use them in other applications such as music composition, sound design, and timbre research. This work describes how to morph musical instrument sounds with the sinusoidal model using the sound morphing toolbox (SMT), a freely available and open-source piece of software. The text describes the audio processing steps required to morph sounds with the SMT using a step-by-step example to illustrate the need for and the result of each step. The SMT contains implementations of a sound morphing algorithm in MATLAB ® that were designed to be as easy as possible to understand and use, giving the user control over the result and full customization.

Keywords: Sound morphing · Musical instruments · Sinusoidal model · Musical timbre

1 Introduction

Sound morphing has found creative, technical, and research applications in the literature. In music composition, sound morphing allows the exploration of the sonic continuum [32]. Notable examples include Jonathan Harvey's *Mortuos Plango, Vivos Voco* [18], Michael McNabb's *Dreamsong* [22], and Trevor

Electronic supplementary material The online version of this chapter (https://doi.org/10.1007/978-3-030-70210-6_31) contains supplementary material, which is available to authorized users.

R. Kronland-Martinet et al. (Eds.): CMMR 2019, LNCS 12631, pp. 481–503, 2021.
https://doi.org/10.1007/978-3-030-70210-6_31

Wishart's *Red Bird* [32]. These morphs were achieved by hand. Ideally, given the input sounds, sound morphing should allow automatically setting input parameters that control the morph to achieve the desired result [28]. Sound morphing is also used in audio processing, sound synthesis, and sound design. Tellman *et al.* [30] proposed a sound morphing technique based on sinusoidal modeling (SM) that is intended to improve the performance of a sample-based synthesizer by morphing between sounds of the same instrument to obtain intermediate pitches, dynamics, and other effects. Fitz *et al.* [12] use an SM called *Loris* to morph sounds. Sound morphing techniques have been used to investigate different aspects of timbre perception. Grey and Gordon [16] investigated the perceptual effect of exchanging the shape of the spectral energy distribution between pairs of musical instrument sounds. More recently, Carral [10] used spectral morphing to determine the just noticeable difference in timbre for trombone sounds. Siedenburg *et al.* [27] investigated the acoustic and categorical dissimilarity of musical timbre with morphing. However, these results are difficult to reuse, re-purpose, and build upon because seldom do we find freely available or open-source implementations of the morphing algorithms used in the literature.

Currently, there are commercial morphing implementations available, such as Symbolic Sound's *Kyma*[1], SoundMorph's *Time Flux*[2], Melda Production's *MMorph*[3], and Zynaptic's *Morph*[4]. These commercial products typically have stable and bug-free implementations that can be controlled via a graphical user interface (GUI). However, besides the price, disadvantages such as little flexibility (i.e., control) and scarce technical information prevent their wider adoption in academic circles. A notable exception is *Kyma*, an implementation of the SM dubbed Loris [12] integrated in a full-fledged sound design environment. However, composers and researchers alike need to be able to understand the algorithms employed and control several parameters of the transformation. There also exist closed-source implementations based on algorithms whose technical details can be found in publications. Ircam's *Diphone Studio*[5] uses the SM to morph between sounds. Trevor Wishart's *Sound Loom*[6] also allows morphing sounds. These are controlled via a GUI and the manuals typically contain little technical information because composers are the target user.

There are freely available open-source morphing implementations, such as Google Magenta's *NSynth*[7], Mike Brookes's *Voicebox*[8], and Hideki Kawahara's *STRAIGHT*[9] and *SparkNG*[10]. However, these find limited use in musical instrument sound morphing. NSynth uses a neural network synthesizer trained on a

[1] http://kyma.symbolicsound.com/.
[2] https://www.soundmorph.com/product/24/timeflux.
[3] https://www.meldaproduction.com/MMorph.
[4] http://www.zynaptiq.com/morph/.
[5] http://anasynth.ircam.fr/home/english/software/diphone-studio.
[6] http://www.trevorwishart.co.uk/slfull.html.
[7] https://magenta.tensorflow.org/nsynth-instrument.
[8] http://www.ee.ic.ac.uk/hp/staff/dmb/voicebox/voicebox.html.
[9] https://github.com/HidekiKawahara/legacy_STRAIGHT.
[10] https://github.com/HidekiKawahara/SparkNG.

dataset with sounds from commercial sample libraries instead of recordings from acoustic musical instruments. Voicebox, STRAIGHT, and SparkNG were optimized for speech and their performance with musical instrument sounds remains untested. Dedicated sound models usually perform poorly on other acoustic sources.

This article describes the sound morphing toolbox (SMT), which contains MATLAB ® implementations of modeling and transformation algorithms used to morph musical instrument sounds. The SMT is open-source and freely available[11], making it highly flexible, controllable, and customizable by the user. The contribution of this work is the use of a practical example to illustrate the audio processing steps in the SMT to less technically inclined users (such as composers or researchers without the technical background) so these users understand the impact of technical decisions (i.e., parameter values) in the final result. This manuscript is an extended version of [7] presented at CMMR 2019[12]. The figures have been updated along with the text to provide more detailed information about the SMT and the algorithms within. The next sections take the reader through the audio processing steps involved in morphing with the SMT, which are illustrated with figures and citations to the reference implementations. Section 2 presents an overview of the SMT and the source and target sounds used throughout the rest of the text. Section 3 shows the time-scaling algorithm, Sect. 4 describes the sinusoidal model used, Sect. 5 describes parameter interpolation, followed by resynthesis in Sect. 6 and finally morphing in Sect. 7.

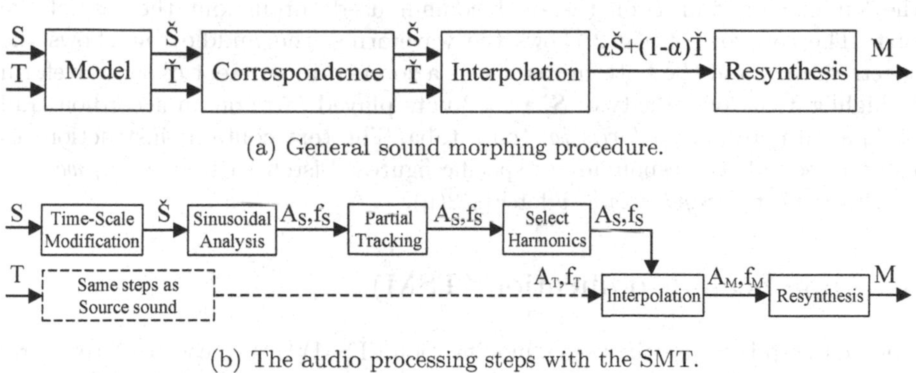

(a) General sound morphing procedure.

(b) The audio processing steps with the SMT.

Fig. 1. Overview of the morphing procedure in the SMT

2 Overview

Figure 1 shows an overview of sound morphing with the SMT. Figure 1(a) shows the general morphing procedure and Fig. 1(b) shows the audio processing steps in

[11] https://github.com/marcelo-caetano/sound-morphing.

[12] https://cmmr2019.prism.cnrs.fr/.

the SMT. The SMT automatically morphs between a source sound S and a target sound T by setting the morphing parameter α that varies between 0 and 1. Only S is heard when $\alpha = 0$, whereas only T is heard when $\alpha = 1$. Intermediate values of α correspond to morphed sounds M with different combinations of S and T. For example, setting $\alpha = 0.5$ produces a morph that is halfway between S and T. Figure 1(a) shows that, firstly, S and T are modeled to obtain a parametric representation $\check{S}$ and $\check{T}$. Next, correspondence between $\check{S}$ and $\check{T}$ is established, followed by interpolation and resynthesis.

In Fig. 1(b), we see a representation of the audio processing operations behind these steps in the SMT. First, both S and T are time-scaled to the same duration. Next, the SMT performs sinusoidal analysis of $\check{S}$ and $\check{T}$, producing the sets of parameters $\{A_S, f_S\}$ and $\{A_T, f_T\}$, namely, the amplitudes A and frequencies f of the sinusoids corresponding to $\check{S}$ and $\check{T}$. Correspondence in the SMT requires *partial tracking* and only the *harmonics* are interpolated because S and T are assumed to be nearly harmonic musical instrument sounds. The SMT establishes correspondence between harmonics of the same order and interpolates the amplitudes A and frequencies f using α to obtain $\{A_M, f_M\}$, which are used to synthesize the morphed sound M.

2.1 Source and Target Sounds

In what follows, the signal processing steps in the SMT corresponding to Fig. 1(b) are explained and illustrated with an example for $\alpha = 0.5$. Figure 2 shows S on the left column and T on the right column used throughout the rest of the text. The top row of Fig. 2 shows the waveforms, the middle row shows the spectrograms, and the bottom row shows a zoomed-in segment of the waveform to highlight the periodicity of S, a C#3 note played *forte* on an accordion, and of T, a C3 note played *fortissimo* on a tuba. The text contains instructions to listen to sounds corresponding to specific figures. Listen to *source_orig.wav* for Fig. 2(a) and to *target_orig.wav* for Fig. 2(b).

3 Time-Scale Modification (TSM)

The first step is to use time-scale modification (TSM) [11] to establish temporal correspondence between S and T, which simply guarantees that both have the same duration. In the SMT, the TSM algorithm implemented is *synchronized overlap-add with fixed synthesis* (SOLA-FS) [19]. SOLA-FS uses local waveform similarity with an adaptable analysis step and a fixed synthesis step (see [19] for details). Figure 3 illustrates the result of performing TSM with the SOLA-FS algorithm by comparing the original waveforms against two transformations, namely a time stretch by a factor of two and a time compression by the same factor, which can be expressed as $1/2$. The purpose of Fig. 3 is to show that the waveforms are preserved whether the duration is doubled or halved. More importantly, with the exception of the sound duration and other time-varying attributes such as the attack time, *tremolo* and *vibrato*, the overall sound quality

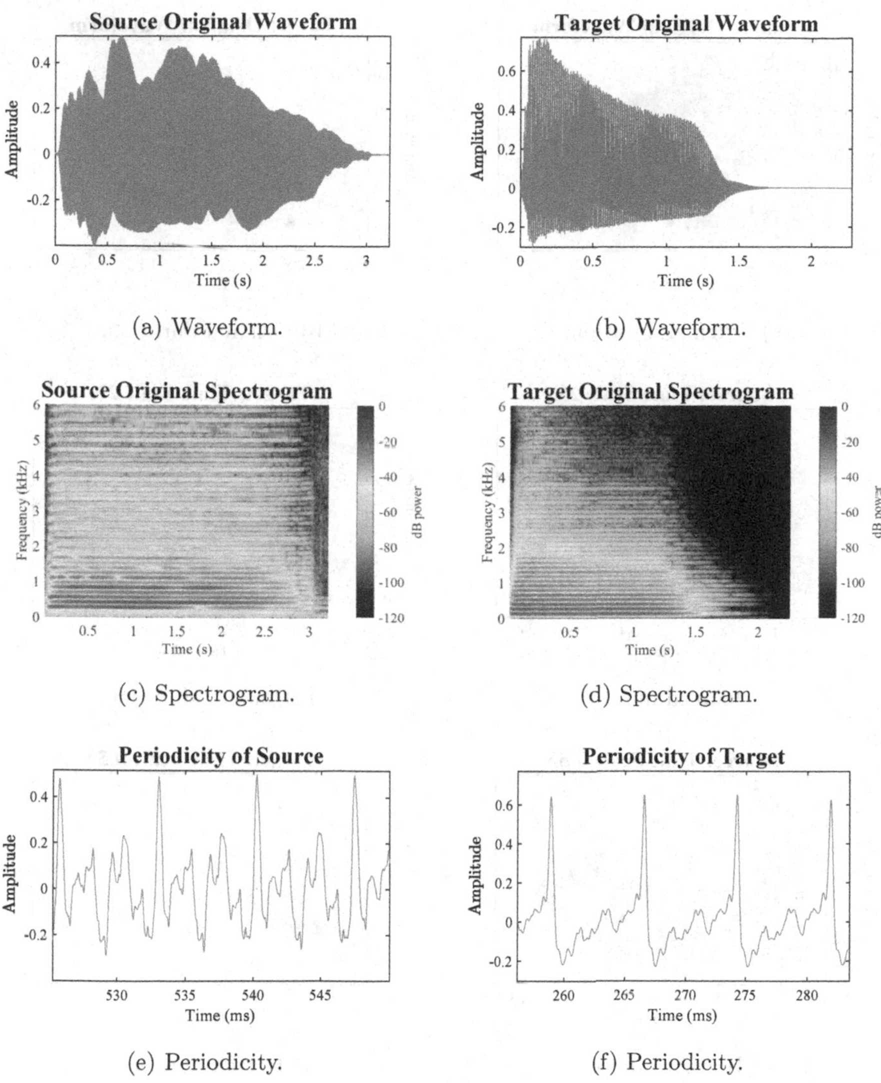

(a) Waveform.

(b) Waveform.

(c) Spectrogram.

(d) Spectrogram.

(e) Periodicity.

(f) Periodicity.

Fig. 2. Source (Accordion C#3 *forte*) and Target (Tuba C3 *fortissimo*) sounds used throughout the text to exemplify the audio processing steps in the SMT.

is preserved after the transformations. Listen to the sounds *source_tsm2X.wav* and *target_tsm2X.wav* for the doubled sounds, and *source_tsm05X.wav* and *target_tsm05X.wav* for the halved sounds.

In the SMT, the morphing parameter α sets the final duration of the morphed sound (see [6] for details). Here, $\alpha = 0.5$ so the duration of M will be halfway between that of S and T, as shown in Fig. 4. Figures 4(a) and 4(b) show $\check{S}$ and $\check{T}$ respectively, which are S and T time-scaled. Note that the duration of both $\check{S}$

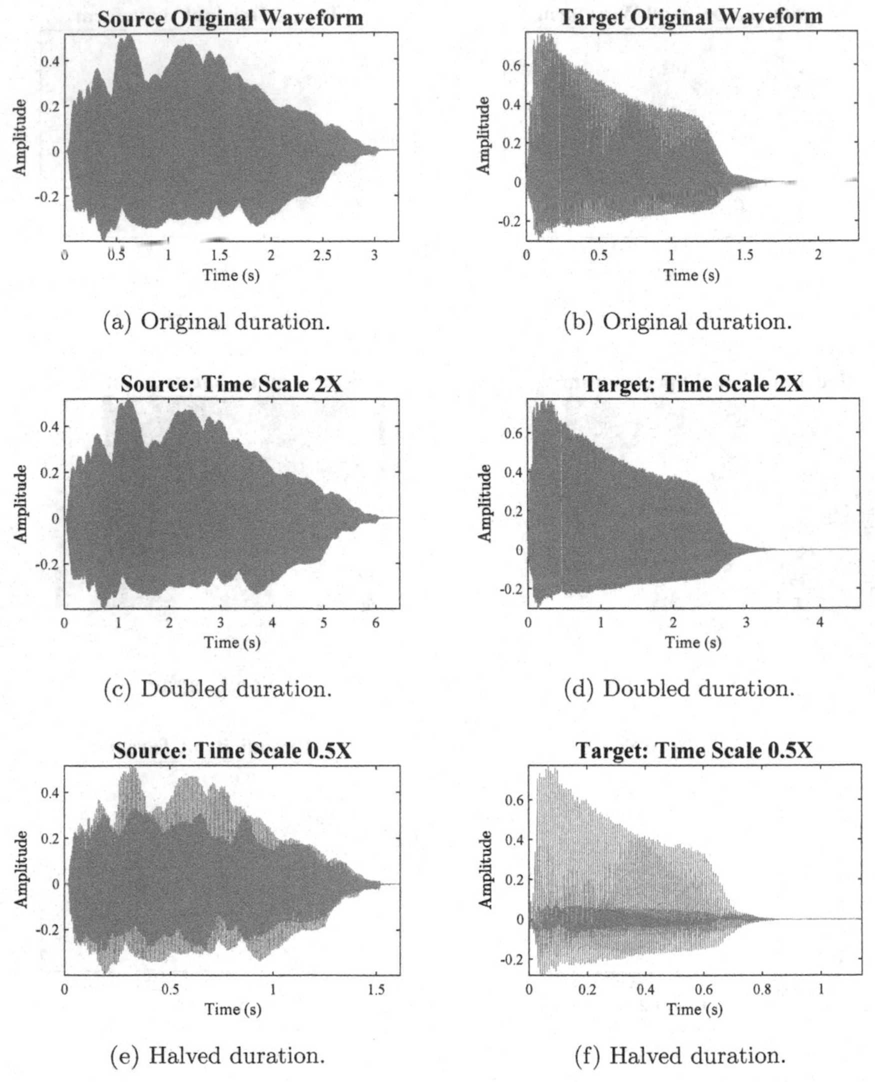

(a) Original duration. (b) Original duration.

(c) Doubled duration. (d) Doubled duration.

(e) Halved duration. (f) Halved duration.

Fig. 3. Illustration of the SOLA-FS time-scale modification algorithm.

and $\check{T}$ is the same. Listen to *source_tsm_alpha.wav* and *target_tsm_alpha.wav* and compare with the original sounds. The next step is to use sinusoidal modeling (SM) to represent the oscillatory modes of $\check{S}$ and $\check{T}$.

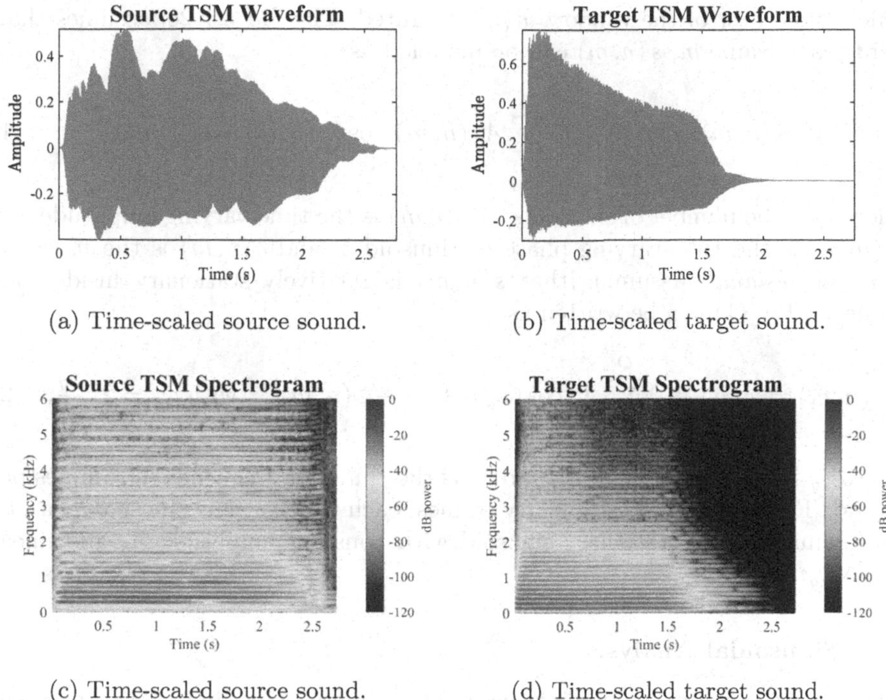

(a) Time-scaled source sound. (b) Time-scaled target sound.

(c) Time-scaled source sound. (d) Time-scaled target sound.

Fig. 4. Time-scaled versions $\check{S}$ of the source sound and $\check{T}$ of the target sound.

4 Sinusoidal Modeling (SM)

Currently, the SMT represents musical instrument sounds with the SM, which models a waveform as a sum of time-varying sinusoids parameterized by their amplitudes A, frequencies f, and phases θ [21,26]. The time-varying sinusoids, called partials, represent how the oscillatory modes of the musical instrument change with time, resulting in a flexible representation with perceptually meaningful parameters. The parameters completely describe each partial, which can be manipulated independently. So the original waveform is represented by the set of time-varying A, f, and θ for each partial, greatly reducing the amount of information required to represent it. The estimation of parameters is called sinusoidal analysis and the process of recreating a waveform from the parameters of sinusoidal analysis is called sinusoidal resynthesis. After the analysis step, sound transformations can be performed as changes of the parameter values prior to resynthesis. In what follows, the mathematical formalization of the SM is described.

The waveform of a sound is represented as $s(n)$, where n is the sample index and there are L samples in total. Then, sound $s(n)$ is divided into frames with a window function $w(n)$ with D samples, so D is the length of the frame and usually $D \leq L$. Inside each frame m, the waveform $s(n,m) = w(n-m)\,s(n)$ is $s(n)$ seen through $w(n-m)$, where m is the integer number of samples by which the center of the window $w(n)$ is shifted. The SM [21,26] assumes that, inside each frame m, $s(n,m)$ can be modeled as

$$s(n,m) = w(n-m)\sum_{q=1}^{Q} A_q(n,m)\cos\theta_q(n,m) + e(n,m), \tag{1}$$

where Q is the number of sinusoids, $A_q(n,m)$ is the time-varying amplitude and $\theta_q(n,m)$ is the time-varying phase of sinusoid q, and $e(n,m)$ is the *modeling error* or *residual*. Assuming that $s(n,m)$ is relatively stationary inside each frame m, Eq. (1) can be written as

$$s(n,m) = w(n-m)\sum_{q=1}^{Q} A_q\cos(\omega_q n + \phi) + e(n,m), \quad \text{with } \omega_q = 2\pi\frac{f_q}{f_s}, \tag{2}$$

where f_q is the frequency in Hz and f_s is the sampling frequency in samples per second. Therefore, inside stationary frames, each time-varying sinusoid q can be approximated by a stationary sinusoid with constant amplitude A_q and linear phase $\omega_q n + \phi$.

4.1 Sinusoidal Analysis

The aim of sinusoidal analysis is to use a set of time-varying sinusoids to represent the waveforms $\check{S}$ and $\check{T}$ when added together (hence the name *additive synthesis* [29]). In the SMT, sinusoidal analysis uses spectral modeling [21,26], which comprises *peak picking* and *parameter estimation.* Prior to sinusoidal analysis, the short-time Fourier transform (STFT) is calculated as the discrete Fourier transform (DFT) of each frame m of $s(n,m)$ [24]. For each of these frames, the peaks of the magnitude spectrum (peak picking) are associated with underlying sinusoids whose parameters are estimated (parameter estimation) and later connected across frames in the *partial tracking* step. The DFT $s(n,m)$ from Eq. (2) is

$$S(k,m) = \sum_{q=1}^{Q} A_q W(\omega_k - \omega_q) + E(\omega), \tag{3}$$

where $W(\omega_k)$ is the DFT of the window $w(n)$ and $E(\omega)$ is the DFT of the modeling error $e(n,m)$. Therefore, in the frequency domain, each sinusoid appears as the DFT of the window $w(n)$ scaled in amplitude by A_q and shifted in frequency by ω_q. The magnitude of $W(\omega_k)$ has a main lobe used to estimate A_q and ω_q and side lobes that introduce spectral distortion and estimation bias [17].

An important requirement to estimate A_q and ω_q using Eq. (3) is *spectral resolution* [17,26]. Spectral resolution is the requirement that each individual sinusoid appear as an independent spectral peak. Two sinusoids with frequencies f_1 and f_2 can be individually resolved in the magnitude spectrum if the frame size D obeys

$$D \geq B\frac{f_s}{f_1 - f_2}, \tag{4}$$

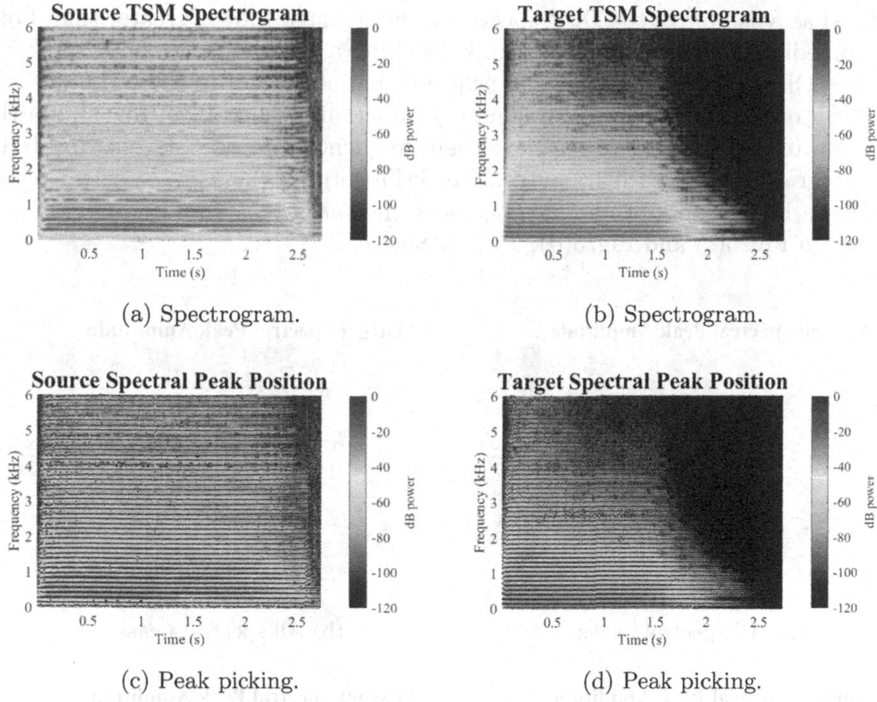

(a) Spectrogram.

(b) Spectrogram.

(c) Peak picking.

(d) Peak picking.

Fig. 5. Illustration of the peak picking algorithm.

where D is the length of the analysis window in samples, f_s is the sampling frequency in samples per second, and B is the bandwidth of the window, or simply the width of the main lobe in samples (see [17] for more information and tabulated values for several commonly used analysis windows). In practice, D must be large enough to ensure spectral resolution. Nearly harmonically related sinusoids have the property that $f_h \approx h f_0$, where f_0 is the fundamental frequency in Hertz and h is an integer that defines the partial number. Thus, adjacent harmonics are separated by f_0 and the condition in Eq. (4) becomes

$$D \geq B \frac{f_s}{f_0}. \tag{5}$$

For the Hann window, $B = 4$ bins [17]. In the SMT, the fundamental frequency f_0 is estimated with SWIPE [9]. In the example, C3 $\approx$ 131 Hz and C#3 $\approx$ 138 Hz and $f_s = 44.1$ kHz, so $D = \max\{1279, 1347\}$ samples. The size of the DFT was $N = 2048$ (the power of two immediately greater than D, achieved by zero padding), and the hop size $H = D/2$ (50% overlap).

Peak Picking. In practice [21,26], A_q and ω_q are estimated from peaks in the magnitude spectrum $|S(k)|$, where the frame index m has been omitted to simplify the notation. A peak is a local maximum of the magnitude spectrum [26], defined as a sample of the DFT spectrum whose magnitude is greater than both its immediate neighbors. At DFT bin k, $|S(k)|$ is a peak if $|S(k-1)| < |S(k)| > |S(k+1)|$. Figure 5 illustrates the peak-picking algorithm in the SMT [21,26]. The top row shows the spectrogram of $\check{S}$ and $\check{T}$ and the bottom row shows the position of the spectral peaks (i.e., their frequencies f) as dots on top of the spectrogram. Inside each frame m, the SMT returns the $P_{\max}$ spectral peaks with the highest amplitude, so $P_{\max}$ sets the *maximum number of peaks* per frame. In Fig. 5(c) and Fig. 5(d), $P_{\max} = 80$.

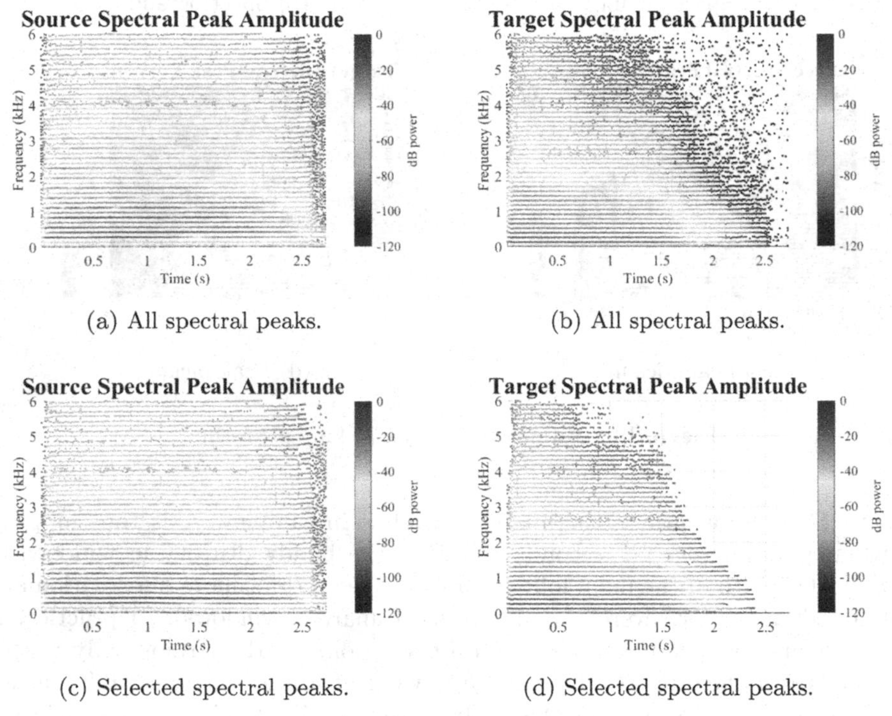

Fig. 6. Illustration of the peak selection step.

Peak Selection. After peak picking, the information used to represent the magnitude of the STFT is greatly reduced from N frequency bins per frame to $P_{\max} = 80$ peaks per frame. This can be visually confirmed by comparison of Fig. 5 with Fig. 6. The spectrogram shown in Fig. 5(a) and Fig. 5(b) is reduced to the spectral peaks shown in Fig. 6(a) and Fig. 6(b) as the peak frequencies f with their corresponding amplitudes A. The spectrogram of Fig. 5 illustrates the magnitude of the STFT. When both the magnitude and the phase (or equivalently the real part and the imaginary part) of the STFT are used, the STFT can be inverted to recover the original waveform (i.e., the forward and inverse

STFT form an identity transform pair [24]). When only the spectral peaks are kept, the rest of the information is lost. Figure 6 only illustrates the peaks of the magnitude spectrum, but Sec. **Parameter Estimation** below explains how the corresponding phase values are retrieved. Section 6 explores in more detail how to resynthesize a waveform using only spectral peaks with the SM. At this point, we will assess the perceptual impact of removing all this information from the STFT. Listen to *source_sin_allpeak_synthPI.wav* and *target_sin_allpeak_synthPI.wav* and compare with the original sounds.

Additionally, the SMT allows to further reduce the information in the representation with two different thresholds that set the minimum amplitude level (in dB) of the selected peaks. Across all frames, peaks below the *absolute threshold* ϱ are removed. Inside each frame, the *relative threshold* ρ removes peaks whose amplitude is ρ below the maximum level of the frame. In Figs. 6(c) and 6(d), $\rho = -76$ dB and $\varrho = -96$ dB. Visual comparison of Figs. 6(a) and 6(b) shows the difference. Note, however, that there is virtually no perceptual difference. Listen to *source_sin_thres_synthPI.wav* and *target_sin_thres_synthPI.wav* and compare first with *source_sin_allpeak_synthPI.wav* and *target_sin_allpeak_synthPI.wav* and then with the original sounds.

Parameter Estimation. In the SMT, the values of the parameters of the SM (A, f, and θ) are estimated using either *nearest-neighbor* estimation [21] or refined by interpolation. The estimation of the amplitudes A and frequencies f is refined by *quadratic interpolation* [26,29] of the peaks of the magnitude spectrum over a *linear* [26], a *logarithmic* [29], or a *power* [31] scale. The estimation of the phase θ uses *linear interpolation* [29] over the unwrapped phase spectrum. Figure 7 illustrates quadratic interpolation, which fits a parabola to each spectral peak in the magnitude spectrum to refine the estimation of A and f. Linear interpolation is shown in Fig. 8 as fitting a straight line to the unwrapped phase spectrum to refine the estimation of θ at the refined frequency estimation f.

Magnitude Scaling. Figure 7 shows the main lobe of the Hann window [17] (zoomed-in on the right) modulated by a sinusoid with $A_q = 1$ and $f_q = 2100$ Hz under linear magnitude scaling in Fig. 7(a) and Fig. 7(b), log magnitude scaling in Fig. 7(c) and Fig. 7(d), and power magnitude scaling in Fig. 7(e) and Fig. 7(f). The column on the left of Fig. 7 shows that the shape of the main lobe of $W(\omega_k)$ changes radically under these different scalings. The column on the right emphasizes how the parabolic fit changes under the different scales. In Fig. 7, the solid line represents the main lobe of the window (in a continuous frequency representation such as the discrete-time Fourier transform), the vertical dotted lines mark the position of the frequency bins k, and the DFT samples are illustrated as * where the bins k cross the main lobe. The spectral peak will be notated as $\hat{S}(k)$ to simplify the notation. Nearest-neighbor estimation [21] uses $A_q = \hat{S}(k)$ and $f_q = \frac{k}{N} f_s$, where N is the size of the DFT. In practice, the frequency bin corresponding to the spectral peak is used, as illustrated in Fig. 7 by *. The DFT samples are discrete frequency values f_s/N Hz apart whereas the analyzed

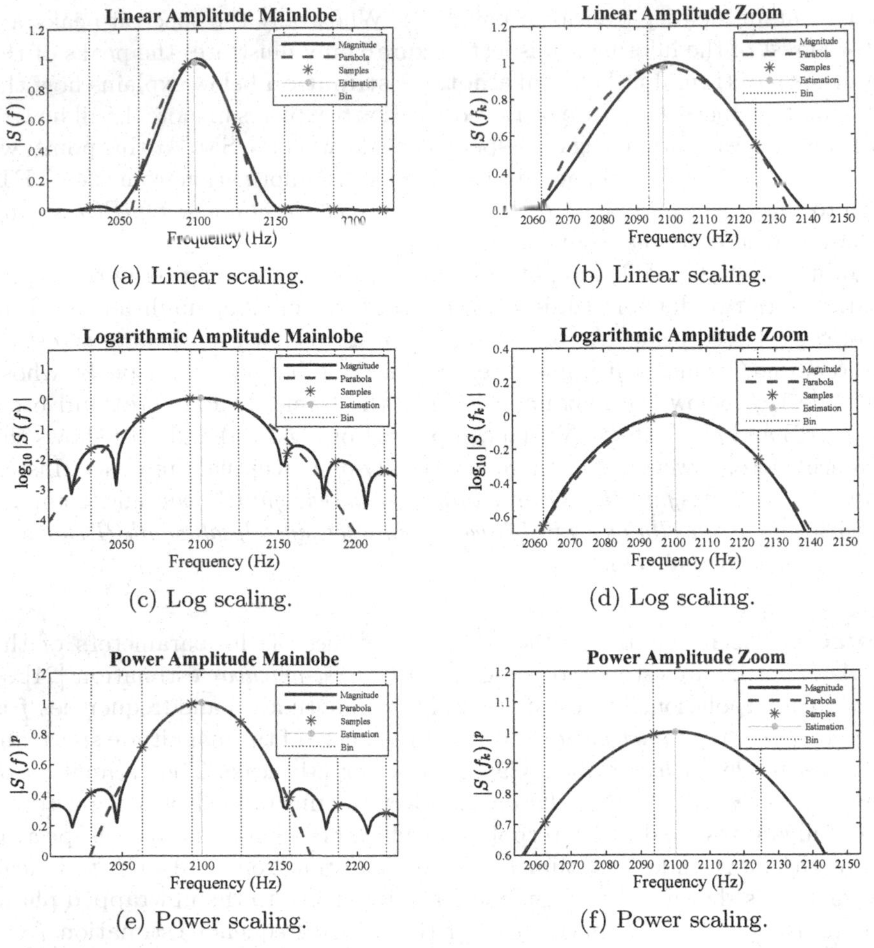

(a) Linear scaling. (b) Linear scaling.

(c) Log scaling. (d) Log scaling.

(e) Power scaling. (f) Power scaling.

Fig. 7. Illustration of quadratic interpolation of amplitude and frequency. The figure shows the effect of scaling the magnitude spectrum in the estimation of the amplitudes and frequencies of the underlying sinusoids.

frequency f_q is continuous. In practice, f_q can be anywhere between two samples of the DFT, resulting in *spectral leakage*, which is basically the appearance of a spectral peak in more that one bin of the DFT (the lobes in Fig. 7 are typical illustrations of spectral leakage). Consequently, nearest-neighbor estimation leads to estimation errors of up to half a bin [26,31] with the DFT. The SMT uses quadratic interpolation of spectral peaks to address the bias inherent in nearest neighbor estimation [1].

As shown in Fig. 7, quadratic interpolation fits a parabola (dashed line in Fig. 7) to $[k-1, k, k+1]$ and $\left[\hat{S}(k-1), \hat{S}(k), \hat{S}(k+1)\right]$. Quadratic interpolation improves the accuracy of estimation of both A_q and f_q by using the vertex of the parabola as refined estimation. Linear scaling uses $\hat{S}(k) = |S(k)|$, log scaling uses $\hat{S}(k) = \log_{10}|S(k)|$, and power scaling uses $\hat{S}(k) = |S(k)|^p$. Figure 7(c) shows that the parabola fits the log-scaled main lobe better than the linear case in Fig. 7(a). However, there is still frequency and amplitude estimation error. Figure 7(e) visually confirms the finding that power scaling improves the fit over log scaling [31]. However, power scaling is currently limited to $D = N$ with N being a power of two, which limits the selection of D. The example in this article uses log magnitude scaling and selection of D according to Eq. (5).

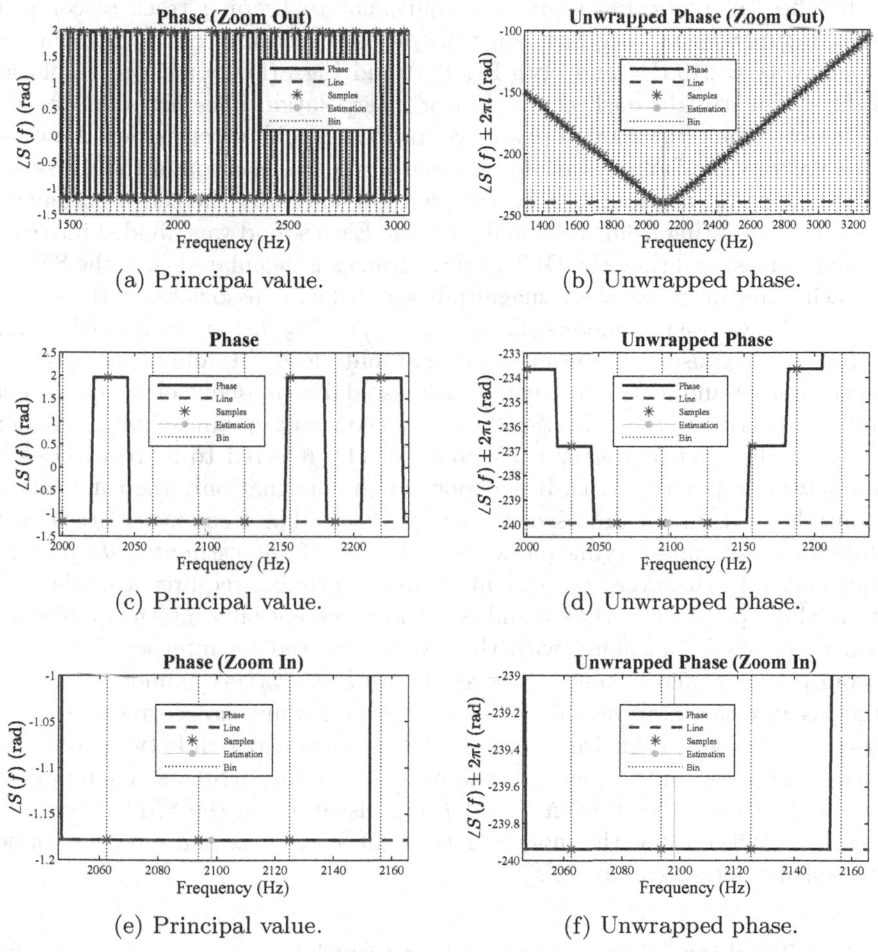

(a) Principal value. (b) Unwrapped phase.

(c) Principal value. (d) Unwrapped phase.

(e) Principal value. (f) Unwrapped phase.

Fig. 8. Illustration of linear interpolation of phase. The figure shows the effect of unwrapping the phase in the estimation of the phases of the underlying sinusoids.

Phase Unwrapping. Figure 8 shows the phase spectrum of the modulated zero-phase Hann window from Fig. 7. The left column of Fig. 8 shows the principal value of the phase $-\pi < \vartheta \leq \pi$ and the right column of Fig. 8 shows the unwrapped phase $\theta = \vartheta \pm 2\pi l$, where $l \in \mathbb{N}$. The solid line in Fig. 8 represents the phase spectrum (principal value and unwrapped), the vertical dotted lines mark the position of the frequency bins k, the DFT samples are illustrated as *, and the dashed line shows the linear fit. As Fig. 8(a) shows, the principal value of the phase is discontinuous because it is confined to the interval $-\pi < \vartheta \leq \pi$. Phase unwrapping, shown in Fig. 8(b), corrects the phase ϑ by adding multiples of $\pm 2\pi$ whenever the discontinuity ξ is $\xi \geq \pi$. Note that there is no linear phase component because the analysis window is zero phase [25], so the effect of phase unwrapping is equivalent to keeping track of complete cycles. Figure 8(c) and Fig. 8(d) show the phase spectrum around the estimated frequency $f_0 \approx 2100$ Hz and both Fig. 8(e) and Fig. 8(f) zoom in to emphasize the fit of the straight dashed line. Linear interpolation does not seem to visually improve the estimation of phase over nearest-neighbor estimation. However, phase unwrapping is important for an accurate representation of the phase θ.

At this point, the sounds $\check{S}$ and $\check{T}$ are represented by the set of parameters A, f, and θ resulting from sinusoidal analysis. Each sound was divided into overlapping frames, and then the DFT of these frames is calculated (i.e., the STFT). For each frame m, peaks of the magnitude spectrum are associated with underlying sinusoids whose parameters $A_q(m)$, $f_q(m)$, and $\theta_q(m)$ are estimated. Across the frames m, sinusoids with time-varying amplitude $A_q(n)$ and phase $\theta_q(n)$ can be synthesized and added to create the sinusoidal component of $\check{S}$ and $\check{T}$ separately as described in [21]. Section 6.1 shows the resultant sinusoidal component as well as the modeling error $e(n)$ from Eq. (1), referred to as resynthesis by parameter interpolation (PI). It is important to note that only the time-varying amplitudes and phases are used in PI resynthesis. The frequencies are used to reconstruct the time-varying phase with the aid of the estimated $\theta_q(m)$ used as anchors [21]. However, as Fig. 1 illustrates, morphing requires a single set of intermediate parameters that would result in a perceptually intermediate sound upon resynthesis. Morphing with the SM is achieved by interpolating A and f from $\check{S}$ and $\check{T}$ across time. However, the anchors $\theta_q(m)$ cannot be interpolated because the interpolated time-varying phase would not correspond to the interpolated time-varying frequency [3,4,23], so the mismatch between temporal variation of phase and frequency would result in audible artifacts. Therefore, the estimated phase values θ from $\check{S}$ and $\check{T}$ are discarded in the SMT. Section 6.2 provides details on how the morph M is resynthesized via phase reconstruction by frequency interpolation [20].

Partial Tracking. The spectral peaks returned from the peak-picking step (after further parameter estimation) do not result in a set of *continuous* partials because there is no mechanism to ensure temporal continuity. Figure 9 shows the final peaks returned from the parameter estimation step connected by lines. Inside each frame, spurious spectral peaks appear and later disappear (due mainly to interference by nearby peaks and sidelobe interaction), resulting in the discontinuous "spectral lines" in Figs. 9(c) and 9(d). The SMT uses a *partial tracking* algorithm to convert the discontinuous spectral lines seen in

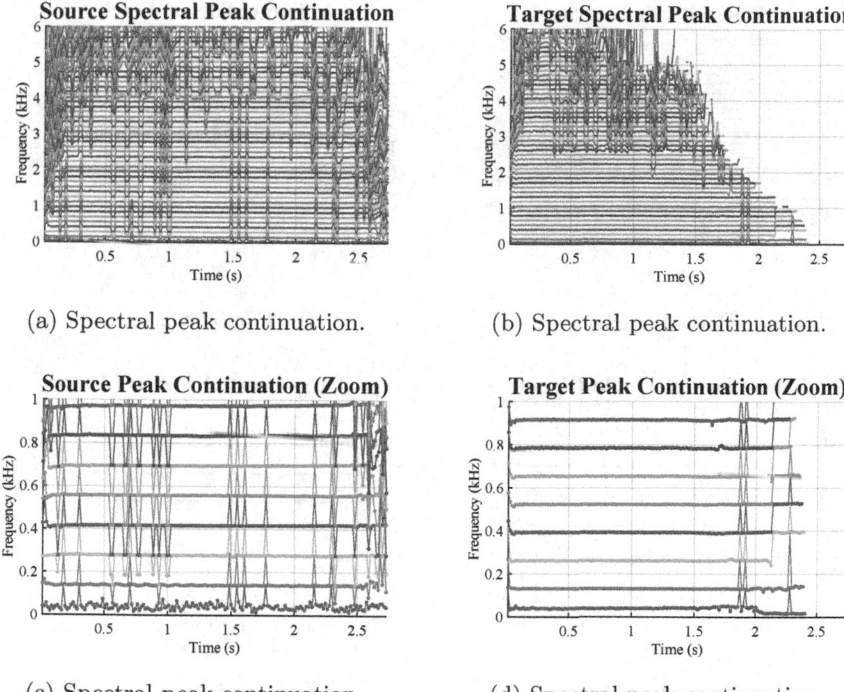

(a) Spectral peak continuation.

(b) Spectral peak continuation.

(c) Spectral peak continuation.

(d) Spectral peak continuation.

Fig. 9. Spectral peak continuation prior to partial tracking. The top row shows the spectral peaks connected by lines to illustrate the temporal discontinuity. The bottom part shows a zoomed-in part of the top row.

Fig. 9 into the continuous partial tracks shown in Fig. 10. The partial tracking algorithm implemented in the SMT is based on the peak continuation algorithm proposed by McAuley and Quatieri [21], so it simply collects peaks within a frequency threshold Δ_p into continuous tracks. In Fig. 10, $\Delta_p = f_0/4$, where f_0 is the fundamental frequency of $\check{S}$ or $\check{T}$. Note the difference between Figs. 9 and 10, especially the zoomed-in panels on the bottom. After partial tracking, the partials present continuous temporal trajectories, seen as fairly straight horizontal lines across. Once again we might want to assess the perceptual impact of the partial tracking algorithm. Listen to *source_sin_partrack_synthPI.wav* and *target_sin_partrack_synthPI.wav* to hear the result of resynthesis using the original phase θ and all the partial tracks. Compare with *source_sin_thres_synthPI.wav* and *target_sin_thres_synthPI.wav*, which use essentially the same information (i.e., the selected spectral peaks) but not yet organized into partial tracks.

4.2 Harmonic Selection

The next step after partial tracking is to select the harmonics of the fundamental frequency f_0. The *harmonic selection* step eliminates mainly the partials

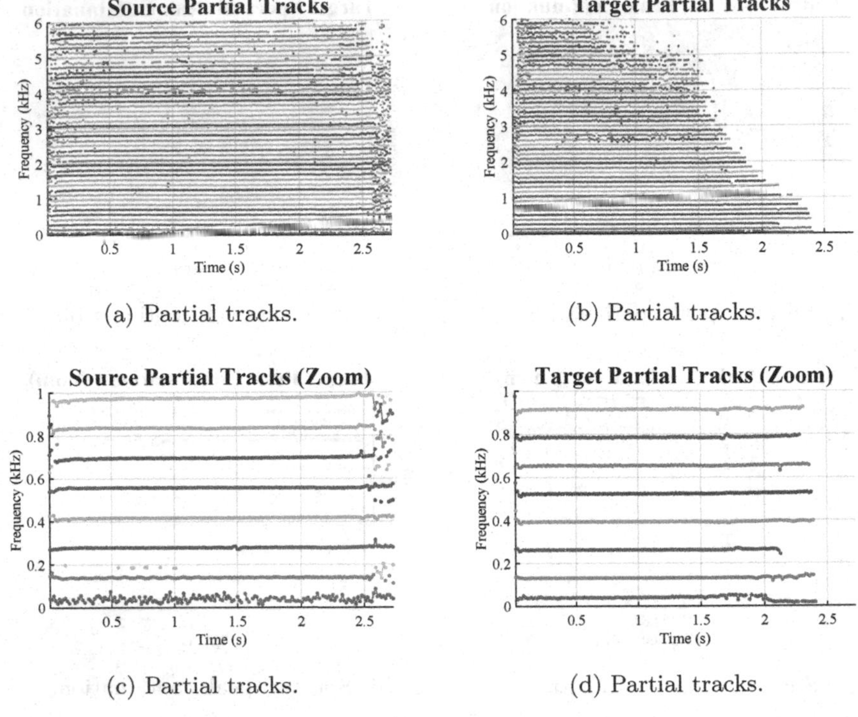

(a) Partial tracks.

(b) Partial tracks.

(c) Partial tracks.

(d) Partial tracks.

Fig. 10. The result of partial tracking. The top row shows the spectral peaks from Fig. 9 reorganized as partial tracks. The partial tracking algorithm ensures temporal continuity, as illustrated by the zoomed-in regions on the bottom row.

resulting from spurious frequency peaks while keeping the harmonically related partials, called *harmonics*. In the SMT, harmonics are the partials whose median frequencies over time are harmonically related to the fundamental f_0 within an interval Δ_h. This nearly harmonic relation can be expressed as $f_h = hf_0 \pm \Delta_h$, where f_h is the harmonic of order h. Figure 11 shows the result of harmonic selection on the partial tracks from Fig. 10 with $\Delta_h = 10\,\text{Hz}$. Listen to *source_sin_harm_synthPI.wav* and *target_sin_harm_synthPI.wav* to hear the result of resynthesis using the original phase and only the harmonics.

5 Interpolation

Prior to interpolation, the SMC establishes correspondence between harmonics using the harmonic number h. Then, the frequencies are interpolated in cents (see [6] for details) and the amplitudes can be interpolated linearly or in decibels. The interval in cents c between two frequencies f_1 and f_2 is $c = 1200\log_2(f_1/f_2)$, so an intermediate frequency f_α is given by

$$f_\alpha = f_1 2^{(1-\alpha)\log_2\left(\frac{f_2}{f_1}\right)}. \tag{6}$$

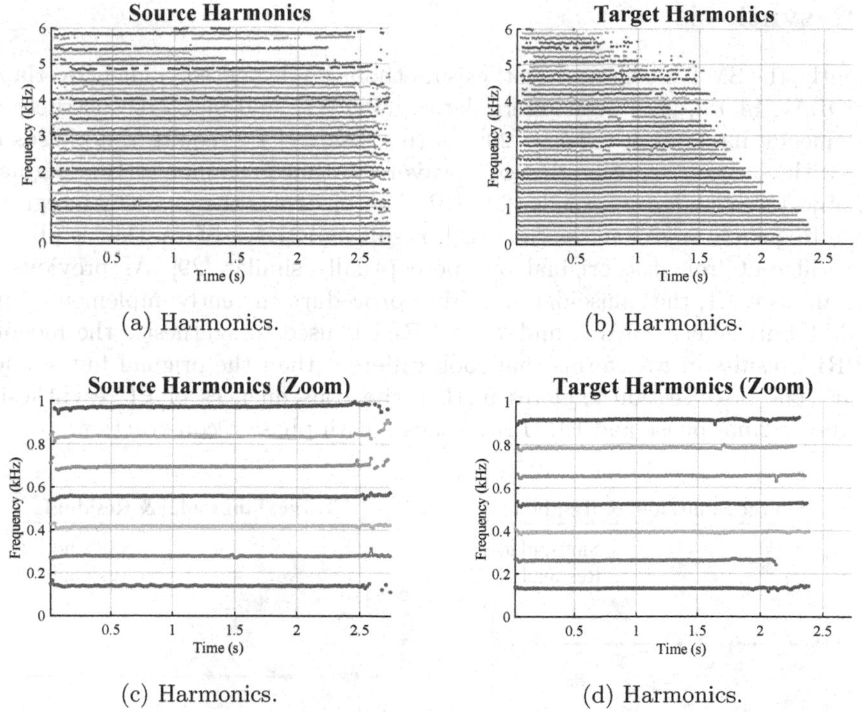

(a) Harmonics. (b) Harmonics.

(c) Harmonics. (d) Harmonics.

Fig. 11. Only the partials whose frequencies are nearly harmonically related to the fundamental remain. Compare with Fig. 10. See text for details.

Equivalently, f_α can be obtained as

$$f_\alpha = f_2 2^{\alpha \log_2 \left(\frac{f_1}{f_2}\right)}. \tag{7}$$

Both Eqs. (6) and (7) yield the same value for f_α, so either one may be used. Naturally, they can also be combined as in [7]. Similarly, for the amplitudes, the interval in dB between A_1 and A_2 is $\text{dB} = 10 \log_{10} \left({}^{A_1}/_{A_2}\right)$ and an intermediate amplitude A_α is given by

$$A_\alpha = A_1 10^{(1-\alpha) \log_{10} \left(\frac{A_2}{A_1}\right)} \tag{8}$$

or

$$A_\alpha = A_2 10^{\alpha \log_{10} \left(\frac{A_1}{A_2}\right)}. \tag{9}$$

Again, these expressions are equivalent and can also be combined as in [7]. Linear interpolation of amplitudes is achieved as $A_\alpha = \alpha A_1 + (1 - \alpha) A_2$. In the example, logarithmic interpolation of amplitudes from Eq. (8) was used. After all frequencies and amplitudes have been interpolated, the set of interpolated harmonics is resynthesized to obtain the final morph.

6 Resynthesis

Currently, the SMT has three resynthesis methods implemented, namely overlap-add (OLA) [14,15], parameter interpolation (PI) [21], and phase reconstruction by frequency integration (PRFI) [20]. Both OLA and PI require the phases θ along with A and f to re-synthesize a waveform that is similar to the original both objectively and perceptually [29]. PRFI reconstructs the phase by integrating the frequency tracks across time [20], resulting in a waveform that is objectively different from the original but perceptually similar [29]. As previously stated in Sect. 4.1, the sinusoidal morphing procedure currently implemented in the SMT only interpolates A and f, so PRFI is used to synthesize the morph M. PRFI results in waveforms that look different than the original but sound similar. The next section explores further the consequences of PI resynthesis with the original phase and PRFI resynthesis with phase reconstruction.

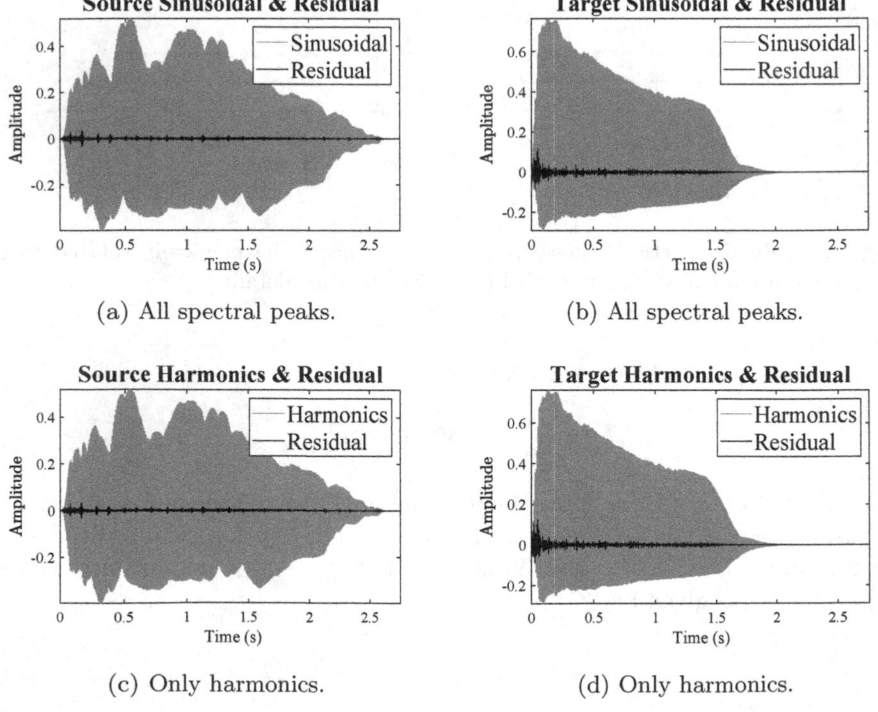

(a) All spectral peaks.

(b) All spectral peaks.

(c) Only harmonics.

(d) Only harmonics.

Fig. 12. Source sound is Accordion C#3 *forte* and Target Sound is Tuba C3 *fortissimo*

6.1 Resynthesis with the Original Phase

Figure 12 shows a comparison of the waveforms of S (on the left) and T (on the right) resynthesized with the original phase θ (PI resynthesis) using all spectral peaks (top row) or only the harmonics (bottom row). Each panel of Fig. 12 shows both the sinusoidal component (in gray) and the residual (in black). The residual is simply the subtraction of the sinusoidal component from the original waveform. Thus, the residual results from the information in the original waveform missed by the sinusoidal component. The energy present in the residual is an indication of how well the sinusoidal model captures the oscillatory behavior of S and T, where the lower the residual energy the better the model. The modeling residual is commonly assumed to be noise that was not captured by the sinusoidal component because sinusoids are not a compact representation of noise [8]. For musical instrument sounds, the residual commonly captures noise from the sound production mechanism such as the hammer striking the strings on the piano, the plectrum plucking the strings on the harpschord, bowing on the violin, blowing into the flute, among many other vibration mechanisms. Mechanical noise is intrinsic to the sounds produced by acoustic musical instruments, so the residual is commonly modeled as filtered white noise and added back into the sinusoidal component. Caetano *et al.* [8] investigated if there is oscillatory energy left in the residual from sinusoidal analysis and concluded that the residual is not perceptually equivalent to filtered white noise, further noting that the differences may lie in the phase spectrum.

Figure 12 reveals that, visually, the difference between using all spectral peaks and only the harmonics is barely noticeable. Naturally, the perceptual difference is also important, so listening to the sounds might reveal perceptual differences that are not visible in the waveforms shown in Fig. 12. The sinusoidal component of Fig. 12(a) corresponds to *source_sin_thres_synthPI.wav* and the residual to *source_res_thres_synthPI.wav*. The original residual *source_res_thres_synthPI.wav* is much softer than the sinusoidal component, so *source_res16dB_thres_synth.wav* is the same sound normalized to −16 dB RMS. Similarly, for Fig. 12(b), the sinusoidal component is *target_sin_thres_synthPI.wav* and the residual is *target_res_thres_synthPI.wav*, normalized in *target_res16dB_thres_synth.wav*. Finally, for the harmonic resynthesis of Fig. 12(c), listen to the sinusoidal component *source_sin_harm_synthPI.wav* and the residual *source_res_harm_synthPI.wav* (normalized in *source_res16dB_harm_synthPI.wav*). For Fig. 12(d), listen to the sinusoidal component *target_sin_harm_synthPI.wav* and to the residual component *target_res_harm_synthPI.wav* (normalized in *target_res16dB_harm_synthPI.wav*).

6.2 Resynthesis via Phase Reconstruction

Figure 13 shows a comparison of the resynthesized waveforms of S and T with the original phase θ (PI resynthesis) and via phase reconstruction (PRFI resynthesis). The left column shows the source sound $\check{S}$ and the right column shows the target sound $\check{T}$. The top row shows both $\check{S}$ and $\check{T}$ resynthesized using all spectral peaks and the bottom row shows resynthesis using only the harmonics. In all panels, the grey waveform uses the original phase θ (PI resynthesis) and the black waveform uses PRFI. Figure 13 illustrates the role of the original phase in the SM. For example, Fig. 13(a) and Fig. 13(b) show that the resynthesized waveform is different when the original phase θ is discarded and a

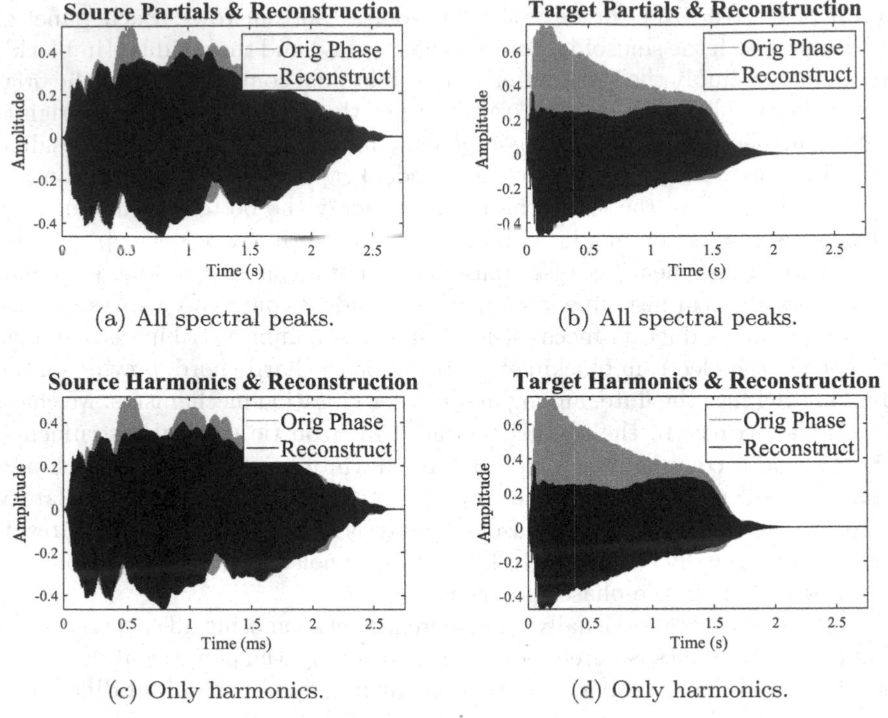

(a) All spectral peaks. (b) All spectral peaks.

(c) Only harmonics. (d) Only harmonics.

Fig. 13. Comparison of different resynthesis methods in the SMT.

new phase $\hat{\theta}$ is reconstructed by integrating the time-varying frequencies of the partials [20]. For sound morphing, it is more important to determine if PRFI resynthesis results in a waveform that is perceptually different from the one using the original phase. Listen to *source_sin_thres_synthPI.wav* for the resynthesis with the original phase and to *source_sin_thres_synthPRFI.wav* for the resynthesis with the reconstructed phase in Fig. 13(a). Similarly, for Fig. 13(a), listen to *target_sin_thres_synthPI.wav* and to *target_sin_thres_synthPRFI.wav*.

Additionally, Fig. 13 shows the impact of *harmonic selection* in the SMT. Most pitched musical instruments are designed to present clear modes of vibration that are nearly harmonic [13]. The piano is a notorious exception where the stiffness of the strings results in slightly inharmonic notes [2]. Nevertheless, the majority of pitched acoustic musical instruments produces sounds with most of the oscillatory energy concentrated around harmonics of the fundamental frequency. Therefore, the harmonic selection step is not expected to result in perceptually different sounds than keeping all spectral peaks. Listen to *source_sin_harm_synthPI.wav* and *source_sin_harm_synthPRFI.wav* to compare the waveforms shown in Fig. 13(c). For the waveforms shown in Fig. 13(d), listen to *target_sin_harm_synthPI.wav* and to *target_sin_harm_synthPRFI.wav*.

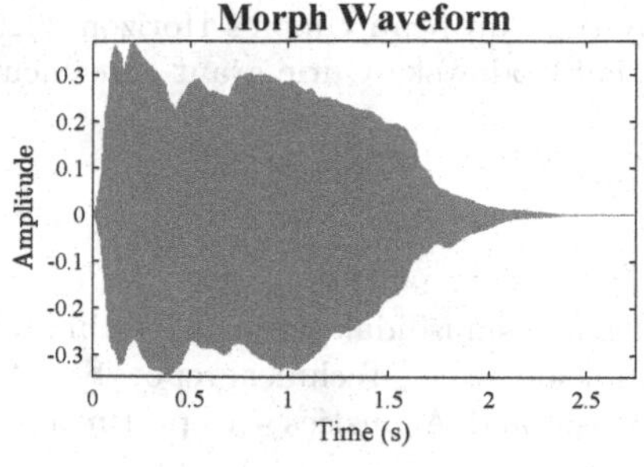

(a) Waveform of morphed sound.

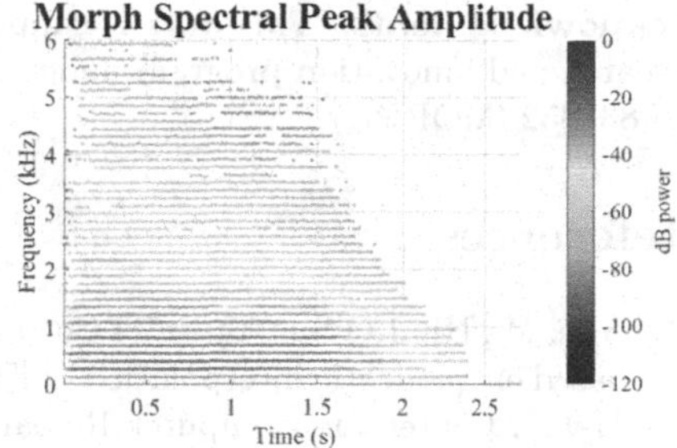

(b) Spectrogram of morphed sound.

Fig. 14. Morphed musical instrument sound. The left-hand side shows the waveform and the right-hand side shows the spectral peaks with their corresponding amplitudes.

7 Morphing

Finally, the morph is achieved by resynthesizing the set of interpolated parameters M with PRFI, as shown in Fig. 14. Figure 14(a) shows the waveform and Fig. 14(b) shows the spectral peaks of the morph. Visually, it is more intuitive to use the spectral peaks than the waveforms to confirm that M is indeed intermediate between S and T. For example, it is not visually intuitive that the waveform of Fig. 14(a) is perceptually halfway between those of Fig. 2(a) and Fig. 2(b). However, visual comparison between Fig. 14 and Fig. 6 reveals that the spectral peaks in Fig. 14(b) correspond to intermediate peaks between those of Fig. 6(c) and Fig. 6(d). Naturally, for sound morphing, the perceptual comparison is more important than the visual intuition. Listen to the original sounds *source_orig.wav* and *target_orig.wav* and then to *accordion_tuba_morph_alpha05.wav* to assess if M is indeed perceptually intermediate between S and T.

8 Conclusions and Perspectives

This work has described how to use the Sound Morphing Toolbox (SMT) to morph musical instrument sounds with the sinusoidal model. The audio processing steps were illustrated with figures and citations to the reference implementations. The SMT is open-source and freely available under a GNU3 license. Time-varying morphs [6] will be incorporated into a future version. Future development of the SMT will also add a GUI and an implementation of the hybrid source-filter model and the sophisticated sound morphing algorithm that uses it [5]. Finally, the SMT is currently an *alpha release* with possible bugs in the code due to limited testing. Adoption and use of the SMT by the community is encouraged to provide usability testing and bug corrections that might lead to a *beta release*.

Acknowledgments. This work is supported by the European Union's Horizon 2020 research and innovation program under the Marie Skłodowska-Curie grant agreement No 831852 (MORPH).

References

1. Abe, M., III, J.O.S.: CQIFFT: Correcting bias in a sinusoidal parameter estimator based on quadratic interpolation of FFT magnitude peaks. Technical report STAN-M-117, Center for Computer Research in Music and Acoustics - Department of Music, Stanford University (2004)
2. Bader, R., Hansen, U.: Modeling of musical instruments. In: Havelock, D., Kuwano, S., Vorländer, M. (eds.) Handbook of Signal Processing in Acoustics, pp. 419–446. Springer, New York (2009). https://doi.org/10.1007/978-0-387-30441-0_26
3. Boashash, B.: Estimating and interpreting the instantaneous frequency of a signal I. Fundamentals. Proc. IEEE **80**(4), 520–538 (1992)
4. Boashash, B.: Estimating and interpreting the instantaneous frequency of a signal. II. Algorithms and applications. Proc. IEEE **80**(4), 540–568 (1992)
5. Caetano, M., Kafentzis, G.P., Mouchtaris, A., Stylianou, Y.: Full-band quasi-harmonic analysis and synthesis of musical instrument sounds with adaptive sinusoids. Appl. Sci. **6**(5), 127 (2016)
6. Caetano, M., Rodet, X.: Musical instrument sound morphing guided by perceptually motivated features. IEEE Trans. Audio Speech Lang. Process. **21**(8), 1666–1675 (2013)
7. Caetano, M.: Morphing musical instrument sounds with the sound morphing Toolbox. In: Proceedings of the 14th International Symposium on Computer Music Interdisciplinary Research, CMMR 2019, Marseille, France, pp. 171–182, October 2019
8. Caetano, M., Kafentzis, G.P., Degottex, G., Mouchtaris, A., Stylianou, Y.: Evaluating how well filtered white noise models the residual from sinusoidal modeling of musical instrument sounds. In: Proceedings of the IEEE Workshop on Applications of Signal Processing to Audio and Acoustics (WASPAA), New Paltz, NY, pp. 1–4, October 2013
9. Camacho, A., Harris, J.G.: A sawtooth waveform inspired pitch estimator for speech and music. J. Acoust. Soc. Am. **124**(3), 1638–1652 (2008)
10. Carral, S.: Determining the just noticeable difference in timbre through spectral morphing: a trombone example. Acta Acustica united with Acustica **97**, 466–476 (05 2011)
11. Driedger, J., Müller, M.: A review of time-scale modification of music signals. Appl. Sci. **6**(2), 57 (2016)
12. Fitz, K., Haken, L., Lefvert, S., Champion, C., O'Donnell, M.: Cell-utes and flutter-tongued cats: Sound morphing using loris and the reassigned bandwidth-enhanced model. Comput. Music J. **27**(3), 44–65 (2003)
13. Fletcher, N.H., Rossing, T.D.: The Physics of Musical Instruments, 2 edn., Springer, New York (1998). https://doi.org/10.1007/978-1-4612-2980-3
14. George, E.B., Smith, M.J.T.: Speech analysis/synthesis and modification using an analysis-by-synthesis/overlap-add sinusoidal model. IEEE Trans. Speech Audio Process. **5**(5), 389–406 (1997)
15. George, E.B., Smith, M.J.T.: Analysis-by-synthesis/overlap-add sinusoidal modeling applied to the analysis and synthesis of musical tones. J. Audio Eng. Soc. **40**(6), 497–516 (1992)

16. Grey, J.M., Gordon, J.W.: Perceptual effects of spectral modifications on musical timbres. J. Acoust. Soc. Am. **63**(5), 1493–1500 (1978)
17. Harris, F.J.: On the use of windows for harmonic analysis with the discrete Fourier transform. Proc. IEEE **66**(1), 51–83 (1978)
18. Harvey, J.: "Mortuos Plango, Vivos Voco": a realization at IRCAM. Comput. Music J. **5**(4), 22–24 (1981)
19. Hejna, D., Musicus, B.R.: The SOLA-FS time-scale modification algorithm. Technical report BBN (1991)
20. McAulay, R., Quatieri, T.: Magnitude-only reconstruction using a sinusoidal speech model. In: Proceedings ICASSP, vol. 9, pp. 441–444 (1984)
21. McAulay, R., Quatieri, T.: Speech analysis/synthesis based on a sinusoidal representation. IEEE Trans. Acoust. Speech Signal Process. **34**(4), 744–754 (1986)
22. McNabb, M.: "Dreamsong": the composition. Comput. Music J. **5**(4), 36–53 (1981)
23. Picinbono, B.: On instantaneous amplitude and phase of signals. IEEE Trans. Signal Process. **45**(3), 552–560 (1997)
24. Portnoff, M.: Implementation of the digital phase vocoder using the fast Fourier transform. IEEE Trans. Acoust. Speech Signal Process. **24**(3), 243–248 (1976)
25. Serra, X.: Musical sound modeling with sinusoids plus noise. In: Poli, G.D., Picialli, A., Pope, S.T., Roads, C. (eds.) Musical Signal Processing, pp. 91–122. Swets & Zeitlinger, Lisse, Switzerland (1996)
26. Serra, X., Smith, J.O.: Spectral modeling synthesis: a sound analysis/synthesis based on a deterministic plus stochastic decomposition. Comput. Music J. **14**, 12–24 (1990)
27. Siedenburg, K., Jones-Mollerup, K., McAdams, S.: Acoustic and categorical dissimilarity of musical timbre: evidence from asymmetries between acoustic and chimeric sounds. Front. Psychol. **6**, 1977 (2016)
28. Slaney, M., Covell, M., Lassiter, B.: Automatic audio morphing. In: Proceedings ICASSP, vol. 2, pp. 1001–1004 (1996)
29. Smith, J.O., Serra, X.: PARSHL: an analysis/synthesis program for non- harmonic sounds based on a sinusoidal representation. In: Proceedings ICMC, pp. 290–297 (1987)
30. Tellman, E., Haken, L., Holloway, B.: Timbre morphing of sounds with unequal numbers of features. J. Audio Eng. Soc. **43**(9), 678–689 (1995)
31. Werner, K.J., Germain, F.G.: Sinusoidal parameter estimation using quadratic interpolation around power-scaled magnitude spectrum peaks. Appl. Sci. **6**(10), 306 (2016)
32. Wishart, T.: On Sonic Art, 1st edn. Routledge, New York (1996)

Mapping Sound Properties and Oenological Characters by a Collaborative Sound Design Approach – Towards an Augmented Experience

Nicolas Misdariis[1(✉)], Patrick Susini[1], Olivier Houix[1], Roque Rivas[1], Clément Cerles[1], Eric Lebel[2], Alice Tetienne[2], and Aliette Duquesne[2]

[1] STMS Ircam-CNRS-SU, Paris, France
nicolas.misdariis@ircam.fr
[2] Maison KRUG, Reims, France

Abstract. The paper presents a specific sound design process implemented upon a collaboration with an important stakeholder of the wine (Champagne) industry. The goal of the project was to link sound properties with oenological dimensions in order to compose a sonic environment able to realise a multisensory experience during the wine tasting protocol. This creation has resulted from a large scale methodological approach based on the semantic transformation concept (from wine words to sound words) and deployed by means of a codesign method – after having shared respective skills of each field (sound and oenology). A precise description of the workflow is detailed in the paper, The outcomes of the work are presented, either in terms of realisation or conceptual knowledge acquisition. Then, future perspectives for the following of the work are sketched, especially regarding the notion of evaluation. The whole approach is finally put in the broad conceptual framework of 'sciences of sound design' that is developed and argued in the light of this study.

Keywords: Sound design · Codesign · Taste · Methodology · Tools

1 Introduction

The present project comes within the broad scope of crossmodal correspondences, i.e. the synesthetic associations that people tend to operate between different sensory modalities. In the literature, several studies aimed at describing or investigating the psychological mechanisms and the rationale of such associations [1]. The global aim of most of them is finally to understand how the percept in one modality can be interpreted or altered by sensory information given in another modality.

In the auditory domain, examples addressing that issue can be described, among others, with the following questions: what is the sound of a big/small or sharp/rounded objects? (e.g., the 'booba-kiki' effect studied by McCormick [2]). How does blue, red or yellow sound (e.g., the music/color correspondence, especially formalized by Kandinsky [3])? To what musical timbre a given flavor can be associated with (e.g., *bitter* paired with the French horn and *sweet* with the clarinet [4, 5]). Or, quoting Charles Spence, can

R. Kronland-Martinet et al. (Eds.): CMMR 2019, LNCS 12631, pp. 504–516, 2021.
https://doi.org/10.1007/978-3-030-70210-6_32

you taste the music? In other words, how music can influence the experience of taste, and change the personal emotional state?

In that domain, the "complex tasting experience that is drinking wine" [6] is especially focused. Not long ago, some works studied different interactions between what we drink and what we hear, among which the effect of different music styles on basic sensations (fresh, powerful, soft) during the taste of wine [7], or the perceptual and cognitive mechanisms underlying sensory modulations due to cross-modality [8].

In that scope, we recently conducted a long-term project (2017–18) with a famous French Champagne producer: Maison Krug. The goal of the project was to realize a mapping between sound properties and oenological characters in order to guide a sound design process and create an augmented multisensory tasting experience. This experience associates sound pieces with different types of wine coming from different regions. The challenge here was to understand the oenological concepts and transcribe them into sonic properties used, afterwards, for sound composition.

To do that, we worked in collaboration with members of the Krug winemaking team (Eric Lebel, the *Cellar Master* or *Chef de Caves*, and Alice Tetienne, *Winemaker*) and a music composer (Roque Rivas). Moreover, the project aimed at being implemented in a dedicated room – *La Salle des 400 vins* – where a specific multi-channel sound diffusion system has been designed and installed in order to render spatial properties of the sound production (see Fig. 1 and Sect. 4.2 for details).

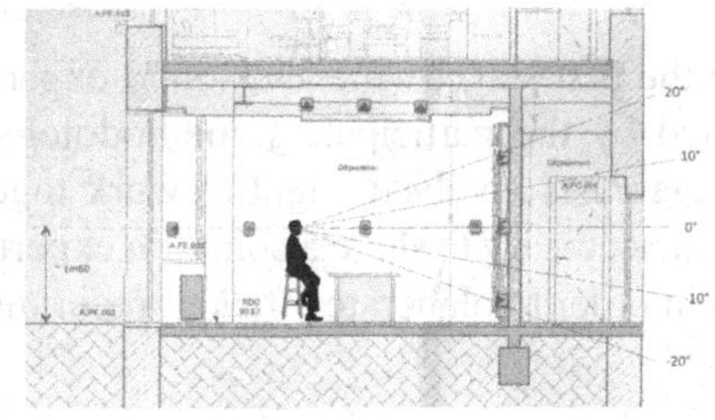

Fig. 1. Krug tasting room (Reims) equipped with a 32-loudspeaker system (right, ©O.Warusfel), and the "400 wines wall" representing the 400 'vins clairs' held in the Krug wine library (left, ©P.Susini)

The main claim of this work concerns the concept of semantic transformation and one dedicated mean to achieve it, the collaborative design approach.

Semantic transformation is a concept that has been initially formalized in the visual domain by Karjalainen and Snelders [9]. It is a translation operation that addresses the issue of transcription of intentions. It relies on the association between words attached to given intentions (e.g. Brand identity) and words able to deliver design insights. Usually, semantic transformation are supported by mediations tools [10] like moodboards, card sets, etc. and are implemented within methodological frameworks.

Collaborative design – or *codesign* – can precisely be a relevant method to implement semantic transformation. It is a creative methodology based on a participatory approach that started to emerge in the late nineties [11, 12]. It starts from the assumption that end-users are the experts of their own activity, so that they should be actively involved in the design process [13]. It is applied in several domains going from engineering to education, through design or arts [14].

In the sound design domain, semantic transformation and codesign have recently been studied and applied in a long-term research within a sound branding issue. In that frame, tools and methods were developed to convey sound identity and build corporate sounds [15, 16]. That work aimed at making a link between the semantic definition of a Brand (*Brand-words*) and semantic descriptions of sound characteristics (*sound-words*), in order to provide sound design recommendations.

The present study is directly inspired from this process. It tends, this time, to implement a semantic transformation between oenological identities (*wine-words*) and *sound-words*, in order to give insight to sound design composition.

The article relates the workflow implemented to conduct this project. In a first stage, two expert groups (wine and sound) learnt from each other and passed on their respective knowledge and skills (Sect. 2). In a second stage, a codesign process is implemented and resulted in mapping strategies between *wine-words* and *sound-words* (Sect. 3). In a third stage, *sound-words* are transformed into composed sound pieces to illustrate oenological characters and transcend the tasting experience (Sect. 3). Then, after a conclusion, we open to perspectives, especially regarding evaluation, and finally reposition the whole project into a global conceptual framework.

2 Expertise Sharing

During the first stage, wine and sound experts learnt from each others. This stage was motivated by the participatory methodology implemented in the project. In fact, as the protagonists involved ought to work together within a collaborative framework, it appeared necessary to share a common expertise and language to speak about wines and sounds in order to elaborate efficient recommendations for the sound creation.

2.1 Speaking About Wine

Vocabulary used to describe wine characteristics is quite huge. This is first due to the fact that wine tasting involves several sensory modalities corresponding to different sensory operations: we look at wine (sight), we smell it (smell) and we taste it (taste).

Each step brings specific information on wine. For instance, sight informs on color, intensity or viscosity (superficial aspects), smell informs again on intensity but also on flavors, and taste informs on mouth flavors (aroma, bouquet, etc.), balance or length in mouth. Each of these dimensions gets specific terminology and represents a semantic profile by itself. The visual analysis uses words like clear/blurry, brilliant/dull, fluid/thick, pale/intense, etc., together with all the shades of red (purple, burgundy, ruby, …) or white (colourless, yellow, golden, …) colors. The olfactory analysis uses words like closed/opened, poor/strong, etc. together with all the families of odors. The gustatory analysis uses words like soft/nervous, bitter, flexible/heavy, fleshy, velvet, short/long, etc. together with all the families of flavors.

This massively polymorphic character of wine comes mainly from the fact that it results from complex mechanisms (terroir, soil composition, sunshine, fermentation, conservation, etc.) occurring all through the production of the liquid that will become, *in fine*, a wine or a Champagne. Precisely for Champagne – and especially in the Krug traditional process – this complexity is amplified by two elements: *i)* at early stage of production, a Champagne is a blend of several elementary wines – called '*vins clairs*' – that the Chef de Caves mixes together to build the Cuvées of the year; *ii)* vinification, and especially effervescence (formation of bubbles), takes at least seven years to be completed, a period during which the liquid inside the bottle goes on evolving according to its oenological nature.

On that basis, it was really ambitious and utopic to learn how to speak and taste about wine in the frame of the project – also considering that it takes a life of learning and practice to become a professional winemaker! Nevertheless, the Krug team made the task easy by, first, opening the doors of an internal tasting session and, second, delivering a simplified (but relevant) nomenclature of their oenological references.

The tasting session was a regular meeting of the Krug team (5 winemakers) dealing with the characterization of 15 yearly samples of 'vins clairs'. This kind of session is done twice a year: from October to December, after the grape harvest, and from February to March, before the Champagne creation. It is done for all the 'vins clairs' collected in that particular year, each of them corresponding to a specific grape variety ('*cepage*'), vineyard ('*cru*'), and even parcel ('*parcelle*'). All the tasting notes are registered in a repository document (the 'Krug *black book*') that also compiles notes from previous years. It is used during the blending process as a reminder of tasting notes (gustatory sensations) that have been previously produced.

The simplified nomenclature concerned the gross regions of growing included in the overall certified Champagne Region (East of France, around the city of Reims). In fact, after the first steps of the project, it was assumed with the Chef de Caves that this level of description was a good compromise between relevance (regions with indeed specific characters) and feasibility (number of regions compatible with sound design capability and sensitivity). Thus, 10 regions were defined (e.g. '*Montagne Reims Nord*', '*Cote des Blancs*', etc.) and specified with words in a 3-class typology: *i)* oenological cursors, i.e. six words that forms a standard grid for the oenological tasting at Krug (e.g., '*structure*' or '*expression*'); *ii)* additional terms, i.e. words that can be freely added by anyone in the winemaking team (e.g., '*roundness*' or '*liveliness*'); ii) additional marks, i.e. words that rather correspond to metaphoric associations or affective evocations. For that latter category, it is worth noticing that musical/instrumental metaphor were often used (e.g., violin, trumpet, marimba, etc.).

Outputs of this first section was then a table of 10 regions, each described by a group of words (20 in average) structured in 3 categories going from standard dimensions to free metaphors or associations, and a sound design team – including the composer R. Rivas – that was less novice about the semantic world and process of wine tasting.

2.2 Speaking About Sounds

The second section consisted in the dual approach: learn novices in sonic issues (the Krug team) how to listen to sound and speak about them.

For that, we started from the research undertaken by Carron (2016) in the domain of sound branding and from which the present study is inherited [16]. In fact, based on an analysis of several articles related to sound semantic description, Carron et al. (2017) proposed a list of common words related to sound features independent of the meaning, the process that produced the sound, or its location. Words are related to the sound itself, its acoustical characteristics and timbre features rather than illustrative analogies. Then, a lexicon – called afterwards *SpeaK* – that includes a list of 37 words was developed as an application displaying each word with a definition and sound examples in different categories (musical instruments, voices, environmental sounds, etc.). Within Carron's work, this operational tool was used as a training environment before a sound indexing task but also as a support for codesign sessions [17].

In the present work, the *SpeaK* tool was precisely used to introduce the wine experts (Krug team) to the world of sounds, and its related words. Beforehand, the tool was improved in the light of the collaboration with the composer R. Rivas. A preliminary workshop was organized in order to refine, and if needed extend, the lexicon.

This session actually gathered two composers (R. Rivas and Frederic Le Bel), three researchers (the 3 first authors of the article) and the sound designer who initially composed sound examples for the first version of *SpeaK* (Thomas Rotureau). During the session, the 22 semantic scales of the lexicon (15 bipolar scales +7 single words) were methodically discussed with regard to the precision of the definition and the relevance of the sound examples. According to the latter point, the two composers were previously asked to prepare and bring for this session, alternative examples able to complement or improve the existing ones.

The global outcome of this session was a new release of *SpeaK* with 3 new elements: *i)* a simpler and user-friendly interface; *ii)* a 5-class generic structure of the sound examples (music, voice, environment, sound effects and basic synthesis); *iii)* if need be, new sound examples able to improve the quality of the illustration.

This current version of *SpeaK* was then used during a training session with the Krug team directly involved in the project: two members of the winemaking team – among whom the 'Chef de Caves' –, and the international marketing and communication director who also contributed to the collaborative process throughout the project.

The learning stage was inspired from Carron's experimental approach [16], and especially used the same training sound corpus. After some adjustments, the learning test included 4 exercises. An ownership period (45 min.) by a free browsing inside the lexicon. A first individual task (20 min.) that consisted in choosing one sound among five (5-AFC) with regard to a given semantic attribute – e.g. "choose the sound that is the most *fluctuant*". A second individual task (20 min.) that consisted in selecting one attribute among 10 words (a reduced list of the 37 words) with regard to a given sound. Answers from these two tasks were collectively discussed in order to share everyone's view. Finally, a third collective task (20 min.) consisted in the free description of a sound with 3 to 5 words from the lexicon. This last task allows the participants to agree on the perceptive qualities associated with a term in the lexicon.

Outputs of this second second learning section was, firstly, an adopted tool to support the semantic description of sounds, that will be used thereafter supporting the codesign session (Sect. 3), and secondly, a group of wine experts provided with expert language on sound which should refine perceptive capacities, enriches sensory exploration, and facilitates information selection, identification and comparison.

3 Collaborative Design

Then, after having investigated successively the wine and sound world (and words), we implemented a collaborative sound design (codesign) approach that basically consisted in going from the *wine-words* to the *sound-words* with a methodological process. This was done to give insights to the sound designer, so that he would be able to create and arrange the most relevant sound matters and forms.

3.1 Apparatus

The codesign environment was also transposed from Carron's work [16] and was formerly inspired by specific design approaches like *Kansei* [18]. Discussions were mediated by series of cardsets and the area of reflexion was materialized with a board, by analogy with a standard board game or role play. Supporting that, the *SpeaK* lexicon played the role of help to which anyone can refer during the session.

Three series of cardsets were built. They corresponds to the 10 wine regions, the 44 *wine-words* extracted from Krug terminology (6 oenological cursors +38 additional terms) and the 37 *sound-words* of the lexicon, organized in 3 gross categories (General, Morphology, Timbre). Cardsets got a color chart to make their handling easier. Moreover, two things were added to facilitate the session proceedings: blank cards to possibly introduce new terms, and a trash bin to put aside non relevant words.

The board was configured with concentric circles considering that the bull's-eye (middle) was the region and its oenological description, and that the rim could be used to organise, and in case hierarchise, the corresponding sound properties (Fig. 2).

3.2 Protocol

After a warm-up stage (*SpeaK* browsing and exercise), the codesign session went as follows: one region is chosen, the Krug team fixed its oenological properties and placed the corresponding cards on the board. Then, semantic transformation is processed by discussing and placing cards around the target. At someone's request, examples or definition attached to a particular *sound-word* may be given by means of the lexicon. After a while, the instrumental metaphor is delivered to revitalize the debates and launch a new round of card handling. When all the participants agreed, the semantic portrait of the region is finalized and fixed (Fig. 2).

The processing of one region took approximately 30 min and systematically involved the same 7 persons. One of them, from the research team, played the role of mediator who opened the discussion and led or chased up the dialogue. The whole codesign stage (for 10 regions) occurred in 2 consecutive half-days.

At the very end, the semantic portraits were reconsidered to adjust descriptions in light of global coherence. Besides, few words were instinctively added to reach affective or emotional character of each region, such as 'serious', 'happy', 'warm', 'shy', etc. This additional contribution came out of the initial methodological frame, and was motivated by the composer who felt the need to collect more sensitive and complex dimensions than the basic sound properties given by the lexicon (Fig. 2).

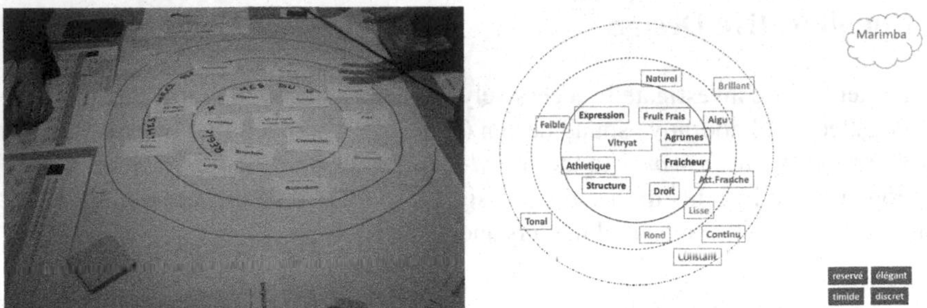

Fig. 2. Illustrative elements of the codesign sessions. The environment was formed of cardsets representing the different semantic spaces and board with concentric circles (left). At the end of each round, a semantic portrait of an oenological region is formed by associating wine-words – et the center – and sound-words – in concentric circles. In each portrait, the musical metaphor is recalled and some additional affective or emotional words are added (right). (©N.Misdariis)

3.3 Outcomes

The main outcome of the codesign stage was 10 semantic portraits respectively of the 10 oenological regions (Fig. 2 gives an example on 'Vitryat'). From that, a synthesis was done, by trying to highlight global coherence and local differences among regions. For example, we tended to reveal global characteristics related to the Montagne Reims that were common to the 3 sub-areas (Reims Nord, Sud and Ouest), and local differences to discriminate between these same areas.

A reflexive look at this approach can also form another outcome of this stage. In fact, methodological elements can be usefully extracted from this experiment. They especially concern the role and the status of the mediator, the position of the composer – as the ultimate sound expert and potential session leader – or the use of extended sound examples, especially from musical/instrumental databases, able to feed the discussion and enlighten or consolidate raw ideas. These statements may certainly help us to improve the collaborative sound design approach which seems to be a rather specific practice within the general frame of codesign (see also Sect. 5.1).

4 Composition and Implementation

After the apprenticeship and codesign parts (Sect. 2 and 3), the third link of this project was mainly dedicated to composition and implementation of sonic transcriptions of concepts and words that have been handled, up to then. This part addresses two main issues: an artistic one dealing with the way to create sound sequences on the basis of words describing basic properties of sound or emotions; and a methodological one dealing with the way to transpose the work done in studio to the location where the sound design pieces were intended to be played – *a fortiori* if the sound diffusion system is technologically complex and massively multi-channels.

4.1 From Description to Composition

The composition started from all the semantic tags produced during the codesign session, plus the composer's personal notes. During the composition process (nearly 2 months), R. Rivas was also fed by some listening feedbacks (from the working team) that guided him for semantic interpretations and Krug's expectations on aesthetics.

The transcription work – from *sound-words* to sounds – is a challenge that contains a non-negligeable part of artistic intuition and, here, that sometimes forced the composer to read into root notions – *wine-words* or evocations – in a personal manner. Nevertheless, he tried to rationalize his approach by translating *sound-words* into the three fundamentals sonic dimensions: frequency, time and space.

Frequency and time were generally informed by the basic *SpeaK* vocabulary and gave rise to specific spectral contents or temporal envelopes. For instance, notions like 'low/medium/high', 'crescendo/decrescendo', 'brilliant/dull' or 'fluctuating' get nearly direct correspondences in the acoustic domain. Here, the main difficulty came from the need to combine several basic notions, make them physically compatible and musically relevant. Back to root notions, as evoked above, terms like 'complexity' (oenological cursor), or 'lemony' (additional term) can respectively be related to a dense multi-layer mix of several sound textures or high-pitched and rough elements – like the sound of the harmon trumpet mute that Miles Davis used to play.

On this point, the notion 'natural/artificial' used for some portraits also drove R. Rivas for the choice of specific sound synthesis paradigms. But for that, he also relied on the instrumental metaphor attached to each region by the Krug team (e.g., violin, marimba, horn, etc.). These essential references gave the color of each piece while staying subtile and integrated by means of sound transformations or complex mixing.

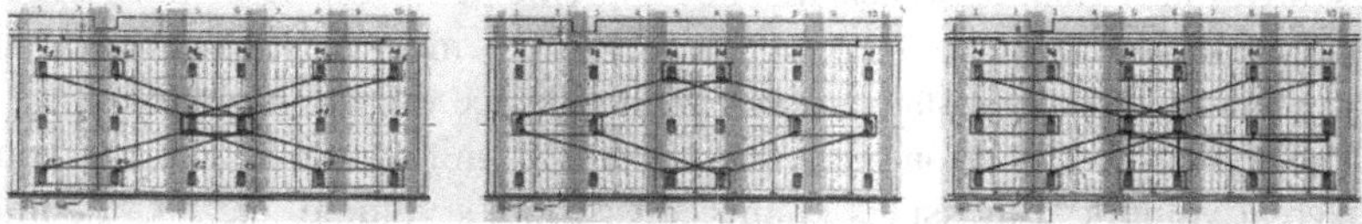

Fig. 3. Depiction of spatial sketches as stated by the composer R. Rivas in the composition phase. The background plane represents the '400 wines wall' and its 18-loudspeaker device and the drawings represent sound localisation or trajectories designed inside this grid.

Space was also fully used by R. Rivas to get another degree-of-freedom in the transcription process. In fact, thanks to the multi-channel device attached to the project, a real 3D-soundscape could have been designed in order to convey sound properties like 'close/far' or illustrate complex notions like 'aerial' or 'powerful'.

These spatial effects were able to be developed either in the frontal plane of the device (18-loudseaker wall) or in the surrounding space of the room by mainly dealing with opening, localisation, dynamic trajectories (Fig. 3), or in case, immersivity and envelopment.

4.2 From Studio Work *to Location Specific* Mastering

The specificity of this project lies also in the sound diffusion system it is associated with. This is a 32-loudspeaker system, split in 3 parts: 3 lines of 6 speakers associated with the '400 wines wall', 6 loudspeakers placed in circle around the audience, 6 speakers integrated in the ceiling and 2-subwoofers (Fig. 1). This device – developped by Amadeus[1] upon design specifications made by the Ircam/EAC team –, offers a rather unique configuration for diffusing the sound pieces created in the project. But, added to specific acoustic conditions of the tasting room (glass or plaster walls, tiles floor), it also addresses sound engineering issues related to the mastering practice.

This being, *in situ* setting sessions were set. They mainly consisted in: *i)* tuning the the audio mix quality, potentially altered by resonances or reflections due to room acoustics or electroacoustic response; *ii)* adjusting the 3D-soundscape with regard to the room dimensions and behavior. These operations were directly done in the audio sessions made in the studio and resulted in a multi-channel bounce for each of the 10 pieces, dedicated to be played back by a direct-to-disk device.

This part of the work points out a crucial practice in sound design: the *location specific* mastering. In fact, mastering is the final step of standard music production that aims at optimizing listening conditions in as many diffusion systems as possible. Sound design practices are commonly faced at specific mastering issues because of the diversity of sound devices usually used in this domain – from few (cheap) buzzers or loudspeakers placed in non conventional rooms (e.g. an automotive cockpit) to a lot of diffusion sources placed in large hall, such as a museum or a commercial hall[2]. One way to deal with this problem is to use audio simulation strategies based on 3D impulse response (IR) measurements that – by a deconvolution process – are able to render the effect of a given source diffused in the given room.

Presently, this virtual approach was not implemented for sake of time and project phasing. Instead, the composer and sound engineers (Clement Cerles and Colin Lardier), worked in studio either in a standard monitoring device or with a *pseudo-* '400 wines wall'. This system was built on purpose with similar unit sound devices and complied with the real volumic dimensions (wall's area, room's volume, etc.). In addition, as mentioned above, *location specific* mastering sessions were set and resulted in several modifications (EQs, internal balance of the mix, panoramic, tight filtering, etc.) that significantly improved the listening quality of the sound pieces.

5 Conclusions and Perspectives

To conclude, we conducted a long term project (nearly 2 years) that led us into the unexplored territory of wine industry and Champagne know-how. The main goal of the project was to design sound pieces informed by the knowledge of semantic correspondences between wine and sound worlds.

---

1 https://amadeusaudio.fr/en/.

2 https://www.ircam.fr/article/detail/mastering-hors-du-studio-trois-experts-en-design-sonore-decryptent-des-nouvelles-pratiques-1/.

The research and creation team was formed with researchers in auditory perception and sound design, a composer and a sound engineer who also played the role of a computer music designer [19]. The industrial collaboration was mainly interfaced with the Krug winemaking team and the marketing/communication department.

The project implemented the concept of semantic transformation and unfolded a participatory approach within a collaborative design (codesign) process. Moreover, it leaned on a methodological tool – previously developed and improved in the present frame: a sound lexicon (*SpeaK*) built as a dictionary collecting the major words used to describe sound properties, together with definitions and sound examples.

Within this frame, the project got four main stages in order to successively learn how to speak about wines, speak about sounds and collectively implement the semantic transformation from *wine-words* to *sound-words*. The fourth stage was dedicated to sound design (creation) and aimed at translating *sound-words* into sounds and musical composition that finally resulted in ten 1-min sound pieces diffused by a multi-channel sound device placed in a dedicated room: the Krug tasting room.

5.1 Perspectives

In the light of its originality and complexity, the Krug's project brings into front an emblematic approach. As a research process, it leads to open perspectives that should be further investigated in order to complement the project outputs. These perspectives mainly concern two components: codesign methodology and evaluation. As a sound design research, this project may also contribute to enhance our knowledge on the discipline and be part of a conceptual framework called sciences of sound design [20].

The codesign methodology applied to sound design seems to be quite encouraging and promising. As in its first implementation [16], the lexicon that supported the approach confirmed to be an efficient and relevant tool able to help communication and understanding on sounds. Nevertheless, the current codesign implementation showed some weakness that should be investigated and, may be, improved.

For instance, whereas the preliminary training exercises appeared to be unmissable, some uncertainties arose according the relevancy of the sound examples dedicated to these exercises and especially their ability to express just one basic property. Attention must be paid on the selection of these sounds and their polysemic content.

This precise issue is also addressed to the lexicon itself. In fact, on behalf of its rather 'encyclopedic' status, *SpeaK* must provide irrevocable and unequivocal specimens of sound examples illustrating sound attributes. This effort goes through the re-design of most of all examples from all categories. This work has yet started with the voice category by means of a recording campaign conducted by the composer R. Rivas; it will soon produce high quality and controlled vocal samples.

Indeed, concerning *SpeaK*, a more conceptual issue appeared during the Krug experiment: the fact that the list of pre-defined words were not sufficient enough to describe an oenological identity and that the composer needed high level descriptions (emotions, evocations, character) to be able to translate ideas into composition.

Finally, and more globally, we observed the fact that the experimental apparatus (board, cardsets, lexicon) prevented from describing dynamic changes of a semantic portrait as it often occurs in sound perception, but also wine tasting! This may force us to imagine new paradigms that would also consider the temporal dimension of sounds which is not equally relevant in other domains (e.g. graphics).

On the other hand, whereas the PDS research group used to promote a 3-step sound design model (Analysis, Creation, Validation) [21], the evaluation stage is, right now, rather completely missing from the project proceedings – except few informal (and positive) feedbacks from the first tasting sessions at Krug. This point addresses an interesting and controversial issue that the project itself could help to investigate.

In fact, this asks the following fundamental questions: why should we evaluate and how can we proceed an evaluation? A rational answer to the first question could be: to verify the match between solutions and specifications, or to ensure the usefulness, usability, and desirability of the user experience produced by the solutions [22]. As for evaluation procedures, they should to be inspired, as usual, by the experimental psychology discipline with physiological, perceptual or cognitive measurements.

But, transposed to the current use case, the previous rationale appears to be more complex to argue and implement. In fact, in that case, the main specification to evaluate could be the perception of the wine characters into the sound composition. In other words, does one recover the basic oenological attributes of a region into a 1-min sound piece experience? Or more globally, is the semantic transformation finally valid, i.e. does it help the composer to create a relevant sound content and the listener to recognize the wine identity that intended to be illustrated? Or, alternatively, what does all of this bring to the tasting experience? All these questions address methodological issues in terms of experiment (what/how to measure?) but also in terms of contextualization (how to put the participants into controlled – and ethically acceptable – tasting conditions?). These issues form a work-in-progress reflexion that we hope to investigate and implement in a near future.

By listing all these outcomes and perspectives, we can observe that the Krug project brings considerable knowledge on the sound design discipline itself, its protagonists, its process and even its production. In that way, and even if it initially targeted a direct application – sound pieces composition for a tasting experience –, this project could finally be seen as a potential research project implementing a *research-through-design* approach that aims at producing knowledge instead of only solutions [23].

This precisely comes into the conceptual frame we recently tried to make emerge and promote, in accordance with the three research loci of Nigel Cross' formalization on design research: people, process and products [24]. In fact, transposed to the discipline of sound design, we look at laying the foundations of sciences of sound design that will investigate simultaneously the character of the sound designer, the sound design process, tools or methods and the status of the designed sound, i.e. what sound design produces *in fine* [20]. Then, to some degree, we can expect that the present project may have helped – and will help – to inform this approach and, by quoting Cross (2001) [25] give some elements to answer to the seminal question: is there a designerly way of knowing, thinking and acting in sound design?

Acknowledgments. The authors – namely the Ircam group – are sincerely thankful to Maison KRUG (Maggie Henriquez, and the last three authors of this paper) for their fruitful collaboration and flawless welcome. All authors would also like to thanks Cyril Beros, Jeremie Henrot (Ircam PROD), Olivier Warusfel (Ircam STMS EAC), Gaetan Byk (Amadeus) and Emmanuelle Zoll for their contributions to the study.

References

1. Spence, C.: Crossmodal correspondences: a tutorial review. Attention, Percept. Psychophys. **73**(4), 971–995 (2011)
2. McCormick, K., Kim, J., List, S., Nygaard, L.C.: Sound to meaning mappings in the bouba-kiki effect. In CogSci, vol. 2015, pp. 1565–1570, July 2015
3. Kandinsky, W.: Du spirituel dans l'art. Denoël/Gonthier.
4. Crisinel, A.-S., Spence, C.: As bitter as a trombone: synesthetic correspondences in nonsynesthetes between tastes/flavors and musical notes. Attention Percept. Psychophy. **72**, 1994–2002 (2010)
5. Crisinel, A.-S., Spence, C.: A sweet sound? Exploring implicit associations between basic tastes and pitch. Perception **39**, 417–425 (2010)
6. Spence, C., Wang, Q.J.: Wine and music (II): can you taste the music? Modulating the experience of wine through music and sound. Flavour **4**(1), 33 (2015)
7. North, A.C.: The effect of background music on the taste of wine. Br. J. Psychol. **103**(3), 293–301 (2012)
8. Spence, C., Wang, Q.J.: Wine and music (I): on the crossmodal matching of wine and music. Flavour **4**(1), 34 (2015)
9. Karjalainen, T.M., Snelders, D.: Designing visual recognition for the brand. J. Prod. Innov. Manag. **27**(1), 6–22 (2010)
10. Boujut, J.F., Blanco, E.: Intermediary objects as a means to foster co-operation in engineering design. Comput. Supp. Cooper. Work (CSCW) **12**(2), 205–219 (2003)
11. Kvan, T.: Collaborative design: what is it? Automation in construction, **9**(4) (2000)
12. Sundblad, Y.: UTOPIA: participatory design from scandinavia to the world. In: Impagliazzo, J., Lundin, P., Wangler, B.: History of Nordic Computing 3, IFIP Conference on History of Nordic Computing. Springer, Heidelberg (2010)
13. Darras, B.: Design du codesign Le rôle de la communication dans le design participatif. MEI Médiation et information, n 40: Design et communication, 141 (2017)
14. Côté, N., Dubus, B., Fruleux, A., Roche, C.: Utilisation du Codesign dans la formation d'ingénieurs: exemple de projets en acoustique. In: Proceedings of the CFA 2014 (2014)
15. Carron, M., Dubois, F., Misdariis, N., Talotte, C., Susini, P.: Designing sound identity: providing new communication tools for building brands corporate sound. In: Proceedings of the 9th Audio Mostly: A Conference on Interaction with Sound, p. 15. ACM (2014)
16. Carron, M. : Méthodes et Outils pour Définir et Véhiculer une Identité Sonore (Doctoral dissertation, Université Paris 6 (UPMC) (2016)
17. Carron, M., Rotureau, T., Dubois, F., Misdariis, N., Susini, P.: Speaking about sounds: a tool for communication on sound features. J. Design Res. **15**(2), 85 (2017)
18. Gentner, A., Bouchard, C., Badoil, A., Favart, C.: Kansei cards: a visual tool supporting the investigation; discussion; and representation of the Kansei-related intentions of a product to be designed. In: KEER2014 Proceedings. Linköping; Sweden, June 2014
19. Zattra, L., Donin, N.: A questionnaire-based investigation of the skills and roles of Computer Music Designers. Musicae Scientiae **20**(3), 436–456 (2016)

20. Misdariis, N.: Sciences du design sonore. Approche intégrée du design sonore au sein de la recherche en design. HDR thesis, Université de Technologie de Compiègne (2018)
21. Susini, P., Houix, O., Misdariis, N.: Sound design: an applied, experimental framework to study the perception of everyday sounds. New Soundtrack **4**(2), 103–121 (2014)
22. Robare, P.: Sound in Product Design (Doctoral dissertation, Master thesis in Interaction Design. Pittsburgh, USA: Carnegie Mellon University School of Design) (2009)
23. Findeli, A.: La recherche-projet en design et la question de la question de recherche: Essai de clarification conceptuelle. Sciences du design **1**, 45–57 (2015)
24. Cross, N.: Designerly Ways of Knowing. Springer, London (2006)
25. Cross, N.: Designerly ways of knowing: design discipline versus design science. Des. Issu. **17**(3), 49–55 (2001)

Kinetic Design
From Sound Spatialisation to Kinetic Music

Roland Cahen(✉)

Centre de Recherche en Design (CRD), Ensci les Ateliers – École Normale Supérieure Paris-Saclay, Paris, France
roland.cahen@ensci.com

Abstract. This paper explores the process of kinetic music design. The first part of this paper presents the concept of kinetic music. The second part presents the sound design and compositional process of this type of music. The third part presents some excerpts from the composition logbook of a piece called *Kinetic Design* to illustrate the process of kinetic design as work in progress. This paper focuses on the question of sound spatialisation from a theoretical, as well as an empirical, point of view, through the experience and experiments of an electroacoustic music composer trying to make the imaginary concept of kinetic music real. It is a form of research by design, or research by doing. The kinetic design project examined here is the first time an experimental approach of research by design has been applied to kinetic music.

Keywords: Sound spatialisation · Kinetic design · Kinetic music · Electroacoustic music · Sound design · Design process · Composition

1 Introduction

Kinetic music aims to produce sound choreography where the sound is diffused. Hence, it uses sound spatialisation in such a way that both the composer and the listener focus on kinetic aspects of sound, in opposition to using spatialisation only illustratively, or for rendering effects. In kinetic music, like theatre, dance or visual arts, each zone, position or direction can take on a musical value, a form of density that the sound space itself embodies. Kinetic music wishes to add a new form of expression and compositional methods to existing spatial music concepts and techniques. Sound spatialisation has already been the subject of abundant literature, the focus of this paper is to demonstrate the specificity of kinetic music. Of the literature on spatial sound, much has been written on the subject, such as generalities (principles, philosophy of space and music, history) numerous tools and techniques, analyses of musical intentions and abstractions about spatial figures, but very little has concentrated on the auditory experience, spatial sound aesthetics and none on the design process.

This article explores the hypothesis of kinetic music as a new process of composition and analyses its compositional process using my piece, *Kinetic Design*. The term design is used hereafter in relation to the creation process. The creative process explored here

R. Kronland-Martinet et al. (Eds.): CMMR 2019, LNCS 12631, pp. 517–530, 2021.
https://doi.org/10.1007/978-3-030-70210-6_33

is 'research by design' or research by doing [6]. This form of research has a long legacy and is not novel in music. Indeed, Pierre Schaeffer developed his experimental approach by 'doing and listening'[1]. However, the kinetic design project examined in this paper is the first application of an experimental approach to kinetic music. By exploring the different motivations that drove the project, the successful and less successful experiments, and looking at extracts from my composition logbook, this paper tries to shed some light on some of the basic concepts and methods for kinetic sound design and composition. Kinetic Design was commissioned by INA-GRM, composed in octophony and performed on the acousmonium for the first time on January 20th 2019 at the MPAA Saint Germain (Paris).

2 The Characteristics of Kinetic Music

Kinetic Music aims to shape empty space with a choreography of sounds. However, a body of sounds would obviously be a kind of simulacrum[2], quite different from the human body or existing material objects. Composing and listening to kinetic music means focusing attention on spatial differences and similarities, as essential parts of kinetic musicality. Kinetic music adds new values to orchestration: spatial plasticity, incarnation and corporality, bringing an *orchestralisation*[3] of electroacoustic sounds. Kinetic music could be a breakthrough for electroacoustic/acousmatic music, anticipating new formal experiences and enabling new musical styles to emerge. However, to achieve these beautiful promises, the audibility of kinetic effects must be guaranteed.

2.1 Spatial Sound and Music Existing Work

There is a vast literature about sound spatialisation in the domain of music technology, electroacoustic music and perception. New rendering techniques procure nowadays a better sensation of sound incarnation thanks to new techniques such as WFS, High Order Ambisonics, dynamic pan and routing and room simulation. Simultaneously, spatialisation tools, editors such as the Ircam Spat, Panoramix, ICST Ambisonics, MaxMSP mc., and animation tools such Music Space, Acousmodules, Iosono Animix, GRM Tools (Spaces) and Iannix give most multichannel DAWs (digital audio workstations) and 3d real-time game editors (such as Unity3d) facilities for editing and automating sound source positions and motion. At the same time more international scientific, artistic and audio production centres are working on large multichannel sound devices to experiment with lines, arrays, matrix, domes and other sets of speakers. The existing literature about sound spatialisation describes perception, concepts, descriptors and techniques[4]. Object based formats allow to give sound sources 3D(xyz) theoretical positions, that can be rendered to any standard multichannel soundfile format and in any real space, independently

[1] Musical research approach by Schaeffer [11].

[2] Simulacrum refers to representation in ancient Greek literature and philosophy. This term was also used in XX century by Schaeffer [12].

[3] A neologism meaning making something orchestral which was not originally.

[4] Blauert, Bregmann, Rumsey, Jot, Warusfel, Pachet/Delerue, Cadoz/Luciani, Brümmer, Duchenne, Pottier, Vandegorne, Schumacher, Schacher, Baalman, Orlarey etc.

of the number and positions of the speakers. The SSMN Spatialization Symbolic Music Notation is an abstract and geometry toolkit for writing spatialised sound movements on instrumental scores. Spatial interactions with physical gestures are also explored at CIRMMT[5] and at Ircam[6].

2.2 Audibility as a Premise

Most spatial music rests on so-called trajectories, easily visible on sound editors' interfaces, but rarely audible in situ. However, spatial shapes, i.e. the compositional building block of kinetic music, should be clearly audible in order to be operational. Even if music can be heard when spatial sound shapes are not obvious, it is no longer kinetic music. What we could call *kineticality*, as a measurement of kinetic audibility, could be defined by how many audible elements of kinetic sound content or qualia[7] are lost in the spatial reduction process[8]. Unfortunately, musical audibility is more difficult to measure than individual sound-effect audibility. Spatial sound and music audibility can change a lot from one listening context to another and from one listener to another, for example because of the hotspot effect,[9] which some techniques, such as real source positioning[10] and linear panning[11] can reduce[12] (Table 1).

2.3 Kinetic Design Qualia

Here is a short list of kinetic qualities experienced in *Kinetic Design*. It is difficult to separate concepts, sensations or experiences from sound shapes.

- Immersion, position distribution, sound mobility.
- Punctual sounds and impulses: position (referent / changing), position blur, motion by re-iterations, motion by elementary transition, referent positioning, accentuation.
- Sustained sounds: motion by transitions (trajectory) between positions, spatial accentuation.

[5] Schumacher with OMPrisma lib for open music.

[6] Bevilaqua, Schnell, Lambert CoSiMa project.

[7] See the kinetic music qualia below.

[8] The reduction process consists of downmixing or converting multichannel sounds to stereo or mono.

[9] Only listeners placed in the hotspot position can hear the spatial effects properly, e.g. equidistant from the surrounding speakers.

[10] Real source positioning, as opposed to virtual positioning, techniques consist in placing each sound element on only one track / speaker. It has been used since the very beginning of spatialisation (multiple mono) and considered theoretically as a spatial compositional approach by various artists such as Pierre Boeswillwald in Octophonie Delta P (1991–94) with the concept of "octuor" or Benjamin Thigpen [13].

[11] Linear panning stands for panning between two next in line speakers, works also for a circle where the azimuth controls the position.

[12] The necessity to listen to spatialised sounds from a small point in the center of the device. The hotspot effect is more important when using virtual source positions than with real source positions.

Table 1. Easily audible kinetic sounds/elements vs. hardly kinetic ones.

Audible	Inaudible (or less audible)
Recorded/synthesised impulses/attacks	Sine waves or tonic sounds with poor spectral complexity
Various noise dynamic modulations (filtering, granularity…)	Soft attacks are less precisely positioned
Tonal sound with rich complexity	Spatial complexity blurs kinetic sense
Reduced spatial complexity up to 2/3 voices	Complex movements

- Movements: pointed, traces drawn through space, rhythm, oscillation, swing, bouncing, hold and release, etc.
- Mass: extension/diversity, deployment/folding, spatial resolution.
- Plasticity, incarnation, sound corporeality.
- Explicit visual reference (visualisation) vs. Implicit or metaphorical (materialisation, kinaesthetic shape, imagination).

In order to better understand where this typology comes from and how it has been established, Sect. 3 will present some of the concepts of kinetic design qualia through the process of experimentation and composition, referring to the composition logbook of *Kinetic Design*.

2.4 Visual Imagery

Designing geometrical patterns of sounds, such as a sound trajectory, is not sufficient to produce kinetic sensation, but our imagination seems nevertheless to shape our representation of kinetic sounds. On the one hand, imagining these spatial sound shapes, our natural inclination is to project a visual grid on the auditory perception and to try to draw sound in space. However, by doing this, we might risk distracting the listener from the auditory experience. The act of hearing a sound should be sufficient in itself, and it is necessary to keep it at a distance from visual design, or tools for visualisation, so as to privilege audibility, i.e. auditory experience and sensation. On the other hand, "kinetic sound design" refers to visual imagery. Some visual metaphors are realistic and obvious, such as the big swing, or the little soldiers (Table 2) marching around the listener], others are more abstract, such as diversity variations or positional contrapuntal impulses (Table 2 Dots & Lines). This is why kinetic sound design belongs to the discipline of design, since sound shapes emerge from the sound itself referring to our spatial representation of the world, which is mostly visual.

In this article the term design is also used in relation to the creation process which this article presents through a "research by design' approach.

3 Composition Device, Design Process and Workflow

A description of a kinetic design and compositional process follows. This enquiry encompasses theoretical and then applied research. Since Sect. 4 contains a presentation of my experience and methods of kinetic design composition, as a concrete illustration of this process, an outline of the composition follows in order to help the reader situate the different sections of *Kinetic Design* discussed below. The workflow depicted below is only one among others, but it focuses on i) kinetic audibility and ii) spatial composition and spatial authoring possibilities at every stage of the compositional process from its conception to performance (Fig. 1).

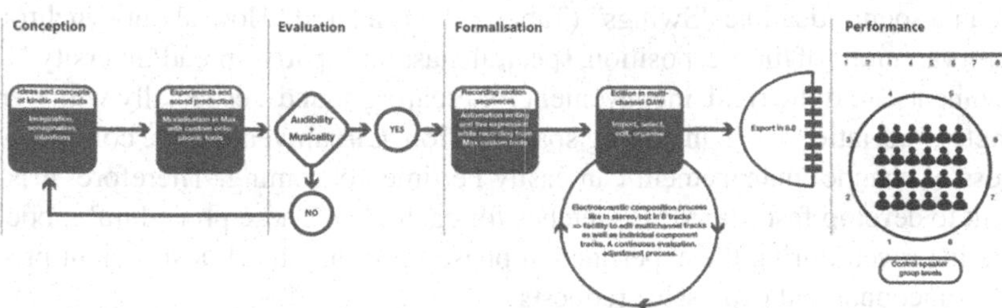

Fig. 1. This schematic offers an overview on the design / compositional process. The conception phase consists of imagining audio kinetic ideas and making sound sketches or Max models for experimenting with them. Only elements with kinetic musicality and audibility are kept for composition. Otherwise ideas are improved or abandoned. This evaluation, which also happens at further stages, is the condition of existence of kinetic music. Formalisation is the proper compositional part of the project, where sound elements are performed, recorded and organized into a music composition. During this part of the process, it is essential to facilitate modifying the sound elements.

3.1 Ideation

Planning the kinetics from the very beginning of a composition project enables us to put movement at the heart of a project, whether the kinetic plan concerns sound design or the whole composition. Adding spatialisation once the whole composition is finished, or even once sound elements are recorded, is generally too late to achieve kinetic creation consistency. Design ideation techniques exist and flourish in design thinking literature. Some can partly be applied to art creation as well as functional design. Here are two complementary methods which can be used to sonagine[13] kinetic sound objects:

i) An inductive method which starts from an imaginary metaphor. For example, “Swings” (see Table 2) inspired by Edgar Allan Poe’s the pit and the pendulum, imagining a giant pendulum, whistling by passing near with trajectory. Here the idea is typically physical or visual.
ii) An experimental derivational process which imagines an abstract tool for moving any sound source materials. By experimenting with various sound sources and perfusing the tool, it is possible to produce lots of musical materials, out of which the most interesting can be kept for creating musical sequences.

[13] Sonagination is a neologism invented by sound designers to draw a distinction between visual imagination and auditory imagination.

Ideas can sometimes reveal themselves as being well sonaginated, but also other times less so because they are totally abstract and unrealistic, too visually oriented or inappropriate. In reality these two methods are often used successively or combined.

3.2 Experimentation and Sound Production in Max MSP Custom Octophonic Tools

How can a sound idea like "Swings" (Table 2) be rendered? How about synchronising between variations of timbre, position, spectral mass and spatial spread/diversity? DAWs environments are quite rigid, inconvenient for creating sounds, especially with dynamic parameters' variation when including spatialisation. Circumventing the complexity and haziness of channel management can easily be time consuming. Therefore, it is more efficient to develop fast MaxMSP sketches for each idea. These procedural models can also be improved during the experimental phase until they reach a sufficient precision to fulfil functional and expressive requests.

Two examples are described here:

- *OctoLine* allows to control a set of parameter's variations for a single stream, using break point functions to modify dynamically the following: volume, position, a filter cut-off frequency, spread and spatial diversity[14]. Octoline therefore produces variations in spatial extension. It uses mostly noise or simple generators the instances of which can be easily differentiated.
- *KDvector* launches polyphonic spatialised sound vectors triggered by MIDi notes. Time dynamic parameters or parametric vectors can be set before launching them, such as sound type volume curve, position curve, filter cut-off frequency, filter quality and spread. Diversity is ensured by multiplying vectors units.

3.3 Recording Sound Elements

During the process of developing MAXMSP patches and producing kinetic shapes, sequences of octophonic sound are recorded. Each sequence is performed live or automatized to produce the desired kinetic sound. All elements are recorded in multichannel with their spatialisation embedded and will be manipulated later on in multichannel.

3.4 *Kineticality* Evaluation of Sound Elements

Before going further in the composition *kineticality*[15] is evaluated to validate sounds the kinetic expressivity of which are audible and thus to exclude those that are not[16]. A proper evaluation would require a large listener panel, but a simple listening evaluation is

[14] Spatial diversity is the desynchronization, or the originality, of the different voices. It has been used by Charles Verron [14] in his PhD thesis to simulate natural immersive sounds such as rain. Diversity equals 0 when 8 sound voices are mixed together and played on one or more speakers according to the spread value. Diversity equals 1 when a different sound voice plays on each speaker. Between 0 and 1, positions spacing of 8 the sound voices vary continuously.

[15] See Kinetic audibility Sect. 2.2, above.

[16] Nevertheless, all the sounds of a kinetic music are not necessarily kinetic.

better than nothing. Therefore, waiting a few days before re-listening helps to step back and allows us to forget the original perception. François Bayle use to say *"il faut faire fonctionner l'oubli"*[17], in order to recover primary unbiased musical sensation. Such a subjective evaluation would not satisfy scientific evaluation criteria[18] but seems good enough for creating music for which the main evaluation is the final performance.

3.5 Editing and Assembling Pre-recorded Octophonic Elements in a Multichannel DAW[19] to Compose Musical Sequences

Once sound elements are recorded and their *kineticality* validated, a selection of sequences or parts of them are imported in the DAW. This is where the main composition is achieved. It is important that DAWs allow the following features:

- Accept mono, stereo and multichannel audiofiles
- Edition of multichannel tracks: splitting, editing and merging. This essential feature, which allows to modify easily and precisely previously spatialised sound elements, does not exist as such in most DAWs.
  - Splitting for edition: easy switch from grouped tracks to individual tracks
  - Easy edition of the individual tracks
  - Merging edited elements: easy backwards switch from individual tracks to grouped tracks after edition
- Multichannel effects and in/out routing for multichannel effects
- In place offline multichannel effects

In Avid Pro Tools HD for example, it is easy to move multitrack clips to n mono tracks and to edit individual tracks, but in order to bring back the elements to a multitrack clip after being edited, the group must be consolidated and then moved back to its original multitrack.

In other professional environments, such as Steinberg Nuendo, it is possible to route any kind of track to a High Order Ambisonic bus and monitor the rendering on any number of channel outputs. But a splitting and merging process is not available unless whole tracks are duplicated for splitting again when merging (Fig. 2).

3.6 Performance: On Groups of N Speakers and Effects on an Ensemble of Speakers (Acousmonium, Sound Dome or Any Other Concert Diffusion Device)

In order to obtain the best possible kinetic perception in diffusion for all the audience, a few criteria should be taken into account:

---

[17] 'One should use the function of forgeting' (my translation).

[18] It should be tested by non-expert listeners using proper perceptive evaluation methods.

[19] DAW is an abbreviation of Digital Audio Workstation.

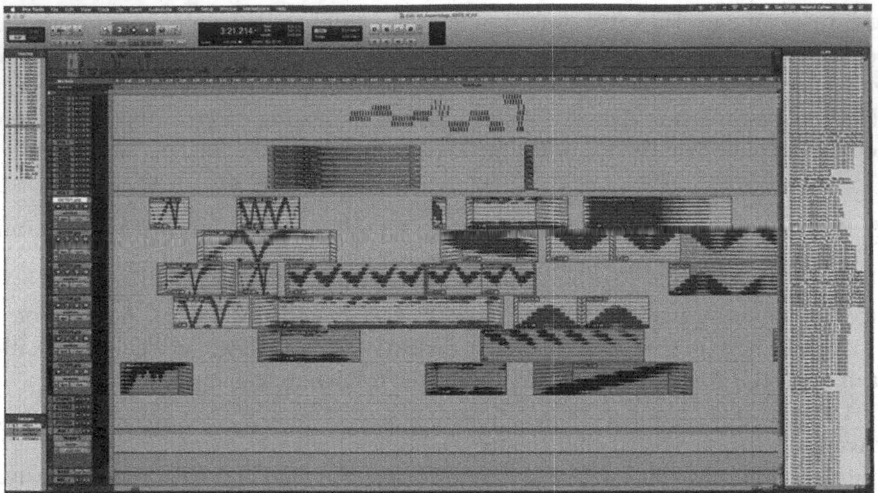

Fig. 2. Example of *Kinetic Design* Pro Tools HD Cession with kinetic multitrack elements (octophonic tracks) and mono elements in mono tracks (on top tracks).

- The acoustic of the venue should be non-resonant: muffled venues, studios or open air are preferable to empty resonant rooms or churches.
- Speakers are organised by groups of n, corresponding to the number of channels in the music or its master soundfile e.g. 8 channels => one or several groups of 8 speakers.
- Listeners are not too near the next speaker. A distance of a few meters allows to reduce the blinding effect[20]

Diffusion Setup

The octophonic (8.0) octal diffusion format[21], which is an interesting work format because it is efficient and accessible as lots of multichannel devices work by 8, can be used. Track numbering from back left to back right allows i) to avoid an automation break in front of the listener ii) to switch and transit easily from a circular to a linear front screen distribution[22] (Figs. 3 and 4).

20 Blinding effect in electroacoustic concerts happens when as a listener you mostly hear the speaker next to you.

21 8.0 is a common format but not a market standard, but it is compatible with 7.1 SDDS.

22 Some parts of the music composition would avoid 1/8 transitions in order to be performed on a linear speaker array instead of a circular one. During performance, it is possible to avoid jumps when swapping from a circular to line, or line to circular, diffusion device by choosing the nearest speakers to ensure continuity e.g. 4–5. (Fig. 6.).

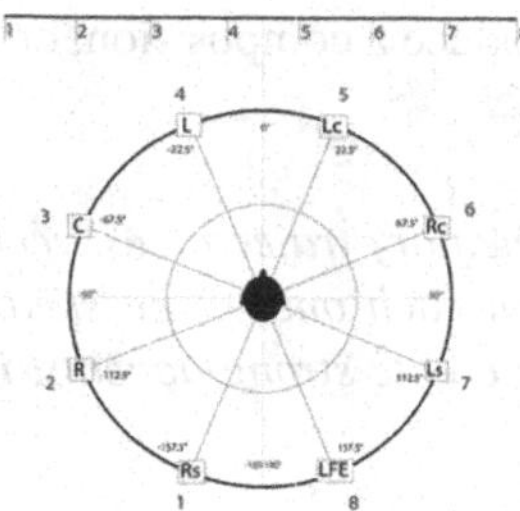

Fig. 3. Octal or circular 8.0 distribution allowing: 1 - a geographic allocation corresponding to spatial intuition 2 – the possibility to switch easily from circular to linear diffusion 3 - rejects automation hedges values in the back (instead of in the front in standard formats) 4 – a simple compatibility with 7.1 SDDS standard format: L, Lc, C, Rc, R, Ls, Rs, LFE.

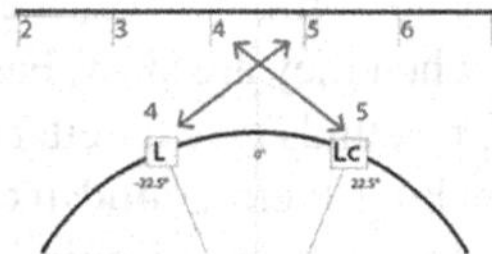

Fig. 4. Circular-linear transitions in performance

4 Excerpts of Kinetic Design Composition Logbook

Table 2. Kinetic Design is composed of 12 chained movements. (This table is presented here to simplify references).

	Time	Title	Duration
1	0:09	Stretching - Extension	1′ 45″
2	1:54	Swings	2′ 21″
3	4:15	Dots & Lines	3′ 10″
4	7:25	Pulsed	2′ 54″
5	10:19	Untied - Incises	2′ 35″
6	12:54	March	55″
7	13:49	OtoGliss_1	1′ 26″
8	15:15	Little Soldiers	4′ 19″
9	19:34	Wave breathing	1′ 06″
10	20:40	OtoGliss_2	1′ 47″
11	22:27	*Laché*	2′ 14″
12	24:41	*Final Balancé*	1′ 43″

Thursday 19th July 2018

I am in the process of finishing the first part of my research to create *Kinetic Design.*

My original intention was to produce a composition, or "ballet" made up of "lines" and "dots":

- *Lines between speakers: elementary trajectories, vectors or curves.*
- *Dots or punctual elements on each one of the speakers themselves, either to start and end the musical lines, to create strong accents, impulses in the music, points of support or clicking effects.*

Although the idea works, the result does not fit with what I imagined (or more accurately sonagined). To maximise spatial precision, I choose to work with two categories of sounds: impulses and sustained noise. I will refer to these figures as impulse and sustained noise spatial vector[23] (or NoiseVect).

My NoiseVect lack musicality, quickly becoming boring to the ear, almost like a dancer stretching her arms back and forth. Worse, they do not validate the idea of a line, segment or trace, especially when they are slow. Faster motion and shorter swishes, such as mechanical pistons or whip sounds give a better idea of a directional movement. But I could not find a way of making them sound like lines starting from a position and finishing on another. And if we can hear whipping sounds crossing through space, the sounds also carry a dramatic and ridiculous musical connotation. It even seems that line/trace impression are inversely proportional to spatial precision. In other words, the more accurate a position, the more noise the sound must carry. However, noise is perceived as large and blurred and not as a line. On the contrary, sustained sounds, reduced in mass (FN), such as pure tones, which better suggest lines, can hardly be heard at a precise position in space. This leads me to having to choose between Scylla and Charybdis (Fig. 5).

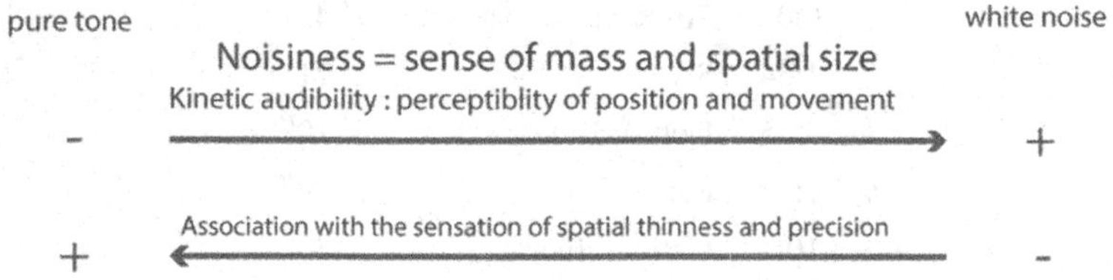

Fig. 5. Impression of a trace thinness being inversely proportional to spatial resolution.

Impulses placed at a precise position on one single speaker (track) are situated well in their position, but neither give the idea of points. They sound rather like events marked in time and space. When an impulse is attached to a *NoiseVect*, at the begining or end, it sometimes appears grouped together, sometimes not[24]. But even when impulses and *NoiseVect* merge together in time and timbre, impulses are not perceived as being beginning and ending positions of a Noise*Vect*, since the positions do not seem to merge. Spatial perception thus seems to keep separate from the sound stream. Further research

[23] Vectors are elementary directional trajectories going from one speaker to another.

[24] As established by Albert Bregman's grouping principles [4].

could be done on merging spatial and sound content perceptions. Fortunately, as soon as rhythm and musicality inhabit these sounds, I enter as a listener into an astonishing and new sound universe. Like a sorcerer's apprentice, I feel incapable of understanding exactly what I manipulate. I can hear some effects, artefacts, bursts, spreads, folding and unfolding, but I cannot manage any of these elements precisely. While writing this, I am reminded of Pierre Schaeffer, whose *journal de la musique concrete* [10] has been an inspiration for me.

Monday 27th August

Capping/unplugging effect: difficult to achieve with simple clicks, try breaking an infra-bass hold sound with a strong distributed click. Try curtain effects from mass of scattered grains passing from one side to the other opening and closing a background.

- MAKE SILENCE, rarefy, nuance, intensify differences.

Mobility takes its value only in contrast with stationary moments. Look for motion variation control.

- For the swings: hold the balance in a position creating tension, then release. Try Ping-Pong rhythms on the origin and the destination of the pendulum (Table 2).

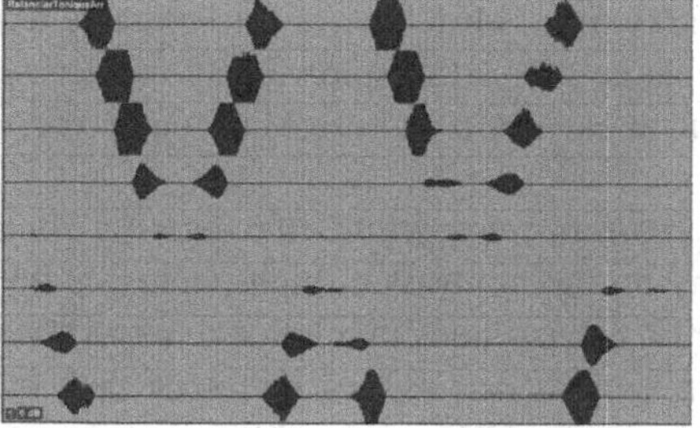

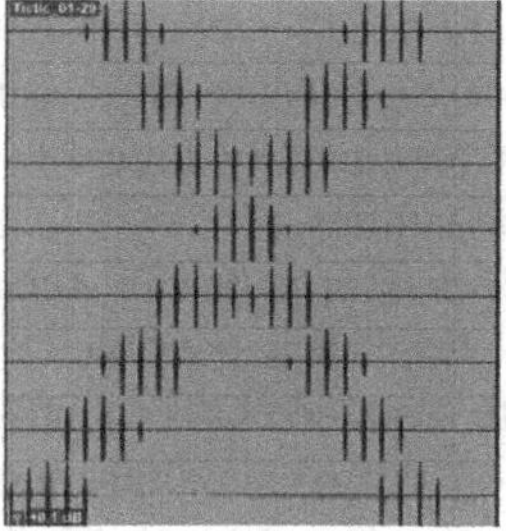

Fig. 6. Transitions (Left) Rear swing: transition from 8 to 1 happens in the middle of the movement - (Right) Two identical iterative sounds in opposite direction, starting from the rear, crossing forward and ending at the back gives this amusing picture (1 to 8 + 8 to 1)

Note that the intersection of the two iterative sound movements is not in the centre but on channel 4. If the crossing happened in the middle, the sound would be played on speakers 4 and 5 with a bad spatial focus and would reduce the spatial resolution to only 7 points. With 8 channels this kind of asymmetry is inevitable, but on the other hand, odd numbers of channels would bring other asymmetries, e.g. rhythmical ones. Twelve channels would be a very good working module but unfortunately not standard and more expensive.

Tuesday 28th August

The GRM studio-A is comfortable and beautifully equipped[25]. The acoustics are excellent, the sound awesome, the computer powerful. A shelter from the outside world in a hidden basement, where there are no distractions. Perfect!

I have tried many musical concepts, recording hours of octophonic sequences using different models: plots, whips, swings, spatial loops, variation of position, diversity, polyphony and spatial amplitude, with various sound materials: dynamically filtered white noise, various wave generators and samples. On the whole there are some remarkable figures, but I am struggling. Once these sound movements are produced, it is difficult to assemble them. I tend to regress, replaying musical approaches of the late 70′s called "*séquence jeu*", where the same set of gestural sounds are repeated with pattern variations, quickly becoming monotonous. Trying other formal approaches, I combine different parts of the composition as if they were sediments, layers of a landscape, as if each one of the parts of the work were stacked on top of one another. I play with transitions, creating geological faults in the landscape, planes and protrusions, leaving glimpses into the future or flashbacks into the past.

I realize that my sampled loops are spatially shifting because of a scheduling drift between the signal and data, which I then correct. At last, each sound element in a sample or loop now plays in sync and always comes through on the right speaker allowing me to make kinetic rhythms. I can also precisely control the position of each component.

I have created my own instruments with Max, which gives me a lot of possibilities, but the difficulty with Max is that I develop and add new features all the time, and the patches are never stabilized. Each time I try to add a new feature to the patch, new bugs appear, and I need to debug from time to time. Moreover, it is impossible to memorize the best presets because after each change the settings previously memorized become obsolete. Consequently, I record audio at each step and use Max "pattr" presets only as setting-up facilities.

Kinetic masking effect and kinetic pattern segregation - the masking effect[26] acts at the spatial level. It is possible to play on the contrast of high-pitched moving sounds mixed with sustained bass sounds, or on close planes in relation to more distant planes. But as soon as two simultaneous movements or positions are exceeded, independent movements become quite difficult to hear, except with very different or complementary or eccentric sounds. Hence the use of very eccentric registers, e.g. the infra-bass only slightly disturb the spatial perception of other sounds. Maximising temporal, spectral, dynamic and of course spatial differences helps to separate the patterns.

Playing with the diversity parameter - diversified sound masses, i.e. composed of 8 independent sound sources, but of the same nature (e. g. 8 different white noises on each track versus the same white noise on the 8 tracks), allow me to stabilize the movements of sounds and give our ears a rest. They create a sensation of breadth and richness, like open-air soundscapes.

MAKE CLEARER - spatial complexity and diversity must be undressed, flattened or lightened, the movements should stop. More static and monophonic moments would

[25] The studio is equipped with 8 Genelec 8250 monitors placed around the central working position.

[26] Auditory masking effect occurs when the perception of A is affected by the presence of sound B. It also concerns simultaneity, frequency, spectrum and directional masking.

reinforce the spatialised ones. Should I do this in the composition or during the performance? Both probably. Unfortunately, the possibilities to reduce complexity without losing content during the performance are limited.

Thursday 27th December

I am at the end of the project. The composition is more Baroque and more dramatic than originally expected. Many bass and infra-bass sounds, clinging clicks and stridencies provoking inner ear interferences. Treble strident sounds are heard as they saturate the ear itself. Strange feeling, It seems as if the sound was produced by the ear itself, often mixed up with provoked otoacoustic emission, I do not think they are the same phenomenon. They happen when treble sine which are distributed in frequencies and space and are modulated slowly, typically between 1 and 4 kHz. At the end of listening, the ear is physically tired, yet the listener has travelled to unusual places and sensations.

I believe I have succeeded in my challenge to create kinetic music, where spatialisation plays a central role, constitutive of the musicality. There is a lot of imagination and variety in kinetic configurations allowing new sounds and musicality to emerge. There is hopefully more to explore in order to create music with new sounds, finding their own expressiveness. There is also humor in there, like the grotesque walk of the little soldiers, both burlesque and tragic, ridiculous and terrifying at the same time.

It is difficult to find the right balance between movement and immobility. Like watching a dancer on stage, and appreciating the choreography, it is easier if the stage and the spectator do not move too much themselves. Here there are sometimes too many unnecessary swirls, but I have a hard time deciding which ones to cut in order to stop the movement in the right place, moment and positions. Two approaches are possible: either: i) starting from fixed sounds and building the movement at the time of the compositional process, which means adding a disconnected movement on top of an existing playing sample; ii) or pre-constructing the movement inside the sound materials themselves and then reducing or fixing them afterwards, with the inconvenience that the movement is fixed and attached to the sound. I mostly used the second method.

I have moved on from the idea that sounds have to be noisy or contain noisy attacks to be precisely positioned, while tonic and sustained sounds are difficult to locate. That is still true, but intermediaries also work. It is an important compositional choice that the positions be clear and precise for some sounds, less for others. Trajectories require a fairly high spatial precision, unless listeners simply feel that spatialisation has changed, but without perceiving kinetic qualia. Spectral, temporal, pattern complementarity is also a major tool for distinguishing kinetic qualia. For example, impulses are very easily positioned on top of sustained sounds and seem to appear at the forefront. This complementarity is a key to access musical complexity.

Kinetic design is a composition that must be listened loud enough but not to the point of needing ear protectors. Physiologically speaking, it is very demanding for the listener's ears. At the end of listening to it, listeners may start to feel this composition has made them work in various unusual registers but without pain or hearing fatigue.

5 Conclusion

This design process has proved efficient in a number of ways. A large part of the audience who listened to *Kinetic Design* said they had a singular experience of spatialisation. For the first time, they could really hear the movement of the sound. The spatialisation was effective and impressive. They also said that it was a show of sound, the plasticity of the sound was expressive and constituted a novel listening experience. However, does this mean that there is a new musicality, a kinetic music, a new genre in music? The answer is more nuanced. Some other composers working in the same field who listened to the performance were quite critical and said that the music did move but they could not feel any particular significance in the movement, nor a specific kinetic musicality. Any evaluation from listeners' experience is only representative of a sample; it is bound to be subjective and must therefore be relativised and treated with caution. The question whether kinetic music can be developed into a new expressive genre or is only a fictive construction to push spatialized expressivity forward to its limits, still remains of interest and needs to be explored further with more experimentation, applied research and experimental creation. New tools and design processes also may help to improve kinetic music experience.

References

1. Baalman, M.: On Wave Field Synthesis and Electro-Acoustic Music, with a Particular Focus on the Reproduction of Arbitrarily Shaped Sound Sources. Ph.D. thesis, Technische Universität Berlin (2008)
2. Baalman, M.: Spatial composition techniques and sound spatialisation technologies. Organ. Sound **15**(3), 209–218 (2010)
3. Blauert, J.: Spatial Hearing. The MIT Press, Cambridge (1997)
4. Bregman, A.S.: Auditory Scene Analysis: The Perceptual Organization of Sound. Bradford Books, MIT Press, Cambridge (1990)
5. Cahen, R.: Octophonie DeltaP-Cahen. Compte rendu de recherche pour Octophonie Studio Delta P La Rochelle (1994)
6. Hauberg, J.: Research by Design – a research strategy
7. Macedo, F.: Phenomenology, spatial music and the composer: prelude to a phenomenology of space in electroacoustic music. In: Proceedings of the International Computer Music Conference 2011, University of Huddersfield, UK, 31 July–5 August (2011)
8. Merlier, B.: Vocabulaire de l'espace en musiques électroacoustiques DELATOUR France, p. 230. Hal shs-0051174 (2006)
9. Pottier, L.: La Spatialisation Des Musiques Électroacoustiques. Université Jean Monnet-Saint-Etienne. Edited by C.I.E.R.E.C Travaux ; Musique et Musicologie 157. Saint-Étienne: Publications de l'Université de Saint-Étienne (2012)
10. Schaeffer, P.: De l'expérience musicale à l'expérience humaine. La Revue musicale n°274–275. Paris, Richard-Masse (1971)
11. Schaeffer, P.: Traité des objets musicaux essai interdisciplines. Éditions du Seuil, Paris (1977)
12. Schaeffer, P.: Machines à communiquer Tome 1 Genèse des simulacres
13. Thigpen, B.: Spatialization Without Panning. eContact! 11.4 Symposisum électroacoustique de Toronto CEC (2009). https://econtact.ca/11_4/thigpen_spatialization.html. Accessed 20 Apr 2019
14. Verron, C.: Synthèse immersive de sons d'environnement. Thèse de doctorat en acoustique Université Aix-Marseille (2010)

Sonic Interaction for Immersive Media - Virtual and Augmented Reality

Designing Soundscapes for Alzheimer's Disease Care, with Preliminary Clinical Observations

Frédéric Voisin[1(✉)], Arnaud Bidotti[2], and France Mourey[3]

[1] Saint Mesmin, France
[2] Laboratoire Psy-DREPI EA-7458, Bourgogne - Franche-Comté University, Besançon, France
[3] Laboratoire CAPS (Cognition, Action et Plasticité Motrice), UMR INSERM U1093, Dijon, France
france.mourey@u-bourgogne.fr

Abstract. Acoustic environment is a prime source of conscious and unconscious information which allows listeners to place themselves, to communicate, to feel, to remember. Recently, there has been a growing interest to the acoustic environment and its perceptual counterparts of care facilities. In this contribution, the authors describe the process of designing a new audio interactive apparatus for Alzheimer's Disease care in the context of an active multidisciplinary research project led by a sound designer since 2018, in collaboration with a residential longterm care (EHPAD) in France, a geriatrician, a gerontologist, psychologists and caregivers. The apparatus, named «Madeleines Sonores» in reference to Proust's madeleine, has been providing virtual soundscapes for two years 24/7 to elderly people suffering from Alzheimer disease. The configuration and sound processes of the apparatus are presented in relation to Alzheimer Disease care. Preliminary psychological and clinical observations are discussed in relation to dementia and to the activity of caring to evaluate the benefits of such a disposal in Alzheimer's disease therapy and in caring dementia.

Keywords: Sound design · Soundscapes · Alzheimer's Disease · Mental Health Care

1 Introduction

Nowadays, Alzheimer's disease (AD) is the main cause of dementia. AD usually starts slowly and gradually worsens over time with brain damages and main effects on memory, cognition and behavior: short-term and procedural memories are progressively affected until severely damaged, with severe spatio-temporal disorientation, when long-term memory becomes impaired later [1, 2]. When different hypothesis may explain the causes of AD, there is no known validated pharmacologic therapy. Nevertheless, the research effort present promising results. Non-drug therapies are adapted to flatten or compensate the AD effects by stimulating cognitive and sensorimotor activities such as

F. Voisin—Independant Researcher.

R. Kronland-Martinet et al. (Eds.): CMMR 2019, LNCS 12631, pp. 533–553, 2021.
https://doi.org/10.1007/978-3-030-70210-6_34

music practice and dance, which convene neural plasticity processes [3]. Playing and listening to music all together stimulate social forms of cognition, emotion and participate to re-entrainments of implicit and procedural memories affected by AD [4–6].

In the context of residential longterm care (EHPAD), these recent results encourage group musical activities led by music therapists in a variety of non-drug therapies for AD. Nevertheless, in such a longterm care context, musical activity may be too rare and the benefits for each victim of AD are difficult to evaluate individually, particularly when the latter may present different forms of dementia.

In addition, as a geriatrician may observe in his own practice in such a context [7] and as recent research suggest [8, 9], too little attention is generally given to sonic environment which include not only music but various oral communications, various noises, audio productions… And silences, all that actually defines the actual standard of a living and social place in residential longterm care. Some residential longterm care inner sound environment may not be adapted to AD victims: during the day, various caring activities mixed to loud radio or TV-shows play for a long time in individual or collective rooms make a continuous flow of information that has mostly become incomprehensible in the studied cases of dementia. At night, wanderings are usual in deep silence with no landmarks, no surprise, nowhere to go when the way back may be already lost in anonymous and closed halls, etc.

However, sonic interactions may be able to recall facts from subjects' trivial (long term) memory, and reach the subcortical circuits spared by the disease, in particular those that are related to emotion as well as hearing [10]. At a different level of cognition, the significance of sound for selfhood and social relationship for people living with dementia in longterm care facilities have been recently focused [11].

In 2016, an experimentation by Dr Jeannin with AD victims showed that some peculiar sounds can help recall long-term memories and emotions, when the listener's performance shows no relation with standard cognitive tests such as Mini Mental State Examination (MMSE) and Neuro-Psychological Inventory (NPI) [7]. Dr Jeannin also demonstrates how long such an experience of auditory memory with simple sounds implies a knowledge of the biography of the listener: this biographical knowledge may facilitate the activity of caring by, for instance, sparking some conversation. When sonic interactions may focus on the caring activity in a clinical perspective, a question may be: how would sound directly take part in AD caring?

It is with this prospect that the Grégoire Direz Residence (EHPAD) at Mailly-le-Château (France), has welcomed a sound design research action in their unit specially equipped for AD victims. The longterm care facility, its geriatric physician (Dr Pierre Jeannin) and its caregivers work together with a gerontologist (Prof. France Mourey) on scientific aspects while the sound designer (Frédéric Voisin) on conceiving and carrying out the sound device on location: the «Madeleines sonores» [12].

In a clinical perspective, we presumed that from a functional and systematic point of view, not only music but every sound may involve various cognitive and emotional circuits [13, 14]. Our hypothesis was that as soon as emotions and long-term memory are still strong in later stages of AD—when alexithymia appears late [1], not only music but any sound, if well chosen sounds, may participate in the care of patients with AD: being in situ (i.e. on location), attention, social processes as well as emotion—i.e. some ability to spark motion—can be called upon as much through the music as from a variety of familiar or merely recognized sounds. Where, when and how sounds occur seem to be relevant questions to AD and dementia in a longterm care facility: the acoustic environment has to be designed for the residents and caregivers [8, 9] and, insofar as it is heard or even listened to, it has to form a soundscape according to the International Organisation for Standardisation (ISO) definition [17]. In other words, from a sound design perspective and to the extent that our approach differs from music therapy for Alzheimer's disease since we do not consider music in its most common acceptance, we suggest considering that soundscapes, as long as they are specifically designed for patients with AD, may not only participate in the quality of life, but also in their care from a therapeutic perspective[1].

2 Designing Soundscapes for Alzheimer's Disease Victims

We suggest designing soundscapes adapted not only to different stages of dementia due to AD, i.e. to different mind states and beliefs, but also to physiological effects of aging such as a visual and hearing impairments, altered movement control, relative perceptions of time, etc.

Considering ecological aspects of soundscapes and theoretical frameworks devoted to soundscapes and mental health [8–12], and rare references to some experiments on environmental sounds for AD victims (when starting the project, see discussion below) [10, 14], we decided at first to shape the time and space of the Alzheimer's Unit and, then, to focus on anxiety phenomena that a sound environment may generate in certain conditions, particularly with elderly people.

After observations a few days and nights of observation in the Alzheimer's Unit, the sound designer decided to design the common areas of the Unit first, i.e. the places where residents spend most of their time standing, moving around, doing some activity or resting. The first sounds to be produced had to be congruent with the physical environment: big rooms, corridors, impersonal furniture, windows overlooking beautiful gardens and, in the distance, a village… They also had to be congruent with the immediate perception and beliefs the residents may have, residents who are affected by (various forms of) dementia but who also bravely bear the various marks of now ancient times! To address the various perceptual disorders of residents (vision, audition, proprioception), the sound designer started by reinforcing the reality of the immediate environment and its neighbourhood from both an ergonomic and ecological perspective. This is the context in which, afterwards, sounds were supposed – tactfully – to encourage each one's imagination of former memories, collectively as well as individually, ordinary as well as extraordinary. This was achieved by means of reterritorialised sound samples through a realistic staging.

---

[1] Considering here the term "therapeutic" in its definition from Ancient Greek which refers to «the art of giving a care» (θ ε ρ α π ε υ τ ι κ η). On the subject of intentionality, it seems interesting to note that the French terms "soigner" (to care) and "songer" (to think), which have been used in many spellings in Old French, probably have a common Latin origin (cf. https://www.cnrtl.fr/etymologie/songer, last accessed 2020/5/7).

A great variety of sound effects may partake in the staging of different sound realities and their modeling. With that prospect, we suggest understanding the notion of sound effect with an emphasis on a logic of meaning, between the cause and the event itself, "in a dimension that is altogether that of event and of situation", through the "demonstration of a phenomenon that supports the [assumed] existence of the object" [18]. Therefore, the staging of this particular hospital space, that has become the canvas of a "film for the ear", must be as much part of the scripting as of the content of the generated sound flows. By the way, the digital audio processing used in the actual disposal are not numerous: some peculiar synthesizers and peculiar sound players with volume controls, fading, filters and a reverb. On the contrary, the logical and stochastic effects are much richer and are the subject of the original computer coding.

In the map above (see Fig. 1), sounds produced from realistic sources from outside are supposed to be welcome in such a hospital's closed space: at its extreme borders, synthesized sounds of (virtual) bells give night and day to the listeners the (real) hours… or a landmark, as well as a short but regular game for cognitive stimulation (counting the strokes). In the patio, a granular audio synthesizer produces a continuous but varying waterfall sound, congruent with the beautiful but silent view, when the windows cannot be opened for security reasons.

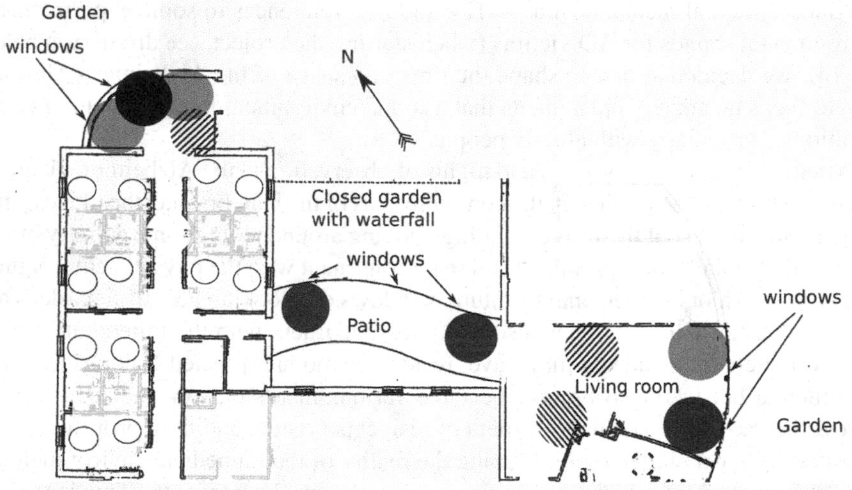

Fig. 1. Layout of the loudspeakers in the common spaces of the Alzheimer's Unit: 1) the broadcasting points of the landmarks: bells and waterfalls (black circles), can also play geophonic and biophonic sequences; 2) the broadcasting points of sounds for geophony or biophony and occasional human sonic activities from outside (grey circles); and 3) the broadcasting points of human audio activities, mostly from inside (dashed circles). The bedrooms have two broadcasting points each (smaller empty circles): only six of them are shown on this map.

This very first signals appear to be strong enough as landmarks to allow some algorithmic variations, depending on a mix between the actual and virtual place, on both the weather and the rhythm of the caring activity: when the sound quality of the waterfall or of the bells can change according to the outside temperature, or to the amount of humidity in air, their loudness intensity varies according to the care activity as well as to the cosmological events. Periods of days and seasons are also marked by a variety of geophonic sounds such as rain and wind which vary according to the actual weather… On the biophonic side, animal populations and their audio activity also change according the actual season, weather and ethological data. In the same way, the biophonic production is in relation with the precise location of the broadcasting of sound: birds that might come – whether in reality or virtually – to the waterfall in the patio are not the same ones as those that can be heard in the little living room on the North side, neither are they the same as those that can be heard in the big living on the South side.

The time-length of the animal sound sequences is approximately twenty minutes long, depending on weather conditions. Their intensity and density, therefore the duration of silences, depend on season and weather. Thus different tones continuously blend while they «naturally» diversify, as the algorithm gives the sound of birds in the rain, that would be more often crows in winter and tits in spring. When the sonorous broadcasting through loudspeakers is allowed for by the layout, audio spatialisation effects may be produced, with moderation, to render movements coming from the wind, trees, birds, mammals…

Sounds that are distinctive to human activity, more variable and arbitrary, are broadcast in other (more infrequent) places of the common space. In the area of the dining room sounds may suggest meal preparation. In this case, aiming at realism, and especially at respecting a multimodal congruence (here audition vs. taste and/or vision), the choice of sound samples can be made consistent with the menu, which is online, or with the season and outdoor temperature. For instance, the sound of a pressure cooker become much more frequent in winter than in spring and, at the contrary of sounds of fried potatoes, etc.

Very simple, repetitive, soft and evocative sounds may have a soothing effect: an initial observation, along with the care team, showed that the warm, slow and regular sound of a grandfather clock's pendulum, slowed down to an every-two-second impulse, seems to ease the sleeping phases and allow for a better sleep, at least in common spaces. Such observations are still, at this point of experimentation, to be confirmed experimentally: the rooms are in the process of being empirically and progressively fitted with sound. We hope that, in the long run, such an experimentation may enable to elaborate a precise questionnaire, based – for example – on a guided listening of sounds which are defined beforehand, that better allows to characterize each resident's sensitivity to different sounds.

Each broadcasting point being independent, several sequences can partly overlap in various places. The number of simultaneous voices in the same location remains, however, voluntarily limited so as not to saturate the sound space, without, for that matter, preventing more or less fortuitous sounds meeting. Silences also allow, depending on what sounds are conjured up by the context, various effects that can concern sometimes a feeling of expectation (calls), at other times relief (response), mirroring the shape of a rhythm.

When the soundscapes broadcast in the common spaces take their inspiration from a shared reality, the design of sound atmospheres broadcast in private spaces (bedrooms) is personalized. For these, the design strategy consists to invoke the residents' episodic memory while avoiding to cause confused states that would take place in particular moments that the care team would help define. The choice of sounds and their staging here has to answer the congruence with a reality perceived in a state of dementia – which needs to be diagnosed in the best possible way – as well as the life story of the listener. We also have to admit that such diagnoses are not often enough made, with regards the evolution of the disease. Different protocols, based on the above-mentioned principles, are being considered.

Extreme attention is given to the sound pressure intensity with a concern for the continuously exposed audience. Calibrated measures of acoustic pressure are underway. At day time, in the common spaces that are the noisiest, the acoustic pressure produced is unevenly distributed. Periods of silence (the acoustic pressure being of roughly 30 dBA) are frequent, except in the patio that overlooks the inner garden and its waterfall whose sound is continuous, though variable during long periods depending on time and weather conditions (minimum pressure of roughly 40 dBA). From the little living room on the north side, some sounds are broadcast loud enough to be heard as we arrive from the corridors that lead to it. In this more isolated place than the others, that leads to meditation or strolling, periods of silence alternate with active periods (with an acoustic pressure of 70 dBA and peaks at 80 dBA). Until now, as confirmed by the written notes taken by the care team, voiced complaints from residents have never been about sound pressure. On the contrary, it even seems that over time, sounds tend to not be noticed consciously, at least by the health care workers. As a result, the general sound pressure has even been reinforced in agreement with the caregivers and the physician, in particular to compensate for the residents' eventual hearing loss.

3 Digital Architecture for Live Soundscapes

The soundscapes are systematically generated and mixed in real-time using a distributed architecture with a principal generator that can be described as a server hosting the sound database and a set of routines periodically executed by its operating system scheduler (the «Soundscape generator», in Fig. 2) that can be described as a server hosting the sound database and a set of routines periodically executed by its operating system scheduler[2]. These routines, written in Lisp language and Unix-like shell scripts, compute different kinds of mapping, empirically developed, relevant to the environmental data as modelled, to its inner virtual population and to individual data (biographies). They finally control 24 on-board computers[3] fixed in the ceiling of the common and private spaces and hosting their own digital signal processing (DSP) and loudspeakers (the «Players», in Fig. 2).

All the soundscapes are generated in real-time as a remix of short sound samples (lasting from a few seconds to a few dozens of seconds) and using realistic sound synthesizers models specially adapted from [19]. The sound samples, specially recorded or adapted from open sound collections to represent various places, activities, animals

[2] Cf. Cron programs in Unix-like operating systems (see: https://en.wikipedia.org/wiki/Cron).

[3] All computers operating systems are GNU-Linux based. The on-board ARM based computers are Raspberry Pi3-B + with audio boards IQaudio Pi-DigiAMP + and in-ceiling 6.5″ loudspeakers QI 65C/St by QAcoustics (70 Hz to 16 kHz ± 3 dB, up to 90 dBA max pressure level). DSP is built using Pure Data open-source software [24].

and machines from the 40's to the 60's, are retrieved from a large database with thousands of items indexed by myself. Periods of silence between sound samples or synthesizers are more or less short and always irregular. They define the density of virtual events that occur depending on each resident's sensitivity and the general context: according to daytime periods, the year, the care provided, etc.

In the individual rooms, the soundscapes are rendered using two equivalent monophonic loudspeakers placed across the room, one close to the window and the other facing the bed. The activation of the soundscapes entirely depends on the explicit approval of whom concerned: the individual, himself, herself or their family when he or she cannot agree for clinical reasons and, obviously, by the caring team (doctors, psychologists, nurses).

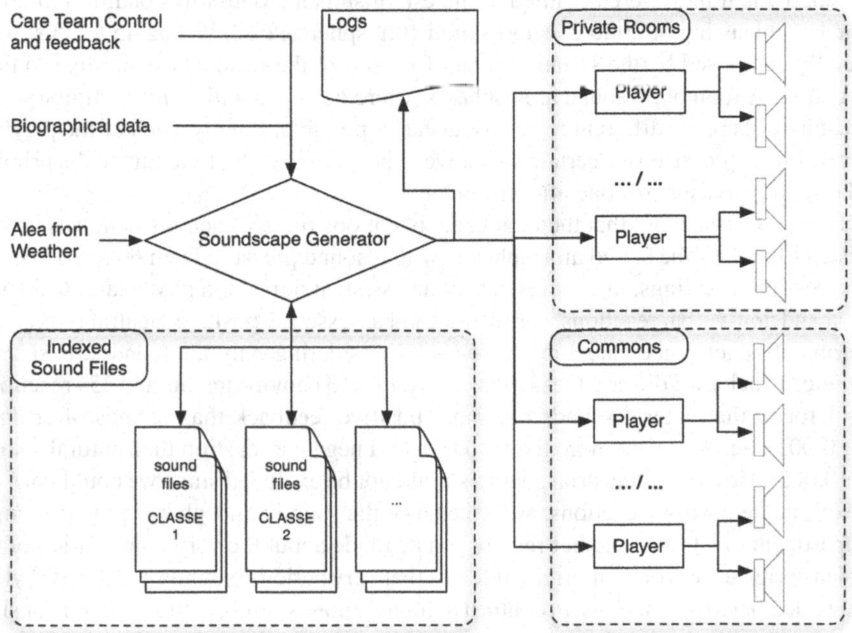

Fig. 2. A Digital architecture for the «Madeleines Sonores».

All hi-level instructions, play-lists, sound filenames, pressure levels, etc. are systematically locally logged. The overall disposal can be remotely controlled and monitored thru a standard secured connection (SSH) on internet, using any Unix-like terminal. Confidentiality is ensured in particular by the entire anonymity of the digitized data).

4 Personalized Sound Atmospheres for Individual Care

On the occasion of a clinical neuropsychology study undertaken in 2020[4], we decided that, in addition to the soundscapes broadcasted in the common areas 24/7, individualized sound diffusion should be limited only to the time of individual care in the morning and,

[4] Thanks to Mélinda Cherruault-Anouge, Master student in neuropsychology and clinical psychology at Lumière University Lyon 2 (Laboratoire des Mécanismes Cognitifs).

possibly, for falling asleep at bedtime. This decision is also consistent with the observations made regarding the effects of the system on health care practices, as discussed below.

A protocol for the clinical evaluation of the effects of such individualized sound diffusion on each of the 14 residents with Alzheimer's disease has been developed[5] and has begun to be implemented[6]. Our working hypotheses were essentially based on the reminiscence processes, on the one hand, and of core affect, arousal and appraisal [14, 20] on the other, the latter being considered as reflecting to reflect the most fundamental dimensions underlying emotional states [21].

A first step was to evaluate the effects on each resident of different soundscapes specially chosen to evoke an ancient period of their lives, as reported in a questionnaire submitted when they were admitted to the establishment. With this condition in mind, a playlist consisting of 20 to 25 short sound atmospheres, each lasting 45 to 75 s, were specially composed by the sound designer for each of the residents, according to their life-course. A total of 36 sound atmospheres where designed with some common sound atmospheres kept for different residents, as far as possible. Finally, each of the playlists has been arranged to have a certain evocative coherence in order to facilitate the priming of the sound atmospheres one after the other.

Then, after checking that their ear canal is not obstructed, each resident was invited to listen to each of the sound atmospheres, with a sound pressure from 60 to 70 dB, and to express their feelings, in the presence of an assistant nurse or a physician. Resident's verbal and non-verbal reactions were scored and assessed as positive, neutral or negative in terms of beneficence (see Table 1 below). Considering only all sound atmospheres presented to at least 4 different residents, i.e. a total of 31 environments and 254 reactions, it was found that natural sounds had more positive feedback than sounds of artifacts ($p < 0.001$), and these are more likely to trigger a negative reaction than natural sounds ($p = 0.002$). However, industrial sounds should not be excluded since we could miss out on exploitable positive reactions, as for instance the sound atmosphere in the passenger compartment of a train. Another remark can be made about the very composition of the ambiences regardless of their origin. It seems that very periodic sounds with a fast rhythm do not elicit positive reactions, in contrast to monotonous sounds with a moderate or slow tempo, such as the sound of waves or a train. These observations about the periodicity of sounds related to AD certainly require further study on core affect in relation to appraisal, as suggested other studies [8–10, 16].

Finally, we note that among the ten or so atmospheres that significantly elicited the most positive feedback, half of these atmospheres elicited a negative or even very negative reaction, or no reaction at all, from one or two different people. This is the case of the farmyard waking up and for the see waves, with many positive reactions but a negative reaction from one of the residents when, for the same person, the sound of the

[5] On the advice of the "Emeraude 58" Ethics Committee seized in March 2020 (Emeraude 58, 49 Ter rue des Hôtelleries, 58400 La Charité sur Loire, France — website: https://www.emeraude-58.com, last visited in may 2020).

[6] Unfortunately the application of this protocol was suspended during the covid-19 health crisis, which is why we present here only preliminary results. In addition, one resident did not take part in the experience because of his state of health.

Table 1. Quality of 13 residents' reactions of the sound atmospheres. Ratings range from black (detrimental effect) to orange (beneficial effect), with an X for a neutral reaction and a blank cell when a not submitted atmosphere.

Sound atmospheres	Qualities of residents' reactions												
Pigeons of Paris													
Cattle market													
Pastoral with cuckoo			X										
Wake up at the farm												X	
Horses that go by and hail													
Church bells												X	
See waves													
A calm street in Paris												X	
Purring cat		X			X								
Sound of rain	X								X			X	
Jean Gabin is talking												X	X
In the train							X						X
A dog barks in the distance						X			X				
Lapping of the lake				X						X			
Canoeing	X												
Small creek	X			X	X							X	
Calm wind	X											X	X
Curtains in the theatre								X					
Steam locomotive	X												
Simmering dish					X								
Manual coffee grinder					X				X	X			
Carpenter's work									X				
Playtime at school			X										
Tractor passing					X								
Chimney fire					X			X			X		X
Crickets				X	X		X	X		X		X	
In the chef's kitchen	X							X			X		
At the market							X		X		X		
Sewing machine	X				X				X				
Airport ambiance (60's)													
In the subway (60's)								X		X		X	
Cocotte-minute		X											
Typewriter													X
Rural watch													

rain had a positive effect. Thus the design of sound environments dedicated to individual care, even if it is explicitly inspired by the life experiences of each patient, requires prior and systematic experimentation with the people concerned.

5 Preliminary Observations About Behavioral Disorders

As part of the clinical trial protocol described above, a voluntary interruption of the virtual soundscapes in the common areas of the Alzheimer Unit welcoming 14 residents was carried out for three weeks (21 days, from February 17 to March 8, 2020)[7]. This interruption of the soundscapes caused an increase in the activity of the healthcare team, as reported by the nurse manager about an increase in behavioral disorders among the residents.

A lexical analysis of the anonymous so-called "transmission" reports—which are usually and systematically carried out by the caregivers—made possible to assess more precisely the evolution of behavioral disorders. As shown in Table 2 below, the daily frequency of the lexical forms used by the Medical-Psychological Assistant (MPA) during the interruption of sound broadcasting, compared to those recorded during the

Table 2. Variations of lexical forms extracted from the MPA transmission reports when the virtual soundscapes were carried out from the Alzheimer Unit, in comparison with a period when virtual soundscapes were broadcasted (English equivalents to French lexical forms are in parenthesis).

Rank	Lexical form	Variation	Rank	Lexical form	Variation
1	asthéni* (astheni*)	1467%	16	couché (lying awake)	284%
2	tape* (hit*)	1243%	17	mécontent (dissatisfied)	236%
3	réveill* (awake)	795%	18	déambul* (wander*)	198%
4	agit* (agitation)	721%	19	trouve* (find*)	147%
5	difficile (hard)	571%	20	agress* (agressiv*)	124%
6	énerv* (excit*)	571%	21	allong* (lying down)	124%
7	violen (violen*)	571%	22	apais* (relax*)	124%
8	relev* (get up)	515%	23	cri* (scream*)	124%
9	emport* (rage*)	348%	24	frapp* (strik*)	124%
10	évit* (avoid*)	348%	25	renvers* (spill*)	124%
11	griff* (scratch*)	348%	26	répliqu* (rispost*)	124%
12	lent* (slow*)	348%	27	triste (sad)	124%
13	opposant* (opposing)	348%	28	verbalis* (verbaliz*)	124%
14	partir (leave)	348%	29	altération (alteration)	100%
15	vomi* (vomit)	348%	30	angoiss* (anxiety/anxious)	100%

[7] The restoration of the soundscapes was carried out one week before the start of the containment imposed by the covid-19 crisis.

immediately preceding period (47 days, from January 1st to February 16), demonstrates an increase in the lexical forms used to describe behavioral disorders.

Reports related to asthenia has become 14 times more frequent, words describing slowness 3 times more frequent and wandering 2 times more frequent. Reports related to agitation and aggressive behavior was both much more numerous and significantly more frequent. The daily frequency of words used to report hits went up 12 times, awakening 8 times, agitation 7 times, etc. And, as shown in Fig. 3 below, reported aggressive behaviors increased significantly as soon as the sound broadcast was discontinued, even if reports are totally missing for two days at the beginning of this period.

Of course, a clinical evaluation of the beneficial effects of the device on the behavioral disorders of residents with AD must show opposite results. The hypothesis that the diffusion of soundscapes reduces behavioral disorders remains to be proven. The clinical evaluation protocol is already planned to be developed for this purpose. Although such mining of data from the staff's reports was not originally planned, it not only corroborates the observations made by the Coordinating Physician, but also appears to be a valuable indicator in the clinical assessment of the effects of sound environment.

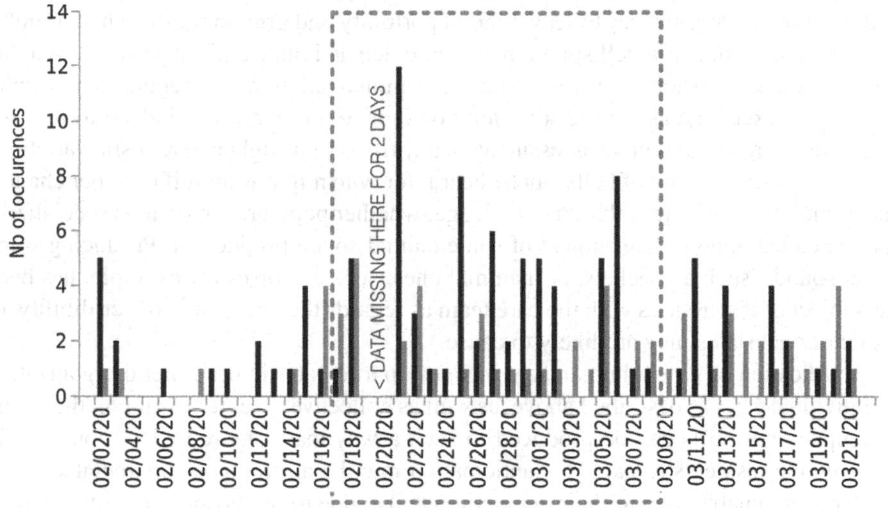

Fig. 3. Evolution of the number of instances of lexical forms denoting agressive behavior (black columns) and depressive behavior (grey columns) in the observations noted by the medical-psychological assistant. Dotted lines in the graph mark the interruption of the audio broadcast, from February 17th to March 8 included. Data are missing on 18 and 19 February (only) due to medical-psychological assistant absence.

Missing data for two days at the beginning of the soundscape interruption draw our attention to the need to involve all staff in the process of the protocol. In this case, we assume that the absence of data is only due to the absence of the medical-psychological assistant. Nevertheless, reports noted from psychologists, nurses and auxiliaries can complement those of the MPA. The actual data also focus our attention on the need to extend observations at night: for instance, if lying awake and wandering has been reported twice as often during the day time, it may be assumed that more instances would be made if some reports were made at night, when there are usually fewer caregivers.

6 Soundscapes for Caregivers

Obviously, some sounds that are part of the soundscapes can cause difficulties in relation to states of dementia. In particular with off-field sounds, when the perception of some sounds implies as a reflex the viewing of their origin, their separation from their real or imaginary cause may create confused states: to avoid such a case, the help of a caregiver is useful to explain the origin of such a sound and to finally have—as expected—some conversation that situates the sound.

Then, conceiving a sound environment and its dynamics necessarily involves the health care team. Sound must help and support caring activity, not interfere with. It may help the patient in directly addressing him or her while addressing the care team as well. With their assent and their complicity, oral conversations may be engaged in and sounds adopted. For example, in the very first days following the beginning of the setup (in July 2018), nursing auxiliaries asked me for the new and virtual bell tower placed in the commons areas never to leave: the opportunity and ergonomics of such a multi-functional sequence of a bell sound, repeated twice an hour (at 2′ interval), 24 h a day allows to mark a territory, to recall an hour common to all, to be the regular opportunity for a social exchange as well as a training of short-term memories, indeed to become part of spontaneous cognitive assessment, at any time. And slight and realistic variations in the synthesized sound of bells can be heard, for who might want it if only per chance. Furthermore, more or less shared knowledge, whether popular, personal or specialized, may be called upon on the subject of some animal sound production. Producing some insect sounds, such as crickets, or mammal ones, such as horses for example, has been the subject of discussions with the care team as regards their realism[8], the cridibility, or the emotional states they are likely to cause.

Sonification of virtual human activities may participates in the general organization of individual care, as described above, as well as collective care: for example, the sound accompanying meals can be produced in such a way that it more or less consciously prepares the residents to eat. This anticipation may be all the more appreciated when residents are unable, due to their dementia but also due to the hospital facility context, to know that it is time for dinner. Such an effect is most certainly welcome when it contributes to the support of demented people in the absence of any other clue that would be obvious and familiar to them, in a hospital context.

In complement to the study of the effects of individualized soundscapes in individual care must be validated, as part of the clinical protocol envisaged above, the effects of the device on the caregivers have been the subject of another study.

In this perspective, we undertook a psycho-sociological study on the links between sonic environment, the soundscapes, and care. In a first step, after a review of the scientific

---

[8] During this experiment, we noted that the question of the realism of sounds arises as much for sampled sounds as for synthesized sounds. As mentioned above, this complex issue stems both from the temporal dynamics of the sounds, from the context of their diffusion and from the state of mind in which they are perceived.

literature on the subject of caregiving in longterm care facilities [8, 9, 16], and having observed the sound system in its context, a student in social psychology (the second author) drew up a guide for interviews with the Alzheimer Unit's caregivers. Secondly, on the basis of this interview guide, he conducted 4 interviews of an average duration of 30 min each. He then carried out a thematic analysis [22, 23] on each interview to understand the central topics related to the soundscapes, and extracted the most recurring and important words according to their themes. With the different themes that emerged from these interviews, he created questions related to each of the themes, so that the questionnaire adheres as closely as possible to the reality on the ground in relation to the soundscapes, as described by the caregivers. And finally, the questionnaire was slightly reworked by the team in order to correspond even better to the empirical study of the effect of the soundscapes on the relationship between caregivers and their residents. The resulting questionnaire, consisting of 44 questions, is set out below (see Annex: A questionnaire for caregivers on soundscapes at work).

This questionnaire has been presented first (in French) in june 2020 to the caregivers, with a short written introduction that preceded it to set the context for this research and the necessary precautions. Because of staff turnover, only half of the ten caregivers working in the Alzheimer's Unit responded anonymously to the questionnaire. An analysis of the responses on a case-by-case basis allows an initial assessment of the effects of the «Madeleines sonores» on the caregivers[9] in the Alzheimer's unit.

On the issue of well-being at work, among the 5 caregivers, 2 of them admit to a rather good well-being at work, and 3 to a rather average well-being. Only one considers that the soundscapes seem to make his work more pleasant, when the others consider that the soundscapes seem to have no impact. Four caregivers nevertheless find the sounds moderately pleasant or rather pleasant and, at least, never unpleasant or only slightly unpleasant for four of them, and moderately unpleasant for one. On the issue of the care practice, two caregivers consider that the soundscapes help them from time to time, more rarely for two others and never for one of them. But four out of the five caregivers seem to see rather positive effects of the sound device in the long term, and one of them envisages future effective work in connection with.

At this stage of the project, a longitudinal survey seems to be essential in order to assess the effects of the soundscapes over time, particularly when individualized sound diffusion at the time of individual care in each single room has become systematic. It would also be relevant to compare the results of the caregiver/resident relationship in specialized units of the same type in different facilities with the same sonic device. These initial observations also show the need to raise awareness of the noise environment among health care professionals [8, 9], which will necessarily have to be done as soon as sound broadcasting is systematically part of care in single rooms.

7 Discussion

The work presented here is only the beginning of a long conceiving process in an emerging activity within the field of sound design, mental health and care. Its actual state is an

[9] The garegivers who responded to the questionnaire were a nurse, a nurse assistant or a medical-psychological assistant.

action-research led in the fields of sound art, human and health science, and technology. This work, which began in July 2018 and was presented and published for the first time in October 2018, now benefits from contemporary and surprisingly comparable work carried out as part of the Acusticare project in Belgium, which elaborates on some of the aspects addressed in the present study [12].

Our first observations are encouraging: the behavior of part of the residents suggest that not only the residents appreciate the variety of the soundscape in the common spaces and, as we observed for ourselves, they tend to place themselves closer to the audio sources to recollect or to meditate, whether consciously or not (see Fig. 4 below). Then,

Fig. 4. A resident is meditating at the closest place to the audio source mounted at the ceiling.

in common spaces, while the design of the soundscape must adapt to the architecture and to the neighbourhood of the facility, the spaces and furniture must be arranged to facilitate their perception and appropriation by the residents.

So far, it has only been possible to assess the effects of the soundscape in common areas on residents indirectly and empirically. The lexical analysis of systematic (and anonymous) reports from the caregivers about behavioral disorders observed among the residents seems to be an interesting indicator within the framework of a protocol for the evaluation of the effects of the sound device. Its relevance remains to be evaluated experimentally. The questionnaire carried out for the caregivers indicates a moderate and more rarely good contribution of the soundscape to the quality of care. Certain details certainly remain to be done in the generation of the soundscape and its algorithms. The demands of the "public" are all the greater as it is exposed all day and all year round. The variety of sounds can always be enriched, the mixing effects multiplied and the spatialisation games of the sounds developed. However, these initial observations need to be validated with a larger number of care personnel, and they suggest that the appropriation of this device in the practice of care may require specific training.

In this case, particular attention must be paid to the choice of sound atmospheres. Indeed, although the population of residents actually studied is still small, it appears that although natural source sounds (geophonic or biophonic) are best appreciated by residents when broadcast individually, this is not the case for all natural source sounds even though they are supposed to evoke an ancient period of the resident who is listening to them. When certain sounds resulting from human artifacts (anthropophony) are likely to create a positive reaction.

Finally, there is also the question of assessing the quality of the reactions to the sound atmospheres, whether beneficial, neutral or detrimental to the residents. As with some neuropsychological evaluation tests, such an assessment may require the observation of at least two observers. As noted by the geriatrician with whom we have collaborated, reactions that may be judged as negative may, on the contrary, prove beneficial in that they recall an old memory that is part of the patient's identity. It is up to the caregivers to be able to address such reactions in their own care practice.

At this time, the whole plan of action is operating as a multimedia work of art for sound and computer that falls within the altogether artistic, scientific and clinical perspective that federates different social and economic players in a humanistic dynamic of research and innovation.

Acknowledgement. We are particularly thankful to Dr Pierre Jeannin for his benevolence, his logistic and voluntary support, and of course to the charity Castel-Mailletaise that welcomed this project, and the care team that is closely involved in it.

Annexe: A Caregiver's Questionnaire on Soundscape at Work

Here is a series of questions about you, your activity at work and your perception of the sound device «Madeleines sonores». Please answer carefully and as spontaneously as possible: there are no right or wrong answers, just tick the box that corresponds to what you think.

	Very low	Low	Neither high nor low	high	Very high
1. I am in spirits...	☐	☐	☐	☐	☐
2. My confidence in the future is generally...	☐	☐	☐	☐	☐

	All the time	A lot	Sometimes	Rarely	Never
3. I feel stressed by my work...	☐	☐	☐	☐	☐
4. I feel like I break down because of my job...	☐	☐	☐	☐	☐
5. I feel burned out by my work...	☐	☐	☐	☐	☐

	Very hard	Hard	Neither easy nor hard	Easy	Very easy
6. Concerning the efforts of reflection or attention that I have to provide my work is...	☐	☐	☐	☐	☐
7. Concerning the efforts to control my emotions (don't get angry, get along with others, ...) my job is...	☐	☐	☐	☐	☐

	Annoys me	Doesn't suit me	I deal with	Suits me	Contrib- utes to my fulfilment
8. The physical characteristics of my work environment (space, sound, light, etc.)...	☐	☐	☐	☐	☐
9. The layout of the place where I work	☐	☐	☐	☐	☐
10. The general appearance of the places where I work...	☐	☐	☐	☐	☐
11. Overall, my physical work environment...	☐	☐	☐	☐	☐

	Upset me	Doesn't suit me	I deal with	Suit me	Contributes to my fulfil- ment
12. The interest I find in my work...	☐	☐	☐	☐	☐
13. The variety of what I do in my job...	☐	☐	☐	☐	☐
14. The usefulness of what I do...	☐	☐	☐	☐	☐
15. The diversity of contacts that my work brings with it	☐	☐	☐	☐	☐

	Not a all	Rather no	Neither yes nor no	Rather yes	Ut- terly
16. I like my job.	☐	☐	☐	☐	☐
17. Overall, I feel good about my work environment.	☐	☐	☐	☐	☐

	Not at all	Rather not	Modera-tly	Very much	Strongly
18. How enthusiastic are you about the "madeleines sonores" project ?	☐	☐	☐	☐	☐
19. The new system of "madeleines sonores" recreates everyday sounds, are you receptive to this type of sound environment ?	☐	☐	☐	☐	☐
20. To what extent is the "madeleines sonores" system soothing for you ?	☐	☐	☐	☐	☐
21. In your opinion, to what extent is the "madeleines sonores" system soothing for residents?	☐	☐	☐	☐	☐
22. As a whole, do you like the "madeleines sonores" system?	☐	☐	☐	☐	☐
23. In its entirety, is the "madeleines sonores" system pleasant for residents ?	☐	☐	☐	☐	☐
24. As a whole, is the system of the "madeleines sonores" unpleasant for you ?	☐	☐	☐	☐	☐
25. In its entirety, is the "madeleines sonores" system pleasant for residents ?	☐	☐	☐	☐	☐

	Never	Rarely	Some-times	Often	Over and over
26. Overall, do the "madeleines sonores" help you in your work and in your relationship with the residents ?	☐	☐	☐	☐	☐
27. How often do you interact with residents in relation to the "madeleines sonores" ?	☐	☐	☐	☐	☐
28. How often do you interact with residents based on their own reactions to the "madeleines sonores" system ?	☐	☐	☐	☐	☐
29. In your opinion, to what extent do the boadcast sounds arrive at the right times of the day ?	☐	☐	☐	☐	☐

	Never	A quarter of the time	Half the time	Three quarters of the time	Always
30. In your opinion, how much time in the day should be set aside for silence to improve your relationship with the resident ?	☐	☐	☐	☐	☐

	Detrimental	Rather negative	Neutral	Rather positive	Positive
31. What are the effects of the "madeleines sonores" system on your appeasement in your work (stress reduction) ?	☐	☐	☐	☐	☐
32. What effects does the new sound system have on the working atmosphere within the team (e.g. through jokes or discussions related to "madeleines") ?	☐	☐	☐	☐	☐

	Not at all	Mostly no	Neutral	Mostly yes	A lot
33. In your opinion, does the design of "madeleines sonores" contribute to your motivation in your work ?	☐	☐	☐	☐	☐

	Detrimental	Rather negative	Neutral	Quite beneficial	Beneficial
34. In your opinion, what will be the effects of using the "madeleines sonores" system as a tool in the future?	☐	☐	☐	☐	☐

	Strongly disagree	Rather disagree	Indifferent	Rather agree	Strongly agree
35. The "madeleines sonores" are useful.	☐	☐	☐	☐	☐
36. The sounds of the "madeleines sonores" reduce residents' anxiety or nervousness.	☐	☐	☐	☐	☐
37. The sounds of the "madeleines sonores" are artificial.	☐	☐	☐	☐	☐
38. With the "madeleines sonores", I feel better in my work.	☐	☐	☐	☐	☐
39. The sounds of the "madeleines sonores" help me in my relationship with the resident.	☐	☐	☐	☐	☐
40. The "madeleine sonore" system improves my daily work.	☐	☐	☐	☐	☐
41. The "madeleines sonores" are a beneficial innovation for our work.	☐	☐	☐	☐	☐
42. In order to help and soothe, the sounds of "madeleines sonores" should rather be sounds of nature.	☐	☐	☐	☐	☐
43. In the future, I would like to use the "madeleines sonores" as a tool.	☐	☐	☐	☐	☐

44. Please note below any comments you would like to make about this questionnaire or the "madeleines sonores" system.

References

1. Eustache, F.: Langage, vieillissement et démences. In: Eustache, F., Lechevalier, B. (eds.) Langage et Aphasie, Séminaire Jean-Louis Signoret. De Boeck Université, Bruxelles (1993)
2. Dubois, B., et al.: Revising the definition of Alzheimer's disease: a new lexicon. Lancet Neurol. **9**, 118–127 (2010)
3. Chancellor, B., Duncan, A., Chatterjee, A.: Art therapy for Alzheimer's disease and other dementias. J. Alzheimer's Disease **39**, 1–1 (2014)
4. Guétin, S., et al.: Effect of music therapy on anxiety and depression in patients with Alzheimer's type dementia: randomised, controlled study. Dement. Geriatr. Cogn. Disord. **28**, 36–46 (2009)
5. Moussard, A., Bigand, E., Clément, S., Samson, S.: Préservation des apprentissages implicites en musique dans le vieillissement normal et la maladie d'Alzheimer. Revue de neuropsychologie **18**, 127–152 (2008)
6. Mofredj, A., Alaya, S., Tassaioust, K., Bahloul, H., Mrabet, A.: Music therapy, a review of the potential therapeutic benefits for the critically ill. J. Crit. Care **35**, 195–199 (2016)
7. Jeannin, P.: Projet Hippocampe: les madeleines sonores (essay). https://fredvoisin.com/IMG/pdf/pierre_jeannin-projet_hippocampe.pdf. Accessed 7 May 2020
8. Van den Bosch, K.A., Andringa, T.C., Başkent, D., Vlaskamp, C.: The role of sound in residential facilities for people with profound intellectual and multiple disabilities. J. Policy Pract. Intellect. Disabil. **13**, 61–68 (2016)
9. Devos, P., et al.: Soundscape design for management of behavioral disorders: a pilot study among nursing home residents with dementia. In: Proceedings of the INTERNOISE 2018 Conference, Chicago, USA, pp. 26–29 (2018)
10. Nagahata, K., Fukushima, T., Ishibashi, N., Takahashi, Y., Moriyama, M.: A soundscape study: what kinds of sounds can elderly people affected by dementia recollect? Noise Health **6**, 63 (2004)
11. Graham, M.E.: Re-socialising sound: investigating sound, selfhood and intersubjectivity among people living with dementia in long-term care. Sound Stud. **5**(2), 175–190 (2019)
12. Voisin, F.: Designing virtual soundscapes for Alzheimer's disease care. In: Aramaki, M., Derrien, O., Kronland-Martinet, R., Ystad, S. (eds.) Proceedings of the 14th International Symposium on Computer Music Multidisciplinary Research (CMMR 2019), pp. 222–231. The Laboratory PRISM, Marseille, France (2019)
13. Westerkamp, H.: Linking soundscape composition and acoustic ecology. Organised Sound **7**(1), 51–56 (2002)
14. Andringa, T.C., Lanser, J.J.: How pleasant sounds promote and annoying sounds impede health: a cognitive approach. Int. J. Environ. Res. and Public Health **10**, 1439–1461 (2013).
15. Schafer, R.M.: The Tuning of the World. Knopf, New-York (1977)
16. Devos, P., et al.: Designing supportive soundscapes for nursing home residents with dementia. Int. J. Environ. Res. Public Health **16**(24), 4904 (2019)
17. ISO 12913-1: Acoustics—Soundscape—Part 1: Definition and Conceptual Framework; Technical report. International Standardisation Organisation, Geneva, Switzerland (2014)
18. Augoyard, J.F., Torgue, H.: Sonic Experience: A Guide to Everyday Sounds. McGill-Queen's Press-MQUP, Montreal (2014)
19. Farnell, A.: Designing Sound. The MIT Press, Cambridge (2010)

20. Smith, C.A., Lazarus, R.S.: Appraisal components, core relational themes, and the emotions. Cogn. Emot. **7**(3–4), 233–269 (1993)
21. Russell, J.: Core affect and the psychological construction of emotion. Psychol. Rev. **110**, 145–172 (2003)
22. Osgood, C.E.: The representational model and relevant research method. In: de Sola Pool, I. (ed.) Trands in Current Analysis, pp. 33–88. Universty of Illinois Press, Urbana (1959)
23. Negura, L.: Content analysis in the study of social representations (L'analyse de contenu dans l'étude des représentations sociales), SociologieS (2006). Theory and research, https://journals.openedition.org/sociologies/993. Accessed 7 May 2020
24. Puckette, M.: Pure data. In: Proceedings of the International Computer Music Conference (ICMC 1996), pp. 269–272. ICMA, Hong-Kong (1996)

ARLooper: A Mobile AR Application for Collaborative Sound Recording and Performance

Sihwa Park(✉)

Media Arts and Technology, University of California, Santa Barbara, Santa Barbara, CA 93106, USA
sihwapark@mat.ucsb.edu

Abstract. This paper introduces ARLooper, an AR-based iOS application for multi-user sound recording and performance, that aims to explore the possibility of using mobile AR technology in creating novel musical interfaces and collaborative audiovisual experience. ARLooper allows the user to record sound through microphones in mobile devices and, at the same time, visualizes and places recorded sounds as 3D waveforms in an AR space. The user can play, modify, and loop the recorded sounds with several audio filters attached to them. Since ARLooper generates the world map information through iOS ARKit's tracking technique called visual-inertial odometry which tracks the real world and a correspondence between real and AR spaces, it enables multiple users to connect to the same AR space by sharing and synchronize the world map data. In this shared AR space, the user can see each other's 3D waveforms and activities, such as selection and manipulation, as a result, having a potential of collaborative AR performance.

Keywords: Augmented reality · AR · Mobile music · Mobile instrument · Mobile performance · Collaboration

1 Introduction

Advances in mobile computing and technology have affected the field of computer music in terms of the exploration of musical interfaces and performance paradigms. Before smartphones with touchscreens emerge, the relevant beginning of this history can be referred to a body of pioneering work that experimented the active use of mobile phones, which were just ordinary consumer electronic devices, in creating interfaces for musical performance that allow audiences to participate in a part of performance or in making new forms of musical instruments that expand performers' musical expression. Along with these experiments and applications of mobile computing in music technology, a concept of mobile music was also suggested by Gaye et al. [12], emphasizing the mobility and collaborative aspects of mobile music.

R. Kronland-Martinet et al. (Eds.): CMMR 2019, LNCS 12631, pp. 554–562, 2021.
https://doi.org/10.1007/978-3-030-70210-6_35

Since the emergence of smart devices such as smartphones and tablets, there has been various research that explores possibilities of using consumer electronic devices as New Interfaces for Musical Expression (NIME) by utilizing diverse sensors embedded in these devices, such as GPS, cameras, gyroscopes, accelerometers, touchscreens, wireless sensors, etc., expanding the field of mobile music technology. Many of examples are well documented by Essl et al. [11].

Mobile augmented reality (AR) technology has also evolved in this context of mobile computing [2]. Especially, advances in tracking physical objects and environments without any prior information and fusing virtual content with the real world without 2D fiducial markers or images have been significantly contributing to mobile AR research since seminal works of researchers including Davison [9], Klein and Murray [14] were introduced. Agilely adopting these advancements, major companies such as Google and Apple have been leading mobile AR by releasing and updating their own development frameworks, e.g., ARCore and ARKit, for mobile AR applications that can be running on commonly accessible devices. The markerless mobile AR, however, has been yet not enough explored in the fields of mobile music technology and NIME. It has a potential to devise novel and collaborative interfaces for musical creativity in an AR space and create unique musical experience for both performers and audiences.

As an initial study on this promising exploration, this paper introduces ARLooper, an AR-based mobile interface for multi-user sound recording and performance. ARLooper allows the user to record sound through microphones in mobile devices and, at the same time, visualizes and places recorded sounds as 3D waveforms in an AR space. The user can play, modify, and loop the recorded sounds with several audio filters attached to them. ARLooper employs ARKit's tracking technique, which is called visual-inertial odometry to track the real world and a correspondence between real and AR spaces by combining information from camera sensor data with the device's motion sensor data, so that the multiple users of ARLooper can connect to the same AR space in which the recorded sounds are shared and can see each other's activities, such as selection and manipulation of sound waveforms.

2 Literature Review

Considering that ARLooper tries to investigate the possibility of state-of-the-art mobile AR in designing mobile music interfaces, it is reasonable to review the context of prior research for mobile phone-based music making and collaborative performance.

In addition to Levin's Dialtones (A Telesymphony) [17], which is considered as one of the pioneering works harnessing the mobile phones of audiences as part of musical performance, early attempts to re-purpose a variety of built-in sensors of consumer mobile electronics and to utilize the mobility of the devices for NIME have been actively made and well documented by several researchers [10,12].

On top of the focus of using mobile devices in making musical interfaces, paradigms for collaborative mobile music-making and performance also have been explored and suggested. Tanaka [24] created an early system with PDAs of which performers collaborate in controlling audio streams over mobile wireless networks, thereby creating a piece of music together in real time. Performers of CaMus2 [21], which used the built-in camera of mobile phones to track maker sheets as visual references for musical interaction, shared their interaction parameters through Bluetooth communication to control and generate sound by transforming sensor data into MIDI messages. While these systems created sound in remote computes, the Stanford Mobile Phone Orchestra (MoPho) [18] took the advantage of iPhone's capability in synthesizing sound in local mobile devices by running the custom software MoMu Toolkit, introducing a new paradigm for mobile phone performances from their own perspective. Alessandro [3] and Lee et al. [16] also demonstrated a possibility of collaborative music-making with mobile devices by utilizing networking functionality. Salazar et al. [22] documented various performances using Auraglyph, a sketch gesture-based iPad music application, as the extended paradigm of mobile music performance.

It is also noteworthy that AR technology has evolved to support environments for Computer Supported Cooperative Work (CSCW). Since the first collaborative AR projects, such as the Studiersube [23] and Shared Space [5], emerged in the mid-nineties, there have been a lot of examples of collaborative AR applications that support remote or co-located user contexts. Some of the remarkable examples are well-reviewed by Zhou et al. [25]. One of the interesting advances in AR is that fundamental environments for collaborative AR research have changed from surface projection-based systems, e.g., Rekimoto and Saitoh's Augmented Surfaces [20], to handheld or wearable devices with see-through displays, e.g., Emmie [7] and ARTHUR [6], thereby enabling 3D virtual information to be overlaid anywhere in the real world in ways that would be otherwise impossible.

Compared to the abundant AR research for CSCW, there are a few AR research works that have been conducted for Computer Mediated Musical Collaboration (CMMC) [1]. Poupyrev et al. [19] presented Augmented Groove, an AR musical interface using head-mounted displays and 2D fiducial markers, of which the users play music together by controlling physical cards where 3D virtual controllers and images are attached to. Similar to Augmented Groove, Berry's The Music Table [4] used marker cards as musical sources in a compositional process in which the user arranges the cards on a table. While these systems work in a way that the users share the physical markers on a single table, YARMI [15], a multi-user, networked musical instrument, operates on multiple tabletops based on a client-server architecture, presenting a shared AR space for performers as the concept of a synchronized ensemble. The reacTable [13] that uses networked multiple tabletop interfaces for collaboration also could be considered as one of AR musical systems in terms of augmenting physical objects with virtual information, although it only overlays 2D graphics below the objects placed on tabletop screens. Clouth [8] suggested an AR version of the reacTable that works on mobile devices, attempting to use AR as a control mode for the reacTable but without a feature for collaboration.

3 Design

3.1 ARKit and AudioKit

ARLooper is an iOS application developed with ARKit[1], Apple's AR development toolkit for iOS devices, and AudioKit[2], a sound synthesis, processing, and analysis framekwork for the operating systems running on Apple's products, such as iOS, macOS and tvOS.

(a) Recordingn UI

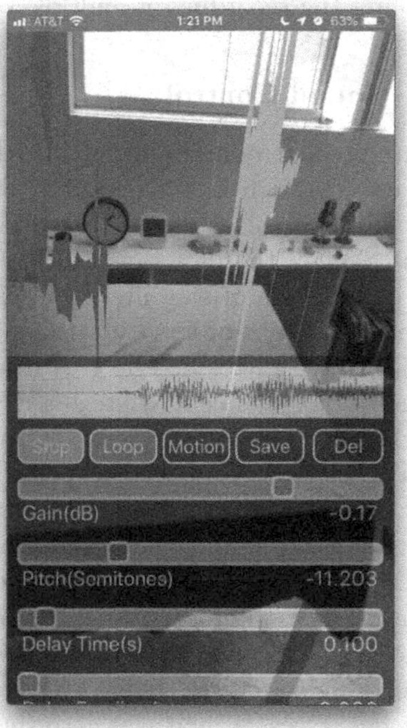

(b) Control UI

Fig. 1. Screenshots of ARLooper. (a) A sound being recorded is visualized as a 3D waveform at the screen center. The recording button at the bottom also indicates it is currently recording. (b) When a waveform is tapped, a bounding box appears and the sound control GUI is presented. The cyan color of the waveform means the waveform is currently playing. (Color figure online)

[1] https://developer.apple.com/arkit/.

[2] https://audiokit.io/.

3.2 AR-Based Sound Recording and Visualization

ARLooper allows the user to record sound incoming through the microphone of a device in real time by presenting a recording GUI button as shown in Fig. 1a. The recording interaction is similar to 3D line drawing with real-time audio data. When the user presses the button, it immediately begins to record a sound and at the same time, visualizes the currently recording sound as a 3D waveform in an AR space in a way that the height of 3D waveforms represents amplitudes of recorded sound samples. While the recording is in progress, the x and z positions of the 3D waveform are determined by the position of the device which the user holds and moves around in a space. As a result, the user can perform 3D drawing interaction in an AR space by easily understanding this real-time audio recording and 3D visualization. This recording process continues until the button is pressed again and is possible to repeat upon the user's intent, enabling the recording of multiple sound sources being used later.

3.3 Sound Control

For audio control and playback, ARLooper uses AudioKit's various sound filters and effects, such as pitch shifter, delay effect, low pass filter, reverb, tremolo, and gain control. A set of these filters and effects are attached to each recorded sound. When the user taps a 3D waveform, ARLooper presents a GUI to control parameters of the filters and effects. The GUI also has a conventional 2D waveform viewer of the recorded sound and buttons for playback, looping, and deletion (See Fig. 1b). The GUI disappears when the user re-taps the 3D waveform or taps a space where no AR waveform object exists. If a waveform is selected, its bounding box is shown in orange color to indicate that the waveform is selected. To distinguish the control status of a waveform, three colors are uses: red, orange, and cyan. Red means the availability of the waveform. Orange means it is selected, whereas cyan color represents it is playing.

On top of the GUI-based sound manipulation, ARLooper also provides a gesture-based interaction method on a touchscreen, thereby supporting direct audiovisual manipulation. It has two types of gestures: pinch and rotation. When the user pinches a selected 3D waveform inward or outward, the size of the waveform decreases or increases correspondingly. Along with the visual size change, its sound gain is simultaneously modulated in the same manner. In case of rotation, the pitch of the sound shifts according to the rotation of the waveform. As a result, with the gesture interaction, the user can more intuitively control the gain and pitch of a sound, not through GUI sliders.

3.4 Collaborative AR Mode

ARLooper utilizes ARKit's tracking technique, visual-inertial odometry that fuses information from camera sensor data with the iOS device's motion sensor data. It recognizes feature points in a visible scene captured from the camera of the device and infers the device's position and motion in a space. Based on

(a) iPhone user's screen (b) iPad user's screen

Fig. 2. Multi-user mode. (a) The iPhone user can see the iPad user's activity along with shared waveforms. (b) The iPad user is playing one of the waveforms.

this process, ARKit generates a world-mapping data called ARWorldMap that can be used as a frame of reference in building a shared AR space for a multi-user AR experience. Using the iOS Multipeer Connectivity framework that supports the discovery of nearby devices and the data communication among the devices, ARLooper follows two steps to create a shared AR space among users. First, one user starts as a host with ARLooper, finds a reference plane, and places a virtual plane with additional adjustment. Other users then join a shared AR space as guests by requesting and obtaining an ARWorldMap instance from the host user. Here the guests have to find a similar view of the frame of reference in the space to re-localize to the received AR world map.

Once the AR session for multiple users is established, it is possible to share virtual content or information about user interaction. When a user creates a 3D waveform, its visual data is shared with others in real time so that everyone in the same AR space can see each other's recording activity (See Fig. 2). Also, information about the user's manipulation such as playback, parameter control, and gesture interaction is synchronized among all participants in the session. One important aspect to be considered in this shared sound AR space is a protocol for isolating the manipulation of a waveform according to who is a dominant user; ARLooper allows only one user to play or control a waveform by preventing others from having access to operate the waveform at the same time until the user deselects the waveform.

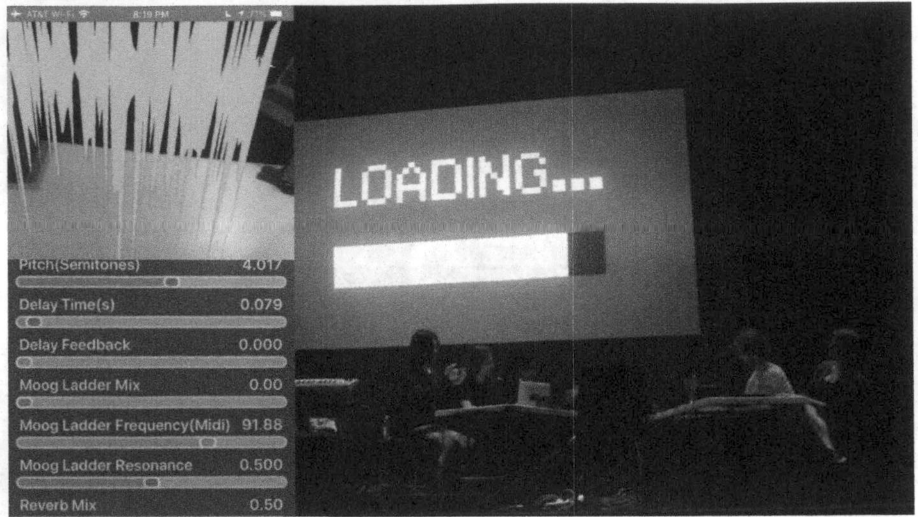

Fig. 3. ARLooper in the UCSB CREATE Ensemble performance, "Loading... (2018)". In this performance, I used ARLooper in single-user mode. The left is a screenshot of ARLooper running on my iPhone. The right is an image of the CREATE members improvising with their own instruments.

4 Discussion and Future Work

As the initial prototype of a long-term project, ARLooper shows the possibility of exploiting the recent mobile AR technology in creating novel musical interfaces and collaborative audiovisual experience in an AR space. As shown in Fig. 3, I have tested and used the single-user mode of ARLooper in a couple of actual music performances as a member of the UCSB Center for Research in Electronic Art Technology (CREATE) Ensemble[3]. ARLooper, however, still needs to be more stabilized in sharing real-time visual and sound data to use the multi-user mode in music performances. Considering that AR-based musical interfaces and performances are not common, this research should consider relevant use scenarios and a performance paradigm. Especially, since the AR technology is affected by a lighting condition in tracking objects from captured images, finding the best stage setup for performances will be one of the essential aspects to be deliberated. For a better user experience, it is also necessary to improve user interaction in manipulating AR waveforms. For example, a feature for loading and placing pre-recorded audio files in an AR space, an additional UI for selecting the playback range of a recorded sound in a 2D waveform viewer, and multi-touch based direct parameter control over AR waveforms. Reflecting that AR waveforms are positioned in a physical space, it would be interesting to spatialize recorded sounds in playback according to the direction and distance between AR waveforms and users. Also, it would be worth attempting to find an aesthetically

[3] http://www.create.ucsb.edu/.

better way to visualize recorded sound in 3D. Finally, it is imperative to conduct quantitative and qualitative user tests of ARLooper which will give invaluable insights to improve its usability.

References

1. Arango, J.J., Giraldo, D.M.: The smartphone ensemble. Exploring mobile computer mediation in collaborative musical performance. In: The New Interfaces for Musical Expression Conference, Brisbane, Australia, pp. 61–64 (2016)
2. Arth, C., Grasset, R., Gruber, L., Langlotz, T., Mulloni, A., Wagner, D.: The history of mobile augmented reality. arXiv preprint arXiv:1505.01319 (2015)
3. d'Alessandro, N., Pon, A., Wang, J., Eagle, D., Sharlin, E., Fels, S.: A digital mobile choir: joining two interfaces towards composing and performing collaborative mobile music. In: the International Conference on New Interfaces for Musical Expression. University of Michigan, Ann Arbor (2012)
4. Berry, R., Makino, M., Hikawa, N., Suzuki, M.: The augmented composer project: the music table. In: the 2nd IEEE and ACM International Symposium on Mixed and Augmented Reality, pp. 338–339. IEEE (2003)
5. Billinghurst, M., Weghorst, S., Furness III, T.: Shared space: an augmented reality interface for computer supported collaborative work. In: Proceedings of CVE, vol. 96 (1996)
6. Broll, W., et al.: ARTHUR: a collaborative augmented environment for architectural design and urban planning. J. Virtual Reality Broadcast. **1**(1), (2004)
7. Butz, A., Hollerer, T., Feiner, S., MacIntyre, B., Beshers, C.: Enveloping users and computers in a collaborative 3D augmented reality. In: The 2nd IEEE and ACM International Workshop on Augmented Reality, pp. 35–44. IEEE (1999)
8. Clouth, R.: Mobile augmented reality as a control mode for real-time music systems. Universitat Pompeu Fabra, Barcelona (2013)
9. Davison, A.J.: Real-time simultaneous localisation and mapping with a single camera. In: ICCV, vol. 3, pp. 1403–1410 (2003)
10. Essl, G., Rohs, M.: Interactivity for mobile music-making. Organ. Sound **14**(2), 197–207 (2009)
11. Essl, G., Lee, S.W.: Mobile devices as musical instruments - state of the art and future prospects. In: Aramaki, M., Davies, M.E.P., Kronland-Martinet, R., Ystad, S. (eds.) CMMR 2017. LNCS, vol. 11265, pp. 525–539. Springer, Cham (2018). https://doi.org/10.1007/978-3-030-01692-0_35
12. Gaye, L., Holmquist, L.E., Behrendt, F., Tanaka, A.: Mobile music technology: report on an emerging community. In: the International Conference on New Interfaces for Musical Expression, Paris, France, pp. 22–25 (2006)
13. Kaltenbrunner, M., Jorda, S., Geiger, G., Alonso, M.: The reacTable*: a collaborative musical instrument. In: The 15th IEEE International Workshops on Enabling Technologies: Infrastructure for Collaborative Enterprises, pp. 406–411. IEEE (2006)
14. Klein, G., Murray, D.: Parallel tracking and mapping for small AR workspaces. In: The 6th IEEE and ACM International Symposium on Mixed and Augmented Reality, pp. 1–10. IEEE Computer Society (2007)
15. Laurenzo, T., Rodríguez, E., Castro, J.F.: YARMI: an augmented reality musical instrument. In: the New Interfaces for Musical Expression Conference, Pittsburgh, PA, USA, pp. 268–269 (2009)

16. Lee, S.W., Srinivasamurthy, A., Tronel, G., Shen, W., Freeman, J.: Tok!: a collaborative acoustic instrument using mobile phones. In: the International Conference on New Interfaces for Musical Expression. University of Michigan, Ann Arbor (2012)
17. Levin, G.: Dialtones (A Telesymphony) (2001). http://www.flong.com/projects/telesymphony/. Accessed 05 Mar 2019
18. Oh, J., Herrera, J., Bryan, N.J., Dahl, L., Wang, G.: Evolving the mobile phone orchestra. In: The International Conference on New Interfaces for Musical Expression, Sydney, Australia, pp. 82–87 (2010)
19. Poupyrev, I., et al.: Augmented groove: collaborative jamming in augmented reality. In: ACM SIGGRAPH 2000 Conference Abstracts and Applications, vol. 17, no. 7, p. 77 (2000)
20. Rekimoto, J., Saitoh, M.: Augmented surfaces: a spatially continuous work space for hybrid computing environments. In: the SIGCHI Conference on Human Factors in Computing Systems, pp. 378–385. ACM (1999)
21. Rohs, M., Essl, G.: CaMus 2: collaborative music performance with mobile camera phones. In: The International Conference on New Interfaces for Musical Expression, pp. 190–195 (2007)
22. Salazar, S., Pipepenbrink, A., Reid, S.: Developing a performance practice for mobile music technology. In: The International Conference on New Interfaces for Musical Expression, pp. 59–64. Virginia Tech, Blacksburg (2018)
23. Szalavári, Z., Schmalstieg, D., Fuhrmann, A., Gervautz, M.: "Studierstube": an environment for collaboration in augmented reality. Virtual Reality **3**(1), 37–48 (1998)
24. Tanaka, A.: Mobile music making. In: The International Conference on New Interfaces for Musical Expression, Hamamatsu, Japan, pp. 154–156 (2004)
25. Zhou, F., Duh, H.B.L., Billinghurst, M.: Trends in augmented reality tracking, interaction and display: a review of ten years of ISMAR. In: The 7th IEEE/ACM International Symposium on Mixed and Augmented Reality, pp. 193–202. IEEE Computer Society (2008)

Singing in Virtual Reality with the Danish National Children's Choir

Stefania Serafin, Ali Adjorlu(✉), Lars Andersen, and Nicklas Andersen

Multisensory Experience Lab, Aalborg University Copenhagen, Copenhagen, Denmark
{sts,adj}@create.aau.dk

Abstract. In this paper we present a Virtual Reality (VR) system that allows a user to sing together with the Danish National Children choir. The system was co-designed together with psychologists, in order to be adopted to prevent and cope with social anxiety. We present the different elements of the system, as well as a preliminary evaluation which shows the potential of the system as a tool to help coping with social anxiety.

1 Introduction

Fig. 1. A panoramic view of the studio at Danish Radio in Copenhagen, Denmark, where the recordings took place.

Social anxiety concerns the fear and subsequent avoidance of social situations. In a person suffering from anxiety, this negatively affects the participation in social situations (e.g., attending school), the forming of social relationships, and overall reduces quality of life. If the anxiety persists through adulthood, a person is less

R. Kronland-Martinet et al. (Eds.): CMMR 2019, LNCS 12631, pp. 563–574, 2021.
https://doi.org/10.1007/978-3-030-70210-6_36

likely to become a contributing member of society by finishing an education and getting a job. As a consequence, people suffering from anxiety tend to isolate themselves and live a life of lost opportunities.

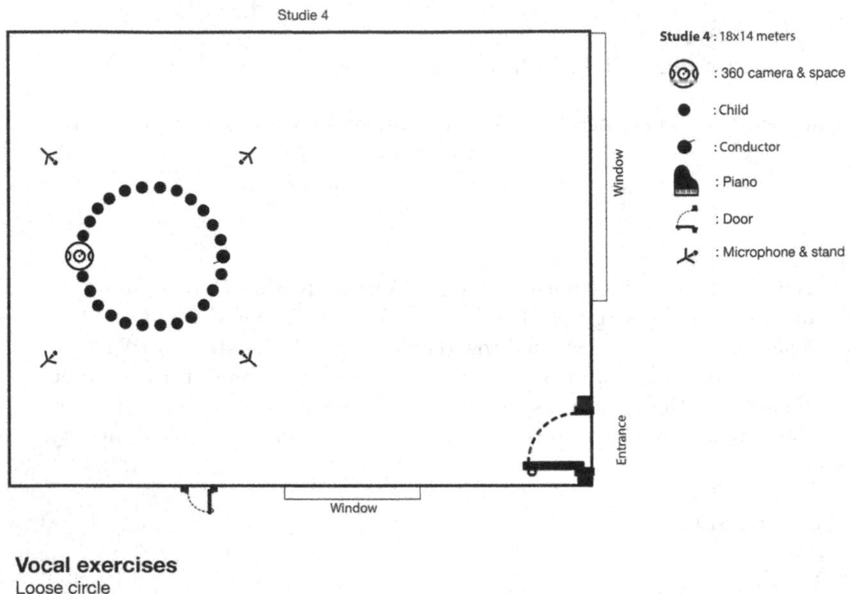

Fig. 2. The placement of camera, microphone and children during the vocal exercises: children placed in a loose circle.

A commonly used method for treating phobia and anxiety is exposure therapy, where the patient is exposed to the object that induces the anxiety. Exposure therapy has been shown to be effective with anxiety disorders, and was first used for social phobia in the mid-1980s. This is due to the fact that exposure to realistic social situations is very difficult to conduct and organise [2].

Lyneham and colleagues have developed a cognitive behavioral therapy tool for children called Cool Kids [9]. Cool Kids Program is a scientifically based and effective anxiety treatment program. The program was developed in Australia and translated into Danish at the Anxiety Clinic for Children and Youth at Aarhus University. In a Cool Kids group course, children and parents are introduced to concrete methods and strategies that can make it easier to overcome and deal with anxiety in everyday life. Cool Kids Program is based on principles of cognitive behavioral therapy and can be implemented either individually or in groups with other children and their parents. The program has been developed throughout more than 15 years of research and has some evidences that a fraction of the children completing the program are diagnosis-free or markedly improved.

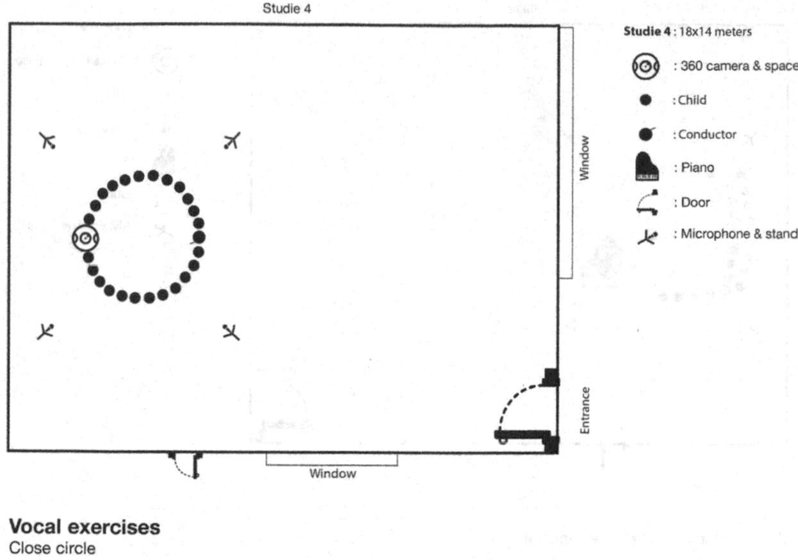

Fig. 3. The placement of camera, microphone and children during the vocal exercises: children placed in a closed circle.

Virtual Reality (VR) has become a popular platform used in interventions, and research has delivered successful results in areas including social and cognitive training exercises combined with exposure therapy [1,7,11,12]. While VR headsets are not in most homes currently, the development is going in that direction due to lower cost and wider availability.

The use of VR in the treatment of anxiety is grounded in emotional processing; fear memories can be constructed as structures that contain information regarding stimuli, responses and meaning [5]. VR is presumed to activate the fear structure by immersing the individual in the feared situation and to modify the fear structure through the processes of habituation and extinction.

Since the use of VR in social and cognitive training is a relatively new area of exploration, to our knowledge there are no applications to music or sound therapy for social anxiety. An exception is the work presented in [8].

Singing, and especially singing within a choir, can have psychological benefits for individuals with chronic mental health issues, with research indicating a reduction in anxiety and an increase in positive emotions and relaxation, which translates to maintained and extended mental well being [3,4]. However, empirical research in this area is in its infancy, with an acknowledged need for robust interdisciplinary studies [6]. From the technical perspective, no system exists that is capable of creating responsive 360° experiences, enabling to sing with a virtual choir and interact with a virtual audience. However, research exists into the technologies and principles enabling such a system. Recent advances allow for capturing and rendering 360° videos, boosting research in so-called

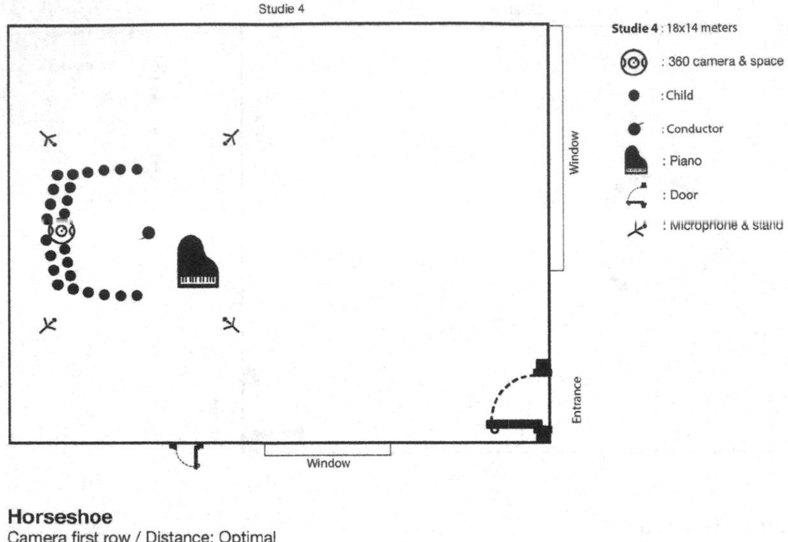

Fig. 4. The placement of camera, microphone and children while performing the songs.

cinematic VR. This includes surround visual displays as well as spatial sound, particularly important to direct user's attention to a specific locations of the screen [10]. Such solutions, however, have reduced interactivity, mostly limited to the possibility to turn the head in 360°. The full interactive potential of VR has usually been adopted using 3D graphics computer rendered scenes. In this paper, we present the first prototype of a VR exposure therapy system, which combines 360° video footage with the possibility of interaction and feedback. In the system, the users experience the venue of the original performance from the viewpoint of a singer, including visual and auditory feedback, and are able to hear themselves in that space as they sing live with the recorded performance. This system is intended to test the benefits of singing in a group in order to help coping with social anxiety. The system consists of a user singing while wearing an HMD.

2 Capturing the Choir

During the Spring 2019, we had the possibility of recording the Danish National Children choir in one of their studios, shown in Fig. 1. A subset of 25 children from the choir were recorded while performing a warmup session and singing two songs from the repertoire of a day called *Skolernessangdag*[1]. This day is an event where several danish schools, for a total of around 200.000 children, learn different traditional danish songs, and sing them all together while the Danish

[1] The material from the day can be found here: https://skolernessangdag.dk/.

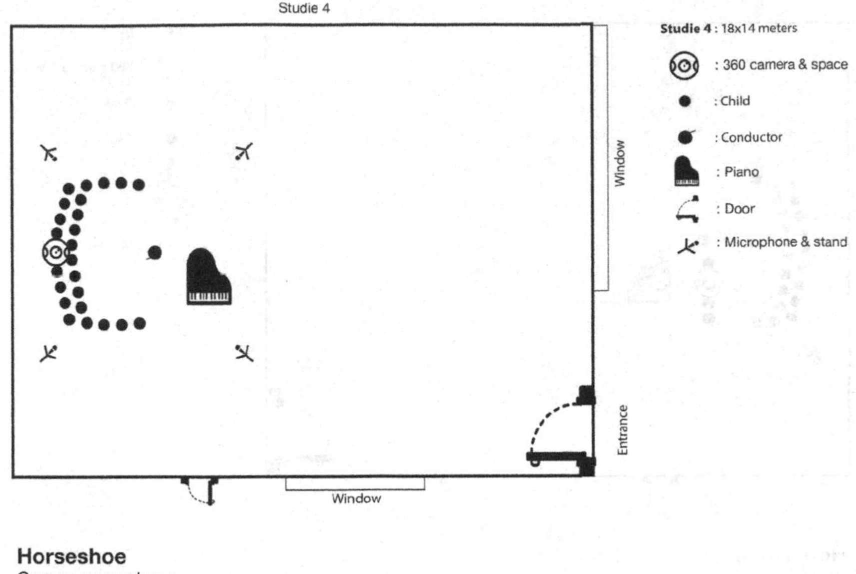

Fig. 5. The placement of camera, microphone and children while performing the songs.

National Children choir is streamed from the Danish radio concert hall. It is a very cozy event that promotes singing and being together.

We recorded the experience from different viewpoints, as shown in Fig. 2, 3 and 4, 5, 6. rated from inducing high anxiety towards inducing lower anxiety. Specifically, Fig. 2 and 3 show the position of camera, microphones and children during vocal exercises. As can be seen from the figure, the children were placed in a circle. Two scenarios were captured, from a first scenario where the camera was very close to the children, to another scenario where the camera was far from the children. The two scenarios represented a situation with higher and lower social anxiety respectively. The recordings consisted of capturing the vocal exercises that the children usually perform at the beginning of a session.

Figure 4, 5 and 6 show the placement of the children while performing two songs. Specifically, the chosen songs were two famous danish songs named *Hvis jeg var en cirkushest* and *Tarzan Mamma mia*. Three situations were captured, from a situation inducing less anxiety (with the camera placed in the second row and with a large distance from the other children) to a situation inducing higher anxiety (where the camera is placed in the first row and very close to the other children).

Visuals were captured using an Insta 360 Pro Camera, while the sound was captured by the ambisonic microphone Ambeo by Sennheiser, as well as clip mics placed on the conductor.

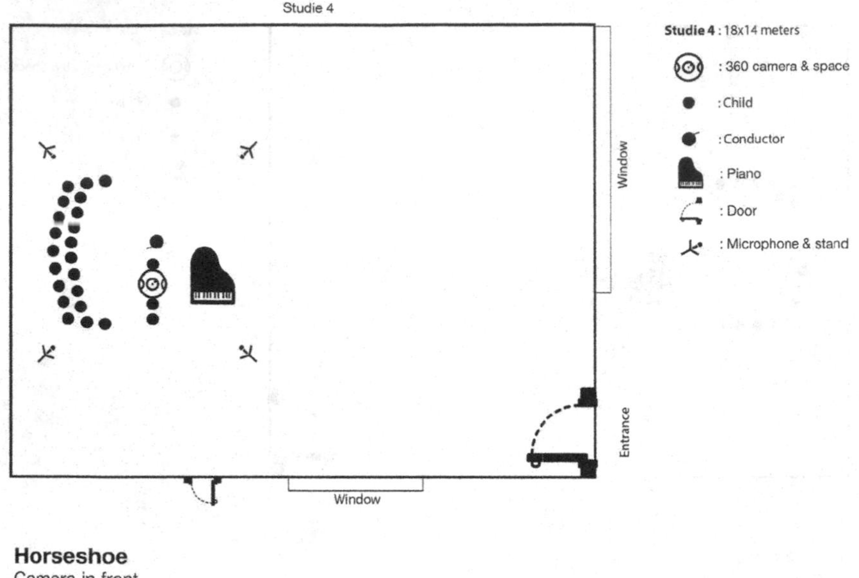

Fig. 6. The placement of camera, microphone and children while performing the songs.

3 Audio-Visual Rendering

The virtual reality experience consisted of the captured footage from the Danish national children choir, together with 3D rendered relaxation rooms.

The captured videos were rendered in Unity and delivered using an Oculus head-mounted display.

Figure 9 shows the 3D rendered relaxation spaces. The goal of these relaxation spaces is to design virtual environments where the child can go to and take a break from the singing experience, in case it becomes too overwhelming. The spaces were designed after consultation with a psychologist, who described the need to take a break from the experience when it becomes too overwhelming.

From top to bottom, left to right, the spaces show a beach, and empty and a filled room, and then a forest. The spheres that can be seen in the figure are the different cinematic singing experiences. Such experiences can be grabbed by the user using the Touch controllers from Oculus, and are ordered according to the level of anxiety they induce.

The user's singing is captured in real-time by a microphone, where is it processed by the reverberation characteristics of the desired simulated space (Fig. 7).

Fig. 7. A screenshot from the captured footage during the warmup exercises.

4 Evaluation

A preliminary qualitative evaluation of the system was performed with two psychologists using the Cool Kids method and two interns who had suffered social anxiety and therefore used the Cool Kids method. The goal of the evaluation was to test how a psychologist can work with the child in VR through three phases for exposure therapy (readiness, action, integration). The goal was to find design solutions for the phases. In the different phases there are also different design solutions to be found. The evaluation therefore tested: readiness phase, which belongs to a safe zone. This safe zone should help the children to relax and get ready for both VR and getting into a social scenario. For the psychologists they must be able to help the children relax and also choose which scenario to use played. This should lead on to a conversation topic on which functions the psychologist needs and how best to get the child to relax. Action phase, which belongs to the social scenarios. Here the different functionalities should be investigated. This space can be used by the psychologists to help them perform their work. For the children it is important to give them the commitment to participate and, if so, where their anxiety becomes too violent, they must be able to relax again. The sound in the action phase, which is being feedback to the player, must empower a child to sing further (Fig. 8).

The integration phase, which belongs to safe zone or outside VR. Here the psychologist should be able to talk with the child about the experience they have been through. The psychologist intends to use VR to integrate the experience into a positive way for the child.

Fig. 8. A screenshot from the captured footage during the performance of one song, with the camera placed on the second row.

5 Method

The test was set up as a role-playing game where the psychologist and the child come in VR through the developed prototype. The evaluation was a qualitative evaluation based on feedback from the users. We first gave the psychologists the opportunity to talk about how they perform exposure therapy, in order to compare traditional methods with our VR solution. Since think out loud does not work well with people who do not have experience with VR, because they may have trouble putting words on what they want, it is important to be able to ask questions while they are in VR, if they do not say anything for a while. This must be done without putting words into their mouths but hopefully starting a conversation about opportunities. The questions asked along the way were used as a springboard for a small conversation. By keeping it semi-structured, we could dive deeper into their thoughts and hopefully get them propose some solutions that would not otherwise have been said.

A joint discussion at the end, with all the test subjects, gave the participants the chance to talk about ideas, bouncing ideas between each other and gave us a chance to elaborate some of the things we ask about in the role-play scenario. Observations were taken along the way so that we have a basis for building questions in one joint discussion at the end. The observations looked at:

1. How could they use the digital space and integrate it into their daily process?
2. How will they interact with the system and with the child?
3. What do we expect them to do in relation to what they actually do?
4. What performance do they repeat?
5. What problems do they face?

Fig. 9. The four different relaxation environments built for the application.

The evaluation took place at the psychologists' clinic. A screenshot from the evaluation can be seen in Fig. 10. In the screenshot, one of the two psychologists is wearing an head mounted display from Oculus while experiencing the simulation in his office, and providing think aloud feedback.

When asked to describe an ideal relaxation room, the first subject, a 19 years old girl with previous experience in anxiety, said she would like a homely environment with toys and books.

She also commented how the beginning of the experience was too loud and should be fixed. She suggested to implement fading in and out amplitude curves.

The second test user, a psychologist from the clinic, started by describing the importance of gradual exposure therapy. He then commented on the content of the waiting room. He suggested a place with more lively actions, for example the beach could have a seagull, or the forest could have birds and insects. He liked the implementation of several options, since each child is different and likes different forms of relaxation.

The third test user, an intern at Cool Kids, suggested to have the relaxation room look like the cafe' from the clinic, in order to create a virtual safe and comfortable environment.

She also found that the different levels on anxiety worked, e.g., she could perceive the difference in anxiety between performing from the second row to being in front of the other children where you feel placed on the spotline.

The last subject was the head of the clinic. He stressed how it is important to create a plan that goes through different steps in order to reach the child's goal. Improvisation and deviation are expected and the psychologist is prepared to do so. This plan also helps both parties for the different phases, as there is an

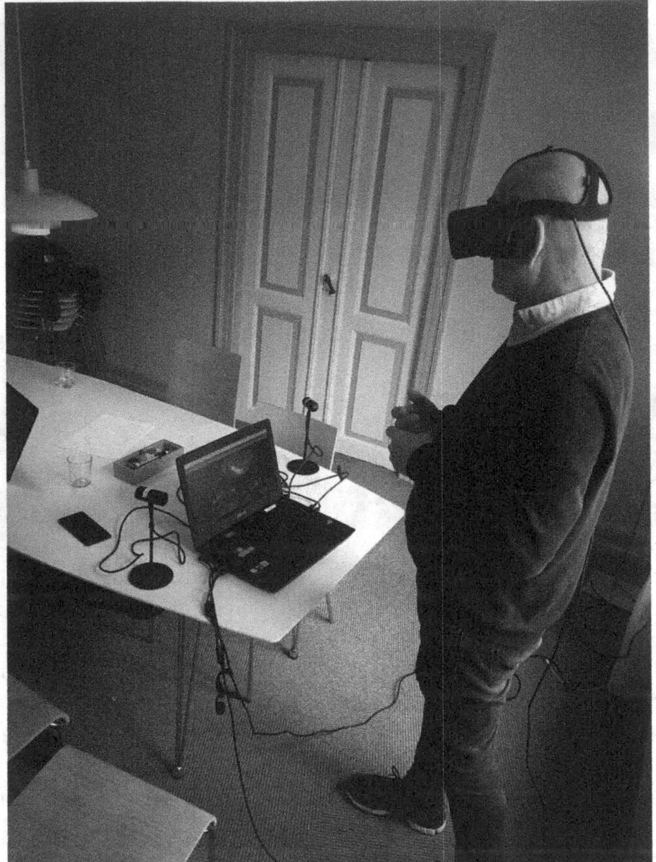

Fig. 10. One of the psychologists testing the application.

expectations on both sides what the current session is about - control is a key component from both parties.

Regarding the readiness room, he was impressed and liked the metaphor of the beach, a zen-like places where there is no to little interruptions. Each recorded session was represented as a tiny ball that can be interacted with, grabbed and thrown. It is a way to normalize what is about to happen, and gives a trust/interaction with the child. Expressiveness is a must in order to fully read the emotional and physiological state of the child, and if it's possible to transit to the next phase. Drawing, scales, or a dashboard to express themselves could be some possibilities. Visual expressive tool is a necessity, but should correlate to the surrounding environment. Simplistic seems to be a keyword for a readiness phase, where there is a possibility to reduce the incoming stimuli and find one self. Interaction is a necessity. Søren, the psychologist sees a lot of possibilities using just the first recordings over more sessions - inactive, active but only movement, active movement and singing. Then go to the next scene, where you are in the front row, do the same and go to the last position that is in front of the choir. Agrees there is an increasing social anxiety in the dataset A. Must be a possibility for the child to mark, point towards what can be a fearful factor. Time and time again it is necessary for the child to express their emotions and malaise. Complete control for the psychologist - play, pause, rewind, forwind etc. with the sessions, environment etc. Back and forth between scenes could also be a possibility. The child should not necessarily control the important, but should be able to express itself. Natural physiological body language.

Again as previously stated, it all depends on the child. Some might find it easier to integrate in VR, while others not so much. It is important to understand that this is a tool, and should not replace reality. Some evaluating tools in VR could be a fun way to try and integrate what we learned in the session.

6 Conclusion

In this paper, we presented a prototype and a primary evaluation of a VR experience that allows singing in a choir to prevent or help to cope with social anxiety. The purpose of this evaluation was to gather some information on how to further develop the application to make it more useful for professionals working with children suffering from social anxiety. During the evaluation, two clinicians and two interns at the clinicians who had suffered from social anxiety tried out the application and provided us with some valuable feedback.

The head of the clinic pinpointed the importance of enabling the opportunity to improvise during the VR exposure therapy, as he does during the traditional in-vivo exposure therapy sessions. One way to allow the clinicians to improvise during VR exposure therapy sessions is to let him pause, start or stop the application, as well as giving him the ability to change the volume of the choir members or the choir instructors. Additionally, the ability to change scenes can be added to the application, giving the psychologist even more control of his patients experience.

The psychologists also pointed at the importance of interaction between the psychologist and the patient during exposure therapy sessions. During the traditional in-vivo exposure therapy sessions, the psychologist is present and can communicate to the patient about the anxiety-inducing experience, guiding him in how to cope with the situation. In VR, when the patient is immersed in another environment using the head-mounted display, communicating with the outside world becomes less efficient. Therefore, future iterations of the application can try to bridge the communication gap between the psychologist and the patient when using the VR exposure therapy application.

Via a microphone, the voice of the psychologist can be broadcasted in the virtual environment, while the volume can be adjusted so that it is loud and clear for the user. It is even possible to create a version of the application where the psychologist can log in to the VR exposure therapy together with the patient using a head-mounted display where they both can see, talk to and interact with each others using their avatars. Future studies should investigate how to design VR exposure therapy interventions that provide the ability to control the sessions while enabling them to improvise. Interaction schemes required to achieve this must be intuitive as the clinicians should not spend their cognitive capabilities on figuring out how to interact with the program and instead use it to help their patients.

Acknowledgments. We would like to thank Susanne Wendt and Clara Smedegaard, conductors at Danish National children choir, and the children for preparing a dedicated rehearsal session and allowing us to record their rehearsal. We would also like to thank the psychologists from Cool Kids who provided us with design suggestions as well as dedicated time to test our prototype.

References

1. Anderson, P., Rothbaum, B.O., Hodges, L.F.: Virtual reality exposure in the treatment of social anxiety. Cogn. Behav. Pract. **10**(3), 240–247 (2003)
2. Butler, G.: Exposure as a treatment for social phobia: some instructive difficulties. Behav. Res. Ther. **23**(6), 651–657 (1985)
3. Clift, S., Hancox, G., Morrison, I., Hess, B., Kreutz, G., Stewart, D.: Choral singing and psychological wellbeing: quantitative and qualitative findings from English choirs in a cross-national survey. J. Appl. Arts Health **1**(1), 19–34 (2010)
4. Dingle, G.A., Williams, E., Jetten, J., Welch, J.: Choir singing and creative writing enhance emotion regulation in adults with chronic mental health conditions. Br. J. Clin. Psychol. **56**(4), 443–457 (2017)
5. Foa, E.B., Kozak, M.J.: Emotional processing of fear: exposure to corrective information. Psychol. Bull. **99**(1), 20 (1986)
6. Gick, M.L.: Singing, health and well-being: a health psychologist's review. Psychomusicol. Music Mind Brain **21**(1–2), 176 (2011)
7. Gorini, A., et al.: Virtual reality in anxiety disorders: the past and the future. Expert Rev. Neurother. **8**(2), 215–233 (2008)
8. Kearney, G., Daffern, H., Thresh, L., Omodudu, H., Armstrong, C., Brereton, J.: Design of an interactive virtual reality system for ensemble singing. In: Interactive Audio Systems Symposium, York, UK (2016)
9. Lyneham, H.J., Wuthrich, V., Rapee, R.M.: Cool Kids: Child & Adolescent Anxiety Program Adaptation for Supported Bibliotherapy Therapist Manual. Centre for Emotional Health (2010)
10. MacQuarrie, A., Steed, A.: Cinematic virtual reality: evaluating the effect of display type on the viewing experience for panoramic video. In: 2017 IEEE Virtual Reality (VR), pp. 45–54. IEEE (2017)
11. Opriş, D., Pintea, S., García-Palacios, A., Botella, C., Szamosközi, Ş., David, D.: Virtual reality exposure therapy in anxiety disorders: a quantitative meta-analysis. Depress. Anxiety **29**(2), 85–93 (2012)
12. Rizzo, A., Shilling, R.: Clinical virtual reality tools to advance the prevention, assessment, and treatment of PTSD. Eur. J. Psychotraumatol. **8**(sup5), 1414560 (2017)

Musical Interaction: Embodiment, Improvisation, Collaboration

Embodied Cognition in Performers of Large Acoustic Instruments as a Method of Designing New Large Digital Musical Instruments

Lia Mice(✉) and Andrew P. McPherson

Centre for Digital Music, Queen Mary University of London, Mile End Road, London E14NS, UK
{l.mice,a.mcpherson}@qmul.ac.uk
http://instrumentslab.org/

Abstract. We present The Large Instrument Performers Study, an interview-based exploration into how large scale acoustic instrument performers navigate the instrument's size-related aesthetic features during the performance. Through the conceptual frameworks of embodied music cognition and affordance theory, we discuss how the themes that emerged in the interview data reveal the ways size-related aesthetic features of large acoustic instruments influence the instrument performer's choices; how large scale acoustic instruments feature microscopic nuanced performance options; and how despite the preconception of large scale acoustic instruments being scaled up versions of the smaller instrument with the addition of a lower fundamental tone, the instruments offer different sonic and performative features to their smaller counterparts and require precise gestural control that is certainly not scaled up. This is followed by a discussion of how the study findings could influence design features in new large scale digital musical instruments to result in more nuanced control and timbrally rich instruments, and better understanding of how interfaces and instruments influence performers' choices and as a result music repertoire and performance.

Keywords: Embodied cognition · Digital Musical Instruments

1 Introduction and Background

When interacting with an interface not only does the performer move their body to control the interface, the interface design and affordances control the way the performer moves their body. This paper introduces The Large Instrument Performers Study, an interview-based study with performers of various large acoustic instruments, and discusses the results, analysed through the thematic analysis methodology. The study findings are analysed in terms of embodied music cognition, affordances and idiomatic writing to show ways that size-related

R. Kronland-Martinet et al. (Eds.): CMMR 2019, LNCS 12631, pp. 577–590, 2021.
https://doi.org/10.1007/978-3-030-70210-6_37

aesthetic features of large acoustic instruments shape the performer's choices while improvising, composing and performing repertoire.

Through elucidating the ways in which the size of large instruments influence performance, instrument designers can learn about the ways large instruments are more than small instruments scaled up, and consider the impact of size-related affordances when designing new instruments. Now that DMIs can be any shape and dimension, and performed with virtually any gesture, exploring the impact of instrument scale on performers choices is useful for Digital Musical Instrument (DMI) designers when deciding what size to create instruments. As music production increasingly takes place in the home (due to faster consumer computers capable of running professional grade digital audio workstations), there is a trend in commercial DMI design of scaling down instruments and interface dimensions, resulting in smaller and smaller 'desktop' instruments such as the Korg Volca series of miniature synthesizers. But what is lost when an instrument is scaled down? More research is needed to understand the true impact of an instrument's scale and dimensions on music creation and performance.

Leman's embodied music cognition theory provides an interesting framework for exploring the impact of an instrument's scale and dimensions on music creation and performance, arguing that our bodily interactions shape our perception of music [9]. In the context of musical instrument performance, the body's 'vehicle' for mediation is musical gestures, which *"have an important experiential component that is related to intentions, goals, and expression."* [10] Not only are musical gestures linked to musical intentions, they are also linked to cognitive processing of the sounds they create, and in this way physical interaction with instruments involving gesture/action consequences changes our performance gestures and choices, and therefore our thinking.

Expanding or contracting the physical dimensions of an instrument results in changes to the musical gestures. In the taxonomy of affordance theory [6,14,17], it could be said that the size of an instrument influences its affordances, that is the possibilities, such as the gestural language for performance. Additionally, as De Souza argues, affordances offer the performer 'distributed cognition' in that an instrument may 'know' things for the performer [5]. In this way, the performer does not need to know every detail about the instrument to play it. As Magnusson [11] illustrates, the piano knows a pitch class represented by each of its keys. By only offering the tones created by pressing the piano keys, and not all the microtones in between, the embedded knowledge contained in a piano forms a 'script' that influences compositions created on the instrument. It follows that 'distributed cognition', or as Magnusson [12] calls it 'material epistemology', not only offers affordances but also constraints, and it is therefore through both that instruments elicit influence on performer's choices.

Tuuri et al. [18] argue that an interface enforces 'experiential control' on a user through 'push' effects (in which the user feels their tacit bodily movement is constrained by an interface) and 'pull' effects (in which the interface enables the user's tacit and spontaneous movements). Jack et al. [8] provide evidence of 'push' and 'pull' effects of a DMI's design on musical gestural interaction, showing that performers optimise their gestures to correspond with the sensing modalities of the instrument.

It can therefore be argued that the gestural language for performing an instrument is governed by the 'push' and 'pull' effects of the instrument's affordances and constraints. De Souza explores the link between affordances and distributed cognition, proposing 'idiomatic music' as those compositions which feature *"characteristic patterns that cannot be predicted by grammatical rules alone"*, arguing these characteristic patterns are the result of players interacting with the affordances of the instrument, composing not on a note-by-note basis but also through selection of 'ready-made sequences' on offer [5, page 77]. This music that is *"suited, adapted, and optimised for an instrument"* is what Tanaka [16] refers to as 'idiomatic writing', and is therefore the result of the physical affordances of the instrument. Huron and Berec [7] show that idiomatic writing for an instrument can become less idiomatic if the circumstances change, observing that trumpet players find it more difficult to perform trumpet repertoire that is shifted in key or tempo so as to alter key fingerings and duration of breath.

The size of the instrument changes its relationship to the body and therefore its affordances, and in turn influences the idiomatic music of the instrument. However, more research is required to fully understand the extent of this influence as well as other factors that may be at play. In particular, the preceding references raise the questions of what circumstances DMI designers can control and change, and the resulting impact on DMI repertoire and performance.

2 The Study

The Large Instrument Performers Study was designed to explore the possible impact an instrument's scale and dimensions may have on the performance of composed and improvised repertoire on the instrument by identifying affordances specific to large acoustic instruments, and how these affordances impact the performer's choices. The study consisted of one-on-one interviews with seven instrument performers who are trained on physically large instruments (see Table 1). Some participants were trained on more than one instrument of an instrument family in which one instrument is larger than the other, for example baritone saxophone and tenor saxophone. The interviews lasted up to one hour. During the interviews, questions about performance technique and repertoire were asked and participants were encouraged to perform their instrument(s) as examples arose. The interviews were videoed and took place either in a professional music studio, on campus at Queen Mary University, or over Skype.

The participants were asked questions designed to reveal how the performers respond to effects introduced by the large scale of the instrument, such as physical navigation challenges, the additional physical effort required to perform larger instruments, and the relative changes in tone, timbre, volume and intensity encountered when performing repertoire on a large instrument versus a smaller similar instrument.

Table 1. Study participants.

Participant number	Primary large instrument played	Other instruments played	Primary style
P1	Contrabassoon	Bassoon, double bass, electronics	Contemporary, ambient
P2	Contrabass clarinet	Clarinets (soprano, bass, alto), flute, guitar, piano, saxophones (soprano, alto, tenor, baritone)	Contemporary classical, experimental
P3	Organ	Piano, soprano clarinet, voice	Classical, renaissance
P4	Contrabass flute	Flutes (bass, alto, concert, piccolo), recorder, piano	Contemporary
P5	Gyil	Percussion, drum kit, piano, guitar	World jazz
P6	Tuba	Guitar, gong, self-designed mechanical instruments	Metal
P7	Baritone saxophone	Saxophones (alto, tenor, soprano)	Jazz

Specific questions asked included: Which techniques/patterns require you to move the most? Which techniques/patterns require you to move the least, or require microscopic precision? How long can you perform the instrument before you are too tired to continue? What causes the fatigue? How do you think the instrument influences the music you make when improvising? Would you improvise in the same way on a different instrument? What is an example of well written music for your instrument? How would it change if you performed it an octave higher or on another instrument?

The performers were also shown repertoire composed for cello, "Cello Suite no. 1 in G Major" (all movements) by J. S. Bach, and asked what issues they would encounter if they attempted to perform it on their instrument.

The videos were manually transcribed and the transcription data analyzed following a thematic analysis methodology [4]. Codes emerged through an iterative process that took a theory-driven approach [15], in that the raw interview data was examined for trends and correlations that relate to the theories of embodied music cognition, affordances and idiomatic writing. Four iterations of coding were performed resulting in a codebook that was updated and refined at each coding iteration.

3 Results

3.1 Thematic Analysis Codebook and Overarching Themes

The codes that emerged from the thematic analysis methodology were organised by the grouping of codes that shared a theme. Table 2 presents an overview of the codebook structure and which participants commented on each code.

At a high level, we noticed a differentiation in the themes between those that describe instrument characteristics, and those that illustrate performer reactions to those characteristics.

In the context of how size-related affordances impact performer choices, the codes reveal both trends and individual insights that illustrate how large acoustic instruments impose fatigue issues on the performer influencing their decision of how long or whether to perform the instrument at all; how timbral variations across registers influence choices performers make when improvising on the instrument; and how micro-level control and design of large instruments can result in substantial changes to the sound, influencing new performance techniques.

The interview content relating to techniques and repertoire performed on large instruments was categorised under three themes: idiomatic, easy and natural; unidiomatic, difficult and unnatural; and virtuosic or impressive composition. Comparing the comments that fell into one or more of these themes resulted in interesting insights into the differentiation between what is easy, natural, idiomatic and/or virtuosic in the context of idiomatic writing for large instruments.

3.2 Influence of Size and Weight on Performance Fatigue

Six out of the seven interviewees identified the cause of performance fatigue to be uniquely related to the instrument size. Causes included the instrument weight, the posture required to play the instrument due to its size, and extreme use of diaphragm/core muscles to support the air column and air pressure required to perform large scale woodwind instruments. As a result, five out of seven of the participants use a device or performance method designed to minimise performance fatigue caused by the instrument's weight.

The methods of compensation range from altering their performance method once fatigue sets in, to using commercially available or self-created devices, such as a harness or strap for tuba, baritone saxophone and contrabass, and the performer-designed belt clip for supporting the weight of the contrabassoon. Contrabassoon performer P1 describes the inception of the belt clip and how it has improved the issue of weight-induced performance fatigue: *"I was finding that I was using my left arm too much so I was locking my muscles up to the point where playing the notes became difficult. And I thought with saxophones and so on there's a harness, and you really need it for a heavy instrument, and so just by complete chance, I thought what about if I clip it onto me and that's it, I now don't use my arms to support my instrument. This has allowed me to*

Table 2. Thematic analysis codebook.

Code mentioned by participants	P1	P2	P3	P4	P5	P6	P7
Impact of size, weight or fatigue of large instruments on performers							
Which technique/passage makes the performer move the most	×	×	×		×	×	×
Fatigue	×	×	×	×	×		×
Weight		×		×		×	×
Strength required to perform large instrument	×	×	×		×	×	
Size		×					
Timbral variation across registers in large instruments							
Choosing difficult techniques for sonic gratification	×						
Effects of variation across register on repertoire arrangements		×	×			×	×
Effect of playing in different registers on idiomaticity	×	×		×		×	
Influence of timbral variation on repertoire	×	×	×	×			×
Instrument is designed to have a strong bottom register	×		×	×			
Micro scale within macro scale of large instruments							
Microscopic design that has a large effect	×						
Microscopic gestures that have a large effect	×			×		×	
Improvising or composing on large instruments							
The feel of the instrument changes how I improvise		×					
What the performer doesn't play when improvising		×		×			
What the performer plays when improvising		×		×			
Idiomatic, easy, natural to perform on large instruments							
Idiomatic techniques		×	×	×			
Performance of idiomatic music	×	×			×	×	×
Composition relating to idiomaticity	×	×	×	×	×	×	×
What is easy to play on the instrument	×	×		×	×		
What makes music idiomatic for this instrument	×			×		×	×
Unidiomatic, difficult or unnatural to perform on large instruments							
What is difficult to play	×					×	
What makes a composition unidiomatic	×	×		×		×	×
Examples of unidiomatic compositions		×	×	×		×	×
Performances of unidiomatic compositions		×		×		×	×
What is more difficult to play than it seems		×		×			
Virtuosic or impressive compositions for large instruments							
Video of virtuosic composition	×					×	
Examples of virtuosic or impressive writing	×	×	×	×			
What makes a composition virtuosic for this large instrument		×	×	×			
Performing a different instrument's repertoire on large instruments							
Performing repertoire intended for a different instrument is possible		×	×	×	×		
Performing repertoire intended for a different instrument is not possible	×	×	×	×	×	×	

play the instrument for a lot longer because I am not using my body to carry the instrument in any way."

Gyil performer P5 identified maintaining a grip on heavy sticks through long and rapid performance as a major cause of performance fatigue as the sticks used for performing Gyil are heavier than sticks used for performing smaller tuned percussion instruments (such as glockenspiel), and as such require more muscle use and control. Her method of pushing through performance fatigue is changing her grip on the sticks. P5 elaborates *"I can feel after a few hours of playing 'I can't hold my sticks!' and I start using the back of my hands. So I've got ways. It's a mental thing."*

In some cases the instrument's size and/or weight influences whether the performer chooses to perform the instrument at all. P4 commented she often opts not to perform with the contrabass flute at improvisational concerts because carrying the contrabass flute limits her ability to travel with more than one flute, whereas if she selects a smaller flute such as alto flute she can also carry another flute such as concert flute or piccolo, offering her greater options at the concert. P6 said he seldom performs tuba in concert due to environmental concerns related to the need to transport such a large instrument by car.

3.3 Timbral Variation Across Registers in Large Wind Instruments

Beyond identifying the aforementioned obvious size-related affordances of large instruments, the study identified a less obvious influence of the size of large wind instruments on composed and improvised repertoire. Large acoustic wind instruments are often designed to have a rich tone in the lower register. This feature is a result of the instrument having a very large pipe/sound chamber. Activating the entire chamber will result in the lowest, most resonant tone. Playing in higher registers uses smaller sections of the chamber, resulting in more airy, frail tones in the higher registers. These unusual upper tones are more difficult to perform in tune because more air pressure is required (due to the instrument's size). Maintaining a steady pressure at the intensity required is a difficult task for even the most advanced players.

Although a byproduct of the instrument's design, the unusual tones in the upper registers can become an interesting aesthetic resource to draw on when composing and improvising on the instrument. The study results indicate that the unique tones of both the upper and lower registers influence performer choices through embodied cognition and 'push' effects.

All performers interviewed improvise on their instrument. When asked what they often play when improvising, four out of seven interviewees mentioned drawing inspiration from the timbral variation across registers. Composing and performing improvisations that are influenced by this aesthetic is an example of embodied cognition, as the performers are making specific choices based on the instrument's affordance of different tone colours at each register.

Contrabassoon performer P1 described performing the same passage an octave higher as having *"not the same feel at all... the more of the instrument you're using the more of the resonance is in the sound."*, noting that as notes are performed in higher and higher registers *"the notes begin to get weaker"*, creating an unstable, *"alien"* timbral quality that he makes use of when composing. *"In an orchestral setting, unless you want to specifically exploit this change in timbre in taking the instrument up an octave it might be better to write (the same part) for a bassoon instead... In my own music however I swap octaves a lot specifically to introduce this slightly more frail sound. When you take the instrument up very high it takes on this very different quality."* By extending his compositions into the higher register for the purpose of utilising this 'frail' tone (rather than other compositional choices such wanting an ascending melody), P1 is revealing the 'push' effects of the timbral aesthetic of the high register. This is an example of embodied cognition in that P1's compositional choices are changed by interacting with the instrument.

P2 is also drawn to the timbral variation across registers on the largest version of the instrument he performs. He mentioned that the E-flat clarinet is designed to have a uniform tone across all registers. By contrast the contrabass clarinet is not, hence it affords more tonal options to the performer. He said the contrabass clarinet *"has a lot richer sounds and things that I can really do with it, whereas the clarinet has more of a certain kind of sound and it doesn't have the same richness and variation."* When asked to name a composition that feels natural to play on the contrabass clarinet, P2 nominated 'Dark Light' by Thanos Chrysakis [3] because it *"highlights the capabilities of the instrument."* Composed for contrabass clarinet, 'Dark Light' features long tones in both the low and high registers. P2 later mentioned that performing contrabass clarinet in the higher registers is more difficult and less precise than performing in the lower registers. *"The higher you go the more notes I have on a single fingering... so I can't move between them as quickly as I have to do it with my mouth rather than with my fingers, so the precision isn't the same."* We find it interesting that even though performance of contrabass clarinet is more difficult for tones in the higher register, P2 indicated the most natural composition to perform on the instrument (in Tanaka's terminology, an example of 'idiomatic writing' for contrabass clarinet) features many complicated tones in the higher registers.

Similarly, P4 said that performing the same part in different registers on the contrabass flute *"would probably make it more difficult. If it was going higher it would make it harder to play in tune."* P4 said this difficulty in performing the higher register in tune is a byproduct of the contrabass flute design, which was designed to optimise the lower register tone at the expense of the higher register tone. *"The smaller (flutes) are deliberately made to make them as even as possible. Whereas the bigger ones are deliberately made not to do that. Because for example if you're playing a bass flute and you're playing in a flute choir, what you want is a really strong bottom octave... (On the contrabass flute) you get much better resonance in the low register, but it's possibly a bit weaker and a bit out of tune in the higher register where you're not going to use it very much."*

Aside from causing tuning issues, P4 indicated that performing the same passage in different registers of the contrabass flute would result in changing the character of the music. P4 said *"the character between the octaves changes quite dramatically. They each have a very different tone colour... I think if you put it in a different octave it would definitely change the character of the music."* When asked what types of sounds and passages she performs when improvising on contrabass flute, her responses included *"slow melodic material, possibly in the different octaves."*

Notably, it is not only the weaker, higher register that influences the performer's choice to perform a tone despite its difficulty. P1 said *"What I love on the instrument (contrabassoon) is holding the low notes for a long time. But that is very difficult."* He explained that unlike performing a long bass tone on another instrument such as the piano which would require the relatively easy gesture of pressing a key with one finger, performing a long bass tone on the contrabassoon requires precise core control. *"When I started playing this instrument it took me several years of doing nothing other than just playing long tones, and learning how to use one's core muscles... The lower you get, the more control you need over a consistent flow of air."* Yet despite the effort, what P1 enjoys performing the most on the instrument is long sustained bass tones. He regularly features them in compositions, commenting *"if you're using that with something on top that is such a brilliant foundation."* When asked why he prefers to use the contrabassoon rather than for example an electronic instrument for sustaining long bass tones, P1 said *"The performative and aesthetic element is important to me. I like using big effort instruments to make relatively reduced music. I have been using smaller instruments for ease of travel and using pitch shifting pedals to take them down an octave and although the end result is almost the same sonically as playing on a bigger instrument, it changes the essence of the music."* That P1 prefers to perform such a difficult technique on the contrabassoon instead of an easier technique on a different instrument is another example of embodied music cognition as he believes that creating the (almost) identical tone on a different instrument *"changes the essence of the music"*, implying that the instrument, not the tone, is changing his perception of the music.

3.4 Microscopic Performance Techniques on Large Instruments

Three out of five of the performers of large scale brass and woodwind instruments commented that microscopic changes in the embouchure and air pressure can result in huge changes in the sound and tone quality.

On the contrabass flute, a millimetre change in air angle can result in large changes and even the sound being lost altogether. P4 said *"it's really critical that the air goes in at the right angle. So because the instrument is so big, the air has to travel, so even something very simple like changing octaves needs very precise control of the air stream. And the distance between the octaves feels much bigger than it would do on a smaller instrument. So if you're playing a normal flute it takes a lot less air, and also the notes feel much closer together because the tube length is so much smaller. So because of that, all of those intervals, everything gets expanded. So I think from that point of view you're using a lot of precision of the airflow all of the time... Literally, if the air goes one millimetre in one way you'll lose the sound or change the sound."*

Similarly, minute alterations to the contrabassoon reed can cause large changes to the instrument's tone. P1 said *"If we want a soft reed we can sandpaper that down for ten seconds, that's going to get the instrument to behave in a completely different way from not really very much of a change. So yes even though it's very big, some of the small changes can have a profound effect on the instrument."*

As a contrabassoon part maker, P1 has discovered ways certain microscopic design changes can influence the overall character of the instrument. When creating his own crooks (also known as bocals, the thin s-shaped tapered tube that the reed connects to), P1 discovered microscopic changes to the angle of the taper result in each crook having a unique sound. When comparing one self-designed crook to another, P1 said that in one *"the inside gets bigger quicker than the other one. So this has the capability to play higher notes more reliably."* While the other crook may be less reliable in the upper tones, P1 noted that it has its own characteristic that can be desirable for certain repertoire. *"The trade off is this one has more fundamental in the low notes."* By refining his crook-making process he can now design characteristics into the tone of the instrument. *"If I know I want a darker sound I know what to change to make that."*

P6 described a microscopic tuba technique he uses when playing in unison with others to create a beating sound. *"Other players will play a solid note and then I'll slightly bend the pitch of my note to create beats and that's done by a minor change in the lipping. It's really subtle. It's probably a bit to do with the air pressure as well but it's mostly a small deviation in the lip."* The result is a perceived effect of the tone rhythmically starting and stopping even though each performer is playing one long tone.

3.5 Influence of Difficulty and Virtuosity on Idiomatic Writing

Interview data relating to improvisation, repertoire, gestural performance techniques and performing repertoire intended for different instruments revealed interesting insights into what makes a technique, pattern or composition more or less difficult, idiomatic, virtuosic or impressive to perform on large instruments. In many cases the results offered insights that contradict common preconceptions of idiomatic writing, such as the assumptions that idiomaticity is synonymous with ease of performance, and virtuosity is synonymous with difficulty of performance. The compositions P2 and P5 regard as the most idiomatic and/or natural to perform on their instruments also contain performance techniques they consider the most difficult. P5 said the most idiomatic music for the Gyil is the polymetric Degaari traditional music, elaborating *"holding both metres and being able to play between them - that's hard for me and I don't think that's virtuosic... And if people thought that it was hard when they're listening to me then I'm not doing it right."* We find it interesting that the factors that impress audiences about this music, such as its speed and use of the full range of the instrument, are not what make it difficult to perform, and the mental challenge posed by the polymetric groove is not necessarily a factor that makes it virtuosic.

4 Discussion

Current ongoing trends in DMI performance research include effortfulness [1], physicality and whether controllerism/laptop music engages audiences [2]. We argue that while large DMIs engage more with the body and are more physical and visible than their smaller counterparts, more research is required to fully understand ways in which their size influences DMI music and performance.

Keeping in mind Magnusson's [11] notion of 'scripts' and 'material epistemologies', the hidden knowledge embedded in instruments that shape idiomatic writing, DMI designers can draw inspiration from the detail and variation of sonic features of acoustic instruments when creating sound design that inspires virtuosic composition on DMIs. The interviews with contrabass flute and contrabass clarinet performers show that the varying timbral qualities afforded by large wind instruments influence performers' choices when improvising on the instrument, as well as their decision of whether to perform the instrument at all (in place of performing the smaller version with a more uniform tone across all registers). This indicates that non-uniformity of tone across registers is a strong aesthetic resource for compositional inspiration. DMI designers could consider implementing this characteristic in not only large DMIs but DMIs of all sizes.

The observations from the Large Instrument Performers Study show that the 'push' effects of timbrally varied tones across registers influenced performers to make use of multiple registers while improvising and composing. That the participants chose to perform within the more difficult registers, even at the risk of discomfort or error, shows the extent to which performers value these tones. We argue these findings should encourage designers of DMIs of all sizes to consider the value of offering simultaneous access to multiple registers and varied sound design across registers, as well as microscopically precise gestural controls - even those initially unnatural or difficult to perform.

In light of the study findings that reveal large wind instruments respond to microscopic changes in gestural control and micro-scale design details, we argue that to reach new frontiers of virtuosic digital instrument performance and repertoire, large DMI designers should take into account the microscale within the macroscale. Scaling up the DMI to be larger is only the first step. Until large scaled DMIs match or exceed the nuanced precision of large acoustic instruments, large DMIs we will not reach their musical and performative potential.

Exploring human interaction with an instrument too large and complex to master was an approach taken by the group Sensorband (Atau Tanaka, Zbigniew Karkowski and Edwin van der Heide) with their architectural scale instrument SoundNet [16]. In the context of researching embodied cognition and idiomaticity, we argue there is more to be discovered from musical interactions with instruments designed to overwhelm the performer with its physicality. One physically overwhelming instrument discussed in The Large Instrument Performers Study was the contrabass flute, which requires so much breath support the performer can become dizzy. P4's expert insight into performing such a physically overwhelming instrument illuminated our discussion by providing a perspective from the extreme end of acoustic instrument performance.

Table 3. Suggested guidelines for implementing findings into DMI design.

Study results	DMI design choices influenced by study results
Impact of size, weight or fatigue on performers	
Weight	Consider ways the DMI design may decouple size from weight, such as the use of light-weight materials or a design that packs down into travel cases
Strength required to perform instrument	Consider how a DMI that requires physical strength to perform influences the material epistemological scripts of the instrument, and what is idiomatic to perform on it, for example resulting in slower tempos or recurring clusters of tones located near one another
Size	Consider ways to avoid the size-related constraints of large DMIs such as open spaces/layouts that the performer can see past, or translucent materials
Timbral variation across registers	
Choosing difficult techniques for sonic gestures at the very limit gratification	Consider designing in 'easter egg' tones accessible via the most difficult to perform of what is performable
Effects of variation across register on repertoire arrangements	Consider assigning one register as the most resonant and weaker tones in other registers; offer access to many registers at once via many tones or choice of a scale with fewer tones per octave
Effect of playing in different registers on idiomaticity	Consider the ways that implementing sound design that varies across registers results may create scripts of idiomatic music for the instrument
Instrument is designed register with a strong bottom	Consider whether the DMI is intended for performance as a solo instrument or in ensembles
Microscale within macroscale	
Microscopic gestures that have a large effect	Consider DMI designs that allow for microscopic gestures to result in a large sonic effect on the overall tone or performance of the DMI
Improvising/Composing on large DMIs	
Feel of the DMI changes improvisations	Consider how the strength and effort required to perform the DMI may influence the performances or compositions created on the DMI
What is idiomatic, easy or natural to perform on large instruments	
Idiomatic techniques	Consider the impact of the 'push' and 'pull' effects of what tones or passages are created by the easiest to perform techniques

4.1 Guidelines for Implementing Findings into DMI Design

Drawing on the findings of the study, Table 3 outlines a series of design features that DMI designers could consider when designing new large DMIs. These guidelines take into account the insights offered by the participants when discussing the positive aspects of performing large acoustic instruments, such as the timbral variation across registers and the microscale within the macroscale, as well as the negative impacts such as size, weight and fatigue, and offer considerations for how these aspects can be appropriated or avoided when designing large DMIs.

We as designers are using these guidelines while designing a family of instruments for an ongoing study to understand the impact of an instrument's size and layout on the emergence of new gestural languages and the qualities of the music performed [13]. The study monitors classically trained musicians interacting with one of two versions of a new large DMI. The instrument is two metres wide and two metres high and features twenty performable pendulum pipes that create twenty discrete tones. In response to the guidelines, the instrument design decouples size from weight by using as the primary material light weight PVC plastic pipes painted to look metallic, rather than much heavier metal pipes. Inspired by the microscale within the macroscale, the instrument captures audio-rate signals from accelerometers on each pendulum and processes them through a sound model that changes in timbre with increasing strength of hits - a much more sensitive sound producing technique than for example a sample trigger mechanism that therefore allows for a greater range in gestural control. During the musicians' first encounter with the new instrument, we observed that the idiomatic gestures and patterns that emerged were strongly dependant on the relationship between the instrument's physical layout (a combination of the tonal layout and size) and the human body.

5 Conclusion and Future Work

We presented a study to examine the affordances of large acoustic instruments and their effect on performers choices. This study has shown us that large scale instruments are more than just small instruments scaled up; rather they are highly detailed, precise instruments that in many cases offer different sonic affordances than their smaller counterpart of the same instrument family. The findings revealed a series of interesting aesthetic design features of large acoustic instruments, such as the timbral variation across registers and the microscopic precision of control, that have a strong influence on performers choices through embodied music cognition and 'push' effects. More research is required to understand the full impact of instrument size and scale on musical performance and composition, however this research offers initial insights to consider when designing new DMIs of all sizes.

Acknowledgments. Research supported by EPSRC under grants EP/L01632X/1 (Centre for Doctoral Training in Media and Arts Technology) and EP/N005112/1 (Design for Virtuosity).

References

1. Bennett, P., Ward, N., O'Modhrain, S., Rebelo, P.: DAMPER: a platform for effortful interface development. In: Proceedings of International Conference on New Interfaces for Musical Expression, NIME, New York, pp. 273–276 (2007)
2. Bin, S. M. A., Bryan-Kinns, N., McPherson, A. P.: Hands where we can see them! investigating the impact of gesture size on audience perception. In: Proceedings of International Computer Music Conference. ICMC, Shanghai (2017)
3. Chrysakis, T.: Dark Light. London (2017)
4. DeCuir-Gunby, J.T., Marshall, P.L., McCulloch, A.W.: Developing and using a codebook for the analysis of interview data: an example from a professional development research project. Field Methods **23**(2), 136–155 (2011)
5. De Souza, J.: Music at Hand. Oxford University Press, New York (2017)
6. Gibson, J.J.: The Ecological Approach To Visual Perception. Houghton Mifflin, Boston (1979)
7. Huron, D., Berec, J.: Characterising idoimatic organisation in music: a theory and case study of "musical affordances". Empir. Musicol. Rev. **4**(3), 103–22 (2009)
8. Jack, R. H., Stockman, T., McPherson, A. P.: Rich gesture, reduced control: the influence of constrained mappings on performance technique. In: Proceedings of International Conference on Movement and Computing, pp. 15:1–15:8. ACM, New York (2017)
9. Leman, M., Maes, P.J., Nijs, L., Van Dyck, E.: What is embodied music cognition? In: Bader, R. (ed.) Springer Handbook of Systematic Musicology, pp. 747–760. Springer, Heidelberg (2018). https://doi.org/10.1007/978-3-662-55004-5_34
10. Leman, M.: Musical gestures and embodied cognition. In: Dutoit, T., Todoroff, T., d'Alessandro, N. (eds.) Actes des Journees d'Informatique Musicale, pp. 5–7 (2012)
11. Magnusson, T.: Of epistemic tools: musical instruments as cognitive extensions. Organised Sound **14**(2), 168–176 (2009)
12. Magnusson, T.: Designing constraints: composing and performing with digital musical systems. Comput. Music J. **34**(4), 62–73 (2010)
13. Mice, L., McPherson A.: From miming to NIMEing: the development of idiomatic gestural language on large scale DMIs. In: Proceedings of International Conference on New Interfaces for Musical Expression. NIME, Birmingham (2020)
14. Norman, D.A.: The Psychology of Everyday Things. Basic Books, New York (1988)
15. Ryan, G.W., Bernard, H.R.: Techniques to identify themes. Field Methods **15**, 85–109 (2003)
16. Tanaka, A.: Musical Performance Practice on Sensor-Based Instruments. In: Wanderley, M., Battier, M. (eds.) Trends in Gestural Control of Music, pp. 389–405. IRCAM-Centre Pompidou, Paris (2000)
17. Turvey, M.T.: Affordances and prospective control: an outline of the ontology. Ecol. Psychol. **4**(3), 173–187 (1992)
18. Tuuri, K., Parviainen, J., Pirhonen, A.: Who controls who? Embodied control within human-technology choreographies. Interact. Comput. **29**(4), 494–511 (2017)

Augmentation of Sonic Meditation Practices: Resonance, Feedback and Interaction Through an Ecosystemic Approach

Rory Hoy(✉) and Doug Van Nort

DisPerSion Lab, York University, Toronto, ON M3J1P3, Canada
rorydavidhoy@gmail.com, vannort@yorku.ca,
http://dispersionlab.org/

Abstract. This paper describes the design and creation of an interactive sound environment project, titled dispersion.eLabOrate. The system is defined by a ceiling array of microphones, audio input analysis, and synthesis directly driven by this analysis. Created to augment a Deep Listening performative environment, this project explores the role that interactive installations can fulfill within a structured listening context. Echoing, modulating, and extending what it hears, the system generates an environment in which its output is a product of ambient sound, feedback, and participant input. Relating to and building upon the ecosystemic model, we discuss the benefit of designing for participant incorporation within such a responsive listening environment.

Keywords: Interactive audio · Sonic ecosystem · Deep Listening

1 Introduction

In contrast to fixed-media works for concert, the generation of a sonic environment for an installation context invites participants to traverse a space, wherein their action has amplified potential to modulate generated sound through manipulation of devices, interfaces, and the ambience of the room itself. The systematic formation and implementation of these interactive works is dependent upon the role of participants within the space (or lack thereof). Techniques range from a linear system flow where in participant action directly drives generated output to a sonic ecosystem approach, where in feedback mechanisms establish autonomous and self sustaining sonic activity.

This paper will explore the formation of *dispersion.eLabOrate*, an interactive sound environment which began as an augmentation on the form of the "Tuning Meditation", a text piece found within the practice of *Deep Listening* [6]. This meditative and performative context informed the aesthetic and design considerations employed within the system's development, due to its need to function as a collaborative member of the piece, rather than distracting from the focused

R. Kronland-Martinet et al. (Eds.): CMMR 2019, LNCS 12631, pp. 591–599, 2021.
https://doi.org/10.1007/978-3-030-70210-6_38

listening context in which it was deployed. The system was developed with the design metaphor of an "active listening room" in mind, reacting both to participants and its own generated audio. The relationships established between human, machine, and ambient environment led to exploration of the ecosystemic approach presented by Agostino Di Scipio [3]. Contending with boundaries put in place by the classical ecosystemic approach, *dispersion.eLabOrate* presents a model in which the human and the machine can act together in the generation of an ecosystem such that the blending of agency is achieved through the system's self/ambient observing behavior and the participant's ability to be present in this observation. We will discuss the need to bridge between methodologies for interactive sound environments, presenting an approach that extends the capabilities of a sonic ecosystem dynamically through participant input, resulting in spatially distributed parameter changes. These localized changes can be thought of as generating diverse locations within the sonic ecosystem, with input conditions resulting in distinct perceptual effects for both participants and the ambient sensing of the system.

2 Related Works

2.1 Ecosystemic Framework

Undertaken in Di Scipio [2], the challenge of generating a sonic ecosystem is engaged by questioning the nature of interactivity, by exploring the limits of "where and when" this occurs. Di Scipio notes that the majority of interactive systems employ a linear communication flow in which a participant's action is the singular cause of output. Di Scipio then presents an alternate approach in which the principal aim is the creation of a dynamical system which can act upon and interfere with the external conditions that define its own internal state. This approach decentralizes the primal importance of human agency in the space (apart from ambient noise) and grants the ability of self-observation to the system. Di Scipio describes this ability as "a shift from creating wanted sounds via interactive means, towards creating wanted interactions having audible traces"; and it is through these traces that compelling sonification can occur. This ideation of an audio ecosystem culminates in Di Scipio's Audible Eco-Systemic Interface project (AESI) project. This machine/ambience interrelationship is paramount and understood to function as "interaction", rather than the typical human/machine relationship. AESI emits an initial sound that is captured by two or more microphones in the room. Relevant features are extracted from this capture, which are then used to drive audio signal processing parameters. Measurements on differences between microphone signals are used as additional control values, and the internal state of the AESI is set through functions defined by this ecosystemic concept. The four functions achieving this are compensation (active counterbalance of amplitude with the ambient environment), following (ramped value chasing given a delay time), redundancy (supporting a predominant sound feature), and concurrency (supporting a contrasting or competing predominant feature).

These defining ecosystemic characteristics of equilibrium and adjustment are explored by Haworth [4], who suggests the need to update the ecosystemic model to reflect current broader thoughts on ecosystems, de-emphasizing stability and highlighting imbalance and disorder. Haworth identifies two distinct models, stemming from Di Scipio and Simon Waters. Di Scipio's form is a cyclical closed system in which traditional control structures of linear systems in interactive audio works are dismantled in favor of a self-regulated ambient sensing. Meanwhile, Waters moves away from tendencies to instrumentalise technology, instead highlighting the role of human attention upon relations formed between each of the components within a generated ecology. Waters posits, "The notion of Performance Ecosystem enfolds all three concepts (performer, instrument, environment) and allows room for the undecideabilities of the virtual domain" [7], depicting this interrelated nature of ecosystemic components as primary over their intersection with the "virtual domain". While an extended examination of these two positions is beyond the scope of this paper, for the purposes of this discussion it is suitable to work from this relatively high-level distinction between the two. In so doing, the modified understanding of the ecosystemic model posed by Haworth [4] and the situated performance ecology of Waters [7] are most applicable to the system design of *dispersion.eLabOrate*. Incorporating aspects of system self-observation while explicitly designing around participants' attentional dynamics, the generated sonic ecosystem deals with the blending of influence between the system and environmental actors.

2.2 Deep Listening

The practice of Deep Listening was developed by composer Pauline Oliveros in the 1970's and refined into the 2000's. It is described by Oliveros as "a practice that is intended to heighten and expand consciousness of sound in as many dimensions of awareness and attentional dynamics as humanly possible" [6]. With a focus on embodied listening to internal and environmental stimuli, the practice integrates somatic awareness and energy exercises, listening meditations, and sound-making exercises that build upon an initial set of text-based pieces Oliveros created known as Sonic Meditations, with the Tuning Meditation (TM) being one of the earliest and most widely-practiced. The Deep Listening community has grown through regular workshops to include thousands of past and current practitioners, and is kept alive through certified Deep Listening instructors, including the second author.

3 System Description

The project was created in the DisPerSion Lab at York University in Toronto, an interdisciplinary research-creation space outfitted with a multichannel audio system. For *dispersion.eLabOrate*, 12 channels mounted on floor stands were employed, with positions chosen in order to mitigate extraneous feedback, while facilitating intended feedback between the generated audio and the array of ceiling mounted microphones. The array of 3 × 3 omnidirectional microphones ensures participant input is evenly sensed throughout the space. The TM asks participants to inhale deeply, exhaling on a note/tone of their choice for one full breath. On the following exhalation, participants will then match a tone that another has made. Next, a new tone should be held that no one else has made. This alternation between matching others and offering new tones repeats until a natural end point is reached, as determined by the group listening dynamic. In this project we also allowed participants to choose between noise or tone at each cycle. As this was the primary context in which the project was intended, all major aesthetic considerations and testing revolved around ensuring the piece could be performed without distraction. The role of the system is to extend the potential for the piece, rather than overtake it as a singular focus (Fig. 1).

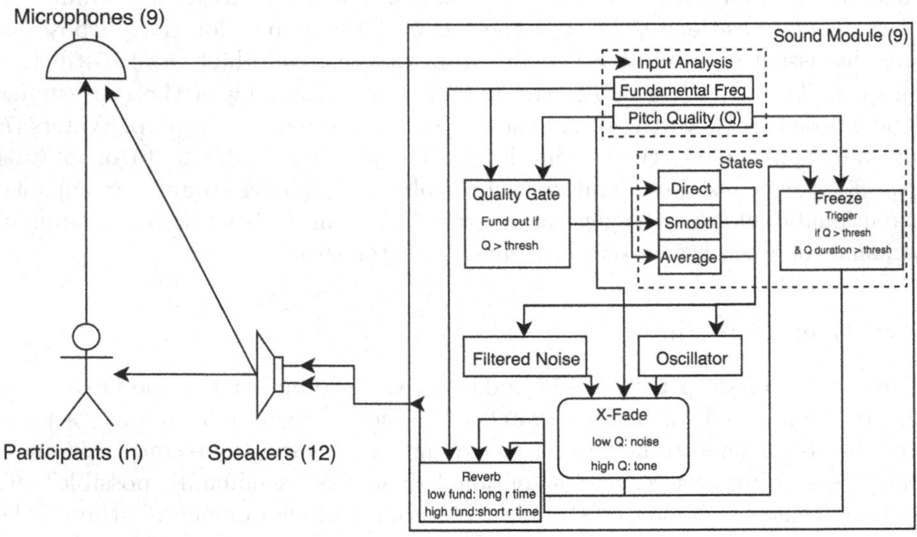

Fig. 1. System diagram of *dispersion.eLabOrate* depicting signal and data flow from microphones, through pitch analysis, to audio generation, and output to room.

The audio is received by the computer via an audio interface connected to the microphones. Incoming audio is then accessed by Max/MSP, where the analysis and audio generation occurs. The system is comprised of 9 modules, one for each of the microphones in the array. Each module consists of a sinusoidal oscillator, as well as a white noise generator that is fed into a bandpass filter. The system's output is located spatially with regards to the location of the microphones within the room, placing each of the 9 output signals in relation to their input source. This placement promotes feedback at the localized level between a modules output and accompanying microphone, while additionally influencing adjacent output and microphone pairs. The modules contain states which alter the behavior of audio generation and its listening parameters. The four states are, *direct*, *smooth*, *average*, and *freeze*. These states differ in the way they map values to the module's oscillator and filter, and change parameters for data thresholding. States can be set individually for each module, allowing varied behavior within localized areas of the room. Each audio input is analyzed for fundamental frequency, and pitch quality (an estimation of analysis confidence). Fundamental frequency is calculated by the zsa.fund method [5] and pitch quality estimation is extracted using the yin algorithm [2]. Yin was not used for fundamental frequency tracking as it was found to increase feedback past a desired level, hence the use of the FFT-based method. The 9 separate modules receive the fundamental frequency and pitch quality from their respective microphone, which are then sent to the module's oscillator and filter. The fundamental is used as the desired frequency for the oscillator as well as the centre frequency for a resonant bandpass filter. Values are only sent if a defined threshold for pitch quality is passed (default 0.2), and pairing this quality gate with a noise gate on the original microphone signal avoids having unintentional ambient stimulus/noise as input. Moving between ostensibly simple states results in a potentially drastic difference of behavior for the system's output. *Direct* causes the analyzed fundamental frequency to be immediately reflected in the oscillator and filtered noise. *Smooth* sends values to the output sources ramped over time (default 50ms). *Average* sends out values to the sources after calculating a running mean during a given time window (default 200 ms). *Freeze* implements spectral freeze and sustain techniques [1], triggering them when input passes a set pitch quality threshold and pitch quality duration (default 1s). In addition to gating data flow, the pitch quality value is used to crossfade between the two audio generation sources of each module. Low pitch quality is perceptually tied to "noisy" input stimulus, while high pitch quality will result from clear tones. When the quality value is low, output will be closer to the filtered noise. If the quality is high, output will be towards the generated pure tone of the oscillator. Thus the resulting output of a module is congruous with the timbral quality (ranging from tone to noise) at any given mic. Reverb was added to accentuate the spatial aspects of the audio generation and was also controlled by the analyzed fundamental frequency at the module level. Low frequency was mapped to a long reverb time, while high frequencies were mapped to a short reverb time.

4 Evaluation and Discussion

4.1 Tuning Meditation User Study

To systematically examine the perceived influence of *dispersion.eLabOrate* across its four states, a user study was conducted with five volunteers joining the two authors, for a total of seven participants. The TM ran five times in a row: first without *dispersion.eLabOrate*'s sensing to establish a "ground truth". The four following runs implemented the system states, moving through *direct*, *smooth*, *average*, and *freeze* Participants were allotted time to write personal comments and rest in between each run. A survey was completed after the final run and before group discussion, to avoid biasing personal reflections on the experience.

The survey utilized a five-point Likert scale, with the following questions for each run: Q1: During this piece/experiment, could you differentiate any electronic sound output from that of human performers? Q2: During this piece/experiment, could you recognize any tones/noises being matched (either yours or another person's) by another human performer? Q3: During this piece/experiment, could you recognize any tones/noises being matched (either yours or another person's) by electronic sound output? Q4: How confident are you about your recollection of run N and related ability to answer these questions?

The responses show a trend in participants reporting less ability to recognize tones being matched by fellow humans (Q2) in successive runs. This may be a product of becoming more comfortable with the system as another participant/agent within the piece. This is supported by participant comments: noting in run 3 that the "electronics faded in background - less interested in triggering the electronics than using it as a source for unique tones" and in run 5 that "the electronics lost novelty (and) acted more as (a) participant in my mind". The same participant noted of run 3 that "the electronics held (the) same importance as other performers", whereas they earlier reported that they "spent (the) first few breaths figuring out what tones would trigger the electronics". Another participant noted in run 3 that "the machine felt like it was part of the sound field, but in a different way to the rest of the participants" whereas by run 5 they noted that the run "had a very satisfying ending when the machine faded out with the group", pointing to its collaborative place within the piece. While the surveys required a recollection of every run from the 1.5 h session, each participant reported high confidence in this recollection across every run. The general trend of recognizing less human matching (from the quantitative data) and increasing regard for the interactive system as an agent to be listened and responded to (qualitative comments) is quite interesting. This certainly must be related to an increasing familiarization with the system, but it also may be related to the specific ordering of the states: while all system output was normalized to the same volume (balanced to blend with group sound), state changes from runs 2–5 correlated with an increased sustain of system output due to state behavior. This greater sustain, and related self-regulatory feedback, seemingly contributed to the increased sense of presence reported, with participants noting that the sound was "less chaotic" and contributed to the larger environmental context of the experience. This additionally speaks to the influence of the ecosystemic design on perceived agency. Future research conducted with this system will address this bias in sustain weighting, incorporating multiple trials of varied state orders (Fig. 2).

4.2 Discussion

The "Tuning Meditation" Deep Listening piece is itself an emergent dynamical process that could be seen as an acoustic form of an interactive sonic ecosystem. When intersected with *dispersion.eLabOrate*, the result is a piece positioned within the ecosystemic model through shared human/technological influence.

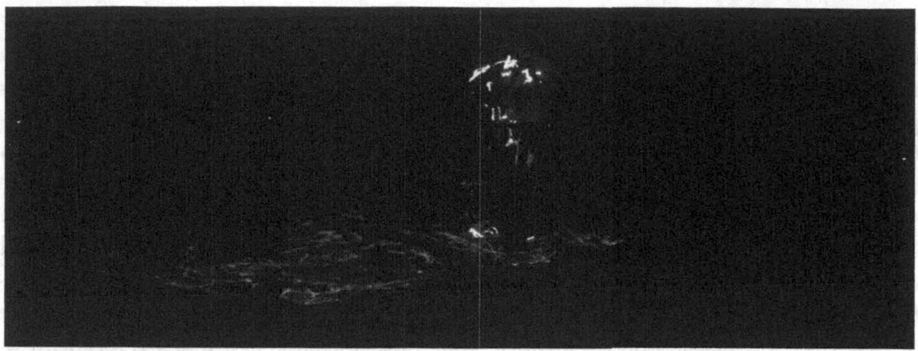

Fig. 2. System diagram of *dispersion.eLabOrate* was developed in the context of a project that explored different input sensing, media output displays and interaction designs for augmenting sonic meditations.

Due to the flexible number of participants that may take part in a performance/session of the TM, variances in voice density may be quite apparent or perceptually unnoticeable due to aligning breath cycles. "Feedback" is inherently present through the act of matching another's output and the ambient qualities of the piece are established by all participants acting to form a self-regulating system. Additionally the piece is ran until collective stimuli concludes, further positioning the importance of ambient content to drive the output of the human "system" established between participants, noted in the user study through the comments of the "machine" ending the piece in run 5. All of these participant interrelationships are extended through the addition of the generated audio of *dispersion.eLabOrate*, as behaviors not typically found in the original piece and "vocalizations" not achievable due to human physical constraints emerge from the system. This was evident in the user study through comments that regarded the environment as another agent, and has been further apparent to the authors across test sessions. Incorporating behaviors such as *freeze*, the system is able to sustain tones across gaps in participant stimuli, allowing continuous output to take place in the piece even within small groups. This was shown to have a noticeable positive effect on group coherence, with participants noting that the "interactive sound became more meaningful". While these extensions of human ability are present within the system, an important design consideration was that output was still bound to the activity provided by participants. System output is reliant on a "communal breath", as the cyclical deep exhalations on unique or matched tones drives the system's audio input. The system is at once an actor taking part in the meditation along with the other participants, as well as the generator of the environment in which it resides. Each of the system's states presents a different possible form that sonic ecosystems can take within an interactive audio environment. Where the direct state results in the real time modulation of input audio mapped to output found in systems that employ a linear communication flow, *smooth*, *average*, and *freeze* move the system's behavior away from this one-to-one mapping. *Smooth* results in a behavior that is clearly linked to, but perceptually disjointed from participant input. This state results in "audible traces", where generated output hangs in the environment and is perceivable over a duration of time. These dynamic gestures of sound lack stable forms and fluctuate around the system's input (to varying degrees given a certain delay time). Audible traces continue within both the *average* and *freeze* states. *Average* behaves similarly to *smooth* as its calculation window begins, and upon receiving a number of samples will begin to reach a steady-state and settle around a small range of tones. At the end of the averaging window, the system's output may jump drastically to the current input fundamental. This cycle of progressively static and eventually collapsing forms is again self-referential in relation to feedback detected by the microphones, modulated and informed by the input of participants within the space. *Freeze* became arguably the most consistently intriguing of the states, as hanging tones and rhythmic sustained patterns were formed as a product of a surpassed pitch quality threshold, in combination with surpassed specified quality duration. The frozen tones were also spatialized to the location of the microphones detecting them, placing the live system output and spectral capture of sound within the same point of emanation. Generated output possibilities including beating waves and cyclical "following" behaviors caused by new frozen tones being generated from past output, given their proximity to adjacent microphones and source positions.

Reverb acted in facilitating positive feedback within *dispersion.eLabOrate*, allowing the system to further obtain the self-observing behavior that is characteristic of sonic ecosystems. Reverberation time is tied to the incoming analyzed frequency of each of the microphones, where low frequency content results in a high reverberation time and high frequencies cause a very short reverberation time. If a continuous low tone were to be captured by the system, the reverb time would be quite large (10 s). This continuous tone could then be disturbed by input at a higher frequency than previously generated, causing the output of the system to spike in frequency, reducing the reverberation time, and collapsing the generated sonic structure. This behavior reflects Haworth's perspective on sonic ecosystems, "which de-emphasizes stability and regulation in favour of imbalance, change and disorder" [4].

5 Conclusion and Future Work

Created as a system to augment the sonic output of the Deep Listening "Tuning Meditation", *dispersion.eLabOrate* drew upon an ecosystemic design approach in its methodology, aesthetic output, and system considerations. Approaching perceived sonic agency as a symbiotic relationship between human and machine output, the work succeeds in placing human actors as integral to and active in the analyzed room ambience. This active participation within the environmental ambience is reliant on the generated output from the system, informed by chosen states for varied or uniform system response. Through the states *direct*, *smooth*, *average*, and *freeze*, *dispersion.eLabOrate* sculpts the environment participants are engaged within, while becoming an active participant itself within the framing of the piece. Cycling through these module states illustrates the potential for multiple interaction paradigms and system outputs from simple mapping changes within a single environment, highlighting the complex role of collective human action in the presence of feedback as found within the ecosystemic approach. Currently the system has the capability to define localized behavior within the sonic ecosystem through it individual modules which are related to each of the microphones in the space. The dry/wet content of reverb was not connected to any input analysis feature for this project, yet incorporating a reactive nature to this parameter could yield perceptually interesting variations for dynamically defining the shape of the sonic ecosystem at a localized level. This could also be applied to the function and assignment of states at the module level, defining multiple sonic locations in which output and systemic behavior varies, yet their collective output and proximity coalesce into a cohesive sonic ecosystem. This could allow autonomous reactive changes to occur as a result of decision making from the system, as determined by the structure of an exercise such as a sonic meditation, or through participant input. Such dynamic localized behaviour (either pre-set conditions or reactive) points towards exciting applications of sculpted, diverse, and mutating sonic ecosystems for use through augmenting participatory listening/sounding pieces such as those found within the Deep Listening tradition.

References

1. Charles, J.-F.: A tutorial on spectral sound processing using Max/MSP and jitter. Comput. Music J. **32**(3), 87–102 (2008). https://doi.org/10.1162/comj.2008.32.3.87
2. de Cheveigné, A., Kawahara, H.: YIN a fundamental frequency estimator for speech and music. J. Acoust. Soc. Am. **111**(4), 1917–1930 (2002)
3. Di Scipio, A.: Sound is the interface: from interactive to ecosystemic signal processing. Organised Sound **8**(3), 269–277 (2003). https://doi.org/10.1017/S1355771803000244
4. Haworth, C.: Ecosystem or Technical System? Technologically-Mediated Performance and the Music of The Hub. Electroacoustic Music Studies Network, Berlin (2014)
5. Malt, M., Jourdan, E.: Zsa. descriptors: a library for real-time descriptors analysis. In: Sound and Music Computing Conference, Berlin (2008)
6. Oliveros, P.: Deep Listening: A Composer's Sound Practice. iUniverse, Lincoln (2005)
7. Waters, S.: Performance Ecosystems: Ecological approaches to musical interaction. Electroacoustic Music Studies Network, Leicester (2007)

Gesture-Timbre Space: Multidimensional Feature Mapping Using Machine Learning and Concatenative Synthesis

Michael Zbyszyński[1(✉)], Balandino Di Donato[2], Federico Ghelli Visi[3], and Atau Tanaka[1]

[1] Department of Computing, Goldsmiths, University of London, London SE14 6NW, UK
{m.zbyszynski,a.tanaka}@gold.ac.uk

[2] Informatics Department, University of Leicester, University Road, Leicester LE1 7RH, UK
balandino.didonato@leicester.ac.uk

[3] (GEMM) Gesture Embodiment and Machines in Music, School of Music in Piteå, Luleå University of Technology, Snickargatan 20, 941 63 Piteå, Sweden
mail@federicovisi.com

Abstract. This chapter explores three systems for mapping embodied gesture, acquired with electromyography and motion sensing, to sound synthesis. A pilot study using granular synthesis is presented, followed by studies employing corpus-based concatenative synthesis, where small sound units are organized by derived timbral features. We use interactive machine learning in a mapping-by-demonstration paradigm to create regression models that map high-dimensional gestural data to timbral data without dimensionality reduction in three distinct workflows. First, by directly associating individual sound units and static poses (anchor points) in *static regression*. Second, in *whole regression* a sound tracing method leverages our intuitive associations between time-varying sound and embodied movement. Third, we extend interactive machine learning through the use of artificial agents and reinforcement learning in an *assisted interactive machine learning* workflow. We discuss the benefits of organizing the sound corpus using self-organizing maps to address corpus sparseness, and the potential of regression-based mapping at different points in a musical workflow: gesture design, sound design, and mapping design. These systems support expressive performance by creating gesture-timbre spaces that maximize sonic diversity while maintaining coherence, enabling reliable reproduction of target sounds as well as improvisatory exploration of a sonic corpus. They have been made available to the research community, and have been used by the authors in concert performance.

Keywords: Gestural interaction · Interactive machine learning · Reinforcement learning · Sonic interaction design · Concatenative synthesis · Human-computer interaction

R. Kronland-Martinet et al. (Eds.): CMMR 2019, LNCS 12631, pp. 600–622, 2021.
https://doi.org/10.1007/978-3-030-70210-6_39

1 Introduction

The performance of synthesized sound by means of musician gesture poses several compositional challenges. The association of performer input to sound synthesis output is typically framed as a mapping problem [13]. However, in creating a mapping, a composer has authored neither gesture nor sound, only an abstract association between the two. If we focus on creating gesture and a sound that goes with it, or a synthesizing a sound and finding a gesture that goes with that, we arrived at two ways to think about a problem that might otherwise be thought of as a "chicken or egg" problem. Do we design gesture to sound, or do we design sound to gesture? Mappings in both these cases can then be inferred, creating an opportunity for machine learning techniques. Given that performance is a temporal medium and that gestures and sounds are both time varying phenomena, capturing the evolution of one in association with the other becomes a central challenge. This becomes doubly important when techniques such as signal feature extraction or neural network regression may not have a notion of time in their internal representations. In this chapter we present a series of three systems of increasing complexity where we address questions of gesture design, sound design, and workflows of associating the two by means of machine learning. We introduce a method for creating a regression mappings between gesture input and sound output in a multidimensional feature space. We experiment with techniques for making the information space robust, and providing feedback between machine agent and human user through reinforcement learning.

The systems we describe enable musicians to explore and perform with a multidimensional audio space using multimodal gesture sensing as the input. The input takes features extracted from electromyography (EMG) and inertial sensors, and uses machine learning through regression modeling to create a contiguous gesture and motion space. EMG sensors on the forearm have demonstrated [32] potential for expressive, multidimensional musical control, capturing small voltage variations associated with motions of the hand and fingers. Our approach allows musicians to quickly create an association between points and trajectories in a gesture feature space and units in a timbral feature space. The spaces can be explored and augmented together, interactively, offering the potential for new expressive interactions that extend beyond the initially defined gestures [38].

We used granular synthesis and corpus-based concatenative synthesis (CBCS). Granular synthesis enables manipulation of the time/frequency morphology of sound by dividing recorded audio into grains [18]. CBCS is an extension of granular synthesis where grains, or units, are automatically generated and are cataloged by auditory features by the use of music information retrieval and the timbral descriptors it generates. CBCS [23,25] creates longer sounds by combining shorter sounds, where units can be recalled by query with a vector of those features. The actual sound to be played is specified by a target and features associated with that target. The target may be of the same or different modality than the corpus. In speech synthesis, the target is text. In audio resynthesis and "mosaicing" applications, the target can be another sound. In digital musical instrument (DMI) performance, the target is sensor data or some representation of performer action, or gesture, and it may have the same or different feature dimensionality than the corpus.

CBCS performance systems until now have, on the whole, been implemented using dimensionality reduction. A subset of corporal features are projected onto a low dimension space, typically Cartesian, and performance input is constrained to those dimensions (Fig. 1). The dimensionality reduction acts as funnel that does not provide access to the complete feature space of the corpus and may forsake the richness of performance input. Could we provide a way to preserve that richness? Could we create tools to allow musicians sensibly create mappings between multidimensional spaces? Could a regression model be harnessed to carry out multidimensional feature mapping from the input domain (gesture) to the output domain (sound)?

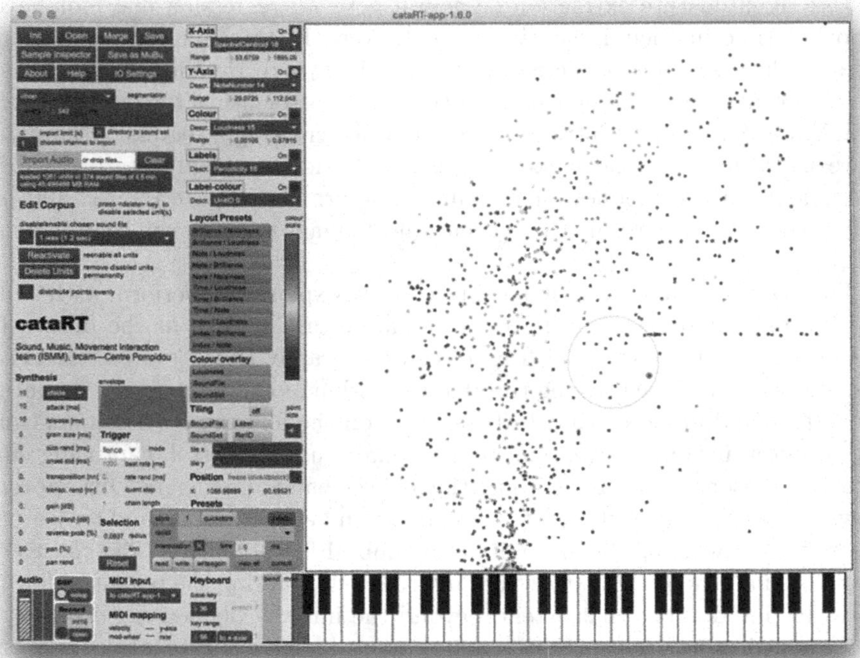

Fig. 1. A graphical interface for CataRT, showing a performance space generated through dimensionality reduction. Three audio features can be selected and projected onto x, y, and color.

We use an interactive machine learning (IML) approach to allow users to quickly customize interactions by demonstration, encoding intuitive knowledge about performance gestures into trained machine learning models. Fails and

Olsen [8] define IML as a machine learning paradigm with a workflow that features rapid, iterative cycles of a user training a model, evaluating its performance, and modifying the model to improve its performance. Fiebrink et al. [9] developed Wekinator to facilitate implementation of real-time, interactive machine learning in creative and musical systems. It provides a high-level interface to the Weka API[1], supporting sensor mapping between applications using Open Sound Control (OSC). Our pilot study uses Wekinator. A similar IML paradigm has been implemented in the RAPID-MIX API [3], part of which is employed in our later studies. Such human-centered machine learning tools have been shown to support creative interaction design, allowing musicians to leverage advances in computation in support of complex musical goals [10]. This approach is characterized by small data sets, relative to classical machine learning and deep learning that rely on big data. In the simplest case, users can interact with the machine learning process by iteratively providing new training examples, such as a specific physical states or motions that should be associated with a specific set of timbral or synthesis parameters. Our follow-up study extends this workflow by employing autonomous agents and reinforcement learning [30].

This chapter is structured as follows. We first review related work on concatenative synthesis in performance. We then describe the architectures (Sect. 3) and technical implementations (Sect. 4) of three systems: a pilot, the main study, and a follow up system. We present user workflows to associate gesture with granular and CBCS synthesis sound via different strategies of regression. Machine learning models are generated interactively, using supervised learning or via reinforcement learning. In the discussion, we provide a critical assessment of these approaches and point out perspectives for future work before concluding.

2 Related Work

Aucouturier and Pachet [1] used concatenative sound synthesis to generate new musical pieces by recomposing segments of pre-existent audio recordings, in a form of audio "mosaicing." They developed a constraint-satisfaction algorithm for controlling high-level properties like energy or continuity of the new track. They presented an example where a musician controls the system via MIDI, demonstrating an audio engine suitable for building real-time, interactive audio systems.

Stowell and Plumbley's [29] work focused on building associations between two differently distributed, unlabeled sets of timbre data. They implemented a regression technique that learns the relations between a corpus of audio grains and input control data. In evaluating their system, they observed that such an approach provides a robust way of building trajectories between grains, and mapping these trajectories to input control parameters.

An example of gestural control of concatenative synthesis is the project *Luna Park* by G. Beller [2]. He uses one accelerometer on top of each hand to estimate

[1] https://www.cs.waikato.ac.nz/ml/weka/.

momentum variation, hit energy, and absolute position of the hands. Two piezoelectric microphones responded to percussive patterns played in different zones of his body (one near the left hip and the other one near the right shoulder). Sensor data were then mapped to audio engine parameters to synthesize and interact with another performer's recorded speech.

Schwarz [26] used his CataRT CBCS implementation controlled through a 2D GUI in live performance taking five different approaches: (i) re-arranging the corpus in a different order than the original one, (ii) interaction with self-recorded live sound, (iii) composing by navigation of the corpus, (iv) cross-selection and interpolation between sound corpora, and (v) corpus-based orchestration by descriptor organization. After performing in these five modes he concludes that CataRT enables musicians to produce rich and complex sounds while maintaining precision in the gestural control of synthesis parameters. It presents itself as a blank canvas, without imposing upon the composer/performer any precise sonority.

Savary et al. [20,21] created *Dirty Tangible Interfaces*, a typology of user interfaces that favour the production of very rich and complex sounds using CataRT. Interfaces can be constantly evolved, irreversibly, by different performers at the same time. The interface is composed of a black box containing a camera and LED to illuminate a glass positioned above the camera, where users place solid and liquid materials. Material topologies are detected by the camera, where a greyscale gradient is then converted into a depth map. This map is then projected onto a 3D reduction of the corpus space to trigger different grains.

In a later work Schwarz et al. [24] extended interaction modes and controllers (2D or 3D positional control, audio input). They concluded by stating the need for machine learning approaches in order to allow the user to explore a corpus by the use of XYZ-type input devices. They present gestural control of CataRT as an expressive and playful tool for improvised performance.

The second and third studies we present both use CataRT as its CBCS synthesis engine and respond to the challenges identified by these researchers in their previous work. Our system allows the mapping of one multidimensional feature space to another without going through a dimensionality reduction stage. It uses machine learning as a way to enable the user to explore the corpus, and reinforcement learning to suggest new mappings connecting input gesture to output sound.

3 Mapping Systems and Workflows

We describe three systems of increasing complexity: First a granular synthesis system in a gesture-design workflow where we examine different strategies for introducing temporality into regression techniques; second, a CBCS system that enables multidimensional mapping of gesture and timbral features; and third, a system that reorganizes the sound corpus by means of self-organizing maps and proposes gesture-sound mappings through reinforcement learning.

3.1 Pilot Study: Regression Anchor Points

The first system uses a procedure based on sound tracing, where participants design gestures to articulate time-varying sound using granular synthesis (Fig. 3). Classical sound tracing typically studies evoked gestural response to sound [4]. Sound tracing has been used as a starting point for techniques of "mapping-by-demonstration" [11]. While these studies look at the articulation of gesture in response to sounds, they focus on evoked gesture. In the field of sonic interaction design, embodied interaction has been used to design sounds. This includes techniques applying interactive technologies to traditions of Foley, or by vocalization [6] and invoke the body in the design of sounds.

We extend the mapping-by-demonstration paradigm to enable gesture-sound reproduction by training machine learning models to enable exploratory gestural performance, articulating expressive variations on the original sound. A gesture is designed in response to a given time-varying sound. A neural network then trains a regression model on the evoked gesture to the original sound. Granular synthesis reproduction of the source sound then enables variations on the sound to be performed by gestures that are similar to, or go outside the bounds of the original sound trace.

We propose four strategies for modeling the time-varying nature of the gesture with the corresponding evolving sound morphology by creating different forms of manual and automated segmentation. These four approaches are called: *whole regression*, temporal modeling, *static regression* and *windowed regression*. The first approach, *whole regression*, uses a neural network trained on whole stream of gestural data and synthesis parameters recorded during exercising the sound-tracing (Fig. 2a).

The second approach, *static regression*, requires the user to design a gesture through the sound-tracing exercise and segment the gesture into four discrete poses, or anchor points. These poses are then associated with sound synthesis parameters at these points in time. This approach, and the next, use machine learning differently than *whole regression* because both the gesture and the sound are segmented temporally. A regression model comprising gestural data and fixed synthesis parameters is trained to establish a continuous gesture-sound model. This model creates new connections between the disparate segments in the training data, regenerating or replacing their original temporal relationships. Participants can then explore the sound through continuous gesture (Fig. 2b). In the third approach, *windowed regression*, the gesture is automatically segmented by our software during the sound-tracing exercise through a windowing process. Four temporal windows centered around the four fixed anchor points in the sound, will generate a data set comprising gestural and sound synthesis features within these windows. A regression neural network is then trained on this data set (Fig. 2c).

As a reference, we implemented a technique in our last method that, by nature, encodes time. Temporal models are built by Hierarchical Hidden Markov Models (HHMMs) implemented with MuBu [22]. HHMM allows an automatic segmentation of the gesture into equal-sized states (ten, in this case), each represented by a Gaussian Mixture Model. In a hierarchical HMM, both short- and long-term temporal dependencies can be modeled through a hierarchy of hidden states [12]. When running a model reports the probability of a gesture being in each state, and allows the original series to be recreated. Gesture and sound are associated through this probabilistic temporal representation (Fig. 2d).

3.2 Main Study: Interactive Machine Learning and CBCS

The second system extends the regression-based control of parametric synthesis from the first study to create a mapping from gesture features to timbral features. We adopt CataRT CBCS, enabling the user to perform the sound's corpus in real time, using variations on an original sound tracing gesture to articulate new sounds.

Figure 4 shows the architecture of the second system. The user first selects a sound, importing it into CataRT. The sound is automatically analyzed and segmented into a corpus. Two forms of segmentation are proposed: onset-based segmentation generating units of varying length and "chop," which divides the sound into equal-sized units. It is significant that long-term temporal data is separated from timbral data at this point. There are features that describe short-term behavior inside of a unit, but a unit's position in the original sound is not directly accessed by our regression models.

The first way of interacting with audio units is to play an entire file from the first to the last unit, recreating the original sound. This corresponds to the *whole*

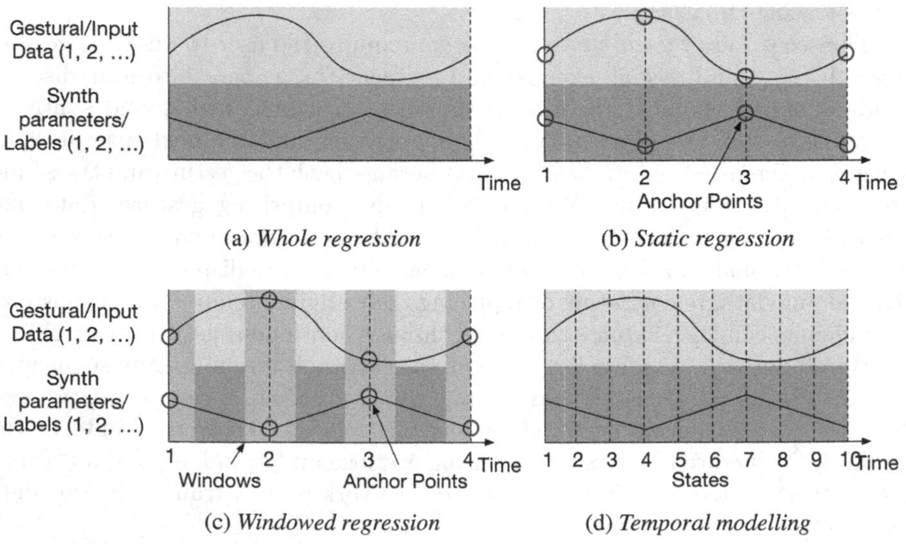

Fig. 2. Pilot study Machine Learning approaches

Fig. 3. A workshop participant, performing a sound tracing exercise in study one.

gesture regression mode from our previous work, and enables the sound tracing workflow. Performers can listen to the whole sound and design the appropriate gesture to accompany that sound. Once that gesture has been designed, they can perform their gesture synchronously with sound playback. As each unit passes in order, a recorder captures associated timbral data in conjunction with the gestural data at that moment. These data form a training set that is used to train a regression model.

A second form of interaction recreates the *static regression* method from the first study. Performers may listen to individual units by selecting the buffer index (which file the unit is from) and data index (which unit in that file). The analyzed timbral features associated with the selected unit are displayed (Fig. 5). In order to associate gestural features with the selected timbral features, they press the *record* button in the machine learning column of the GUI, which automatically captures 500 ms of sensor data during a pose and associates it with the selected unit data.

Once a set of training data has been recorded, users train the neural network. When training has finished, the system enters run mode. At this point, incoming gestural data is sent to the trained regression model. This model outputs a vector of target timbral features which is sent to a k-nearest neighbors algorithm that outputs the buffer and data indices of the unit that most closely matches those features. The CataRT engine receives the indices and plays the requested unit. In this way, we have coupled the multilayer perception (MLP) model of gestural and timbral features to a k-NN search of timbrally defined units the corpus. This

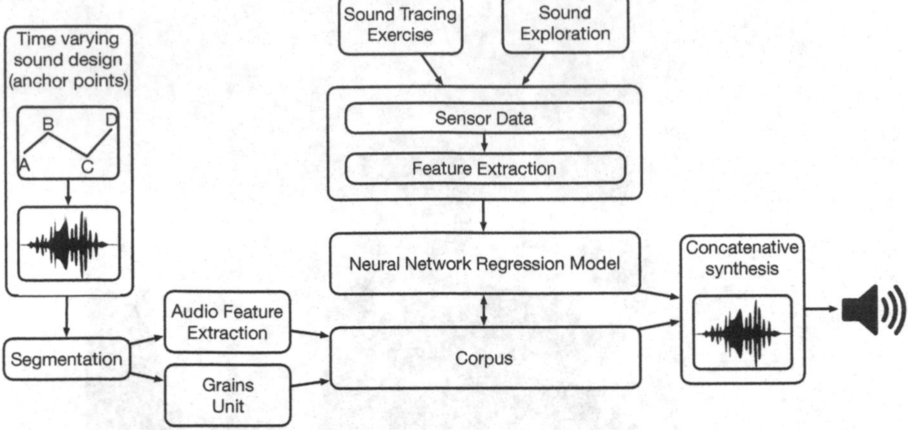

Fig. 4. System architecture for IML+CBCS in the main study.

process allows musicians to explore the gesture-timbre space and perform with it in real time.

When creating models, we encountered potential problems of sparsity of the corpus feature space. There is no guarantee that there will be a unit in the corpus that is closely related to the timbral features generated by the neural network in response to a given set of target gesture features. This is addressed in the third system and described in Sect. 4.4.

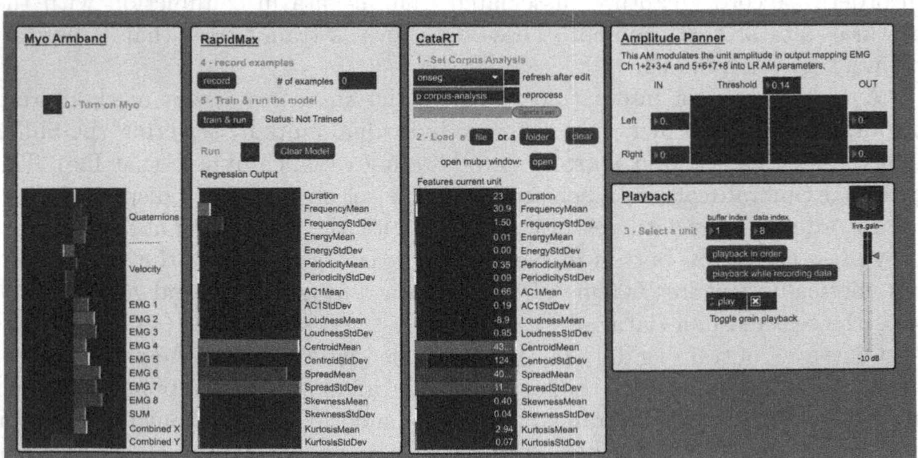

Fig. 5. Graphical-User Interface of the system in the main study.

3.3 Follow-Up Study: Assisted Interactive Machine Learning

Testing of the system revealed a number of strengths and weaknesses that are discussed, below, in Sect. 6. Large, highly-dimensional sound corpora offer opportunities for timbral exploration. But, exploring the numerous sonic articulations afforded by these vast sound spaces is challenging when using a gesture mapping approach that relies exclusively on supervised learning. Based on these preliminary considerations, we developed a system that employs deep reinforcement learning for the purpose of exploring the many, non-obvious ways in which the domains of gesture and timbre can be interfaced. We refer to this interaction design approach as Assisted Interactive Machine Learning (AIML) [35].

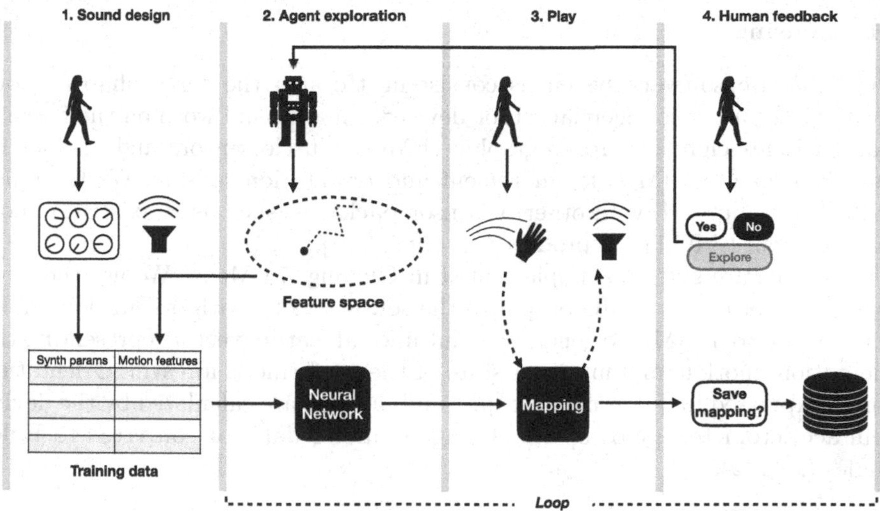

Fig. 6. Assisted Interactive Machine Learning workflow.

Reinforcement learning is an area of machine learning in which artificial agents are programmed to take actions in an environment defined by a set of parameters. Their goal is to maximize the positive feedback – or rewards – they are given by a human (or by another algorithm) observing the outcome of their actions. Deep reinforcement learning approaches, such as the Deep TAMER algorithm, leverage the power of deep neural networks and human-provided feedback to train agents able to perform complex tasks [36]. Recently, Scurto et al. [28] implemented the Deep TAMER algorithm to design artificial agents that allow performers to interactively explore the parameter spaces of software synthesizers.

In our AIML system (Fig. 6), we made use of deep reinforcement learning to explore different mappings between an input device and a sound synthesis engine interactively. The agent first proposes a mapping of gesture features to sound synthesis parameters. The user plays sound using the mapping, and gives feedback to the agent on whether they liked the mapping or not. Based on this feedback, the agent then generates another proposed mapping. The procedure iterates.

The main difference from the workflow described in Sect. 3.2 is that, in AIML, sensor data for training the machine learning model is provided by the artificial agent and not by the user. Rather, the user can give positive or negative feedback to the artificial agent about the proposed mapping while playing, and try new mappings on the fly. Mappings can be saved for later use, and the process can be repeated multiple times in order to co-explore the gesture-sound articulations afforded by the coupling of the sound corpus with a gestural interface.

4 Implementation

4.1 Sensing

The hardware/software system is consistent through the three phases of our research. We use a commercial sensor device[2], an armband worn on the forearm that packages eight electromyographic (EMG) muscle sensors and an inertial measurement unit (IMU) for movement and orientation sensing. We have also verified our approach with other biosensor packages, such as Plux's BITalino[3], and a custom EMG board produced in our lab [7].

The software system is implemented in Cycling '74 Max[4]. We use the `myo`[5] object to capture raw EMG output of the sensors along with orientation angles from the on-board IMU to generate a multimodal feature vector representing the orientation, motion, and muscular state of the performer's forearm. Orientation can be expressed in quaternions (x, y, z and w) that are calculated by the device from accelerometer, gyroscope, and magnetometer data, or converted to Euler Angles (x, y, z).

4.2 Feature Extraction

Because raw EMG signals are intrinsically noisy, we do not include them in our feature vector. From EMG we calculate gesture power [5] from muscle exertion, by tracking the amplitude envelope from each EMG channel with a Bayesian filter [19] to probabilistically predict the amplitude envelope. In addition to orientation, we take the first-order difference between the current orientation frame and the previous frame (e.g., x_d, y_d, z_d, w_d) to represent the motion of the forearm. This is an important feature because hand gestures can be performed ballistically or in a more static fashion, causing different patterns of muscular activation even though the resulting gross movement may seem similar. This also adds a temporal dimension our example points, since this feature incorporates data from the previous frame.

---

2 https://developerblog.myo.com/.
3 https://bitalino.com/.
4 https://cycling74.com/products/max.
5 https://github.com/JulesFrancoise/myo-for-max.

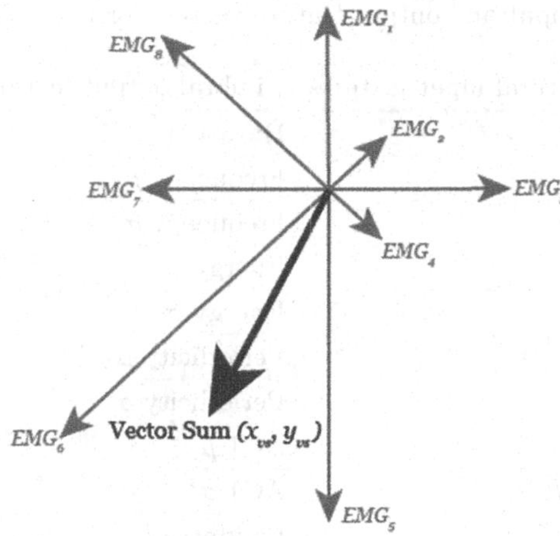

Fig. 7. A sample vector sum, in blue, drawn with the component EMG vectors in grey. (Color figure online)

In the pilot study, (Sect. 3.1)we used Euler Angles (x, y, z) from the device's IMU, as well as calculating first order differences. In addition we derived amplitude envelopes for four of the eight EMG sensors.

In the main study (Sect. 3.2), we used a larger gestural feature vector. We used amplitudes from all eight electrodes in the armband. The sum of all amplitude envelopes is also included in the input feature vector, along with a new feature we have developed called "vector sum." Vector sum (Fig. 7) is a representation of the fact that the forearm muscles are situated around the periphery of the arm in such a way that they can oppose or reinforce the action of other muscles. To calculate the vector sum, we model each electrode as representing a vector pointing away from the center of a circle, evenly spaced every 45°. The direction for each electrode vector does not change and the magnitude is proportional to the amplitude calculated by the Bayesian filter. The eight vectors are summed, and the resulting vector is related to the overall direction of force represented by all of the electrodes. When compared to the sum of all electrodes, the vector sum can distinguish gestures where muscles are opposing one another isometrically. This is a useful feature, since joint movement might be minimal in such gestures but the subjective perception of effort is high. The vector sum is reported as a pair of Cartesian coordinates, which are better suited to regression than polar coordinates because they do not wrap around at zero degrees. See Table 1 for a list of the full gestural and timbral feature vectors. Where relevant, we took the average (μ) and standard deviation (σ) of each timbral feature over the whole audio unit.

The follow-up study (Sect. 3.3) makes use of the *modosc* library [33] for feature extraction and OSC data handling, taking advantage of the OSC-based multi-paradigm programming enabled by the *odot* extensions for Max [14]. While initially designed for the purpose of processing motion capture data in real time,

Table 1. Input and output feature vectors for regression models

Gestural input features	Timbral output features
x	Duration
y	Frequency μ
z	Frequency σ
w	Energy μ
x_d	Energy σ
y_d	Periodicity μ
z_d	Periodicity σ
w_d	AC1 μ
EMG_1	AC1 σ
EMG_2	Loudness μ
EMG_3	Loudness σ
EMG_4	Centroid μ
EMG_5	Centroid σ
EMG_6	Spread μ
EMG_7	Spread σ
EMG_8	Skewness μ
EMG_{sum}	Skewness σ
$vectorSum_x$	Kurtosis μ
$vectorSum_y$	Kurtosis σ

modosc has been recently extended to handle also IMU and EMG data from various devices including the Myo. This allowed us to obtain a more structured OSC namespace, where input features are organized hierarchically, and can be easily retrieved and sent to machine learning and sound synthesis modules. This approach to feature extraction and OSC data handling is exemplified in *GIMLeT*[6], a Max pedagogical toolkit for interactive machine learning.

4.3 Machine Learning

In the pilot study, we used Wekinator [9] as an outboard machine learning application, with communications taking place between sensing and sound synthesis in Max over OSC. OSC messages were constructed in *sendrcv*, a Max abstraction that serves as a modular scripting system, enabling parallel and bi-directional scaling and mapping of sensors and audio synthesis data between Wekinator and our software. On input, it allows the user to select gesture features to be recorded by Wekinator. On output, each instance makes a bridge between a parameter in the synthesizer and the model output.

[6] GIMLeT – Gestural Interaction Machine Learning Toolkit: https://github.com/federicoVisi/GIMLeT.

For the main study, we brought the regression algorithm into Max using an external object called `rapidmax` [17]. This object implements basic machine learning algorithms, such as multilayer perceptrons, k-nearest neighbor, and dynamic time warping, to allow Max users to quickly employ machine learning for regression or classification tasks. It is a Max wrapper around RapidLib [39], a C++ and JavaScript library for creative, interactive machine learning applications in the style of Wekinator [9]. Here we use a multilayer perceptron (MLP) neural network with one hidden layer to create models that perform regression based on user-provided training examples. This particular implementation uses a linear activation function on the output layer, allowing for model outputs that go beyond the numerical range of the provided examples, extending the interpolation typically carried out by mapping to a form of *extrapolation*, to create a larger and potentially more interesting generative space for aesthetic exploration. In our main workflow (Sect. 3.2), training examples are created manually by associating inputs—gesture feature vectors—with outputs: vectors of timbral features. Through the use of supervised machine learning, performers can record example interactions, associating positions and gestures with sounds to build an exploratory and performative gesture-timbre space.

The extended AIML workflow (Sect. 3.3) employs reinforcement learning to help performers discover new interaction mappings. The AIML architecture features interaction with an artificial agent for the purpose of generating training data and train regression models using rapidmax. For the agent, we used *Co-Explorer*[7], a Python deep reinforcement learning agent proposed by Scurto et a. [28] and based on the Deep TAMER algorithm [36]. Bidirectional communication between the agent and Max is done through OSC. Human feedback to the agent can be given in different ways. For the first prototype of the system, [35] we used a custom touch interface designed in TouchOSC[8] and implemented on an iPhone; whereas for a performance piece [34] we opted for a simpler design using a 3-button remote control.

4.4 Sound Synthesis

In the pilot study, we used SCP for Max by Manuel Poletti, and controlled a breakpoint envelope-based playback system to design sounds that transition between four fixed anchor points of synthesis parameters in SCP's granular synthesis module. Envelopes interpolate between these points. The temporal evolution of sound is captured as different states in the breakpoint editor whose envelopes run during playback. Any of the parameters can be assigned to breakpoint envelopes to be controlled during playback.

For the main study, we use the CataRT engine implemented using the MuBu[9] library of Max objects. The `mubu.process` object performs segmentation and auditory feature analysis, `mubu.knn` retrieves the closest matching unit to a given

[7] https://github.com/Ircam-RnD/coexplorer.
[8] https://hexler.net/products/touchosc.
[9] https://forumnet.ircam.fr/product/mubu-en/.

set of auditory features, and the `mubu.concat~` object is used for synthesizing the unit once recalled (see Sect. 3.2).

When a sound file is imported into MuBu, it is automatically segmented into units, either of a fixed length or determined by an onset detection algorithm (Fig. 8). A vector of auditory features (Table 1) is derived for each unit. These vectors of auditory features are associated with sensor feature vectors to train a neural network, and roughly represent a high-dimensional timbral similarity space.

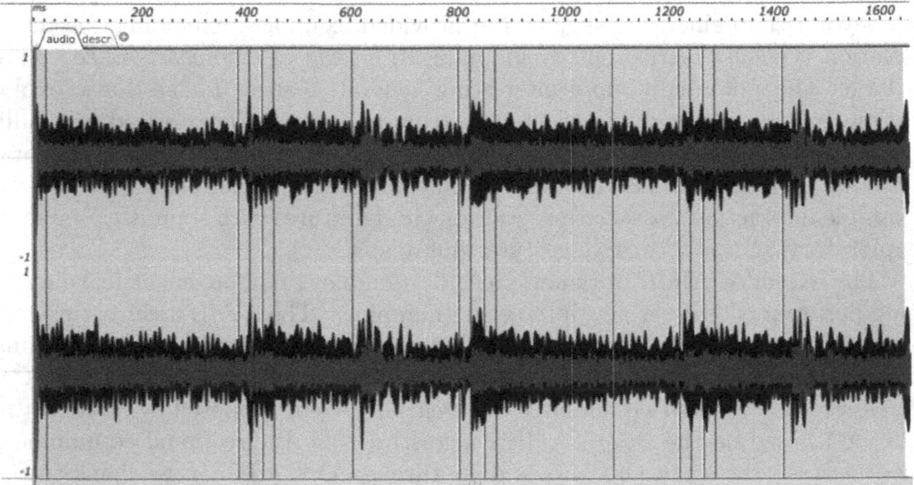

Fig. 8. A sound file imported into a MuBu buffer, using the **onseg** algorithm. Unit boundaries are shown as vertical, red lines. (These lines would be equally spaced if segmented in chop mode.) (Color figure online)

During playback, the amplitude and panning of the output are controlled by an amplitude panner (Fig. 5, upper right panel). The EMG sensors are divided into two groups and their amplitude envelopes are summed. The sum of each group is used to control the overall amplitude of the audio output in the left and right channels, respectively. When there is no muscular activation, both channels have near-zero gain, giving the performer a natural method to make the instrument silent when they are not putting any energy into the system.

In the AIML system, we retained CataRT. Interaction with corpus-based concatenative synthesis was further refined by adopting the method based on self-organizing maps (SOM) by Margraf [16]. This allowed us address the problem of corpus sparseness described earlier in Sect. 3.2, and to have more control over the spatial characteristics of sound corpora, i.e. how grains are distributed in their feature space. Distributing grains in a Cartesian space using audio descriptors as coordinates may lead to sparse corpora in which some regions are much more dense while others are nearly empty, as shown in Fig. 9a. This is a major drawback when using exploratory approaches like AIML, as exploring nearly empty areas of the corpus would result in poor sound variety. SOM allows us to address this issue, resulting in sound corpora that are more evenly distributed and built using multiple descriptors (Fig. 9b).

5 Results

The pilot study was conducted in a workshop-based scenario to teach non-specialists gesture design without needing technical knowledge of machine learning [31]. Participants were able to explore new timbres using the four approaches described in Sect. 3.1 and one of three pre-designed sounds. The regression algorithm allowed them to scrub to different granular parameters in the stimulus sound. Participants were interested in going beyond reproducing the sound trajectory they had traced, exploring the expressivity of a given technique and responding to variations of gesture within and outside the designed gesture. Three out of five participants preferred the windowed regression technique. Participants felt that this technique enabled them to reproduce the sound accurately but at the same time also to explore new sonic possibilities. Interestingly, participants thought that the HMM temporal modeling was too "choppy" for exploration outside the designed gesture. Static regression was found to be a precise way to recreate the designed gesture/sound relationship, while whole regression was found by participants to be "embodied" [31].

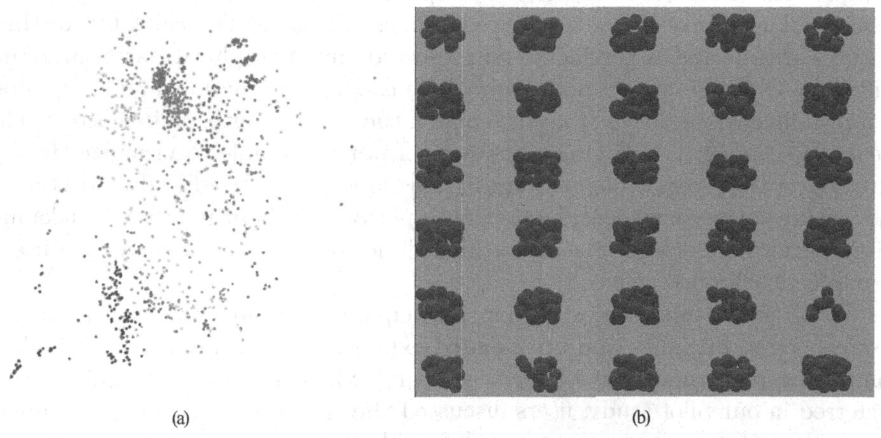

Fig. 9. Spatial distribution of sound corpora with and without self-organizing maps. *A* (left) shows an example corpus from [27] where grains are mapped using three features: spectral centroid (x), periodicity (y), note number (color). *B* (right) shows a sound corpus mapped on a bidimensional space using 19 descriptors and self-organizing maps.

Of the proposed four segmentation approaches introduced in this study, we retained two of them, *whole* and *static*, for the subsequent work with the concatenative audio engine.

For the second study, we assessed the strengths and weaknesses of the system and explored its affordances by using it in our creative practice. The system has been used as the substructure for a series of compositions called *Delearn* by Tanaka where each version uses different source audio and selection of key units, to be performed live where the process of associating poses with sound units, training and running the neural network is exposed as the dramaturgy of the concert performance[10,11,12].

In the third study, the reinforcement learning system was presented in a symposium demo session on a mobile phone. This fed into a design iteration of the system that was then used with the EMG sensors. A prototype of this process – schematized in Fig. 6 – has been demoed and evaluated at the Human Data Interaction (HDI) workshop *Art, AI-created content, & industrial/cultural effects* [35]. Visi composed and performed a musical work using the system, *"You have a new memory"* [34].

6 Discussion

Concatenative synthesis is described in terms of a target that one tries to synthesize by navigating a corpus. In an audio-audio mosaicing task, the "target" is an example sound that one is trying to resynthesize with the corpus. In cases using interfaces for live controllers [20,24], mappings between gesture and sound have, until now, taken place in reduced dimension spaces. Typically, two or three features are selected as pertinent and projected onto a graphical Cartesian representation. Our system does not require dimensionality reduction, and the number of input dimensions does not need to match the number output dimensions. This creates a seeming disadvantage, however, of not being able to visualize the feature space. However, while Schwarz in [24] finds seeing a reduced projection of the feature space convenient, he prefers to perform without it. Both Tanaka and Visi's performances take place in a high dimensional space without the use of visual feedback onstage.

We observed from our workshop participants in study one that a balance between reproducibility and open-ended exploration was important to make a compelling performance system. In selecting which regression technique they preferred in our pilot study, users discussed the trade-offs between determinacy and exploration. Anchor points were defined by breakpoints in the granular synthesis parameters, and encouraged users to decompose the continuous tracing gesture they had made in response to the sound into salient postures corresponding to the anchor points. By breaking apart the temporal relationships of both

[10] https://cmmr2019.prism.cnrs.fr/programArtistic.html.

[11] http://newmusic.org/media/vnm-festival-2019-resonances-atau-tanaka/.

[12] https://www.eegsynth.org/?p=2682.

the sound and the gesture, the machine learning system was afforded the opportunity to open up new pathways through the sound space. Sound tracing was a useful impetus for gesture design, but once the gesture-sound relationship was established, users were interested in varying the gesture or changing it altogether to make the source sound musically expressive.

Schwarz describes exploratory performance as a DMI application of CBCS that distinguishes it from the more deterministic applications of speech synthesis or audio mosaicing [24]. He provides the example of improvised music where the performer uses an input device to explore a corpus, sometimes one that is being filled during the performance by live sampling another instrumentalist. This creates an element of surprise for the performer. Here we sought to create systems that enable timbral exploration, but that would be reproducible, and useful in compositional contexts where both sound and associated gesture can be designed *a priori*.

The main study shifted from gesture design to sound design, automating aspects of audio feature extraction. Anchor points were defined by the user when they selected interesting sounding CBCS units during the playback of the source sound. These points were associated with poses. We were also able to perform the sound tracing gesture to reconstruct the original sound. This shows that the generation of time-varying sound sources from our parametric synthesis program was faithfully reproduced by CataRT in this playing mode.

While this was ostensibly temporal (in that the units came in sequence through the evolution of the sound), they also identified points in the auditory feature space outside of time. In performance, arriving at one of the anchor poses reliably recalled the unit associated with it. Continuous gesture through these anchors (or not) in effect allowed the performer to explore the timbral information space. In this sense, retaining a notion of time was, in our work, connected to the reproducibility of an original gesture-sound relationship. While this was established in the first study and shown to be possible in the second study, the multidimensional feature space mapping also provided an affordance that enabled exploration out of time. By situating sonic units in a timbral space, the second system allowed users to perform in a way that either reproduced the temporal relationship between units or generated completely new relationships. With machine learning handling the gestural and timbral features, performers were able to explore the temporal dimension of the corpus freely. The third study then, proposed gesture-sound mappings that were not time-based at all. Did we somehow respond to our workshop participants from study one, who established exploration as an emerging theme, by making subsequent systems where temporal representation disappeared?

In the main study, the association of gesture and sound operates at two levels. First, the timbral distance from the anchor units was provided by the k-NN algorithm within the CBCS engine. Second, regression models mapped multiple gestural feature dimensions to destination timbral features, whether or not a sound unit of those features existed. The timbral distance measure served to nominate a unit for playback. Self-organizing maps, in the final study, aided in distributing units evenly across the audio corpus, reducing large gaps between the hypothetical audio features specified by the neural network and the existence of an corresponding sound unit.

Supporting expressive performance implies the need to create gesture-timbre spaces that maximize sonic diversity. When a performer navigates through gesture space, the outcome is considered more expressive if a diverse range of individual units is activated. However, there also needs to be some coherence across the diversity for the result to be musically meaningful. Nuances of gesture are sonically meaningful if the gestural trajectory has a fine-grained sonic result. This was not always the case in the workflow from the main study, especially where the user chooses individual units and associates them with specific poses. It is here that corpus sparseness becomes apparent and where the distribution of units in the high-dimensional space is not even. In a typical corpus, there will be areas with large clusters of units and other units that are relatively isolated. When musicians chose individual units to use for gesture mapping, there was a tendency for them to choose units that had the most character. The very fact that the selected units had "character" means that these units were often outliers in the feature space. Outlier units represent the edges of the timbral space of a corpus. Regression between units on opposite edges of the space will seek a wide range of hypothetical intermediate units. However, it is also possible that a gestural path between two interesting units does not pass near any actual units in the corpus. While the regression may specify features for a unit that might exist, corpus sparseness means that there may be a void in this part of the timbral space. When this happens, the resulting space performs more like a classifier, allowing the performer to play one unit or another without any transitional material between them. It is in this case that the self-organizing map aids in redistributing the timbral space to fill it more consistently and allow more "hits" as a performer gesturally explores between previously identified anchor units

The AIML workflow in the third study uses reinforcement learning in addition to the SOM to help performers find interesting mappings in the gesture-timbre space. In this case, we have moved from the gesture-design focus of the first study, through the sound-design focus of the second, to arrive at an agent assisted mapping-design where the system proposes exploratory gesture-sound associations that may not have been evident even in a *mapping-by-demonstration* paradigm. The trial with mobile phones afforded a quick, fun workflow that was perceived as useful in providing unexpected mappings. The full system led to a rewarding creative process during the development of new musical work that has been performed in concert [34]. More time needs to be spent exploring a consistent system to expose its affordances and constraints clearly, leading to a better understanding of the *ergodynamics* [15] of assisted interactive machine learning as a sonic interaction design paradigm situated in musical practice.

The systems we have presented enable mapping across multidimensional spaces without dimensionality reduction. Other ways to use multidimensional gesture-timbre mapping could be to generate feature mapping using one corpus of sounds, and then either augment that corpus or swap it with an entirely different corpus – moving the timbral trajectory of a gesture space into a new set of sounds. This can be fruitful when units in the new corpus intersect with the existing gesture space, but it is difficult to give users an idea about whether or not that will be the case. One idea we are exploring is "transposing" a trajectory in timbral feature space so that it intersects with the highest number of units in a new corpus. This could be accomplished using machine learning techniques, such as Dynamic Time Warping (DTW), to calculate the "cost" of different ways to match a specific trajectory to a given set of units, and find the optimal transposition. We know from Wessel's seminal work on timbre spaces [37] that transposition in a low dimensional timbre space is perceptually relevant. Automatically generating these transpositions in a high dimensional space, or suggesting multiple possible transpositions, has the potential to generate novel musical phrases that are perceptually connected to the original training inputs.

7 Conclusion

We have presented a series of systems that combine regression-based machine learning with sound synthesis. They grow from a pilot study where a sound tracing workflow was used to design gestures to articulate time-varying sounds. Gesture input from EMG and IMU sensors was associated with a pre-designed sound as a means to explore gesture design. We coined the notion of *anchor points* to generate training data for a neural network. Workshop participants used these anchor points to reproduce the source sound and to explore novel results in areas between and around the points.

The main study focused more sharply on sound-design by using corpus-based concatenative synthesis to catalog sound units by timbral features. Our regression-based mapping approach allowed us to model complex mappings that preserve the high-dimensionality defining the sound units in a corpus. We were able to reproduce original sound tracings and afford improvisational exploration. However, distribution of units in a corpus could be uneven and may result in stepped unit output that does not correspond to the continuous gesture input.

The third system uses self-organizing maps to address the corpus sparsity problem. A reinforcement learning agent proposes mappings between gesture and timbre spaces, automating the design of mappings that are no longer based on temporal evolution as its basis. There is no longer any source to reproduce, only gesture-sound spaces to explore. Self organizing maps served to even out the distribution of units in a corpus, making it more likely that a performed gesture will engage a wide pallet of sonic units. Increasing the "hit rate" is important, because in this system mappings are proposed by an automatic agent. The performer evaluates mappings dynamically, feeding their preferences back into the system. This Assisted Interactive Machine Learning (AIML) workflow allows for a fluid process of mapping design, helping musicians discover mappings that fit their aesthetic needs by keeping them directed towards the interaction at hand, rather than numerical parameters or features that inform the underlying algorithms.

Together, these systems explore the potential of regression-based association of performance gesture and sound synthesis. They offer associated techniques to situate the regression model at different points in a musical workflow, be it focused on gesture design, sound design, or mapping design. These systems have been made available to the research community, and have been used by the authors in concert performance.

Acknowledgments. The research leading to these results has received funding from the European Research Council (ERC) under the European Union's Horizon 2020 research and innovation programme (Grant agreement No. 789825).

References

1. Aucouturier, J.J., Pachet, F.: Jamming with plunderphonics: interactive concatenative synthesis of music. J. New Music Res. **35**(1), 35–50 (2006). https://doi.org/10.1080/09298210600696790
2. Beller, G.: Gestural control of real time speech synthesis in Luna Park. In: Proceedings of Sound Music Computing Conference, SMC, Padova, Italy (2011)
3. Bernardo, F., Zbyszyński, M., Grierson, M., Fiebrink, R.: Designing and evaluating the usability of a machine learning API for rapid prototyping music technology. Front. Artif. Intell. **3**(a13), 1–18 (2020)
4. Caramiaux, B., Bevilacqua, F., Schnell, N.: Towards a gesture-sound cross-modal analysis. In: Kopp, S., Wachsmuth, I. (eds.) GW 2009. LNCS (LNAI), vol. 5934, pp. 158–170. Springer, Heidelberg (2010). https://doi.org/10.1007/978-3-642-12553-9_14
5. Caramiaux, B., Donnarumma, M., Tanaka, A.: Understanding gesture expressivity through muscle sensing. ACM Trans. Comput. Hum. Interact. (TOCHI) **21**(6), 31 (2015)
6. Delle Monache, S., Rocchesso, D.: To embody or not to embody: a sound design dilemma. In: Machine Sounds, Sound Machines. XXII Colloquium of Music Informatics, Venice, Italy (2018)
7. Di Donato, B., Tanaka, A., Zbyszyński, M., Klang, M.: EAVI EMG board. In: Demo of International Conference on New Interfaces for Musical Expression. NIME 2019, Federal University of Rio Grande do Sul, Porto Allegre, Brazil, June 2019
8. Fails, J.A., Olsen Jr, D.R.: Interactive machine learning. In: Proceedings of the 8th International Conference on Intelligent User Interfaces, pp. 39–45 (2003)
9. Fiebrink, R., Cook, P.R.: The Wekinator: a system for real-time, interactive machine learning in music. In: Proceedings of the International Society for Music Information Retrieval Conference, ISMIR 2010, Utrecht, Netherlands (2010)
10. Fiebrink, R.A., Caramiaux, B.: The machine learning algorithm as creative musical tool. In: Dean, R.T., McLean, A. (eds.) The Oxford Handbook of Algorithmic Music, vol. 1, pp. 181–208. Oxford University Press (2018). https://doi.org/10.1093/oxfordhb/9780190226992.013.23
11. Françoise, J.: Motion-sound mapping by demonstration. Ph.D. thesis, UPMC Université Pierre et Marie Curie, Paris (2015)
12. Françoise, J., Caramiaux, B., Bevilacqua, F.: A hierarchical approach for the design of gesture-to-sound mappings. In: 9th Sound and Music Computing Conference, SMC, Copenhagen, Denmark (2012)

13. Hunt, A., Wanderley, M.M.: Mapping performer parameters to synthesis engines. Organ. Sound **7**(2), 97–108 (2002)
14. Maccallum, J., Gottfried, R., Rostovtsev, I., Bresson, J., Freed, A.: Dynamic message-oriented middleware with open sound control and Odot. In: International Computer Music Conference, ICMA, Denton, United States (2015). https://hal.archives-ouvertes.fr/hal-01165775/document
15. Magnusson, T.: Introduction: on objects, humans, and machines. In: Sonic Writing. Bloomsbury Academic (2019). https://doi.org/10.5040/9781501313899.0006
16. Margraf, J.: Self-organizing maps for sound corpus organization. Master's Thesis. Audiokommunikation - Technische Universität Berlin (2019). https://www2.ak.tu-berlin.de/~akgroup/ak_pub/abschlussarbeiten/2019/Margraf_MasA.pdf
17. Parke-Wolfe, S.T., Scurto, H., Fiebrink, R.: Sound control: supporting custom musical interface design for children with disabilities. In: Proceedings of the International Conference on New Interfaces for Musical Expression, NIME 2019, Porto Alegre, Brazil (2019)
18. Roads, C.: Microsound. The MIT Press, Cambridge, MA (2002)
19. Sanger, T.D.: Bayesian filtering of myoelectric signals. J. Neurophysiol. **97**(2), 1839–1845 (2007)
20. Savary, M., Schwarz, D., Pellerin, D.: Dirti–dirty tangible interfaces. In: Proceedings of the International Conference on New Interfaces for Musical Expression, NIME 2012, Ann Arbor, Michigan (2012). http://www.nime.org/proceedings/2012/nime2012_212.pdf
21. Savary, M., Schwarz, D., Pellerin, D., Massin, F., Jacquemin, C., Cahen, R.: Dirty tangible interfaces: Expressive control of computers with true grit. In: CHI 2013 Extended Abstracts on Human Factors in Computing Systems, CHI EA 2013, Paris, France, pp. 2991–2994. ACM (2013). https://doi.org/10.1145/2468356.2479592
22. Schnell, N., Röbel, A., Schwarz, D., Peeters, G., Borghesi, R.: MuBu & friends - assembling tools for content based real-time interactive audio processing in Max/MSP. In: Proceedings of the International Computer Music Conference, ICMC, Montreal, Quebec, QC, pp. 423–426 (2009)
23. Schwarz, D.: Concatenative sound synthesis: the early years. J. New Music Res. **35**(1), 3–22 (2006). https://doi.org/10.1080/09298210600696857
24. Schwarz, D.: The sound space as musical instrument: playing corpus-based concatenative synthesis. In: Proceedings of the International Conference on New Interfaces for Musical Expression, NIME 2012, Ann Arbor, Michigan (2012). http://www.nime.org/proceedings/2012/nime2012_120.pdf
25. Schwarz, D., Beller, G., Verbrugghe, B., Britton, S.: Real-time corpus-based concatenative synthesis with CataRT. In: 9th International Conference on Digital Audio Effects, DAFx 2019, Montreal, Canada, pp. 279–282 (2006). https://hal.archives-ouvertes.fr/hal-01161358
26. Schwarz, D., Cahen, R., Britton, S.: Principles and applications of interactive corpus-based concatenative synthesis. In: Journées d'Informatique Musicale. JIM, Albi, France (2008)
27. Schwarz, D., Tremblay, P.A., Harker, A.: Rich contacts: corpus-based convolution of contact interaction sound for enhanced musical expression. In: Proceedings of the International Conference on New Interfaces for Musical Expression, pp. 247–250 (2014). http://www.nime.org/proceedings/2014/nime2014_451.pdf
28. Scurto, H., Van Kerrebroeck, B., Caramiaux, B., Bevilacqua, F.: Designing deep reinforcement learning for human parameter exploration. ArXiv Preprint (2019). http://arxiv.org/pdf/1907.00824.pdf

29. Stowell, D., Pumbley, M.D.: Timbre remapping through a regression-tree technique. In: Proceedings of the Sound Music Computing Conference, SMC (2010)
30. Sutton, R.S., Barto, A.G.: Reinforcement Learning: An Introduction. MIT Press, Cambridge (2018)
31. Tanaka, A., Di Donato, B., Zbyszyński, M.: Designing gestures for continuous sonic interaction. In: Proceedings of the International Conference on New Interfaces for Musical Expression, NIME 2019, Porto Alegre, Brazil (2019)
32. Tanaka, A., Ortiz, M.: Gestural musical performance with physiological sensors, focusing on the electromyogram. In: Lesaffre, M.L., Maes, P.J., Leman, M. (eds.) The Routledge Companion to Embodied Music Interaction. Routledge, London (2017)
33. Visi, F., Dahl, L.: Real-time motion capture analysis and music interaction with the modosc descriptor library. In: Proceedings of the International Conference on New Interfaces for Musical Expression, pp. 144–147 (2018). https://github.com/motiondescriptors/modosc
34. Visi, F.G., AQAXA: "You have a new memory". In: ICLI 2020 - the Fifth International Conference on Live Interfaces, Trondheim, Norway (2020)
35. Visi, F.G., Tanaka, A.: Towards assisted interactive machine learning: exploring gesture-sound mappings using reinforcement learning. In: ICLI 2020 - the Fifth International Conference on Live Interfaces, Trondheim, Norway (2020)
36. Warnell, G., Waytowich, N., Lawhern, V., Stone, P.: Deep TAMER: interactive agent shaping in high-dimensional state spaces. In: 32nd AAAI Conference on Artificial Intelligence, AAAI 2018, pp. 1545–1553 (2018). http://arxiv.org/abs/1709.10163
37. Wessel, D.L.: Timbre space as a musical control structure. Comput. Music J. 45–52 (1979)
38. Zbyszyński, M., Di Donato, B., Tanaka, A.: The effect of co-adaptive learning & feedback in interactive machine learning. In: ACM CHI: Human-Centered Machine Learning Perspectives Workshop, Glasgow, UK. ACM (2019)
39. Zbyszyński, M., Grierson, M., Yee-King, M.: Rapid prototyping of new instruments with codecircle. In: Proceedings of the International Conference on New Interfaces for Musical Expression, Copenhagen, Denmark, pp. 227–230 (2017). http://www.nime.org/proceedings/2017/nime2017_paper0042.pdf

Developing a Method for Identifying Improvisation Strategies in Jazz Duos

Torbjörn Gulz[1,2], Andre Holzapfel[2(✉)], and Anders Friberg[2(✉)]

[1] KMH Royal College of Music, Stockholm, Sweden
gulz@kth.se
[2] KTH Royal Institute of Technology, Stockholm, Sweden
{holzap,afriberg}@kth.se

Abstract. The primary purpose of this paper is to develop a method to investigate the communication process between musicians performing improvisation in jazz, and to apply this method in a first case study. In jazz, applied improvisation theory usually consists of scale and harmony studies within quantized rhythmic patterns. There is a need to expand the concept of theory to include areas related to communication and strategic choices. To study improvisational strategies we recorded duos performed by the first author at the piano together with different horn players. Backing tracks were provided by prerecorded material from an ensemble with piano, bass and drums The duo recording was transcribed using music production software. The resulting score and the audio recording were then used during an in-depth interview of the horn player to identify underlying strategies. The strategies were coded according to previous research and could be classified according to five different categories. The paper contributes to jazz improvisation theory towards embracing artistic expressions and choices made in real-life musical situations.

Keywords: Jazz improvisation strategies · Musical interaction · Horn players

1 Introduction

Improvising is an activity that raises great interest in many disciplines. There are several questions concerning improvisation that need to be answered. What or who defines free improvisation? When is prior knowledge required for improvisation? What kind of knowledge do we need and how do we acquire it? How much of the knowledge in improvisation is explicit?

The ethnomusicologist Bruno Nettl [9] summarizes how the term improvisation has been treated historically in music research. He describes how improvisation for a long time was ignored and how it later on, based on a Western music tradition, was used as an opposite activity to composition. The improvisation

Electronic supplementary material The online version of this chapter (https://doi.org/10.1007/978-3-030-70210-6_40) contains supplementary material, which is available to authorized users.

R. Kronland-Martinet et al. (Eds.): CMMR 2019, LNCS 12631, pp. 623–635, 2021.
https://doi.org/10.1007/978-3-030-70210-6_40

was then to be considered as the musician's way of putting a personal touch to the music through interpretation. Björn Alterhaug [2] argues that the changed social and economic structures during the 19th century changed the view of improvisation as an important means of musical expression. The composers became the creators of music and the musicians their tools.

Since composed music had higher status and was treated as more serious, the boundary between composition and improvisation becomes an exciting field, as Carlos Guedes [8] argues. He also discusses how a comparison between composed and improvised music can be used as a quality concept, with well-performed composed music being perceived as improvised and vice versa.

Jazz has become one of the music styles most associated with improvisation since the very core of jazz music is the musician's ability to improvise in a given context [3]. As jazz music includes several different styles and has evolved relatively fast over the last 100 years, the *context*, according to style, is what primarily differentiates jazz musicians' way of dealing with improvisation. In older jazz from the 1920s to the 1950s, it is clear how rules for improvisation have been developing rapidly. From mainly embellishing the melody of the tunes, the musicians started to create a pile of phrases linked to the harmony of the compositions. Several trend-setting musicians during this period stress the possibilities of expressing themselves through improvisation, which leads to an ever-increasing repertoire of phrases. The vocabulary of jazz is replenished, but this new way of relating to jazz improvisation thus leads to a more advanced context where the risk of playing "wrong notes" increases. Although much of the jazz improvisation studies have been based on listening, transcribing, and playing with solos from recordings, an elaborated theory of jazz improvisation began to take shape. In the mid-1940s pure jazz education was even beginning to emerge in competition with the previous programs, which only dealt with classical music [3]. A large part of the jazz theory taught nowadays refers to this period of the 1940–50s and is considered a foundation for young musicians to build their personal sound upon.

Around 1960 there was a breaking point in jazz history when new ways of treating harmony and new playing techniques were broadly introduced. Harmonically, the previous function-based harmony was replaced by modal-harmony based on scales. The introduced scales were, on the one hand, scales inspired by classical composers such as Debussy, Scriabin and Bartok, but also scales transferred directly from other cultural contexts. As jazz was in a rapid development phase at that time, even the ordinary modal scales were soon supplemented or replaced by improvisation related to open structures [3]. Through this transformation of underlying material and practice, improvisation in jazz had become looser and was transformed from a phrase-based improvisation practice.

A musician requires years of preparation to bring forward the tools and individual language suitable in his musical sphere, as Marcel Cobussen [5] emphasizes in his book "The field of musical improvisation". According to Cobussen, improvisation cannot occur without preparation, where part of the preparation consists of being able to meet the unexpected. Because a considerable part of a musician's reality also means being dependent on other musicians and their ability to improvise, it is of great value to have a large range of reactions and approaches at one's disposal. There are different ways for jazz musicians to practice improvisation, from developing the traditional form of storytelling [3,4] that is mostly built on the practice-based vocabulary of phrases [6] mentioned earlier, until the free jazz language with extended degrees of freedom [7]. Analyzing the horizontal lines as melodies by using tools from melody analysis is one way to acquire some of the basic knowledge in jazz improvisation, and therefore there are many transcriptions of famous jazz musicians' solos available. In addition to books with transcriptions, there are also large projects such as the Jazzomat [11] project with a very extensive database of solo transcriptions. Such improvised melodies are related to an implicit chord structure based on a song or a composition, in which the chord pattern repeats during the soloist's performance.

The present study embraces the diversity of improvisation styles by incorporating a continuum from chord progressions to more open musical contexts into a novel, explorative method for investigating improvisation strategies. The British musicologist and guitar player Thomas Williams makes the following definition of improvisation in jazz that is useful in this study:

> *"Improvisation in jazz is an extemporaneous activity in which performers navigate complex mental processes to produce musical utterances that aim to be at once novel, spontaneous and interesting and also communicative (both to the wider ensemble and audience), well-structured and familiar* [12]."

A subject specifically addressed in this study, which is potentially useful for an extended jazz theory, are the strategies used by experienced musicians, who have overcome the first barriers of limited instrument skills and insufficient knowledge of basic jazz theory. With a starting point in Norgaard's [10] categorization of improvisation strategies, Williams [12] has developed five main categories of strategies on which this study is based:

1. Rhythmic (timing, placement, density)
2. Pitch (chord scales, melody, harmony)
3. Timbral (i.e. instrument sound, effects, articulation)
4. Physical (physical cliche's, phrases)
5. Dialogical (interaction - with fellow musician or audience)

The purpose of this study was mainly to design and evaluate a methodology to uncover strategies in an unprepared jazz improvisation setting. Participants and the first author of the study were involved in a duo improvisation session, which was recorded and subsequently analyzed. The results from the analysis were obtained in interviews between the participant and first author, and the transcribed outcomes were adapted to the coding system by Williams [12]. We will discuss the advantages and shortcomings of this coding system, with the goal to extend and apply it in an upcoming study with Swedish professional jazz musicians. The advantage of the proposed method lies in its stylistic openness and its ecologically valid performance settings, which produce analytically as well as artistically expressive outcomes.

2 Experiment

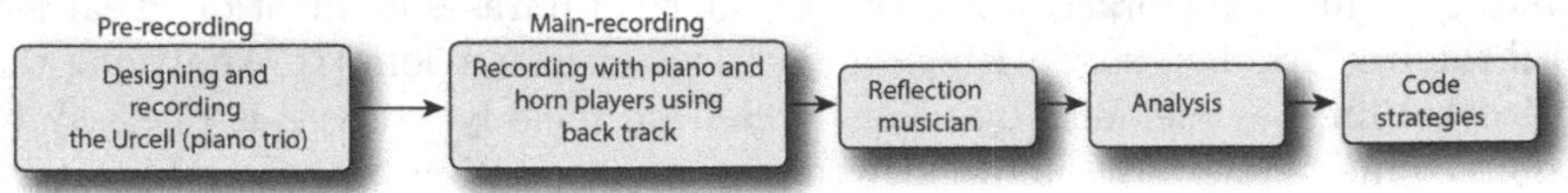

Fig. 1. Method applied in this study.

Figure 1 illustrates the process that underlies the study presented in this paper, which will be explained in the following parts of this section.

2.1 Music Material

Prerecording. In the preparatory stage five different piano trio schematic scores, called Urcells (Fig. 2), were performed and recorded, which later served as backing tracks for the duo improvisations (main recording). The label Urcell is used through this paper to define the musical center of the experiment. The only instructions available in the score were implicit instructions, based on few chords or scales for the different six parts that lasted about one minute each. The five Urcells were deliberately composed with both easier and more difficult passages according to chord and chord scales. The studio recording with the piano trio was performed in a authentic recording environment by professional musicians. After the recording, the audio signals from the double bass were mixed down to a single track, and all drums were mixed down to a stereo track, whereas the piano was muted. The six parts of the Urcells were:

1. Rubato, with one chord scale.
2. Rubato, harmonic movement with four chord scales.
3. A tempo, with one chord scale.
4. A tempo, harmonic movement with four chord scales.
5. A tempo, atonal.
6. Rubato, atonal.

Main Recording. The main recording was performed without visual contact between the musicians. The center of the music was the six-minute Urcell, based on the prerecorded material. The first four minutes of the main recording – before entering the Urcell – a freely improvised part without given conditions was played. This first part was merely for letting the musicians enter the music gradually. The Urcell, together with the free introduction, was to be seen as a whole composition-form. It was important, even though the recording was part of a research study, to strive for a truly artistic result. The recording environment resembled the situation within a real recording session.

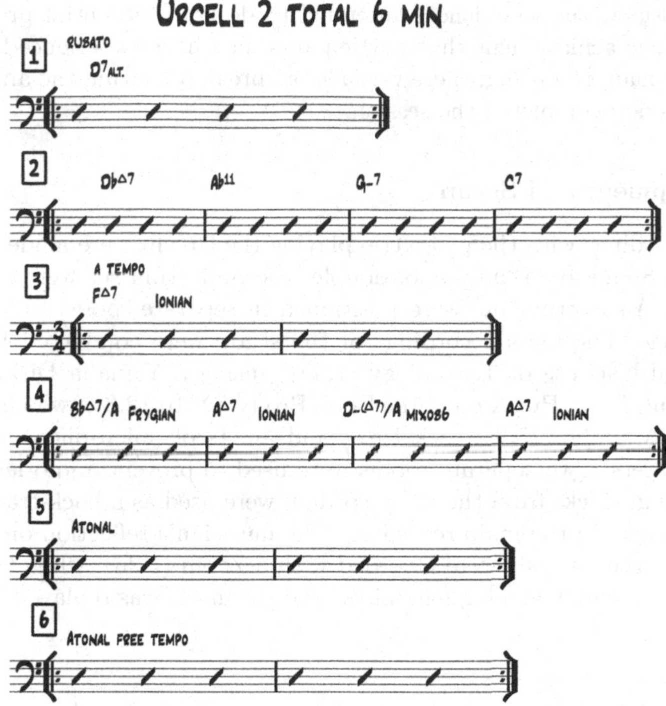

Fig. 2. Example of the score from one of the Urcells used.

2.2 Participants

The participants in the study were four male advanced music students (age 22–26 years) from the jazz department of the Royal College of Music (KMH) in Stockholm, Sweden. The students were selected based on musical skills and their interest in contributing to the research study. All students were horn players, and the four instruments used were trumpet, clarinet, alto saxophone, and trombone. In addition to these students, the first author played the grand piano to complete the duo in the main recordings.

2.3 Procedure

The students faced an unprepared musical situation except for information about the aims of the experiment. A short introduction concerning practical details over the recording was equally crucial for creating a comfortable situation concerning the physical and social circumstances. All participants filled in a consent form and were then informed about the basic idea of the experiment setup. The participants were also informed that a subsequent reflection would follow. Before initiating the main recording, some less complicated music was played, such as a standard composition or other suitable music. The brief rehearsal of a simple piece of music at the soundcheck intended to decrease potential pressure concerning artistic achievement that participants may have experienced. After the ten minutes main recording, there was a short break preparing the analysis. The 40 min reflection completed the session.

2.4 Equipment and Setup

The pre-recordings with the piano trio playing the Urcells were made in a studio at KMH. A Steinway grand piano, double bass and drum set were recorded on multi-track. All instruments were positioned in separate rooms to avoid audio signal leakage. The main recordings of the study were conducted in a studio at the Royal Institute of Technology (KTH), using a Yamaha Disklavier with MIDI Output, Logic Pro X on a MacBook Pro (OSX 10.12.6), two-channel USB sound card M-audio (Fast Track Pro), and an Aston microphone (Spirit) for the horn players. Two separate rooms were used to prevent audio leakage. The bass and drum tracks from the pre-recording were used as a back-track for horn and piano player in the main recording. The musician's reflection on the studio material and the analysis were recorded with a Zoom (H2n), while the analysis (score) was presented on a large monitor, and the music was replayed in an audio system.

2.5 Data Analysis

Recording the piano part in the main recording via midi facilitated an accurate transcription of the piano using the built-in functions of Logic Pro X. The virtual sound of the grand piano (East-West, piano platinum [1]) was found indiscernible from the acoustic sound by the participants. However, in the study, it was an advantage to use a Disklavier grand for a more real-life experience while recording instead of using a master MIDI-keyboard. Built-in features of Logic Pro X were used to obtain a simplified notation from the acoustic recordings of the horns. The functions are inside the Flex Pitch module and are mostly used for pitch correction, but in this case, these functions were used as a transcription/visualization tool. Finally, the interpretation of the pitches was transformed into a MIDI-track, and the score was presented. Unfortunately, the piano trio in the pre-recording was recorded without a click track, which increased the effort needed for the analysis.

This analysis was done immediately after the main recordings and was accompanied by some transcription errors. Most of them were possible to adjust within the Flex Pitch window by listening and transcribing traditionally by ear. The obtained score was found to be sufficient as a starting point for reflection on the musician's strategies. The Flex Pitch window also offered other vital information about such as micro pitch, bend, and vibrato, which also was useful during the reflection over improvisation strategies.

2.6 Reflection (Musician)

The reflection was performed in front of a computer screen, and the principal focus was on the score of the horn player. The piano score was mainly used as a reference together with chord or scale instructions from the Urcell. The score – in sync with the audio from the recording – provided information for the reflection, and the ability to stop and rewind the music while checking the score.

Only limited guidance was provided for the reflection, in order not to influence the participant's reflection. The goal was to have the participants carry out the reflection on their own. To interrupt a possible silence, the researcher could make comments like: How did you think when you played there? Do you remember what you related to in the surrounding music? Do you experience your music playing differently now than at the time of recording? The reflection was recorded with a Zoom H2n and manually transcribed. Each reflection lasted for about 40 min.

As a complement to the reflection, participants filled in a survey with general questions regarding musical experience and background. The questions in the survey are shown in Table 1:

Table 1. The questions in the survey.

	Questions	Interval	Mean	Range
1	At what age did you start to be interested in improvised music?		11	4–15
2	When did you start playing your instrument (age)?		9.25	5–15
3	How necessary do you consider knowledge in traditional jazz theory to be during improvisation?	[1–5]	2.75	1–4
4	Rank your knowledge in traditional jazz theory	[1–5]	3.75	3–4
5	How useful is advanced relative pitch when you improvise in jazz?	[1–5]	4.75	4–5
6	Rank your relative pitch.	[1–5]	3.75	3–4

3 Results

The main results of the study concern method development. The method proposed here can, of course, be refined and further developed, which is on the agenda for the continued research. Overall, the experimental situation was well adapted to describe some of the improvisation strategies in jazz, and specifically in treating how the improvisation output changes direction when conditions change. In this study, the conditions differed due to the design of the Urcell.

Within this study, we also categorize strategies within jazz improvisation. The methods in previous work [10,12] were used as a starting point for identifying possible strategies and classify into main categories (Rhythmic, Pitch, Dialogical, Timbral, and Physical). The participants were able to identify personal strategies by playing and then reflecting on their musical choices. Still, they were not presented to the main categories in advance. Below, several examples[1] are provided of different strategies that have emerged during the study through the reflections by the participants.

a) Half step: the participant recognized that the note sounded "out of the scale" and rapidly changed the note a half step up. In this case, the student discussed whether he actually perceived the note as the minor third in a D$^\flat$-chord, perceived it as a half step below the major third, or just changed note because it sounded wrong, see Fig. 3. This strategy belongs to the Pitch category.

Fig. 3. Example of changing notes by a half step to arrive in the chord scale. (Clarinet score, non transposed)

b) Chromatic: the participant played chromatic melodic movements to postpone the resolution according to the chord scale, G-dorian, see Figure 4. There were almost two bars of chromatic searching before reaching the target note, B$^\flat$. This strategy belongs to the Pitch category but also to the Physical category if the chromatic searching is to be considered as a cliche.

Fig. 4. Example of using chromatism to postpone the resolution. (Clarinet score, non transposed)

[1] Examples available at https://bit.ly/2YiNw9o.

c) Pentatonic: the participant played two pentatonic scales. The pentatonic scales are commonly used within the chord scale as well as outside the chord scale due to the distinct sound. This type of pentatonic scales belongs to what jazz musicians practice, attributing this strategy to the category Physical, see Fig. 5.

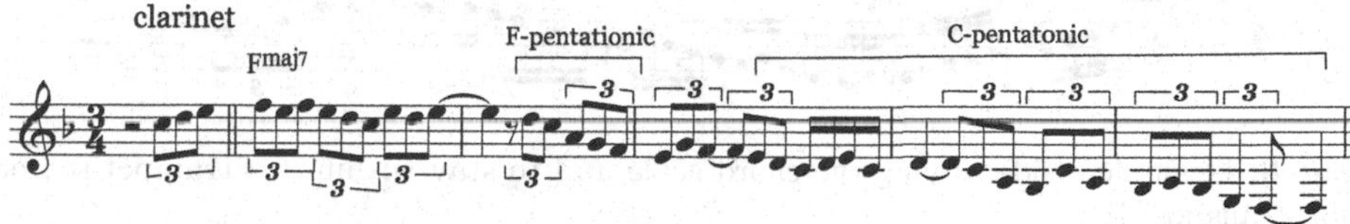

Fig. 5. Example of using pentatonic phrases to be able to play inside or outside the chord scale. (Clarinet score, non transposed)

d) Tied notes: the participant kept to the same note when the chord changed, and one strategy was to rapidly identify the function of the note. In this case, the participant immediately noticed that the note (E♭) change from being the ♭9 in the D-altered scale to the 9th in the new chord D♭maj7, see Fig. 6. This strategy belongs to the Pitch category, and a combination of a good ear and explicit knowledge of music theory is needed.

Fig. 6. Example of how to understand the new function of the withheld note when the chord scale changes. (Clarinet score, non transposed)

e) Reduced number of notes: the participant decided to play a few notes that belong to all chord scales in the example. The scales differed widely from A Phrygian to A major, but the note E was a familiar note in both scales, see Fig. 7. This strategy shares attributes with both the Pitch and the Rhythmic categories.

Fig. 7. Example of the participant reducing number of notes and only using notes connecting chord scales. Instead, the focus was to use rhythmical variation. (Trombone score)

f) Scale-wise: the participant quickly identified the scale, here C-Lydian, and was able to play pre-produced patterns or even new ones, see Fig. 8. This strategy attributes the Pitch category, and also to the Physical strategy.

Fig. 8. Example of identifying the chord scale and to stay within it. (Trumpet score, non transposed)

g) Copied notes: in this case the participant copied one note, A, from the piano and repeated it, see Fig. 9. This strategy belongs to the Pitch category regarding relative pitch and a good ear but also to the Dialogical category according to the interaction with the fellow musician.

Fig. 9. Note copying via Dialogical interaction (Alto saxophone and piano scores, non transposed)

h) Idiomatic: the participant produced instrument-specific sounds by a continuous glissandi, see Fig. 10.

Fig. 10. Idiomatic playing (Trumpet score, non transposed)

Table 2. Strategies from the examples were grouped and put into categories.

Categories	Strategies
Rhythmic	e) Reduced notes
Pitch	a) Half step, b) Chromatic, d) Tied notes, e) Reduced notes, f) Scale-wise, g) Copied notes
Dialogical	g) Copied notes
Timbral	h) Idiomatic
Physical	b) Chromatic, c) Pentatonic, f) Scale-wise

All strategies that emerged from the reflections in the previous examples were grouped according to Williams [12] as follows, see Table 2:

The categories are described earlier in Sect. 1. There is, however, a reason to review the categories, and to decide how to represent an individual strategy that falls under various categories.

One of the interesting results from the survey was that the participants considered traditional jazz theory to be not that essential, but, thus, ranked their ability high in the subject. Another result was how unanimous the participants valued sufficient capacity regarding perfect pitch, see Table 1.

4 Discussion

The central motivation of this pilot study has been methodological development since there are few previous studies that may serve as starting point. This method will be applied on a larger scale in an upcoming study with Swedish professional jazz musicians.

When designing experiments that involve human participants into creative processes it will always be essential to create a positive experience, especially as the design of recordings can be perceived as demanding both in an artistic and a technical sense. Therefore, it is essential to introduce the study to the participant. This introduction includes – apart from oral instructions – soundcheck and rehearsal of some music not included in the experiment. This music might be a standard tune or even a simple composition directly from a score. The surrounding environment can affect participants' motivation for the experiment, such as the atmosphere in the recording room, social disturbance, coffee break, etc. It is often discussed among musicians how an optimal recording environment would look and work, and several of the thoughts were directly transferable to this study. The students who participated in the pilot study were predominantly positive to the study. Above all, it was noticed how the method developed, in which the participants' performance was carefully analyzed and discussed, provided great opportunities for further development of the participants' musical progress. The method can, thus, potentially be used as a teaching method.

During the composition/construction process of the Urcell, the whole "piece" needed to obtain a functional musical form. At the same time, it was important not to create too protracted forms in order to ensure full concentration of the musician during the performance and analysis. On the other hand, enough time for the data collection of the experiment had to be available for each part. The structure with an Urcell consisting of six one-minute parts was found to be a reasonable length during the pilot study, and the four minutes of free improvisation at the beginning of the recording helped the musicians to relax.

The elements that were based on simple scales have, in most cases, been experienced as easy to decipher but have also provided an opportunity for a looser musical language where the musician took off from a safe harmonic environment. The playing of parts that were moving faster from one chord scale to another led to more considerable uncertainty and a more pending outcome. In all Urcells, where there was a change of chords, there was a sequence of four chords that repeated, which was not always perceived by the participant.

The accuracy of the analysis was high in this study compared to only listening to the recorded music. The reflections did not – as it is often the case when discussing jazz improvisation – primarily land on a meta-level but were also concrete and directly linked to the practice. One of the most interesting insights from the reflections and the survey was the impact that proper ear training has on the participants' self-confidence, which in turn seems to lead to a broader palette of strategies.

5 Conclusion

To improvise in jazz is complex. This study shows the possibility of using a structured analysis of a musician's improvisation strategies through a method that provides a flexible framework but also retains space for the musician's freedom to create. The result offers a palette of strategies that move in several areas, from music theory to individual choices. The main categories developed by Williams [12] seem well suited to this study. Still, they will be further improved when conducting an extensive study with more experienced jazz musicians where the frequency of occurrence of the various strategies will be investigated. The musical core of the recording, the Urcell, will be instrumental in these future experiments to bring to light the dependence of various strategies on how complex the parts are with respect to rhythm and harmony.

References

1. EastWest/Quantum Leap. http://www.soundsonline.com/pianos
2. Alterhaug, B.: Improvisation on a triple theme: creativity, jazz improvisation and communication. Studia Musicologica Norvegica **30**(3), 97–117 (2004)
3. Berliner, P.F.: Thinking in Jazz: the Infinite Art of Improvisation. University of Chicago Press (1994)
4. Bjerstedt, S.: Storytelling in Jazz Improvisation: Implications of a Rich Intermedial Metaphor. Ph.D. thesis, University of Lund (2014)

5. Cobussen, M.: The Field of Musical Improvisation. Leiden University Press (2017). http://oapen.org/search?identifier=637220
6. Crook, H.: How To Improvise: An approach to practising improvisation. [SI]: Advance Music (1991)
7. Crook, H.: Beyond time and changes: a musician's guide to free jazz improvisation. Advance Music (2006)
8. Guedes, C.: Music Technology with Swing, vol. 11265. Springer (2018). https://doi.org/10.1007/978-3-030-01692-0. http://link.springer.com/10.1007/978-3-030-01692-0
9. Nettl, B.: Contemplating the concept of improvisation and its history in scholarship. Music Theory Online **19**(2), 4–7 (2018)
10. Norgaard, M.: Descriptions of improvisational thinking by artist-level jazz musicians. Ph.D. thesis, University of Texas (2008)
11. Pfleiderer, M., Frieler, K., Abeßer, J., Zaddach, W.G., Burkhart, B.: Inside the Jazzomat: New Perspectives for Jazz Research. Schott Campus (2017)
12. Williams, T., Mermikides, M., Barham, J.: Strategy in contemporary jazz improvisation: theory and practice. Ph.D. thesis, University of Surrey (2017)

Instruments and Sounds as Objects of Improvisation in Collective Computer Music Practice

Jérôme Villeneuve(✉), James Leonard, and Olivier Tache

Univ. Grenoble Alpes, CNRS, Grenoble INP, GIPSA-Lab, 38000 Grenoble, France
jerome.villeneuve@gipsa-lab.fr

Abstract. Collective forms of improvisation are at the heart of numerous creative processes today, in a vast range of cultures, practises and artistic disciplines, each one bearing its own definitions, traditions and customs. In this contribution, we raise the question of collective sound improvisation involving digital technologies on two levels: first, by discussing the possible nature of improvisation in relation to digital artistic creation as a transversal notion that permeates through multiple fields of scientific research and artistic practise, raising fundamentally different questions than those of traditional musical improvisation. Then, by presenting a practise-based study on an emergent collective computer music improvisation project involving the authors. Subjective experiences, interrogations and remarks from this shared practise are confronted on the one hand with traditional literature regarding musical improvisation, and, on the other hand, placed within a broader scope of improvisation involving digital technologies. In particular, we will elaborate on using the computer instrument as a means to improvise both tools and sounds in one continuous flow.

Keywords: Computer music · Free improvisation · Collective experimentation · Instrument and sound improvisation · Live patching · Digital arts

1 Introduction

1.1 Improvisation in Digital Arts

This paper introduces preliminary research initiated by the authors regarding the study of emerging creative processes in the field of digital arts. We define the latter in the broadest sense possible, i.e. any artistic processes involving the significant use of digital technologies in any manner at any point of the chain. Such practises have indeed largely multiplied and diversified in the last thirty years, drawing on (and often blurring the lines between) the fields of visual arts,

O. Tache—Independent Researcher

R. Kronland-Martinet et al. (Eds.): CMMR 2019, LNCS 12631, pp. 636–654, 2021.
https://doi.org/10.1007/978-3-030-70210-6_41

music, plastic arts, scenography and theatre, in performative contexts as well as installations.

Amongst these creative processes renewed, altered or extended by the incursion of digital tools, we propose to discuss those pertaining to collective improvisation. Ideally, to do so, one would have to extensively consider the variety of what improvisation means among the various fields of Arts [3,14] (such as in dance [6,22], in music [1,2] or in theatre [7] for instance), sometimes even within each of their own currents, and, to be perfectly thorough, one should not forget how all of that will differ from one culture to another. Furthermore, and this is of the most prominent interest, one would have to consider how improvisation processes adapt to hybrid forms of performances. Obviously, even if narrowed to the specific cases where digital technologies are involved, this landscape is vast, and hoping to address it frontally and extensively in a single effort would be unrealistic.

Still, field observations in this area[1] reveal that more and more artists, especially "digital" ones, gathered in ephemeral or more durable collectives, find themselves exploring new ways to create together, almost on the spot, interlacing aesthetics and creative strategies in unusual and largely undocumented fashions. While the use of digital technologies in various art forms is now indisputably present in our everyday lives, the literature regarding improvisation with such technologies remains scarce, and generally grounded on the use of technology to augment improvisation in one domain by translating or mapping it to another (e.g. augmenting a dancer's motion with real-time sonification or generating reactive visuals from a real-time sound performance). We believe that digital technologies *in themselves* constitute a singular prism through which a broader form of improvisation may be studied.

This area of research does not aim to establish a frontal comparison of practises with and without digital tools, nor to assert the idealised virtues of technological innovation in creative processes that, upon inspection, are often the complete antithesis of digital determinism. Nor is this the place to reach for tools or technological specifications to encourage, facilitate or further hybridise collective improvisation practises. On the contrary, we begin from the simple observation that digital tools are already heavily incorporated in artistic practises, and permeate into the fields of collective improvisation alongside additional (digital or other) tools, in various and often heterogeneous aesthetics. From this initial observation, we believe in the necessity of a first analysis: to identify and document multiple practises within the scope of digital tools, in order to possibly establish certain correlations and invariants among them.

It is important to clearly position the present paper as a preliminary work, the first contribution to the larger scope described above. The authors decided to initiate it in the field of contemporary musical creation. This choice was guided

[1] In particular concerning the artistic programs of "Digital Arts" or Art and Technology festivals and venues, or more generally considering the fields of popular electronic music, contemporary arts and academic research and creation. A thorough referencing of these contexts, artists and pieces will be the subject of another paper.

partly by the inspiring context offered by the "14th International Symposium on Computer Music Multidisciplinary Research (CMMR)" special calls, and partly by the authors' own artistic, technological and scientific experiences, which will be extensively explained hereafter.

1.2 Computer Music and Improvisation

Transversality of Computer Music Practises. The field of Computer Music originates from the close relationships between music academia and technological research as early as the 1950s, resulting in over half a decade of scientific and artistic breakthroughs. While the ties to musical institutions are as strong today as ever, recent years have seen an increasing tendency of computer music artists to overflow out of strictly musical considerations, by interveawing various media forms, providing multimodal and/or immersive experiences for audiences, as well as exploring the interaction between the user and one or several digital artefacts as a central element of the creative process, including in live performance and improvisation settings. Thus, one could arguably state that the practises of many composers, electronic musicians and sound artists today are very close in nature to those of digital artists, and that they share many of the same interdisciplinary concerns.

Musical Improvisation is covered extensively in the literature through (often complementary) musicological, social, epistemological, aesthetical or philosophical standpoints, several of which will be discussed further in the paper. These positions generally pertain to a certain cultural heritage: improvisation certainly bears a different meaning whether one is interpreting a baroque score, improvising in a jazz ensemble, taking part in an Indian raag, or performing John Cage's works involving indeterminacy. A common point is however that, to our knowledge, the majority of such theoretical frameworks and studies are carried out in regards to a traditional and stabilised instrumentarium[2]. While this may certainly comprise electronic instruments, it rarely accounts for a broader definition of digital instruments, tools and workflows.

Improvisation with Digital Technologies poses numerous additional and fundamental questions, to which certain answers may be found in a variety of communities ranging from Human-Computer Interaction (HCI) to Computer Music or Motion and Computing [19]. The meaning of the word *improvisation* in itself is manifold in these contexts, depending on the end-goal: a possibly restrictive but operational categorisation may be to separate cases in which the computer is considered as an artefact, or instrument, with which the user may

[2] This may be a consequence of the common conception that improvising requires a high level of mastery of an instrument, which is only possible on stabilised instrument designs. This, in turn, could justify why few studies have addressed extensive improvisation with novel or digital musical instruments.

interact with in order to yield creative results in an artistic setting, and those considering the computer as an improviser in itself, capable of co-articulating a performance with the user (such as teaching the computer the appropriate rules in order to improvise jazz music, or using artificial intelligence to create real-time computer generated motion in tandem with a dancer).

In our work, we will concentrate on the former category, considering digital technologies as new elements that may stimulate new user-driven creative processes. In [26], the philosophical concepts of affect and assembly (introduced by Deleuze and Massumi) are employed to illustrate and qualify interactions between users and artefacts in creative interactive digital systems. This theoretical framework is then exemplified by a collaborative musical improvisation scenario employing such technologies. Jay Silver et al. describe the accessible Makey user interface prototyping tools as a *"platforms for improvising tangible user interfaces"* [9]. In works such as Sergi Jordà Puig's dissertation [17], the notion of "Digital Lutherie" is introduced to address the design systems and interfaces for new music performance and improvisation. Finally, improvisation practises may be employed as a metric to evaluate the design of new digital tools such as Digital Musical Instruments [15].

1.3 Our Hypotheses

We propose to discuss collective improvisation in the context of digital technologies by analysing and decomposing the creative process of a Computer Music improvisation trio composed of the authors, taking a step back from a purely music-based (and by extension computer music-based) framework. Our hypotheses are that:

- The core questions that arise from this process, both in terms of creative human-computer interaction improvisation with digital tools, are shared by many creative digital practises (as discussed above).
- The computer constitutes a singular dynamically re-configurable instrument, that may offer an expanded approach to improvisation that encompasses the instrument *itself.* We exemplify this through the analysis of synchronous improvisation of instruments and sound during collective Computer Music performance.

Such bold hypotheses can obviously not be validated or disproved through a single practise-based report, especially one with such strong ties to computer music, and one directly involving the subjective perception by the authors of their own artistic practise. This scope does however allow us to ground our reflections by drawing on musicological literature as a starting point, an anchor against which we may draw parallels and underline differences, thus painting the first initial strokes on the vast canvas for an epistemological analysis of creative processes including digital technologies, especially in improvised and collective settings. As such, the paper is both a subjective testimony and a first attempt to deconstruct our shared practice in light of existing works as well as our musical and technological backgrounds.

2 A Brief Presentation of Our Study Material: Orcæ

Orcæ[3] is a trio of musicians composed of the authors that practices free collective music improvisation using mainly computers. Each of us has a different history of musical practices, including such diverse styles as heavy metal, jazz, reggae, *chanson française*, rock or electro-dub. Although we had never played music together before forming the band, we have a common experience as researchers in Computer Music and Digital Arts, having prepared PhDs and worked in the same team during a 5-to-10-year period. Two of us are still actively involved in Computer Music research, with an expertise in physical modelling for sound synthesis and sensory immersion (force feedback interaction with virtual musical instruments, spatial audio, etc.). After several discussions regarding playing music together over the years, the project was initiated in January 2017.

2.1 Beginnings and Gravitation Towards Free Improvisation

The initial purpose of Orcæ was to combine the authors' instrumental practices - namely guitar, keyboards and drums - with the idea of playing and performing post-rock music. Some songs were written beforehand, whereas other ideas were to emerge through recorded improvisation sessions, then to be transcribed and progressively fixed into song format. However, after recording and noting down a few improvised structures, attempts to reproduce them at a later time proved rather fruitless and frustrating: we all felt that something was "lost in translation" and that re-exploring the same sounds was never as fun and exciting... Gradually, the electronic drumset became evermore drowned in post-processing and effects, before being abandoned in favour of a simple laptop. Similarly, fixed

Fig. 1. Photo of a live performance in May 2018. Live-coded visuals were generated by Maxime Bouton and Emile Greis

[3] An online repository of Orcæ's music productions is available at the following link: http://orcaescapes.github.io.

Table 1. Profiles of the three players: musical and technical backgrounds, prior experience with musical improvisation and configuration used within Orcæ.

Player A	
Musical experience & training	Self-taught guitarist, formerly focused on heavy rock and metal: written music, rehearsed regularly and rendered "as is" live. Short spell in the Grenoble Conservatory's composition class
Background	Software engineer & Computer Music PhD. Also sound engineer (mostly producing bands from punk to metal)
Link to improvisation	Small amount of jazz improvisation during first years of guitar playing - a skill now completely lost
Instruments used in Orcæ	Electric guitar and various effect pedals Max/MSP patches with control surface
Player B	
Musical experience & training	Self-taught musician, has successively played guitar, drums and keyboards in a now-defunct electro-rock band, before turning to solo electronic music production
Background	Software engineer, PhD in Computer Music, former Pure Data / DAW teacher
Link to improvisation	Has practised some free collective improvisation with his previous band (non-public jam sessions) and one-person improvisation as a way to compose electronic music
Instruments used in Orcæ	Reason, and very recently Max/MSP
Player C	
Musical experience & training	Formal education: percussion, drums and piano, then jazz school. Drummer in various projects (ska-punk, big-band, raeggea, chanson française and Klezmer). Confidential electronic music composition
Background	Computer Music PhD with a background in physics
Link to improvisation	Systematic tendency to improvise when sitting behind drums, regardless of rehearsal or public contexts
Instruments used in Orcæ	Ableton Live, always starting from the default patch at the beginning of an Orcae session. Zero external controllers

keyboard virtual instruments were replaced by a modular sound-synthesis environment, and the guitar became accompanied (and often replaced) by a laptop running sound transformation patches. Not only the music couldn't be written, but the instrument line-up itself was constantly evolving, sometimes expanding, other times shrinking. The progressive mutation was never planned, never completely grasped and never formally discussed by the players. After approximately 6 months of weekly sessions, our practice started to stabilise into the current workflow (Fig. 1).

The players each have different musical backgrounds and relationships towards improvised music (see Table 1). It is worth noting that although we all come from a sound-synthesis technical background, most of our musical activity has been in current popular music genres (exception made of one or two electroacoustic fixed-piece compositions) and that only one of us had any significant prior experience - or real interest - in free form (or *self-idiomatic*) improvised musical practice before this project. The music production tools used by each member within Orcæ also differ: Player A relies on *Max/MSP*[4], Player B creates mostly using *Reason*[5], and finally Player C uses *Ableton Live*[6].

2.2 Workflows and Practices

Private Sessions start as soon as each member has connected their instrument to the main sound card and has a pair of headphones on. There are usually no directives exchanged between the members: we just start playing. One of us may occasionally propose a specific constraint (e.g. "let's not use any distortion today"), but most of the time such constraints are self-imposed as a way to avoid repetition and foster creativity. The session usually ends by an implicit common agreement, after anything from 40 min to well over an hour: sounds fade out, then one of us takes his headphones off, quickly followed by the others.

Public Sessions or performances were envisaged later (after nearly a year of playing together) and are handled a little differently. Before each performance, members usually exchange a few words about the global mood that the music may aim to achieve (although we rarely manage to stick to what we discuss beforehand). We are usually not aware of what other members have prepared (or have in mind) for the performance, and enjoy having a few "tricks up our sleeves" for the others. Additionally, it is quite common for us to communicate verbally during public performances (e.g. "let's slow down") - while we hardly ever do so in private sessions - particularly when trying to plan a "come down" for the closing minutes of the performance, as there are generally strict time limitations.

Multi-track Recording is systematic and has been since the very beginning of Orcæ, for both public and private sessions. This material is exploited to produce fixed audio tracks that we publish on the internet. The production process is kept as simple as possible so that the results resemble what can be heard live during a session, while filtering out certain inevitable moments were we are in more of a sonic research process than in a musical one. This work mostly consists in listening to raw material, selecting interesting portions and preparing them with limited editing and mixing as a stereo file (generally lasting from 3 to 15 min). We rarely desynchronise tracks, in order to keep the energetic cohesion from the collective improvisation. We are also rather attached to listening to the raw unedited recordings of our sessions, and have published a small amount of them, usually from public performances.

[4] A modular patching environment for music and digital creation: cycling74.com/products/max.

[5] The digital audio workstation (DAW) developed by Reason Studios: https://www.reasonstudios.com/.

[6] Arguably the most popular DAW for producing electronic music: www.ableton.com/en/live/.

Collaborations have occurred regularly since the earliest stages of the project, through additional players occasionally performing with us as guests. We have worked with musicians and vocalists, video makers (in the context of producing spontaneous soundtracks for a short film playing in a loop during the session, or someone improvising live with us using a wide range of pre-recorded video capsules) and even live coders for real-time image generation. The latter have been a steady collaboration (during both private and public sessions).

3 Collective Computer Music Performance and Improvisation

In the following section, we will use Orcæ's creative process as a basis for analysing fundamental questions of performance and improvisation in collectively-practised Computer Music. We propose to reflect upon these elements by combining various positions and results from the corresponding literature with interrogations and observations related to our personal practice. Although the acts of performance and improvisation are highly linked in this case, they will first be treated separately, as each bring forward a number of specific questions.

3.1 Performance

Performed Computer Music can designate any number of things. Our background lies in experimental music and academia. However we will consider here any public representation in which music is (at least seemingly) produced in the presence of a computer - englobing everything from electroacoustic contemporary music, to popular DJs, underground artists, to Laptop Orchestras and NIMEs[7].

Authenticity. Computer Music performance in many of these contexts can spark a certain degree of confusion or scepticism among audiences since, as Andrew Schloss [24] remarks, it is not always possible for spectators to *"understand the performance from a direct/physical standpoint"*. It is indeed not trivial for an audience to know if all or part of the sounds that they are hearing are being generated through live performance or if they are simply pre-recorded and then played back. To Schloss, this situation is deceitful: *"Tape music was boring to watch, but at least it was honest, with no false expectations of performance"*. He decries *"knob twiddling"* and other computer performance gestures that display no visual effort as things that should be either predetermined beforehand or discretely (and anonymously) performed behind the mixing desk.

[7] New Instruments for Musical Expression - conference: www.nime.org.

Role of a Human Performer. Schloss' primary focus is to bring back certain *theatrics* of effort and of corporeal causality from gesture to sound, a goal shared by much of the academic research on NIMEs, and by most of today's popular electronic music performers. One could argue that the question of ergonomics allowing the performer to finely control a Digital Musical Instrument is sometimes superseded by the need to convey "readable" gestural efforts for the sake of the observer/audience. One way or the other, designing meaningful corporeal links from gesture to sound in modern music is often problematic as a) one-to-one gesture-sound mappings are easily understandable but rarely sufficient for the musical discourse and b) complex gesture-sound mappings (e.g. triggering complex sound processes by means of relatively simple gestures) can generate even more frustration from the observer, who is a spectator to seemingly abstract gestures, perceptively unlinked to the sonic result.

For Guy Garnett [13], the human performer harbours more fundamental aesthetic consequences, such as the gestural nuance generally associated with human instrumental performance, rarely present in electroacoustic tape music:

it is more difficult to incorporate "performative" inflection into tape music, and therefore, for practical reasons, it becomes less likely to occur. [...] because [these subtleties] are difficult to produce, there is a definite tendency to avoid them.

Garnett also underlines the physical and cognitive constraints of human performance that affect the composer, the performer and the listener:

The performance gestures [...] must be cognizable: the performer must be able to get their mind around them in some way. The composer without physical limitations of performance can more easily convince himself or herself that they have created something real and comprehensible, whereas what they have may be an unhearable ideal. It is relatively easy to create algorithms that generate sounds whose qualities as music are inscrutable, beyond the cognitive or perceptive abilities of listeners.

One can therefore conclude that human performance in Computer Music is not only a question of adding readability to a restitution by expliciting (possibly caricatured) musical gestures, primarily directed towards an audience. Rather, human performance factors can be considered as fundamental structuring elements in the writing (or *thinking*, in the case of improvisation) of interactive Computer Music. As such, they are both meaningful and relevant even in the absence of performance, during any individual or collective creative processes.

Contexts and Expectations. Considerations such as those presented above stem at least partially from heterogeneous conceptions of what could be identified as a *performance* according to composers, interprets or the audience - and, by extension, what each considers important or acceptable as a Computer Music performance. They certainly result in distinct expectations from each party towards the others. These co-expectations will tend to match if the context of the gathering is clearly specified: is it entertainment? A formal representation pertaining to a strongly-codified music genre? A scientific and technical proof of concept? An exploratory approach? An organic and open artistic journey?

We are, of course, in no position to judge of the relative artistic validity of any of these contexts, however, finding which context Orcæ's performances "fit into" and which expectations we will confront has been a matter of trial and error.

Orcæ's Concerns. Given that our public performances are constituted entirely of spontaneous real time improvisation, an inherent aspect of trust must be installed between the audience and us. We invite them to embark on an open sound exploration, knowing fully well that it could be transcendental... or uncomfortable... or just very boring.

That being said, two recurring questions still obsess us and remain largely unanswered. The first, regularly expressed by the audience is: "who is doing what?". The subsequent second question then becomes: "what should we explain to the audience beforehand, or what should we show, of what actually goes on during our performances?". Should we stick to a purely acousmatic listening experience and hide behind curtains? Should we face the audience even though we barely seem to move during the whole session? Should we visually project parts of our tools/screens (as a Causal augmentation) or should we go all out and build a complete dynamic scenography and audio-visual counterpart (as an abstract augmentation)?

We seek for simplicity, and if we were to consider only ourselves (as is the case during private sessions - which in the end are simply performances in which we are both the performers and the listeners), we would not even think about anything but the sound for itself, disembodied of its producers. The fact that the performance aspect might not be seen at all or even known from the audience makes little difference to us. But it clearly does for the audience. And while the literature largely states that fact, each one of our performances has been an occasion to measure it. We have played in various contexts and configurations (music only or working in collaboration with visual artists, playing on stage or amidst the listeners, fantastic to disastrous listening conditions, etc.) to various audiences, each time expliciting the bare minimum of our process (if we did so at all). Sometimes, the expectations of the audience converged with ours, some other time they did not. And the questions remain.

Further still, while the essence of our music may not have changed (too) drastically depending on these performance contexts, our subjective experience of each of them undeniably differs from the experience of private sessions. In other words, we don't feel any need to be considered as performers, however being put in a performing position/context significantly impacts our process.

3.2 Improvisation

In this section, we will not address the notion of improvisation in regards to the notion of composition. While the historical interest accorded to each has been very uneven (with a clear emphasis on composition, at least in western culture), numerous works have since proposed ways to formalise their relative positioning (see Sarath [23], Smith and Dean [25], Andy Hamilton [16]). We will restrain ourselves to the matter of musical improvisation involving computers. This specific field has seen distinct kinds of practices emerge and develop since the earliest ages of computer sciences. The first one would be to consider the *Computer-as-improviser*, able to generate structured musical information (e.g. MIDI then rendered by synthesizers). The second practice considers the *Computer-as-instrument* and emerges from the possibility of calculating real-time streams of synthesised or transformed audio data [10].

The practice of the authors within Orcæ is clearly positioned in resonance with the latter, in the sense that the computer is not perceived as an agent whose role is to respond creatively to the player's input (for instance by following procedural rules) but is instead considered as an extensively controllable and re-configurable instrument that allows for each parameter of each sound-producing process to be observable, editable or even stoppable at any given time[8].

Below, we will contextualise our approach and practice of computer music improvisation. From there, in the next section, we will posit that this context brings forth a second level of improvisation, referring to real-time design/de-construction/re-construction of computer-based instruments.

Orcæ's Improvisational Process can be identified as pertaining to the codes of *self-idiomatic* music, as defined by Michael Bullock [4] (building upon Derek Bailey's term of *non-idiomatic* music):

> *self-idiomatic music is the concentration on sound-making actions for their own productive potential rather than in the service of representation of an external, received idiomatic identity.*

There is generally no prior agreement between players regarding any thematic, musical or stylistic directions, be it harmonically (no set key or preference for tonal or atonal material) or rhythmically (no shared tempo or clock synchronisation between machines). Sessions pass without any form of communication other than the sound itself.

Active listening is pivotal to collective improvisation[9] and may be even more so in this case, as each player's gestures are essentially limited to clicking, occasionally typing, and of course the infamous "knob twiddling". In other words, the sound is the only communication vector between players and the only means

[8] This doesn't mean that we don't use emergent or chaotic sound processes (i.e. strongly nonlinear systems or feedback loops) but we don't consider the computer to be *improvising* in these cases - an electric guitarist controlling amplifier feedback is still a musician playing an instrument, even if the instrumental system is no longer passive in the mechanical/electrical sense.

[9] Marcel Cobussen [8]: "the constant process of decision-making that takes place during an improvisation is for a large part based on the listening attitude of the musicians involved."

for developing a collective musical discourse[10]. As a result, the *who-is-doing-what* can occasionally become totally blurred, resulting in moments in which each individual sound component dissolves into a greater entity and none of us are certain of the sound that we are each contributing.

Specificities of Public Improvisation. Marcel Cobussen [8] states that *"The possibility of failure is an intrinsic element of all improvised music"*, and while we certainly fail as much in private sessions as in public ones, the former feels much safer than the latter (at least for two of the three players). We tend to aim for a more "controlled" experience during public performances, often restraining our exploration of more "extreme" sonic territories, partly because there is a risk of producing uncomfortable sounds for the audience - but possibly because certain fears and inhibitions reappear in a public setting.

Conversely, being in front of an audience yields a strong tension that develops focus and the feeling of flow, and as a result time seems to fly during public performances, to the point where it can be very hard for us to remember what actually happened[11].

Another consideration is that it may be difficult for a member of the audience to know, based solely on our performance, if the music is improvised or not - especially since we are not concerned with effort-based control gestures. Knowledge about how a piece of music was or is being produced has a significant impact on the listener's judgement [5], therefore we do ask ourselves if performances should start with a little disclaimer (*"be nice, it's impro!"*). Nevertheless, doing so may result in the audience focusing on us as performers, on what we are doing, how we are controlling sounds... whereas our aim is for the sound to be the object of interest in and for itself. As of yet we choose to say nothing beforehand.

Increasing Risk - Alleviating Failure. One thing is for certain, for the audience as for ourselves: improvising computer music demands for perpetual richness, variety, curiosity and surprise. It seems that this posture must be considered on two different time-frames:

First, there is the time of the performance, during which we try to build an interesting exploration path for (with?) the audience. As expressed in Sect. 3.1, the ability to match the expectations of an audience is of first common interest. This matter turns out to be even more crucial in the context of a free improvisation with computers. It leads Mazierska to express the following advice: "*[...] current electronic musicians are free to improvise, but if they want to keep*

[10] The degree of engagement and pleasure experienced during a public performance is then highly dependant on the quality of sound monitoring. Proper channels for this communication have to exist and low end systems can easily lead to frustration or even jeopardise the whole process.

[11] Ed Sarath [23]: *"The improviser experiences time in an inner-directed, or'vertical' manner, where the present is heightened and the past and future are perceptually subordinated"*.

their audience interested, they have to balance this need with the requirement to work with templates and observing traditions" [20]. This statement brings us back to the inherent necessity of a (possibly unconscious) *common language* between performers, and between performers and audience. Nevertheless, we find it important to emphasise on the widest possible interpretation of what these traditions or templates might refer to. We feel that they may include those from codified music, but also those closer to natural or evolving cultural hearing, such as our inherent tendency to relate to organic or artificial sounds through their potential to evoke the physical world, ambiences or even individuals.

Secondly, there is - mostly for us, but maybe also for our most die-hard fans (if we have any) - a need to explore new creative fields on a wider time scale, from one collective public or private session to the next. This need was never defined as a prerequisite of our work together, it simply emerged from the fact that at some point, one of us would identify a routine coming from another (a recurring sound, effect, pattern, or way to respond to or place himself in the macro form, etc.). For some reason, being spotted was spontaneously felt as a personal failure in contributing to the collective effort of improvisation, and it progressively pushed each of us to rethink and reinvent our improvisation processes. This ultimately led to deconstruct the very notion of "musical instrument" and widen the scope of improvisation from sound only, to the low-level elements allowing us to produce it. In other words, one of our common practices now consists in starting from an entirely blank page/patch at the beginning of every session. As if the significant increase in risk was somehow the safest way not to fail our pairs or the audience.

4 Synchronous Improvisation of Instruments and Music

4.1 Plasticity of the Computer Instrument

On the topic of the use of computers in improvised music, Frisk [12] expressed:

> *A computer does not have a sound but rather comprises the possibility of (nearly) any sound [...] to say that any sound is possible is not quite true [...] the kind of minute variation and dynamic change that constitute the very notion of a musical sound is still difficult to achieve on the computer. This is a programming challenge, a need to further develop synthesis techniques, but it is also a question of the interface between musician and computer.*[12]

Despite the ambiguous notion of *musical sound*, this statement relates directly to Orcæ's posture towards tools for Computer Music, and the need to investigate new paradigms of *improvising these tools.* The computer constitutes a highly reconfigurable instrument, that may be shaped and twisted to express any number of sonic possibilities.

Indeed, since the late nineties research in software environments and programming languages for Computer Music has led to several tools - both high and

[12] This resonates directly with what Max Mathews stated at the dawn of Computer Music: the perspective of infinite possibilities versus our ability to explore them in a sensible way.

low level - that allow performers to program and produce sound in real-time. The strongest movement that inherently carries such possibilities is live coding: *"Live coding is the writing of rules in a Turing complete language while they are followed, in order to improvise time based art such as music, video animation or dance"* [21]. It brings together a large community of performers/developers (for the most part academics or close to academy) around tools such as SuperCollider and Chuck.

Another tool worth mentioning is the Reactable [18], a - potentially collective - hardware interface that engraves physical objects with logical functions to be assembled on a visual display. In fact, it stands as a tangible version of visual programming environments such as PureData and Max/MSP, which allow for what can be called *live-patching*, although it is not their most frequent use-case. And, finally another very interesting work relying on lower-level programming is the UrSound audio and multimedia engine [11].

Although the listing of these dedicated and often expert environments is relevant, luckily one does not need to graduate in computer sciences in order to explore this path. Numerous free or commercial solutions allow synthesising, controlling and manipulating live audio without requiring intricate knowledge of software or digital signal processing.

4.2 Instrument Improvisation in Orcæ

A schematic representation of the typical workflow during an Orcæ improvisation session is given in Fig. 2. Below, we discuss certain technical aspects and offer personal insights on the synchronous improvisation of both computer instruments and sonic material.

In-Session Tool Improvisation is mostly practised by players B and C, as they generally start with blank *Live* or *Reason* workspaces. Although these environments possess advanced mapping possibilities for control surfaces, the players use almost exclusively the mouse and keyboard. Indeed, control mapping is usually employed when performing with pre-structured musical environments, whereas player B and C's processes are qualitatively different in that they consist in creating work/creation environments in real time. To this day, the classic mouse and keyboard combination remains the most effective way to perform such operations.

Pre-session Tool Improvisation is practised by Player A, whose main tool is Max/MSP. Live-patching entire instruments from scratch during sessions is rather tricky, so they are often (although not always) conceived beforehand. However, we still refer to them as improvised tools as they are often devised rapidly in the days or hours preceding a session, and are experimented in a *work-in-progress* state, tweaked, broken and fixed on the fly. The few of these experiments that stabilise over time into reusable tools are generally mapped to a control surface in order to facilitate exploration of the offered parameter space.

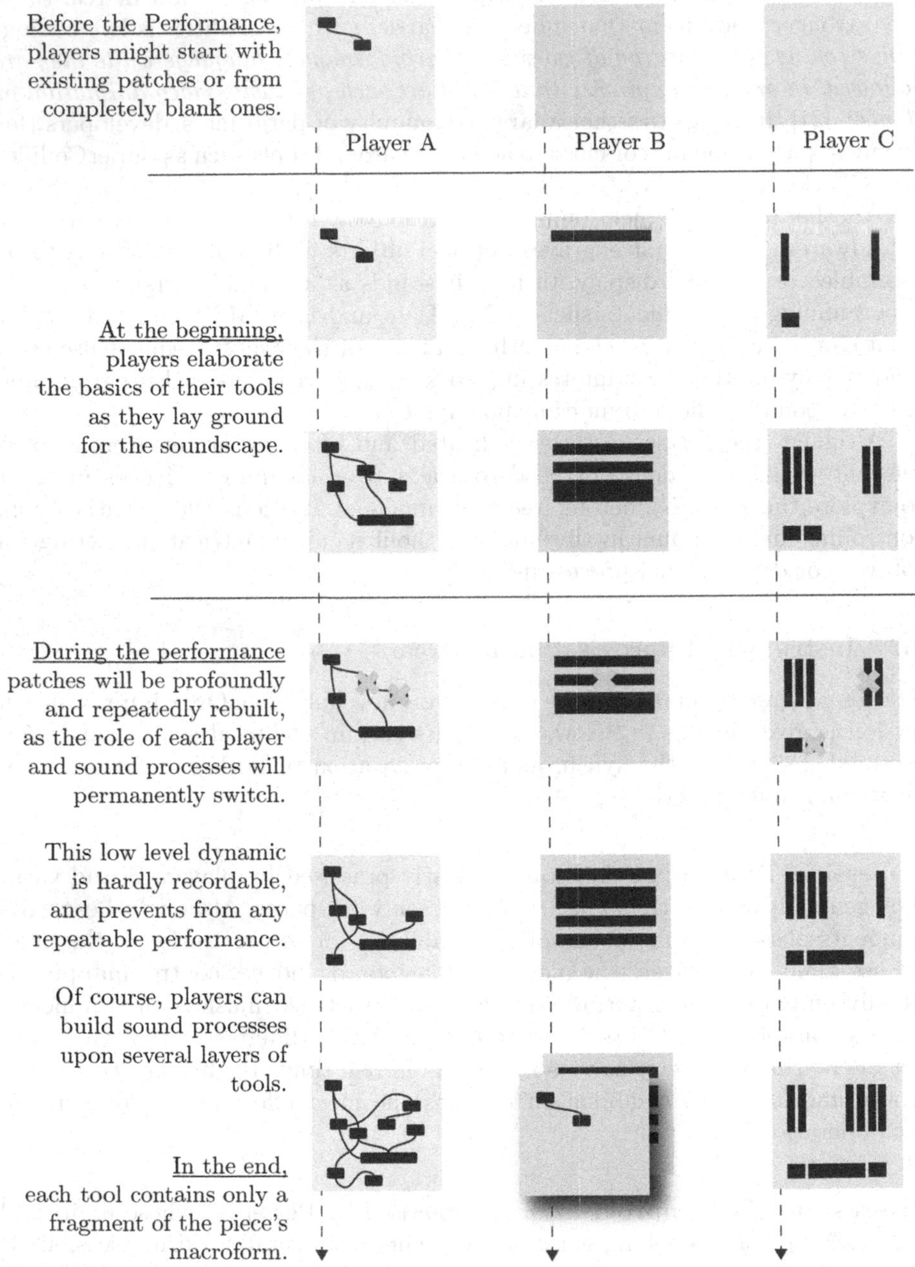

Fig. 2. Symbolic representation of changes on computer instruments (hence sounds) during the performance. This occurs without any interruption in sound and in a continuous flow of music. Each player handles his own set of tools (generally modular environments). No digital data circulates between the players.

Imperfect Digital Tools. In each of the above, one of the factors that drew us towards improvising Computer Music tools is the fascination for imperfections, a term often cited as a central aspect of musical improvisation [16]. Discovering unexpected properties (and possible artefacts) of live-patched audio chains or synthesis processes and exploring how to put them to use in a collaborative setting is a large part of Orcæ's creative process. In this sense, our approach is very tolerant to imperfections and faults, with no prescription even to phenomena such as hard audio-clipping or harsh digital artefacts.

4.3 Relationship Between Player and Computer Instrument

Regarding musician and instrument in improvisation, Cobussen states:

The instrument does not simply yield passively to the desires of the musician. Likewise, he does not just bend it to his own will with no consideration to the resistance it offers. Rather musician and instrument meet, each drawing the other out of its native territory.

Embracing the computer instrument as part of the improvisation process precisely offers a means to perpetually renew this play of resistance and exploration. In our case, novelty and personality in improvisation do not stem from virtuosity developed in relation to a given computer-instrument - something we see as difficult and possibly restrictive given the diversity and rapid evolution of available tools - but in systematically "*(re)discovering the specific characteristics of their instrument, its unique and perhaps unexpected possibilities*". Rather than acquiring a form of virtuosity, we would say that this perpetual renewal of the player/instrument relation fosters a form of agility over time: one learns to embrace the state of musical flow, and to bounce back when faced with unpredicted scenarios without breaking this flow. This brings forth another crucial element, developed hereafter: the means for interacting with such volatile computer instruments.

Mapping Strategies for Evanescent Instruments. Mapping strategies are of course a major concern in New Interfaces for Musical Expression and Digital Musical Instruments. Regardless whether the mapping strategy is formalised before, during or after designing the gestural control and sound synthesis sections of a digital instrument, it is assumed that the instrument will stabilise into fully mastered key functionalities, audio processes, parameter ranges, etc.

In our case, the sound generating process can be ephemeral, evanescent, ever changing. Hence, any mapping strategy will either have to preexist, as a very generic and versatile system, or will have to be created on the spot, remaining "raw", minimalist and low-level. As expressed in Table 1, Orcæ players have different approaches and we can easily observe a balance between the modularity/persistence of their sound processes and their need/capacity to map them to external controllers. Player A does use external controllers and will generally begin a performance with a loosely rooted mapping, of which he will progressively increase the scope. Player B will use at most an external keyboard, using the standard MIDI rooting to trigger notes in his patches. Player C refrains from using any external controller other than his laptops' mouse and keyboard. In any case, the mapping strategies remain empirical and very far from a natural interaction paradigm, with a necessity of looseness and effectiveness, and an acceptance of imperfection. All of these features appear to us (in our subjective experience) as inherent conditions for expressiveness, richness and surprise during our collective musical performances.

Causal Relationship with Evanescent Instruments. As we interact - and dynamically condition the modalities through which we interact - with the instrument, it responds. Usually, this visual and/or haptic and/or auditory feedback closes the loop, establishing the most intimate and causal relationship between an instrument and its player. In the classic scenario of an unchanging instrument, the player will (extensively) explore the response domain(s) of the instrument in order to progressively build a mental representation of causes and effects, and develop an expressive language. In the case of ever-changing instruments, the time in which a mental image of control-to-sound causality can be inferred is extremely constricted, imposing different exploration methodologies. Hence, the causal bond between actions and effects, which still exists in a particularly thrilling way, has to be dynamically and efficiently captured, even if it is only partially, and put into practice.

These very "un-intimate" or superficial relationships actually work for the best when it comes to Orcæ's general approach. But if we had to find it one negative consequence, it would be the sometimes occurring scenarios of the "lost sound(s)" or even of the "is this mine?". This effect is very specific to a collectively improvised performance where nothing else exists than a merged auditory feedback. In this case, it may be impossible for a player to isolate the sound that he produces, or even be able to observe other players' movements as a way to infer a causal relationship between a part of the sounds that are heard, and the "owner" of these sounds. Ultimately, each player has his own strategies to undoubtedly establish the paternity of a sound and recover a certain amount of control over it. Interestingly though, the situations of confusing, entangled, hardly tamable masses of sounds are amongst the most exhilarating experiences for us as players, often perceived as a climax or high point during a session.

5 Discussion

Through this work, we have offered a brief introduction to the transversal concerns that may arise when addressing improvisation with digital technologies in the scope of digital artistic practises. We have illustrated this position by a practise-based report of our own shared practise of collective Computer Music improvisation. Although the positions advanced in this work inevitably fall into the domain of subjective evaluation and self-analysis of our own artistic process, it seems to us that the freely-improvised Computer Music context constitutes a unique and intriguing object of study. We believe that this improvisation scenario differs significantly from improvising with traditional musical instruments and that, in addition to the vast creative potential that it harbours, it brings forth enticing interrogations as to multilayered improvisation paradigms and the creative exploration that occurs during the interaction between users and digital artefacts. We are convinced that further insight into this area can be gained by addressing the question of improvisation with digital technologies as a broader and more general notion, encompassing a variety of artistic disciplines and interdisciplinary scientific topics.

The format of this first attempt has led us to skim over a number of key considerations such as multi-modal collective improvisation and performance. This seems to be the obvious next step in pursuing this work. Indeed, collaborations with visual artists have taken place in several of our private and public performances (with movie makers for short-film sound-tracks, with visual live-coders and visual jockeys for full-live audio-visual performances) and bring forth many new questions and concerns regarding how to achieve the best possible collective creative process, how to co-articulate a constructive dialog between the different media, but also how one media may take predominance over another, both for participants and for audiences. Further investigation and analysis of these aspects is one of many long-term objectives in the larger research scope described in the introduction of this paper.

In parallel with a direct continuity of this work, we aim to initiate two other (hopefully converging) ramifications oriented towards a more exhaustive coverage of the scientific literature, artistic pieces and artists/collectives pertaining to collaborative improvisation involving digital technologies in the fields of Dance and Theatre. This perspective will (and must) be instigated through collaborations with experts in these two fields, and by observing and analysing related artistic creative processes, for instance through prolonged research/creation residencies.

References

1. Alperson, P.: On musical improvisation. J. Aesthetics Art Crit. **43**(1), 17–29 (1984)
2. Bailey, D.: Improvisation: Its Nature and Practice in Music. Da Capo, New York (1993)
3. Bresnahan, A.: Improvisation in the arts. Philos. Compass **10**(9), 573–582 (2015)
4. Bullock, M.T.: Self-idiomatic music: an introduction. Leonardo Music J. **43**, 141–144 (2010)
5. Canonne, C.: Listening to Improvisation. Eastern Division Meeting American Society Aesthetics, Philadelphia (2017)
6. Carter, C.: Improvisation in dance. J. Aesttics Crit. **58**(2), 181–90 (2000)
7. Charton H.: Alain Knapp et la liberté dans l'improvisation théâtrale - Canaliser ou émanciper. Classiques Garnier, coll. "Études sur le théâtre et les arts de la scène", Paris (2017)
8. Cobussen, M.A.: Improvisation. an annotated inventory. New Sound **32**, 9–22 (2008)

9. David, S., et al.: Makey Makey: improvising tangible and nature-based user interfaces. In: Proceedings of the Sixth International Conference on Tangible, Embedded and Embodied Interaction (2012)
10. Dean, R.T.: Envisaging improvisation in future computer music. In: Dean, R.T. (ed.) The Oxford Handbook of Computer Music, pp. 133–147. Oxford University Press, New York (2009)
11. Essel, G.: UrSound, live patching of audio and multimedia using a multi-rate normed single-stream data-flow engine. ICMC 2010 Proceedings, Lisbon (2010)
12. Frisk, H.: Improvisation, computers, and primary process: why improvise with computers? New Sound **32**, 107–118 (2008)
13. Garnett, G.E.: The aesthetics of interactive computer music. Comput. Music J. **25**(1), 21–33 (2001)
14. Garry, H.: Improvisation in the arts. J. Aesttics Crit. **58**(2) (2000)
15. Ghamsari, M., Pras, A., Wanderley, M.M. : Combining musical tasks and improvisation in evaluating novel digital musical instruments. In: Proceedings of the International Symposium on Computer Music Multidisciplinary Research, pp. 506–515 (2013)
16. Hamilton, A.: The art of improvisation and the aesthetics of imperfection. British J. Aesthetics **40**(1) (2000)
17. Jorda, S.: Digital lutherie crafting musical computers for new musics' performance and improvisation. Ph.D. dissertation. Universitat Pompeu Fabra (2005)
18. Kaltenbrunner, M., Geiger G., Jordà S.: Dynamic patches for live musical performance. In: Proceedings of 2004 NIME Conference, Singapore (2004)
19. Liu, L., Long, D., Gujrania, S., Magerko, B. : Learning movement through human-computer co-creative improvisation. In: Proceedings of the 6th International Conference on Movement and Computing (2019)
20. Mazierska, E.: Improvisation in electronic music—the case of Vienna Electronica. Open Cultural Stud. **2**, 553–561 (2018)
21. McLean, A., Wiggins, G.: Live coding towards computational creativity. In: Proceedings of 2010 Conference, Lisbon (2010)
22. Midgelow, V.: Oxford Handbook of Improvisation in Dance. Oxford Handbooks, Oxford University Press, Oxford and New York (2019)
23. Sarath, E.: A new look at improvisation. J. Music Theory **40**(1), 1–38 (1996)
24. Schloss, A.: Using contemporary technology in live performance: the dilemma of the performer. J. New Music Res. **32**, 239–242 (2003)
25. Smith, H., Dean, R.T.: Improvisation, Hypermedia and the Arts since 1945 (Performing Art Study). Harwood Academic Publishers, Amsterdam (1997)
26. Swift, B.: Becoming-sound: affect and assemblage in improvisational digital music making. In: Proceedings of the SIGCHI Conference on Human Factors in Computing Systems (2012)

Jean-Claude Risset and Beyond

Jean-Claude Risset's Paradoxical Practice of Interdisciplinarity: Making Inseparable Both Activities of Scientist and Musician, While Resolutely Distinguishing the Two Fields

Vincent Tiffon(✉)

Aix Marseille Univ, CNRS, PRISM, 31 Chemin Joseph Aiguier, CS 70071, 13402 Marseille Cedex 09, France
tiffon@prism.cnrs.fr

Abstract. In 2017, Jean-Claude Risset gave his archives to the PRISM laboratory. Thereby the researchers' community will have soon at their disposal a fund, especially interdisciplinary art and science oriented. For the moment, the archives are divided into two main parts: one within scientific research and one within artistic creation activity. More specifically, Jean-Claude Risset's own story shaped major interdisciplinary orientations: first of all, his pioneering research at Bell Labs, then back to "French reality" (his half-failure with Ircam and his difficulties concerning Marseille-Luminy), afterwards his quest for solutions as a political lever, especially through the Art-Science-Technology's report in 1998, and finally his turning point with his CNRS 1998 Gold Medal, consequently increasing conferences and mostly concerts. In addition, the study of material aspects (sharing activities between the laboratory and his home, place and content of documentation, etc.) is also necessary to understand "Risset's practice" of interdisciplinarity.

Keywords: Musicology · Archives · Science & art

1 Introduction

First of all, I would like to thank Richard (Kronland-Martinet), and through him the PRISM laboratory, for their welcome when arrived last June 2019. I would also like to warmly thank Nemanja Radivojevic, PhD student from the University of Bern (in Switzerland), who came at the end of July 2019 to consult the Risset's fund, and helped me a lot in organizing it, notably in July 2020. Finally, I would like to thank Tanguy Risset for his trust and his help during these two years (2019–2020).

The physician and composer Jean-Claude Risset gave his archives to the PRISM laboratory in 2017, in association with the INA-Grm in Paris for extracting and securing the scores, the audio-supports and digital documents (correspondences, patches, etc.). Thereby the researcher's community will have soon at their disposal (when it will be organised) a fund especially interdisciplinary art and science oriented. More precisely, the study of these archives will help all of us to better understand how Risset organised

R. Kronland-Martinet et al. (Eds.): CMMR 2019, LNCS 12631, pp. 657–664, 2021.
https://doi.org/10.1007/978-3-030-70210-6_42

his double activity as a researcher in science and as a composer. It will also make it possible to evaluate in detail the way Risset conceived interdisciplinarity. Incidentally, these archives will also make it possible to work on the analysis of composition processes, in a perspective of TCPM conferences (Tracking the Creative Process in Music). Indeed, these archives could be a kind of workbook to implement interdisciplinarity within a team or across teams.

After a quantitative presentation of the collection (for the moment relatively approximate because the process is ongoing), we will propose a first qualitative approach, aiming to suggest some hypotheses on Jean-Claude Risset's own choices concerning Art/science interdisciplinarity.

2 Quantitative Content

With about 80% of the archives retrieved, we can describe its content as follows. These figures are a low estimate.

- 38 original manuscripts (other manuscripts are also being processed at l'INA-Grm from Paris). The number of Jean-Claude Risset's works is 77. Yann Geslin (ex. INA-Grm) and I are finalizing the definitive catalog of Jean-Claude Risset's musical works. In these 77 works, some opus are different versions of the same work; for example *Little Boy* exists in four versions, including two versions for incidental music, added to a version based on an excerpt from the incidental music version, and finally a version for solo tape; *Phases* is offered in a version for large orchestra, but also in a reduction of the third movement realized by Bernfried Pröve; *Contre nature* (in three movements,) also exists in four movements under the title of *Nature-Contre-nature*; *Resonant Soundscapes* for 2 tracks is available in a 8 tracks version spatialized by Laurent Pottier's Holophon at the GMEM of Marseille
- Sketches, drafts and various documentation of 75 works ranging from 1963 to 2016. This part of the archives is particularly rich for musicological research in sketch studies, as well as for musicians who wish to play Jean-Claude Risset's musical works. If all this works do not have the same level of documentary richness, especially in terms of sketches, the main works or those judged as such by the artistic community are widely documented. This section also contains several projects of unfinished works (at least 3), as well as numerous sketches of fragments of works, or various compositional essays
- Notebooks (more or less dated, from 1971 to 2016), schedules (from 1958 to 2014), 1959 and 1965 are missing years
- Near 2.5 linear meters of archives about early research (for examples "Bell labs in 1964–1965", "1967", "JCR Trumpet Report catalogue in 1966 and 1968", "Trumpet Analyses", "Pitch Paradoxes", "Music IV Programmer's Manual", "JCR Sound Catalogue: Manuscript & original Printout", etc.) and scientific topics or, for example auditory perception, "hot articles" on perception, auditory illusions, historical articles on synthesis, motricity and musical performance, Ircam (1973–1979), quadraphonic spaces, voice, hearing, correlation, filtering, heuristic creativity intelligence, wavelets, math and music, etc.

- 2–4 linear meters of archives about administration of research (reports, evaluations, project reports, laboratory staff administration, careers, etc.)
- 3–5 linear meters of archives of conferences and/or concerts
- 2 linear meters of archives of projects of talks or/and papers, drafts of talks or/and papers and articles
- Between 2 and 4 linear meters of documentation about works performed in concert
- 7 linear meters of drafts, sketches and runs by Music IV, Music V, screenshot of Max-MSP patches (for works with Disklavier/Yamaha)
- 1 linear meter of class notes (when he was student)
- 44 linear meters of books, of which we can make a rough division between

  a) the fields of Art-science, perception, psychoacoustics, cognitive sciences, computer and music… (22)
  b) music and musicology (19)
  c) other scientific fields (3) Books not related to the professional activities of Risset remained in the private domain of Jean-Claude Risset's heirs.

- 1.5 linear meters of correspondence
- Undetermined number of recordings [not yet stripped] (concert recording, concert master).

3 Qualitative Content

3.1 Material Perspective

The question of the combination of scientific and musical activities naturally depends on the places where these activities have been carried out, whether or not they have been correlated. Here again, we will distinguish different periods in Jean-Claude Risset's professional life.

On one hand, the "Bell Labs" (1964–65, 1967–1969) and "Ircam" (1975–1979) periods are times of clearly joint activity, precisely because of the claimed interdisciplinary nature of these two institutions. Resident invitations to the CCRMA (1971, 1975, 1982, 1986, 1998), Dartmouth College or the MIT Media Lab (1987, 1989) belong to the same kind of interdisciplinarity (for a synthetic visualization of Jean-Claude Risset's institutional itinerary, cf. Fig. 1). The close combination of theoretical research, technological development, musical "craftsmanship", collaborative work with teams, at the heart of the interdisciplinary approach defended by Anglo-Saxon researchers in those years, had a very strong adhesion in Jean-Claude Risset's mind. If we assimilate Ircam (in Paris, France) to this American environment, it is because this institution wanted by President Pompidou for the composer Pierre Boulez (for a long time "exiled" from France) was created based on the model of Stanford, in order to produce the same supposed effects. For this reason, Pierre Boulez called Risset to head the computer department at the very beginning of the foundation of the institution.

On the other hand, his activity within the LMA (Laboratoire de Mécanique et d'Acoustique, CNRS, Marseille, between 1971 and 1975, then from 1979 to his death), reveals a more strong division between the scientific work, carried out within the laboratory's premises (Luminy, then CNRS-Aiguier campus), and his artistic activity, rather made from home. This dichotomy is corroborated by the researchers' testimonies who knew Risset at that time, as well as his family, notably Tanguy Risset, his son. These first findings, which we will have validated them through a series of interviews (using the "oral history" method) with direct witnesses of his Marseille activity, interviews that I intend to conduct in 2021. In a rather obvious and logical way, it can be recalled that the sound synthesis on the Music software is carried out in the CNRS laboratory because it requires heavy equipment before the Personal Computers technological mutation, and the parts of graphic writing for instruments (for mixed music) or the writing of purely instrumental works have been made rather at home. This point has been confirmed by Tanguy Risset (Jean-Claude Risset's son). By "home", we refer to Marseille, or in summer in Bénodet in Britain, West of France.

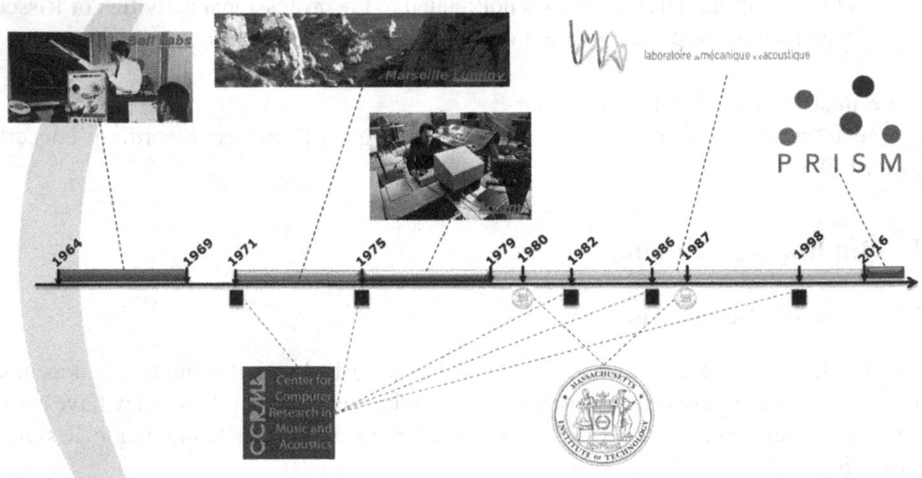

Fig. 1. Jean-Claude Risset's institutional itinerary

The observation of the existing documentation at his home—articles, and especially books, excluding books outside the artistic and scientific fields—shows the predominance of musicological books, and the fields of cognitive sciences, computer music and sound perception, many of which have been already there in the LMA laboratory (now PRISM laboratory). A more in-depth study of the home documentary collection moved by the Risset's family to the PRISM lab still to be undertaken.

By material perspectives, and in accordance with the genetic method "à la française", in other words the analysis of compositional processes as developed at IRCAM in the APM team [8, 9] and in a more anthropological perspective than the sketch studies do, we mean the composer's workshop, i.e. the set of material conditions constituting the composer's workshop. Thus, more than just the workplace, available tools for successive generations of computers (with their specific constraints, usual problems of obsolescence, etc.) and laboratory equipment will have to be the topic or subject matter of an in-depth study, in order to understand their place in the creative process. This type of study must also involve a comparison between the workshop of the composer/scientist Risset and that of the other composers/scientists, although Risset's posture is relatively unique, at least in France.

Back to the documentary sources of Risset's archives, the process involves also to pay attention not only to different types of paper supports used (format, grid or not, binding of the notebooks, etc.), but also to specific methods of note-taking such as use of abbreviations and notes comments. For instance, we know Risset used to take a large number of notes during colloquia, congresses, PhD dissertations, and sometimes even in concerts. All of this provides us with information on the one hand about his scientific and musical interests, on the other hand about his thoughts' evolution, about the development of certain themes, his ideas emergence... Finally, usual work in the field of sketch studies also covers attention to the way Risset proposed germinal ideas to himself, how those germinal ideas result or not from his own contemporary scientific research or from the scientific community, how they are transformed with different iterations (total or partial drafts copying, use of layers or not, back and forth with the dedicatory or creative interpreter(s) of the world premiere), how these transformations depend or not on scientific aspects (without forgetting techno-scientific constraints, in exactly the same order), etc.

3.2 Disciplinary Perspective

"Both science and art are ways of understanding the world beyond the individual subjective view of reality" said Jean-Claude Risset [4, 18]. And Risset to precise: "According to Jacques Mandelbrojt [6], science is good at describing reality itself ("en soi"), while art is more apt to express or translate reality in us ("en nous"): its exquisite sensitivity and its extreme quest of subjectivity capture human universals and archetypes" [4, 18]. For the record, Jacques Mandelbrojt is both painter artist and theoretical physician.

Beyond the common vocation of science and art to create knowledge, the interdisciplinarity according to Risset was first and foremost a radical mastery of each of the two disciplines. "I am a composer and a researcher. Inseparably, while never having confused [scientific] research with [artistic] creation" [4, 173]. Testimonies of this assumed dichotomy, at the edge of schizophrenia, are numerous in Risset's writings and interviews. However, these assertions need to be factually verified. Also, Risset mentioned difficulties encountered with this dichotomy: "If my research has nourished my creation, I have nevertheless experienced the conflict between different activities in their aims, methods and tempo. This conflict is transposed to the institutional level" [1, 175]. These are also areas that are largely different and even often opposed, by their goals (revealing mechanics vs. Inventing new sound and musical forms), their methods (theory and experiential vs always experimental), their inclusion in the social ecosystem: "The scientific work is collective, ascertainable, provisional or temporary: it is subject to correction (adjustments), obsolescence and incorporation into the progress of science. The artistic work, on the other hand, is individual, subjective and sustainable." [1, 179] "[Science] proceeds by tests superimposed one on the other and whose dark thickening slowly shows at the level of the true. Nothing similar in art. 'Art is not successive, art is once and for all', said Victor Hugo [2, 29], 'real presences' according to George Steiner

[3].” This vision, close to the thinking of the physician Jean-Marc Levy-Leblond [5], a vision that no one could suspect of being too positivist, emphasizes the notion of alloy rather than that of identity.

Risset said: “There is no need to recall that music has benefited from science and technology. However, the inspiration which music has brought to science and technology is largely under-estimated. Music has a special kindship with scientific disciplines. According to Jon Appleton, ‘music inspires the kind of rational thoughts necessary to produce scientific work’” (4, 13). However, we suggest that the reading of the draft articles, sketches of theoretical works, as well as some of Risset’s texts show that Jean-Claude Risset participated very largely in fighting against this asymmetry, he was in favor of cross-fertilization between art and science.

Finally, this dual activity is also expressed in the writing of reports and other evaluations, many of which have been found in the archives. Jean-Claude Risset’s extreme generosity meant that, when he was asked to take part in a PhD defense or HDR juries (HDR means French new thesis after the PhD thesis to obtain authority to conduct individual or collective research), he did not hesitate to switch from an expertise in musicology to acoustics physics, from aesthetics to signal studies, and so on. Many texts (papers or talks) –including a few excerpts cited here– show a constant self-assessment process, or more precisely, introspection into his practices. He acted as if his own meta-position had to be shared with potential multidisciplinary community suggest us “good practices”. Additionally, the very large number of correspondences, scrupulously preserved but totally fragmented in his various activities, show once again the crosswise dimension of his scientific, artistic, intellectual, and even political relations (but more rarely). A careful study of his correspondence could again allow us to understand some of the mechanisms of interdisciplinary activity.

3.3 Historical Perspective

Jean-Claude Risset’s own story shaped major interdisciplinary orientations: first of all, his pioneering research at Bell Labs, then back to “french reality”, afterwards his quest for solutions as a political or institutional lever, and eventually his turning point with his CNRS 1998 Gold Medal, consequently increasing conferences and mostly concerts. As Risset himself admitted, the Bell Laboratories offered him perhaps the only moment of interdisciplinarity to his own person. “I have myself worked as a researcher (at CNRS), as a composer (at IRCAM) and as both (at Bell Laboratories).” [4, 22]. And indeed, according to Jean-Claude Risset, Bell Labs seemed to be a model: “It must be said that the hosting of American laboratories, not only the material capacity, but also the open-minded and interdisciplinary affordability, were quite large and, in my opinion, quite exemplary, and this is not the case here [in France]. That is to say, in this great extraordinary scientific laboratory at the time called Bell Laboratories, we were involved in information theory, that is, we discovered the background noise of the Big Bang, we discovered the theory and practice of the transistor, we would never stop recalling the extraordinary contributions. There was an extraordinary atmosphere of openness where mathematicians, artists, psychologists, physicists, computer scientists, could work together. And so I was able to do both research for music there, and then even music where I stayed as an artist in residence in a laboratory. In France, it is a difficult concept…"[1].

In fact, second period, is a return to the "French reality". We must remember his half failure at Ircam (1975–1979). The requested and insistent injunction of "artistic production" was incompatible, according to Risset, with the longtime of scientific research. What do the archives say? It was a time of great musical production with Inharmonique, Passages and works around the emblematic Songes (Profils. Moments Newtoniens, etc.) Hence Risset's remark mentioned above that his Ircam's activity was essentially related to musical composition.

But the return to France was also the initial enthusiasm for the creation of an interdisciplinary department (art-science) within the Science Faculty of Marseille-Luminy, under the impetus of the physicist Daniel Kastler (son of the Nobel Kastler Prize winner) and the support of Mohammed Mebkhout, for four years (between 1970 and 1975). The Ircam parenthesis (1975–1980) being closed, his scientific activities were only within the LMA. The archives show both the richness of the correspondence with these Marseilles precursors of the introduction of interdisciplinarity in France, but also the administrative difficulties which Risset faced. The lack of understanding of the CNRS's supervision at the time, which only recognized research results, not musical activity, hindered cross-fertilization. And yet, "It is for musical reasons that our computer music team [IM means "Informatique Musicale" - LMA, CNRS Marseille] has contributed since 1984 to the development of the possibilities of wavelet transformation" [1, 7], to cite just one example.

Afterwards, Risset's quest for solutions as a political, institutional and academic education lever, especially through the Master ATIAM (Acoustic, Signal processing and Computer Science Applied to Music) at Ircam in Paris from 1993, and the Art-Science-Technology's report in 1998, commissioned by the Minister of "Education Nationale" in France [10]. This report is a landmark in the French environment aiming to try to catch up with Anglo-Saxon research by relying on political dynamics. The archives are particularly rich in files mentioning numerous contacts at a national level, for the implementation of the ATIAM Master's degree, then the broad consultation with the main actors of the art-science-technology in France (following the creation in 1983 of an association, "Collectif pour la Recherche en Informatique Musicale"), and finally the AST report.

The turning point with his CNRS 1999 Gold Medal, consequently increased conferences and mostly concerts. Concerning this period, the archives are extremely abundant (numerous invitations, especially outside France), combining talks or keynotes and concerts (monograph or isolated pieces). Jean-Claude Risset scrupulously kept all the drafts of the talks, the correspondence for the preparation of the concerts, and other more tourist details. Interdisciplinarity is no longer so much productive as it is militant. This is an opportunity for Risset to bear witness to the way in which cross-fertilization has taken place in his life. Studying the archives shows Risset's concern with going and testifying in different networks, sometimes closed networks: he could thus respond to requests for Keynotes during conferences in his disciplinary field as well as meetings of musicologists, festivals for composers, or more institutional meetings. However, this period is

[1] Interview with Jean-Claude Risset by Jean-Yves Bosseur, France Culture, «Opus», 17/04/1999.

characterized by a strong compositional activity, probably at the expense of his personal research, without sacrificing his team leadership activity. It is a kind of handover period. This period also ends with the realization of one of Jean-Claude Risset's great dreams, namely the creation in Marseille of a laboratory dedicated to art-science interactions: several annotated preparatory documents have been found in the archives (around 2015) about the creation of the laboratory, PRISM (Perception, Representations, Image, Sound, Music), a creation representing concretization of his efforts since his return to France.

4 Conclusion

"I think that interdisciplinarity never works as good as when it is embodied in the same person. There are already communication difficulties within myself between the musician and the scientist, even though I can be both but not necessary at the same time. But then if it's about getting around a table… For instance, interdisciplinarity with specialists if each one of them doesn't go part of the others' way, it seems extremely heavy to me"[2]. Interdisciplinarity is not so frequent, neither at the individual level, nor at the institutional level. Concerning Jean-Claude Risset, the study of archives (for the moment superficially) seems to indicate that Risset as a composer is more the inspiration of Risset as a researcher (than the opposite). Thus, Risset's work seems to seek to rebalance frequent tropism in the field of art and science, according to which scientific discoveries inspire artists, rather than the opposite. Therefore, musical ideas can largely provoke new fields of research and knowledge.

In other words, Jean-Claude Risset's practice of interdisciplinarity is a way to make inseparable the activities as a scientist and as a musician, while resolutely distinguishing the two fields.

References

1. Risset, J.C.: Recherches au-dessus de tout soupçon. In: Autrement, n°158 (1995)
2. Hugo, V.: Art et science. Paris, Acte Sud (1985) – issue de William Shakespeare (1864)
3. Steiner, G.: Reel Presences. Is there anything in what we say? Faber and Faber, London (1989)
4. Risset, J.C.: Science, technology and art as mutual inspirations: the computer as an interface. In: SAT 2006, pp. 13–23 (2006)
5. Levi-Leblond, J.M.: La science n'est pas l'art: brèves rencontres. Paris, Hermann (2010)
6. Mandelbrojt, J.: Les cheveux de la réalité – autoportraits de l'art et de la science. Nice (1991). Alliage (ed.)
7. Kronland-Martinet, R., Morlet, J., Grossmann, A.: Analysis of sound patterns through wavelet transforms. Int. J. Pattern Recogn. Artif. Intell. **1**, 273–302 (1987)
8. Donin, N., Traube, C.: Tracking the creative process in music: new issues, new methods. Musicae Scientiae **20**(3), 283–286 (2016). Special Issue
9. Donin, N.: Empirical and historical musicologies of compositional processes: towards a cross-fertilization. In: Collins, D. (ed.) The Act of Musical Composition – Studies in the Creative Process. Ashgate, Farnham/Aldershot (2012)
10. Risset, J.C.: Arts-Science-technologie, rapport, Ministère de l'Education nationale, de la recherche et de la Technologie (France) (1998). https://media.education.gouv.fr/file/95/6/5956.pdf

[2] Interview with Jean-Claude Risset by Philippe Boulanger, France Culture, "la Science et les hommes", 10/07/1991.

Machine Learning for Computer Music Multidisciplinary Research: A Practical Case Study

Hugo Scurto[1(✉)] and Axel Chemla–Romeu-Santos[1,2]

[1] STMS IRCAM–CNRS–Sorbonne Université, Paris, France
{scurto,chemla}@ircam.fr

[2] Laboratorio d'Informatica Musicale, Università degli Studi di Milano, Milan, Italy

Abstract. This paper presents a multidisciplinary case study of practice with machine learning for computer music. It builds on the scientific study of two machine learning models respectively developed for data-driven sound synthesis and interactive exploration. It details how the learning capabilities of the two models were leveraged to design and implement a musical interface focused on embodied musical interaction. It then describes how this interface was employed and applied to the composition and performance of *ægo*, an improvisational piece with interactive sound and image for one performer. We discuss the outputs of our research and creation process, and expose our personal reflections and insights on transdisciplinary research opportunities framed by machine learning for computer music.

Keywords: Machine learning · Interface design · Composition · Performance · Transdisciplinarity

1 Introduction

Machine learning is a field of computer science that studies statistical models able to automatically extract information from data. The statistical learning abilities of the models induced a paradigm shift in computer science, which reconsidered mechanistic, rule-based models, to include probabilistic, data-driven models. Recent applications of machine learning led to critical advances in disciplinary fields as diverse as robotics, biology, or human-computer interaction. It also contributed to new societal representations of computers through the loosely-defined notion of Artificial Intelligence (AI).

Computer music also witnessed an increased interest in machine learning. Research has mostly been scientific in focus, using and studying models to automatically analyse musical data—*e.g.*, extracting symbolic information related to pitch or timbre from audio data. This led to technical advances in the field of music information retrieval [12], while also benefiting the field of musicology,

H. Scurto and A. Chemla-Romeu-Santos—Equal contribution.

R. Kronland-Martinet et al. (Eds.): CMMR 2019, LNCS 12631, pp. 665–680, 2021.
https://doi.org/10.1007/978-3-030-70210-6_43

notably through large-scale computational analysis [15]. In parallel, machine learning also enabled the building of many automatic music generation systems, which are currently being invested by the industry in the wave of AI [6].

Importantly, these scientific investigations of machine learning have also enabled the birth of new musical practices. For example, gesture modelling, as a scientific challenge, opened new design perspectives on body-based musical interfaces that adapts to one's way of playing it [4]. Similarly, symbolic sequence modelling created new human-machine improvisational situations where the machine learns to imitate a musician's style [2]. Reciprocally, artistic investigations of machine learning began taking a complementary approach, using the models themselves as material for composition of sound [11] and image [1].

We are interested in adopting a *joint scientific and musical approach* to machine learning research. We are inspired by the computer music pioneer Jean-Claude Risset [18], whose research and creation approach to computer science enabled new scientific understandings of sound as a physical and perceptual phenomenon, jointly with an artistic commitment toward computing aesthetics. His work and personal approach gave insight to both scientists—ranging from formal science to humanities—and artists—ranging from composers and performers to interface designers. Our wish is to perpetuate his multidisciplinary impetus toward contemporary computer music issues related to machine learning.

The work that we present here is a step toward this direction. We led a *scientific* investigation of two machine learning models that jointly frame new data-driven approaches to sound synthesis. We then adopted a *musical* approach toward these models, leveraging their interactive learning abilities to design a musical interface, for which we created an improvisational piece. Rather than seeking general abstractions or universal concepts, our wish was to test these models through a practical case study to develop a personal reflection that inquires, or even challenge, their current applications to computer music. Our hope is that our idiosyncratic research and creation process will help open new perspectives for computer music multidisciplinary research on machine learning.

The paper is structured as follows. We start by the scientific foundations of our work, describing the two models that we developed for two musical issues—sound analysis-synthesis, and sonic exploration. Next, we present the design of our musical interface, describing its embodied musical interaction workflow and implementation. We then describe *ægo*, an improvisational piece with interactive sound and image for one performer, which we created for our interface. Finally, we discuss our research and creation process, and share our personal reflections as computer music practitioners and researchers to draw insight on contemporary machine learning from crossed science, design, and art perspectives.

2 Scientific Modelling

In this section, we describe our two machine learning models, based on *unsupervised learning* and *reinforcement learning*, from a computer science perspective. We explain how they respectively address two specific musical issues: sound synthesis-analysis and sonic exploration.

2.1 Unsupervised Learning for Sound Analysis and Synthesis

Musical Issue. Most sound analysis-synthesis techniques, such as the phase vocoder [19] or the wavelet transform [14], are based on invertible transforms that are independent of the analyzed sounds. Such transforms provide frameworks that can be applied regardless to the nature of the signal, but in return impose a determined structure such that the extracted features are not corpus-dependant. Conversely, could we think about a method retrieving continuous parameters from a given set of sounds, but rather aiming to recover its underlying structure?

Model. The recent rise of *unsupervised generative models* can provide a new approach to sound analysis-synthesis, by considering each item of a given audio dataset $\{\mathbf{x}_n\}_{n\in 1...D}$—here, a collection of spectral frames—as draws from an underlying probability distribution $p(\mathbf{x})$ that we aim to recover. The introduction of latent variables $\mathbf{z}$ allows us to control a *synthesis* process by modelling the joint distribution $p(\mathbf{x},\mathbf{z}) = p(\mathbf{x}|\mathbf{z})p(\mathbf{z})$, such that these variables act as parameters for the generative process $p(\mathbf{x}|\mathbf{z})$. The full inference process, that would here correspond to the *analysis* part, leverages the Bayes' rule $p(\mathbf{z}|\mathbf{x}) = \frac{p(\mathbf{x}|\mathbf{z})p(\mathbf{z})}{p(\mathbf{x})}$ to recover the distribution $p(\mathbf{z}|\mathbf{x})$, called the posterior.

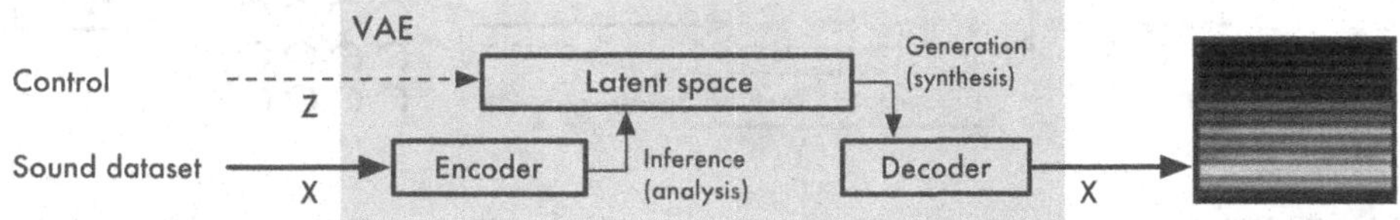

Fig. 1. Unsupervised learning for sound analysis and synthesis. The variational auto-encoder (VAE) encodes a sound dataset into a high-dimensional latent space, which can be parametrically controlled to synthesize new sounds through a decoder.

To improve expressiveness of inference and generation, we propose to investigate variational learning, a framework approximating the true posterior $p(\mathbf{z}|\mathbf{x})$ by a distribution $q(\mathbf{z}|\mathbf{x})$, such that both inference and generative processes can be freely and separately designed, with arbitrary complexity. The variational auto-encoder (VAE) is representative of such methods [13]. In this model (Fig. 1), inference and generation processes are held by two jointly trained separated networks, respectively the *encoder* and the *decoder*, each modelling respectively the distributions $q(\mathbf{z}|\mathbf{x})$ and $p(\mathbf{x}|\mathbf{z})$. The inherent Bayesian nature of variational learning enforces the smoothness of the *latent space*, a high-dimensional, non-linear sonic space, whose parametric dimensions can be freely explored in the manner of a synthesizer.

In related work, we show how this latent space can be regularized according to different criteria, such as enforcing perceptual constraints related to timbre [9]. We refer the reader to the latter paper for technical details on the model and quantitative evaluation on standard sound spectrum datasets.

2.2 Reinforcement Learning for Sonic Exploration

Musical Issue. Sonic exploration is a central task in music creation [25]. Specifically, exploration of digital sound synthesis consists in taking multiple steps and iterative actions through a large number of technical parameters to move from an initial idea to a final outcome. Yet, the mutually-dependent technical functions of parameters, as well as the exponential number of combinations, often hinder interaction with the underlying sound space. Could we imagine a tool that would help musicians explore high dimensional parameter spaces?

Model. We propose to investigate *reinforcement learning* to support exploration of large sound synthesis spaces. Reinforcement learning defines a statistical framework for the interaction between a learning agent and its environment [22]. The agent can learn how to act in its environment by iteratively receiving some representation of the environment's state S, taking an action A on it, and receiving a numerical reward R. The agent's goal, roughly speaking, is to maximize the cumulative amount of reward that it will receive from its environment.

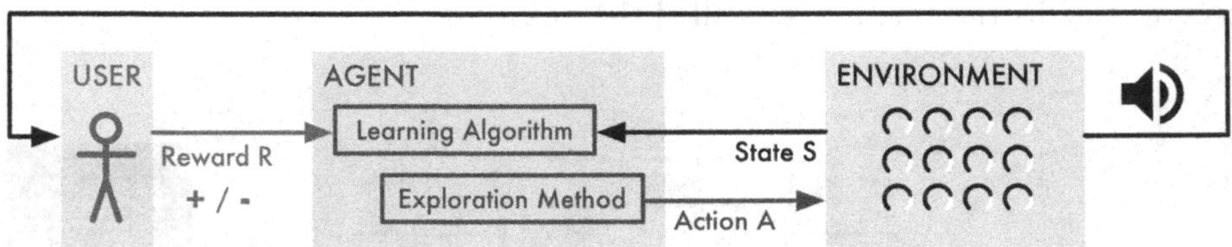

Fig. 2. Reinforcement learning for sonic exploration. The agent learns which actions to take on a sound synthesis environment based on reward given by the musician. The agent implements an exploration method to foster discovery along interaction.

For our case of sonic exploration, we propose that the musician would listen to the agent exploring the space, and teach it how to explore by giving reward data (Fig. 2). Formally, the environment's state is constituted by the numerical values of all synthesis parameters. The agent's actions are to move one of the parameters up or down at constant frequency. Finally, the musician communicates *positive or negative reward* to the agent as a subjective feedback to agent actions. We implemented a deep reinforcement learning model to support learning from human reward signal in high-dimensional parametric spaces [24].

A crucial requirement for reinforcement learning agents is to *autonomously explore their environment*, to keep on discovering which actions would yield the most reward. We developed a statistical method, based on intrinsic motivation, which pushes the agent to "explore what surprises it". The resulting interactive learning workflow was found to be useful to relax musicians' control over all synthesis parameters, while also provoking discoveries by exploring uncharted parts of the sound space. We report the reader to [20, 21] for technical details on the model and qualitative evaluation from expert sound designers.

3 Interface Design

In this section, we present our musical interface that combines our two models and leverages their learning capabilities from a design perspective. We describe how interaction design was framed in joint coordination with hardware and software engineering to support embodied musical interaction.

3.1 Interaction Design

Motivation. Our main design motivation was to use our reinforcement learning agent to support musical exploration of high-dimensional latent sound spaces built by our unsupervised learning model.

Specifically, our aim was to exploit the exploration behaviour of our reinforcement learning agent to support *improvisation by feedback* inside the spaces. Instead of acting as a tool, we used machine learning as an expressive partner [2] that would be playable by musicians using positive or negative feedback.

A complementary aim was to use the generative abilities of our unsupervised learning model to support *customization* of synthesis spaces. Instead of accurately modelling sounds, we used machine learning as a creative interface [10] supporting experimentation with the intrinsic non-linearities of latent spaces.

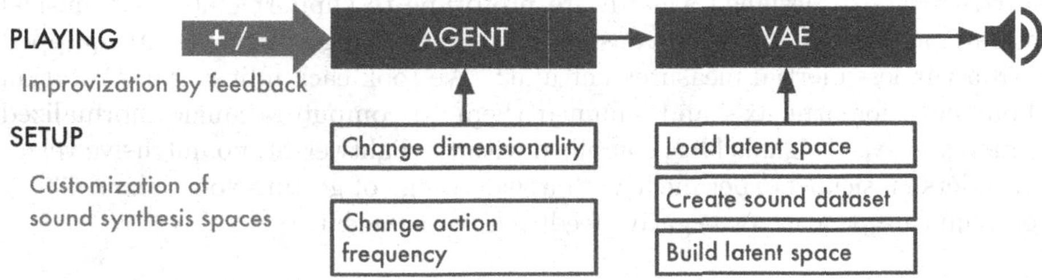

Fig. 3. The interactive workflow that we designed for our interface.

Workflow. We designed a two-phase interactive workflow, shown in Fig. 3.

The *setup* phase allows musicians to configure the interface. They can create a customized sound dataset for the unsupervised learning model, experiment with various training parameters, or also load a previously-built latent sound space. They can also change dimensionality of the reinforcement learning agent to explore specific dimensions of the latent sound space, as well as the frequency at which it would take actions inside the latent space.

The *playing* phase allows musicians to improvise with the agent by means of feedback. The agent produces a continuous layer of sound from the spectrum output of the VAE. Musicians can either cooperate with its learning to attain a sonic goal by giving consistent feedback data. Or, they can obstruct its learning to improvise in sonic exploration by giving inconsistent feedback data.

3.2 Engineering

Implementation. Technically (see Fig. 4), the reinforcement learning agent receives a representation of the environment's state S as a position in the latent space $\mathbf{z}$. Then, it takes an action A corresponding to a displacement along some dimension of the latent space. The resulting position has the unsupervised learning model generate a sound spectrum $\mathbf{x}$. Based on the sound, the musician would communicate reward R to the agent. The latter would progressively learn to explore the latent space in relation to the musician's feedback data.

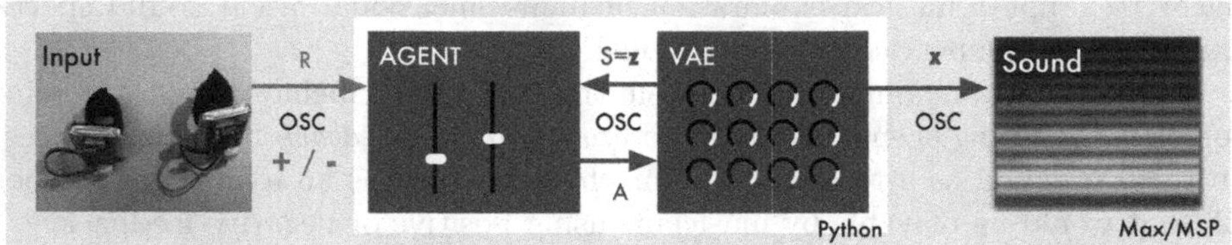

Fig. 4. Schematic representation for the engineering of our interface.

Hardware. We designed a hardware prototype to support embodied musical interaction (see Fig. 4, left). It consists in two velcro rings, each of them equipped with a wireless inertial measurement unit[1]. We took each unit angular rotation about each forearm axis and summed them to compute a single, normalized numerical reward signal. This, combined with the lightweight, nonintrusive velcro rings, lets musicians experiment with a wide range of gesture vocabulary [23] to communicate positive or negative feedback to the agent.

Software. We implemented our two machine learning models as Python libraries[2,3]. We developed a Max/MSP patch to implement a user interface for the setup phase, as well as a hardware data converter for the playing phase. We leveraged the OSC protocol to bridge hardware data, reinforcement learning agent, unsupervised latent space, and sound spectra together into the patch.

4 Musical Artwork

In this section, we present *ægo*, an improvisational piece that we created for our musical interface, premiered at the *14th International Symposium on Computer Music Multidisciplinary Research* on 16 October 2019, in Marseille, France. We describe how its aesthetics intend to challenge current views on AI and music, and detail how composition and performance were handled within our interface.

[1] http://ismm.ircam.fr/riot/.

[2] https://github.com/domkirke/vschaos_package.

[3] https://github.com/Ircam-RnD/coexplorer.

4.1 Description

Intention. Our artistic intention for *ægo* was to emphasize the human learnings that machine learning could enable toward sound and music—rather than the opposite, as is often framed in contemporary AI applications.

We opted for a performance format showing a human and a machine improvising together—respectively using feedback, and an exploration method—to learn to interact with latent sound spaces—on an embodied level for the performer, and on a computational level for the machine. The slow-paced spectromorphologies, synthesized and projected in real-time over the stage and the performer, encourages meditation on this joint human-machine learning.

Crucially, we directed the performance so that the human would progressively relinquish communication of accurate feedback to the machine, thus leaving the machine's learning indeterminate on purpose. Released from the obligation of teaching and controlling its artificial alter ego, the human is allowed to let his or her embodied mind unify with sound, eventually learning to interact with music.

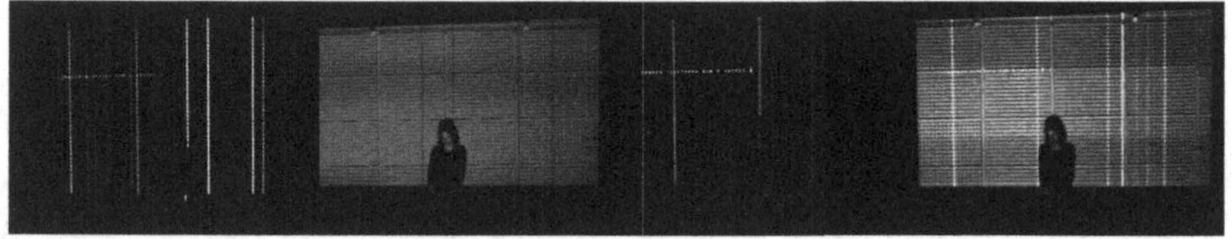

Fig. 5. Pictures taken from *ægo*.

Aesthetics. The piece's aesthetics result from two artistic choices, which conceptually and technically intertwine sound, body, and image (see Fig. 5).

Our first choice consisted in exploiting *artifacts of sound synthesis* produced by the unsupervised learning model to compose unheard-of timbral spaces for the piece. We built latent sound spaces using datasets of sounds that were commonly used in pioneering works of computer music to accentuate audience perception of sonic artifacts produced by learning. In addition, we projected the spectrogram image over the stage and the performer in real-time to provide the audience with a visual representation of artifacts. The blending of sound and performer representations symbolically accounts for the unification of performer and sound.

Our second choice consisted in creating *indeterminacy of composition* using the exploration behaviour of the reinforcement learning agent. We used the performer's body as a symbolic element to communicate kinesthetic information to the audience on how indeterminacy may be experienced while performing with sound. We also added raw textual information on the machine's learning at top left of the projected image to reinforce audience perception of machine's unpredictability. The indeterminacy pushes the performer to relinquish control over the machine's learning to fully focus on sound and its timbral attributes.

4.2 Writing

Composition. The piece was composed at three temporal scales (see Fig. 6).

The first scale is that of *exploration*. It consists in the improvisational paths taken by the reinforcement learning agent in response to performer's feedback data. We set the frequency of agent actions between 30 and 100 ms. This choice resulted in slow and continuous evolution of spectromorphologies, which let the performer improvise at similar temporal scales than the agent.

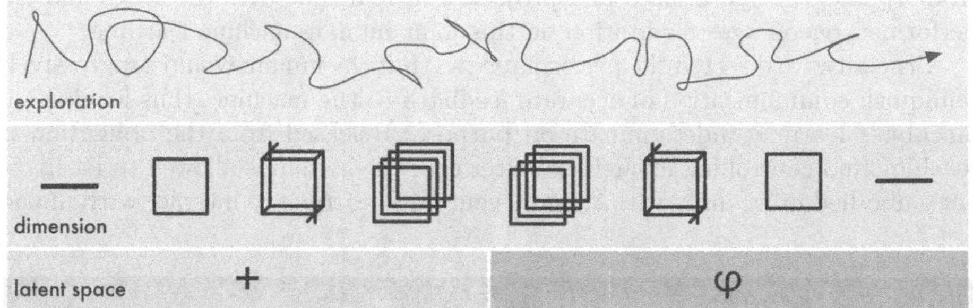

Fig. 6. Temporal structure composed for the piece.

The second scale is that of latent space *dimensionality*. It consists in defining the axis of the latent spaces that the reinforcement learning agent will explore. We set the dimensions to 1, 2, 4, and 8, respectively. This allowed us to write a specific kind of musical form inside the latent space: the more dimensions we open to the agent, the more sonic variance the performer and audience may experience—the harder it may be for the performer to teach the agent.

The third scale is that of latent space itself. It consists in connecting the reinforcement learning agent to another type of latent space. We built two latent spaces using synthesis sounds (additive and frequency modulation) and one using physical instruments recordings (flute, saxophone, piano, violin, bassoon [3]). This enabled us to build a narrative through the use of different soundscapes (here, going from elementary sinusoidal spectra to richer instrumental timbres).

Performance. While the piece is intended to be improvised, our sole direction toward the stage performer is that she or he may perform with the machine with deep attentiveness toward sound[4]. We proposed that the performer would start the piece facing the audience, relaxed, using small wrist rotations to communicate feedback through our interface. As the piece unfolds, the performer would freely adapt its gestures in response to sound, possibly forgetting the presence of the machine, as well as the mapping between gesture and feedback.

A second contributor is required to manage the two remaining temporal scales of the piece—*i.e.*, changing dimensionalities, and switching latent spaces.

[4] See these video excerpts from early rehearsals: https://vimeo.com/418787133.

5 Discussion

In this section, we discuss our research and creation process, starting by providing contextual information about our case study. We then expose our personal reflections emerging from music practice with machine learning, and present insight for future multidisciplinary and transdisciplinary approaches to computer music practice and research.

5.1 Contextual Information About Our Case Study

Process. The work presented here relates a practical case study with machine learning in the frame of computer music. We leveraged both conceptual and technical aspects of machine learning to jointly produce *scientific knowledge* with our two models for sound synthesis, as well as *musical creations* through the design of our interface and the writing of our improsivational piece. In this sense, our work emerged from a research and creation process, in which we closely articulated a creation project within a research methodology.

We followed a sequential multidisciplinary agenda (see Fig. 7, solid lines and arrows). We started by the scientific modelling of sonic exploration and sound synthesis, which took us two years to date. We then planned a one-month residency to design the interface and write the musical piece. This research and creation agenda was opted for because our work occupation at that time—doctoral researchers in machine learning applied to computer music—required a more important focus on computer science than on music creation.

While many researchers of our laboratory were involved in scientific modelling, we (the two coauthors) managed interface design and musical artwork as a pair. Importantly, both of us have professional experience in music composition and performance, and followed a dual training in science and music. These dual skills were central to individually work, as well as to effectively collaborate, on conceptual and technical aspects related to music and machine learning throughout the process.

Output. The relatively short period dedicated to music creation pushed us to take pragmatic decisions about the form of outputs, notably by relinquishing certain technical developments. For example, using the unsupervised learning model to learn temporal features of sound spectrums could have improved the dynamical richness of the generated sounds, as well as supported other musical forms than slow spectral evolution. Other agent parameters could have been used to create quicker or more discontinuous exploration behaviours, as well as other commands than feedback data to give the performer more control over reinforcement learning. Finally, many other musical forms could have been conceived, using other sound datasets—*e.g.*, voice corpora or environmental sounds—and investigating other temporal writings for dimensionality and exploration. Future continuation of our work may consider addressing these research questions to evolve the created outputs. Meanwhile, we do believe that interesting insights have already thrived out of the present case study.

5.2 Authors' Personal Reflections on Practicing with Machine Learning for Computer Music

Beyond the created outputs, the process of practicing with the two machine learning models gave us insight on the particular interests that they may have for computer music. In the next two sections, we successively share our personal reflections on composing with unsupervised learning (Axel Chemla–Romeu-Santos), and performing with reinforcement learning (Hugo Scurto). We use first-person narratives to make it clear that our personal approaches as musician-researchers will be exposed here, rather than general analyses or evaluations.

Axel Chemla–Romeu-Santos. *(On composing with unsupervised learning.)* The topic of my doctoral work, initiated in September 2016, targeted the investigation of machine learning-based generative models as a novel method of sound synthesis. This project was innovative, as most approaches developed so far were mainly focused on symbolic generation, due to the challenging density of audio signals. However, such symbolic approaches were rather aiming to model specific genres or authors and had, to my opinion, modest creative interests and ambiguous motivations. We decided to rather address the generation of audio signals, positing that the high-capacity modelling capacity of neural networks could disclose a novel approach with sound synthesis, nonconflicting with existing musical practises. This postulate hence enforced the use of representation-based methods, such as variational auto-encoders, allowing to directly control the generation through higher-order features, used as automatically extracted synthesis parameters (contrary to systems like adversarial methods, whose generation were initially only based on sampling). This choice was also partly inspired by my parallel practice of composition in electroacoustics, where I discovered among various composition processes (fortunately non-exclusive) the specificity of what I would call an *experimental* approach. This approach can be described by focusing on a physical (mechanical, analogical, digital...) or abstract (symbolic systems, generation rules...) object, and realizing them into whether compositions (hence allowing an iterative workflow, delineating composition and realization times) or performances (entangling composition and execution time, emphasizing the reflective interaction between involved agents). This approach, mandatory for the research and creation process I was coveting, drove my activity during the three years of the doctoral work.

This positioning, jointly with the musical interest aroused by the development of these methods, motivated simultaneously the writing of this paper and the composition of the piece. Hence, using these models to conceptualize a musical performance raised two ontological questions: first, how to *compose* with the developed models (distributing musical elements through time), and how to *interact* with it. Hugo and I quickly drew the conclusion after some initial experiments that the architecture of the variational auto-encoding system presented an inner *explorational* creativity (in the sense of Boden [5]), proposing a generative space that could be interestingly navigated by an agent (human, machine, or hybrid as we did in our performance). Hence, we chose to let the navigation of the latent space to the performer (Hugo), the compositional aspect then consisting in the dynamical determination of the performance *frame*. Therefore we had to split architectural decisions between, from the one hand the *free parameters* that can be handled through time, and from the other hand the *fixed parameters* that are kept fixed among the performance. We left free the decisions that we found most decisive for both the diversity and the morphology of the produced output: the amount of explored dimensions, that had a direct impact on the complexity of the space (and hence on the performer's choices), and the explored models, trained on different datasets and then providing different spectromorphologies. This step, quite common in experimental music (that we can call *setup design*), then drove the subsequent experiments about the precise composition of the piece. We adopted a recursive compositional process, first by exploring generative spaces and several projections "at hand", and then including the navigation with the exploratory agent. This procedure naturally led us to a distribution of live actions between the performer and an operator, setting the refreshment rate of the agent and triggering the transitions between the successive episodes, then amounting to a three-agent improvisational setup. This choice has been made to extend the flexibility of the piece, allowing to dynamically adapt the frame of the improvisation to its realization, but also to face hypothetical technical issues arising from the prototype interface.

Hence, the compositional process adopted in this piece was rather close to the *experimental* method I described, first crafting models that were trained on different datasets, exploring their properties jointly with the performer, and giving the composition a macro-structure distributing in time the parameters considered as the most determining for the performance. If we analyze the shift that recent machine learning techniques proposed in the domain of scientific knowledge, that we can describe as modelling functions by with automatic determination techniques rather than an explicit formulation of targeted dependencies, what would mean the transposition of this shift in musical practises? Clearly, our work is more based on the *objectisation* of these techniques for its use in existing musical paradigms (that I call here experimental), rather than a compositional processed based on automatic generation of musical content through high-level attributes. I think that this question would be very interesting to investigate more deeply into artistic and scientific communities, in order to reconcile "AI-luthery" with "high-level composition" approaches.

Hugo Scurto. *(On performing with reinforcement learning.)*

> Then the answers, instead of coming from my likes and dislikes, come from chance operations, and that has the effect of opening me to possibilities that I hadn't considered. Chance-determined answers will open my mind to the world around. (John Cage, 1982 [16])

Rather than a fortunate introduction, this quote on composition and indeterminancy by John Cage actually embodies my very own reflections on performing with reinforcement learning—that is, switching from instrumental control of sound to *spiritual unification with music.* These reflections drove the artistic direction of our musical artwork—showing a human favouring unification with sound over the control of a machine's learning—, and were further fostered through improvisational practice with reinforcement learning. Below is an attempt to describe how these reflections progressively crystallised for me through experimentation within the setup designed with Axel.

Reinforcement learning enables humans to interact with sound using positive or negative feedback—a standardized form of likes and dislikes. The agent may explore and learn how to synthesize sound based on this feedback data, eventually providing humans with a certain degree of instrumental control over sound. In relatively small parameter spaces (for example the one- and two-dimensional spaces composed for our musical artwork), I was able to rapidly teach the agent my preferences toward sound, and gain control over the synthesis process. In spaces of higher dimensions (where the agent needed more feedback data to properly learn to behave), I was not necessarily able to tell whether I could teach the agent, or if it was acting by chance toward a desired sound—thus convincing myself of having some influence, instead of control, over sound synthesis.

This "mind game", as I would call it, pushed me to open my expectations as a performer away from gaining instrumental control over sound. I began mindfully listening to timbral attributes of generated sound, as timbre was the only clue for me to actually know if the agent was learning from my likes and dislikes. Entering this state of heightened listening, I observed myself oscillating between two mental postures toward sound: one that was performative—where I attempted to grasp control over timbre by producing very precise feedback—, and one that was meditative—where I carefully listened to sound as if it existed by itself, detached from my very own influence. In both cases, heightened listening almost had me forgetting about the technicality of the agent for the benefit of sound and its timbral attributes. This mental exercise eventually freed my physical movements from the task of being performative toward feedback, which unexpectedly let me contemplate new bodily sensations in relation to timbre over time—such as the apparent interdependence between my inner breathing motions and the perpetual unfolding of sound.

The enabling of these mental and physical practices by reinforcement learning paved the way, I believe, to a spiritual practice that I regularly undertake within musical performance, which I may refer to as *unification with music.* Unification with music seeks to relinquish instrumental control of sound in performance and cultivate awareness that its organisation over time is already part of one's self—echoing Cage's definition of music as an "affirmation of [the very] life" that we are living [7]. Of course, unification with music may be witnessed and practised through performance and improvisation with many other interactive music systems. However, I would argue that the intrinsic operations of reinforcement learning facilitate awakening in unification with music, compared to the logical, verbal, and embodied operations conventionally used in interactive music systems—*e.g.*, parametric, note-based, or gestural control of sound synthesis.

By releasing my mind from technical conventions, feedback allowed me to experiment with basic forms of nonverbal communication with sound. Reflecting on the symbolic and performative aspects of these communication forms, I ended up thinking of them as *invocation rituals for sound*, which may be characterized by the following sequence: first, focusing the mind on timbral attributes, then using the body to summon acoustic presence, and eventually letting one's self identify with sound. In a complementary manner, by systematically yet unpredictably responding to my acts of communication, the reinforcement learning agent—*i.e.*, its algorithmic operations and exploration methods—helped me awaken to the *affirmation of an external agency* in the organisation of sound over time. Assuming that reinforcement learning remained a tool for performing a piece of music, I learned from this awakening that music *was* that actual affirmation of agency. Through invocation of a rapport with this agency—*i.e.*, through feedback on sound synthesized by the agent—I was able to witness and cultivate unification with music in ways I had not experienced in performance yet.

On a lighter note and to come full circle, I must agree that performing with reinforcement learning certainly opened my mind to the world around.

5.3 Insight for Computer Music Transdisciplinary Research

Our personal reflections gave us insight on the artistic, design, and scientific aspects of computer music research on machine learning (see Fig. 7, dashed arrows), whose multidisciplinarity may be rethought as transdisciplinary.

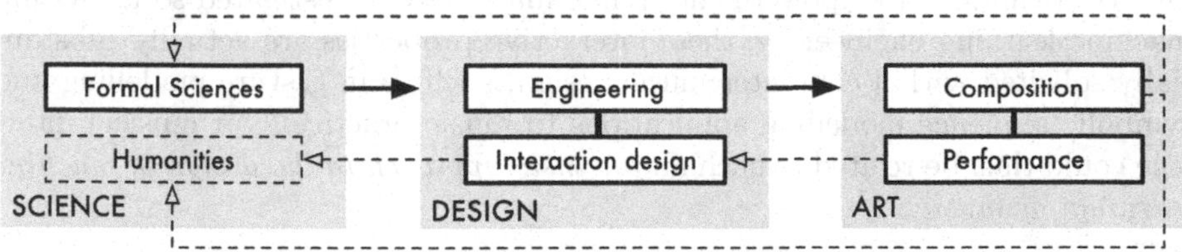

Fig. 7. Our case study. Solid arrows: The sequential research and creation process that we took to lead multidisciplinary research on machine learning. Dashed arrows: Insight gathered for a transdisciplinary approach in the frame of computer music.

Critical Music Practices with Machine Learning. Composition and performance of our musical artwork (see Sect. 4) allowed us to challenge current applications of machine learning to computer music, in a way that could have not been experimented within the standard scientific approach. Many applications of AI to music arguably seek to produce impressive results in terms of automatic generation of music, often leaving musical and aesthetic aspects behind. Conversely, our unconventional use of machine learning in our improvisational piece was intentionally deceptive toward these shared expectations. We deliberately composed with sound synthesis artifacts produced by unsupervised learning, as well as with the indeterminacy of reinforcement learning, to realise novel musical forms linked to our personal spiritualities before seeking to obtain innovative scientific results through the lens of machine learning. Also, we purposefully displayed a music performer progressively relinquishing control over a machine's learning to promote attentive musical listening over the fast-paced quest for technological progress typical of many contemporary AI applications to music. Our artistic choices could thus be described as *critical music practices with machine learning*, inquiring the musical representations and experiences that the formalism of machine learning models may implicitly encapsulate.

Intrinsic Design of Machine Learning for Music. Designing our musical interface let us reflect on our peculiar design approach to machine learning for music (see Sect. 3). Standard engineering of machine learning usually employs quantitative evaluation frameworks, mostly focused on measuring a model's performance regarding a set of explicit tasks, generally also involved in the training—and then raising legitimate suspicions about their intrinsic tautology. Such evaluations, that we call *extrinsic*, tend to prune out the emergent behavior of the trained system in favor to a measurable idea of efficiency, hence denoting a certain statistical materialism that is regularly castigated in this new trend of computer science. At the opposite, our use of latent spaces as customizable sound spaces, as well as our use of feedback as modality for improvisation, rather employed the *intrinsic* properties of such models, hence redefining their original purpose. Such qualitative, creativity-oriented evaluations targeted different interaction design properties, detached from the idea of measurable efficiency, but rather fostering high-level attributes—*e.g.,* expressiveness, compliance, richness, or empowerment. While marginally investigated so far within machine learning engineering, these interactive properties are actually substantially solicited within computer music design, such as in gesture modelling and symbolic sequence modelling applications to music practice. Our musical interface could thus be related to such an *intrinsic approach to the design of machine learning for music.*

The Formal and Humanistic Dimensions of the Sciences of Computer Music. In the present case study, we took a multidisciplinary approach to machine learning, successively assuming the roles of scientists, engineers, designers, and musicians along research. As a consequence, we do not pretend to provide a formal, quantitative, or universal evaluation of machine learning for computer music, as we did in our two scientific modelling studies (see Sect. 2). Rather, we believe that our research approach does constitute one example of machine learning research led by specific computer music practitioners—a complementary type of qualitative and humanistic evaluation, perhaps sharing similarities with the joint scientific and musical approach to computers of Jean-Claude Risset [17]. We hope that the present paper convinced the reader of our diligence toward switching these roles and approaches throughout research and creation.

More generally, we believe that this multidisciplinary approach to machine learning could be likened to a *transdisciplinary* approach to computer music research, considering the current social and industrial context surrounding AI. Historically, multidisciplinary collaboration between engineers and musicians has enabled discoveries and innovations that jointly benefited scientists and computer musicians [18]. Nowadays, rapid advances in digital technology—especially in machine learning engineering—put strong infrastructural pressures on computer musicians, arguably not leaving substantial time for equitable scientific and musical contributions as framed by standard multidisciplinary collaboration.

As researchers in computer science upon leading this case study, we took a modest step toward countering this trend, by letting our computer music practices and personal reflections reassign the scientific ontology of machine learning models, possibly at the expense of standard evaluation approaches of computer science and engineering. Without depreciating nor seeking to relinquish multidisciplinary collaboration at all, we believe that such transdisciplinary approaches are increasingly becoming crucial nowadays, not only to build new practices for the development and evaluation of machine learning models, but also to construct a collective discourse about these technologies that critically considers their ecological integration in human practices—and philosophically speaking, a phenomenological understanding of their behavior. We hope that these insights will resonate with other computer music practitioners and researchers wishing to further contemporary cultivation of the *formal and humanistic dimensions of the sciences of computer music.*

6 Conclusion

We presented a practical case study of machine learning for computer music. We studied two machine learning models, from which we designed a musical interface, and wrote a musical piece for it. We discussed our research and creation process and our personal reflections and insight as computer music practitioners and researchers. Future work may explore transdisciplinary music research approaches that complement computer music multidisciplinary collaboration.

Acknowledgments. We thank Frédéric Bevilacqua, Philippe Esling, Gérard Assayag, Goffredo Haus, and Bavo Van Kerrebroeck for their broad contributions to scientific modelling.

References

1. Akten, M., Fiebrink, R., Grierson, M.: Deep meditations: controlled navigation of latent space. Goldsmiths University of London (2018)
2. Assayag, G., Bloch, G., Chemilier, M., Cont, A., Dubnov, S.: OMax brothers: a dynamic topology of agents for improvization learning. In: Proceedings of the 1st ACM Workshop on Audio and Music Computing Multimedia (2006)
3. Ballet, G., Borghesi, R., Hoffmann, P., Lévy, F.: Studio online 3.0: an internet "killer application" for remote access to IRCAM sounds and processing tools. In: Journées d'Informatique Musicale (JIM) (1999)
4. Bevilacqua, F., Zamborlin, B., Sypniewski, A., Schnell, N., Guédy, F., Rasamimanana, N.: Continuous realtime gesture following and recognition. In: Kopp, S., Wachsmuth, I. (eds.) GW 2009. LNCS (LNAI), vol. 5934, pp. 73–84. Springer, Heidelberg (2010). https://doi.org/10.1007/978-3-642-12553-9_7

5. Boden, M.A.: Computer models of creativity. AI Mag. **30**(3), 23 (2009)
6. Briot, J.-P., Hadjeres, G., Pachet, F.: Deep learning techniques for music generation-a survey. arXiv preprint arXiv:1709.01620 (2017)
7. Cage, J.: Experimental music. In: Silence: Lectures and Writings, vol. 7, p. 12 (1961)
8. Chowning, J.M.: The synthesis of complex audio spectra by means of frequency modulation. J. Audio Eng. Soc. **21**(7), 526–534 (1973)
9. Esling, P., Chemla-Romeu-Santos, A., Bitton, A.: Bridging audio analysis, perception and synthesis with perceptually-regularized variational timbre spaces. DAFx2018 (2018)
10. Fiebrink, R., Caramiaux, B., Dean, R., McLean, A.: The Machine Learning Algorithm as Creative Musical Tool. Oxford University Press, Oxford (2016)
11. Ghisi, D.: Music across music: towards a corpus-based, interactive computer-aided composition. Doctoral dissertation, Paris 6 (2017)
12. Hamel, P., Eck, D.: Learning features from music audio with deep belief networks. In: 11th International Society for Music Information Retrieval Conference (2010)
13. Kingma, D., Welling, M.: Auto-encoding variational Bayes. arXiv preprint arXiv:1312.6114 (2013)
14. Kronland-Martinet, R.: The wavelet transform for analysis, synthesis, and processing of speech and music sounds. Comput. Music J. **12**(4), 11–20 (1988)
15. Meredith, D. (ed.): Computational Music Analysis, vol. 62. Springer, Cham (2016). https://doi.org/10.1007/978-3-319-25931-4
16. Montague, S.: John Cage at seventy: an interview. Am. Music **3**, 205–216 (1985)
17. Risset, J.C., Wessel, D.L.: Exploration of timbre by analysis and synthesis. In: The Psychology of Music, pp. 113–169. Academic Press (1999)
18. Risset, J.-C.: Fifty years of digital sound for music. In: Proceedings of the 4th Sound and Music Computing Conference (SMC) (2007)
19. Rodet, X., Depalle, P., Poirot, G.: Speech analysis and synthesis methods based on spectral envelopes and voiced/unvoiced functions. In: European Conference on Speech Technology (1987)
20. Scurto, H., Bevilacqua, F., Caramiaux, B.: Perceiving agent collaborative sonic exploration in interactive reinforcement learning. In: Proceedings of the 15th Sound and Music Computing Conference (SMC) (2018)
21. Scurto, H., Kerrebroeck, B.V., Caramiaux, B., Bevilacqua, F.: Designing deep reinforcement learning for human parameter exploration. ACM Trans. Comput.-Hum. Interact. (TOCHI) **28**(1), 1–35 (2021)
22. Sutton, R.S., Barto, A.G.: Reinforcement Learning: An Introduction. MIT Press, Cambridge (2018)
23. Tanaka, A., Donnarumma, M.: The body as musical instrument. In: The Oxford Handbook of Music and the Body (2018)
24. Warnell, G., Waytowich, N., Lawhern, V., Stone, P.: Deep TAMER: interactive agent shaping in high-dimensional state spaces. In: Thirty-Second AAAI Conference on Artificial Intelligence, April 2018
25. Ystad, S., Aramaki, M., Kronland-Martinet, R.: Timbre from sound synthesis and high-level control perspectives. In: Siedenburg, K., Saitis, C., McAdams, S., Popper, A.N., Fay, R.R. (eds.) Timbre: Acoustics, Perception, and Cognition. SHAR, vol. 69, pp. 361–389. Springer, Cham (2019). https://doi.org/10.1007/978-3-030-14832-4_13

Iterative Phase Functions on the Circle and Their Projections: Connecting Circle Maps, Waveshaping, and Phase Modulation

Georg Essl(✉)

University of Wisconsin – Milwaukee, Milwaukee, US
essl@uwm.edu

Abstract. In memoriam of Jean-Claude Risset's recent passing, we revisit two of his contributions to sound synthesis, namely waveshaping and feedback modulation synthesis as starting points to develop the connection of a plenthora of oscillatory synthesis methods through iterative phase functions, motivated by the theory of circle maps, which describes any iterated function from the circle to itself. Circle maps have played an important role in developing the theory of dynamical systems with respect to such phenomena as mode-locking, parametric study of stability, and transitions to chaotic regimes. This formulation allows us to bring a wide range of oscillatory methods under one functional description and clarifies their relationship, such as showing that sine circle maps and feedback FM are near-identical synthesis methods.

1 Introduction

Jean-Claude Risset's legacy contains wide-ranging contributions to the field of computer music, sound perception, composition, and sound synthesis. While all these aspects warrant detailed engagement, in this paper[1] we engage only with aspects of his work in sound synthesis. The general range of early contributions of Risset to sound synthesis is staggering and catalogued in his seminal work *An Introductory Catalogue of Computer Synthesized Sounds* [29].

One of Risset's most enduring influences in sound synthesis is seeding ideas of nonlinear functional distortion for sound synthesis (see [29] #150) now known as *waveshaping.* The history of waveshaping is not only intricately tied with an early proposal by Risset, but also with his coming to Marseille. There he would facilitate Daniel Arfib to join, who in turn would develop waveshaping into a full fledged synthesis method [1], an effort that was independently also pushed

[1] This article is an expanded version of a paper presented by the author at CMMR 2019 in Marseille with the title "Connecting Circle Maps, Waveshaping, and Phase Modulation via Iterative Phase Functions and Projections". The present paper is primarily distinguished from its predecessor by the addition of Sect. 5 and contains occasional improvements elsewhere.

R. Kronland-Martinet et al. (Eds.): CMMR 2019, LNCS 12631, pp. 681–698, 2021.
https://doi.org/10.1007/978-3-030-70210-6_44

forward by Le Brun at Stanford University [23]. A number of other contribution helped shape this topic along the way [24,34,38]. For an early unifying review of these developments see Roads [31].

Somewhat less widely recognized [42] though equally foundational, Risset also was part of the group of researchers who pioneered the use of feedback and proposed what would later be coined feedback amplitude modulation synthesis [19,29,32]. Risset himself would credit Arthur Layzer, a colleague at Bell Labs for suggesting the idea (see [29] #510 and #511) though Roads would later attribute the overall development to Layzer, Risset, Matthews, and Moore [32, pp. 244–245]. Since then, feedback has come to play an important role in a range of techniques, such as feedback FM [32,40] and their variations [21].

Finally, Jean-Claude Risset was undoubtedly fascinated by chaos theory as expressed in his 2014 Keynote at ICMC/SMC in Athens, Greece [30] and the use of fractal and chaos theoretic ideas in his pieces *Phases*, *Strange Attractors* as well as *Pentacle.* Chaos theory can be understood as the most flashy aspect of the study of certain deterministic dynamical systems, of which iterative maps are perhaps the most widely considered form in computer music and sound synthesis [2,3,6,8,10,13,15,25–28,33,37,41].

The goal of this paper is to develop explicit connections between many established techniques, such as waveshaping, modulation techniques, and a certain class of chaotic oscillators called circle maps [10,11], hence tying these three strands of Risset's ideas and interests together. Some interrelationships between oscillatory synthesis methods are known, such as the relationships waveshaping [23], phaseshaping [20], frequency [4] and phase modulation and distortion techniques [16,20,22]. Some connections between the chaos theory of dynamical systems and classical synthesis methods have already been unearthed. Di Scipio describes his discovery of interesting nonlinear iterative maps and the relation to chaos through the repeated application of waveshaping [36, footnote 16]. It is also known that feedback frequency modulation (FM) [40] can be driven into chaotic regimes [37]. While experimenting with cascaded and feedback FM, Schottstaedt noted that the output will transition into chaos for certain parameter choices [35]. Some of the ideas presented here have already been sketched out but not fully developed earlier [10,11]. A uniform formulation of all these methods with respect to iterations connects the established sound synthesis literature with the dynamical systems literature and will clarify the individual relationships of different synthesis methods as well as contribute to a broader program to classify synthesis methods with respect to mathematical structure [9].

2 An Iterative Dynamics View of Oscillators on Circles

First we develop a general way to look at oscillatory synthesis algorithms through the lense of dynamical systems. Iterative processes are at the heart of much of dynamical systems theory. But there are a number of further building blocks that add insight into iterative formulations of familiar algorithms. Ultimately we are looking to give the following interpretation of generally familiar phase-centric formulations of oscillators, and interpret them as generalized projections from dynamics on the circle to itself:

$$\underbrace{y_n}_{\text{Time Series}} = \underbrace{p}_{\text{Projection}} \underbrace{(x_n = f(x_{n-1}) \overbrace{\text{mod } 1}^{\text{Circle Topology}}\ )}_{\text{Iterative Phase Function}}$$

This will provide a joint view of oscillatory synthesis and the dynamics of iterated functions, which we will explore in more detail as follows.

2.1 Circle Domains as Topological Spaces

Take a circle and any function acting on the circle returning to another position on the circle. It is easy to see that this is a natural, yet general way to think about any sufficiently low-dimensional oscillatory process.

We can write the general form of the circle map as a mapping of the circle $\mathcal{S}^1$ onto itself. It is a general result in topology that quotients of the real line are equivalent to the circle topologically, and this in turn is equivalent to mapping from the repeated interval $[0,1)$ into itself. Hence, we get three topologically equivalent ways to denote general mappings from the circle onto itself:

$$f : \mathcal{S}^1 \to \mathcal{S}^1 \qquad f : \mathbb{R}/\mathbb{Z} \to \mathbb{R}/\mathbb{Z} \qquad f : [0,1) \to [0,1)$$

This final two equations regarding quotients $\mathbb{R}/\mathbb{Z}$ and unit intervals $[0,1)$ should look already very familiar to anybody who works with sinusoidal oscillators. Equations of the argument of a trigonometric function are periodic with respect to 2π. For example the sine function has the following property $\sin(x) = \sin(x + 2\pi n)$ for all $n \in \mathbb{Z}$. If we divide out the 2π factor we arrive at functions that are periodic on the unit interval $[0,1)$. This normalization is convenient and will be used through our discussion.

Choosing a topologically closed domain such as a circle provides a domain-induced stability for the data on the domain [10]. All data is bounded to this topology, hence there is no escape, overflow, or explosion possible. This is one reason why, numerically, circle maps are attractive over other chaotic maps, where certain parameter ranges or computational inaccuracies can lead to blowups. Practically, one can induce stability of phase computations by taking the modulo the repetition of the phase. This is a general idea and can be used to stabilize a wide range of synthesis algorithms (see [5] for an example) and will apply to all phase computations in this paper.

2.2 Time-Series from Dynamical Systems via Projections

It is common to define a sound synthesis algorithm through giving an equation or algorithm. Our purpose here is to clarify the relationships of different aspects of these equations in the light of general mappings from the circle to the circle.

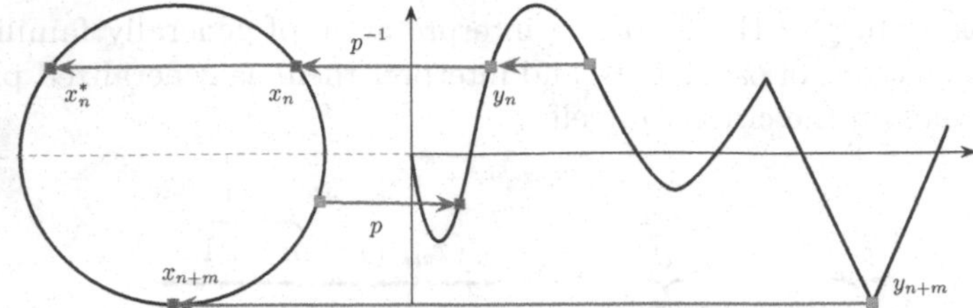

Fig. 1. Projection p and inverse projection p^{-1} between positions on a circle domain and a waveshaped time series. For most values the inverse projection is a two-valued function, hence an additional choice needs to be made to relate a given waveshape to a phaseshape.

So we will look to give strong intuitions of the origins of the aspects of the algorithms in the light of the given topological domain. The formulation of circle maps allows to be precise about the relationship between stable topological space and the dynamics on it one the one hand, and the construction of the resulting time series on the other. Here we will discuss how we extract a time series y_n from an iterative dynamical system x_n. As an illustrative example, let us consider a constant step Ω around the circle [10,14,17][2]:

$$x_n = x_{n-1} + \Omega \mod 1 \tag{1}$$

Notice that there is a choice involved in how we treat this iteration as a time series. One is to simply interpret x_n as a sample and write $y_n = x_n$ leading to linear ramps. If we however consider sinusoidal choices such as:

$$y_n = sin(2\pi x_n) \qquad y_n = cos(2\pi x_n) \qquad y_n = sin(2\pi x_n + \psi)$$

Geometrically we can interpret these as three different choices of orthogonal projection of the motion on the circle onto a line domain (see Fig. 1) and we recover sinusoidal oscillation. The rightmost case describes the general orthogonal projection from the circle under the choice of projection angle ψ. Using this intuition we will refer to mappings from a potentially higher dimensional dynamical system onto a discrete time line as *projection*, even if this mapping does not have a clear geometric meaning, and denote this function as $p(\cdot)$.

This is not the only choice of projection. A second projection that will be important in our discussion uses the phase function directly as output. It may appear trivial to explicitly point out the presence of a function that performs the identity operation $y_n = x_n$ but it serves the important recognition that this is a choice of how to interpret a dynamical system as time series. Some readouts of dynamical systems use linear transformations of the identity to rescale values and add offsets. For simplicity of discussion we will call all these cases *trivial projection* and we will use the symbolic notation $p(\cdot) = 1\cdot$.

[2] Throughout this paper the mod operation is applied to the whole expression.

Waveshaping as Modifying Projections: Waveshaping is the modification of a sine oscillator with a transfer function [1,23]:

$$y_n = f(\sin(2\pi t_n)) \tag{2}$$

$f(\cdot)$ has some general restriction such as they it should be bounded between $(-1, 1)$ for inputs of $(-1, 1)$ in order to not exhibit gain. It is straightforward to interpret waveshaping as a composite projection $p(\cdot) = f(sin(2\pi\cdot))$. And an arbitrary choice of projection $p(\cdot) = f(\cdot)$ is a direct interpretation of the *phase-amplitude mapping* of a form of synthesis called *direct digital synthesis* in the context of digital hardware waveform generation [39]. A linear phase accumulator ϕ_n is directly fed into a wavetable lookup containing an arbitrary waveshape:

$$y_n = f(\phi_n) \qquad \phi_n : x_n = x_{n-1} + \Omega \mod 1 \tag{3}$$

Phaseshaping from Waveshaping: We can construct phaseshapes from waveshapes via the use of inverse projections. The goal is to find a phase-shaped function $f^*(\cdot)$ such that $y_n = f(p(x_n)) = p(f^*(x_n))$ or in short $f \circ p = p \circ f^*$ (compare [17]). The specifics of this construction for an orthogonal projection is shown in Fig. 1. Notice, that in most cases any back projection is a multivalued function. Except for normalized phases 0.25 and 0.75, there are two possible phases on the circle that can achieve any individual (forward) projection. To select a unique case, one can add a further criterion, such as the phase that is closest to a previous phase. The language of projection gives geometric meaning to this constructions, providing a template for generalizing these ideas in higher-dimensional cases, such as higher dimensional versions of phaseshaping [18].

2.3 Iterative Phase Functions

Next we seek to motivate *iterative phase functions.* When convenient we will abbreviate this to simply *phase functions* throughout this paper. These will be the main vehicle for connecting synthesis methods that have relations to oscillation. A simple definition of the iterative phase function is an iterative process that computes a discrete point x_n on a circle domain from a previous position on the circle x_{n-1} through some given mapping.

We have already encountered the simplest example of a phase function in Eq. (1). If we walk around a circle with constant phase steps Ω and project out through $sin(2\pi\cdot)$ we get the simple sinusoidal oscillator. Phase function (1) is sometimes called the *bare circle map* in the dynamical systems literature [14].

Synthesis algorithms are often given in terms of a time parametrization. To understand the reformulation from time-parametric to phase-iterative functions, let us again consider the sine oscillator with frequency ω over discrete time t_n:

$$y(t_n) = sin(2\pi\omega t_n) \tag{4}$$

We can convert this time-parametric version of the sine oscillator into a time-iterative version by writing a time step t_n as increment from a previous time step t_{n-1}:

$$t_n = t_{n-1} + \Delta t$$

To arrive at a phase iterative version, and hence the phase function for the sine oscillator of Eq. (1) we interpret our incremental changes as change in phase x_n with each iteration n. The frequency ω of Eq. (4) relates to phase increment Ω of Eq. (1) up to scale in time to phase dimensions. If a sample frequency ω_s and a fundamental frequency ω_0 are given, we can compute our phase increment as follows $\Omega = \omega_0/\omega_s$ [17].

From this individual mapping we construct a dynamical system by considering repeated iteration. The nth functional iteration $x_n = f(x_{n-1})$, along with some initial phase x_0, then is computed as follows (compare [36]):

$$x_n = f^n(x_0) = \underbrace{f \circ f \circ \cdots \circ f}_{n \text{ times}}$$

3 Oscillatory Synthesis Methods via Phase Functions

Next we will derive the phase functions for a range of oscillatory synthesis methods. In some cases, we will find that phase formulations are immediate, or have been provided in the prior literature. We will start with methods involving nonlinear feedback and follow with techniques absent nonlinear feedback such as modulation techniques. The cases of the sine oscillator has already been given in Eq. (1). Waveshaping and phase-amplitude mappings are not defined by the choice of phase function hence is treated in our discussion of projections in Sect. 2.2.

3.1 Phase Functions with Nonlinear Feedback

Circle Maps: Circle maps have been proposed as candidates for providing chaotic oscillation for sound synthesis [10–12]. The most general form of circle maps refers to all mappings from the circle to itself [10]. Here we will restrict this to a perturbative form of the linear oscillator defined as follows:

$$x_n = x_{n-1} + \Omega + Hf(x_{n-1}) \mod 1 \tag{5}$$

$f(\cdot)$ refers to a nonlinear function. Throughout this paper a function is considered linear if it has the form $ax_{n-1} + b$ over the whole range of values $[0, 1)$ where $a, b \in \mathbb{R}$ are constants. All other functions we will call *nonlinear*. Hence, piecewise linear functions (linear only over a subset of $[0, 1)$), impulses, quadratic functions in x_{n-1}, trigonometric functions are all nonlinear functions. H is the strength of the nonlinearity[3] . If H is 0 then the map reduces to the phase function of the sine oscillator of Eq. (1). The choice of the nonlinear function $f(\cdot)$ provides a significant source of variation [11,12] not unlike general waveshaping. To distinguish this form

[3] Much of the dynamical systems literature uses $H = -\frac{k}{2\pi}$ for the nonlinearity constant, as the sine circle map becomes non-invertible at $k \geq 1$ [10].

of the circle map from those where a specific function $f(\cdot)$ has been chosen, we will refer to this form as *general circle maps*[4]. It can be intuitively described as a one-parameter nonlinear perturbation of the sine oscillator.

Sine Circle Maps and Feedback Frequency Modulation: One of the most widely studied circle map uses a sine function $f(\cdot) = \sin(2\pi\cdot)$ as nonlinear perturbation and we will call this particular instance of the circle map the *sine circle map* [14]:

$$x_n = x_{n-1} + \Omega + H \sin(2\pi x_{n-1}) \mod 1 \tag{6}$$

It turns out that this phase function has appeared as a synthesis method, though the connection, as best as we know, has not been recognized so far. Consider the phase in the range of $[0, 2\pi)$ of the Feedback Frequency Modulation method [40, Eq. (1)], keeping the notation of the original:

$$y = x + \beta \sin y \tag{7}$$

Clearly if we choose $\beta = H$, $x = \Omega$, and normalize to the range of $[0, 1)$ by dividing by 2π, this equation is identical to the sine circle map (6). For simplicity of the feedback in hardware the output projection of feedback FM was chosen to be $p(\cdot) = sin(2\pi\cdot)$. Hence we see that *feedback FM and sine circle maps are identical* when a sine projection is chosen, and they are closely related otherwise. Hence, we can immediately apply the literature on sine circle maps to understanding feedback FM.

Modulated Sine Circle Maps: A straight forward generalization of the sine circle map (aka feedback FM) is the introduction of a "modulation" frequency ω_m. This is not modulation in the sense of a fixed frequency, but a multiplicative change to a feedback frequency, which takes the same position as modulation frequency would in a construction without feedback:

$$x_n = x_{n-1} + \Omega + H \sin(2\pi\omega_m x_{n-1}) \mod 1 \tag{8}$$

It is a special case of the nonlinear perturbation by a Fourier series discussed in [11] where only one frequency is present. If the perturbation function is a general function rather than the sine, we arrive at the *modulated circle map*:

$$x_n = x_{n-1} + \Omega + H f(\omega_m x_{n-1}) \mod 1 \tag{9}$$

Reciprocal Frequency Modulation as Additively Modulated Sine Circle Maps: Medine has proposed a method he calls reciprocal frequency modulation [26, Figure 4]. It differs from the modulated sine circle map by having a set modulation carrier that is perturbed additively by the feedback:

$$x_n = \Omega + H \sin(2\pi(\Omega_m + x_{n-1}) \mod 1 \tag{10}$$

In the language of circle maps this is an *additively modulated sine circle map.*

[4] *Perturbative circle maps* might be an advisable alternative nomenclature.

Functional Iteration and Nested Phaseshaping: Removing the term $x_{n-1} + \Omega$ and omit the scaling factor H from general circle map of Eq. (5) reduces to the following form:

$$x_n = f(x_{n-1}) \mod 1 \quad (11) \qquad x_n = \sin(2\pi\omega_m x_{n-1}) \mod 1 \quad (12)$$

This approach has been introduced to sound synthesis by DiScipio under the name *functional iteration synthesis* (FIS) [36] and has been specifically studied using the sine function $f(\cdot) = \sin(2\pi\omega_m\cdot)$ [7,30]. In his formulation it was not viewed as a phase function but was directly used as output. Hence we need the trivial projection $p(\cdot) = 1\cdot$ to retain our phase interpretation from the original proposal. A natural generalization is to use alternative projections. The projection $\sin(2\pi\cdot)$ is used in the context of nested phaseshaping [17], which is another generalization allowing the change of the phaseshaping functions between iterations. Hence, we get a more general understanding of iterated phaseshaping and functional iteration synthesis as nonperturbative nonlinear feedback iterations.

3.2 Phase Functions Without Nonlinear Feedback

Phaseshaping: Phaseshaping are classical sound synthesis techniques [16,17, 20,22] and it can be generally written as follows:

$$y_n = \sin(2\pi f(\phi(t_n))) \qquad \phi(t_n) = \omega t_n$$

where $\phi(t_n)$ is a linear phase accumulator [39]. It is critical to note that t_n and y_n are independent in this formulation, hence there is no cascade or feedback in this construction. This can be formulated as phase function by introducing an independent iteration z_n as follows:

$$x_n = f(z_{n-1}) \qquad z_n = z_{n-1} + \Omega \mod 1 \qquad (13)$$

Formulated as deviation from a sine oscillator, we get *perturbative phaseshaping* as follows:

$$x_n = x_{n-1} + \Omega + Hf(z_{n-1}) \qquad z_n = z_{n-1} + \Omega \mod 1 \qquad (14)$$

Observe that if $z_0 = x_0$ and we set $H = 1$ then x_n becomes can be computed from a single function f that includes a additive term $+n\Omega$. Hence this first formulation and second formulation differs only in the content of the lookup table of the phaseshape. In Eq. 14 it contains the change in phase position relative to the previous phase position, whereas in Eq. (13) it contains the phase indexed by a linear phase accumulator, and these two formulations are closely related. The perturbative formulation allows a straightforward comparison to modulation techniques.

Frequency and Phase Modulation: Angle modulation techniques, of which frequency and phase modulation are closely related examples, are among the most successful oscillatory synthesis methods. A phase incremental formulation of frequency and phase modulation was given by Schottstaedt [35] that can be trivially unified into our notation for a sinusoidal modulation signal as follows:

$$x_n = x_{n-1} + H\sin(z_{n-1})\Omega \qquad z_n = z_{n-1} + \Omega_m \mod 1 \tag{15}$$

H is the modulation index. Ω_m is the phase increment associated with the modulation frequency. For general modulating functions $f(\cdot)$ we note that FM differs from perturbative phaseshaping of Eq. (14) only in the shape of the modulator function is arbitrary.

Table 1. Phase functions and projections of oscillatory synthesis methods.

Synthesis Method	Chaos	Projection	Phase Function $x_n, z_n = \dots$ mod 1	Equ
General Circle Map	✓		$x_{n-1} + \Omega + Hf(x_{n-1})$	(5)
Sine Circle Map	✓		$x_{n-1} + \Omega + H\sin(2\pi x_{n-1})$	(6)
Feedback FM	✓	$\sin(2\pi\cdot)$	$x_{n-1} + \Omega + H\sin(2\pi x_{n-1})$	(7)
Modulated Circle Map	✓		$x_{n-1} + \Omega + Hf(\omega_m x_{n-1})$	(9)
Modulated Sine Circle Map	✓		$x_{n-1} + \Omega + H\sin(2\pi\omega_m x_{n-1})$	(8)
Reciprocal FM	✓	$\sin(2\pi\cdot)$	$x_{n-1} + \Omega + H\sin(2\pi(\Omega_m + x_{n-1}))$	(10)
Functional Iteration	✓	$1\cdot$	$f(x_{n-1})$	(11)
Iterative Phaseshaping	✓	$\sin(2\pi\cdot)$	$f(x_{n-1})$	(11)
Iterated Sine Map	✓	$1\cdot$	$\sin(2\pi\omega_m x_{n-1})$	(12)
Phaseshaping		$\sin(2\pi\cdot)$	$f(z_{n-1}), z_{n-1} + \Omega$	(13)
Perturbative Phaseshaping		$\sin(2\pi\cdot)$	$x_{n-1} + \Omega + Hf(z_{n-1}), z_{n-1} + \Omega$	(14)
Frequency Modulation		$\sin(2\pi\cdot)$	$x_{n-1} + \Omega + H\sin(2\pi z_{n-1}), z_{n-1} + \Omega_m$	(15)
Sine Oscillator		$\sin(2\pi\cdot)$	$x_{n-1} + \Omega$	(1)
Waveshaping		$f(\sin(2\pi\cdot))$	$x_{n-1} + \Omega$	(2)
Phase-Amplitude Mapping		$f(\cdot)$	$x_{n-1} + \Omega$	(3)
General Modulated Circle Map	✓		$x_{n-1} + \Omega + Hf(x_{n-1}, z_{n-1}, \omega_m)$	(16)

4 Discussion and Generalization

Table 1 shows all oscillatory synthesis methods formulated with phase functions in the previous section. From it we can observe which changes transform one method into another. For simplicity we use $f(\cdot)$ whenever an unknown function can be used. It is important to keep in mind that these are not identical between different cases and methods and can have quite different interpretations. Furthermore we will choose the sine projection $p(\cdot) = \sin(2\pi\cdot)$ for sinusoidal oscillators, even if some other orthogonal projection is used (such as cos or some sine oscillation with phase offset). If the method is usually discussed without a specific projection in mind (as is typical for the dynamical systems literature), the entry is omitted from the table. Methods that are capable of exhibiting chaotic behavior are indicated in the table. The right-most column references the equation numbers from the discussion of these methods in this paper.

There are a few main differences between synthesis methods in Table 1. One difference is the absence or presence of the iterative constant phase increment $x_{n-1} + \Omega$ that corresponds to the simple sinusoidal oscillator from Eq. (1). Independent of the projection this term corresponds to a linear phase increase over time, also known as phase accumulator [39]. If another term is also present, then we can interpret the phase function as a *perturbation* to the linear phase case and under projection, as a perturbation to the sinusoidal oscillator. We see that a number of synthesis methods have been formulated perturbatively, while non-perturbative version has also been proposed. For example, Functional Iteration Synthesis (FIS) is a non-perturbative General Circle Map.

A second distinction is the use of the previous iteration x_{n-1} within a non-linear function $f(\cdot)$ (which may be $\sin(\cdot)$) or alternatively some independent iterative constant phase increment $z_n = z_{n-1} + \Omega$. In the former case we have *feedback*, whereas in the former case the nonlinear function does not depend on the output. Notice that the presence of a past phase x_{x-1} is not sufficient here, as even the sine oscillator is computed from the past value of the phase. We see that for example the General Circle Map differs from Perturbative Phaseshaping only in the presence of feedback, as is the case for the difference of Phaseshaping and Functional Iteration.

The third distinction is the presence of a second frequency. Modulated Circle Map, Reciprocal FM, Iterated Sine Map, and Frequency Modulation have this property in our comparison. We note that this is a different property than an independent variable. If the independent variable z_n uses the same increment as the overall phase function it serves to protect the phase progression from the interference of a nonlinear function in the iteration. It does not introduce a second frequency.

Now we can write down the general form of an iterative equation that encompasses all methods discussed here by allowing each variation to be possible. It is important to note that this iteration is more powerful given that it allows arbitrary mixing between modulation and feedback aspects within an arbitrary function. We call this method *General Modulated Circle Map* to stay in line with other naming choices made:

$$x_n = x_{n-1} + \Omega + Hf(x_{n-1}, z_{n-1}, \omega_m) \mod 1 \tag{16}$$

Note, that we can convert this into a form absent the constant phase increment $x_{n-1} + \Omega$ by requiring that $\Omega = 0$ and that $f(x_{n-1}, z_{n-1}, \omega_m)$ contains the term $-\frac{1}{H}x_{n-1}$.

5 Qualitative Differences of Maps

Next we will seek to give some broad characterisations of the different methods from their output behavior in response to changes in their parameters. The goal is to give a base level intuition of similarities and differences in the method.

In order to give a sense of the relationship of these maps, we will utilize renderings of their parameter spaces with perceptually inspired measure for comparison [12]. These parameter planes represent broad spectral characteristics encoded in one color-range value for each local parameter pair. Hence it allows a broad overview of the impact of parametric change over a range of parameters at once. This approach of visualizing dynamical behavior has a long history in the theory of dynamical systems. The general process is flexible but for our purpose it can be summarized as follows: For each parameter pair, compute the iterative map with projection for a sufficient time to achieve steady state, compute the spectrum on the steady state portion, and then using a measure in R to capture properties of interest of the spectrum. This is then used to color-code a local pixel in the rendering of the plane. Details can be found in [12].

We will use the log-scale PeakSparcity measure [12] to compute the local color in all our plots in the parameter plane. This measure is designed to quantify the sparcity of peaks in the spectrum while being insensitive to the location of the peaks within the spectrum, hence it does not respond to pitch or harmonicity properties and is well suited to compare spectral content of a wide range of sounds.

We will use a normalized frequency sweeps on the interval $[0, 1)$ for the x-axis in all plots. Frequency sweeps may be over Ω or any modulation-related frequency parameter (Ω_m, ω_m) of Table 1. To simplify our notation we will use Ω_m and hence remove the distinction between additive and multiplicative modulation for this discussion. The y-axis will correspond to an increase in the parameter H from our equations of Table 1. This parameter has been rescaled to conform to standards in the dynamical systems literature, captured by the parameter $K = 2\pi H$. This rescaling leads to the sine circle map losing invertibility at $K > 1$ [11,12]. This point is marked in all parameter plane renderings even if it does not carry the same meaning for the particular map under consideration. For low to moderate modulation regimes we will use a linear sweep of K from 0 to 1.5, whereas for high modulation (high nonlinearity, if applicable) regimes we will use a linear sweep of K from 0 to 15. The figures are rendered to allow direct comparisons to existing depictions of parameter planes of the general and sine circle maps [12].

5.1 Oscillators Without Feedback

Three maps without nonlinear feedback are depicted in Fig. 2. The left figure shows the sine oscillator, followed by standard FM using a sinusoidal modulator function, and then followed by perturbative phaseshaping, which alternatively we can think of as FM with a non-sinusoidal modulator function. The modulation function used is a triangular function (compare [11]):

$$f(y_n) = \begin{cases} 4 \cdot y_n & \text{if } 0 \leq y_n < 1/4 \\ (1/4 - y_n) \cdot 4 + 1 & \text{if } 1/4 \leq y_n < 3/4 \\ (y_n - 3/4) \cdot 4 - 1 & \text{otherwise.} \end{cases}$$

All our rendering of non-sinusoidal functions in place of f in our equations will use this functional shape. Hence all comparisons will be between sinusioidal

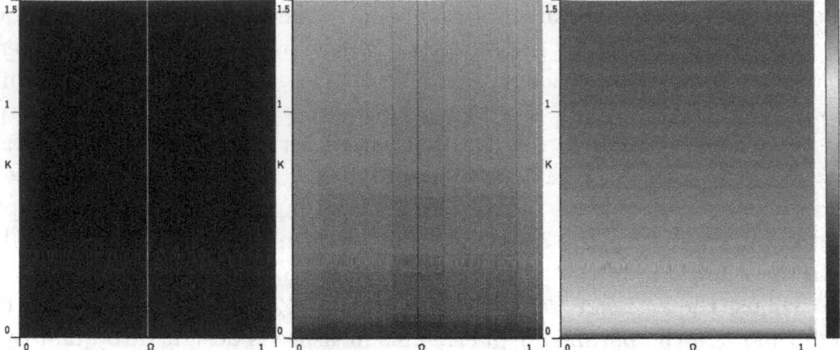

Fig. 2. Oscillators without nonlinear feedback. Linearity assures that frequencies remain undisturbed under variation of a possible modulation index (if applicable). (left) Sine (center) Frequency Modulation (right) Iterative Phaseshaping with triangular modulation oscillation. $\omega_m = 0.103$. The spectral content gets richer from left to right.

and triangular functions (as modulators, phase shapers and so forth). We restrict ourself this way to further our aim for comparison and it does not capture the rich tapestry of effects, specifically in the nonlinear feedback case that the choice of the function effects (see [11,12] for illustrations of further cases).

A main characteristic of linearity is that frequencies remain unaltered but are merely rescaled and added. We can see in all three cases that with increasing parameter H (and hence K) which in the FM literature is called *modulation index* [35] the spectrum does get richer, but frequencies remain stable over all parameters. The triangular modulator injects substantially more spectral content than the sinusoidal modulator.

5.2 Oscillators with Nonlinear Feedback

Figure 3 shows three maps which involving nonlinear feedback. The three examples all have a perturbative formulation hence they each reduce to a linear oscillator with frequency Ω if $K = 0$. On the left we show the sine circle map (also known as feedback FM) (see [10–12] for more details). It displays a range of nonlinear feedback effects including mode locking (represented by the widening "tongue-like" triangles, the dependence of output frequency on the strength of the nonlinearity. The center of the figure shows the modulated circle map with sine modulation function, and the right shows the modulated circle map with a triangular modulation function. It is well-known that features like mode-locking are robust aspects of nonlinear feedback [12] as is the parameter dependency of output frequency. The most obvious effects of changing modulation functions in these depictions is the impact on the shape of mode-locking and fixed-point regions.

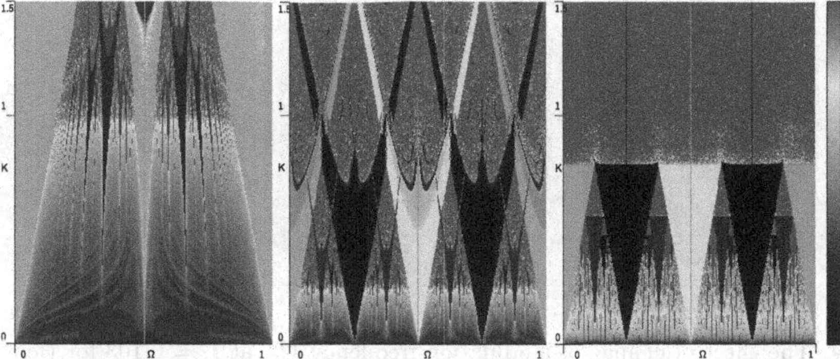

Fig. 3. Oscillators with nonlinear feedback iterations. Linearity is no longer preserved, hence frequencies are no longer stable under change of the modulation index. (left) Sine circle map (feedback FM) (center) modulated sine circle map $\omega_m = 4$ (left) general modulated circle map $\omega_m = 4$ with a triangular modulation oscillation. The modulation function changes the behavior of fixed-point regions and the shape of frequency shifts.

This figure also serves to provide some comparison with respect to methods without nonlinear feedback. The three renderings in Fig. 3 are analogous to the ones depicted in Fig. 2. The sine circle map without is the feedback generalization of the sine oscillator, the modulated sine circle map is a feedback version of FM, and the modulated circle map using a triangular nonlinearity is the feedback version of iterative phaseshaping with a triangular phaseshaper. Given the perturbative nature of the feedback maps, the figures are similar in the very low nonlinearity regime (H is close to 0).

5.3 Effect of Change in Modulation Frequency

Observe that Figs. 2 and 3 were rendered at different modulation frequencies ($\Omega_m = 0.103$ and $Omega_m = 4$ respectively). Hence it remains to be explained how the modulation frequency impacts each maps output to make this comparison valid. Taking FM as a prototype, it is well understood, that the modulator frequency does not impact the presence of spectral content, just their relative placements with respect to the carrier frequency [35]. Hence we expect the PeakSparcity measure to be unaffected by changes in modulation frequencies for standard FM, this and the case of the triangular modulation function is verified via the left two parameter planes in Fig. 4. The case on nonlinear feedback maps is more complicated. The right two planes in Fig. 4 shows effect of changing modulation frequency in the presence of feedback. Hence we can always align the modulation frequencies of maps without nonlinear feedback to those of maps with such feedback but we cannot assume that we will be able to perform the inverse.

Figure 5 shows two parameter planes for reciprocal FM. While the overall behavior of the map with respect to base frequency changes is near identical to

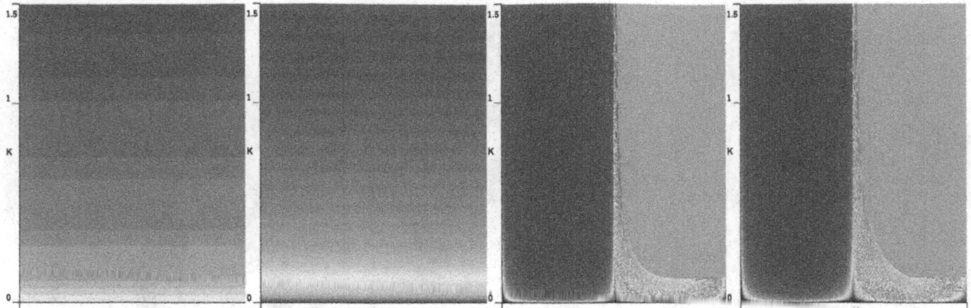

Fig. 4. The effect of change of modulation frequency Ω_m at $\Omega = 0.103$ for (left) FM (center left) iterative phaseshaping with triangular modulation function (center right) modulated sine circle map and (right) modulated circle map with triangular modulation function.

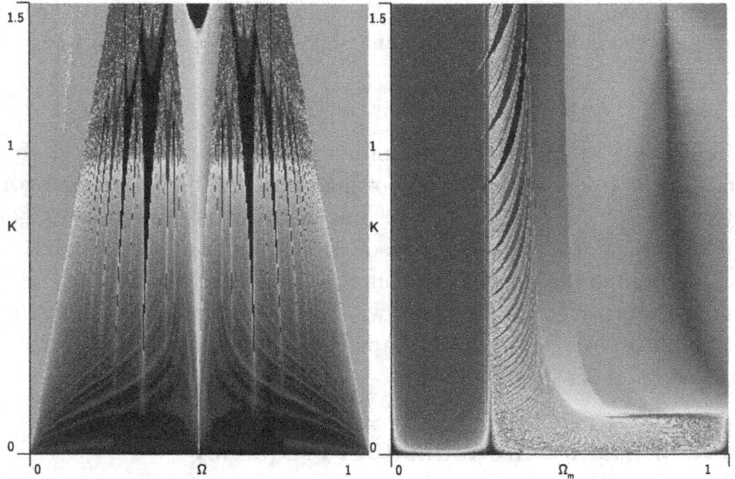

Fig. 5. Reciprocal frequency modulation (left) variation of the base frequency with a modulation frequency of $\Omega = 0.103$ (right) variation of the modulation frequency with a base frequency of $\Omega = 0.103$.

that of the sine circle map (compare Fig. 3), notice that additive modulation leads to a widening of the transitional behavior under change of modulation frequency.

5.4 Nonlinear Feedback and the Effect of Perturbative Formulations

The iterated sine map is an example of a non-perturbative nonlinear feedback map with a frequency parameter Ω_m. Figure 6 shows this map with a frequency sweep over its frequency parameter for the same range as other figures on the left, as well as for high values of H on the right. The red area on the lower left of both

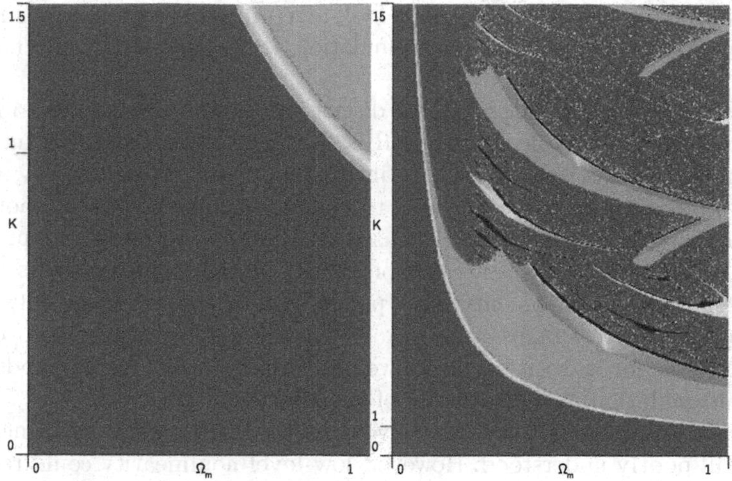

Fig. 6. Iterated sine map for an initial value of $x_0 = 0.25$. (left) mild nonlinearity $K = [0, 1.5)$ (right) strong nonlinearity $K = [0, 15)$.

figures correspond to fixed point regions of the map. Hence the map only creates meaningful output for large parameters and then the transition into chaotic regimes is quite rapid. Furthermore, the map is particularly susceptible to fixed points in response to initial values. In particular, an initial value of $x_0 = 0$ leads a fixed point solution over all parameter choices. Hence mild nonlinearity effects such as mode-locking and mild spectral alterations [11] are not observed in non-perturbative nonlinear feedback maps, and the perturbation from the nonlinear map has the further effect of reducing fixed-point solutions for a large range of the parameter plane (compare Figs. 6 and 3). In general, perturbative versions of nonlinear feedback maps are easier to control and relates to well-understood methods when the nonlinearity small.

6 Conclusions

In this paper, we have shown how many oscillatory synthesis methods can be understood as different instances of iterative phase functions that are broadly understood as mappings from the circle to itself, clarifying in particular when one should expect the possibility of chaotic behavior in the presence of nonlinearities. Furthermore, it allows relating of these synthesis methods, understanding them as generalizations or special cases. We have shown that feedback FM and sine circle maps as near identical methods, we have given a phase perturbative version of phaseshaping, clarified the relationship of functional iteration and nested phaseshaping, and formulated a unifying generalization that include all discussed methods.

We have presented a range of numerical computations leading to visualizations of many of the discussed methods using parameter planes of local spectral information. This has provided a first look at comparing the methods not only with respect to their algorithmic formulation, but also with respect to their output properties.

Two of the main components of our discussion, nonlinearity and feedback, are inextricably linked with Jean-Claude Risset's foundational research into sound synthesis methods as well as his later interest in chaos. More broadly, we hope that this work gives an easier pathway to understanding the use of chaotic oscillation within the context of widely used oscillatory methods and provides a stronger connection between waveshaping, modulation type synthesis methods and chaotic dynamical systems. This paper can, however, be sensibly read as a proposal that circle maps form a good candidate for inquiry into chaos in sound synthesis for its relationship to well-established synthesis methods and its intuitive formulation as perturbation of the sine oscillator.

There are numerous interesting avenues for future work. Nonlinear feedback is still poorly understood. However, low-level nonlinearity could readily be exploited, specifically in the context of mildly perturbing well-understood methods. The development of concrete projection strategies for higher dimensional oscillators is another exciting topic of future inquiry.

Acknowledgement. The author would like to thank Bill Schottstaedt for providing helpful information during the preparation of this work. Feedback of anonymous reviewers proved helpful and is much appreciated. Part of this work was made possible by a fellowship of the John Simon Guggenheim Memorial Foundation.

References

1. Arfib, D.: Digital synthesis of complex spectra by means of multiplication of nonlinear distorted sine waves. J. Audio Eng. Soc. **27**(10), 757–779 (1979)
2. Berdahl, E., Sheffield, E., Pfalz, A., Marasco, A.T.: Widening the razor-thin edge of chaos into a musical highway: connecting chaotic maps to digital waveguides. In: Proceedings of the International Conference on New Interfaces for Musical Expression, pp. 390–393 (2018)
3. Bidlack, R.: Chaotic systems as simple (but complex) compositional algorithms. Comput. Music J. **16**(3), 33–47 (1992)
4. Chowning, J.M.: The synthesis of complex audio spectra by means of frequency modulation. J. Audio Eng. Soc. **21**(7), 526–534 (1973)
5. Collins, N.: Even more errant sound synthesis. In: Proceedings of the Sound and Music Computing Conference (SMC) vol. 6 (2012)
6. Di Scipio, A.: Composition by exploration of non-linear dynamic systems. In: Proceedings of the International Computer Music Conference, pp. 324–327 (1990)
7. Di Scipio, A.: Synthesis of environmental sound textures by iterated nonlinear functions. In: Proceedings of the 2nd COST G-6 Workshop on Digital Audio Effects (DAFx99) (1999)
8. Dobson, R., Fitch, J.: Experiments with chaotic oscillators. In: Proceedings of the International Computer Music Conference. Banff, Canada, pp. 45–48 (1995)
9. Essl, G.: Mathematical structure and sound synthesis. In: Proceedings of the International Conference on Sound and Music Computing. Salerno, Italy (2005)

10. Essl, G.: Circle maps as a simple oscillators for complex behavior: I. Basics. In: Proceedings of the International Computer Music Conference (ICMC). New Orleans (2006)
11. Essl, G.: Circle maps as a simple oscillators for complex behavior: II. Experiments. In: Proceedings of the International Conference on Digital Audio Effects (DAFx). Montreal (2006)
12. Essl, G.: Exploring the sound of chaotic oscillators via parameter spaces. In: Proceedings of the International Conference on Digital Audio Effects (DAFx). Birmingham (2019)
13. Gogins, M.: Iterated functions systems music. Comput. Music J. **15**(1), 40–48 (1991)
14. Hao, B.L., Zheng, W.M.: Applied Symbolic Dynamics and Chaos. 2nd edn. World Scientific, New Jersey (2018)
15. Holopainen, R.: Self-organised sound with autonomous instruments: Aesthetics and experiments. Ph.D. thesis, University of Oslo (2012)
16. Ishibashi, M., et al.: Electronic musical instrument (Apr 21 1987). US Patent 4,658,691
17. Kleimola, J., Lazzarini, V., Timoney, J., Välimäki, V.: Phaseshaping oscillator algorithms for musical sound synthesis. In: Proceedings of the 7th Sound and Music Computing Conference (SMC) (2010)
18. Kleimola, J., Lazzarini, V., Timoney, J., Valimaki, V.: Vector phase shaping synthesis. In: Proceedings of the International Conference on Digital Audio Effects (DAFx) (2011)
19. Kleimola, J., Lazzarini, V., Välimäki, V., Timoney, J.: Feedback amplitude modulation synthesis. EURASIP J. Adv. Sign. Process. **2011**(1), 434378 (2010)
20. Lazzarini, V., Timoney, J.: New perspectives on distortion synthesis for virtual analog oscillators. Comput. Music J. **34**(1), 28–40 (2010)
21. Lazzarini, V., Timoney, J., Kleimola, J., Välimäki, V.: Five variations on a feedback theme. In: DAFx 09 Proceedings of the 12th International Conference on Digital Audio Effects, Politecnico di Milano, Como Campus, Sept. 1–4, Como, Italy, pp. 1–7. Department of Electronic Engineering, Queen Mary University of London (2009)
22. Lazzarini, V., Timoney, J., Pekonen, J., Välimäki, V.: Adaptive phase distortion synthesis. In: DAFx 09 Proceedings of the 12th International Conference on Digital Audio Effects, Politecnico di Milano, Como Campus, Sept. 1–4, Como, Italy, pp. 1–8. Department of Electronic Engineering, Queen Mary University of London (2009)
23. Le Brun, M.: Digital waveshaping synthesis. J. Audio Eng. Soc. **27**(4), 250–266 (1979)
24. Letowski, T.: Difference limen for nonlinear distortion in sine signals and musical sounds. Acta Acustica United Acustica **34**(2), 106–110 (1975)
25. Mackenzie, J., Sandler, M.: Modelling sound with chaos. In: Proceedings of IEEE International Symposium on Circuits and Systems (ISCAS), pp. 93–96 (1994). https://doi.org/10.1109/ISCAS.1994.409534
26. Medine, D.: Dynamical systems for audio synthesis: embracing nonlinearities and delay-free loops. Appl. Sci. **6**(5), 134 (2016)
27. Mikelson, H.: Mathematical modeling with csound: from waveguides to chaos. In: Boulanger, R. (ed.) The Csound Book, pp. 369–384. MIT Press, Cambridge (2000)
28. Mudd, T.: Nonlinear dynamics in musical interactions. Ph.D. thesis, The Open University (2017)

29. Risset, J.C.: Catalog of Computer Synthesized Sound. Bell Telephone Laboratories, Murray Hill (1969)
30. Risset, J.: Sound and music computing meets philosophy. In: Joint Proceedings of the 40th International Computer Music Conference, ICMC, and the 11th Sound and Music Computing Conference, SMC (2014)
31. Roads, C.: A tutorial on non-linear distortion or waveshaping synthesis. Comput. Music J. **3**(2), 29–34 (1979)
32. Roads, C., Strawn, J.: The Computer Music Tutorial. MIT Press, Cambridge (1996)
33. Rodet, X., Vergez, C.: Nonlinear dynamics in physical models: simple feedback-loop systems and properties. Comput. Music J. **23**(3), 18–34 (1999)
34. Schaefer, R.A.: Electronic musical tone production by nonlinear waveshaping. J. Audio Eng. Soc. **18**(4), 413–417 (1970)
35. Schottstaedt, B.: An Introduction to FM (2006). https://ccrma.stanford.edu/software/snd/snd/fm. Retrieved on March 31 2019
36. Scipio, A.D.: Iterated nonlinear functions as a sound-generating engine. Leonardo **34**(3), 249–254 (2001)
37. Slater, D.: Chaotic sound synthesis. Comput. Music J. **22**(2), 12–19 (1998)
38. Suen, C.: Derivation of harmonic equations in nonlinear circuits. J. Audio Eng. Soc. **18**(6), 675–676 (1970)
39. Symons, P.: Digital Waveform Generation. Cambridge University Press, Cambridge (2013)
40. Tomisawa, N.: Tone production method for an electronic musical instrument (Feb 10 1981). US Patent 4,249,447
41. Truax, B.: Chaotic non-linear systems and digital synthesis: an exploratory study. In: Proceedings of the International Computer Music Conference, pp. 100–103 (1990)
42. Valsamakis, N., Miranda, E.R.: Iterative sound synthesis by means of cross-coupled digital oscillators. Digit. Creativity **16**(2), 90–98 (2005)

Mathematics and Music: Loves and Fights

Thierry Paul[1,2P (✉)]

[1] Centre de Mathématiques Laurent Schwartz, CNRS and Ecole Polytechnique, 1128 Palaiseau Cedex, France
thierry.paul@upmc.fr

[2] Laboratoire Jacques-Louis Lions, CNRS, Sorbonne Université 4 Place Jussieu, 75005 Paris, France
http://ljll.math.upmc.fr/paulth

Abstract. We present different aspects of the special relationship that music has with mathematics, in particular the concepts of rigour and realism in both fields. These directions are illustrated by comments on the personal relationship of the author with Jean-Claude, together with examples taken from his own works, specially the "Duos pour un pianiste".

Keywords: Music · Mathematics · Rigour · Philosophy · Jean-claude risset

Prelude: In Memoriam

October 3rd 2016, I attended the Italian premiere of "Oscura". It was in Rome, with Maureen Chowning singing and John Chowning at the mixing board.

Unfortunately Jean-Claude couldn't come but I exchanged with him the following emails, alas the last ones.

Cher Jean-Claude,
je sors du concert au conservatorio à Rome, où ton absence nous a surpris et ta presence beaucoup manqué. Ton œuvre est très belle.
(...)
Très amicalement,
Thierry.
.

Cher Thierry,
Je te remercie vivement pour ton message de Rome : j'avais escompté assister au concert de Rome, mais j'ai dû rester à Marseille pour des examens un peu énigmatiques.

R. Kronland-Martinet et al. (Eds.): CMMR 2019, LNCS 12631, pp. 699–708, 2021.
https://doi.org/10.1007/978-3-030-70210-6_45

Ton message amical m'a fait très plaisir.
Bien à toi,
Jean-Claude

1 Introduction

Jean-Claude Risset used to say: "[for example] *in music, we don't even have a Heisenberg principle, yet*".

This complain might seem strange, coming from a composer who used all along his life a lot of physics and mathematics in his action of composing. And on the other side, how not to imagine a bit awkward such a sentence in the mouth of a "pure" researcher other than Jean-Claude? This reference to the quantum uncertainty relations - which, by the way, is a (mathematical) theorem - is also very interesting if one thinks that quantum mechanics brought a deep change of paradigm in our way of seeing the world, which could be put in correspondence with the big changes we got from music - between the loss of tonality to nowadays music inseparable from computer sciences - in our way of hearing the sound [7].

If there are many examples of very famous mathematicians interested in music, such as Euler and his famous "Tentatem Novae Theoriae Musicae" from 1739 (see Fig. 1), one has to admit that there were also a lot of missed occasions of fruitful interactions between mathematics and music. How not to find astonishing to think that the d'Arezzo system of musical notation, a robust system still operating more than thousand years after its invention, didn't impulse the creation of the analytic geometry invented much later in seventieth century by Descartes?

Representing the two parameters - height and time to be played - by a single point in the plane isn't it basically the same as associating to a point two Cartesian coordinates? How to imagine that none of the mathematicians reading and playing fugues since the seventieth century, with their translated, inverted, augmented subject and all this counterpoint "machinery", didn't read in this practice the mathematical theory of groups invented two centuries later?

Nowadays, music consumes a lot of mathematics, at least trough computer sciences. But as pointed Jean-Claude Risset in the aforementioned quotation, music certainly misses some important scientific recent discoveries, such as quantum mechanics (the reader interested by this point can look at [7]). And, on the other side, I wouldn't be surprised that mathematics of the following centuries "rediscover" object used in nowadays music.

But it seems to me that there is more in the relation between math and music Much more (and much less studied) than the link between the d'Arezzo notation and Descartes analytic geometry (much later), much more than group theory versus inversions, dilations, translations in the art of composing or improvising fugues (much earlier, again). Exactly like there is more than this analogy between wavelets and music scores, an analogy more pleasant to (some) mathematicians than to (any) musician. One discovers, according to me. Stronger links between mathematics and music when one addresses the following question:

what is common and different

in the processes of

(music) composition and (math) research?

TENTAMEN
NOVAE THEORIAE
MVSICAE
EX
CERTISSIMIS
HARMONIAE PRINCIPIIS
DILVCIDE EXPOSITAE.
AVCTORE
LEONHARDO EVLERO.

PETROPOLI, EX TYPOGRAPHIA ACADEMIAE SCIENTIARVM.
cIↄIↄCCXXXIX.

Fig. 1. Cover of Euler's "Tentatem Novae Theoriae Musicae"

A first important peculiarity to notice is that both use a **proper language**. In fact they are the only ones, among fundamental sciences and arts, to do so. At least in an intrinsic and efficient way: even more than a language, they use somehow their own proper alphabet. That is to say:

they share the property of having their own proper type of *kinematics*.

More than that: we will see that they both use extensively **rigour**:

they have in common a *dynamics* driven by rigour.

Indeed, one of the deeper links between math an music, which also reveals fundamental differences, is located for me in the concept of rigour. Both mathematicians and musicians are rigorous in their action. No need to talk about the yoke that constitutes the obligation for the mathematician to prove things. Choosing a tonality, later a series, now a set of patches also consists in fixing some constraints which tie the composer in an a priori quite rigid frame. But this use, sometimes abuse, of rigour - and we claim that this is the same type or rigour which is truly used in both domains, a fact which characterizes them in between other sciences and art - is performed in very different places in music and in mathematics. As an a priori for the composer who feels free, in fine, to "cheat" with the constraints (in the same way with respect to tonality as to dodecaphonism). And, at the contrary, as a final achievement for the mathematician.

Rigour versus reality is another concept I would like to see math and music to share. In fact the famous (and for me a bit "has been") debate on mathematical Platonism - to put it in a nutshell, do mathematicians invent or discover theorems? - has some resonances in music: after all, any sound belongs (already(?)) to the nature, can one say naively. A comparison between (what one can call) realism in mathematics and music deserve, according to me, to be exhibited.

I will first discuss the position of rigour in both actions of doing mathematics and doing (composing) music: a priori for musicians, in fine for mathematicians. I believe Jean-Claude was a perfect illustration of this, and his works continue to illustrate this way of handling this quite schizophrenic bridge between math and music.

Then I will briefly discuss the duality rigour/realism, and the tied concept of emergence in music and illustrate it by the "Duos pour un pianiste", this fantastic work by Jean-Claude where the unplayable rings real piano sounds.

2 Rigour in Mathematics and in Music: Confluences and Divergences

Let us start by two anecdotes concerning rigour and its perceptions by mathematicians and musicians.

The first one concerns the famous mathematician Claude Chevalley[1] who, during a talk on algebraic, "very abstract", mathematics forgot part of a proof. In order to recover the missing argument. he draws a little picture on the blackboard. But he makes sure nobody in the audience can see it, and eventually erases it before to continue its "rigorous" demonstration. Pictures, schemes are fundamental in the process of research in mathematics, but they are not rigorous. They just show examples, very often emblematic of a general situation, but they cannot constitute a proof. Nevertheless they provide tools as useful for the audience of a talk than for the mathematician at work, and shouldn't be absent of a conference.

The second story concerns Stravinsky and is about his Movements for piano and orchestra [14]. This is very late piece by Stravinsky, belonging to the period where he (finally!) discovered and used Viennese serialism. It seems [1] that Stravinsky claimed that it is impossible to recover the series from the score[2]. And was much happy about this success in the direction of hidden serialsim.

These two anecdotes show clearly that, first, rigour is important in both mathematical and musical fields, and, second, that something is inverted in the perception of rigour by mathematicians and musicians.

[1] The same anecdote has been also told to me with another main character in place of Chevalley.

[2] Boucourechliev [1] claims that Stravinsky is wrong and that is possible but, actually, doesn't give the recovered series.

In a nutshell:
mathematicians like to hide *non-rigorous aspects*,
musicians like to hide *too rigorous aspects*.

But, according to me, they also reveal some more historical important features. The fact that the music of the fifties (period of full and strict serialism) was more or less disapproved by their own creators, for the argument that they represent a "passage obligé" to be hidden afterall[3], might have had a true responsibility in a certain form of disinterest of nowadays audiences for contemporain music. The public also has the right (the duty) to reach (and feel) the "limites du pays fertile"[4]

To conclude:
the rigour is either too emphasized (in mathematics) or too hidden (in music)

A natural question arises then: why is it so? Why the concept of rigour, present in the two fields considered here, is expressed, perceived in such different forms in mathematics and in music? We shall now try to give al answer to this question.

Let us summarize: music shares with mathematics a particular mandatory use of rigour. This is obviously, intrinsically true in mathematics. But it is also true for music, at least a certain kind of, as choosing tonality, series, a certain use of randomness, numerical patches, are constraint which constitute, according to me, a full tool box of rigour.

Composing, as proving, are actions very rigour consuming. But, at the contrary, the action of proving uses also a lot of other behaviours that escape completely from rigour. This is, this time, obvious for music, as everybody knows the disaster that created, in the past, a too rigid way of composing. But this is also true for mathematicians, who pass most of their time outside of rigour, being wrong.

Let us illustrate briefly these two common points for mathematics and music, namely the rigour and the loss of it, by the famous article "... wie die Zeit vergeht ..." by K. Stockhausen [13] and by looking at examples of writing (and I believe thinking) mathematics in an article by H. Poincaré published in the early twentieth century and a book by É. Goursat in the thirties (see [8] for more details.

In [13], Stockhausen makes the radical bet that one can compose by using in the same manner all the (very) different time scales (from the time of rythm (or even more, of the concert) to the one of timbre). This - in a certain sense quite natural - remark, very embedded in the rigorous serialism philosophy of music in the fifties, constitutes a starting point, a way of starting inside some

[3] Pierre Boulez comdans voluntary the third part of "Structure I for two pianos"[2] for the argument that "a computer could have composed it in a few minutes". Et alors ?.

[4] Let us remark that, at the same period, Bourbaki's attempt to constrict what could be called a kind of absolutely pure mathematics was offering a vision of mathematics where the only figures are commuting diagrams, which by the way are not figures but just notations.

very rigorous rules. Rules that the musician will be free to abandon during the process of composing.

At the contrary, in 1912, Poincaré [12] "defines" the famous Dirac δ function (a function equal to zero except at the origin where it takes an infinite value) in a significant but highly nonrigorous way. Strictly speaking the definition is empty. But it gives the whole flavour of what it should be, using a non defined notion of "infinitesimal small", a concept that Gourçat defines in a very floppy way[5] [6] twenty years later. In fact, one had to wait twenty years more to have a rigorous definition of δ, much after its extensive effective use. On sees that, here, rigour enters the game after nonrigorous considerations, much after.

In fact the initial data are of the same type for the two fileds: an original material (a chord, a theme, a patch, an equation, a conjecture, an equality), but the way that have musicians and mathematicians to "honour their material" [4] are very different: limiting the imagination by strong constraints for the musician, fishing ideas outside any rigour for the mathematician. Eventually, the musicians will free themselves from this rigorous straitjacket (sometimes quite quickly [5]) in the name of musicality and the mathematician will put some strict rigorous order in the different arguments necessitated by the constitution of the final proof.

Therefore, if mathematics and music share both the use of rigour and the loss of rigour, we arrive to the conclusion that there is a fundamental difference between them. In the action of doing mathematics and composing music, the musician start with rigour and eventually get rid of it by a typical artistic gesture. In the contrary of the mathematician, who starts outside any rules, fishing ideas, and end up with a perfectly rigorous situation produced by a typical scientific gesture[6]. In a nutshell:

Music: one starts with rigour (tonality, series, algorithms)
and leave over things
for *musical arguments.*

Mathematics: one starts freely in order to get ideas
and select rigorous things
for *mathematical reason.*

The composer changes at the last minute
or wait long for a musical fact.

The mathematician proves till the end
and might wait long for a simple rigorous lemma[7].

[5] "On dit qu'un nombre variable x a pour limite un nombre fixé a, ou tend vers a, lorsque la valeur absolue de la différence $x-a$ finit par devenir et "rester" plus petite que n'importe quel nombre positif donné à l'avance. Lorsque $a=0$, le nombre x est dit "un infiniment petit".", Gourçat [6].

[6] The reader interested in the concept of rigour in mathematics, philosophy and music, might consult the proceedings [3] of the conference RIGUEUR held in Paris, July 2 and 3 2019, to be published by Spartacus editions (Paris).

[7] Though wrong proofs are usaully very beautiful.

In conclusion, musicians and mathematicians both need rigour, but at different times in their process of creation.

Before finishing this section, let us ask the following question: Is there a Mathematical equivalent to the (famous) question: "What is musical?"?

A too naive and fast (and actually wrong) answer would claim :

What is mathematical is what is rigorous.

In mathematics, rigour is not a "fin en soi":

"Ce qui limite le vrai, ce n'est pas le faux, c'est l'insignifiant."[8] [15]

This famous quotation will lead us naturally to questioning in the next section the concept of realism in math and music, and, as a kind of by-product, to some remarks on Jean-Claude's "Duo pour un pianiste" which will close this article.

3 Rigour Versus Realism, and All That

What is real in mathematics, and in music? After having discussed the fundamental role of rigour in the processes of proving and composing, the aforementioned question concerns more the result of the production both in math and in music. Of course, the answer seems easier in music: what is real is the execution of the work during a concert.

There are no concerts in mathematics. Mathematical results are exchanged mostly through articles in specialized journals and discussions between experts. The diffusion of mathematics to non-mathematicians is something else, something apart, considered as non fundamental for the evolution of the field mathematics. What questions realism in mathematics is generally circumscribed to the notion of mathematical Platonism. Mathematical Platonism [10] states the problem of knowing if the contents of theorems are truly invented by mathematicians, as coming from a "nowhere", or, at the contrary, if mathematicians "just" discover their production in a "somewhere else" susceptible to contain everything.

There is a temptation [10] to consider that this "somewhere else" should be incarnated in music by the concert, a place of reality for music. But the situation seems to me less simple that it appears. Indeed: which concert? Which interpretation of the piece? And which "realization" in the case of an open work? Placing realism in music too close to the acoustic event is, according to me, problematic.

I also strongly believe that the Platonistic debate in mathematics is a bit "has been" and that there is no "somewhere else": mathematics are just the result of their own construction. And I also think that realism in music doesn't seat in the place of concert: what is more real concerning the "Valses nobles et

[8] What limits the true is not the false, it is the insignificant.

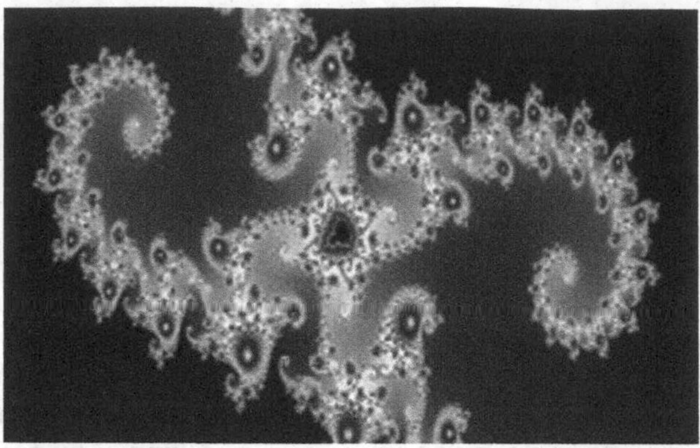

Fig. 2. Fractal

Fig. 3. Jean-Claude Risset

sentimentales"? The version for orchestra or the version for piano? What is real in "Duos pour un pianiste"?

Let us go a bit further: What is real in mathematics, in a fractal for example?

Certainly not this picture, which represents a naive (though beautiful) finite image of an infinite multi-scale (that is why the picture is an image of a fractal) rigorous mathematical process (Fig. 2)[9].

And : What is real in music, in "Duo for a pianist" for example (Fig. 3)?

Is it what we listen, or what we imagine could emerge from a potentially infinite virtuosity of the Disklavier? Is "Duo pour un pianiste"

a Computer assisted live music

or

a Mind assisted computer music?

[9] Like a calisson shaped box of calissons where all calissons are replaced by ... a box of callisons where all calissons are replaced by ... a box of callisons...etc.

In fact, putting realism in music inside the execution of a piece is by far too naive. It seems to me that realism emerge in music as a consequence of, among other things but necessary including it, the rigour present in the process of composing. Reading a fugue without playing it is a real experience, after all. And conversely, considering that the mathematical realism calls only the rigorous part of mathematics is too simple, too reductive.

The conclusion of this short section could be expressed by saying that, both in music and in mathematics, the rigour has the role of providing a kind of "emergence of realism".

Postlude: Solo for a Scientist and a Musician

This conclusion will be an homage to Jean-Claude Risset, who all along his too short life, played continuously and successfully a permanent duo between him physicist and him musician [11].

"Duos pour un pianiste", which, together with this postlude, has a quite surrealistic but rigorous title, illustrate marvellously this duality. First of all, the work addresses the issue of the limits of virtuosity, a very musical one. These limits will be overcome thanks of the use of a computer, a evry mathematical object. Not by a computer creating electroacoustic sounds, but by a computer playing, through a precise and rigorous reaction to what the pianist just played, a piano Disklavier. And the only limit of virtuosity for the computer will be the one of the acoustic instrument.

Nobody knows really who, during the execution, is more influenced by the other: the pianist and the computer. Once again, rather than a computer assisted piece of music, it is more of a mind assisted Nancarrow studies style piece.

Only the double-hatted mind of Jean-Claude could achieve such a miracle.

Acknowledgment. This work has been partially carried out thanks to the supports of the LIA AMU-CNRS-ECM- INdAM Laboratoire Ypatie des Sciences Mathématiques (LYSM).

References

1. Boucourechliev, A.: Stravinsky. Fayard, Paris (1982)
2. Boulez, P.: Structures I Pour Deux Pianos. Universal Edition, Vienna (1952)
3. Paul, T., Schmidt, M. (eds.): RIGUEUR. Spartacus, Paris (2021). https://indico.math.cnrs.fr/event/4602/, http://ljll.math.upmc.fr/paulth//phenomath/
4. Drouin, G.: Les deux moments de la rigueur du compositeur. In: [3]
5. Giavitto, J.L.: Formalisme, Exactitude, Rigueur. In: [3]
6. Goursat, É.: Cours d'Analyse Mathématique. Gauthier-Villars, Paris (1933)
7. Paul, T.: Des sons et des Quanta. In: Alunni, C., Andreatta, M., Nicolas, F. (eds.) Mathématique/Musique/Philosophie. Collection "Musique/Sciences" IRCAM-Delatour, Paris (2012)
8. Paul, T.: Rigueur-contraintes: mathématiques-musique. Gaz. Mathématiciens **139**, 71–77 (2014)

9. Paul, T.: platonisme - intrication - aléa (mathématique - physique - musique), à la mémoire de Jean-Claude Risset, magicien des sons impossibles. In: Hautbois, X., Laliberté, M., Stransky, L., Stransky, V. (eds.) L'émergence en musique - dialogue des sciences, Delatour, Paris, pp. 37–52 (2019)
10. Paul, T.: Mathematical entities without objects, on the realism in mathematics and a possible mathematization of the (non)Platonism - Does Platonism dissolve in mathematics? Eur. Rev. **29**(2), 1–21 (2021)
11. Paul, T.: In memoriam. http://ljll.math.upmc.fr/paulth/inmemoriamtp.pdf
12. Poincaré, H.: Sur la théorie des quanta. J. Phys. Théorique Appl. **2**, 5–34 (1912)
13. Stockhausen, K.: ...wie die Zeit vergeht.... Die Reihe, 3 (1957) In: French: ...comment passe le temps.... Analyse musicale 6 (1987)
14. Stravinsky, I.: Movements for Piano and Orchestra. Boosey and Hawkes, London (1959)
15. Thom, R.: Prédire n'est pas Expliquer. Eshel, Paris (1991)

Zero-Emission Vehicles Sonification Strategy Based on Shepard-Risset Glissando

Sébastien Denjean[1,2(✉)], Richard Kronland-Martinet[2], Vincent Roussarie[1], and Sølvi Ystad[2]

[1] Groupe PSA, Paris, France
{sebastien.denjean,vincent.roussarie}@mpsa.com
[2] Aix Marseille Univ, CNRS, PRISM, Marseille, France
{kronland,ystad}@prism.cnrs.fr

Abstract. In this paper, we present a sonification strategy developed for electric vehicles aiming to synthetize a new engine sound to enhance the driver's dynamic perception of the vehicle. We chose to mimic the internal combustion engine (ICE) noise by informing the driver through pitch variations. However, ICE noise pitch variations are correlated to the engine's rotations per minute (RPM) and its dynamics is covered within a limited vehicle speed range. In order to provide the driver with extended pitch variations throughout the full vehicle speed range, we based our sonification strategy on the Shepard-Risset glissando. Such illusory infinite ascending/descending sounds enable to represent accelerations with significant pitch variations for an unlimited range of speeds. In this way, it is possible to conserve the metaphor of ICE noise with unheard gearshifts. We tested this sonification strategy in a perceptual test in a driving simulator and showed that the mapping of this acoustical feedback affects the drivers' perception of vehicle dynamics.

Keywords: Sonification · Automotive acoustics · Multisensory perception

1 Introduction

Car manufacturers are widely expanding their production of electric vehicles, commonly called 'Zero Emission Vehicles' (ZEV), to reduce greenhouse emission gases. If the development of electric motorizations can help improve the automotive environmental footprint, these quieter motorizations also lead to a radical change in the acoustic feedback due to the loss of the engine noise.

This issue has largely been studied in the case of outside feedback alerting pedestrians that a vehicle is approaching [1, 2, 4, 8, 10]. At low speeds, when wind and rolling noises are very low, the loss of Internal Combustion Engine (ICE) feedback makes electric vehicles inaudible for pedestrians, leading to potentially dangerous situations. Standards are now imposed to car manufacturers to equip their vehicles with Acoustic Vehicle Alert System (AVAS) in order to generate sounds that enable pedestrians to hear such vehicles.

R. Kronland-Martinet et al. (Eds.): CMMR 2019, LNCS 12631, pp. 709–724, 2021.
https://doi.org/10.1007/978-3-030-70210-6_46

In the present study, we will focus on inside acoustic feedback. The reduced noise level in the passenger compartment has become a strong selling argument for ZEV, being associated with passenger comfort. However, the ICE noise is the most significant source of information for the driver and its loss can be detrimental for driving. Horswill and Plooy [11] indeed showed that drivers underestimate their speed when the acoustic feedback loudness is reduced. Quieter motorizations can thus deteriorate the drivers' perception of speed and encourage them to drive faster. We also showed in a previous work that the loss of ICE noise could affect the drivers' perception of acceleration [6]. ICE noise is indeed the main acoustic information related to the vehicle dynamics and its loss may influence the driver's motion perception. It has also a strong emotional power and its loss can have a negative impact on the perceived sportiness, driving pleasure and brand identity of the vehicle [22].

With the development of electric motorizations, we thus loose a significant part of the dynamic and emotional acoustical information. To compensate this loss, we developed a sonification strategy to synthetize a new engine sound for electric vehicles to replace the information usually conveyed by engine noise in ICE cars.

2 Sonification Strategy

Adaptive sonification is a powerful tool to inform the user in an action-perception loop [3, 5, 12, 14, 20, 24], and especially in a driving task in which the sight must be dedicated to the road. We used sonification to inform the driver about the vehicle dynamics to enhance his/her motion perception. With the vanishing of internal combustion engine (ICE) noise, zero emission vehicles (ZEV) also become an amazing playground to shape the soundscape of these quiet(er) vehicles with sonification. Thanks to the freedom offered by sound synthesis, we can design sounds that give character to the vehicle, with a technological or even futuristic dimension. Sonification is therefore becoming a key for car manufacturers to develop acoustic brand identities and tools to enhance the perceived quality inside the cabin.

As a first step, we chose to set aside the esthetic dimension to work on the dynamic feedback and the acoustics invariants of vehicle dynamics. We built our sonification strategy by mimicking time-varying acoustic attributes of the ICE noise to achieve a natural and intuitive way of informing the drivers.

2.1 Objectives

We decided to inform the driver through pitch variations, similarly to the ICE noise behavior, in order to convey information on vehicle dynamics through the same levers as ICE noise, but with its own 'electric' personality. In the case of an ICE noise, the pitch is correlated to the engine rotations per minute (RPM) which describes a piecewise linear function of vehicle speed. During acceleration, the pitch grows up to the higher RPM of a given gear ratio before falling down at each gearshift. The ICE pitch range is thus covered several times over the whole vehicle speed range and remains quite limited within a pitch range of around 2.5 octaves.

In the case of electric vehicles, the situation is different, since there are no gearshifts, as if the whole vehicle speed range was covered by only one gear. In this case, RPM is proportional to vehicle speed. We chose to directly map the pitch to speed, which seemed more relevant for drivers. However, the pitch-based sonification strategy cannot be directly transferred from RPM-dependency in ICE vehicles to speed-dependency in ZEV for several reasons:

- creating frequency drops to simulate gearshifts despite physical reality would be confusing for the driver (Fig. 1(1)),
- keeping the pitch range of an ICE noise to cover the whole vehicle speed range, would infer too low pitch variations for low accelerations and provide information to the driver that would not be sufficiently precise to estimate the vehicle acceleration (Fig. 1(2)),
- duplicating the pitch variation of an ICE noise 5 times to 'unwrap' the pitch and cover the whole vehicle speed range would ensure precise information for low accelerations, but would give too high-pitched sounds at high speeds (Fig. 1(3)). Choosing a 2.5 octave range for around 30 km/h would even lead to inaudible sounds.

We answered this issue by using the Shepard-Risset glissando illusion of continually ascending or descending pitch. With these peculiar sounds, we can produce large pitch variations to precisely inform the driver, even for low vehicle accelerations while keeping a constrained pitch for the whole speed range of the vehicle.

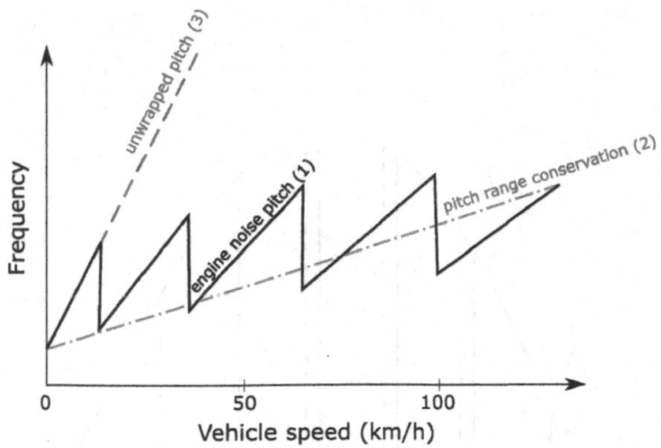

Fig. 1. Schematic representation of the evolution of fundamental frequency of ICE noise over vehicle speed (1). (2) and (3) represent the pitch strategies of pitch range conservation and unwrapped pitch to map pitch to vehicle speed in ZEV.

2.2 Shepard-Risset Glissando Based Sonification Strategy

Principle

Previous experiences within both the visual and auditory domain have revealed the importance of perception of local motion that can be exploited to create both visual and auditory illusions. A well-known example of this effect in the visual domain is Penrose's endless staircase [15]. In the auditory domain Shepard [23] was the first to create this illusion by synthesizing a bank of complex tones and applying a fixed, bell-shaped spectral envelope that determined the amplitudes of the harmonics.

Shepard tones [23] are made of a sum of ten sinusoidal components each separated by an octave interval. For instance, for a tone corresponding to a C, the tone will consist of the frequencies C1, C2, …, C10. The amplitudes of the components are determined by a fixed, raised cosine function that covers the whole frequency range (10 octaves in Shephard's experiment) as represented in Fig. 2. This amplitude function is linked to the log frequency. From these tones, we can construct a scale by shifting all the sinusoidal components by a certain fraction towards higher octaves without moving the amplitude window as represented by the dashed lines in Fig. 2. We thus will get a C# with a 1/12 octave shift of each component, a D with another 1/12 octave shift, etc. At the last step, when the comb has been shifted by one octave, the cycle will start again with the C, and the first nine components will replace the components which were one octave higher before shifting (C1 becomes C2, C2 becomes C3…). The previously highest component (C10) drops out the envelope and a new component is introduced one octave below the previously lowest component (C10 thus becomes C1). A shift of one octave thus leads to the exact same note, forming a cyclic scale. Due to the window shape, intermediate frequencies (in the middle of the window) will always dominate while the higher and lower frequency components gradually taper off (vertical solid lines, Fig. 2) so that the repetitions are not perceived.

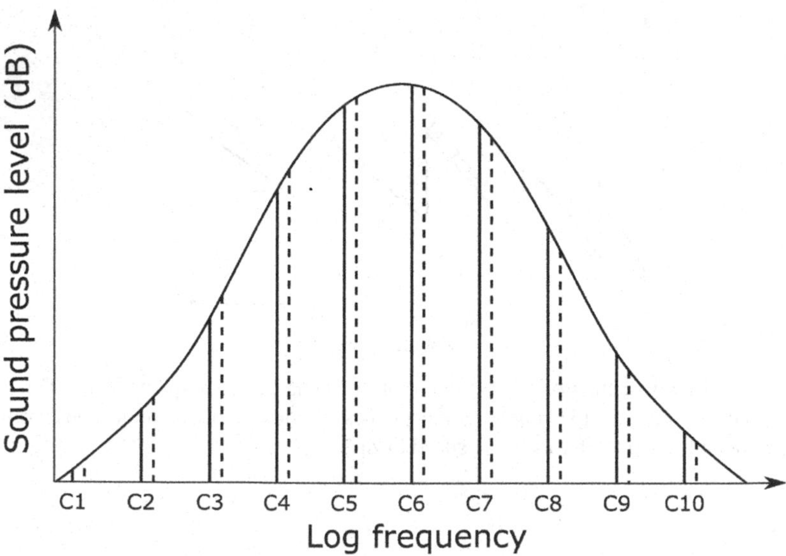

Fig. 2. Construction of a Shepard tone.

With the peculiar construction of his tones, Shepard built the illusion of a cyclic scale that can be played up and down "infinitely".

Pitch perception has two dimensions. If pitch is correlated to the log frequency of the sound as described for instance by the mel scale (pitch height), we can also notice a circular dimension well known in music (pitch class) representing a strong perceptual proximity of tones in an octave relationship. Pitch is thus often represented as a helix to illustrate these two dimensions, with a complete turn by octave to ensure spatial proximity of tones separated by an octave (Fig. 3). With his tones, Shepard managed to scramble these two dimensions. By constructing a scale of ten of these complex tones dividing one octave into ten equal intervals on a scale in log frequency, and turning around the chromatic scale, he showed that listeners felt the pitch growing while playing up this scale, but also while looping this scale from the last tone of the scale to the first. These tones preserve pitch class but cannot be ordered with respect to height. The exact same tone can be perceived at different heights depending on the preceding sequence.

Risset further used this illusion to create an infinite glissando with continuous transitions between tones and played with the two pitch dimensions to choose opposite directions for spectral envelope movements and pitch class movements, hereby creating sequences that ascended and descended at the same time [18, 19].

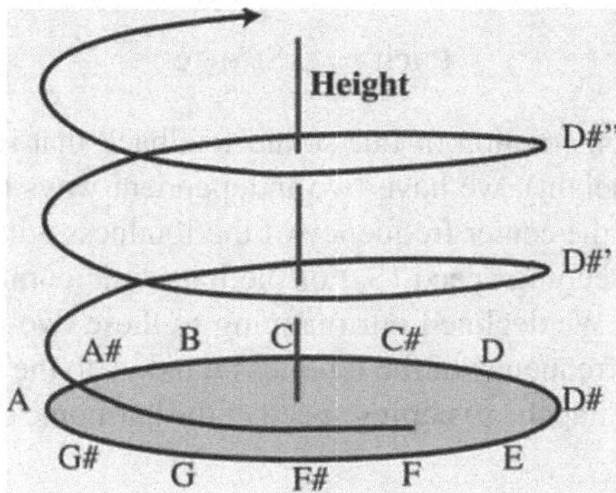

Fig. 3. Helical representation of pitch, varying linearly in the vertical dimension (pitch height) with frequency and describing a circular dimension of pitch class on the musical scale, showing spatial proximity of tones in an octave relation (from [7])

In the present study, we adapted this illusion to our sonification application and made it possible to control both pitch dimensions. We reduced the bandwidth of the window to few octaves to be able to move this window in the frequency domain to change the pitch height through the central spectroid of the generated sounds. But this reduction of bandwidth mechanically leads to the reduction of the number of sinusoidal components of the tone and can weaken the illusion. We thus chose to modify the Shephard tones by adding some components between the sinusoidal components that originally were separated by one octave. Adding more components in a different relation than an octave creates the sensation of chords and also opens new design possibilities related to the pitch class that conveys the desired identity with this sound feedback.

Synthesizer Development

We developed a synthesizer in Max/MSP to generate these sounds and map our feedback to the vehicle speed and acceleration in real-time. The sine wave components are hereby tuned to form the time-varying scale and the raised cosine function is configured to set the loudness window.

Harmonic Comb: The user can create the chord-like tone by selecting the components to be added between the octaves that originally separate the components that form the Shephard tone. These components are then duplicated to each octave to generate the complete harmonic comb. The frequencies of the components of this harmonic comb are controlled by a saw tooth function that browses the scale periodically. The amplitude of each component is defined by the loudness window.

Loudness Window: The shape of this window corresponds to a raised cosine function and defines the amplitude of each harmonic component of the comb. The user can define its bandwidth, which may span over one or several octaves, and its central frequency which determines the pitch height of the perceived scale.

Mapping: We mapped the pitch height of the generated sounds to the vehicle speed. We chose a generic linear mapping between the pitch and the vehicle speed (S_V):

$$\text{Pitch} = kS_V + c \tag{1}$$

With the specific construction of our sound feedback that relies on two attributes, (pitch class and pitch height), we have two independent ways to vary the pitch of the generated sounds: with the center frequency of the loudness window (F_c), i.e. the pitch height, and with the sweeping speed (S_S) of the harmonic comb (i.e. the frequency of the sawtooth function). We declined our mapping to these two parameters, linking the logarithm of the center frequency of the loudness window to the vehicle speed (S_V), and deriving this formula to map the sweeping speed of the harmonic comb to the acceleration (A_V) (Fig. 4.).

$$\log(F_c) = k_1 S_V + c_1 \tag{2}$$

$$S_S = k_2 A_V \tag{3}$$

Information Feedback

The sweeping speed of the harmonic comb informs the driver on the vehicle acceleration. As for the ICE noise, the faster the frequency variation, the larger the acceleration is perceived by the driver. It is interesting to notice that our glissando is controlled by a sawtooth function. As for the pitch of the ICE noise, the frequency of the generated sound increases during acceleration before decreasing to its original frequency, like it does in ICE noise at gearshift (Fig. 1(1)). With the Shepard-Risset glissando illusion, we thus kind of reproduce 'unheard' gearshifts that enable large pitch variations even at low accelerations, but with a constrained pitch range in the whole vehicle speed range.

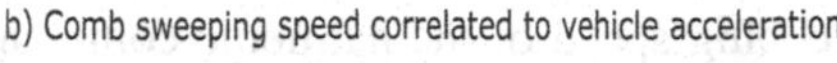

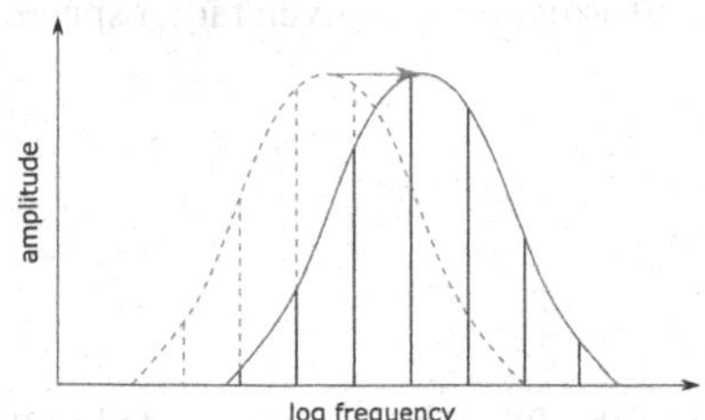

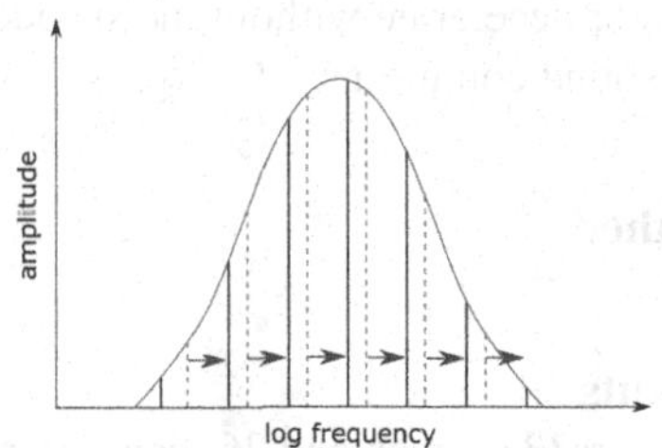

Fig. 4. Representation of the mapping of pitch with vehicule dynamics. The pitch height is controlled through the center frequency of the loudness window mapped to the vehicle speed (a) while the pitch class is mapped through the sweeping speed of the harmonic comb mapped to the vehicle acceleration

In addition to this ICE noise metaphor, we also added a second vehicle speed information (i.e. the height attribute of the pitch) by enabling the control of the center frequency of the loudness function.

We tested this sonification strategy in a perceptual test in a driving simulator to evaluate the impact of this pitch attribute on the drivers' perception of vehicle dynamics.

3 Impact of Shepard-Risset Based Sonification Strategy on the Drivers' Perception of Vehicle Speed and Acceleration

ICE noise represents an important feedback on vehicle acceleration for drivers. This information is useful in the perception of vehicle dynamics and particularly important in speed maintenance. We thus focused our strategy on acceleration feedback through the sweeping speed of the harmonic comb. To evaluate the impact of the proposed sonification strategy on drivers' perception, we ran a perceptual test in a driving simulator.

3.1 Experiment Objectives

The main goal of this experiment was to evaluate the impact of the sonification strategy on the drivers' perception of vehicle dynamics through their perception of the vehicle speed. Speed perception indeed strongly depends on the preceding acceleration [17, 21].

We designed our sonification strategy relying on this information. The proposed sound, based on the Shepard-Risset glissando, is well suited to give strong acceleration information with the variation of pitch, but can give fuzzy information about absolute speed with its paradoxical pitch, even if we correlate the spectral centroid to vehicle speed. We assumed that the sonification mapping would affect the drivers' perceived acceleration, and thus their speed production. In particular, we hypothesized that increased pitch variations would induce stronger perceived acceleration among the drivers, hereby inciting them to produce slower speeds.

To validate this hypothesis, we focused on the mapping between the sweeping speed of the harmonic comb and the vehicle acceleration. We fixed the mapping between the filtering window displacement and the speed, and tested different mappings between the sweeping speed of the harmonic comb and the acceleration. We asked participants to accelerate or decelerate without the speedometer information to a given target speed in different sound conditions.

3.2 Method

Participants

29 volunteers (3 women and 26 men), employees of the PSA group, participated in this study. They all held a valid driver license and declared to have normal or corrected to normal vision and normal audition.

Experimental Device

We chose to run this perceptual experiment on a driving simulator to control the stimuli presented to the participants and ensure their repeatability. For this experiment, we used a fixed-based driving simulator composed of the front half of a car disposed in front of a hemi-cylindrical screen. The scene used for the simulation represented a straight two-lane urban road. A picture of the driving simulator and an extraction of the scene are presented in Fig. 5.

Fig. 5. Picture of the driving simulator and the driving scene used for the perceptual study.

The vehicle noise played to the participants in the driving simulator was based on recordings in an actual car with a binaural dummy head. It was replayed using granular synthesis as a function of the vehicle speed, and our sonification proposals were mixed with this noise. This global mix was reproduced in the simulator thanks to a five-loudspeaker sound system.

Experimental Variables

Vehicle Speed and Acceleration: Participants had to reach 2 target speeds, 50 and 70 km/h, either accelerating from 30 km/h below the target (acceleration condition) or decelerating from 30 km/h above the target (deceleration condition). The acceleration was controlled and fixed to 2 values in the acceleration and deceleration conditions: +/− 0.75 m/s^2 or +/− 1.5 m/s^2. We thus tested 4 acceleration and 4 deceleration conditions.

Sonification Parameters: To focus on the impact of the harmonic comb speed variation on the perceived dynamics, all the other sonification parameters were fixed. The harmonic comb was composed of a major triad (tonal, major third and fifth) duplicated to the other octaves and served as a basis for the sound feedback. This harmonic comb was filtered with a 4-octave length Gaussian window (see Fig. 2) with a central frequency varying exponentially with vehicle speed from 120 Hz at idle to 660 Hz at 130 km/h (approximately 1 octave every 55 km/h).

The mapping between the sweeping speed of the harmonic comb and the vehicle acceleration, was tested with 3 linear mappings with three different values of the constant k_2 ($k_2 = 0.04$, 0.08 and 0.16). In the rest of this paper, we will use the mapping with a constant $k_2 = 0.08$ as reference (mapping1) and refer to the other mappings as mapping 0.5 ($k_2 = 0.04$) and mapping 2 ($k_2 = 0.16$). It should be noted that we will encounter situations in which the sound feedback is the same at different visual accelerations, with mapping 1 at 0.75 m/s^2 and mapping 0.5 at 1.5 m/s^2, or mapping 1 at 1.5 m/s^2 and mapping 2 at 0.75 m/s^2.

The influence of this mapping can be observed in Fig. 6 in which we represented the spectrogram of the sounds obtained during a constant acceleration from 0 to 90 km/h. The loudness window is moving from 120 Hz at idle to around 450 Hz at 90 km/h and the harmonic comb sweeping speed is mapped to acceleration with low constant (mapping 0.5, Fig. 6a) or high constant (mapping 2, Fig. 6b).

We also added a control condition without sonification to the 3 previous conditions.

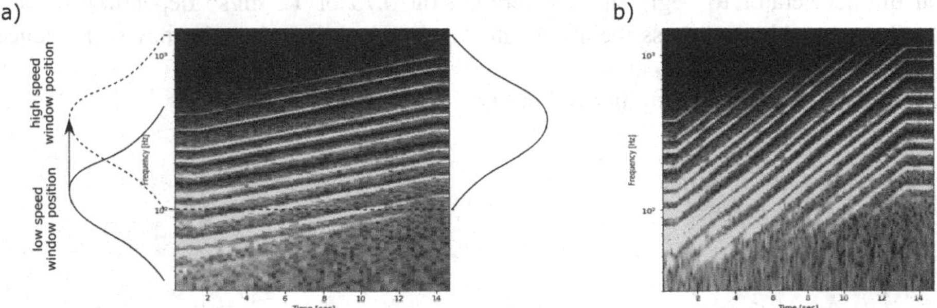

Fig. 6. Spectrograms of two sounds given by our sonification strategy with the same constant vehicle acceleration from 0 to 90 km/h. The central frequency of the loudness window is increasing linearly with speed from 120 Hz at idle to 450 Hz at max speed in both figures. The harmonic comb sweeping speed is mapped with a low constant to vehicle acceleration (mapping 0.5) in (a) and high constant (mapping 2) in (b)

Experimental Variables Summary: These experimental variables that are summed up in Table 1 have been crossed into a full factorial design. Each stimulus has been repeated 3 times, leading to a complete experimental design of 96 stimuli.

Procedure

Participant Tasks: Participants were to perform a symmetric task during the acceleration and deceleration conditions.

Table 1. Experimental variable summary. All variables were crossed in a complete experimental design and each stimulus was repeated 3 times leading to 96 stimuli tested by each participant.

Use case	Target speed	Acceleration level	Sound feedback
Acceleration	50 km/h	± 0.75 m/s^2	Mapping 0.5 ($k_2 = 0.04$)
			Mapping 1 ($k_2 = 0.08$)
Deceleration	70 km/h	± 1.5 m/s^2	Mapping 2 ($k_2 = 0.16$)
			Electric vehicle (no sonification)

During acceleration, subjects were launched at a constant speed (20 or 40 km/h) depending on the target speed (50 or 70 km/h). The driving simulator regulated the vehicle speed and the driver did not press the accelerator pedal in the constant speed situation, as if a speed regulator was used. When entering the acceleration zone, the subject pressed the accelerator pedal to accelerate. The vehicle acceleration was regulated by the simulation (at 0.75 or 1.5 m/s^2) and the driver had to stop the acceleration by releasing the pressure on the accelerator when he/she thought the target speed had been reached. After the acceleration, the vehicle speed was kept constant by the driving simulator.

In the deceleration condition, the task was symmetrical, and the participants were asked to press the accelerator pedal to keep the speed constant (at 80 or 100 km/h depending on the target speed). When they were ready to start, they reduced the pressure on the accelerator to begin the deceleration (at 0.75 or 1.5 m/s^2 depending on test condition) and had to press the accelerator again when they thought they had reached the target speed.

Both conditions are summarized in Fig. 7.

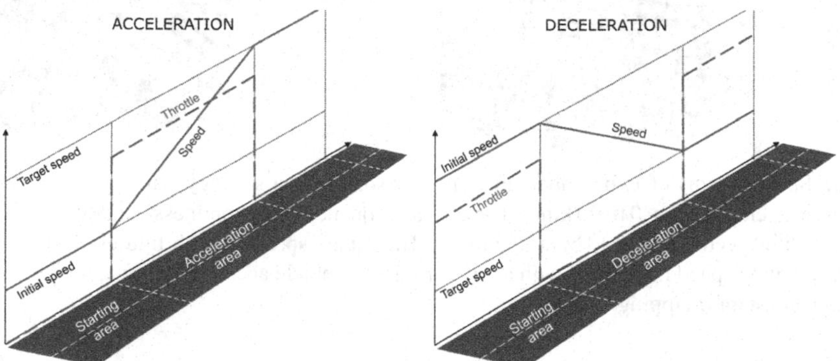

Fig. 7. Test procedure for acceleration and deceleration conditions.

Test Sessions: Stimuli were divided in two blocs by the acceleration/deceleration condition. To avoid learning effects, half of the participants began with the acceleration condition and the other half with the deceleration condition. The whole test lasted for approximately 1 h 45.

At the beginning of the test session, the experimenter presented the experiment to the participant. The experimenter explained that the participant would have to evaluate the vehicle speed without a speedometer feedback at different speeds. He also explained that different acoustic feedbacks would be provided, but without mentioning the nature or the type of control of these sounds.

Before the beginning of the test, the participants underwent a training phase. The first training phase aimed to familiarize each participant with the driving simulator: the participant drove freely within roads on the map used for the test. During this phase, the speedometer was visible and the participant could calibrate his/her speed perception without the sonification, with only the natural electric vehicle acoustic feedback *i.e.* in the sound control condition. When the participant felt comfortable with the driving simulator, the test began.

Each test bloc (acceleration and deceleration) began with a task-learning phase. The experimenter explained the subject's task and a couple of additional tasks were tested to make sure the participant fully understood the task. Stimuli corresponding to the different acceleration intensities, target speeds and sounds were presented with a pseudo-randomized experimental design based on a Latin-square to reduce learning effects.

3.3 Results

We recorded the speed reached by the participants after the acceleration/deceleration phase and considered it as their perceived target speed. We calculated the error between the speed reached by the driver and the target speed to compare the results between the two target speeds tested.

Analysis of Variance (ANOVA) was ran on acceleration and deceleration conditions to determine the experiment parameters that had a significant impact on the speed reached by the drivers in each condition.

Acceleration Condition

Sound Condition: In the case of acceleration, the ANOVA showed a significant effect of the sound condition ($P < 0.001$). A Scheffé post-hoc test separated these four conditions (3 mappings and one electric – without sonification - condition) in three groups:

- Mapping 2 (Mean Error −1.6 km/h),
- Mapping 1 (Mean Error −0.1 km/h) and Electric Condition (Mean Error 0.8 km/h),
- Mapping 0.5 (Mean Error 1.1 km/h) and Electric Condition.

Intensity of Vehicle Acceleration: The intensity of the acceleration had a significant impact on the speed reached by the drivers ($p < 0.001$), with a speed error of −2.8 km/h during acceleration and 3 km/h during deceleration.

Target Speed: We can notice a significant effect of the target speed ($p < 0.001$) with a mean error of 0.9 km/h at 50 km/h and −0.7 km/h at 70 km/h.

Repetition: Repetitions showed significant effects ($p < 0.001$) with a mean speed error of −0.7 km/h for the first repetition, 0 km/h for the second and 1 km/h for the third repetition.

Interactions: No interaction between these parameters reached a significance level of 5 %.

Deceleration Condition

Sound Condition: The sound condition had a significant effect on the speed reached by the drivers ($p < 0.001$) and Scheffé post-hoc test sorted the conditions in three groups:

In the deceleration condition, the ANOVA showed the same significant effects.

- Mapping 0.5 (Mean Error 8.5 km/h),
- Mapping 1 (Mean Error 10.2 km/h) and Electric Condition (Mean Error 10.6 km/h),
- Mapping 2 (Mean Error 12.4 km/h).

Intensity of Vehicle Acceleration: We can notice a significant effect of the intensity of the acceleration ($p < 0.001$) with lower speeds reached at higher decelerations (mean error of 7.5 km/h at -1.5 m/s^2 and 13.3 km/h at -0.75 m/s^2).

Target Speed: The target speed significantly influences the speed reached by the participants ($p < 0.001$), with a mean error of 10.8 km/h at 50 km/h and 10 km/h at 70 km/h.

Repetition: As for the acceleration condition, repetition also has a significant influence on mean speed errors of 11 km/h for first, 10.6 km/h for the second and 9.6 km/h for the third repetition.

Interactions: No interaction between these parameters reached a significance level of 5 %.

3.4 Discussion

Speed Perception and Influence of Acceleration

In Fig. 8, we plotted the mean speeds reached by the participants in the acceleration and deceleration conditions for target speeds of 50 km/h and both acceleration intensities 0.75 and 1.5 m/s^2.Consistently with the literature on speed perception, this study highlighted a global overproduction of speed by the participants, suggesting that they compensated their underestimation of the speed by reaching higher speeds than the target [16]. We can notice that this underestimation of the speed is higher at lower speeds, in line with [9, 13, 16, 17], with a mean speed of 56 km/h reached for a target speed of 50 km/h (Fig. 4) and 77 km/h for a target speed of 70 km/h.

We also notice that the speed reached by the participants is modulated with the intensity and sign of the acceleration.

Regarding the sign of the acceleration, we can see that the drivers tend to reach higher speeds when decelerating than when accelerating, suggesting that they tend to overestimate their acceleration (Fig. 8). This overestimation of the acceleration makes them think that they accelerated (resp. decelerated) more than they actually did and stopped the acceleration (resp. deceleration) before they should, inducing them to reach lower (resp. higher) speeds.

Regarding the intensity of the acceleration, we can notice that the situation is symmetrical. In the acceleration condition, the drivers tended to reach lower speeds at lower accelerations (Fig. 8). Focusing on speed, we can infer that drivers underestimate their speed more after stronger accelerations, consistently with the study of Salvatore [21]. However, during deceleration, the opposite effect can be observed, with lower speeds reached with higher decelerations. This symmetrical result suggests that drivers tend to overestimate their acceleration and even more when its intensity its lower. Drivers thus tend to reach higher speeds at strong accelerations and lower at high decelerations.

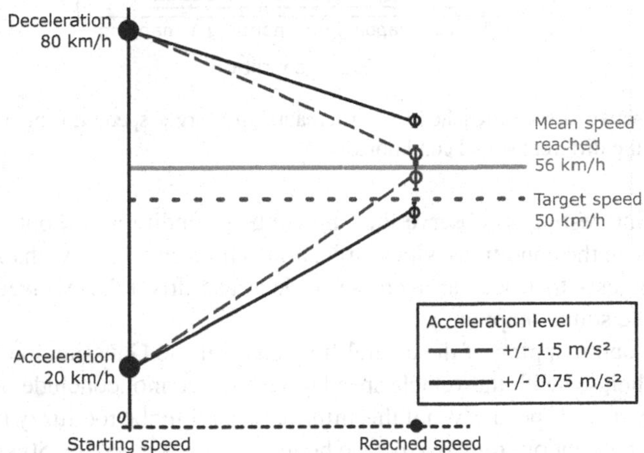

Fig. 8. Mean speeds reached by participants for a 50 km/h target speed during acceleration and deceleration for both acceleration levels.

This result confirms the major role of acceleration in drivers' speed perception.

Influence of Sound Feedback

Our sonification strategy based on the Shepard-Risset illusion is particularly well suited to inform on vehicle acceleration. More than the association of a pitch to a particular speed, this feedback enables to control the variation of the pitch according to vehicle acceleration.

We assumed that this feedback could modify the perceived acceleration among drivers and modify their speed production. The plot of speeds reached by participants in the different sound conditions (Fig. 9) confirms this hypothesis. Similarly, to the effect of the intensity of acceleration, we can notice that the effect of sound mapping is symmetrical during acceleration and deceleration. During acceleration, drivers tended to reach lower speeds with a sound mapping that had a faster comb sweeping. In deceleration, they reached higher speeds with faster comb sweeping.This result suggests that the sound information influenced the perceived acceleration among participants, with a perception of acceleration that increased with the comb sweeping.

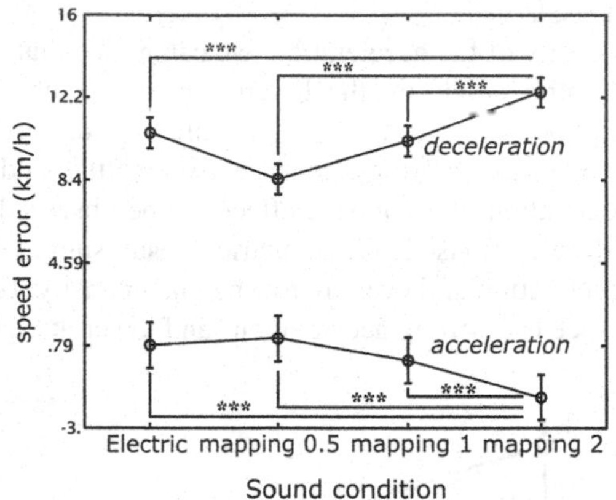

Fig. 9. Errors between speed reached by participants and target speed during acceleration and deceleration in the different sound conditions

It is also interesting to observe that the control condition without sonification is included between the conditions with sonification. The comparison with the sonification conditions suggests than we can increase or decrease drivers' perceived acceleration according to the sound mapping.

With only one mapping of the central frequency of the Gaussian loudness window (i.e. the pitch height) with the vehicle speed tested, we cannot conclude on its effect on the drivers' perceived speed. Even if this information might be too fuzzy to improve the drivers' speed perception (only one octave height change for around 50 km/h), it might contribute to increase the effect of the comb sweeping, i.e. the pitch class increase, when pitch height is linearly mapped to speed as in the present study. However, we can also imagine different mapping strategies of the Gaussian window's central frequency with the vehicle speed to enhance the information, for instance with piecewise mapping functions to more clearly influence typical speeds for city, road or highway driving.

Even if the effect of our sonification strategy is naturally lower than the effect of the vehicle acceleration intensity, it can contribute to change the drivers' perception of the vehicle dynamics. We saw that the drivers tend to overestimate their acceleration and mostly at low acceleration intensities. An exponential mapping can then be used to reduce this overestimation for low accelerations, hence adjusting the mapping to the way acceleration is perceived.

4 Conclusion

The development of quieter electric motorizations changes the soundscape perceived by drivers in their vehicles, and this "silence" is often praised for these zero emission vehicles (ZEV). However, Internal Combustion Engine (ICE) noise is an important feedback for drivers. It gives precious information about vehicle dynamics and has an important impact on the emotional level, since it contributes to the evocation of sportiness and driving pleasure.

In this study we developed a sonification strategy to enhance drivers' perception of vehicle dynamics and improve the pleasure of the driving experience in electric vehicles. We decided to focus on speed and acceleration information, which are of major interest for driving control. The proposed strategy is based on the engine noise metaphor, with a pitch that increases with acceleration, to provide natural and intuitive feedback to the driver. We found that the Shepard-Risset glissando illusion was perfectly suited for this aim. We used both height and pitch class variations to inform respectively on speed and acceleration.

Acceleration has been shown in literature to have a strong impact on speed perception. We thus focused our sonification strategy to enhance this information, giving more information to the variation of the parameter of interest than to this parameter itself. We mapped the infinite glissando speed proportionally to the vehicle acceleration to give salient information to the driver. With this illusion, we could precisely provide information on the vehicle acceleration with fast pitch variations that could be maintained over the whole speed range of the vehicle.

This is, to our knowledge, the first time that the Shepard-Risset illusion has been used as a sonification strategy in an action-perception loop. With the two dimensions of pitch (height and pitch class) which can be controlled independently, this illusion can also be a very powerful tool to investigate human perception and cognition in an action-perception loop with two independent aspects linked to the same sensation. In our application, we used both dimensions consistently to provide information on speed and its derivative through a new and original sonification strategy.

We tested different mappings of this sonification strategy with vehicle dynamics and showed that this had an impact on the drivers' acceleration perception and speed production. This sonification strategy can also be designed to generate more technological sounds than ICE noise and is particularly well suited to answer the issue of interior sonification of ZEV.

Acknowledgements. This work was partly supported by the French National Research Agency (ANR-10-CORD-0003, MetaSon, "Métaphores sonores", https://metason.prism.cnrs.fr).

References

1. Altinstoy, E.: The detectability of conventional, hybrid and electric vehicle sounds by sighted, visually impaired and blind pedestrians. In: Internoise 2013, Innsbruck (2013)
2. Ashmead, D.H., et al.: Auditory perception of motor vehicle travel paths. Hum. Fact. J. Hum. Fact. Ergon. Soc. **54**(3), 437–453 (2012)
3. Bressolettte, B., Denjean, S., Roussarie, V., Aramaki, M., Ystad, S., Kronland-Martinet, R.: Harnessing audio in auto control: the challenge of sonifying virtual objects for gesture control of cars. IEEE Consum. Electron. Mag. **7**(2), 91–100 (2018)
4. Chamard, J.C., Roussarie, V., et al.: Design of electric or hybrid vehicle alert sound system for pedestrian. In: Acoustics 2012, Nantes (2012)

5. Danna, J., et al.: The effect of real-time auditory feedback on learning new characters. Hum. Mov. Sci. **43**, 216–228 (2015). https://doi.org/10.1016/j.humov.2014.12.002
6. Denjean, S., Velay, J.L., Kronland-Martinet, R., Roussarie, V., Sciabica, J.F., Ystad, S.: Are electric and hybrid vehicles too quiet for drivers? In: Internoise 2013, Innsbruck, pp. 3081–3090 (2013)
7. Deutsch, D.: The paradox of pitch circularity. Acoust. Today **7**, 8–14 (2010)
8. Emerson, R.W., Kim, D.S., Naghshineh, K.: Blind pedestrians and the impact of quieter vehicles on mobility decisions. In: Internoise 2013, Innsbruck (2013)
9. Evans, L.: Automobile-speed estimation using movie-film simulation. Ergonomics **13**(2), 231–237 (1970)
10. Garay-Vega, L., Pollard, J.K., Guthy, C., Hastings, A.: Auditory detectability of hybrid electric vehicles by blind pedestrians. Transp. Res. Rec. J. Transp. Res. Board **2248**(1), 68–73 (2011)
11. Horswill, M.S., Plooy, A.M.: Auditory feedback influences perceived driving speeds. Perception **37**(7), 1037 (2008)
12. Merer, A., Aramaki, M., Ystad, S., Kronland-Martinet, R.: Perceptual characterization of motion evoked by sounds for synthesis control purposes. Assoc. Comput. Mach. Trans. Appl. Percept. (TAP) **10**(1), 1–24 (2013)
13. Miloševic, S., Milic, J.: Speed perception in road curves. J. Saf. Res. **21**(1), 19–23 (1990)
14. Parseihian, G., Gondre, C., Aramaki, M., Ystad, S., Kronland-Martinet, R.: Comparison and evaluation of sonification strategies for guidance tasks. IEEE Trans. Multimedia **18**(4), 674–686 (2016). https://doi.org/10.1109/TMM.2016.2531978, ISSN: 1520–9210
15. Penrose, L.S., Penrose, R.: Impossible objects: a special type of visual illusion. Brit. J. Psychol. **49**, 31–33 (1958)
16. Recarte, M.A., Nunes, L.M.: Perception of speed in an automobile: Estimation and production. J. Exp. Psychol. Appl. **2**(4), 291 (1996)
17. Recarte, M.A., Conchillo, A. and Nunes, L.: Traffic and transport psychocology. In: Perception of Speed and Increments in Cars, pp. 73–84. Elsevier (2004)
18. Risset, J.C.: Pich control and pitch paradoxes demonstrated with computer-synthesized sounds. J. Acoust. Soc. Am. **46**, 88 (1969)
19. Risset, J.C.: Paradoxes de hauteur. Technical report, IRCAM, 1978 (1978). https://articles.ircam.fr/textes/Risset78a/
20. Rozé, J., Aramaki, M., Kronland-Martinet, R., Ystad, S.: Assessing the effects of a primary control impairment on the cellists' bowing gesture inducing harsh sounds. IEEE Access **6**, 43683–43695 (2018). https://doi.org/10.1109/ACCESS.2018.2856178
21. Salvatore, S.: Estimation of vehicular velocity under time limitation and restricted conditions of observation. Technical report, Transportation Research Board (1967)
22. Sciabica, J.F., Bezat, M.C., Roussarie, V., Kronland-Martinet, R., Ystad, S.: Timbre Characteristics of Interior Car Sound, Auditory Display, pp. 377–391. Springer, Heidelberg (2010)
23. Shepard, R.N.: Circularity in judgments of relative pitch. J. Acoust. Soc. Am. **36**(12), 2346–2353 (1964)
24. Thoret, E., Aramaki, M., Bringoux, L., Ystad, S., Kronland-Martinet, R.: Seeing circles and drawing ellipses: when sound biases reproduction of visual motion. PLoS ONE **11**(4), e0154475 (2016). https://doi.org/10.1371/journal.pone.0154475

Author Index

Printed in the United States
by Baker & Taylor Publisher Services